THE NEW OXFORD HISTORY
OF ENGLAND

General Editor · J. M. ROBERTS

The Mid-Victorian Generation

1846–1886

K. THEODORE HOPPEN

CLARENDON PRESS · OXFORD
1998

Oxford University Press, Great Clarendon Street, Oxford OX2 6DP

Oxford New York
Athens Auckland Bangkok Bogota Bombay
Buenos Aires Calcutta Cape Town Dar es Salaam
Delhi Florence Hong Kong Istanbul Karachi
Kuala Lumpur Madras Madrid Melbourne
Mexico City Nairobi Paris Singapore
Taipei Tokyo Toronto Warsaw
and associated companies in
Berlin Ibadan

Oxford is a trade mark of Oxford University Press

Published in the United States by
Oxford University Press Inc., New York

British Library Cataloguing in Publication Data
Data available

Library of Congress Cataloging in Publication Data
Hoppen, K. Theodore, 1941–
The mid-Victorian generation, 1846–1886 / K. Theodore Hoppen.
p. cm. — (New Oxford history of England)
Includes bibliographical references and index.
1. Great Britain—History—Victoria, 1837–1901. I. Title.
II. Series.
DA560.H58 1998 941.081—dc21 97—18126 CIP

ISBN 0–19–822834–1

1 3 5 7 9 10 8 6 4 2

Typeset by Pure Tech India Limited, Pondicherry
Printed in Great Britain by
Bookcraft Ltd., Midsomer-Norton
Nr. Bath, Somerset

For
Martha
Katherine
&
Theo

General Editor's Preface

The first volume of Sir George Clark's *Oxford History of England* was published in 1934. Undertaking the General Editorship of a *New Oxford History of England* forty-five years later it was hard not to feel overshadowed by its powerful influence and well-deserved status. Some of Clark's volumes (his own among them) were brilliant individual achievements, hard to rival and impossible to match. Of course, he and his readers shared a broad sense of the purpose and direction of such books. His successor can no longer be sure of doing that. The building-blocks of the story, its reasonable and meaningful demarcations and divisions, the continuities and discontinuities, the priorities of different varieties of history, the place of narrative—all these things are now much harder to agree upon. We now know much more about many things, and think about what we know in different ways. It is not surprising that historians now sometimes seem unsure about the audience to which their scholarship and writing are addressed.

In the end, authors should be left to write their own books. None the less, the *New Oxford History of England* is intended to be more than a collection of discrete or idiosyncratic histories in chronological order. Its aim is to give an account of the development of our country in time. It is hard to treat that development as just the history which unfolds within the precise boundaries of England, and a mistake to suggest that this implies a neglect of the histories of the Scots, Irish, and Welsh. Yet the institutional core of the story which runs from Anglo-Saxon times to our own is the story of a state-structure built round the English monarchy and its effective successor, the Crown in Parliament, and that provides the only continuous articulation of the history of peoples we today call British. It follows that there must be uneven and sometimes discontinous treatment of much of the history of those peoples. The state story remains, nevertheless, an intelligible thread and to me appears still to justify the title both of this series and that of its predecessor.

If the attention given to the other kingdoms and the principality of Wales must reflect in this series their changing relationship to that central theme, this is not only way in which the emphasis of individual volumes will be different. Each author has been asked to bring forward what he or she sees as the most important topics explaining the history under study, taking account of the present state of historical knowledge, drawing attention to areas of dispute and to matters on which final judgement is at present difficult (or, perhaps, impossible) and not merely recapitulating what has recently been the fashionable centre of professional debate. But each volume, allowing for its special approach and proportions, must also provide a comprehensive account, in which politics is always likely to be prominent. Volumes have to be demarcated chronologically but continuities must not be obscured; vestigially or not, copyhold survived into the 1920s and the Anglo-Saxon shires until the 1970s (some of which were to be resurrected in the 1990s, too). Any single volume should be an entry-point to the understanding of processes only slowly unfolding, sometimes across centuries. My hope is that in the end we shall have, as the outcome, a set of standard and authoritative histories, embodying the scholarship of a generation, and not mere compendia in which the determinants are lost to sight among the detail.

J. M. ROBERTS

Preface

The approach I have adopted in writing this book is explained in the Introduction. As my work proceeded I became ever more aware of the high quality of the publications of my fellow historians and of my own heavy dependence upon the results of their labours. I have tried to give credit where it is due and hope that I will be forgiven for any unintentional lapses in that respect.

I also have some more specific debts to acknowledge. Without the support of the University of Hull—and more especially, over the years, of colleagues in the Hull History Department—I could never have completed the task. Three other institutions made it possible for me to devote uninterrupted periods to sustained writing and research. The National Humanities Center of Research Triangle Park in North Carolina appointed me a fellow for the academic year 1985–6. Sidney Sussex College, Cambridge, elected me a visiting fellow for the Easter Term 1988. The British Academy awarded me a Research Readership in the Humanities for the years 1994–6. I am deeply grateful to them all.

C. H. Feinstein and W. D. Rubinstein were good enough to answer queries on particular points. Tim Blanning of Cambridge and four colleagues at the University of Hull—Rod Ambler, Howell Lloyd, David Omissi, and Michael E. Turner—read individual chapters in draft to my very great benefit. Michael J. Turner of the University of Reading helped with the Bibliography. The general editor, John Roberts, asked me to write the book and thereafter supplied perfectly calibrated help and encouragement as he reacted to the evolving text. Colin Matthew, with extraordinary kindness, also read the whole work in draft and provided just that combination of criticism and reassurance which nervous authors so badly need. It will be all too obvious that I have sometimes been too stubborn or too imperceptive to take the advice I so often sought and so generously received.

As with everything that I have written since the happy day of our marriage in 1970 this book owes an immeasurable debt to my wife, Alison, whose love, help, and scholarly sympathy have sustained me in bad times and good. The dedication to our three children recognizes their salutary talent for reminding me of the imperatives of a more recent generation than that of the mid-Victorians.

K. T. H.

Contents

PART III   MONEY AND MENTALITIES

PART IV   ENGLAND AND BEYOND

xiv CONTENTS

Plates

Maps

Tables

Acknowledgements to the Illustrations

Plates 1 and 6 are from Hulton Getty.

Plate 2 is from Topham.

Plate 3 is from the Victoria & Albert Picture Library.

Plate 4 is from Manchester City Library, Local Studies Unit.

Plate 5 is from the National Library of Ireland, Dublin (Lawrence Collection, Ref. no. Royal 1367).

Plate 7 is from the Scottish National Portrait Gallery. Photograph by Thomas Annar.

Plate 8 is from Towneley Hall Art Gallery and Museum (Burnley Borough Council), © Bridgeman Art Library.

Maps 1 to 3, and 7, are adapted from E.J. Evans, *The Forging of the Modern State: Early Industrial Britain 1783–1870* (2nd edn., Addison-Wesley Longman Ltd., 1996).

Map 4 is adapted from P. S. Bagwell, *The Transport Revolution from 1770* (Batsford Ltd., 1974); and came originally from H. J. Dyos and D. H. Aldcroft, *British Transport from the Seventeenth Century to the Twentieth* (Leicester University Press, 1969).

Map 5 is adapted from J. Clapham, *An Economic History of Modern Britain: Free Trade and Steel 1850–1886* (Cambridge University Press, 1932).

Map 6 is from B. J. Graham and L. J. Proudfoot (eds.), *An Historical Geography of Ireland* (Academic Press, 1993, based on the map by K. M. Davies in T. W. Moody, F. X. Martin, and F. J. Byrne (eds.), *A New History of Ireland* ix. *Maps, Genealogies, Lists* (Oxford University Press, 1984)).

Map 8 is adapted from J. A. R. Marriott, *England since Waterloo*, 15th edn. (Methuen & Co., 1954).

Map 9 is adapted from J. B. Conacher, *Britain and the Crimea 1855–56: Problems of War and Peace* (Macmillan Ltd., 1987).

Map 10 is from C. C. Eldridge, *Victorian Imperialism* (Hodder & Stoughton, 1978).

Map 11 is from T. O. Lloyd, *The British Empire 1558–1983* (Oxford University Press, 1984).

Introduction

Sir Robert Ensor's fine volume in the first 'Oxford History' series was simply entitled *England 1870–1914*. Though I think it is no longer possible to concentrate as exclusively as Ensor did upon England alone, I have emulated him at least in choosing a plain title. Books deliberately written to delineate past periods as, for example, ages of reform or revolution or reaction, as ages of rising middle classes or collapsing aristocracies, of expansion or contraction, of new regimes or of old, whatever they may gain in invigorating coherence, too often achieve their effects by a species of historical brigandage or (worse still) of historical myopia. An approach appropriate for monographs examining one comparatively self-contained topic imposes an unduly partial influence upon more general works such as this. To designate a whole period under a single word or phrase inevitably makes it necessary to render so many recalcitrant matters invisible—by distortions both subtle and unsubtle—that the resulting landscape can often seem grossly underpopulated, sometimes, indeed, hardly populated at all. C. S. Lewis wrote in 1954 (when the exclusive use of the masculine gender was more common than today) that

Some think it the historian's business ... to grasp in a single intuition the 'spirit' or 'meaning' of his period. With some hesitation, and with much respect for the great men who have thought otherwise, I submit that this is exactly what we must refrain from doing. I cannot convince myself that such 'spirits' or 'meanings' have much more reality than the pictures we see in the fire ... The 'canals' on Mars vanished when we got stronger lenses.[1]

None of this means that the only alternative is that of an extreme empirical nihilism in which the 'facts' are somehow supposed to be able to 'speak for themselves'. In the first place, it should be possible to offer a

[1] C. S. Lewis, *English Literature in the Sixteenth Century excluding Drama* (Oxford, 1954), 63–4.

series of linked interpretations which do as little violence to the essentially
ragged and confused nature of the past as is compatible with understanding
and good sense. In the second, while the whole idea of 'periods' (let alone
their staccato description) may well be a mischievous conception, it is
also—as Lewis himself realized—a methodological necessity. Thus even
the term 'mid-Victorian generation' suggests something more than a mere
slice of time, and might, indeed, be taken to constitute almost a psychological category (though one best applied to different individuals in very
different ways). For the historian, therefore, eternal vigilance is required,
though it is easy to nod off during the dark watches of the interpretative
night (as doubtless I have done more often than I should).

The four decades with which this book deals stretch from the repeal of
the Corn Laws in June 1846 to the defeat of Gladstone's first Home Rule
Bill in June 1886. In political terms it is tempting to see them as marking a
high point of Liberal dominance with the Tories out of office for three years
in every four. But because the Liberal administrations in power during
these years owed so much to Peel's particular kind of Conservatism, it can,
in fact, be highly misleading to denominate the governing political ideologies of the time in simple and straightforward party terms. Again,
confident assertions of Liberal ascendancy can all too easily be coupled
with arguments that see the Great Exhibition of 1851 as an unequivocal
sign of growing confidence regarding the United Kingdom's role as a world
power in economic, political, cultural, and imperial terms. And it is, of
course, true that aristocrats, businessmen, clerks, skilled workers, and
many others too flocked to the Crystal Palace to revel in the modernity of
the age, in its progress, its enlightenment, its expansiveness. Yet the very
same year also witnessed one of nineteenth-century Britain's greatest outbursts of anti-Catholicism, with the Protestant nation—worshippers and
non-worshippers alike—united in a mighty orgy of nervous, worried, and
entirely unconfident outrage against the threats posed by the 5 or 6 per cent
of the British (and perhaps just over 20 per cent of the United Kingdom)
population that could be regarded as adhering in some way or other to the
Church of Rome. And just as the Great Exhibition attracted enthusiasm
from almost all sections of society, so too did the anti-papist outburst of
1850–1, with the Prime Minister, Lord John Russell, leading the fray. Both
of these public manifestations of private feelings were, however, equally
'authentic' as expressions of the manner in which members of the mid-
Victorian generation saw themselves and regarded the world in which they
lived. That, in retrospect, some might think the one pointed to the future
and the other to the past—though even that is far from clear—should not
disguise the historical importance of their close temporal juxtaposition.

This book is, therefore, quite deliberately not constructed around a single overarching thesis. None the less, it has, equally deliberately, been written with three very general themes or contexts in mind. The first might be called the context of 'established industrialism': that at virtually all levels of society men and women increasingly realized that factory life and manufacturing had come to stay (even though factories long remained small and many people continued to earn their living by other means) and that, as Peel put it in 1842, 'we cannot recede'.[2] In one way or another this theme informs a good deal of what follows, though here too there are exceptions—as Chapter 15 on Ireland makes clear.

The second context might be called that of 'multiple national identities': that, beneath the shell of a unitary state, there flourished separate and overlapping national traditions which make it necessary sometimes to speak of England and Wales, Scotland, and Ireland, sometimes of England, Wales, Scotland, and Ireland, sometimes of Britain and Ireland, sometimes of the United Kingdom, sometimes of the British Empire. Not only that, but the ubiquitous use, then and since, of the word 'England' to mean any combination of these terms (not least in the title of the series to which this book belongs) says much about the location of power and wealth in mid-Victorian as in more recent times and about the attitudes which have been engendered thereby. This is not to deny that certain shifts had taken place in the late eighteenth and early nineteenth centuries towards the fashioning of something like a 'British' consciousness,[3] merely to insist that this added to, rather than replaced, a whole series of existing and still developing allegiances of a Scottish, Irish, Welsh, and (by no means least) English kind—and, indeed, of a more restricted and regional kind also. This book is, therefore, not just about England, but about the United Kingdom taken both as a whole and as an aggregation of individual administrative units and national identities.[4]

The third context might be called that of 'interlocking spheres' or the manner in which the public culture of the period (as of almost all periods) was generated, not by a series of influences operating separately, but by

[2] To J. W. Croker, 27 July 1842, C. S. Parker, *Sir Robert Peel from his Private Papers*, 3 vols. (London, 1891–9), ii. 529.

[3] L. Colley, *Britons: Forging the Nation* (New Haven, 1992).

[4] Acts of Union with Wales (1536), Scotland (1707), and Ireland (1800) had created a constitutional situation in which legally and (for most purposes) administratively England and Wales, Scotland, and Ireland were treated as units. Legislatively, however, the Union parliament at Westminster controlled statutory acts. It also contained MPs representing the whole of the United Kingdom on a (roughly) equal basis. Scotland and Ireland (but not Wales) enjoyed an executive status of their own, each dependent upon whatever executive government was able to sustain a majority in the House of Commons.

means of developments resonating reciprocally—and perceived to be so resonating—between the spheres of politics, economics, science, literature, and art. But because these three contexts or themes do not, of course, illuminate or 'explain' everything, I have tried to apply them with a light touch. By the same token, I have written individual chapters on certain major topics, but not on all. In particular, the experiences of mid-Victorian women ranged so widely that I thought it best to discuss them at a number of different points.

The seventeen chapters that follow have been assigned to four larger 'Parts' in an attempt to make the book's overall organization and arguments clearer and more distinct, without, it is hoped, blurring that sense of inter-connectedness so necessary if historical writing is to be credible and inter-esting. The first three chapters in Part I constitute a kind of blueprint of the social architecture of the mid-Victorian United Kingdom. Architecture, of course, tends to presuppose upper and lower levels, basements and pent-houses, but equally its constructs tend to contain staircases and elevators connecting such locations with one another in sometimes unusual and complicated ways. Thus, although mid-Victorian economic distinctions clearly were central to mid-Victorian social distinctions, to rely on econom-ics alone as a determinant of hierarchy and ignore all other links connecting one body of persons with another obscures more than it reveals. While, therefore, the headings I have chosen for these three chapters carry distinct economic overtones, they are not exclusively economic in character or intent. The nature of the 'agrarian interest', for example, was determined more by place, tradition, kinship, and perception than by exclusively economic congruities. In some circumstances farmers and landlords acted together; in others they did not. Agricultural labourers, though clearly workers by hand, were so different from those employed in factories that—despite much justified distrust of their 'superiors'—they, too, often seemed to see themselves, first and foremost, as countrymen and women with all that that implied. In towns things, unsurprisingly, followed differ-ent, though not totally distinct, paths. Neither the middle sort of people nor manual workers formed a single closely integrated and homogeneous social group. Both, however, were more and more obviously beginning to see themselves as members of broad social categories in which common inter-ests could sometimes, though by no means always, overcome the fissipar-ousness characteristic of relationships at the personal and microscopic level. These three chapters attempt, therefore, to set down the broad outlines of a highly complex set of social structures, in particular by addressing such key questions as Who? and How many? (A third question—What did they do?—though more directly discussed in Chapter 10, also receives some preliminary attention in Part I, especially with regard to standards of living and group relationships.) And because the middle sort of people, workers by hand, and the members of the agrarian interest all found themselves living under particular arrangements of government which clearly affected their everyday lives and because these arrangements were, in turn, influenced by the different degrees of power such groups were able to exercise, the fourth and last chapter of Part I examines the nature of the mid-Victorian state: what contemporaries thought it should do and what it actually did.

Part II is devoted to political and closely associated developments during what roughly amounts to the first half of our period, 1846–68. Chapters 5 and 7 consist essentially of political narrative interwoven with discussions of party relationships, political leadership, and imperial and foreign affairs. Because the political and administrative developments of the mid-1850s were so closely (if briefly) marked by two significant military outbreaks, I thought it proper to examine the Crimean War and the Indian Mutiny in some detail in Chapter 6. In a rather different manner, the politics of the mid-1860s also turned much on questions of franchise reform. Chapter 8, therefore, seeks to place the whole matter of reform and the passage of the Reform Acts of 1867–8 both into a parliamentary context and into the broader electoral framework of the time.

The five chapters of Part III deal with fundamental economic, behavioural, and intellectual aspects of mid-Victorian life. Although the findings of economic history have not proved as conclusive as its practitioners might once have hoped, there can be no doubt that many of the most vigorous and important insights into modern British history have come from that source. These insights are, however, not always easy to understand and there is undoubtedly some truth in the jibe that economic historians have too closely followed the exhortation 'If it moves, leave it out'. But difficulties are there to be overcome, and it seemed to me mere cowardice in the face of danger to omit the analysis offered in Chapter 9 of economic developments in the mid-Victorian years. This, then, leads to Chapter 10 which acts—as has already been indicated—as a pendant to Chapters 1 to 3 by examining the life experiences of those who did, indeed, 'move' and often in remarkably vigorous and impressive ways. Not least did an increasing number of mid-Victorians colonize what might broadly be called the field of 'high culture'. This is always a difficult topic to deal with in books of this kind where limitations of space can easily turn any treatment of literature, painting, and the like into little more than breathless lists of the good and the great. In an attempt to avoid this, I have devoted Chapter 11 to an examination of the close relationships which existed in the

Victorian period between art and art producers of all kinds, on the one hand, and hard cash, on the other: How much were they paid? Who earned the most? Did relative rewards change over time? This will, I hope, provide a link between literary and artistic developments and those of a more general—and in this case predominantly financial—kind (without, however, implying that the former should be interpreted only in such terms). But if Mammon always played a large part on the mid-Victorian stage, so too did God. Chapter 12, therefore, explores the denominational land-scapes of the time and tries to shed some light on the people who inhabited them. Closely related to religious beliefs—their rise, decline, rearrange-ment, and impact—was the growing mid-century importance of the natural sciences. In particular, the whole idea of evolution and Darwin's specific contributions to that idea furnished educated mid-Victorians with perhaps the most beguiling of all the analytical tools in their intellectual armoury. Not only did organisms of every kind begin more and more to be seen in evolutionary terms, but so, too, did human and natural history in general. This being the case, it is in Chapters 11 and 13 that the context of 'interlocking spheres' is most obviously and directly addressed.

Part IV, in turn, is substantially, though by no means entirely, devoted to the context of 'multiple national identities'. The experiences of mid-Victorian Scotland and Wales are set side-by-side in Chapter 14 and those of Ireland—the least integrated part of the United Kingdom—are ex-amined in Chapter 15. The last two chapters return to a broadly political narrative, in this case of the years between 1868 and 1886, with Chapter 17 concluding with a discussion of the increasingly intrusive and important question of Irish Home Rule.

Finally, I am well aware that there are matters with which this book does not deal or deals with only in passing. Some have been deliberately omitted because no book can include everything: hard choices have to be made. Some have been deliberately omitted because I was—possibly not often enough—aware of my lack of relevant expertise. In this latter respect, I am especially ashamed of an inability even to begin to be able to engage with the work of Darwin's equal—perhaps more than equal—scientific contem-porary, the physicist, James Clerk Maxwell (1831–79), whose profoundly important advances, above all the creation of the electro-magnetic theory of light, constitute achievements in pre-quantal theoretical physics compar-able only with those of Newton in dynamics and Einstein in relativity. Some matters, however, have doubtless simply been overlooked: *mea culpa*.

PART I

Society and the State

CHAPTER I

The Agrarian Interest

1. AGRICULTURAL UPS AND DOWNS

Mid-Victorians were less dominated by the aristocracy and landed gentry than their forefathers had been. Equally, they were less subject than later generations to dictation from the upper middle-class gladiators of modern capitalism. Instead, they lived at a time when a variety of social and economic interests contended for mastery, sometimes overtly, often not. In this process, not only were all sections of society changed, but—just as important—the way in which each section was perceived by the others changed also. For none was this more true than those who owned the soil, the men (they were mostly men) who had long piped tunes for others to dance to.

Despite some exceptions, most mid-nineteenth-century landed families were becoming quite as Victorian as everyone else. In literary terms, the novels of R. S. Surtees, with their sometimes absurd, almost surrealist, portraiture of landowners old and new, represent a final genuflection to a fading world. Once feelings of real unease had begun to break the surface of events, then their particular kind of extreme and knowing comedy (Surtees was himself a landed gentleman) ceased to be possible. And although in a certain idiosyncratic sense Surtees may well have regarded himself as a kind of 'realist', the notion of what constituted realism was undergoing perceptible change during the quarter-century before his own death in 1864.[1] George Eliot's *Adam Bede* (1859) is typical of this transitional phase during which rural communities tended to be represented, not as pastoral never-never lands, but as active societies engaged in the earning of livelihoods. Not that this invariably obliged contemporary readers to put sentimentalism entirely to one side. Indeed, Queen Victoria commissioned two watercolours by E. H. Corbould based on scenes in *Adam Bede* in which village life is portrayed as unproblematically wholesome, gentle, and—above all—

---

[1] For an interpretation of Surtees as, indeed, a 'very un-Victorian man', see N. Gash, *Robert Surtees and Early Victorian Society* (Oxford, 1993).

clean.[2] Only later, with Thomas Hardy, is the countryside subjected to unmistakably sombre visions, which, however partial and exaggerated, were at last capable of emphasizing the bleaker aspects of rural life with sustained power and effect (and, of course, in a manner especially congenial to modern minds). However, long before this occurred Surtees's bizarre characters had already given way to those of Anthony Trollope—worthy and plainly recognizable, slimy perhaps, but tediously mundane sinners on the whole.

By participating in, indeed, by helping to orchestrate, so signal a metamorphosis, the landed gentry and aristocracy of the United Kingdom not only succeeded in acquiring that most admired of all mid-Victorian virtues, respectability, they also helped to ensure that their own political power would survive (in however diminished a form) for longer than some at least of their enemies might have hoped. The Janus-faced nature of the processes involved in this complicated transformation were strikingly reflected in the character of the most impressive political personality of the age, William Ewart Gladstone. For, just as he was in many respects the great public icon of Victorian middle-class respectability, so Gladstone—though one of the very few prime ministers to die plain 'Mr'—was one of the greatest of all Victorian venerators of hereditary land tenure and of the social system that accompanied it. 'I am', he noted in 1878, 'a firm believer in the aristocratic principle ... I am an out-and-out *inequalitarian*'.[3]

Such attitudes were the more possible because the social and economic arrangements of the nineteenth-century countryside stood apart from those of the towns. It was not so much that the men and women engaged in and dependent upon agriculture belonged to groups innocent of class distinctions, rather that the divisions between landowners, tenant farmers, and landless labourers, although they carried echoes of urban patterning, were in many respects unique.

The repeal of the Corn Laws in 1846 constituted the political and economic grid upon which subsequent agrarian developments were laid out. High fixed duties on grain imports had been imposed in 1815 and replaced by a more moderate sliding scale in 1828 which was itself lowered by Sir Robert Peel in 1842 as part of a move towards greater freedom of trade. Agriculturalists believed that protection was essential to rural prosperity. Peel, on the other hand, thought that high food prices increased the tensions within society and threatened the stability of power relationships.

[2] M. Laski, *George Eliot and her World* (London, 1973), 60–1 (where the paintings are reproduced).
[3] H. C. G. Matthew, *Gladstone 1875–1898* (Oxford, 1995), 356; J. Morley, *The Life of William Ewart Gladstone*, 3 vols. (London, 1903), ii. 582.

This above all motivated his actions, though a belief in free trade as such, a contempt for the red-faced country gentlemen who provided the bulk of his parliamentary following, and the sudden appearance of famine in Ireland all helped to encourage them. The vociferous activities of the Anti-Corn Law League founded in 1839 were important as a model for later middle-class agitations, but had little impact upon the decisions made in cabinet or even in parliament. For Peel the whole business was undertaken to 'fortify the established institutions of this country, to inspire confidence in the equity and benevolence of the Legislature... and to discourage the desire for democratic change'.[4] As in 1832, so in 1846, concessions were offered with the conservative aim of preserving the fabric of traditional authority. But, despite a certain appearance of stasis in the 1850s and early 1860s, as far as the agrarian interest was concerned—indeed as regards the rural world generally—things would never be the same again.

The story of British agriculture in the second half of the nineteenth century was one of relative decline at a time when the industrial and service sectors were assuming a growing importance. This did not necessarily signify 'decline' in any pejorative sense, since the change could well have resulted simply from greater specialization in international trade. Indeed, the value at current prices of agriculture's contribution to national income grew consistently from £76.0m in 1821 to £130.4m in 1871 (and thereafter never dropped below the level of 1841, when it stood at £99.9m). But in proportionate terms there was an equally steady fall, from 26.1 to 8.6 per cent over the seventy years ending in 1891.[5] Although, therefore, the initial dramatic swing towards industrialization had taken place by the beginning of our period, the relative trend away from agriculture was to continue throughout the rest of the century. As regards manpower the process was also pronounced, though somewhat slower. As the population and the overall labour force continued to grow, so those employed in agriculture came to constitute a smaller and smaller proportion of the total. Yet the size of the British agricultural labour force did not reach its absolute peak of some 2.1 million until 1851 when almost twice as many people were still working in fields as in factories or mills. By 1891 numbers had fallen to about 1.6 million, though in percentage terms the reduction was far steeper, from 21.7 to 10.5 per cent of the occupied population as a whole.[6] Thus,

[4] *The Times*, 17 July 1847.
[5] P. Deane and W. A. Cole, *British Economic Growth 1688–1959*, 2nd edn. (Cambridge, 1967), 166. For developments in the century before 1850, see G. E. Mingay (ed.), *The Agrarian History of England and Wales*, vi (Cambridge, 1989). At the time of writing, the volume dealing with 1850–1914 is still awaited.
[6] Deane and Cole, *British Economic Growth*, 142–3.

while in 1851 agriculture was still the single most important British 'industry' from an employment point of view, twenty years later more people were finding work as domestic servants than as workers on the land. By the end of the century, if not a little earlier, countrymen and women had ceased to be the representative figures they had been since time immemorial.

All of this was of course closely related to contemporary shifts in the distribution of people between countryside and town. Although the distinctions involved are necessarily artificial, the best estimates suggest that the 'rural' population in England and Wales (those living outside settlements of more than 2,500 inhabitants) changed as shown in the table. Not only, however, was this rural population shrinking (at first in relative and later also in absolute terms) but the 'countryside' itself was steadily becoming less and less agrarian in character, in the sense that the proportion of its inhabitants directly employed in agriculture fell continuously from 54.2 per cent in 1851 to 45.4 per cent in 1891 and to even lower levels thereafter.[7] Although to some extent this must have been caused by the rise of suburbia beyond civic boundaries, such figures cast doubt upon arguments which suggest that the decline in the number of rural artisans and craftsmen brought about by the economic difficulties of the late Victorian period was so great that eventually little save agriculture was carried on in rural areas. Certainly many mid-century villages boasted an impressive range of occupations—Binbrook in the Lincolnshire wolds had 109 craftsmen among its 1,269 inhabitants in 1851, as well as doctors, solicitors, architects, and surveyors.[8] But trades such as those of the blacksmith, wheelwright,

	000s	% of total population
1801	5,883	66.2
1841	8,211	52.7
1851	8,240	46.0
1861	8,282	41.3
1871	7,910	34.8
1881	7,794	30.0
1891	7,402	25.5

[7] C. M. Law, 'The Growth of Urban Population in England and Wales, 1801–1911', *Transactions of the Institute of British Geographers*, 41 (1967), 125–43; F. D. W. Taylor, 'United Kingdom: Numbers in Agriculture', *Farm Economist*, 8 (1955), 36–40.

[8] F. M. L. Thompson, 'Free Trade and the Land', in G. E. Mingay (ed.), *The Victorian Countryside*, 2 vols. (London, 1981), i. 115; G. E. Mingay, *Rural Life in Victorian England* (London, 1977), 181; P. Horn, *The Rural World 1780–1850* (London, 1980), 226–7.

and saddler continued to flourish as long as horses remained predominant in traction and local transport (that is, until the Great War), while any decline that took place among tailors, shoemakers, and the like was made good by a growth in retailing and by the influx of prosperous people from towns anxious and now able to dwell in rustic surroundings. Indeed, by becoming in this fashion more closely intermingled with the economy as a whole, the agrarian sector in effect disguised its relative decline, delayed recognition of that decline, and ensured that its traditional preoccupations remained more central to national concerns than might otherwise have been the case.

Yet it cannot be denied that the repeal of the Corn Laws signified a defeat for the agricultural interest. While individual landowners remained politically powerful, landowners as a body were no longer able to determine the political agenda as they had done even during the early days of industrialization. Economically, too, the transformations that followed 1846 were to prove real enough. While the so-called golden age of British agriculture between the 1850s and the mid-1870s may have obscured the effects of repeal, the underlying character of agriculture began to undergo deep changes almost at once, in part at least in direct or indirect reaction to free trade operating within a context of changing consumption patterns among the people as a whole. Wheat prices remained relatively stable after 1852 (though stable along a gradually declining curve) only because rising consumption was able to absorb rising imports and because these imports were in any case held in comparative check by high transport costs, lack of full prairie exploitation in North America, and supply crises produced by wars in the Crimea and the United States. But with about half of domestic wheat consumption already being met by imports in 1873–5 as opposed to a quarter just after repeal, the traditional role of wheat cultivation had ceased to be secure.[9] This was not in any case the kind of future that had been envisaged in 1846. Both protectionists like Disraeli and free traders like Bright had predicted an immediate and lasting fall in wheat prices, leading (by the former's analysis) to agricultural ruin and (by the latter's) to cheaper bread. Neither happened. Nor is there any evidence that repeal, by releasing domestic demand, stimulated manufacturing industry or that higher imports produced, through the foreign-trade multiplier, any direct bilateral additional demand for British goods from wheat-supplying countries abroad.

[9] C. Ó Gráda, 'British Agriculture, 1860–1914', in R. Floud and D. McCloskey (eds.), *The Economic History of Britain since 1700*, 2nd edn., 3 vols. (Cambridge, 1994), 166–70; J. Clapham, *An Economic History of Modern Britain*, 3 vols. (Cambridge, 1930–8), ii. 3; W. Ashworth, *An Economic History of England 1870–1939* (London, 1960), 54.

The major agricultural consequence of repeal was that an existing price swing away from grain and towards animal products was sustained. Increasing prosperity led to a growing demand for proteins at the expense of cheaper starches such as bread. As a result, the prices of meat, butter, cheese, milk, and the like rose faster than those of grain in general and wheat in particular. Farmers began to move decisively away from 'corn' and towards 'horn', Between 1846/50 and 1876/80 (when overall prices went up by about 7 per cent) prime beef and mutton recorded increases of 49 and 37 per cent respectively, but English wheat a fall of 8 per cent.[10] Within the mixed farming system common in the 'arable' areas of the east and south of England more and more emphasis was placed on livestock (which could utilize the fodder produced by four-crop rotation and which also provided dung). Indeed, the prosperity of the golden age was built upon the twin pillars of rising animal prices and expanding wheat yields. With the pasture areas of the north and west being maintained and even extended, the overall result was a shift away from wheat. Because reliable British agricultural statistics only began to be collected in the late 1860s, the immediacy of these changes is difficult to demonstrate. Ireland, however, led the field in statistical matters and there the early appearance of the process is both obvious and unambiguous (Table 1.1).

TABLE 1.1 *Index of grain acreage and cattle numbers in Britain and Ireland, 1849–1893* (Ireland, 1849–51 = 100; Britain, 1867–9 = 100)

	Wheat acreage	All grain acreage	Cattle numbers
Ireland			
1855–7	82	85	128
1861–3	57	81	114
1867–9	46	69	128
1873–5	29	61	143
1885–7	12	50	145
1891–3	12	48	155
Britain			
1873–5	98	100	115
1885–7	66	87	125
1891–3	60	82	130

Source: Based on material in B. R. Mitchell, *British Historical Statistics* (Cambridge, 1988), 186–206.

[10] A. Sauerbeck, 'Prices of Commodities and the Precious Metals', *Journal of the Statistical Society*, 49 (1886), 642–3.

By the 1890s the animal sector had, indeed, come to supply the clear preponderance of gross farm output in England at current prices: 63.1 per cent for 1894–8 as opposed to 49.6 per cent for 1867–71.[11]

Without Corn Law repeal certain branches of agriculture would have suffered more seriously than they did from the depression which began to intensify during the late 1870s as expanding grain imports pushed down prices at the very time when a series of bad harvests drastically reduced domestic output. Livestock producers, for example, were able to benefit from cheaper feed and to do comparatively well in an environment of generally falling prices throughout the economy as a whole. Some other farmers too proved adept in making the most of changed circumstances, either by moving into milk which was free from foreign competition or by extreme caution over the supposed benefits of mechanization. Those who had invested most heavily in capital-intensive arable farming did, however, suffer grievously, and many went to the wall to be replaced by less grandiosely ambitious operators (often from Scotland) who knew how to farm light and to skim the soil without too much risk to its essential qualities. What was new was the persistence of bad times after the mid-1870s, though as always different parts of the country were affected very differently. Indeed, behind the immediately visible and much-reported gloom the overall level of farm output at constant factor cost held up remarkably well, while output per head (given the shrinking agrarian population) actually recorded a modest rise.[12] Even so, an average annual productivity growth rate of 0.4 per cent between the 1860s and the 1910s, though very like that of 1700–1850, compared badly with those achieved by agrarian sectors in other countries such as the United States and Japan.[13]

2. RURAL SOCIETY

Such briefly was the economic context of the agricultural interest, a context heavily influenced by the abolition of protection in 1846. At the apex of that interest stood the landlords. Radical criticisms and tendentious census returns (which in 1861 purported to show that there were 30,766 'landed proprietors' in England and Wales, over half of them, supposedly, women) persuaded the government to mount an official investigation eventually

[11] T. W. Fletcher, 'The Great Depression of English Agriculture 1873–1896', *Economic History Review*, 13 (1961), 432.
[12] A. Howkins, *Reshaping Rural England: A Social History 1850–1925* (London, 1991), 150; C. H. Feinstein, *National Income, Expenditure and Output of the United Kingdom 1855–1965* (Cambridge, 1972), T118.
[13] Ó Gráda, 'British Agriculture', 148–9.

published in 1873 and generally known as the 'New Domesday Book'. To
the delight of some and the annoyance of others this showed that land was
concentrated in remarkably few hands. Certainly no other rural élite in
nineteenth-century Europe owned so large a part of their nation's soil.
What is less clear is whether (as some claimed) there had been a trend
towards increased concentration during the previous hundred years or
whether things had more or less remained the same. Plain enough, however, were facts such as these: (a) that more than two-fifths of the land in
England and Wales belonged to less than 1,700 persons while about 4,200
with more than 1,000 acres each owned well over half, (b) that in England
363 individuals owned over 10,000 acres each and almost a quarter of all the
land, (c) that more than four-fifths of the surface of the United Kingdom
belonged to some 7,000 proprietors.[14] Broad indeed may have been the
acres, but few were the gentlemen and ladies to whom they belonged.

Below them the NCOs and the privates of the agrarian army consisted,
respectively, of farmers and labourers, with the former, if sufficiently
successful, occasionally allowed to enter (though not to join) the lower
end of the officers' mess. By 1831 there were approximately one million
adult males engaged in English agriculture, with about 5.5 labourers for
every farmer who gave employment.[15] The remarkable stability in the
number of farmers—there were 249,000 in England and Wales in 1851
and 229,000 sixty years later—suggests that it was above all the system of
land tenure that helped to determine the size of farms. The dramatic fall in
the agrarian population after the middle of the century was entirely brought
about by a loss of hired hands. Their number in England and Wales shrank
from 1,268,000 in 1851 to 650,000 in 1901, with the result that farmers
became more and more prominent demographically as the ratio of workers
to farmers declined: 5.1:1 (1851), 4.0:1 (1871), 3.6:1 (1891), 2.9:1 (1901). In
Scotland (and in Wales taken alone) the trend was much the same, while in
Ireland the Great Famine of 1845–9 so reduced the army of landless
workers that there too the relative numerical and cultural importance of
the farmer community was substantially enhanced.[16]

[14] F. M. L. Thompson, *English Landed Society in the Nineteenth Century* (London, 1963),
25–44, 109–50; J. Bateman, *The Great Landowners of Great Britain and Ireland*, 4th edn.
(London, 1883; repr. Leicester, 1971).
  [15] E. A. Wrigley, 'Men on the Land and Men in the Countryside', in L. Bonfield, R. M.
Smith, and K. Wrightson (eds.), *The World we have Gained* (Oxford, 1986), 305.
  [16] Taylor, 'Numbers in Agriculture', 36–40 ('farmers' relatives' and 'others' excluded).
The addition of (mainly female) relatives and the like greatly increases numbers (E. Higgs,
'Occupational Censuses and the Agricultural Workforce in Victorian England and Wales',
Economic History Review, 48 (1995), 700–16).

Not that farmers as a group were economically or socially homogeneous. The line between men with little land, on the one side, and those with fifty acres or more, on the other, was clear enough. Above it, styles of life became steadily more comfortable until the wealthiest could afford to live like minor landed gentlemen. By continental standards English farms were large, though the trend towards enlargement came to an end in the 1860s. There were, however, wide regional variations, with farms in pastoral Lancashire and Cheshire much smaller than in arable Suffolk or Essex. What official statistics for England and Wales first revealed in 1851 was that, although most farmers were men of comparatively modest degree, the land as such was dominated by those who worked on an extensive scale. This was confirmed by more accurate data in 1885 which showed that, of 338,715 holdings above five acres in size, the 83,632 above 100 acres encompassed 71 per cent of all cultivated soil. And, because the very largest operators were few in number—only 573 occupied more than 1,000 acres— it was precisely those with 'intermediate' holdings who now formed a dominant economic core.[17] Yet even within a single county the nature and income of the 'typical' farmer could vary dramatically from one district to another. While, therefore, in Lincolnshire as a whole the 'average' mid-century farmer was a man with about 120 acres of poorly drained clay soil, employing perhaps three or four workers, attending market once a week in his chimney-pot hat, and living in tolerable but plain comfort, in the Fens and the Marsh and in the Isle of Axholme ten-acre holdings were the norm and the families of many smallholders lived rough, hard, poverty-infested lives.[18]

The great majority of farmers were tenants standing in a direct financial relationship with the owners of the soil. Most held by annual agreements, the declining use of leases (something which urban radicals complained much about) being widely accepted because, when times were hard, leases made it difficult to obtain rent reductions or to escape quickly from complete financial collapse. By the end of Victoria's reign the proportion of land held by owner occupiers amounted to less than an eighth, some of it in the form of landlords' home farms, untenanted land, or parsons' glebes. Owner farmers—or yeomen as they were often called—were in any case heavily concentrated in areas such as Cumberland, Westmorland, and parts

[17] Clapham, *Economic History*, ii. 264–5; *Agricultural Returns of Great Britain*, H[ouse of] C[ommons Paper] 1870 [C 223], lxviii. 363–438; *Agricultural Returns of Great Britain*, HC 1886 [C 4847], lxx. 1–236; D. Grigg, 'Farm Size in England and Wales, from Early Victorian Times to the Present', *Agricultural History Review*, 35 (1987), 179–89.

[18] R. J. Olney, *Rural Society and County Government in Nineteenth-Century Lincolnshire* (Lincoln, 1979), 54–5.

of Lincolnshire. Mortgage rather than rentpayers, they found life especially
hard during the difficult years after 1875.

In political terms farmers constituted the key group within rural county
constituencies. In mid-century Lincolnshire, for example, though only a
tenth of the population, they supplied half the electorate because, in so
prosperous a county, enfranchisement began with holdings as small as
thirty acres in the period 1832–67 and five acres thereafter. County politics
were, as a result, predominantly farmer politics revolving around protection, local taxation, the malt tax, and similar matters.[19] Although those with
small farms relied exclusively on family assistance, and at the lower levels
were sometimes (notably in Scotland, Ireland, and Wales) barely distinguishable from regularly employed labourers, the rest occupied a distinctive and middling position within rural society. And where landowners were
thin on the ground, the more prosperous tenants did duty as leaders of
opinion and local society, having, in some cases, been able to accumulate
considerable fortunes, take up shooting, build comfortable houses, and
educate their children at tolerable schools. Unlike the gentry, however,
they tended to divide their property at death among all their children and to
maintain political and cultural perspectives in which wider horizons
counted for little. Above all, they stood apart from the bulk of the urban
middle classes in their very different notion of capital and of the entrepreneurial ideal, in their protectionist Conservatism, and in their deep distrust
of city life.

For their part, agricultural labourers—the countryside's working class—
were comparatively slow to emerge as a coherent social group and retained
longer than landlords and farmers a lingering sense of being involved in
some kind of comprehensive rural community. Eventually, however, the
increasing impact of the market and the decline of much of the casual
paternalism of former times brought such misunderstandings to an end.
In many areas their circumstances were no better than those of slum
dwellers in the towns, as James Caird found when visiting Northumberland
in 1850.

Wretched houses piled here and there without order—filth of every kind scattered
about or heaped up against the walls—horses, cows and pigs lodged under the
same roof with their owners, and entering by the same door—in many cases a
pigsty beneath the only window of the dwellings—300 people, 60 horses and 50
cows, besides hosts of pigs and poultry—such is the village of Wark.[20]

    [19] R. J. Olney, *Lincolnshire Politics 1832–1885* (Oxford, 1973), 78, 82, 243; id., *Rural
Society*, 149.
    [20] Mingay, *Rural Life*, 92.

Living conditions depended, however, not only upon the rewards provided by farmers but also on whether labourers lived in 'closed' villages dominated by one or two powerful proprietors or in 'open' villages where property was more widely distributed. Dwellings in the former were generally superior, but their availability was strictly limited by landlords as anxious to keep their rate bills down as to make their cottagers conform to deferential social disciplines of a generally rebarbative kind. Open settlements, on the other hand, though often overcrowded and dirty, allowed greater social, political, and religious freedoms. Although the distinctions between the two were not always as clear as this, they were widely recognized by contemporaries as real and significant. Different parts of the country sustained different patterns, with open villages commoner in the north-west and south-west than in the central districts, though even adjacent counties like Leicestershire (with more than half its townships open) and Lincolnshire (with only a third) could vary substantially.[21] A notable sign of the 'modernization' of rural society and its increasing dependence upon the cash nexus was the decline in the number of so-called indoor farm servants, especially in England. These lodged and often ate with the farmer, obtained regular work and substantial fringe benefits, and tended, therefore, to enjoy some sense of affinity with their employers. They were commonly unmarried—many were female—and were most frequently to be found in Scotland and in counties like North Yorkshire. But in a period of only ten years after 1851 their presence among agricultural workers in England and Wales fell from almost a quarter to barely a sixth. Thereafter it declined further still.[22]

Between 1851 and 1891—when the overall population of England and Wales rose by more than three-fifths—the number of agricultural labourers fell by almost two-fifths, not primarily because of the introduction of mechanized farming, but because urban employment became more attractive. Something approaching a labour shortage ensued, with the result that wages rose. And although national data disguise a host of regional variations, it is possible to indicate the orders of magnitude involved by means of indices of both 'money' earnings (including quantifiable non-cash benefits) and real earnings adjusted for the cost of living (Table 1.2).

Following the bad experiences of labourers during the decades immediately after 1815, the second half of the century witnessed undoubted improvements. The violent discontents of the 'Swing' riots of 1830–1

[21] D. R. Mills, *Lord and Peasant in Nineteenth-Century Britain* (London, 1980), 77, 117; J. Obelkevich, *Religion and Rural Society: South Lindsey 1825–1875* (Oxford, 1976), 12–13.
[22] Horn, *Rural World*, 244.

TABLE 1.2 Indices of earnings and real earnings of agricultural labourers
in England and Wales, 1840–1889 (1830–4 = 100)

	Earnings	Real earnings
1840–9	99	99
1850–9	107	105
1860–9	116	109
1870–9	143	139
1880–9	123	139

Source: Based on A. L. Bowley's index in B. R. Mitchell, *British Historical Statistics* (Cambridge, 1988), 157–8, adjusted (for real earnings) by the Rousseaux price index (ibid. 722–3).

eventually gave way in England to formal rural trade unionism and this in turn confirmed the simultaneous growth among labourers of greater group cohesion and of rising expectations. The processes involved in this transformation were, however, neither linear nor unambiguous. Rural crime did not, for example, suddenly disappear after 1831. Indeed, it reached its highest peak in the British countryside as a whole in the 1840s, remained at a high level until the early 1850s, and thereafter still experienced occasional sharp rises as in the late 1860s and early 1880s. Not only that, but crimes of violence (which formed between a tenth and a fifth of rural offences) continued to worry the authorities more or less persistently until the mid-1860s and from time to time in later years also.[23] The people most often targeted were farmers, land agents, gamekeepers, Poor Law officials, and policemen (landlords were too well protected). This was true of all parts of the United Kingdom. In Ireland, for example, though rural violence undoubtedly declined during the quarter-century after the Great Famine (only to rise again during the Land War of 1879–82), it neither vanished nor ceased to be primarily an expression of the tensions which had long existed between men with access to land (farmers) and those with nothing to offer but their sweat and their strength (labourers).[24] In East Anglia, too, the long local tradition of incendiarism—of setting a torch to the property of unpopular and exploitative farmers and landowners—continued well into the 1860s, with eight fires taking place in November 1870 alone, all of them in villages notorious for unrest and burnings for half a century and more.[25] And it is of course highly probable that some at least

[23] D. Jones, 'Rural Crime and Protest', in Mingay (ed.), *Victorian Countryside*, ii. 571.

[24] K. T. Hoppen, *Elections, Politics, and Society in Ireland 1832–1885* (Oxford, 1984), 341–435 (though W. E. Vaughan takes a somewhat more sanguine view of rural violence in mid-century Ireland in *Landlords and Tenants in Mid-Victorian Ireland* (Oxford, 1994), 138–76).

[25] J. E. Archer, *By a Flash and a Scare: Incendiarism, Animal Maiming and Poaching in East Anglia 1815–1870* (Oxford, 1990), 119–25.

of the decline in crime after about 1850 had as much to do with better policing as with improvements in the relationships within rural society as a whole.

Certainly Joseph Arch's National Agricultural Labourers' Union and the various independent unions that sprang up during the prosperous years of the early 1870s still found much combustible material upon which to work. But while their activities helped to give collective vent to a good deal of pent-up rage—'England was a happy England when there was not a farmer in the land'—they achieved little in terms of hard cash save in the shortest of runs. None the less, their success in attracting, however fleetingly, the support of so many agricultural labourers (possibly 115,000 in England and Wales alone or an eighth of the male labour force) unquestionably helped to bring about gradual but significant changes in the outlook and behaviour of those who worked upon the land.[26]

In absolute terms the farm workers' lot remained miserable. When the Earl of Yarborough died in 1875, his stock of cigars was sold for £850—or more than eighteen years' income for the agricultural labourers who lived on or near his estate. As late as 1892 regional wage levels ranged from as low as 14s. 9d. to no more than 19s. 2d. a week. Indeed, the whole of the cash increase gained by English labourers between the mid-1820s and 1898 came to the great sum of 5s. a week for those fully employed.[27] Although housing improved and men's work became more regular, hours remained long and women and children found it harder to earn money than before. Average real incomes never rose much above half those in industry throughout our period and farm labourers received a much lower proportion of the wealth they helped to create than ever their urban counterparts did.[28]

Yet the reality of relative improvement cannot be doubted. While during the 1850s and early 1860s British farmers' incomes rose in percentage terms more than those of landlords and labourers, thereafter it was the labourers who recorded the largest proportional increase, though of course, in their case, starting from very low levels and almost entirely the result of continuing large reductions in the total number of those employed. Proprietors were the clearest losers on the agricultural merry-go-round of late Victorian

[26] J. P. D. Dunbabin, *Rural Discontent in Nineteenth-Century Britain* (London, 1974), 75–6, 249; G. R. Boyer and T. J. Hatton, 'Did Joseph Arch raise Agricultural Wages?', *Economic History Review*, 47 (1994), 310–34.

[27] A. Armstrong, *Farmworkers: A Social and Economic History 1770–1980* (London, 1988), 133; C. S. Orwin and B. I. Felton, 'A Century of Wages and Earnings in Agriculture', *Journal of the Royal Agricultural Society of England*, 92 (1931), 231–57.

[28] J. R. Bellerby, 'Distribution of Farm Income in the United Kingdom, 1867–1938', in W. E. Minchinton (ed.), *Essays in Agrarian History*, 2 vols. (Newton Abbot, 1968), ii. 271; W. A. Armstrong, 'The Workforce', in Mingay (ed.), *Victorian Countryside*, ii. 505.

times, most of the (25 per cent or so) rent rise in England and Wales between the middle of the century and the onset of the depression being simply 'bought' by landlords spending unrealistic amounts on fencing, new buildings, and other improvements. Even in the prosperous mid-century decades arable land yielded no more than 2 to 3 per cent a year or about half that available in banking, commerce, and industry. Prestige clearly counted for more than the maximization of returns.[29] Rents reached their peak in the mid-1870s. By 1894–6 they had fallen back by 29 per cent on the levels of 1873–5.[30] While landlords, therefore, had made substantial permanent gains during the French Revolutionary Wars, increases after 1850 proved transient. As always, national statistics disguise local variations, especially after 1875 when rents in arable areas fell substantially while those in live-stock and dairying districts either declined less or not at all. Although landlords too benefited from the deflation of the late nineteenth century, in the sense that they could obtain more for each pound spent, theirs was relatively an unhappy experience, made worse by a decrease in land prices and a shortage of buyers. Land values as measured in years' purchase (that is, the number of years' rent needed to equal the purchase price of an estate) moved roughly from about 25 in the 1830s and 1840s to 35–40 in the late 1860s and then down to 20–5 by the end of the century. Thus, while in 1870 an estate yielding an annual gross rental of £1,000 might have sold for about £40,000, by 1900 the price had virtually halved. Yet, partly by choice and partly because farmers, in turn, found it difficult to raise the mortgages required for purchasing land, most owners managed to hold on to their properties. Mansions and moors were let to businessmen with rustic tastes, but really big sales did not become widespread until just before the out-break of the Great War.[31]

As their investment behaviour shows, British landlords were not in general 'economic' men. Farmers have greater claims to that distinction. In 1881 the Earl of Derby listed the five 'objects which men aim at when they become possessed of land': political influence, social importance, power over tenantry, residential enjoyment, and, very much last, 'the money return—

---

[29] Thompson, *English Landed Society*, 247–55. Some drainage schemes, however, gave reasonable returns, especially on large estates (A. D. M. Phillips, *The Underdraining of Farmland in England during the Nineteenth Century* (Cambridge, 1989), 206–46).

[30] R. J. Thompson, 'An Inquiry into the Rent of Agricultural Land in England and Wales during the Nineteenth Century', *Journal of the Royal Statistical Society*, 70 (1907), 592–5; H. A. Rhee, *The Rent of Agricultural Land in England and Wales 1870–1943* (1949), 37 ff.

[31] F. M. L. Thompson, 'The Land Market in the Nineteenth Century', *Oxford Economic Papers*, NS 9 (1957), 294; id., 'Free Trade and the Land', i. 115; J. Habakkuk, *Marriage, Debt, and the Estates System: English Landownership 1650–1950* (Oxford, 1994), 662–70.

the rent'.[32] 'Land', as Trollope had Archdeacon Grantly say, 'gives so much more than rent. It gives position and influence and political power, to say nothing of the game.' But much depended on the amount and value of the land owned, while outlook, temperament, and behaviour also helped render complicated and distinct the members of a group who, seen from afar, could present a picture of misleading uniformity.

Thus the marginal and mortgaged landlord limping along on a gross income of £1,000 a year inhabited a physical and psychological universe light years away from that illuminated by the Duke of Westminster whose balances increased by £1,000 a day.[33] And even if proprietors resembled one another by the mere fact of owning land and by a common (but by no means universal) interest in country pursuits, the differences between them could be as great as the similarities. As the reformer, Bernard Cracroft, put it in 1867,

A and B are cousins, landowners, county Members. Both are Etonians, both Oxonians, both Guardsmen, both have married daughters of peers. But one is a member of the Carlton [i.e. a Tory], the other of Brooks's [i.e. a Whig]. One is a Protectionist, the other a Freetrader. One hugs primogeniture, the other thinks it better that land should be as saleable as a watch. One is an enthusiastic defender of the Protestant faith in Ireland, the other thinks that the Irish Church would be best swept off the face of the earth.[34]

Given that this was so, it is possible to slice up landed society in a multitude of kaleidoscopic ways. There were untitled squires who did almost nothing but hunt, some of them poor, some of them as rich as any earl. There were extravagant spenders who went down to ruin and insolvency. But there were also those who, like the 6th Baron Monson, scraped and saved to rescue their estates from bankruptcy and hand on an inheritance to their sons, who invested almost nothing in improvements, lived cheaply far away from their properties, and squeezed their tenants until the pips squeaked. And while Monson, for example, was a hater of parsons—indeed of organized religion generally—his close Lincolnshire neighbour, Sir Charles Anderson, was a High Churchman, an attender to local business of every kind, an improver, a resident landlord, and a passionate hunter of foxes and slayer of birds. Yet, Monson and Anderson also shared certain outlooks and traditions which, in turn, separated them from other landed proprietors. Because both, for example, belonged to families that

[32] 'Ireland and the Land Act', *Nineteenth Century*, 10 (1881), 474.
[33] D. Cannadine, *The Decline and Fall of the British Aristocracy* (New Haven, 1990), 22.
[34] B. Cracroft, 'The Analysis of the House of Commons, or Indirect Representation', in *Essays on Reform* [ed. A. O. Rutson] (London, 1867), 168-9.

had once been richer and more prominent, their great consciousness of rank and social position—as well as a joint interest in antiquarianism—sprang, to a large extent, from a touchy awareness of straitened circumstances. Both, as a result, distrusted 'new' money and made their distrust obvious to all.[35]

Not only, however, did family and personal habits generate a widely divergent range of attitudes and behaviour, but the very patterning of landownership itself varied substantially between regions and even within individual counties. Thus, while half the land in Northumberland was held within estates of 10,000 acres and more, in Essex the proportion was less than a tenth. Equally diverse was the distribution of substantial country houses, their density ranging from 1 to 31,000 acres in Rutland to 1 to 449,000 acres in Westmorland.[36] Again, though many men possessed properties in Ireland, Scotland, or Wales as well as in England, the circumstances of landownership were far from uniform throughout the United Kingdom as a whole. Some Scottish estates covered enormous tracts of desolate land, the Duke of Sutherland owning 1,176,459 acres—or not far short of 2,000 square miles—in the county from which he took his title. In Ireland, where most landlords were Protestants and most tenants Catholics, tenurial relationships were often so tense, not to say violent, that the notion of a comparatively comprehensive and stable agrarian interest remained almost entirely a fictional one. And while landlords in England enjoyed a tolerably favourable image throughout most of the nineteenth century, those in Ireland (sometimes of course precisely the same men) were frequently pilloried as nothing more than bloodsucking exploiters of the poor. Indeed, it was symptomatic of the low esteem in which Irish proprietors had come to be held that during and immediately after the Great Famine there was much excited, if entirely unrealistic, talk to the effect that they alone should be made to bear the cost of relieving Irish hunger and distress.[37] Not only, therefore, did the agrarian interest of mid-Victorian times consist of broadly distinct groups such as landowners, farmers, and labourers, but each of these groups was itself composed of diverse individuals who, though held together by an affinity to land, differed greatly in numerous other respects.

What, perhaps more than anything else, drove proprietors of old lineage like Monson and Anderson into bouts of apoplectic rage was the belief—

[35] Olney, *Rural Society*, 22–45.
[36] Thompson, *English Landed Society*, 30–2.
[37] J. S. Donnelly, jun., ' "Irish Property Must Pay for Irish Poverty": British Public Opinion and the Great Irish Famine', in C. Morash and R. Hayes (ed.), *'Fearful Realities': New Perspectives on the Famine* (Dublin, 1996), 60–76.

based more on apprehension than fact—that hordes of rich parvenus were throwing money about in an attempt to buy their way into local 'society'. In reality, the British system of primogeniture and strict settlement[38] meant that estates tended to pass intact between generations and that it was difficult for large numbers of outsiders to enter the landed class. Of course there had long been some interchange between the worlds of landowner-ship and of banking, commerce, trading, and professional life. But the view that the British landed class was especially open to fresh blood from below is in need of some qualification.[39] If anything, things became more exclu-sive during the half-century after Waterloo. Fewer fortunes were to be made in the law, strict settlement strengthened its grip, land prices made purchase an ever more expensive undertaking. At the very top, the peerage remained closed to manufacturers until 1885. Such direct contacts as did exist were based either on the downward drift of younger sons into the politer reaches of commercial life—though the church, the armed forces, and the civil and colonial services provided more congenial prospects—or on some form of involvement in mineral exploitation and urban develop-ment. But though minerals and town property were financially important to the landed super-rich (in the 1870s eighteen of the forty-odd families with gross valuations of £60,000 or more derived their chief revenues from such sources), they counted for much less among the generality of owners with more typical incomes.[40] In any case, even the commercial investments of the great, like those of the Duke of Devonshire at Barrow-in-Furness or Lord Bute in the Cardiff Docks, often proved unwise, being driven, as often as not, by that same search for prestige and popularity which induced other proprietors to join the costly agricultural improvement frenzy of the 1850s and 1860s. The fact that families like the Derbys, the Ramsdens, the Seftons, the Norfolks, the Fitzwilliams, the Bedfords, and the Westmin-sters owned large parts of Liverpool, Huddersfield, Sheffield, and London in no way diminished their essential 'landedness'. Even Lord Cranborne,

[38] A general term used to describe legal and customary procedures designed to prevent the alienation of land outside families by turning each successive landowner into a 'life tenant' precluded from selling all or part of the land and required to pass it on intact to the next heir.

[39] W. D. Rubinstein, 'New Men of Wealth and the Purchase of Land in Nineteenth-Century Britain', *Past & Present*, 92 (1981), 125–47; F. M. L. Thompson, 'Life after Death: How Successful Nineteenth-Century Businessmen Disposed of their Fortunes', *Economic History Review*, 43 (1990), 40–61; W. D. Rubinstein, 'Cutting up Rich: A Reply to F. M. L. Thompson', ibid. 45 (1992), 350–61; F. M. L. Thompson, 'Stitching it Together Again', ibid. 362–75.

[40] D. Cannadine, 'The Landowner as Millionaire: The Finances of the Dukes of Devonshire, c.1800–c.1926', *Agricultural History Review*, 25 (1977), 92.

who in 1866–7 impartially denounced Gladstone and Disraeli for weakening the agrarian interest, showed no objections to becoming a fully paid-up member of the urban property club on succeeding his father as Marquess of Salisbury in 1868.

Such comparative exclusiveness rendered the proprietorial class, whatever its differences, numerically small. All the more remarkable, therefore, was the comparative (though diminishing) success with which landowners kept their hands on the tillers of local and national affairs. In this respect there was a clear distinction between the lesser gentry, whose social and political influence was confined to their own neighbourhoods, and wealthier men with wider concerns. In most counties only estates of 3,000 acres of decent land guaranteed significant local standing, with 10,000 acres being required for 'automatic pre-eminence'.[41] Locally the magistrates' bench (which exercised administrative as well as judicial authority) was the prime platform for landed solidarity and upon it the gentry and their allies maintained a strong grip well into the 1880s and beyond. By contrast, the parliamentary seats still controlled by patrons—some sixty-two in England and Wales as late as 1868 and rather more in the 1840s—were almost exclusively in the hands of larger magnates, though even in such places truly unpopular candidates could not simply be forced down the county voters' throats.[42] In the Commons of 1865 there were 326 more or less 'aristocratic' MPs and another 120 who belonged 'substantially . . . to the same class'. More than two-thirds of the members shared, therefore, a 'common freemasonry of blood, a common education, common pursuits, common ideas, a common dialect, a common religion, and—what more than any other thing binds men together—a common prestige'.[43] Indeed, since the Reform Acts of 1832 the proportion of MPs who were bankers, merchants, and manufacturers had hardly changed, remaining steady at a little over a fifth. And even when landed numbers did eventually begin to decline, landed men continued to form the most significant and stable element within the Conservative-Unionist alignment and to dominate all cabinets until 1905, perhaps even until 1919.[44] More tenaciously still did they maintain a grip upon the outlying citadels of power, as ambassadors and viceroys, generals and admirals, as bishops, as key members of the Civil Service. Not, however, that closeness of kinship necessarily entailed either

[41] Olney, *Rural Society*, 22–3, 27.
[42] H. J. Hanham, *Elections and Party Management: Politics in the Time of Disraeli and Gladstone* (London, 1959), 412; N. Gash, *Politics in the Age of Peel: A Study in the Technique of Parliamentary Representation 1830–1850* (London, 1953), 438–9.
[43] Cracroft, 'Analysis of the House of Commons', 160, 171–2.
[44] Cannadine, *Decline and Fall*, 207, 711.

political harmony or party collaboration, unity being reserved for the hunting field and the magistrates' bench. Individual families were split over Corn Law repeal in the 1840s as they had been before and were to be thereafter. Several late nineteenth-century politicians like Harcourt, Campbell-Bannerman, and Edward Stanhope all had brothers on the opposite side of the Commons. But though both major parties received considerable landed support, the club affiliations of those with British estates worth at least £5,000 a year indicate that in 1880—that is, before the Home Rule split—less than one out of every three such men still thought of themselves as Liberals.[45]

Yet despite their comparative success in holding on to the sweets of office, landed proprietors in general encountered deep-seated problems of various kinds long before the onset of agricultural depression in the 1870s, though a mortgaged Indian summer in the 1850s for a time persuaded many of them that all was for the best in the best of all possible worlds. That the political rhythms of mid-Victorian county constituencies still responded to landed influence now depended more upon the unthinking and transient survival of old habits than upon the tangible reality of power relationships and common identities. The enormous differences in wealth, outlook, status, and temperament long characteristic of the proprietorial class were beginning to exercise an increasingly splintering impact upon the political effectiveness of the class as a whole. Though some landowners remained electorally active, many simply gave up the fight. And even those who continued to exert themselves began to find that traditional conventions of deference were no longer sufficient by themselves to secure political con-formity.[46] In large measure this was because English tenant farmers (the situation in Scotland and Wales was rather, in Ireland very, different) had always tended to vote more in a broadly geographical and communal than in a merely tenurial context. They voted, in other words, primarily for a local interest rather than simply for a particular proprietor.[47] The repeal of the Corn Laws, by removing the foundations upon which this state of things had chiefly become based, set in train the gradual erosion of those landlord–tenant congruities which only local interest had been able to generate and sustain.[48] In this sense 1846 marks the crucial 'point of no return', the sentence of death ready to be carried into execution when next agri-culture experienced difficult times.[49] But already well before the late 1870s and the 1880s the deployment of those forms of paternalism upon which

---

[45] Hoppen, *Elections*, 127.   [46] Olney, *Lincolnshire Politics*, 48.   [47] Ibid. 44–5.
[48] D. C. Moore, 'The Gentry', in Mingay (ed.), *Victorian Countryside*, ii. 392.
[49] Thompson, *English Landed Society*, 272.

political influence depended far more than upon naked coercion was becoming increasingly patchy in nature and extent, as also was proprietorial involvement in the duties of rural administration and local government generally.[50] Landed control over borough constituencies had suffered a severe blow in 1832, landed influence in county constituencies began to erode after 1846.[51] Electoral managers, once able to forecast the outcome of county elections with informed precision, from the 1850s onwards found themselves all at sea, as farmers no longer responded predictably to the political imperatives of those who owned the land.[52]

This does not mean that the political community of rural England fell to pieces immediately on—or very soon after—the repeal of the Corn Laws in 1846. Indeed, even in Ireland landlords succeeded in orchestrating a good deal of electoral success in the decade or so following the Great Famine.[53] What, however, it does mean is that landlord power was becoming a fading asset, occasional displays of firework effectiveness notwithstanding. If, therefore, the day of economic reckoning did not finally arrive until the mid-1870s and that of electoral reckoning not until the reforms of 1884–5, proprietorial overdrafts had been accumulating on both accounts for thirty years and more.

As the cohesion of the agrarian interest was slowly unravelling two things helped to keep a select number of landed men close to the centre of political influence. The first was a willingness to whistle at least a selection of the tunes favoured by the middle classes of the towns. The second was money, for, well into the second half of the century, landowners predominated among the ranks of Britain's really wealthy men. Indeed, until 1880 they constituted the great majority of those leaving half a million pounds or more at death and even between then and the end of the century they constituted well over two-fifths.[54]

After 1846 the main thrust of radical attack on the wealth and influence of rural landowners took the form of land reform movements through which it was hoped to reduce proprietorial power, give increased rights to tenants, and break up the great estates by outlawing strict settlement. But though these started with brave salvos to the effect that the 'citadel'

---

[50] J. V. Beckett, *The Aristocracy in England 1660–1914*, revised edn. (Oxford, 1989), 360–1, 369, 374–402.

[51] K. T. Hoppen, 'Roads to Democracy: Electioneering and Corruption in Nineteenth-Century England and Ireland', *History*, 81 (1996), 553–71; Beckett, *Aristocracy in England*, 428–35, 438–48, 460–3.

[52] D. C. Moore, *The Politics of Deference: A Study of the Mid-Nineteenth Century English Political System* (Hassocks, 1976), 292–3, 320.

[53] Hoppen, *Elections*, 89–170.

[54] W. D. Rubinstein, *Men of Property: The Very Wealthy in Britain since the Industrial Revolution* (London, 1981), 60–6.

(protection) having now been taken, 'the axe must be laid at the root of the tree'[55] and despite some modest parliamentary enactments, little was at first achieved. British farmers remained aloof and rarely translated frustration over the game laws into support for land reform in general. (Irish farmers behaved very differently.) Though the Settled Land Act of 1882—the most substantial piece of relevant legislation—did indeed follow hard on the heels of economic depression and farmer discontent, its passage was secured primarily because landlords, having themselves come to favour greater flexibility in estate management, now saw the measure more as a protective than a threatening device.

It was, in short, a combined process of economic and political change and internal loss of nerve largely set in motion by the events of 1846 that eventually reduced the power of the landed classes to a shadow of its former self, not—in any important sense—the pin-prick attacks of contemporary radicalism. From 1875 onwards the widening of the financial gap between the great magnates and the smaller proprietors brought about by the depression further reduced the ability and willingness of the latter to continue the political fight. It had, in any case, always been the wealthiest families that had shown the greatest commitment. For the bulk of the gentry, politics had been at best a casual pursuit and London more interesting as the annual home of 'Society' than as the location of parliament. Amidst the colour and excitements of mid-nineteenth-century electioneering it is easy to forget how difficult it often was to persuade suitable candidates to stand at all. By the 1880s estates needed closer management and the hunting field and grouse moor offered greater attractions than a parliament containing too many cultural and class enemies—uncouth Irish obstructionists, atheists, and Jews. Many, probably the majority, of landed gentlemen had always been narrowly self-centred in their interpretation of what was required to protect their interests.[56] A broader franchise, increasingly recalcitrant farmers, tensions over Home Rule, attacks on property, and the eventual imposition of death duties combined to make political commitment seem ever more tedious and unprofitable. And with the increasing shift in the 1880s of all kinds of property towards the Conservative Party, the gentry could now rely on tough-minded urban politicians to fight the good fight on their behalf.

It is clear, therefore, that between the 1840s and the 1880s the nature and importance of agriculture and of the agrarian interest experienced many

[55] J. Beal, *Free Trade in Land* (London, 1855), 64.
[56] F. M. L. Thompson, 'Landowners and the Rural Community', in Mingay (ed.), *Victorian Countryside*, ii. 458.

transformations. Surface continuities—generally the products of nostalgia rather than reality—veiled the extent of change. The continuing expansion of a mass industrial and urban society drove the countryside's economy away from the centre of the stage. The proprietorial class, though maintaining a remarkable grasp upon the political levers, was beginning to enter into real retreat. Agricultural labourers declined sharply in number, and, though registering an increase in earnings, still limped behind their industrial counterparts. Farmers—even though their troubles filled official reports in the 1890s no less than in the 1880s—consolidated their cultural as well as their demographic position. Their share of total agricultural incomes, having fallen between the 1860s and the mid-1890s, then began to rise very substantially indeed.[57] While at the end of our period tribulations and hard times certainly still lay ahead, in the longer run of all those belonging to the agrarian interest it was the farmers who were to prove the most successful masters of their fate.

[57] Ó Gráda, 'British Agriculture', 146; A. Offer, 'Farm Tenure and Land Values in England, c.1750–1950', *Economic History Review*, 44 (1991), 17.

CHAPTER 2

The Middle Sort of People

1. NUMBERS, EXPERIENCES, ANXIETIES

The first inheritors of the new urban society were those who employed, organized, and sold, those who argued in the courts or tried (mostly without success) to cure the sick. They were, in other words, the great middle class. Despite much heated debate, it is perhaps most sensible to see class and class consciousness as phenomena of oscillating intensity. Like umbrellas during a shower they came out rapidly in times of hardship and were as rapidly put away again once economic sunshine reappeared.

Yet the obvious fact that people were not constantly at one another's throats cannot disguise the appearance of important changes within the deep structures of British society. With a growing realization among certain—but by no means all—groups connected with industry that aristocratic government had not always been sympathetic to their concerns, there came a growing sense of communal disadvantage. The manner in which a landed parliament had imposed the Corn Law of 1815 and resisted franchise reform until 1832 helped give political edge to economic and social discontents. As a result, the middle class was the first of all the classes to be discovered by those with contemporary axes to grind. Sir James Graham in 1826 hailed those 'removed from the wants of labour and the cravings of ambition' as constituting the 'seat of public opinion', while in 1831 Lord Brougham equated the 'middle classes' with 'the wealth and intelligence of the country, the glory of the British name'.[1] And, indeed, the campaign against the Corn Laws, which more than anything gave sections at least of the middle class a real sense of missionary identity, was profoundly constitutional. Cobden might denounce the 'citadel of privilege' and the Manchester Chamber of Commerce insist that 'the inalienable right of every man freely to exchange the results of his labour for the productions

[1] A. Briggs, 'Middle-Class Consciousness in English Politics, 1780–1846', *Past & Present*, 9 (1956), 65–74.

of other people' was an 'eternal principle', but behind such rhetoric lay landscapes of more limited ambition.[2]

Only on the surface did the business ideal of free trade and competition in everything have much reality, for even amidst the Corn Law battles of the 1840s there were to be found cotton manufacturers combining demands for cheap imported raw materials with opposition to the export of advanced machinery and the emigration of skilled operatives. In the world of action as opposed to that of words, industrialists displayed no impetuous desire to undermine the aristocratic constitution. Many were timorous and conservative, local in their interests, deferential to their 'betters'.[3]

Entrepreneurs and professional men, shopkeepers and clerks, were not all stamped out of identical moulds. They were not all thirsting for revenge upon the aristocracy and the agricultural interest. A significant minority of businessmen were either open protectionists or free traders in no extreme sense of the term. Many loved a lord and were happy, as 'one of the greatest industrialists' told a French visitor in the 1860s, 'to leave the government' in aristocratic hands.[4] Professional men, in their turn, depended on a wide variety of face-to-face clients, and for this and other reasons stood a little apart from the economic nexus that bound industrialists together. That with all these differences and distinctions, the middle sort of people still formed a recognizable force in society constitutes perhaps their most remarkable and lasting achievement.

Who exactly they were and how many of them can be counted are of course key questions. For practical purposes it is, in the first place, most useful to be able to identify a large group standing just above the level of manual workers and excluding only the agrarian interest broadly interpreted, in other words, a long chain of propertied opinion stretching from the wealthiest financiers and industrialists down to modest shopkeepers whose incomes depended upon the erratic earnings of working people. Property in some form lay at the heart of the matter, even if, as lower white-collar occupations expanded, this defining mark can no longer be universally relied upon. In the end, however, despite a myriad of subtle gradations, not only did an undoubted gulf exist between workers by hand and workers by brain, but the social (if not always the psychological) interplay between successful industrialists and the landed élite was usually cool and always circumscribed.

[2] J. Morley, *The Life of Richard Cobden*, 2 vols. (London, 1881), ii. 53; A. Prentice, *History of the Anti-Corn-Law League*, 2 vols. (London, 1853), i. 87.

[3] A. Howe, *The Cotton Masters 1830–1860* (Oxford, 1984), 235; P. Adelman, *Victorian Radicalism: The Middle-Class Experience, 1830–1900* (London, 1984), 26–7.

[4] *[H.] Taine's Notes on England*, ed. E. Hyams (London, 1957), 155.

Various methods exist for producing estimates of middle-class numbers, all of them defective, few of them valueless. It is possible to look at census reports and winnow out those occupations that might reasonably fall under the appropriate umbrella, an approach which makes it possible to establish the broadest limits of what might be called the 'inclusive' middle class, here taken to encompass shopkeepers and their assistants, clerks, administrators, professional men, as well as employers of all kinds (Table 2.1).

TABLE 2.1 *Number of males in England and Wales in non-agricultural middle-class occupations and the percentages these constituted of the total occupied non-agricultural population, 1851 and 1891*

	1851		1891	
	000s	%	000s	%
Professions and administration	183	4.0	289	3.6
Commerce, clerks, miscellaneous	121	2.7	514	6.5
Dealers and assistants	483	10.7	769	9.7
Other employers	129	2.8	190	2.3
TOTAL	916	20.2	1,762	22.1
Total occupied non-agricultural male population	4,526		7,967	

Increase in occupied non-agricultural middle-class males: 92.4%
Increase in all occupied non-agricultural males: 76.0%

Source: 1891 from A. L. Bowley, *Wages and Income in the United Kingdom since 1860* (Cambridge, 1937), 128; 1851 from rough estimates in C. Erickson, *British Industrialists: Steel and Hosiery 1850–1950* (Cambridge, 1959), appendix F, though the figure for total occupied male population in C. Booth, 'Occupations of the People of the United Kingdom, 1801–81', *Journal of the Statistical Society*, 49 (1886), 314–435, is preferred. Male farmers and agricultural labourers have been 'removed' on the basis of figures in F. D. W. Taylor, 'United Kingdom: Numbers in Agriculture', *Farm Economist*, 8 (1955), 36–40.

These figures suggest that the non-agricultural middle class interpreted in its broadest sense constituted about a fifth of the population and was probably growing somewhat more quickly than other urban groups (though the bulk of this growth was clearly taking place among the ranks of clerkdom and lower white-collar employment generally). Fuller and more reliable data in the census for 1911 suggest that little had changed since the end of our period. Following roughly the same occupational categories—but this time for males and females in Great Britain—it emerges that an 'inclusive' middle class constituting 20.7 per cent of the non-agricultural population was made up of: higher professionals 1.1 per cent, lower professionals 3.3 per cent, employers excluding farmers 5.9 per cent, managers and administrators 3.7 per cent, clerical workers 5.3 per cent, foremen and supervisors 1.4 per cent.[5] In other words, the 'inclusive' middle class consisted of two broad components: a more affluent half made up of higher professionals, employers, and managers, and a lesser one of lower professionals, foremen, and clerks.

Another way of laying bare the divisions in society is to use income as the dissecting tool. By adapting the valuable (if speculative) estimates of the Victorian statistician, Dudley Baxter, it is possible to derive figures for all 'income receivers' in England and Wales in 1867, without, however, in this case being able to exclude the agricultural sector (Table 2.2). From this it is clear that those with about £100 or more a year probably corresponded fairly closely to the occupational groups already identified as making up a large and 'inclusive' middle class which reached much further down the income scale than stereotypical images of wealthy manufacturers and sleek lawyers might suggest. Indeed, even in 1911–12 (when more accurate information becomes available) only 2.0 per cent of all employees and professional persons in Britain were earning as much as £200 a year.[6]

There are, of course, yet other ways of trying to assess the size of the Victorian middle class. All cast light on certain matters while obscuring others. Contemporaries like Edward Baines argued that the borough elect-

TABLE 2.2 *Income recipients in England and Wales, c.1867*

	000s	% of income recipients	Total income £000s	% of total income
£5,000 and above	4,290 ⎫	0.3	90,384 ⎫	23.4
£1,000–£5,000	25,200 ⎭		75,544 ⎭	
£300–£1,000	90,000	0.9	79,296	11.2
£100–£300	510,300	5.2	101,976	14.4
'Near' £100	1,422,860	14.5	106,715	15.1
Upper and middle class	2,052,650	20.9	453,915	64.1
Other income recipients	7,785,360	79.1	254,729	35.9

Source: Data in R. D. Baxter, *National Income: The United Kingdom* (London, 1868) recalculated by P. H. Lindert and J. G. Williamson, 'Reinterpreting Britain's Social Tables, 1688–1913', *Explorations in Economic History*, 20 (1983), 94–109. Baxter does not give equally detailed information for Scotland and Ireland, though what he does provide could be taken to suggest that similarly defined Scottish and Irish middle classes would have constituted just over and just under a sixth of income recipients respectively.

[5] G. Routh, *Occupation and Pay in Great Britain 1906–79*, 2nd edn. (London, 1980), 5–7.
[6] Ibid. 48.

orate and the middle class were more or less coterminous. If this was so, then in England and Wales between the first and second Reform Acts about 20 per cent of the population would have been middle class (the equivalent Scottish and Irish figures being 17 per cent and 15 per cent respectively), with the proportions in individual towns varying greatly—that for Leeds in 1841 would have been no more than 12.5 per cent.[7] Less abstract criteria are supplied by two key middle-class imperatives—privacy and servants— neither as common as might be imagined at a time when 'possession of an entire house' was hailed by the Registrar-General as 'strongly desired by every Englishman'.[8] For example, the percentage of households in 1871 containing no lodgers, no one save the immediate family and at least one servant, fell as low as 4.9 and 6.0 in industrial towns like Bolton and Coventry, reached 6.6 in Lincoln, and rose to all of 14.9 even in genteel Hastings.[9] With an income of £200 considered the minimum for engaging a single maid-of-all-works and with so few on such an income, the efforts of the less well-off to maintain appearances in this respect were as bitter as the wages they paid were low. The impoverished curate, Josiah Crawley, in Trollope's *The Last Chronicle of Barset* (1867) struggled to keep a maid on £130 a year amidst ragged carpets and shabby furniture. And although England had relatively more domestic servants than any other major European country, their presence in particular places was less common than the overall size of the 'inclusive' middle class might suggest. In 1851 the percentage of households employing any servants ranged from 6.7 in Bradford through 11.7 in Nottingham to 20.0 in York. Thirty years later, while Bath could boast one servant to every nine inhabitants, agricultural Suffolk registered only one to twenty-one and industrial Lancashire one to thirty.[10]

National data do, indeed, assume a different aspect when measured against the state of things in particular towns. In 1859–60 the proportion of the 2.1 million adult males living in English and Welsh parliamentary boroughs who paid income tax (and thus enjoyed incomes of at least £100 a

[7] K. T. Hoppen, 'The Franchise and Electoral Politics in England and Ireland', *History*, 70 (1985), 210; R. J. Morris, 'The Middle Class and British Towns and Cities of the Industrial Revolution, 1780–1870', in D. Fraser and A. Sutcliffe (eds.), *The Pursuit of Urban History* (London, 1983), 287–8.

[8] *Census of Great Britain 1851: Tables of the Population and Houses*, H[ouse of] C[ommons Paper] 1851 [1399], xliii, p. xxxvi.

[9] B. Preston, *Occupations of Father and Son in Mid-Victorian England*, Reading University Geographical Papers, 56 (1977), 11–12.

[10] A. Elliott, 'Social Structure in the Mid-Nineteenth Century', in D. G. Wright and J. A. Jowitt (eds.), *Victorian Bradford* (Bradford, 1981), 107–8; P. Horn, *The Rise and Fall of the Victorian Servant* (Dublin, 1975), 27.

year) was 20.6 per cent, a figure remarkably close to most other estimates of the size of the 'inclusive' middle class.[11] Locally, however, the picture was much more varied, with barely one-twentieth of adult males liable to income tax in Leicester but well over a third liable in London. Indeed, what such tax statistics above all demonstrate is the extraordinary importance of Victorian London for the middle sort of people, its lack of heavy industry and its chronic underemployment being more than made up for by the vast size of its white-collar and professional sectors. By contrast, boroughs with low proportions of middle-class taxpayers included most of the classic northern industrial towns, especially those which depended upon manufacturing to the virtual exclusion of all else and where class relationships were often at once bitter, direct, and uncomplicated. The proportion paying income tax in places like Oldham, Preston, Blackburn, Bolton, Bury, Stockport, Wigan, Warrington, and Sheffield was in every case less than a tenth. And even though centres like Manchester (15.3 per cent), Birmingham (14.2 per cent), and Leeds (10.3 per cent) seem to have been marginally more affluent, their social structures were very distinctly less bourgeois (in the sense of polite and well-heeled) than those of places like Brighton (23.1 per cent), Cambridge (22.1 per cent), and York (20.0 per cent).

A similar picture emerges from quite different statistics dating from the late 1840s concerning so-called 'assessed' taxes, which confirm that personal wealth was concentrated in those parts of the country with more traditional economies and was particularly thin on the ground in towns heavily dependent upon modern industry.[12] If, therefore, in some cities with comparatively diverse economies industrialists occupied the upper reaches of wealth (Birmingham, Bristol, and Manchester—though not Glasgow—are examples), in most single-industry towns (such as Bradford) the tax-paying élite was dominated, not by industrialists at all, but by professionals and rentiers of various kinds.[13]

---

[11] Calculated from information in W. D. Rubinstein, 'The Size and Distribution of the English Middle Classes in 1860', *Historical Research*, 61 (1988), 65–89, and on additional material kindly supplied by the author.

[12] A. D. M. Phillips and J. R. Walton, 'The Distribution of Personal Wealth in English Towns in the Mid-Nineteenth Century', *Transactions of the Institute of British Geographers*, 64 (1975), 35–48. Assessed taxes were levied on luxury expenditure of various kinds.

[13] H. Berghoff, 'British Businessmen as Wealth-Holders, 1870–1914: A Closer Look', *Business History*, 33/2 (1991), 222–40; S. Nenadic, 'Businessmen, the Urban Middle Classes, and the "Dominance" of Manufacturers in Nineteenth-Century Britain', *Economic History Review*, 45 (1991), 67–74; T. Koditschek, *Class Formation and Urban-Industrial Society: Bradford, 1750–1850* (Cambridge, 1990), 138–9.

What all this meant was that, in some quite substantial towns, the size of the business and professional élite could be remarkably small. Mid-century Oldham, for example, contained only 300 men (3 per cent of the total) who could realistically claim to be major businessmen or upper and middling professionals and of these 300 only seventy counted for much in political terms. And in Rochdale less than 550 adult males (again 3 per cent of the total) even lived in houses valued above the comparatively modest sum of £30.[14]

Really big wealth was, in any case, concentrated in the financial and commercial communities from which came the majority of non-landed millionaires, half-millionaires, and those leaving at least £100,000 on death in the period up to the 1890s.[15] Already in the 1840s Joseph Pease had argued that the greatest fortunes were being made in trading rather than making, a view supported by probate records which show typically prosperous Victorian industrialists leaving fortunes in the £100,000 range—large certainly but modest compared to those bequeathed by their financial counterparts. For example, among well-known politician-industrialists W. E. Forster left £81,000 in 1886 and John Bright £86,000 in 1889, amounts which, though entirely representative of their order, were much lower than those accumulated by the metropolitan bankers and merchant princes of the time.[16] But while, paradoxically, industrialists enjoyed great contemporary prominence, the financial and mercantile super-rich were generally invisible, especially in the political sphere.

Whether very wealthy or only moderately so, few Victorian manufacturers came originally from the world of manual labour, fewer still from the broad acres of landed property. During the century after 1750 perhaps four out of every five had been born to a father himself in business or active in that social borderland where shopkeepers, farmers, craftsmen, and small traders flocked together. The vaunted mid-Victorian notion (associated especially with the writings of Samuel Smiles) that self-made men ruled British industry was true only in the qualified sense that being an 'industrialist' was a more elevated thing than being a draper.[17] While, therefore,

[14] J. Foster, 'Nineteenth-Century Towns: A Class Dimension', in H. J. Dyos (ed.), *The Study of Urban History* (London, 1968), 284; J. Garrard, *Leadership and Power in Victorian Industrial Towns 1830–80* (Manchester, 1983), 13–14.

[15] W. D. Rubinstein, *Men of Property: The Very Wealthy in Britain since the Industrial Revolution* (London, 1981), 60–7; id., 'British Businessmen as Wealth-Holders, 1870–1914: A Response', *Business History*, 34/2 (1992), 75.

[16] W. D. Rubinstein, *Elites and the Wealthy in Modern British History* (Brighton, 1987), 23. The umbrella-cloth manufacturer and political theorist, Friedrich Engels, left £25,000 in 1895.

[17] F. Crouzet, *The First Industrialists: The Problem of Origins* (Cambridge, 1985), appendices.

the typical self-made man may often have been the 'architect of his own fortune', he was rarely the offspring of unskilled labourers or factory drudges. Although credit was easy to obtain, power generators and buildings easy to hire, and work could initially be done on commission, the costs of setting oneself up were not low. Even in the relatively 'cheap' cotton-weaving business they could amount to £28,000 for 800 looms, while an 80,000-spindle spinning undertaking required £100,000.[18]

For a variety of reasons industrial enterprises remained small. Of the 677 engineering firms making (admittedly incomplete) returns in 1851 only fourteen employed 350 workers or more, over two-thirds less than ten. The average number of employees per cotton mill was 188 in 1850 and 190 in 1878. In 1841, out of 1,105 primary process cotton producers in Lancashire only eighty employed over 500 hands, though from the workers' side things looked rather different in that almost two out of every five operatives laboured in mills of this kind.[19] Steam power too spread slowly. By 1870 over half of it was still concentrated in textiles alone. All the evidence suggests that behind a few really wealthy manufacturers there marched a corps of smaller men whose businesses were subject to rapid rise and collapse, who made strenuous efforts to keep their firms under private family control, and whose profits were probably erratic and rarely—after the middle of the century—productive of riches beyond the dreams of avarice. Information about profits is scanty and difficult to interpret, though it seems that they were lower in the half-century after 1825 than in the previous half-century and that something around 10 to 15 per cent (taken to include a 5 per cent return on capital) was considered 'normal'. In the light of interest rates on consols or other safe securities, such figures— given the risks involved—are hardly dramatic. Not that comfortable livings were unavailable to men of enterprise. For example, two partners in a medium-size London building firm managed to increase their joint capital from £30,000 in 1877 to £56,500 in 1896 having each drawn £4,567 a year (or £182,680 in total) out of the business in net profits—a return far greater than would have been available from the secure investments of the time.[20]

[18] S. J. Chapman and F. J. Marquis, 'The Recruiting of the Employing Classes from the Ranks of the Wage-Earners in the Cotton Industry', *Journal of the Royal Statistical Society*, 75 (1912), 293–306.

[19] S. G. Checkland, *The Rise of Industrial Society in England 1815–1885* (London, 1964), 134; C. H. Lee, 'The Cotton Textile Industry', in R. A. Church (ed.), *The Dynamics of Victorian Business* (London, 1980), 173; V. A. C. Gatrell, 'Labour, Power, and the Size of Firms in Lancashire Cotton in the Second Quarter of the Nineteenth Century', *Economic History Review*, 30 (1977), 96–8.

[20] E. W. Cooney, 'The Building Industry', in Church (ed.), *Dynamics*, 158–9.

In many cases, however, bad years could seriously damage margins and it is clear that the rise in real wages towards the end of the century put a substantial number of employers under considerable strain.

Changes in the relative economic position of the higher sections of British society—amid which the smaller 'exclusive' middle class of merchants, industrialists, bankers, professionals, rentiers, and the like found itself—are not, however, easy to pin down accurately. A number of heroic attempts to demonstrate that the first half of the nineteenth century witnessed a dramatic growth in inequality and the second half a gradual decline have been shown to rest on faulty foundations.[21] Indeed, the best conclusion that can be drawn from the very imperfect evidence available is that the century after 1815 constituted, not a period of fluctuations in inequality, but one of broad stability in the ratio of skilled to unskilled pay and in the distribution of earnings as a whole, a pattern that conforms neither to Marx's continuous drive towards inequality nor to the egalitarian optimism of Victorian statisticians like Giffen and Porter who believed that the industrial revolution was lifting more and more individuals towards closer economic relationships.

What is certain is that, in one way or another, almost everybody complained that incomes were rising too slowly to match expenditure. In the case of the lower middle class—the clerks, the white-collar workers of little status—arguments of this sort may well have been to the point: more people were entering such occupations, but their relative share of the cake was diminishing. But for prosperous business and professional men complaints probably had more to do with rising perceptions of what was 'necessary' than with relative movements in objective standards. Indeed, calculations with respect to the number of times fully occupied cotton-spinners and agricultural labourers would have had to multiply their earnings to equal those of Anglican clergymen or elementary schoolmasters in 1835, 1851, and 1881 suggest that income relativities changed little over these years.[22] This did not stop the better-off from feeling sorry for themselves and in a famous article published in 1875 an essayist with a business background told sad tales, 'the substantial truth of which cannot be denied', to the effect that the life of the 'vast proportion of the middle

---

[21] C. H. Feinstein, 'The Rise and Fall of the Williamson Curve', *Journal of Economic History*, 48 (1988), 699–729. It is, however, possible that a rise in inequality may have taken place in the period 1750–1815 (P. H. Lindert, 'Unequal Living Standards', in R. Floud and D. McCloskey (eds.), *The Economic History of Britain since 1700*, 2nd edn., 3 vols. (Cambridge, 1994), i. 381).

[22] J. G. Williamson, 'The Structure of Pay in Britain, 1710–1911', *Research in Economic History*, 7 (1982), 48.

classes' was becoming 'more difficult and more costly' by the year. The prices of servants, rent, meat, and other necessary items had allegedly risen by 'a quarter' since 1850. Worse still, the pressure to spend money on the extravagant lifestyles demanded by new cultural imperatives was, it seems, creating an intense sense of being crushed 'between the upper and the nether millstones of a prosperous and well-paid labouring class and the lavish expenditure of the noble or ignoble opulent'.[23] In reality, prices since 1850 had probably gone up by about 18 per cent, for pretty well everyone. Two things, however, persuaded the middle sort of people of 1875 that something worse was in train: first, the fact that half of this rise had been generated during the recent and intense boom of 1868–73,[24] second, that manual workers had, during these years, managed to obtain better rewards. Unsurprisingly, the articulate were the first to complain, though their post-boom sufferings were by no means especially severe. Illusions, as so often, were doing sterling duty for reality.

2. PROFESSIONAL PERSONS

At something of a tangent to the business community, though undoubtedly belonging to the 'exclusive' middle class, stood the members of the professions. These were an amphibious group, gentlemanly and respectable in the main, but working for a living, handling dusty briefs, their patients' insides, other people's souls. As late as 1800 only the Anglican clergy and a few hundred physicians and barristers had counted as fully professional (army and, to a lesser extent, naval officers belonging more properly to the landed interest). By the second half of the nineteenth century a far wider range of occupations was coming to be marked by the presence of independent practitioners, qualifying and disciplinary associations, specialized knowledge, a self-conscious identity, and sometimes even legal monopoly over practice. Though, in truth, very much products of the industrial revolution, Victorian professionals, with their closed and restrictive practices, were among its least dutiful children. Small wonder that craft trade unions were sufficiently green with envy to declare their own desire—the words are those of the leaders of the Amalgamated Society of Engineers founded in 1850—to 'exercise the same control over that in which we have a vested interest as the physician who holds a diploma or the author who is protected by his copy-

---

[23] W. R. Greg, 'Life at High Pressure', *Contemporary Review*, 25 (1875), 623–38.

[24] A. L. Bowley, *Wages and Income in the United Kingdom since 1860* (Cambridge, 1937), 121–2. C. Feinstein offers an improved index (but only from 1870) in 'A New Look at the Cost of Living 1870–1914', in J. Foreman-Peck (ed.), *Essays in Quantitative Economic History 1860–1914* (Cambridge, 1991), 170–1.

right'.[25] By the middle third of the century many key professional bodies were already firmly in place and firing on all cylinders. The Inns of Court protected barristers and regulated entry. The Society of Apothecaries and the Royal College of Surgeons were creating a new class of general medical practitioners. Engineers of various kinds, as well as architects and veterinary surgeons, were extending their domains. Most striking of all, the Law Society and the British Medical Association were already well on the way to bringing off that sleight of hand by which what are, in effect, trade unions have long been able to pass themselves off as 'professional bodies'.

The numbers involved are, as always, difficult to pin down, for so much depends on who is to be included and who not. The Census Commissioners operated a lucky-dip by which the ancient professions of church, medicine, and law were casually augmented by the admission of schoolmasters, actors, musicians, and civil engineers in 1861, architects in 1881, but accountants not until after the Great War. If, instead, one picks out members of the three ancient professions, on the one hand, and then, on the other, all those who might reasonably be classed (and were so by the late Victorian social inquirer Charles Booth) as belonging to the 'public service and professional sector', the resulting picture is that presented in Table 2.3.

TABLE 2.3 *Male numbers in the professions in England and Wales, 1851–1891*

	1851	1861	1871	1881	1891
	Numbers (000s)				
Law	15.8	15.2	17.4	19.1	22.0
Medicine	19.2	18.0	19.2	21.2	20.8
Church [of England]	17.3	19.2	20.7	21.7	24.2
A: total of above	52.3	52.4	57.3	62.0	67.0
B: other public service and professional	148.6	330.9	372.0	397.7	496.0
A + B	200.9	383.3	429.3	459.7	563.0
	% of occupied male population				
A	0.9	0.8	0.8	0.8	0.8
B	2.6	5.2	5.3	5.1	5.6
A + B	3.5	6.0	6.1	5.9	6.4

Source: C. Booth, 'Occupations of the People of the United Kingdom, 1801–81', *Journal of the Statistical Society*, 49 (1886), 314–435, as reworked and extended to 1891 in W. A. Armstrong, 'The Use of Information about Occupation', in E. A. Wrigley (ed.), *Nineteenth-Century Society* (Cambridge, 1972), 226–83.

[25] A. Briggs, *The Age of Improvement 1783–1867*, 2nd impression (London, 1960), 405.

In relative terms, therefore, the ancient professions increased not at all, while the rest experienced, first a sharp rise, and then a period of stability. Thus, while the 900 or so engineers of 1850 had grown to 15,000 forty years later, the number of medical practitioners only increased from 14,415 in 1861 to 15,091 in 1881—an actual decline from 1 for every 1,392 potential patients to 1 for every 1,721.[26] Making all due allowances, it is, in any case, unlikely that the proportion of adult males engaged in what might be called the recognized professions ever exceeded 2 per cent or thereabouts. This made it easy for those involved to form small tightly knit élites: in 1861, for example, the half a million people in Birmingham and Leeds (together with those living roundabout) made do with the services of 275 lawyers and 232 medical men of all kinds.[27]

As members of the 'exclusive' middle class most professionals shared that group's economic experiences. Enormous incomes for the top practitioners in law and medicine—between 1809 and 1899 ten professional men died worth more than half a million pounds—stood at the head of a long chain which moved down through the prosperous at £1,000 or more a year to the palpably hard-pressed. In general, professional earnings do not seem to have gone up dramatically during the second half of the century. At the bar real rewards rose only among leading men and much the same was true of medicine. Solicitors experienced something of an economic decline when late century incomes faltered as dips in the property and building cycles reduced the demand for conveyancing work. Not, however, until 1913 do we have tolerably reliable information on the incomes of particular professions as opposed to single individuals. By then the earnings of the top quarter and the averages for all those receiving professional fees were as shown in the table.[28]

	Top 25 per cent	Average
Barristers	£680	£478
Solicitors	£790	£568
Doctors	£700	£395
Engineers	—	£292

[26] R. A. Buchanan, 'Gentlemen Engineers: The Making of a Profession', *Victorian Studies*, 26 (1983), 428.

[27] E. P. Hennock, *Fit and Proper Persons: Ideal and Reality in Nineteenth-Century Urban Government* (London, 1973), 350–2.

[28] Routh, *Occupation and Pay*, 60–3. Figures are for males in Britain.

Such averages were of course dragged down by an army of less well-to-do practitioners. Books of advice to parents on their sons' choice of career talked dolefully of how the law was 'a sinking profession', how only 500 of the 4,035 barristers in the 1850s were prospering, how almost all professions were grossly overcrowded.[29] And certainly there were plenty of seedy doctors who scraped a thin living, obsessed by the size of their shilling fees, jealous of their consultant 'colleagues', and (as Booth found in late Victorian London) sending their children to local elementary schools. Many lawyers too had a hard time of it. However, as the same books pointed out, it was generally agreed that 'in pursuit of social position the professions have vastly the superiority over the business world' because their members formed the true 'head' of the 'great English middle class' and maintained 'its tone of independence [and] ... morality'.[30]

Not that high status was automatically accorded once a diploma had been obtained. Outside the consultant élite, Victorian medical men were not especially well regarded. Country surgeons in particular were looked down upon by rector and squire and usually found themselves obliged to enter the houses of better-off patients by the tradesman's door. In 1892 one angry Leeds alderman denounced the presence of 'publicans, licensed victuallers, architects, a doctor, members of other professions' on the benches around him, while in 1859 a witness before a select committee expressed the hope that rating qualifications would be kept high enough to ensure that 'the parish doctor ... could not get on to the town council'.[31] Though the wonderfully precise sentiments of Miss Marrable in Trollope's *The Vicar of Bullhampton* may have been a little dated by 1870, they probably reflected an outlook which had not entirely died away.

She always addressed an attorney by letter as Mister, raising up her eyebrows when appealed to on the matter, and explaining that an attorney is not an esquire. She had an idea that the son of a gentleman, if he intended to maintain his rank as a gentleman, should earn his income as a clergyman, or as a barrister, or as a soldier, or as a sailor. Those were the professions intended for gentlemen. She would not absolutely say that a physician was not a gentleman, or even a surgeon; but she would never allow to physic the same absolute privileges which, in her eyes, belonged to law and the church. There might also possibly be a doubt about the Civil Service and Civil Engineering; but she had no doubt whatever that when a

[29] H. B. Thomson, *The Choice of a Profession: A Concise Account and Comparative Review of the English Professions* (London, 1857), 29, 96, 162; F. Davenant, *What Shall my Son Be? Hints to Parents on the Choice of a Profession or Trade; and Counsels to Young Men on their Entrance into Active Life* (London, 1870), 16, 151, 196.
[30] Thomson, *Choice of a Profession*, 5, 16.
[31] Hennock, *Fit and Proper Persons*, 324–6.

man touched trade or commerce in any way he was doing that which was not the work of a gentleman.[32]

But if such comments point out the important truth that there was a hierarchy of professions, they also highlight the still more crucial fact that in many eyes the most significant criterion of relative middle-class status was involvement or lack of involvement in 'trade'. And from any taint of trade, however remote, professional men tried hard to keep themselves aloof. Perhaps this is why the majority of them seem to have voted Tory whether they lived in metropolitan Manchester or provincial Exeter.[33] While, therefore, the professions also threw up many of the leading middle-class critics of Victorian society—the lights of liberalism, the denouncers of mass production, even a few worshippers of the proletariat—these were generally either maverick dissidents or second-generation rentiers, qualified perhaps as lawyers or the like, but lacking the need to earn their own livings.

Given the size of even the 'exclusive' Victorian middle class, there were surprisingly few openings available to those who aspired to dwell within its ranks. Between 1830 and 1900 about 600 ordinands entered the Church of England ministry each year, so that the number of clergymen—though it rose from 17,463 in 1851 to 24,374 in 1891—did not keep pace with the rising population. Commissions in the infantry and cavalry hovered around 300 a year between 1871 and 1885 and in the army as a whole no more than 600 were available annually in the period 1886–90.[34] Most clergymen and military officers were, in any case, relatively poorly paid. And though occasional positions with attractive remuneration were available (especially in the church), their existence merely confirms the 'jackpot' nature of professional life: high rewards for a handful, comfort for a minority, frugality for many more. In the 1860s few curates received above £100 a year. In 1891 more than 70 per cent of parishes were worth less than £300. As *The Times* put it in 1867

The Church will always remain more or less like the Army. The value of a living is like the value of a commission. The standing, the authority, the opportunities which are given by an incumbency or a captaincy are actually worth the sacrifice of

[32] A. Trollope, *The Vicar of Bullhampton* (1870), ch. 9.

[33] V. A. C. Gatrell, 'Incorporation and the Pursuit of Liberal Hegemony in Manchester 1790–1839', in D. Fraser (ed.), *Municipal Reform and the Industrial City* (Leicester, 1982), 40; R. Newton, 'Society and Politics in Exeter, 1837–1914', in Dyos (ed.), *Study of Urban History*, 308; J. R. Vincent, *Pollbooks: How Victorians Voted* (Cambridge, 1967), 18–19, 73, 75, 84, 85 etc.

[34] A. Haig, *The Victorian Clergy* (London, 1984), 1–3; E. M. Spiers, *The Army and Victorian Society 1815–1914* (London, 1980), 3–4.

money... Officers do not expect to live upon their pay, and incumbents, in the same way, do not expect to live upon their tithes or stipends.[35]

Yet there were plenty of aspirants for both careers. Almost two-thirds of ordinands in the 1860s were Oxford or Cambridge graduates. Between 1854 and 1899 all but one in seven senior army officers possessed a background of land, soldiering, church, or professional life, the abolition in 1871 of the commission purchase system having little effect in this respect because pay levels were not increased.[36]

Nor did the reform of Civil Service recruitment procedures in the 1850s and 1870s have much immediate effect. The same kinds of people that had previously entered by patronage now had themselves drilled in public schools or cramming establishments for the new written examinations. Here too the number of openings with prospects of substantial remuneration was limited and rose only slowly, not least because total complements (including even lowly messengers) in key departments of state remained extremely small. In 1851 the Board of Trade managed with 103 men, the Foreign Office with 85, and the Treasury with 96. In 1868 one authority estimated that in the United Kingdom as a whole there were 1,173 Civil Servants of 'professional' standing earning average incomes of £831, 1,801 of 'superior' grade at £512, and about 10,000 in the 'general body of clerks' with something between £100 and £200.[37] The reforms of 1870, which introduced compulsory competitive examinations for the domestic Civil Service, did nothing to increase the number of positions. Indeed, between 1870 and 1881 only 117 posts in the new 'higher division' became available, less than a dozen a year. Of course the Indian Civil Service, which had pioneered competitive entry, offered additional openings and attracted highly talented candidates from a wider range of backgrounds. But its recruitment was also modest in absolute terms: eighty were admitted in 1860, but well under forty in most other years.[38] Hence the sense of worry and frustration increasingly to be found in certain middle-class households, the anxieties concerning income, status, and prospects, the fears that there were altogether too few loaves and fishes to go round.

[35] Haig, *Victorian Clergy*, 223, 294; *The Times*, 5 Sept. 1867.

[36] Haig, *Victorian Clergy*, 32; Spiers, *Army and Society*, 8.

[37] H. Mann, 'On the Cost and Organization of the Civil Service', *Journal of the Statistical Society*, 32 (1869), 38–60. See also below Ch. 4, s. 3.

[38] W. J. Reader, *Professional Men: The Rise of the Professional Classes in Nineteenth-Century England* (London, 1966), 94–6; [Anon.], 'Effects of Competitive Appointments in the Civil Service of India', *Journal of the Statistical Society*, 24 (1861), 586–9; E. Chadwick, 'On the Economical, Educational, and Political Influences of Competitive Examinations', ibid. 21 (1858), 18–51.

3. LOWER BORDERLANDS

Whatever the worries of businessmen about profits and professional men about prospects and incomes, anxiety was keenest and most pervasive among the lower middle groups whose substantial increase in numbers was so notable a feature of the period. The precise boundaries between them and the rest of the middle class and between them and manual workers are difficult to establish. Barristers were gentlemen, cotton masters were not, but both belonged to a recognizable 'exclusive' middle class. By the same token, while clerks shared attributes of respectability with many skilled artisans (and sometimes earned less), there were undoubted distinctions of outlook and perception between the two. In England and Wales the number of male white-collar workers (taken to include clerks, commercial travellers, office employees in national and local government, teachers, and so forth) rose very roughly from about 130,000 (plus 69,000 women) in 1851 to 500,000 (plus 194,000 women) in 1891 or from 2.3 to 5.7 per cent of all occupied men.[39] To be found especially in London and the larger cities, their rapid increase alone suggests that the majority must have come from working-class backgrounds helped on their way by the improving literacy and education of the times. Indeed, if social mobility (an escalator that went down as well as up) is to be found anywhere in this period it is to be found round and about the blurred but eagerly patrolled borders that separated white-collar workers from those who laboured with their hands. Although the majority of the lower middle class shared many things with manual workers—they went to the same schools, sprang from the same parents, spoke (despite themselves) in much the same kinds of accent—they, none the less, *felt* themselves to be very different indeed. Not only that, but a nagging sense of insecurity and comparative marginality rendered them perhaps the most concentrated repositories of so-called 'classic' Victorianism—a belief in respectability, merit, competition, money, hierarchy, privacy, and success. It also, however, seems to have helped to make them, and here, for reasons that remain obscure, they differed markedly from their counterparts in countries like Germany and France, politically characterless and submerged.

Clerks in particular were a defensive and far from optimistic breed. Male clerks in England and Wales numbered about 129,000 in 1871 and 461,000 in 1901. They were in general poorly paid. A few earned £200 or more a year, were able to keep a servant of sorts, and worked mostly in banking,

---

[39] W. A. Armstrong, 'The Use of Information about Occupation', in E. A. Wrigley (ed.), *Nineteenth-Century Society* (Cambridge, 1972), 226–83.

insurance, and the Civil Service. The majority struggled on sums that could easily fall below £100: in one firm of solicitors in the 1870s employing twenty-nine clerks twenty-one received less than £2 a week. Working in small groups they found it difficult to present a united front when it became obvious that supply was outrunning demand. 'Clerks as clerks', wrote one in 1870, 'are at a discount. There are swarms of them glad to engage at £180 a year and less. Clerks as clerks never will be in a better position.'[40] With women taking over many office functions (the 1,446 female clerks of 1871 had by 1901 become 57,736) male anxieties increased and good wages became harder to find. At the higher end of clerkdom—as George and Weedon Grossmith's *The Diary of a Nobody* (1892) inimitably shows—life could be pleasant enough: the Pooters enjoyed modest comfort, occasional bottles of 'Jackson Frères' champagne, and were eventually even able to afford the 'chimney-glass for the back drawing-room, which we always wanted'. But this was far from universal. Even if many other clerks, commercial travellers, and salesmen probably lived better than their parents had done, many also lived in that misery which only penury combined with aspirations to respectability can create. And almost all of them feared that things were likely to get worse.

Schoolteachers (apart from masters in public schools) fell into much the same category. Taking men and women together (and the latter were in a substantial majority) their numbers in England and Wales rose from 94,900 in 1851 to 218,000 in 1891. Although their salaries probably rose modestly over the same period, they too found it difficult to make respectable ends meet. After comparatively generous treatment beginning with the establishment of the 'certificated teacher' system in 1846, their pay suffered attrition after the introduction in 1862 of the Revised Code and 'payment by results'. In 1875 the average annual salary of male certificated teachers (and many were not so qualified) was £109, of females £65. They were all treated like docile automata, a government minister likening the notion of consulting teachers about what should be taught to 'asking chickens with which sauce they would be served'.[41]

Occupying a distinct middle-class niche of their own were those central figures of Victorian town and village life, the shopkeepers. Fixed-shop retailing has a long history and it is probable that the main expansion of shops per head of population occurred in the first half of the century. The ratio for six northern towns moved as follows: 1801 = 1 shop to 136

[40] Letter from a clerk in F. Davenant, *What Shall my Son Be?*, 188–201.

[41] A. Tropp, *The School Teachers: The Growth of the Teaching Profession in England and Wales* (London, 1957), 18–40; A. M. Carr-Saunders and P. A. Wilson, *The Professions* (Oxford, 1933), 252.

persons, $1821 = 1$ to 71, $1851 = 1$ to 57, $1881 = 1$ to 56.[42] However, the actual numbers employed in 'dealing' (including shop assistants) never stopped rising: in 1851 it was 546,000 in England and Wales alone or 6.7 per cent of the occupied population, in 1891 it was 1,149,000 or 9.1 per cent.[43] Shopkeepers sat less completely within the lower middle class than did clerks or teachers. Their earnings covered a great range. The most prominent occupied positions of local—and in W. H. Smith's case even of national—influence. Those in dingy and temporary premises were poorer than any clerk. But though shopkeeping remained overwhelmingly the preserve of small operators, retailing in general became an increasingly complex business, wide enough to encompass, at one end, the department stores and multiples of late Victorian Britain and, at the other, the tiny hole-in-the-wall sweetie shops to be found at the corners of so many nineteenth-century streets. And even if as late as 1900 co-operatives, department stores, and multiples together were still probably generating no more than 10 to 13 per cent of all sales,[44] this was quite enough to persuade many shopkeepers that their own traditional skills were being rendered redundant by increasing standardization in the packaging, advertising, pricing, and presentation of goods.

It was, therefore, above all during the mid-Victorian period that comparatively well-to-do retailers standing above widow shopkeepers and below the advancing tycoons were able to make their most effective contribution to urban life. Known to contemporaries as the 'shopocracy', they owned substantial premises in the best areas, possessed distinctive values and attitudes, and were perhaps the most notable beneficiaries of the franchise reforms of 1832. Indeed, until 1867 retailers of all kinds constituted over a third of the borough electorate.[45] Characterized by a special kind of tight-fisted meanness, they fought their way on to town councils in order to restrain the 'extravagances' of other élites. Not themselves generally aspiring to office beyond their localities, they provided some of the key electoral shock-troops that helped make Gladstonian Liberalism a powerful political force. And in this respect at least they had perhaps more in common with the many labour aristocrats who responded so enthusiastically to Gladstone's particular mixture of retrenchment and

---

[42] G. Shaw, 'The Role of Retailing in the Urban Economy', in J. H. Johnson and C. G. Pooley (eds.), *The Structure of Nineteenth-Century Cities* (London, 1982), 174; M. J. Winstanley, *The Shopkeeper's World 1830–1914* (Manchester, 1983), 13.

[43] Armstrong, 'Use of Information', 226–83.

[44] J. B. Jeffreys, *Retail Trading in Britain 1850–1950* (Cambridge, 1954), 18–29.

[45] T. J. Nossiter, *Influence, Opinion and Political Idioms in Reformed England* (Hassocks, 1975), 165–7; R. J. Morris, *Class, Sect and Party: The Making of the British Middle Class, Leeds 1820–1850* (Manchester, 1990), 133–7; Winstanley, *Shopkeeper's World*, 19–27.

rectitude than with some at least of those who stood above them in the urban middle-class hierarchies of the time.[46]

4. URBAN CONTEXTS

If farmers are excluded, the middle class was of course predominantly urban. Towns provided the context for its members' political as well as economic and social experiences. Urban society, however, varied enormously. The dramatic appearance of large industrial centres should not obscure the fact that, until well into the third quarter of the century, places like York, Exeter, and Lincoln were as 'typical' of England (let alone anywhere else) as Oldham and Dewsbury. In cathedral and market towns small-scale industry survived and the atmosphere was one in which political tensions existed but class consciousness remained ephemeral, as Trollope discovered when he stood as a Liberal candidate in the East Riding market town of Beverley in 1868. While in 1871 two-thirds of occupied men in Coventry and Bolton worked in manufacturing and only one in twenty-five was a professional person, in Hastings and Lincoln the proportions were quite different—between a fifth and two-fifths in manufacturing and between an eighth and a twelfth in the professions.[47]

One reasonably uniform system of occupational categorization has been applied to nineteenth-century towns. This divides the occupied population into five social 'classes', of which the first consists of professional and similar occupations, the second of 'intermediate' occupations between the first and the skilled workers of the third, with semi-skilled and unskilled workers consigned to the fourth and fifth. Its main defect is that almost all 'dealers' find themselves in Class III which, for this and other reasons, becomes unhelpfully large. However, various countervailing tendencies ensure that Class I emerges as something very close to the 'exclusive' middle class already identified, while Classes I and II taken together approximate roughly to the larger 'inclusive' middle class. Although various scholars have applied the system somewhat differently, the scattered results available give an unusually precise indication of the social architecture of mid-Victorian towns (Table 2.4).

What emerges most clearly from such data is that an inverse relationship seems to have existed between the extent of industrialization and the numerical presence of a middle class: York and Hull, therefore, had more middle-class citizens than Bradford and Wakefield. But not all differences

[46] E. F. Biagini, *Liberty, Retrenchment and Reform: Popular Liberalism in the Age of Gladstone, 1860–1880* (Cambridge, 1992), 84–138.
[47] Preston, *Occupations of Father and Son*, 7.

can be so easily explained, not least the substantially divergent social structures that could exist in small towns situated only a few miles apart.[48] In such cases only detailed local studies can even begin to recover the truths which broadly based generalizations inevitably miss.

TABLE 2.4 *Heads of households and social 'classes' in nine English towns, 1851–1871*

	Heads of Household (%)		
	Class I	Class II	Classes III–V
Bradford 1851	2	12	86
Cardiff 1851	3	8	89
Chorley 1851	5		95
Hull 1851	5	12	83
Nottingham 1851	3	12	85
York 1851	8	14	78
Wakefield 1861	8	6	86
Liverpool 1871	1	15	84
Wolverhampton 1871	14		86

Source: R. J. Morris, *Class and Class Consciousness in the Industrial Revolution 1780–1850* (London, 1979), 35; A. Elliott, 'Social Structure in the Mid-Nineteenth Century', in D. G. Wright and J. A. Jowitt (eds.), *Victorian Bradford* (Bradford, 1981), 105–6; R. Dennis, *English Industrial Cities of the Nineteenth Century* (Cambridge, 1984), 189. A rather differently constructed set of five 'classes' has been applied to London and produces %s for 1861 (for working males in this case) in Class I of 8.3 and Class II of 18.8 (G. S. Jones, *Outcast London: A Study in the Relationship between Classes in Victorian Society* (Oxford, 1971), 397).

The most untypical of all the nineteenth-century urban agglomerations was London, the 'infernal wen' as William Cobbett had called it in 1822. To an important—but by no means an exclusive—extent this was a function of its size. In 1841 the area that might best be called Greater London contained 2.24 million people or 14.1 per cent of all those living in England and Wales. By 1891 these figures had risen to 5.64 million and 19.4 per cent respectively. Yet, if anything, London's distinctiveness diminished rather than increased over these years, as much because other places began to achieve a critical urban mass and imitate the processes of suburbanization and occupational rearrangement which London had inaugurated as because London itself changed in any deeply qualitative way. Although, therefore, London's enormous growth continued to attract nostalgic complaints—like those of a writer in the *Builder* of 1870 who grieved that 'all before you, and

[48] S. A. Royle, 'Aspects of Nineteenth-Century Small Town Society: A Comparative Study from Leicestershire', *Midland History*, 5 (1979–80), 50–62.

around you, to a quadrant of the compass, were [once] fields, gardens, and farms, with breezy Hampstead up the hill on the right, and the pleasant village of Kilburn away on the left'[49]—the place's essential character continued to retain many features inherited from former times. These, in almost every case, were themselves the products of London's long political and administrative importance.[50] No other Victorian centre depended so much upon the presence of old forms of capitalism, old institutions, old trades. What this meant was that a consciousness of status long remained more significant than a consciousness of class, especially so given the unique importance in London of a substantial body of persons dependent, on the one hand, upon employment in what might be called 'individual/familial' organizations such as banks, merchant houses, and shops, and, on the other, upon those professions drawing sustenance and profit from the proximity of central government, the lawcourts, the Civil Service, and wealthy clients of every kind.

Not the least remarkable characteristics of mid-Victorian London were its administrative confusions and political invisibility. Until 1855 there was no administrative authority (except, from 1829, that of the Metropolitan Police) covering the whole, or even a large part, of its population. Within the square mile of the 'City' the Corporation exercised unpredictable sway. Elsewhere a chaotic jumble of authorities—some mildly democratic, many completely undemocratic, some mildly efficient, most notably incompet-ent—grappled ineffectively with the giant problems of the greatest city in the world. And even when in 1855 the Metropolis Management Act introduced certain reforms, London's inhabitants were still left with thirty-eight different authorities covering some 74,000 acres, which, together with the City Corporation, were now made jointly responsible for a central Metropolitan Board of Works. That this board did, indeed, take less than twenty years to complete the first and greatest of its allotted tasks, the construction of a system of main sewerage, owed more to the dynamic genius of its chief engineer, Joseph (from 1874 Sir Joseph) Bazalgette, than to the local government structures laid down by parliament in 1855.[51]

There were two principal reasons why mid-Victorian London was accorded such fragmentary administrative machinery. The first was the fear of centralization so widespread among the contemporary political élite. Indeed, Sir Benjamin Hall, who was largely responsible for the legislation

---

[49] D. J. Olsen, *The Growth of Victorian London* (London, 1976), 196.

[50] See W. D. Rubinstein's thought-provoking essay 'Charles Dickens, R. Austin Free-man and the Spirit of London', in his *Elites and the Wealthy*, 304–38.

[51] F. Sheppard, *London 1808–1870: The Infernal Wen* (London, 1971), 23, 279–84.

of 1855, thought himself dangerously radical in reducing the number of authorities to as low a figure as thirty-eight and had only been persuaded to do so by the manifest weaknesses of the existing system when faced with a cholera outbreak in 1854.[52] The second reason was the extraordinary inconspicuousness of the capital's electoral profile. In 1861 the London parliamentary boroughs (which contained about two-thirds of all those living in the conurbation as a whole) returned only eighteen MPs (out of 656), each of whom 'represented' an average population of 118,668 and an average electorate of 6,870 as compared to averages of 42,390 people and 1,880 voters in the case of members sitting for constituencies elsewhere.[53] It was not, indeed, until 1885 (when fifty-seven seats were allocated to the London boroughs) that the capital of the empire even began to receive the electoral representation which its size, population, and wealth so clearly deserved. During our period the metropolis remained, for most politicians, a dangerous and, above all, a mysterious place, the only readily available guide-books to its secrets being provided by the at best intermittently reassuring novels of Charles Dickens. Though politicians of course lived in London for much of the year, its mercantile, banking, commercial, and proletarian worlds long remained too complicated and too idiosyncratic for ministers or back-benchers to comprehend. By contrast, the new industrial order of the northern towns and the old rural order of the countryside at least shared the merits of greater social simplicity and transparency. Best then, to leave London alone.

Although in some parts of the United Kingdom it was occasionally possible for those without the vote to influence the formal political life of their communities as rioters, customers, agitators, and the like, the public political class—in London as in the provinces—consisted largely of those admitted within the pale of the constitution by the various franchise acts of the time. The period during which the borough electorate was most closely—though by no means entirely—coterminous with the middle class was that between the Reform Acts of 1832 and 1867–8. However, different social and economic circumstances and the vagaries of voter registration procedures meant that levels of enfranchisement varied from place to place. The fact that in 1846, for every 100 householders qualified to vote by a rate assessment of £10–£15, there were thirty-six with values over £100 in

[52] D. Owen, *The Government of Victorian London 1855–1889* (Cambridge, Mass., 1982), 31–46.

[53] Calculated from F. W. S. Craig, *British Parliamentary Election Results 1832–1885* (London, 1982), 3–21; *McCalmont's Parliamentary Poll Book: British Election Results 1832–1918*, ed. J. Vincent and M. Stenton (Brighton, 1971), 1–344; B. Walker, 'The Irish Electorate, 1868–1915', *Irish Historical Studies*, 17 (1973), 356–406.

Manchester, but only twenty-five in Leeds, twelve in Birmingham, and seven in Blackburn, not only says something about economic relativities, but also clearly affected the size of the electorate in each place.[54] Official estimates were made in the mid-1860s of the proportion of borough voters in England and Wales that might then reasonably be described as belonging to the 'working classes', most of them skilled artisans, modest shopkeepers, and non-factory operatives. Although the data are not without their problems, it would seem that the working-class element within the borough electorate was somewhat larger (and the middle-class element somewhat smaller) in towns with middling populations than in either substantial cities or smaller and more traditional settlements (Table 2.5).

TABLE 2.5 *Electoral class representation in English and Welsh borough constituencies (excluding London), 1865–1866*

	Cities (n=11)	Large towns (n=18)	Medium towns (n=50)	Small towns (n=113)
Population	100,000+	50,000–100,000	20,000–50,000	Under 20,000
Total population 1861	2,211,075	1,321,667	1,615,323	1,048,069
Total Electorate	109,469	62,111	91,639	83,577
Average	9,952	3,451	1,833	740
Middle class %	78.0	72.0	68.2	79.0
Working class %	22.0	28.0	31.8	21.0

Source: Return of the Several Parliamentary Cities and Boroughs in England and Wales, arranged in order according to the Proportion of Electors belonging to the Working Classes, H[ouse of] C[ommons Paper] 1866 (170), lvii. 47–51; also Electoral Returns, Boroughs and Counties 1865–66, HC 1866 [3626], lvii. 215–532.

The precise reasons for this are unclear. Undoubtedly most of those working men who managed to obtain the vote before 1867 were not factory operatives but independent or small-workshop craftsmen. Yet many medium-sized towns were heavily industrialized, while pre-industrial artisans were not confined to London and continued to flourish in a variety of urban centres elsewhere. Whatever the cause, it is clear that the middle-class voters of the first Reform Act period were confronted by comparatively smaller groups of enfranchised working men in the largest cities and the smallest centres than in that spectrum of sixty-eight intermediate boroughs with between 20,000 and 100,000 inhabitants each.

[54] Gatrell, 'Incorporation', 20–1.

More detailed examination suggests that even such generalizations disguise a multitude of peculiarities, especially with regard to the urban
middle class's own success in infiltrating the electoral registers. In other
words, not only were working-class communities in certain towns more
widely enfranchised than in others, but it is a mistake to rely too generally
upon a belief that all adult male members of the middle class possessed the
vote before 1867. Calculations based upon a comparison of the fivefold
social categorization already discussed and the 1866 official *Return* of working men in borough electorates show how much things could vary from
place to place. In the case of four boroughs with no freemen voters it
emerges that, while almost all adult middle-class men in Bradford and
Wakefield had the vote in the mid-1860s, in Oldham and South Shields the
proportions were only about a half in each case. In four other boroughs,
where freemen (and therefore working-class) voters were better represented, one finds Hull, Nottingham, and York in the higher category, but
Cardiff clearly in the lower.[55] Why this should have been so remains to be
discovered. That, however, it was so provides further evidence of the
profound differences that distinguished individual towns, differences of
social structure, employment, wealth, and political culture.

In almost all places, however, the socially similar middle-class groups
which contended for control of town councils generally did so by clothing
their disputes in language designed to appeal to working men, though to
working men as spectators first and negotiators second. And because the
municipal household franchise established in 1835, however generous in
theory, was practically more restrictive than the £10 level set for the
parliamentary vote in 1832, such groups had little difficulty in achieving
their ends. As a result, businessmen, professionals, and rentiers ('gentlemen') imposed an iron control in most places, yielding from time to time
only to the demands of retailing interests anxious to hoist cheese-paring
banners yet higher still.[56] Although the precise nature of such oligarchies
may have varied a little, they all shared a desire to combine politics with
business (easier on councils than at Westminster) and a sense of localism so

[55] 'Middle class' has here been taken to consist of Classes I and II of the fivefold model
used in Table 2.4. As regards electoratal statistics, it is the remainder left after the removal
of the working-class element recorded in the official 1866 *Return* cited in the source note
to Table 2.5. For a more detailed discussion of franchise and electoral matters, see below,
Ch. 8.

[56] A. Elliott, 'Municipal Government in Bradford in the Mid-Nineteenth Century', in
Fraser (ed.), *Municipal Reform*, 142–3; Garrard, *Leadership*, 14–20; Howe, *Cotton Masters*,
144–5. A more 'negotiating' relationship is proposed in M. C. Finn, *After Chartism: Class
and Nation in English Radical Politics, 1848–1874* (Cambridge, 1993).

intense that it rendered the upswelling of any single national middle-class consciousness a very halting and sporadic affair indeed.

By the 1850s large elements within the middle class had, in any case, begun to have enough of reform. Free trade did not seem to be producing the quick industrial bonanza some had expected. Changing patterns of trade in the cotton sector were making it easy for Lancashire businessmen to respond with enthusiasm to Palmerston's combination of bellicosity and liberalism. Gun boats, it was hoped, might find new markets where free trade had failed. The poor showing of Radical candidates at the general election of 1857 constituted the first fruits of this shift in opinion. Professional men as a group had never been Radical. Businessmen could be seen cooling in ardour by the year as they sought to defend the *juste milieu* baptized in 1832 and confirmed in 1846. 'I am one', wrote a Manchester free trader to Gladstone in 1852, 'of a considerable and daily increasing class who belong to the Liberal party by early connections, long and active association and by many surviving opinions also, who are yet decidedly conservative in all that relates to the further infusion of the democratic elements into our constitution.'[57] Of course not all felt this way: but the degree to which the middle class was prepared to undermine existing arrangements had always been limited. No longer was there any hard and fast line of demarcation at Westminster 'between aristocrats and others in respect of most of the issues Parliament was concerned with'.[58] Rather than raising high the roofbeams over triumphant structures of middle-class power, the removal of protection in 1846 had instead knocked down the wall separating land and trade and thus allowed the aristocracy, the farmers, and the middle sort of people of the towns to begin—slowly at first and then more rapidly—to coalesce in defence of property, whether that property took the form of acres, factories, warehouses, or professional monopolies. In the longer run the fires lit by Peel in 1846 consumed, not—as first seemed likely—the Conservative Party, but many of the rivalries which had once fragmented those with something to lose.

---

[57] D. Fraser, *Urban Politics in Victorian England* (Leicester, 1976), 262.
[58] W. L. Burn, *The Age of Equipoise: A Study of the Mid-Victorian Generation* (London, 1964), 319.

CHAPTER 3

Workers by Hand

I. NUMBERS, WORK, POVERTY

Four out of every five mid-Victorians were manual workers or the dependants of manual workers,[1] their lives for the most part shaped by two related influences: industrialization and urbanization. By 1851 about 54 per cent of the people of England and Wales lived in settlements with more than 2,500 inhabitants. Fifty years later over half lived in places with more than 50,000. Between 1801 and 1891 the urban population increased sevenfold, the rural only by a quarter. In no other country did as high a proportion of people live in towns as in England, Scotland, and Wales.[2] Urban conglomerations were beginning to form the conurbations characteristic of industrial societies. By 1881 Greater London had 4.77 million people, South-East Lancashire 1.69 million, the West Midlands 1.13 million. If some mid-Victorians mourned what had been lost, few denied the extent and permanence of the change. 'We cannot', a Birmingham manufacturer noted in 1869, 'revert to rural felicity, to green fields, to rough and manly and ignorant squires, to independent yeomanry, to ill supported and superstitious and serf-like hinds.'[3]

The move into towns and away from agriculture provided a greater variety of new occupational opportunities for manual workers than for the middle classes. Already by 1841 about 47.3 per cent of the British male labour force worked in industry and only 28.6 per cent in agriculture, with the balance in the service sector.[4] Nineteenth-century 'industry', however, ranged wider than might be supposed. In 1851 slightly more

[1] See above Chs. 1 and 2.
[2] C. M. Law, 'The Growth of Urban Population in England and Wales, 1801–1911', *Transactions of the Institute of British Geographers*, 41 (1967), 130. For Scotland and Wales, see also below, Ch. 14.
[3] W. L. Sargent, *Essays of a Birmingham Manufacturer*, 4 vols. (London, 1869–72), i. 3.
[4] N. F. R. Crafts, *British Economic Growth during the Industrial Revolution* (Oxford, 1985), 62–3.

men in England and Wales worked in the tailoring, shoe, and umbrella 'industries' (397,500) than in the whole of the woollen and cotton industries combined (393,500). And even if the two major textile sectors together employed the bulk of women *factory* workers (393,700), this was less than the number of women who worked as dress, shirt, and glove makers (471,200). Forty years later, though the relativities had changed, there were still 505,200 female dressmaking and tailoring workers as opposed to 526,800 women in cotton and wool manufacturing, while male tailors (119,500) still outnumbered men working to produce all kinds of woollen cloth (114,300).[5]

Textile mills apart, mechanization and the factory system did little to increase job opportunities for women, and even in textiles the best-paid jobs were reserved for men. Indeed, as a proportion of all women in England and Wales, those in waged employment probably fell from 28.5 per cent in 1851 to 25.4 per cent forty years later (if domestic service, much the largest female sector, is excluded, the figures drop to 23.4 and 20.2 per cent respectively).[6] With the collapse of handicraft trades there was—apart from domestic service, agricultural work, textiles, stitching, and washing— little open to women of any class before the final decades of the century.[7] The whole ethos of Victorian culture was antagonistic to the notion that married women with children should work for money at all, though (hidden from the statisticians' gaze) many of them augmented family budgets by means of part-time undertakings of various kinds. However, probably no more than a tenth of married women held waged jobs at any particular moment, and full-time female employment was dominated by those who were young or single or both at once.[8]

In what might be called the second phase of industrialization, economics and culture together combined to restrict the incomes of most families to those of a male breadwinner alone. As Henry Broadhurst—stonemason, union official, and from 1880 'Lib.-Lab.' MP for Stoke-on-Trent—told the Trades Union Congress in 1875, the goals of the labour movement included the creation of conditions where 'wives and daughters would be in their proper sphere at home, instead of being dragged into competition

[5] W. A. Armstrong, 'The Use of Information about Occupation', in E. A. Wrigley (ed.), *Nineteenth-Century Society* (Cambridge, 1972), 255–81.

[6] E. Higgs, 'Women, Occupations and Work in the Nineteenth Century Censuses', *History Workshop*, 23 (1987), 75. These figures are based on some rather heroic adjustments to census data.

[7] E. Richards, 'Women in the British Economy since about 1700', *History*, 59 (1974), 349.

[8] W. Seccombe, 'Patriarchy Stabilized: The Construction of the Male Breadwinner Wage Norm in Nineteenth-Century Britain', *Social History*, 11 (1986), 53–76.

for livelihood against the great and strong men of the world'. One simple device for preventing such competition was to keep female wages low. And as late as 1906 (when the first useful information becomes available) women in *industrial occupations* earned on average well under half (43.7 per cent) as much as men, while over the economy as a whole the proportion was probably lower still.[9]

Shrinking job opportunities for women increased the attractions of domestic service. According to the usually accepted sources, female domestics in England and Wales numbered almost a million in 1851 and 1,487,700 twenty years later when a higher proportion of occupied women (46.4 per cent) are known to have worked as servants than ever before or since.[10] The great majority (more than nine in ten) worked in households with two servants or less, very few in plutocratic establishments. Most were young and single, but precisely because marriage (by generally bringing domestic employment to an end) made continuous recruitment necessary, the experience of service at some stage in life was widespread, touching (according to one estimate) as many as one in three of all adult women in our period.[11] The popularity of domestic service in the second half of the nineteenth century was not, however, merely a result of limited alternatives. Contrary to much received wisdom, not only did cooks and maids (save in the very meanest one-servant households) receive relatively attractive emoluments, but their rewards probably grew faster than those of women working in industry or of industrial workers generally.[12]

Clearly, then, industrialization had a distinctly patchy effect upon the occupational contours of society. The initial thrust lay in the direction of saving capital (which was in comparatively short supply) rather than labour (which was not). By 1841 less than one in five occupied males in Britain worked in industries revolutionized since 1760 or thereabouts. And though the proportions varied from one part of the country to another, they

[9] S. Boston, *Women Workers and the Trade Union Movement* (London, 1980), 16; A. L. Bowley, *Wages and Income in the United Kingdom since 1860* (Cambridge, 1937), 51; D. Levine, 'Industrialization and the Proletarian Family in England', *Past & Present*, 107 (1985), 179.

[10] Higgs, 'Women, Occupations and Work', 74. Higgs (p. 75), however, produces much lower revised estimates of 'true' domestic servants and reaches a figure for 1871 of 714,100 (or 21.7% of all occupied females).

[11] M. Anderson, 'Households, Families and Individuals', *Continuity and Change*, 3 (1988), 427–8; T. McBride, ' "As the Twig is Bent": The Victorian Nanny', in A. S. Wohl (ed.), *The Victorian Family* (London, 1978), 53.

[12] M. Ebery and B. Preston, *Domestic Service in late Victorian and Edwardian Britain*, Reading University Geographical Papers, 42 (1976), 93; W. T. Layton, 'Changes in the Wages of Domestic Servants during Fifty Years', *Journal of the Royal Statistical Society*, 71 (1908), 515–24.

exceeded a third only in Lancashire (where, however, no less than 55,000 handloom weavers were still at work as late as 1851) and in the West Riding of Yorkshire.[13] Even in 1861 only about 30 per cent of the labour force was employed in activities that had been radically transformed in technique over the previous eighty years.[14]

That by 1850 Britain had become the *workshop* of the world is, therefore, quite literally true. Manual power lay at the heart of the productive process, assisted often by only the simplest of mechanical equipment. Human beings were cheaper to install than steam engines and much more adaptable in their behaviour than a self-acting stamp or press. 'When they broke down, the master did not have to pay them for repairs; when they made a mistake he could fine them; when there was no work for them to do he could give them the sack.'[15] Even cotton factories—the most advanced manufacturing units—were rarely very large. In 1841 only a third of Lancashire cotton operatives worked in firms with more than 500 employees, more than a fifth in the 714 firms (out of 1,105) with less than 150.[16] And much the same was true of the other major textile sectors. In worsted production, the average number per factory only rose from 160 in 1850 to 175 twenty years later, while woollen mills remained smaller still, with, on average, forty-six employees in 1838 and seventy in 1871.[17]

The typical British worker in the mid-Victorian period was not a machine operator in a factory at all but a traditional artisan or labourer or domestic servant. And even the great majority of those who worked in manufacturing were employed, not by great capitalists in great factories, but by small-scale entrepreneurs in small-scale workshops. In 1898–9 the average British workshop still employed less than thirty male workers.[18] One such place differed subtly, perhaps substantially, from another. A myriad of specialized activities was pursued in different kinds and sizes of factories and outside factories altogether. The extent to which the work-

[13] Crafts, *British Economic Growth*, 4–5; G. Timmins, *The Last Shift: The Decline of Handloom Weaving in Nineteenth-Century Lancashire* (Manchester, 1993), 109.

[14] D. N. McCloskey, 'The Industrial Revolution 1780–1860', in J. Mokyr (ed.), *The Economics of the Industrial Revolution* (London, 1985), 58.

[15] R. Samuel, 'Workshop of the World: Steam Power and Hand Technology in Mid-Victorian Britain', *History Workshop*, 3 (1977), 58.

[16] A. Howe, *The Cotton Masters 1830–1860* (Oxford, 1984), 5; V. A. C. Gatrell, 'Labour, Power, and the Size of Firms in Lancashire Cotton in the Second Quarter of the Nineteenth Century', *Economic History Review*, 30 (1977), 98.

[17] E. M. Sigsworth, 'The Woollen Textile Industry', in R. Church (ed.), *The Dynamics of Victorian Business* (London, 1980), 191, 197.

[18] R. McKibbin, *The Ideologies of Class: Social Relations in Britain 1880–1950* (Oxford, 1990), 6.

force felt a sense of sameness, of unity, of being involved in one great coherent industrial culture is, therefore, likely to have been limited.

The complexities of class and class consciousness are also starkly revealed by the fact that one of the greatest divisions in Victorian society—that between the 'poor' and the rest—did not occur at any obvious point of class separation at all, but within the working class itself. As usual, problems of definition hover menacingly in the air. What is poverty? Is it an absolute or a relative concept? Does it differ from one district to another, as between town and country, as between those 'born to' and those 'reduced to' its embrace? One category almost all articulate Victorians recognized was that which John Bright in the late 1850s dubbed 'the residuum', though even here there was disagreement. Some talked of a substantial group of very poor people thoroughly broken by chronic distress, those William Booth (the founder of the Salvation Army) called the 'submerged tenth' (perhaps three million people in England and Wales). And, indeed, Booth's estimate bears some relation to the numbers which the (inadequate) statistics of the period 1850–85 suggest were being relieved under the new Poor Law of 1834.[19] But the Poor Law, however it functioned in practice, had been designed for the sick and aged and to force the unemployed back to work, not for a totally demoralized 'residuum' alone. This last, therefore, soon came to be regarded as consisting of comparatively small groups living in 'badlands' or 'rookeries' beyond the reach of law or civilization. And though it is now generally held that no rigid distinction can be sustained between a dishonest criminal class and a poor but honest working class, many at the time believed otherwise. Even the humanity of Henry Mayhew, the most brilliant social observer of the mid-century period, drew the line at criminals notable for their 'high cheek-bones and protruding jaws', while Thomas Wright, the famous self-improving 'journeyman engineer', was once, when down on his luck, shocked to see neighbours in bed at midmorning, 'loafing about street-corners during the afternoon, and in publichouses until a late hour at night'. In similarly superior vein, a Birkenhead Poor Law officer defined the residuum as consisting simply, if rather eclectically, of 'thieves on the look out, low prostitutes, beggars of both sexes and all ages, hawkers of petty articles, . . . ballad singers, travelling tinkers, china menders, umbrella repairers'.[20]

---

[19] W. Booth, *In Darkest England and the Way Out* (London, n.d.), 17; J. H. Treble, *Urban Poverty in Britain 1830–1914* (London, 1979), 111; M. E. Rose, *The Relief of Poverty 1834– 1914*, 2nd edn. (London, 1986), 15–16, 50.

[20] C. Emsley, *Crime and Society in England 1750–1900* (London, 1987), 61, 64, 133; 'The Journeyman Engineer' [Thomas Wright], *The Great Unwashed* (London, 1868), 137; G. K. Behlmer, 'The Gypsy Problem in Victorian England', *Victorian Studies*, 28 (1985), 233.

Most contemporary estimates of the numbers clinging to the extremest margins of Victorian society were no more than educated guesses. Cobbett in 1826 thought there were 30,000 English 'tramps and beggars'. Eighty years later the Salvation Army declared the legion of 'homeless, wandering idlers living on the labour of others' to be 60,000 strong and growing fast. By the 1880s the extent of poverty in London was being talked about in increasingly frightened tones as the well-to-do began to fear an alliance between a 'criminal' residuum and all those many more who suffered from bad housing and unemployment.[21] Towards the end of the decade a more accurate investigation claimed that in London as a whole there were no less than 37,545 who could be described as 'the lowest class of occasional labourers, loafers, and semi-criminals'.[22] But as these constituted less than 1 per cent of the population, the limits of 'poverty' clearly spread far wider, to encompass, at the very least, men like the tubercular tailor interviewed by Mayhew in 1849.

I went on for two years working away, though I was barely able, and at last, five weeks ago, I was dead beat. I couldn't do a stitch more, and was obliged to take to my bed. Since then we have been living on what we pawned. . . . I have come down to my very last now, and if I don't get better in health what will become of us all I don't know. We can't do without something to eat. My children cry for victuals as it is, and what we shall do in a little while is more than I can say.[23]

The two major (and surprisingly late) Victorian attempts to delineate the statistics of poverty were made during the 1880s and 1890s: in London by the wealthy shipowner, Charles Booth, and in York by a member of the chocolate aristocracy, Benjamin Seebohm Rowntree. Both were anxious to discover the 'facts', but while Booth (who subsequently approved of Rowntree's work) disliked philanthropy and 'undoubtedly expected' that his 'investigations would expose exaggerations', Rowntree did not.[24] Combining detailed (if indirect) methods of inquiry and a good deal of impressionistic guesswork Booth came to the conclusion that 18s. to 21s. a week was the minimum sufficient 'for a moderate family' to be considered 'poor' rather than 'very poor' (anything more lifted one 'above the line of poverty'), that some 1,292,433 individuals or 30.7 per cent of London's

---

[21] Behlmer, 'Gypsy Problem', 233; G. S. Jones, *Outcast London: A Study in the Relationship between Classes in Victorian Society* (Oxford, 1971), 282–4.

[22] C. Booth, *Life and Labour of the People in London: First Series: Poverty*, 4 vols. (London, 1904 edn.), ii. *Streets and Population Classified*, appendix, p. 60; and i. *East Central and South London*, 33.

[23] *The Unknown Mayhew: Selections from the 'Morning Chronicle' 1849–1850*, ed. E. P. Thompson and E. Yeo (London, 1971), 216.

[24] R. O'Day and D. Englander, *Mr Charles Booth's Inquiry* (London, 1993), 3–97; A. Briggs, *A Study of the Work of Seebohm Rowntree 1871–1954* (London, 1961), 25–45.

inhabitants fell below this line, while manual worker families with incomes of more than 21s. a week constituted a further 51.5 per cent. Booth's total working-class element came, therefore, to just over four out of every five Londoners and of these well over a third were classified by him as indisputably 'poor'.[25]

Booth saw irregular employment and 'questions of circumstances' (illness, old age, large families) as far more important in pushing people towards poverty than 'questions of habit' (drink, a thriftless wife, and so forth).[26] Rowntree went further and injected a dynamic element into his analysis by relating poverty to a five-stage working-class life cycle of 'alternating periods of want and comparative plenty': poverty during early childhood for all save the children of skilled workers; then an improvement when the children themselves could go to work; poverty again once their own children were born 'perhaps for ten years, i.e. until the first child is fourteen years old and begins to earn wages'; then prosperity once more; followed by poverty in old age. The message was clear. 'The proportion of the community who at one period or other of their lives suffer from poverty to the point of physical privation is therefore much greater ... than would appear from a consideration of the number who can be shown to be below the poverty line at any given moment.'[27]

Rowntree also defined two types of poverty: 'primary', or 'families whose total earnings are insufficient to obtain the minimum necessaries for the maintenance of merely physical efficiency', and 'secondary', or 'families whose total earnings would be sufficient for the maintenance of merely physical efficiency were it not that some portion ... is absorbed by other expenditure, either useful or wasteful'.[28] Together the two encompassed 27.8 per cent of York's population, a proportion tolerably close to Booth's 30.7 per cent for London a decade before. Although subsequent studies of other towns have shown how the diversity of labour-market conditions could produce different levels and causes of poverty and although the manner in which Rowntree and Booth collected and handled their data is not beyond reproach, their surveys undoubtedly helped to puncture the impact of more optimistic contemporary commentaries such as those published by Sir Robert Giffen and Leone Levi in 1883 and 1885.[29]

[25] Booth, *Life and Labour: First Series*, i. 33; ii, appendix, p. 60.
[26] Treble, *Urban Poverty*, 91–3.
[27] B. S. Rowntree, *Poverty: A Study of Town Life*, revised edn. (London, 1922; 1st publ. 1901), 169–72.
[28] Ibid. 117–18.
[29] R. Giffen, 'The Progress of the Working Classes in the Last Half Century', *Journal of the Statistical Society*, 46 (1883), 593–622; L. Levi, *Wages and Earnings of the Working Classes* (London, 1885).

Using official national data rather than locally collected information the Victorian statistician, Dudley Baxter, provided useful insights into the structure of the manual labour class about the year 1867. He divided the relevant population into three major groups—for Ireland and Scotland as well as for England and Wales (Table 3.1). Here again we have figures for the lowest group which, this time on a national basis, appear to bear out the subsequent findings of Rowntree and Booth. Scotland, it seems, differed comparatively little from England and Wales, though Ireland's many poor farmers and agricultural labourers stand out both within the manual labour class and the population as a whole.

TABLE 3.1 *The 'manual labour class' in the United Kingdom, c.1867*

	Higher skilled labour	Lower skilled labour	Agriculture and unskilled labour	TOTAL (%)
England and Wales				
'Net annual earnings'	£60–£73	£46–£52	£20–£41	
% of population	11.4	38.8	28.9	79.1
% of manual lab. class	14.4	49.1	36.5	100.0
Scotland				
'Net annual earnings'	£56–£68	£41–£48	£16–£32	
% of population	9.8	40.0	30.6	80.4
% of manual lab. class	12.2	49.7	38.1	100.0
Ireland				
'Net annual earnings'	£50–£62	£35–£41	£10–£26	
% of population	3.4	28.5	50.6	82.5
% of manual lab. class	4.1	34.6	61.3	100.0
United Kingdom				
% of population	9.8	37.1	33.0	79.9
% of manual lab. class	12.3	46.4	41.3	100.0

Source: R. D. Baxter, *National Income: The United Kingdom* (London, 1868), 40–66. Baxter's 'net annual earnings' take account of periods of unemployment, short-time, and the like as (heroically) estimated by himself.

However defined, the line of poverty clearly ran *through* the working class. Though the frequency with which workers could find themselves, now above, now below it, must have exposed large numbers of people to broadly similar, if differently paced, experiences of life, many other boundaries, some closely some only distantly connected to income, also separated individuals and groups in all sorts of complicated and equivocal ways. The 'real social divide', it has been argued, 'existed between those who, in earning daily bread, dirtied hands and face and those who did not',[30] a distinction which emphasizes the gulf between the best-paid skilled artisans and the lowest-paid clerks, though the latter may well have earned less than the former. But even systematic observers like Booth found it difficult to 'draw the line' between the lower middle class 'and so-called working men'. ' "What is a working man?" is a question to which no very clear answer can be given. In theory, dealers and small master men would be excluded, but in practice ... the central mass of the English people consort together in a free and friendly way.'[31] So numerous, indeed, are the instances when the really important disparities seem to have occurred between different kinds of manual workers—as, for example, in matters such as diet and rates of mortality[32]—that it becomes difficult to believe in the mid-Victorian existence of one overarching economically (let alone politically) coherent working class, as of course Marx himself recognized.

2. RESPECTABILITY, ADJUSTMENT, AUTONOMY

Much has also been made of the Victorian concept of 'respectability'. 'Here was the sharpest of all lines of division ... a sharper line by far than that between rich and poor, employer and employee, or capitalist and proletarian.'[33] However, unlike the contrast between employer and employee, respectability has always been a slippery affair, easier to recognize than to describe. Appearances and immediate impressions deceive as well as illuminate in an age when cleanliness of clothing was difficult to achieve for the 'respectable' poor, and speech at all levels of society retained strong regional variations of accent, vocabulary, and usage.[34] And precisely because respectability was at least as much a matter of presentation, style, and perception as of purely economic distinctions, it could be put on and taken off almost at will. More a congeries of adopted roles than a fixed characteristic, respectability sometimes involved little more than the muttering of a few acceptable passwords to secure immunity from the badgering of charity workers or the police. It could stretch down near the poverty line as well as

[30] R. Roberts, *The Classic Slum: Salford Life in the first Quarter of the Century* (Manchester, 1971), 6.
[31] Booth, *Life and Labour: First Series*, i. 99.
[32] A. Armstrong, *Stability and Change in an English County Town: A Social Study of York 1801–51* (Cambridge, 1974), 134–9; D. J. Oddy, 'Working-Class Diets in late Nineteenth-Century Britain', *Economic History Review*, 23 (1970), 318–21.
[33] G. Best, *Mid-Victorian Britain 1851–1875* (London, 1971), 260.
[34] P. J. Waller, 'Democracy and Dialect, Speech and Class', in Waller (ed.), *Politics and Social Change in Modern Britain* (Brighton, 1987), 22; W. H. Fraser, *The Coming of the Mass Market, 1850–1914* (London, 1981), 59.

far above it; but it was not universal, save perhaps in the widespread feeling that only a 'proper' funeral would 'do'. And though its haunts—friendly societies devoted to thrift, co-operative stores, trade unions—were not confined to the top of the working-class tree, they were far from being open to all.

Mid-Victorian working people, like mid-Victorians generally, found it easy to sustain a variety of overlapping identities determined by—among much else—age, gender, earnings, respectability, size of family, level of skill, intelligence, religion, health, region, sometimes (in Scotland, Ireland, and Wales) by language, let alone accent or dialect. Local wage differences were enormous: late nineteenth-century Britain has to be divided into thirteen distinct areas to make sense of the situation.[35] Nor is there much evidence of collaboration between workers in different industries. Indeed, the existence of occupational hierarchies at individual workplaces put serious barriers in the way of collaboration even within a single industry. Dock and riverside work on the Thames provides an extreme but not uncharacteristic example, with unions in the 1880s having to submit separate pay claims for deal porters, lumpers, stevedores, overside corn porters, quay corn porters, steamship workers, weighers and warehouse-men, granary corn porters, and many more. Ship workers looked down on shore workers, permanent labourers despised 'casuals'.[36]

The gap between skilled and unskilled workers was large both in status and remuneration. Mayhew in 1849 put it only a little too starkly when he noted that 'in passing from the skilled operative of the West End to the unskilled workman of the eastern quarter of London' the 'moral and intellectual change' was 'so great that it seems as if we were in a new land and among another race'.[37] The census commissioners of 1861 identified over a thousand separate occupations, some very large, some tiny (though it is hard to believe that England could support only a single public execu-tioner, perhaps most of the rest were part-time). Units of employment remained small, and even if this did not necessarily mean more relaxed conditions, it did mean less uniformity and less opportunity for the creation of common identities.[38] This was also the effect of the late nineteenth-

[35] E. H. Hunt, *Regional Wage Variations in Britain 1850–1914* (Oxford, 1973).

[36] S. Pollard, 'The New Unionism in Britain', in W. J. Mommsen and H.-G. Husung (eds.), *The Development of Trade Unionism in Great Britain and Germany, 1880–1914* (London, 1985), 36; G. Crossick, *An Artisan Elite in Victorian Society: Kentish London 1840–1880* (London, 1978), 63.

[37] E. H. Hunt, *British Labour History 1815–1914* (London, 1981), 99.

[38] J. A. McKenna and R. G. Rodger, 'Control by Coercion: Employers' Associations and the Establishment of Industrial Order in the Building Industry of England and Wales, 1860–1914', *Business History Review*, 59 (1985), 203–31.

century growth of the service sector which reinforced differences between those manual workers who made things and those who did not. For every activist aspiring to overthrow capitalism, there were dozens of individuals preoccupied with saving for better furniture, a seaside holiday, or simply against a rainy day. Nor do studies of spending and saving point to a more homogeneous working class than do the more numerous studies of production and work, quite the reverse. While both reveal the existence of a world of competition and struggle, it was often one of competition and struggle between manual workers rather than between workers and capitalists as such.[39]

While, therefore, militancy of various kinds was common enough, its character was often diffuse and its aims unfocused. Even Chartism, however dramatic and significant in the 1830s and 1840s, was never big enough or wide enough to generate those fundamental changes in working-class attitudes with which it is sometimes credited. The drive of 1839 and 1842 was never recaptured. The geographical spread, though impressive, was always patchy. For London artisans, Chartism provided a road to political equality. In Wales it possessed a nationalist tinge, in Scotland an ethical one, in East Anglia it mingled with long-established forms of agrarian protest.[40] Even in its heyday (as a Dundee Chartist recalled) it remained a collection of tendencies: 'Repealers and anti-Repealers, anti-Poor Law men and Malthusians, O'Connorites, O'Brienites, Cobbettites, Churchmen, Dissenters, or no Church at all men... differing in their views of political economy, morals and religion, wide as the poles asunder'.[41]

And much the same can also be said of mid-Victorian trade unionism. Most unions remained small and restricted to skilled workers, almost all of them men. Informed contemporaries talked of 600,000 members in 1859, 'not short of half a million' in 1865, perhaps 800,000 in 1867, 1.6 million in 1876 (though this seems high).[42] Trade unionists, in other words, remained a distinct minority—as late as 1891 only one among every seven working men.[43] Though quite prepared to adopt militant strategies from time to

---

[39] P. Johnson, *Saving and Spending: The Working-Class Economy in Britain 1870–1939* (Oxford, 1985), 10; id., 'Conspicuous Consumption and Working-Class Culture in Late-Victorian and Edwardian Britain', *Transactions of the Royal Historical Society*, 5th ser. 38 (1988), 41.

[40] K. D. Brown, *The English Labour Movement 1700–1951* (Dublin, 1982), 123.

[41] A. Wilson, *The Chartist Movement in Scotland* (Manchester, 1970), 187.

[42] W. H. Fraser, *Trade Unions and Society: The Struggle for Acceptance 1850–1880* (London, 1974), 16.

[43] J. Lovell, *British Trade Unions 1875–1933* (London, 1977), 21; B. R. Mitchell, *British Historical Statistics* (Cambridge, 1988), 137, 104, assuming that (as in 1896) 8.8% of union members were women. Figures are for Britain.

time, their main interests long lay in preserving craft restrictions and pay differentials and doing so within a distinctly local framework in which branch matters counted for more than anything else.

Large amounts of ink have been spilt in attempts to explain comparative working-class quiescence during the 1850s and 1860s after a deal of turbulence in the 1840s. Possible explanations fall under a number of headings: structural, economic, psychological, conspiratorial. The first depends on the argument that manual workers continued to be divided into conflicting interest groups separated by income, residence, ethnic origin, religion, occupation, and so forth. However true, this cannot provide support for any slowing down of conflict, presupposing, as it does, continuance rather than caesura. The economic argument is disarmingly simple: people became better off after the late 1840s, had less to complain about, less need to see a distinct working-class identity as necessary for material salvation. But here too there are problems. The timing and the degree of improvement are far from clear. Poor Law statistics and the work of Booth and Rowntree reveal the continuance of large pools of distress. Working people in towns experienced little improvement as to health, sanitation, and housing before the 1870s at the earliest.[44] Indeed, the economy of the 1850s and 1860s provided a distinctly roller-coaster experience, with spells of rising, falling, and stable prices, of stagnant and then rapidly rising real wages, of labour shortages and sudden unemployment. Far from constituting one continuous boom, the 'prosperity' of the third quarter of the century (during which regional income differentials widened) was fragile, patchy, and limited.[45]

The psychological and conspiratorial explanations for mid-century reductions in militancy are not unconnected. According to the latter, the working class was now fragmented in a new way, the upper section becoming a 'labour aristocracy' increasingly willing to be used by the workers' enemies to spread bourgeois values and false consciousness among working people as a whole. The former, while also involving matters of perception, puts more—and more convincing—emphasis upon a self-generated realization that capitalism had come to stay and that certain behavioural patterns such as thrift and respectability did not belong exclusively to the middle sort of people.

The difficulty with the 'labour aristocracy' theory is simply this: that although it was clearly a concept—though not a phrase—which many

[44] F. B. Smith, *The People's Health 1830–1910* (London, 1979), 197–203, 223–6; Hunt, *British Labour History*, 94–5.
[45] R. A. Church, *The Great Victorian Boom 1850–1873* (London, 1975), 71–3, 78.

mid-Victorians recognized, neither they nor later students of the period have found it possible to agree as to who exactly the aristocrats in question were. A classic article by E. J. Hobsbawm refers to the distinctive higher 'strata of the working class, better paid, better treated and generally regarded as more "respectable" and politically moderate than the mass of the proletariat'.[46] Few, however, agree about the upper and lower boundaries of any such group or about the criteria which most clearly distinguished its members. Some emphasize income, others control over work processes. Some see the labour aristocracy emerging from those industries where craft skills remained important (shipbuilding, printing, engineering), others look in quite the opposite direction, at a breakdown of craft control in the 1840s leading to the emergence of labour aristocrats as a segment of production workers involved in management. Even if Hobsbawm's suggestion that 10 per cent of workers might be called labour aristocrats is accepted, these can never have constituted a fixed assemblage. Trades of all kinds—and as different as cabinet making, flint glassmaking, baking, and pottery—were marked by endless ranks and by vast regional differences. Shipbuilding was notable for complex levels of sectional fragmentation. Even in industries where grades were strictly defined, membership of such grades changed constantly as skills were picked up on the job or old age brought about their decay, while in sectors with less individual fluidity there was, instead, much overlap in the distribution of earnings as well as large ranges of pay within each grade.[47]

The idea that the bourgeoisie deliberately used its industrial power to split the labour force and bribe its upper layers into docility, though not without some substance (the framers of the Liberal Reform Bill of 1866 certainly had something like this in mind), none the less exaggerates the effectiveness of the former and the servility of the latter. Respectable working men and women (a much larger group than the 'labour aristocracy') desired respectability not because they were ordered to do so but because they disapproved of shiftless and improvident ways. Indeed, it was precisely Gladstone's emphasis upon retrenchment, low taxation, and probity in government expenditure which turned so many of them into supporters of the Liberal cause. The institutions and practices which

[46] E. J. Hobsbawm, 'The Labour Aristocracy in Nineteenth-Century Britain' (1st published 1954) in Hobsbawm's *Labouring Men* (London, 1964), 272.

[47] K. McClelland and A. Reid, 'Wood, Iron and Steel: Technology, Labour and Trade Union Organization in the Shipbuilding Industry, 1840–1914', in R. Harrison and J. Zeitlin (eds.), *Divisions of Labour: Skilled Workers and Technological Change in Nineteenth Century England* (Brighton, 1985), 179; R. Harrison, 'Introduction', ibid. 1–7; A. Reid, 'Class and Organization', *Historical Journal*, 30 (1987), 232–3.

underpinned respectability were generated by working people themselves, though their willingness to do this may well have owed something to the manner in which a rising tide of nationalist feeling in the 1850s was helping to bring together working-class and middle-class Radicals as never before.[48] If, in one sense, mid-Victorian workers did indeed view labour and capital as bound together in a single project, many also still adhered to the simple idea so long important in radical and revolutionary thinking, namely, that labour constituted the true basis of wealth.

At the 1867 annual dinner of the Cardiff branch of the Amalgamated Society of Carpenters a picture was placed over the president's chair 'portraying the friendship between employer and workman, by their cordially shaking hands'. 'By commerce we live' read banners carried by miners marching from St Hilda's colliery in South Shields in 1873. 'Masters', remarked the Tyne and Wear secretary of the Chain Makers' Union in 1861, 'always had the right for a fair profit upon their capital invested, and remuneration also for their business capacity'.[49] Not for one moment, however, did any of this prevent such men or such unions from pursuing bitter strikes when the need arose. All believed that fairness to employers took a poor second place to their own claims. Resentment was never far below the surface. 'We are told', said an ironworker's wife during a lockout in 1866, 'of the extravagance, wickedness, and immorality of the working classes, and how we have kept ourselves "quiet and peaceable during these trying times", just as if we were some species of wild beast'.[50]

Naturally the better-off rejoiced to see working people becoming more respectable (though respectability was hardly the most obvious quality possessed by those many *middle-class* swindlers who throng the pages of Dickens, Trollope, Surtees, and Thackeray). Admonitions about punctuality and submission to authority characterized ceaseless campaigns to 'improve' popular leisure activities (less violence, less drinking, less dirt) and to extend noseyparkerism in general (larger police forces). But, more often than not, the outward conformity these evinced disguised a high

[48] M. C. Finn, *After Chartism: Class and Nation in English Radical Politics, 1848–1874* (Cambridge, 1993), 142–87; E. F. Biagini, 'Popular Liberals, Gladstonian Finance and the Debate on Taxation, 1860–1874', in Biagini and A. Reid (eds.), *Currents of Radicalism: Popular Radicalism, Organised Labour and Party Politics in Britain, 1850–1914* (Cambridge, 1991), 134–62.

[49] E. J. Hobsbawm, 'Artisan or Labour Aristocrat?', *Economic History Review*, 37 (1984), 362; K. McClelland, 'Time to Work, Time to Live: Some Aspects of Work and the Re-Formation of Class in Britain, 1850–1880', in P. Joyce (ed.), *The Historical Meanings of Work* (Cambridge, 1987), 185, 189.

[50] T. R. Tholfsen, *Working Class Radicalism in Mid-Victorian England* (London, 1976), 247.

degree of disrespectful independence. Despite concerted middle-class efforts to elevate the tone of working-men's clubs, 'good order' and sobriety were invariably subverted by the fug of tobacco smoke and clatter of glasses created by members resentful at being told how to behave. From the point of view of its recipients, the financial support of the wealthy for working-class recreations could, without difficulty, be seen as providing something for (almost) nothing. And if at times this involved wearing—as certain cricketers had to do—belts inscribed 'the prince and peasant by cricket are united' then its main effect was to provide new reasons for moving rapidly into the greater independence of professional sport.[51]

Behind impressive ramparts working-class culture was developing along predominantly self-generated lines. Working men knew the middle-class cult of respectability for what it was. To the better-off respectability meant deference to superiors; to artisans it meant independence. Workers were not cowed, and to see the period 1850–75 as one of unusual industrial peace is misleading. That trade-union militancy was common is shown by the widespread engineering strikes and lockouts of 1851–2, the Preston textile dispute of 1853–4, bitter unrest in the building industry in 1859, by conflict in Lancashire in 1861, 1867, and 1869, strikes and lockouts among Yorkshire and Staffordshire miners and ironworkers in 1864, among Dewsbury woollen workers in 1865, among masons and ironworkers in the north-east and shipworkers along the Clyde in 1866, and by the great wave of industrial unrest in 1871–3 involving colliers, plumbers, carpenters and joiners, shoe and bootmakers, ironworkers, engineers and fitters, masons, and many more. And if some disputes were the products of hard times or of attempts to cut wages (1854, 1861, 1867), others took place during booms when workers felt able to act from a position of strength. But whatever the precise circumstances, such events hardly indicate the existence of a population transformed into horny-handed clones of Samuel Smiles.

Quite apart from sustaining indigenous concepts of respectability, working people proved increasingly adept at turning weapons designed to muzzle them into weapons of defence. Thus, when mid-century Bradford employers began to use voluntary associations to extend middle-class values, in the hope that this would produce social integration, almost at once the same strategy was taken up by factory operatives in order to resist such pressures. Indeed, it may well have been the workers' very commitment to self-improvement which encouraged them to repudiate the kinds

[51] P. Bailey, *Leisure and Class in Victorian England* (London, 1978), 122; H. Cunningham, *Leisure in the Industrial Revolution c.1780–c.1880* (London, 1980), 119–28.

of behaviour their masters were trying to foist upon them.[52] Yet even then their aims often remained sectional and local: hence the different nature of class relationships in individual towns. What was the case in Sheffield or Manchester or London continued to have at least as much to do with the peculiarities of particular industries, the distribution of property, and the social patterning of streets and districts, as with any general impact of capitalism and industrialization as a whole.

The 1850s and 1860s were, then, ambiguous decades during which strategies and tactics on all sides took on a decidedly chameleon-like character. The same individuals could pursue moderate policies and affirm their responsibility and respectability while adopting the language of class. The same union leaders who, on public platforms, pictured themselves as speaking for a coherent class, battled furiously for the maintenance of rigid demarcation lines at their places of work.[53] Negotiation, giving as well as taking, shadow-boxing as well as outright war, dissimulation as well as bluntness, all played their part in a period which was neither one of dramatic movement towards a more class-based society nor one in which positions previously gained were simply rubbed away.

A similar picture emerges from those many modern studies of urban social segregation which have tried to establish the existence or non-existence of distinct class barriers 'on the ground'. If by the 1840s it had become something of a fashion to see large industrial towns as rigidly segregated—Edwin Chadwick, perambulating the slums of Glasgow and Edinburgh in 1842, had famously recorded the 'astonishment' of their 'inmates' who had not 'for many years witnessed the approach or the presence of persons of that condition near them'[54]—this was, in general, a perception that owed more to fear than to discriminating insight. Of course economic differences did exist and with them at least a certain degree of segregation, if at a very local, almost house-to-house, level. Indeed, it is only when one examines streets or clusters of streets rather than whole districts that a developing process of separation stands out with any consistency: 'streets notoriously had right sides and wrong sides to inhabit, their best ends and worst ends'.[55] No town, however, was exactly like another. Smaller places such as Oldham or Stourbridge maintained more uniform social arrangements than did, for example, Edinburgh or

---

[52] T. Koditschek, *Class Formation and Urban-Industrial Society: Bradford 1750–1850* (Cambridge, 1990), 445–83.

[53] Fraser, *Trade Unions and Society*, 224–5.

[54] E. Chadwick, *Report on the Sanitary Condition of the Labouring Population of Great Britain* (1842), ed. M. W. Flinn (Edinburgh, 1965), 397.

[55] P. J. Waller, *Town, City, and Nation: England 1850–1914* (Oxford, 1983), 115.

London. Not until the last quarter of the century did developments in transport allow really substantial numbers of people to move far away from their places of work. Of London's 2.7 million inhabitants in 1854 only 50,000 travelled daily to work by means of omnibus, boat, or train. Even in the 1870s a place like Manchester (with 351,000 people in the city proper) could still be crossed by foot in less than an hour. Only with the arrival of steam trams in the 1880s and 1890s did changes in travel facilities seriously begin to affect the social layout of the larger urban areas.[56]

Housing was, in any case, only one of the elements which shaped communities. The impact of clubs, pubs, factories, and union branches cut across the relationships created by residential propinquity. Not all streets functioned as units simply because their inhabitants lived cheek by jowl. Complicated social alliances or ethnic, religious, and workplace distinctions could matter as much as housing patterns determined by income levels. And even when earnings and other influences reinforced one another—as with the Irish in Victorian towns—the degree of segregation often seemed greater than it was because groups like the Irish (and later the East European Jews) were particularly easy to identify. Segregation was, therefore, at best a rough-and-ready affair. Few streets before the appearance of one-class suburbs in the 1880s were homogeneous in character. Within quite small areas lived people bent on self-improvement and education and others 'approximating to the navvy life-style', with many gradations between.[57] If the boundaries between the middle class and manual workers were the most noticeable, this may have been more a matter of perception than of objective residential hierarchies. Mid-Victorian towns were, quite simply, so riddled with status and economic differences that the concept of segregation possesses analytical purchase only at the most local and microscopic of levels.

3. STANDARDS OF LIVING

Complications, though of a different kind, also beset discussions of that other crucial aspect of working-class history, the standard of living. Did incomes generally increase or decrease for those who laboured with their

[56] T. C. Barker and M. Robbins, *A History of London Transport*, 2 vols. (London, 1963–74), i. 57–8; C. G. Pooley, 'Choice and Constraint in the Nineteenth-Century City', in J. H. Johnson and Pooley (eds.), *The Structure of Nineteenth-Century Cities* (London, 1982), 203; R. Dennis, *English Industrial Cities of the Nineteenth Century* (Cambridge, 1984), 119–25.

[57] H. McLeod, *Class and Religion in the late Victorian City* (London, 1974), 44; Dennis, *English Industrial Cities*, 223–33, also 34–41; R. Swift, 'The Outcast Irish in the British Victorian City', *Irish Historical Studies*, 25 (1987), 264–76.

hands? Did they change in real as well as in nominal money terms? To what extent, indeed, can income levels capture the totality, or even the greater part, of a person's experience of life? These questions have long aroused impassioned debate, especially in relation to the period classically regarded as that of the industrial revolution—the last quarter of the eighteenth and the first half of the nineteenth century. And even though our own period lies later, it is impossible to understand what happened then without some knowledge of what had gone before.

Any analysis must begin with nominal incomes and these can be calcu-lated either from the top downwards (by computing national income data and dividing the total by the number of income earners) or from the bottom upwards (by collecting wage series for various occupations and producing indices for the working population as a whole). Both approaches depend upon heroic statistical assumptions: the former produces very broad-brush information, the latter can only yield *earnings* (as opposed to *wage*) data after yet further adjustments have been made for levels of unemployment, sickness, and so forth. However that may be, attempts to shed light upon the earnings experiences of particular groups or regions have necessarily relied upon the wage-series approach, prone though that is 'to lead not so much to a dead end as to country so open that no wholly satisfying answers suggest themselves'.[58] The whole debate has, in addition, been deformed by a good deal of ideological gunfire—with 'pessimists' coming largely from the left and 'optimists' from the right of the political spectrum. Nor are matters made easier when, as is of course essential, attempts are made to translate money incomes and wages into real incomes and wages by com-paring purchasing power at different dates and over long periods. Informa-tion on food costs is, for example, less satisfactory than might be supposed and usually relates to wholesale prices or the prices paid by workhouses or charities. As regards important items such as clothing and rent only the smallest lamps illuminate a general gloom: for example, a famous cost of living index for 1781–1850 bases national rent movements entirely on the rents of a few dozen cottages in Trentham, Staffordshire.[59] Also problem-atic are regional differences in living expenses and the changing composi-tion of those baskets of commodities which families in various conditions of life might 'typically' have purchased at different places and times.

The Victorians themselves were confused about the matter. The less numerate they were, the more they inclined to a pessimistic view of the

[58] A. J. Taylor, 'Introduction', in Taylor (ed.), *The Standard of Living in Britain in the Industrial Revolution* (London, 1975), p. xlii.

[59] P. H. Lindert and J. G. Williamson, 'English Workers' Living Standards during the Industrial Revolution', *Economic History Review*, 36 (1983), 9.

effects of industrialization. Carlyle, Chartists, and romantic Young Englanders all took the gloomy side. Prominent statisticians like Sir Robert
Giffen and Leone Levi (writing somewhat later) believed that enormous
advances were being made: the rich were becoming more numerous, the
poor less so, and those who remained poor were by 1880 twice as well-off as
they had been half a century before.[60] Some, indeed, thought that a
consistent transition from low to high wages and from 'incessant toil to
comparative leisure' was, by the 1870s, bringing about a severe moral
deterioration 'in the working classes' exemplified by rising sales of beer
and spirits and (so Levi claimed) by 'miners indulging in Champagne wine,
and ... puddlers purchasing for themselves sealskin waistcoats'.[61]

Within this jungle there are few certainties, though a careful dissection of
what is at stake makes some agreement possible. Thus, as regards the
period up to about 1850, it is helpful to distinguish between three major
questions: (a) 'Whether, given some set of exogenous changes [that is,
changes outside the system being studied], the working classes were better
off than they would have been in the absence of industrialization',
(b) 'Whether, given the industrial revolution, it would have been possible
for there to have been some set of policies which would have permitted the
working classes to have been better off than they actually were',
(c) 'Whether the working classes improved their standard of living over
the period of the industrial revolution'.[62] The first alone has elicited an
almost united response. Few serious scholars now maintain that Britain
would have been better off without an industrial revolution. As long ago as
1948 T. S. Ashton pointed to the inhabitants of China and India, 'plague-
ridden and hungry', living the desperate lives of those who increase their
numbers without industrialization.[63] A much nearer example is that of
Ireland, overwhelmed in the late 1840s by the same potato blight from
which rural populations in, for example, Scotland and the Low Countries
were better protected because of the more industrial nature of the economies in which they found themselves. The second question is closely
bound up with the third but carries with it perhaps the greatest political
charge. This is because many of the commonly expressed reservations are
not concerned with industrialization as such but with capitalism in general
and the form of capitalism adopted during these years in particular.

[60] See above, n. 29.

[61] A. E. Dingle, 'Drink and Working-Class Living Standards in Britain, 1870–1914',
Economic History Review, 25 (1972), 615–16.

[62] R. M. Hartwell and S. Engerman, 'Models of Immiseration: The Theoretical Basis of
Pessimism', in Taylor (ed.), *Standard of Living*, 193–4.

[63] T. S. Ashton, *The Industrial Revolution 1760–1830* (London, 1948), 161.

The period around 1820 tends to feature so prominently in discussions of this kind because, amidst a welter of other differences, something like a consensus (though even it is not total) has emerged to the effect that it was in these years that the real wages of working people began to experience substantial improvement. With, broadly speaking, real wages growing in line with real national income per head, the application of revised cost of living indices produces a more optimistic picture than was once the case (Table 3.2). But although the new indices are undoubtedly an improvement (they capture more goods, relate more specifically to manual workers, and make some attempt to include rent and clothing), further work remains to be done in a field where it is extremely unlikely that absolute certainty will ever be attained. These figures suggest two things: first, that living standards did not rise very quickly before the 1820s; secondly, that real wage growth was probably not held below the overall rate of economic growth (as those who believe that inequalities were increasing at this time have proposed).[64]

TABLE 3.2 *Growth of manual workers' real wages and real consumption per caput, 1760–1850* (%, p.a.)

	Real wages	Real consumption per caput
1760–1800	−0.17	0.25
1780–1820	0.56	0.47
1820–1850	1.27	1.24
1780–1850	0.88	0.80

Source: N. F. R. Crafts, 'Real Wages, Inequality and Economic Growth in Britain, 1750–1850', in P. Scholliers (ed.), *Real Wages in 19th and 20th Century Europe* (Oxford, 1989), 80. Real consumption per head is derived from the consumption part (the other parts are investment, government spending, and exports) of the nation's real national income per head, eliminating inflation.

Clearly such a chronology fits uneasily with accepted notions about the hardness of the times in the second quarter of the century—the period of Chartism, the new Poor Law, the hungry 1840s. And certainly some proponents of wage take-off have claimed a great deal: a near doubling of real wages 1820–50, with the 'average worker' better off in any decade from the 1830s on than in any decade before 1820 and the same true for all major groups of earners, whether labourers, artisans, or middle class.[65]

---

[64] Crafts, *British Economic Growth*, 104; P. H. Lindert, 'Unequal Living Standards', in R. Floud and D. McCloskey (eds.), *The Economic History of Britain since 1700*, 2nd edn., 3 vols. (Cambridge, 1994), i. 368–72.

[65] Lindert and Williamson, 'Living Standards', 11–12.

Wage-rate data are not, however, the same as earnings data. The latter depend crucially upon unemployment levels and it is possible that shortages of work during these years may have had a retarding effect upon actual incomes received, though it has also been argued—in the face of studies revealing savage unemployment rates in particular districts—that no conceivable level of unemployment could have cancelled the substantial gains made between 1820 and 1850.[66] What seems to have happened is that industrialization increased the spatial differentiation of wages by redistributing national income in favour of the industrializing districts of the Midlands and North. But while the broad pattern laid down by 1800 remained largely intact for the succeeding hundred years, the differentials between regions narrowed, possibly from 1850 and certainly from 1870 onwards. Nor were these merely money-term differences, for the cost of living was geographically far more uniform than wages.[67] What does, however, seem to have been the case is that throughout the nineteenth century working-class living standards in Britain were higher than elsewhere in Europe. They were certainly higher than in Ireland. To move from studies of the nineteenth-century Black Country where, it is claimed, 20 per cent of the people 'lived almost perpetually below the minimum level necessary to maintain life' (this being computed as including, for two adults and two small children, 2 lb. of meat, 1/2 lb. of bacon, and a dozen eggs weekly, as well as three hundredweight of coal, a gallon of beer, an ounce of tobacco, and money for newspapers, postage, entertainment, and holidays) to a survey of a parish in Donegal which showed 4,000 people sharing ten forks, five beds, two watches, and 10 square feet of window glass, is to cross a very dramatic and visible boundary indeed.[68]

Given that all previous history might have suggested that a rising population would lead to falling incomes per head, what was truly extraordinary about the industrial revolution was how '*better* land, *better* machines, and *better* people so decisively overcame diminishing returns'.[69] Many reservations, however, still stand between the (inadequate) data and the enunciation of confident conclusions. The comment of one historian

[66] Lindert and Williamson, 'Living Standards', 13–16; G. J. Barnsby, 'The Standard of Living in the Black Country during the Nineteenth Century', *Economic History Review*, 24 (1971), 220–39.
[67] Hunt, *British Labour History*, 101–2; id., *Regional Wage Variations*, 4, 59–60, 79; id., 'Industrialization and Regional Inequality: Wages in Britain, 1760–1914', *Journal of Economic History*, 46 (1986), 935–66.
[68] G. J. Barnsby, 'Standard of Living', 228, 233; T. P. O'Neill, 'Poverty in Ireland 1815–45', *Folk Life*, 11 (1973), 26–7.
[69] McCloskey, 'Industrial Revolution', 57.

that different combinations of tolerably respectable real wage series are capable of producing results 'anywhere from an increase of 150 per cent between 1750 and 1850 down to no increase at all' is not without a certain haunting power.[70] So much depends upon the definition of terms and the analysis of confusing evidence. The highly technical approach of econometric historians, though it has yielded interesting results, can be criticized for failing to take account of all that should be encompassed. Apart from difficulties when faced with unemployment, short-time working, overtime earnings, and regional differences, it has rarely succeeded in making much sense of family and women's earnings, child labour, or, indeed, of the changing life span over which earnings are accumulated. And it has tended also to concentrate on the incomes of adult males in full-time jobs, even though family living standards depended, then as now, upon much else besides.

As long ago as the 1950s 'an *unambiguous* increase in the average standard of life' during the years of the classic industrial revolution was announced by one party at much the same time as another argued that 'no strong basis' existed 'for the optimistic view, at any rate for the period from *c*.1790 or 1800 on until the middle 1840s'.[71] Those who dislike capitalism and statistical techniques in fairly equal measure have found it easy to see the 'average' working man's share in the 'benefits of economic progress' at this time as consisting only of 'more potatoes, a few articles of cotton clothing for his family, soap and candles, some tea and sugar, and a great many articles in the *Economic History Review*'.[72] And, indeed, by looking critically at the many workers for whom wage data are virtually non-existent, by adopting an agnostic view of the price information upon which so much of the claimed improvement of the second quarter of the century depends, by emphasizing the meagre extent of the 'modern' sector in these decades, and by examining the consumption patterns of luxuries like sugar and tea, a case can be made for seeing little increase in the incomes of the poorest two-thirds of the population much before the middle of the 1840s when our period begins. At the very least, therefore, the character of the evidence available should caution against any uncritical acceptance of the arguments

---

[70] G. N. von Tunzelmann, 'Trends in Real Wages, 1750–1850', *Economic History Review*, 32 (1979), 48.

[71] R. M. Hartwell, 'Interpretations of the Industrial Revolution in England', *Journal of Economic History*, 19 (1959), 248; E. J. Hobsbawm, 'The British Standard of Living, 1790–1850', in Hobsbawm, *Labouring Men: Studies in the History of Labour* (London, 1964), 87 (revised version of a paper 1st published in 1957).

[72] E. P. Thompson, *The Making of the English Working Class*, revised edn. (Harmondsworth, 1968), 35.

of those who insist that real wages doubled during the thirty years before 1850, powerful though these arguments undoubtedly are.[73]

There is more agreement about the course of events in the second half of the century. But even though substantial improvements in the real wages of working people seem to have taken place in these years, trends were never uniform and periods of increase were interrupted by periods of decline. At the general level there was, from the early 1860s onwards, an increase in the proportion of the national income going to earnings at the expense of profits, the share of wages in the sum of profits plus wages rising from 52.3 per cent in 1870–4 to 62.2 per cent in 1890–4.[74] While nominal wages rose but fitfully, changes in price levels and a greater stability in employment helped to produce significant improvements in real terms. This is not to say that the upward movement of real wages during the depression traditionally supposed to have begun in the mid-1870s was simply caused by a fall in prices. No less important was the ability of wage earners to force wages up above prices in boom years and to maintain a money wage plateau in between. But while real wages did rise, they hardly showed much significant change until the mid-1860s. Only then does a marked, though still discontinuous, upward trend become unmistakable, a chronology which makes it virtually impossible to ascribe any detectable reduction in class antagonisms in the mid-century decades to improvements in the material standards experienced by working people as a whole.

Although it remains important to retain a critical stance, the improved data of the second half of the century make it possible to present a plausible index of real wages for the period beginning in 1850. This shows that substantial increases were achieved from the mid-1860s onwards and especially so from the mid-1880s, just as our period comes to an end (Table 3.3).

Such averages do, however, conceal many industrial, regional, and occupational variations. Wage receivers who also earned money from part-time self-employment were clearly able to boost their incomes above the levels recorded by most indices.[75] Although all workers endured cyclical troughs, some cycles were nigh universal (1857–8, 1862–4, 1866–7, 1878–9, 1884–7), others (such as those in shipbuilding) were confined to particular industries or particular parts of the country. To individual

---

[73] J. Mokyr, 'Is there still Life in the Pessimist Case? Consumption during the Industrial Revolution, 1790–1850', *Journal of Economic History*, 48 (1988), 69–92; id., 'Has the Industrial Revolution been Crowded Out?', *Explorations in Economic History*, 24 (1987), 293–319.

[74] C. H. Feinstein, *National Income, Expenditure and Output of the United Kingdom 1855–1965* (Cambridge, 1972), T44.

[75] J. Benson (*The Working Class in Britain, 1850–1939* (London, 1989), 52–3) suggests

TABLE 3.3 *Real wages for manual worker adult males in full-time employment in Britain 1850–1899 (1850 = 100)*

1850–4	101	1875–9	128
1855–9	99	1880–4	129
1860–4	99	1885–9	140
1865–9	107	1890–4	154
1870–4	116	1895–9	164

Source: N. F. R. Crafts and T. C. Mills, 'Trends in Real Wages in Britain, 1750–1913', *Explorations in Economic History*, 31 (1994), 181–2.

workers it was the short (often the very short) run that mattered, something historians too easily forget. More often than not, increases in living standards occurred by irregular jumps punctuated by sudden declines, rather than by steady growth. Age, health, and size of family remained as important as ever in affecting the experiences of those earning wages and salaries. And for manual workers especially, actual incomes received in any year continued to depend crucially upon the availability of work. But comprehensive employment statistics were not collected until the 1920s and even the word 'unemployment' did not appear in the language of political economy until the late 1880s, when, indeed, it was identified by *The Times* (in 1888) as 'the fundamental problem of modern society'.[76] Classical economists, after all, had long denied that any general imbalance between supply and demand could ever exist. For them unemployment—or to use their terminology 'inconstancy of employment'—was a temporary and self-correcting phenomenon produced by the idleness of working people. Only gradually were a few more pragmatic commentators beginning to look beyond moral delinquency and short-term disequilibriums. 'None but those who have examined the facts', wrote Dudley Baxter in 1868, 'can have any idea of the precariousness of employment in our large cities, and the large proportion of time out of work [so that] . . . for loss of work from every cause . . . *we ought to deduct fully 20 per cent from the nominal full-time wages*'.[77]

The much used trade-union unemployment statistics for the second half of the century have serious defects. Initially they covered very few workers:

that overall it would be reasonable to assume that earnings from self-employment equalled 10% of money wage earnings in the later 19th century.

[76] J. Burnett, *Idle Hands: The Experience of Unemployment, 1790–1990* (London, 1994), 145.

[77] R. D. Baxter, *National Income: The United Kingdom* (London, 1868), 46–7 (Baxter's italics). This deduction also took account of what Baxter called the 'non-effectives up to 65 years of age', i.e. those too infirm or ill to work.

less than 100,000 before 1872. Workers subject to cyclical unemployment (in shipbuilding, engineering, and the metal trades) were over-represented, those vulnerable to seasonal unemployment (dressmakers, cobblers, building workers) were under-represented. Many of the losses suffered by those in sectors like mining and textiles (where short-time working was a common response to economic difficulties) were simply not captured at all.[78] Small wonder then that contemporaries differed violently about the mathematics of unemployment, especially when political issues were at stake. As late as 1895, when data were becoming less unreliable, Keir Hardie could argue that unemployment in the United Kingdom affected, at its peak, 1.7 million members of the labour force, while the Revd W. Tozer, standing on different ideological ground, put the total at 280,000 or (deducting 'the old, the infirm, the physically and mentally handicapped, and the idle and the intemperate') perhaps only half that number.[79] None the less, the union returns are not entirely without value, especially after corrections have been made to overcome the excessive weight given to the engineering, shipbuilding, and metal trades. Because five-year averages (matching the real wage index in Table 3.3) smooth out occasional dramatic changes from one year to another, it is necessary also to provide annual figures, as in Table 3.4.

TABLE 3.4 *Percentages unemployed of the working population in the United Kingdom, 1855–1894*

1855	3.7		1860	1.8		1865	1.8	
1856	3.2		1861	3.7		1866	2.6	
1857	4.2	4.2	1862	6.0	3.6	1867	6.3	4.7
1858	7.3		1863	4.7		1868	6.7	
1859	2.6		1864	1.9		1869	5.9	
1870	3.7		1875	2.2		1880	5.2	
1871	1.6		1876	3.4		1881	3.5	
1872	0.9	1.8	1877	4.4	5.4	1882	2.3	4.3
1873	1.1		1878	6.2		1883	2.6	
1874	1.6		1879	10.7		1884	8.1	
1885	9.3		1890	2.1				
1886	10.2		1891	3.5				
1887	7.6	6.8	1892	6.3	5.3			
1888	4.9		1893	7.5				
1889	2.1		1894	6.9				

Source: B. R. Mitchell, *British Historical Statistics* (Cambridge, 1988), 124.

[78] W. R. Garside, *The Measurement of Unemployment: Methods and Sources in Great Britain 1850–1979* (Oxford, 1980), 16–19.
[79] Treble, *Urban Poverty*, 53.

From this the cyclical depressions stand out, with comparatively high rates in 1858, 1862, 1867–8, 1878–9, 1884–7, and 1892–4, as also do the booms, with low rates in 1859–60, 1864–6, 1871–5, 1882–3, and 1889–90. What is, however, especially remarkable is that, in the whole of the period 1855–94, recorded national unemployment exceeded 10 per cent in only two years (1879 and 1886) and that only one four-year period can be found (1884–7) in which it stood consistently above 7.5 per cent. Of course the local impact upon earnings varied far more than such averages suggest. Just as wages seem to have been highest in areas of greatest factory penetration, so high unemployment in the later nineteenth century was 'primarily a feature of the industrial areas of northern England and Ireland, and, from the 1880s, Scotland; the lowest levels... were consistently found in southern and eastern England'.[80] During, for example, the bad year of 1879 (when the national rate was 10.7 per cent) the Amalgamated Society of Engineers recorded, for the month of July, percentage rates for those in membership of 11.3 overall, 14.7 in West Yorkshire, 14.6 in South Clydeside, but only 3.2 in the districts around London. Of the union's fifty-seven branches with over 300 members, fourteen (including Lincoln, Southampton, and Swindon) reported less than 5 per cent out of work, while sixteen (including Leeds, Halifax, Preston, and Bury) reported 15 per cent or more.[81]

The time people actually spent at work was affected not only by unemployment but by changes in the number of hours demanded in various industries and occupations. The evidence here is difficult to quantify. The ten-hour day common in the middle of the eighteenth century may well have lengthened during the subsequent hundred years (especially in textiles) to something like twelve hours, with perhaps also a more widespread insistence that six full days be worked each week. Despite, therefore, the survival well into the second half of the nineteenth century of the custom of Saint Monday (by which many workers simply took that day off), it has been suggested that over the course of the century from 1750 to 1850 the working year for those in full employment rose from 2,500 to 3,000 hours or thereabouts. Others, however, believe that by 1850 things had generally begun to fall back from the high levels of the early industrial period, though more slowly in mining, agriculture, and domestic service than elsewhere.[82]

[80] H. R. Southall, 'The Origins of the Depressed Areas: Unemployment, Growth, and Regional Economic Structure in Britain before 1914', *Economic History Review*, 41 (1988), 256.

[81] H. Southall, 'Regional Unemployment Patterns among Skilled Engineers in Britain, 1851–1914', *Journal of Historical Geography*, 12 (1986), 275–8.

[82] D. A. Reid, 'The Decline of Saint Monday 1766–1876', *Past & Present*, 71 (1976), 76–101; N. L. Tranter, 'The Labour Supply 1780–1860', in R. Floud and D. McCloskey (eds.), *The Economic History of Britain since 1700*, 1st edn., 2 vols. (Cambridge, 1981), i. 220–1;

Subsequent reductions in hours came in a series of sudden declines (especially in the 1870s and again after the Great War) as workers were able to use their collective strength during good times, not only to increase wages (always the prime concern), but to protect themselves against future unemployment. For what it is worth, the best estimate available indicates that average full-time hours worked per week fell from 65 to 56 between 1856 and 1873 and then remained at about that level for a further forty years. Allowing for holidays, sickness, and strikes, the equivalent average hours worked per year were 3,185 in 1856, 2,744 in 1873, and 2,753 in 1913.[83] But if, by the 1870s, the nine-hour day was being widely conceded (as the Saturday half-holiday had been somewhat earlier), huge differences remained. For example, in Scotland in the early 1890s Fife miners worked a 44-hour week, Lanarkshire miners one of 50 hours, employees in bakers' shops worked 83 1/2 hours, those in china shops only 69 1/2.[84] Whereas by the 1880s the big London stores were closing at 2 p.m. on Saturdays and at 6.30 p.m. during the week, small drapery shops often stayed open until 9.30 p.m. and beyond.[85] One bricklayer in Gateshead, who happened to keep records, worked 31 hours a week in 1885, but 49 in 1889, with the result that his average weekly earnings could range from 20s. 7d. to 33s. 1d. And while factory production undoubtedly brought about greater standardization of work patterns, large numbers of workers in towns like Birmingham (with its many very small enterprises) remained exempt from rigid time disciplines until well after the end of our period.[86]

The 'standard of living' in its most comprehensive form has to encapsulate qualitative as well as quantitative data. Indeed, any evaluation of industrialization and its aftermath raises large questions about the desirability or otherwise of certain developments associated with modern society: urbanization, factory working, regular time-keeping, greater geographical mobility, changes in the size of families, and so on. Here only the most tentative assessment is possible, and sometimes not even that. Undoubtedly,

H. Cunningham, 'Leisure and Culture', in F. M. L. Thompson (ed.), *The Cambridge Social History of Britain 1750–1950*, 3 vols. (Cambridge, 1990), ii. 280–1.

[83] R. C. O. Matthews, C. H. Feinstein, and J. C. Odling-Smee, *British Economic Growth 1856–1973* (Oxford, 1982), 565–71.

[84] T. C. Smout, *A Century of the Scottish People 1830–1950* (London, 1986), 101–2.

[85] W. B. Whitaker, *Victorian and Edwardian Shopworkers* (Newton Abbot, 1973), 89, 203; G. Cross, *A Quest for Time: The Reduction of Work in Britain and France, 1840–1940* (Berkeley, Calif., 1989), 81–92.

[86] K. Burgess, 'Did the Late Victorian Economy Fail?', in T. R. Gourvish and A. O'Day (eds.), *Later Victorian Britain, 1867–1900* (London, 1988), 259; E. Hopkins, 'Working Hours and Conditions during the Industrial Revolution', *Economic History Review*, 35 (1982), 52–66.

the physical aspects of many towns—houses, alleyways, sewers, smells, squalor—were often dreadful. Undoubtedly, too, many handworkers were reluctant to move into factories, though this was not always so. But claims that family ties were 'weakened', that homes were dirtier and more cramped, that factory work required more exertion than other forms of labour, tend to overlook the fact that pre-industrial (and contemporary rural) conditions were often no better and sometimes very much worse.

Although, therefore, some evidence exists to suggest that in certain large towns the density of people per house was rather higher in 1870 than a century before, there is widespread agreement that outside London and Scotland the quality of housing in most towns slowly improved during the second half of the nineteenth century. This improvement had less to do with legislation than with a general growth in effective demand. While absolute standards remained low, from 1850 onwards new housing was being provided at a slightly faster rate than that by which the population was growing.[87] The trend in English working-class housing during the second half of the century was towards a separation from neighbours outside and a separation of function within. Houses came to have particular rooms for particular purposes. And as this occurred, so the facilities available improved.[88] In Scottish cities, however, tenements continued to be built and styles of working-class living remained closer to the continental pattern of fewer undifferentiated rooms. In 1861 over a third of all Scottish dwellings had only a single room, and nearly two-thirds of the people lived in two rooms or less. Even twenty-five years later, one in three Glasgow families still occupied only one room.[89] If many of the buildings put up in these years were not especially pleasing to the eye, at least the parallel lines of terraced housing and a standardized monotony of design often went hand in hand with those new amenities which made it possible for more people to regard their dwellings, not simply as shelters, but as homes.

All this cost money. Very few working people owned their own houses, almost all rented from private landlords.[90] And rents constituted the major

---

[87] J. Burnett, *A Social History of Housing 1815–1985*, 2nd edn. (London, 1986), 141; C. H. Feinstein and S. Pollard (eds.), *Studies in Capital Formation in the United Kingdom 1750–1920* (Oxford, 1988), 382–3.

[88] M. J. Daunton, 'Public Place and Private Space: The Victorian City and the Working-Class Household', in D. Fraser and A. Sutcliffe (eds.), *The Pursuit of Urban History* (London, 1983), 226.

[89] Smout, *Scottish People*, 33–5. This was almost certainly worse than the situation in England: in 1891 one-third of Londoners but two-thirds of Glaswegians lived two or more to a room (ibid.).

[90] The level of owner occupation varied widely, e.g. Durham City 1850 = 17%; Leicester 1855 = 4% (Dennis, *English Industrial Cities*, 142–3).

exception to the stability and even decline of late Victorian living costs. It is estimated that the rent of a 'typical' working-class house rose by about two-fifths (and the overall cost of living by less than a tenth) between 1850 and 1880.[91] In fact, urban rents probably went up even faster, one index showing a rise of no less than a quarter between 1870 and 1893 when prices overall were actually falling. Indeed, it might be argued that increased expenditure on housing, the growth of home-based consumption, and the development of a culture of domesticity were predictable accompaniments to a period of rising real wages. Inevitably the poor spent a much higher proportion of their incomes on housing than the well-to-do. Whereas, for much of the century an average of about 16 per cent of income was spent on rent, for the middle class the figure was 8–10 per cent, for workers 16–25 per cent, and for the very poor about 30 per cent. If anything, such differentials were increasing. Already by the mid-1880s a royal commission on housing estimated that in London 85 per cent of workers paid at least one-fifth and almost one in two between a quarter and a half of their incomes on rent.[92] But if this placed additional burdens on the very lowest sections of society, the rest undoubtedly benefited from the simultaneous reduction in other costs and the greater space and better facilities which their payments were now able to buy.

In contrast, the proportion of average working-class budgets spent on food fell from almost three-quarters before 1850 to perhaps a half at the end of the century. Here again, the poor spent proportionately the most, with Board of Trade returns from the late 1880s indicating that those with annual incomes in the range £28–£40 devoted 87 per cent to food (though how they could then also have devoted 30 per cent to rent is unclear!), while those with £40–£50 devoted only 56 per cent to food.[93] If there was little dietary advance in the period 1820–48 (now generally identified as a time of substantial real wage growth), thereafter, though many regional and income-level differences remained, standards almost certainly improved. The consumption of bread and potatoes fell, that of meat and fats rose. Between the 1860s and the 1890s meat consumption may actually have doubled at a time when the population was rising by just over two-fifths. An analysis of individual daily nutrient intake as recorded in a range of family budgets suggests that, whereas levels hovered around 2,000/2,100

[91] Benson, Working Class, 81.

[92] R. Rodger, Housing in Urban Britain 1780–1914 (London, 1989), 10; id., 'Political Economy, Ideology and the Persistence of Working-Class Housing Problems in Britain, 1850–1914', International Review of Social History, 32 (1987), 111–12.

[93] Hunt, British Labour History, 81; Fraser, Coming of the Mass Market, 34. Thus the very poor had little if anything left to spend on clothing and wore mostly cast-offs and rags.

'calories' (more correctly, kilocalories) in the late eighteenth and early nineteenth centuries, from the 1840s onwards they rose to about 2,250/ 2,600. Yet in absolute terms malnutrition remained rife and calcium deficiency was common in Britain until well into the twentieth century.[94] Increasing real wages were not, in any case, always translated (or indeed translatable) into equivalent improvements in diet. Adult male breadwinners continued to get the lion's share, while wives and children went without. And the quality of food for many poor families was further constrained by the dearness of fuel, the lack of easily accessible water supplies, and the inadequacy of most kitchen ranges (gas cookers become common only towards the end of the century). Nor was it always possible to benefit from the falling food prices of the 1870s and 1880s when shopping in the retail outlets of the poorer districts where very small quantities were bought and adulteration was rife. In addition, some at least of the additional spending power went on items of little nutritional, though considerable psychological, value. Tea consumption went up enormously from 1.61 lb. a head in the United Kingdom in 1841–50 to 4.92 lb. in 1881–90. Cigarette smoking also increased. In 1888 Wills introduced their 'Woodbine' penny-for-five packets, with the result that by 1891 126 million cigarettes of all kinds were being sold by this one firm alone.[95]

That significant improvements in diet, as in environmental matters, had begun to have a widespread effect by the end of the century can be seen in the great transition inaugurated in the 1880s from the age-old pattern of mass morbidity and mortality occasioned by infectious diseases, poor nutrition, and hard labour towards our own accumulation of functional disorders, viral diseases, and bodily decay associated with old age. The annual mortality rate for England and Wales began to fall: 23.0 (per thousand) in 1863–7, 22.2 in 1868–72, 21.4 in 1873–7, 20.3 in 1878–82, 19.4 in 1883–7, 19.0 in 1888–92, down to 14.2 just before the Great War (1908–12).[96] To match this, the expectation of life at birth in Britain

[94] D. J. Oddy, 'Food, Drink and Nutrition', in Thompson (ed.), *Cambridge Social History*, ii. 269–75; J. Burnett, *Plenty and Want: A Social History of Diet in England from 1815 to the Present Day*, 3rd edn. (London, 1989), 60–1. In the 1930s the lowest 10% of the income range averaged 2,317 kilocalories per head per day. See also below, Ch. 10, S. 3.

[95] Oddy, 'Working-Class Diets', 314–23; J. Burnett, *A History of the Cost of Living* (Harmondsworth, 1969), 274; id., *Plenty and Want*, 15–16, 114–15; B. W. E. Alford, 'Penny Cigarettes, Oligopoly, and Entrepreneurship in the U.K. Tobacco Industry in the Late Nineteenth Century', in B. Supple (ed.), *Essays in British Business History* (Oxford, 1977), 49–68. Cigarettes were introduced into Britain by soldiers returning from the Crimea where they had acquired the habit from their French comrades-in-arms. The first branded (hand-made) cigarette was Wills's 'Bristol' introduced in 1871.

[96] Mitchell, *British Historical Statistics*, 57–8. The Scottish rate moved from 24.2 in 1863–7 to 20.2 in 1888–92.

increased during the nineteenth century from the mid-thirties to the upper forties, with the bulk of the rise occurring towards the end of the period.[97] All this was evidence of a general improvement in living standards, though the death rate for the most vulnerable (infants under one year of age) did not decline until the early twentieth century and all rates continued to vary substantially between the most favoured areas and the least. Already, indeed, by 1861 those living in many rural districts were experiencing life expectancies that the 'average person' would not attain for another sixty years.[98]

More surprising was the decline in the birth rate which began to be noticed at much the same time. After having hovered (in England and Wales) around 35 births per thousand persons since the 1830s, it now fell: to 32.4 in 1881–90, 29.9 in 1891–1900, 27.0 in 1901–11.[99] The reasons remain mysterious. Perhaps the effects of economic betterment on real incomes and patterns of consumer expenditure encouraged people to think, not merely in terms of *actual*, but also of *desired* living standards. As incomes rose so also did the expectations of parents for their own and their children's futures, and the greater these expectations became the more likely it was that people would worry about the cost of large families. The very question 'How many children should we have?' was a new one for most Victorians and may well have been brought to their attention by the depressed times so many thought they were experiencing during the last quarter of the century. Changing behaviour patterns towards family limitation also began to appear at this time, a development given further impetus by the reduction in child mortality, increased education and literacy (especially among women), even perhaps by the gathering secularization of late Victorian society. All these influences created an atmosphere in which having no more than two or three children came to be thought respectable. Though most couples almost certainly used the well-tried 'techniques' of coitus interruptus and abstinence, the advent of mass-produced rubber contraceptive devices in the 1880s probably played some part in the matter and may subsequently have helped to give permanence to a phenomenon which might otherwise have proved less lasting or less marked.[100]

---

[97] R. Woods, *The Population of Britain in the Nineteenth Century* (London, 1992), 57.

[98] R. Woods, 'The Structure of Mortality in Mid-Nineteenth Century England and Wales', *Journal of Historical Geography*, 8 (1982), 391.

[99] N. L. Tranter, *Population and Society 1750–1940* (London, 1985), 59.

[100] R. Woods, 'Approaches to the Fertility Transition in Victorian England', *Population Studies*, 41 (1987), 309–11; W. Seccombe, 'Starting to Stop: Working-Class Fertility Decline in Britain', *Past & Present*, 126 (1990), 151–88; J. Peel, 'The Manufacture and Retailing of Contraceptives in England', *Population Studies*, 17 (1963), 113–25.

The decline in fertility seems to have affected all occupational groups at much the same time and there is now little support for the once much-canvassed 'social diffusion' model, according to which the professional middle classes inaugurated a downward movement from about the middle of the century which was then successively taken up by manual workers of various kinds. Though fertility distinctions remained considerable, even within the working class it is difficult to discover any obvious patterning. In the vanguard of family-size limitation were most railwaymen, but not engine drivers; most domestic servants, but not gamekeepers; most textile workers, but not cotton-spinners. Clearly something more complex than social diffusion was at work: private feelings, attitudes, and emotions no longer recoverable.

The nature and the effects of these changes were unprecedented. Had the rate of growth of the early 1870s continued, the population of England alone by the year 2000 would stand at 110 million, roughly double the prospective total for that date. For a time Britain became a land of fewer 'dependent' people, though only so long as the falling proportion of children outstripped the rising numbers living into old age. More generally, traditional assumptions about the relationship between economic and demographic changes were beginning to disintegrate. With rising living standards there was every reason to suppose that death rates would fall, which indeed they did and to an unprecedented degree. But population growth rates did not rise. Greater prosperity did not lead to either earlier or more universal marriage. If anything, age at marriage rose and celibacy increased down to the outbreak of the Great War. Men and women were turning away from the marriage patterns of earlier generations according to which a continued rise in real wages should have pulled fertility back up to the very high levels sustained, for example, in the early decades of the nineteenth century. This process represents a clear break with what had been the case for centuries, 'a demographic revolution' to match that which had taken place in manufacturing. Only in Ireland, with its predominantly agricultural economy, did things pursue a less novel path. There the Great Famine of the late 1840s was followed by population decline produced by a combination of emigration, a steep fall in the marriage rate, and a rise in the age of marriage. This was the traditional logic of families fitting the means of subsistence. In 1841 almost one in three United Kingdom citizens lived in Ireland. Sixty years later barely one in ten did so.

The conclusion that real living standards probably rose during the thirty years after 1820 and certainly rose in the second half of the nineteenth century has much to recommend it. But sceptics and the more pessimistically inclined have long expressed doubts as to the reliability of the wage and cost of living indices upon which this picture is based and questioned whether such data (even if perfect) can ever adequately capture the totality of physical, let alone psychological, experience. More recently an alternative approach has been attempted which, while not without its own problems, avoids many of the difficulties of previous methodologies. Put simply, this involves measuring changes in the heights of large samples of individuals over long periods on the well-attested assumption that stature constitutes a useful surrogate for what biologists term 'nutritional status', that is, the state of the human body as it balances nutrient intake with growth, work, and the defeat of disease. Although measurement of height provides no instant solution to the standard of living debate, it possesses the advantage of concentrating a wide range of environmental and other influences within the compass of a single set of figures.

While the findings can only be summarized here they certainly throw an explosive grenade into analyses based mainly upon wage and price levels. For most of the period 1750–1850 the height data indicate substantial, though gradual, improvements in living standards which would have been hard to detect on the evidence of mortality, morbidity, diet, or housing alone. However, for people born after 1830 the data support those historians who have found at best little improvement in living conditions, at worst actual deterioration.[101] This then runs counter to claims that real standards experienced a significant rise from about 1820 onwards. Not that the proponents of the improvement thesis themselves overlooked the argument that income increases in the quarter-century after 1820 might in fact have been overwhelmed by countervailing deteriorations in environmental conditions. In particular, they have tried to calculate in monetary terms the negative value of the various disamenities (poor sanitation, bad housing, air pollution, less leisure, etc.) which industrialization and urbanization brought in their wake in these years. As, however, the result of such calculations has been a suggested reduction of at most 10 per cent in real growth, how then, they ask, does one explain the origin and persistence of 'the urban-quality-of-life-deterioration myth?'[102] But while some parts of this 'myth' (such as the idea that industrialization caused more suicides) have indeed been satisfactorily laid to rest,[103] the height data do suggest

---

[101] R. Floud, K. Wachter, and A. Gregory, *Height, Health and History: Nutritional Status in the United Kingdom, 1750–1980* (Cambridge, 1990), 304.

[102] J. G. Williamson, *Did British Capitalism Breed Inequality?* (London, 1985), 26; id., 'Urban Disamenities, Dark Satanic Mills, and the British Standard of Living Debate', *Journal of Economic History*, 41 (1981), 75–83; Lindert and Williamson, 'Living Standards', 1–25.

[103] O. Anderson, 'Did Suicide Increase with Industrialization in Victorian England?', *Past & Present*, 86 (1980), 149–73. In fact, suicide rates (highest at this time among the old)

that, 'even if there were substantial gains in real income or in real wages for the working class in the second quarter of the nineteenth century, these were more than outweighed by other features of the environment—urbanisation, disease, diet and possibly work intensity'.[104] Of course the connection between height and income per head should not be pushed too far. For example, parallel findings that before the Great Famine the Irish were, if anything, slightly taller than the English do not necessarily mean that they were 'better off' in the traditional sense of economic welfare: perhaps the English simply 'preferred, say, a diet of toast and tea to healthier foods'.[105]

More radical still are the implications of the new approach for the second half of the century which almost no serious scholar has ever seen as anything but a period of material improvement for all sections of society. This is because the decline in heights which started in the 1830s persisted well into the 1860s and because mean heights did not recover the levels reached by the cohort of the 1820s until just before the outbreak of the Great War.[106] The implication is that it was not until the very end of the century that improvements in real incomes and in public health and other sanitary measures effectively compensated manual workers for the horrors of urban and industrial life during the thirty or so years after Waterloo.[107] In short, Victorian working people neither lived nor died nor prospered nor decayed by wages alone, but according to an intricate conjuncture of earnings, diet, shelter, air quality, clothing, work, disease, and much else besides.

While historians love categories, agglomerations, and patterns, the inhabitants of the past have laid wonderfully beguiling traps for those bent on making simple sense of their affairs. Rigid and deterministic notions of class (its growth and striving towards some foreshadowed goal), of class conflict, of direct relationships between economic cause and social and political effect, disguise more than they reveal. Certainly by the end of the century it is possible to identify developments which have traditionally been held up as generators of class and class consciousness: the growth of an industrial workforce, its concentration in large plants, its subjection to general economic fluctuations, its organization into national trade unions, and so on. But the proportion of people employed in very large undertakings is, for

were often quite low in industrial towns, even allowing for their comparatively youthful populations.

[104] Floud, Wachter, and Gregory, *Height, Health, History*, 305.
[105] J. Mokyr and C. Ó Gráda, 'Poor and Getting Poorer? Living Standards in Ireland before the Famine', *Economic History Review*, 41 (1988), 228.
[106] Floud, Wachter, and Gregory, *Height, Health, History*, 306.
[107] Ibid. 319.

example, easy to exaggerate and was still probably much less than half of the whole.[108] And just as there was no single focus for the discontents of that great variety of mid-Victorians who worked with their hands, so neither did the conflicts in which those discontents were expressed require constant oxygenation from militant class consciousness before being able to burst into flame.

[108] McKibbin, *Ideologies of Class*, 12.

CHAPTER 4

The Nature of the State

I. WHAT SHOULD THE STATE DO?

The Victorian state remains elusive. Little has been found in the way of a corpse, so that analysis must largely be confined to a study of tracks and footprints. Contemporaries developed no definitive view, let alone theory, of the 'state' as a coherent entity. Instead, 'government'—its proper limits and functions—was the focus of their concerns. What cannot be doubted is that the scope and character of government in its economic, social, and bureaucratic manifestations changed during the Victorian period. What remains open to interpretation is the significance of these changes, their extent, nature, inspiration, and effect.

Notwithstanding Adam Smith's claims to the contrary, the eighteenth-century state had largely confined itself to defence, external affairs, the regulation of trade, law and order, the raising of revenue, and to a few residuals of an older and increasingly anachronistic paternalism such as the Elizabethan Poor Law and the Statute of Labourers. Whether this small territory was thereafter expanded under the impress of pragmatic contingency or in reaction to a body of a priori ideas is a question that has been much discussed and still remains in doubt, as does the assumption that 'a revolution in government' took place at some stage during Queen Victoria's reign. Change there certainly was, development too; revolution probably not. Yet even change and development do not appear ready-armed from the void. Large urban populations, the growth of factories, modulating social relationships did not in themselves become 'problems' until certain values had convinced people they should perceive them as such. However, the very complexity of the new social and economic environment and the comparative caution of mid-Victorian élites meant that comprehensive and drastic solutions rarely seemed attractive, let alone plausible. Not only that, but, as J. S. Mill put it in 1842, 'Existing evils, it seems to me, lie too deep, to be within reach of any one remedy, or set of remedies . . . their removal, I conceive, can only be accomplished by slow degrees, and through many successive efforts.'[1] Ideology, in turn, must not be placed in a vacuum, if only because, at the very least, it generally constitutes a crystallization of the accepted understandings and previously unexpressed assumptions of large numbers of people. And the ideology which spoke most powerfully to the condition of the new industrial society was that which had first sprung from the so-called classical economists and then been filtered through the utilitarianism of Jeremy Bentham and his disciples.

This ideology did not, however, provide an automatic remedy applicable with procrustean rigour to every problem. Indeed, the variety of responses to the question 'What should be the role of mid-Victorian government?' derived as much from the Janus nature of the 'ideology in office' as from the changing demands of practical circumstances. It is vulgar error to see anything approaching unadulterated *laissez-faire* (the view that the state should play virtually no social or economic role) as the dominant belief of either classical economics or Benthamite utilitarianism. Beginning with Adam Smith virtually all those involved admitted the state's right, even duty, to 'interfere' in certain matters: usually—as in Smith's case—to enforce the law, combat monopolies, furnish services no individual could run, provide a stable monetary framework, and exercise 'unavoidable paternalism' by, for example, protecting children against exploitation and abuse. The difficulty lay, however, in the fact that not all of these duties were invariably reconcilable, so that Smith, for one, was prepared to contemplate state ownership in order to prevent private monopoly and even temporary monopoly in order to provide services which would otherwise not exist.

Be that as it may, there can be little doubt that even 'refined' *laissez-faire* of this kind had no room for differential excise duties, import, capital, and price controls, public housing, minimum wage legislation, resale price maintenance, or major nationalizations—none of them embraced with any ardour until the nineteenth century had itself passed into history. What, however, all who adopted such an approach were agreed upon was that there must be exceptions to any rule—save only (they would quickly have added) to the great rule of free trade. And with the arrival of utilitarianism, which measured the usefulness of actions not from the perspective of a priori natural rights (as Smith had largely done), but according as to whether or not they led to increased happiness in individuals as such or individuals in the mass (society), the whole principle of

[1] *Collected Works of John Stuart Mill*, ed. J. M. Robson and others, 33 vols. (Toronto, 1963–91), xiii. 550.

non-intervention was placed on less rigid and more contingent foundations. Thus, for an economist like Nassau Senior, the rational and proper functions of government lay in expedient pursuit of the community's general benefit. Already by the 1840s he had come to believe that 'the most fatal of all errors would be the general admission of the proposition that a government has no right to interfere for any purpose except for that of affording protection, for such an admission would prevent our profiting by experience'. J. R. McCulloch, in turn, baldly announced in 1848 that to appeal to *laissez-faire* 'on all occasions savours more of the policy of a parrot than of a statesman or a philosopher', while J. E. Cairnes, perhaps the last of the classical economists, insisted that the notion was only 'a *practical rule*, and not a doctrine of science; a rule in the main sound, but like most other sound practical rules, liable to numerous exceptions'.[2]

This general plasticity allowed different analysts to adopt different and even contradictory views of particular issues. Adam Smith defended the usury laws, Bentham opposed them; Nassau Senior was one of the architects of the new Poor Law of 1834, McCulloch upheld the traditional system of local control; J. S. Mill supported the idea of limited liability on grounds of non-intervention, McCulloch opposed it on grounds of individualism. By the same token, practising politicians also wove an uneasy path between general principles and practical applications. Cobden was consistently fierce against trade unions and against interference with 'trade and industry', but accepted state interference in less developed economies like that of India, welcomed Peel's Bank Charter Act of 1844 which gave the Bank of England a quasi-monopoly, distinguished between the state's proper protection of child and female workers (neither held capable of perceiving their own best interests) and its improper protection of adult males, and (like Smith and, for most of his career, Bright) believed in the idea of a national network of state schools.[3] Viscount Howick (later the 3rd Earl Grey) contributed to the parliamentary debates of 1844 on the Factory Bill by simultaneously attacking 'restrictions imposed upon industry, with the visionary hope of increasing a nation's wealth' and upholding 'those of which the aim is to guard against evils, moral or physical, which it

[2] N. W. Senior, *Industrial Efficiency and Social Economy*, ed. S. L. Levy, 2 vols. (New York, 1928), ii. 302; J. R. McCulloch, *Treatise on the Succession to Property Vacant by Death* (1848) cited L. Robbins, *The Theory of Economic Policy in English Classical Political Economy*, 2nd edn. (London, 1978), 43; J. E. Cairnes, *Essays in Political Economy, Theoretical and Applied* (London, 1873), 251.
[3] W. H. Greenleaf, *The British Political Tradition: The Ideological Heritage* (London, 1983), 39; D. Read, *Cobden and Bright: A Victorian Political Partnership* (London, 1967), 177–81, 209–18.

is apprehended that the absence of such precautions might entail upon the people'.[4]

What allowed many to square the circle was the belief that state interference was permissible if designed to strengthen individual liberties by helping place all citizens in an initial condition of equality in the struggle of life. Once all were lined up under starter's orders, then competition and struggle might properly be allowed to take their course. Hence education, better health, industrial safety, and minimal poor relief could be seen as ensuring that individuals were in a position to maximize their own happiness. State intervention, in other words, though rarely achieving good of itself, could properly be used to remove specific abuses in order to allow the free market to work its miracles of growth. Thus, for Gladstone, the tariff-reducing Anglo-French Commercial Treaty of 1860 was admirable precisely because it gave the people a weapon for 'enlarging their means without narrowing their freedom'.[5] But, unlike later Individualists such as Herbert Spencer, most utilitarians saw liberty, not as an independent principle, but as a subordinate element in proper government. None, however, save J. S. Mill (who in later life moved towards an idiosyncratic socialism), truly perceived the inconsistency between the idea of individual freedom (which involved a tendency to non-intervention) and the principle of utility (which in important ways was neutral on the matter).

From this a conviction ensued that *laissez-faire* should be the 'general rule', but that utility could admit the introduction of exceptions on particular points. For Bentham *'Be quiet* ought on those occasions to be the motto, or watch word, of government'. For Cairnes *'laissez-faire'* as a 'practical rule' was 'incomparably the safer guide'. For J. S. Mill it should 'be the general practice: every departure from it, unless required by some great good, is a certain evil'.[6] But Mill himself soon admitted a burgeoning army of 'exceptions' concerning child protection, education, poverty, and a whole army of matters of 'general convenience'. In the political world, too, Lord John Russell, while clinging to a feeling that 'the interference of the State' deadened 'private energy', none the less supported a number of notable interventionist measures when in government.[7] While, therefore,

---

[4] *Hansard*, lxxiv. 643 (3 May 1844). Grey was a cabinet minister under Melbourne 1835–41 and Russell 1846–52.

[5] *Hansard*, clvi. 871 (10 Feb. 1860).

[6] *Jeremy Bentham's Economic Writings*, ed. W. Stark, 3 vols. (London, 1952–4), iii. 333; Cairnes, *Essays*, 251; J. S. Mill, *Principles of Political Economy*, 4th edn., 2 vols. (London, 1857), ii. 542.

[7] To Duke of Leinster, 17 Oct. 1846, *The Later Correspondence of Lord John Russell 1840–1878*, ed. G. P. Gooch, 2 vols. (London, 1925), i. 157.

a flag emblazoned 'laissez-faire' certainly flew over the mid-Victorian battlements, it was a flag saluted with the loyalty of broad belief rather than with that of invariable compliance.

That Benthamite utilitarianism laid at least some of the eggs which later hatched into interventionist chickens can hardly be doubted. The Victorian state aligned itself, if only loosely, to the blueprint laid down in Bentham's *Constitutional Code* of 1830, with the Poor Law Commission of 1834, the Education Committee of 1839, and the Board of Health of 1848 representing dim and imprecise reflections of Bentham's Ministries of Indigence, Education, and Health. Above all, Bentham offered models for both the processes and the institutions of reform in the shape of public inquiries, reports, specialist legislation, and inspection. Although even inspection was not entirely novel, the dynamic twist given it by utilitarian hands overcame opposition on the part of populist Tories like Richard Oastler who had in large measure been responsible for the original agitation over factory conditions but possessed no mechanism for putting proposals into effect. And even if a good deal got lost as ideas were translated into realities, the manner in which Bentham became 'the avatar of the single-minded' ensured that it was not long before his disciples were to be found strategically placed at many levels of government.[8] Key Civil Servants like Edwin Chadwick and James Kay-Shuttleworth rigged inquiries in order to produce 'correct' findings, orchestrated press campaigns with carefully timed articles, and distributed enormous numbers of free copies of suitable official reports (10,000 in the case of Chadwick's Sanitary Report of 1842 alone).[9] Indeed, the second generation of utilitarians became distinctly more authoritarian in their use of the state as time went on.

Some reforms, among them those produced by the Passenger Acts regulating emigrant traffic, the Alkali Acts against chemical pollution, and much of the health legislation of the 1860s, owed little to utilitarianism. Others, however, owed a great deal, notably those connected with factory and mines inspection in the 1830s and 1840s, the new Poor Law of 1834, the first General Board of Health of 1848, the education grants and inspectorates of 1833 and 1839, and the Civil Service innovations of 1855 and 1870. Indeed, having once infiltrated important sections of political and administrative opinion, utilitarianism, now tempered by the imperatives of practical government, became important, not simply for such power as its

[8] J. Hart, 'Nineteenth-Century Social Reform: A Tory Interpretation of History', *Past & Present*, 31 (1965), 42–3; G. H. Le May, *The Victorian Constitution: Conventions, Usages and Contingencies* (London, 1979), 10.

[9] S. E. Finer, 'The Transmission of Benthamite Ideas 1820–50', in G. Sutherland (ed.), *Studies in the Growth of Nineteenth-Century Government* (London, 1972), 21–7.

original and rigorist postulates still possessed, but for the manner in which its truths could be used to justify exceptions to the very rules of non-interference itself.

Other influences also played an important role, not least plain decency in the face of poverty, disease, and exploitation. Men like Oastler made factory reform a life's mission because 'I saw young and helpless neighbours dying excruciatingly...I heard their groans, I watched their tears; I knew they relied on me'.[10] Others, like Lord Palmerston, were sometimes simply less hard-boiled than they seemed.

He really thought that to have little children of from eight to twelve years of age brought out on a drizzling winter's morning at five, or half-past five, when they perhaps lived three or four miles distant from the place where they worked... with, perhaps, snow on the ground, was a practice which must entail such evils that no one could be surprised at the extreme mortality among the children of factory operatives.... It was said that to limit the number of hours... for the employment of children, would indirectly tend to limit the employment of persons of more advanced age; but all he could say was, he thought it was so essential to protect these children from being overtasked that he could not consider the results which it might be imagined would flow from it.[11]

Directly religious motivations varied with the individual and the nature of the belief. Anglican clergymen in the north of England were prominent for factory reform (partly because they disliked Dissenting manufacturers). Their colleagues elsewhere (who knew few such manufacturers) tended to adhere to a more rigid faith in the rights of commercial property. Non-conformist ministers (with Primitive Methodists a notable exception) generally opposed state interference. Especially deep fissures existed in the 1840s and 1850s between, on the one hand, those Evangelicals who (both within and outside the Church of England) believed that providence operated 'generally' and predictably through natural and immutable laws and that society, in harmony with this, should also operate without external interference, and, on the other, those of a more millenarian and extreme cast of mind—the reformer Lord Shaftesbury prominent among them—who saw providence operating 'specially' in an *ad hoc* and *ad hominem* manner and concluded that particular protection should therefore be afforded to the weakest and most vulnerable in society.[12]

Overall, however, the temporal patterning of the state's social and economic interventions does not allow neat divisions to be made between

[10] J. T. Ward, *The Factory Movement 1830–1855* (London, 1962), 425.

[11] *Hansard*, cxxviii. 1269 (5 July 1853). Palmerston was speaking as Home Secretary.

[12] B. Hilton, 'The Role of Providence in Evangelical Social Thought', in D. Beales and G. Best (eds.), *History, Society and the Churches* (Cambridge, 1985), 215–33.

periods of government growth and periods of quiescence, though the abandonment of protection in 1846 was certainly a step of very considerable importance. Undoubtedly many of the crucial interventionist break-throughs occurred in the 1830s and 1840s, not least because it was in these decades that an influential group of high Whigs, much exercised by notions of *noblesse oblige*, succeeded in pushing through a series of social reforms against the opposition of Peelite Tories and *laissez-faire* Radicals alike. Emphasizing the importance of 'citizenship', high Whigs like Russell, Morpeth, Duncannon, and Ebrington believed that if *laissez-faire* (however admirable in extending economic independence) obstructed its exercise, then citizenship should come first. Ultimately it was better—they argued in advocating state interference in the hours of labour—'for working people to work less and think more'.[13] And though not all the interventionist legisla-tion of this period was their doing, their success in reasserting the idea that parliament could significantly improve the lot of the people was certainly effective in the short term, and perhaps in the long term also.

The Factory Acts of 1833, 1844, and 1847 placed restrictions upon the employment of women and children in most textile enterprises, that of 1842 did the same for mines. The introduction of the new Poor Law in 1834 and the reorganization of its central machinery in 1847 injected an element of centralization where none had existed before. The Metropolitan Police Force was established in 1829; in 1835 boroughs were required to set up forces; in 1839 counties were permitted (though not compelled) to do the same. Education grants were made to voluntary societies from 1833 onwards and a system of inspection was set up in 1839 as part of that general move towards the establishment of minimum conditions to which the setting-up of factory (1833), mines (1842), and prisons (1835) inspect-orates also belonged. Voluntary provision for smallpox vaccination was made in 1840 and a Public Health Act passed in 1848 which, though it possessed some sharp teeth, proved a disappointment to those most anxious to extend the state's central responsibilities.

Much of this was important more for the way in which it marked a symbolic acceptance of change than for the impact—often rather limp—of the measures themselves. Factory legislation was long confined to parts of the textile sector and the ten-hour limitation of 1847 remained open to easy circumvention by employers until 1853. The new Poor Law system was a jumbled mixture of tradition and innovation. As late as 1856 there were still 2.25 million people in England and Wales living in pre-1834 administrative

---

[13] P. Mandler, *Aristocratic Government in the Age of Reform: Whigs and Liberals, 1830–1852* (Oxford, 1990), 33–43.

units that had not yet been reorganized, while the intended abolition of assistance outside workhouses proved impossible and outdoor relief continued even for able-bodied males well into the last quarter of the century.[14] The grants given to elementary schools in England and Wales remained below £200,000 a year during the 1840s, though in Ireland (as so often) more was spent, more quickly, and to greater effect.[15] In 1850 a reforming MP noted that 'A Harlequin's jacket was of a consistent colour in comparison with the variety and discrepancies of the so-called [prison] system which prevailed in this country'. Public health, in turn, long remained little more than a battlefield for ideological interest groups despite, perhaps even to some extent because of, Chadwick's sanitary revelations of the 1840s.[16]

If the interventions of the 1830s and early 1840s were more circumscribed than is often supposed, those of the immediately succeeding period were perhaps somewhat more extensive—an unconscious counterweight, perhaps, to the introduction of free trade in 1846. An important series of so-called 'model clauses' acts was passed in 1847 dealing with gasworks, town police, waterworks, and so forth, in an attempt to lay down guidelines for local emulation. The Public Health Act of 1848, despite all its failures in reducing mortality and the erosions of its central administration in 1854 and 1858, set a trend which was eventually to prove irresistible.[17] Important acts relating to indictable offences and summary jurisdiction were also passed in 1848. The revolutionary Irish Encumbered Estates Act of 1849 broke through (in that country at least) centuries of restrictive property law. Mines inspection, merchant shipping, and burial grounds were subjected to reform in 1850, criminal justice administration and procedure in 1851. And though it is of course possible to draw up similar lists for other periods, it seems clear that—despite much individualistic rhetoric—the mid-century generation was certainly keeping up the good work. New areas of concern were addressed, such as food adulteration and industrial pollution in the 1860s, and existing ones extended by, for example, the spread of workplace legislation beyond textiles and beyond factories narrowly defined. Those who stood in the way, especially if they were vulnerable and unpopular, were—some quickly, others slowly—ground down by the

[14] V. D. Lipman, *Local Government Areas 1834–1945* (London, 1949), 48–9.

[15] E. J. Evans, *The Forging of the Modern State: Early Industrial Britain 1783–1870*, 2nd edn. (London, 1996), 336; D. E. Akenson, *The Irish Education Experiment: The National System of Education in the Nineteenth Century* (London, 1970), 136, 276–7.

[16] Charles Pearson in *Hansard*, cvii. 704 (11 Feb. 1850); A. Brundage, *England's 'Prussian Minister': Edwin Chadwick and the Politics of Government Growth, 1832–1854* (University Park and London, 1988), 133–72.

[17] J. Prest, *Liberty and Locality: Parliament, Permissive Legislation, and Ratepayers' Democracies in the Mid-Nineteenth Century* (Oxford, 1990), 28–36.

millstones of moral and financial righteousness: 'life-fellows of colleges, trustees and masters of decayed grammar schools, the vendors and purchasers of army commissions, parish vestrymen, the men who bribed and took bribes at elections, the convicts, the prostitutes, the habitual criminals'.[18]

Undoubtedly parliament still preferred specific to general legislation and liked to devolve a good deal of power to the localities. But so long as it could be argued that innovation 'supposes no theory, rests on no pledge, makes no party', then even the most cautious of Liberals had little difficulty in accepting it as 'the proper work of an unpledged legislature'.[19] Admittedly the fundamental drive was still towards the elimination of abuses rather than the creation of 'positive good'. Admittedly several crucial areas, notably housing, long remained almost untouched. Admittedly the tendency was by no means always linear, as can be seen in the case of vaccination policy, which, after experiencing strong moves towards state compulsion in the 1850s, registered a decline into breakdown and collapse in the years after 1883.[20] Admittedly, too, the mid-century years saw a continuing commitment to minimal intervention in the strictly economic and fiscal fields. Overall, however, the momentum established in the 1830s was maintained.

It was not, however, much accelerated. The legislation of Gladstone's energetic first ministry (with the partial exception of that concerned with Ireland) slaughtered few sacred cows. And behind the much-trumpeted social reforms of the Conservative government of 1874–80 lay a series of distinctly modest and permissive acts of a type neither very substantial nor very new, such as those passed between 1874 and 1877 concerning education, merchant shipping, public health, food and drugs, river pollution, and friendly societies. Despite a good deal of debate, party distinctions did not, generally speaking, count for a great deal in such matters, as the history of the parliament subjected to the most rigorous examination in this respect (that of 1841–7) shows.[21] Shifting alliances appeared and disappeared in response to particular issues and campaigns. The factory movement, for example, attracted sympathy and opposition from virtually every political

[18] W. L. Burn, *The Age of Equipoise: A Study of the Mid-Victorian Generation* (London, 1964), 226.

[19] A. Briggs, *The Age of Improvement*, 2nd impression (London, 1960), 436.

[20] R. J. Lambert, 'A Victorian National Health Service: State Vaccination 1855–71', *Historical Journal*, 5 (1962), 1.

[21] W. O. Aydelotte, 'The Conservative and Radical Interpretations of early Victorian Social Legislation', *Victorian Studies*, 11 (1967), 225–36; id., 'The House of Commons in the 1840s', *History*, 39 (1954), 249–62.

group, the one occasion on which Tory MPs gave it *unequivocal* backing (the Ten-Hour Bill of 1847) having more to do with their hatred of Peel for having introduced free trade than with the issue in hand. Some Tory squires could join Radicals in supporting Poor Laws on the grounds of economy, but oppose education grants on the very unradical grounds that schooling the poor would encourage the spread of dangerous ideas. On public health legislation, the parliamentary lines of division were different again, those in favour consisting of certain Radicals and a few philanthropic Tories, those against of the 'commercial interest' and the bulk of the landed gentry.[22]

Although prominent middle-class politicians like Cobden, Bright, and Hume were highly vocal in their opposition to state interventionism, the middle sort of people generally registered considerable gains during a mid-Victorian period characterized, not only by a belief in personal 'liberties' and low taxation, but—no less strongly—by the development of substantial new state protections for property by means of police, prison, and legal reform. In the happy and unusual position of being able to enjoy the best of all worlds, such people found it easy to persuade themselves that all was fairness and equity, that, indeed, 'There is now no monopoly in this land. There is no class legislation'.[23] In reality, many reforms had class-specific overtones and even intentions. Divorce reform in 1857, not only favoured men over women, but favoured men with money over men without. Cholera, which affected all classes, was dealt with more firmly than typhus which tended to confine its attentions to the poor. The Civil Service reforms of the 1850s and 1870s were undertaken in the clear hope that they would encourage greater recruitment from the upper middle class. The vested interests of 'old corruption' so energetically attacked by Radicals tended to be those from which the new men of property had least to lose, while moral reforms such as the Gambling Act of 1845 or attempts to control the sale of alcohol were aimed either at dissolute aristocrats or horny-handed sons and daughters of toil. By the same token, certain matters, notably housing, were for long excluded from the reformist pantheon because they touched too closely upon the raw nerve of private property, in this case the property of the urban middle class. But if it was obviously easier to aim coercive legislation against criminals, social outcasts, and labouring people generally (MPs could be supposed not to keep common lodging houses or consign their wives and daughters into prosti-

[22] U. R. Q. Henriques, *Before the Welfare State: Social Administration in early Industrial Britain* (London, 1979), 131.

[23] The words of Baron Bramwell in a Court of Exchequer judgement of 1867 (*The Annual Register . . . for the Year 1867* (London, 1868), 'Chronicle', p. 214).

tution), intervention in such fields as the adulteration of food, workshop conditions, and agricultural labour (all tackled in the 1860s) involved less blatantly class-specific considerations. Indeed, in a few cases legislation actually followed revelations of middle-class misbehaviour, as when the Apprentices and Servants Act of 1851 obliged masters to provide servants or apprentices with food and clothing after a scandalous case in which a lawyer and his wife had assaulted and starved an 18-year-old maid in their employ.[24]

The class tendency of much interventionist legislation makes the cautious and often hostile reactions of many working people easy to understand. Mobs singing 'Britons Never, Never, Never Shall Be Slaves' reflected the survival of that anarchistic chauvinism which had long constituted a strand of thinking among the poor and could still issue forth as a species of radical libertarianism—as evidenced in the support given in the 1870s and 1880s to the Vigilance Association for the Defence of Personal Rights by the agricultural trade unionist Joseph Arch, the secularist G. J. Holyoake, and the ex-Chartist Benjamin Lucraft.[25] Opposition to the new Poor Law formed a general backdrop to working-class distrust of the state, with even outdoor relief often regarded as degrading. Factory legislation too aroused a good deal of hostility because parents often depended on the earnings of their children and because some of the early officials were anything but even-handed. And although the first mines inspector, H. S. Tremenheere, was critical of the masters' undue reliance on mere cash relationships and of the *laissez-faire* attacks on inspection by Cobden and Bright, his own deep suspicion of the operatives' drinking habits, lack of cleanliness, sensuality, brutal sports, liking of 'pernicious literature', and attempts to restrict output, inevitably created distrust among the colliers and their families. As late as the 1860s the Employment Commissioners (of whom Tremenheere was one) considered that 'against no persons do the children of both sexes require so much protection as against their parents'. Indeed, it was only mechanization (see Plate 6) that finally persuaded politicians that workers in industries other than textiles and coal should also be accorded the benefits of factory laws.[26]

The education provisions of the Factory Acts and, indeed, education provisions generally were also widely resented as imposing burdens upon the poor in the shape of loss of earnings and the payment of fees, so that

[24] Burn, *Age of Equipoise*, 154–61.
[25] B. Harrison, 'State Intervention and Moral Reform', in P. Hollis (ed.), *Pressure from Without in Early Victorian England* (London, 1974), 298.
[26] R. K. Webb, 'A Whig Inspector', *Journal of Modern History*, 28 (1955), 356–7, 361–2; G. Best, *Mid-Victorian Britain 1851–1875* (London, 1971), 114.

both masters and operatives connived at their evasion. Hostility was similarly generated by the 1832 Anatomy Act (which allowed corpses in poorhouses and hospitals to be supplied to medical schools), by the spread of compulsory vaccination after 1853 (because only the well-to-do could afford to pay fines for non-compliance), by Chadwick's Board of Health of 1848 (which refused to accept that diseases might be aggravated by poverty and grandly advised those vulnerable to cholera to follow a 'temperate diet' and keep warm), by the Contagious Diseases Acts of the 1860s (perceived as yet another attack on the most marginal in society, in this case prostitutes), and by all legislation designed to restrict the sale of alcohol (seen as an attempt to diminish the attractions of that central institution of working-class life, the pub). Again, when some tentative housing reforms were at last introduced in the 1870s, the demolition of slums tended to be undertaken without much concern for those left homeless thereby. Rehousing, the President of the Board of Trade, Joseph Chamberlain, told the Royal Commission on the Housing of the Working Classes in 1884, could 'safely be left to private enterprise'.[27]

Only rarely, however, did working people respond with universal and unambiguous hostility even to the more obviously 'interfering' legislation of the mid-Victorian state. Respectable parents soon found they had little to fear from magistrates trying prosecutions under the Factory Acts.[28] While the new police forces (see Plate 4) certainly generated a good deal of sullen discontent, it was not long before artisan householders, small shopkeepers, and the like began to see the police as protectors against the ravages of crime.[29] And the few skilled operatives who managed to get themselves elected to town councils generally feared 'taxes more than filth' and were often to be found among the ranks of those anxious to keep the rates as low as possible.[30]

Ambivalence seems, therefore, to have been the order of the day. Legislation purportedly designed to create 'freedom' by restricting monopolies or procuring an open labour market could produce very uneven playing

---

[27] *First Report of Her Majesty's Commissioners for Inquiring into the Housing of the Working Classes*, H[ouse of] C[ommons Paper] 1884–5 [C 4402], xxx. 533.

[28] A. E. Peacock, 'The Successful Prosecution of the Factory Acts, 1833–55', *Economic History Review*, 37 (1984), 200.

[29] D. J. V. Jones, 'The New Police, Crime and People in England and Wales, 1829–1888', *Transactions of the Royal Historical Society*, 5th ser. 33 (1983), 165–6; R. D. Storch, 'The Plague of Blue Locusts: Police Reform and Popular Resistance in Northern England, 1840–57', *International Review of Social History*, 20 (1975), 66, 69, 72; B. Weinberger, 'The Police and the Public in Mid-Nineteenth-Century Warwickshire', in V. Bailey (ed.), *Policing and Punishment in Nineteenth Century Britain* (London, 1981), 66–9.

[30] Henriques, *Before the Welfare State*, 147.

fields indeed. The Railway Acts and much Poor Law legislation are cases in point, while the Medical Act of 1858, though it did not make unregistered practice illegal, gave enormous powers to a new and highly anti-competitive General Medical Council. Vigorous compulsion over vaccination was combined with permissive vagueness with regard to sewerage, drainage, and nuisance removal. Temperance reform posed the same problems, while in the case of trade-union law it was often unclear whose rights and whose liberties were being protected or attacked. In fact, the very weakness of union attempts to generate monopoly conditions in labour meant that a species of economic *laissez-faire*, a partial tolerance of unions, a growing recognition of the legal rights of workers, and a degree of social collectivism were all in evidence at more or less the same time.

The Company Acts of 1855, 1856, and 1862 also received support and condemnation from all sides of the interventionist debate.[31] The same people could be at once individualists and collectivists and many of the movements of opinion which contained collectivist elements—old Tory-ism, middle-class reformism, working-class radicalism—also contained their opposites. Experience could turn Benthamite individualists like Chadwick and Kay-Shuttleworth into Benthamite collectivists, and tradi-tionalists like Tom Taylor at the Local Government Act Office into reluctant but crusading advocates of administrative centralization. Just as bodies like the Public Health Associations of the mid-1840s cut across neat ideological divisions and included Whigs and Tories, secularists and sec-tarians, protectionists and free traders, Benthamites and philanthropists, so it was possible for opposition to public health legislation to come from a curious alliance of reactionary squires and 'wide boy' property devel-opers.[32] A staunch critic of expenditure like the Radical MP, Joseph Hume, could dart hither and thither with eye-deceiving rapidity, now supporting a government role with regard to prisons, poor laws, charities, education, public health, medicine, emigration, police, railways, mines, tithes, enclosures, and the supervision of lighthouses, now opposing it with regard to lace mills, framework knitting, adult factory labour, omni-buses, London bakers, chimney-sweeps, dog carts, merchant shipping, and coolie workers in Mauritius. Even the most outrageous haters of the state had chinks in their armour: Colonel Sibthorp, the parliamentary enemy of

---

[31] Burn, *Age of Equipoise*, 211; S. Checkland, *British Public Policy 1776–1939: An Economic, Social and Political Perspective* (Cambridge, 1983), 120–1; P. S. Atiyah, *The Rise and Fall of Freedom of Contract* (Oxford, 1979), 376; J. Saville, 'Sleeping Partnership and Limited Liability, 1850–1856', *Economic History Review*, 8 (1956), 418–33.

[32] O. MacDonagh, *Early Victorian Government 1830–1870* (London, 1977), 143; Henri-ques, *Before the Welfare State*, 253.

all things modern from water closets to investigatory commissions, loudly demanded government inspection of the newfangled railways he so much despised.[33] Perhaps the most eloquent attack on the quiescent state came from Samuel Smiles, usually (if not quite correctly) identified as the high priest of unaided self-help:

Nobody adulterates our food. Nobody poisons us with bad drink. Nobody supplies us with foul water. Nobody spreads fever in blind alleys and unswept lanes. Nobody leaves towns undrained...Nobody as a theory, too—a dreadful theory. It is embodied in two words: *Laissez-faire*—Let alone...When people live in foul dwellings, let them alone. Let wretchedness do its work; do not interfere with death.[34]

2. CENTRE AND LOCALITIES

Similar cross-currents informed the relationship between central and local government. Again and again centralization was attacked as foreign to the national spirit. The new police seemed to *The Times* an instrument 'for the purposes of arbitrary aggression upon the liberties of the people'. During the passage of the 1856 Constabulary Bill parliament was warned against tampering with old free county institutions, the bill itself denounced as fit only for Naples.[35] Lord Shaftesbury, though once an admirer of Napoleon III, pronounced in 1858 that centralization was something 'to which Englishmen very strongly object'. The National Association of Factory Occupiers asked in 1855 how factory inspectors differed from 'mere spies and informers'. The opposition to public health legislation in 1847–8 relied heavily on denunciations of centralized despotism as alien to the constitution.[36] 'Unlike the Irish and the French, who call on the Government to do everything for them, we warn', wrote one user of the royal pronoun in 1869, 'against any intermeddling with what we regard as our own affairs.'[37] As Mr Podsnap put it in Dickens's *Our Mutual Friend* (1864–5), 'Centralization. No. Never with my consent. Not English'.

[33] D. Roberts, 'The Utilitarian Conscience', in P. Marsh (ed.), *The Conscience of the Victorian State* (Hassocks, 1979), 62; id., *Victorian Origins of the British Welfare State* (New Haven, 1960), 97.
[34] S. Smiles, *Thrift* (London, n.d.), 357–8 (1st publ. 1875).
[35] *The Times*, 10 Jan. 1842; T. A. Critchley, *A History of Police in England and Wales*, rev. edn. (London, 1978), 117; Burn, *Age of Equipoise*, 171.
[36] R. M. Gutchen, 'Local Improvements and Centralization in Nineteenth-Century England', *Historical Journal*, 4 (1961), 85; E. J. Evans (ed.), *Social Policy 1830–1914* (London, 1978), 57; Henriques, *Before the Welfare State*, 131.
[37] [W. R. Greg], 'Scientific versus Amateur Administration', *Quarterly Review*, 127 (1869), 42–3.

The mid-Victorian period might, indeed, be seen as one during which arguments about the proper role of the state were debated primarily in terms of centre and locality. Localist polemics, like most polemics, operated well beyond the boundaries of practical possibility. 'The Saxon system', announced one critic of the Poor Law Commission, 'was to multiply the centres of government, so that the energies of all were called into play ... We hold all centralisation to be objectionable, and only to be tolerated in cases of absolute necessity.'[38] In 1847 religious Dissenters believed that proposals to expand the power of the Education Committee were 'against liberty, against national spirit', while the *Economist* in the same year condemned that 'engrossing centralisation, which is in truth absorbing all things into itself, and dwarfing down the whole nation to the poor standard of ministerial capacity'.[39] And Disraeli, who in 1847 preached against the 'enervating system of centralisation, which, if left unchecked will prove fatal to the national character', was, on this matter at least, little different from Bright.[40] Here too, however, exceptions were implicitly, sometimes even explicitly, admitted, and even so doughty a mid-century champion of administrative devolution as Toulmin Smith—coiner of slogans such as 'Centralisation is only Communism in another form'— never denied that Whitehall might properly exercise at least an enabling and advisory role in the execution of social policy.[41] The clever politicians were those who knew how to bend with the wind. Thus the Constabulary Bill of 1854 failed while that of 1856 succeeded in large part because the latter paid greater obeisances to notions of local autonomy. The Prisons Bill of 1865 did the same, while Henry Labouchere, as President of the Board of Trade, cunningly told the Commons that his Merchant Marine Bill of 1850 'would prevent any system of undue centralisation, and would at the same time ensure an effectual check against local abuses'.[42] While, therefore, all realized that pure administrative localism was practically impossible, it was best to pretend otherwise.

This approach and the variability of the many local acts of parliament introduced about this time injected a high degree of practical diversity into

[38] [Anon.], 'Delenda est Carthago: The Poor-Law Commission must be Determined', *Fraser's Magazine*, 23 (1841), 388.

[39] A. Wells, *On the Education of the Working Class* (London, 1847) cited Roberts, *Victorian Origins of the British Welfare State*, 60; *Economist*, 10 July 1847, p. 780.

[40] W. F. Monypenny and G. E. Buckle, *The Life of Benjamin Disraeli*, 6 vols. (London, 1910–20), iii. 21.

[41] J. Toulmin Smith, *Local Self-Government and Centralization* (London, 1851), 54–69; E. T. Stokes, 'Bureaucracy and Ideology: Britain and India in the Nineteenth Century', *Transactions of the Royal Historical Society*, 5th ser. 30 (1980), 142.

[42] *Hansard*, cxii. 111 (20 June 1850).

the pattern of social reform. The Birmingham Act of 1851 extended the authority of constables to arrest on suspicion and developed the law of blackmail. Local powers were granted to stop the building of houses without privies (Newcastle upon Tyne and Burnley 1846), for the provision of public conveniences (Northampton 1843, Southampton 1846), for ensuring that rooms had ceilings at least 8 feet high (Liverpool 1842, Belfast 1845), for the erection of public gardens (Chester 1845, Leicester 1846), and so on and so forth. The effectiveness of general statutes often depended heavily on the extent of local adoptions. Although even after five years towns with a combined population of no more than two million had completed the procedures required by the Public Health Act of 1848,[43] by the 1860s local authorities were to be found actively requesting central assistance in sanitary matters and responding enthusiastically to suggestions that vaccination facilities be expanded and improved.[44] Indeed, when the purses of powerful interests stood to gain, demands for strong central action could sometimes prove unexpectedly fierce, as in the case of the cattle plague of 1865–6 when the government found itself besieged by demands from landed back-benchers that compensation be given to the owners of slaughtered animals.

Overall there can be little doubt that the quarter-century after 1850 marks a high point of local power and that this occurred at the precise moment when the structure of local government was itself undergoing a set of highly complex and uncoordinated developments. Outside the boroughs there were comparatively few elected bodies at all. London operated in an administrative fog in which (even after the establishment of the Metropolitan Board of Works in 1855) many functions remained the responsibility of vestries of parishes. 'Nothing', as one witness before the 1870 Select Committee on Local Taxation remarked, 'in London is under anybody'.[45] Apart from the creation of new Poor Law unions after 1834 and some consolidation of highway responsibilities after 1862, no significant swing towards a concentration of authorities or districts took place during our period. Instead, the almost continuous creation of special bodies for particular functions parcelled out the growth of government into pockets exceeding small. By 1869 the public health of a rapidly growing town like Merthyr Tydfil came under the supervision of the local board of health, two burial boards, the board of poor law guardians,

[43] B. Keith-Lucas, *English Local Government in the Nineteenth and Twentieth Centuries* (London, 1977), 14–15; Henriques, *Before the Welfare State*, 141.

[44] R. J. Lambert, 'Central and Local Relations in Mid-Victorian England', *Victorian Studies*, 6 (1962), 134, 147; id., 'Victorian National Health Service', 7–8.

[45] *Report from the Select Committee on Local Taxation*, HC 1870 (353), viii. 68.

the superintendant and district registrars, and the inspector of factories.[46] After 1870 boroughs could be served by town councils, guardians, school boards, and improvement commissioners; rural areas by parish vestries, guardians, boards of health, school boards, county police authorities, and highway boards, all separate and distinct, all levying rates directly or by precept. So complicated was this that it is not easy to draw up a complete list of the relevant bodies and units of local administration, though one attempt for 1870 has collected the following bag for England and Wales alone:[47]

65	County units (together with 97 Quarter Session Boroughs) with their magistrates
224	Municipal Borough Councils
667	Poor Law Unions under Boards of Guardians
852	Turnpike Trusts
117	Bodies of Improvement Commissioners
637	Local Boards of Health
404	Highway Authorities in rural areas
15,414	Parishes, townships, and the like
335	Burial Boards
	Together with numerous School Boards shortly to be set up under the Education Act of 1870.

Innovation led, therefore, not to the implementation of any master plan, but to the multiplication of bodies and the division of power. And just as *ad hoc* structures were created for specific activities, so *ad hoc* franchises were created for specific structures—when, that is, elections were held at all. Parliamentary franchises differed from the municipal franchise; local boards of health and boards of guardians maintained their own arrangements; the school board franchise of 1870 was also *sui generis*. Even the passing of the County Councils Act in 1888 (which at last introduced the elective principle into English county government) did not end the chaos, for not until 1894 (and in London not until 1900) were the most serious problems of overlapping responsibility and administrative diffusion brought to an effective end. In 1846, when total central expenditure on civil government for the United Kingdom amounted to £5.4m, the sum of £6.8m was being raised locally from poor rates in England and Wales alone. In 1886 English and Welsh local government expenditure (£44.5m)

---

[46] *First Report of the Royal Sanitary Commission, with the Minutes of Evidence up to 5th August 1869*, HC 1868–9 [4218], xxxii. 646.
[47] N. Chester, *The English Administrative System 1780–1870* (Oxford, 1981), 347–8.

amounted to more than twice the cost of civil government for the United
Kingdom as a whole (£19.2m).[48]

3. WHAT THE STATE DID

The effect of social reforms was muffled, therefore, not only by diffusion of
responsibility, but also by the vagueness of statutes and the modesty of the
means allocated for their implementation. The early Factory Acts contained substantial loopholes, in part because manufacturing interests
quickly realized that guerrilla warfare on particular points would produce
greater concessions than outright opposition. Just as the Reform Acts of
1832, 1850 (Ireland only), and 1867–8 were loosely drawn and produced
administrative chaos, so legislation in the field of health—notably the
centralizing act of 1866—often proved useless until heavily amended and
defined. In the same way, the Prisons Act of 1865, which laid down the
duties of gaolers in enormous detail, had a much more limited impact than
its framers expected.[49] Grand proposals could not, it seems, be easily
transformed into grand realities. A classic example is that of the statutes
of 1834, 1840, 1864, and 1875 designed to control the employment of
children as chimney-sweeps (one of the most emotional of Victorian social
issues): all promised improvement, but none significantly affected practice
at the workplace at all.[50]

As a direct operator the state was doing little more in 1865 than in 1790
and still confined itself largely to the Post Office, the Ordnance, and naval
shipbuilding. The burst of local authority involvement in gas, electricity,
and transport did not become significant until the 1880s at the earliest. As
late as 1870 only four-fifths of all Poor Law unions had built workhouses
under legislation then more than thirty-five years old. By 1861 considerable
towns such as Bury (population 87,563), Birkenhead (41,649), and Chatham (36,177) had still not got round to incorporating themselves under the
Municipal Reform Act of 1835. Not until the Shops Act of 1886 were
working conditions in the retailing sector brought under the umbrella of
factory legislation going back more than fifty years. Despite parliamentary
provision for police in 1829, 1835, 1839, and 1856, it was still possible in
1876 for Cornwall to maintain nine separate forces, eight of them with less

[48] B. R. Mitchell, *British Historical Statistics* (Cambridge, 1988), 587–8, 605, 612. The
other main items in total UK central government expenditure were military costs and debt
charges. Scottish local authority receipts in 1886 amounted to £8.1m (ibid. 623).

[49] Lambert, 'Central and Local Relations', 121–50.

[50] P. W. J. Bartrip, 'State Intervention in Mid-Nineteenth Century Britain', *Journal of
British Studies*, 23 (1983), 67.

than seven men each. Nor was the collection of income tax centralized until 1868.[51]

In the area of government inspection—often hailed as the Victorian state's most significant new departure—practical realities fell far short of the expectations aroused or the claims first made. Although a central Factory Office was set up in 1844, individual inspectors continued to go their separate ways, while the mines inspectorate long lacked any central clearing house at all. In any case, by no means all inspectors were stern administrative imperialists. Men like Alexander Redgrave (appointed factory inspector in 1852), Sydney Turner (industrial schools 1857), and Vivian Majendie (explosives 1875) happily followed the minimalist and localist proclivities of Home Secretaries such as Sir George Grey (1846–52, 1855–8, 1861–6) and Sir William Harcourt (1880–5), Majendie firmly announcing that 'all state interference in industrial life is absolutely contrary to the first principles of economical science'. Nor were the early constabulary inspectors appointed in 1856 prepared to stand up against local traditions or idiosyncrasies.[52] And even when firm interventionism was preferred, action was often circumscribed by the meagreness of the resources that were made available.

By 1875 twenty-two major inspectorates had been set up in the years since 1832. Yet the total inspecting staff still came to no more than 497 and in only seven cases—factories, mines, tithe commutation, education, public health/local government, mercantile marine, and contagious diseases in animals—had it reached double figures.[53] And though numbers *had* increased, they had not kept pace with growing responsibilities: in 1874 fifty-four factory inspectors were each required to deal with far more premises and employees than their nineteen predecessors of 1844 had been. As late as the early 1880s, the combined cost of the factory, mines, alkali, and explosives inspectorates for the whole of the United Kingdom amounted to £60,975 each year.[54] Such paucity of means set strict limits on what could be done. For example, although there is no evidence that the magistrates adjudicating Factory Act prosecutions were generally reluctant to convict, the average number of prosecutions brought each year by the inspectors in the period 1835–55

---

[51] Evans, *Forging of the Modern State*, 235; Best, *Mid-Victorian Britain*, 38; Burn, *Age of Equipoise*, 175; H. C. G. Matthew, 'Disraeli, Gladstone, and the Politics of Mid-Victorian Budgets', *Historical Journal*, 22 (1979), 629.

[52] J. Pellew, *The Home Office 1848–1914: From Clerks to Bureaucrats* (London, 1982), 146–7, 179; Critchley, *History of Police*, 92, 130; C. Steedman, *Policing the Victorian Countryside: The Formation of English Provincial Police Forces, 1856–80* (London, 1984), 38–41.

[53] P. W. J. Bartrip, 'British Government Inspection, 1832–1875', *Historical Journal*, 25 (1982), 607.

[54] Ibid. 613–14; id., 'State Intervention', 70, 76–7.

against both employers and operatives came to no more than 131, while total annual fines amounted to £940 or something like 0.001 per cent of the net value of textile output as a whole.[55]

The Civil Service in general grew only slowly in size and changed only slowly in temperament. In 1870 the Home Office, then responsible for eight inspectorates, employed no more than thirty-three permanent officials and clerks, its Domestic and Criminal Departments (which looked after most of the inspectorates, police, prisons, criminal law, and so forth) together making do with fourteen of these thirty-three. The Board of Trade, which developed rapidly after 1830 from an almost purely advisory committee into a ministry collecting statistics, registering companies, administering schools of design, and supervising railways and merchant shipping, was in 1855 handling all of these functions with seventy administrative Civil Servants. In 1851 the Foreign Office's total complement came to eighty-five, that of the Treasury (without the Commissariat) to 105. The aggregate salaries required for all United Kingdom public departments remained small: £0.75m in 1846, £2.4m in 1886.[56]

The number of those engaged in public employment is difficult to pin down, for not only are the sources unclear, but much depends upon definition and categorization. In 1846 the statistician, William Farr, estimated that 16,353 persons were 'permanently on the establishment in situations liable to assessment under the Superannuation Act', of whom no less than 13,331 were in the Customs, Excise, Coast Guard, and Post Office. In 1869 another expert, Horace Mann, thought there were 16,701 Civil Servants in the United Kingdom, though only 1,173 of these occupied what he called 'superior' and another 1,801 what he called 'professional' grades.[57] The census of 1851 for England and Wales returned a mere 1,628 persons as being engaged in the 'civil departments of the government for general purposes'. Figures collected by Charles Booth—also for England and Wales—indicate that the number of men and women employed in central administration, local government, sanitary supervision, and the police and prison services did not begin to show any appreciable increase in relation to population until after 1881.[58]

[55] Peacock, 'Successful Prosecution', 197–9; C. Nardinelli, 'The Successful Prosecution of the Factory Acts: A Suggested Explanation', *Economic History Review*, 38 (1985), 429.

[56] Pellew, *Home Office*, 6, 22–3, 30; R. Prouty, *The Transformation of the Board of Trade 1830–1855* (London, 1957), 99, 110–11; Chester, *Administrative System*, 168; Mitchell, *British Historical Statistics*, 587–8.

[57] W. Farr, 'Statistics of the Civil Service', *Journal of the Statistical Society*, 12 (1849), 106–7; H. Mann, 'On the Cost and Organization of the Civil Service', ibid. 32 (1869), 50.

[58] W. A. Armstrong, 'The Use of Information about Occupation', in E. A. Wrigley (ed.), *Nineteenth-Century Society* (Cambridge, 1972), 255–81.

Nor was the history of the Victorian Civil Service one of consistently increasing dynamism. To some extent growing professionalization and a widening separation of political and administrative functions actually reduced the extent to which senior Civil Servants could make a creative impact upon events. The pioneering social reforms of the middle third of the century depended heavily on the energy and influence of a small number of 'war lords' prepared to engage in public disputes of an openly political kind such as Edwin Chadwick, James Kay-Shuttleworth, John Simon, Southwood Smith, and Charles Trevelyan. But already by 1859 Gladstone was reflecting a growing consensus when he claimed that 'references from the opposition bench to opinions of the permanent officers of the government, in contradiction to the Minister who is responsible in the matter at issue, were contrary to rule and to convenience'.[59] By the early 1870s the war lords were almost extinct, Simon, the last of their order, feeling himself so constricted by the new atmosphere that he resigned from government service in 1876. Indeed, from then almost until the end of the century, the picture is one of a bureaucracy gently ossifying, keeping its head down, and concerning itself primarily with pushing out again the paper that was coming in.

All this rather cuts the much-vaunted Civil Service reforms of 1855 and 1870 down to a comparatively modest size. The famous report presented in 1853 by Sir Stafford Northcote and Sir Charles Trevelyan, though allegedly based on close study of individual departments, was more a brilliant airing of preconceived ideas than the result of careful inquiry. Its main recommendations—for competition in recruitment, promotion by merit, and a clear separation between 'intellectual' and 'mechanical' work—were at first only very partially implemented. A Civil Service Commission was indeed established, but departments continued to arrange their own standards for entry. Early competitions were, in any case, largely artificial: of the 9,826 certificates of competence issued by the Commission between 1855 and 1868, 7,033 related to men appointed without any competition at all, 2,763 to entrants who had been subjected to very limited forms of competition, and all of twenty-eight to those who had emerged from competitions open to all.[60] The greatest long-term effects flowed, not from the stated intentions of 1855, but from a hidden, though privately acknowledged, subtext to the effect that a closer nexus should be established between a reformed university system (Oxford and Cambridge were

[59] G. Kitson Clark, ' "Statesmen in Disguise": Reflexions on the History of the Neutrality of the Civil Service', *Historical Journal*, 2 (1959), 24.

[60] R. A. Chapman and J. R. Greenaway, *The Dynamics of Administrative Reform* (London, 1980), 48.

the subjects of legislation in 1854, 1856, and 1871) and a reformed government service. In 1854 Chadwick had talked disparagingly about the backgrounds of some of those hitherto recruited by patronage: he instanced cases of prize fighters and dog fanciers. In the same year, Gladstone, as Chancellor of the Exchequer, had pointed out that 'one of the great recommendations of the change in my eyes would be its tendency to strengthen and multiply the ties between the higher classes and the possession of administrative power'. As MP for Oxford University he was especially hopeful that the new division of intellectual and mechanical responsibilities would 'open to the highly educated class a career and give them a command over all the higher parts of the civil service'.[61] And if such was to be the case at home, all the more was it to be the case with regard to the better-paid Indian Civil Service, that great Victorian provider of jobs for the choicest products of the ancient universities. In 1853 open competition was, therefore, introduced into the ICS with the proviso that all examinations be held in London (a location rather more convenient for British than for Indian candidates).

Arguments similar to those of Gladstone in the 1850s lay behind the attempts of a later Chancellor, Robert Lowe, to extend the work of reform. Lowe's Order in Council of 4 June 1870 was designed to make open competition the norm for the domestic Civil Service and ensure that a differentiated system of recruitment would finally impose the intellectual/mechanical distinction which many believed essential. Like Gladstone, Lowe made no secret of his ambition to seek out those trained in 'the best education that England affords'.[62] Not all, however, were convinced. The Foreign Office remained aloof and certain specialized departments (notably those concerned with education) continued to recruit 'technical' staff entirely by nomination until at least the second decade of the twentieth century. Three large-scale investigations into the Civil Service between 1870 and 1914 all showed how difficult it was to classify positions according to a uniform intellectual/mechanical distinction without giving rise to numerous anomalies. Only in the attachment of a new aristocracy of talent to the old aristocracy of breeding were the intentions of Gladstone and Lowe more or less carried out, with the result that the senior reaches of the service—once open to a rag-bag of idiosyncratic individualists—were transformed into a virtually exclusive hunting ground for those trained at

[61] E. Hughes, 'Civil Service Reform 1853–5', *History*, 27 (1942), 58; V. Cromwell, *Revolution or Evolution: British Government in the Nineteenth Century* (London, 1977), 139–40.

[62] *Third Report from the Select Committee on Civil Service Expenditure*, HC 1873 (352), vii. 672.

Oxford and Cambridge in the literature, philosophy, and history of ancient Greece and Rome.

External defence and internal order represented other areas in which the state was rendered physically manifest. The first had long been accepted as a central responsibility, the second came increasingly to be seen as such. Defence remained, not only a prime political concern, but also the single largest element in central public expenditure, of which it absorbed 25.8 per cent in 1841–5, 28.9 per cent in 1846–50, and as much as 31.3 per cent towards the end of our period in 1881–5.[63] The military could not be treated with the brisk contempt ladled out, for example, to the poor. And, indeed, the limited changes introduced before the Crimean War of 1854–6 (shorter terms of engagement in 1847, attempts to consolidate military departments in 1833, 1838–9, and 1849–50, the introduction of better weapons—notably in 1850) had more to do with pressure from within the machine itself than from without. As a result, the mid-Victorian army continued to be an administrative jungle in which the Horse Guards (where the Commander-in-Chief held sway), the War Office, the Ordnance, the Commissariat (a Treasury department), and even the Home and Foreign Offices were all entitled to hack through the undergrowth.

Although a certain degree of consolidation was imposed during the Crimean War, responsibilities remained confused and the relative power of the various departments unclear.[64] Even the well-known reforms introduced by Edward Cardwell—reorganization of the War Office and shorter engagements in 1870, the abolition of the purchase of army commissions in 1871, and the so-called localization of forces in 1872—were at best partial, at worst ineffective. Like so much of the work of Gladstone's first ministry, they promised more than they proved able to deliver. No planning department was established and no chief of staff appointed to set out the purpose and strategy of the army as a whole because politicians, Civil Servants, and soldiers all proved reluctant to take seriously the idea that Britain could ever again be involved in a large-scale European war.[65]

Above all, the desire for economy underlay Cardwell's actions as it did governmental attitudes to defence in general. Purchase abolition, which did little—and was not intended—to alter the social composition of the officer

---

[63] Mitchell, *British Historical Statistics*, 587–8.

[64] H. Strachan, 'The Early Victorian Army and the Nineteenth-Century Revolution in Government', *English Historical Review*, 95 (1980), 782–809; O. Anderson, *A Liberal State at War: English Politics and Economics during the Crimean War* (London, 1967), 54–68.

[65] A. V. Tucker, 'Army and Society in England 1870–1900: A Reassessment of the Cardwell Reforms', *Journal of British Studies*, 2 (1962), 110–41; E. M. Spiers, *The Late Victorian Army 1868–1902* (Manchester, 1992), 1–28.

corps, was presented as a device to save money.[66] The introduction of short service reduced the need for pensions. A more coherent War Office, it was firmly hoped, would reduce costs. The valuable joint manœuvres held in 1871, 1872, and 1873 under the impress of the Franco-Prussian War were suspended as too expensive and not held again until a quarter of a century later in 1898.

Perhaps the arena into which the Victorian state spread its influence most dramatically was that of law and order. Until the second quarter of the century the prevention of crime and of disturbances had been undertaken by inefficient groups of watchmen and parish constables backed by draconian punishments, with the military available as a long-stop in cases of severe riot and discontent. The reform of the criminal law which began in the 1820s—after 1838, and for the rest of the century, no person was hanged save for murder or (up to 1861) attempted murder—was matched by the gradual introduction of a modern system of police. Although the army was still called out 'to aid the civil power' on twenty-four occasions between 1869 and 1910, except in Ireland its use as an agent of crime prevention became steadily less frequent.[67] Fears about ordinary crime, not political disorder or threatened disorder, constituted the chief inspiration for the invention of the modern constabulary.

The Metropolitan force established in 1829, though owing a good deal to Irish models, conformed essentially to a pattern of administrative Benthamism in the way it combined government control (under the Home Secretary) with a paid professional service. Later developments, however, proved less obviously centralist in character and operated on the basis of partnership between local authorities and Whitehall, with a gradual (though always limited) shift towards the latter as the century wore on. In part this was the result of a suspicion of professional policing common to virtually all sections of society, in part the result of ministerial reluctance to become too involved in matters of detail and potential complexity. Change proceeded along its usual crab-like path. The Municipal Reform Act of 1835 required incorporated boroughs to establish police forces under the control of local watch committees made up of town councillors. Initially 178 towns were involved, though the number grew as additional places obtained municipal charters. Yet as late as 1856 a hard core of thirteen still lacked forces and were thus ignoring requirements then more than twenty years old. Not only that, but police numbers remained low: by the mid-

[66] *Hansard*, ccv. 137 (16 Mar. 1871).

[67] E. M. Spiers, *The Army and Society 1815–1914* (London, 1980), 219; K. T. Hoppen, 'Grammars of Electoral Violence in Nineteenth-Century England and Ireland', *English Historical Review*, 109 (1994), 597–620.

1850s the ratio of borough constables to population was still only half that of the metropolitan area.[68]

The predominantly rural counties were tackled in a still more delicate fashion. The County Police Act of 1839, though it laid down stricter guidelines than the Municipal Act—the Home Secretary had to approve the appointment of each chief constable and the size of forces was not to exceed one policeman for every thousand inhabitants—was entirely permissive. By 1851 forces had been set up in only half the fifty-six counties of England and Wales.[69] Eventually in 1856 all counties were required to establish forces and the crown was empowered to appoint three national inspectors to assess efficiency. Particularly noteworthy was the way in which the act cunningly combined deference to local sentiment and central supervision by providing that the Exchequer should henceforth pay a quarter (after 1876 a half) of the cost of wages and clothing, but only to those forces certified efficient and serving populations of not less than 5,000.

Although much remained to be done—in 1881 there were still thirty-one borough and county forces with less than six men each[70]—much had undoubtedly been achieved (Table 4.1). In Ireland, where British politicians were usually prepared to adopt a sterner mode, matters took a different and numerically still more impressive course. There an act of 1836 established a national paramilitary constabulary, armed, mobile, and living in barracks. There too, despite Gladstone's complaints, cost seems to have been no object at all, so that by 1871 there were relatively more than *four* times as many men in uniform in Ireland as in England and Wales (1:195 persons as opposed to 1:828).[71]

While, however, the impact of the police and the state's apparatus in general upon crime and disorder in Ireland remains obscure, it seems to have been the case that in England the Victorians proved remarkably successful in containing and even reducing crime at a time of broadly growing prosperity, when, according to much received modern wisdom, the opposite should have occurred. Although criminal statistics are notoriously opaque, there is strong evidence to suggest that the peak of nineteenth-century crime came in the early 1840s and that this was followed by

[68] Critchley, *History of Police*, 62–7; J. Hart, 'Reform of the Borough Police, 1835–1856', *English Historical Review*, 70 (1955), 418–21. For Manchester constables in the 1850s, see Pl. 4.

[69] Critchley, *History of Police*, 88–9; C. Emsley, *The English Police: A Political and Social History* (Hemel Hempstead, 1991), 42–8.

[70] J. Hart, 'The County and Borough Police Act, 1856', *Public Administration*, 34 (1956), 408.

[71] K. T. Hoppen, *Elections, Politics, and Society in Ireland 1832–1885* (Oxford, 1984), 414.

TABLE 4.1 *Police strength in England and Wales, 1851–1891*

	Total	County	Borough	London
Number of police				
1851	c.13,400			
1861	20,750	7,829	6,135	6,786
1871	27,425	9,468	7,571	10,386
1881	32,032	10,855	9,140	12,037
1891	39,673	12,425	11,287	15,961
Population per policeman				
1851	c.1,344			
1861	937	1,489	792	504
1871	828	1,348	800	420
1881	810	1,286	792	466
1891	731	1,192	758	421
Annual cost (£000s)				
1861	1,579			
1871	2,243			
1881	3,157			
1891	3,971			

Source: 1861–91 from V. A. C. Gatrell, 'The Decline of Theft and Violence in Victorian and Edwardian England', in Gatrell, B. Lenman, G. Parker (eds.), *Crime and Law: The Social History of Crime in Western Europe since 1500* (London, 1980), 275; 1851 from T. A. Critchley, *A History of Police in England and Wales*, rev. edn. (London, 1978), 146, with an estimated addition of 6,000 for London (taken throughout to include both the Metropolitan force and the City force set up in 1838).

a fairly steady decline until the end of the century. For all indictable offences (a class heavily dominated by larcenies) the annual rate per 100,000 people in England and Wales moved from 276.7 in 1857–65 to 194.0 in 1886–95, while that for more serious indictable offences against the person fell from 13.4 in 1841–5 to 8.6 in 1896–1900.[72] Although the reasons for this are complex and must have included certain broad cultural adjustments, it seems improbable that the growth of policing did not play some important part in the process.

If the history of the police represents an unusually successful mixture of Benthamite inspiration and pragmatic adjustment to circumstances, that of the Victorian judiciary shows how enthusiastic implementations of fashionable theories could sometimes prove powerful enough to survive

[72] V. A. C. Gatrell, 'The Decline of Theft and Violence in Victorian and Edwardian England', in Gatrell, B. Lenman, and G. Parker (eds.), *Crime and Law: The Social History of Crime in Western Europe since 1500* (London, 1980), 282–3.

the explosion of the theories themselves. A remarkable case in point is furnished by the mid-Victorian judicial adoption of individualism and *laissez-faire* as a basis for new interpretations of the law of contract. Whereas Hanoverian judges had been prepared to assess contracts in the light of 'public policy' and protect the weaker partners (misled customers and the like), by the middle third of the nineteenth century an altogether narrower interpretation had become the norm. In particular, a new tone was set by Court of Exchequer judges sympathetic to the individualist ideas of the political economists and the interests of commercial enterprise. All parties to a bargain, it was now assumed, gave full and informed consent, for, after all, were all parties not fully intent upon maximizing their own happiness? This withdrawal into a realm of abstract general principle raised the notion of *caveat emptor* into a species of immutable rule. The decision of the 'body of judges' in the 1853 case of *Egerton* v. *Brownlow* to uphold the validity of a will which specified that the beneficiary become a marquess or duke within a certain time (though overturned by the House of Lords) came to be regarded as stating the correct attitude to issues of public policy: that every person could lay down almost any conditions as long as they were not illegal.[73]

In 1867 Baron Bramwell told some London tailors who had come before the court in connection with strike action that 'every body knows that the total aggregate happiness of mankind is increased by every man being left to the unbiassed, unfettered determination of his own will' and that trade unions and strikes were nothing other than attempts to 'create a set of corporate guilds which were very useful in times gone by ... but which are quite otherwise in these enlightened times'.[74] As Master of the Rolls, Sir George Jessel (a merchant's son and Gladstone's Solicitor-General 1871–3), drove the notion of freedom of contract to its limits in the cases of *Printing and Numerical Co.* v. *Sampson* (1875) and *Bennet* v. *Bennet* (1876). In the latter he upheld a moneylending transaction entered into at 60 per cent interest by a palpable alcoholic, on the grounds that, as far as the law was concerned,

a man may agree to pay 100 per cent if he chooses. There is no reason why a man should not be a fool ... Suppose [the deceased] had gambled on the Stock Exchange, or at the gaming table, or had spent his substance in debauchery. A man may be a foolish man to do that, but still the law does not prevent him from being a fool.[75]

[73] Atiyah, *Freedom of Contract*, 384–5.
[74] *The Annual Register ... for the Year 1867* (London, 1868), 'Chronicle', 214.
[75] Atiyah, *Freedom of Contract*, 387–8.

The shift which this represented from the ideas of mercy and equity towards those of fixed principle culminated in the Judicature Acts of 1873–5, which (despite certain noises to the contrary) marked the virtual demise of equity as a separate source of discretionary justice for several decades to come. Although equity mounted a slow revival in the 1890s and although the strict application of *caveat emptor* in sale of goods cases eventually diminished its hold, judicial attitudes showed little sign of movement until well into the twentieth century. Unperturbed by changes in either ideology or circumstances, the judges continued to expound the true faith long after the church itself had crumbled into dust.

Of course neither practical nor theoretical responses to the constant nineteenth-century question 'What should government do?' proved simple or unequivocal. Advance in one sector was matched by inactivity, even retreat, in another. Few generalizations have withstood qualification or dilution. Even the suggestion that social affairs attracted a more considerable intervention than economic or financial affairs has been criticized.[76] Yet that particular distinction is perhaps one of the few that deserves a measure of qualified assent. Gladstone's (and Peel's) legacy of free trade, balanced budgets, low taxation, sound banking, and a self-regulatory currency remained broadly in place until the Great War. Contrary views, such as the proto-Keynesianism of the Tory *Blackwood's Review* in the 1820s or of Cornewall Lewis's budgets of the 1850s, made no lasting impression. As regards banking and finance, anything other than self-regulation was feared for its potential complexities. Monetary crises in 1847, 1857, and 1866 notwithstanding, strong exports (and hence strong sterling), the injection of new gold into the world system, and low public borrowing requirements absolved Victorian governments from having to think about developing mechanisms for controlling the money supply. As a result, politicians as different as Cobden, the 3rd Earl Grey, and the 8th Duke of Argyll all clearly believed that—in matters of government—the distinction between the economic and the social spheres was the most important distinction of all.[77]

Not that the frontier between the two was always completely impassable or precisely defined. Just as certain areas of social concern were long innocent of effective intervention, so the Bank of England did exercise some control over credit by buying and selling government securities, while 'economic' topics like patent rights and limited liability were not entirely abandoned to the laws of natural harmony. But as a working device the

[76] Evans (ed.), *Social Policy*, 5.

[77] Greenleaf, *British Political Tradition: The Ideological Heritage*, 39–41 (Cobden), 146–7 (Argyll); *Hansard*, lxxiv. 643 (3 May 1844) (Grey—then Viscount Howick).

distinction remains useful, especially when it is remembered that the Victorian state made no attempt to regulate the economy as a whole. Whether the country prospered or whether levels of employment went up or down—though much discussed—remained matters for private decisions only lightly affected by government.[78]

Things were different in the social sphere because circumstances could so easily undermine cash limits, not because of any general desire to throw money about. Indeed, there existed an army of public men ever ready to warn against extravagant expenditure and 'excessive' taxation: hence the modest size of inspectorates, hence the attempts to constrain the cost of poor relief, hence the preference for reforms that were cheap, hence too the dislike of spending without immediate returns. Gladstone's reformulation of Peel's notion of economy as public virtue was widely accepted and admired. Even Disraeli, notwithstanding occasional deviations, was a kind of economizer. Certainly in the 1870s his attacks on the rising burden of local taxation were almost as colourful as his hymns to imperialism and social reform.[79] However, unlike Cobden, Bright, and Gladstone, who, by the 1850s, had come to the conclusion that only a wider franchise would ensure the total triumph of retrenchment,[80] Disraeli made no close connections between the nature of the electorate and future budgetary control.

Yet however much Gladstone kept good housekeeping in mind, his two main weapons—setting up a Public Accounts Committee in 1861 and appointing a Comptroller and Auditor-General in 1866—proved less successful in containing expenditure than he had hoped. The Treasury still found it difficult to reduce spending. So often did ministers heading powerful departments obtain extra funds by appealing directly to the cabinet that in 1871 the permanent head of the Treasury did 'not know who is to check the assertions of experts when the government has once undertaken a class of duties which none but such persons understand'.[81] Indeed, the improved efficiency of government may in some respects have actually helped to increase expenditure by defusing those traditional attacks on waste and mismanagement that had formerly exercised a strong restraining hand.

---

[78] S. Pollard, *Britain's Prime and Britain's Decline: The British Economy 1870–1914* (London, 1989), 235–56.

[79] P. Smith, *Disraelian Conservatism and Social Reform* (London, 1967), 162–3; P. R. Ghosh, 'Disraelian Conservatism: A Financial Approach', *English Historical Review*, 99 (1984), 268–96.

[80] Read, *Cobden and Bright*, 152–3; Matthew, 'Politics of Mid-Victorian Budgets', 630.

[81] Lambert, 'Victorian National Health Service', 16; M. Wright, 'Treasury Control 1854–1914', in Sutherland (ed.), *Growth of Government*, 195–226.

Retrenchment, none the less, remained a potent political force well into the last quarter of the century. It entered into discussions of the relative merits of the 'silent' and 'separate' prison systems. It helped determine the comparative lowness of the original constabulary grant of 1856. So closely did retrenchment touch the Civil Service reforms of the 1850s that the Peelite, Sir James Graham, was persuaded to hope that the opening of the lower grades to elementary school pupils would help to effect 'the cheap and the real mode of encouraging the education of the people without ruinous assistance from the public purse'.[82] The Revised Code of 1862, by which teachers were paid 'by results', was hailed by the responsible minister with brutal frankness: 'If it is not cheap it shall be efficient; if it is not efficient it shall be cheap.'[83] Indeed, so petty could the obsession become—in 1848 the Treasury's permanent head found time to denounce the Home Office's extravagant use of a 'very fine description of paper'[84]—that pounds must sometimes have been ignored so that pennies might be saved.

It is not, therefore, altogether surprising that the actual statistics of central public spending resemble nothing so much as a hall of mirrors. As late as 1886 the total cost of 'civil government' for the United Kingdom came to a mere £19.2m at a time when defence (also of course paid for out of taxation) absorbed no less than £29.7m. And of this £19.2m only £2.4m was spent on the salaries incurred by public departments. Such figures undoubtedly look tiny to modern eyes, but they had grown substantially since 1846 when civil government had cost £5.4m and salaries £0.75m. It is also true that the proportion of total public spending devoted to civil government rose from 12.0 per cent in the late 1840s to 21.2 per cent forty years later. However, closer examination reveals these 'increases' to have been illusory. In the first place, civil government's proportion of total public expenditure had risen largely because careful housekeeping had reduced the proportion needed to meet debt charges, from 50.2 to 28.5 per cent.[85] In the second place, spending *per head of the population* showed only a small increase and, in some respects, no increase at all (Table 4.2).

A favourite mid-Victorian piece of self-congratulation involved contrasting Britain's lack of extensive and expensive government machinery (and of the bureaucrats needed to operate it) with the situation in the rest of Europe. There, it was claimed, the people were hounded by political police, harassed by an army of petty officials, subjected to all-pervasive systems of intrusive control. The conclusion of the Newcastle Commissioners inquiring into educational matters in 1861 was entirely typical in detecting 'a

[82] Hughes, 'Civil Service Reform', 64.   [83] *Hansard*, clxv. 229 (13 Feb. 1862).
[84] Pellew, *Home Office*, 10.   [85] Mitchell, *British Historical Statistics*, 587–8.

TABLE 4.2 *Annual United Kingdom per caput expenditure on total central government and on 'civil government', 1846–1890*

	Total	'Civil'
1846–50	£2.0	£0.2
1851–5	£2.1	£0.3
1856–60	£2.6	£0.3
1861–5	£2.4	£0.4
1866–70	£2.3	£0.4
1871–5	£2.2	£0.4
1876–80	£2.3	£0.5
1881–5	£2.4	£0.5
1886–90	£2.4	£0.5

Source: B. R. Mitchell, *British Historical Statistics* (Cambridge, 1988), 587–8.

material difference ... between the political and social circumstances of our own country and those of countries where the central administration wields great power over a people but recently emancipated, habituated to the control of a searching police, and subjected to the direct action of the Government'.[86] And, indeed, there is much to commend the view that 'no industrial economy can have existed in which the State played a smaller role than that of the United Kingdom in the 1860s'.[87] Certainly it seems to have been the case that, even during the last quarter of the century, central and local government bodies in the United Kingdom employed a somewhat smaller proportion of the labour force (and of the total population) than was the case in France, Germany, Belgium, or the Netherlands.[88] Certainly, too, the idea that 'government' and 'economy' should be treated as quite separate entities was fiercely insisted upon, not least by Gladstone who feared for the nation's future whenever politicians with laxer fiscal principles or different economic theories held sway.[89] In this respect, the innovative budget presented by Cornewall Lewis in 1857 attracted especial wrath for having (so Gladstone thought) 'utterly reversed' his own 'fifteen years' of labour to reduce public expenditure and taxation. By 1873/4 he had even come to believe that ideas of 'economy, or what I call economy'

---

[86] *Report of the Commissioners appointed to Inquire into the State of Popular Education in England. Vol. I*, HC 1861 [2794-1], xxi/1, 215; B. Porter, ' "Bureau and Barrack": Early Victorian Attitudes towards the Continent', *Victorian Studies*, 27 (1984), 407–33.

[87] H. C. G. Matthew, *Gladstone 1809–1874* (Oxford, 1986), 169.

[88] P. Flora and others (eds.), *State, Economy, and Society in Western Europe 1815–1975: A Data Handbook*, 2 vols. (Frankfurt and London, 1983–7), i. 193–243.

[89] Matthew, *Gladstone 1809–1874*, 114–15.

had been out of fashion for twenty years (that is, since 1853): 'the political pulse is low and the spirit of action and (especially) of economy feeble, as it seems to me in all ranks and classes'.[90]

Given the modest range of services provided by the mid-Victorian state, Gladstone's anxieties might seem exaggerated. However, information with regard to public expenditure and taxation (in 1874 Gladstone was once again planning to abolish the income tax altogether) suggests that in these matters the differences between the United Kingdom and other European countries were less dramatic during the last three decades of the nineteenth century (when the relevant information becomes available) than is some-times supposed. Although comparative international data are never without their problems, it would seem that taxes as a proportion of Gross Domestic Product were no lower in the United Kingdom in the years after 1868 than in, for example, Germany, Norway, Sweden, and Denmark—indeed, they were probably higher than in the first two of these.[91] Nor did public expenditure generally constitute a lower proportion of national income than was the case elsewhere (Table 4.3).

TABLE 4.3 *Central public expenditure as a percentage of national income in various European countries, 1871–1895*

	UK	Italy	Denmark	Norway	Sweden	Germany
1871–5	5.4	10.0	7.0	3.8	n.a.	6.6
1876–80	6.0	10.5	6.2	6.5	n.a.	4.2
1881–5	6.2	11.5	5.9	5.9	5.9	4.0
1886–90	6.1	12.8	6.8	6.2	6.7	5.6
1891–5	6.2	13.3	6.3	7.1	6.4	6.2
1871–95	6.0	11.6	6.4	5.9	—	5.3

Source: B. R. Mitchell, *European Historical Statistics 1750–1975*, 2nd edn. (London, 1981), 734–5, 817–18; B. R. Mitchell, *British Historical Statistics* (Cambridge, 1988), 588. The national income data are at current prices and exclude capital formation. The UK, Italian, and Danish data are for Gross National Product, those for Norway and Sweden for Gross Domestic Product (not very different for most countries). The German data are for Net National Product. Because until 1895 the German public expenditure figures include the expenditure of public enterprises net of receipts, the 1896 relative shift in the figures has been used to adjust the initial percentages obtained in an upward direction. Note that the first German figure is for 1872–5.

Leaving aside the aberrant case of Italy, the central sector in the United Kingdom was, it seems, neither especially large nor especially small in

---

[90] *The Gladstone Diaries*, ed. H. C. G. Matthew and M. R. D. Foot, 14 vols. (Oxford, 1968–94), v. 197; viii. 278–9, 439.

[91] Flora and others (eds.), *State, Economy, and Society*, i. 264.

THE NATURE OF THE STATE

international terms. Perhaps, therefore, mid-Victorians deceived themselves when they believed their state to be quantitatively as well as qualitatively unique. Not only that, but perhaps Gladstone was not entirely wrong in seeing the twenty years before 1873 (for more than thirteen of which he was himself Chancellor of the Exchequer or Prime Minister) as ones during which public 'economy' proved easier to extol than enforce. Of course it might be said that comparisons with countries like Denmark and Sweden ignore the fact that the United Kingdom necessarily operated on a larger scale. But Germany too was now a great power. And in any case, the fact that the United Kingdom was still the richest country in Europe—British income levels per head in 1870 were not matched until 1890 in Belgium, 1900 in Denmark, Germany, and Holland, and 1910 in France[92]—meant that identical percentages of national income devoted to public expenditure would tend to produce a relatively larger and grander public sector in the United Kingdom than elsewhere.

By concentrating upon central (and in some countries, regional) expenditure, statistics of this kind do, however, resemble *Hamlet* without the prince, for it was in the field of local government that many of the largest Victorian social developments took place. Perhaps the most important innovatory principle introduced by men like Chadwick was the separation of control (central) and execution (local), a development which may well have made lower levels of central expenditure possible than might otherwise have been the case. To some extent this was merely a species of sleight of hand, though it was also seen by economists like Nassau Senior as increasing the pressure for local financial restraint and efficiency. For a time Gladstone too (as well as the Treasury in general) came to believe that statutory changes such as the 1870 Education Act were acceptable so long as the costs remained a local responsibility. However, already by the mid-1870s it had become evident that local taxation would have to be augmented by central government grants or 'doles' as Gladstone despondently called them.[93] The extent of local expenditure in the United Kingdom is, in any case, difficult to assess, especially before 1868, and international comparisons are virtually impossible. Such calculations as have been made do, however, indicate a considerably faster rate of growth at the local than the central level. Thus, as a proportion of the sum of the two, local expenditure rose from 21 per cent in 1840 to 41 per cent in 1890 and 50 per cent in 1910.[94]

[92] N. F. R. Crafts, *British Economic Growth during the Industrial Revolution* (Oxford, 1985), 59.
[93] Stokes, 'Bureaucracy and Ideology', 140–1; Matthew, *Gladstone 1809–1874*, 215–25.
[94] J. Veverka, 'The Growth of Government Expenditure in the United Kingdom since 1790', *Scottish Journal of Political Economy*, 10 (1963), 119.

Of course in the longer perspective the state had, by the 1880s, advanced only a modest distance down the road which it was to travel over the next hundred and more years. Yet however great the differences between 1846–86 and the present, the physical manifestations of government in the mid-1880s already pointed more clearly to the future than to the past. Small wonder that by the end of the century the very term 'state' was being employed more generally and more polemically than before. In 1832 it had made no appearance at all in a work (by a future Chancellor of the Exchequer) devoted specifically to *The Use and Abuse of Some Political Terms*.[95] By the 1880s it had become almost universal coin, in large part because many of those who so admired Gladstone's minimal image of the state had begun to worry that things were taking a more collectivist turn, not least because of some of Gladstone's own more recent activities. With the 1850s and 1860s now being seen by such critics as 'the Paradise Lost of Liberalism', talk of the state and the dangers or benefits to be derived from increasing its domain became at once ubiquitous and fierce. On the one side were ranged the Individualists who looked to Herbert Spencer's *The Man versus the State* (1884) as a key text, on the other the New Liberals who argued that it was the duty of government to accept responsibility for the positive welfare of its citizens.[96] And although both sides energetically distorted the history of the decades that had gone before, the intensity of their debate and the changing intellectual ground upon which they now ranged themselves are evidence that the image and the reality of the state were beginning to develop in new and not altogether expected ways.

[95] G. C. Lewis, *Remarks on the Use and Abuse of Some Political Terms*, new edn. by R. K. Wilson (Oxford, 1877; 1st publ. 1832).

[96] M. W. Taylor, *Men versus the State: Herbert Spencer and Late Victorian Individualism* (Oxford, 1992), 1–35.

PART II

The Fabric of Politics

CHAPTER 5

Parties, Governments, Policies 1846–1855

I. CORN LAW REPEAL

The repeal of the Corn Laws in June 1846 marked a decisive step in the process of reform inaugurated by the franchise concessions of 1832. By its drama and parliamentary excitement it gathered to itself deep feelings of movement, transition, and order. It was, in short, the central rite of passage of mid-Victorian politics.

That in 1846 Sir Robert Peel should have faced criticism within the Conservative Party was not remarkable. That almost one in three Conservative MPs supported repeal, while the number of Liberals voting against could—despite the Whigs' landed proclivities—be numbered on the fingers of two hands, was very remarkable indeed. Such solidarity among Liberals flowed no doubt in part from an anxiety to make good Lord John Russell's failure to form a ministry in December 1845. No doubt too some Conservatives favoured repeal largely for the old-fashioned reason that the royal government must be carried on. Yet, when all is said and done, the numbers trooping through the lobbies with Peel were significantly greater than short-term self-interest, social background, or inherited traditions alone can account for.

Peel himself had been convinced of the correctness of the free trade case for more than twenty years. However, not until he became Prime Minister for the second time in 1841 was he able to consolidate his convictions into a great moral imperative and to attach them to economic and financial adjustments which went far beyond corn.[1] In this new context the lowering of import duties in the budgets of 1842 and 1845, the Bank Act of 1844, and the reintroduction of the income tax in 1842 all helped to establish an agenda in which the repeal of the Corn Laws could be understood, not simply as good in itself, but as another logical—indeed necessary—step in a grand project of national progress and efficiency.

---

[1] B. Hilton, 'Peel: A Reappraisal', *Historical Journal*, 22 (1979), 585–614.

For Russell to find himself deprived of his reformist image and inheritance was wounding and destabilizing, and to it can be ascribed in large measure the erratic path he was to follow after 1846 as he sought to recover what had been lost. It was especially galling that Peel's new 'progressive' clothes seemed to hide their wearer's consistent opposition to franchise reform, to the limitation of factory hours, to attempts to render the Protestant Church of Ireland less anachronistic, and to educational measures designed to diminish Anglican exclusivity (indeed, in 1834 Peel had gone so far as to describe the Dissenters' request to be admitted to Oxford and Cambridge as 'the most extravagant demand which has been advanced in modern times').[2] His criminal law reforms of the 1820s had been less effective than Russell's in the 1830s and his administration's reactions to Chartist disorders in 1842 less balanced than Russell's in 1839. More striking still, even in financial management (Peel's great field of expertise) the Conservative leader's claim to have turned a Whig deficit into a surplus by means of tariff reductions was at best exaggerated, at worst untrue.[3] Small wonder, therefore, that Russell's all too vivid awareness that 'Peel had guided the ship by the charts left by the Whigs in the cabin'[4] should have made that sensitive man more tetchy and difficult still.

No less aggravating was Peel's resignation speech of 29 June 1846 (delivered after his government's defeat by a combination of Liberals and Protectionist Tories on an Irish coercion bill), marked as it was by two statements, one politically mischievous, the other addressed to a wider constituency already moving within earshot. The first was the suggestion that it was above all Cobden who deserved the credit for repeal, something not only wrong (because Peel's decision to abolish protection on grain had almost nothing to do with the activities of the Anti-Corn Law League) but unhelpful, for it increased Whig suspicions and needlessly antagonized the Protectionists beyond even their existing state of hysteria. The second was the famous peroration, and the hope

That I shall leave a name sometimes remembered with expressions of good will in the abodes of those whose lot it is to labour, and to earn their daily bread by the sweat of their brow, when they shall recruit their exhausted strength with abundant and untaxed food, the sweeter because it is no longer leavened by a sense of injustice.[5]

[2] D. Beales, 'Peel, Russell and Reform', *Historical Journal*, 17 (1974), 880; *Hansard*, xxii. 704 (26 Mar. 1834).
[3] R. Stewart, *The Politics of Protection: Lord Derby and the Protectionist Party 1841–1852* (Cambridge, 1971), 41.
[4] J. Prest, *Lord John Russell* (London, 1971), 218.
[5] *Hansard*, lxxxvii. 1040–55 (29 June 1846).

Here Peel touched most closely upon the changing currents of the time, because such remarks—however lugubrious—were more than mere 'clap-trap about cheap bread',[6] reflecting as they did Peel's belief in an ethical imperative for free trade derived from certain views concerning the operation of providence as revealed above all in the contemporary visitation of famine in Ireland. Indeed, it is in them that his claim to be the chief architect of the mid-Victorian equipoise must lie rather than in administrative competence or in the attachment of money and business to the landed establishment, for not until his final gesture of repeal and consequent political demise did he even begin to be able to persuade 'the toiling masses that there was a moral energy at the centre of the state which was not indifferent to their fears and aspirations'.[7]

One of the results of this was further to compound the problems of the Chartists, the major contemporary exponents of unrest, in trying to sustain a coherent political message at a time when—the brief commercial crisis of 1847 excepted—economic conditions no longer created the receptive audiences of former years. While only discontent with the limited nature of the franchise reforms of 1832 had ever united Chartists as a whole—on factory legislation, the poor laws, and other social matters their opinions differed—so long as the state could consistently be pictured as hostile to working people this had not mattered greatly. During the 1830s the new Poor Law, municipal reform for the benefit only of those who had already benefited in 1832, and more efficient policing had made sweeping critiques of those in power at once possible and convincing. However, by 1838–9 the comparatively mild reactions of Melbourne's government to Chartist activity had signalled a change, soon to be reinforced by legislation in the 1840s regarding working conditions and health and by the reduction of taxes on consumption. The comprehensive rigour of the Chartist argument had thus begun to unravel well before prosperity and economic stability made it difficult to orchestrate the kinds of mobilization which alone made the spread of that argument possible.[8]

The failure of Chartist agitation in 1848 is, therefore, hardly surprising. Nor can revisionist attempts to extend Chartist vitality well beyond that year disguise the fact that almost everything was soon to run into the sands of greater public harmony and narrowly focused campaigns. Although the widespread continental revolutions of that year formed a backdrop to

[6] *The Greville Memoirs 1814–1860*, ed. L. Strachey and R. Fulford, 8 vols. (London, 1938), v. 329 (4 July 1846).

[7] Hilton, 'Peel: Reappraisal', 614.

[8] G. S. Jones, 'The Language of Chartism', in J. Epstein and D. Thompson (eds.), *The Chartist Experience* (London, 1982), 3–58.

events in Britain, no major Chartist leader saw himself in truly revolutionary terms. As in 1839 and 1842 so the agitation of 1848 grew from
domestic and not imported roots. A Chartist convention assembled on 6
April, not long after distress rioting had broken out in Glasgow, Birmingham, and other towns. Four days later a mass meeting was held on
Kennington Common in south London which Chartist leaders hoped
would mobilize opinion behind their presentation of yet another great
petition to parliament. Undoubtedly there was a good deal of propertied
alarm. Unimportant politicians like Lord John Manners and Lord Campbell fell into panic and the Earl of Malmesbury called up five armed
gamekeepers to attend upon him in London. But the government was
well informed and both the Prime Minister (Russell) and the Home
Secretary (Sir George Grey) remained calm. Over 8,000 troops and army
pensioners were deployed, the 4,000-strong Metropolitan Police was put on
alert, and about 85,000 special constables were enrolled. These last, among
them Gladstone and the still-exiled Louis Napoleon Bonaparte, were
mostly middle-class, for, though some working men were ordered in by
their employers, few actually volunteered.[9] The exact numbers attending
the Kennington meeting remain mysterious, though there must have been
at least 15,000 (and there may well have been many more) on the Common
to hear Feargus O'Connor combine violence of language with firm instructions to abandon a threatened procession to Westminster.[10]

In June another mass meeting was held at Bonner's Field attended by
5,000 troops and more than 4,000 police. There were also disturbances in
the North and much talk of a linked set of provincial outbreaks in some way
co-ordinated with revolution in Ireland (where a minor rising took place in
July). Far more remarkable, however, than the demonstrations themselves
was the speed with which those in charge of the minimal mid-Victorian
state were able to put together a substantial repressive apparatus of soldiers,
police, volunteers, and legislation (notably the Treason-Felony Act of
1848) to protect both their own interests and the 'settlement' of 1832.[11]

While violence did not altogether disappear, it now retreated to its
traditional heartlands of populist mayhem, sectarian conflict, and election-

---

[9] The number of special constables was then and has since been variously estimated, with
figures ranging as high as 200,000. D. Goodway's maximum of 85,000 seems convincing
(*London Chartism 1838–1848* (Cambridge, 1982), 72–4, 131).

[10] Goodway (*London Chartism*, 139–40) criticizes the suggestion by D. Large ('London in
the Year of Revolutions, 1848', in J. Stevenson (ed.), *London in the Age of Reform* (Oxford,
1977), 192) that no more than 54,560 could *possibly* have squeezed into the 13,640 square
yards of available ground by pointing out that the Common was in fact much larger, but he
does not suggest a better figure. O'Connor's various claims ranged as high as 500,000.

[11] J. Saville, *1848: The British State and the Chartist Movement* (Cambridge, 1987), *passim*.

eering, with occasional forays in support of particular strikes in particular industries and areas. Indeed, the fierce London working-class agitation of 1855 against attempts to restrict Sunday trading generated mass meetings in Hyde Park substantially larger than that which O'Connor had managed to assemble in April 1848.[12] But if Chartism collapsed as a direct threat, the political education it had given working people did not disappear. A vigorous egalitarian strand survived within urban politics, which, in the form presented by men like William Norton of the Engineers' Society in 1852 ('every Town or Parliamentary Borough should have its Operatives' Election Committee, composed of and representing both electors and non-electors'),[13] was soon to constitute an important part of those footloose forces gradually sliding into attachment with the Liberal Party in parliament. What, however, Peel and Russell had done was to torpedo the Chartist critique of the state without obliging industrialists and the like to make any significant changes in the capitalist conditions of production. Manifestations of calmer social relationships were at once evident and emphasized: at the Great Exhibition held in Hyde Park between May and October 1851 only two miles from Kennington Common, during pioneering visits by Queen Victoria to industrial towns, by crowds in Manchester cheering Royal Fusiliers on their way to kill Russians in 1854 along streets where the Grenadier Guards had marched with fixed bayonets to suppress the Plug Riots of 1842. As a celebration of private enterprise, the Great Exhibition evoked the enthusiasm, not only of lawyers, managers, and gentlemen, but of operatives too; just as operatives too subscribed their pennies to help pay for those many statues of Peel erected throughout the country after his death following a riding accident in July 1850.[14]

2. PARTIES

Although 117 Conservative MPs voted or paired in favour of repealing the Corn Laws in 1846, it soon became apparent that, generally speaking, permanent departure from the party was to be more a matter of leaders than followers. The number of Peelites or 'Liberal Conservatives' (that is, Conservatives who followed Peel in supporting free trade) fell substantially after the general election of 1847: after that of 1852 the true hard core stood revealed as little more than three-dozen strong. Nor did the gut beliefs

[12] J. Stevenson, *Popular Disturbances in England 1700–1870* (London, 1979), 275–93; B. Harrison, 'The Sunday Trading Riots of 1855', *Historical Journal*, 8 (1965), 219–45.

[13] M. Bentley, *Politics without Democracy: Great Britain, 1815–1914* (London, 1984), 146.

[14] D. Read, *Peel and the Victorians* (Oxford, 1987), 287–312.

dividing the major parties change much. The positions that had been characteristic of Whigs and Tories during the first few decades of the century—the latter cleaving to the Church of England, the former prepared to recognize Dissent, support Catholic Emancipation, and contemplate certain reforms—were still (in however transmuted a form) recognizable in the 1850s and even beyond. If (as one scholar has said) party be defined as 'a body of politicians with a coherent organization and a rudimentary philosophy of action, who provided the legislative foundations either for a Ministry or for an Opposition aiming at its replacement',[15] then in terms of party history what happened in 1846 was adjustment as well as discontinuity. Despite Russell's fears, the Liberals suffered no considerable defections apart from a brief away-trip by Radicals in 1848–9. Disraeli's endless attempts to seek realignments in parliament failed because party proved too strong to allow much shifting about. (And it is noteworthy that Disraeli's first ideas in 1846 had envisaged a 'Grand Junction Ministry' uniting all shades of Tory opinion, led in the Commons by himself and Gladstone, rather than anything more novel.)[16] No identifiably Liberal front-bencher became a Protectionist Tory or vice versa in the two decades after repeal. Once a politician had been in office he was expected to behave as a party man and usually did. It is of course true that the administration led by Russell between 1846 and 1852 enjoyed no clear and stable majority and was obliged to avoid 'difficult' topics so as to be able to catch a wind from other parts of the Commons: on protection and commercial questions it tended to act with Peelites, on religion with Protectionists against Peelites. But it is likely that, should the voting behaviour of MPs ever be analysed for the period 1847–52 as it has been for 1841–7 and 1852–7, then these years would not—in parliamentary terms—stand out as anything more than moderately fluid or passingly unstable.[17]

Fluidity, indeed, was severely circumscribed, and 'unnatural' alliances (such as that between Liberals, Protectionists, and O'Connellites which brought down Peel's government) rarely lasted beyond a single division unless the matter in hand related to social or religious issues upon which MPs often split in rather unusual ways. But on the majority of political

---

[15] N. Gash, *Reaction and Reconstruction in English Politics 1832–1852* (Oxford, 1965), 126.

[16] *Benjamin Disraeli Letters*, ed. M. G. Wiebe and others, 5 vols. to date (Toronto, 1982–), iv. 383.

[17] W. O. Aydelotte, 'The House of Commons in the 1840s', *History*, 39 (1954), 249–62; id., 'Voting Patterns in the British House of Commons in the 1840s', *Comparative Studies in Society and History*, 5 (1963), 134–53; id., 'Parties and Issues in Early Victorian England', *Journal of British Studies*, 5 (1966), 95–114; J. R. Bylsma, 'Party Structure in the 1852–1857 House of Commons: A Scalogram Analysis', *Journal of Interdisciplinary History*, 7 (1977), 617–35.

questions, voting in the Commons followed patterns which matched (though they never precisely coincided with) the formal labels of the day. Members defined themselves (most overtly in their annual entries in *Dod's Parliamentary Companion*) according to fairly standard party/issue conjunctures; Conservatives most commonly mentioning religion and protection, Liberals free trade and franchise reform. Because leaders tended to adopt more moderate positions than the bulk of their followers and because there were so many silent and inactive MPs,[18] there is a temptation to exaggerate the amount of cross-party consensus as well as the degree of independence among back-benchers. It was a temptation contemporaries did not resist. Greville talked in 1854 about the 'total dissolution of party ties and obligations'. Sir Charles Wood, a regular member of Liberal cabinets, declared in the same year that 'any leader of the liberal party must be prepared to reconcile himself to conduct on the part of his supporters which never could have occurred in old *party* times'. Gladstone too, in an article on 'The Declining Efficiency of Parliament' in the *Quarterly Review* for 1856, as well as in earlier unpublished writings, compared (what he saw as) existing and ineffective vaguenesses with the creative cohesions of 1835–45.[19] But such comments place altogether too great an emphasis upon Peelite tergiversations and probably flowed more from a need to blame villains for a lack of political dynamism than from real efforts at accurate analysis.[20]

'Modern' notions of what party should represent were undoubtedly being propagated by leading politicians, though Disraeli was grinding several axes at once when he insisted during the Corn Law debates that 'it is only by maintaining the independence of party that you can maintain the integrity of public men, and the power and influence of Parliament itself'.[21] But even less exotic figures such as Aberdeen in 1847 and Cornewall Lewis in 1851 were saying much the same when they identified parties (and the restriction of individual opinion which their successful operations

[18] Bylsma, 'Party Structure', 617–35; *Disraeli, Derby and the Conservative Party: Journals and Memoirs of Edward Henry, Lord Stanley 1849–1869*, ed. J. Vincent (Hassocks, 1978), 110–11, 122.

[19] *Greville Memoirs*, ed. Strachey and Fulford, vii. 56 (14 Aug. 1854); Wood to Russell, 7 Dec. 1854, J. B. Conacher, *The Aberdeen Coalition 1852–1855* (Cambridge, 1968), 499; Gladstone in *Quarterly Review*, 99 (1856), 521–70; J. B. Conacher, 'Party Politics in the Age of Palmerston', in P. Appleman, W. A. Madden, M. Wolff (eds.), *1859: Entering an Age of Crisis* (Bloomington, Ind., 1959), 164.

[20] The view that the 1850s House of Commons was notable for the presence of 'independent' MPs has, however, been given a new twist in M. Taylor, *The Decline of British Radicalism, 1847–1860* (Oxford, 1995), 19–25.

[21] W. F. Monypenny and G. E. Buckle, *The Life of Benjamin Disraeli*, 6 vols. (London, 1910–20), ii. 356–7.

now required) as the only viable 'means of government'.[22] Certainly in the constituencies political conflict followed distinct party lines, and it is a mistake to perceive the sort of local concerns important in some places—immediate, tangible, material, often corrupt—as somehow less serious and less 'political' in party terms than those of the Westminster élite.

While for a time there were, indeed, more parliamentary groupings than before, party solidarity remained formidable. Not only did the Peelites call themselves Liberal Conservatives rather than Independents, but no more than a dozen of the 654 MPs elected in 1852 failed to give themselves a party label in the relevant issue of *Dod*. And even if Russell picked up some curious temporary supporters between 1846 and 1852 and the Aberdeen coalition managed to attract the votes of about thirty Conservatives in the period 1853–5, this constituted at most a minor and passing slackening of loyalties, for even in Peel's heyday there had always been a handful of unreliables. Edward Stanley's informed estimate of February 1851 that 'in the entire House there are not 40 members ... who can be styled really independent' makes it clear that, whatever else happened after 1846, no major lurch into unpredictability was under way.[23]

The backwash of repeal presented all parliamentary groupings with new problems. The 270 or so 'Protectionists'—or Conservatives as they soon once again styled themselves—were faced with difficulties respecting both policy and leadership. As regards the former, continued opposition to free trade, while music to back-bench ears, could only lead to office if the political nation as a whole could be persuaded to see the error of its ways. As regards leadership, there was simply a shortage of talent so severe that at first only one man, Lord Stanley (from June 1851 the 14th Earl of Derby), commanded universal respect. In the Commons there was no one at all. Admittedly Lord George Bentinck (younger son of the Duke of Portland) had undergone a Pauline awakening and turned himself from an indolent back-bencher into a dedicated hounder of Peel and all his works (even to the extent of selling his string of horses in order to concentrate on politics). But Bentinck suffered from two great defects: uncontrollable rage and an obstinate attachment to liberal views on religious matters, the latter in part a relic of his earlier Canningite Toryism, in part an affirmation of loyalty to the only other leading Commons figure in the party, Benjamin Disraeli, with whom he had shared the task of attacking Peel throughout the first half of 1846. Both men were energetic masters of abuse, but while Bentinck

---

[22] Gash, *Reaction*, 126–7.

[23] *Disraeli, Derby*, ed. Vincent, p. 36; also D. Beales, 'Parliamentary Parties and the "Independent" Member, 1810–1860', in R. Robson (ed.), *Ideas and Institutions of Victorian Britain* (London, 1967), 1–19.

(whose chief objection to repeal was summed up in the remark 'What I cannot bear is being sold') was ultimately prepared to accept electoral defeat in order to preserve 'traditionary' Toryism, Disraeli (perhaps rather too obviously) never lost sight of the fact that parliamentary politics—to be effective—must be addressed to the acquisition of power in government. This was not because Disraeli possessed an unusually deep sense of immediate political realities, but because nationally representative and responsible (and therefore more constrained) figures like Stanley and Bentinck, having made a great fuss over protection in 1846, were in no position simply to drop the cause in order to regain power, as Disraeli (who held few strong views on the matter) wanted them to do.[24]

By the end of 1847 Bentinck no longer commanded trust and was obliged to resign because his patent lack of balance, his support for the admission of Jews into parliament (later exotically memorialized by Disraeli)[25] and his refusal to join in the favourite Tory game of anti-Catholicism rendered him unacceptable to what was still the 'Church of England party'. Because the relatively parvenu Disraeli could hardly step straight into Bentinck's shoes, the party spent the next few years pretending that he could do the work without receiving formal title or recognition. A nonentity, Granby, was elected Commons leader in February 1848, only to resign three weeks later. For the rest of the session Stanley tried to lead from the Lords, though Bentinck and Disraeli continued to do most of the speaking until the former's sudden death in September 1848 at the age of 46. In December Stanley desperately alighted upon the superannuated J. C. Herries, the only Protectionist (apart from himself) who had ever held cabinet office. Herries, however, declined. Then in January 1849 a curious joint Commons leader-ship was set up consisting of Herries, Granby, and Disraeli, a triumvirate which reminded Aberdeen of 'Sieyès, Roger Ducos, and Napoleon Bona-parte'.[26] Although Disraeli did not formally assume sole control until 1851–2, he was now Commons leader in all but name and it is noteworthy that in 1849 the Protectionists for the first time acted with real vigour against Russell's government. Bentinck's departure not only meant that one of the chief obstacles to Conservative reunion was removed, but that some of the more exotic policies which Bentinck had supported—notably, large grants for building railways and paying Catholic priests in Ireland—were

[24] A. Macintyre, 'Lord George Bentinck and the Protectionists', *Transactions of the Royal Historical Society*, 5th ser. 39 (1989), 149–50.
[25] B. Disraeli, *Lord George Bentinck: A Political Biography*, 4th edn. (London, 1852), 482–514.
[26] Monypenny and Buckle, *Disraeli*, iii. 139. The reference is to the appointment of three consuls after Bonaparte's *coup* of 18 Brumaire (9 Nov.) 1799.

abandoned. Disraeli, never a friend of central government expenditure, found it easy to hoist the flag of retrenchment in order to keep the bulk of his supporters happy and possibly attract a little Radical support as well. Soon he was even making efforts to seem grave and to suppress his customary jeering rhetoric, though not until June 1850 was he rewarded by Stanley with a letter beginning 'Dear Disraeli' rather than 'My dear Sir'.[27]

Stanley's vision of the future was more ambiguous than Disraeli's. On the one hand, he had a greater desire for reunion with the Peelites, on the other, a greater awareness of the dangers of angering his followers by any sudden dilution of protectionist principles. Until the last twelve months of Russell's ministry he seems, indeed, to have followed Wellington's notion of the late 1830s that true Toryism lay in keeping the Whigs in power where they could be controlled by careful opposition rather than in setting up weak Conservative governments which might galvanize the latent forces of Radicalism into irritated life. Nor was this approach entirely barren of results, as can be seen in Russell's early caution and (more specifically) in the 1847 act setting up a new Anglican bishopric in Manchester, in larger grants for denominational schools, and in refusals to reform the Church of Ireland or allow Dissenters to enter England's ancient universities. By 1849, however, though Russell was still making some crab-like approaches to the Protectionists (as well as to the Peelites), a shift of gear becomes apparent. On the issue of repealing the Navigation Laws (the continuation of Peel's remedies) Stanley at last mounted a real attack in the Lords against further moves towards free trade which the government only defeated on 8 May by 175 votes to 165. This certainly restored morale. But it also undermined the possibility of Conservative reunion and rendered Disraeli's efforts to talk less about protection singularly ineffective, at least in the short run. And while Protectionist approaches to the Peelites continued with unconvincing frequency, they all foundered, not just upon Peelite and Peel's own *amour propre* and disinclination, but because protectionist issues were once again being brought to national prominence by a sharp drop in wheat prices during the four years beginning in 1849.

Disraeli, however, could not simply relax and wait for better days—in essence Stanley's strategy—but began in 1849 to embark seriously upon the task of persuading his party that compensation for, rather than reversal of, free trade must constitute the basis of its politics. His annual motions for the relief of agricultural distress (which proposed a kaleidoscope of reme- dies in the shape of reduced local taxation, sinking funds, and other palliatives) started to attract growing support and signalled at least a

[27] Stewart, *Politics of Protection*, 136, 158.

muffled and tentative acceptance of repeal. Though the dodging and weaving forced upon him by back-bench opinion showed how strong the party's traditions and attachments continued to be, the Liberal government's majorities on the distress motions certainly declined: 282 to 191 in 1849, 273 to 252 in 1850, 281 to 267 in 1851.

Stanley was a more subtle if less busy political operator. Not until early 1849 did he give any earnest thought to the possibility of a Protectionist administration and then only in the most melancholy way. When in February 1851 Russell resigned because of a sudden unrepresentative defeat in a thin House, Stanley at last made some serious, if reluctant, efforts to form a government. But when no leading Peelite would join and the Queen refused a dissolution, he gave up. His public announcement of failure was brutally frank. The party, he declared, 'though it no doubt comprises men of talent and intellect, yet contains within itself, I will not say no single individual, but hardly more than one individual, of political experience and versed in official business'.[28]

Though Disraeli (not for the first or last time) was disappointed, Stanley had at least ensured that, should another opportunity arise, the Queen could hardly again refuse a dissolution. And she did not do so when in February 1852 Russell again resigned, this time after Palmerston had engineered a successful parliamentary *coup* in retaliation for his own dismissal the previous December. However, Derby (as Stanley had now become) fought the elections that ensued in a curiously half-hearted way, by seeming to ask the voters for guidance rather than offering leadership. He even thought Disraeli's tortuous election speech in Buckinghamshire insufficiently vague in suggesting that 'if the country has chosen to abrogate that system [protection], and if the majority of the people of this country are of opinion it would be unwise to recur to it, I say we must seek by other means, and in another direction, to place the cultivators of the soil in a fair and just position'.[29] With most back-bench candidates still fulminating against free trade, no one could divine what the party really believed. Although it is difficult to compare the results straightforwardly with those of 1847, the numbers come out more or less as in the table on p. 138.[30]

The subsequent story of the Conservative Party in the 1850s and 1860s revolved around the task of finding some kind of distinct but potentially rewarding role after the effective burial of protection in the autumn of 1852. Here Derby played the key part, on the one hand loudly protesting

---

[28] *Hansard*, cxiv. 1008 (28 Feb. 1851).   [29] *The Times*, 15 July 1852.

[30] The disfranchisement of St Albans for corruption reduced the total number of seats by two between 1847 and 1852.

	1847	1852
Protectionists	c.227	c.291
Peelites	c.100	c.40
Liberals of all kinds	c.329	c.323
	656	654

attachment to ancient Tory verities, on the other, being prepared to enter minority office in 1852, 1858–9, and 1866–8 in order to give his flock a glimpse at least of the promised land. Disraeli, for his part, supplied the 'movement', sometimes fruitful, always inventive, often self-defeating. His budget of 1852 gave tangible proof of the party's return to the mainstream of national politics. His fruitless search for allies, often from unlikely points of the compass, revealed the nakedness of minority status and the need for some powerfully dramatic stroke with which to square the circle of more or less permanent opposition. What it did not, however, indicate was any substantial softening in Disraeli's attachment to the aristocratic constitution. As the 1850s unrolled, so the desire for Peelite support faded into nothingness. Gladstone in particular, though still being approached, was now so rebarbative to back-bench opinion that his return to a Conservative cabinet (where he had been as recently as June 1846) would have caused massive discontent. Indeed, by 1855 people were convinced that Gladstone needed the Conservatives rather more than they needed him. Not that Derby's foot soldiers showed much interest in movement, let alone innovation: that, after all, was why they had opposed Peel. As Disraeli put it in February 1853 with some, but only some, exaggeration, 'They could not be got to attend to business while the hunting season lasted... They... wanted culture: they never read: ... they learnt nothing useful, and did not understand the ideas of their own time.'[31]

The Peelites, for their part, resembled highly strung athletes too nervous to respond decisively to the starting pistol. At the outset, the least hesitant had been Peel himself. While now simply refusing to acknowledge the existence of party, he was, none the less, quite prepared to nudge MPs into regular support for Russell's ministry. Not that so striking a combination of fastidious integrity and patent partisanship did his standing much good. Indeed, had his death come later than July 1850 his reputation could hardly have stood the strain. Most other Peelites oscillated between individual atomism and a desire that their orphaned condition be brought to an end. But even though men like Gladstone, Lincoln, Cardwell, Goulburn, and Herbert were less terrified by thoughts of Conservative reunion than

---

[31] *Disraeli, Derby*, ed. Vincent, p. 96.

Graham and Peel, they were never willing to meet the Protectionists quarter- let alone half-way. Though prepared to vote against Russell—on dismantling the preference given to West Indian sugar in June 1848 only five Peelites (among them Graham and Peel) supported the ministry—they always saw such votes as passing episodes. When approached by either of the main parties for some more secure connection, they found endless and ingenious excuses for saying No.

In the end, however, a sense of frustration that, as Gladstone put it, the Peelites did not 'exercise any considerable degree of permanent influence as a body'[32] finally pushed the remaining three dozen true believers into coalition with the Liberals in December 1852. And their massive share in the spoils of office on that occasion—six out of thirteen cabinet posts— showed that they had in fact played the political game more rewardingly than anyone else. Not only had they made themselves indispensable, but they had succeeded in rendering those much-vaunted gifts of progress, efficiency, and broad-minded earnestness which they claimed to bring with them seem greater than in reality they were. As wizards of administrative competence their reputation rested on the impressive but select shoulders of Peel (now dead), Gladstone, and Graham, which may have been the reason for their comparatively small contribution to the important matter of Civil Service reform in the mid-1850s, the famous Northcote-Trevelyan Report being the work of, respectively, a Conservative (who had, admit- tedly, once been Gladstone's private secretary) and a Whig. Their broad- mindedness, too, had its limits. As a group they more usually opposed than supported Russell's annual bills to admit Jews into parliament, Herbert (so often depicted as little short of a saint) attacking Disraeli in November 1852 in a speech which sneeringly ascribed the difficulty of Jews in making converts to the 'surgical operation' involved in circumcision.[33] Yet none of this seemed to matter very much and of course in some respects—an example is Graham's fiercely brave attack on the Ecclesiastical Titles Bill of 1851—the Peelites did match actions to reputation. Overall, however, their success in persuading others of their corporate importance was very remarkable. When in April 1853 Newcastle (as Lincoln had then become) baldly claimed that 'Peelism—if I may still use the word—is really the more advanced form of Liberal opinion, cleared of that . . . oligarchic tendency of the old Whigs'[34] there were still some in politics too awed to laugh.

[32] J. Morley, The Life of William Ewart Gladstone, 3 vols. (London, 1903), i. 351.

[33] D. Southgate, The Passing of the Whigs 1832–1886 (London, 1962), 204–5; R. Blake, Disraeli (London, 1966), 337.

[34] Lord E. Fitzmaurice, The Life of Granville George Leveson Gower, Second Earl Gran- ville, 2 vols. (London, 1905), i. 79–80.

To Russell all this was hemlock, for there was a good deal of truth in his aphorism that the word 'Whig' said better in one syllable what the Peelite ascription 'Liberal Conservative' said in seven. Speaking very generally the Whigs still represented those landed elements that were not Tory. They defined themselves by talking of Charles James Fox, religious liberty, reform, and stability. Their function was to provide leadership, and in general they had done this very well. Indeed, throughout the 1830s they had supplied much of the impetus for movement and change.[35] None the less, Russell's cabinet of 1846 was the last truly Whig cabinet in British history and it was all too obvious that its members knew this to be so. The Whigs had always been the most exclusive political group, dependent as much on family connection as anything else, and the relevant families were no longer breeding with their old efficiency. Already in the mid-1840s Lord Clarendon could be found musing that Whiggery was 'guided by past historical reminiscences rather than by present public opinion'.[36] In 1851 it seemed to another observer that 'there is not in existence a young Whig'.[37] Not only was Russell's following becoming less Whig in charac-ter—consisting, as it now did, predominantly of 'commonplace wealthy Englishmen whose political actions were bound neither by affiliation to great houses nor by theoretical intransigence'[38]—but the Whigs' own rural power base was becoming narrower: in 1852 Liberals of all kinds held only twenty-nine English county seats compared to 104 in 1832.

Because the Liberal tone was being increasingly set to suit the aspirations of this new central group of 'commonplace wealthy Englishmen' the Radical wing of the party was also losing rather than gaining influence. From the start, Radicals had been dissatisfied with Russell's failure to press on with reform and annoyed that Cobden had not been included in the cabinet of 1846. After making some gains at the 1847 election, in early 1848 they set up what purported to be a separate organization under the nominal leadership of Joseph Hume, in effect the Westminster arm of the Parlia-mentary and Financial Reform Association established that year to agitate for retrenchment and further franchise reforms.[39] But Radicalism, even in

---

[35] R. Brent, *Liberal Anglican Politics: Whiggery, Religion, and Reform 1830–1841* (Oxford, 1987); I. Newbould, *Whiggery and Reform, 1830–1841: The Politics of Government* (London, 1990); P. Mandler, *Aristocratic Government in the Age of Reform: Whigs and Liberals 1830–1852* (Oxford, 1990).

[36] H. Maxwell, *The Life and Letters of George William Frederick, Fourth Earl of Clarendon*, 2 vols. (London, 1913), i. 265.

[37] *Disraeli, Derby*, ed. Vincent, p. 55.

[38] J. Vincent, *The Formation of the Liberal Party 1857–1868* (London, 1966), p. xxxiv.

[39] N. C. Edsall, 'A Failed National Movement: The Parliamentary and Financial Reform Association, 1848–54', *Bulletin of the Institute of Historical Research*, 49 (1976), 108–31.

its parliamentary manifestation, was seriously split, most notably between a Manchester School under Cobden and Bright and an increasingly vociferous nationalist persuasion of which J. A. Roebuck was the leading spokesman. By July 1849 it had become clear that, with divisions on humanitarian issues like factory reform, on religious matters, on education, on foreign policy, any 'combined system of Radical action' was now impossible.[40] Although powerful anti-aristocratic feelings surfaced once again during the Crimean War, these found little political purchase, not least because the implicit assumption by Bright and Cobden that Britain was *always* in the wrong did little to spread acceptance of their cause. At the same time Cobden himself had—ironically enough—begun to see the aristocratic leadership of the then Prime Minister, Lord Aberdeen, as the best bulwark against the populist bellicosity of the nation out of doors.[41]

3. GOVERNMENTS

The survival of Russell's 1846–52 ministry for almost six years was, in the circumstances, a considerable achievement. If the cabinet was recruited from a distinctly exclusive circle—of the twenty-one men who served in this period, twelve were sons of aristocrats and five heirs to baronetcies, while half the original team of 1846 were close relatives—as departmental administrators, Palmerston at the Foreign Office, Lord Grey at the Colonial Office, Sir George Grey at the Home Office, Wood as Chancellor, and Auckland and Baring at the Admiralty were not notably less talented than their Conservative counterparts of 1841–6 had been. Russell, though he failed to provide the important central control so characteristic of Peel, possessed sporadic tactical skills and succeeded, at least until 1849, in obtaining surprisingly large parliamentary majorities for a legislative programme of considerable bite. Important extensions to free trade were secured in the shape of reductions in colonial preferences on significant commodities like sugar and the repeal in 1849 of the Navigation Laws which had restricted the carriage of goods to British or colonial ships. In 1847 the government made Fielden's bill to limit child and female factory work to ten hours a day an open question, with Russell—though well aware that *laissez-faire* principles were being undermined because adult males would also benefit—giving the measure his support. Predictably enough, Radicals of both Manchester and 'patriotic' persuasions disagreed and voted against, while Peel—with almost Gladstonian convolution—declared

[40] R. E. Leader, *Life and Letters of John Arthur Roebuck* (London, 1897), 230.
[41] *Hansard*, cxxix. 1806 (16 Aug. 1853).

that, in the unlikely event of it being decisively shown that the measure would 'tend to the moral and intellectual improvement [and] to the general social welfare of the labouring classes', he would at very best be 'tempted' to abandon his opposition to it.[42] But because the bulk of the Protectionists, acting from humanitarian motives or out of simple hatred of Peel, took a different view, Fielden's important bill was passed into law. In the same year the Poor Law Commission of 1834 was transformed into a Board, two of whose three members were now to sit in parliament, a clever manœuvre which seemed to promise something to almost everybody—old-fashioned humanitarians hoped for less harshness, new-fashioned Radicals for less expenditure, Protectionists that traditional units of local government would count for more, Whigs that parliamentary control would increase. A similar three-man Board was also set up under the provisions of the Public Health Act of 1848. And on education, although matters were made extraordinarily complicated by the kaleidoscopic nature of denominational attitudes, the government was able to make modest changes in 1847 allowing state money to be spent not only on schools but on schoolteachers as well.

It did not, however, prove possible to sustain the ministry's initial burst, with the result that after 1849 its record becomes something of a blank. Even before this, great strains had been caused by the severe famine in Ireland that had followed the failure of the potato crop—on which the majority of the Irish population depended—in the autumn of 1845. In dealing with the famine Russell and his cabinet managed to get the worst of all worlds: an English reputation for massive expenditure, an Irish one for mean-minded stinginess, their constant Scrooge-like rhetoric rendered ridiculous rather than humane by occasional cascades of cash.[43] Just as Charles Trevelyan, the head of the Treasury, gave lectures on political economy to representatives sent by the Viceroy in Dublin to plead for assistance, so Russell presented relief deputations with extracts from the fifth chapter of Adam Smith's *Wealth of Nations*. 'We cannot', he tersely announced in October 1846, 'feed the people'.[44] State interference in the food trade would, he told parliament three months later, so undermine 'all private enterprise' that eventually 'everything' would be 'abandoned to the care of the Government'.[45]

However, the sheer totality of the potato failure, the disease, the deaths, the realization that many parts of Ireland lacked a private retailing sector capable of distributing food even to those with money to buy, forced

[42] *Hansard*, xc. 815 (3 Mar. 1847).
[43] K. T. Hoppen, *Ireland since 1800: Conflict and Conformity* (London, 1989), 53–8. See below, Ch. 15, s. 2.
[44] Prest, *Russell*, 240–1, 246.   [45] *Hansard*, lxxxix. 138–9 (19 Jan. 1847).

ministers into a (temporary) change of mind. Within weeks of Russell's lecture on private enterprise the Navigation Laws and the remaining corn duties (not originally supposed to expire until 1849) were suspended, imported corn was purchased out of state funds and taken to the West of Ireland in government ships, and a decision was made to establish a network of soup kitchens which would do exactly what had earlier been declared impossible, that is, 'feed the people'. By July 1847 three million persons were getting daily rations, mostly free of charge. By the middle of 1848 some 800,000 were receiving outdoor relief and many others were being relieved within workhouse walls. As always there was a quid pro quo, in this case in the shape of the Irish Poor Law Extension Act of 1847 which forbade the giving of relief to anyone holding more than a quarter of an acre of land in the hope that the most indigent and desperate farmers would rapidly transform themselves into wage labourers and thus help align the social structures of the Irish countryside to the most approved models of rural England. However, death and disease—greater social engineers by far than mid-century governments—hit the poorest agricultural labourers hardest of all and thereby ensured that something very like the opposite occurred.[46]

By 1850 the worst was over. Out of an Irish population of over eight million, more than one million died and about a million emigrated as a result of the famine.[47] The government performed the last legislative rites with a dramatic Encumbered Estates Act in 1849 which facilitated the sale of bankrupt properties and introduced the principles of free trade into the Irish (but not the British) land market. More important still (though this was not realized at the time) was the Franchise Act of 1850 which changed the whole nature of electoral politics in Ireland and thus constituted a key legislative preparation for the later campaigns of the Home Rule Party under Charles Stewart Parnell.[48]

Though the famine blew Wood's budgets off course and undermined the ministry's reputation for financial competence, it did not itself threaten Russell's position at Westminster because creative alternatives regarding Ireland were in distinctly short supply. Indeed, what is so interesting about

[46] J. S. Donnelly, jun., 'The Soup Kitchens' and 'The Administration of Relief, 1847–51', in W. E. Vaughan (ed.), *A New History of Ireland, Ireland under the Union*, i. *1801–70* (Oxford, 1989), 307–15 and 316–31.

[47] J. Mokyr, *Why Ireland Starved: A Quantitative and Analytical History of the Irish Economy, 1800–1850*, rev. edn. (London, 1985), 263–8.

[48] W. L. Burn, 'Free Trade in Land: An Aspect of the Irish Question', *Transactions of the Royal Historical Society*, 4th ser. 31 (1949), 61–74; K. T. Hoppen, *Elections, Politics, and Society in Ireland 1832–1885* (Oxford, 1984), 17–33.

the reactions of British politicians to the famine is their practical congruity. Whigs, Liberals, Radicals, Peelites, and Protectionists argued mightily amongst one another, but, when it came to taking action, they differed little. If anything, the severity of the famine helped Liberal politicians of various kinds to resolve their initial waverings between public-works programmes (an interventionist policy) and non-interference in the market (a *laissez-faire* policy) in favour of the latter. As expenditure rose, they became more and more disillusioned with interventionism, a process aggravated by widespread and unvarnished contempt for the Irish themselves ('Incapable of the honest exertion, the prudence, and the integrity, which were characteristics of the poor of this country', as—rather less stridently than many others—R. V. Smith MP for Northampton put it in June 1847).[49] By encouraging a wider and a deeper commitment to non-intervention on the part of Whigs, middle-of-the-road Liberals, and Radicals alike, the famine helped to set Westminster politics as a whole firmly into the mould created by Peel. The Whigs grew less adventurous with regard to the actions and responsibilities of the state. The Peelites had never been very adventurous. Within a few years Protectionist leaders too began to adopt similar grammars of non-intervention even if the actual words 'free trade' had to be avoided for fear of causing apoplexy among their more stubborn back-benchers. Without starvation in Ireland this political triumph of the principles of 1846 would have been less speedy and probably very much less complete.[50] And because almost everyone at Westminster also agreed that the Irish had been treated with a generosity beyond their deserts, nobody wanted to hear from them again for a very long time indeed.

The emergence of a broad consensus about the famine and its implications did not, however, save Russell from having to live in constant fear that some—almost any—new issue might suddenly overcome the opposition's confusions and disunities. And eventually in 1850 events did, indeed, take a distinct turn for the worse. Disraeli's agricultural distress motions were attracting more support. The colonial and foreign policies of Lords Grey and Palmerston were under fierce attack. Budgets were being badly mauled and reversals on minor issues becoming embarrassingly frequent. Even when the government was able to snatch victory from the jaws of defeat—most notably in the Don Pacifico debate of June 1850 (see below, section 4)—the benefits tended to accrue, not to Russell or even to the ministry as a whole, but to Palmerston. In these circumstances Russell,

[49] *Hansard*, xcii. 1423 (1 June 1847).
[50] G. L. Bernstein, 'Liberals, the Irish Famine and the Role of the State', *Irish Historical Studies*, 29 (1995), 513–36.

with few alternatives left to him, embarked upon a dramatic shift from emollient caution to abrasive boldness. From the start this was a high-risk strategy. And its eventual failure brought about not only the defeat of the government, but something very like the final ruin of Russell's own reputation for political creativity and competence.

The Prime Minister's new departure revolved around issues of religion and the franchise. Anti-Catholicism had long played an important part in British public life, having last surfaced politically in 1845 in connection with Peel's proposal to increase the government's grant to the Catholic seminary at Maynooth in Ireland. Its next major inflammation, the so-called 'Papal Aggression' of 1850–1, was prompted by Pope Pius IX's decision to restore a full hierarchy of bishops to replace the vicars-general who had controlled Catholic affairs in England and Wales since the 1580s.[51] Clauses in the Catholic Relief Act of 1829 forbade non-Anglican ecclesiastics to take the titles of sees already occupied by bishops of the established church. And though in 1846 Russell himself had told the Commons that 'nothing could be more absurd and puerile than to keep up such a distinction',[52] when, in the autumn of 1850, Rome appointed its new bishops, he eagerly joined the wild popular protests which ensued (even though no Anglican diocesan names had in fact been appropriated). In particular, the high-octane abuse of his letter to the Bishop of Durham (made public in November) gave official sanction to the still more extreme outbursts of lesser men. 'No foreign prince or potentate', he grandly observed, 'will be at liberty to fasten his fetters upon a nation which has so long and so nobly vindicated its right to freedom of opinion … a nation which looks with contempt on the mummeries of superstition, and with scorn at the laborious endeavours which are now making to confine the intellect and enslave the soul'.[53]

The irony was that Russell (whose religious views were Erastian and broad) had long argued for the removal of Catholic disabilities. Words like 'mummeries' had, however, also for years been common in his own aristocratic family circle,[54] and he clearly found it impossible to keep calm when faced with resurgent Catholicism in the shape of poor Irish immigrants and triumphant clerics hot from Rome. More worrying still, for him and for many others, was the recent Anglo-Catholic revival within the Church of England: as he reminded the Queen, while a Roman Catholic was at least an

[51] J. Wolffe, *The Protestant Crusade in Great Britain 1829–1860* (Oxford, 1991), 198–289; D. G. Paz, *Anti-Catholicism in Mid-Victorian England* (Stanford, Calif., 1992), 197–223.
[52] *Hansard*, lxxxiii. 501 (5 Feb. 1846).
[53] Text in E. R. Norman, *Anti-Catholicism in Victorian England* (London, 1968), 159–61.
[54] Prest, *Russell*, 320.

enemy 'in uniform', the Anglo-Catholic was 'an enemy disguised as a spy'.[55] And even if Russell's motives are no longer fully recoverable, it seems likely that they also included a keen desire to increase his own and his government's standing by means of some sudden, bold, and popular stroke. In order, therefore, to give legislative shape to the outbursts of 1850, Russell brought forward an Ecclesiastical Titles Bill the following year making it illegal for Catholic bishops to attach any British or Irish place-names to the titles of their sees.

Throughout all this huffing and puffing Disraeli remained well aware that Russell, however hard he tried, could never outrun the Conservatives in the bigotry stakes. Indeed, Conservative ultras thought the bill too weak, while Irish Catholic MPs were so enraged that twenty of them voted for Disraeli's agricultural distress motion in February 1851, thereby reducing the government's majority to fourteen (281 to 267). Not only that, but the bill was also fiercely opposed by Peelites like Graham and Gladstone (who eventually repealed the ensuing act in 1871) and by Radicals as different as Cobden, Bright, Roebuck, and Hume. In truth, many Liberals and even some Conservatives quickly became shamefaced about the whole business, which, in the end, did Russell's reputation nothing but harm.[56] Henceforth Peelites simply muttered the phrase 'Ecclesiastical Titles Act' when declining invitations to join or support the ministry. Catholic Irish members became positively hostile. Protectionists had been shown nothing to make them move towards the government: indeed it was they who gained seats at the election of 1852 and did so in many cases on a religious cry.

Nor was the second leg of Russell's dash for freedom any more success-ful. In June 1848, though long associated with the idea that the Reform Acts of 1832 must be considered 'final', Russell suddenly persuaded himself to blame these very measures for having 'reduced . . . too much . . . the great variety of voting which existed under the former constitution' (the exact argument that Peel had used *against* change and *against* Russell in 1830–2).[57] However, a strong cabinet faction under Palmerston still opposed almost any advance. In August 1850 Russell, now determined to out-manœuvre Palmerston, drew up a plan to reduce the borough franchise to £6 and the occupation franchise in the counties to £20, which, augmented by a redistribution of seats and the creation of so-called 'fancy' franchises for 'safe' groups such as taxpayers and depositors in savings banks, was to form the basis for all his subsequent initiatives on the matter. Throughout the following winter ministers unenthusiastically batted his proposals back

---

[55] Russell to Queen Victoria, 25 Oct. 1850, *The Letters of Queen Victoria: First Series*, ed. A. C. Benson and Viscount Esher, 3 vols. (London, 1907), ii. 326.

[56] *Disraeli, Derby*, ed. Vincent, p. 58.   [57] *Hansard*, xcix. 929 (20 June 1848).

to base. So confused did everyone become that some thought it had been decided to postpone things for a year while others believed that no decision of any kind had been made. Then, during a debate in February 1851 on Locke King's regular motion to assimilate the county to the borough qualification (a direct attack on the landed interest), Russell, in an attempt to stave off defeat, suddenly promised to bring in an official measure in 1852. When even this failed to yield a majority, he decided to force the issue by resigning the next day. There followed a confused interval during which 'everybody went to call upon everybody'.[58] The Queen sent for Stanley who advised that Russell be asked to lead a Whig-Peelite coalition. When this proved impossible, Stanley himself tried to form a ministry, but without success. Eventually, in early March Russell, now politically feebler still, resumed his original place. The implications of what had happened soon became clear. While the Protectionists had at least put down a marker for the future, Russell had fluffed his last realistic chance to place himself at the head of a coalition government.

When the ministers returned to office they were more discontented than ever. Most thought the resignation had been frivolous and out of all proportion to its alleged cause. From now on the government became provisional in all but name. Disraeli, who confined his comments on Russell's franchise proposals to vague nothings in defence of proper 'territorial preponderance',[59] was happy enough to let the Liberal pot boil under its own steam. In the last months of 1851 a cabinet committee of Minto, Carlisle, Wood, and Russell meanderingly sought some common denominator on reform. In December a measure of agreement was reached just as Palmerston was being sacked as Foreign Secretary for his unauthorized approval of Louis Napoleon's recent *coup* in France. Whatever Palmerston was up to at this time, he could hardly have been much surprised by Russell's blunt assertion that 'misunderstandings perpetually renewed, violations of prudence and decorum too frequently repeated' had 'marred the effects which ought to have followed from a sound policy and able administration'.[60] A Reform Bill was eventually presented by Russell in February 1852. Only days later a vengeful Palmerston succeeded in engineering the defeat of the government on an amendment to the Militia Bill. In his attempts to find a way out of political impotence, Russell had committed a fatal trinity of errors: the Ecclesiastical Titles Act had offended many Peelites, Radicals, and Irish; the reform proposals had offended many Whigs; the dismissal of Palmerston brought matters to a final shuddering halt.

[58] *Punch*, 20 (8 Mar. 1851), 100.   [59] *Hansard*, cxv. 939 (2 Apr. 1851).
[60] Russell to Palmerston, 17 Dec. 1851, Prest, *Russell*, 337.

Derby's ensuing minority administration has gone down in history as the 'Who? Who?' ministry because the aged Duke of Wellington kept repeating that question when the obscure names of its members were read to him. It lasted as long as it did (from February to December 1852) largely because a general election was necessary before the various elements within the opposition could begin to sort themselves into the coherence necessary for power. And although the July election was a confused affair, it certainly showed that unreconstructed protectionism was no longer viable. At the same time, however, it also confirmed Derby and Disraeli as leaders of the party Peel had abandoned, and allowed Disraeli, by means of new financial strategies (however unsuccessful these were to prove in immediate budgetary terms), to point his followers once more towards the mainstreams of national political life. In the mean time, although Gladstone and Herbert were at first reluctant to enter into a Liberal-Peelite coalition and Graham expressed his usual gloomy doubts, their fellow Peelite, Lord Aberdeen, turned out to be both a charming and an effective matchmaker. Eventually in December Gladstone's fierce attack on Disraeli's budget made formal union possible.

When Aberdeen succeeded Derby as Prime Minister in the last days of 1852 he showed himself capable of somewhat more toughness than had been expected. Though anxious to soothe Russell's wounded pride, he made few concessions on the composition of the cabinet, which emerged with six Peelites, six Whigs, and a single Radical (Molesworth). Russell was left not only understandably annoyed that his numerous troops had been given so few commissions, but markedly isolated within a cabinet where few of the other Whigs could be counted his reliable friends. To make matters worse, he had wavered long and tediously over the offices he himself should hold. Aberdeen wanted him to be Leader of the House and Foreign Secretary. Russell thought this too strenuous, but, being anxious to confine Palmerston to domestic affairs, accepted on condition that he could soon resign the Foreign Office to Clarendon and hold the leadership alone. Although many, not least the Queen, thought such arrangements unprecedented, Russell was indulged, resigning the Foreign Office in February 1853 and holding cabinet rank without portfolio until June 1854 when he took on the (not very onerous) office of Lord President of the Council. Aberdeen had also— vaguely and incautiously—led Russell to believe that in due course he would resign the prime ministership in Russell's favour. When the advent of the Crimean War made this impossible, Russell's feelings of anger and sense of having been cheated grew stronger still.[61]

---

[61] Prest, *Russell*, 353–4, 359–61; M. E. Chamberlain, *Lord Aberdeen: A Political Biography* (London, 1983), 446.

On taking office Aberdeen announced a mixed Conservative/Liberal programme on the grounds that, as a Peelite, he considered 'both qualities to be essentially necessary'.[62] And, indeed, belief in cautious reform was to prove the keynote of his administration. The 1853 session was certainly more productive than its two immediate predecessors had been. As Home Secretary, Palmerston tightened up the limitation of hours laid down in the Factory Act of 1847. The education grant was increased. The government of India received attention. Merchant shipping law was reformed. As it happened, Palmerston had been well served by becoming Home rather than Foreign Secretary. He achieved a good deal of minor though useful legislation on employment, prisons, sewage, and health, while remaining largely untouched by the unfavourable fall-out produced by the government's handling of relations with Russia and the outbreak of the Crimean War. All in all the cabinet worked well together in 1853 and such splits as did occur rarely followed party lines.

In order to understand the new ministry's financial policies (which, initially at least, seemed to constitute the jewels in its crown) it is necessary to return to the late 1840s when leading Peelites were already denouncing Russell's Chancellor of the Exchequer, Sir Charles Wood, for allowing government finances to be blown off course by the costs of famine relief in Ireland and thereby squandering the great budgetary legacy of Peel himself whose heirs in such matters they naturally considered themselves to be. Nor, in Peelite eyes, did Wood's performance improve. In 1848 he found himself humiliatingly obliged to withdraw proposals to increase the income tax. Two years later his plans were again badly mauled with defeats on stamp duty adjustments (which would have hit larger landed proprietors), the window tax, and other details. In 1851 things got even worse when the income tax (ostensibly a temporary impost after its revival by Peel in 1842) was renewed for only one year (Wood had suggested three) because Protectionists wanted it abolished and Radicals wanted it made permanent but along new lines involving 'differentiation' or the levying of different rates on incomes according to their source—higher on 'regular' incomes such as rents, lower on 'transient' incomes such as professional fees. Gladstone, who was strongly opposed to differentiation, refused to serve on a select committee appointed to look into the matter. He also attacked renewal, on the grounds that, to be acceptable in Peelite terms, it should be both temporary and matched by certain large reductions in the taxes on consumption and industry.

It fell to Disraeli, as Chancellor of the Exchequer in Derby's government, to try his luck in 1852. Why he was appointed to that office is unclear,

<hr />

[62] *Hansard*, cxxiii. 1726–7 (27 Dec. 1852).

though it may have been because chancellors had little contact with the
court where Disraeli was then much less popular than Gladstone. When he
nervously confessed to a lack of expertise, Derby nonchalantly replied 'You
know as much as Mr Canning did. They give you the figures.'[63] In fact,
Disraeli had for some time been educating himself in financial matters and
his proposals were by no means devoid of merit, though flawed in a number
of technical details. Because no more than a holding operation was required
before the general election, the full budget was postponed until December.
This meant that Disraeli was obliged to draw up figures well before the end
of the financial year (5 April 1853) and before it was possible to produce
even relatively reliable estimates of income and expenditure. Matters were
rendered still more difficult by last-minute increases in defence costs and by
the insistence of Treasury officials (who admired Disraeli for his competence) that pessimistic forecasts of income be laid before parliament. All
Derby could offer was cheerful advice: 'Put a good face on it ... and we
shall pull through. L'audace—l'audace—toujours l'audace'.[64]

In this light it is the coherence and creativity of Disraeli's budget which
demand recognition rather than its defects. By halving the taxes on malt
and hops he tried to conciliate the agricultural interest, while a substantial
reduction in tea duty over six years marked a continuation of Peel's
approach. As regards income tax there was to be a partial extension to
Ireland (hitherto exempt), a lowering of the existing £150 exclusion limit to
£100 for 'industrial' and £50 for 'property' incomes, with special exemp-
tions for farmers, as well as differentiation in the shape of a new lower rate
of $5\frac{1}{4}$d. (as opposed to 7d.) in the pound for trade, farm, and professional
incomes only. Especially interesting—at least to modern minds—was Disraeli's almost Keynesian gloss on an expected reduction in government
income of £3.7m following cuts in various indirect taxes and duties to the
effect that the revenue of the country 'shall mainly depend on the consuming power of the people'.[65] Though some like Macaulay saw the whole
thing as 'nothing but taking money out of the pockets of people in towns,
and putting it into the pockets of growers of malt',[66] the real reason for the
budget's eventual defeat lay in the way in which it allowed the Peelites, and
above all Gladstone, to denounce its provisions—on both substantive and
illusory grounds—as dangerous, incompetent, and (worse still) unsound.
In addition, the Irish were offended by the income tax proposals, while,
apart from a handful of Radicals, all denounced differentiation.

---

[63] Monypenny and Buckle, *Disraeli*, iii. 344.   [64] Blake, *Disraeli*, 338.
[65] *Hansard*, cxxiii. 874 (3 Dec. 1852).
[66] G. O. Trevelyan, *The Life and Letters of Lord Macaulay*, 2 vols. (London, 1876), ii. 330.

Disraeli might well have succeeded with more modest proposals, but he was rightly convinced that only a successful *and* dramatic budget could keep the minority ministry afloat. Fatally, however, he also gave Gladstone a perfect opportunity to commence the construction of a reputation for financial brilliance and expertise. In an ostensibly impromptu speech, which had in fact been fomenting within him for days, Gladstone demolished the budget. He rose from his seat 'choked with passion'[67] and produced a two-hour onslaught of sustained power and destructive energy. All was grist to his mill: the undoubted inadequacies of Disraeli's grasp of the various schedules under which income tax was paid, the unfair benefits awarded to agriculture, the horrors of differentiation, the juggling which had been required to make petty reductions in tax seem bold and important. The speech killed, as it were, two birds with one stone, being both a repayment for Disraeli's vicious assaults on Peel in 1846 and a presentation of the view that nothing financially wholesome could be expected from a mind so sullied by chicanery and a brain so innocent of high economic truth. In short, the budget was simply 'the most subversive in its tendencies and ultimate effects which I have ever known submitted to this House'.[68] It was defeated by 305 votes to 286 and over its broken back the various opposition forces which had been so long and energetically negotiating were at last able to ride into coalition and into office.

Gladstone, for whom financial probity had become a powerful generator of energy, was the new administration's inevitable choice as Chancellor. His first budget of April 1853 was to be everything that had been lacking since 1846. Not only were circumstances more favourable than they had been for Disraeli, in that income had proved greater and expenditure less than forecast, but Gladstone's seriousness and grasp of detail made a good budget seem great, even heroic. In a speech of four and three-quarter hours ('my strength stood out well thank God'),[69] he followed Disraeli in reducing the tax on tea as well as on a number of other articles. Legacy duty was extended, and the abolition of excise duty on soap appealed to those who believed that cleanliness was next to godliness. The crowning glory was a plan for the total repeal of the income tax by means of successive reductions from the existing rate of 7d. in the pound, to 6d. in 1855, 5d. in 1857, and zero in 1860. In the mean time the tax was to be fully extended to Ireland in return for the cancellation of remaining famine debts, and the threshold lowered from £150 to £100. This combination of immediate increase and

---

[67] *Disraeli, Derby*, ed. Vincent, p. 89.   [68] *Hansard*, cxxiii. 1691 (16 Dec. 1852).
[69] *The Gladstone Diaries*, ed. H. C. G. Matthew and M. R. D. Foot, 14 vols. (Oxford, 1968–94), iv. 519 (18 Apr. 1853).

promised disappearance was a brilliant stroke made possible by the buoyant economy of 1853.[70]

What Gladstone was above all anxious to show was that at last someone had emerged capable of continuing Peel's work of master professionalism.

One thing I hope this House will never do, and that is, nibble at this great public question. Don't let them adopt the plan of reconstructing the income tax to-day, and saying, 'If that does not work well, we'll try our hands at it again to-morrow'. That is not the way in which the relations of classes brought into the nicest competition one with another under a scheme of direct taxation, are to be treated.[71]

A few years before his death Gladstone claimed that, if providence had endowed him 'with anything which can be called a striking gift', then this consisted of 'an insight into the facts of particular eras, and their relations one to another, which generates in the mind a conviction that the materials exist for forming a public opinion, and for directing it to a particular end'. On only four occasions, he believed, had such a conjuncture occurred, the first of them in relation to 'the renewal of the income tax in 1853'.[72]

While the budget was a brilliant political success, it did not immediately establish Gladstone's reputation as financial magus once and for all. Within twelve months worrying signs began to appear that not everything had been competently done. The extended legacy duties were yielding less than Gladstone had anticipated and the scheme for debt conversion, brought forward in 1853 to reduce the cost of government borrowing, was not producing the expected results.[73] Not only that, but the budget of 1854 —introduced as Britain was about to declare war on Russia—necessarily constituted something of a reversal. Income tax rates were doubled, at first for six and then for twelve months, and additional revenue was raised from increases in stamp duty and in duties on spirits, sugar, and malt. All this was reasonable enough, though disappointing. What, however, soon became less plausible was Gladstone's insistence that military costs should be entirely met out of revenue rather than borrowing. 'The expenses of war', he told the Commons in a characteristic phrase, 'are the moral check

[70] Of course income tax was never abolished, so that the practical consequence of Gladstone's actions was to leave the tax 'both permanent and unreconstructed' (H. C. G. Matthew, 'Disraeli, Gladstone, and the Politics of Mid-Victorian Budgets', *Historical Journal*, 22 (1979), 631, also 615–43 generally).

[71] *Hansard*, cxxv. 1383–4 (18 Apr. 1853).

[72] H. C. G. Matthew, *Gladstone 1875–1898* (Oxford, 1995), 92. The others were 'The proposal of religious equality for Ireland in 1868', 'The proposal of Home Rule for Ireland in 1886', and 'The desire for a dissolution of Parliament in the beginning of 1894'.

[73] F. W. Hirst, *Gladstone as Financier and Economist* (London, 1931), 150; Conacher, *Aberdeen Coalition*, 77.

which it has pleased the Almighty to impose upon the ambition and the lust of conquest that are inherent in so many nations.'[74] Unfortunately, a mere six weeks after this ringing declaration the Treasury found it necessary to offer £6m of Exchequer Bonds for sale, which, though technically repayable in 1858–60, were later added to the funded debt (indeed in 1860 Gladstone himself was responsible for remitting taxation rather than redeeming them). Worse still, shortly before his resignation from Palmerston's successor ministry in February 1855 Gladstone was obliged to draw up plans for yet another war loan, this one twice as large as that of the previous year.[75] Small wonder, then, that by 1857 Gladstone was being widely regarded as something of a financial crank.

Overall, 1854 was a year of decline for the Aberdeen coalition. Though at first the Crimean War (for which, see Chapter 6) took up little parliamentary time, the discontents it generated directed public attention to the many legislative proposals failing to reach the statute book: on the franchise, the Poor Law, education, the police, the admission of Jews to parliament. When eventually on 23 January 1855 the bellicose Radical, Roebuck, gave notice of a motion for appointing a committee to inquire into the conduct of the war, Russell, feeling that he could not defend the issue, at last resigned from the cabinet—unapplauded and alone. On 29 January Roebuck's motion was carried by 305 votes to 148, with more than eighty Liberals voting in the majority. 'There was no cheering, but a slight, incredulous laugh: the extent of the victory had astonished one party and stunned the other.'[76] No one gained politically, except Palmerston, who soon succeeded Aberdeen as head of what was at first almost an unchanged ministry. For his part Aberdeen, now seen primarily as a failed war leader, had suffered the fate that had overtaken Addington in 1804 and was to overwhelm Asquith in 1916.

4. IMPERIAL AND FOREIGN AFFAIRS

In imperial terms the mid-century period was marked both by significant extensions to empire and by the development of new systems of association between some of the major colonies and the 'mother country'. Historians have tied themselves in knots in doomed efforts to find some overarching principle behind the pattern of overseas acquisition. At one time it was supposed that the end of the Napoleonic Wars had ushered in a

[74] *Hansard*, cxxxi. 376 (6 Mar. 1854).
[75] O. Anderson, *A Liberal State at War: English Politics and Economics during the Crimean War* (London, 1967), 193–7.
[76] *Disraeli, Derby*, ed. Vincent, p. 129.

half-century of self-denial during which the adoption of free trade not only rendered empire irrelevant but produced a widespread desire to abandon territory already held. Then revisionists argued that free trade was itself profoundly imperialistic, though in a manner that led free traders to prefer a policy of 'informal' control and adopt direct rule only when informality had obviously failed to provide satisfactory trading environments. Subsequent debates have, however, dissolved many such neat generalizations into a complicated chiaroscuro made up of particular events and unique occurrences.

That the 'events and occurrences' of colonial and foreign policy were rarely perceived at the time without (though not always handled with) a measure of long-term ministerial coherence owed much to the development of what has been called an 'official' view of Britain's place in the world, a view enshrined in a kind of informal case-law regarding individual problems and territories filed away for future reference if need be in the archives of the appropriate departments of state. The chief elements making up this view were separately unambiguous but collectively contradictory (or at least potentially so). The most important were a strong belief in the superiority of white peoples, and especially of the 'English race', and a conviction that overseas expansion should be fuelled by commercial enterprise but should not necessarily exclude all involvement by the state. Lord Clarendon put the second point forcefully some years before becoming Foreign Secretary for the first time in 1853. 'I look', he told Palmerston, 'only to what may be for the honor [*sic*] and advantage of England, and to what offers the fairest prospect of extending her commercial relations and the sphere of her influence and power'.[77] And if the Cobdenites objected that the exercise of power by government would interfere with the expansion of trade, practical Victorian statesmen had no difficulty in finding that the two worked closely together.[78]

Such broad-brush principles undoubtedly seeped into the institutional consciousness of both the Colonial and the Foreign Office. Senior Civil Servants became their guardians and gave them substance by recommending their application in detailed and particular ways. When a minister required information, the files would be consulted, and not just the files, but the keepers of the files, some of whom remained so long in post that their pronouncements and interpretations acquired almost oracular power. The library at the Foreign Office, for example, 'belonged' to the Hertslet family

[77] Memorandum in Clarendon to Palmerston, 14 Mar. 1840, Maxwell, *George William Frederick*, i. 188.

[78] R. Robinson and J. Gallagher, *Africa and the Victorians: The Official Mind of Imperialism* (London, 1961), 4.

throughout almost the whole of the nineteenth century. Lewis Hertslet became deputy librarian in 1801, librarian in 1810, and retired in 1857 in favour of his son, Edward, who soon came to possess 'a more intimate knowledge than perhaps any other man living of the literature of diplomacy' and did not himself leave office until 1896.[79] However, the rigid division of duties within departments meant that the 'official mind' tended to become disaggregated and compartmentalized as time went on. Thus in the Colonial Office very few—less than half a dozen—men had any influence on matters outside their own narrowly defined responsibilities.[80] Ministers, of course, did try to interpret the national interest in a wider manner. But, while obviously themselves the most complete individual embodiments of the mid-Victorian 'official mind' in foreign and colonial matters and while often remarkably dogged in the pursuit of particular aims—some of Palmerston's activities in overseas affairs remind one of Gladstone's tenacity at the Treasury—together they were capable of surprisingly innovative and deviant behaviour when the occasion arose, behaviour by no means predictable on the basis of a pre-existing 'official mind'. The most notable example of this occurred when, having for years been reluctant to become more than glancingly involved in the African continent, ministers suddenly decided in the 1880s that the protection of the Indian empire demanded the urgent putting together of an entirely new empire in Africa.[81] In other words, the 'official mind', dour and consistent as it generally was in each small thing, lacked a similar consistency in larger matters (or, indeed, when attempting to generate policies applicable to a multitude of small things).

It would, of course, also be idle to deny that purely economic considerations played a part in colonial developments. The United Kingdom at mid-century was a commercial power like no other. In 1860 she generated about a quarter of all world trade, more than twice as much as the next most important country, France. And a far higher proportion of this was done outside Europe, so that her commercial interests were inevitably spread more widely that those of continental powers.[82] Indeed, the very fact that

[79] C. R. Middleton, *The Administration of British Foreign Policy 1782–1846* (Durham, NC, 1977), 284; R. Jones, *The Nineteenth-Century Foreign Office: An Administrative History* (London, 1971), 19. Two other members of the family also worked in the Foreign Office Library in these years.

[80] J. W. Cell, *British Colonial Administration in the Mid-Nineteenth Century: The Policy-Making Process* (New Haven, 1970), 20; B. L. Blakeley, *The Colonial Office 1868–1892* (Durham, NC, 1972), pp. x, 6.

[81] Robinson and Gallagher, *Africa*, 464.

[82] W. Woodruff, *Impact of Western Man: A Study of Europe's Role in the World Economy 1750–1960* (London, 1966), 313–30; R. Davis, *The Industrial Revolution and British Overseas Trade* (Leicester, 1979), 88–125.

Victorian capitalism was global in nature could be used to justify a policy of isolation from the rest of Europe in favour of broader involvements in more distant parts of the world. What, above all, Britain's leading position allowed was the riskless presentation of rhetoric favouring 'fair and open' trading conditions. Contemporary administrations were telling no lies when they claimed to want equality for all in every market because of course this meant that the advantage in the game must continue to lie with the strongest player, namely Britain. However, once individual business-men ceased to believe that free trade would crush foreign industries, they were ready enough to adopt strategies which had little to do with fairness, however interpreted.[83] Because most adopted free trade as a pragmatic response to changing circumstances, few had much time for the pacific internationalism of Cobden and Bright who opposed colonial expansion and believed that free trade would automatically produce equitable rela-tions throughout the world. Hence the enthusiastic response of many Lancashire cotton masters to Palmerston's policies in the 1850s: gunboats, they hoped, would open new markets where free trade had failed.[84]

Free trade was, in any case, a broad church big enough to include Little Englanders as well as expansionist belligerents like the Manchester busi-nessman and Governor of Hong Kong, Sir John Bowring, who believed that 'Jesus Christ is Free Trade and Free Trade is Jesus Christ'.[85] Not that it is at all easy to discover 'economic motives' in the specific *details* of government action. What is clear is that successive ministries tended to adopt those solutions which cost the least. Where threats alone (the cheap-est solution) could secure 'fair' trade, as in South America, threats alone were employed. Where minor wars were necessary, then minor wars were mounted, like those against China in 1839–42 and 1856–60. Where only annexation would serve, then the paintbox was resorted to and red put on the map. But even broad categories like these represent no more than a hierarchy of intention. Some things fit in. Others do not. The many formal annexations of the first sixty years of the century—among them Australia, New Zealand, the Cape Colony, parts of the Gold Coast, Aden, Lagos, Singapore, Malacca, parts of India and Burma, Hong Kong, Labuan, and the Falkland Islands—follow no clear pattern. Some places were taken for military and strategic reasons, some for commercial reasons, some merely because a few enterprising individuals on the spot decided to act as semi-

---

[83] D. C. M. Platt, 'Further Objections to an "Imperialism of Free Trade", 1830–60', *Economic History Review*, 26 (1973), 85.

[84] G. R. Searle, *Entrepreneurial Politics in Mid-Victorian Britain* (Oxford, 1993), 12, 45–6, 49, 126–7.

[85] R. Hyam, *Britain's Imperial Century 1815–1914* (London, 1976), 58.

independent buccaneers. The complicated game of advance and withdrawal played out in southern Africa virtually defies explanation. What New Zealand had in common with the small island of Labuan off the Borneo coast is difficult to discover. Lagos was seized in the early 1850s because the British man-on-the-spot, John Beecroft, having got himself into a tangle over relations with local rulers, swept into action long before the arrival of Palmerston's famous note of February 1851 reminding the Kosoko of Lagos that his territories ran 'near to the sea, and that on the sea are the ships and cannon of England'.[86]

India, the richest possession of all, provides the most striking exception to the idea that free trade and *laissez-faire* exercised a direct impact upon the nature of imperial growth. Though in 1823 the Governor-General had been told to avoid further expansion, the decades leading up to the Revolt of 1857 (see Map 10) were very expansionary ones indeed. Parts of Burma were taken in 1824 and Sind was conquered in 1843. Under the governorship of Lord Dalhousie (1848–56) a policy of vigorous annexation was followed, especially in relation to local states where the rulers had no legitimate heirs—'lapsing' as it was called. Seven states lapsed between 1848 and 1854, while the Punjab was conquered in 1849 and the rich province of Oudh annexed in 1856. Just as striking was the fact that in India mercantilism remained the order of the day. Tariffs were manipulated to benefit British cotton exports, something that would never have been possible had India not been a formal possession. The government even involved itself in the building of a communications network to the extent of guaranteeing the interest rates paid to investors in the railway system. Occasional reproofs notwithstanding, the administrators of India were effectively allowed to pursue almost autonomous military and political goals, and, being so allowed, seem to have thought annexation, expansion, and intervention to be solutions of first rather than last resort.

Neither in India nor elsewhere was there much sign of that 'retreat from empire' once thought to have characterized the middle third of the nineteenth century. No leading British statesman ever seriously argued against the proposition that existing colonies should be retained. In 1849 Russell told his Colonial Secretary, Lord Grey, that 'the loss of any great portion of our Colonies would diminish our importance in the world, and the vultures would soon gather together to despoil us of other parts of the Empire'.[87] The following year he declared in the Commons that, just as everybody

[86] M. Lynn, 'Consul and Kings: British Policy, "The Man on the Spot", and the Seizure of Lagos, 1851', *Journal of Imperial and Commonwealth History*, 10 (1982), 150–67. See Map 11 for the empire's extent in the 1890s.

[87] W. P. Morrell, *British Colonial Policy in the Age of Peel and Russell* (Oxford, 1930), 208.

admitted 'the value of that commerce which penetrates to every part of the globe', so all should remember that 'many of those colonies give harbours and security to that trade, which are most useful in time of peace, but are absolutely necessary in time of war'.[88] In other words, almost any justification could and would be wheeled out to meet each particular case.

Occasional exasperated outbursts, like that of Disraeli in 1852 about 'these wretched colonies' being 'a millstone round our necks', lose their bite when placed in context, for almost all of them were uttered in annoyance over the endless problems of British North America.[89] Nor did the few withdrawals that *were* made amount to much. Java and Sumatra were returned to the Dutch in 1816 and 1824 as a coda to the post-Napoleonic settlement. The Orange River Sovereignty was granted a form of independence after having been a crown colony between 1848 and 1854. No overarching pattern was involved, simply a series of pragmatic responses to unconnected circumstances, though each carried with it an internal logic of its own.[90] Even among Radicals, those who actively opposed expansion (let alone supported diminution) were a tiny and isolated group, not least because the so-called 'Colonial Reformers' like Molesworth, Buller, and Wakefield (who saw the empire as a great sponge for mopping up surplus population and thereby preventing domestic revolution and economic collapse) successfully attached many other Radicals to a version at least of the imperial idea.

The major constitutional development of the decade beginning in 1846 was the granting of a substantial measure of local autonomy to colonies of white settlement. This was done by establishing 'representative' government in the shape of elected bodies and then 'responsible' government by making executive councils answerable to legislative assemblies. The most important proponent of this approach was Lord Elgin, Governor-General of Canada between 1847 and 1854. British North America had long been a troublesome possession: unremunerative, quarrelsome, and ethnically divided. Granting responsible government would make it liable for its own military and administrative costs and thus serve the interests of retrenchment—in contemporary eyes the first cousin of free trade. Responsible government was, therefore, granted to Nova Scotia and Canada proper in 1848, to Prince Edward Island in 1851, and to New Brunswick in 1854.

[88] *Hansard*, cviii. 546 (8 Feb. 1850).
[89] S. R. Stembridge, 'Disraeli and the Millstones', *Journal of British Studies*, 5/1 (1965), 122–39.
[90] B. A. Knox, 'Reconsidering Mid-Victorian Imperialism', *Journal of Imperial and Commonwealth History*, 1 (1973), 158–9.

As soon as Lord Grey (who had followed a cautious policy) left the Colonial Office in 1852, some colonies were actually forced to take the new medicine whether they liked it or not. In 1853 New South Wales was given a constitution containing provisions for responsibility, even though the local political élite was at best lukewarm; and full responsible government followed in 1856–9 for all Australian states save Western Australia (1890). Not only that, but some of the authorized constitutions included such extraordinarily progressive provisions (for manhood suffrage, the ballot, and triennial parliaments) that it almost seemed as if the Chartists were receiving government-sponsored resurrection in the Antipodes. New Zealand, too, obtained a representative system in 1854, responsibility being added shortly afterwards with a casual alacrity which began to look foolhardy when the Maori Wars started up again in 1860.[91] Nor was this all. The 1851 constitution of the Cape Colony stopped only just short of responsibility, the Ionian Islands had their partly representative system further extended in 1849, while an approximation to responsible government was tried in Jamaica in 1853 only to be withdrawn after the risings of 1865. And even though it was not long before Canada began to spit in the free-trade church by signing a reciprocity treaty with the United States in 1854 and in 1859 imposing heavy import tariffs on certain manufactured goods, her example was not widely followed. Overall, indeed, the whole business—the abandonment of expensive direct administrative responsibilities and their replacement by looser imperial controls—turned out to be a brilliant pragmatic success. In one major territory, however, there was not so much as a whisper of such things. India was another country: they did things differently there.

Foreign, as opposed to colonial, affairs necessarily followed a more narrowly European path. Although the highly visible and experienced Lord Palmerston (Foreign Secretary 1846–51 under Russell, and as Home Secretary under Aberdeen 1852–5 influential beyond his departmental brief) played a key role, policy itself was determined as much by the immediate imperatives of economic, strategic, and political considerations as by the character of individuals. Like many of his contemporaries Palmerston was much given to talking about the 'balance of power', by which he and they generally meant the preservation—more or less regardless of ideological considerations—of the territorial balance created between the five great powers by the Vienna settlement of 1815. While, therefore, the differences between constitutional Britain and France, on the one hand, and

[91] P. Burroughs, 'Colonial Self-Government', in C. C. Eldridge (ed.), British Imperialism in the Nineteenth Century (London, 1984), 60.

autocratic Russia, Austria, and Prussia, on the other, could hardly be wished away, they were not supposed or expected to play any discordant or unbalancing role. And, indeed, France sided with the autocratic powers over Spain in 1822 but with Britain in 1834, Britain with Russia against France on the eastern question in 1840 but with France against Russia in 1854, while Austria, though welcoming Russian help in Hungary in 1849, moved closer to Britain and France in 1855. Because British politicians were almost entirely satisfied with the settlement of 1815, they had a particular interest in its maintenance, something best achieved by the avoidance of major wars. But their 'pacifism' in this respect was never a policy of simple denial, nor was it an absolute principle. It was a matter of self-interest. Wars in Europe were expensive and disturbing. Minor wars further afield could and did repay the modest investments they required.

Palmerston was well aware of such things. Already as Foreign Secretary in 1836 he had noted that 'England alone cannot carry her points on the Continent; she must have allies as instruments to work with', a theme he continued to elaborate throughout his life, not always, however, with the means necessary to translate theory into practice. 'When people ask me', he remarked rather ungrammatically in 1856, 'for what is called a [foreign] policy, the only answer is that we mean to do what may seem to be best, upon each occasion as it arises, making the Interests of Our Country one's guiding principle'.[92] Such opinions were, in any case, commonplace in official circles. Russell, for example, put precisely the same point to Queen Victoria in December 1851 when he defined 'the traditionary policy of this country' as the avoidance of 'engagements, unless upon special cause shown'.[93] Splendid as all this sounded, it could only gain the required leverage abroad if underpinned by something more than diplomatic skill, namely, military power. And military power in the European sense was precisely what had been lacking ever since 1815. Britain had a navy of repute—its repute increasingly based on memories rather than efficiency—which, though useful in relation to geographically peripheral countries like Spain, Portugal, and Greece, had no role to play in Lombardy or the central European plains. As for land forces, national tradition and the exigencies of the minimalist mid-Victorian state meant that the army was a modest affair, spread thinly over the globe and rarely in peacetime more than 100,000-strong. Such limitations greatly increased the need for alliances—as was generally recognized. They also and too often obliged British ministers to

[92] C. Webster, *The Foreign Policy of Palmerston 1830–1841*, 2 vols. (London, 1951), i. 414; H. Temperley and L. M. Penson (eds.), *Foundations of British Foreign Policy from Pitt (1792) to Salisbury (1902)* (Cambridge, 1938), 88.

[93] *Letters of Queen Victoria*, ed. Benson and Viscount Esher, ii. 427.

conduct foreign policy largely by means of smoke, mirrors, and sleight of hand.

Palmerston was the most prominent (though not always the most successful) performer of such necessary conjuring tricks. His operations functioned at a number of distinct and only loosely connected levels: that of rationality where practical interests alone were pursued, that of principle where liberal rhetoric created a large domestic following, that of reality where it was a matter of winning here and losing there. The most immediate problem which faced him on entering office in 1846 was that of relations with France. His immediate predecessor at the Foreign Office, Aberdeen, had gained a considerable reputation as the architect of an entente cordiale between the two countries. Though Palmerston was to gain one for ruining this happy state of affairs, the entente had, in reality, never amounted to much, relations between Aberdeen and his French opposite number (Guizot) having been bedevilled by differences over the slave trade, control of Tahiti, and by clashes regarding Greece, Morocco, and Spain. Indeed, Aberdeen's initial desire for friendly coexistence in 1841 had, already by 1844, been whittled down to a mere determination to avoid war, almost at any price.[94]

In 1846 the attentions of France and Britain were focused especially on Spain where neither wanted the other to gain an advantage by any marriages which might be contracted by the teenage Queen Isabella and her younger sister, the Infanta Louisa Fernanda. Although Aberdeen and Guizot had come to some informal understanding on the matter (the crux of which seems to have been that the Infanta would not wed a French prince until the Queen had married a Spanish cousin and produced an heir), the details of this were vague and remembered rather differently by the two men. Palmerston's first dispatch to Bulwer, the minister in Madrid, gave prime place among the Queen's three leading suitors to Leopold of Saxe-Coburg-Gotha (generally regarded as the 'British' candidate). Although Palmerston actually showed the letter to the French ambassador in London, Guizot was more than ready to decipher sinister meanings between the lines. In Madrid, where complex intrigues were the order of the day, the Queen-Mother, Christina, ignored Palmerston and arranged a double wedding in October 1846: Isabella married her cousin, the (supposedly impotent) Duke of Cadiz, the Infanta married the French King's son, the Duke of Montpensier. Though in the end France gained little from its success, Palmerston stumbled again when a dispatch of his to Bulwer in

---

[94] M. E. Chamberlain, *'Pax Britannica': British Foreign Policy 1789–1914* (London, 1988), 88–91.

March 1848 ordering the latter to read a lecture on constitutionalism to the Spanish government resulted in Bulwer's expulsion—an unusual and extreme act according to the conventions of the time. In London the cabinet was taken by surprise. Wood and Lord Grey led the attack on Palmerston who promised to submit future dispatches to the Prime Minister for approval, a promise which, not for the first or last time, he entirely failed to keep.[95]

Much more serious and potentially explosive was the situation created by the continental revolutions of 1848. Here, though Palmerston again succeeded in alienating foreign statesmen, his record was more successful given the feebleness of the cards in his hands. As revolutions engulfed almost all of Europe outside Russia and Britain, so Palmerston kept certain key principles in view: the maintenance of Austria as a first-class power, the avoidance outside Italy of substantial boundary changes, the prevention of large-scale war. While he accepted the assurances of the new republican government in France that it desired no substantial adjustments to the Vienna settlement, the declaration of war by Charles Albert of Piedmont against Austria (which then still occupied Lombardy and Venetia) presented him with considerable problems. On the one hand, he believed that Austria would in fact ultimately be strengthened by the loss of its Italian territories, on the other, he was fearful that, in the short term, Austrian weakness would allow France to establish a powerful position in the region. He, therefore, deployed his usual technique for constraining potentially hostile powers: an offer of joint mediation with, in this case of course, France itself. As so often in diplomacy, the unexpected happened. While the French dithered, the Austrians succeeded in defeating Charles Albert, not just in 1848 but again in 1849 after he had foolishly declared war a second time. He then abdicated and the Austrians imposed a comparatively gentle peace on his successor, Victor Emmanuel, which broadly restored the status quo. Continental conservatives persuaded themselves that this was a defeat for Palmerston and for the constitutionalist rhetoric to which he was so partial. In fact, Palmerston's basic (and more limited) objective of preventing any settlement seriously inimical to British interests had been secured.[96]

The essential 'realism' of Palmerston's policies was more starkly revealed in the case of Hungary where an aristocratic uprising in 1849 (the politics of which he supported—indeed he compared its principles to those of the

[95] K. Bourne, *The Foreign Policy of Victorian England 1830–1902* (Oxford, 1970), 58–60, 293–4; Prest, *Russell*, 312–14.

[96] D. Southgate, *'The Most English Minister...': The Policies and Politics of Palmerston* (London, 1966), 201–42.

'Glorious Revolution' of 1688) gravely threatened the ability of the Habsburg Empire to remain an important factor in the central European balance of power. Here, in effect, Palmerston supported the intervention of autocratic Russia to suppress the revolt on Austria's behalf, and he did the same when Russia put down disorders in the Danubian Principalities (then still technically part of the Turkish dominions). Only when the Hungarian revolt had been finally crushed did he indulge in condemnations of Russian and Austrian severity and support Ottoman refusals to deport Hungarian and Polish refugees who had sought sanctuary in the East. In Germany he displayed even less enthusiasm for sudden change. Though he favoured some limited consolidation of boundaries, he feared that any greater measure of German unity might well prove dangerous. When, in an aberrant moment of liberal enthusiasm, the Prussians in April 1848 talked about some national reorganization of their Polish territories, he was quick to oppose the idea and tell Berlin 'to abstain from any proceeding which could justifiably be regarded by Russia as aggressive'.[97]

Only when situations had stabilized was Palmerston usually prepared to make those pronouncements which continental liberals so liked and continental reactionaries found so irritating. Nor was this entirely hypocritical, for Palmerston believed the existing balance of power to be, not only in Britain's practical interests, but a force for real and effective, as opposed to illusory, liberalism. Thus for him it was the balance of power that made suppression of the Hungarian revolution 'right' and part of a fundamentally liberal strategy, however true it might be that liberalism could also be served by Austria following less coercive policies at home. 'The argument was involved, but entirely logical—and of course highly convenient.'[98]

On the surface, however, things sometimes looked rather different. Although there can be no doubt that Palmerston was convinced—as he told the British minister in Munich—that the most significant struggle of 1848 was 'one between those who have no property and those who wish to keep it' (a remark reminiscent of his famous pronouncement on Irish affairs that 'tenant right' was 'equivalent to landlords' wrong'),[99] yet the language of 'progress' he so often deployed and the brusqueness with which he lectured the autocracies gave him a high international reputation for sympathy with liberal causes. The more continental reactionaries assailed

[97] W. J. Orr, jun., 'British Diplomacy and the German Problem, 1848–1850', *Albion*, 10 (1978), 212; R. W. Seton-Watson, *Britain in Europe 1789–1914* (Cambridge, 1937), 265–71.
[98] B. Porter, *Britain, Europe and the World 1850–1986: Delusions of Grandeur*, 2nd edn. (London, 1987), 25.
[99] M. E. Chamberlain, *British Foreign Policy in the Age of Palmerston* (London, 1980), 63; *Hansard*, clxxvii. 823 (27 Feb. 1865).

him—as when in December 1851 the Austrian Foreign Minister, Schwarzenberg, tartly noted that the oppressor of Ireland had best 'spare himself the trouble of advising us on the subject of Lombardy'[100]—the more did liberals count him as a friend. At home too, Palmerston's spasmodic belligerence as Foreign Secretary (invariably directed against minor powers who could easily be bullied by the Royal Navy) tended to engender a good deal of popular support. When in 1850 he sent ships to Greece to support the ludicrous demands for compensation made by a shady Portuguese merchant named Don Pacifico (born in Gibraltar and on that account claiming British citizenship) whose furniture had been pillaged by an Athenian mob, matters came to a head. Not only had Palmerston offended the Greeks and their Russian backers, he had also annoyed the French by effectively ignoring their efforts to mediate. For once the leading Peelites presented a completely united front and opposed Russell's government in the debate on the incident held in June. Though voting in the Commons followed party lines, the ministry's victory by 310 to 264 was above all seen as a victory for Palmerston himself. Not only did mainstream Whigs tend to approve of his posturings abroad, but so did those many rank-and-file Radicals who wished to assert the strength of the Liberal Party in the Commons, who saw him as an aristocratic reformer lending weight to the people's party, and who no less crucially believed that he possessed statesmanlike qualities which Russell lacked.[101] What has, however, always been best remembered about the Don Pacifico debate, and what gave Palmerston's subsequent career a rather greater reputation for bellicosity than was strictly deserved, was the confident and jaunty insistence that 'as the Roman, in days of old, held himself free from indignity, when he could say *Civis Romanus sum*; so also a British subject, in whatever land he may be, shall feel confident that the watchful eye and the strong arm of England, will protect him against injustice and wrong'.[102]

However much Russell, who in fact generally supported Palmerston's policies if not always their presentation, might now have wished to rid himself of so troublesome and threatening a subordinate, the political balance of power was shifting decisively away from him. In the autumn of 1851 Palmerston was only with difficulty persuaded not to receive the visiting Hungarian rebel, Kossuth, something which would have greatly angered the Austrians. In November he chose to accept an Address from voters in which the Emperors of Russia and Austria were called 'odious and

[100] A. J. P. Taylor, *The Italian Problem in European Diplomacy 1847–1849* (Manchester, 1934), 190–1.
[101] M. Taylor, *Decline of Radicalism*, 150–7.
[102] *Hansard*, cxii. 444 (25 June 1850): note '*British* subject', but 'strong arm of *England*'.

detestable assassins'. In December he rode roughshod over cabinet policy by telling the French ambassador that he entirely approved of Louis Napoleon's recent *coup*. When the Queen demanded blood, he was dismissed, only to help engineer the government's downfall in February 1852.[103]

That in Aberdeen's coalition Palmerston held the Home rather than the Foreign portfolio only added to his reputation, for it placed him well away from the Crimean flames. In broad terms there was in any case no great discontinuity between the diplomatic manœuvrings pursued by the various administrations of the time, as Aberdeen himself confirmed on becoming Prime Minister in December 1852.[104] Even in the case of relations with the United States, where Aberdeen had achieved a considerable settlement in 1846 over the vexed questions of Texas and the Canadian boundary, the Clayton-Bulwer Treaty of 1850 (by which the two countries agreed to desist from colonizing central America) was more a continuation than a new departure.[105] What *was* new under the Aberdeen coalition was a shift from the dominance of a single individual (Palmerston) to the formulation of policy by endless and often inconclusive debate.

Although the Crimean War of 1854–6 had almost nothing to do with the growth of nationalist movements, these undoubtedly flourished in the atmosphere it helped to create. Here as elsewhere the arrival on the scene of a revived Bonapartist Empire in France constituted a crucial break with the immediate past. No doubt Napoleon III was sincere in claiming that he preferred peace to war, but he also represented a new force with a real interest in upsetting the settlement of 1815. The Crimean War allowed him to obscure his support in 1849 for an illiberal pope by now waging war against an illiberal tsar. And by thus finally demonstrating that liberalism and nationalism were quite separate things, he helped to make the latter even more dynamic and destabilizing than it already was. What this meant for Britain in the field of European relations was that smoke, mirrors, and a bit of bluff had pretty well had their day.

Already Palmerston's bluff had failed at least once, in the case of Schleswig and Holstein in 1848–9. These duchies (the former partly Danish in population, the latter almost entirely German) were attached to Denmark only because all three shared the same ruler. When in 1848 a real possibility that divergent succession laws might soon sever that attachment coincided with a clash between Danish and German nationalists (and, in consequence, between Denmark and Prussia) Palmerston found it difficult

---

[103] Southgate, *Most English Minister*, 285–93.
[104] *Hansard*, cxxiii. 1724 (27 Dec. 1852).
[105] Bourne, *Foreign Policy*, 51–3, 57, 86–7.

to influence events. Those who did have something to say were those in a position to deploy troops in the area: the Danes, the Prussians, the Austrians, the Swedes, the Russians. Although in 1852 the status quo was briefly restored by the Treaty of London, the Schleswig-Holstein problem did not disappear. Palmerston's lack of bayonets was now becoming obvious to all. Over the next two decades, as Britain's military weakness grew more and more apparent, British foreign policy was kept from complete disintegration only by benign combinations of circumstance and rhetoric. When, however, in 1864 the duchies once again surfaced into diplomatic prominence, Palmerston (then Prime Minister) found himself entirely bereft of influence.[106] By then, indeed, Britain had ceased, in any real sense, to be a great *European* power at all.

With regard to domestic politics Palmerston was, by contrast, able to construct an altogether more solid and less flashy reputation by drawing to himself those important elements in society which had achieved all they wanted to achieve and believed him to be a more effective guarantor of stability than Derby, Disraeli, and the Conservatives. He also proved surprisingly successful in attracting support from those many Radicals who had, by the 1850s, become as fearful of Russia as they were tired of Bright's pacific internationalism.[107] And with public opinion coming to count for more, a new premium was being placed (not least by newspapers) upon the kind of conspicuous political energy which Palmerston so clearly possessed.

In short, Palmerston had made himself the embodiment of a very wide spectrum of opinion both within and outside the restricted government circles of the time. He had done so by being in many respects the most modern politician of his day: by cultivating the press, appealing to public opinion on grounds of national pride, taking his policies—however indirectly—to 'the people'. He had done so too by sheer professional skill. Though as a minister he abandoned just as many bills and turned just as many somersaults as Russell ever did, yet he somehow never cut the same sorry or inconsistent figure. As an orator he could reach considerable, though unpredictable, heights. His progressive rhetoric abroad and support for enough reform to distance himself from complete reaction at home allowed him to achieve a unique place in political life. By early 1855 he had so clearly become the only possible Prime Minister that for many mid-Victorians the whole period 1846–55 was beginning to assume almost the character of a rehearsal for the Palmerstonian decade that was to come.

[106] K. A. P. Sandiford, *Great Britain and the Schleswig-Holstein Question* (Toronto, 1975), 105–20.

[107] A. Taylor, 'Palmerston and Radicalism, 1847–1865', *Journal of British Studies*, 33 (1994), 157–79.

CHAPTER 6

Crimean War and Indian Mutiny

I. WAR AGAINST RUSSIA

The 1850s were warlike. Two of the three major British military endeav-ours between Waterloo and the Great War, besides two of those 'minor' campaigns—in Persia and China—which regularly punctuated the Victor-ian age, took place then. It was almost as if, by some curious act of compensation, a period of comparative social calm at home had to be balanced by death and destruction beyond the seas. However, although both the Crimean War and the Indian Mutiny involved substantial mobil-izations and intense public concern, the differences between the two were more striking than the similarities. Yet their close temporal conjunction meant that the eventual victories of the Mutiny—in essence a very grand version of the small-scale colonial engagements in which the post-Napoleonic British army specialized—helped to block out many of the lessons that should have been learnt from the earlier and militarily far more significant battles in the Crimea.

As an armed engagement between major European powers, the Crimean War of 1854–6 constituted the kind of conflict which British statesmen thought the Vienna settlement of 1815 had rendered virtually impossible. Although the pattern of events created by the revolutionary outbreaks of 1848 had not at first seemed to contradict such complacent optimism, a major new element of instability was added to international relationships by the coming to power in France of Louis Napoleon, first as elected President in 1848 and then, after a *coup* in late 1851 and a plebiscite eleven months later, as the Emperor Napoleon III. Simply by choosing that particular numeral Napoleon gave notice that his was to be a revisionist regime determined to unravel the settlement of 1815 and construct a new world order in its place.

That this unravelling should begin in the East was largely the result of Napoleon's desire to kill as many birds as possible with a single stone. It needed no genius to notice that the Ottoman Empire provided the most readily available theatre for innovatory diplomatic activities. In particular, Napoleon hoped that renewed concern for France's traditional 'rights' with respect to the Holy Places of Palestine (then part of the Sultan's dominions) would both increase his general prestige and help make him less unpopular with conservative and Catholic elements at home. But if the Holy Places were little more than a convenient point of entrance for Napoleon, their location and their history meant that his actions would inevitably antagonize Russia (the chief patron of Orthodox Christianity), irritate powerful elements in Constantinople (understandably resentful at foreign interference in an area under Ottoman suzerainty), and inject a new tension into old and familiar anxieties about Eastern instability. As recently as 1841 a formal convention—by which Britain, Austria, Russia, Prussia, and a reluctant France had agreed that the Straits be closed to non-Turkish warships in time of peace—had provided a degree of equilibrium as well as something like an international guarantee for the Ottoman Empire. It had also, however, left the French with resentful feelings against British bullying, Tsar Nicholas I with lively visions of imminent Turkish dismemberment, and Palmerston with the belief that knocking foreign heads together could solve almost anything.[1]

In the course of conversations in early 1853 with Sir George Hamilton Seymour, the British ambassador at St Petersburg, Nicholas delivered himself of wide-ranging plans for dealing with the dissolution of the Ottoman state. Russell, the Foreign Secretary, responded by supporting international co-operation and denying that Turkish collapse was imminent. This failed to impress the Tsar, who, in the mean time, had sent a mission to Constantinople under Prince Menshikov to press for a 'rectification' of the situation created by recent Turkish concessions to Latin Christians and their French patrons. Menshikov's demands were extreme and unwarranted by any formal agreement, for he insisted that Russia be given unprecedented rights, not simply as regards clergymen and places of worship, but with respect to the substantial body of Orthodox believers as a whole.[2] By an unconvincing combination of bullying and ungracious moderation Menshikov gained the worst of all possible worlds. Not only did he offend the Turks, but he gave them time to call for support from the British and French governments, both of which viewed Russian expansionism and the disintegration of the Ottoman Empire with considerable alarm. For Turkey's 'intransigence' the Russians blamed Britain's ambassador in

[1] M. A. Anderson, *The Eastern Question 1774–1923* (London, 1966), 106–7; K. Bourne, *The Foreign Policy of Victorian England 1830–1902* (Oxford, 1970), 42–3; A. P. Saab, *The Origins of the Crimean Alliance* (Charlottesville, Va., 1977), 3.
[2] N. Rich, *Why the Crimean War? A Cautionary Tale* (Hanover, NH, 1985), 35–8.

Constantinople, Lord Stratford de Redcliffe, whose activities remain controversial, but whose public reputation as an old Ottoman hand rested in 1853 more on past glories than upon any great confidence placed in him by ministers at home.[3]

In May 1853 Menshikov left Constantinople and effectively broke off diplomatic relations with the Porte (as the Ottoman government was known). Stratford urged the cabinet to take a strong line, advice which earned the enthusiastic support of Palmerston, who, with Russell, represented the militant tendency within Aberdeen's administration. Already Palmerston (who as Home Secretary successfully combined energetic comments on overseas affairs with a lack of direct responsibility) had told Clarendon, the new Foreign Secretary appointed in February 1853, that 'the policy and practice of the Russian Government has always been to push forward its encroachments as fast and as far as the apathy or want of firmness of other Governments would allow it to go, but always to stop and retire when it was met with decided resistance'.[4] And, indeed, over the months that followed it was Palmerston, with increasing if unfocused support from other members of the cabinet, who proved the chief force for movement on the British side. Stratford, by contrast, generally sought to exercise a moderating influence, though the mere presence in Constantinople of a man of his experience and reputation was bound to give encouragement to those Turks looking for military support against Russia from the West.[5]

The Russians reacted to Menshikov's failure by announcing that they would occupy the principalities of Moldavia and Wallachia (roughly modern Romania), which, though more or less autonomous, were formally under Ottoman suzerainty subject to certain rights given to Russia by the Treaty of Adrianople of 1829. In response, Britain joined France in moving naval forces to Besika Bay just outside the Dardanelles and ministers gave Stratford authority to call ships to Constantinople should he think it necessary. In July 1853 Russian troops occupied the principalities, with—so Nicholas thought—tacit support from Austria. The Austrians, however, knew well that any conflict in the region might upset the unstable equilibrium upon which the integrity of the multinational Habsburg Empire so crucially depended. They therefore embarked upon a search for peace

---

[3] D. M. Goldfrank, *The Origins of the Crimean War* (London, 1994), 147–61, 240–7.

[4] E. Ashley, *The Life and Correspondence of Henry John Temple Viscount Palmerston*, 2 vols. (London, 1879), ii. 273.

[5] J. L. Herkless, 'Stratford, the Cabinet and the Outbreak of the Crimean War', *Historical Journal*, 18 (1975), 497–523; Saab, *Origins of Crimean Alliance*, 123–6; Rich, *Why the Crimean War?*, 70–3.

through negotiation that was to dominate their diplomacy for the next three years.

In August, Russia actually accepted the so-called 'Vienna Note' which Britain, France, and Prussia had joined Austria in drawing up the previous month. This provided that the Sultan should promise to observe his existing treaty obligations towards Russia regarding the Orthodox Church and that no changes in such matters should be made without the agreement of Russia and France. The Turks, however, proved unresponsive. The situation became more serious still when in September it emerged that the Russian Foreign Minister, Count Nesselrode, seemed to believe that the Note granted Russia a general right of intervention on behalf of Orthodox Christians as a whole. In fact, this so-called 'violent interpretation' was less extreme than excited reactions in London and Paris implied.[6] None the less, Aberdeen and Clarendon ordered the fleet to Constantinople without consulting the cabinet. Aberdeen still hoped for peace, but Clarendon, who had hitherto adopted a wavering attitude, wrote at once to Stratford that 'the only real likelihood ... now is war'.[7]

It is rarely acknowledged that the Vienna Note was simply unacceptable to almost every element in Turkish political life. British public opinion has often been given much weight as part of the context within which war was eventually joined. Yet the arrogance of Western historians has disguised the fact that in the Ottoman Empire 'public opinion' (the term is not of course without its obscurities) was no less important than elsewhere.[8] And in this sense Turkey was at least as active a player in the unfolding drama as Russia, France, or Britain. Indeed, by the autumn of 1853 the Porte was dragging the Western powers in its wake and doing so with no little skill and diplomatic dexterity, its resolve greatly strengthened by dispatches from the Ottoman ambassador in London, whose ministerial contacts were confined to Palmerston and an increasingly militant Clarendon at the Foreign Office.[9]

Turkey's eventual declaration of war on Russia on 4 October was, therefore, the outcome of developments both at home and abroad. On the last day of November the Russians destroyed a Turkish fleet near the Black Sea port of Sinope. This perfectly legitimate act of war cranked the Russo-

---

[6] Goldfrank, *Origins of Crimean War*, 194–7; Rich, *Why the Crimean War?*, 80–1.

[7] H. Temperley, 'Stratford de Redcliffe and the Origins of the Crimean War: Part II', *English Historical Review*, 49 (1934), 277.

[8] Saab, *Origins of Crimean Alliance*, 95–6; Herkless, 'Stratford and Outbreak of War', 497–523.

[9] Saab, *Origins of Crimean Alliance*, 74–5, 90–1. The ambassador also sent numerous clippings from the British press which still survive in the Istanbul archives.

phobia of much of the British press to new heights of excitement, with the result that 'public opinion' became an ever sharper debating sword in the hands of those members of Aberdeen's cabinet most determined to resist Russia by preserving the integrity of the Ottoman Empire. On 3 January 1854 the British and French fleets entered the Black Sea and began to behave in a belligerently anti-Russian fashion. Early in February St Petersburg broke off diplomatic relations with London and Paris. On 12 March, Britain and France signed an alliance with Turkey and finally declared war on Russia just over a fortnight later.

In all these manœuvres, not one of the governments involved exhibited any consistent and unambiguous determination for war—not autocratic Russia, imperial France, despotic Turkey, or quasi-democratic Britain. Indeed, the hesitations and shifting balances which marked the history of the Aberdeen coalition were, in this respect, no more than constitutional versions of a universal indecisiveness. Yet the very fact that responsible cabinet government was the British way of doing things, not only gave a particular patterning to the exercise of power in London, but made it possible, perhaps even necessary, for the chief actors there to present their arguments within a framework of public rhetoric and party relationships.

Almost all of these actors knew what they wanted. Aberdeen wanted peace, Palmerston wanted to render Russia harmless for decades to come, Russell wanted to assert Britain's moral superiority. Only Clarendon lacked resolve: his genius lay in drafting dispatches rather than developing strategies. It was not, therefore, a case of men operating without clear aims, though the energy, skill, and persistence with which their aims were pressed differed greatly. Aberdeen, in particular, though a man of ability and experience, allowed policy to slip away from his initial determination to remain wary of French 'revolutionary' designs and keep the 'unspeakable' Turk at arm's length. Palmerston, by contrast, mounted a confident defence of the Ottoman Empire and, as time went on, moved more and more into alignment with popular notions both inside and outside parliament.[10]

Initially the coalition cabinet functioned smoothly enough and until early September 1853 Aberdeen's moderate line appeared to be paying dividends. Yet already Palmerston's consistency and Clarendon's talk of growing Russophobia out of doors were allowing the initiative to slide into Turkish hands.[11] By October it was clear to all with eyes to see (and Queen

[10] D. Wetzel, *The Crimean War: A Diplomatic History* (Boulder, Colo., 1985), 68; M. Chamberlain, *Lord Palmerston* (Cardiff, 1987), 85–6.

[11] J. B. Conacher, *The Aberdeen Coalition 1852–1855* (Cambridge, 1968), 173; P. W. Schroeder, *Austria, Great Britain, and the Crimean War* (Ithaca, NY, 1972), 63–8.

Victoria's eyes proved sharper than most)[12] that the cabinet was proving entirely unsuccessful in distancing itself from the imperatives of the Porte. At a crucial meeting early that month it became obvious that Aberdeen was losing control. After Palmerston and Russell had demanded that the fleet be sent at once to support the Turks, 'we came at last', Aberdeen noted, 'to a sort of compromise; our great difficulty being how to deal with the question of entering the Black Sea. I consented to this being done, provided it was strictly in defence of some point of attack on Turkish territory . . . We have thus assumed a strictly defensive position.'[13] Such arguments were, however, little more than self-delusion and their deployment did nothing at all to diminish anger over the events at Sinope on 30 November—quite the reverse.

Although Palmerston and Russell represented the most active proponents of 'movement' in the cabinet they developed their policies quite independently of one another. Indeed, Russell, who was always self-centred, never saw himself as supporting 'Palmerston's policy', but rather as creating his own, which generally, but never completely, happened to coincide with that of the Home Secretary.[14] For Palmerston it was predominantly a matter of implementing a particular interpretation of the balance of power, which he explained as meaning 'only this—that a number of weaker States may unite to prevent a stronger one from acquiring a power which should be dangerous to them . . . It is the doctrine of self-preservation. It is the doctrine of self-defence.'[15] Russell, by contrast, operated in a context at once grander and more circumscribed. While his desire to regain the premiership was probably no greater than Palmerston's ambitions, he proved altogether less able to hide behind a disguise of geniality. Nor did sweeping assertions of Britain's manifest destiny— 'We, Sir, who are following the maxim which, since the time of William III has governed and actuated the councils of this country . . . believe it is our duty to throw our weight into the scale in these conflicts'[16]—strike the right note: blunter claims carried greater weight.

In December 1853 Palmerston resigned on the franchise question. When he came back to office almost at once, the coincidence of his reappearance with the excitements caused by Sinope rendered his position stronger still. The peace party in the cabinet began to melt away. It had always been strongest among the Peelites (Aberdeen, Graham, Herbert, and Gladstone), though Whigs like Wood and semi-detached Peelites like Argyll had also provided notable support. In the final analysis, the triumph, if one

[12] Saab, *Origins of Crimean Alliance*, 100.   [13] Conacher, *Aberdeen Coalition*, 195.
[14] Ibid. 266.   [15] *Hansard*, cxxxii. 279 (31 Mar. 1854).
[16] *Hansard*, cxxxii. 213 (31 Mar. 1854).

can call it that, of Palmerston, Russell, Lansdowne, and (to a lesser extent) Clarendon showed that Whiggery could still show 'Liberal Conservatism' a clean pair of heels. The Peelites had been much given to condemning 'drift' without actually doing much to reverse the tendency they deplored. Now some of them, in particular Graham and Newcastle, became more belligerent. From January 1854 the business of preparing for war began to dominate ministerial correspondence. The fact that by February Protectionist leaders were also arguing in parliament that there had been too much drift, that, as Derby declared, 'we are not at war, not at peace, and we are not neutral', merely served to encourage such trends.[17]

Much historical energy has been devoted to games of 'might-have-been' concerning Britain's entry into the Crimean conflict. It has been suggested that a more consistent line—almost any kind of consistent line—would have prevented war.[18] Certainly Aberdeen regretted until the end of his days his failure to push more strongly for peace. Palmerston, too, ever armed with instant self-justifications, was already in January 1854 declaring that if only 'the measures now tardily resolved upon had been taken when I first recommended them six or eight months ago, much of the present difficulty would have been averted'.[19] Yet the whole business involved so many unstable elements, both at home and abroad, that all such claims should be seen more as examples of Anglocentric myopia than of retrospective insight of any kind.

Once the conflict was under way the politics of war became subsidiary to the war itself. The government remained in power because the war had to be pursued, though it was at first pursued without the benefit of much parliamentary attention. And when the coalition was eventually brought down in early 1855 (and Palmerston became Prime Minister) it fell because the advanced Liberals abandoned it once military deficiencies became apparent and not (or at least not chiefly) because of internal disagreements within the cabinet itself. A curious paradox lay at the heart of all this: as Prime Minister Palmerston continued to beat the Russophobe drum by demanding ever further military extensions and doing his best to prevent Britain from being drawn into any of Austria's plans for a compromise peace, yet he actually made no substantial contribution to the war effort at any but the most general of levels. Palmerston, in fact, proved insignificant as a war leader in the Churchillian mould. His government formed in February 1855 survived for as long as it did, first, because the passage of time allowed it

---

[17] *Hansard*, cxxx. 628 (14 Feb. 1854).

[18] See K. Bourne, *Foreign Policy*, 75, and L. Woodward, *The Age of Reform 1815–1870*, 2nd edn. (Oxford, 1962), 263–4 (where is to be found a long catalogue of 'ifs').

[19] *The Letters of the Third Viscount Palmerston to Laurence and Elizabeth Sulivan 1804–1863*, ed. K. Bourne, Camden 4th ser. 23 (London, 1979), 308.

to benefit from military reforms already under way, secondly, because the early resignation of three Peelite cabinet ministers pleased Liberal back-benchers, and, finally, because Palmerston, unlike Aberdeen, worked with rather than against the grain of existing party allegiancies.

The Peelites, for their part, proved awesomely successful in getting the worst of all worlds. By resigning when they did they set in marble an irredeemable association with the early chaotic phase of the war. No doubt this was unfair. But those who had long thought them 'prigs' or (as Clarendon put it) no more than 'a little bank of conceited colonels without general officers and no rank and file' were more than happy to let the cup of *Schadenfreude* run over. That, none the less, Gladstone could still insist in April 1855 that there was 'scarcely one among them who was not, for one reason or another, much above par as a Member of Parliament' merely showed that, for the Peelites, the learning process had scarcely begun.[20]

As regards military matters, Britain's forces in 1854 were not so much badly prepared as prepared for the wrong kind of war. This owed much to the manner in which successive governments had looked—and continued to look—to the royal navy as the prime military guarantor of Britain's role as a colonial and world power, with the possibility that the army might be involved in engagements on the European continent always a lesser concern. But if the 'primacy' of the navy was frequently asserted by contemporaries, its physical embodiment had, by mid-century, become more impressive in legend and perception than in reality. Because no foreign power was pre-pared to spend substantial sums on its own sea-going forces during the sixty or so years after 1815, the Treasury was able to cut the cost of the royal navy beyond what might otherwise have been possible.[21] Indeed, one of the most surprising aspects of nineteenth-century government expenditure is that it was not until 1896 (when the so-called 'Blue Water School' was in the ascendant) that more money began to be spent on the navy than on the army.[22] This remarkable fact does rather cut the navy's much-vaunted 'primacy' down to size. What it meant was that both branches of the armed services suffered. The army, though more costly (and more fashionable among the élite), was always seen as essentially an ancillary force, important certainly, but not central to Britain's global interests. The navy, though granted the prestige of 'primacy', was never given the funds or accorded the expertise which such a role demanded and deserved.

[20] A. Hawkins, *Parliament, Party and the Art of Politics in Britain, 1855–59* (London, 1987), 15, 286.
[21] P. M. Kennedy, *The Rise and Fall of British Naval Mastery* (London, 1976), 149–202; C. J. Bartlett, *Great Britain and Sea Power 1815–1853* (Oxford, 1963), *passim*.
[22] B. R. Mitchell, *British Historical Statistics* (Cambridge, 1988), 587–9.

At least the administration of the navy had experienced a certain amount of reorganization in 1832. By contrast, that of the army remained a striking example of the early Victorian preference for checks and balances in matters of bureaucracy. So many ministers and officials were involved that even contemporary experts became lost in the maze. The Secretary for War and the Colonies was invariably a member of the cabinet and spent most of his energies on colonial affairs while also exercising political oversight of all line and reserve troops outside the United Kingdom. The Secretary at War looked after financial and legal matters. The Commander-in-Chief (always a senior military man) saw to discipline, appointments, promotions, and the army's general state of professional readiness, though his overall authority suffered great decline once soldiers had gone abroad. The distribution of the regular troops in Britain itself had to be approved by the Home Secretary, who also administered the yeomanry and the militia. The engineers and artillery came under the Ordnance which had both military and civil branches. The Commissariat, a department of the Treasury and staffed by civilians, saw to supplies and transport. The list could be extended almost indefinitely.

Contrary to much accepted wisdom, criticism of this 'system' had been widespread during the quarter-century before 1854.[23] In particular, the commission appointed in 1837 at the instigation of the then Secretary at War, Lord Howick, had recommended wide-ranging changes designed to consolidate responsibility in fewer hands. But a combination of tolerable success in colonial campaigns, fears about the creation of an overpowerful military authority, bureaucratic inertia, and dedication to cheese-paring generally ensured that little was done.

The Duke of Wellington was Commander-in-Chief in 1827–8 and 1842–52, and even when not in that position he exercised an almost hypnotic authority over military affairs. Although not entirely opposed to new ideas, his influence was deployed on the side of tradition and parsimony. As a result, Britain maintained an army which, leaving India aside, rarely exceeded 100,000 men, of whom about two-fifths were usually on colonial station and therefore unavailable for rapid deployment should any European crisis arise. In addition, a common and by no means unwarranted perception on the part of army officers that calls for reform were really no more than calls for further economies substantially diminished the internal constituency for change. While, therefore, the cost of the armed services invariably constituted a very large proportion of total central government

---

[23] H. Strachan, *Wellington's Legacy: The Reform of the British Army 1830–54* (Manchester, 1984); J. Sweetman, *War and Administration: The Significance of the Crimean War for the British Army* (Edinburgh, 1984).

expenditure—that of the army alone consistently exceeded the amount devoted to all branches of civil administration—it was never enough to provide the sinews for continental war. Given that this was so it is not the failures but the comparative successes of the military machine in the Crimea which should elicit surprise.

Of course not all had remained the same since 1815. Conditions for the ordinary soldier, though still harsh, had improved. An attempt was made in 1847 to introduce enlistment for limited periods. Military education was extended. In the early 1850s the partial adoption of the Minié rifle (which was more accurate and had a much longer range than the musket it replaced) and the holding of field manœuvres at Chobham represented a notable increase in energy. The first was initiated by Wellington, the latter occurred under his successor, Lord Hardinge, who was to hold office during the Crimean War itself. Yet, despite signs of growing professionalism among sections of the officer corps, actual experience of command was necessarily confined to colonial wars. Little attention was given to 'grand strategy' in any of its forms: handling large forces in the field, co-ordinating their activities, or, perhaps more important still, thinking about the relationship between war, politics, and administration. That commissions in the infantry and cavalry were available for purchase (though, especially in time of war, not all promotions were so determined) was a lesser problem. At least younger men—however inexpert—could thereby obtain middle-ranking commands, whereas in the navy and artillery a rigid seniority system ensured that only dead men's shoes provided a route to higher things. And though gunnery and engineering officers were generally trained, they were also invariably very ancient indeed.

At the highest level antiquity was universal. On entering the Crimean War the commander of the British land forces, Lord Raglan, was 66. Only one of his five infantry divisional commanders was under 60 (and he was the Queen's 34-year-old cousin who had never seen action before). The chief engineer, Sir John Burgoyne, was 72. The only admiral worth considering for command of the Baltic fleet formed to attack Russian shipping and fortifications in that area was the 68-year-old Sir Charles Napier. Age is of course no automatic obstacle to either ability or determination (Burgoyne, the oldest of all, was generally considered competent), but an army commanded entirely by such men would needs be very lucky to experience much in the way of innovation or flexible leadership.[24] Nor can there be

[24] Note, however, that Field-Marshal Radetsky was well into his eighties when he so brilliantly led the Austrian forces against the Sardinians in 1848–9 and that Blücher was 72 at Waterloo.

much doubt that the senior officers chosen were the best available. Raglan, in particular, had admirable qualities of tact and diplomacy. Vision and ruthlessness, however, were in distinctly short supply.

British and French contingents began to arrive at the Dardanelles in April 1854. The initial intention was to protect Constantinople. Once that had been achieved, a move northwards was intended, to assist Turkish forces for some time engaged in indecisive encounters with Russian troops in the eastern Danube area. With this in mind the allied armies embarked for Varna (on the Black Sea coast of what is now Bulgaria) on 28 May. Then in June the (non-combatant) Austrians, without consultation, demanded that Russia evacuate the principalities forthwith. The Russians did this in August, and distrusted the Austrians from that moment onwards. Their withdrawal also left the allies at Varna with nothing to do (see Map 9).

Although the idea of attacking the Crimea and in particular the great fortress at Sebastopol had been discussed by British ministers for months— Palmerston had often mentioned it and Graham with his naval responsibilities saw it as a key element in Britain's overall Mediterranean strategy— it had never been analysed with any rigorous eye to the practical difficulties involved.[25] The British commanders were, therefore, astonished when first informed of what London had in mind. The account given by the commander of the Fifth Division, Sir George Brown, of Raglan's receipt of the order to attack Sebastopol reveals much about the contemporary military mind. 'I naturally enquired', wrote Brown,

what information he [Raglan] had in regard to the strength of Sebastopol, and what force he expected might be opposed to him in the Crimea. His answer was, that he had no information whatever! . . . 'You and I', I said, 'are accustomed, when in any difficulty . . . to ask ourselves how the Great Duke would have acted . . . Now, I tell your Lordship, that without more certain information . . . that great man would not have accepted the responsibility of undertaking such an enterprise as that which is now proposed to you. But notwithstanding that consideration, I am of opinion that you had better accede to the proposal and come into the views of the Government, for this reason, that it is clear to me . . . that they have made up their minds to it at home, and that if you decline to accept the responsibility, they will send some one else out to command the army, who will be less scrupulous, and more ready to come into their plans'.[26]

Led thus by unhappy generals and armchair strategists at home, some 27,000 British, 28,000 French, and 7,000 Turkish troops disembarked at

[25] H. Strachan, 'Soldiers, Strategy and Sebastopol', *Historical Journal*, 21 (1978), 312.
[26] G. Brown, *Memoranda and Observations on the Crimean War, 1854–5* (Elgin, 1879), 15–16.

Calamita Bay some twenty miles north of Sebastopol on 14 September 1854 (see Plate 3).

Three major battles were fought in quick succession. On 20 September the allies drove the Russians back at the Alma river. The army then moved south and further engagements took place at Balaclava on 25 October and Inkerman on 5 November, the first famous for the charge of the Light Brigade, the second more a series of separate skirmishes than a 'battle' as usually understood. All this gave the Russians time to improve Sebastopol's defences and it took another ten months of bombardment and attack before they were eventually driven out in September 1855. Because it was never made clear who precisely was in overall charge of the allied forces the feeble leadership of the various senior commanders was rendered feebler still. The allies succeeded in the end because their equipment was better, their soldiers more skilful, and because Russian lines of communication were stretched and Russian commanders (with a few prominent exceptions) were notably below par.

Efforts to make the war a global one, though at times ambitiously formulated, never amounted to much.[27] An allied fleet sent to the Baltic achieved little save the destruction of fortifications on the Aaland Islands. Minor naval engagements also took place in the White Sea and the Pacific where the allies attacked a Russian base on the Kamchatka peninsula. More significant were two episodes at the very end of the war: the allied capture of Kinburn, a fortified place at the end of the long peninsula enclosing the estuary of the Dnieper to the north-west of the Crimea and the Russian victory over the Turks at Kars in Asia Minor, a last-minute success which enabled them to enter the peace conference less naked than they might otherwise have been.

Apart from certain famous deeds of valour, the Crimean War is, from the British point of view, best remembered for confusions over supply, chaos in Balaclava Harbour, disease, inadequate medical services, and the—somewhat overinflated—activities of Florence Nightingale. The torments suffered by soldiers during the early winter of 1854–5 were intense and elicited much contemporary denunciation. A description by another forceful woman of wounded men being thrown into ships at Balaclava was neither extreme nor inaccurate:

The dignified indifference of the medical officer, who stood with his hands in his pockets, gossiping in the hospital doorway,—the rough and indecent way in which

[27] A. D. Lambert takes a different view and—the title of his book notwithstanding—prefers to use the term 'Russian' War (as did some at the time); see next note and Lambert's *The Crimean War: British Grand Strategy, 1853–56* (Manchester, 1990).

the poor howling wretches were hauled along the quay, and bundled, some with one, and others with both legs amputated, into the bottom of a boat...was truly an edifying exemplification of the golden rule, 'Do to others as you would be done by'.[28]

Such things were the products of a myriad of financial, administrative, and moral defects. Mid-Victorian army medical services attracted the least competent and most callous members of a notably callous profession. No one had been prepared to spend either money or time in planning for something which no one had ever expected to happen. Raglan recorded how 'it did not occur to me to suppose that Her Majesty's Government would be willing to form establishments upon a large scale, which could not at once be got up in the midst of the active operations of a campaign'.[29] The decision to use Balaclava Harbour to disembark supplies was a terrible mistake and a storm in November 1854, which destroyed much shipping, added further to the army's woes.

Yet it is remarkable how quickly the situation was rectified, in large measure because those in charge of government already knew that improvements were needed. From its earliest days the Aberdeen coalition had discussed bureaucratic reform, though action had been hampered by differences between those who, like Russell, wanted complete 'consolidation' of departments and those (in particular Herbert) who insisted that co-ordination by 'one single authority' would prove more effective.[30] Decisions to divide responsibility for 'war' and 'the colonies'—thus creating a fourth secretary of state—and to transfer the Commissariat from the Treasury to the War Department were taken in May 1854. As early as January 1855 the worst supply problems had been overcome and the lines of command between London and the Crimea improved. By the time the war ended the duplication of responsibility for military finance and supply had been substantially erased. And even if the new arrangements proved less neat in practice than they looked on paper, important strides had undoubtedly been made towards a more rational system of military administration.[31]

The one thing that was not in short supply during the war was money. Peacetime spending on the army and navy in 1853 amounted to £15.3m or 27.7 per cent of total central government expenditure including debt charges, a proportion not generally much less than that incurred by other

---

[28] Mrs Henry Duberly, *Journal kept during the Russian War* (London, 1855), 143–4.

[29] J. B. Conacher, *Britain and the Crimea, 1855–56* (London, 1987), 85.

[30] O. Anderson, *A Liberal State at War: English Politics and Economics during the Crimean War* (London, 1967), 33–69.

[31] Sweetman, *War and Administration*, 6–7, 128.

countries (save Russia). By 1856, however, Britain was spending £46.7m (or 50.2 per cent of total central government expenditure) on its military machine.[32] As Chancellor of the Exchequer, Gladstone cranked up taxes and announced that everything must be paid for out of revenue, though he worried that overreliance on income tax would exempt the poorer classes from paying their share. That such a hope could even be entertained showed how rich a country Britain had become, though in the event Gladstone was obliged to borrow. However it was done, the Crimean forces were well supplied, even if initially the means of distribution were deficient. By 1855 the army and the navy had more than doubled in size and cumulative war expenditure had reached something around £70m, of which just under half was eventually met by additions to net public borrowing.[33]

Palmerston came out of it all with undeserved good fortune. The outcry which had greeted revelations about the inadequacies of supply during the winter of 1854–5 began to recede just as he took over as Prime Minister in February 1855. In this sense, but in few others, public opinion played a significant role, in shifting gear just as Palmerston was reaching the top of the greasy pole. Of course the fact that the Crimean War was the first conflict to be observed by special correspondents (notably W. H. Russell of *The Times*) who were able to telegraph their stories home more efficiently than the generals could contact Whitehall undoubtedly helped to create a special kind of public atmosphere. (Soldiers had suffered as greatly in previous campaigns, but few civilians had known or much cared.) However, in other respects newspapers exercised less influence on policy than is often claimed, not least because many of the leading ministers—Clarendon, Aberdeen, and Palmerston in particular—manipulated the press far more successfully than the press ever manipulated them.

Public opinion in these years is, in any case, much more interesting for what it reveals about the preoccupations and obsessions of the 'thinking classes' than for any practical impact upon parliamentary politics or the governmental machine. Particularly noteworthy is the manner in which manifestations of religious concern and class rhetoric helped not only to identify villains, but to create a sense of expectation and change. Evangel-

---

[32] Mitchell, *British Historical Statistics*, 588; J. Gooch, *Armies in Europe* (London, 1980), 54–5; M. Messerschmidt, 'Die politische Geschichte der preussich-deutschen Armee', in G. Papke and W. Petter (eds.), *Handbuch zur deutschen Militärgeschichte*, iv/1 (Munich, 1975), 184; R. Holmes, *The Road to Sedan: The French Army 1866–70* (London, 1984), 159–60; G. E. Rothenberg, *The Army of Francis Joseph* (West Lafayette, Ind., 1976), 10. The Russian government spent two-fifths of its income on the military (J. S. Curtiss, *The Russian Army under Nicholas I* (Durham, NC, 1965), 99).

[33] Anderson, *Liberal State at War*, 201–2.

ical millenarians like Lord Shaftesbury (Palmerston's stepson-in-law) saw the war as yet another milepost along the road to the comparatively imminent end of the world. A good deal of nimble footwork was undertaken to show that the Sultan was a greater friend of Protestant truth than the Tsar (indeed, not the least of Peelite sins was a Tractarian interest in Eastern Orthodoxy). 'The Turk', declared one Evangelical authority, 'was not an infidel. He was Unitarian. As to the Russian Greeks or Greek Christians, he said nothing against their creed, but they were a besotted, dancing, fiddling race.'[34]

In general the religiously inclined were united in seeing the war as a judgement imposed by the Almighty upon a sinful nation (and official 'fast days' emphasized the point). Those who believed that providence operated by means of 'special' visitations to punish individuals or nations were also disposed to canvass the necessity of special and specific actions of a reforming character. In this respect their approach, though coming from a very different source, had certain points of similarity with the brief but intense campaign mounted by the Administrative Reform Association of 1855 which contrasted aristocratic bungling with the triumphs of contemporary commerce and urged that business-like procedures be applied to government and administration. Throughout the war, indeed, it was the most respectable members of the middle class who led the attack on the established order of things and did so 'under the inspiration of a distinctive middle-class set of values which had been developing since the 1820s'.[35] All the more ironic, therefore, that it should have been Palmerston (later the recipient of so much middle-class adulation) who, alone among ministers, had the nerve to point out that the most serious breakdowns had taken place 'not where the gentry were, not where the aristocracy were, but where there were persons belonging to other classes of the community—in the medical department, the Commissariat department, the transport service, which have not been filled by the aristocracy or the gentry'.[36]

The war only came to an end when enough points had been established to render further conflict superfluous. This, rather than the ceaseless efforts of Austria, made the Peace of Paris possible. Nicholas I died in March 1855 and his successor, Alexander II, though less emotionally wedded to the war, took time to appreciate the actual damage that was being caused to the Russian economy and the possible damage that continued fighting might do to autocratic power in general. Napoleon III, for his part, was coming to the conclusion that, unless the conflict could be broadened well beyond its

---

[34] O. Anderson, 'The Reactions of Church and Dissent towards the Crimean War', *Journal of Ecclesiastical History*, 16 (1965), 209–20; Saab, *Origins of Crimean Alliance*, 149.
[35] Anderson, *Liberal State at War*, 108.   [36] Conacher, *Britain and the Crimea*, 18.

present confines to encompass a more general revision of boundaries (such as those of Poland and Italy), then it was best to call a halt. While, therefore, Palmerston continued to seize every opportunity to encourage belligerence, France now embarked upon a determined effort to end the war.[37] Already it was beginning to become clear that the Anglo-French alliance of the Crimea might well turn out to be an aberration—something which the Orsini plot of 1858 and the subsequent hysteria about a possible French invasion were soon to make clearer still. But although Napoleon consistently supported Russia against Palmerston's demands for harsher terms at the Peace Congress which opened in Paris in February 1856 this did not mean that the dividing line between victors and vanquished was blurred beyond ready recognition or that the treaty signed on 30 March represented anything but a considerable Russian defeat. Turkey was admitted 'to participate in the advantages of the public law and system (concert) of Europe'—a declaration at once grand and opaque. Russia lost its rights in the principalities which remained under Turkish suzerainty but were guaranteed virtual independence. The amount of territory confiscated in Bessarabia, though less than the British demanded, was enough to exclude Russia from the Lower Danube area. The most important clause was that relating to the Black Sea. Here Russia was obliged to eat humble pie by agreeing to complete neutralization and the destruction of all its naval bases along the coast.

Certainly the Russians believed they had been dealt a severe blow, and in the sense that no major crises occurred in the Near East over the next twenty years the war might be accounted a modest international success. But, by effectively transforming Russia into a revisionist power (that is, one hoping to overturn the status quo), a very heavy investment in future instability had been made. As Russia for a time withdrew eastwards and as the concert of 1815 was finally destroyed, so the European continent was delivered, first, into the hands of Napoleon III, and then into those of Bismarck.[38] Austria was the biggest loser of all, its refusal to support Russia being deeply resented in St Petersburg. When the 1815 settlements were next challenged (in Italy in 1859 and Germany in 1866) Austria found itself isolated and alone.

While the inefficiencies revealed by the war undoubtedly reduced the prestige of Britain abroad as well as that of the political and economic relationships which she exemplified, at home the effect was altogether less dramatic. Enough (potentially reformable) scapegoats—aristocratic priv-

---

[37] Conacher, *Britain and the Crimea*, 141.
[38] A. J. P. Taylor, *The Struggle for Mastery in Europe 1848–1918* (Oxford, 1954), 82.

ilege, administrative muddle, a narrow franchise—had been identified and just enough victories won to sustain a belief that the heart of the system was still sound. The subsequent withdrawal from continental troubles at once resulted from and reinforced such beliefs, while within months new battles on the Indian subcontinent were, for no very good reason, to restore domestic confidence in Britain's military might.

2. REVOLT IN INDIA

Although the Crimean War was essentially a European conflict, it is not surprising that Asian subplots were also sometimes written into the script. These revolved around Russia's eastward expansion and the potential threat this might one day pose to the security of India (which until 1858 remained under the, increasingly diluted, authority of the East India Company). In this respect the Afghan War of 1838–42 had represented an inconclusive military overture, after which Palmerston (who had been Foreign Secretary between 1835 and 1841) seldom missed an opportunity to tell colleagues of the importance of keeping such matters in mind. Indeed, within eight months of the Treaty of Paris, Britain declared war on Persia and dispatched an expedition from India to drive the Persians (seen by many as Russia's surrogates) out of Afghanistan. This was achieved with little difficulty and in the process a new treaty of alliance was signed with Dost Mohammed of Afghanistan whose friendship—guaranteed with the help of liberal subsidies—secured peace on the North-West frontier during the turbulent events that were soon to occur in India itself.

It looked almost as if Palmerston's government was falling into the habit of war when, in October 1856, its forces bombarded Canton in punishment for the Chinese having impounded a small boat flying (improperly as it turned out) the British flag. Palmerston persuaded the cabinet that, whatever the rights of the situation, British prestige demanded firmer action still. In the Commons Disraeli sarcastically urged the Prime Minister to go to the country on the slogan 'No Reform! New Taxes! Canton blazing! Persia invaded!' When Palmerston did more or less exactly that, the Conservative joke turned sour, not because Palmerston's victory at the general election of April 1857 was based upon any clearly articulated national enthusiasm for bellicosity as such, but simply because victory (however obtained) allowed Palmerston to continue at the centre of affairs and, when the need arose, to sustain a 'national' response to the 'mutiny' which broke out in India a month after the election results had been declared.[39]

[39] Hawkins, *Parliament*, 63–75.

On 10 May 1857 Indian soldiers (sepoys) at Meerut in the North-Western Provinces rose against their British officers, killed a number of them, set the cantonment alight with the help of local inhabitants, and then departed rapidly southwards. The next day they captured Delhi and, together with the regiments stationed there, placed the 82-year-old pensioned King of Delhi (the descendant of the Mogul emperors) at the head of their movement. Within weeks, serious unrest spread over much of the surrounding regions as suppressed discontents of many kinds affected soldiers and civilians alike. For several months a corridor 200 miles wide stretching from Meerut to Benares (some 400 miles to the south-east and thus half-way to Calcutta) was largely under rebel control with small groups of Europeans besieged in places like Cawnpore and Lucknow.[40] (See Map 10.)

Perhaps the single most surprising aspect of the whole affair is the sense of complete astonishment with which those in authority reacted to the events at Meerut and their aftermath. Even without the advantage of hindsight, it should have been clear that long-term developments and certain occurrences immediately before 1857 pointed to the probability of trouble ahead. Although all of these were ultimately political or strategic, their immediate points of leverage touched upon more general concerns—cultural, religious, economic.

The half-century before the 'Mutiny' (Revolt is a better word) had witnessed both a decline in the independent power of the East India Company and a general extension of British control. The Company's monopolies of trade with India and China were abolished in 1813 and 1833 respectively, while in 1853 even its patronage over administrative appointments was effectively withdrawn, so that it became little more than a subcontractor for the London government. Yet the vast distances involved, the many filters through which instructions were still required to pass, and the necessity of local decision-making continued to ensure that metropolitan policies experienced a good deal of transmission loss on their way to the East. Forceful instructions in the early 1820s that no further territories should be taken from local princes and that a period of peace was urgently desired seemed unrealistic to many men on the spot, sometimes simply because circumstances had changed, sometimes because such men had always nurtured contrary ideas of their own. Thus parts of Burma were acquired in 1826, while the huge territories of Sind (1843) and the Punjab

---

[40] J. A. B. Palmer, *The Mutiny Outbreak at Meerut in 1857* (Cambridge, 1966), 70–128. I have preferred Anglicized versions of well-known place-names such as Cawnpore (for Kanpur) and Oudh (for Awadh).

(1849) were annexed after wars of the most dubious 'necessity'.[41] Nor did the ideological baggage shipped from Britain—predominantly, by the second quarter of the nineteenth century, utilitarianism and Evangelical-ism—survive the journey in any more pristine condition. Theories of *laissez-faire*, for example, wilted rapidly under the tropical sun by being manipulated so that cotton manufacturers in Lancashire could receive protection against Indian imports while facing minimal barriers for their own exports to the subcontinent. Whatever the effects of this upon large-scale Indian industrial enterprises, and these are a matter of dispute,[42] smaller craftsmen were just as hard hit as their counterparts in the United Kingdom. By such means too was India rendered predominantly an exporter of agricultural produce and an importer of manufactured goods of all kinds.

The effects of attempts to 'reform' Indian culture, though often derived from utilitarian and Evangelical attitudes, are more difficult to assess. Here the Governor-Generalship of Lord William Bentinck between 1828 and 1835 furnished the major initial thrust, for these years saw vigorous attacks on such 'traditional' Hindu customs—though some were in fact neither ancient nor universal—as suttee (or widow-burning) and the quasi-religious murders undertaken by wandering bands of robbers known as 'thugs'.[43] Combined with the introduction of Western educational concepts, judicial and revenue novelties, increased state involvement in the economy, and the activities of Christian missionaries (who had been largely excluded before 1813), such things inevitably suggested that the more cautious policies of former times were being abandoned with enthusiastic zeal.[44]

Yet the outcome of many of these developments was sometimes small and generally rather different from what had initially been intended. Even land reforms—probably the most intrusive—were often subtly modified as British district officers found themselves obliged to compromise with the aspirations of local society.[45] Still, there can be little doubt that the collision between British notions of land tenure based upon individual alienable ownership and those very varied Indian practices according to which

[41] R. J. Moore, 'India and the British Empire', in C. C. Eldridge (ed.), *British Imperialism in the Nineteenth Century* (London, 1984), 64–84.

[42] N. Charlesworth, *British Rule and the Indian Economy 1800–1914* (London, 1982), 56–67.

[43] C. A. Bayly, *Indian Society and the Making of the British Empire* (Cambridge, 1988), 122.

[44] P. Spear, *The Oxford History of Modern India 1740–1947* (Oxford, 1965), 130–7; T. R. Metcalf, *The Aftermath of Revolt: India, 1857–1870* (Princeton, 1965), 3–30.

[45] E. Stokes, 'The First Century of British Colonial Rule in India', *Past & Present*, 58 (1973), 146–8.

ownership was a diffuse concept, and a whole hierarchy of individuals possessed 'rights', caused increasing friction as time went on.

Because land tax revenues furnished by far the largest element in the Indian government's income—indeed their incidence caused widespread complaint—much contemporary attention was focused on matters of tenure and tax liability. The approach adopted in the three presidencies into which British India was divided differed substantially. In Madras to the south the actual cultivators of the soil were identified as the primary group when it came to taxation and tenurial rights. In the Bengal Presidency to the north and east various more elevated individuals, who went under a variety of local names such as *zamindar* or *talukdar* and might loosely be described as 'landlords', were preferred. In Bombay to the west a compromise between these two methods was adopted.[46] It was the Bengal Presidency centred on Calcutta which experienced the most widespread agrarian discontents and which, to some extent because of that, provided the epicentres of revolt in 1857.

So direct an equation cannot, however, be sustained without a good deal of local modification. It is simply too sweeping to suggest that entire classes of the population were caught up in any kind of unified or universal response to British 'reforms'. To suggest, without qualification, that 'the Brahmin challenged by a new educational system, the aristocrat deprived of his ancestral lands, the prince shorn of his state ... all readily joined in a common effort to overthrow the British raj'[47] distorts the kaleidoscopic nature of Indian politics and social relationships.

Undoubtedly the innovation of making landholding rights alienable under due process of law allowed the quick-witted to benefit economically—sometimes by astute estate management, sometimes by mere force— and it was such men who tended to side with the British. Those who had lost out went the opposite way. And when this occurred the power actually exercised by the former and still popularly accorded to the latter ensured that the peasants adopted a similarly divergent set of attitudes and actions. This, above all, explains why a declining and aggrieved aristocracy could lead into open and sustained revolt districts which were suffering much less severely than certain loyal areas from the economic and social dislocations of British rule.[48]

[46] Metcalf, *Aftermath of Revolt*, 36–91; id., 'Rural Society and British Rule in Nineteenth Century India', *Journal of Asian Studies*, 39 (1979), 111–19; E. Stokes, *The Peasant and the Raj: Studies in Agrarian Society and Peasant Rebellion in Colonial India* (Cambridge, 1978); id., *The Peasant Armed: The Indian Revolt of 1857*, ed. C. A. Bayly (Oxford, 1986).

[47] Metcalf, *Aftermath of Revolt*, 62.

[48] E. Stokes, 'Traditional Elites in the Great Rebellion of 1857', in E. Leach and S. N. Mukherjee (eds.), *Elites in South Asia* (Cambridge, 1970), 16–32; Bayly, *Indian Society*, 188–94.

The greatest nineteenth-century upheavals in the land system in the north of India probably took place during the two or three decades before 1857. In particular, the activities of Lord Dalhousie, as Governor-General 1848–56, cranked up the ratchets of change over virtually all areas of governmental concern. Dalhousie, one of the most energetic of all British rulers of India, arrived determined to modernize and to Westernize. Though not always able to carry the fullness of his intentions into effect he showed little regard for local traditions, whether in cultural, social, or economic matters. By refusing to acknowledge the traditional practice of allowing princes without sons to adopt heirs he took under British rule no less than seven Indian states by means of his so-called doctrine of 'lapse'. Then in 1856, throwing any pretence at legality to the winds, he annexed the populous kingdom of Oudh, whose ruler, though incapable of efficient government and the centre of a network of graft and self-indulgence, had none the less proved himself almost embarrassingly deferential and loyal.

And it was in Oudh that the Revolt received much of its most energetic support, not least because the so-called 'Summary Settlement' of 1856–7 had there reapportioned taxation in such a way that those who suffered most from its impositions could now add the anger of monetary loss to the hurt pride produced by annexation and the dethronement of their king.[49] Discontent in Oudh was also marked by social and cultural characteristics, for districts where relations between *talukdars* and peasants most obviously possessed elements of mutual co-operation provided both the largest number of (increasingly fractious) sepoy recruits and the highest levels of armed resistance in 1857–8.[50] By causing an upheaval in the rural world, the imposition of British rule in Oudh assaulted traditional views of social, political, and religious norms and obligations. As one *talukdar* put it to a British official at the time:

Your countrymen came into this country and drove out our King. You sent your officers round the districts to examine the titles to the estates. At one blow you took from me lands which from time immemorial had been in my family. I submitted. Suddenly misfortune fell upon you. The people of the land rose against you. You came to me whom you had despoiled. I have saved you. But now,—now I march at the head of my retainers to Lakhnao to try and drive you from the country.[51]

Despite the development of feelings of this kind the actual outbreak of revolt in May 1857 depended as much upon the fortuitous conjuncture of comparatively minor accidents as upon the wider context of discontent and uncertainty created over the previous decades. The fact that neither army

---

[49] R. Mukherjee, *Awadh in Revolt 1857–1858* (Delhi, 1984), 32–63.
[50] Ibid. 22–4, 78, 95, 133, 157, 164.   [51] Ibid. 81.

mutiny nor serious civil disorder was unknown in early nineteenth-century India helped to blind the authorities to the possible implications of increasing unrest in parts of the Bengal army during late 1856 and early 1857.[52] In the past the two phenomena had generally occurred separately. On this occasion a sepoy mutiny was to prove merely the prelude to a more general uprising.

The military forces available to the Governor-General in 1857 amounted to about 232,000 Indian and 45,000 European troops, the latter so few because of withdrawals for the Crimean and Persian campaigns. Of these, 135,000 and 24,000 respectively belonged to the Bengal army most immediately affected by the Revolt. As was not the case elsewhere, the Bengal Native regiments included large numbers of high-caste Indians who, until recently, had often been tacitly allowed to impose their own individual superiorities upon the strict hierarchies of military rank. Refusals by Brahmin and other soldiers to serve abroad—crossing the sea was held to injure the integrity of caste—had, however, led the authorities to introduce a stricter discipline and (by means of the General Service Enlistment Order passed by Dalhousie's successor, Lord Canning, in August 1856) gradually to withdraw the Bengal army's privilege of not being required to serve overseas. The fact that nearly a third of the sepoys of Bengal were recruited from Oudh, and thus closely connected with disaffected relatives in that recently annexed kingdom, provided further grounds for discontent.

The matches that actually set such tinder alight were the cartridges supplied for use with the new Lee-Enfield rifle. These were greased in order to keep the powder dry and it soon became widely believed (and probably not without cause) that both pork and beef fat had been used in their manufacture—the former deeply repugnant to Muslims and the latter to Hindus. Demonstrations against the cartridges began in February 1857 and it was the failure to meet these with anything more than brute force or (despite much effort) to provide replacement cartridges quickly enough that led directly to the mutiny at Meerut on 10 May. Rumour played an especially large part in spreading discontent. Wave upon wave of reports about greased cartridges, flour polluted by bone-meal, forcible conversions to Christianity, the disarming of Indian soldiers, the imminent coming of a 'deliverer' all merged into 'one gigantic rumour', which in turn helped to transform disparate elements of popular grievance into a widespread sepoy and peasant war.[53]

[52] M. Chamberlain, *Britain and India* (Newton Abbot, 1974), 89; S. B. Chaudhuri, *Civil Disturbances during the British Rule in India (1765–1857)* (Calcutta, 1955).

[53] R. Guha, *Elementary Aspects of Peasant Insurgency in Colonial India* (Delhi, 1983), 255.

The paucity of European troops—the only forces upon which the government could totally rely—meant that British reactions were at first extremely slow. As a result, sepoy mutinies took place throughout the North-Western Provinces and Oudh (as well as in some adjacent areas) and rapidly unleashed a formidable revolt among significant sections of the civil population. By the end of June much of the region was no longer effectively in government hands, Delhi had been captured by the rebels, and a small force of Europeans had surrendered and been slaughtered at Cawnpore. In Lucknow (the capital of Oudh) the British flag still flew, though for how long those besieged there could hold out was far from clear. It was, in the event, to take another year to break the back of the rebellion and longer still before its last flickerings had been crushed.

The events of 1857–8 are commonly described as the *Indian* Revolt or Mutiny. This obscures the crucial point that the great bulk of the sub-continent remained peaceful throughout. The Madras Presidency was almost entirely quiet and isolated mutinies and disturbances in Bombay were easily contained. Even in Bengal it was really only in the North-Western Provinces and Oudh, the western parts of Bihar, and certain areas in the Central India Agency (notably Jhansi) that the British substantially lost control.[54] In particular, most Punjabis, who distrusted various regional rivals more than they did their recent British conquerers, remained 'loyal'. Yet the effects upon the Bengal army were severe. Some 70,000 sepoys joined the Revolt at different times, another 30,000 provided invaluable support to the British, while the remaining 30,000 deserted or took no active part one way or the other.[55]

What is surprising is not that the unrest was eventually crushed, but that it lasted as long as it did and over so large and important an area, for almost every circumstance rendered the task of sustaining the Revolt extremely difficult. There was very little co-ordination between different areas. A primitive communications network amongst rebel regiments and the issuing of grandiose proclamations urging solidarity between Muslims and Hindus were no substitutes for a central authority. Apart from a feeling that the Mogul Empire should be restored, even in the matter of aims coherence was maintained only at a very high level of generality. Less debilitating—though often remarked upon—was the rebels' lack of 'positive' ideas or of a blueprint for tomorrow consisting of anything more than a return to yesterday, for counter-revolutions have, after all, succeeded often enough. Rather, it was the lack of any one explicit and universal cause

[54] Though even in the area around Delhi British power was never *completely* eliminated (Bayly, *Indian Society*, 181).
[55] S. N. Sen, *Eighteen Fifty-Seven* (Calcutta, 1957), 406.

which helped to produce a state more accurately described as a series of local revolts than a single rebellion as such.

Private vendettas were pursued with dynamic zeal. In some places moneylenders were attacked, in others traders were the chief targets, in yet others official records were ransacked and burnt.[56] Nor were the leaders thrown up by the events of 1857–8 either a united or an impressive group. The 'Emperor', Bahadur Shah, was an unwilling octogenarian, Nana Sahib an unstable and dispossessed adopted son of a deposed chief of the Maratha Confederacy, while the Ranee of Jhansi and Kunwar Singh, though more able and energetic, lacked any widespread basis for authority or influence.

Just as in other great *bouleversements*, many people desperately pursued a cautious and neutral path, only throwing in their lot with one side or the other when some kind of decision could no longer safely be withheld. In many of the disturbed areas the adoption of an armed vigilance—reminiscent of that maintained by the 'clubmen' during the Civil War in seventeenth-century England—was dictated both by prudence and self-interest. Ugly communal riots between Muslims and Hindus were also far from uncommon, especially when elements among the former talked openly of holy wars.[57]

The rebellion was most effectively sustained by the fighting qualities of the sepoys themselves. Even when not especially well led they fought with dedication, skill, and tenacity. However, for white men and women it was absolutely necessary that the suppression of the Revolt be portrayed as a total success, something rendered easier by the fact that, unlike the Crimea, the North-Western Provinces were not swarming with war correspondents. Distance, therefore, could be allowed to render enchantment (and horror) to events which, more closely and dispassionately observed, might well have assumed a different moral colouring. The undoubted atrocities committed by the rebels were seized upon with enthusiasm as providing *carte blanche* for every kind of counter-cruelty. The events at Cawnpore in June and July 1857 when, despite a safe-conduct, British soldiers were shot and some 200 women and children hacked to pieces caused an outcry and a revulsion unusual even in so emotional an age. Nana Sahib was at once held responsible, though his precise role in the matter may well have been less active than vivid British imaginations liked to suppose.[58]

[56] H. Chattopadhyaya, *The Sepoy Mutiny, 1857: A Social Study and Analysis* (Calcutta, 1957), 159–66; R. C. Majumdar, *The Sepoy Mutiny and the Revolt of 1857*, 2nd edn. (Calcutta, 1963), 394.

[57] Majumdar, *Sepoy Mutiny*, 403–4; S. B. Chaudhuri, *Civil Rebellion in the Indian Mutinies (1857–1859)* (Calcutta, 1957), 79, 89, 109, 112, 115–17, 157—but see also pp. 69, 209, 281–2 for more harmonious tendencies.

[58] R. Mukherjee, ' "Satan Let Loose upon Earth": The Kanpur Massacres in India in the Revolt of 1857', *Past & Present*, 128 (1990), 92–116.

Atrocities on the British side were no less extreme. Well before news of Cawnpore had become known, officers like Colonel Neill were busily wielding the sword of Christian righteousness on the march from Calcutta to the centres of revolt further to the west and north. Like some latter-day Cromwell, Neill sought biblical justification for what he was about. Around Allahabad he instituted a reign of terror. No attempt was made to separate the guilty from the innocent. Perhaps as many as 6,000, 'their corpses hanging by twos and threes from branch and sign-post all over the town', were done to death.[59] And this was just the beginning, for many of Neill's colleagues and many of the European rank and file had little hesitation in following his example. There was, indeed, a fearful inevitability about such conduct once the Revolt had begun to establish itself. Although some British officials and military men, especially in the remoter districts, had for years sustained comparatively decent relations with 'native' peoples, racial tension had never been far below (and often well above) the surface of everyday attitudes and behaviour. Even the far from radical Duke of Cambridge as Commander-in-Chief thought many officers guilty of 'treating the men and especially the Native Officers with contempt, in fact looking down upon them, calling them niggers etc.'[60]

To the British it seemed as if the jaws of a pagan hell had been opened before them with the express aim of destroying both colonial rule and Christian civilization. The initial reaction in the press demanded more rather than less severity. 'The country', wrote Lord John Russell's father-in-law, 'is running wild ... with passion and regards the natives of India (the few allowed to survive) as monsters only to be held in slavish subjection by the sword.'[61] Newspapers dwelt lovingly upon every atrocity and were adept at discovering rape where none had taken place. Given such an atmosphere it is not surprising that the Governor-General's famous 'Resolution' of 31 July 1857 (for which he earned the derogatory title of 'Clemency' Canning), insisting that careful distinctions should be made between rebels and others among the sepoy soldiers and that no civil punishment be administered for desertion alone, was met with widespread denunciation and abuse in London and Calcutta alike. Only towards the end of the rebellion, as indiscriminate killing continued, did a few observers like *The Times* correspondent, W. H. Russell (who arrived on the scene very late in the day), begin to recognize the long-term dangers of what was taking place.

[59] M. Edwardes, *The Red Year: The Indian Rebellion of 1857* (London, 1973), 80–9.
[60] E. M. Spiers, *The Army and Society 1815–1914* (London, 1980), 122.
[61] A. Hawkins, 'British Parliamentary Party Alignment and the Indian Issue, 1857–1858', *Journal of British Studies*, 23/2 (1984), 80.

All these kinds of vindictive, unchristian, Indian tortures, such as sewing Mahomedans in pig-skins, smearing them with pork-fat before execution, and burning their bodies, and forcing Hindoos to defile themselves, are disgraceful, and ultimately recoil on ourselves. They are spiritual and mental tortures to which we have no right to resort, and which we dare not perpetrate in the face of Europe.[62]

Behind the public relief and adulation which greeted eventual British victory lay a reality of confusion and a good measure of incompetence as well. While the press contrasted the skills of military leadership in India with the failures of the Crimea, the truth was less reassuring.[63] After all, the campaigns mounted during the Revolt were precisely those for which the army *had* been prepared, so that many of the Crimean excuses were simply irrelevant. The forces involved were not enormous: frequently no more than a couple of thousand European troops with some loyal sepoys in support. Had generals like the much-praised Havelock (who marched from Allahabad to Cawnpore with 2,000 men) been obliged to conduct affairs on a Crimean scale their success would have been very much less certain. What appealed to the public was the fact that men such as Havelock, Neill, Nicholson, and Campbell had not advanced their careers by patronage and wealth. Havelock, indeed, was a devout Baptist, a godly soldier, who had worked in India unsung and unrewarded before, at the age of 62, being matched with a sudden and unexpected hour of fame and of death.

An unimpressive picture emerges from the disastrous initial delays which occurred before any serious campaigning was undertaken. There were simply too few European troops available and substantial reinforcements—by the end the number of British soldiers had doubled—took all too long to arrive. Commissariat and transport difficulties, despite the small forces involved, were considerable. The system of moving troops was appallingly slow because the government had disbanded the Military Transport Establishment three years earlier and now depended on the uncertain services of Indian contractors. The railway from Calcutta only ran a hundred miles to the town of Raniganj and even this, as Neill found to his rage, was far from efficiently operated.[64] The medical services were no better than those of the Crimea, and in a climate where even seasoned European soldiers found it hard to survive on campaign, it proved difficult at first to replace those incapacitated by disease.

[62] W. H. Russell, *My Diary in India, in the Year 1858–9*, 2 vols. (London, 1860), ii. 46.
[63] Spiers, *Army and Society*, 132.
[64] Edwardes, *The Red Year*, 80–1; Metcalf, *Aftermath of Revolt*, 50.

Even in the matter of numbers a good deal of creative accounting was employed to make it seem as if minuscule British forces were regularly defeating vast hordes. In fact the estimates of the various rebel armies still often presented in the literature are almost always exaggerated. To oppose Havelock's 2,000-strong column at Fatehpur on 12 July 1857 the rebels could put only 3,500 men into the field, of whom less than three-fifths were regulars. Four days later, at the decisive battle for Cawnpore, Nana Sahib's effective army numbered only a quarter of the 20,000 nominally under his orders. Grosser still were the inflations made by British sources regarding the final attack on Delhi, where, far from mustering the 35,000 sepoys plus another 20,000 'fanatics' widely mentioned at the time, the rebel leaders had only about 10,000 to 12,000 fighting men at their disposal against a British army of 9,000 effectives assisted by another 3,000 men supplied by the Rajas of Kashmir and Jhind.[65]

In the end it was the middle-ranking officer corps which held firm when all else failed on the British side, when the nerves of generals broke and infantrymen were driven beyond endurance. Although many generals emerged with enhanced (if sometimes posthumous) reputations, in the longer perspective, this was fully deserved only in the case of Sir Hugh Rose, who, with no Indian experience at all, took command of the Central India Field Force in December 1857 and over the next six months defeated the rebellion in the most southerly regions of its active existence. A soldier of intelligence and dash, he dressed his men in khaki and took care to carry with him an adequate baggage-train. He captured Jhansi and Gwalior in turn, at the latter of which the Ranee of Jhansi was killed in action and thereby entered the pantheons of both Indian and feminist heroism. Rose later called her 'the bravest and best of the military leaders of the rebels', which, considering the expertise displayed on both sides, was probably less of a compliment than it seemed.[66]

By the time peace was officially proclaimed by the Governor-General on 8 July 1858, although guerrilla warfare continued into the next year, the Mutiny-Revolt had been effectively crushed. As regards domestic politics, its effects were rather different from those of the Crimea, that is to say, they were entirely negligible. Because difficulties and failures were so decisively swallowed up by military success, Palmerston was able to ensure that the Indian question would acquire the aspect of one needing administrative reform (over which the government could retain the initiative) rather than of one capable of generating demands for a difficult post-mortem into the cabinet's handling of the crisis.[67]

[65] Stokes, *Peasant Armed*, 57–8, 93–4.　　[66] Edwardes, *Red Year*, 118–26.
[67] Hawkins, *Parliament*, 85.

During the summer recess of 1857 hardly any ministers thought it necessary to remain at their posts and even the emergency parliamentary session in December was almost entirely concerned with the commercial crisis that had recently blown up. In opposition, the Conservatives were divided on India. Only Disraeli and Lord Ellenborough (a former Governor-General) wanted to make anything of the issue, and neither elicited much support. Disraeli did, however, make a remarkable speech in the Commons on 27 July in which he offered a sustained condemnation of Britain's clumsy interference with the established customs of Indian society, a speech which, in many respects, laid the foundations for most later criticisms of the rashness and insensitivity deployed by, for example, Bentinck in the 1830s and Dalhousie twenty years thereafter.[68]

Yet in every important sense Palmerston's government succeeded in presenting the Revolt as a 'national crisis' to be treated in the light of 'patriotic duty'. Whereas the Crimean 'national crisis' had eventually transformed itself into a 'political' one and in 1855 had brought about the fall of Aberdeen's ministry, the prevailing circumstances at Westminster in 1857 prevented such a metamorphosis from taking place. Russell believed that the franchise offered greater opportunities than India for power-mongering, while Derby as Conservative leader preferred (and for good reason) to adopt a policy of masterly inactivity. By alighting on the idea of abolishing the East India Company in the autumn of 1857 Palmerston was able to concentrate attention upon administrative 'improvements' rather than upon military affairs.[69] When, for reasons that had nothing to do with India, the Conservatives succeeded in forming a short-lived minority administration in February 1858 they did little more than continue where Palmerston had left off. The India Bill passed by Derby was based upon enlightened recommendations from Ellenborough. And even when the latter was obliged to resign from the cabinet after an embarrassing mix-up concerning Canning's hasty Oudh Proclamation of 20 March 1858 (declaring certain 'proprietary rights in the soil' of that province forfeit to the British government), he was succeeded by Derby's eldest son, Lord Stanley, who was more enlightened still.

In India itself a slowing down of the kind of policy associated with men like Dalhousie followed the Revolt. This was far more important than the largely cosmetic changes in governmental machinery introduced by the India Bill of 1858—for the imposition of direct rather than Company rule was little more than a formal recognition of what had already become a practical reality. The Indian princes, who had almost all proved loyal, were

---

[68] *Hansard*, cxlvii. 440–81 (27 July 1857).   [69] Hawkins, 'Party Alignment', 79–105.

rewarded with titles, honours, and hard cash. Those most shabbily treated were the few Westernized Indians who had responded to earlier calls to 'modernize' and were now, without explanation or excuse, left beached upon the shores of an abandoned philosophy. Henceforth, in everything save the manipulation of economic relationships and occasional thrusts along the North-West frontier, the British were to adopt a more cautious approach than before 1857. The separate local army was abolished and all soldiers brought under direct crown control. The proportion of European to Indian troops was substantially increased from about 1:9 before the Revolt to 1:2 in Bengal and 1:3 in Madras and Bombay thereafter.[70] The artillery became almost entirely British, no important station was ever left without a complement of British troops, and the recruitment of Brahmins was reduced in favour of Gurkhas and Punjabis (especially Sikhs). Yet despite all such precautions, white men were beginning to look over their shoulders more anxiously than before. Expatriate merchants had long been hostile to anything save repression. Now the administrators, too, though more moderate, increasingly stressed both the thanklessness of the task and their own indispensability.[71] As British rule in India entered the era of later Victorian imperial grandeur, so the white man's burden seemed heavier than ever to men driven by the reality of rebellion to encase themselves within new attitudes of watchful fatalism.

India, though vast and self-contained, was of course only part of a greater empire. The strategies adopted by its British rulers in the middle of the nineteenth century had reverberations elsewhere. This was especially the case as regards land policy, where the parallels and contrasts with what was happening in, for example, Ireland were at once striking and widely recognized at the time. British attempts before the Revolt, particularly in the Bengal Presidency, to introduce more clearly defined notions of alienable ownership, and thus bring about at least the beginnings of a free market in land, matched contemporary efforts to denigrate the Irish peasants' claims to some measure of quasi-proprietary 'interest' in the farms they rented from landlords.[72] And in both countries administrators in the 1850s made strenuous, though largely unsuccessful, efforts to replace bankrupt and inefficient landowners with 'new' and more commercially minded operators.[73]

---

[70] I owe these figures to the kindness of David Omissi.

[71] B. Porter, *The Lion's Share*, 2nd edn. (London, 1984), 43–4.

[72] S. B. Cook, *Imperial Affinities: Nineteenth Century Analogies and Exchanges between India and Ireland* (New Delhi, 1993), 9–80.

[73] Metcalf, *Aftermath of Revolt*, 63–6, 158–60, 204–18; Chaudhuri, *Civil Rebellion*, 20–1; C. A. Bayly in Stokes, *Peasant Armed*, 232–3; J. S. Donnelly, jun., *The Land and the People of Nineteenth-Century Cork* (London, 1975), 131.

Throughout the middle decades of the century it seems to have been the case that Indian ryots or peasants often enjoyed better legal protection than their Irish counterparts, above all because of the existence of 'fair rent' principles unknown in Irish statutes until 1881. In addition, the policies of the Indian government remained subject to much greater adjustment and modification at the local level than was the case in Ireland. Thus in 1859, when the free-market wonders of the Irish Encumbered Estates Act of 1849 were being widely canvassed in India, one District Officer—after noting how all attempts to undermine a similar approach in Rohilkhand seemed to involve 'the anomaly of declaring that what is the highest wisdom in Ireland (a country in many respects resembling India...) is the highest folly in India'—still decided that political economy 'must bend before the force of local and national circumstances'.[74]

Perhaps the most important element producing a different governmental approach in the two countries was the fact that many British landlords owned substantial estates in Ireland but not in India. Thus Lord Mayo, himself an Irish landlord, proved, when Viceroy of India between 1869 and 1872, simultaneously a strong opponent of unfettered proprietorial rights in that country and a bitter critic of Gladstone's Irish Land Act of 1870, on the grounds that it would reduce precisely those powers he was himself attempting to diminish in India.[75] Indeed, in 1867 Isaac Butt (the future leader of the Irish Home Rule Party) tried to explain what he believed to be the more favourable treatment of the Indian peasantry by pointing out that in Ireland 'we have the fiction of an identity with England. The owner of the soil is a "landlord", not a "zemindar"—the occupier is a "tenant", and not a "ryot"'.[76]

In the military sphere the successes eventually achieved in India dampened down the movement for change. The administrative reforms introduced during the Crimean War still left many important questions of authority and procedure unresolved. In particular, the relationship between the Secretary for War and the Commander-in-Chief remained shrouded in dangerous ambiguity. It was not that there was any widespread reluctance to pick over the entrails. Indeed, in the twelve years after 1856 no less than seventeen royal commissions, eighteen select committees, nineteen internal War Office inquiries, and thirty-five committees of officers dealt in some manner with military administration. It was simply that precious little was actually done. Even the Staff College set up in 1858 was a very modest

[74] Metcalf, *Aftermath of Revolt*, 212.

[75] Ibid. 201; E. D. Steele, 'Ireland and the Empire in the 1860s: Imperial Precedents for Gladstone's First Irish Land Act', *Historical Journal*, 11 (1968), 69–70.

[76] I. Butt, *The Irish People and the Irish Land* (Dublin, 1867), 268.

affair, while efforts to improve living conditions for ordinary soldiers in the early 1860s ran all too rapidly into the buffer of government 'cuts'.[77] The introduction in 1864 of breech-loading rifles, though obviously important, was no more dramatic a sign of sustained concern than had been the (pre-Crimean) adoption of the muzzle-loading Minié rifle thirteen years before.

The American Civil War of 1861–5—a people's war like no other before it—provoked a good deal of interest in British military circles but little effective analysis. Apart from specialized developments relating to artillery and fortifications, most British experts dismissed the novel tactics and techniques developed in America as aberrations arising from unique circumstances.[78] And while the Franco-Prussian War of 1870–1 undoubtedly left a deep impression upon certain British officers, it neither provided the immediate impetus for the army reforms of the early 1870s nor persuaded their author, Cardwell, to look to Prussia as any kind of model for his own plans.[79]

The close temporal proximity of the Crimean War and the Indian Revolt was, therefore, significant precisely because the army's apparent success in the latter so quickly wiped out the slate of dissatisfaction drawn up between 1854 and 1856. Even if the universal conviction that Britain would not soon again be involved in a European war was by no means fanciful, the almost total failure to adjust to the new military realities revealed in 1861–5 and 1870–1 betokened a very grand kind of complacency. That Britain's luck held thereafter for as long as it did, that for more than fifty years no British general was required to control the number of troops commanded by Raglan—let alone the huge forces disposed of by Grant and Lee or by Moltke and MacMahon—was just as well, for, as the Boer War was to show, even the modest lessons provided by the Crimea and India were soon forgotten, assuming, that is, they had ever been learnt at all.

[77] Sweetman, *War and Administration*, 131–2; B. Bond, *The Victorian Army and the Staff College 1854–1914* (London, 1972), 73–4; Spiers, *Army and Society*, 157–62; A. R. Skelley, *The Victorian Army at Home: The Recruitment and Terms and Conditions of the British Regular, 1859–1899* (London, 1977), *passim*.

[78] J. Luvaas, *The Military Legacy of the Civil War: The European Inheritance* (Chicago, 1959), 46.

[79] Spiers, *Army and Society*, 186–8.

CHAPTER 7

Palmerston and After, 1855–1868

I. PALMERSTON AT LAST

The most natural outcome of the collapse of Aberdeen's coalition in late January 1855 was the emergence of Palmerston as Prime Minister. Derby and Russell had both very publicly failed to construct administrations. Russell's efforts had been dismissed by almost everyone because few were prepared to grant their author absolution for his part in bringing about the coalition's collapse.[1] Derby in turn had given up in the face of refusals from Palmerston, Gladstone, and Herbert to join a Conservative-dominated ministry. Being the natural successor did not, however, mean that every crooked thing was suddenly made straight or that Disraeli's comments of February 1855 about the 71-year-old Prime Minister were not widely shared: 'He is really an imposter, utterly exhausted, and at best only ginger-beer, and not champagne, and now an old painted pantaloon, very deaf, very blind, and with false teeth, which would fall out of his mouth when speaking if he did not hesitate and halt so in his talk.'[2] 'Progressive' Conservatives like Derby's son, Lord Stanley, believed Palmerston 'would break under the weight of the premiership' while Cobden expressed the Radicals' view that 'to call in an exploded sham to master a crisis like this is merely proof that we as a nation are in a state of collapse'.[3] Indeed, Palmerston's position in parliament was never secure during the whole of his first ministry. He survived partly by luck and partly because his own undoubted political skills were rarely put to the test by an opposition as cautious as it was disunited.

Ironically things got off to what can, at least in retrospect, be seen as a promising start when, less than a month after the new government's

[1] J. B. Conacher, *Britain and the Crimea 1855–56* (London, 1987), 5–8.
[2] W. F. Monypenny and G. E. Buckle, *The Life of Benjamin Disraeli*, 6 vols. (London, 1910–20), ii. 567.
[3] *Disraeli, Derby and the Conservative Party: Journals and Memoirs of Edward Henry, Lord Stanley 1849–1869*, ed. J. Vincent (Hassocks, 1978), 132 (30 Jan. 1855); Cobden to Bright, 11 Feb. 1855, Cobden Papers, British Library MS 43650.

formation, the leading Peelite members of the cabinet—Graham at the Admiralty, Gladstone at the Exchequer, and Herbert at the Colonial Office—resigned. The ostensible reason was Palmerston's refusal to veto the appointment of a committee of inquiry into the conduct of the Crimean War. In reality the Peelites were having second thoughts about attaching themselves to a politician who had long constituted one of their main targets of attack. If this necessitated some rather tedious hunting for replacements—Russell (who had previously refused) came in as Colonial Secretary, Cornewall Lewis became Chancellor, while the third vacancy went to the uninspiring R. V. Smith—it had the merit of ensuring that Palmerston's administration no longer looked like the coalition of 1853–5.[4] Russell, however, continued to cause trouble though, fortunately for Palmerston, revelations about his diplomatic activities in Vienna during the Crimean War forced him on to the back-benches once more in the summer of 1855.

Palmerston excelled at turning things to his advantage: the Crimean War, the Indian Mutiny, and later the matter of Italy. While Aberdeen had fallen over the Crimea, Palmerston succeeded in transforming the Indian Mutiny into a 'national' rather than a 'political' crisis. And yet he depended upon almost precisely the same body of support as Aberdeen had done in a parliament notable for both strong party feelings and political instability.[5] The trick was done by avoiding official proposals which might cause disruption. And though this did not mean that Palmerston's governments did nothing—accusations along such lines are wide of the mark—the chief business of the late 1850s tended to turn on matters which, while certainly capable of causing rows, did so in ways too complex to threaten the ministry.[6] An Order in Council in May 1855 showed how Whig traditions of patronage could be used to defuse the Northcote-Trevelyan proposals on Civil Service reform. The Cambridge University Act of 1856 was merely a matching twin to the Oxford Act passed two years before. Much time, not least Gladstone's, was devoted to discussing an unsuccessful, and in party terms 'unpolitical', Deceased Wife's Sister Bill in 1856 (one of nineteen occasions between 1849 and 1907 when legislation was put forward to allow a husband to marry his dead wife's sister contrary to certain interpretations of Holy Writ) and to a successful Matrimonial

---

[4] P. M. Gurowich, 'The Continuation of War by Other Means: Party and Politics, 1855–1865', *Historical Journal*, 27 (1984), 608.

[5] A. Hawkins, 'British Parliamentary Party Alignment and the Indian Issue, 1857–1858', *Journal of British Studies*, 23/2 (1984), 80–6; J. R. Bylsma, 'Party Structure in the 1852–1857 House of Commons', *Journal of Interdisciplinary History*, 7 (1977), 629–30.

[6] E. D. Steele, *Palmerston and Liberalism, 1855–1865* (Cambridge, 1991), 45–107.

Causes (or Divorce) Bill the following year. Previously divorce had been possible only by special Acts of Parliament, which were extremely expensive and therefore rare (about one or two a year). The 1857 act (which did not extend to Ireland) set up a new court where proceedings, though cheaper, still cost £100 or thereabouts—enough to prevent an unseemly rush (by 1872 only about 200 decrees were being granted annually).[7] Gladstone was inconsolable none the less, lashing the bill in the Commons with all the rhetorical whips at his disposal, intervening seventy-three times, devoting long speeches to the horrors of bringing divorce to the doors of all classes.[8] His listeners exchanged knowing looks and whispered about lack of judgement. Palmerston (in some respects a less conservative man than Gladstone)[9] must have taken a good deal of pleasure from telling MPs 'We shall return and sit here day by day, and night by night until this Bill be concluded.'[10] Predictably enough, the act itself was biased towards men; whereas they could petition on grounds of adultery alone, wives could only do so if their husbands had indulged in bestiality, bigamy, incest, rape, or cruelty as well. Even so, it was not entirely devoid of reforming content with respect to women's rights, granting, as it did, additional protection over the control of property to separated, divorced, and deserted wives—a modest step which eventually led to the Married Women's Property Act of 1882.

If the Matrimonial Causes Act involved a loosening of existing restrictions, 1857 saw the introduction of another statute having the opposite effect. This was Lord Campbell's Obscene Publications Act, which (amplified by Mr Justice Cockburn's definition of obscenity in *Regina* v. *Hicklin* (1868) as the tendency 'to deprave and corrupt those whose minds are open to such immoral influences and into whose hands a publication of this sort might fall') remained the ruling legislation until 1959. At a time when criticisms of 'intrusive' policing were commonplace, it is noteworthy that, in the matter of pornography, parliament was prepared to give the constabulary sweeping powers to enter and search premises and to seize and burn offending materials. And even if the act was never consistently

---

[7] M. L. Shanley, ' "One Must Ride Behind": Married Women's Rights and the Divorce Act of 1857', *Victorian Studies*, 25 (1982), 361; L. Holcombe, *Wives and Property: Reform of the Married Women's Property Law in Nineteenth-Century Britain* (Oxford, 1983), 95–6; O. Chadwick, *The Victorian Church*, 2 vols. (London, 1966–70), i. 484.

[8] R. Shannon, *Gladstone 1809–1865* (London, 1982), 343–4.

[9] He favoured life peerages, wished to ennoble industrialists, was more prepared to attack 'property' on matters such as cheap housing for working people (E. D. Steele, 'Gladstone and Palmerston 1855–65', in P. J. Jagger (ed.), *Gladstone, Politics and Religion* (London, 1985), 136–9).

[10] Holcombe, *Wives and Property*, 98.

enforced and caused no problems for wealthy collectors of erotica, its appearance marked a significant shift towards a new kind of public moralism, the harbinger of those laws affecting male homosexuality, prostitution, and indecent advertising passed in 1885, 1889, and 1898.[11]

Two much-cited remarks have given an unduly listless air to the legislative achievements of Palmerston's administrations. The future 3rd Marquess of Salisbury claimed in 1864 to believe that Palmerston deserved praise for encouraging parliament to do 'that which it is most difficult and most salutary for a Parliament to do—nothing'. Palmerston himself, in the penultimate year of his long life, is supposed to have responded to an enquiry about the government's plans by 'rubbing his hands with an air of comfortable satisfaction' and saying 'There is really nothing to be done. We cannot go on adding to the Statute Book *ad infinitum*.'[12] Neither comment should be taken too seriously. Salisbury was being mischievous and clever; Palmerston was putting on that cloak of jovial insouciance with which he disguised the seriousness of his deeper political life. Achievement has, in any case, been too exclusively equated with the dramatics of franchise reform, agricultural protection, factory laws, and the like. On such matters Palmerston's ministries had little to contribute. Yet divorce reform, limited liability in 1856, the great consolidating Companies Act of 1862, Poor Law changes in 1865 ending the old restrictions on settlement, the Constabulary Act of 1856, a set of six acts consolidating and reforming criminal law in 1861, the Bankruptcy Act of the same year relieving private debtors, as well as important advances in public health, constituted a harvest of considerable importance to both the economy and the people at large. Leaving aside, therefore, such highly unusual—though not necessarily more effective—bursts of lawmaking as those of the early 1840s and 1869–73, Palmerston's ministries were by no means especially deficient in either the quality or the quantity of their legislative output.[13]

The parliamentary instability of Palmerston's first years as Prime Minister was made manifest by a sudden squall which led to resignation and a general election in the spring of 1857. Remarkably this involved censure of that belligerence overseas which had hitherto proved a distinct political asset. In October 1856 the Chinese authorities at Canton had arrested a

---

[11] M. J. D. Roberts, 'Morals, Art, and the Law: The Passing of the Obscene Publications Act, 1857', *Victorian Studies*, 28 (1985), 627; J. Weeks, *Sex, Politics and Society: The Regulation of Sexuality since 1800*, 2nd edn. (London, 1989), 83.

[12] [Lord R. Cecil], 'The House of Commons', *Quarterly Review*, 116 (1864), 245; *Lord Goschen and his Friends*, ed. P. Colson (London, [1946]), 58.

[13] The number of public acts passed did not drop under Palmerston: 1853 (137), 1854 (125), 1855 (134), 1856 (120)—*Disraeli, Derby*, ed. Vincent, p. 150.

small sailing vessel or *lorcha* called the *Arrow*, even though the ship had (as it later turned out improperly) been flying the British flag. The Governor of Hong Kong demanded restitution and an apology. When these were not produced in a sufficiently grovelling manner he ordered the bombardment of Canton. The news reached London in February 1857. Most cabinet ministers were uneasy but agreed with Palmerston that British prestige was now so fully at stake that there could be no turning back.

Then, more rapidly than anyone could understand, the Chinese issue provided the grain around which the pearl of anti-Palmerstonianism found itself able to coalesce. Derby contrasted 'menacing, disrespectful, irritating, and arrogant' British actions with the 'forbearing, courteous, and gentle-manlike' behaviour of the Chinese.[14] Despite—or perhaps because of—this, the Lords backed Palmerston by 146 to 110. In the Commons, however, a motion by Cobden produced a dramatic government defeat in a large House by 263 votes to 247 because the Conservatives remained solid and enough Radicals and what was left of the Peelites deserted Palmerston in his hour of need.

Although the vote was an unexpected triumph for Derby's general policy of masterly passivity, the affair was so very odd that the eventual failure of the disparate victors—Derby, Disraeli, Gladstone, Russell, Cobden, and so forth—to sustain any kind of permanent relationship was entirely predict-able. That Palmerston's was as yet neither an automatic nor a secure control was, none the less, now clear, even though the shift in voting patterns had been less extreme than that which had brought down Aberdeen in January 1855.[15] Dented too was the notion that Palmerston had merely to replay his Don Pacifico speech of 1850 and all criticism would melt away. Indeed, even one of his most memorable phrases to the effect that for Cobden and the Radicals 'everything that was English was wrong, and everything that was hostile to England was right' failed to prevent his speech on China from being judged 'very dull in the first part, and very bow-wow in the second'.[16]

Immediately after the division the government obtained a dissolution and mounted an appeal to popular belligerence. Although behind the scenes Palmerston's approach to foreign affairs was never as crude as his public pronouncements suggest and while as Prime Minister he was always very careful to avoid major wars that might disrupt the economy and increase social tensions, he had become something of a past master at deploying hectoring abuse against other peoples and nations. On this

[14] *Hansard*, cxliv. 1181 (24 Feb. 1857).

[15] Bylsma, 'Party Structure', 633.

[16] *Hansard*, cxliv. 1812 (3 Mar. 1857); *The Greville Memoirs 1814–1860*, ed. L. Strachey and R. Fulford, 8 vols. (London, 1938), vii. 276 (4 Mar. 1857).

occasion he briskly overruled the high-minded protests of his Chancellor of the Exchequer, Cornewall Lewis, and launched two fiercely chauvinistic rockets against the variegated forces lined up against him.[17] In a Mansion House speech on 20 March he declared an inability to 'envy the feelings of those men who could witness with calmness the heads of respectable British merchants on the walls of Canton', while an address to his Tiverton constituents blamed everything upon 'insolent' barbarians who had 'violated the British flag, broken the engagements of treaties, offered rewards for the heads of British subjects . . . and planned their destruction by murder, assassination, and poisons'.[18]

Palmerston's tactics achieved only partial success. He did, indeed, come back after the general election of April 1857 with a modestly increased paper majority. But as the *Arrow* division had shown and as events in early 1858 were to show again, mid-century paper majorities could easily blow away. The election was not, in any case, simply a Palmerstonian plebiscite. The topics discussed in candidates' addresses included much besides China—education, local matters, religion, reform. That was why, although some notable Radicals lost their seats, Radical numbers overall suffered little attrition.[19] Even so, of all Palmerston's parliamentary followers, it was the Radicals who now seemed to face the most uncertain future. As every month passed it became clearer that the repeal of the Corn Laws had been a much greater triumph for free trade than for Radical free traders. Although entrepreneurial Radicals still exercised a certain amount of leverage and were eventually able to break into government under Russell (1865–6) and Gladstone (1868–74), the failure of Radicals generally to produce and then unitedly support coherent political programmes greatly reduced their influence. Many were now finding it difficult to say what exactly, in any particular instance, even *laissez-faire* itself meant. Some opposed all import duties, others (like Cobden) only those of a 'protective' nature. While bodies like the Administrative Reform Association hoped that competitive examinations would allow the middle classes to take over the running of the state, others pointed out that businessmen themselves placed no reliance on examinations. Nor was it easy in important fields like education to decide, on strictly *business* grounds, whether one should be a voluntaryist (because free schools complemented the free market), a secularist (because compulsory minimum standards in secular subjects created an efficient workforce)

[17] Steele, *Palmerston and Liberalism*, 57–9, 245–316.
[18] *The Times*, 21 and 24 Mar. 1857.
[19] A. Hawkins, *Parliament, Party and the Art of Politics in Britain, 1855–1859* (London, 1987), 64–5, 311; M. Taylor, *The Decline of British Radicalism, 1847–1860* (Oxford, 1995), 275–9.

or even a denominationalist (because using existing church schools was the cheapest option of all).[20]

For Peelites, in turn, it was aggravating to find that the sky did not fall in when Gladstone (whose 1853 budget had, they believed, ushered in a new fiscal dawn) resigned in February 1855. Palmerston, far from seeming concerned, casually hawked the Chancellorship of the Exchequer around, first to the Peelite Cardwell, then to the superannuated Whig, Sir Thomas Baring (who had held the post in ancient times, 1839–41), and only after both had refused to Sir George Cornewall Lewis.[21] Lewis, though an intellectual to his finger tips, had spent his early years as a Poor Law administrator and knew how to manage large organizations. He had served as Financial Secretary to the Treasury between 1850 and 1852 and, on losing his seat in the latter year, become editor of the *Edinburgh Review*. He returned to Westminster just in time to fill the post that nobody else seemed to want. Whereas Gladstone was inclined to passionate intensity, Lewis, though not devoid of self-deprecating humour (his dictum that 'life would be tolerable but for its amusements' became famous), was calm, grave, and undemonstrative. He was also formidably clever as his brilliant book *On Local Disturbances in Ireland* (1836)—still one of the best analyses of rural discontent in that country—testifies. Although some unbiased contemporaries thought little of his financial talents, these were in fact considerable, free from fads and, above all, capable of sustained political articulation. In particular, his budgets of 1855, 1856, and 1857 showed a greater and more flexible creativity in dealing with the problems of war finance than Gladstone had revealed in 1854.[22]

Lewis refused to follow Peel and Gladstone in seeing the budget as an instrument of political and economic morality. It was a practical business—no more and no less. He also belonged to the (then unfashionable) school which believed that heavy taxation was more damaging to the economy than state borrowing. In 1855 the manifest logic of his proposals ensured parliamentary acceptance. Nor in 1856 did Gladstone's barbed hope that 'we shall not set the pestilent example of abolishing taxes and meeting the expenditure of the country with borrowed money' make much of an impact.[23] Gladstone's most remarkable Commons ally on the matter turned

[20] G. R. Searle, *Entrepreneurial Politics in Mid-Victorian Britain* (Oxford, 1993), 268–9, 50, *passim*.

[21] D. Southgate, *The Passing of the Whigs 1832–1886* (London, 1962), 285.

[22] *Disraeli, Derby*, ed. Vincent, p. 149 (13 Feb. 1857); O. Anderson, *A Liberal State at War: English Politics and Economics during the Crimean War* (London, 1967), 195–216.

[23] *Hansard*, cxxxvii. 1561 (20 Apr. 1855); A. Hawkins, 'A Forgotten Crisis: Gladstone and the Politics of Finance during the 1850s', *Victorian Studies*, 26 (1983), 296–7.

out to be Disraeli, by then a rather embarrassing acolyte in questions of finance. The budget of 1857 was, therefore, greeted by the unusual spectacle of Disraeli joining a furiously agitated Gladstone (who had privately consulted Derby on budgetary matters) in defence of Peel's fiscal principles.[24] Lewis took no notice. While the early conclusion of the Crimean War allowed him to present an uncontroversial budget which reduced the income tax to Peel's original fixed rate of 7d. and even to reiterate Gladstone's plans for abolition by 1860, he did not hesitate to make clear his distaste for one of the central verities of Peel-Gladstone orthodoxy by declaring that a good system of taxation should bear lightly on an infinite number of points and heavily on none.[25]

Gladstone's reactions were notable more for anger than good sense. Shifting the point of criticism so frequently that he made it seem as if nothing could elicit his approval, he accused Lewis of throwing overboard 'everything for which we have been labouring during the last fifteen years'.[26] However, the presence of forty-two Conservative MPs among the government's majority of eighty served notice on Disraeli that any kind of co-operation with Gladstone would receive an extremely frosty reception from those sitting on the benches behind him.[27]

Gladstone did not forget, nor did he forgive. In April 1858 he extended a friendly welcome to the budget presented by Disraeli as Chancellor in the Conservative minority administration of 1858–9.[28] A year later, when at last he had persuaded himself to sup with the devil and enter a Palmerston ministry, he insisted on getting the Chancellorship—with the result that Lewis was moved to the Home Office and in July 1861 to the Colonial Office. Even so, Gladstone's rehabilitation was slow and he long remained an object of distrust. As late as April 1862 the future Lord Acton (then himself an MP) was convinced that Gladstone would not be able to hold the government 'together for a week if Palmerston were to die because of his genius, of his principles, and of his pugnacity. The only man who could disarm the opposition... would be Lewis, who has gained wonderfully of late.'[29] Lewis's exclusion from the Exchequer in 1859 and his death in April

[24] P. Ghosh, 'Disraelian Conservatism: A Financial Approach', *English Historical Review*, 99 (1984), 268–96; *The Gladstone Diaries*, ed. H. C. G. Matthew and M. R. D. Foot, 14 vols. (Oxford, 1968–94), v. 196 (11 Feb. 1857); R. Blake, *Disraeli* (London, 1966), 373–4; W. D. Jones, *Lord Derby and Victorian Conservatism* (Oxford, 1956), 215–16.
[25] Hawkins, 'Forgotten Crisis', 307. This was contrary to Gladstone's insistence on 'simplification'.
[26] *Hansard*, cxliv. 986 (20 Feb. 1857).   [27] Hawkins, 'Forgotten Crisis', 311–12.
[28] Shannon, *Gladstone*, 351.
[29] Acton to R. Simpson, 30 Apr. 1862, *The Correspondence of Lord Acton and Richard Simpson*, ed. J. L. Altholz, D. McElrath, J. C. Holland, 3 vols. (Cambridge, 1971–5), ii. 293.

1863 at the age of 56 meant that an important view of finance was deprived of a hearing for years to come. As it was a view which did not consider retrenchment transcendently important, did not worship at the shrine of balanced budgets, gave especial emphasis to the role of investment, and yet looked to the interests of consumers as well as producers and sellers, this was to prove a deprivation of considerable, perhaps even of damaging, significance.

Despite the 'success' of the 1857 election the government was really no more secure at Westminster than it had been before. A severe commercial crisis in the autumn of 1857 did nothing to increase confidence in 'the authorities'.[30] A sense of unease infected the cabinet, some of whose members were beginning to express worries over the inadequacies of the forthcoming India Bill, the looming possibility that reform might once again become an issue, indeed, about Palmerston's leadership generally. And then on 14 January 1858 an Italian, Felice Orsini, threw a bomb at Napoleon III in Paris. When it became known that the plot had been hatched in England and revolvers and explosives obtained there, the French demanded that action be taken to prevent similar conspiracies. Palmerston's ministry thought this reasonable, but Francophobe public opinion did not. A bill was introduced to extend existing Irish legislation throughout the United Kingdom by making conspiracy to murder a felony punishable by penal servitude, regardless of where the intended crime was to be committed. The first reading passed by 299 votes to 99 and all seemed set fair (though, ominously, Russell had voted in the minority). Then a brilliant piece of drafting produced an amendment in the name of the Radical Milner Gibson which so successfully combined universal appeal and a capacity to wound that the ministry went down to defeat on 19 February by 234 to 215, largely because the bulk of Conservatives changed sides. In short, Palmerston had found it impossible to continue preventing the formation of that coalition against him which had been on the agenda since 1855. Even a speech declaring Milner Gibson's record to be one of 'crouching to every foreign Power with which we have had any differences'[31] could not blind MPs to the delicious irony that, on this occasion at least, it was the great apostle of Anglo-Saxon primacy who seemed to be 'truckling' to foreigners and selling short the liberties of free-born Englishmen.

---

[30] J. R. T. Hughes, 'The Commercial Crisis of 1857', *Oxford Economic Papers*, 8 (1956), 195.
[31] *Hansard*, cxlviii. 1838 (19 Feb. 1858).

2. CONSERVATIVE INTERLUDE

At last the Conservatives had been given an opportunity to break out of the strait-jacket of being obliged to 'oppose' a man (Palmerston) who was an ideological and perhaps even a future parliamentary ally. Yet the very unexpectedness of the defeat ('Disraeli's face', recorded Malmesbury, 'was worth anything—a mixture of triumph and sarcasm that he could not repress')[32] showed that combinations against Palmerston depended too heavily upon chance to have much potential for either coherence or permanence. Derby, however, saw the importance of seizing the moment and— Palmerston having resigned—agreed to form a minority administration. And even if his 1858–9 government is best remembered for having provided the immediate occasion for Liberal consolidation, there can be no doubt that the overall cohesiveness of Conservative MPs was greatly improved by a dose of power and patronage, however fleeting and short-lived.[33]

As had become almost a tradition, Derby approached Gladstone and Newcastle as well as the Whig Lord Grey with offers of ministerial rank. No one was surprised when they refused. Gladstone continued to play the game of *noli me tangere*, punctuating it only with an occasional enigmatic tease, as when in October 1858 he bizarrely accepted appointment as Special Commissioner to the Ionian Islands (which run down the west coast of Greece and had been a British protectorate since 1815). In every sense—not least that of sorting out Gladstone's immediate party loyalties— it proved a strange and barren interlude. Gladstone spent almost three months in the islands, during which he thought much of Homer, kissed the rings of Orthodox bishops (to the scandal of Protestant opinion), failed to deal with the 'Risospast' (union with Greece) movement, produced constitutional plans of striking impracticability,[34] and perhaps unconsciously laid the grounds for a later and more prolonged engagement with a not dissimilar congeries of problems concerning land, nation, and faith, namely, the Irish Question.

Despite Derby's failure to attract non-Conservative ministers, a progressive programme enabled him to obtain support from individual Radicals and Liberals who preferred Tory jam today to Palmerstonian jam tomorrow. Certainly there was no great dissimulation in his promise to parliament in March 1858 that 'we shall not hesitate to propose and support

---

[32] Earl of Malmesbury, *Memoirs of an Ex-Minister* (London, 1885), 417 (20 Feb. 1857).

[33] R. Stewart, *The Foundation of the Conservative Party 1830–1867* (London, 1978), 319.

[34] B. Knox, 'British Policy and the Ionian Islands, 1847–1864: Nationalism and Imperial Administration', *English Historical Review*, 99 (1984), 503–29; H. C. G. Matthew, *Gladstone 1809–1874* (Oxford, 1986), 162–5; Shannon, *Gladstone*, 365–73.

measures of undoubted improvement and progress ... There can be no greater mistake than to suppose that a Conservative Ministry necessarily means a stationary Ministry. We live in an age of constant progress—moral, social, and political.'[35] In little over a year the minority government patched up relations with France, introduced a budget of Gladstonian rectitude, and produced indubitably progressive legislation affecting the administration of India, Thames drainage, municipal affairs, and the constitutional status of British Columbia. Then, by agreeing to abolish the property qualification required of MPs, Derby secured the distinction of being the first Prime Minister to grant one of the Chartists' six main demands of 1838. Of equal symbolic importance was the admission in 1858 of Jews into parliament. Although a few Tories had long given sporadic support to Jewish Emancipation—notably Lord George Bentinck (who did so entirely on grounds of principle and heartily wished all Jews 'back in the Holy Land') and Disraeli (whose record was patchy and who based his arguments, not on liberal grounds, but on Christianity's Jewish origins)—it remains remarkable that it should have been under a government dependent upon Conservative back-benchers that the question was finally laid to rest. One disgruntled Tory MP, Charles Newdegate, had no doubts as to what was *really* behind it all—a Talmudic conspiracy directed from Rome by the Jesuits to destroy the free constitution and religion of Protestant Englishmen.[36]

The history of the Reform Bill presented by the Conservatives early in 1859 constitutes a minor foreshadowing of the more dramatic events of 1866 and 1867. It was proposed to leave the borough franchise at £10, lower the county franchise to the same level (but stop supposedly Radical urban freeholders from voting in counties), give the vote to those with savings deposits, degrees, and the like (the so-called 'fancy' franchises), and introduce a very small measure of redistribution. The modesty of all this resembles the initial ideas of 1866. Yet on neither occasion was it enough to prevent cabinet resignations—with Spencer Walpole, the Home Secretary, and J. W. Henley, the President of the Board of Trade, going in 1859. And, just as Derby and Disraeli in 1867 eventually settled upon an 'intelligible' and 'permanent' principle (namely 'household suffrage'), so in 1859 they settled on 'assimilation', that is, aligning the rural franchise to that of the towns.[37] There was, however, one crucial difference between the two

[35] *Hansard*, cxlix. 41 (1 Mar. 1858).

[36] A. Gilam, *The Emancipation of the Jews in England 1830–1860* (New York, 1982), 98, 155–71; M. C. N. Salbstein, *The Emancipation of the Jews in Britain* (London, 1982), 230, 241–2.

[37] A. Hawkins, *Art of Politics*, 197–217.

episodes: in 1859 the Liberals held steady, with the result that on 31 March the government lost its bill by 330 votes to 291.

At the general election that followed—notable for the high level of uncontested constituencies—the Conservatives made modest gains but still remained in a distinct minority. At first most wise observers did not think that Palmerston would become Prime Minister again. Russell patronizingly agreed that he had 'done good service to the country, and should be respected while he is quiet'.[38] Peelites like Herbert and Graham confidently declared coherent parties things of the past, 'broken into fragments' and incapable of being 'pieced together again'.[39] But the longer the Conservatives clung to office the less attractive became the extremes of Derby, on one side, and Russell, on the other, while the growing prominence of foreign affairs—France, Austria, and Sardinia were now at war in northern Italy—inevitably strengthened Palmerston's claims.

Soon it became clear that just about enough had occurred—guilt over Liberal disunity, annoyance over a period of Tory rule, an international crisis—to allow a grand conciliation gathering of Liberals, Peelites, and Radicals: it was called for 6 June at Willis's Rooms in London. Some 280 MPs attended and, with inconsiderable exceptions, all was sweetness and light. Palmerston and Russell more or less agreed that each would serve under the other, as the Queen chose. Herbert 'preached union'. Bright rather vaguely promised support. There was a general feeling that franchise reform might now once again be pursued, the French alliance maintained, and non-intervention remain the lodestar of foreign policy. Five days later Derby's government was defeated in a large House along clear party lines by 323 votes to 310 (with Gladstone recording a silent retrospective vote on the ministry's behalf). Since 1846 the Conservatives had remained a generally coherent entity. Now the Liberals too adopted a less fissiparous mode, with Whigs, Radicals, a handful of Peelites, and a great central core of moderation beginning to co-operate in new and more effective ways.

3. PALMERSTON AGAIN AND GLADSTONE RISING

Queen Victoria, desperate to avoid the 'dreadful old men', as she was soon to call Palmerston and Russell, turned to Lord Granville to form a government. Predictably he failed. She then approached Palmerston. This left Russell with little choice but to come along and keep his spirits up by insisting upon the Foreign Office (which left the experienced Clarendon

[38] Ibid. 170.
[39] D. F. Krein, *The Last Palmerston Government* (Ames, Ia., 1978), 10.

out in the cold). There was, indeed, a good deal of shuffling about all round, some of it caused by another important development—the appointment of Gladstone as Chancellor of the Exchequer. While the unravelling of motives is always difficult, not least in this particular case, it seems clear that Gladstone's acceptance of office was undertaken at two distinct levels of cogitation. At the more conscious level there was a conviction that the kind of reasoned and flexible conservatism which now constituted the kernel of Gladstone's politics—the belief in tradition tempered by reform, and the desire to harness forces of change to the maintenance of established society—would henceforth find a happier home among Liberals than Conservatives.[40] At the more instinctual level Gladstone must have known no less clearly that this would be his last chance of leaving the wilderness and that both the Italian Question and actuarial considerations—Palmerston was 74 and Russell 67, Disraeli however was 54 (only five years older than Gladstone himself)—pointed strongly in a Liberal direction. While Palmerston badly needed a powerful speaker on the front bench, Gladstone, despite a long-nurtured distaste for Palmerstonianism, needed office even more.

In some respects Palmerston's cabinet looked much like that of Aberdeen: four or five 'Peelites', nine or ten Whig/Liberals, two Radicals. Indeed, nine of its sixteen members had actually served in Aberdeen's cabinet and another two had been junior ministers in the coalition. The crucial difference lay, however, in the fact that the new administration was not a coalition at all, but simply a Liberal government with former Peelites more or less fully on board. And although Palmerston was to have many differences with Gladstone it is noteworthy that his initial concern was to ensure the isolation of the chiefest and purest of the Whigs, namely, Russell. As he cheerfully told Granville: 'A pretty mess I would have been in with Johnny...[on my own], and objecting to all his proposals with no one to back me up.'[41]

What Palmerston had done was to resolve the problem of government for the Liberal Party. This, much more than any immediate reconciliation between the various forces now ranged under his leadership, was the real achievement of 1859. In particular, Palmerston's second premiership saw the effective (though not fully formed) appearance of the kind of cabinet-centred administration which was to become the hallmark of Gladstone's own years as Prime Minister. Ministerial control within parliament

[40] D. M. Schreuder, 'Gladstone and Italian Unification 1848–70: The Making of a Liberal?', *English Historical Review*, 85 (1970), 499.

[41] D. Beales, *England and Italy 1859–60* (London, 1961), 86; Hawkins, *Art of Politics*, 265.

increased. Liberal assumptions about the correct operation of government moved away from a Whig-Radical faith in parliamentary sovereignty towards a greater confidence in disinterested executive government backed by party loyalty in the House of Commons.[42] Not only was Palmerston a greater pioneer than Peel of the kind of executive control later associated with Gladstone, he also did much to launch those public and carefully choreographed overtures to provincial opinion that were later to become so characteristic an aspect of Gladstone's political style. Already in 1847 Peel had made restrained efforts to stand well with the middle classes of Liverpool by, for example, proposing to 'chat on 'Change' and attend mercantile dinners. Nine years later Palmerston was behaving far more energetically—mixing with businessmen in Manchester and proclaiming the district a 'hive of industry', 'the cradle and nursery of genius'.[43] Over the decade that followed he was to go, among other places, to Leeds, Sheffield, and Bradford, greeted by cheering crowds, addressing large audiences, making it clear that he was quite as concerned to ingratiate himself with his hosts as they were to impress upon him their loyalty and support. And where Gladstone tended to lecture the middle classes, Palmerston flattered them, in a conscious attempt to foster general feelings of Liberal solidarity.[44]

In such respects, as in others, the elderly Prime Minister was, indeed, a much more modern political figure than is sometimes supposed or than he himself often liked to pretend. Over his long career no other politician could match his staying power and few could match his capacity for hard work. His relations with the Queen became better as time went on, not least because he possessed the ability (which Gladstone was later so obviously to lack) of smoothing over disagreements with ample helpings of tact, flattery, firmness, and social ease. He also became more patient with age and more popular, though he remained capable of substantial—and sometimes surprising—errors of judgement. That in 1863, in his late seventies, he was cited as a co-respondent in a divorce petition brought by a Mr O'Kane merely seemed to add to his indestructible charm. If polite society soon rang to a new joke—'While the lady was certainly Kane, was Palmerston Abel?'—most people spoke it in an affectionate, perhaps almost a slightly jealous, vein. Gladstone, the only other man ever to reach the premiership with anything like Palmerston's experience, was not, however, among them.

[42] Taylor, *Decline of Radicalism*, 326–31; T. A. Jenkins, *The Liberal Ascendancy, 1830–1886* (London, 1994), 88–90.

[43] D. Read, *Peel and the Victorians* (Oxford, 1987), 252; G. R. Searle, *Entrepreneurial Politics in Mid-Victorian Britain*, 134–8.

[44] Steele, *Palmerston and Liberalism*, 35–6.

After 1859 Derby's reversion to a policy of inaction represented the least bad solution as far as the Conservatives were concerned. Though discipline remained relatively intact, there was a good deal of passivity on the back-benches, some of it merely indolent in character, some generated by a feeling that Palmerston deserved support. Disraeli's endless fishing expeditions—in February 1861 he declared that 'the union of the R. Catholics with the Conservative party' had 'been his object for twenty years'—were gradually assuming more the character of habit than of expectation.[45] What few realized was how well Derby was playing the dingy hand which fate had dealt him. If the death of protection had left his party without a rationalizing principle then Derby made a virtue out of necessity by using the very absence of a 'watchword' to prevent the raising of issues inimical to party unity. Even the semi-formal agreements made with Palmerston from 1860 onwards, to the effect that the Conservatives would support the Prime Minister against Radical demands in return for moderation in all things, were put together with as much hostile intent as the circumstances would allow.[46]

The administration of 1859–65 was marked by a slide towards impotence abroad, some energetic scrapping between Gladstone and Palmerston over defence, and a modest amount of thoroughly useful legislation. Significant by its absence was any continuation of that interest in franchise reform which in 1858–9 had provided a vehicle for Liberal revival. The collapse of Russell's Reform Bill of 1860—a reprise of what had been put forward in 1852 and 1854—caused neither the Commons nor most of the cabinet much anxiety.[47] In any case, contrary to the Prime Minister's own initial expectations, the chief split was to come between Palmerston and Gladstone on finance rather than between Palmerston and Russell over reform.

As Chancellor, Gladstone was determined to restore fiscal probity after the 'excesses' of the Crimean War. Unfortunately his return to office coincided with a revival of hysteria about possible invasion from France. Increased spending on the French navy and coastal defences by Napoleon III, British chauvinism over the Orsini affair, memories of the Emperor's

[45] *Disraeli, Derby,* ed. Vincent, pp. 167, 227; K. T. Hoppen, 'Tories, Catholics, and the General Election of 1859', *Historical Journal,* 13 (1970), 48–67.
[46] Jones, *Lord Derby,* 264–8; Monypenny and Buckle, *Disraeli,* iv. 293–4; *Disraeli, Derby,* ed. Vincent, p. 170; Earl of Malmesbury, *Memoirs,* 534; Gurowich, 'Continuation of War', 625.
[47] C. Seymour, *Electoral Reform in England and Wales: The Development and Operation of the Parliamentary Franchise, 1832–1885* (New Haven, 1915), 242–7; Krein, *Last Palmerston Government,* 27–8; J. Prest, *Lord John Russell* (London, 1972), 389–90.

uncle, and the existence of a good deal of semi-automatic Francophobia combined to create widespread excitement among high and low alike. Already in 1858 Clarendon at the Foreign Office had been 'haunted' by the prospects of invasion while Derby's government of 1858–9 had lost no time in finding money 'for the reconstruction of the British navy'. A quasi-spontaneous Volunteer movement sprang into being and received official sanction. By mid-1860 there were about 100,000 volunteers, by February 1862 as many as 160,000.[48] Tennyson caught the mood with 'Riflemen Form' published just as the chief actors on the Italian stage—Austria, France, and Sardinia—were about to go to war.

> Let your reforms for a moment go!
> Look to your butts, and take good aim!
> Better a rotten borough or so
> Than a rotten fleet and a city in flames!
> Storm, Storm, riflemen form!
> Ready, be ready against the storm!
> Riflemen, Riflemen, Riflemen, form!

Small wonder that Gladstone found himself 'very *lonely*' in the cabinet 'on the question of Military Estimates'.[49]

Far from reducing public alarm, the achievement of partial Italian unification by force of French bayonets did quite the reverse. Napoleon's acquisition of Nice and Savoy from Sardinia as payment for services rendered seemed evidence of expansionist cunning. Although an Anglo-French commercial treaty based on unofficial negotiations undertaken by Cobden was signed in January 1860, suspicions remained. Gladstone's view that the mutual abolition of a range of import duties guaranteed a pacific future was not universally shared.[50]

All this strengthened Palmerston's ceaseless demands for additional military expenditure. With even Peelites like Herbert at the War Office demanding more money in 1860, with Cornewall Lewis proving himself a 'formidable and grimly unforgiving' opponent of retrenchment, with Russell in 1862 insisting that the army was 'miserably insufficient', Gladstone was reduced to fighting a series of dogged rearguard actions on behalf of

[48] B. Porter, *The Refugee Question in Mid-Victorian Politics* (Cambridge, 1979), 173; M. J. Salevouris, *'Riflemen Form': The War Scare of 1859–1860 in England* (New York, 1982), 72, 165, 213.

[49] *Gladstone Diaries*, ed. Matthew and Foot, v. 442 (30 Nov. 1859).

[50] Matthew, *Gladstone 1809–1874*, 113; Beales, *England and Italy*, 139; E. Ashley, *The Life and Correspondence of Henry John Temple Viscount Palmerston*, 2 vols. (London, 1879), ii. 446; P. H. Scherer, 'Partner or Puppet? Lord John Russell at the Foreign Office, 1859–1862', *Albion*, 19 (1987), 368.

economy and thrift.[51] Robert Lowe, who actually managed to reduce the amount devoted to education, alone stood shoulder to shoulder with the Chancellor. But Lowe was not in the cabinet and when it came to defence, an aristocratic ministry had little trouble in rejecting middle-class demands for cuts. On the two front benches sustained support came only from Disraeli, though whether comments by him on 'bloated armaments' in May 1862 or 'economical' behaviour when he himself was Chancellor in 1866–8 gave much comfort to Gladstone is highly improbable.[52]

The fact remains that a higher proportion of central government expenditure (39.4 per cent) was devoted to defence during the period 1861–5 than at any other time of peace during the whole of the nineteenth century.[53] Despite all his arguments, despite his regular diary references to imminent resignation, despite setting up the Commons Public Accounts Committee in 1861 (a toothless bulldog when it came to biting the military departments), Gladstone failed to develop an effective critique of defence spending. A belief in executive power and an inability to accept the anti-colonialism of the Manchester School (which might have rendered some defence expenditure unnecessary) reduced him to conducting a series of poorly co-ordinated retrenchment campaigns on disparate issues, while remaining, as Cobden complained, the fueller of imperialism.[54]

If Gladstone, as Palmerston delightedly told the Queen in July 1860, could do little more than pursue a course of 'ineffectual opposition and ultimate acquiescence',[55] he was none the less able to cover his nakedness with the help of a buoyant economy and increasing revenues. This made it possible to bring down the income tax from 10d. (on incomes over £150) in 1861 to 4d. five years later. But while Gladstone was certainly a pioneer of what later became known as 'Treasury orthodoxy', such reductions were no more than pale shadows of his earlier plans to abolish income tax entirely. It was precisely, indeed, the comparative *failure* of his financial hopes which first led him, during the winter of 1863–4, to turn over in his mind the possibility of giving the vote to thrifty artisans as a means of strengthening the economical wing of the Liberal Party.[56] By beginning to consider the

[51] Salevouris, '*Riflemen Form*', 261–2; Shannon, *Gladstone*, 445; *The Later Correspondence of Lord John Russell 1840–1878*, ed. G. P. Gooch, 2 vols. (London, 1925), ii. 299.

[52] Shannon, *Gladstone*, 403, 522; *Hansard*, clxvi. 1403–28 (8 May 1862); Blake, *Disraeli*, 428–9; Ghosh, 'Disraelian Conservatism', 286–8.

[53] H. C. G. Matthew, 'Disraeli, Gladstone, and the Politics of Mid-Victorian Budgets', *Historical Journal*, 22 (1979), 633.

[54] Ibid. 632.

[55] B. Connell, *Regina v. Palmerston: The Correspondence between Queen Victoria and Her Foreign and Prime Minister 1837–1865* (London, 1962), 292.

[56] Matthew, *Gladstone 1809–1874*, 128.

benefits that might flow from mutually sustaining connections between plebeian Radicalism and virtuous finance, Gladstone was eventually able to create a new kind of Liberal consensus. If, ironically, this enterprise turned out to be a continuation of Palmerston's popular Liberalism by other means, its political success depended heavily upon the basic simplicity of Gladstone's own particular approach to finance. His businesslike mottoes of 'small profits and quick returns' and leaving 'money to fructify in the pockets of the people' were easy to understand and so popular that it was not long before industrious Radicals began to hail Gladstone as—in the words of George Howell—the first Chancellor 'to discover how to increase the receipts by reducing the burthens'.[57] While, therefore, Disraeli's pilgrimage to parliamentary reform began (and ended) with the desire to achieve and remain in office, from the very beginning Gladstone's had as much to do with economic as with political considerations.

Although Palmerston was able to have his way over defence, budget-making allowed Gladstone to regain some of the ground which a reputation for crankiness in the late 1850s had undermined: hence the long disquisition in his four-hour budget speech of 10 February 1860 upon the financial evils of the immediate past.[58] Hence too the triumphant claims that it was only the combined benefits of free trade and a return to rectitude and technical mastery in finance which now made it possible to cancel tariffs on a vast range of articles and abolish the paper duty, the last of those 'taxes on knowledge' which had been progressively withdrawn since the 1830s and especially rapidly so since 1853.[59]

Paper duty abolition, however, caused much difficulty, partly for fiscal reasons—Palmerston did not want to forgo revenue—and partly because the last thing many MPs wished to do was encourage newspaper circulations to rise. Gladstone took no notice and hailed the recent growth of Liberal and Radical papers as 'highly creditable to the conductors of what is called the cheap press'.[60] The House of Lords at first blocked the plan, to the public delight of Palmerston, even though the constitutional propriety of its rejecting a financial measure passed by the Commons was already questionable. In the following year Gladstone responded with a stroke of

[57] E. F. Biagini, 'Popular Liberals, Gladstonian Finance and the Debate on Taxation, 1860–1874', in Biagini and A. J. Reid (eds.), *Currents of Radicalism: Popular Radicalism, Organised Labour and Party Politics in Britain, 1850–1914* (Cambridge, 1991), 134–62.

[58] *Hansard*, clvi. 812–72 (10 Feb. 1860); *Gladstone Diaries*, ed. Matthew and Foot, v. 464 (10 Feb. 1860).

[59] Advertisement duty was lowered in 1833 and abolished in 1853, stamp duty lowered in 1836 and abolished in 1855, paper duty lowered in 1836 and abolished in 1861.

[60] *Hansard*, clvi. 860 (10 Feb. 1860).

tactical genius. He bundled all his budget proposals (including paper duty abolition) into a single bill which the Lords reluctantly passed, thereby postponing a collision on finance between the two Houses for no less than forty-eight years.

Gladstone's enthusiastic references to the press reveal the direction of his own political travels and highlight the development of newspapers in general. The abolition of various duties between 1853 and 1861 made it possible to produce tolerable dailies for a penny, with the result that *The Times* (still charging 3d. in 1870) lost its pre-eminence in circulation. Yet in many respects the new 'popular' press was at first neither very new nor excessively popular. Literate working people still read mostly on Sundays and were specifically provided for by papers such as the *News of the World* and the more radical *Reynold's News*. Nor did removing taxes have much effect upon the typographical appearance of mid-Victorian dailies. Cross-headings, shorter paragraphs, and larger headlines lay in the future—as did 'human interest' stories. Unsurprisingly, therefore, the London and provincial papers of the 1860s still catered for a largely middle- and upper-class readership or, as a contemporary put it, for 'the governing classes—aristocratic, official, parliamentary, financial and commercial'.[61] By the early 1870s *The Times* was selling about 67,000 copies a day compared to the 150,000 of the *Daily News* and the 190,000 of the *Daily Telegraph*. Yet even the *Telegraph* (the most striking product of changes in taxation and printing techniques) succeeded more by making shrewd adjustments to the slowly changing mores of middle-class Liberalism than by undertaking anything dramatically new. And much the same was true of the provinces where expanding circulations and the arrival of new publications proceeded along sporadic and highly localized lines and where success depended upon the political circumstances of particular towns rather than on superior technology, reductions in taxation, or canny marketing.[62]

Palmerston combined aristocratic distrust of journalists with a willingness to make the most of any opportunity that might come along. At various stages of his career he exercised influence over (and made anonymous contributions to) the *Morning Chronicle* and the *Morning Post*. By the late 1850s even the Peelite *Times* had grown to love him. Gladstone cultivated Thornton Hunt of the *Telegraph*: they met and corresponded over a hundred times between 1864 and 1868.[63] Cobden and Bright instinctively

[61] A. J. Lee, *The Origins of the Popular Press in England 1855–1914* (London, 1976), 38.

[62] L. Brown, *Victorian News and Newspapers* (Oxford, 1985), 52–3; Taylor, *Decline of Radicalism*, 356–66.

[63] S. Koss, *The Rise and Fall of the Political Press in Britain*, i. *The Nineteenth Century* (London, 1981), 77–84; Brown, *Victorian News*, 171–2.

adopted beneficial relationships with the growing provincial daily press which by 1864 had an aggregate circulation almost twice as large as that of the metropolitan dailies.[64] Indeed, it is clear that mid-Victorian politicians, with the significant exception of Russell whose old-fashioned Whiggism now lacked flexibility, influenced newspapers quite as much as the latter influenced politics. One acted upon the other and if the *Telegraph* later helped to turn Gladstone into the 'People's William' he, for his part, did much to draw up the agenda upon which it and the rest of the press could flourish and expand. The dominance of the Liberal newspapers simply became more evident than before. By 1868 there were twenty-six Liberal, nine Conservative, and eight independent provincial dailies—and the situation in London was much the same.[65] However, the long-term political implications of such developments were anything but straightforward: in 1874, in the heyday of the Liberal newspaper, Gladstone was defeated at the polls, while in 1906, when the Liberals were extremely anxious about the press, the party enjoyed one of its greatest electoral victories.

Palmerston became so strongly entrenched after 1859 not so much because of a large formal majority in the Commons but because he managed to keep almost everyone happy and took care never to antagonize more than one group at a time. If in foreign affairs his policies lacked teeth, no one in parliament had any viable popular alternatives to suggest. Rank-and-file Tories saw him as more cautious on franchise matters than any other Liberal, more cautious even than leading men on their own side. Radicals were kept quiet by extensions of free trade, a liberal (if largely ineffective) foreign policy, and unflamboyantly significant legislative measures at home.

Not that squalls were unknown, with the year 1864 proving especially turbulent. Within a period of a few months the government's majority sank to single figures in connection with two notorious débâcles: the unwitting involvement of the Radical, James Stansfeld, a junior Admiralty minister, in a Mazzinian plot against Napoleon III and a confused and unsuccessful campaign against the Ashanti in West Africa. On the more important matter of the ministry's handling of the Schleswig-Holstein Question the majority (eighteen) was almost as low. Yet even in that case Palmerston was able to avert disaster by, as the Austrian ambassador put it, 'making an immense draft on his old popularity' and reminding the House that under him taxes had been lowered, large resources had been devoted to defence, foreign trade had greatly increased, a deficit in India had been turned into a

[64] Koss, *Political Press*, 121.
[65] Lee, *Origins*, 287, 291. The big circulations were also on the Liberal side.

surplus, and Britain had remained at peace.[66] Nor did the man himself seem at all jaded. After the debate in which these claims were made a baffled Disraeli admiringly noted how Palmerston had 'scrambled up a wearying staircase to the ladies' gallery' to see his wife, 'and they embraced! An interesting scene, and what pluck! To mount those dreadful stairs at three o'clock in the morning and eighty years of age!'[67]

If parliament was occasionally prepared to snap at Palmerston's heels the electorate was less antagonistic. When, therefore, a general election took place in July 1865 the government gained about a dozen seats. For his part Gladstone—now becoming 'the central figure in our politics ... his importance is far more likely to increase than to diminish'[68]—was unsurprisingly surprised when certain opaque but threatening pronouncements that he had recently made on the franchise persuaded the fiercely reactionary voters of Oxford University to dispense with his services as their MP. Palmerston was not pleased: 'Keep him in Oxford, and he is partially muzzled; but send him elsewhere, and he will run wild.'[69]

Gladstone at once moved to the constituency of South Lancashire where he famously told an audience that he came among them 'unmuzzled'.[70] The truth was more complex. He had expected a Liberal defeat and persuaded himself that this would slow the pace of political movement and allow great progressive constitutional complexities like the Irish established church and franchise reform to be avoided for another decade, perhaps for another generation.[71] His realization that electoral success had now foreshortened so leisurely a time-scale created considerable uneasiness of mind.

4. PERTURBATIONS, 1865–1868

For long no one in the select world of high politics had been in any doubt that Palmerston's death would dissolve many of the certainties which had been lingering while he lived. When at last it took place in October 1865 the 'truce' of parties ended and the Liberals found themselves deprived of steady leadership. 'Our quiet days are over; no more peace for us' remarked

---

[66] D. Southgate, '*The Most English Minister ...*': *The Policies and Politics of Palmerston* (London, 1966), 519; *Hansard*, clxxvi. 1272–87 (8 July 1864).

[67] Monypenny and Buckle, *Disraeli*, iv. 405.

[68] *Disraeli, Derby*, ed. Vincent, p. 233 (26 July 1865).

[69] E. Hodder, *The Life and Work of the Seventh Earl of Shaftesbury* (London, 1892), 604.

[70] This had become the word of the moment ever since 26 June when Derby had compared the abolition of special parliamentary oaths for Catholic MPs with unmuzzling a dog and thereby (?deliberately) undermined Disraeli's efforts to attract Catholics to the Conservative Party (*Hansard*, clxxx. 790).

[71] Shannon, *Gladstone*, 551.

Sir Charles Wood at the funeral. Russell, now well into his seventies—and since 1861, as Earl Russell, a member of the House of Lords and as quirky as ever—was the obvious successor. Determined to make his mark before he too departed the scene he quickly disinterred the question of reform (more fully discussed, especially with regard to the Second Reform Acts, in Chapter 8 below) even though Gladstone for one could discern no sudden feeling for it among his Lancashire constituents.[72] Together he and Gladstone bungled things by being at once too cautious and too precipitate and by treating their followers with disengaged hauteur. In June 1866 the government was defeated and replaced by Derby's third minority administration. And although Disraeli's brilliantly pragmatic handling of parliament greatly helped both to shape the eventual nature and secure the eventual passage of Reform Bills for England and Wales, Scotland, and Ireland in 1867–8, the success of the Tory enterprise as a whole owed almost everything to Derby and to the policies he had been pursuing with dogged determination for twenty years. No other politician had, or has subsequently, held the leadership of a great party for so long (1846–68). Few have suffered so many disappointments. Yet under Derby the Conservative Party was able, not only to reshape itself, but to develop the most sophisticated electoral apparatus of the time.[73] His obsessive interest in the turf and in rural pursuits—so useful for a leader of red-faced country gentlemen—was matched by sharp political insight, brilliant oratory, and a more lively interest in classical literature than commonly found among slaughterers of game.[74] It is, indeed, among the more satisfying ironies of history that it should have been the sober 'administrative' Peel who wrecked his party and the spirited mercurial Derby who, with truly Fabian patience, put it back together again.

Failure and departure from office in 1866 prompted Gladstone to move beyond reform and to begin turning a very recent interest in Irish affairs into a sovereign method for reuniting the fractured forces of Liberalism. At first he was inclined to give priority to the Irish land question and actually introduced a bill on the matter. However, its collapse persuaded him that a measure to disestablish the Anglican Church of Ireland (to which only a tenth of the Irish population belonged) would exercise a more emollient

[72] J. Morley, *The Life of William Ewart Gladstone*, 3 vols. (London, 1903), ii. 198.

[73] A. Hawkins, 'Lord Derby and Victorian Conservatism', *Parliamentary History*, 6 (1987), 294; Stewart, *Foundation*, 325–39; K. T. Hoppen, *Elections, Politics, and Society in Ireland 1832–1885* (Oxford, 1984), 286–91.

[74] Derby's translation of Homer (published in 1864 and sold out in a week) was exceedingly literal, Gladstone's *Studies on Homer and the Homeric Age* (1858) exceedingly idiosyncratic.

and unifying effect upon Liberal MPs. As usual he began with some oracular observations. 'Ireland', he informed an audience at Stockport, 'is at your doors. Providence placed her there; law and Legislature have made a compact between you; you must face these obligations: you must deal with them and discharge them.'[75] What all this was leading up to was what John Morley later designated 'one of the heroic acts' of Gladstone's life,[76] namely, the introduction from the opposition benches in March 1868 (only a month after Disraeli had succeeded a tired Derby as Prime Minister) of three Commons Resolutions to the effect that the Church of Ireland should cease to exist as an establishment. The first was carried by 65 votes on 30 April, upon which the rest went through without a division.

Disraeli managed to hang on until the autumn by arguing that it would be senseless to hold elections until the new franchise established by the Reform Acts of 1867–8 had come into force. But already it was Gladstone who actually seemed to be in command, with his Irish Resolutions, his activity over the abolition of church rates (something which later generations long incorrectly believed was the work of a Liberal administration),[77] and his introduction of a Suspensory Bill for the Irish Church all suggesting that he was in office rather than opposition. Yet it remains mysterious precisely why Gladstone decided to take up Irish matters at this moment. Certainly the unfolding of his engagement does not match the development of serious unrest in Ireland. Probably he realized that Ireland would allow him to divert attention from more divisive issues. Not only that, but he had also come to understand that it was above all matters of church and religion and their relationship to the state which divided even the most reactionary Whigs and anti-reforming Liberals from the Conservatives. It was an insight of pure genius and one which Disraeli, with his notorious inability to treat religious questions seriously, never managed either to understand or take into sufficient account.[78]

At the general election held in November and December 1868 the Liberal majority rose to about 110. Gladstone, having led the Liberals since 1866, was called to Windsor on 3 December—where he found the Queen 'kind, cheerful, even playful'—to accept the royal commission to form a government. Although (after Palmerston) the most ministerially experi-

---

[75] Matthew, *Gladstone 1809–1874*, 145–6, 134.

[76] Morley, *Life of Gladstone*, ii. 246.

[77] O. Anderson, 'Gladstone's Abolition of Compulsory Church Rates', *Journal of Ecclesiastical History*, 25 (1974), 185–98.

[78] J. Vincent, 'Gladstone and Ireland', *Proceedings of the British Academy*, 63 (1977), 200; J. P. Parry, *Democracy and Religion: Gladstone and the Liberal Party 1867–1875* (Cambridge, 1986), 10.

enced man ever to become Prime Minister, there was, as one of his twentieth-century successors as Chancellor of the Exchequer has noted, nothing *réchauffé* about him. In the context of the time he was, indeed, almost a new man, 'full of elemental and even dangerous force'.[79]

After having put together a strong cabinet, Gladstone wrote a fifty-ninth birthday entry in his diary on 29 December: 'I descend the hill of life. It would be a truer figure to say I ascend a steepening path with a burden ever gathering weight. The Almighty seems to sustain and spare me for some purpose of His own deeply unworthy as I know myself to be.'[80] But if in some respects the age of Palmerston already seemed very far away, in others (notably foreign and colonial affairs) the policies which had marked its conclusion were to be pressed into service for many years to come.

5. IMPERIAL AND FOREIGN AFFAIRS

During the 1850s and 1860s the empire continued to grow in no consciously controlled or monocausal way and politicians continued to find it difficult to decide whether or not it was necessary to acquire territory in order to expand trade. Palmerston was no more consistent than anyone else.[81] But while his comments on the commercial effects of direct rule were contradictory, he knew that force could achieve a good deal, as the catalogue he drew up in 1864 of the steps to be followed when opening up new markets outside Europe so frankly reveals. 'First—agreement for Trade, next Breach of Engagement, Injustice and outrage—Then Redress demanded and refused—Then Reparation enforced by Hostility. Then temporary acquiescence—Then renewed endeavours to break engagements—Then successful display of superior strength and then at last peaceful and settled commercial Intercourse.'[82]

Although by the early 1860s the overseas empire already covered 9.5 million square miles and included 148.4 million people (94 per cent of them in India),[83] a series of mid-century difficulties and complications gave some renewed weight to the arguments of those apostles of retrenchment who

[79] *Gladstone Diaries*, ed. Matthew and Foot, vi. 645; R. Jenkins, *Gladstone* (London, 1995), 291.

[80] *Gladstone Diaries*, ed. Matthew and Foot, vi. 654.

[81] R. Hyam, *Britain's Imperial Century 1815–1914* (London, 1976), 54; J. D. Hargreaves, *Prelude to the Partition of West Africa* (London, 1963), 36–7.

[82] J. Ridley, *Lord Palmerston* (London, 1970), 543.

[83] L. E. Davis and R. A. Huttenback, *Mammon and the Pursuit of Empire: The Political Economy of British Imperialism, 1860–1912* (Cambridge, 1986), 27–8. For the extent of the empire in the 1890s see Map 11.

had long criticized the imperial enterprise. In South Africa the costly policy of pacification by annexation and settlement was temporarily abandoned and some territory given up after Sir George Grey left the Colonial Office in 1855.[84] Palmerston's own disillusionment with the annexation of Lagos in 1861 was deepened when a British expedition against the Ashanti, overcome by incompetence and malaria, was forced to withdraw in May 1864. The resulting debate in parliament was a dramatic event, first, because the government's majority fell to seven (233 to 226), and secondly, because Sir John Hay (whose brother had perished in the campaign) delivered a speech of high-octane power and vituperation. Raking over incidents many had hoped to forget he asked

Who is to blame? The men who have alienated France and irritated Russia. Who is to blame? The men who have convulsed China and devastated Japan; the same men who ten years ago sent a British army to perish of cold, of hunger, and of want of shelter in a Crimean winter, and have now sent British troops to perish of fever, of thirst, and of want of shelter on the burning plains and fetid swamps of Western Africa. These men cling to that front Bench with wonderful tenacity, and they send other men to die with wonderful courage.[85]

One year later a select committee on West Africa strongly advised against 'all further extension of territory or assumption of Government, or new treaties offering any protection to native tribes' and expressed the hope that Britain would eventually withdraw from all but a handful of settlements in the area.[86] That disengagement, even from so economically marginal a region, was, however, to prove no more than a pious aspiration, shows how difficult it had become to put the colonial juggernaut into reverse.

Nor were attempts to reduce imperial commitments and costs in other ways any more successful. Though the recommendation of the Select Committee on Colonial Military Expenditure that self-governing colonies should 'undertake the main responsibility for providing their own internal order and security, and ought to assist in their own external defence', was accepted by the Commons in March 1862 without a division, most colonies simply found new ways to avoid paying up.[87] In New Zealand, for example, renewed warfare with the Maoris in the 1860s over land rights—that commonest of all matters of local colonial dispute—made it difficult for

---

[84] B. Porter, *The Lion's Share*, 2nd edn. (London, 1984), 56–7; C. C. Eldridge, *Victorian Imperialism* (London, 1978), 55.

[85] *Hansard*, clxxv. 1962 (17 June 1864).

[86] *Report from the Select Committee on Africa (Western Coast)*, H[ouse of] C[ommons Paper] 1865 (412), v, p. iii.

[87] Eldridge, *Victorian Imperialism*, 84.

London to avoid substantial military expenditure even though self-government had been granted in 1856.[88]

Clearly, therefore, the development in the 1840s and 1850s of the concept of self-government had not produced the immediate cash dividends many had expected. Canada continued to soak up money, not least because the potentially destabilizing impact of the American Civil War (1861–5) required the dispatch of additional troops. Gladstone was not alone in complaining that, here as elsewhere, the problems of defence had 'separated the burdens of freedom from the spirit of freedom'.[89] The British North America Act of 1867 setting up a Canadian Federation along what became known as dominion lines was, therefore, among much else, a determined attempt to reduce calls upon the imperial exchequer. But while it was not without some modest successes in that respect, neither Canada nor the other colonies or dominions of white settlement were ever to show much enthusiasm in the Victorian period for shouldering the burdens of freedom in the way Gladstone and many others thought they should.

From Britain's point of view, therefore, all talk of imperial retrenchment proved illusory. The same House of Commons that worshipped at the altar of economy went on voting increased budgets for the army abroad and also, indeed, for fortifications at home. Even the two actual cases of territorial cession in this period were idiosyncratic acts of no general significance. In 1852 the tiny Bay Islands off the Caribbean coast of Central America were acquired by the Colonial Office without the Foreign Office knowing about it. In retaliation the Foreign Office, without telling the Colonial Office, made a treaty transferring them to Honduras in 1861.[90] The Ionian Islands—the second case—were not technically a colony at all having been placed under British 'protection' in 1815. After the failure of Gladstone as Special Commissioner in 1858–9 to defuse their inhabitants' desire for union with Greece, ministers grew increasingly irritated at being accused (not least by Irish Catholic MPs anxious to defend the Pope's temporal sovereignty against liberal attack) of denying the Ionians precisely those principles they insisted upon in the case of Italy. When, therefore, a Greek revolution overthrew the unsavoury King Otho in 1862, the cabinet lost no time in marking the accession of a tolerable successor by dispatching the islands into his hands. King George I (a Dane) ascended the throne in

---

[88] D. K. Fieldhouse, *The Colonial Empires* (London, 1966), 261.

[89] Eldridge, *Victorian Imperialism*, 87.

[90] D. Waddell, 'Great Britain and the Bay Islands, 1821–61', *Historical Journal*, 2 (1959), 59–77.

March 1863 and the islands were transferred to Greece in the following year.[91]

Attempts to loosen colonial ties by introducing responsible government and cutting military costs received an especially dramatic set-back when a revolt in Jamaica became the focus of one of the most violent mid-century debates over an imperial matter. A minor black uprising in October 1865 was put down by the Governor, Edward Eyre, with brutal savagery. Talking wildly of the Indian Mutiny he introduced martial law: 439 persons were killed, 600 flogged, 354 court-martial sentences passed, and a thousand homes burnt down.[92] Within weeks, opinion in England had become polarized between those who condemned Eyre as a racialist brute and those who hailed him as a defender of all that was best in Christian civilization. Angry debates took place within and outside parliament. And the affair, by uncovering one of the deepest fault lines bisecting the educated classes, and indeed society as a whole, rapidly assumed an importance running well beyond the confines of Jamaica in particular or the idea of colonialism in general.

On returning to England, Eyre was enthusiastically greeted by large working-class demonstrations and by support from a bevy of notables. The latter predictably included Carlyle (whose views on the 'nigger question' were of ancient vintage), but also, more unexpectedly, Kingsley, Ruskin, Tennyson, and Dickens. Kingsley, formally abandoning an earlier belief in equality, declared that the realities of life demonstrated how 'differences of race are so great, that certain races, e.g. the Irish Celts, seem quite unfit for self-government'.[93] Ruskin denounced attacks on Eyre as hypocrisy because poor white Englishmen at home required help more than did black Africans abroad. Tennyson was convinced that the Indian Mutiny had provided 'a warning to all but mad men against want of vigour and swift decisiveness'. While the men of letters mobilized in defence of Eyre, the scientists were strong on the other side, with Darwin, Huxley, Spencer, and Lyell attaching themselves to the Jamaica Committee set up by a number of Radicals with the support of J. S. Mill and politicians such as Bright and Edward Baines.[94] A royal commission was appointed to inquire into the matter. Though its report in 1866 was cautious, its

[91] *Hansard*, clxii. 1676 (7 May 1861); C. C. Eldridge, 'The Myth of Mid-Victorian "Separation": The Cession of the Bay Islands and the Ionian Islands in the early 1860s', *Victorian Studies*, 12 (1969), 331–46; Knox, 'Ionian Islands', 503–29.

[92] Hyam, *Imperial Century*, 75.

[93] [F. E. Kingsley], *Charles Kingsley: His Letters and Memories of His Life*, 2 vols. (London, 1877), ii. 242–3.

[94] B. Semmel, *The Governor Eyre Controversy* (London, 1962), 62–5, 108–15.

acceptance of some at least of the atrocity stories diminished the enthusiasm of all but Eyre's most blinkered partisans.

The Eyre controversy reached such peculiar heights because it intermeshed with two other contemporary preoccupations. The more immediate was increasing concern about parliamentary reform. Eyre's friends included many who believed that reform would unleash at home those 'primitive' horrors displayed in black Jamaica and Fenian Ireland. The anti-Eyre forces, which represented a regrouping of those who had supported the Union during the American Civil War, wanted to extend the franchise not only on grounds of principle but because a refusal to do so might encourage precisely that violence which their opponents also feared. More generally the Jamaican revolt occurred at a time when harsh racial attitudes were achieving a wider prominence. Older beliefs in humanity's basic perfectibility were fading under the impress of missionary pessimism, ethnographical theories ranking peoples in a 'scale of civilization', false readings of Darwin, strident claims by 'experts' like Dr James Hunt that the inferiority of blacks could be 'proved' by craniology, and a growing willingness to draw parallels between African 'savages' and the inhabitants of British slums.[95] While, however, such developments undoubtedly produced a new contempt for blacks in colonial lands, they also reinforced the belief that withdrawal was now impossible and that the white man's burden could not simply be put down. In such a context anti-imperialism remained a toothless phenomenon. The so-called 'crisis' of 1869–70 when Gladstone and his Colonial Secretary, Lord Granville, are supposed to have tried to dismantle the empire, was no more than an unusually zealous attempt to revive the flagging idea of retrenchment. And while there would long continue to be a sizeable body of imperial 'minimalists' on the Liberal side, not even they were prepared to call for the actual dissolution of the empire as a whole.

There was an irony in all this because the economic argument of the mid-Victorian critics of Empire that the whole ramshackle edifice represented a great haemorrhage for the British economy, and above all for Britain's poor, may well have been correct. Certainly some modern calculations, though complex and not undisputed, suggest that many of the things which supposedly made the empire worthwhile—emigration, high returns on capital investment, increased trade—were not in the end sufficiently powerful to transform a vast expenditure upon administration and defence

---

[95] Hyam, *Imperial Century*, 37–40; D. A. Lorimer, *Colour, Class and the Victorians: English Attitudes to the Negro in the Mid-Nineteenth Century* (Leicester, 1978), 131–61, 178–200.

into an overall balance of financial gain.[96] Throughout the late nineteenth century the United Kingdom was more highly taxed on a per caput basis than any comparable country—more highly taxed too than either the dominions, the colonies proper, or India—largely because of the defence costs imposed by imperial responsibilities. In addition, all parts of the empire benefited from a variety of other 'subsidies': cash grants, cheap services of various kinds, favoured access to London capital markets, and so forth. Only India paid for its own defence, while the dominions contributed so little that they were able to spend far more upon welfare and health than would have been possible had they been independent states.[97]

This is of course to talk in aggregate terms (though it certainly suggests that the Victorian state was perhaps less 'minimal' than is sometimes supposed). For certain individuals and certain groups the empire undoubtedly proved splendidly rewarding, with the result that in imperial terms the prosperous classes, especially financiers, merchants, shippers, and the like, did well, while the majority of the people continued cheerfully and even proudly to shoulder the tax costs of an empire from which they obtained little in the form of material gains, though—from time to time—a good deal in terms of emotional satisfaction.[98] Yet perhaps in the longer run, when war broke out in 1914 and colonies and dominions came to Britain's aid in battles fought almost entirely in Europe, the 'excessive' expenditure of the previous century suddenly turned out not to have been quite so 'excessive' after all.

If mid-Victorian ministers found it difficult to follow a consistent line in imperial matters, in foreign affairs they behaved with rather greater decisiveness, but also with rather less success. After the end of the Crimean War and the Peace of Paris of 1856 there were more countries determined to undermine than to uphold the balance of power established forty years before. Napoleon III wanted to revise the European map along national lines. Austria was more anxious than ever. Russia felt humiliated by the arrangements of 1856. Prussia was no longer the last and weakest of the five great powers—not that outside Prussia many recognized the fact.

The first big problem that confronted European statesmen in this new and unstable environment was that of Italy. With Russia following a policy

---

[96] Davis and Huttenback, *Mammon, passim*; P. K. O'Brien, 'The Costs and Benefits of British Imperialism 1846–1914', *Past & Present*, 120 (1988), 163–200. But see the critique of this view in A. Offer, 'The British Empire, 1870–1914: A Waste of Money?', *Economic History Review*, 46 (1993), 215–38.

[97] O'Brien, 'Costs and Benefits', 187–9.

[98] P. J. Cain and A. G. Hopkins, *British Imperialism: Innovation and Expansion 1688–1914* (London, 1993), 107–225.

of consistent hostility to Austria, and Prussia resentful of Austria's linger-ing hegemony in Germany, Napoleon III was able to deploy his bayonets and Palmerston and Russell their verbosities in the cause of unifying Italy around the core of the existing Sardinian state. After July 1858 when Napoleon and the Sardinian Prime Minister Cavour met at Plombières and agreed on joint military operations against Austria (which still occupied large parts of northern Italy) armed conflict became likely. In April 1859 Austria fell into the trap, invaded Sardinian territory, and within weeks was defeated by the allies at the battles of Magenta and Solferino. At precisely the same time Westminster was witnessing the replacement of Derby's administration by that of Palmerston. The confusions of this latter process rather than any significant change in approach (for there was none) gave an added touch of uncertainty to British policy during these crucial months. Malmesbury, the Tory Foreign Secretary, was not really more pro-Austrian than his successor, Russell, though he was sometimes considered so. His personal dislike of Cavour and King Victor Emmanuel—'an Italian attorney and a tambour major' as he once famously called them—had no effect on policy.[99] Devious enough to dangle vague promises in front of Pope Pius IX when seeking Catholic support for Tories in Ireland during the general election of June 1859 he none the less fully shared contempor-ary Protestant dislike for the Pope's temporal sovereignty over large parts of central Italy.[100]

Queen Victoria was a more active friend of Austria. But though she managed to tone down the language of dispatches, Palmerston and Russell were usually able to have things their own way.[101] What rendered the British position so complicated was the fact that, while only Napoleon could push Italian unity along, he also represented a potential threat to British interests in all sorts of ways. And, indeed, the necessity of reconcil-ing anti-French sentiments with pro-Italian attitudes inevitably produced tensions within the cabinet and gave British policy a reactive rather than a creative character, especially when the speed of events in Italy itself took almost everyone by surprise. Palmerston famously claimed that he was 'very Austrian north of the Alps, but very anti-Austrian south of the

---

[99] F. A. Wellesley (ed.), *The Paris Embassy during the Second Empire* (London, 1928), 175; Beales, *England and Italy*, 44–5.

[100] Hawkins, *Art of Politics*, 192–3; C. T. McIntire, *England against the Papacy 1858–61: Tories, Liberals and the Overthrow of Papal Temporal Power* (Cambridge, 1983), 107–8; Hoppen, 'Tories, Catholics', 48–67.

[101] H. Hearder, 'Queen Victoria and Foreign Policy: Royal Intervention in the Italian Question 1859–60', in K. Bourne and D. C. Watt (eds.), *Studies in International History* (London, 1967), 172–88.

228 THE FABRIC OF POLITICS

Alps',[102] by which he meant that a geographically central power on the continent without territorial ambitions, whose material interests did not clash with those of Britain, was a splendid thing, but that Austria's governance of northern Italy was abominable. Yet however logical and convenient such an analysis might be, it carried with it equally logical consequences regarding Austrian power and Italian unification which its author was slow to grasp. Gladstone, for his part, looked to racial explanations and publicly wanted to know 'whether anywhere in Christendom there be an instance corresponding with the Austrian power in Italy; an instance where a people glaringly inferior in refinement rule . . . over a race much more advanced'.[103]

Such philo-Italianism was of course common currency among contemporary political and intellectual élites. It suffused almost all versions of liberalism, had much to do with the regard in which educated Victorians held the ancient classics, was part, indeed, of that 'Mediterranean passion' so characteristic of the age.[104] It also, for some at least, drew particular nourishment from a distrust of Catholicism, with the new anticlerical Italy of Cavour welcomed as a potential antidote to the benighted superstitions of Rome and the Popes. But while most British politicians wanted more constitutionalism in Italy and perhaps even a reduction in the number of separate states, none wanted any accretion of power to the French and few, to begin with, wanted complete unity. Indeed, as late as August 1859 Russell still thought that a single united Italy would 'make a despotism instead of a free government'.[105] Not until Garibaldi's campaign in Sicily and the southern mainland was well under way (the Straits of Messina were crossed on 18/19 August 1860) did British policy-makers become wedded to the concept of a united Italy as the best solution in the circumstances. And it was only then, too, that Gladstone began to move from his initial support in 1859 for a North Italian kingdom in amicable relationship with Austria to his later view of 1866 that the process towards complete unification had been perhaps 'one of the noblest works of recent times'.[106]

Even the news which became public in March 1860 that Napoleon was to receive Nice and Savoy from Sardinia in payment for services rendered,

---

[102] Palmerston to Granville, 30 Jan. 1859, Lord E. Fitzmaurice, *The Life of Granville George Leveson Gower Second Earl Granville*, 2 vols. (London, 1905), i. 325.

[103] 'War in Italy', *Quarterly Review*, 105 (1859), 549–50.

[104] R. Jenkyns, *The Victorians and Ancient Greece* (Oxford, 1980); J. Pemble, *The Mediterranean Passion: Victorians and Edwardians in the South* (Oxford, 1987).

[105] R. W. Seton-Watson, *Britain in Europe 1789–1914* (Cambridge, 1937), 411–12; Beales, *England and Italy*, 95–6.

[106] *Hansard*, clxxxiv. 1242 (20 July 1866); K. A. P. Sandiford, 'Gladstone and the Liberal-Nationalist Movements', *Albion*, 13 (1981), 30–1.

though it fuelled Francophobe sentiment, failed to dampen the new-found enthusiasm for unification under the auspices of Cavour and Victor Emmanuel. Italy, indeed, became a kind of theatre within which British Liberals could declaim their lines in a manner as pleasing to themselves as to their Italian admirers (who in the mean time were rigging referendums in Modena, Parma, Tuscany, and the Romagna with an enthusiasm that made the Catholic clergy of Ireland—invariably accused by British politicians of electoral 'interference'—seem the merest amateurs).[107] Russell's famous dispatch of 27 October 1860 provided the final and public seal of approval. Sent to the minister at Turin with Palmerston's agreement (but without that of the cabinet) it announced the pleasure of 'Her Majesty's Government' at 'the gratifying prospect of a people building up the edifice of their liberties and consolidating the work of independence, amid the sympathy and good wishes of Europe'.[108]

This was, indeed, a far more revolutionary document than Lamartine's celebrated circular of March 1848 (which had merely denounced the Vienna settlement in the name of France and not, as Russell was doing, in the name of any people who might feel themselves strong enough to overthrow it). For traditionalists like the Russian ambassador in London the equation of 'Europe' with peoples rather than monarchies was no more than a crude joke.[109] For Russell, with his Whig historical sense, it was simply the logical working out on a continental stage of the Glorious Revolution, an episode of such mystic significance for him that he could not restrain himself from lecturing even the Queen about how 'the right of deposing princes who violate their word, and subvert the fundamental laws' had been 'fought for, bled for, and established by the Revolution of 1688'.[110]

Events in Italy in 1859–60 seemed to confirm the belief of ministers that ringing declarations by Britain could achieve results for which lesser nations required gunpowder and shot. But because 'prestige' is a wasting asset if not physically augmented and renewed, Italy turned out to be a British triumph in only the very shortest of runs. A revealing insight into the contradictions involved was provided by Garibaldi's visit to England in

---

[107] McIntire, *England against the Papacy*, 184–7, K. T. Hoppen, 'Priests at the Hustings: Ecclesiastical Electioneering in Nineteenth-Century Ireland', in E. Posada-Carbó (ed.), *Elections Before Democracy: The History of Elections in Europe and Latin America* (London, 1996), 117–38.

[108] Seton-Watson, *Britain in Europe*, 409.

[109] A. J. P. Taylor, *The Struggle for Mastery in Europe 1848–1918* (Oxford, 1954), 124; Earl of Malmesbury, *Memoirs*, 529.

[110] Russell to Queen Victoria, 12 Jan. 1860, *Later Correspondence of Russell*, ed. Gooch, ii. 255.

April 1864. Huge crowds—500,000 said some—turned up to greet him at the railway station. Whig and Tory leaders (with the notable exception of Disraeli) thronged to meet him as they might a new arrival at the zoo. 'His face', recorded Lord Stanley, 'is manly and pleasant: his habits not equally so: he smokes in the house, spits abundantly, goes to bed when he pleases, and breakfasts before any one else is up.'[111] It was not long before the hero became an embarrassment, the personification of revolution close at hand seeming altogether less attractive than the idea of unification far away. As enthusiasm among the populace and in extreme radical circles increased, so Gladstone, Palmerston, and others worked frantically to put their guest upon the next ship home. Eventually they 'persuaded' him to abandon a provincial tour and, pleading ill health, to retire sooner than planned from the land of liberty, liberalism, and the Revolution of 1688.[112]

If Italian affairs gave the impression that, on the British side, declarations could do perfect duty for actions, the American Civil War of 1861–5 reinforced the feeling that a refusal to become involved militarily was the best policy in an increasingly shark-infested world. The fact that neutrality was accompanied by recognition of the belligerent rights (though not the independence) of the Confederate States angered the North. The fact that Britain did not prevent the North from blockading Southern ports (even though the blockade was so feeble it could hardly be considered legal in international law) angered the Confederacy. In July 1862 the Southern commerce raider *Alabama* was allowed to leave Birkenhead to embark upon a devastating career destroying Union shipping. Eight months earlier, transatlantic war had seemed nearer still when Lincoln's navy had stopped the British steamer *Trent* and removed from it two Confederate agents, Mason and Slidell. Such matters were rendered the more dangerous because the Northern Secretary of State, W. H. Seward, was rabidly anti-British and, until late in 1862, Palmerston, Russell, and Gladstone all believed the Confederacy would win. Gladstone in particular favoured the South and made a notorious speech at Newcastle in October 1862 in which he declared that 'Jefferson Davis and other leaders of the South have made an army; they are making, it appears, a navy; and they have made what is more than either, they have made a nation.'[113] Fortunately Palmerston, who never shared Gladstone's contempt for the readiness of what the

---

[111] *Disraeli, Derby*, ed. Vincent, p. 213.

[112] D. Beales, 'Garibaldi in England: The Politics of Italian Enthusiasm', in J. A. Davis and P. Ginsborg (eds.), *Society and Politics in the Age of the Risorgimento* (Cambridge, 1991), 184–216.

[113] Krein, *Last Palmerston Government*, 62–76; Morley, *Life of Gladstone*, ii. 79.

latter called 'negrophilists' to 'sacrifice three white lives in order to set free one black man',[114] saw sense before it was too late.

In the end Britain managed to keep to the least bad path through the diplomatic minefields of the Civil War, partly by good sense, mostly by good fortune. And if the war provided Gladstone with an undoubted banana skin—he was never allowed to forget the Newcastle speech—it also supplied one of those 'insights' essential to his continuing metamorphosis from Peelite to popular Liberal politician, in this case the belief that Lancashire textile operatives had stoically endured the cotton famine created by the Civil War with, as Gladstone put it, 'no murmuring against the dispensations of God; no complaining against man; no envious comparison of their case with the case of their employers'.[115] Although such sentiments certainly involved a good deal of wishful thinking, working-class Lancashire's supposed reactions to the American Civil War undoubtedly provided Gladstone with a pearl of great political price, namely, the conviction that skilled working men were fit to enter within the constitution's pale.

While the American War had been handled with some success, European events continued to reveal the increasingly mirage-like nature of Britain's influence abroad. A Polish rebellion against Russian rule in early 1863 set off those rhetorical fireworks that had, at all levels, now become Britain's characteristic mode: confident condemnations of tsarism combined with a distinct refusal to offer tangible aid should Napoleon III decide to launch military operations to help the rebel forces. Briefly Poland became a fashionable cause. Catholic MPs supported fellow-Catholics. Palmerston disliked Russia. Disraeli told the Commons that the movement for Polish independence possessed 'all the elements of a sound cause, the love of country, the memory of a glorious past, and . . . the inspiration of a triumphant future'.[116] Palmerston and Russell handled the matter with singular ineptitude: when one was prepared to act sensibly, the other would not. Palmerston especially nurtured fantastical expectations of Polish success and seems to have hoped that Napoleon could somehow be persuaded to do all the hard work and then allow Britain to bask in any victories that might ensue.[117] Even the normally cynical Lord Robert Cecil (the future 3rd Marquess of Salisbury) could not tear himself away from the notion that 'protests' and 'declarations' were a sovereign remedy for foreign troubles. 'The idea of war', he told the Commons, 'was absurd. This country could

[114] *Disraeli, Derby*, ed. Vincent, p. 219 (23 June 1864).
[115] Shannon, *Gladstone*, 476.   [116] *Hansard*, clix. 943 (27 Feb. 1863).
[117] Krein, *Last Palmerston Government*, 98–118; W. E. Mosse, 'England and the Polish Insurrection of 1863', *English Historical Review*, 71 (1956), 28–55.

not reach Poland . . . But the great point in this matter was that we were bound to record our protest against a great violation of public law.'[118]

If Britain's reactions to the Polish rebellion revealed that the moral force diplomacy which Palmerston and Russell had applied with seeming success in Italy was at bottom a hollow thing, subsequent events drove the message home. In the Polish drama Bismarck (Minister-President of Prussia since 1862) had played no more than a supporting part. In the revival in 1864 of that other hardy perennial, the matter of Schleswig-Holstein, he cast himself in an unambiguously leading role, though contemporaries differed as to whether it was that of German hero or demon king.

Neither the Germans nor the Danes had shown much loyalty to the principles enshrined in the Treaty of London of 1852. The props underpinning that settlement—jealousy between Prussia and Austria, Anglo-Russian co-operation in northern Europe, the goodwill of France—had, one by one, been knocked away by the Crimean War, the Italian Question, and the Polish revolt.[119] Buoyed up by illusions of nationalist grandeur the Danes promulgated a separation of the two duchies (united to Denmark only because they happened to share the same ruler) by fully incorporating the more northerly Schleswig into Denmark itself in March 1863—an act of folly and undoubted illegality. British ministers desperately tried to mount a mediation. Not only, however, did Napoleon reject any kind of co-ordinated action, but a common fear of diplomatic isolation and possible French expansion eastwards drew Prussia and Austria into temporary but effective alliance against Denmark. In July 1863 Palmerston (without consulting the cabinet) told the Commons that those threatening the 'integrity' of Denmark 'would find in the result, that it would not be Denmark alone with which they would have to contend'.[120] Although this was less important in bolstering Danish belligerency than is sometimes supposed, it certainly rendered Britain foolish when, in December 1863, troops under the control of the German Confederation occupied Holstein (which actually belonged to that curious entity) and, even more so, when shortly thereafter joint Austrian and Prussian forces moved northwards into Schleswig as well.

Caught between a pacifically minded cabinet and a resolutely pro-German Queen, on the one side, and an excited pro-Danish public opinion, on the other, Palmerston and Russell squirmed uneasily between strong words and a realization that, in the face of French refusals, strong actions

[118] *Hansard*, clxix. 920 (27 Feb. 1863).

[119] K. A. P. Sandiford, *Great Britain and the Schleswig-Holstein Question 1848–64* (Toronto, 1975), 30–66.

[120] *Hansard*, clxxii. 1252 (23 July 1863).

were no longer even remotely practicable. Palmerston in particular was finding it almost impossible to adjust his policies to meet the first intimations of the new Bismarckian age. 'If no diplomatic action was ever to take place', he told the cabinet in January 1864, 'unless there was beforehand a formed intention to follow it up by force there would be an end to all negotiation.'[121] But, though this was perhaps reasonable enough as a general comment, it was no more than a bewildered excuse in circumstances in which its author had not even begun to confront the strategic realities of the day.

An international conference on Schleswig-Holstein began its deliberations in London towards the end of April 1864. In mid-June it broke up in confusion, Prussia having played a clever and Denmark a remarkably foolish part in undermining the various solutions put forward. As war began anew, Russell proposed all sorts of pro-Danish bellicosities if Austria and Prussia refused arbitration. Not only, however, did the Queen and the majority of ministers firmly reject such ideas, but Palmerston, having decided that only Danish concessions could now save anything from the wreckage, would have nothing to do with them either.[122] Britain, in truth, had simply become irrelevant. In June an armistice was agreed and in October 1864 Christian IX ceded his rights over the duchies to Prussia and Austria jointly.

At home the opposition (whose own behaviour during the crisis had been no more percipient than that of the government) sensed that attack might at last yield greater dividends than inactivity. Already in February Derby had lashed Russell for presiding at the Foreign Office over a policy of 'meddle and muddle', of 'lecturing, scolding, blustering, and retreating', of making it clear that for all his roaring he was 'no lion at all, but only Snug the joiner'.[123] Now Disraeli, with all the easy skill of being wise after the event, lampooned the London Conference for lasting 'as long as a Carnival' and, like a carnival, for having been no more than 'an affair of masks and mystifications'.[124] Such comments did not, however, address the central issue: that Britain's gambit of seeking to exercise influence on the cheap had been tested and found wanting. As Lord Robert Cecil put it in July

As long as the public fancied that we could obtain the aid of Russia or France in a Baltic war, the war feeling ran breast high for Denmark; but as soon as the fact dawned upon them that some sacrifice might be necessary to save their friends,

---

[121] Krein, *Last Palmerston Government*, 139.
[122] L. D. Steefel, *The Schleswig-Holstein Question* (Cambridge, Mass., 1932), 203–43; Sandiford, *Schleswig-Holstein Question*, 109.
[123] *Hansard*, clxxiii. 28 (4 Feb. 1864).   [124] *Hansard*, clxxvi. 743 (4 July 1864).

they contented themselves with what Lord Palmerston euphemistically calls 'honourable sympathies'.[125]

No wonder that, less than two months later, Count von Moltke came to the conclusion that 'England is as powerless on the Continent as she is presuming'.[126]

Not only, however, was the foreign policy of British governments in the 1860s affected by the conjuncture of armed weakness and post-Crimean fatigue, but ministers—like so many others in Europe—were slow to grasp the extent to which international relativities were being changed by the growth of Bismarckian Prussia. Almost without exception they continued to regard France as the greatest continental power. Palmerston never ceased to believe that this was so and insisted only days before his death that

Prussia is too weak as she now is to be honest or independent in her action; and, with a view to the future, it is desirable that Germany, in the aggregate, should be strong, in order to control those two ambitious and aggressive powers, France and Russia, that press upon her west and east. As to France, we know how restless and aggressive she is, and how ready to break loose for Belgium, for the Rhine, for anything she would be likely to get without too great an exertion.[127]

But while Russell (and indeed many others) held similar views, British ministers entirely failed to develop any consistent or viable policy towards France in these years. Friendly overtures were interrupted by invasion scares and fear was so often mingled with contempt that the description of Napoleon III offered by the ambassador in Paris might as readily, in this respect at least, have been applied to Palmerston himself. 'I do not', wrote Lord Cowley in 1862, 'believe the Emperor to have any fixed policy at all. He [merely] has certain ideas and desires floating in his mind which turn up as circumstances seem favourable.'[128]

When in 1866 Bismarck turned on his erstwhile partner and inflicted a crushing defeat upon Austria at Königgrätz (Sadowa) on 3 July, the cabinet persuaded itself that as 'neither English honour nor English interests' were involved it would be best to allow the new continental 'realism' to develop unchecked.[129] It mattered little who was in office. Indeed, the tired frankness of Clarendon's remark of May 1866 that 'we are willing to do anything

---

[125] 'The House of Commons', Quarterly Review, 116 (1864), 276.

[126] A. A. W. Ramsay, Idealism and Foreign Policy: A Study of the Relations of Great Britain with Germany and France, 1860–1878 (London, 1925), 143.

[127] Palmerston to Russell, 13 Sept. 1865, Ashley, Life of Palmerston, ii. 446.

[128] Scherer, 'Partner or Puppet?', 347–71; Wellesley (ed.), Paris Embassy, 237.

[129] Clarendon to Queen Victoria, 31 Mar. 1866, The Letters of Queen Victoria, 2nd ser., ed. G. E. Buckle, 2 vols. (London, 1926), ii. 315.

for the maintenance of peace except committing ourselves to a policy of action'[130] was raised by Stanley, his Tory successor at the Foreign Office, into a virtual theology of non-intervention. In November he went so far as to exclude entirely the affairs of Western Europe from the eight chief matters 'under discussion' in the Foreign Office, while throughout the following year negotiations with the United States worried him far more than the possibility of 'a war between France and Germany', which, 'though disagreeable would not for us be dangerous'.[131]

Towards the end of his career Palmerston had come more and more to resemble a poker player who regularly and predictably outbids the value of his cards. Stanley went further by actually revealing the feebleness of his hands to anyone who cared to look. This might of course be seen as an acceptance of the inevitable and it is true that Stanley displayed a welcome honesty in realizing that without reliable allies and a substantial army a high degree of circumspection could hardly be avoided. But it was the uninspired way he handled affairs and the manner in which he unerringly found plausible justifications for doing nothing that rendered a weak inheritance weaker still. The government's impotent fastidiousness reached a pinnacle in May 1867 at the conclusion of the London Conference called to discuss France's claim for 'compensation' (more precisely Luxembourg) to balance Prussian gains the previous year. On 11 May a treaty was signed by the major powers guaranteeing Luxembourg's neutrality. Almost immediately Derby (who was both Prime Minister and Stanley's father) publicly disabused those who might think that this amounted to anything more than shadows. 'The guarantee', he explained, 'is not a joint and separate guarantee, but is a collective guarantee, and does not impose upon this country any special and separate duty of enforcing its provisions.'[132]

Clarendon, who took over as Foreign Secretary again in December 1868 as a member of Gladstone's first administration, had more finesse, slightly more sympathy for France, but no more international influence. Bismarck's later claim that had Clarendon lived beyond June 1870 his efforts might have prevented war between Prussia and France was little more than mischief-making.[133] His successor, Lord Granville, had the confidence

---

[130] R. Millman, *British Foreign Policy and the Coming of the Franco-Prussian War* (Oxford, 1965), 21.

[131] *Disraeli, Derby*, ed. Vincent, p. 269 (1 Nov. 1866) and p. 326 (31 Dec. 1867).

[132] *Hansard*, clxxxvii. 379 (13 May 1867).

[133] H. Maxwell, *The Life and Correspondence of George William Frederick Fourth Earl of Clarendon*, 2 vols. (London, 1913), ii. 366; J. L. Herkless, 'Lord Clarendon's Attempt at Franco-Prussian Disarmament, January to March 1870', *Historical Journal*, 15 (1972), 455–70.

of the Queen, generous supplies of feline tact, and a talent for trailing behind events. His efforts to mediate between a Napoleon III bent on making dramatic material gains and a Bismarck equally determined to unite Germany around the Hohenzollerns could hardly, in any case, have succeeded even if undertaken by a statesman of measureless skill and dexterity. As it was, the actions which he and the cabinet eventually took were more suited to solving a dispute over fishing rights than a major controversy between two great European powers like Prussia and France.

On the very day of the Battle of Königgrätz in 1866 Disraeli offered a commentary upon England's position in the contemporary world. 'It is not', he declared,

that England has taken refuge in a state of apathy, that she now almost systematically declines to interfere in the affairs of the Continent of Europe. England is as ready and as willing to interfere as in the old days, when the necessity of her position requires it. There is no Power, indeed, that interferes more than England. She interferes in Asia, because she is really more an Asiatic Power than a European. She interferes in Australia, in Africa, and New Zealand.[134]

As so often with Disraeli, the rolling phrases contained both truth and illusion. The illusion was the belief that, despite a changing Europe and Britain's lack of military might, one could still make significant choices in the handling of continental problems and continental powers. The truth sprang of course from the growth of the empire. Here certainly there was a makeweight for Britain's decline as an international force, and—best of all perhaps from Disraeli's point of view—one that offered enough scope for 'interference' to satisfy even the most enthusiastic disciples of meddlesomeness.

[134] Monypenny and Buckle, *Disraeli*, iv. 467.

CHAPTER 8

Reform and Electoral Politics

I. QUESTIONS OF REFORM

In the twenty years before 1865 the cause of franchise reform, though it generated sporadic bouts of ill-coordinated activity, came at times to resemble nothing so much as a corpse on the dissecting table. Its supporters—bereft of influence, cohesion, and staying power—remained rich only in the ability to irritate and to bore. After the collapse of Chartism as a major political phenomenon in 1848 there was no general or effective reform movement. Under Sir Joshua Walmsley, and with occasional support from Cobden and Bright, the Parliamentary and Financial Reform Association organized a strikingly unsuccessful campaign between 1849 and 1852. The announcement in 1848 by Lord John Russell that he no longer thought the reforms of 1832 'final' failed to arouse the nation.[1] Only Westminster seemed at all keen. Some seventy Radical MPs doggedly supported motions brought forward by members like P. J. Locke King aimed at assimilating the county to the more generous borough franchise and introducing the secret ballot. Official bills issued forth from Russell's Liberal administration in 1852, Aberdeen's coalition in 1854, Derby's Tory government in 1859, and Palmerston's Liberal government in 1860. All sank beneath the waves. Indifference rather than opposition stood in the way. Almost no significant leader was completely opposed. Some, like Russell, were committed. Some, like Derby and Disraeli, hoped to revive party fortunes with superficially bold but practically anodyne proposals. Some, like Palmerston, were at least prepared to take up the question as a flag of truce towards more radical elements. But while a growing body of MPs wanted reform, they did not want it very much and could not agree as to the shape it should take. The nation, however, seemed apathetic. In 1856 Cobden thought one 'might as well call out for the millennium'.[2] Even the

---

[1] But see R. Quinault, '1848 and Parliamentary Reform', *Historical Journal*, 31 (1988), 831–51.
[2] D. G. Wright, *Democracy and Reform 1815–1885* (London, 1970), 127.

one substantial piece of reform legislation from these years—the Irish Franchise Act of 1850 (which greatly altered the nature of the electorate in Ireland)—was passed, not because of public pressure or official enthusiasm, but because the Great Famine had so reduced the number of voters that something simply 'had to be done'.[3]

What is most significant about the way in which the franchise was handled after 1848 is that at the level of theory and of potential practice the question was treated with a crab-like mixture of sympathy and anxious reservation. The three most prominent contemporary writers on the matter appeared in print in the late 1850s. Thomas Hare's *Machinery of Representation* (1857) pushed the idea of proportional representation. Earl Grey's *Parliamentary Government* (1858) argued that only an adequate presence in parliament of the various 'interests' in society brought about by means of specially reserved seats could ensure efficient administration. John Stuart Mill's *Thoughts on Parliamentary Reform* (1859) extended Hare's ideas and demanded more cerebral government and an end to corruption. Such writers shared two important characteristics: they saw change in terms of tying up the loose ends of 1832 and they denied that citizens possessed any 'natural rights' to the vote. Thoroughgoing opponents of reform said little. Two dull Tory ministers (Henley and Walpole) resigned in protest over Disraeli's bill of 1859. The rest, very effectively in the circumstances, relied upon a silence as unintentionally cunning as it was intellectually appropriate. Only in the heat of constituency electioneering did the mask of indifference occasionally slip—as at the Sheffield hustings of 1857 when a voter's shout of 'The more [voters] the better' was met with a brisk 'I say the more the worse'.[4]

The thread running through almost all arguments for reform between 1848 and 1865 was that of caution. Common to every serious proposal was the question of numbers: how many additional voters should be admitted, who should they be, how would they behave? It is sometimes suggested that the electorate grew markedly after 1832 as inflation eroded the money values laid down as the basis for enfranchisement by the Reform Acts of that year. This is to confuse totals with proportions, for, while the number on the electoral registers in England and Wales rose from 652,777 in 1833 to 1,056,659 in 1866 and while this increase was somewhat greater than the rise in overall population, the changing age structure of the people meant that voters (allowances being made for duplicate and plural entries) moved

[3] K. T. Hoppen, *Elections, Politics, and Society in Ireland 1832–1885* (Oxford, 1984), 16–18.
[4] *Sheffield Independent*, 21 Mar. 1857.

undramatically from about 17.2 per cent of all adult males to about 18.4 per cent over the same period. In Scotland and Ireland the proportions (13.4 per cent in both countries in 1861) were lower still.[5] Only to a very limited extent, therefore, did growing prosperity impair the key franchise barriers set up in 1832: occupation of a £10 house in boroughs, and in counties the possession of a 40s. freehold or payment of £50 a year in rent (with somewhat different requirements in Ireland and very different ones in Scotland where a system of feudal property law produced complications of high impenetrability).

After 1848 only a handful of marginal extremists advocated complete manhood—let alone universal—enfranchisement. Most reformers played variations on the numbers game. Russell in 1853 wanted to include only such as had given 'a proof of prudence'. In 1860 he hoped his bill would admit 'that large number of the working classes who, by their knowledge, their character, and their qualifications, are fitted to exercise the franchise freely and independently'.[6] What no one, Liberals and Tories alike, wanted was the admission of the 'residuum', that elastically defined 'class of persons' inhabiting 'the corners of the streets of the Seven Dials...the hordes of Irish labourers...the class who, in common parliamentary language, was designated as the dangerous class'.[7] So-called 'fancy' franchises were devised to admit respectable men with deposits in savings banks, university degrees, dividend incomes of £10 a year—the permutations were endless. In 1852 and 1854 the borough franchise was to be £6. In 1859 it was to remain at £10. In 1860 Russell reverted to £6. In 1866 Gladstone opted for £7. Caution was further enshrined in the modesty of the proposals for redistributing constituencies brought forward in 1854, 1859, and 1860 (there were none at all in 1852), all designed to do no more than cut out a few small boroughs and increase the number of MPs in a few under-represented counties.

Though the reform movement remained noisy enough, it failed to mobilize support from traditionally responsive parts of the country such as the manufacturing north-west and metropolitan London.[8] None the less, most leading politicians favoured some kind of reform. The practical

[5] C. Seymour, *Electoral Reform in England and Wales: The Development of the Parliamentary Franchise, 1832–1885* (New Haven, 1915), 533; K. T. Hoppen, 'The Franchise and Electoral Politics in England and Ireland 1832–1885', *History*, 70 (1985), 202–17.

[6] F. B. Smith, '"Democracy" in the Second Reform Debates', *Historical Studies*, 11 (1964), 306; *Hansard*, clvi. 2052 (1 Mar. 1860).

[7] George Leeman (a supporter of the secret ballot) in *Hansard*, clxxxii. 2127 (26 Apr. 1866).

[8] M. Taylor, *The Decline of British Radicalism 1847–1860* (Oxford, 1995), 159.

reasons for this are not easy to discover. The electoral behaviour of those few constituencies which already had working-class majorities in their electorates (because of the survival of so-called 'ancient' franchises) yielded no clear message as regards morality or partisan benefit.[9] Indeed, few strong party preferences could or can be discovered among the various social gradations in the electorate before 1867. What most probably kept the reform cause on the political agenda and gave its mid-century manifestations their characteristic air of mild but persistent solicitude was a change in the way those involved in the formal institutions of the state regarded working people in general. Many began to believe that the heat was being taken out of social antagonisms; that, occasional strikes notwithstanding, physical force and revolution were giving way to gradualism under the impress of prosperity. Self-congratulation was to be heard throughout the land, particularly in the shape of the so-called 'Rochdale' argument—named after the town famed for its co-operative movement and for an electorate which, while returning a steady stream of Radicals to parliament, actually contained one of the smallest working-class elements of any in the nation. Heartening statistics recorded the growing enthusiasm of small investors for savings banks: the amount per head on deposit rose from £1. 6s. 2d. in 1841–5 to £2. 16s. 5d. in 1881–5. Good behaviour during the shilling days at the Great Exhibition of 1851 caused much gratification and surprise. Newspapers thought working men 'more intelligent, more self-reliant, more energetic . . . ashamed of their former prejudices'. In 1865 Edward Baines—ardent Liberal MP, Congregationalist, teetotaller, voluntary educationist, and owner of the *Leeds Mercury*—rhapsodized at a meeting of Yorkshire artisans about the distance travelled since the 1830s when working men had indeed been 'ignorant and destitute of education and intelligence'. A Bradford Radical in 1867 was not alone in feeling sure that working men would repay any concessions 'by cherishing a feeling of gratitude, which would make them all feel that they were brethren in the land, and that it was no longer a nation divided against itself'.[10]

At the core of such attitudes lay the belief that skilled manual workers were abandoning the suspicions and violence of earlier decades in favour of

[9] According to an official inquiry a majority of voters in eight boroughs supported 'themselves by daily manual labour' usually as non-industrial artisans and the like (*Return of the Several Parliamentary Cities and Boroughs in England and Wales, arranged in order according to the Proportion of Electors belonging to the Working Classes*, H[ouse of] C[ommons] Paper] 1866 (170), lvii. 47–51). Of the fourteen seats at stake, nine went Liberal in 1859 and nine Tory in 1865—on both occasions rather against trends.

[10] T. R. Tholfsen, 'The Transition to Democracy in Victorian England', *International Review of Social History*, 6 (1961), 230–1; id., *Working Class Radicalism in Mid-Victorian England* (London, 1976), 317–21.

cultural alignment with the middle class. Whatever the defects of the so-called 'labour aristocracy' argument (see Chapter 3), growing mid-century perceptions that people of this kind were now dominating formal worker politics as they had not done during the more desperate moments of the Chartist agitation probably played a significant part in bringing a new political atmosphere into being. So also did the shift in employment away from depressed handicraft trades: the number of handloom weavers in Lancashire (the centre of the cotton industry) fell from 165,000 to less than 30,000 in the forty years after 1821.[11] By 1871 towns like Blackburn, with over half their working populations employed as factory operatives, were physically, economically, and culturally dominated by the factories they contained. This affected both sides of industry. On the one hand, a significant number of employers, though hostile to aggressive unionism, began to welcome organized bargaining. On the other, a growing realization that industrial capitalism had come to stay began to shape factory workers' attitudes to employers in particular and political action in general.[12]

At the same time the whole system of the law, however biased it undoubtedly remained in a social sense, was slowly beginning to take on the character of a potential instrument of class mediation. Once factory legislation, free trade, and fiscal reforms had started to diminish the bitterness of political and economic conflicts, it became possible to perceive the law as territory in which labour leaders might hope to make significant gains.[13] Middle-class Radicals responded by a new willingness to see respectable workers as allies in the greatest struggle of all, the fight against 'aristocratic domination'. For their part, artisan leaders like the shoemaker, George Odger (prominent in trade-union circles and in the Reform League of the 1860s), proudly wove into their statements of worker solidarity sentiments plucked from the same mid-century bran-tub that furnished Samuel Smiles with his notions of individual effort and self-improvement: 'Rely upon yourselves! Self-reliance,—that rising, animating, soul-stirring, heart-inspiring quality which whispers to a man;—no matter whether he be a shoemaker . . . a bricklayer or a mason . . . "Look up! There's a brighter and happier future before you" '. Even opponents of class collaboration like the 'physical force' Republican, G. J. Harney, and the London cobbler,

[11] A. E. Musson, 'Class Struggle and the Labour Aristocracy', *Social History*, 3 (1976), 335–56; G. Timmins, *The Last Shift: The Decline of Handloom Weaving in Nineteenth-Century Lancashire* (Manchester, 1993), 108–11.

[12] P. Joyce, *Work, Society and Politics: The Culture of the Factory in later Victorian England* (Brighton, 1980), 106.

[13] E. F. Biagini, *Liberty, Retrenchment and Reform: Popular Liberalism in the Age of Gladstone, 1860–1880* (Cambridge, 1992), 1–28.

George Murray, expressed themselves in this kind of language, which, by its increasingly widespread appeal, at once reflected and helped to reinforce the changing political relationships of the time.[14]

While such developments persuaded contemporaries to think of franchise reform as possible, sensible, and safe, the tentative and collusive nature of the accommodations involved might almost have been designed to keep the question from exploding into effective life. What eventually did the trick was the impact of certain developments abroad. In particular, excitement over the unification of Italy became widespread in 1859–60 and gave additional encouragement to class collaboration of various kinds. In 1862 enthusiasm for Garibaldi was attracting all sections of society. MPs hailed his endeavours for freedom and unity. Former Chartists supported anti-Catholic rallies in his honour in northern temperance halls. When the hero came to England in 1864 he was greeted, not only by enthusiastic crowds, but by leading politicians of all persuasions. The collaboration of a Working Man's Garibaldian Fund Committee and a middle-class City of London Demonstration Committee led to joint action in favour of franchise and other reforms. Similar interlocking groups supported the Northern States during the American Civil War of 1861–5 and the Poles who rebelled against Russian rule in 1863. Indeed, revolutions almost anywhere outside Britain—save in Ireland—invariably generated widespread enthusiasm and did so in a way that made Britons of all kinds feel that they had a good deal in common after all, not least a sense of superiority over lesser peoples beyond the seas.

Out of these Italian excitements the Reform League was established in February 1865. Its general ethos was that of the skilled working class, though it depended for financial support upon a few wealthy manufacturers who were not without a restraining influence. Already a series of reform initiatives in the North of England had resulted in the formation at Manchester in March 1864 of the more middle-class Reform Union, the true successor of the Anti-Corn Law movement. The League, at its peak, had some 600 branches (100 of them in London) and the Union about 150.[15] In May 1865 Robert Lowe delivered the first of his great parliamentary speeches against reform in response to a motion by Baines. The matter seemed at last to be finding a place upon the political agenda. Two developments helped give the final push: Gladstone's jerky move towards reform throughout the early 1860s and Palmerston's death in October 1865.

---

[14] R. Harrison, *Before the Socialists: Studies in Labour and Politics 1861–1881* (London, 1965), 207; Tholfsen, *Working Class Radicalism*, 308–15.

[15] Harrison, *Before the Socialists*, 80, 139.

Gladstone was the figure around which the events of reform gathered and found their centre. Though consistent in his High Church defence of organic societies, he was, none the less, unusually prepared to allow particular moral passions to modify long-cherished assumptions about political behaviour and innovation. As regards reform itself he was a late convert with credentials a good deal less convincing than those of Russell. Yet in the course of the 1860s he was able—partly indeed by his very involvement in reform—to turn himself into a public figure of a new and dramatic kind. In 1859 he voted in favour of the mild Tory Reform Bill for the very conservative reason that it would preserve those small boroughs which opponents of extreme reform like himself had long defended as 'nurseries of statesmen'.[16] Indeed, a nostalgic tenderness towards electoral tradition remained at the core of Gladstone's being until the very end, surfacing most notably in his lingering reluctance over the secret ballot in the early 1870s, his defence of two-member boroughs at the time of the Third Reform Bills of 1884–5 (when he was surprised at Salisbury's want of 'respect for tradition'), and his consistent lack of interest in party organization.[17] On joining Palmerston's administration in 1859 he was not much concerned with the franchise at all, but rather with the import- ance of pressing home a certain kind of financial revolution and restraining defence expenditure while furthering as far as was safe the cause of Italian unity. Admittedly in 1860 he supported Russell's Reform Bill with preg- nant remarks about 'that body of our working men' whose conduct was 'good enough to entitle them to a share in the privileges of Parliamentary representation'—remarks nobody seems to have taken much notice of.[18]

If, however, Gladstone never took the high road to reform, his interest in finance and in foreign affairs provided him with an equally serviceable low road. Repeal of the paper duties and other financial activities in 1860–1 allied him with the Radical cause as also, to a certain extent, did his reactions to events on the European continent. Throughout the early and mid-1860s he seems, indeed, to have been actively engaged in marking out much of his later political territory: attracting Dissenters with votes on the Burials Bill in 1863 and against compulsory church rates in 1866, dropping hints about the Irish state church, making gnomic references to reform, talking to the public in new ways. The very rapidity of his evolution as a popular leader meant that he was momentarily able to associate himself with 'the conflicting aims of half the great interests of the country', with

[16] *Hansard*, cliii. 1055–9 (29 Mar. 1859).
[17] *Hansard*, cciii. 1028–34 (27 July 1870); *The Diary of Sir Edward Walter Hamilton 1880–1885*, ed. D. W. R. Bahlman, 2 vols. (Oxford, 1972), ii. 741.
[18] *Hansard*, clviii. 633 (3 May 1860).

those of the serious aristocracy and High Churchmen (his long-standing friends), of industrialists (who liked his commercial treaties), of the press (which liked his removal of its taxes), and of Radicals and Dissenters (who responded well to gestures aimed particularly at them).[19] And though his utterances invariably contained tortuous reservations, his audiences heard what they wanted to hear.

In October 1862 Gladstone undertook the first of those provincial tours—in this case to Tyneside—which were to help transform the remote parliamentarian of former years into the remote popular hero of late Victorian Liberalism. Instinctively he now found the materials for this process all about him: 'the great multitude of people', the way in which his six speeches in as many hours were 'admirably borne', the 'daring and comprehensive' engineering works along the Tyne, all united to generate 'circumstances... I do not in any way deserve'. Mrs Gladstone recalled his triumphal progress. 'Oh, I shall never forget that day! It was the first time, you know, that *he* was received as he deserved to be.'[20] Eighteen months later Gladstone was so impressed by the respectability of the trade-union delegation which had called on him as Chancellor of the Exchequer in connection with the Annuities Bill that he began (amid renewed wrangles with Palmerston over defence) to believe that modest suffrage extension might force parliament to reduce expenditure by admitting voters of a frugality similar to his own.[21]

Then came the famous speech of 11 May 1864 on Baines's Borough Suffrage Bill, a speech so convoluted and qualified that it actually went no further than Disraeli, for example, had done in 1859. Its unwarranted welcome as not only a deep insight into Gladstone's mind, but a sign of dramatic change at the top of the political tree, reflects the important position which Gladstone had begun to occupy with the public at large. What he actually said was this:

Every man who is not presumably incapacitated by some consideration of personal unfitness or of political danger is morally entitled to come within the pale of the Constitution. Of course, in giving utterance to such a proposition, I do not recede from the protest I have previously made against sudden, or violent, or excessive, or intoxicating change... What are the qualities which fit a man for the exercise of a

[19] J. Vincent, *The Formation of the Liberal Party 1857–1868* (London, 1966), 227–8.

[20] *The Gladstone Diaries*, ed. H. C. G. Matthew and M. R. D. Foot, 14 vols. (Oxford, 1968–94), vi. 152 (7 and 8 Oct. 1862); G. Battiscombe, *Mrs Gladstone: The Portrait of a Marriage* (London, 1956), 126.

[21] E. F. Biagini, 'Popular Liberals, Gladstonian Finance, and the Debate on Taxation, 1860–1874', in Biagini and A. J. Reid (eds.), *Currents of Radicalism: Popular Radicalism, Organised Labour and Party Politics in Britain, 1850–1914* (Cambridge, 1991), 134–62.

privilege such as the franchise? Self-command, self-control, respect for order, patience under suffering, confidence in the law, regard for superiors ... I admit the danger of dealing with enormous masses of men; but I am now speaking only of a limited portion of the working class ... a select portion.[22]

Later the same year Gladstone toured Yorkshire and Lancashire and made some more of the (comparatively few) outdoor speeches on which his popular reputation was soon to rest. Throughout his subsequent career, while working people *en masse* always remained obscure and dangerous to him, whenever they were presented 'in an organized and particularized form, his reaction was almost always enthusiastic'.[23] Gladstone's language to them may have been carefully qualified, but he courted his new audience by broader means, by the very fact of coming to the places where they lived.

The general election of July 1865 reflected the ambivalent nature of contemporary politics. Reform was not ignored and appeared in many candidates' addresses. But it was given little priority: government expenditure, foreign policy, church rates, and the malt tax all counted for more. The election was violent without being contentious in any national sense. The Queen's Speech hardly mentioned reform and the new parliament's first concerns turned out to be the cattle plague and Governor Eyre's activities in Jamaica. It was Palmerston's death in October that gave matters a new twist. For five years Derby and the Tories had agreed to support Palmerston against internal dissension so long as reform was left untouched. Now, not only was the truce at an end, but the Liberals themselves were deprived of effective leadership. All agreed that changes would take place, and Gladstone, in particular, was not slow to tell the Prime Minister, Russell, that any government now to be formed could not 'be wholly a continuation, it must be in some degree a new commencement'.[24] Russell, now well into his seventies and since 1861 in the House of Lords, was especially anxious to regain the image of a great reformer. On many issues—the franchise, the Irish state church, Irish land, education—he held many of the views for which Gladstone was beginning to become known, and he had held them longer, with greater consistency, and less agonizing. Yet his personality had again and again dashed the cup of recognition from his lips. He was now determined to make his mark, so much so that Gladstone (on the whole his most eager lieutenant) soon became fearful at 'Lord Russell's rapidity'.[25]

---

[22] *Hansard*, clxxv. 324–5 (11 May 1864).
[23] H. C. G. Matthew, *Gladstone 1809–1874* (Oxford, 1986), 131.
[24] S. Walpole, *The Life of Lord John Russell*, 2 vols. (London, 1891), ii. 422.
[25] J. Morley, *The Life of William Ewart Gladstone*, 3 vols. (London, 1903), ii. 154.

2. REFORM ACTS, 1867–1868

By 1865, the year in which Russell took office as Prime Minister for the second time, the vagaries of the electoral system established in 1832 (see Map 8) had come to be widely acknowledged. Sixty-seven boroughs had populations below 10,000, twenty-six populations above 50,000. The five small towns of Honiton, Totnes, Wells, Marlborough, and Knaresborough together contained less than 23,000 people but returned as many members as the 1.5 million inhabitants of Liverpool, Manchester, Birmingham, Sheffield, and Leeds. The 334 English and Welsh borough members each 'represented' 26,000 people, the 162 county members no less than 70,000 each. But if the greatest anomalies related to the distribution of constituencies, it was to the more exciting matter of the franchise in England and Wales (Scotland and Ireland were, as in 1832, to be dealt with separately and later) that the government first addressed itself. Russell's initial idea was to go for a rating franchise—that is, one based on the property valuations made in each locality for poor-rate purposes and, therefore, allegedly more 'scientific' than the existing system—set at £12 in counties and £6 in boroughs because it was believed that working people were virtually unrepresented in the electorate and should now be admitted to a modest and respectable degree. When, however, official statistics began to show that over 26 per cent of borough voters were already working men, the cabinet took fright.[26] Anxious meetings in early 1866 became more anxious still as enquiries revealed enormous local variations in value and the strong probability that any rating franchise would be highly uneven and capricious in its effects.

Cabinet disputes continued as Gladstone (the Liberal leader in the Commons) introduced a raggedly constructed bill on 12 March 1866 which now proposed a *rental* qualification of £14 in counties and £7 in boroughs coupled with the granting of the vote to supposedly 'safe' (but numerically mysterious) groups like £10 lodgers and £50 savings-bank depositors. Gladstone characteristically used statistics more to persuade himself than convince others. What he thought they seemed to suggest was that, notwithstanding the unexpected presence of horny-handed electors on the existing registers, his new proposals would still leave six middle- and upper-class voters for every four from the working class. A decade earlier he had thought an annual income of £100 (the starting-point for income tax

---

[26] *Return of the Several Parliamentary Cities and Boroughs*, HC 1866 (170), lvii. 47–51; *Electoral Returns: Boroughs and Counties, 1865–66*, HC 1866 [3626], lvii. 215–532. The criteria used by the compilers to assess which electors were 'working class' are not without ambiguity.

established in his budget of 1853) the dividing-line 'between the educated and the labouring part of the community'. He now sliced a modest third off that figure, reassuring himself that no one could pay £7 in rent every year on an income below 26s. a week, that such a sum was 'unattainable by the peasantry or mere hand labourer', and that only a select portion of skilled workers could possibly earn as much.[27] His figures, he rather unconvincingly insisted, were based on fine and accurate statistical tuning: a rental franchise of £8 would be too exclusive, £6 would produce a working-class majority, £7 alone would admit the respectable while still leaving the bulk of male working-class householders without the vote.

These were mild proposals, though Gladstone's very willingness to play so defensive a numbers game created more suspicion than it allayed. Indeed, some employer MPs, though self-proclaimed Radicals, were in such 'great terror of the amiable working class' that they actually wanted a lower franchise in the hope that this would 'reach a Class of W'm more under their Masters' influence'. Others, however, objected 'altogether to the use of the word "class" as applied to the working men of this country ... There are as many divisions and subdivisions amongst them as there are amongst any other part of the community'.[28] What eventually doomed the government was the manner in which all this unease on the Liberal benches was organized by Lord Elcho and expressed through the oratory of Robert Lowe. These two formed the core of the so-called Cave of Adullamites (Bright likened the Liberal skulkers to those the Bible, at 1 Samuel 22: 1–2, described as inhabiting the 'Cave Adullam' where 'every one that was discontented, gathered themselves'), a group which, properly speaking, never numbered more than about a dozen MPs but which was able to attract the shifting support of a much wider penumbra of back-benchers. Lowe provided speeches of rebarbative power: pessimistic, utilitarian, mesmeric in their heroic frankness. 'I shall', he announced in a famous outburst in March 1866,

say exactly what I think ... If you want venality, if you want drunkenness, and facility for being intimidated; or if, on the other hand, you want impulsive, unreflecting, and violent people, where do you look for them? ... Do you go to the top or to the bottom? ... The effect [of the bill] will manifestly be to add a large number of persons to our constituencies of the class from which if there is to be anything wrong going on we may naturally expect to find it.[29]

---

[27] *Hansard*, cxxxvii. 1592 (20 Apr. 1855) and clxxxii. 54–5 (12 Mar. 1866).
[28] F. B. Smith, *The Making of the Second Reform Bill* (Cambridge, 1966), 61; *Hansard*, clxxxii. 1439 (16 Apr. 1866).
[29] *Hansard*, clxxxii. 147–8 (13 Mar. 1866).

And all this flowed, not from Tory presuppositions, but from a kind of high-minded élitist Liberalism: franchise extension would lead to corrupt government, bellicose foreign policy, administration without vision, contempt for long-term considerations, the rule of the lowest. What is surprising is not that a core of Palmerstonians should have proved distrustful of reform proposals however mild, but that a dozen key Adullamites were at one time or another able to attract the support of about a hundred MPs— among them some who thought the bill did not go far enough. Discontent spread to every corner of the Liberal Party, its very lack of intellectual cohesion reflecting the fact of its being bound together as much by distrust of Gladstone's leadership as by dislike of reform. It was, indeed, not a doctrinal rebellion at all, but the sudden disintegration of a coalition which only the successful ambiguities of Palmerston had managed to hold together.[30]

Derby and Disraeli were astute enough to allow the Adullamites to do their work for them. Disraeli, in particular, proved remarkably successful in smashing vital sections of the government's legislation without giving the appearance of opposing all reform. Apart from Lord Cranborne (the future Prime Minister and 3rd Marquess of Salisbury, in 1866–7 a kind of Tory Lowe), Conservatives never mounted a sustained attack on the working classes as such. This left Disraeli—whose sensitivity to back-bench opinion contrasted with Gladstone's aloofness—with considerable room for manœuvre. By May 1866 Gladstone was in desperate straits: as Leader of the Commons and Chancellor of the Exchequer he had fourteen hours a day of 'other work' to do and was actually trying to sleep in the House.[31] Eventually the government was defeated on 18 June by 315 votes to 304 on an amendment moved by the Adullamite, Lord Dunkellin, aimed at substituting a rating qualification for the £7 rental in the original bill, a change which would have reduced the size of the new borough electorate. Few, however, understood the technicalities. Disraeli even defended rating (which he had rejected in his own bill of 1859) on the ludicrous grounds that the system of valuation had recently improved. On 28 June Derby became Prime Minister for the third time, once again at the head of a minority administration, with Disraeli taking over from Gladstone as Commons Leader and Chancellor of the Exchequer.

During the ensuing lull the agitation orchestrated by a number of recently founded reform movements at last took off. Disturbances in

---

[30] M. Cowling, *1867 Disraeli, Gladstone and Revolution: The Passing of the Second Reform Bill* (Cambridge, 1967), 298–9.

[31] J. Prest, *Lord John Russell* (London, 1972), 411.

Hyde Park in July caused damage to railings and flower-beds but, despite later assuming almost mythical proportions, involved much less violence than many individual constituencies had experienced in the way of rioting during the general election of the previous year. While Disraeli was unperturbed, parliamentary sceptics were, however, driven to the conclusion that the whole business was not going to disappear.

With the parliamentary session due to end in early August, the main advantage enjoyed by the new administration was that nothing much needed to be done publicly until sittings resumed in February 1867. In any case, Disraeli's first impulse was to do as little as possible because he realized—as Gladstone had not—that premature precision was likely to damage party unity. In a public show of seeming activity he and Derby drew up a series of 'Resolutions' (rather than an actual bill) for presentation to the Commons. These were anodyne and went no further than Gladstone had done. Knowing, however, that more would eventually be needed, Derby and Disraeli also cast about for some kind of franchise idea—almost any kind of franchise idea—that would mollify their followers, gain some support from Liberals, and keep the new government afloat. As early, indeed, as December 1866 Derby first hazarded the notion that 'Of all possible Hares to start I do not know a better than the extension of household suffrage, *coupled with plurality of voting*' (or giving more votes to richer than to poorer householders). Disraeli then worked on this idea and in due course managed to gain agreement for a form of household suffrage so hedged about with 'safeguards' that it amounted to very little at all. Even the obdurate General Peel (Secretary for War) proved, as Disraeli reported to his chief, on most points 'very placable, except on the phrase "household suffrage", when his eye lights up with insanity'.[32]

Disraeli introduced the Resolutions on 11 February 1867 in a speech that bored the House. Three days later, however, he misunderstood a question from a Tory back-bencher and fumbled his way into promising an immediate bill. At first Disraeli managed to fox cabinet ministers with some brisk statistical juggling into accepting rather fewer safeguards than they had expected, though plural voting based on property remained in place. But when Cranborne's sums produced very different answers, he, Carnarvon, and Peel threatened a joint resignation. Upon this the cabinet reverted to a pathetic imitation of Gladstone's bill, with £6 rating in boroughs, £20 in counties, and no plurality at all. In the House this was quickly shot down and a meeting of back-benchers came out for what was hoped would be a truly permanent settlement, namely, household suffrage limited by the

---

[32] Smith, *Second Reform Bill*, 139, 148.

requirement that voters be personal ratepayers and should have had no less than three years' residence in the same place.

What the bulk of Tories wanted was not any dramatic extension of the suffrage, but a successful Reform Bill which would set safe and lasting limits to the number of those entitled to vote. In the words of a typical back-bencher, there was 'one Principle of Vital Importance, *One* Barrier against *Manhood* Suffrage, namely, *"Personal* Rating". Upon some one Firm Basis we *must* make a stand against "Democracy"'.[33] What this referred to was the fact that in many constituencies a large number of voters, mostly of the poorer sort, did not pay their rates personally but 'compounded' to do so through their landlords who then settled with the appropriate authorities. This procedure had great fiscal advantages but virtually excluded compounders from the existing £10 franchise under which personal payment was required. Attempts had been made, and an act passed in 1851, to allow compounders to opt for personal payment and thus obtain the vote, but as this meant the loss of a useful discount, the great majority of compounders preferred to remain as they were. What Tory back-benchers and the Adullamites wanted, therefore, was to confine the new franchise only to those householders who paid their rates directly and had lived in the same place for three years rather than the one year required by existing legislation. During an angry cabinet meeting Disraeli managed to push his proposals through, with the result that Cranborne, Carnarvon, and Peel carried out their threat and resigned on 2 March.

The history of the Conservative Reform Bill is complicated in detail but simple in fundamentals. Gladstone recalled the most salient points in some autobiographical notes of old age. In the first place, 'the government... bowled us down' by the force of the phrase 'Household Suffrage' which gave the proposals a superficial coherence they did not initially possess. Secondly, 'to keep to the *drapeau* was the guiding motion... The governing idea of the man who directed the party seemed to be not so much to consider what ought to be proposed and carried as to make sure that whatever it was it should be proposed and carried by those in power'.[34] When on 18 March Disraeli finally introduced his bill he made much of the 'manliness' of household suffrage in contrast to the weasel-like ideas of the former government. His task was made easier because Gladstone was already caught upon the horns of a very real dilemma. Realizing that Disraeli would jettison one, perhaps all, of his 'safeguards' if advantage was thereby to be gained,

[33] Smith, *Second Reform Bill*, 160.
[34] *The Prime Ministers' Papers: W. E. Gladstone*, ed. J. Brooke and M. Sorensen, 4 vols. (London, 1971–81), i. 91–5.

Gladstone felt unable to accept household suffrage at all, even as a preliminary idea. For their part, bemused Tory MPs simply wanted the government to remain in power and pass a bill. Once again Liberal defections—this time in the shape of the so-called 'Tea-Room Revolt' of April—sabotaged Gladstone's initial success in puncturing Disraeli's numerical prophecies. Tories followed Disraeli out of respect for Derby, out of a desperate belief that only a Tory bill could ensure the party's survival, out of eagerness to humiliate the Liberals, and because they believed the bill's mild county proposals would keep rural constituencies safe. Some Liberals supported the bill because they disliked their leaders' abandonment of Palmerstonianism. Some Radicals did so in reaction against Gladstone's feeble efforts of 1866, because they liked the bill more and more as it proceeded, and because they feared their own side could not pass so good a measure. Gladstone's defeat was finally secured when a crucial division on 12 April went 310 to 289 in the government's favour. Forty-five Liberals voted or paired against their own side, seventeen were absent, only six Tories voted with the opposition. Gladstone recorded it 'a smash perhaps without example', though what was smashed was less his own position as Liberal leader in the Commons than his attempt to prevent reform from exceeding certain carefully defined limits.[35] Disraeli's position within his own party suddenly became much stronger. On the night of 12 April he was toasted at the Carlton Club as 'the man who rode the race, who took the time, who kept the time, and who did the trick!'[36]

All the uncertainties of a government staggering from Resolutions to a 'small' bill and then to a 'big' bill with safeguards were forgotten as Disraeli dazzled MPs with a sang-froid he did not always feel. Soon even most of the safeguards were abandoned in the desperate search for elusive majorities. First to go was the original residence requirement, which was reduced to one year. Then Disraeli accepted a lodger franchise which he had previously rejected from Gladstone and which ran a coach-and-horses through the supposedly crucial safeguard that all voters be personal ratepayers. It was oppressively hot, the smell of the Thames blew through the Commons chamber. Gladstone slept on the benches and others sweated and scratched in their heavy clothes. The complications associated with compounding proved especially troublesome until, on 17 May, Grosvenor Hodgkinson, an obscure Liberal back-bencher, moved an amendment which seemed to cut the Gordian knot by the simple device of outlawing compounding

[35] Matthew, *Gladstone 1809–1874*, 141–2.
[36] W. F. Monypenny and G. E. Buckle, *The Life of Benjamin Disraeli*, 6 vols. (London, 1910–20), iv. 533.

altogether. Disraeli accepted this without cabinet approval, thereby almost casually allowing as many as half a million additional voters on to the registers. By this time few cared much about the figures. The various safeguarding fancy franchises were ditched. Cumulative voting in the twelve new three-member constituencies (that is, allowing electors only two instead of three votes in an attempt to help minority parties) was accepted. J. S. Mill, then MP for Westminster, even managed to muster a respectable seventy-three votes in favour of female suffrage.

In two important areas Disraeli was, however, able to draw the line, partly by luck partly by design. First, the county franchise was only reduced from the originally proposed £15 to a still-formidable £12. And secondly, though fifty-two seats (mainly in small two-member boroughs) were abolished, only seventeen of these involved the disfranchisement of whole constituencies. Seven of the fifty-two were given to Scotland, twenty-five went to English counties, one to London University, and a mere nineteen to large and predominantly Liberal towns such as Birmingham, Manchester, and Leeds. These provisions constituted the most truly conservative aspects of the whole affair. A Reform Bill for Scotland and a mouse-like one for Ireland were passed in 1868 amidst the parliamentary boredom which—when no violence was involved—generally attended discussions of affairs in the outlying lands.

The real losers were the Whigs, who could no longer claim to be progressive simply by pointing to the Tories, and the Adullamites now left with nothing but their pessimism. Radicals could console themselves with the thought that they had in the end achieved a reform which in some respects lay closer to their own hopes and expectations than to those of any other significant group. Tory MPs had at last, after twenty years of frustration, achieved a real success. They were not yet in sight of the Promised Land. But at least manna had fallen from the heavens to give them sustenance for the journey ahead.

Intellectuals like Matthew Arnold and Thomas Carlyle and intellectual politicians like Cranborne and Lowe thought the world had come to an end. Arnold made the Hyde Park demonstrations a symbol of disorder in *Culture and Anarchy* (1869). Carlyle sulphurously indulged his gift for splenetic abuse: ' "Manhood Suffrage" . . . universal "glorious liberty" . . . count of Heads, the . . . Devil-appointed [way] . . . "the equality of men", any man equal to any other; Quashee Nigger to Socrates or Shakespeare; Judas Iscariot to Jesus Christ'.[37] If few Conservatives shared such fears, fewer still—and least of all Derby and Disraeli—entertained hopes of winning

---

[37] 'Shooting Niagara: And After?', *Macmillan's Magazine*, 16 (1867), 321.

many more working-class voters to their cause. Amidst much tactical flexibility, Disraeli's strategy had remained clear—to retain as best he could those aspects of the electoral system which had traditionally supported the Conservative Party. He had simply written off the majority of the boroughs as Liberal strongholds where it would do no harm to expand the electorate. While, therefore, the number of borough voters in England and Wales rose by 138 per cent from 514,026 to 1,225,042, the number of county voters did so by less than 46 per cent from 542,633 to 791,253. Between 1861 and 1871 the percentage of adult males on the electoral registers rose from 16.9 to 23.8 in the counties but from 19.7 to no less than 44.7 in the boroughs.[38] What Disraeli had rather fitfully if, in the end, quite successfully been trying to do was not to make more voters vote Conservative, but to construct a system in which Conservative voters counted for more.

During the Reform Bill's final stages Derby famously said that they had been 'making a great experiment and "taking a leap in the dark"' while expressing the 'greatest confidence in the sound sense of my fellow-countrymen'.[39] But while the former sentiment certainly reflected the Prime Minister's real views, the latter was no more than a pious hope. Disraeli, too, was soon to announce his faith in the working man. Most of this was mere persiflage, for neither Derby's nor Disraeli's broad opinions and expectations had really changed. In so far as anything now sustained them it was the belief that the electoral system still remained sufficiently anomalous, sufficiently 'unbalanced', sufficiently undemocratic, to give their party a chance to benefit from the new and mysterious changes they had introduced. Nor was this a totally unrealistic belief. Most of the new voters were corralled within the largest towns. Many boroughs with populations below 20,000 continued to return MPs. In almost eighty constituencies seats were still controlled by patrons.[40] Boroughs and counties remained clearly distinct in franchise terms. The residence qualification (even at one year) still kept a large number of men off the registers. Of all males aged 21 and above little more than a third now enjoyed the vote in England and Wales, just under a third in Scotland, and just under a sixth in Ireland. For Derby and Disraeli it was such things, not visions of urban Toryism, which gave immediate and partisan justification to what they had done.

[38] Smith, *Second Reform Bill*, 236; Hoppen, 'The Franchise', 210, 215.

[39] *Hansard*, clxxxix. 952 (6 Aug. 1867).

[40] H. J. Hanham, *Elections and Party Management: Politics in the Time of Disraeli and Gladstone* (London, 1959), 405–12.

3. ELECTIONS AND THE ELECTORAL SYSTEM

The general election of late 1868 that followed the Reform Acts was profoundly traditional, despite the Liberal Chief Whip's prediction that all would be 'new & changed & large'.[41] Although Gladstone pulled his party together with great skill, the Liberals hardly improved on their position in 1865. The ability of the Tories to hold on—not the 'ingratitude' of the electorate towards Disraeli—was the most striking aspect of the result. In retrospect it is clear that, while Gladstone would have won in 1868 with or without a Reform Act, Disraeli's success in 1874 would not have been possible had the franchise remained unchanged. Reform League agents were distressed to find voters no less venal than before and no less subject to purely local enthusiasms.[42] Few Conservatives issued clarion appeals to the newly enfranchised working men, and the Tories failed, on the whole, to attract the bulk of new voters save in parts of Lancashire, where, for example, they held Blackburn even though (and possibly because) the working-class element in that town's electorate had risen from 16 to 75 per cent.[43] By contrast, three-fifths of Tory seats were still supplied by the counties, though well under half of all MPs sat for county constituencies. Of the 114 borough seats in constituencies with more than 50,000 inhabitants, only twenty-five went to the Conservatives. No working man was elected to parliament. Such straws as did flutter in the wind, though discernible with benefit of hindsight, were few and fugitive: Conservative successes in Lancashire (with Gladstone defeated in the new South-Western constituency), some signs of middle-class movement in Greater London, a modestly increased impact in some of the largest industrial towns.

Legislation was, however, only one among many influences upon the pattern and development of electoral politics, not least because mid-Victorian constituencies (see Map 8) ranged along a lengthy continuum from comparatively straightforward deference communities to provincial capitals sustaining something close to the free exercise of political judgement. At one extreme stood the agricultural counties where property was concentrated in few hands and economic interests were comparatively uniform. Rather different, though sharing similar characteristics of influence and patronage, were the many small boroughs with compact, largely pre-

---

[41] A. F. Thompson, 'Gladstone's Whips and the General Election of 1868', *English Historical Review*, 63 (1948), 189.

[42] Harrison, *Before the Socialists*, 159–62.

[43] J. C. Lowe, 'The Tory Triumph of 1868 in Blackburn and in Lancashire', *Historical Journal*, 16 (1973), 733–48; Joyce, *Work, Society, Politics*, 203–7; R. L. Greenall, 'Popular Conservatism in Salford 1868–1886', *Northern History*, 9 (1974), 123–38.

industrial, and often bribable electorates. At the other extreme, the large
metropolitan cities had much in common with urbanized county constituencies like Staffordshire, Cheshire, and the West Riding of Yorkshire.

Yet even the most rural counties were, in electoral terms, more complicated places than is sometimes supposed. Deference—a much misused
notion—was effective as much for voluntary as for directly coercive reasons.
Landowners evoked loyalty because of their local standing and behaviour,
not simply because they were rich. Tenant farmers voted in a local as much
as in a tenurial context. They voted with their neighbours as well as for their
proprietors.[44] On the basis of strict self-interest it is difficult to see why they
remained so overwhelmingly Tory for so long. If the party of Peel had done
little for farmers, that of Derby and Disraeli did less. 'The broad but
intangible truth is that the "heavy" agriculturalists . . . and particularly the
arable farmers, suffered from Conservatism almost as an occupational disease. They seemed to inhale it from the very furrows that they ploughed.'[45]
And, indeed, the Conservative Party's ability to masquerade as an embodiment of the 'agricultural interest' sprang from a congruence of attitudes
among landlords and farmers operating most effectively at the level of
instinctive reactions and half-realized ideas. For such men, the countryside
was a world of its own, and their highly exclusive view of rural society helped
to keep the merchants and manufacturers of market towns safely inside the
Liberal camp—their 'general ideas' being, as one Tory squire noted in 1882,
'so different; their social position so vastly appart [sic]'.[46]

Disraeli's caution regarding redistribution ensured that small boroughs
remained electorally important. Between 1867 and 1885 106 of the 263
English borough members sat for towns with less than 20,000 inhabitants.
While Liberals in such places tended to represent 'the essence and core of
the town—business, shopkeeping, and craftsmanship', Tory strength
depended on a coalition of those under the hegemony of the countryside:
lawyers, doctors, clergy, schoolmasters, and so on.[47] Because Disraeli's
franchise legislation greatly increased the number of employed persons
entitled to vote, the nature of electoral behaviour may well have become
somewhat, but only somewhat, more uniform than before. In particular, the
electoral importance of vendor–customer relations in small and middling
boroughs seems to have faded as the influence of employers increased. In

[44] D. C. Moore, *The Politics of Deference: A Study of the Mid-Nineteenth Century English
Political System* (Hassocks, 1976), 19–133.
[45] R. J. Olney, *Lincolnshire Politics 1832–1885* (Oxford, 1973), 249.
[46] J. Howarth, 'The Liberal Revival in Northamptonshire, 1880–1895', *Historical Journal*, 12 (1969), 98–100, 107–8.
[47] J. Vincent, *Pollbooks: How Victorians Voted* (Cambridge, 1967), 14–15.

Lancashire especially, textile mills began to function rather like urban versions of landed estates, with many of the newly enfranchised factory workers voting either for or with their employer, because they knew him, because they respected him, because the livelihood of so many depended on his goodwill that his interests seemed the same as theirs, because they realized that the world of the factory had come to stay.[48]

With industrial towns now numerically dominated by factory workers, the culture of the mill became central to local political life. Already in 1868 one acute observer noted how the 'deeds of prowess performed' by the voters in each factory were 'proudly rehearsed by every man and boy, by every woman and girl, attached to the establishment'. At the 1874 election another found that 'in some of the factory districts they vote by mills and wards in the spirit in which schoolboys play cricket or football by "houses"'.[49] Of course crude coercion was also common, just as on landed estates, but in virtually all circumstances electoral influence proved more effective when exercised with tact than with big sticks. For many people voting as they did was a matter of the expected and the understood, a matter ultimately of common sense more than ideological discrimination. In all kinds of constituencies, poor voters gave canvassers an impression not so much of either hostility or enthusiasm, as of a kind of ill-informed but knowing suspiciousness. One Conservative canvasser kept coming across voters who 'expressed surprise when I said the Liberals had been governing the country for the last five years, and had thought, because their own member was a Conservative, that the Conservatives had been in office all that time'. Electors of this kind responded best to appeals comprehensible within their own immediate experiences. Rising prices or unemployment could influence them, so could local loyalties or antipathies. Little else mattered much.[50]

Large cities were electorally important in our period more for the way in which they sustained the beginnings of a system of mass politics than for their impact upon the composition of the House of Commons. Apart from Greater London, which returned eighteen MPs before and twenty-two after 1867, there were in 1861 only six boroughs with 200,000 inhabitants or more in the whole of the United Kingdom (two of them outside

---

[48] Joyce, *Work, Society, Politics*, 158–239; A. Russell, *Political Stability in Later Victorian England* (Lewes, 1992), 91–179.

[49] W. A. Abram, 'Social Condition and Political Prospects of the Lancashire Workmen', *Fortnightly Review*, NS 4 (1868), 439; F. Harrison, 'The Conservative Reaction', *Fortnightly Review*, NS 15 (1874), 303.

[50] Howarth, 'Liberal Revival', 109; C. E. L. Rayleigh, 'Canvassing Experiences in an Agricultural Constituency', *National Review*, 7 (1886), 180.

England). Even in 1881 there were only ten. In this handful of places there was certainly less paternalism than elsewhere—though manifestations of the art were not unknown, especially in parts of London. Broadly speaking, the upper professional groups in such constituencies were strongly Conservative, the merchants and manufacturers divided, the craft and retail trades strongly Liberal.[51] That their economic élites were often rather different from those elsewhere (commercial rather than landed or industrial) did not, however, make much impression on national political life because, from a parliamentary perspective, the United Kingdom consisted so overwhelmingly of broad acres, small-to-middling towns, and—increasingly as time went on—of the spatchcock haunts of suburbia.

Locally, involvement in electoral politics tended to mean action and ritual (often violent action and ritual) rather than decision-making. Posters and cartoons showed political leaders in sporting contests, horse and bicycle races, as pugilists. Even the fastidious John Bright was nonchalant about rioting at the Rochdale by-election of 1865. *The Times* thought 'a good fight at intervals of four or five or six years is very well'. A Liberal journalist recorded more than twenty riots involving personal injuries at the general election of 1880. In 1885 things were more exciting still—and this even though electoral riots in England were generally considered to have passed their peak and were certainly much less murderous than those of contemporary Ireland.[52] Some were, in any case, quite artificial, paid for by cash on the nail and, as such, part of the great business of electoral corruption, a business as culturally remarkable as it was broadly neutral in party-political effect.

Until the Corrupt Practices Act of 1883, contested elections were often fearsomely expensive. The official returns of cost could be striking enough—£25,781 spent by four candidates fighting for the favour of South-East Lancashire's 26,037 voters in 1880—but usually record only a fraction of what was actually spent.[53] 'Nursing' constituencies between elections added to the expense. In the Irish borough of Cashel one candidate in the 1860s ostentatiously spent £2,000 on local charities in order to

[51] D. Fraser, *Urban Politics in Victorian England* (Leicester, 1976), 228; M. B. Baer, 'Social Structure, Voting Behavior, and Political Change in Victorian London', *Albion*, 9 (1977), 227–41.

[52] D. C. Richter, *Riotous Victorians* (London, 1981), 63–71; K. T. Hoppen, 'Grammars of Electoral Violence in Nineteenth-Century England and Ireland', *English Historical Review*, 109 (1994), 597–620; *The Times*, 9 Dec. 1885.

[53] Hanham, *Elections*, 251; K. T. Hoppen, 'Roads to Democracy: Electioneering and Corruption in Nineteenth-Century England and Ireland', *History*, 81 (1996), 553–71; also C. O'Leary, *The Elimination of Corrupt Practices in British Elections 1868–1911* (Oxford, 1962) and W. B. Gwyn, *Democracy and the Cost of Politics in Britain* (London, 1962).

stand well with its 200-odd voters when next an election was called. And it was in small constituencies like this, where tightly knit groups of electoral *condottieri* were able to hold candidates to ransom, that the cost per voter was highest—occasionally as much as £40 a head. Little wonder then that in the period 1865–84 something between a third and a half of all English boroughs experienced corrupt practices on a scale sufficient to attract sustained public, and often official, notice.[54] Yet in party terms much of this was more vaporous than electoral investors liked to admit. Only a very few boroughs seem to have tuned their results to cash with quite the briskness of the Dorset town of Poole—Liberal in 1865, but then (against all trends) Tory in 1868, Liberal in 1874, and Tory again in 1880.[55] Indeed, precisely because in so many cases money was a commonplace and expected part of electoral life, the varied and colourful efforts of rival candidates—direct cash bribes, treating voters to food and drink, supplying the elderly with winter coal, getting jobs for voters and their relatives—often simply tended to cancel each other out.

Another area in which the Reform Acts of 1867–8 made little impact was the social composition of the House of Commons. Eagerly fought elections give the impression that men were itching to sit at Westminster. The truth was otherwise. In agrarian counties there had never been much competition to stand: more often it was a question of impressing his public duty upon some less than willing victim. Elsewhere the slowness of industrialists and the like to make much of an appearance as candidates had less to do with opposition from traditional élites than with the fact that it was much easier for such men to combine their business interests with local than with national government.[56] The well-known (if rather confusing) statistics produced in 1867 by the reformer Bernard Cracroft indicate that, while 246 borough members were primarily associated with land, only thirty-one of the remaining 150 appear to have been connected primarily with manufacturing. In addition, all but a handful of the 262 county members were from aristocratic and other landed families. Not only had this been the case for many years, but it remained so for twenty years more. The proportion of bankers, merchants, and manufacturers in the Commons—24 per cent in 1831 before the First Reform Acts—was still 24 per cent in 1874 and did

[54] Hoppen, *Elections, Politics*, 74–85; Hanham, *Elections*, 263.

[55] For mid-century electioneering in Poole, see T. A. McDonald, 'Religion and Voting in an English Borough', *Southern History*, 5 (1983), 221–37.

[56] Olney, *Lincolnshire Politics*, 231–2; J. Garrard, 'The Middle Class and Nineteenth Century National and Local Politics', in Garrard, D. Jary, M. Goldsmith, A. Oldfield (eds.), *The Middle Class in Politics* (Farnborough, [1978]), 35–66; G. R. Searle, *Entrepreneurial Politics in Mid-Victorian Britain* (Oxford, 1993), 4–9.

not rise significantly until 1885.[57] Indeed, not until 1880 did the first *active* manufacturer become a cabinet minister, when Gladstone appointed Joseph Chamberlain to the comparatively inconspicuous office of President of the Board of Trade.

In all sorts of ways, therefore, the legislative changes of 1867–8 proved less dramatic than they at first appeared. Such realistic glimpses into the future as they offered revealed few revolutionary landscapes ahead. In particular, the behaviour of those householders who had received the vote in a few constituencies which, though technically boroughs, actually consisted of large tracts of open countryside, gave little promise of sensational happenings should household suffrage be extended to the county constituencies themselves.[58] Among boroughs as a whole Disraeli's franchise arrangements ironed out some anomalies, while his redistribution exacerbated others. Most of the new voters went to the largest towns, without, however, bringing many new seats with them, so that city Radicals merely had more heads to count and more persons to organize and manage. At the same time the boundaries between boroughs and counties grew wider still. Artisans could vote in Warrington Borough but not in nearby St Helens. Miners could vote in Morpeth but not in the surrounding county. And because the law concerning voter registration was handled with singular incompetence it became more rather than less difficult to discriminate between those who should have the vote and those who should not.[59] Even the (Secret) Ballot Act of 1872, though it rendered bribery a more haphazard affair, proved less dramatic than expected. In small towns it may somewhat have reduced the power of the voteless to bring pressure to bear on enfranchised grocers, drapers, publicans, and the like. In rural districts, where it was not accompanied by any immediate change in existing economic and political relationships, its effects were marginal.[60] In the biggest cities it made almost no difference at all.

Given that this was so, it is not surprising that national party organization on both sides remained puny and ineffective, with local leaders still as sovereign in the constituencies as national leaders were at Westminster.

[57] W. L. Guttsman, *The British Political Elite* (London, 1963), 41, 82.

[58] The four 'boroughs' in question—Aylesbury, Shoreham, Cricklade, and East Retford—together covered 856 square miles and experienced an average increase of 182% in their electorates between 1865 and 1868.

[59] J. Davis, 'Slums and the Vote, 1867–90', *Historical Research*, 64 (1991), 375–88; J. Davis and D. Tanner, 'The Borough Franchise after 1867', *Historical Research*, 69 (1996), 306–27.

[60] B. L. Kinzer, *The Ballot Question in Nineteenth-Century English Politics* (New York, 1982), 245–9; M. Hurst, 'Ireland and the Ballot Act of 1872', *Historical Journal*, 8 (1965), 326–52.

Liberal initiatives came entirely from the provinces because Gladstone preferred to transmit his appeals to voters through oratory rather than organization. Chamberlain's Birmingham-based National Liberal Federation (established in 1877) formalized the local activities of the National Education League which had orchestrated the complex School Board electoral system set up by the Education Act of 1870. It had a theoretically democratic structure: ordinary members were represented by committees which shrank steadily in size the nearer they approached the seat of power. However, because as late as 1884 the majority of borough associations (110 out of 198) were not even affiliated, it was only in a few of the largest towns that the Federation achieved much success.[61] What it did best was provide local worthies with impressive political roles, involve an element of the working-class electorate in highly circumscribed contacts with Liberal politicians, give formal recognition to the attachment of popular opinion to the Liberal Party, and—perhaps most obviously—furnish Chamberlain with a platform and a base. Yet the actual power of the 'Caucus', as it was called, was small. As regards national policies it remained a cypher in our period. Entrenched MPs with strong local backing had little to fear from the party 'machine'—or from the party leadership for that matter. Indeed, the greatest Liberal successes at the 1880 election occurred in county constituencies where working-class Radicals had taken control of the party but where the Caucus had almost no standing at all.[62]

Altogether more important from the Liberal Party's general point of view were the steadily increasing attachment of Dissent and the growing prominence of Scotland, Wales, and Ireland, whether in the form of Liberal or (in the case of Ireland) Home Rule MPs. Gladstone announced as much in 1868 when he said that 'our three *corps d'armée*, I may almost say, have been Scotch presbyterians, English and Welsh nonconformity, and Irish Roman catholics'.[63] And again, after the victory of 1880 he acknowledged that Nonconformists had put 'their own views into the shade in order that they may not interfere with the success of the cause in which they believe their particular idea is included and absorbed'.[64] However, there were also times when the alliance could become brittle, not to say unstable—over Parnell's divorce scandal in 1890 or, in a rather different way, over the so-called Newcastle Programme of 1891 when the Dissenting tail pretty well succeeded in wagging the Liberal dog.

On the other side of the party divide, the National Union of Conservative and Constitutional Associations established in November 1867 was

---

[61] Hanham, *Elections*, 139.   [62] Biagini, *Liberty, Retrenchment, Reform*, 328–37.
[63] Morley, *Life of Gladstone*, ii. 259.   [64] Hanham, *Elections*, 124.

neither influential nor encouraged from on high. As with Chamberlain and the Liberal Federation, so the Union was primarily a platform for the ambitions of one man, John Gorst, who in 1870 became Principal Agent to the recently established Conservative Central Office. What was new about Gorst was not organizational skill—here he represented no advance on Peel's political agent, Francis Bonham—but the realization that Tory strength might be enhanced by means of strictly controlled mobilizations through a wider (but by no means unlimited) social range. Disraeli, however, remained ambivalent, even suspicious. His famous speeches at Manchester and the Crystal Palace in 1872 said little to the point. Apart from a stress on empire all was, as so often, left relentlessly vague.[65] Small wonder that in 1877 Gorst handed in the first of what was to become a long series of resignations.

When the question of 'Tory Democracy' came once more to the surface in the early 1880s it did so primarily in connection with Lord Randolph Churchill's bid for a central role in leadership. In so far as it moved beyond this it raised the issue of parliamentary influence for urban notables, not that of the development of policies with which the masses might be won. Gorst, now a member of Churchill's so-called Fourth Party, was again Principal Agent (as well as MP for Chatham) and again aimed his efforts almost entirely at middle-class Conservative activists in large cities and towns.[66] That in the end so many industrialists as well as other members of the middle class came to join what had long been the party of landed property had more to do with feelings of being pushed out of Liberalism than with a positive response to the virtues of the other side. While, therefore, Salisbury lost few opportunities of announcing that the Conservatives were now the only reliable defenders of all kinds of property and even undertook a number of provincial speaking tours to drive the message home, it was Gladstone himself who eventually proved to be Toryism's most effective recruiting sergeant.[67]

This is not to say that the move of the 'villa' vote (as Salisbury derisively called it) towards the Conservative Party was purely and simply reactive in character, for, at the local level, Tories had throughout the 1860s and 1870s often shown themselves better than Liberals at responding to politics as a

[65] E. J. Feuchtwanger, *Disraeli, Democracy and the Tory Party* (Oxford, 1968), 45; id., 'The Conservative Party under the Impact of the Second Reform Act', *Victorian Studies*, 2 (1959), 303.

[66] Feuchtwanger, *Disraeli, Democracy*, 170–2; R. F. Foster, *Lord Randolph Churchill: A Political Life* (Oxford, 1981), 58–97.

[67] E. H. H. Green, *The Crisis of Conservatism: The Politics, Economics and Ideology of the British Conservative Party, 1880–1914* (London, 1995), 78–119.

participatory and inclusive set of activities. Nor, with ritual and symbol the mother tongues of the party of unspoken tradition, was this altogether surprising. The Primrose League established in 1883 as rather casual fall-out from the Fourth Party soon became the most important political organization in the constituencies. It drew in women members (for whom Liberals found little to do) and its fêtes, garden parties, and smoking concerts provided general entertainment, hierarchical ordering, and an opportunity for the middle classes to mingle with one another and occasionally with party notables.[68] Increasingly, too, Conservatism adopted those tenets of 'freedom' and individualism which had formerly constituted the natural stock-in-trade of English Liberalism and in so doing gave them an even more distinctly property-orientated character than they had hitherto possessed. This meant that, by the 1880s, the party was in a position to welcome regiments of middle-class supporters without having either to alter its existing power structures or do much to change its policies. If, by 1884, Salisbury was being driven to comment that his epitaph would be 'Died of writing inane answers to empty-headed Conservative Associations', this was a small price to pay for so substantial and so unexpected a gift.[69]

As social fault lines widened during these years the culture of the middle sort of people proved active and combative, that of manual workers increasingly defensive and enclosed. Irritated Radicals were dejected to discover in 1874 that there was 'a Conservative working man' and that 'throughout Yorkshire and Lancashire, the Conservative candidates represent the working man's cause'.[70] The number of working men standing as Liberal candidates fell from eleven in 1874 to six in 1880. And even if in parts of the industrial North, Dissent still underpinned the Liberalism of skilled artisans, in London (electorally of growing importance) working-class culture was becoming more docile and less aggressive, its focuses not trade unions, friendly societies, or politics, but amusements, hospitality, public houses, and sport.[71]

Although the Conservative electoral success of 1874 marked a real breakthrough, the results in 1880 and 1885 at first looked worryingly like

---

[68] M. Pugh, *The Tories and the People 1880–1935* (Oxford, 1985), 15–69.

[69] Lady G. Cecil, *Life of Robert Marquis of Salisbury*, 4 vols. (London, 1921–32), iii. 108; also R. Shannon, *The Age of Salisbury 1881–1902: Unionism and Empire* (London, 1996), 109–22.

[70] H. W. McCready, 'British Labour's Lobby, 1867–75', *Canadian Journal of Economics and Political Science*, 22 (1956), 156.

[71] G. S. Jones, 'Working-Class Culture and Working-Class Politics in London, 1870–1900', *Journal of Social History*, 7 (1974), 460–508; R. McKibbin, *The Ideologies of Class: Social Relations in Britain 1880–1950* (Oxford, 1990), 101–66.

reversions to the long period of failure which had begun in 1846. Yet both for Conservatism and for party politics in general the 1880s proved a fulcrum decade. Individual judgement was beginning to grow less politically significant than the expression of great social forces. The trend towards national opinion and national patterns of party support accelerated, especially after 1885. 'There is always', remarked A. J. Balfour in 1880, 'a local reason to be found for every defeat: the singular thing being that the local reasons are all on one side.'[72] And even if this was still something of an exaggeration, a slow, erratic, and uneven move away from the predominantly regional and local politics of the mid-century was undoubtedly under way. The election of 1880 witnessed unprecedented public participation by party leaders. Not only Gladstone (during his second Midlothian campaign), but also Bright, Hartington, and Salisbury all spoke so often to large audiences that it was claimed that more speeches by cabinet and ex-cabinet ministers were delivered than in all previous parliamentary recesses combined.[73] The Conservatives lost because of agricultural and industrial depression and more immediately because Disraeli's dissolution in 1880 was as inept as Gladstone's had been in 1874. In terms of votes the Conservatives did a little better than in 1868 and moved significantly ahead in the very largest constituencies. In London especially they held their ground, their eight seats (out of twenty-two) in 1880 contrasting with ten in 1874, two in 1868, and none at all in 1865. Among the forty-three seats in the Home Counties of Kent, Middlesex, Surrey, and Sussex they pushed their total of twenty-two in 1868 up to thirty-five.[74]

Although the question of further franchise reform attracted little excitement in 1880, it none the less received a certain amount of official support on the Liberal side because Gladstone himself had, since 1873, come to believe 'the extension of the Household Suffrage to counties to be one which is just & politic in itself, & which cannot long be avoided'.[75] When eventually he turned to the matter in 1883 his general approach was similar to that of 1866–7, though his handling was far superior. On the one side, he isolated the more cautious Whigs who lost on every issue they held dear— fewer seats for Ireland, the retention of small boroughs, fierce opposition to moving from a system in which almost all constituencies returned two members to one in which single-member constituencies would predominate.

[72] T. Lloyd, *The General Election of 1880* (Oxford, 1968), 140.

[73] Ibid. 13–14.

[74] Feuchtwanger, *Disraeli, Democracy*, 82–3; J. P. D. Dunbabin, 'Parliamentary Elections in Great Britain, 1868–1900', *English Historical Review*, 81 (1966), 88–9; Lloyd, *General Election of 1880*, 150.

[75] *Gladstone Diaries*, ed. Matthew and Foot, viii. 359.

On the other, he managed to keep Radicals like Dilke and Chamberlain with him, the latter more hesitantly than the former. While the parliamentary debates never reached the heights of 1866–7, the same arguments were put through the same paces over much the same course. By agreeing at an early stage that the extension of household suffrage to the counties would constitute the 'hinge of the whole Bill', the cabinet was able to put forward a single principle, which, like Disraeli's in 1867, could be widely touted as simple and comprehensible.[76] Salisbury, however, conducted the Tory side of the argument with great skill. In a cool and bold move (cooler and bolder than Disraeli would have risked) he encouraged the Lords to reject the bill in July 1884 in order to ensure that an acceptable scheme of redistribution would accompany the franchise changes that were being proposed. Eventually it was agreed in November 1884 to hold private meetings between party chiefs because the leading experts—Dilke for the Liberals and Salisbury himself for the Tories—had independently concluded that a drastic redistribution based on single-member constituencies would benefit each of their respective sides.[77]

While Dilke favoured the adoption of single-member divisions because uniformity and numerical even-handedness were well-established Radical principles, Salisbury did so not only for the traditional Tory reason that rural areas might thus be best protected against urban intrusion, but because single-member divisions carved out of large socially mixed boroughs might, if sufficiently middle-class, return Tory members where none had been returned before. Gladstone characteristically emerged as a more effective defender of tradition than Whigs like Hartington, though equally characteristic was the manner in which his defence now encompassed only minor matters. While insisting that no attempt was being made 'absolutely to efface all inequality from our representative system . . . at the application of a single hard mathematical rule',[78] in practice he confined himself to securing, on historic grounds, the retention of a handful of two-member constituencies amongst towns of middling size.

Gladstone was right when he claimed that total uniformity was still a distant goal. Yet the collection of items commonly called the 'Third Reform Act' constituted a giant step along the road, not least because the strict expenditure limits of the 1883 Corrupt Practices Act—no more than £470 per candidate in, for example, boroughs with 5,000 electors—had

---

[76] *Hansard*, cclxxxvi. 1181–1252 (31 Mar. 1884) and cclxxxv. 111 (28 Feb. 1884).

[77] M. E. J. Chadwick, 'The Role of Redistribution in the Making of the Third Reform Act', *Historical Journal*, 19 (1976), 665–83; Lord Salisbury, 'The Value of Redistribution: A Note on Electoral Statistics', *National Review*, 4 (1884), 145–62.

[78] *Hansard*, ccxciv. 373 (1 Dec. 1884).

already inaugurated an era of unpaid election workers and comparative financial probity. The 1884 Representation of the People Act itself was not only the first of its kind to apply more or less equally to all parts of the United Kingdom, but, by broadly aligning borough and county franchises, it reduced traditional electoral distinctions between country and town. Although the percentage increase in voters was less than in 1867–8, the numerical growth was greater. In England and Wales the 2,618,453 voters of 1883 became 4,376,916. In Scotland numbers rose from 310,441 to 560,580, in Ireland (where the franchise had changed little since 1850) from 224,018 to 737,965. The overwhelming majority of voters were now qualified on occupation (rather than ownership) franchises: in England and Wales some 95 per cent in boroughs and 80 per cent in counties. Boroughs with populations below 15,000 were disfranchised and those below 50,000 reduced to one member. A Redistribution Act in 1885 allocated the 150 seats thus made available: twelve went to Scotland and sixty-six to county and seventy-two to borough divisions in England and Wales.

To contemporaries all this seemed very dramatic and, indeed, to some extent it was. The proportional disadvantage of the concentrated centres of population and industry largely disappeared. There was less deviation from the numerical mean. While the over-representation of the south of England as a whole was ended, the under-representation of the metropolis was only partly redressed by increasing the number of its MPs from twenty-two to fifty-nine. The Boundary Commissioners sliced up the old boroughs along what amounted to class lines. In Leeds, for example, they ignored local ward boundaries 'in view of the great difference in the character of the population in different parts' and firmly put all the prosperous villa dwellers into the northern division. The result was that redistribution may well have enabled the urban middle classes previously submerged in large multi-member constituencies to translate their increasingly Tory votes into additional Tory seats (although the impact of this is easier to detect at the general election of 1885 than at those held thereafter).[79]

Complacency soon settled in. Tories wanted little more. Chamberlain in his Radical Programme of 1885 announced that 'government of the people by the people ... has at last been effectively secured'. Sir Henry Maine's widely read *Popular Government* (1885) talked, quite inaccurately, of 'unmoderated democracy'. Ten years later Keir Hardie believed there

[79] H. Pelling, *Social Geography of British Elections 1885–1910* (London, 1967), 292; J. Cornford, 'The Transformation of Conservatism in the Late Nineteenth Century', *Victorian Studies*, 7 (1963), 35–66; J. P. D. Dunbabin, 'Some Implications of the 1885 British Shift towards Single-Member Constituencies', *English Historical Review*, 109 (1994), 89–100.

was no longer any need 'to fight the battle of the franchise'.[80] Such afflations, however, tell us more about attitudes than about realities. By 1891 still only about three in every five adult males (62.2 per cent) had the vote in England and Wales, the proportions in Scotland (56.0 per cent) and Ireland (58.3 per cent) being lower still.[81] This meant that working men broadly defined, though now certainly in a majority, remained heavily under-represented in electoral terms. Numerically significant groups such as paupers, living-in servants (except in Scotland), most sons residing with parents, and lodgers with unfurnished rentals below £10 were entirely excluded. Registration law continued to make it difficult for people who moved house a good deal to obtain the vote on the household and lodger franchises, something which principally affected working men (like the Liverpool railway porter who notched up a dozen recorded moves within a single decade as his family grew and circumstances changed).[82] That, indeed, the new enfranchisements struck few shafts into the lowest social structures of all is made clear by the modest rise in the proportion of English and Welsh voters designated illiterate: 1.3 per cent in 1880, 2.2 per cent in 1885. At the same time the new system, by greatly increasing the number of constituencies, augmented the advantages enjoyed by those middle-class electors who, on the basis of ownership franchises, were able to vote in more than one. These were often businessmen or men of rural property who could also, if graduates, vote at elections for university MPs whose number had been increased from six to nine in 1868.

The general election of 1885, as it turned out, constituted something of a false start. The Liberals benefited from the fact that the bulk of additional county seats had gone to the least rural areas and from the enthusiasm with which the newly enfranchised agricultural labourers voted against the farm- ers who had long exploited them. Not since 1832 had Liberals won a majority of English county seats: only in 1906 were they ever to do so again. The labourers, however, proved unreliable outside East Anglia and the gains made were totally eroded by the Home Rule split of 1886 and the ensuing collapse of landed support. On the other hand, the equally surprising Conservative success in winning just over half the English borough seats in 1885 did foreshadow the shape of things to come. The Liberals had failed to appeal sufficiently strongly to working-class electors, a significant min- ority of whom consistently voted Conservative during the years of Tory

---

[80] H. C. G. Matthew, R. I. McKibbin, J. A. Kay, 'The Franchise Factor in the Rise of the Labour Party', *English Historical Review*, 91 (1976), 724.

[81] Hoppen, 'The Franchise', 217.

[82] P. J. Waller, *Democracy and Sectarianism: A Political and Social History of Liverpool, 1868–1939* (Liverpool, 1981), 70.

electoral hegemony between 1886 and 1906.[83] A new electoral geography was developing in which Conservatism was triumphant in a great triangle, the apex of which lay in West Lancastria and the base of which ran from the River Exe in the west to Margate in the east (with extensions into rural Yorkshire). Liberals now dominated only scattered fiefs in Wales, East Scotland, and the industrial citadels of the West Riding and the North-East. With this change came a slow shift towards forms of electoral politics in which broad considerations of class assumed a more important—though by no means an exclusive—role. The process was uncertain and uneven. Only gradually and at different local rates did the politics of culture give way to the politics of class: in the West Riding possibly in the 1880s, in Lancashire probably not until the twentieth century. Clusters of deep and unconscious attitudes were involved and these do not change by abrupt jumps. Certainly Dissent still helped in many areas to hold the Liberal Party together and religion generally retained a place near the centre of electoral life, even though attachment to its institutions and dogmas was now sometimes casual to the point of invisibility. But despite the lasting importance of sectarian and local considerations, class was having more and more to say. Above all was this true in England (rather than Scotland or Ireland) and in England above all was it true in London and in the districts within and surrounding some of the great cities of the Midlands and the North.

The move towards class politics was, however, set in motion more by the well-to-do than by those who worked with their hands. In the shift of 'property' from a diverse to a committed party position the various groups involved—the gentry, the intellectuals, the men of commerce and industry, the new lower middle class—all moved at more or less the same time. Although the Tory Party had long enjoyed some business support (even textile masters were never entirely Liberal let alone Radical),[84] the increasing size of enterprises and the appearance of public limited companies in the later nineteenth century favoured precisely the kinds of businessmen—those with apparently unearned elements in their incomes rather than owner-managers—who came to form the nucleus around which middle-class Conservatism could most easily expand.[85] Already in the 1850s and 1860s moderate businessmen had been attracted to Palmerstonianism as a

[83] J. Lawrence, 'Class and Gender in the Making of Urban Toryism, 1880–1914', *English Historical Review*, 108 (1993), 629–52.

[84] R. H. Trainor, *Black Country Elites: The Exercise of Authority in an Industrialized Area 1830–1900* (Oxford, 1993), 112–19; A. Howe, *The Cotton Masters 1830–1860* (Oxford, 1984), 98–132.

[85] H. Perkin, 'Land Reform and Class Conflict in Victorian England', in Perkin, *The Structured Crowd: Essays in English Social History* (Brighton, 1981), 103.

kind of surrogate Conservatism because Palmerston's domestic caution and foreign confidence appealed to them and because there was good reason for finding Palmerston's politics commercially attractive.[86] This had led a few unusually clever Tories to see that manufacturers were more and more becoming 'material for Conservative principles to work upon' and that the towns were full of 'Conservative opinion, disguised as Moderate Liberalism'.[87] But while the shedding of 'right-wing' Liberals to the Conservatives was a phenomenon as old as the Liberal Party itself, the rate of departure undoubtedly accelerated during the 1870s (though less so in the north-east of England than elsewhere) and sharply so during the 1880s.

Too much should not perhaps be read into the trail-blazing triumphs in 1868 of Tory candidates at Westminster and suburban Middlesex where no Tory had been successful since 1841. Although years later Lord George Hamilton (the Middlesex victor) ascribed it all to the 'rapid extension of suburban railroads and the outpouring of professional men, tradesmen, and clerical employees into the rural outskirts of London', it is interesting to note that the Tories won the seat only after the county's most suburban district had been taken out and transformed into the separate constituency of Chelsea, which then remained predominantly Liberal until 1886.[88] None the less, by the end of Gladstone's first ministry most middle-class grievances had been met. Sated themselves, moderate voters wanted an end to the feast. As early as 1861 Bright had predicted that the 'inveterate flunkeyism which pervades nearly all the newly rich' would eventually turn them 'against us'. In 1868, just as the business vote was really beginning to slide towards the Conservatives, John Morley used the pages of the *Fortnightly Review* to denounce the arrival of a 'new feudalism' busily transforming the (in his view) rugged Liberal industrialists of former times into owners of mansions with feelings 'as of blue blood' and a 'motto in old French'.[89] Disraeli, by some now imperceptible and probably largely passive process, was more and more successful in making the Liberal Party seem dangerous to men of property. He realized that Gladstone's restlessness meant the end of Palmerstonianism, that all he needed to do was wait and avoid anything too consistently rebarbative to those who unprompted seemed increasingly eager to join his crew.

[86] Searle, *Entrepreneurial Politics*, 126–65.

[87] Lord Stanley's words of 1853 and 1860, cited P. Smith, *Disraelian Conservatism and Social Reform* (London, 1967), 22, 24.

[88] G. Hamilton, *Parliamentary Reminiscences and Reflections 1868 to 1885* (London, 1916), 11; Baer, 'Social Structure', 238–9.

[89] Vincent, *Formation*, 173–4; J. Morley, 'The Chamber of Mediocrity', *Fortnightly Review*, NS 4 (1868), 690.

By the mid-1870s many Liberals were reading the runes with growing anxiety. Concern for the rights of property was giving Conservatism a new appeal in places like Manchester and Bradford. A. J. Mundella, the Nottingham lace manufacturer and MP for Sheffield, noted just before the 1874 election how 'numbers of the middle-class Liberals' were preparing to join the Tories. Edward Baines ascribed his defeat in Leeds to the fright taken by 'a great number of the middle classes'. Frederic Harrison looked at the election results in 'the City of London, in Westminster, in Middlesex, in Surrey, in Liverpool, Manchester, Leeds and Sheffield, in the metropolitan boroughs and in the home counties, in all the centres of middle-class industry' and deduced the 'one unmistakeable fact, that the rich trading-class, and the comfortable middle-class has grown distinctly Conservative'.[90] Prominent individuals adopted new cultural as well as new political wardrobes. W. H. Smith exchanged Palmerstonian Dissent for Conservative Anglicanism. Sir Robert Fowler, Tory MP for the City of London, abandoned the Religious Society of Friends in favour of the Church of England. The wealthy Rylands of Warrington moved in three generations from Nonconformist Liberalism in the 1840s, through Anglican Liberalism and Liberal Unionism, to ardent Church Toryism at the century's end.

The results of the general election of 1880 showed how strong the Tory grip now was in the wealthy south-east of England, with almost two-thirds of the seats in London, Kent, Surrey, and Sussex going to Conservative candidates. Five years later it was firmer still.[91] The distribution of business MPs in the Commons moved from Liberal majority in the early 1880s to a situation in which the Conservatives and Liberal Unionists could claim two-thirds of business MPs when in office and half even when in opposition.[92] The axiom ascribed by a Liverpool Liberal to future Unionists like G. J. Goschen—'Faith, hope, charity, and property, but the greatest of these is property'—was not untrue for being acidulous.[93] Of course many businessmen and a few Whigs remained loyal Gladstonians to the end. Others, having departed, returned to the fold after no more than day trips away. East London, Lancashire, and Birmingham continued to exhibit voting patterns in which social differences seemed to count for little (to considerable Conservative advantage). In terms of a class electorate, the 1880s were at most a transitional period. Many workers continued to resist

---

[90] Joyce, *Work, Society, Politics*, 38; N. Blewett, *The Peers, the Parties and the People* (London, 1972), 6; Vincent, *Formation*, 125; Harrison, 'Conservative Reaction', 304.
[91] Pelling, *Social Geography*, 85–6.   [92] Perkin, 'Land Reform', 124.
[93] Waller, *Democracy and Sectarianism*, 79.

Liberalism, while the drift of the better-off to the Conservatives, suggestive after 1868 and pronounced after 1885, became emphatic only after 1906.[94]

In the midst of all this the impact of Home Rule, upon which the Liberal Party split so dramatically, is difficult to assess. It used to be thought that the actual issue of Irish devolution mattered little in itself and merely provided a particularly effective excuse for men of property to abandon Gladstone. This is probably untrue (or at least exaggerated), though it remains the case that without the fractures of 1886 the Conservatives could not so quickly or decisively have moved into an electoral majority.[95] Home Rule aborted any possible Liberal realignment based on rural labourers, miners, smallholders, and the like, to offset losses among the middle classes. Certainly in places like Liverpool it really was Home Rule which strangled Liberalism, while the important Conservative revival after 1885 in parts of Scotland also owed much to the Irish Question as such. For Whigs like Hartington it was above all the manner in which Gladstone's Irish proposals so clearly signalled a defeat for what they believed to be their own parliament-driven and 'rational' (as well as entirely Anglocentric) approach to politics that finally persuaded them to resist Home Rule.[96] Indeed, as an efficient conduit for the transmission across traditional party divides of various kinds of opinion, not least those associated with commerce and academic life, Liberal Unionism proved so important a phenomenon largely because Home Rule allowed both politicians and voters to equate desertion of Gladstone with defence of national unity, the empire, even Protestantism. The ninety-four original parliamentary defectors included the purple of Liberal commerce: a Goschen, a Rothschild, a Mildmay of Baring Brothers, a Goldsmid, a Jardine, a Morrison, and a Brown of Brown, Shipley. Where property led intellectuals and writers followed, ready as always to run up cloaks of respectability: A. V. Dicey, J. R. Seeley, J. A. Froude, Henry Sidgwick, Herbert Spencer, Goldwin Smith, Sir John Lubbock, Tennyson, Swinburne, Arnold, and many more. The six university constituencies, some of which had returned occasional Liberals before 1886, now entirely ceased to do so, their graduate electorates the least radical in the nation.

A week before Herbert Gladstone flew the 'Hawarden Kite' in mid-December 1885 and announced his father's conversion to Home Rule, Gladstone himself had pondered upon the state to which his opponents

    [94] P. F. Clarke, 'Electoral Sociology of Modern Britain', *History*, 57 (1972), 49.

    [95] W. C. Lubenow, *Parliamentary Politics and the Home Rule Crisis: The British House of Commons in 1886* (Oxford, 1988), 163–208, 249–89.

    [96] J. Parry, *The Rise and Fall of Liberal Government in Victorian Britain* (London, 1993), 292–303.

had come and the future which now beckoned them. 'Toryism in other days', he noted,

had two legs to stand upon: a sound leg, and a lame leg. Its sound leg was reverence: its lame leg was class interest. Reverence it has almost forgotten. It no longer leans upon that leg. It leans now upon its lame leg, the leg of class interest, more much more; and to mend the matter, as it stumps along, it calls out progress.[97]

However sentimental Gladstone's memories of his own Tory yesteryears may have been, his view of the present was accurate enough: the Conservatives had at last been dealt a winning hand.

[97] *Prime Ministers' Papers: Gladstone*, ed. Brooke and Sorensen, iv. 104.

PART III

Money and Mentalities

CHAPTER 9

A Maturing Economy

I. REVOLUTIONS, CLIMACTERICS, PRODUCTIVITY

At the end of the nineteenth century the United Kingdom was the richest country the world had ever known. Yet accounts of its economy have been dominated by talk of failure, not failure in the sense of slums and poverty, but failure with respect to abstractions, notably overall rates of growth: were these faltering and if so were they faltering in comparison with what had gone before or with what was happening abroad or with both? Britain's subsequent economic woes have, indeed, generated a kind of treasure hunt in reverse—an obsessive search for the precise moment when an age of gold began to tarnish and decay.

For many years it has also been fashionable to express unease about the unambiguous existence of anything as linguistically strident as an industrial *revolution*. In particular, the statistical findings of econometricians (economists who apply sophisticated mathematical techniques in historical contexts) have suggested that overall growth during almost any part of the hundred years beginning about 1750 was far slower than words like 'revolution' tend to suggest. Thus Gross Domestic Product (GDP)[1] may have risen in percentage terms by no more than 0.64 a year in the period 1760–80, 1.38 in 1780–1801, and 1.90 in 1801–31 (with equivalent rises for industrial output alone of something like 1.29, 1.96, and 2.78 respectively), figures which, while not without upswing, do not at first seem to encourage talk of sudden and substantial change.[2] What does seem to have started to happen about the middle of the eighteenth century, and what *was* revolutionary, was the appearance of a number of very specific and limited developments which made unprecedented growth in certain sectors possible, especially in the

---

[1] Gross Domestic Product (GDP) includes only the product generated within a country's territory; Gross National Product (GNP) includes, in addition, net income from abroad. The difference is not generally very important.

[2] N. F. R. Crafts and C. K. Harley, 'Output Growth and the British Industrial Revolution', *Economic History Review*, 45 (1992), 715.

textile and metal industries. For more than a century thereafter Britain sustained a dual economy: one functioning along conventional lines, the other (focused on cotton, iron, engineering, heavy chemicals, and mining) increasingly marked by modern methods, procedures, and rates of growth. Because in 1760 traditional activities still constituted 90 per cent of the economy, the effect upon overall growth of highly dramatic growth rates in the modernizing industries was at first necessarily small. It was also slow: even within the manufacturing sector, the so-called 'new technology' industries did not contribute more than half of total output until about 1850 and not more than three-quarters until just after 1900.[3]

In the end, the industrial revolution can, none the less, be said to have been revolutionary because its effects were sustained. The shackles restraining economic improvement were removed. Despite occasional reversals, the long-term trend now clearly pointed upwards. However, even the most sophisticated litanies of recent scholarship have provided no more than partial explanations for why this should have been so: new ways of regarding innovation, changing patterns of demand, exploitation of mineral deposits, the role of the state, the manner in which technological change was implemented by an unusual alliance between men of learning and men of enterprise. What alone is certain is that it was a complex process in which a series of interactions—between inventions and investment, the worlds of business and agriculture, new sources of energy and their exploitation— provided the dynamic element. 'Examining British economic history in the period 1760–1830', writes one scholar, 'is a bit like studying the history of Jewish dissenters between 50 B.C. and A.D. 50. At first provincial, localized, even bizarre, it was destined to change the life of every woman and man in the West beyond recognition and to affect deeply the lives of others.'[4]

By the second quarter of the nineteenth century Britain had become the home of the first urban industrialized economy in the modern world. And it is the pioneering character of the processes involved (which of course reach back into the previous century) that has established certain points of departure for attempts to assess long-term rates of change and to investigate the location of any possible caesura after which rates of growth began to slow down.

Contemporaries favoured a three-phase model when discussing the period after 1850: boom 1850–73, depression 1873–96, then recovery until

---

[3] P. Bairoch, 'International Industrialization Levels from 1750 to 1980', *Journal of European Economic History*, 11 (1982), 288.

[4] J. Mokyr, 'The New Economic History and the Industrial Revolution', in Mokyr (ed.), *The British Industrial Revolution: An Economic Perspective* (Boulder, Colo., 1993), 131.

1919. This still haunts many textbooks. But while there was certainly much angry talk of hardship in the late 1870s and the 1880s, the imprecisions of the relationship between such complaints and the underlying economic realities of the time highlight the need for caution in accepting the validity of contemporary discontents. For their part, scholars—faced with serious statistical difficulties—have opted for so dazzling a variety of so-called climacteric dates that almost every decade between the 1840s and the Great War has, at some time or another, received nomination as a time of climacteric when growth *rates* (not of course growth itself, which continued throughout) began to fall.[5] However, only two—broadly incompatible— views possess much credibility. Those who hold the first, place the climacteric later than the once-fashionable 1870s and 1880s and identify a break in the growth of GDP as taking place around 1900 or shortly thereafter.[6] By contrast, those who support the second view, find the notion of a late nineteenth-century discontinuity to be misconceived and suggest that, if a major break is indeed to be found, it is most convincingly to be located around the present volume's opening years (the 1840s) rather than at any later date. While the idea that no clear caesura occurred between the 1860s and the 1900s has been canvassed for some time,[7] the identification of the 1840s as a time of climacteric in relation to GDP in general and industrial production in particular is still provisional and requires further analysis. Its proponents have, however, made unusual efforts to avoid some of the pitfalls associated with calculations of growth-rate movements, in particular that created by choosing time-periods in which to gather and present data before obtaining results (the latter being inevitably affected by the

[5] S. Pollard, 'The Dynamism of the British Economy in the Decades to 1914', in M. Mann (ed.), *The Rise and Decline of the Nation State* (Oxford, 1990), 48–50; id., *Britain's Prime and Britain's Decline: The British Economy 1870–1914* (London, 1989), 16–17; P. J. Cain and A. G. Hopkins, *British Imperialism: Innovation and Expansion 1688–1914* (London, 1993), 107–10.

[6] C. H. Feinstein, R. C. O. Matthews, J. C. Odling-Smee, 'The Timing of the Climacteric and its Sectoral Incidence in the U.K., 1873–1913', in C. P. Kindleberger and G. di Tella (eds.), *Economics in the Long View*, 3 vols. (New York, 1982), ii. 168–85; C. H. Feinstein, 'What Really Happened to Real Wages? Trends in Wages, Prices, and Productivity in the United Kingdom, 1880–1913', *Economic History Review*, 43 (1990), 329–55; D. McCloskey, 'Did Victorian Britain Fail?', *Economic History Review*, 23 (1970), 446–59; id., 'Victorian Growth: A Rejoinder', *Economic History Review*, 27 (1974), 275–7; id., 'No It Did Not: A Reply to Crafts', *Economic History Review*, 32 (1979), 538–41.

[7] S. Broadberry, 'ESRC Quantitative Economic History Study Group 1985 Conference', *Journal of European Economic History*, 15 (1986), 384–90; D. Greasley, 'British Economic Growth: The Paradox of the 1880s and the Timing of the Climacteric', *Explorations in Economic History*, 23 (1986), 416–44; S. Solomou and M. Weale, 'Balanced Estimates of UK GDP 1870–1913', *Explorations in Economic History*, 28 (1991), 54–63.

former). If their enterprise eventually succeeds in holding water—and many others have gone down with all hands in what remain turbulent and shark-infested seas—then this would constitute an important advance.[8]

However, even for predetermined periods, revised annual growth-rate estimates for real GDP and real industrial output ('real' values take inflationary and deflationary movements into account) suggest a rise up to the mid-nineteenth century and then a gradual and steady decline, rather than any obvious climacteric in late Victorian or Edwardian times (Table 9.1). And when so-called 'open-ended' procedures (by which fixed time-periods are not determined before calculation) are applied to industrial output the argument for seeing the second quarter of the century as the time of fastest growth would seem to become clearer still (Table 9.2).

If, therefore, the 'Great Depression' of 1873–96 as a general and all-encompassing phenomenon no longer possesses much historical credibility, however strongly some contemporaries talked of hard times, the supposed 'Great Victorian Boom' of 1850–73 has fared even worse. Because, however, *absolute* growth in both total and per caput terms did of course

TABLE 9.1 *British GDP and industrial output growth rates,*
1780–1913 (%, p.a.)

	Real GDP	Real industrial output
1780–1801	1.3	2.1
1801–31	2.0	3.0
1830–60	2.5	3.4
1856–73	2.2	2.8
1873–99	2.1	2.2
1899–1913	1.4	1.6

Source: N. F. R. Crafts, S. J. Leybourne, T. C. Mills, 'Britain' in R. Sylla and G. Toniolo (eds.), *Patterns of European Industrialization in the Nineteenth Century* (London, 1991), 110. This is a rather different picture from that offered in P. Deane and W. A. Cole, *British Economic Growth 1688–1959*, 2nd edn. (Cambridge, 1967), 170.

[8] N. F. R. Crafts, S. J. Leybourne, T. C. Mills, 'The Climacteric in Late Victorian Britain and France', *Journal of Applied Econometrics*, 4 (1989), 103–17; id., 'Trends and Cycles in British Industrial Production, 1700–1913', *Journal of the Royal Statistical Society*, A152/1 (1989), 43–60; id., 'Measurement of Trend Growth in European Industrial Output before 1914', *Explorations in Economic History*, 27 (1990), 442–67; id., 'Britain', in R. Sylla and G. Toniolo (eds.), *Patterns of European Industrialization: The Nineteenth Century* (London, 1991), 109–52; Crafts and Mills, 'Trends in Real Wages in Britain, 1750–1913', *Explorations in Economic History*, 31 (1994), 176–94; id., 'The Industrial Revolution as a Macroeconomic Epoch', *Economic History Review*, 47 (1994), 769–75.

TABLE 9.2 *British trend growth rates of industrial output,*
1784–1913, obtained by open-ended time-period procedures (%, p.a.)

	Trend	Rates
1784–1802	Rising	1.4 to 1.8
1803–18	Rising	1.8 to 3.0
1819–36	Rising	3.0 to 3.4
1837–53	Falling	3.4 to 2.9
1854–74	Falling	2.9 to 2.4
1875–99	Falling	2.4 to 2.2
1900–13	Constant	2.2

Source: N. F. R. Crafts, S. J. Leybourne, T. C. Mills, 'Britain', in
R. Sylla and G. Toniolo (eds.), *Patterns of European Industrialization in
the Nineteenth Century* (London, 1991), 134–5. Similar results can be
obtained for GDP. The statistical techniques used in these calculations
produce somewhat different figures from those in Table 9.1, even for
almost identical periods.

continue throughout the century, it would seem that increases in the British
(though not the Irish) population of more than 10 per cent in every decade
between 1781 and 1911 proved sufficiently large to sustain the growth
process without being so great as to swamp it in the manner Thomas
Malthus had pessimistically predicted.

With the output of industry and services increasing more rapidly than
that of agriculture, the distribution of labour and national product between
the three main sectors of the economy was transformed. Crude estimates
of the percentage of the British labour force in various sectors reveal
continuous decline in agriculture and a substantial rise in industry. And
much the same can be said with regard to the generation of national income
(Table 9.3). However, though Britain was of course the 'first industrial
nation'—perhaps indeed *because* it was the pioneer—this particular patterning of temporal conjunctures has turned out to be unique. All other
countries at the moment when their citizens' level of income reached that
attained at some earlier date in Britain were then still less urban and
industrial and more agricultural than Britain had been at the equivalent
stage.[9] But while in Britain the shift from agriculture was undoubted, that
into industry was not without its ambiguities. On the surface it would seem
that the latter process had virtually played itself out by the beginning of our
period and that mid-century Britain, with two-fifths of its labour force in

[9] N. F. R. Crafts, *British Economic Growth during the Industrial Revolution* (Oxford,
1985), 55–63.

TABLE 9.3 *Distribution of British labour force and national income, 1801–1881* (%)

	Agriculture		Industry	
	Labour force	National income	Labour force	National income
1801	35.9	32.5	29.7	23.4
1841	22.2	22.1	40.5	34.4
1851	21.7	20.3	42.9	34.3
1881	12.6	10.4	43.5	37.6

Source: P. Deane and W. A. Cole, *British Economic Growth 1688–1959*, 2nd edn. (Cambridge, 1967), 142, 166.

industry (by 1951 the proportion was still less than half), had already reached a high level of economic 'maturity'. In reality, much so-called industrial activity long remained small-scale and unaffected by advanced technology, steam power, or managerial innovation. In 1831 manufacturing (strictly defined) still provided only 10 per cent of adult male employment in England whereas retail trade and handicraft provided 32 per cent.[10] While, therefore, it is often said that the crucial shift in the second half of the nineteenth century was not that from agriculture into industry (which had in fact taken place earlier) but that from agriculture either directly or indirectly into a service sector whose share of the occupied population grew from 36 to 45 per cent in the half-century after 1851, such a claim disguises those transfers from traditional to modern subsectors which were taking place within 'industry' itself. Thus, as compared to the situation in 1831, 81 per cent of British industrial employment and 75 per cent of industrial output by 1856 were being sustained by modern manufacturing alone.[11] Not only, therefore, was the service sector growing substantially throughout the second half of the century, but the income and employment structures of industry (and indeed of agriculture) were changing rapidly as well. In particular, though Britain continued to rely heavily upon a handful of major staples—textiles, mining, the production and processing of metals—the earliest 'industrial census' (which was not held until 1907) shows that textiles were clearly contributing a much smaller percentage of the net value of industrial production in 1901 (16.2) than had been the case sixty years before (28.9).[12]

[10] E. A. Wrigley, 'Men on the Land and Men in the Countryside', in L. Bonfield, R. M. Smith, and K. Wrightson (eds.), *The World we have Gained: Histories of Population and Social Structure* (Oxford, 1986), 297.

[11] N. Gemmell and P. Wardley, 'The Contribution of Services to British Economic Growth, 1856–1913', *Explorations in Economic History*, 27 (1990), 301.

[12] F. Crouzet, *The Victorian Economy* (London, 1982), 186–9.

Apart from labour, capital constitutes the other major production input. And here too Britain's experience proved unusual. Capital formation consists of investment in physical assets,[13] most importantly in the case of modern economies in fixed assets used for production over a period longer than the year in which they are acquired. In early industrialization a relatively high proportion of capital formation was devoted to 'circulating' capital, such as unsold stock and work still in progress. With better sales methods, faster distribution, and the decline of the putting-out system the need for circulating capital diminished, so that, by the 1870s, this kind of investment represented at best a tenth of capital formation as a whole.[14]

From the point of view of the overall economy it is the ratio of Gross Domestic Fixed Capital Formation plus net investment abroad to Gross Domestic Product which offers the most revealing insight into patterns of investment over time. Because the relevant calculations involve a good many heroic suppositions, their results should be regarded more as orders of magnitude than precise indicators (Table 9.4). By looking back further into the second half of the eighteenth century it becomes clear that Domestic Fixed Capital Formation as a proportion of Gross Domestic Product took a long time to speed up and rarely at any stage exceeded the 10 per cent

TABLE 9.4 *Investment ratios at current prices, 1831–1900*

	GDFCF as % of GDP	GDFCF + NIA as % of GDP
1831–40	9.6	10.8
1841–50	10.4	11.7
1851–60	8.9	11.9
1861–70	9.3	13.1
1871–80	10.2	14.4
1881–90	7.5	13.7
1891–1900	9.5	12.7

Notes: For GB until 1850, then for UK. GDFCF = Gross Domestic Fixed Capital Formation; NIA = Net Investment Abroad; GDP = Gross Domestic Product.

Source: Calculated from C. H. Feinstein, 'National Savings, 1760–1920', in Feinstein and S. Pollard (eds.), *Studies in Capital Formation in the United Kingdom 1750–1920* (Oxford, 1988), 398 (table 18.4), 427–8 (table I), 462 (table XVII); E. A. Wrigley, *Continuity and Change: The Character of the Industrial Revolution in England* (Cambridge, 1988), 110 (table 4.3); B. R. Mitchell, *British Historical Statistics* (Cambridge, 1988), 836 (table 5A, with estimates for 1851–4 based on information on pp. 831–2, table 5) and 857–8 (table 11, new estimates by Feinstein of GDFCF).

[13] Though in the case of foreign investments both physical assets and portfolio investments are included.

[14] Crouzet, *Victorian Economy*, 135–6.

once considered essential for economic 'take-off'. And even if 'take-off' theories no longer command much respect and the relationship between levels of capital formation and rates of growth remains problematic, the 'low' relativities actually achieved may none the less have played a part in creating the comparatively slow overall growth rates already discussed. Admittedly, it is likely that reductions in the cost of plant throughout the nineteenth century produced a continuous fall in what is called the capital/output ratio, with the result that the percentage of national product that had to be invested to increase production by a given fraction never ceased to decline. But even so, for a country with average incomes as relatively high as mid-Victorian Britain, the ratio of capital formation remained markedly low in international terms.[15]

An economy's output is, however, not simply produced by inputs of labour, capital, and land. It also depends upon the effectiveness with which these inputs are used. Better technology and cost-cutting management techniques can increase output and thus Gross Domestic Product by more than the mathematical sum of the inputs employed. This more or less 'free lunch' is usually called productivity. In historical contexts it has proved difficult to measure with any accuracy, especially for individual industries, although one pioneering estimate sees productivity in cotton increasing between 1780 and 1860 by a multiple of 7.7 and by perhaps half or a third as much in iron.[16] Over the economy as a whole, however, more detailed (though still tentative) calculations have been made based upon the notion of 'Total Factor Productivity' (TFP), defined as the ratio of all outputs to a composite of all inputs. This is often identified as a direct measure of technical progress, which, if it rises, signifies a rise in output relative to inputs—or greater 'efficiency' in common parlance. But, because of its residual nature (it is what remains after weighted inputs are deducted from output), TFP inevitably sweeps in all sorts of errors and aggregation biases on both the output and input sides.[17] Be that as it may, the effect of Total Factor Productivity upon the growth of Gross Domestic Product was not especially impressive during the Victorian period, although it is probable that the largest contribution was registered in the middle years of the century—further confirmation of the suggestion that, if a climacteric did indeed occur, it did so then rather than at any time during the next sixty years. Over the longer term, however, it is hard to dispute the conclusion

[15] Crafts, Leybourne, Mills, 'Britain', 112–13.

[16] D. McCloskey, '1780–1860: A Survey', in R. Floud and McCloskey (eds.), *The Economic History of Britain since 1700*, 2nd edn., 3 vols. (Cambridge, 1994), i. 250–1.

[17] Mokyr, 'New Economic History', 25–6; R. C. O. Matthews, C. H. Feinstein, J. C. Odling-Smee, *British Economic Growth 1856–1973* (Oxford, 1982), 506.

that 'there was no substantial phase in the nineteenth century during which the trend in the rate of growth of TFP was upward': 1801–31 = 0.7 per cent a year, 1830–60 = 1.0 per cent, 1856–73 = 0.8 per cent, 1873–99 = 0.7 per cent.[18]

This does not of course exclude the possibility that more general swings in economic activity took place during the Victorian period and, indeed, cycles of varying length have been identified. However, only those of comparatively short duration (such as the eight- to ten-year British trade cycles) carry much conviction as distinct entities. In particular, the mid-Victorian 'Boom' and the late Victorian 'Depression' have failed to withstand destructive attacks upon the reality of long swings of all kinds. The boom never had much coherence. The years 1850–73 saw no continuous and general rise in prices, merely two inflationary bursts (1853–5 and 1870–3), separated by a stable plateau. Nor was there much unity with regard to industrial production, overall growth rates, fixed capital formation, profit margins, or even business sentiment generally. Only in the growth of overseas trade does the term 'boom' retain any validity and even then only in a qualified manner. For, while exports and imports increased sharply in *value* and Britain became an export economy, the rate of growth in the *volume* of overseas trade showed little change as against that of the immediately preceding period when export prices had fallen substantially. A number of short episodes of high overall growth in the mid-1850s and early 1870s were matched by years in which the opposite was true. Indeed, what was possibly the century's most profound short depression occurred in 1858, with further crises or crashes following in 1861–2 and 1866.[19]

The more loudly heralded Great Depression has fared little better. Certainly prices did fall more or less continuously (save in the 1880s), but this trend began, not in 1873, but in the 1860s, and in some respects became less severe around 1887. Taken in a longer context, the period 1873–96 simply fails to stand out in any general economic sense (though the sharp downturn in prices in late 1873 certainly had important political consequences). There is no readily identifiable pattern with regard to flows of innovation, gold discoveries, investment rates, or movements in the relationship between investment at home and overseas. Many of the trends which persuaded contemporaries to talk of a Great Depression were not confined to these years, most obviously the decline in agriculture. National income, on the other hand, continued to rise faster than population as it

[18] Matthews, Feinstein, Odling-Smee, *British Economic Growth*, 213; Crafts, Leybourne, Mills, 'Britain', 110.

[19] Crouzet, *Victorian Economy*, 54–8; Crafts, Leybourne, Mills, 'Trends and Cycles', 57.

responded to a fall in import prices and to increased receipts from abroad.[20] Even so, the pitch and intensity of contemporary complaints were undoubtedly severe. Why? In part because the explosive boom of 1868–73 quickly came to be regarded as a golden age after which nothing could ever seem as good again; in part because certain brief depressive cycles played themselves out during the quarter-century after 1873; in part because some of the trends of the time were unfavourable to highly articulate groups in society such as the upper- and middle-class businessmen, farmers, and landowners who together secured the appointment of a Royal Commission on the Depression of Trade and Industry in 1885. Especially for such people, the idea of an overall Great Depression was an attractive one because it provided them with a device for making sense of their own particular circumstances. If, therefore, the whole thing was never more than a myth, it was undoubtedly a very useful myth at the time.

2. INDUSTRIES, RAILWAYS, SERVICES

In certain sectors of manufacturing industry a depression of sorts does, however, seem to have characterized much of the last third of the nineteenth century. The decline in cotton prices was unusually severe and prolonged—beginning in 1864 and lasting (with a brief break in 1869–72) until 1898. Cotton production expanded much less rapidly than before and suffered from three major cyclical recessions (in 1877–9, 1884–5, and 1891–3) and from a consistent decline in value.[21] And because textiles, the prime engines of early industrialization, remained important staples, the economy as a whole continued to share in their wavering fortunes and increasingly insecure progress. Indeed, one of the most remarkable aspects of the British economy once the pioneering phase of industrialization had come to an end (as it certainly had by 1850) was its continued reliance upon a limited number of traditional staples. Of course a degree of diversification took place as 'new' industries emerged, transport improved, and services expanded. But, even if expansion in some of these new areas proved substantial, the overall effect was at first undramatic. It was the comparatively slow growth rates in the textile, iron, and coal industries during the half-century after 1850, not the much faster rates in, for example, land and sea transport, which dominated economic performance generally. Given

---

[20] S. B. Saul, *The Myth of the Great Depression 1873–1896*, 2nd edn. (London, 1988), 9–15; P. Mathias, *The First Industrial Nation: An Economic History of Britain 1700–1914*, 2nd edn. (London, 1983), 361–9.

[21] D. A. Farnie, *The English Cotton Industry and the World Market 1815–1896* (Oxford, 1979), 171.

that in 1891 an even higher proportion of the labour force (23.1 per cent) worked in textiles, metal manufacture, and mining than had been the case fifty years before (21.0 per cent), this is hardly surprising.[22]

Britain's continued dependence upon textiles had important results. By the middle of the century the dramatic production gains achieved first in cotton and then wool were almost complete. They proved to be unrepeatable. Indeed, the cotton industry—for reasons which seemed convincing in the circumstances—became technologically unadventurous. It was this, perhaps inevitable, calm after the wonderfully productive storms of the early nineteenth century which played the largest part in pushing down the Total Factor Productivity growth rate of the cotton industry from 4.8 per cent a year in the period 1834–56 to 0.5 per cent between 1856 and 1885. Although wool's technological breakthrough came a little later, the woollen industry too declined into a slower late Victorian maturity.[23] As a result, the annual growth rate of textile output as a whole declined from something like 6 per cent between 1815 and 1837 to 2.3 per cent between 1857 and 1873 and 0.7 per cent between 1873 and 1900.[24]

Yet the economic grip of cotton remained strong. From its earliest years the industry had greatly helped to expand the total volume of external trade by establishing a dynamic relationship between imports of raw cotton, the manufacture of yarn and cloth, and the export of finished goods. And even if its share in the volume of exports declined from a remarkable 45 per cent in the period 1831–50, it remained above 30 per cent until 1889. Cotton continued to be an exporting industry *par excellence*. Indeed, the relative shrinkage of the domestic market made it more and more dependent on exports, with almost four-fifths of its productive value going abroad in 1894–6.[25] Of course all textile exports were hit by the spread of protective tariffs in the last quarter of the century. However, whereas cotton was able to shift more of its output towards the still-open markets of India, wool (less suited to hot climates) was not, with the result that woollen and worsted exports declined by more than half between 1870–4 and 1900–4.[26] By the end of the century, therefore, the textile sector was dominated,

---

[22] D. Fisher, *The Industrial Revolution: A Macroeconomic Interpretation* (London, 1992), 82; B. R. Mitchell, *British Historical Statistics* (Cambridge, 1988), 104.

[23] Matthews, Feinstein, Odling-Smee, *British Economic Growth*, 449–50; Crouzet, *Victorian Economy*, 214–19; E. M. Sigsworth, 'The Woollen Textile Industry', in R. Church (ed.), *The Dynamics of Victorian Business* (London, 1980), 191–3.

[24] P. Deane and W. A. Cole, *British Economic Growth 1688–1959*, 2nd edn. (Cambridge, 1967), 213; Crouzet, *Victorian Economy*, 191; C. H. Feinstein, *National Income, Expenditure and Output in the United Kingdom 1855–1965* (Cambridge, 1972), T114 (table 52).

[25] Farnie, *English Cotton Industry*, 9–10; Deane and Cole, *British Economic Growth*, 187.

[26] Pollard, *Britain's Prime*, 41–2.

to a much greater extent than had been the case fifty years earlier, by the cotton industry, in other words, by an industry already in decline. And because cotton tended to be the first industry established by other countries determined upon economic development, international competition became a reality at precisely the time when domestic demand was starting to fall as late nineteenth-century British consumers moved to other materials. Not only that, but shocks induced by interruptions in raw material supplies during the American Civil War of 1861–5 inflicted longer-lasting difficulties than seemed apparent at the time. Indeed, after 1873 cotton exports grew less quickly than those of non-textile manufactured goods in general.[27]

While iron and steel—the second British staple—experienced more dramatic technical innovations than textiles during the thirty years after 1850, they, too, did not always react with either energy or speed. Whether this was the result of some failure in entrepreneurship or a rational response to local economic and physical circumstances does not affect the fact that Britain's position with respect to other major metal producers weakened dramatically during the years between 1870 and the outbreak of the Great War. Although from the 1830s to the late 1870s Britain was the largest producer of iron in the world and the only significant exporter, in 1886 the United States moved ahead with regard to steel and in 1890 with regard to pig iron production. Germany did the same in 1893 and 1904 respectively and also emerged as a rival exporter of significance. After 1895 the British share of world iron and steel exports shrank rapidly.[28] Therefore, just as metals were replacing textiles as the leading British industrial sector, so both began to share a common experience: absolute expansion combined with a falling away of relative shares of world markets from an (almost certainly) untenable position of initial dominance.

In both sectors too a second wave of technological innovation evoked a less clearly enthusiastic response than the wave which had helped to inaugurate and sustain the early decades of industrialization. Ring spinning, widely used in the American cotton industry from the 1860s onwards, spread slowly in England—sometimes for understandable reasons (highly skilled English operatives could do just as much with the older spinning mules), sometimes for incomprehensible ones. And the same can be said of British reactions to the Bessemer process developed in the early 1860s

---

[27] Matthews, Feinstein, Odling-Smee, *British Economic Growth*, 448.

[28] R. C. Allen, 'International Competition in Iron and Steel, 1850–1913', *Journal of Economic History*, 39 (1979), 911–13; Crouzet, *Victorian Economy*, 241–2; Pollard, *Britain's Prime*, 27–8.

(which made it possible to produce steel at an acceptable price),[29] to the further improvements introduced in the same decade by Siemens in Germany and the Martin brothers in France, and to the invention in 1878–9 of so-called 'basic steel making' procedures capable of utilizing the commoner phosphoric ores. British steel makers, with their tradition of importing non-phosphoric ores and massive investment in older techniques, concentrated—not without some success at first—on attempts to improve existing plant rather than on scrapping and starting anew.[30] In engineering, too, late Victorian Britain proved more successful in older and mature sectors such as steam engines and textile machinery than in newer products like gas and diesel engines. Especially noticeable was the comparative slowness of electrification in both the domestic and industrial spheres.[31]

Coal was the third staple. It was once thought that its record of labour productivity from the mid-1880s onwards indicated a dramatic falling-back after earlier, equally dramatic, improvements. Much debate took place as to whether this flowed from management failures or from the inevitable constraints created by bringing more geologically complex seams into production.[32] However, more reliable data suggest a rather different story. While total annual production rose impressively from an average of 56 million tons in 1845–9 to 180 million tons in 1890–4, the annual compounded rate of growth declined from 4.8 per cent in 1847–54 to 2.5 per cent in 1890–4, though it rose slightly thereafter. At the same time labour productivity did, indeed, experience some of the severe tergiversations central to earlier analyses: a very slow rise to the 1860s, then a sharp increase to 1883, then a brief reversal followed by stability until 1908.[33] But because the total hours worked by each miner fell significantly in the 1870s and again after 1908 (though not the output produced in each hour worked) the effects of stability in labour productivity were not translated directly into output as a whole.

[29] Pig iron is hard but brittle, wrought iron malleable but yielding. Steel combines the advantages of both. It is hard, elastic, and plastic, and can be ground to a sharp edge.
[30] D. S. Landes, *The Unbound Prometheus: Technological Change and Industrial Development in Western Europe from 1750 to the Present* (Cambridge, 1969), 254–9; P. Temin, 'The Relative Decline of the British Steel Industry, 1880–1913', in H. Rosovsky (ed.), *Industrialization in Two Systems* (New York, 1966), 140–55.
[31] Pollard, *Britain's Prime*, 19–25.
[32] A. J. Taylor, 'The Coal Industry', in D. H. Aldcroft (ed.), *The Development of British Industry and Foreign Competition 1875–1914* (London, 1968), 37–70; D. McCloskey, 'International Differences in Productivity? Coal and Steel in America and Britain before World War I', in McCloskey (ed.), *Essays on a Mature Economy: Britain after 1840* (London, 1971), 285–304.
[33] R. Church, *The History of the British Coal Industry*, iii. *1830–1913: Victorian Pre-Eminence* (Oxford, 1986), 3; id., 'Production, Employment and Labour Productivity in the British Coalfields, 1830–1913', *Business History*, 30/3 (1989), 6–27.

And because, in addition, geological problems made it difficult to install modern machinery and thus limited the scope for substituting capital for labour, Total Factor Productivity in mining showed a tendency to decline from the 1880s onwards.[34] Not only that, but British exports—at a time when economies across the world were growing more complex and sophisticated—became steadily more dependent upon coal, a primary product with almost no value added by ingenious machinery or advanced skills. In 1840 only 3.8 per cent of coal production was sent abroad, by 1887 this had risen to 15.3 per cent, by 1903 to 20.4 per cent (or 27.7 per cent if supplies to 'foreign bunkers' for steam shipping are included). In 1830–9 coal exports amounted to 1 per cent of total exports, by 1900–9 they constituted 10 per cent.[35]

It was in those industries closest to the service sector that Britain tended to make its most notable mark during the middle and later years of the nineteenth century. This was true of railway construction and especially so of shipbuilding. The kind of caution already noted regarding the adoption of new technologies proved an entirely rational strategy for British shipbuilders at a time when their German rivals were perhaps investing more than was economically justified. The highly skilled character of the workforce, together with optimal rather than excessive investment, made it possible to keep prices down and to implement a sensible long-term policy during the period before the Great War.[36] More generally, the shipping industry had been responding effectively to changing circumstances since the late 1840s when it had already begun to reverse the decline which had set in after 1815. Intelligent use of mid-century developments in naval construction and steam power made shipping one of the few sectors in which Britain sustained the world dominance after 1870 which it had enjoyed over the whole industrial field in 1850. Earnings from shipping represented by far the largest item among invisible exports (or services sold to other countries) and the United Kingdom's share of world merchant shipping tonnage rose from 29.5 per cent in 1840 to 35.8 per cent in 1890, when its share of steam tonnage reached the extraordinarily high proportion of a half (49.2 per cent). In absolute terms net tonnage increased more dramatically still—from 2.77 million in 1840 to 7.98 million fifty years later—and in 1883, for the first time, total net steam tonnage registered exceeded tonnage under sail.[37] Although, as a classic capital-goods invest-

---

[34] Church, British Coal Industry, iii. 768–9.

[35] Ibid. 19; Mathias, First Industrial Nation, 434.

[36] S. Pollard and P. Robertson, The British Shipbuilding Industry 1870–1914 (Cambridge, Mass., 1979), 6–7.

[37] Crouzet, Victorian Economy, 359–60; H. J. Dyos and D. H. Aldcroft, British Transport: An Economic Survey from the Seventeenth Century to the Twentieth (Leicester, 1969), 232; Mitchell, British Historical Statistics, 536.

ment industry, shipbuilding was subject to violent swings in demand, from the 1830s the underlying trend was relentlessly upwards. But while British ships continued to carry a remarkable proportion of world trade (perhaps half as late as 1912), already by the end of the Victorian period foreign fleets were beginning to mount a serious challenge, especially on short-haul continental and Scandinavian routes.[38]

Railways and rail construction constitute perhaps the most distinctive manifestation of Victorian enterprise. Unlike shipping, they were comparatively unaffected by foreign competition, though rail building also experienced cyclical bursts (notably in the 1840s and 1860s) and considerable lags between planning and completion. The crucial breakthrough came in 1830 with the opening of the Liverpool & Manchester Railway, the first substantial undertaking to rely completely on steam and heavily upon passenger income. Thereafter construction, traffic, and revenue all grew rapidly (Table 9.5).

By 1852 the main arteries of the system had been laid down. London was connected, among many other places, to Plymouth, Southampton, Bristol, Cardiff, Birmingham, Manchester, Liverpool, Norwich, Leicester, Sheffield, Hull, Newcastle, Glasgow, and Edinburgh, and many cross-country lines were open too. By 1870 few towns of any size still lacked a station: even the largest of those that did were insignificant minnows like Shaftesbury and Lyme Regis. But, because many linkages remained to be made and the separate companies all competed energetically to reach new areas, significant building continued until the century's end (see Maps 4, 5,

TABLE 9.5. *Railway development in Britain, 1840–1900*

	Lines open (miles)	Passenger journeys (millions)	Freight loaded (million tons)	Total working receipts (£m)
1840	1,497			
1850	6,084	67		12.7
1860	9,069	153	88	26.4
1870	13,388	322	166	42.9
1880	15,563	597	232	62.8
1890	17,281	796	299	76.8
1900	18,680	1,115	420	101.0

Note: The 1870 'lines open' and 'freight loaded' figures are actually for 1871.

Source: B. R. Mitchell, *British Historical Statistics* (Cambridge, 1988), 541, 545–6.

[38] A. Slaven, 'The Shipbuilding Industry', in Church (ed.), *Dynamics*, 114–15; Dyos and Aldcroft, *British Transport*, 234; Aldcroft, 'The Mercantile Marine', in Aldcroft (ed.), *Development of British Industry*, 328–9.

and 6). The last main line to London, the Great Central, was not built until 1893–9. And though some of these late extensions were poor investments, probably no more than 5 per cent of the railway capital spent in England and Wales between 1870 and 1900 went into unprofitable new companies. Misplaced investment strategies were, therefore, not the major cause of diminishing returns in the later years of the century. Rising costs, government intervention, and competition over quality of service proved far more significant.[39]

The social and cultural impact of the railways was considerable and, in the main, unmeasurable. In terms of mobility and choice, rail travel broke down regional barriers and added a new dimension to everyday life. The means of written communication were transformed. Suburban commuting and trips to the seaside, though not inaugurated by the railways, were given an enormous boost. As trains replaced coaches and then cheap trains replaced expensive ones, so travel ceased to be the preserve of the rich. Local fairs and markets declined as it became easier to travel to the nearest town, with the result that new patterns of retailing emerged. The near— but for some people not immediate—presence of stations encouraged an enormous growth in rural feeder services operated by horse-drawn means. Indeed, the number of horses in non-agricultural use in Britain rose from 535,000 in 1851 to 1,766,000 in 1901.[40] At the beginning of our period the marvels of rail caused universal wonder. Dickens, amazed by an eleven-hour journey from London to Paris in 1851, blessed the South Eastern Company for 'realising the Arabian Nights in these prose days . . . Whizz! Dust-heaps, market-gardens, and waste-grounds. Rattle! New Cross Station. Shock! There we were at Croydon. Bur-r-r-r! The tunnel.'[41] By the end of our period much faster journeys had come to seem commonplace and mundane.

In more narrowly economic terms the impact of railways was no less substantial, though it is important to remember that the regional specializations laid down by the industrial revolution predate rail construction. At the outer margins lay the rippling effects upon engineering techniques, business organization, management methods, and the provision of an expanded range of professional services. More immediate were the demands which huge construction undertakings placed upon raw materials, labour, and capital. During the peak years of building between 1844 and

[39] T. R. Gourvish, *Railways and the British Economy 1830–1914* (London, 1980), 43–7.

[40] F. M. L. Thompson, 'Nineteenth-Century Horse Sense', *Economic History Review*, 29 (1976), 60–81.

[41] C. Dickens, 'A Flight', in *The Uncommercial Traveller and Reprinted Pieces etc.* (London, 1958), 474–84 (1st collected in book form in *Reprinted Pieces*, 1868).

1851 the manufacture of new rails absorbed 18 per cent of total domestic pig iron output. In 1845 740 million bricks were used to build stations, bridges, embankments, and viaducts. Such demand pressures, however, proved short-lived and over the longer period 1850–70 the railways absorbed only 3 to 4 per cent of iron production.[42] As a result, the demand for capital, though considerable, manifested itself in a series of identifiable cycles. Thus between 1845 and 1849 construction consumed about 4.5 per cent of national income and represented perhaps a half of all domestic capital formation. Particular peaks stand out—£11m in 1839, £44m in 1847, £28m in 1865—though railway investment continued to form a sizeable proportion of domestic fixed capital formation even after 1870: 19.6 per cent in 1851–60, 20.3 in 1861–70, 13.7 in 1871–80, 14.2 in 1881–90.[43] Substantial as this was (and in the 1860s it exceeded the expenditure on fixed assets—including buildings—in all sectors of manufacturing), it did not quite amount to that *deus ex machina* which, according to some historians, supposedly 'rescued' British capitalism in the 1840s from certain unspecified disasters that a lack of investment outlets elsewhere might otherwise have generated.[44]

~ In contrast to railways in other European countries, those in Britain and Ireland were built entirely by private enterprise. But although the (highly unusual) provisions for possible state purchase contained in the Railways Act of 1844 (the work of Gladstone while Peel's President of the Board of Trade) were never implemented, a rapid process of amalgamations soon reawakened anxieties about the possible growth of monopoly practices in an industry in which the largest operators were becoming very large indeed. By 1871 twenty-eight companies controlled 80 per cent of the track and thereafter concentration went further still.[45] Indeed, with respect to capitalization, turnover, and numbers of employees (275,000 by 1873) railway companies were by far the biggest concerns to appear in Victorian times. Eventually in 1873 a new Railway Commission was set up to ensure that managements obeyed the law. But because its powers remained relatively

---

[42] P. S. Bagwell, *The Transport Revolution from 1770* (London, 1974), 116–18; Mathias, *First Industrial Nation*, 260.

[43] T. R. Gourvish, 'Railway Enterprise', in Church (ed.), *Dynamics*, 135; Dyos and Aldcroft, *British Transport*, 188; C. H. Feinstein, 'National Statistics, 1760–1920', in Feinstein and S. Pollard (eds.), *Studies in Capital Formation in the United Kingdom 1750–1920* (Oxford, 1988), 300, 313, 441.

[44] Attempts, notably by G. R. Hawke in *Railways and Economic Growth in England and Wales 1840–1870* (Oxford, 1970), to measure the impact of railways on the economy by estimating how much it would have cost to have continued to move passengers and freight by earlier means have failed to produce clear results.

[45] Dyos and Aldcroft, *British Transport*, 144, 159.

weak until 1888, when severe constraints started to be placed upon the fixing of freight rates, the mid-Victorian period can be seen to constitute not only a time when the overall impact of the railways was greater by far than that of any other contemporary economic innovation, but the high point of free enterprise in the transport of passengers and goods alike.

Developments in communications formed a key element in the growth of services in the Victorian economy. During the second half of the century, structural economic change involved above all a shift of resources from agriculture to services, both absolutely and relatively to the rest of Europe.[46] Between 1861 and 1911 the proportion of the labour force working in agriculture fell from 19 to 9 per cent while that in services rose from 27 to 35 per cent and that in manufacturing remained unchanged at 39 per cent. In 1801 about a third of national income came directly from agriculture. By 1851 this had fallen to 20 and by 1901 to 6–7 per cent.[47] So important did services become that at no time was their contribution to growth less than that of industry, though, in geographical terms, their expansion was most unevenly distributed, with the South-East becoming at once richer and more dependent upon service-sector employment than any other region—42.1 per cent of its labour force worked in service employment in 1881 compared to 30.2 per cent in Britain as a whole.[48]

Much less dramatic was Britain's engagement with the so-called 'new' technologically advanced industries which began to become important towards the end of the century, especially in the spheres of chemistry and electricity. Although at first the electrical industry seemed destined for sustained growth, a combination of unhelpful legislation, reluctant local authorities, and the presence of an excellent gas service created so many difficulties that by 1895 it had become little more than an offshoot of American and German enterprises with only a fringe of domestic undertakings.[49] In chemicals Britain actually remained the dominant producer until the 1880s. But thereafter, while the industry continued to expand, the dynamic research and production of new organic chemicals (notably dyestuffs) was to prove very much a German and Swiss preserve, with Britain remaining dominant in more traditional and, in general, technically less

[46] Gemmell and Wardley, 'Contribution of Services', 302.

[47] R. Floud, 'Britain, 1860–1914: A Survey', in Floud and D. McCloskey (eds.), *Economic History*, 2nd edn., ii. 18; Mathias, *First Industrial Nation*, 308.

[48] C. H. Lee, *The British Economy since 1700* (Cambridge, 1986), 101–3, 10, 12, 98; id., *British Regional Employment Statistics 1841–1971* (Cambridge, 1979), Series A: Employment Categories 22–27. The proportions in both cases are swollen by the large number of female domestic servants.

[49] I. C. R. Byatt, 'Electrical Products', in Aldcroft (ed.), *Development of British Industry*, 273; id., *The British Electrical Industry 1875–1914* (Oxford, 1979), *passim*.

sophisticated fields, such as soap, heavy chemicals, coal tar intermediates, and explosives. In particular, British producers proved reluctant to adopt the Solway ammonia soda process first patented in 1861, sticking instead to the older Leblanc process in which they had invested heavily. Until the mid-1880s there were tolerably good reasons for doing this. After then there were not—something that might well have been perceived at the time.[50] More generally, for the most advanced country of the age to be encountering its first serious international challenges not in sectors using cheap labour or exotic resources, but in what would now be called high-technology industries, was at once unexpected and potentially very dangerous indeed.

3. A TRADING NATION

There was, in any case, something at least superficially paradoxical about Britain's advanced economy consistently running throughout our period a deficit on its balance of trade. Rough estimates suggest that international trade as a whole doubled between 1830 and 1850, trebled or possibly quadrupled in the following thirty years, and, in per caput terms, grew at a decennial rate of 33 per cent between 1800 and 1913 with a peak rate of 53 per cent over the period 1840–70.[51] And Britain was by far the largest international trader. Enormous quantities of goods flowed through its ports. In 1840 its general imports (a large part of them later re-exported) constituted perhaps 40 per cent of the exports (by value) of the rest of the world—and in 1872–3 the figure was still 31 per cent. Its share of total world trade reached a peak of about a quarter in the 1860s, while more reliable data for 1876–85 show that Britain's exports of manufactured goods then constituted about 38 per cent of the world's total. And, though the proportion had almost certainly been higher in the years immediately before this, it did not thereafter fall until well into the 1890s.[52] So striking a 'dominance' is unique in modern economic history.

As a result, Britain's became a distinctly trading economy, and in a purely statistical sense our period marks the high point of the ratio between

[50] H. W. Richardson, 'Chemicals', in Aldcroft (ed.), *Development of British Industry*, 278–80; P. H. Lindert and K. Trace, 'Yardsticks for Victorian Entrepreneurs', in McCloskey (ed.), *Essays*, 262–4.

[51] A. G. Kenwood and A. L. Lougheed, *The Growth of the International Economy 1820–1990*, 3rd edn. (London, 1992), 67.

[52] A. H. Imlah, *Economic Elements in the 'Pax Britannica': Studies in British Foreign Trade in the Nineteenth Century* (Cambridge, Mass., 1958), 190; Crouzet, *Victorian Economy*, 8; D. McCloskey, *Enterprise and Trade in Victorian Britain* (London, 1981), 143; S. B. Saul, 'The Export Economy', *Yorkshire Bulletin of Economic and Social Research*, 17 (1965), 12.

foreign trade and national income. From about 10 per cent in the 1830s, this rose to 17 per cent in the 1850s, 27 per cent in the 1860s, and more than 30 per cent in the 1880s and 1890s, after which a slightly lower figure of about 27–8 per cent was sustained until the outbreak of the Great War.[53] The overall payments position is shown in Table 9.6, from which (among much else) it can be seen that the third quarter of the century saw Britain's greatest success as an exporting nation.

TABLE 9.6 *United Kingdom Balance of Trade and Payments, 1831–1900 (annual averages, £m at current prices)*

	Net imports	Exports of UK products	Balance of commodity trade	Net income from services	Net income from dividends etc.	Balance on current account
1831–5	53.6	40.5	−13.1	14.1	5.4	6.4
1836–40	73.8	49.8	−24.0	18.6	8.0	2.6
1841–5	71.0	54.0	−17.0	15.4	7.5	5.9
1846–50	87.7	60.9	−26.8	22.0	9.5	4.7
1851–5	116.4	88.9	−17.5	23.7	11.7	8.0
1856–60	158.0	124.2	−33.8	43.5	16.5	26.2
1861–5	201.2	144.4	−56.8	57.1	21.8	22.0
1866–70	246.0	187.8	−58.2	67.9	30.8	40.5
1871–5	302.0	239.5	−62.5	86.8	50.0	74.6
1876–80	325.9	201.4	−124.5	93.0	56.3	24.9
1881–5	336.6	232.3	−104.3	101.0	64.8	61.6
1886–90	327.4	236.3	−91.1	94.6	84.2	87.6
1891–5	357.1	226.8	−130.3	88.4	94.0	52.0
1896–1900	413.3	252.7	−160.6	100.7	100.2	40.3

Source: P. Mathias, *The First Industrial Nation: An Economic History of Britain 1700–1914*, 2nd edn. (London, 1983), 279.

Yet it was a success based upon a uniquely favourable conjuncture of circumstances that had little to do with free trade and could never be more than temporary. In the first place, growing incomes overseas (and hence the demand for British exports) had not yet come to be based upon significant local industries capable of generating import substitutions, competition in third markets, and finally competition in the British market itself.[54] In the second place, very sharp mid-century changes occurred in the terms of

[53] Saul, 'Export Economy', 5.
[54] Cain and Hopkins, *British Imperialism*, 162; S. B. Saul, *Studies in British Overseas Trade 1870–1914* (Liverpool, 1960), 34.

trade, that is, in the relative prices of exports and imports. Because British manufacturers in earlier years had managed to cut the price of cotton goods by large amounts and European population growth had pushed against supplies of grain, the terms on which Britain had traded her commodity exports for food imports had moved unfavourably from the 1820s to the 1850s. Thereafter, however, the trend was reversed as export prices ceased to fall and even rose, so that, while the rate of growth in the *volume* of exports was only slightly faster in the third than in the second quarter of the century, the rate of growth in export *values* proved very substantial indeed.[55]

The composition of Britain's overseas trade during the heyday of the Victorian and Edwardian open and free trading economy between 1846 and 1914 has, in turn, elicited both contemporary and subsequent censure, not all of it justified. While coal certainly increased its primitive presence on the export side from 1 per cent of total exports in 1830–9 to 10 per cent in 1900–9, a greater dynamic spread was, none the less, achieved, because textiles fell from 72 to 38 per cent of total exports and machinery and iron and steel rose from 1 to 7 and from 11 to 14 per cent respectively. The trend in imports was, however, more worrying. The proportion of imports represented by food rose only slightly between 1840 and 1900—from 40 to 42 per cent of the total—but manufactured goods jumped from 4 to 25 per cent, and raw materials (largely required for domestic industry and the production of exports) fell from 57 to 33 per cent.[56] Nor have the changing *destinations* of exports escaped criticism, largely because the proportion of exports going to Germany and the United States fell from 24 to 13 per cent between 1873 and 1913, while the proportion going to the relatively unsophisticated economies of Africa and Asia rose from 17 to 31 per cent, with India in particular becoming increasingly important as time went on.[57]

This has often been depicted as a damaging withdrawal from difficult advanced markets in favour of simple and relatively backward ones. In reality, the pattern of British trade in the late nineteenth century reflected not merely domestic developments, but changes in world trading as a whole. More food and raw material supplies now came from distant areas which needed textiles and railway iron and those other heavy investment goods in which Britain specialized. Germany and the United States, both of them in deficit to primary-producer countries like India, possessed a

[55] McCloskey, *Enterprise and Trade*, 145; K. Harley, 'Foreign Trade: Comparative Advantage and Performance', in Floud and McCloskey (eds.), *Economic History*, 2nd edn., i. 304–5.

[56] Mathias, *First Industrial Nation*, 434; Deane and Cole, *British Economic Growth*, 33.

[57] Matthews, Feinstein, Odling-Smee, *British Economic Growth*, 452.

competitive advantage, not in the products demanded by these primary producers, but in the products of new industries that were being demanded in developed countries. As a result, exports to the unprotected British market, where consumers wanted such new products, provided the best means by which Germany and America could finance their primary imports, while Britain, in turn, paid off deficits with its industrial competitors through what was becoming an increasingly complex and evolving arrangement of multilateral settlements.[58]

The resulting expansion of trade had the effect of plugging Britain closely into an international system of exchange. However, the fact that domestic exports almost doubled to 22 per cent of national product between the 1840s and 1870s does not itself prove that the bulk of the momentum for growth was coming from foreign trade, even though the impressive juxtaposition of growth and trade persuaded many at the time (not least Gladstone and Peel) and has persuaded many since that this must indeed have been the case. If, as has been argued, Britain's foreign trade is properly viewed as, above all, 'a way of acquiring imports, then the question of the extent of British dependence on trade reduces to a question of how well Britain would have done had this way to imports been blocked'.[59] Now, although calculations in this field are highly speculative, one estimate implies that in 1860 total self-sufficiency (that is, a complete lack of external trade) might well have cost Britain about 6 per cent of national income and certainly not more than 12 per cent. Another suggests that, had an absence of overseas markets halved the size of the British cotton industry in the period 1780–1860, the resulting cumulative loss over eighty years would have amounted to perhaps 9 per cent of national income. While these are not insignificant figures, they fall well short of supporting the bold claims so often made for Victorian Britain's 'dependence' on foreign trade. In reality, the chief constraints upon economic growth seem to have been mostly internal, with trading policy and foreign competition playing no more than minor roles—Rosencrantz and Guildenstern perhaps, nothing more.[60] Nor should it be overlooked that the United Kingdom ran a consistently unfavourable balance of commodity trade throughout the whole of the Victorian period and that the chief engines for turning this, equally consistently, into a favourable balance of payments were invisible exports and (increasingly) earnings from investments overseas (Table 9.6).

Free trade, so much debated at the time and since, cannot, therefore, be said to have had any immediately beneficial impact upon the economy as a

---

[58] Harley, 'Foreign Trade', i. 326–8; Cain and Hopkins, *British Imperialism*, 223–4.
[59] Harley, 'Foreign Trade', i. 304.
[60] Ibid. i. 306; McCloskey, '1780–1860: A Survey', i. 257; id., *Enterprise and Trade*, 150–1.

whole or even upon its trading characteristics. In 1846 and for some time thereafter the repeal of the Corn Laws was more important as a political than an economic event. As part of that continuing British dismantling of protection started in the 1820s and more or less concluded in 1860 (by the Cobden-Chevalier Treaty with France and another tariff-cutting budget from Gladstone), it had long-term rather than sudden effects. And while the 1860s and 1870s certainly constituted a brief international episode of almost-free trade, during which British exports and imports taken together grew steadily, this did not—it seems—have much to do with changes in tariff policy at home or overseas: 4.4 per cent growth a year in 1821–51, 4.6 in 1841–70, 4.1 in 1851–80.[61] If anything, what evidence there is seems to suggest that in certain respects the substantial mid-century tariff reductions made by Britain may well have harmed rather than helped the economy and should, therefore, best be seen as a kind of magnanimous Peelite and Gladstonian gift to the rest of the world.

In 1850 Britain dominated so many international markets in a semi-monopolistic manner, and was the main buyer of so many foreigners' exports, that tariffs might actually have improved her terms of trade by reducing the amount of British manufactured goods which other countries could obtain in return for their exports of food. In other words, just as private monopolists can raise their incomes by withholding some of what they sell, so can a country (and it should be remembered that many tariffs had actually been designed to prevent the *export* of advanced machinery etc. to potential competitors overseas). By largely abandoning tariffs, Britain effectively refused to exploit her position. Paradoxically, however, it was at the end of the century, when the monopoly had gone and Britain's open-door policies may at last have been generating benefits by diverting Germany and other countries away from potentially larger markets elsewhere, that protection began to recover its political appeal, an example of how the synchronization of political imperatives and economic realities can often be inexact, even perverse. While the general return to protection on the part of foreign countries from the late 1870s onwards probably did little to dampen down world trade as a whole, its impact upon British trade was more substantial, if circuitous rather than direct. Thus, instead of affecting overall values, world tariffs seem to have helped to augment the existing tendency of British exports to embrace products which were less profitable and less capable of expansion, such as coal and semi-finished goods. Not

[61] Deane and Cole, *British Economic Growth*, 311; P. Bairoch, 'European Trade Policy, 1815–1914', in P. Mathias and S. Pollard (eds.), *The Cambridge Economic History of Europe*, viii. *The Industrial Economies: The Development of Economic and Social Policies* (Cambridge, 1989), 42.

only was the market for these highly volatile, but their export meant that the profits to be derived from such further fabrication as they might require passed more and more into foreign hands.[62]

4. INVESTING AT HOME AND OVERSEAS

No less opaque in character was the enormous late Victorian rise in investment overseas and hence the receipt of substantial interest and dividend remittances, the impact of which kept the balance of payments in credit until the Great War. Before considering the general effects of this, it is important to reflect upon the role of investment, credit, and banking within the economy as a whole. For both legislative and economic reasons, banks in England moved towards consolidation in the decades after the Bank Charter Act of 1844. Although private and country banks continued to exist, it was the joint-stock banks (the products largely of Acts of Parliament going back to 1826) that began to dominate the scene, so much so that Scottish banking, which had earlier begun to consolidate and develop large branch networks, now came more and more into line with developments south of the border. After 1844 the Bank of England (while remaining a private institution) became a central bank and little else. As deposit taking and cheque transactions expanded and note issuing diminished in importance for the other banks, so economies of scale became more apparent and consolidation more advantageous.[63] The number of private banks in England and Wales fell from 327 in 1850 to 81 in 1900 and the number of joint-stock banks in the United Kingdom from 132 to 103. But the number of bank *branches* in the United Kingdom rose from 0.61 per 10,000 people to 1.52 over the same period, with Scotland still somewhat ahead of the field.[64]

It now seems clear that most of the long-term capital for early manufacturing businesses (which were often small) was raised from the entrepreneurs themselves, their kin, friends, and associates. Banks, however, also played a part, and even if their practice of taking short-term deposits made long-term investment difficult, a willingness to renew loans meant that at least some of their lending soon adopted distinctly long-term characteristics.[65] But while it remains difficult to determine precisely

[62] Kenwood and Lougheed, *Growth*, 73–4.

[63] R. Cameron, 'Banking and Industrialisation in Britain in the Nineteenth Century', in A. Slaven and D. H. Aldcroft (eds.), *Business, Banking and Urban History* (Edinburgh, 1982), 108.

[64] Calculated from M. Collins, *Banks and Industrial Finance in Britain 1800–1939* (London, 1991), 28.

[65] Crouzet, *Victorian Economy*, 335–41; R. Sylla, 'The Role of Banks', in Sylla and Toniolo (eds.), *Patterns*, 52; McCloskey, '1780–1860: A Survey', i. 254.

whether early nineteenth-century bankers did or did not encourage industry, their mid- and late Victorian successors are still often accused of adopting conservative and centralized lending practices antipathetical to the needs of provincial manufacturers and of being so biased in favour of 'easy' investments overseas (where sums were big, turnover high, and dealing profits large) that domestic industry atrophied for lack of capital. The chief accusers have generally been those most determined to identify culprits for Britain's alleged late nineteenth-century industrial 'failure'. And, indeed, the banks' links with industry were not always close and the large gulf between bankers and industrialists was an undoubted feature of Victorian social relationships.[66]

While it may be true that banks became more cautious after the serious liquidity crises which accompanied the 'crashes' of 1847, 1857, 1866, and 1878, there is remarkably little evidence to suggest that British industry ever found it difficult to raise capital. What was lacking was not so much capital as manufacturers urgently demanding it. (Ireland, for example, was awash with capital, but not with those prepared to mop it up.[67]) Until 1914 most British firms remained in family hands, were jealous of their independence, and continued to finance long-term investments out of ploughed-back profits or from informal sources of various kinds. That only 18.7 per cent of the money raised in the City of London between 1865 and 1914 for British-based projects was intended for manufacturing enterprises is, therefore, almost entirely a reflection of lack of demand rather than lack of supply.[68]

It is of course possible that the institutional state of domestic capital markets may have been so deeply misaligned that industrialists, no less than investors, simply lacked the information and confidence upon which to base optimal plans capable of achieving rapid structural change in an increasingly competitive and complex environment. With different institutional

---

[66] Y. Cassis, 'British Finance: Success and Controversy', in J. J. van Helten and Cassis (eds.), *Capitalism in a Mature Economy: Financial Institutions, Capital Exports and British Industry, 1870–1939* (Aldershot, 1990), 4; W. P. Kennedy, *Industrial Structure, Capital Markets and the Origins of British Economic Decline* (Cambridge, 1987), 121–2; P. L. Cottrell, *Industrial Finance 1830–1914: The Finance and Organization of English Manufacturing Industry* (London, 1980), 236–8; Y. Cassis, 'Bankers in English Society in the Late Nineteenth Century', *Economic History Review*, 38 (1985), 210–29.

[67] S. Pollard and D. Ziegler, 'Banking and Industrialization', in Y. Cassis (ed.), *Finance and Financiers in European History, 1880–1960* (Cambridge, 1992), 26.

[68] Cassis, 'British Finance', 5; M. Edelstein, *Overseas Investment in the Age of High Imperialism: The United Kingdom, 1850–1914* (London, 1982), 62–5; Collins, *Banks and Industrial Finance*, 33–4; L. E. Davis and R. A. Huttenback, *Mammon and the Pursuit of Empire: The Political Economy of British Imperialism, 1860–1912* (Cambridge, 1986), 54.

arrangements, it has been suggested, businessmen would have borrowed eagerly, the new technologies would have been more fully exploited, and British per caput incomes would have increased by a remarkable 50 per cent between 1870 and 1914.[69] However, such views remain highly speculative and are almost certainly exaggerated.

Unflattering contrasts are also often drawn with the so-called 'investment banks' of Bismarckian Germany, which invested long-term in industrial firms, played an active part in their management, and encouraged them to move into new technologies. The contrast is, however, overdone. German bankers were themselves well aware that it was precisely the inadequacies of German capital markets which obliged them to adopt a more interventionist role. And, in any case, the English banking system may well have contributed as much to economic growth by pursuing a type of banking which did not lead to serious financial crises as the German banks did by facilitating industrial capital formation and the export of manufactured goods.[70] All in all, therefore, a more impressive case has been made by those who believe that British capital markets probably responded positively to demands for domestic industrial finance throughout the second half of the nineteenth century than by those who take a contrary view.[71]

The workings of mid- and late Victorian stock exchanges tell a similar story. Stock markets in this period were overwhelmingly concerned with raising finance for home and foreign governments and for large public utilities overseas. The proportion of quoted securities devoted to the manufacturing and commercial sectors was small, though it did grow considerably during the quarter-century leading up to the Great War. In 1853 only 1.8 per cent of all (and 7.5 per cent of non-governmental) securities traded on the exchanges related to manufacturing and commercial undertakings. By 1873 the proportions had actually fallen—to 1.1 and 2.8 per cent—though by 1913 they had risen to 7.7 and 14.0 per cent.[72] While the proportion which non-domestic securities constituted of all

[69] Kennedy, *Industrial Structure*, 58–77; id., 'Economic Growth and Structural Change in the United Kingdom, 1870–1914', *Journal of Economic History*, 44 (1982), 105–18; id., 'Capital Markets and Industrial Structure in the Victorian Economy', in van Helten and Cassis (eds.), *Capitalism*, 23–51.

[70] Cottrell, *Industrial Finance*, 239, 244; R. C. Michie, 'The Stock Exchange and the British Economy, 1870–1939', in van Helten and Cassis (eds.), *Capitalism*, 108; C. K. Harley, 'Substitution for Prerequisites', in Sylla and Toniolo (eds.), *Patterns*, 40.

[71] Collins, *Banks and Industrial Finance*, 42–51; Edelstein, *Overseas Investment*, 47–72, 163–70, 288–311; id., 'Realized Rates of Return on UK Home and Foreign Portfolio Investment in the Age of High Imperialism', *Explorations in Economic History*, 13 (1976), 283–329.

[72] Michie, 'Stock Exchange', 104.

securities held in the United Kingdom between 1870 and 1913 increased
from 37 to 48 per cent, so did that of domestic non-railway enterprises which
rose from 4 to 19 per cent.[73] If, therefore, the London Stock Exchange
continued to devote most of its energies to financing governments, railways,
and utilities, its participation in domestic industry was increasing all the
same. Because flotation costs were high, few small manufacturers found it
worthwhile to attempt to raise money in the City of London. But, then,
there is little evidence that they found it difficult to raise all they needed by
other means. In so far, therefore, as problems of industrial finance existed,
they had less to do with financial markets than with industry itself.

   Whatever the requirements of British industry, the growth of investment
overseas was an undoubted fact. Table 9.7 shows the proportion of Gross
National Product that was devoted to total domestic and overseas investment and the proportion contributed by net income from abroad (that is, by
overseas investments). The most striking aspects of this table are the
substantial increase in the rate of new investment abroad after the mid-
1850s (Column 3) and the manner in which the resultant income began
to exceed annual net investment outflows from the mid-1870s onwards
(Columns 3 and 4). The former phenomenon was initially generated by

TABLE 9.7 *United Kingdom domestic and overseas savings and investments,*
1835–1894

	1 GNS % of GNP	2 GDI % of GNP	3 NFI % of GNP	4 NOP % of GNP
1835–44	8.57	7.66	0.91	
1845–54	10.96	10.05	0.92	
1855–64	10.68	8.14	2.55	2.57
1865–74	13.90	9.22	4.67	3.76
1875–84	12.16	9.17	2.99	5.29
1885–94	12.42	7.48	4.94	6.70

Notes:
GNP: Gross Domestic Product at market prices plus income from abroad; GNS: Gross
National Savings = Gross National Investment; GDI: Gross Domestic Fixed Investment
plus changes in inventories; NFI: Net Foreign Investment; NOP: Net Overseas Property
Income.

Source: Adapted from M. Edelstein, 'Foreign Investment and Accumulation, 1860–1914', in
R. Floud and D. McCloskey (eds.), *The Economic History of Britain since 1700*, 2nd edn., 3
vols. (Cambridge, 1994), ii. 175.

[73] M. Edelstein, 'Rigidity and Bias in the British Capital Market, 1870–1913', in
McCloskey (ed.), *Essays*, 83–4.

burgeoning opportunities abroad and then driven ever higher from the 1870s onwards as the falling rate of increase of population in Britain restricted incremental investment opportunities in domestic housing, infrastructure, and so forth. It may also have been the case that a highly unequal distribution of national income, by placing disproportionately large resources in the hands of the well-to-do, at times pushed such people into undertaking unusually energetic attempts to find remunerative outlets for their savings. With increasing investment requirements abroad and static requirements at home helping at once to pull and to push investments overseas, there can be little doubt that it was the demand for finance—not biased capital markets—that generally called the investment tune.[74]

The bulk (perhaps 70–80 per cent) of British savings sent abroad between 1850 and 1914 went into so-called 'portfolio' investments which are defined as either IOUs to governments or the equity and IOUs of private companies in which British investors owned less than 30 per cent of the equity interest. This contrasts sharply with the position before the nineteenth century (and indeed after 1945) when most overseas assets took the form of *direct* investments in or through bodies subject to a large measure of British control. The Victorian bias towards portfolio holdings flowed from the fact that the overwhelming weight of investment took the form of 'social overhead capital' (for railways, docks, and so forth) where the large size of undertakings made it difficult to exceed the 30 per cent level. Indeed, social overhead projects attracted about 70 per cent of total overseas portfolio investment between 1865 and 1914, manufacturing projects no more than 4 per cent.[75]

TABLE 9.8 *United Kingdom overseas investment by region, 1830–1914* (%)

	1830	1854	1870	1914
Europe	66	55	25	5
United States	9	25	27	21
Latin America	23	15	11	18
Empire: India	2	5	22	9
Empire: dominions			12	37
Other regions			3	9

Source: A. G. Kenwood and A. L. Lougheed, *The Growth of the International Economy 1820–1990*, 3rd edn. (London, 1992), 30. The 1914 figure does not total 100% because of rounding.

[74] Edelstein, *Overseas Investment*, 290–301, also 4–8, 194–5; id., 'Foreign Investment and Accumulation, 1860–1914', in Floud and McCloskey (eds.), *Economic History*, 2nd edn., ii. 173–96.
[75] Ibid. ii. 177, 179.

The geographical distribution of these investments followed a number of linear and cyclical patterns. In proportional terms Europe became less important, Latin America went up and down, the United States reached something of a plateau after the 1850s, while the empire (though in a variety of configurations) attracted a higher and higher percentage of funds (Table 9.8).

As the flow of funds overseas continued to increase after the 1850s, so the total amount invested abroad grew to unprecedented heights. As a percentage of Gross National Wealth overseas assets rose consistently if unevenly: 6.0 (1850), 11.9 (1870), 21.1 (1890), 26.2 (1910).[76] At current prices they rose from £0.3bn in 1856 to £1.0bn in 1873 and to £4.2bn in 1913.[77] By 1900 Britain's stock of overseas investments was more than twice as large as those of Germany or France and twenty-four times as large as that of the United States.[78] However, because studies of nineteenth-century rates of return have not yet supplied unambiguous results, it remains unclear whether Victorian investors, in sending so high a proportion of their savings abroad, were in fact following the paths of economic 'rationality' with the close fidelity they so often liked to proclaim.[79]

As the total invested abroad rose, a point was reached some time in the 1870s when the dividends received started to exceed the amount of capital invested each year (Table 9.7). In other words, the overall traffic began to take the form of a net inward rather than a net outward flow. The United Kingdom ceased to be a net lender and began instead to be more than able, as an entity, to finance new loans out of the returns coming from existing ones, so that the build-up of foreign assets was being achieved without any strain on the economy. While this clearly helped to compensate for a consistently negative balance of commodity trade, it was not without actual and potential drawbacks of its own. Britain could deal with the surpluses (or sterling gap) which such a state of things necessarily created in three ways: imports could be increased, exports cut, or further amounts of capital sent abroad. The second alternative seemed undesirable to many. The third was merely a postponement rather than a solution. Even the first, though more attractive (at least in the short run), might well distort market signals,

---

[76] Edelstein, 'Foreign Investment', ii. 175.

[77] Matthews, Feinstein, Odling-Smee, *British Economic Growth*, 128. In *Britain's Investment Overseas on the Eve of the First World War* (London, 1986) D. C. M. Platt argues that these figures are substantially exaggerated. His views have not, however, proved convincing (C. H. Feinstein, 'Britain's Overseas Investments in 1913', *Economic History Review*, 43 (1990), 288–95).

[78] S. Pollard, 'Capital Exports, 1870–1914', *Economic History Review*, 38 (1985), 492.

[79] Edelstein, *Overseas Investment*, 126, 138–40; Davis and Huttenback, *Mammon*, 106–17.

limit the growth of output at home, and exercise a broadly negative effect upon domestic enterprise.[80] Such damage, therefore, as was caused by capital outflows in the late Victorian period was, it seems, the result, not so much of any withholding of capital from domestic industry (which may or may not have occurred), but of increasing import streams and the effects these had upon the growth of output at home.

5. NO LONGER AT FULL STEAM?

The topic of overseas investment also has implications for the much-debated question of whether or not the late Victorian economy exhibited signs of 'decline'. And however much certain findings concerning the temporal location of any possible climacteric might suggest that, in this connection, we look at the middle rather than the end of the nineteenth century, contemporaries so clearly believed that something disturbing was beginning to happen towards the end of our period that the very controversy which their views raised has itself become a matter of substantial historical concern.

   Whatever may have happened to the economy generally in the 1840s and 1850s, industrialization still had some way to go. Although the proportion of workers engaged in manufacturing was already as high in 1841 as it was to be sixty years later, the incremental nature of developments in technology, management methods, and scale of operations meant that—even for the world's greatest industrial nation—much remained to be done. For example, management problems relating to the supervision and co-ordination of large-scale enterprises kept the size of mid-century factories and firms small. Only cotton and the primary metal industries provided exceptions, with some cotton mills employing over 1,000 hands and the Dowlais iron works in 1849 no less than 7,000.[81] But half the population of England and Wales still lived in rural areas and the great majority of 'industrial' workers laboured in trades which had hardly been revolutionized at all.[82] Not until the second half of the century were major sectors such as the food industry touched by significant technological change. Even the mechanization of non-cotton textiles took place chiefly after the 1840s, while clothing was

---

[80] Pollard, *Britain's Prime*, 107–10; id., 'Capital Exports', 511–14.

[81] V. A. C. Gatrell, 'Labour, Power, and the Size of Firms in Lancashire Cotton in the Second Quarter of the Nineteenth Century', *Economic History Review*, 30 (1977), 95–139; R. Lloyd-Jones and A. A. Le Roux, 'The Size of Firms in the Cotton Industry: Manchester 1815–41', *Economic History Review*, 33 (1980), 72–82; Crouzet, *Victorian Economy*, 79.

[82] A. E. Musson, *The Growth of British Industry* (London, 1978), 140–1; Mokyr, 'New Economic History', 15; Crafts, *British Economic Growth*, 4–8.

still only partially a factory industry at the beginning of the twentieth century. Building too used few machines of importance. The biggest machine-based undertakings in the third quarter of the century were not in manufacturing at all, but in transport. By 1850 manufacturing enterprises of all kinds were using steam engines with perhaps 300,000 horsepower. By 1870 this had risen to 977,000. Only then did the big jump come—with 9,650,000 horsepower installed in British industry as a whole by 1907.[83]

Although the main waves of pioneering inventions had made themselves manifest by the 1830s, it took another four decades or more for them to spread beyond their industrial and regional starting-points. Indeed, only during the period 1850–1914 can the industrial revolution be said to have finally and firmly established itself on a national scale.[84] Not only that, but the processes leading to the creation of large-scale enterprises, though pioneered in Britain, proved comparatively slow to take hold domestically, so that, by the end of the century, most of the world's greatest industrial undertakings were to be found elsewhere. Amalgamations did not really get under way in Britain until the 1890s and efforts to set up cartels from the 1880s onwards proved only moderately successful. And even if size alone rarely guarantees efficiency, its absence can limit horizons and lead to lapses in managerial and technological inventiveness. By 1905 the fifty largest firms in Britain and the United States had an average capitalization of £4m and £16.4m respectively. Among the former those in brewing and distilling were the most prominent; among the latter those in iron and steel.[85]

The coincidence of increasing industrial maturity, rapid advances by rivals abroad, and spasmodic bad times in the years after 1873, induced repeated contemporary assertions that the late Victorian economy was somehow in decline. Separately these developments would probably have been dismissed as temporary aberrations. Together they can clearly be seen to have exercised a depressive influence upon the psychologies, not only of industrialists, politicians, and theorists, but of subsequent commentators as well. 'Decline' can, however, be assessed in a variety of ways. Was the economy growing more slowly than before? Yes, it would seem that growth had perhaps already slowed down in the 1850s. Were other countries catching up? Unsurprisingly, Yes. Were they moving into the lead? Up to a point. Was the economy declining in any real sense at all? Relatively

[83] Musson, *Growth*, 166–8.
[84] Ibid. 152; J. Mokyr, 'Technological Change, 1700–1830', in Floud and McCloskey (eds.), *Economic History*, 2nd edn., i. 29.
[85] P. L. Payne, 'The Emergence of the Large-Scale Company in Great Britain, 1870–1914', *Economic History Review*, 20 (1967), 519–42; Mathias, *First Industrial Nation*, 355–61.

yes, absolutely no. Most important of all: was the economy performing up to its full potential? Here no unambiguous answer is possible, though a positive one would of course effectively uncouple the concepts of climacteric and decline.

Decline of some sort was of course inevitable. As other countries industrialized, so Britain could hardly retain her comparative position. Nor could she have sustained the initial growth rates of the industrial revolution, however much these may now seem moderate rather than jet-propelled. After 1873 and even more notably after 1899 British growth rates fell behind those of Germany, the United States, and (for the later period) France and Italy as well. Between 1872 and 1899 Britain's share of the world's manufactured exports fell from 45 to 29 per cent, Germany's rose from 12 to 21 per cent. And while in absolute terms Britain's manufacturing output per head was still in 1913 considerably higher than that of Germany, it had by then already fallen behind that of the United States.[86]

Attempts to explain such changes have revolved around two broad arguments. The first emphasizes Britain's early industrial start, the second the configuration of her social and political circumstances. The early-start interpretation, although played in many keys, amounts ultimately to a single melody, namely, that Victorian businesses were doggedly unwilling to renew outdated equipment, an attitude itself seen as part of a wider conservatism created by pioneering industrialization and typified by attachment to small family firms, belief in 'on-the-job' training, and a suspicion of science and research. A coda is often added in the form of the so-called 'inter-relatedness' argument, which maintains that, once complex industrial systems are established, it becomes difficult to replace the parts in need of renewal without jettisoning those still functioning at optimum capacity.

In terms of economic theory such contentions are nonsensical. Old equipment constitutes a 'free gift' from the past that a rational manager will accept only so long as it offers a superior alternative to buying anew. Apart from the costs of demolishing structures and retraining and relocating employees, past investments do not place established manufacturers (who can always choose to change techniques) at any competitive disadvantage to newcomers. Inter-relatedness too should be a problem only in so far as its implications are left unresolved through lack of entrepreneurial vigour.[87] But however true all this may be, in practice there is little doubt that businessmen in lead countries have all too easily tended to slide into a form of psychological traditionalism from which imperfectly operating

---

[86] Floud, 'Britain, 1860–1914: A Survey', ii. 16; Pollard, 'Dynamism', 53.

[87] Lindert and Trace, 'Yardsticks', 240.

markets have not always been able to 'rescue' them or replace them with
more efficient competitors. Those who none the less argue that the mid-
and late Victorian economy was operating as effectively as it could under all
objective circumstances (notably the restraints imposed by binding
resource limitations of various kinds) have begun to encounter growing
scepticism from commentators who insist that other countries responded to
similar economic environments in different and more successful ways.[88]

In the case of late Victorian Britain, explanations for the character of
such responses have been sought largely in the peculiarities of domestic
social structure and political behaviour, though these too are of course by
no means unconnected with the experience of early industrialization.
Neither the nature of the state nor the governing ideas and mores of the
times were, it is suggested, congenial to an agenda on which the aggressive
development of economic superiority should have constituted the first and
only item. Late Victorian governments are accused of failing to provide the
kind of educational and administrative structures which modernizing
industries require and of 'interfering' in the economy in ways which
many (then and since) have held to be inconsistent with the maximization
of economic success. In particular, the railways were increasingly controlled and pressure was exerted to improve the probity of commercial
life, to support reasonable wage levels, to discourage the growth of monopolies and cartels. Successive governments, in this view, felt it more and
more difficult unambiguously to decide whether the aims of industry
should be rigorously confined to maximizing profits or whether notions
of social provision should also be contemplated. Whatever the effects of all
this may have been at home, in economically dynamic Germany—invariably held up as an example of industrial success—Bismarck did of course
'interfere' very dramatically indeed by forcing insurance and pension
provisions upon employers no more enthusiastic about such things than
were their British counterparts.

Education has been the aspect of government activity most often criticized for failing to support industrial renewal, with (once again) unflattering comparisons made with what was happening in late nineteenth-century
Germany. And in some respects such criticisms do, indeed, possess a
certain force. The Germans undoubtedly achieved a far more productive
marriage between science and industry in, for example, the chemical and
electrical sectors. By 1860 a much higher proportion of German children

---

[88] McCloskey, *Enterprise and Trade*, 94–110; M. Thomas, 'Slowdown in the Pre-World
War One Economy', *Oxford Review of Economic Policy*, 4/1 (1988), 15–16; Mathias, *First
Industrial Nation*, 393; Crafts, *British Economic Growth*, 156–65; Pollard, *Britain's Prime*, 1–57.

(97.5 per cent of those between 6 and 14) went to school and received an education which enabled a sizeable minority to go forward to secondary establishments. By contrast, the fact that Britain's early industrialization had been achieved without advanced educational or scientific provision persuaded many British industrialists that such things were unnecessary, even harmful.[89] When, however, one looks at total spending on science and technology it is clear that in 1870 Britain was still spending more both relatively and absolutely than Germany. What is true is that German spending was more focused, particularly upon the universities and certain areas of research like organic chemistry, and that Germany was able to establish much clearer patterns by which the regular progression of technical training was accepted as a qualification for appropriate promotion levels in industry. But this does not mean that everything was better in Germany. From 1856 onwards, the Department of Science and Art in Whitehall inaugurated a substantial state-aided system of technical education. The number of students involved rose from 500 in 1860 to 187,000 in 1890. Further provision was made by the Royal Society of Arts and the City and Guilds of London Institute.[90] And while the German system was centrally organized and depended upon a high degree of compulsion, the British was more diffuse, harnessed enthusiasts rather than draftees, and was in many ways more flexible. Nor is it clear that the kind of on-the-job training favoured in British industry was inferior to more formal academic methods, particularly when, as was the case in late Victorian Britain, the trainees came from a comparatively literate workforce accustomed to the disciplines of factory life.[91]

At the higher levels, it is also clear that neither the public schools nor the universities in Britain entirely ignored science during the last third of the century, though the late Victorian intellectual élite was hardly scientifically trained in the way that it was governmentally trained (government, after all, was what it was supposed to be for). A new generation of headmasters at schools such as Harrow, Rugby, Winchester, and Clifton encouraged scientific studies.[92] Whereas all the universities in the United Kingdom (not excluding the once-dynamic Scottish foundations) had fallen

[89] Crouzet, *Victorian Economy*, 415; S. B. Saul, 'Research and Development in British Industry from the End of the Nineteenth Century to the 1960s', in T. C. Smout (ed.), *The Search for Wealth and Stability* (London, 1979), 114–38.

[90] Pollard, *Britain's Prime*, 155–6, 172–8.

[91] R. C. Floud, 'Technical Education and Economic Performance: Britain, 1850–1914', *Albion*, 14 (1982), 165–6.

[92] M. Sanderson, *Education, Economic Change and Society in England 1780–1870*, 2nd edn. (London, 1991), 42.

into decay by 1850, the next sixty years were marked by expansion, revival, and reform. Numerous provincial colleges were founded in which science and technology were encouraged. If less than a dozen students were taking the new Cambridge Natural Sciences Tripos in the 1860s, the period between 1880 and 1914 was one during which the 'symbiotic relationship of civic university technological departments and industrial firms was closer than ever before or since'.[93] In England alone the number of university teaching posts in science and technology (excluding medicine) rose from 60 in 1850 to 400 in 1900, the number of specialist graduates from 19 in 1870 to 1,231 in 1910.[94] And in any case, even the most cursory look at the situation in Germany reveals not perfection but a world of endless complaints—about funding, excessive concentration upon classical studies, about the social inferiority of the Technical High School, about, above all, a reluctance to engage in practical scientific research.[95]

If in many respects British science was making significant advances in the years before the Great War, two aspects of its relationship with industry remain problematic. The first concerns the motivation underpinning scientific research. And here, despite endless claims that Britain has generally specialized in theoretical rather than applied research, there can be little doubt that it was the highly utilitarian signals coming from late Victorian industry that played a crucial role in encouraging concentration upon a narrow range of problems which, on closer examination, often turned out to be unproductive or insoluble or both. By believing so doggedly that research should 'pay'—at once and immediately—hard-nosed British businessmen helped to lead science down a series of dead ends. In Germany, on the other hand, strategies were adopted which enabled industry to achieve a staggering superiority in certain fields, not because of any overt and relentless pursuit of applicable results, but because German scientists were allowed to experiment much more widely than their British counterparts. Having done so, they then often found that they could apply their new discoveries in all sorts of useful and unexpected ways.[96] The second aspect concerns the numbers graduating from United Kingdom universities in science and technology. Here too, however, though these were

[93] M. Sanderson, 'The English Civic Universities and the "Industrial Spirit", 1870–1914', *Historical Research*, 61 (1988), 99.

[94] Pollard, *Britain's Prime*, 193.

[95] H. James, 'The German Experience and the Myth of British Cultural Exceptionalism', in B. Collins and K. Robbins (eds.), *British Culture and Economic Decline* (London, 1990), 108–11.

[96] Pollard, *Britain's Prime*, 120–3; P. Alter, 'Science and the Anglo-German Antagonism', in T. R. Gourvish and A. O'Day (eds.), *Later Victorian Britain, 1867–1900* (London, 1988), 271–2; James, 'German Experience', 111.

undoubtedly lower than in Germany, there is no evidence that Victorian industry as a whole expressed any strong desire for more. Indeed, many British science and engineering graduates found themselves obliged to go into teaching or to emigrate for want of industrial opportunities.[97]

Lively, not to say combative, debates have revolved around the performance of those who actually ran late Victorian businesses, even though it is difficult (some would say impossible) to isolate entrepreneurship either from more easily quantifiable economic developments, on the one hand, or from the social and intellectual environment, on the other. For those (contemporaries as well as historians) wedded to the notion of almost total British economic failure, entrepreneurs have long constituted irresistible whipping boys—failing to adopt new inventions and processes, failing to invest in science and research, failing to move from old staples to dynamic and innovative industries, failing to market their goods abroad, failing to organize themselves into aggressive cartels with a view to extracting monopoly profits from the world at large.[98] Because British firms remained relatively small, no managerial class emerged as it did in Germany, so that the traditional attitudes formed by early industrialization led, it is argued, inexorably to technical conservatism. This, in turn, was rendered more enfeebling still by having superimposed upon it a rentier mentality generated by huge inflows of 'unearned' income from abroad. And finally, calculations which suggest that Total Factor Productivity showed no increase at all between 1873 and 1913 have been seized upon to support the notion that contemporary entrepreneurs were quite simply not up to the job.[99]

On the other hand, more detailed examinations of particular industrial and business activities have identified certain positive characteristics. Thus a number of studies—some more successfully than others—have sought to exonerate from entrepreneurial lapses those responsible for a large proportion of British industry: cotton, iron and steel, coal, machine tools, shipbuilding.[100] Another common accusation, that British firms were

[97] Pollard, *Britain's Prime*, 198; Floud, 'Technical Education', 166–7; P. Payne, 'Entrepreneurship and British Economic Decline', in Collins and Robbins (eds.), *British Culture*, 43.

[98] D. Aldcroft, 'The Entrepreneur and the British Economy, 1870–1914', *Economic History Review*, 17 (1964), 113–34; and (generally) D. S. Landes, *The Unbound Prometheus: Technological Change and Industrial Development in Western Europe from 1750 to the Present* (Cambridge, 1969).

[99] Crouzet, *Victorian Economy*, 340–1; Mathias, *First Industrial Nation*, 304, 385–6; Matthews, Feinstein, Odling-Smee, *British Economic Growth*, 16.

[100] L. Sandberg, *Lancashire in Decline: A Study in Entrepreneurship, Technology, and International Trade* (Columbus, Ohio, 1974); McCloskey (ed.), *Essays*, 215–34, 285–304,

unimaginative in marketing their products abroad, has also been rebutted with considerable force and some effect.[101] Nor has the tendency of certain critics to adopt a form of 'heads-I-win-tails-you-lose' analysis strengthened their case: blaming British exporters for cavalier disregard of individual markets *and* for 'meeting the most perverse specifications in order to satisfy the customer's often unreasonable demands'.[102] Businessmen are not prophets and the task of assessing the extent to which they should have been able to anticipate problems which lay in the future might reasonably provoke the pertinent question too rarely asked of those economic historians who detect mighty missed opportunities in past times: 'If you're so clever why aren't you rich?' Of course, Victorian businessmen made mistakes—in the chemical industry, for example, they made very large mistakes—but the notion that their collective errors were of such a magnitude that almost anybody at the time could have identified them and found a way out is to conclude, rather unhelpfully, that contemporary industry was more or less entirely in the hands of fools of the most superfine sort.

Broad cultural attacks upon the entrepreneurial mores of late Victorian Britain have also probably scored more misses than hits. Lurid pictures of third-generation businessmen emerging entrepreneurially castrated from effete public schools, buying large country estates, and devoting little of their fading industrial energies to managing cotton mills, iron works, and coal mines are no less ludicrous than similar grand claims that Victorian élites of all kinds were suffused by the louche values of a backward-looking ruralist romanticism which despised wealth creation and knew only of wealth spending.[103] In so far as it is possible to pin down anything as nebulous as an 'industrial spirit' and to distil a national outlook from the productions of high culture, then Britain's was far and away the most procapitalist society in the whole of nineteenth-century Europe, not least in comparison to that of Germany where the extreme right and extreme left did actually combine to present a powerful attack on industrialization from

313–37; R. C. Floud, *The British Machine Tool Industry, 1850–1914* (Cambridge, 1976); Pollard and Robertson, *British Shipbuilding*; D. McCloskey, *Economic Maturity and Industrial Decline: British Iron and Steel, 1870–1913* (Cambridge, Mass., 1973).

[101] S. J. Nicholas, 'The Overseas Marketing Performance of British Industry, 1870–1914', *Economic History Review*, 37 (1984), 489–506.

[102] P. L. Payne, *British Entrepreneurship in the Nineteenth Century*, 2nd edn. (London, 1988), 52.

[103] Such arguments are presented in M. J. Wiener, *English Culture and the Decline of the Industrial Spirit 1850–1980* (Cambridge, 1981); C. Barnett, *The Audit of War: The Illusion and Reality of Britain as a Great Nation* (London, 1986).

a general anti-urban and anti-technology point of view.[104] Disputes continue as to whether wealthy Victorian businessmen were more or less active in buying landed estates than their predecessors had been—as if it were axiomatic that the purchase of broad acres debarred a man from industrial success.[105] Ironically, it was often German commentators who spoke most admiringly of British businessmen's adherence to the sober habits of the middle class. And, in truth, with the exception of a handful of plutocrats, neither German nor British businessmen ever showed much inclination to adopt traditional aristocratic styles of life.[106] If anything, the movement was the other way, as British aristocrats began to take up increasingly entrepreneurial methods when managing their estates and maximizing their incomes as a whole.

Nor did the public schools exercise the entirely negative influences with which they are often credited. In the first place, their values after 1840 were anything but exclusively aristocratic. In the second place, they simply contained too few pupils: perhaps 7,500 boarders in thirty-four schools in the mid-1860s. In the third place, there is no evidence that they turned the sons of businessmen *en masse* away from business pursuits.[107] In any case, only a very small proportion (possibly as low as 10 per cent in the period 1870–1914) of even the higher business élites in towns like Birmingham, Bristol, and Manchester had attended establishments that could conceivably count as public schools.[108] What all this means is that the cultural critique, whatever truths it may contain for later periods, simply has too little purchase upon reality to carry much conviction when applied to Queen Victoria's reign: there was no general shortage of entrepreneurs, quite the reverse.

And yet, however statistically and intellectually dazzling they are, many of the defences of late Victorian entrepreneurship achieve validity only

[104] James, 'German Experience', 91–128; W. D. Rubinstein, 'Cultural Explanations for Britain's Economic Decline', in Collins and Robbins (eds.), *British Culture*, 59–90; id., *Capitalism, Culture and Decline in Britain 1750–1990* (London, 1993), 45–59.

[105] W. D. Rubinstein, 'New Wealth and the Purchase of Land in Nineteenth-Century Britain', *Past & Present*, 92 (1981), 125–47; F. M. L. Thompson, 'Life after Death: How Successful Nineteenth-Century Businessmen Disposed of their Fortunes', *Economic History Review*, 43 (1990), 40–61; Rubinstein, 'Cutting Up Rich: A Reply to F. M. L. Thompson', *Economic History Review*, 45 (1992), 350–61; Thompson, 'Stitching it Together Again', ibid. 362–75.

[106] H. Berghoff and R. Möller, 'Tired Pioneers and Dynamic Newcomers? A Comparative Essay on English and German Entrepreneurial History, 1870–1914', *Economic History Review*, 47 (1994), 262–87.

[107] Rubinstein, *Capitalism*, 112; Sanderson, *Education*, 44.

[108] H. Berghoff, 'Public Schools and the Decline of the British Economy 1870–1914', *Past & Present*, 129 (1990), 156–7.

when confined to comparatively narrow territories, in particular those delimited by certain economic theories. After all, if one agrees with neo-classical assumptions that in a competitive milieu even a brief period of irrationality will inevitably be brought to an end by the expansion of better managed firms, then—in all but the very shortest of runs—any possible effects that might flow from entrepreneurial failures have more or less entirely been written out of the script.

With this in mind it has been argued that true entrepreneurship consists not simply of maximizing profits within a given situation (something British businessmen did well enough), but in anticipating and creating those changes which secure future success by speedily adjusting to dis-equilibriums of various kinds. According to such views, claims that British businessmen were 'rational' are not enough, because, while 'adequate' levels of entrepreneurial behaviour might well ensure acceptable profits, 'entrepreneurial initiative' depends crucially on adopting useful new tech-nologies and practices *before* profitability is threatened by changing circum-stances. Thus, while managers in coal mining and cotton undoubtedly realized where their immediate advantages lay, they failed to grasp longer term opportunities and to see beyond the constraints of existing organiza-tional methods and labour difficulties. 'Wealth now rather than strength later' was, therefore, too often the conscious choice in Britain. By contrast, German and American businessmen anticipated more successfully and built for the future.[109]

So, in the end, we appear to be left with a hall of historical mirrors in which the true contours of the past are refracted into complex and some-times mutually obliterating shapes. Doubts remain concerning the rate of economic growth throughout the whole of the nineteenth century and the timing of a climacteric. Doubts remain too about the success of British industry in handling the new situation created by the emergence of indus-trialized societies overseas. Early and mid-century entrepreneurs operated amidst uniquely favourable circumstances, with a buoyant domestic market buttressed, notably in cotton textiles, by a flourishing foreign demand in the exploitation of which they enjoyed monopolistic advantages. However, when—as was inevitable—rival industrial economies began to appear, British entrepreneurs found themselves altogether more exposed, their errors potentially more serious, their successes more circumscribed.

---

[109] R. C. Allen, 'Entrepreneurship and Technical Progress in the North East Coast Pig Iron Industry: 1850–1913', *Research in Economic History*, 6 (1981), 35–71; W. Lazonick, 'Industrial Organization and Technological Change: The Decline of the British Cotton Industry', *Business History Review*, 57 (1983), 195–236; B. Elbaum and W. Lazonick (eds.), *The Decline of the British Economy* (Oxford, 1986).

Whether, in such changing circumstances, they deployed their talents less advantageously than did their counterparts abroad or whether they were inherently less talented are questions that, despite much energetic debate, remain unresolved. What is clear is that the experiences of Britain in the twentieth century suggest either that a strong and powerful economic inheritance from Victorian times has subsequently been squandered or that the inheritance (however badly handled) itself contained deep and damaging flaws.

Because such matters are difficult, perhaps impossible, to resolve, some historians have tried to escape from the dilemmas they pose by trying to construct what amounts to a complete alternative past for the British economy as a whole, one in which Britain was never at heart an industrial nation at all but rather a country specializing in commerce, banking, and finance, the home of what has been called 'gentlemanly capitalism'. The neat trick here is that one can then claim that discussions of failure are simply beside the point because, as a commercial and financial economy, Britain has always been a success.[110] Thus, with one blow, defeat is swallowed up in victory. There are, however, serious objections to such an approach. In particular, it is simply misleading to see 'industrial' or 'commercial' or, indeed, 'landed' interests as homogeneous and clearly separate entities: all were internally divided, all had connections one with another. Businessmen of every kind operated within environments determined by complex economic strategies and overlapping economic loyalties.[111] Therefore, however important it is to emphasize the non-industrial strengths of the Victorian economy, it is simply fanciful to claim that the world's first and for a time greatest industrial power was, underneath the furnaces, the mills, the coal heaps, the smoke, and the railway lines, in reality merely Switzerland in disguise.

Curiously, then, it is the most statistical, quantitative, and 'exact' department of the historical sciences (economic history) which ends up by giving forth the most uncertain sounds. We may speculate about the motives which lay behind Gladstone's Irish policy, but at least we know the date on which he introduced his first Home Rule Bill and what the bill's contents were. We do not know with any equal certainty some of the most basic 'facts' concerning the Victorian economy. What we do know are the subsequent outcomes to which the nature of that economy contributed and some at least of the circumstances in which its constituent

---

[110] Rubinstein, *Capitalism*, 1–44; Cain and Hopkins, *British Imperialism, passim*.

[111] M. J. Daunton, ' "Gentlemanly Capitalism" and British Industry 1820–1914', *Past & Present*, 122 (1989), 119–58.

elements functioned and changed. Looking back from our present vantage it is difficult not to feel querulous and let down: for, whatever may be said as to whether politically, socially, or culturally Britain advanced in the half-century after 1850 or whether the mass of the people enjoyed a better life, in terms of the pace of economic progress, the nation as a whole at best trod water, at worst floated rippleless across a sea of opportunities missed.

CHAPTER 10

Living and Spending

1. FAMILIES, SEX, RELATIONSHIPS

The family dominated Victorian life. Few questioned its importance, few comprehended its kaleidoscopic differences. Middle-class observers repeatedly detected threats to its integrities: working wives, youths earning more than was 'good for them', the licentiousness of factory life, bad housing, excessive drinking, religious decline. The talismanic paraphernalia designed to repel such evils—silver-framed photographs, genre paintings of family scenes, mugs and pots exuding cheerful domesticity—cluttered Victorian homes as densely as votive offerings cluttered the sooty popish chapels so despised by Protestant Englishmen. For all but the poorest the notion of 'home' was becoming increasingly associated with ideas of protection and defence. Middle- and upper-class husbands enjoyed the best of all worlds: long absences on 'business' or pleasure, on the one hand, much emphasis upon the virtues of domestic life, on the other. Neither the young Gladstone, simultaneously telling his wife that sadly he could be little with her while eagerly planning a trip to Ireland with two fellow MPs, nor the Revd Edward Miall, leaving his wife and five children for a solo summer in Scotland, were at all unusual. Within the home itself a kind of internal remoteness was condoned, even encouraged. Middle-class wives were praised for sheltering their husbands from the tedium of domestic affairs: 'How wonderfully she looked after him ... everything was arranged ... so that he might do the maximum of work.' The Revd Sabine Baring-Gould (author of 'Onward Christian Soldiers' and begetter of sixteen offspring) asked one small child at a party, 'And whose little girl are you?' She burst into tears: 'I'm yours, Daddy'.[1]

---

[1] D. Roberts, 'The Paterfamilias of the Victorian Governing Classes', in A. S. Wohl (ed.), *The Victorian Family* (London, 1978), 60; J. G. Lockhart, *Charles Lindley Viscount Halifax*, 2 vols. (London, 1935–6), i. 161–2; J. Marchant, *Dr John Clifford, C.H. Life, Letters and Reminiscences* (London, 1924), 171; W. Purcell, *Onward Christian Soldier: A Life of Sabine Baring-Gould* (London, 1957), 2.

The size of families and households (*not* the same thing) varied greatly. There was no 'typical' complement of children, though numbers fell during the half-century after 1850. At the beginning of our period anything less than seven born alive would have been considered 'small'; fifty years later five or six was considered 'large'. By the 1880s and 1890s doctors and clergymen averaged 2.8 and 3.0 children respectively, gamekeepers and railway labourers 5.0 and 5.2 (though there was nothing peculiarly working-class about large families). In 1851 the third or so of households consisting of six or more members actually contained over half the total population, and until the end of the century a majority of persons lived in households which were, by modern standards, 'large'.[2]

The 'classic' extended and mutually supportive working-class family—rare in the pre-industrial countryside where mutual help had been beyond the capabilities of the labouring poor—was an urban and comparatively short-lived phenomenon. As prosperity grew and towns became demographically self-sustaining, so a particular form of family life engendered by the need to assist recent arrivals began to seem less necessary. Indeed, the reality of Victorian kin support for the elderly was neither especially benevolent nor (despite much subsequent myth) especially widespread. While the civil authorities invariably forced parents to maintain children, the requirement of the 1601 Poor Law (not fully repealed until 1948) that grown-up children support elderly parents had become so generally ignored that the great bulk of assistance came, not from kin at all, but from the much-derided English Poor Law system set up in 1834, which, already by the 1840s, was making regular cash payments to two out of every three women in England and Wales aged 70 and above. And even when economic ideologues seized control of the Poor Law system in the 1870s and cut back expenditure, relatives, far from bridging the financial gap, did all they could to avoid supporting their elderly kin. Many of course were poor themselves, but the unprecedented number of prosecutions after 1875 makes arguments for universal working-class mutuality difficult to sustain.[3]

What did not, however, undermine working-class families—as many at the time predicted it would—was the 'working wife'. There is little evidence that the homes of those who went out to earn money were invariably

[2] J. A. Banks, *Victorian Values: Secularism and the Size of Families* (London, 1981), 98–9, 106–7; M. Anderson, 'Households, Families and Individuals', *Continuity and Change*, 3 (1988), 424–5.

[3] J. Benson, *The Working Class in Britain 1850–1939* (London, 1989), 102–3, 110; S. Meacham, *A Life Apart: The English Working Class 1890–1914* (London, 1977), 117–18; D. Thomson, ' "I am not my Father's Keeper": Families and the Elderly in Nineteenth Century England', *Law and History Review*, 2 (1984), 265–86.

neglected, though pregnancy and birth were especially difficult times and, given the opportunity, most wives preferred to stay at home. Hospital records from the 1880s show working-class mothers still turning the mangle after the membranes had ruptured and doing so again within hours of confinement. Baby care among the poor involved relentless physical labour: heating water, carrying heavy buckets, emptying coppers.[4] Already by the late 1870s the overall crude birth rate was beginning to fall: not that the impact of various kinds of contraception (mechanical or otherwise, female- or male-led) is at all clear, though abortion was neither rare nor universally perceived as abhorrent. Pious aristocrats, like Maria Stanley (wife of the 2nd Lord Stanley of Alderley), were relieved to find that 'a hot bath, a tremendous walk, and a great dose' could dispose of an unwanted pregnancy, while working-class women sometimes found abortion less expensive (though more dangerous) than other means of birth prevention. Tightening up the law in 1803, 1828, 1837, and 1861 probably had little effect and the advertising columns of the Victorian popular press attest to the amount of money that could be made from the sale of real or bogus abortifacients.[5]

Marriage remained the ideal. Out of every thousand females aged 15 in England and Wales in 1850–2 no less than 859 could expect to have been married at least once by the time they were 50; and of those aged between 35 and 45, 762 were married and 82 widowed.[6] For most women marriage was perceived as promising a release from dependence on parents. Marriage conferred status, sanctioned legitimate sex, and, with luck, provided companionship, children, perhaps even love. Although a few untypical women grumbled about society's expectation that all should marry (Beatrice Webb spoke memorably about a market carried 'on by parents and other promoters, sometimes with genteel surreptitiousness, sometimes with cynical effrontery'),[7] there was far more concern about those who remained single, the 'surplus woman' question, as it was called. The 1851 census

[4] M. Hewitt, *Wives and Mothers in Victorian Industry* (London, 1958), 75; E. Ross, 'Labour and Love: Rediscovering London's Working-Class Mothers, 1870–1918', in J. Lewis (ed.), *Labour and Love: Women's Experience of Home and Family, 1850–1940* (Oxford, 1986), 78–9.

[5] Henrietta Maria Stanley to Edward Stanley, 9 Nov. [1847], *The Ladies of Alderley*, ed. N. Mitford (London, 1938), 169; A. MacLaren, 'Women's Work and Regulation of Family Size: The Question of Abortion in the Nineteenth Century', *History Workshop*, 4 (1977), 71–2; P. Knight, 'Women and Abortion in Victorian and Edwardian England', ibid. 57–60.

[6] P. Branca, *Silent Sisterhood: Middle-Class Women in the Victorian Home* (London, 1975), 3–4.

[7] B. Webb, *My Apprenticeship* (Cambridge, 1979: 1st publ. 1926), 49; also J. Lewis, *Women in England 1870–1950: Sexual Divisions and Social Change* (Brighton, 1984), 77.

revealed that there were 1.4 million spinsters aged 20 to 40 and 359,969 'old maids' over 40; by 1871 there were two widows and spinsters for every three wives.[8] And although most unmarried women were working-class and worked for a living, it was those from middle-class families who attracted the sustained concern of contemporaries worried equally about 'hysterical' illnesses and social deviancy. Charlotte Brontë's mid-century fictional analysis in *Shirley* (1849) was typical enough in contrasting men's involvement 'in business or in professions' with their sisters having 'no earthly employment, but household work and sewing; no earthly pleasure, but an unprofitable visiting; and no hope, in all their life to come, of anything better'.

Girls from the upper and central reaches of the middle class faced particular problems because severe retribution waited upon those who married outside their own social rank. As horizons became wider and more national, so the personal knowledge adequate in the predominantly local social circles of former times had to be replaced by instantly recognizable badges of marital acceptability: attendance at public schools, membership of certain clubs, commissions in certain regiments. At the pinnacle of such concerns stood the 'Season' and its associated concept of 'Society'. The former had eighteenth-century origins and until the 1870s was as much a political as a social phenomenon. It lasted from April to July and collected the leading families in London for the latter part of the parliamentary session. By the last quarter of the century the number of those formally involved had—at 4,000 or so families—begun to make the kind of face-to-face society of earlier times all but impossible. The presentations at Queen Victoria's 'drawing rooms' (perhaps the best indicator of élite female acceptance) increased by a factor of two-and-a-half between the 1840s and the 1880s and the backgrounds of those presented hint at a slowly growing tolerance for those who made their living in the professional and business worlds.[9] This mattered, because the Season also provided the main marriage market for polite society, a market guarded and orchestrated by women, the mothers of those not yet married themselves.

As a dropped pebble affects still waters, so the influence of the Season and its rituals extended ripple-like into neighbouring social spheres. Maga-

[8] P. Jalland, *Women, Marriage and Politics 1860–1914* (Oxford, 1986), 253–5; M. Anderson, 'The Social Position of Spinsters in Mid-Victorian Britain', *Journal of Family History*, 9 (1984), 377–93.

[9] N. W. Ellenberger, 'The Transformation of London "Society" at the End of Victoria's Reign: Evidence from the Court Presentation Records', *Albion*, 22 (1990), 643, 650, 653; L. Davidoff, *The Best Circles: Society Etiquette and the Season*, new impression (London, 1986), 61. Parliament normally sat from February until early August, with occasional autumn sessions when the press of business was great.

zines dispersed information and misinformation and there was much concern in print (Trollope's *The Way We Live Now* of 1875 is a prime example)
about the moral vulgarity of the times.[10] A formidable body of etiquette—
how to fill in dance cards, conduct oneself at the dinner table, address those
of higher rank—began to preoccupy far more than the charmed 4,000.
Especially important was the cult of 'introductions' and the leaving of cards
as a means of testing the social temperature. Its mostly female votaries paid
'morning calls' (which actually took place in the afternoon), gave 'At
Homes', and chaperoned their daughters at balls. In its own terms this
was distinctly serious work: without it important social frontiers would
have remained unpatrolled, possibly even overrun. Small wonder that, by
the third quarter of the century, the rituals of Society had become accepted
well beyond their own home ground.

Precisely because daughters mattered so much in the lineages of the well-
to-do, ways were found to guard them from the ravages of spouses determined to exploit the common-law doctrine of coverture which held that all
the possessions and earnings of a wife belonged to her husband. Various
complex legal devices made it possible for prosperous fathers to draw up
marriage settlements which enabled a small group of women to control
enormous separate estates after marriage, a large number to own substantial
property of their own, and an even greater number to have private incomes
which their husbands could not touch.[11] As, by definition, poor women had
little money (though even that could legally be filched by their husbands),
the main beneficiaries of the acts of 1870 and 1882 designed to safeguard
the property of all married women were those in the middle and lower-
middle ranges of society. Protection of a different kind was provided by the
Matrimonial Causes Act of 1878 which allowed a wife beaten by her
husband to apply for a separation order (though this was often refused)
and by the abolition, six years later, of the imprisonment penalty for non-
compliance with a writ for restitution of conjugal rights. Less effective was
the much-disputed Divorce Act of 1857 (by which men could sue on
grounds of adultery alone, but wives could only do so if their husbands
had indulged in bestiality, bigamy, cruelty, rape, or incest as well). Few
could afford the costs of the legal proceedings required: in the whole of

[10] Note Gladstone's complaint of 1879 about 'men of rank, men of titles... giving
their names to speculations which they neither understand nor examine, as directors
or trustees' (*Political Speeches in Scotland, November and December 1879* (London, 1879),
238).
[11] M. L. Shanley, *Feminism, Marriage, and the Law in Victorian England, 1850–1895*
(London, 1989), 8–9; Jalland, *Women, Marriage, Politics*, 59; J. Perkin, *Women and Marriage
in Nineteenth-Century England* (London, 1989), 50–75.

England and Wales the average number of divorces each year between 1858 and 1886 was 239, of marriages more than 187,000.[12]

People married for all sorts of reasons, though bonds of the 'purest' affection and entirely mercenary matches existed predominantly in novels. Working-class autobiographies (mostly by men) talk reticently of 'falling in love'. 'For I was as fond of my wife', recorded a countryman in the 1880s, 'Has a Cat is of New Milk'.[13] Yet there could also be a deadpan casualness about relationships—as in a navvy's account of his courtship in the 1850s: 'Well, I left Baldock after a bit, and had never spoken to Anne but once... "So you're out for a walk, young woman?" I says to her. "Yes, I am", says she, and that was all that passed between us'.[14] Among the very poor there was much cohabiting, and some groups (like London coster-mongers and dustmen) were renowned for their lack of sexual fidelity. The actual marriage ceremony was, therefore, far less important than the decision to marry, and weddings involved a good deal less fuss (perhaps a drink in a pub) than did funerals.[15] Among London domestic servants (about whose behaviour unusually much, in this respect, is known) both a good deal of shrewdness and an unsurprising desire for pleasure informed the selection of partners. Courtship could be long and women servants resisted sexual intercourse until they were sure of a man's intentions. 'Dear Jane Watson, I solemnly promise to marry you My dear girl. Yours affec. Alex Hay' smacks of contract as much as of fondness.[16] Given that expecta-tions were modest, not a great deal was looked for on either side: some sort of job, some sort of home, some sort of kindness. Courtship was a time of small joys, pranks, silly deceptions, jaunty confidences. 'Old Gal', wrote a 22-year-old gardener in the 1860s to his chambermaid sweetheart,

Brighter days will come again as the darkest cloud 'as a silver lining cheer up your pecker up Dear... don't fret old Gal as I am coming to Long Acre on Thursday evening so I shall give you a call at 7 at the corner so please be on the look out I hope I shall see the Old Clock out when I come.[17]

[12] Shanley, *Feminism*, 42; B. R. Mitchell, *British Historical Statistics* (Cambridge, 1988), 72–5. The average annual number of divorces obtained in Scotland 1858–86 was 35. Ireland was excluded from the 1857 legislation and continued with the earlier (and even more expensive) individual Act of Parliament procedure.

[13] D. Vincent, *Bread, Knowledge and Freedom: A Study of Nineteenth-Century Working Class Autobiography* (London, 1981), 46–7; Perkin, *Women and Marriage*, 197.

[14] *Useful Toil: Autobiographies of Working People from the 1820s to the 1920s*, ed. J. Burnett, new impression (Harmondsworth, 1984), 61.

[15] Perkin, *Women and Marriage*, 158–62; Meacham, *Life Apart*, 63; Vincent, *Bread*, 48.

[16] J. R. Gillis, 'Servants, Sexual Relations, and the Risks of Illegitimacy in London, 1801–1900', *Feminist Studies*, 5 (1979), 155.

[17] F. Barret-Ducrocq, *Love in the Time of Victoria: Sexuality, Class and Gender in Nineteenth-Century London* (London, 1991), 115–16.

The sexual aspect of such relationships reveals contradictions between public morality and private behaviour, as well as the existence of double standards favouring men as against women. Female chastity and fidelity constituted acclaimed public truths, male indulgence and unfaithfulness commonplace private realities. If among the aristocracy women too were allowed a certain (discreet) licence, male street traders had no time for the niceties of equality. Their 'gals', they insisted, 'axully liked a feller for walloping them. As long as the bruises hurted, she was always thinking on the cove as gived 'em her.'[18] Female prostitutes were physical proof of the disjunction between pose and behaviour. The numbers involved are now beyond accurate assessment, though contemporaries produced a wide variety of figures: the Metropolitan Police never (for London) went above 10,000 'full-time professionals', Mayhew suggested 80,000 in the 1850s, newspapers went as high as 120,000. For England and Wales estimates ranged from 25,000 to 368,000 (the latter, wondrously precise, figure would have made prostitution the fourth-largest female occupation in the country).[19] Most prostitutes were only temporarily 'on the streets'; for them it was a passing phase which in no permanent way separated them from the bulk of the working-class community. Despite venereal disease (which Victorians certainly *thought* was increasing), young prostitutes were probably healthier than fourteen-hour-a-day seamstresses. Should, however, speedy escape prove impossible, then it was not long before exploitation, the decay of physical charm, disease, drink, ageing, psychological breakdown, and poverty began to wreak an inevitable toll.[20]

Justification for prostitution was provided by medical 'experts' who deployed allegedly scientific arguments to prove that, whereas men had strong sexual drives, 'normal' women did not. The leading figure here was

[18] H. Mayhew, *London Labour and the London Poor*, 4 vols. (London, 1861–2; repr. 1967), i. 36.

[19] E. Trudgill, 'Prostitution and Paterfamilias', in H. J. Dyos and M. Wolff (eds.), *The Victorian City: Images and Realities*, 2 vols. (London, 1973), ii. 693–4; E. M. Sigsworth and T. J. Wyke, 'A Study of Victorian Prostitution and Venereal Disease', in M. Vicinus (ed.), *Suffer and Be Still: Women in the Victorian Age* (Bloomington, Ind., 1972), 78–9.

[20] Sigsworth and Wyke, 'Victorian Prostitution', 80; J. Walkowitz, 'The Making of an Outcast Group: Prostitutes and Working Women in Nineteenth-Century Plymouth and Southampton', in M. Vicinus (ed.), *A Widening Sphere: Changing Roles of Victorian Women* (Bloomington, Ind., 1977), 72–93; id., *Prostitution and Victorian Society* (Cambridge, 1980), 21–31; T. C. Smout, 'Aspects of Sexual Behaviour in Nineteenth Century Scotland', in A. A. MacLaren (ed.), *Social Class in Scotland* (Edinburgh, [1976]), 60. The Contagious Diseases Acts of the 1860s which, in certain garrison towns, subjected women suspected of being prostitutes to custody and forcible medical treatment were (after a long campaign) suspended in 1883 and repealed in 1886.

the urologist, William Acton, whose many mid-century publications insisted, with more emphasis than proof, that, while 'happily for them the majority of women are not much troubled by sexual desire', 'numerous husbands' had 'complained' to him 'of the hardships under which they suffer by being married to women who regard themselves martyrs when called upon to fulfil the duties of wives'.[21] Writing in the *Westminster Review* for 1850, W. R. Greg—a kind of all-purpose pundit on everything—thought this 'dormant' female sexuality just as well, for without it, 'sexual irregularities would reach a height, of which, at present, we have happily no conception'.[22] However, even at the time, Acton's views, with their gender differentiation and insistence that masturbation produced physical cripples ('the frame is stunted, the muscles underdeveloped, the eye is sunken and heavy') were by no means universally held, even in medical circles. Indeed, popular works based upon neo-Malthusian principles, such as Richard Carlile's *Every Woman's Book* (1828) enjoyed comparatively wide and continuing sales, and even subterranean publications about impotence, sterility, and the pox spoke as much of the joys of sex as the dangers of 'over indulgence'.[23] Sex before marriage, common below the social élite in the previous century, probably declined among 'respectable' artisans and the like, but less so elsewhere. And local levels of illegitimacy and prenuptial pregnancy not only varied widely, but seem to have done so for no obvious reason, proof perhaps that no single working-class 'sex culture' existed at all.[24]

For their part the middle classes demanded a high degree of premarital chastity from women, an altogether lower one from men. Middle- and upper-class observers expressed particular shock about the way in which the housing of the poor denied privacy and encouraged promiscuity. Sir John Simon agonized about this in his 1865 medical officer's report to the Privy Council; so did the 1884–5 Royal Commission on the Housing of the Working Classes (which talked much about incest); so did Beatrice Webb, who was horrified in the 1880s to hear East End girls openly talking of

[21] *Prostitution Considered in its Moral, Social and Sanitary Aspects* (1858) cited F. Bédarida, *A Social History of England 1851–1975* (London, 1979), 162; *The Functions and Disorders of the Reproductive Organs*, 7th edn. (1875) cited J. L'Espérance, 'Doctors and Women in Nineteenth Century Society', in J. Woodward and D. Richards (eds.), *Health Care and Popular Medicine in Nineteenth Century England* (London, 1977), 115.
[22] 'Prostitution', *Westminster Review*, 103 (1850), 457.
[23] F. B. Smith, 'Sexuality in Britain 1800–1900', in Vicinus (ed.), *Widening Sphere*, 182–98; Sigsworth and Wyke, 'Victorian Prostitution', 83.
[24] Barret-Ducrocq, *Love*, 98; T. C. Smout, *A Century of the Scottish People 1830–1950* (London, 1986), 166; id., 'Aspects of Sexual Behaviour', 67–73; Perkin, *Women and Marriage*, 184–5.

having babies by their fathers and brothers.[25] How common this was is impossible to say. Among all but the very poor there was much verbal reticence about sexual matters. Most young girls, for example, found themselves quite unprepared for menstruation, for which a dictionary of euphemisms was employed: the 'curse', the 'poorly time', the 'relations', the 'dipe', the 'antics', and so forth. Menstruation also continued to be used as an argument against female involvement in education, sport, and politics, and in favour of female inferiority generally. Not until the 1870s did more positive interpretations begin to be canvassed, though these (together with the arrival of expensive disposable sanitary towels in the 1880s) at first affected only a very small number of women indeed.[26]

Generally speaking, Victorian sexual relationships were varied and complex and involved far more than mere brutishness and prudery underpinned by notions of female subjection and male lust. The evidence may be anecdotal and largely confined to polite society, but there is enough of it to suggest that crude caricatures will not do. Detailed studies of particular middle-class families reveal equilibrium rather than angst. Daughters were well aware of the sexual stresses and joys of their parents' lives. Married and unmarried women sustained relaxed and rewarding non-sexual friendships with men outside the family circle. Many of the marriages we know about were marked by mutuality, happy sexuality, similarity of interests, and good cheer. The multi-volume biographies in which so many eminent Victorians were embalmed are full of letters between husbands and wives, letters brimming with confidence, sharing, reflection, and mutual trust.[27] Surely too it is the nineteenth, rather than either the eighteenth or twentieth centuries, which can most accurately be described as the great era of companionate marriages.

The once-standard picture of middle- and upper-class women constantly prone to imaginary invalidism, bored, frustrated, and languid is only very partially true. If anything, some women were quite devastatingly energetic: walking, hiking, climbing, riding, swimming, exploring, playing tennis and

[25] A. S. Wohl, 'Unfit for Human Habitation', in Dyos and Wolff (eds.), *Victorian City*, ii. 613; id., *The Eternal Slum: Housing and Social Policy in Victorian London* (London, 1977), 217–18; J. Weeks, *Sex, Politics and Society: The Regulation of Sexuality since 1800*, 2nd edn. (London, 1989), 31.

[26] F. Harrison, *The Dark Angel: Aspects of Victorian Sexuality* (London, 1979), 62–4; Jalland, *Women, Marriage, Politics*, 140–1; C. Dyhouse, *Girls Growing Up in Late Victorian and Edwardian England* (London, 1981), 21–2; Meacham, *Life Apart*, 66–7; E. and E. Showalter, 'Victorian Women and Menstruation', in Vicinus (ed.), *Suffer and Be Still*, 38–44.

[27] M. J. Peterson, *Family, Love, and Work in the Lives of Victorian Gentlewomen* (Bloomington, Ind., 1989), 67–84; Smith, 'Sexuality in Britain', 187.

cricket, regularly travelling on the new and improved bicycles which appeared in the late 1880s. A physician father, asked for advice by his daughter in 1880, was quite happy to send eminent good sense: 'During your "poorly" times ... *rest* yourself—lying, if convenient on a couch. At other times, when you are *not* poorly, you can take exercise and will be the better for it.'[28] Such fleeting glimpses of intimacy as can be recovered reveal the clergyman novelist, Charles Kingsley, pursuing a mutually ardent and openly sexual courtship of his future wife in the 1840s. They show a young upper middle-class woman writing thus in the 1850s to her lover: 'My night dress was on when you saw me. Would to God you had been in the same attire'. They show too the daughter of a London surgeon in 1892 allowing her betrothed to kiss her 'madly' while sitting upon his lap in her family's Savile Row drawing-room.[29]

Of course, then as now, there were frigid marriages, none more so than that of Mark Pattison, the Rector of Lincoln College, Oxford, whose wife told him frankly in 1876 that she could not overcome a 'physical aversion' which had become 'wholly beyond control'.[30] But the bulk of the evidence goes the other way. Victorian couples slept in double beds. Middle-class women treated pregnancy and childbirth in no prudish manner and certainly did not regard them as illnesses. More often than not their husbands were present while the baby was born—Gladstone noting that his wife endured at least 'six times as much bodily pain as I have undergone in my whole life'.[31] And if rare late nineteenth-century evidence from educated women in New England can be applied to old England also, then the majority of such married women enjoyed frank and enthusiastic sex lives with their husbands in which present enjoyment mattered more than thoughts of future reproduction.[32] Even the major Victorian legislative restriction on sexual practices—Labouchere's clause in the 1885 Criminal

---

[28] Peterson, *Family, Love, and Work*, 58–68.

[29] S. Chitty, *The Beast and the Monk: A Life of Charles Kingsley* (London, 1974), 82–4; Perkin, *Women and Marriage*, 278–9; P. Hunt, *The Madeleine Smith Affair* (London, 1950), 98; Z. Shonfield, *The Precariously Privileged: A Professional Family in Victorian London* (Oxford, 1987), 199.

[30] B. Askwith, *Lady Dilke: A Biography* (London, 1969), 61.

[31] Jalland, *Women, Marriage, Politics*, 133–58; *The Gladstone Diaries*, ed. H. C. G. Matthew and M. R. D. Foot, 14 vols. (Oxford, 1968–94), iii. 33 (3 June 1840). Working-class men were less in evidence and, as medical practitioners intruded more and more, so even middle-class childbirth eventually became less of a family event (J. H. Miller, ' "Temple and Sewer": Childbirth, Prudery and Victoria Regina', in Wohl (ed.), *Victorian Family*, 29–30).

[32] C. N. Degler, 'What Ought to Be and What Was: Women's Sexuality in the Nineteenth Century', *American Historical Review*, 79 (1974), 1487–90.

Law Amendment Act which brought all forms of male homosexual activity, whether public or private, within the scope of the law—may well have been introduced in an attempt to render such legislation ridiculous, an attempt which went badly awry. Undoubtedly the existing sodomy laws, which provided fearsome penalties and were not directed solely at homosexuals, had fallen into disrepute and confusion, as the famous trial of the transvestites Boulton and Park showed in 1871.[33] But it is highly doubtful whether those few MPs who nodded Labouchere's amendment through in August 1885 can have had the slightest idea of what their casual acquiescence would subsequently involve.

As an element in people's lives even sex was overshadowed by health, disease, and death. Victorians were much concerned with improving the first, reducing the second, and delaying the third—and undoubtedly mortality rates fell during the second half of the century. Between the 1840s and the mid-1870s the annual crude death rate in England and Wales hovered around 22 per 1,000 persons in every five-year period; from the mid-1870s it declined fairly steadily from 20.8 in 1876–80 to 17.7 in 1896–1900 and 14.7 in 1906–10.[34] However, the annual *infant* mortality rate (expressed as the deaths of infants under one year per 1,000 live births) showed no consistent reduction until after the century had ended.[35] In all these changes medical science counted for little: of the major epidemic diseases, only smallpox was conquered in the nineteenth century by a scientific discovery. Altogether less clear, however, are the relative effects of public health, improved nutrition, and autonomous reductions in the virulence of disease-bearing micro-organisms and other carriers.

Before the 1880s the chief causes of death among those who survived childhood were infectious diseases, notably typhus (transmitted by body lice and largely confined to the poor), typhoid (which was waterborne and less class-specific—Prince Albert was a distinguished victim), tuberculosis, diphtheria, dysentery, scarlet fever, and (until the 1860s) cholera. Experts were divided between those who believed that such diseases sprang from corruptions of the atmosphere caused by terrestrial exhalations (the miasma

[33] F. B. Smith, 'Labouchere's Amendment to the Criminal Law Amendment Bill', *Historical Studies*, 17 (1976), 165–75. During the preliminary hearings in May 1870 Boulton was described as 'living in drag' and 'this was explained as a slang phrase for living in women's clothes' (*The Annals of our Time*, ed. J. Irving, new edn. (London, 1880), 916). The 1885 act also raised the age of consent for girls (already raised from 12 to 13 in 1875) to 16.

[34] Mitchell, *British Historical Statistics*, 57–8. Scottish data become available only in 1855 and record *broadly* similar levels and trends. Irish figures (from 1864) show generally lower mortality rates until about 1892, but then a slower fall.

[35] England and Wales: 156 (1871–5), 144 (1876–80), 156 (1896–1900), 117 (1906–10). Ibid.

theory) and those who looked to specific and probably animate contagion. At first the big sanitary battalions (such as Edwin Chadwick, Southwood Smith, Florence Nightingale) were on the miasmic side. Not until 1849–54 were William Budd and John Snow able to demonstrate that cholera was caused by the ingestion of a living organism of a distinct species and not until 1883 did Koch isolate the cholera bacillus. Physicians, therefore, possessed neither effective treatment nor relevant theory, and were, in any case, far too expensive for the great mass of the people who, if they consulted anyone, went to herbalists, apothecaries, or local 'wise' women.[36] Ineffective patent medicines were swallowed in vast quantities. Entrepreneurs like Thomas Holloway, Thomas Beecham, and Jesse Boot made fortunes from their sale, but in the process contributed less to health than to the development of modern sales techniques (Holloway's annual advertising expenditure rose from £5,000 in 1842 to £50,000 in 1883). Even the Pharmacy Act of 1868, which made some attempt to control the sale of known poisons, had little effect on the availability of patent medicines or, indeed, on that of opium, which, far from being confined to artistic circles, was widely used in the damp Fenland areas of eastern England in a way which might not seem strange in parts of south-east Asia today. As a cure for tiredness, aching limbs, and despair it was readily obtainable in corner shops, just as, in parts of Ulster, ether was stocked by many grocers and bakers anxious to meet an intense public demand.[37]

If doctors could as yet do little to cure disease, they were beginning to be able to alleviate pain and make surgery something more than a gateway to death. By the mid-1850s operations were almost universally done under anaesthesia, though its use in childbirth (despite Queen Victoria's taking chloroform on giving birth to Prince Leopold in April 1853) was at first less common. Altogether slower was the acceptance of Lister's antiseptic system: although the principles were laid down between 1867 and 1871, Lister's methods were not generally emulated until the 1880s.[38] Indeed, many hospitals—despite slow improvements—continued to be fetid and dirty places until well beyond the end of our period. And as people were now living longer, so they remained open to the onslaught of disease and

[36] V. Berridge, 'Health and Medicine', in F. M. L. Thompson (ed.), *The Cambridge Social History of Britain 1750–1950*, 3 vols. (Cambridge, 1990), iii. 188–90 (henceforth *CSHB*); Smith, *People's Health*, 373; Branca, *Silent Sisterhood*, 65–71.

[37] V. Berridge and G. Edwards, *Opium and the People: Opiate Use in Nineteenth-Century England* (London, 1981), 38–48, 116–30; K. H. Connell, 'Ether-Drinking in Ulster', in Connell's *Irish Peasant Society* (Oxford, 1968), 87–111.

[38] A. J. Youngson, *The Scientific Revolution in Medicine* (London, 1979), 42–72, 214, 120–2, 151–7.

decay well into old age. They had more years during which to fall ill, though their illnesses were less frequently resolved in death. Because, therefore, the risk of falling sick remained stable at most ages, the risk of *being* sick actually increased. In this sense, those who lived through the last thirty years of the century found themselves participants in a great drama—the arrival of an 'age of sickness' in place of an 'age of death'.[39]

This may, in turn, have helped to bring about subtle changes in attitudes towards death itself. There is little evidence that the frequent deaths of children and young people drove Victorians of any class into casual callousness. Five of the seven children of Catharine and Archibald Tait (then Dean of Carlisle) died from scarlet fever in the spring of 1856 and the parents almost broke under the shock. Workers by hand felt no less sorrow, and on occasion expressed it with moving eloquence.[40] If a sense of the immanence of death was never far away and was occasionally dwelt upon with luscious excess, death—when it came—was almost always a surprise, no matter how often it had happened before.[41] Religion offered considerable solace to a considerable number of people. And the numerous descriptions of deathbeds and the accounts of lessons learned ('Truly I know the bitterness of mourning over a first-born son. May I as fully realize and mourn over my own sin against God')[42] meant much to Victorians precisely because death was not seen as the end but as the awful preliminary to divine judgement and then to everlasting bliss or eternal punishment.

Although the slow recession of faith inevitably weakened such impulses, the equally notable fall in mortality rates also seems to have played a part in diluting the mid-Victorian obsession with the paraphernalia of death— funerals, mourning, mourning attire, and so on. All classes wanted a 'decent' funeral, working people especially so after 1832 when the Anatomy Act rendered corpses buried at parochial expense liable to the dissector's knife. But the super-grand funerals of the upper and upper middle classes reached their peak of sumptuousness as early as the 1850s. A comparison of Queen Victoria's funeral of 1901 and the chaotic splendour of Wellington's in 1852 makes the point. Though better organized, it was notably less flamboyant, just as Gladstone's in 1898 was less elaborate than Palmerston's

---

[39] J. C. Riley, *Sickness, Recovery and Death: A History and Forecast of Ill Health* (London, 1989), 171, 176, 192.

[40] Peterson, *Family, Love, and Work*, 110–15; M. Anderson, *Family Structure in Nineteenth Century Lancashire* (Cambridge, 1971), 69.

[41] Vincent, *Bread*, 54–8; J. Walvin, *A Child's World: A Social History of English Childhood 1800–1914* (Harmondsworth, 1982), 29–31.

[42] The words of James Mill, a Caithness doctor, on the death of his 14-year-old son in 1859 (W. L. Burn, *The Age of Equipoise: A Study of the Mid-Victorian Generation* (London, 1964), 45).

in 1865. The mourning observances of the well-to-do softened as time went on and the detailed regulations laid down in magazines were rarely followed in full.[43] Amidst undoubted, though diminishing, excess, bereaved middle- and upper-class Victorians were sustained by networks of family support, by religion, by grieving rituals of every kind—letters of condolence were especially valued and much effort was devoted to writing them.[44] Chronic grieving, like that of Queen Victoria, was rare. Most widowers soon married again, though widows found this more difficult.

As work patterns, death rates, and family structures were transformed, so too was the manner in which children were treated and regarded. By mid-century the appearance of a more deliberate concept of 'childhood' as a distinct period can be detected in literature, in new ways of perceiving education, and in a series of reforms creating a specific category of juvenile crime, special children's Poor Law facilities, reformatories, and industrial and ragged schools.[45] This in turn helped to launch the somewhat later notion of 'adolescence' which first emerged among those prosperous families able to slow down their children's hitherto abrupt entry into adulthood. Overall, however, the experiences of Victorian children were marked more by diversity than uniformity. The contempt towards children shown by some early Victorian aristocrats and gentlemen probably lessened as the century wore on, and for every remote father ('I am always informed when they are born') there was a 'papa' worshipped for being 'great fun'. The growth of Evangelicalism increased the number of concerned middle-class fathers, even if their concern was expressed chiefly through pious admonitions—delivered in person during the holidays, by post during boarding school term.[46] Working-class children found themselves more clearly part of a family community: there were fewer rooms, less physical separation between young and old. Patterns of behaviour probably differed substantially between different strata: decorum reigned at the mealtimes of the labour aristocracy while 'mealtimes' scarcely existed in the poorest homes. Doubtless families had a better chance of becoming affectionate when conditions were comfortable, but there was no simple cause and effect. By the 1850s a minor industry was already well established making

[43] e.g. in 1881 Sylvia's Home Journal recommended that 'Second wives for the parents of the first wife, should wear complimentary mourning for about three weeks' (A. Adburgham, Shops and Shopping 1800–1914 (London, 1964), 64).

[44] P. Jalland, 'Death, Grief, and Mourning in the Upper-Class Family, 1860–1914', in R. Houlbrooke (ed.), Death, Ritual, and Bereavement (London, 1989), 171–87.

[45] L. Davidoff, 'The Family in Britain', in CSHB ii. 108; H. Cunningham, The Children of the Poor (Oxford, 1991), 151–63.

[46] Roberts, 'Paterfamilias', 19, 62–5.

cheap so-called 'Bristol toys' (carts, horses, omnibuses, mostly wheeled) at a penny each for those with just a little money to spare. The autobiographies of working men (by definition not 'typical') display fondness and affection but little desire that adults should live their lives through their children or abdicate their own aspirations in favour of the next generation.[47]

Already by mid-century comparatively few children 'worked', in the sense of being engaged in long and regular hours of paid employment outside the home, although many laboured at tasks such as making match boxes or busking which evaded the official statisticians' net. Acts of Parliament from the 1830s onwards had reduced the hours children could legally work. By 1851 the number aged 10 to 14 'working' was substantially outweighed by the 41 per cent being 'schooled' (by 1871 this had risen to 53 per cent). Probably the commonest strategy for working-class parents was to make their children earn some money before they were 15, but to give them some schooling as well.[48]

The persistence of high infant mortality until the end of the century encouraged a chorus of complaints that proletarian mothers neglected their children. Given the want of money, shortage of food, problems of cleanliness, and sheer ignorance, the existence of what middle-class observers called 'incompetence' is hardly surprising. But health risks to children, while especially intense among the poor, were by no means confined to any one section of society. All alternatives to breast-feeding were, for example, potentially dangerous. Cow's milk was expensive and often infected. Most infants were fed on a pap made of bread and water sweetened with sugar or treacle. The cheaper condensed milks introduced in the 1870s were devoid of vitamins A and D and of fats. Fractious babies were dosed with cordials containing opium, laudanum, and morphia, of which Godfrey's Cordial and Atkinson's Royal Infants' Preservative were the most famous.[49] However, regarding the actual amount of attention mothers could devote to their children, it is worth remembering that, in all sorts of direct and indirect ways, industrialization probably *reduced* the female presence in the formal job market. Official returns (which, however, certainly understate female employment) show a steady decline in the proportion of women in the occupied workforce from 34.1 per cent in 1861 to 31.1 per cent in 1891; indeed, the proportion of all women designated 'occupied'

[47] Meacham, *Life Apart*, 161; Perkin, *Women and Marriage*, 152; Walvin, *Child's World*, 96; Vincent, *Bread*, 44–5.

[48] P. E. H. Hair, 'Children in Society 1850–1980', in T. Barker and M. Drake (eds.), *Population and Society in Britain 1850–1980* (London, 1982), 52.

[49] Hewitt, *Wives and Mothers*, 136–7, 144–52.

was lower in 1891 (25.5 per cent) than it had been forty years before (26.3 per cent).[50] Not only that, but the majority of working women were young and unmarried. Even in the cotton industry, which was constantly accused of luring young mothers away from their infants, probably only a quarter of the female labour force in 1851 was married and of *those* no more than a fifth had children under 1 year old.[51]

Constant contemporary criticisms of bad housekeeping among the poor blithely ignored the difficulties of fighting dirt, the endless washing, the damp, the cold, the raw hands, broken backs, and repeated ill health. Though husbands probably helped more about the house than is often supposed, they had to do so secretly for fear of being ridiculed as 'diddy men'.[52] So also the necessity of wives having to go out to work was not something to boast about and such women were pitied not only because they were poor but because theirs was a life of double drudgery. In any case, the majority of working-class married women would, other things being equal, probably have preferred to confine their activities to the domestic scene. And when the arrival of late century prosperity did eventually make it possible for many to become full-time 'housewives', this had the effect of improving the domestic comfort of their families to such a degree that those married men earning a wage could now do so more productively and thus bring yet larger sums of money into the home.[53] As families became more prosperous so the lives of married women became ever more private, some women positively lashing themselves to the domestic pillar and announcing proudly that 'they never go anywhere... and that they never speak to anyone'.[54] The affectionate term 'mum' itself dates

[50] J. Rule, *The Labouring Classes in Early Industrial England 1750–1850* (London, 1986), 177; E. Richards, 'Women in the British Economy since about 1700', *History*, 59 (1974), 347–9; L. Holcombe, *Victorian Ladies at Work: Middle-Class Working Women in England and Wales 1850–1914* (Newton Abbot, 1973), 213; W. A. Armstrong, 'The Use of Information about Occupation', in E. A. Wrigley (ed.), *Nineteenth-Century Society* (Cambridge, 1972), 281. Revisions by E. Higgs ('Women, Occupations and Work in the Nineteenth Century Censuses', *History Workshop*, 23 (1987), 75) suggest that the proportion of all women who were 'occupied' fell more sharply—from 28.5% in 1851 to 25.4% in 1891.

[51] Holcombe, *Victorian Ladies*, 217; Rule, *Labouring Classes*, 179; Hewitt, *Wives and Mothers*, 101–2.

[52] Meacham, *Life Apart*, 117–18; R. Roberts, *The Classic Slum: Salford Life in the First Quarter of the Century* (Manchester, 1971), 36.

[53] J. Lewis, 'The Working-Class Wife and Mother and State Intervention, 1870–1918', in Lewis (ed.), *Labour and Love*, 105; S. Pennington and B. Westhover, *A Hidden Workforce: Homeworkers in England, 1850–1985* (London, 1989), 21; J. Bourke, 'Housewifery in Working-Class England 1860–1914', *Past & Present*, 143 (1994), 167–97.

[54] J. McCalman, 'Respectability and Working-Class Politics in Late-Victorian London', *Historical Studies*, 19 (1980), 113.

from the 1880s when accounts begin to picture mothers as confident managing women, constantly working and planning for the advantage of their families. What might, indeed, be denoted a deferentially assertive dualism characterized many working-class mothers: a measure of withdrawal into domestic privacy coinciding with accretions of power within the home itself.[55]

Elsewhere in society, however, women generally tended to be portrayed in strictly stereotypical terms, not least by many of the leading writers, artists, and scientists of the day. Herbert Spencer, rummaging among biological and physical ideas, insisted in the 1860s and 1870s that sexual division was a hallmark of social progress and, like the mathematician and biologist, Karl Pearson, and the pioneer sexologists, Patrick Geddes and J. Arthur Thomson (authors of *The Evolution of Sex* of 1889), pressed all kinds of modish scientific research into the service of male dominance.[56] And even if some key literary figures—Ruskin, Tennyson, Coventry Patmore—tempered the harshness of science with acknowledgements of female 'virtues', they did so in a manner that was at once patronizing and unreal. Patmore's long poem *The Angel in the House* (1854–62) alternates between praising women's emotional superiority and asserting the absolute dominion of men. Ruskin, who believed that he was countering traditional male prejudice, urged women in the 1860s to see to the home's 'sweet order' and leave to men (whose intellects were for 'speculation and invention') its 'maintenance, progress and defence'.[57] While a few writers like Browning took a different line, most Victorian painters did not, preferring to highlight female gentleness and sweetness rather than intelligence, sexual directness, or dependable solidity. Indeed, even the 'bohemian' Pre-Raphaelites placed great stress on the idea of what they called 'sacred womanhood'. And it was not until the 1880s that sustained painterly engagement with the problem of cheerless marriages begins to appear in, for example, the work of Sir William Quiller Orchardson.[58]

The actual realities of middle- and upper-class life were a good deal more earthbound than the Pre-Raphaelites would have liked them to be. Because for Victorians charity was no snug little duty restricted to parish jumble sales, gentlewomen (whether welcome or not) went into the streets

[55] E. Ross, 'Labour and Love: Rediscovering London's Working-Class Mothers, 1870–1918', in Lewis (ed.), *Labour and Love*, 73–4; Smith, 'Sexuality in Britain', 187.

[56] J. Conway, 'Stereotypes of Femininity in a Theory of Sexual Evolution', in Vicinus (ed.), *Suffer and Be Still*, 140–54; Lewis, *Women in England*, 83–4.

[57] *Sesame and Lilies* (1865): lecture 2 'Of Queens' Gardens'.

[58] H. E. Roberts, 'Marriage, Redundancy or Sin: The Painter's View of Women in the First Twenty-Five Years of Victoria's Reign' in Vicinus (ed.), *Suffer and Be Still*, 50–63.

of the East End and the homes of the poor, into gaols and brothels too. By
1893 one estimate suggests that perhaps half a million women worked
'continuously, and semi-professionally' in voluntary activities.[59] A close
study of one large upper middle-class professional clan (the Pagets) reveals
few shrinking female violets, few martyrs to hypochondria, few demure
onlookers, but rather Paget wives playing key roles as colleagues and
partners in the work of their husbands. And though such marriages typically remained 'single-career' partnerships with the husbands taking most of
the public credit, just as 'much as among agricultural and working-class
families, there was, in the nineteenth century, a family economy of the
upper-middle class'.[60]

If this was not emancipation, it was not mere subjection either. It is
possible that the largely professional upper middle-class families about
which most is known were unrepresentative. And it is more than possible
that among the 'new' industrial middle class, where shared careers were less
easy to pursue, things went differently. Yet women of all kinds, whether
married or not, were, for example, quite generally to be found dealing with
important questions of family finance. Nor was the political kingdom
entirely closed. In 1834 women householders (that is, ratepayers) became
eligible to vote for Poor Law Guardians and in 1875 the first women stood
for election. In 1869 and 1870 certain women were allowed to vote at
municipal and school-board elections and from 1888 at county council
elections also. When in 1879 the Manchester Suffrage Society organized
meetings for working-class women possessing the right to vote at local
elections, it was surprised at how many 'of all ranks and occupations'
turned up.[61] Even for those whose priorities were entirely home-based,
the management of middle-class households involved substantial organizational skills. Increasing financial surpluses were being invested in better
furniture, diet, and domestic technology, all of it adding to the work
demanded of servants and mistress alike. Mrs Beeton (Coventry Patmore's
contemporary) preferred military to angelic allusions: 'As with the commander of an army, or the leader of an enterprise, so it is with the mistress
of a house'.[62]

[59] Peterson, *Family, Love, and Work*, 138; F. K. Prochaska, *Women and Philanthropy in Nineteenth-Century England* (Oxford, 1980), 224.

[60] Peterson, *Family, Love, and Work*, 166, 33.

[61] Ibid. 120–31; J. Liddington and J. Norris, *One Hand Tied Behind Us: The Rise of the Women's Suffrage Movement* (London, 1978), 72.

[62] Perkin, *Women and Marriage*, 246–9; J. Bourke, ' "The Best of all Home Rulers": The Economic Power of Women in Ireland, 1880–1914', *Irish Economic and Social History*, 18 (1991), 36–7; S. Muthesius, *The English Terraced House* (London, 1982), 38.

2. HOUSES, DOMESTICITY, MAKING ENDS MEET

Different homes demanded different talents. Yet even in the grandest, where money and servants were plentiful, husbands tended to assume their wives would be competent in handling accounts, paying bills, ordering supplies, approving menus, and dealing with crises of the most unexpected sort.[63] In a country-house world in which everyone 'knew their place', the buildings themselves constituted tangible icons of hierarchy, for, as the fashionable architect, Sir George Gilbert Scott, put it in 1857, providence having 'ordained the different orders and gradations into which the human family is divided', it was 'right and necessary' that landed proprietors should display their standing and their wealth in the form of brick and stone.[64] Probably £7,000 to £10,000 was the least for which a 'proper country house' could be built in the mid-Victorian period, though there was no upper limit and initial estimates were almost always exceeded. A good many houses absorbed breathtaking amounts: Eaton Hall (Duke of Westminster) remodelled 1870–82 for £600,000; Alnwick Castle (Duke of Northumberland) remodelled 1854–65 for £250,000; Westonbirt House (R. S. Holford) built 1863–70 for £125,000; Bear Wood (John Walter) built 1865–74 for £120,000.[65] Comprehensive statistics remain elusive given the definitional problems involved, but the standing stock of 'country' houses in the middle of the century was probably about 3,000, with at least 500 built or substantially remodelled between 1835 and 1889.[66] Styles were eclectic—with Gothic less universal than is sometimes supposed—though the cult of the 'domestic' and the associated desire for privacy affected all classes. Victorian planning emphasized segregation, specialization, and comfort. Sometimes this involved features which no middle-class villa could have emulated, such as the 44-yard corridor between dining-room and kitchen at Stoke Rochford Hall in Lincolnshire (1841–5) deliberately designed to prevent cooking smells spoiling meals (an altogether higher priority than the provision of hot food).[67] Often, however, the improvements were simply part of a

---

[63] J. Gerard, *Country House Life: Family and Servants, 1815–1914* (London, 1994), 115–41.

[64] G. G. Scott, *Remarks on Secular and Domestic Architecture* (London, 1857), 140.

[65] J. Franklin, *The Gentleman's Country House and its Plan 1835–1914* (London, 1981), 124; id., 'The Victorian Country House', in G. E. Mingay (ed.), *The Victorian Countryside*, 2 vols. (London, 1981), ii. 405–6; M. Girouard, *The Victorian Country House*, new edn. (London, 1979), 409, 404, 394, 423, 272.

[66] F. M. L. Thompson, *The Rise of Respectable Society* (London, 1988), 154–5.

[67] Franklin, *Gentleman's Country House*, 42, 39; id., 'Victorian Country House', ii. 408. Hence Disraeli's quip when offered champagne at dinner: 'Thank God for something warm' (Franklin, *Gentleman's Country House*, 92).

process undertaken by prosperous people generally—such as that towards the provision of water closets and bathrooms for example.

As railways expanded, so active businessmen started to put up buildings which, while in the country, were not country houses strictly defined. Surrounded by only a few hundred acres, they provided the pleasures of rural life (fresh air, shooting, riding) without its responsibilities (tenants, farming, local administration). One step lower came the rather larger number of substantial villas with gardens, ten bedrooms, and 'libraries' that still remain so visible a legacy of Victorian times. And it was within the long spectrum of houses ranging downwards from such places to Charles and Carrie Pooter's The Laurels, Brickfield Terrace, Holloway (in George and Weedon Grossmith's *The Diary of a Nobody* of 1892) that the Victorian cult of domesticity found its most ardent votaries. Contemporary commentators insisted that happy homes should be 'like a bright, serene, restful, joyful nook of heaven' and were delighted to record that 'Home Sweet Home' had become 'almost our national melody'.[68] For Samuel Smiles, writing in 1871, home was the place where every youth 'imbibes those principles of conduct which endure through manhood . . . Law itself is but the reflex of homes'.[69] In the same decade Lord and Lady Folkestone chose to be painted (by Edward Clifford) actually singing 'Home Sweet Home' alongside their eldest son, while a portrait by H. H. Emmerson of the mighty armaments manufacturer, Lord Armstrong, shows him by the fireplace of Cragside (his Norman Shaw extravaganza of 1869–84 in Northumberland) upon which is incised 'East or West Hame's Best'.[70] Given all this, the increasing tendency of the well-to-do to send their sons away to boarding schools does, however, suggest that the new domestic religion, however fervent its rituals, was not lacking in self-interested heretics.

It was, above all, the design and layout of houses for the prosperous middle class that most clearly reflected the growing emphasis upon domesticity and privacy (although of course not all Victorians lived in Victorian houses). Interior space became more specialized with the provision of distinct spheres for women and children. Upper stories gradually ceased to contain 'public' drawing-rooms and were now devoted entirely to sleeping, dressing, sewing, and other 'private' functions.[71] No single 'style'

[68] A. Briggs, *Victorian Things* (London, 1988), 214–15. The song dates from the 1820s: words by J. H. Payne (an American), music by H. R. Bishop.

[69] S. Smiles, *Character* (London, 1897), 31 (1st publ. 1871).

[70] M. Girouard, *Life in the English Country House* (London, 1978), 270; id., *Victorian Country House*, 314–17.

[71] J. Summerson, 'London, the Artifact', in Dyos and Wolff (eds.), *Victorian City*, i. 317; M. J. Daunton, 'Housing', in *CSHB* ii. 212.

dominated, with provincial backwaters, like Beverley in the East Riding of Yorkshire, still building in the 1860s plain tall narrow red brick houses of a type quite out of fashion elsewhere. At the upper end of the market architects' working drawings were used, but more usually builders relied upon pattern-books containing sample plans and methods for estimating quantities and costs. Prices varied widely according to size, site, and location (though most people rented rather than bought their homes): £300 could buy a modest suburban villa, £2,000 might be needed for a very large town house. Contemporaries agreed that the 'middle classes' normally spent about a tenth of their gross incomes on rent.[72] At the lower end this would secure five rooms including a kitchen (but not a scullery) for about £15 a year; at the £50 rent level one got eight rooms and employed perhaps two servants; at £100 a house in a fashionable London square with an impressive hall and staircase, large drawing- and dining-rooms, a parlour and study, ample kitchen areas, four or five main bedrooms, as well as quarters for five or more servants.[73]

A growing market for household manuals signified both a sense of insecurity and an interest in comfort. Mrs Beeton's famous *Book of Household Management* of 1861, which sold 30,000 copies in three years, was only one among many. Already in 1849 the chef, Alexis Soyer, had produced the *Modern Housewife or Ménagère*, while Eliza Warren's titles include *How I Managed My House on Two Hundred Pounds a Year* (1864) and the equally brisk *How I Managed My Children from Infancy to Marriage* (1865). Changing technologies generated increasing calls on middle-class incomes, not because more was needed to maintain a particular style of life, but because perceptions were changing as to what that style should be. The characteristic mid-Victorian liking for clutter required increasing expenditure on tables, chairs, sideboards, chiffoniers, escritoires, pianos, dumb waiters (all covered with tasselled velvet cloths and runners), upon Staffordshire figurines, Doulton china, brass candlesticks, coal-scuttles, papier-mâché models, vases, stuffed birds, wax fruit, and framed photographs. Rapid fashion changes in something as fundamental as carpets regularly forced the 'up-to-date' into making new acquisitions as the flat-woven body carpets of the 1840s gave way in the 1850s to fitted pile or tapestry carpets, and these in turn in the 1870s to squares on polished wooden floors.[74]

---

[72] J. Burnett, *A Social History of Housing 1815–1985*, 2nd edn. (London, 1986), 25–6, 101, 199–200; J. A. Banks, *Prosperity and Parenthood: A Study of Family Planning among the Victorian Middle Classes* (London, 1954), 57.

[73] Burnett, *Social History of Housing*, 101; Muthesius, *English Terraced House*, 44.

[74] R. Guild, *The Victorian House Book*, 2nd edn. (London, 1991), 195–6; W. H. Fraser, *The Coming of the Mass Market 1850–1914* (London, 1981), 55.

The cost of setting up home depended upon inclination and pocket. Instalment purchase schemes for expensive items became available about the middle of the century: by the 1860s pianos could be bought on the so-called 'three-year system' and monthly instalments had become common by the end of our period.[75] The difficulty of keeping houses clean encouraged even the most modest of the middle class to employ servants who were (when all was taken into account) rarely as cheap as they seemed. Cleaning tools and materials were still primitive. A fair-sized room in a middle-class house could easily take one person more than three hours to clean. Early carpet-sweeping machines redistributed rather than removed dirt, until the American Bissell cleaners became available in the late 1870s. Nor did the location of kitchens in basements help, for it meant that running water (when it first appeared) was only available there or perhaps on the ground floor. Kitchens and sculleries, indeed, absorbed long hours of work. Although coal-burning ranges were improved in the third quarter of the century and the so-called 'close' (that is, closed) ranges of the 1880s were at least safe, they were neither reliable nor simple to operate, while gas cooking made little impact until the 1890s. The preservation of food demanded even greater expertise, something the poor did not need because they never bought enough to store. Meat especially had to be examined daily, the outside scraped clean of mould, and flour rubbed into the scraped areas. Laundry work required heroic stamina and was the first thing which anyone with cash to spare sought to avoid. Small wonder that it was an age of gadgetry. Hand-operated washing machines were widely available (several designs were displayed at the Great Exhibition of 1851), but handle-turning could still be heavy work and some mangles required more effort than wringing clothes manually. Most other devices—for cleaning knives, peeling potatoes, blacking shoes—were mere curiosities. Only the sewing machine, which, despite a long prehistory, first made an effective appearance in the 1850s (Singers opened a factory in Glasgow in 1856), proved a real success.[76]

Such things cost money, as did the installation of the gas lighting common by the 1850s in middle- and upper-class houses in the larger towns, though the effect remained yellow and smoky until the introduction of effective (but expensive) incandescent mantles in the mid-1880s. Primitive and dangerous geysers powered by gas, oil, and coke appeared in the

---

[75] Banks, *Prosperity and Parenthood*, 49–51, 54; C. Ehrlich, *The Piano: A History*, new edn. (Oxford, 1990), 100–4.

[76] C. Hardyment, *From Mangle to Microwave: The Mechanization of Household Work* (Oxford, 1990), 14, 77–8, 113–34, 22–3, 56–60, 47–52; Fraser, *Coming of the Mass Market*, 60.

late 1860s just as plumbing was being steadily extended upstairs. From the 1850s the use of non-porous clay pipes made it possible to install more and more water closets, while improvements in design (especially the introduction of the S bend) had, by the 1880s, produced equipment of a recognizably modern efficiency and design. With matchless synergy, the perforated lavatory paper roll was invented in 1879 by Walter Alcock, though wooden boxes containing scrap sheets long held the day.[77]

Drainage and sanitation were much more primitive in working-class houses. In the poorer areas of Darlington in 1850 one undrained privy commonly served as many as sixty people, while 94 per cent of Middlesbrough houses in 1869 still possessed privy middens. Glasgow's first full-time medical officer of health found the central closes of the 1870s chocked with 'midden-steads' holding 'the entire filth and offal of large masses of people'.[78] Without a reliable water supply little could be done, and although improvements were certainly made (by 1885 two-thirds of Newcastle houses had either indoor or outdoor piped supply), the widespread adoption of water-carried sewerage systems occurred after the end of our period. Official reports noted that in the mid-1880s the inhabitants of London slums were still 'in the habit of depositing their excreta in a newspaper, folding it up, and throwing it with its contents out of a back window'.[79]

That, on average, working people should have spent between 16 and 25 per cent—double the middle-class proportion—of their exiguous incomes on housing was striking and burdensome, especially as the very poorest usually paid relatively most of all. In 1884/5 a royal commission estimated that almost half of all Londoners were paying over a quarter of their incomes in rent.[80] And this was also true of the countryside, where agricultural labourers inhabited the worst houses in the land (see Plate 5). Government reports in the 1890s spoke exactly as had government reports half a century before: the cottage 'floors downstairs ... are almost invariably damp, often indeed reeking with moisture ... and several thicknesses of sacking and mats are laid upon the floor. These have to be removed

---

[77] Guild, *Victorian House Book*, 244; Muthesius, *English Terraced House*, 57–61; *Guardian*, 14 Dec. 1990.

[78] A. S. Wohl, *Endangered Lives: Public Health in Victorian Britain* (London, 1983), 87; D. J. Rowe, 'The North-East', in *CSHB* i. 457; R. A. Cage, 'Health in Glasgow', in Cage (ed.), *The Working Class in Glasgow 1750–1914* (London, 1987), 63–4.

[79] M. J. Daunton, 'Housing', in *CSHB* ii. 207; Wohl, *Endangered Lives*, 87.

[80] E. Gauldie, *Cruel Habitations: A History of Working-Class Housing, 1780–1918* (London, 1974), 164–5; R. Rodger, *Housing in Urban Britain 1780–1914* (London, 1989), 10; A. Sutcliffe, 'In Search of the Urban Variable', in D. Fraser and Sutcliffe (eds.), *The Pursuit of Urban History* (London, 1983), 255.

periodically, as the damp causes them to rot.'[81] A detailed mid-century
inquiry revealed that English single-bedroomed cottages (two-fifths of the
total) averaged four persons in a bedroom of perhaps 10ft by 10ft with a 7ft
ceiling. The resulting sleeping space per person was less than two-thirds of
that legally required in common lodging houses. Only when the population
of the English and Welsh countryside began to fall absolutely after 1861 was
the pressure upon the rural housing stock gradually eased, with the result
that, even without any increase in overall quality, the living conditions of
labourers slowly began to improve.[82]

Despite much justified hand-wringing, urban progress was more
marked, particularly in centres of factory production where relatively
well-paid jobs were available. The average number of persons per house
in England and Wales fell from 5.5 in 1851 to 5.1 sixty years later, though in
1891 one in nine or 3.5 million persons still lived more than two to a
room.[83] In Scotland the situation was worse. There in 1861 a third of all
houses had only a single room, another 37 per cent had two rooms, and
almost two in every three persons lived in such dwellings. In England,
however, the size of rooms was probably smaller than in Scottish tenements—8ft by 10ft was common and ceilings were low—so that space, let
alone privacy, was always at a premium.[84]

Governments acted, at best, as cheer-leaders encouraging (but not obliging) local authorities to impose higher standards. The Local Government
Act of 1858 and the Public Health Act of 1875, for example, contained so-
called 'model' by-laws relating to street width, building practices, drainage,
and so forth which municipal authorities could copy and enforce verbatim,
though many towns also secured special local acts of their own. Not only,
however, was all this voluntary, but many houses built in earlier times still
remained in occupation and local authorities could do nothing to ameliorate
the two most important constraints upon the housing conditions of working
people—poverty and high costs.

The mass of the poor lived in rented rooms or houses, moving frequently
from street to street as family and financial circumstances required. The
word 'slum' in its modern sense appeared in the 1840s and while its precise
meaning remained vague it is reasonable to suggest that something between

[81] *Royal Commission on Labour: The Agricultural Labourer*, i. *England, part v*, H[ouse of]
C[ommons Paper] 1893–4 [C. 6894–v], xxxv. 84 (Report on the Chelmsford and Maldon
Rural Sanitary Districts).

[82] Burnett, *Social History of Housing*, 43, 127–37.

[83] J. K. Walton, 'The North-West', in *CSHB* i. 371–2; Sutcliffe, 'Urban Variable', 253;
Meacham, *Life Apart*, 32–3; Burnett, *Social History of Housing*, 141.

[84] Smout, *Century*, 33; M. Anderson, 'The Social Implications of Demographic Change',
in *CSHB* ii. 58; Gauldie, *Cruel Habitations*, 93; Meacham, *Life Apart*, 34–5.

a tenth and a fifth of the population occupied buildings that might plausibly
have been designated by the term: a proportion of a sixth would in 1881
have meant that—in England and Wales alone—three million people in
towns and one-and-a-quarter million in the countryside were living in slum
housing (see Plate 7).[85] By then their plight was beginning to elicit a
considerable descriptive literature, which, though obviously polemical (as
were the better-known fictional accounts of Dickens and others), was
usually based on first-hand observation. Two examples give the flavour.

Courts reeking with poisonous and malodorous gases arising from accumulations
of sewage and refuse scattered in all directions . . . dark and filthy passages swarming with vermin . . . walls and ceiling are black with the accretions of filth which
have gathered upon them through long years of neglect. [London 1883][86]

In the room below, in which the wood is rotting till it well nigh tumbles of its own
accord, is a man in bed . . . on the remnant of a straw pallet, stupified . . . possibly by
the deadening atmosphere of the yard. Above, in the other room, rented at 1s. per
week, is an old woman. 'You have caught me untidy', she says, 'I was just shifting
my bed a bit'. So we look around . . . till we see the heap of straw in the middle of
the room is the shifted 'bed'. [Hull 1883][87]

And even the drastic remedy of 'slum clearance' usually proved no remedy
at all because little was done to replace the demolished slums with better
housing which the dispossessed could actually afford.

   Poor and decaying homes were equipped with poor and decaying furniture. People made do with boxes; they slept in their clothes; they rarely
washed. Household inventories read much like those of three centuries
before: the most valuable items were still beds and bedding, followed by a
table, a cupboard, a couple of chairs. Two rooms rather than one and the
presence of a few items of display differentiated the poor from the very
poor. The moment one London husband of the 1870s got a job, his wife
spent 3s. 6d. on a set of 'little pictures . . . as the room looked so uncomfortable without them'. 'She had not', reported a horrified observer who had
lent her money, 'yet bought bed or bedding, and I should have said needed
every necessity of life.'[88] 'So long', noted an East End family, 'as we have

[85] H. J. Dyos, 'The Slums of Victorian London', *Victorian Studies*, 11 (1967), 8;
Thompson, *Rise of Respectable Society*, 181; Burnett, *Social History of Housing*, 175. In
Ireland and Scotland conditions were worse.
   [86] [A. Mearns], *The Bitter Cry of Outcast London* (London, 1883), 4.
   [87] J. M. Lambert and others, *Homes of the People: Report of the Conference Held in the
Town Hall, Hull, February 1st, 1884* (Hull, 1884), 60.
   [88] J. Burnett, *A History of the Cost of Living* (Harmondsworth, 1969), 280–1; Roberts,
Classic Slum, 55; G. S. Jones, *Outcast London: A Study in the Relationship between Classes in
Victorian Society* (Oxford, 1971), 474.

our glass shade with its flowers we are in steady work and beyond the reach of want'.[89] And mass production made it ever easier to buy an odd figurine, some linoleum, a tablecloth, and—perhaps symbolically most important of all—a clock, preferably one that worked.

Among labour aristocrats the widely canvassed notion of 'respectability' reached its apogee in shrine-like front parlours—formal settings in which to regulate relationships with outsiders according to established conventions. Here was a big Bible, a birdcage, glass vases containing coral from the Philippines, something from India in fragrant wood, brasswork from Benares, heavy furniture, chairs with antimacassars, perhaps even a piano. Most working-class homes—and there was an infinite variety—fell somewhere between the extremes. Families occupied three or at most four rooms (one of which was often sublet), battled ceaselessly against dirt, tried to improve their surroundings with a pot plant or a cheap picture. Despite everything, British workers were almost certainly better housed than their continental counterparts, even in industrially advanced countries like Belgium and Germany, and, in terms of the proportion of wages devoted to rent, more cheaply housed as well.[90] And even if this was not perhaps a great achievement for so relatively 'rich' a country, it was something all the same.

Rent of course constituted only one aspect of making ends meet. For most working people irregularity as well as inadequacy of income characterized the struggle for survival. Anticipatory saving was confined to a small group: for the rest it seemed utterly remote. Almost three-quarters of those in Edinburgh belonging to the Oddfellows (a mutual-benefit insurance society) during the 1860s and 1870s were skilled artisans and less than one in fifty a semi- or unskilled worker.[91] Everything conspired against those with few resources: they could only buy shoddy clothes which wore out quickly, they could only buy food in small quantities which cost more. Most husbands happily handed over the responsibility of budgeting to their wives, together with as much cash as was 'customary' or simply as much as they fancied. As a result, men were often comparatively isolated from the daily strain of making ends meet—so much so that a widower might well give his wages to his 16-year-old daughter 'who knew what her mother used to do' rather than attempt the task himself.[92]

[89] P. Johnson, 'Conspicuous Consumption and Working-Class Culture in late Victorian and Edwardian Britain', *Transactions of the Royal Historical Society*, 5th ser. 38 (1988), 37.

[90] M. J. Daunton, 'Housing', in *CSHB* ii. 197–8.

[91] R. McKibbin, *The Ideologies of Class: Social Relations in Britain 1880–1950* (Oxford, 1990), 115; R. Q. Gray, *The Labour Aristocracy in Victorian Edinburgh* (Oxford, 1976), 122.

[92] P. Johnson, *Saving and Spending: The Working-Class Economy in Britain 1870–1939* (Oxford, 1985), 97; M. Tebbutt, *Making Ends Meet: Pawnbroking and Working-Class Credit* (Leicester, 1983), 38; Perkin, *Women and Marriage*, 176.

The poorest of all were completely trapped; they never fell into debt because nobody gave them the opportunity, though they could of course steal. For the rest there were (apart from theft) broadly four strategies available: (*a*) not paying, (*b*) shopkeepers' credit, (*c*) pawning, (*d*) borrowing from moneylenders. The first meant doing a 'moonlight flit' and, though not uncommon, involved serious penalties in that it deprived participants of that 'steady record' essential before credit without security could be obtained. The fourth was a desperate resort because moneylenders (who usually operated illegally) charged enormous rates of interest and never let go. Shopkeepers and pawnbrokers played altogether larger roles. Most corner shops gave credit to 'reliable' customers, though of course really reliable customers stood in less need than most. You got 'tick' if you were 'known', so it paid not to move too far away. Contrary to received wisdom many co-operative stores also gave credit, even though the principles of the movement insisted on cash transactions—the pressure from customers was simply too great.[93] Clearly the cost of credit was reflected in higher prices, but the relationship between small shopkeepers and customers was a reciprocal one—each needed the other. Even in rural Ireland, where monopoly retailing was more common, the feared 'gombeenman' (or credit retailer) was no mere parasite upon the local community. Much more expensive, for example, were travelling 'Scotch drapers' and other itinerant salesmen of furniture, footwear, and household goods, who added anything between 50 and 100 per cent to the usual price for their services and for the (admittedly considerable) financial risks they took. Hire-purchase proper was confined to more expensive items beyond the reach of the poor, though informal savings clubs and the development of 'check trading' in the 1880s (which involved specialist companies selling 'checks' on credit which could be redeemed at certain stores) helped those making smaller credit purchases to retain a certain amount of respectability.[94]

Pawnbrokers' shops were ubiquitous in working-class districts. Although, once again, the very poorest were excluded, unofficial pawnbrokers (in England called 'dolly' or 'leaving' shops, in Scotland 'wee pawns') were prepared to give small loans at high rates on the lowest grade of pledge. Most licensed brokers could not, in any case, afford to be all that choosy: in Liverpool in the 1870s almost half the nine million loans made by them each year were for less than 2s. and only 50,000 for more than two

---

[93] Johnson, *Saving and Spending*, 188–92, 133, 145–6. The new grocery chains of the late 19th century (see below) did not give credit.

[94] K. T. Hoppen, *Elections, Politics, and Society in Ireland 1832–1885* (Oxford, 1984), 470–3; Burnett, *Cost of Living*, 278–9; Fraser, *Coming of the Mass Market*, 87–9; Johnson, *Saving and Spending*, 150–2.

guineas. The rates of interest (which, at least in theory, were highly regulated) were often denounced as excessive, but in fact depended more upon client decisions about when and how often to pawn than upon the greed of the broker. As usual, those least able to pay, paid the most, because small short loans carried the highest charges. In 1870 a rough estimate concluded that 'on average, every working-class family in Britain made at least one pledge a fortnight, or something over thirty each year'.[95] Although widely denounced as suppliers of money for drink and debauchery, pawnbrokers performed an extremely useful service by helping to smooth out income irregularities and preventing their clients from becoming completely dependent upon a single source of credit, the local shop.

Charitable help was also available, though most people tried hard to avoid (or avoid being seen) making use of it. Private philanthropy constituted a substantial Victorian enterprise. The 640 or so London charities active in the 1860s spent more each year (between £5.5m and £7m) than the annual cost of poor relief in England and Wales. Giving was not confined to any class, though, as one writer put it in 1849, those were most impelled to give who knew 'that the distress they are called upon to mitigate was their own yesterday, and may be their own again tomorrow'.[96] There were charities for every need, some—like the Christian Excavators Union (1877) and the Christian Police Association (1883)—with highly specialized aims. The combined private and public relief of poverty was on a more generous scale in Britain than in countries such as Germany and France, where, ironically, the very dearth of state relief for the poor may eventually have made it easier to introduce provisions for social insurance of various kinds.

The Poor Law system provided an important adjunct to private charity, particularly as regards support for the elderly who were largely sustained at public expense. Conditions in workhouses were arbitrarily different rather than uniformly dreadful and had certainly improved by the last quarter of the century. The harsh system introduced for England and Wales in 1834 was never completely implemented. The central authorities proved unable to control local generosity (or meanness) and outdoor relief continued on a substantial scale. The Irish Poor Law of 1838 was modelled on the revised English code and proved singularly unsuited to a rural country where poverty existed on an altogether larger scale. Although many workhouses

[95] Johnson, *Saving and Spending*, 170, 186–7; Tebbutt, *Making Ends Meet*, 2, 125.

[96] [W. R. Greg], [Review of] 'Mary Barton', *Edinburgh Review*, 89 (1849), 410; B. Harrison, *Peaceable Kingdom: Stability and Change in Modern Britain* (Oxford, 1982), 217; E. Royle, *Modern Britain: A Social History 1750–1985*, corrected impression (London, 1988), 181–2; F. K. Prochaska, 'Philanthropy', in *CSHB* iii. 358.

were built, the system was overwhelmed by the Great Famine of 1845–9 and thereafter survived as a shadow of what its founders had intended. While Ireland had possessed no system at all before 1838, Scotland's had been merely exiguous. When, therefore, a new Scottish Poor Law was introduced in 1845 with the unusual aim of *increasing* relief, there was so much ground to make up that Scotland remained throughout the century a tight-fisted country as regards public provision for the poor. But while the annual cost of poor relief per head of population in England and Wales remained considerably higher than in Scotland (by a factor, in 1870–4, of 1.45), it is difficult to estimate the precise numbers relieved each year. The least inaccurate suggestion would be that in the period from 1851–5 to 1876–80 between 9.0 per cent and 14.9 per cent of all those living in England and Wales received some indoor or outdoor relief, though the period for which they were so relieved remains unknown.[97] The system's increasing cost—more the result of greater generosity than greater numbers—eventually produced a backlash orchestrated by many of the leading social reformers of the day. In 1869 the Charity Organization Society was formed and began its 'efficiency' campaigns against 'indiscriminate' benevolence, thereby throwing an expert's cloak of justification over the prejudices of those who had demanded retrenchment all along. Two years later its efforts bore fruit and relief was taken under the wing of the Local Government Board which, over the next twenty years, treated the poor according to the most scientifically approved and parsimonious standards of the day.

3. FOOD AND CLOTHES

After rent, the chief items of expenditure for the great majority of people were food and drink. Small wonder, therefore, that their acquisition and the habits associated with their consumption preoccupied Victorians of almost every rank. As the century wore on two contradictory trends became apparent: a growing distinction between urban and rural diets and a slow drift towards homogeneity of taste.[98] As the economic condition of agri-

---

[97] J. H. Treble, *Urban Poverty in Britain 1830–1914* (London, 1979), 139–40; M. A. Crowther, 'Poverty, Health and Welfare', in W. H. Fraser and R. J. Morris (eds.), *People and Society in Scotland*, ii. *1830–1914* (Edinburgh, 1990), 267–72; G. Best, *Mid-Victorian Britain 1851–1875* (London, 1971), 147; M. E. Rose, *The Relief of Poverty, 1834–1914*, 2nd edn. (London, 1986), 15–18, 50.

[98] D. J. Oddy, 'Food, Drink and Nutrition', in *CSHB* ii. 269–71; J. Burnett, *Plenty and Want: A Social History of Diet in England from 1815 to the Present Day*, 3rd edn. (London, 1989), 162–5.

cultural labourers deteriorated in relative terms, so did their diets. These were least bad in Scotland and worst in the south of England. A Wiltshire labourer's family in 1863 made do with: a breakfast of water broth, bread and butter; a dinner for the husband and children of cabbage, bread and butter, and—very occasionally—bacon (the wife only had tea); and a supper of potatoes or rice. Workhouses provided better food. Nor did conditions improve until the 1870s when (despite the agricultural depression) rural workers obtained a little more bargaining power because more and more of them were leaving the land.[99]

Such regional differences as remained did so most strongly among the least well off. Scotland retained a liking for oatmeal, the south of England for the wheaten loaf. The houses of the 'very neediest' in mid-century London smelt strongly of fish, though fish featured less frequently in the provinces. Local distinctions of this kind were, however, overlaid by general trends towards more sugar and less bread at a time when potatoes (formerly unpopular in the bread-eating south) were becoming more evenly established throughout the British Isles. Late nineteenth-century evidence reveals that the calorie intake of individuals in 'moderate' families (two adults, three children) was directly related to income: less than 18s. a week = 1,578 kilocalories daily; between 18s. and 21s. = 1,964; between 21s. and 30s. = 2,113; above 30s. = 2,537.[100] In the East End of London Charles Booth estimated that in the 1880s almost two in every five working people depended on family incomes of less than 21s. a week and ate meals marked by lethargic preparation and dominated by bread and tea: 'remains of food are always about—there is perhaps no cupboard—probably part of a loaf is on the table with a little butter and a much-used knife'. Tiredness, ignorance, and a lack of implements and cooking facilities created a demand for food that required little in the way of skilled handling. Hence the popularity of tea, which gave warmth and comfort, and of fish and chips, by the 1880s a well-established feature of working-class life. Those families with earnings between 21s. and 30s. lived in a different dietary world. Here meals were more regular, meat and vegetables appeared every day, bacon, eggs, and fish from time to time, puddings were not uncommon, and bread was no longer the 'staff of life'. Higher still, among the most skilled, the atmosphere was formal: napkins and napkin rings were used, children were expected to be quiet, meals were an occasion rather than a disordered relay

[99] Burnett, *Plenty and Want*, 143–9; id., 'Country Diet', in Mingay (ed.), *Victorian Countryside*, ii. 558–62.

[100] D. J. Oddy, 'Working-Class Diets in Late Nineteenth-Century Britain', *Economic History Review*, 23 (1970), 319. See also above, Ch. 3, s. 3.

with everyone scrambling for the few chairs, plates, and knives available. Yet in all but the most prosperous working-class homes the husband ate better than the rest, and the wife ate worst of all.[101]

Everyone, however, shared to some degree in the changes brought about from the 1870s onwards by cheaper imports (especially of wheat and meat) and by the accelerating appearance of mass-produced foods as food processing at last began to experience an 'industrial revolution' of its own. Margarine (initially made from animal fats) arrived in the 1870s: by 1876 imports exceeded a million pounds weight. Biscuit, jam, and chocolate production became increasingly mechanized and dominated by a handful of large firms. Well-known companies like Huntley and Palmer (who by 1867 employed over 1,000 people making biscuits in Reading) and the three jam-makers Hartley, Chivers, and Keiller were expanding rapidly. By the 1860s Crosse and Blackwell were producing 27,000 gallons of tomato catsup ('ketchup' was still a 'vulgar barbarism'). Bird's eggless 'custard' powder was being distributed in the 1850s and branded blancmanges appeared twenty years later. Bovril—the second syllable of its name derived from a mysterious energy form called Vril in Bulwer-Lytton's (almost) science-fiction novel *The Coming Race* (1871)—was among the country's most prolific advertisers: one poster featured Pope Leo XIII sipping the drink under the caption 'The Two Infallible Powers'. The physical appearance of the standard loaf altered dramatically as the stodgy, soggy, and dirty-coloured 4lb. and even 8lb. loaf common in the 1850s slowly gave way to the finer white bread made possible by various manufacturing innovations. Eventually, in turn, a reaction against high milling set in led by Victorian health enthusiasts like Dr T. R. Allinson of the Bread Reform League. By 1887 it had become possible to produce wheat-germ flour and twelve years later the Hovis Company began selling its new patented 'healthy' brown loaf.[102]

For the upper and middle classes food had never been simply a necessity, though they too bought the products of the mass-producing age. The very times at which meals were taken had class implications. In the early eighteenth century 2 p.m. had been the fashionable dinner hour, by 1815 this had moved to 4 or 5 p.m., by 1860 to 7 or 8 p.m., though for most working people 'dinner' remained a meal eaten in the middle of the day. By the 1870s high tea had begun to appear: for the middle classes it was initially a

[101] Oddy, 'Working-Class Diets', 320–1; Burnett, *Plenty and Want*, 42–4; Meacham, *Life Apart*, 87–8; Fraser, *Coming of the Mass Market*, 108–9; Oddy, 'Food, Drink and Nutrition', 272–3.
[102] Burnett, *Plenty and Want*, 122–4; Fraser, *Coming of the Mass Market*, 135–9, 164–73, 103.

Sunday evening servantless event, for workers a more general meal featuring fried fish or meat (in Northern England and Scotland it was often called a 'meat tea').[103] The other developments which most affected the culinary habits of the better-off were a declining taste for gargantuan meals and a change in the ways in which meals were orchestrated. The guzzling of the eighteenth century disappeared and, though meals remained large by twentieth-century standards, modern preoccupations about the effects of food were becoming more common. An interest in vegetarianism emerged in the 1830s and 1840s. The upper classes drank less. In the 1860s dieting (or 'banting' after William Banting's *Letter on Corpulence* of 1863) enjoyed a boom. To be fat became old-fashioned and by the end of the century fruit—once thought 'bad' for children—was being more widely eaten. Mrs Beeton's recipes (1861), though not so regarded today, were praised by contemporaries for their comparative simplicity. Shifts in appetite were matched by a shift in food presentation as the fashionable slowly abandoned the old method of putting a large number of dishes on the table at once, from which diners helped themselves, in favour of 'service à la Russe' by which the dishes were placed in turn on the sideboard and distributed individually by servants. This change—which did not become widespread until the 1870s—not only made the menu more flexible but reduced the number of items provided and the time taken to serve them. It also established the pattern which thereafter remained standard in polite English society: soup, fish, entrée, roast, dessert.[104]

Developments in the world of clothing and fashion followed broadly similar lines, though there were some important differences. Few things more strikingly indicated one's place in society than appearance—as Carlyle had perceived in the 1830s when, in *Sartor Resartus*, he had argued that almost the whole power-structure of an age might be reconstructed from its clothing. In that sense clothes signalled social distinctions as clearly as uniforms displayed military rank. From the satin of fine ladies, through middle-class merinos and poplins, there was a recognizable declension towards the prints and aprons of cottagers and the shawls of northern mill girls. And the same was also true of men: a Victorian artisan on Sunday night might wear a suit, yet no one could ever mistake him for anything but an artisan. Only below a certain point did precision melt into undifferentiated raggedness. The very poor probably wore the *most* items (often

---

[103] A. Palmer, *Movable Feasts: A Reconnaissance of the Origins and Consequences of Fluctuations in Meal-Times*, new edn. (Oxford, 1984), 8, 37, 91; L. Davidoff, 'The Family in Britain', in *CSHB* ii. 82; Oddy, 'Food, Drink and Nutrition', 259–60.

[104] Oddy, 'Food, Drink and Nutrition', 259, 267; Burnett, *Plenty and Want*, 69–70, 199–201; J. Walvin, *Leisure and Society 1830–1950* (London, 1978), 39; Davidoff, *Best Circles*, 48.

several layers of each) and spent relatively and absolutely the least on them. The pattern of expenditure was, therefore, quite different from that on food. The latter took up so much of the poor's incomes that little was left over and ragged odds and ends had to be obtained by begging, stealth, cunning, or luck. By contrast, a fashionable young man about town in the 1850s might buy seven different coats a year, seven pairs of trousers, five waistcoats, boots, and other accessories at a minimum cost of £46. But because the poor spent almost nothing at all, as incomes grew, so, up to a certain point, did the proportion spent on clothes.[105] Social investigators like Rowntree estimated that the 'minimum necessary' clothing expenditure for a family of five was 2s. 3d. a week or almost £6 a year. But when he came to examine the *actual* budgets of working people in York he found that families of that size earning under 26s. a week only spent, on average, less than 1s. 3d. or little more than half the 'minimum' amount. Small wonder that second-hand clothes markets were common and that large numbers of badly paid craftsmen 'translated' old boots to serve as new.[106]

As the price of cotton goods fell—perhaps by two-thirds between 1820 and 1845—so more cotton and less wool was worn. While this helped those few willing and able to launder their outer garments (for cotton is easier to wash) it meant that everyone was a good deal less warm. Even the cheapest new clothes made by slop tailors, though shapeless and shoddy, were relatively dear: trousers cost between 9s. 6d. and £1, a waistcoat 10s., a greatcoat £2. 10s. For more prosperous working people appearance was as important as for their 'betters'. On the one hand, there was the gaudy smartness of London costermongers, with their worsted caps, corduroy waistcoats, 'cable and cord' trousers, and silk neckerchiefs; on the other, there were those for whom a presentable and sober Sunday suit constituted the ultimate symbol of respectability.[107]

How much the middle class spent is impossible to gauge accurately: mildly convincing estimates suggest perhaps a ninth or rather more of income. But there was an enormous spectrum, ranging from families who made their own dresses using commercial paper patterns (those by Butterick, who opened their first English branch in 1873, cost from 3d. to 2s. in the 1880s) to families with £2,000 a year who may have spent as much as £400 on two adults and five children. Just as with cookery and household management, so fashions in clothing could be followed in a range of

[105] J. Evans, *The Victorians* (Cambridge, 1966), 49; A. Gernsheim, *Victorian and Edwardian Fashion* (London, 1981), 36; Burnett, *Cost of Living*, 279.

[106] S. B. Rowntree, *Poverty: A Study of Town Life*, new edn. (London, 1922), 141, 289.

[107] Fraser, *Coming of the Mass Market*, 60; Mayhew, *London Labour*, i. 51; Jones, *Outcast London*, 475.

specialist magazines by those anxious to be up to date. There was a spate of new publications in the 1850s and 1860s, some of them emulating *The World of Fashion* (founded 1824) which in 1850 began to carry free paper patterns in each issue.[108] No less than in other areas of consumption, obsessive enthusiasts of various kinds found Victorian clothing a subject of infinite concern. Thus the 'woollen movement' initiated by the German Dr Gustave Jaeger (who maintained that only animal products should be worn next the skin or indeed at all) spread to England in 1883 when L. R. S. Tomalin founded the Jaeger Company to supply the wants of what was fast becoming—at least in the world of 'sanitary woollen underwear'—an international freemasonry of true believers encompassing, among others, Edwin Chadwick, Oscar Wilde, George Bernard Shaw, and the Count von Moltke.[109]

It is not easy to detect overall trends in what was fashionable. Short-term changes could be dazzlingly swift: 'one year everyone is furred up to the nose...the next year the very tightest and airiest of costumes alone are admissible'.[110] Well before 1837 the slim high-waisted 'naked' female fashions of the Napoleonic period had yielded to a seemingly 'Victorian' style: full-skirted, tight-corseted, close-bonneted, shawl-shouldered. New aniline dyes introduced garish colours, especially the bright purplish-pink and fuchsia shades named magenta and solferino in honour of Napoleon III's bloody victories over the Austrians in 1859. By then the crinoline— basically a conical hooped petticoat distender—had become the established female style and was to remain so until the bustle or 'dress improver' (which stuck out at the back only) began its twenty-year reign in the late 1860s. This, in turn, coincided with a general drift towards simplicity, which had, however, less to do with the well-known movements for comfortable female dress led in mid-century by the American Amelia Bloomer and in the 1880s by Lady Harberton and the Rational Dress Society than with comparatively autonomous developments within the worlds of fashion and clothing technology. Fashion in the 1870s and 1880s was dominated by the tailormade dress and costume, an English development propagated in Paris by a number of influential English couture houses notably Worth & Cie. and Redfern & Sons. Although tailor-mades—with their stiff-collared shirt blouses, tight waists, and long

---

[108] Burnett, *Cost of Living*, 342–3; Adburgham, *Shops and Shopping*, 39, 114–15; Briggs, *Victorian Things*, 281.

[109] Adburgham, *Shops and Shopping*, 184–7; Fraser, *Coming of the Mass Market*, 63–4; C. Ford and B. Harrison, *A Hundred Years Ago*, new impression (London, 1994), 52.

[110] Lady Violet Greville, *Faiths and Fashions: Short Essays Republished* (London, 1880), 249.

skirts—were hardly 'emancipated', they had an efficient look which attracted women who wished to seem simultaneously independent and conventional.[111] At the same time technical developments, which since the 1850s had made it possible to mass-produce ready-made clothes, were beginning to have a significant impact. Here the crucial innovation was the band saw capable of cutting several thicknesses of cloth at once, introduced in 1859 at John Barron's Leeds factory. Barron, who was also a pioneer in the use of sewing machines, produced his goods, not (as before) only against orders but in anticipation of his salesmen selling from stock. By the 1880s manufacturers such as Joseph Hepworth were establishing their own chains of shops and ready-made clothes for women as well as men were widely available at all (save the most superior) ends of the trade.[112] However, the few genuine concessions made to comfort and 'rationality' were, unsurprisingly, confined to (better-off) men, notably in the shape of the easy-fitting country clothes of the 1840s and the 'Tweedside' of the 1850s. Called 'lounging suits', these were distinctly informal and comfortable—'ease', as the *Gazette of Fashion* over-optimistically noted in 1861, being 'now looked upon as the desideratum in all articles of dress'.[113]

As happens in almost every period, so the fashions of the mid-Victorian generation were—in all their various manifestations—attacked as too simple, too complicated, too modern, too traditional. Critics, like the popular but formidably respectable novelist, Eliza Lynn Linton, were particularly cross about powder, rouge, hair dyes, and *poitrines adhérentes*, all of which, they claimed, led to decadence, smoking, and the reading of 'risky novels'.[114] On the male side, beards (save for fringes under the chin) had become so distinctly unfashionable by the 1840s for all except revolutionaries, that one enthusiast (W. H. Henshaw) was driven to publishing a pamphlet in 1847 entitled *Beard-Shaving, and the Common Use of the Razor, an Unnatural, Irrational, Unmanly, Ungodly, and Fatal Fashion among Christians*. Yet by the 1860s the most solid Members of Parliament were disguising themselves behind the most enormous growths. Why? Possibly the impact of the Crimean War (when even officers had found shaving difficult), possibly no clear reason at all.

---

[111] Adburgham, *Shops and Shopping*, 53–5, 91–2, 133–4, 185–6, 220–7; Gernsheim, *Victorian and Edwardian Fashion*, 45–54, 72–4; D. Rubinstein, 'Cycling in the 1890s', *Victorian Studies*, 21 (1977), 62–8.

[112] Briggs, *Victorian Things*, 282–4; Adburgham, *Shops and Shopping*, 123–8, 135; Fraser, *Coming of the Mass Market*, 61.

[113] Gernsheim, *Victorian and Edwardian Fashion*, 37.

[114] Rubinstein, 'Cycling', 62; Gernsheim, *Victorian and Edwardian Fashion*, 56–7.

4. SHOPS, PUBS, HAVING A GOOD TIME

What rendered many of the changes in diet and dress so rapid and general was a concurrent revolution in retailing. Fixed shops of all sizes probably increased faster in number than the population as a whole. Six large northern towns registered substantial growth between 1801 and 1821 and then more steady expansion from 146 shops per 10,000 people in the latter year to 178 in 1881. In Manchester and Salford there was one shop for every 83 people by 1871, compared to one for every 146 in 1841.[115] In Ireland too, where of course the population declined during and after the Great Famine, the eight million people of 1841 were served by 2,744 grocers, the five million of 1881 by 11,776. Even a remote place like Scariff in County Clare (with only 952 inhabitants in 1851) moved, in the fifteen years after 1846, from having but 'one little shop of the meanest description' to having 'several thriving and wealthy shopkeepers' stocking 'crinoline, hoops, and other articles of fashionable female attire for the farmers' wives and daughters'.[116]

At the same time shops were in the process of changing from places where goods were finished and packed into mere dispensaries of ready-made articles. Fewer shopkeepers were skilled craftsmen and there was less bargaining over prices. Displaying goods behind plate-glass windows had become common, as had special sales (often of supposedly 'bankrupt stock'). Already the Great Exhibition of 1851 had laid down the principles upon which mass advertising was to be sustained: luxury, ostentation, and drama. At first newspapers were slow to adapt, large type remaining taboo and regular columns sacrosanct until the 1880s.[117] But gradually the labels upon branded products—and in 1875 it became possible to register brands under the Trade Marks Act—were beginning to influence customers more than the advice of the shopkeeper. Lord Randolph Churchill (perhaps the most recklessly 'modern' politician of his time) thought it worth remarking in one of his speeches: 'We live in an age of advertisement, the age of Holloway's pills, of Colman's mustard, and of Horniman's pure tea.'[118]

---

[115] J. B. Jefferys, *Retail Trading in Britain, 1850–1950* (Cambridge, 1954), 14–15; G. Shaw and M. T. Wild, 'Retail Patterns in the Victorian City', *Transactions of the Institute of British Geographers*, NS 4 (1979), 280; R. Scola, 'Retailing in the Nineteenth-Century Town', in J. H. Johnson and C. G. Pooley (eds.), *The Structure of Nineteenth Century Cities* (London, 1982), 160.

[116] Hoppen, *Elections*, 52, 438–9.

[117] Jefferys, *Retail Trading*, 1–6; W. B. Whitaker, *Victorian and Edwardian Shopkeepers* (Newton Abbot, 1973), 31–2; Fraser, *Coming of the Mass Market*, 134–8; Berridge and Edwards, *Opium and the People*, 126–9; T. Richards, *The Commodity Culture of Victorian England* (Stanford, Calif., 1990), 21.

[118] R. Shannon, *The Crisis of Imperialism 1865–1915* (London, 1974), 206.

The pioneers of the new retailing were the department stores and multiple chains. The former came first and, though their origins lie earlier, were essentially a mid- and late Victorian phenomenon. In their initial form they were really indoor bazaars or market halls. Not until 1877 was the first custom-built store opened—the Brixton Bon Marché—at a reputed cost of £70,000. Most began as drapers (Harrod's being a notable exception). Well-established shops like Bainbridges of Newcastle and Kendal Milne of Manchester were joined by, among many others, Burberry's of Basingstoke (1856), Derry & Toms of Kensington High Street (1862), John Lewis of Oxford Street (1864), Bentall's of Kingston upon Thames (1867), and Liberty & Co. of Regent Street (1875). By the end of the century almost every large town boasted its own department store, its quality as much a matter of civic pride as that of the local concert hall, newspaper, or football team. Most famous of all was the enormous store in Westbourne Grove opened by William Whiteley (the 'universal provider') in 1863. Such places offered rest and refreshment rooms (a boon for the female shopper) and a delivery service. Wealthy customers were escorted throughout their visits by well-dressed 'shop walkers', whose hovering presence made it difficult to compare prices for fear of embarrassment. The aim was to offer a 'complete service'—by 1870 Whiteley's had more than 2,000 employees—in surroundings at once comfortable, genteel, and persuasive.[119]

Very different were the new multiple chains active from the 1880s onwards, initially in the food and footwear trades. Thomas Lipton opened his first grocery shop in Glasgow in 1871, and his steady expansion thereafter was soon emulated by firms like the Home and Colonial Stores and the Maypole Dairies. Although such shops catered for a less socially elevated clientele than the department stores their refusal to grant credit excluded the less prosperous members of the working class. With their open plans and identical appearances they foreshadowed the shrinking aesthetic variety which has characterized British retailing ever since. Between the multiples and the corner shops stood the retail co-operative movement. In 1863, when the Co-operative Wholesale Society was founded, membership stood at about 100,000; by 1885 it had risen to more than half a million. Soon the middle classes borrowed the idea. In 1866 the Post Office Supply Association became the Civil Service Supply Association. Six years later the Army and Navy Store opened in Victoria Street disguised as a gentleman's club and in 1874 cost-conscious imbibers

[119] Shaw and Wild, 'Retail Patterns', 284–6; Adburgham, *Shops and Shopping*, 153–7, 169, 231–7, 283–6; Fraser, *Coming of the Mass Market*, 131.

founded the International Exhibition Co-operative Wine Society which still flourishes today.[120]

Whilst all these developments pointed to the future, their impact in Victorian times can be exaggerated. Even in 1900, when the earliest moderately reliable estimates become available, co-ops, multiples, and department stores together conducted at most an eighth and possibly only a tenth of Britain's total retail trade.[121] In other words, about 90 per cent of shopping activity by value (let alone by transaction) took place in either corner shops or firms with only a handful of small outlets. The largest of these carried amazingly variegated stocks encompassing everything from tea and coffee, through sandpaper and black lead, to nails, tools, brushes, and ginger-beer powder. They were open long hours; they offered credit; their profits were usually modest; many regularly went bankrupt. Yet they played a vital role in any community, not only as suppliers of goods but as centres for gossip and exchange. No one, indeed, stood more firmly at the crossroads of everyday relationships than the Victorian shopkeeper and his economic cousin the publican.[122]

Drinking—where and how it was done, what was actually drunk—constituted a major nineteenth-century preoccupation. The average annual consumption of beer per person in the United Kingdom rose from 19.4 gallons in 1845–9 to 33.2 gallons in 1875–9. Spirit drinking remained steadier, at about one proof gallon a head between 1850 and 1900, with a modest peak in the 1870s (though illicit production was common in remoter rural areas). The bulk of drinking undoubtedly took place in public houses of various kinds. In 1830 an attempt had been made to reduce alcohol consumption by legislation encouraging people to drink beer (regarded as virtually a temperance beverage) rather than spirits. But when spirits consumption showed no sustained fall—not even after Gladstone's efforts to create a nation of wine drinkers consuming the cheaper 'Gladstone claret' made possible by the Anglo-French Commercial Treaty of 1860—the experiment was dropped in 1869 and beerhouses were brought under normal licensing controls.[123]

---

[120] Fraser, *Coming of the Mass Market*, 111–18, 122–8; Jefferys, *Retail Trading*, 16; Adburgham, *Shops and Shopping*, 215–18.

[121] Jefferys, *Retail Trading*, 29.

[122] Fraser, *Coming of the Mass Market*, 101, 86, 102; Whitaker, *Victorian and Edwardian Shopworkers*, 35; Roberts, *Classic Slum*, 81; C. P. Hosgood, 'The "Pigmies of Commerce" and the Working-Class Community: Small Shopkeepers in England, 1870–1914', *Journal of Social History*, 22 (1989), 441, 450–9; Meacham, *Life Apart*, 54; M. Winstanley, *The Shopkeeper's World 1830–1914* (Manchester, 1983).

[123] G. B. Wilson, *Alcohol and the Nation: A Contribution to the Study of the Liquor Problem in the United Kingdom from 1880 to 1935* (London, 1940), 335; M. Girouard, *Victorian Pubs*

Although pubs were becoming larger, there was still in 1881 one licensee for every 243 people (of all ages) in England and Wales—which may have been less than the one for every 174 of 1841, but was substantial all the same.[124] Locally pubs could be very thick on the ground indeed. Scotland was especially well provided: in the 1840s Edinburgh had one pub for every thirty families, Dundee one for every twenty-four. On a busy London road it was considered a good concession to have a monopoly of 100 yards either way. In 1882 the takers of an unofficial 'recreation census' of Bristol declared a draw between Christianity and alcohol, with 104,557 customers entering pubs on a particular Saturday night and 116,148 going to church or chapel the next day.[125]

The temperance movement, a substantial but fissiparous force, made little real headway. From 1853 the well-funded United Kingdom Alliance demanded that each locality be allowed to ban the sale of alcohol. But it faced opposition simultaneously from those who disliked all state inter-ference and those who distrusted the Alliance's obviously class-biased character. Even attempts to control opening hours enjoyed only modest success. In 1854 Sunday drinking time was reduced in pubs to match the six hours of the beerhouses. Riots followed and the hours were increased to eight and a half. Weekday closing before midnight arrived during the 1870s in the provinces, though London pubs were still able to open from 5 a.m. to 12.30 a.m. (midnight on Saturday) without a break. In Scotland an act of 1853 enforced Sunday closing and inaugurated the practice whereby 'bona fide' travellers (who were entitled to refreshment if they journeyed three miles) moved from hotel to hotel in order to have a whisky on the Sabbath: 'Glasgow drinkers developed a standard Sunday route—to Yoker, by ferry to Renfrew and back into town by way of Govan—a round trip that could take in as much drinking as anyone could require'.[126] In 1871 a severely restrictive bill was dropped, in the face of outraged opposition, and was succeeded by Bruce's Licensing Act of 1873, an innocuous measure which incomprehensibly drove the trade into equally apocalyptic rage.

By mid-century pubs had become entirely working-class (see Plate 1). In a well-known remark the statistician, G. R. Porter, told the Select Com-mittee on Wine Duties in 1852 that 'no person, above the rank of a

(London, 1975), 34, 53; B. Harrison, *Drink and the Victorians: The Temperance Question in England 1815–1872* (London, 1971), 81–6.

[124] Wilson, *Alcohol*, 236.

[125] W. H. Fraser, 'Developments in Leisure', in Fraser and Morris (eds.), *People and Society*, ii. 241–2; Girouard, *Victorian Pubs*, 38–9; Harrison, *Peaceable Kingdom*, 123.

[126] Fraser, 'Developments in Leisure', 243; Harrison, *Drink*, 197–202, 328–9.

labouring man or artisan, would venture to go into a public-house'.[127] In country towns, farmers still met in pubs on market day, but the old classless village inn (always more prominent in myth than reality) had largely disappeared. Well-to-do people drank at home, in hotels, or clubs. This had two results: it left the working class in possession and increased the social gulf between those responsible for licensing regulations and those affected by them.

Pubs thus became the great social centres of working-class life, their attractions based upon, but also reaching far beyond, the consumption of alcohol. Some turned themselves into informal working-men's clubs where friendly societies, trade unions, and craft societies met in upstairs rooms. Until 1886 (when children under 13 were banned) all ages were welcome, though after 1839 spirits could not be sold to those under 16. Election campaigns were planned in pubs and susceptible voters 'treated' to drinks. Freemasons and dog fanciers met in pubs. Publicans were more often the patrons of local sporting events than parsons or ministers. Pubs constituted the quickest route to oblivion, but they also provided a 'good time'— 'beano', 'spree', and 'blow-out' were all popular mid-Victorian terms. Small wonder that, according to an estimate of 1853, 70 per cent of working men in Derby passed their evenings in pubs.[128] Small wonder that many families must have spent a third and some half or more of all their income on drink, with devastating effects upon health and living standards. Yet small wonder, too, that, despite the growing availability of non-alcoholic beverages, the efforts of reformers to set up temperance tea and coffee houses proved consistently unsuccessful.[129] Despite a certain amount of gaudy 'improvement'—by the 1870s Ruskin was complaining that there was 'scarcely a public-house near the Crystal Palace but sells its gin and bitters under pseudo-Venetian capitals copied from the Church of the Madonna of Health or of Miracles'[130]—the majority of pubs remained drab and modest places. Not unrepresentative was the slum pub observed in late nineteenth-century York: a shabby parlour accommodating ten drinkers, no music, bleak décor—but, despite the presence of thirteen other pubs within five minutes' walk, still able to attract 550 customers

---

[127] *Report from the Select Committee on Wine Duties*, HC 1852 (495), xvii. 543.

[128] Girouard, *Victorian Pubs*, 12; P. Bailey, *Leisure and Class in Victorian England* (London, 1978), 27–8, 89; A. Metcalfe, 'Organized Sport in the Mining Communities of South Northumberland, 1800–1889', *Victorian Studies*, 25 (1982), 484–5; A. Delves, 'Popular Recreation and Social Conflict in Derby, 1800–1850', in E. and S. Yeo (eds.), *Popular Culture and Class Conflict 1590–1914* (Brighton, 1981), 103.

[129] Burnett, *Plenty and Want*, 175–6; Rowntree, *Poverty*, 177; Oddy, 'Food, Drink and Nutrition', 266; Girouard, *Victorian Pubs*, 171–7.

[130] E. T. Cook, *The Life of John Ruskin*, 2 vols. (London, 1912), i. 308.

on a typical day, of whom (pubs were never all-male affairs) only 258 were men.[131]

Just as the pattern of pub life was more influenced by commercial than moral pressures, so was this true of leisure generally. The popular pastimes of the early nineteenth century—cock fighting, bear baiting, prize boxing—attracted increasingly critical attention from reformers. Legislation against cruelty to animals preceded legislation against cruelty to female and child workers. Richard ('Humanity Dick') Martin's 1822 act dealing with live-stock and horses was extended in 1835, 1849, and 1854 to cover most domestic animals. The Society for the Prevention of Cruelty to Animals was founded in 1824. Princess Victoria was an early supporter and, as Queen, gave it the title 'royal' in 1840. Like the majority of temperance enthusiasts, animal reformers reserved their sermons for the working-class. When in 1869 the historian, E. A. Freeman, unleashed a powerful attack on fox hunting ('neither in the infliction of death nor at any other time should any pain be inflicted which real need does not call for') the resulting controversy generated more heat than light and no action at all.[132]

Slowly and unevenly many popular recreations were either outlawed or sanitized or taken over by those who thought 'rational' amusements more suited to a reformed age. As dog fighting was made illegal, so dog breeding and showing—the earliest shows often took place in pubs—were appro-priated by the middle classes who invented the artificial notion of 'breeds' as a subspecies with definable and arbitrarily chosen characteristics (the modern bulldog, the epitome of Britishness, is, for example, largely a nineteenth-century invention).[133] In an age of 'progress' it was becoming incomprehensible that people should amuse themselves with bear baiting or with fairground competitions to see who could strip the wicks out of candles fastest with their teeth. The leading crusaders against such things and against all sorts of local 'superstitions' were Evangelical clergymen, utilitarians, earnest Radicals, the new police, and schoolteachers. From the 1840s onwards raucous harvest-home traditions were being replaced by harvest thanksgiving services. As Sir William Wilde (the eminent Irish surgeon and father of Oscar) put it in 1852: 'The fairies, the whole pantheon of Irish demigods are retiring, one by one, from the habitations of man to the distant islands where the wild waves of the Atlantic ... render their fastnesses inaccessible to the schoolmaster and the railroad engin-

[131] Rowntree, *Poverty*, 371–7.

[132] H. Ritvo, *The Animal Estate: The English and other Creatures in the Victorian Age* (London, 1990), 125–9, 137; D. C. Itzkowitz, *Peculiar Privilege: A Social History of English Foxhunting 1753–1885* (Hassocks, 1977), 143–4.

[133] Ritvo, *Animal Estate*, 93–9, 105, 110–13, 249–51.

eer.'[134] Everywhere calendar festivals and old-fashioned fairs decayed or changed their character: the Stamford bull running on 13 November, Derby 'football' on Shrove Tuesday, the Padstow hobby horse on May Day. Already in 1849 Cornish children being taken to the seaside by a Wesleyan minister were ordered to sing

> We rejoice, and we have reason,
> Though we don't attend the fair;
> Better spend the happy season
> Breathing in the fresh sea air.[135]

Of course the old Adam lingered on, but amidst increasing condemnation and distrust. Election riots and their associated bribery, treating, and carnival were still vigorous well after the middle of the century, though more violently so in Ireland than in England or Scotland.[136] Public executions remained wildly popular occasions until abolished in 1868. The hanging of John Wilson in 1849 attracted huge crowds (some said 100,000) brought by special trains. The 'pirates' of the ship *Flowery Land* were executed in February 1864 to applause, hissing, yells, groans, all watched by those rich enough to hire overlooking rooms at twenty guineas a time. Nine months later Franz Muller's last moments were graced by thousands 'clamouring, shouting and struggling', as *The Times* put it, 'to get as near to the gibbet as the steaming mass of human beings before them would allow'.[137]

Not only did some working people long resist middle-class cultural proselytism, many also reformulated their own leisure priorities in order to preserve these from external attack, an adjustment made easier by the development of commercialized entertainment, not all of it respectable. Fairground amusements, circuses, professional sports, music halls, and seaside holidays all grew in popularity because they did not seem to undermine the existing trinity of sex, alcohol, and gambling. From mid-century onwards a free Saturday afternoon spread from textile factories to other industries. In the 1870s a substantial reduction in working hours—to about nine per day—took place generally and statutory bank holidays were also introduced. The informal practice of taking time off on the first

---

[134] W. R. Wilde, *Irish Popular Superstitions* (Dublin, 1852), 16.

[135] Rule, *Labouring Classes*, 222.

[136] D. C. Richter, *Riotous Victorians* (London, 1981), 63–71; K. T. Hoppen, 'Grammars of Electoral Violence in Nineteenth-Century England and Ireland', *English Historical Review*, 109 (1994), 597–620.

[137] Burn, *Age of Equipoise*, 83; also V. A. C. Gatrell, *The Hanging Tree: Execution and the English People 1770–1868* (Oxford, 1994), 90–105, 589–611.

working day of the week (Saint Monday) was fading away, and mill owners
began to think that a whole week's closure in the summer was preferable to
spasmodic absences. Leisure became not only more accessible but obtainable at precise and predictable intervals, even though *paid* holidays
remained rare among manual workers until well after the end of our
period.[138]

Sports of all kinds constituted epitomes of what was happening to leisure
generally, their varied Victorian histories accurately mirroring the impacts
of commercialization and changes in class structure. Field sports were
socially exclusive and commercial in a special sense; cricket had early
commercial intimations but retained a patina of class collaboration; horse
racing attracted aristocrats and working people not least because of its
heavily commercial gambling side; football soon became commercial and
eventually almost exclusively working-class.

Fox hunting enjoyed a golden age between 1850 and 1875, becoming less
wild and dare-devil, to the regret of earlier enthusiasts like Squire George
Osbaldeston who died in 1866. The middle classes and women too parti-
cipated in ever larger numbers, and in key counties like Leicestershire
hunting gates made it possible to follow hounds without having to do
much jumping at all. It was above all the railways that allowed this to
happen. By the 1850s one could leave Euston at 6.30 a.m., hunt with the
Pytchley in the Midlands, and return to London the same night. Indeed, by
1854 no less than twenty-four packs of foxhounds could be hunted like this
from London, not to mention staghounds and harriers. Disraeli's patron,
Lord George Bentinck, could hunt in Hampshire and get to the House of
Commons for an evening debate, his riding clothes concealed under 'a
light-coloured zephyr paletot'. The number of people hunting grew substantially. Even in so relatively unfashionable a country as the Holderness
in East Yorkshire there was a tenfold increase in the three decades after
1843, while nationally the number of packs grew from 99 in 1850 to 137 in
1877.[139] By 1875 all but three of Ireland's thirty-two counties could boast at
least one of the sixty-six mounted packs operating in an island where hard
riding retained an iron grip. Charles Stewart Parnell kept up hunting—and
cricketing—connections with otherwise hostile Conservative proprietors
throughout the Irish Land War of 1879–82. Not to hunt was 'the certain
sign of a fool or an ass', for, as Lord Dunsany remarked, 'any man who is

---

[138] H. Cunningham, *Leisure in the Industrial Revolution c.1780–c.1880* (London, 1980),
146–8; id., 'Leisure and Culture', in *CSHB* ii. 284–6; P. Bailey, *Leisure and Class*, 80.

[139] Itzkowitz, *Peculiar Privilege*, 51–9; Cunningham, *Leisure*, 133; J. Kent, *Racing Life of
Lord George Cavendish Bentinck*, ed. F. Lawley (Edinburgh, 1892), 7. Friedrich Engels rode
regularly with the Cheshire Hunt in the 1850s.

utterly unconnected with the fox lives a little apart'.[140] Packs operated all over the Empire: in Canada, India, even, it is said, in Gibraltar. In Shanghai the famous Paper Hunt founded in the 1860s pursued, in the absence of suitable animals, a human 'fox' dressed in a red cowl and laying a paper trail.[141]

The other imperial sporting obsession, big game hunting, sprang from a deep Victorian mania for shooting birds and stalking deer. The latter, an invention of the 1840s, was very costly indeed. It attracted not only the gentry but industrialists, some of whom bought large Highland estates and poured money into remote parts of Scotland without hope of financial return. Small game shooting was also (if not quite as) expensive and exclusive. Here too urban businessmen were prominent, though few could have matched the extraordinary bags of aristocratic enthusiasts like the 2nd Marquess of Ripon, who, in the period 1867–1900, supposedly killed 142,343 pheasants, 97,759 partridges, 56,460 grouse, 6,738 assorted other birds, 29,858 rabbits, 27,686 hares, 9,175 'various', 568 deer, plus two rhinos, eleven tigers, twelve buffaloes, nineteen samburs, and ninety-seven pigs—a scarcely credible average of 10,904 animals a year.[142]

Altogether less exclusive was that other equestrian domain—the race-course, home of sport, fashion, and gambling. Even if contemporary claims about all racing men being equal were nonsense, there can be little doubt that the *bonhomie* of the turf helped to protect a sport peculiarly susceptible to attack from rational recreationists. While aristocrats and rougher working men were over-represented, there was no shortage of perfectly conventional middle-class enthusiasts, like the Scottish businessman and Liberal MP John Holms who regularly attended race meetings and lost no opportunity for modest gambling on horses, billiards, and cards.[143] However, for real 'gents' like the 14th Earl of Derby (Prime Minister 1852, 1858–9, 1866–8) the adrenalin tended to flow with altogether greater urgency. 'A few weeks ago he was on the point of being Prime Minister', recorded Greville in April 1851, and 'stood up in the H. of Lords, and delivered an oration full of gravity and dignity', but now, at Newmarket, he was to be

[140] Hoppen, *Elections*, 120–1; L. P. Curtis, jun., 'Stopping the Hunt, 1881–1882: An Aspect of the Irish Land War', in C. H. E. Philpin (ed.), *Nationalism and Popular Protest in Ireland* (Cambridge, 1987), 349–402.

[141] Itzkowitz, *Peculiar Privilege*, 75–9; R. Carr, *English Fox Hunting: A History* (London, 1976), 152–6.

[142] P. Gaskell, *Morvern Transformed: A Highland Parish in the Nineteenth Century* (Cambridge, 1968), 81–118; Duke of Portland, *Men, Women and Things* (London, 1937), 228–9.

[143] Bailey, *Leisure and Class*, 25; W. Vamplew, *The Turf: A Social and Economic History of Horse Racing* (London, 1976), 130–42; H. L. Malchow, *Gentlemen Capitalists: The Social and Political World of the Victorian Businessman* (London, 1991), 267, 278–9.

seen 'in the midst of a crowd of blacklegs, betters, and loose characters of every description, in uproarious spirits, chaffing, rowing, and shouting with laughter'.[144]

Like hunting, but in a much wider sense, racing became more popular during the second half of the century. The number of horses running doubled between 1837 and 1869. A nationwide circuit of major meetings developed. The railways—again—had a profound influence in transporting, first horses and then spectators. By the 1880s crowds of 15,000 were 'not uncommon' and leading fixtures could attract 80,000 to a Bank Holiday event. Courses with more than one meeting a year doubled between 1856 and 1870. The attack on cheating was led by the unlikely figure of Lord George Bentinck (a wild and by no means fastidious gambler) who, in this respect at least, showed himself a Victorian of the sternest water. His rules of 1844 were gradually adopted throughout England and implemented by less colourful though more efficient men in the decades that followed. Increasing (if still only relative) probity encouraged hard-headed commercial interests to invest. After the foundation of Sandown Park in 1875 (a mere thirteen miles from the West End) more and more courses began to charge an entrance fee from every spectator. Hitherto courses had been open to all: some attracting large crowds, others (like Newmarket) adopting a more exclusive style. But by the end of the century only the very largest open meetings still survived, notably at Ascot, Epsom, Goodwood, Doncaster, and York.[145]

Already in the 1840s illegal sweepstakes had given way to bookmakers' betting lists aimed specifically at the urban working class: odds were displayed and bets taken from non-racegoers in amounts as low as 6d. or thereabouts. By the early 1850s 150 betting shops of this type operated in London alone.[146] This was a paradoxical development. On the one hand, 'rational leisure' reformers thought gambling (especially working-class gambling) immoral and socially dangerous. On the other, the betting industry was becoming a thoroughly modern, technologically based, commercial enterprise, that is, a thoroughly 'Victorian' one. The completion of the electric telegraph in the 1850s made results instantly and nationally available, and the growth of a specialized press—the *Sporting Life* was

---

[144] *The Greville Memoirs 1814–1860*, ed. L. Strachey and R. Fulford, 8 vols. (London, 1938), vi. 290–1.

[145] Vamplew, *The Turf*, 33, 37, 136; N. Gash, 'Lord George Bentinck and his Sporting World', in Gash, *Pillars of Government and Other Essays* (London, 1986), 162–75; W. Vamplew, *Pay Up and Play the Game: Professional Sport in Britain 1875–1914* (Cambridge, 1988), 57–8; Cunningham, *Leisure*, 177.

[146] Vamplew, *The Turf*, 41, 203; Itzkowitz, *Peculiar Privilege*, 8–11.

founded in 1859, the *Sporting Times* (the famous 'Pink 'Un') in 1865—facilitated and reflected the substantial expansion of racing and gambling alike. Although the draconian Betting Act of 1853, which outlawed betting *shops* in England and Wales (though Scotland remained untouched until 1874), indicated a degree of middle-class disapproval, it affected the nature rather than the extent of gambling. The well-to-do could still bet either on the course or through clubs or postal bookmakers on a credit basis. Working people resorted to street agents acting as runners for illegal bookies who kept themselves out of sight. By the 1880s at the latest, working-class gambling—still almost entirely confined to racing—had become very widespread indeed. Increasing, though often unreliable, wages made gambling an attractive option for those unable to save but with enough money for small risks at 'reasonable' odds. But while bookies' runners constituted key figures in the culture of working-class neighbourhoods, gambling itself was never confined to any one social group.[147]

Racing's cross-class appeal was less exuberantly reproduced on the Victorian cricket field, where, in this respect, the atmosphere was dominated more by hypocrisy than paradox. Ever since the eighteenth century wealthy amateurs had employed professionals to spice up their teams, usually as bowlers. In 1806 the first match took place between the 'gentlemen' and 'players' (a fixture that was to last until 1962). In the 1840s and 1850s the game's popularity owed much to the activities of entrepreneurs like William Clarke who toured the country with a professional All-England Eleven whose members received £4 a match. But while this established the idea of charging gate money and while even the first overseas tours—of the United States in 1859 and Australia in 1861—were professional events, the 1860s and 1870s witnessed a steady appropriation of the game by the amateur-worshipping middle class, so much so that by the end of our period the professionals had reverted to an entirely subordinate role. The appearance of *Wisden* in 1864, of (an at first very loose) county championship in 1873, of a new type of tour inaugurated by visiting Australians in 1878, and of test matches in 1880, all helped to create the kind of cricket characteristic of the years to come. By the 1880s crowds of 10,000 were not uncommon at county matches, by the end of the century 14,000 was the average gate. The whole business was, however, sustained by low wages and shamateurism: professionals not only tended to receive

---

[147] Vamplew, *The Turf*, 205–9; D. C. Itzkowitz, 'Victorian Bookmakers and their Customers', *Victorian Studies*, 32 (1988), 16; C. Chinn, *Better Betting with a Decent Feller: Bookmaking, Betting and the British Working Class, 1750–1990* (Hemel Hempstead, 1991), 84–117; M. Clapson, *A Bit of a Flutter: Popular Gambling and English Society, c.1823–1961* (Manchester, 1992), 18–32; McKibbin, *Ideologies of Class*, 113–16.

far less than many 'amateurs', but were often treated little better than serfs.[148] The two groups used different facilities, dressed in different pavilions, entered by different gates, travelled in different train compartments. The Bolton Club professional in the 1860s actually bowled in clogs as if to acknowledge his lowly status. Twenty years later his successors acknowledged it too by means of dirty white flannels and invariably visible woollen drawers. Masters of a kind of subversive truculence they may have been, but many died in demeaning poverty all the same. By contrast, certain leading 'amateurs' were paid enormous sums, foremost among them W. G. Grace, who, throughout his cricketing career (1870–1910), probably earned not less than £120,000 in all.[149]

Grace, indeed, earned far more than the most successful professionals in the most popular of all late-Victorian commercial sports, football. Although there were initial connections with cricket—the first cup finals were played at the Oval—a sudden collapse of middle-class domination in the mid-1880s gave soccer an altogether different character. Although the earliest football clubs had often had highly 'respectable' roots (some had been founded by local churches or schools, others by skilled artisans in particular factories or mills) during the 1870s all this began to change.[150] Clubs in major areas of football strength outside London—the Midlands, Lancashire, Yorkshire, and Scotland—began to think that winning mattered more than 'playing the game'. A concentration on long rushes, dribbling, and constant possession was giving way to a more modern passing game, just as the two umpires appointed by each side were giving way to a single neutral referee. The spread of a Saturday half-holiday gave crowds a distinctly working-class character. In the period 1875–9 only six matches attracted more than 10,000 people; by 1880–4 forty-one did so. Early institutional growth had been under firm amateur control, notably the foundation of the Football Association in 1863, the first FA cup competition in 1871, and the establishment of separate associations in Scotland

[148] Cunningham, *Leisure*, 113–14; id., 'Leisure and Culture', 315; T. Mason, *Association Football and English Society 1863–1915* (Brighton, 1980), 70; Walvin, *Leisure and Society*, 91; Vamplew, *Pay Up*, 59; K. A. P. Sandiford, 'Amateurs and Professionals in Victorian County Cricket', *Albion*, 15 (1983), 39–45.

[149] Bailey, *Leisure and Class*, 144–5; Sandiford, 'Amateurs and Professionals', 45–8, 37–8; W. F. Mandle, 'Games People Played', *Historical Studies*, 15 (1973), 528–9; Vamplew, *Pay Up*, 7.

[150] Cunningham, *Leisure*, 115, 127–8; Walvin, *Leisure and Society*, 86–92; Mason, *Association Football*, 24–7. Everton, Aston Villa, and Bolton Wanderers were church-based, Queen's Park Rangers school-based, Stoke City and Manchester United were railway teams, West Ham an iron works team, while Preston North End and Sheffield Wednesday developed out of local cricket clubs.

(1873), Wales (1876), and Ireland (1880). Gradually, however, money came to play a larger part as certain players began to receive small payments for turning out. And at more or less the same time the increasing size of the crowds coming to watch the United Kingdom championship games was doing much to establish new forms of popular nationalism (though the founding in 1884 of the Gaelic Athletic Association gave sport in Ireland a more overtly political character than elsewhere).[151]

In 1883 Blackburn Olympic (fielding three weavers, a spinner, a dental assistant, and various other factory hands) defeated the Old Etonians in the final of the FA cup. After bitter resistance the FA accepted restricted professionalism in 1885 and full professionalism four years after that. Though initial payments were modest, smaller even than in cricket, low wages elsewhere meant that there was never a shortage of working men anxious to become players. Some of them must have appalled the game's public school administrators, not least Nick Ross of Preston North End famed for his discoloured teeth—'almost green near the gums'—through which he unnervingly hissed as he played. The initial middle-class arguments in favour of football, that it improved fitness, built character, reduced drinking, increased social harmony, gave way to working-class imperatives emphasizing a sense of local belonging and of competition (gambling came later). While, therefore, the game may, indeed, have eased class tensions, it also strengthened the idea among working men that they were part of a group with experiences and interests not shared by the bulk of another group, the middle classes. Far more than cricket or any other sport, football not only reflected but helped to reinforce a particularly inward-looking view of how working people lived and, more importantly, how they should live.[152]

If trends were similar overall, individual sports reflected them in individual ways. Rugby, for example, actually fractured under the social strains of the 1890s and split into an amateur Union game and a professional and largely North of England Rugby League. Yet even the former was not without a genuinely popular following, though why this should have

---

[151] Mason, *Association Football*, 210–11, 139, 146, 151–2, 153, 155; Vamplew, *Pay Up*, 62–3; Cunningham, 'Leisure and Culture', ii. 314; K. Robbins, *Nineteenth-Century Britain: Integration and Diversity* (Oxford, 1988), 162–82; W. F. Mandle, 'The I.R.B. and the Beginnings of the Gaelic Athletic Association', *Irish Historical Studies*, 20 (1977), 418–38.

[152] W. J. Baker, 'The Making of a Working-Class Football Culture in Victorian England', *Journal of Social History*, 13 (1979), 243, 246; Mason, *Association Football*, 33, 76, 89–94, 229–42; Vamplew, *Pay Up*, 190–2; Mandle, 'Games People Played', 530. The football clubs themselves were, however, generally owned by local businessmen.

developed so notably in parts of Wales remains mysterious.[153] As the middle classes lost ideological, though by no means always economic, control of mass spectator sports, so they retreated in good order towards what were long to remain the unconquered redoubts of lawn tennis and golf. The rules of the former were patented in 1874 by Major Walter Wingfield. Three years later the All England Croquet Club at Wimbledon (founded 1868) added 'and Lawn Tennis' to its title. Manual workers found no welcome in tennis clubs dedicated to providing excellent opportunities for eligible young men to meet eligible young ladies. Golf too—though its really large-scale English popularity was an Edwardian phenomenon—constituted a social bastion rather than a bridge. Indeed, even in supposedly egalitarian Scotland the pleasures of golf were beyond the purses of the bulk of working people. Its great appeal in England (in 1880 there were twelve clubs, in 1887 fifty, in 1914 no less than 1,200) lay in the way club organization permitted sharp local social boundaries to be drawn and in the individualistic, inner-directed, almost Smilesian, character of the game itself.[154]

Not that individualism as such was unappealing to working men for whom angling and pigeon fancying marked a half-way house between sport and hobby as well as a means of swapping masculine lore and getting away from 'the wife'. Many popular sports in the second half of the century— bowling, quoits, dog racing, handicapped foot races—had extensive followings in particular regions (indeed their attraction lay precisely in their localness). There was obviously also a vast appetite for 'do-it-yourself', especially among the lower middle and upper working classes. Magazines such as *Amateur Work, Illustrated* sold extensively in the 1880s to a readership prepared to attempt the making of cabinets, fire-backs, toys, tea tables, even 'an alarum clock, which being set to any required time, will strike a match, ignite a lamp, boil water, make tea, coffee etc., pour out the same, and afterwards awake the sleeper with a bell'.[155] Allotments for artisans and gardens for the well-to-do were seen as providing perhaps the most rational of all leisure activities: the former yielding vegetables, the latter aesthetic

[153] D. W. Howell and C. Baker, 'Wales', in *CSHB* i. 338; Vamplew, *Pay Up*, 64–5; D. Russell, 'The Pursuit of Leisure', in D. G. Wright and J. A. Jowitt (eds.), *Victorian Bradford* (Bradford, 1982), 214.

[154] Royle, *Modern Britain*, 257; Bailey, *Leisure and Class*, 75; J. Lowerson, 'Scottish Croquet: The English Golf Boom 1880–1914', *History Today*, 33/5 (1983), 26–30; id., *Sport and the English Middle Classes 1870–1914* (Manchester, 1993), 125–53; *Scottish Voices*, ed. T. C. Smout and S. Wood (London, 1990), 185.

[155] E. J. Wiseman, *Victorian Do-It-Yourself* (Newton Abbot, 1976), 4–5, 23, 46, 135; McKibbin, *Ideologies of Class*, 142–4.

Plate i. Leisure: Outside a London pub in the 1870s

PLATE 2. Indubitably prosperous Victorians: The Gladstone family photographed at Hawarden about 1868 with Mrs Gladstone sitting at the table and Mr Gladstone standing behind her

PLATE 3. The Crimean War: Photograph of the camp of the 4th Dragoon Guards outside Sebastopol, with French and British soldiers, taken by Roger Fenton, the first photo-journalist

PLATE 4. Manchester policemen off duty in the 1850s

PLATE 5. Rural poverty in Ireland: An eviction in County Donegal in the 1880s

PLATE 6. Work: Inside an engineering works in 1867

PLATE 7. Urban poverty in Scotland: Saltmarket, Glasgow, in the 1860s.

PLATE 8. Victorians dressed as Romans: *The Picture Gallery* by Lawrence Alma-Tadema
(1874). The man at the centre is Ernest Gambart, the art dealer who commissioned the
picture for £10,000

delight. Nottingham (with a census population of 87,000) had no less than 10,000 allotments in 1871 and all towns boasted numerous horticultural competitions and clubs. Notable too was the capacity of contemporaries to exact moral tribute from leisure activity of every kind. Whether it was Beeton's *Dictionary of Every-Day Gardening* (1862) insisting

> Yes! in the poor man's garden grow
> Far more than herbs and flowers,
> Kind thoughts, contentment, peace of mind,
> And joy for many hours![156]

or the still more unlikely claims of the *Glasgow Herald* in 1869 that croquet inculcated 'patience, courage and calmness under momentary defeat, [and] due subordination of means to ends',[157] there can be no doubting that earnest Victorians believed fun without virtue to be no fun at all.

Music halls, which emerged in a recognizable form during the 1850s at a time when stage entertainment was splintering into a number of distinct types, presented obvious difficulties in this respect. Theatres were becoming more respectable, partly in response to a law of 1843 which restricted them to formal plays, partly in response to the readiness of managements to meet the changing demands of middle-class Victorianism. Singing saloons and shabby 'penny gaffs' catered for the bottom end of the market. Often located in abandoned shops or behind pubs they provided singing, dancing, mimes, 'horrible murder' tableaux, and *poses plastiques*. Beer and tobacco featured prominently, and amidst the fumes could—as a journalist noted in 1861—typically be discerned 'a piano, a seedy gentleman with a violin, [and] a remarkably easy and assured but debauched looking young man who sings comic songs'.[158]

Music halls themselves differed greatly. The opening in 1851 of Charles Morton's Canterbury Hall in Lambeth, with its luxurious fittings, singers of both sexes, excerpts from opera as well as comic songs, food and drink (though these later disappeared) all under the direction of a chairman, is generally taken as the beginning of a new age. By 1870 there were thirty-one 'large' halls in London and perhaps 384 altogether in the rest of Britain. Until the last decade of the century the audiences (with a few Central London exceptions) were predominantly either working- or lower middle class. Despite contemporary and later claims to the contrary, few music

---

[156] S. Constantine, 'Amateur Gardening and Popular Recreation in the 19th and 20th Centuries', *Journal of Social History*, 14 (1981), 391.

[157] Fraser, 'Developments in Leisure', 245.

[158] Cunningham, *Leisure*, 135; M. B. Smith, 'Victorian Entertainment in Lancashire Towns', in S. P. Bell (ed.), *Victorian Lancashire* (Newton Abbot, 1974), 175.

halls were the preserve of the disreputable. They catered for families and not just single men and women. They were not regular venues for prostitutes: most of the single women who patronized them were in steady employment. Shopkeepers and artisans, though they sat in the better seats, attended the same places as those who could only just afford the minimum entrance charges (3d. in the provinces and more in London).[159] To emphasize only the commercial and manipulative aspects of music-hall development is, in any case, to miss the point. Paying customers were as much producers as consumers of a form of social drama in which styles and identities were shuttled to and fro. Although some songs were politically conservative, most were not political at all: mothers-in-law featured far more often than prime ministers. Audiences enforced their own imperatives, whether in the shape of the 'nigger minstrels' popular from the 1850s onwards or pawky Scots humour of the 'Hieland Laddie' variety or the subversive and ribald talents of performers like Marie Lloyd.[160]

A similar sense of social complexity informed the holiday industry which developed in the last third of the century as changing employment patterns began to make it possible to undertake longer absences from home. Until then most resorts were either exclusively upper- and middle-class or, from the 1840s, places to which working people went as day excursionists. Organized factory outings, paid for jointly by workers and industrialists, required from their participants the regular saving of small sums, a habit without which the infant holiday industry could never have developed. They were also highly regimented: 'at the sounding of the trumpet, the whole to return to dinner in the same order' read printed instructions handed out on an outing from a Birmingham pin factory in 1850.[161] As the working week shrank and real wages increased so those in secure skilled employment could graduate from day trips to weekends and even to whole

---

[159] P. Bailey, 'Introduction', in Bailey (ed.), *Music Hall: The Business of Pleasure* (Milton Keynes, 1986), p. x; D. Höher, 'The Composition of Music Hall Audiences, 1850–1900', ibid. 73–92; J. Crump, 'Provincial Music Hall: Promoters and Public in Leicester, 1863–1929', ibid. 53–72; G. S. Jones, 'Working-Class Culture and Working-Class Politics in London, 1870–1900', *Journal of Social History*, 7 (1974), 477–8; Cunningham, 'Leisure and Culture', 311.

[160] Bailey, 'Introduction', in *Music Hall*, pp. viii–xxiii; id., 'Champagne Charlie: Performance and Ideology in the Music-Hall Swell Song', in J. S. Bratton (ed.), *Music Hall: Performance and Style* (Milton Keynes, 1986), 49–69; Smith, 'Victorian Entertainment', 178; E. King, 'Popular Culture in Glasgow', in Cage (ed.), *Working Class in Glasgow*, 170.

[161] Thompson, *Rise of Respectable Society*, 212–13, 289–91; J. K. Walton, 'The Demand for Working-Class Seaside Holidays in Victorian England', *Economic History Review*, 34 (1981), 250–1, 254; id., *The English Seaside Resort: A Social History 1750–1914* (Leicester, 1983), 23; Bailey, *Leisure and Class*, 85; P. E. Razzell and R. W. Wainwright (eds.), *The Victorian Working Class* (London, 1973), 299.

weeks away. Because paid holidays for manual workers were rare until the twentieth century, week-long breaks made their first appearance in the late 1870s and 1880s among textile workers in Lancashire and Yorkshire who (a) had regular jobs, (b) had employers who found it convenient to close their mills completely for a period, (c) were able and willing to save for a week's unpaid leave, and (d) lived close to the places they wished to visit. Blackpool was the queen of working-class resorts. Already in 1879—when a million visitors were using its railway facilities—a rate was being levied to pay for tourist advertising, and during the 'season' (mid-July to early September, plus Whitsun) in 1884 about 40,000 excursionists came each day to augment the 70,000 staying visitors in residence at any one time.[162]

All this required money, and commercial interests were soon spending large sums on facilities of all kinds. The 'take-off' decade was probably the 1860s when pier building became something of a mania (Blackpool's North Pier of 1863 cost £13,500, Brighton's West Pier £30,000 in 1866) and a number of huge and expensive hotels were erected such as the Grand Hotels at Brighton (£160,000) and Scarborough. Until the 1870s the middle and the 'middling' sort of people (shopkeepers, traders, sub-professionals, clerks) constituted the bulk of the customers. Their requirements tended to be low-key. The former wanted fresh sea air (a particular Victorian obsession), promenades, gardens, and quiet, the latter liked donkey rides, punch-and-judy shows, pierrots, and gentility. The really substantial and expensive dance halls, winter palaces, and fairgrounds did not appear until somewhat later when a larger mass market had come into being. By then most resorts had developed distinct flavours: Eastbourne and Bournemouth, for example, excluded funfair-style entertainment, Blackpool knew little else—though even there the North Pier was considered 'superior' to the South Jetty (later the Central Pier).[163] Those few places which still attracted a wider range of visitors, like Brighton and Scarborough, kept them firmly apart either by topographical or seasonal apartheid. The result was a kind of truce, coexistence without harmony, the middle class perhaps surprised by the good (if noisy) behaviour of the mass of holiday makers, the latter—at least until the arrival of rougher young male excursionists in the 1890s—unaggressively pursuing leisure very much on their own terms. Even so, the fastidious among the well-to-do

[162] Walton, 'Seaside Holidays', 252–3, 258–9; id., 'Residential Amenity, Respectable Morality and the Rise of the Entertainment Industry: The Case of Blackpool 1860–1914', *Literature and History*, 1 (1975), 65; id., *English Seaside Resort*, 23, 71; Cunningham, 'Leisure and Culture', 313–14.

[163] Walton, *English Seaside Resort*, 23–5, 157; id., 'Residential Amenity', 68.

were already beginning to flee to the remoter charms of Cornwall, Devon, Pembrokeshire, and abroad.[164]

For superior travellers of this kind the characteristic Victorian combination of commercialism and high tone also created significant new 'products', notably through-ticketing and organized tours. Thomas Cook may have begun in 1841 with 570 socially modest temperance enthusiasts travelling between Leicester and Loughborough by rail, but he soon focused his business predominantly upon the more prosperous. In 1846 he began to provide tours to Scotland at £5 or so (and therefore beyond the means of manual workers) which utilized and extended the Victorians' romantic involvement with Caledonian myth. In 1852 he also sent parties to Ireland where post-Famine Killarney supplied equally mysterious Celtic atmospheres. Three years later Cook colonized Paris and the Rhine, adding Italy, Switzerland, and the United States in the 1860s. Soon he and his rivals were sending 'tourists' (the word had already attained derogatory use) all over the world. Their methods were efficient, very English (Cook spoke no foreign tongue), keenly priced, and opened new horizons. Gladstone certainly thought so when in 1887 he included among the 'humanizing contrivances of the age' the 'system founded by Mr Cook...under which numbers of persons, and indeed whole classes, have for the first time found easy access to foreign countries, and have acquired some of that familiarity with them, that breeds not contempt but kindness'.[165]

It was not, however, as simple as Gladstone implied. Undoubtedly the numbers travelling abroad did increase considerably in the second half of the century, with cross-Channel passenger traffic experiencing something like sixfold growth. In 1850 passports (not required for leaving or entering Britain until 1915 but demanded by certain foreign countries) became much easier to obtain and the subsequent unifications of Italy and Germany reduced bureaucratic delay.[166] Extensive continental railway-building also made travel much easier and more comfortable. In 1871 one could reach Rome from London in fifty-five hours, though not until 1875 was it possible (as a result of Cook's efforts) to send luggage in advance. Inevitably this meant that experienced travellers who had, like the future Cardinal

[164] Walton, *English Seaside Resort*, 213–14; id., 'Seaside Holidays', 252.

[165] W. E. Gladstone, ' "Locksley Hall" and the Jubilee', *Nineteenth Century*, 21 (1887), 9; J. Simmons, 'Railways, Hotels, and Tourism in Great Britain', *Journal of Contemporary History*, 19 (1984), 209; id., 'Thomas Cook of Leicester', *Leicestershire Archaeological and Historical Society Transactions*, 49 (1973–4), 25–6.

[166] R. J. Croft, 'The Nature and Growth of Cross-Channel Traffic through Calais and Boulogne, 1870–1900', *Transport History*, 6 (1973), 128–43; J. Pemble, *The Mediterranean Passion: Victorians and Edwardians in the South* (Oxford, 1987), 33–5.

Manning, taken twenty-five days to get to Rome in 1835 under appalling and expensive conditions, looked down upon the cosseted and often less socially elevated tourists of the railway age. Yet the aims of virtually all who travelled on the continent were curiously similar: culture, scenery, and health. Churches, classical ruins, galleries, antiquities of every kind provided the programmes of Cook's packaged groups in much the same way as they had featured—though perhaps a little more nonchalantly—in aristocratic grand tours. This, therefore, was deeply *serious* travelling, which, especially in the classical lands of the Mediterranean, possessed 'an intellectual patina, a cultural bloom'.[167] Not that the results were always particularly elevated: the curios collected abroad by the Meagles in *Little Dorrit* (1855–7) consisted largely of fake archaeology, bits of lava, strange fans, oil lamps, and rosaries allegedly blessed by the Pope. Every year more and more travel books were published and presumably bought. By the 1880s Florence, Rome, and the Riviera had English hotels, shops, churches, and places to eat, all sustained by little English 'societies' in which calling and card leaving were no less endemic than at home.

For many, however, continental Europe repelled as much as it attracted. There were constant complaints on the part of older travel snobs that the new tourists misbehaved themselves, scratched monuments, talked loudly, argued over bills, made themselves absurd. It is hard to know where the truth lay. On the one hand, there was certainly a good deal of ill-informed xenophobia about; on the other, suspicions of 'abroad' were never indiscriminate (for example, the Dutch were 'nice', Spaniards were 'awful') and by no means invariably based upon crude prejudice.[168] Yet in one important respect visits to certain parts of the continent, the Catholic parts, revealed a good deal of Anglo-Saxon bile and confusion. Above all nothing was so enticing nor yet so repulsive as Rome (ruled by the Pope until 1870). Year after year British Protestants flocked to the Easter and Christmas ceremonies there, used every dodge to obtain admission to the more famous churches, and then behaved horribly, refusing to kneel, chattering, sniggering—a champagne cork was heard to pop during one consecration. The advent of the Oxford Movement in the 1840s had increased anxieties that England might slide towards popedom, while the affairs of Ireland added a persistent edge to sectarian fears. The visiting Baptist, Charles Spurgeon, thought Rome the 'city of Babylon' and prayed for another Luther to strike it down. Many others did the same. Travellers not otherwise notably

---

[167] Pemble, *Mediterranean Passion*, 26, 18–20, 3.
[168] B. Porter, '"Bureau and Barrack": Early Victorian Attitudes towards the Continent', *Victorian Studies*, 27 (1984), 407–33.

deranged, like Fanny Kemble, Nassau Senior, and Frances Eliot, blustered and poured scorn in a flurry of adjectival excess: 'ridiculous', 'absurd', 'pitiful', 'puerile', 'childish', 'hideous', 'grotesque'. What, perhaps, they most resented was that in Catholic Europe Anglicans were outsiders, divorced and sundered from a still mighty and universal church. The insensitive returned home with their prejudices confirmed. The sensitive—who too had learnt about the sins of Rome before departure—were in Rome reminded also of the sins of England. 'In entering such a Church as this', wrote a troubled Gladstone after his first visit to St Peter's, 'most deeply does one feel the pain and shame of the schism which separates us from Rome... May God bind up the wounds of his bleeding Church'.[169]

Travel and holidays, like so many other aspects of Victorian life, encapsulated the divisions of nineteenth-century society. When analysed by scholars dealing specifically with questions of class, the precision of such divisions tends to fade under close microscopic examination. It becomes difficult to identify where one 'class' begins and another ends, to pin down the exact differences between semi-skilled and skilled workers or between labour aristocrats and white-collar clerks. Was it a matter of income (its level and regularity) or of perception or of respectability? Did people move easily between one category and another? Was one city street clearly lower middle and another clearly upper middle class? All these are complicated and sometimes unanswerable questions. Yet, by standing a little back from the close detail, by looking sideways through eyes focused at other more distant views, the whole of the Victorian experience does indeed stand out as one in which people in different social and economic locations pursued different goals and styles of living. Family life meant one thing in Mayfair, another in Edgbaston, something different again in the East End or the slum cellars of Liverpool. The role of women—their independence, their activities outside the home, their power or lack of it—followed no universal norm, the element of subordination varying greatly between the well-to-do and the poor and between different levels of poverty. Marriage and courtship may well have been shaped by certain common human characteristics of affection, love, and calculation, but the mixture varied and the degree of choice open to possible partners was by no means invariably the same. Dress, diet, and the rituals associated with clothes and meals were remarkably class-specific. Wives and mothers who lived in Hampstead were, as wives and mothers, inhabiting a world very different from those of their counterparts in Whitechapel or in the grand houses of the aristocracy.

[169] *The Gladstone Diaries*, ed. H. C. G. Matthew and M. R. D. Foot, 14 vols. (Oxford, 1968–94), i. 462 (31 Mar. 1832); Pemble, *Mediterranean Passion*, 212–14.

Health and life chances had class as well as spatial reference points. By the 1880s one set of persons watched football, quite another played golf. Occasional neutral territories notwithstanding, different strata remained remarkably separate—at work, travelling, on holiday, at play. Just as the astronomer's eyes are damaged by looking directly at the sun, so, by looking only at the strictly economic side of things (wages, salaries, property-ownership, and the like) it is easy to become persuaded by the nearer vision's brightness into seeing only a continuous blur. A more contextual and tangential glance, however, can reveal distinctions as well as continuities, barriers as well as bridges, reveal, indeed, a world in which the recognition and maintenance of hierarchy were woven into the very fabric of daily life. Whether any or all of this meant that Victorian society was a 'class' society in any strictly ideological sense matters much less than that its participants certainly believed themselves to be living in status-based surroundings of an acute and aggressive character.

CHAPTER II

The Business of Culture

I. PRELIMINARY

As industrialization became more pervasive in the second half of the nineteenth century so the imperatives of an increasingly sophisticated commercialism began to affect all aspects of British life. High and low culture enthusiastically embraced what Dickens called a new frankness about 'those little screws of existence—pounds, shillings, and pence'. 'I write for money. Of course I do', noted Trollope, 'It is for money that we all work, lawyers, publishers, authors and the rest.'[1] And while this neither negated nor overwhelmed that internally generated logic which has in all periods given works of art their essential pattern and form, its influence upon the deep structures—as well as the surface appearances—of novels, poems, music, buildings, and paintings is difficult to exaggerate.

Literature, perhaps (from the practitioners' viewpoint) the most atomistic form of all, tended to call the Victorian cultural tune. A painter might see departing emigrants at a London railway station. All of a sudden he would think 'This shall be my great picture, and I will call it "Seeking new Homes"': and soon would emerge a painting that was, in effect, 'a poem on canvas'.[2] That a picture should aspire to the condition of literature was to Victorians admirable. Ruskin, who praised Holman Hunt's *The Awakening Conscience* (1853) for precisely this, thought the canine tearfulness of Landseer's *The Old Shepherd's Chief Mourner* (1837) 'one of the most perfect poems or pictures (I use the words as synonymous) which modern times have seen'.[3]

---

[1] *The Letters of Charles Dickens*, ed. M. House, G. Storey, and others, 9 vols. to date (Oxford, 1965–), i. 57; *The Letters of Anthony Trollope*, ed. N. J. Hall, 2 vols. (Stanford, Calif., 1983), i. 167.

[2] Joseph Hatton, *The Tallants of Barton* (1867) cited M. F. Brightfield, *Victorian England in its Novels (1840–1870)*, 4 vols. (Los Angeles, 1968), ii. 303.

[3] C. Wood, *Victorian Panorama: Paintings of Victorian Life* (London, 1976), 247; G. Reynolds, *Victorian Painting* (London, 1966), 15.

Contemporaries were, indeed, well aware that a concern for creating a modern reality was common to both literature and painting—as could be seen as clearly in Frith's pictures as in the novels of his friend Dickens. Frith's famous *The Railway Station* was described in the *Art-Journal* of May 1862 precisely as a 'painted volume', F. G. Cotman's *One of the Family* by the *Liverpool Echo* in October 1880 as an 'illustrated periodical sort of picture', while Tissot's series depicting 'La Femme à Paris' was, according to the *Portfolio* of January 1886, 'easy reading like a clever, not too profound modern novel'.[4] A distinct narrative thrust not only, therefore, gave Victorian fiction and painting much of their dynamic energy but set up a series of fruitful reverberations between the two. Dickens furnished especially revealing literary models for and counterparts of contemporary pictorial forms. Frith's *Ramsgate Sands* (1853–4) creates the same atmosphere as 'The Tuggses at Ramsgate' in *Sketches by Boz* (1836), while his *The Railway Station* (1862) faithfully captures Mr Dombey going upon a journey in *Dombey and Son* (1846–8). Less subtly, the simple sociological message of novels like Disraeli's *Sybil: Or the Two Nations* (1845) could be, and frequently was, represented pictorially, as in George Clausen's *A Spring Morning, Haverstock Hill* (1881) where the painting is split in two by a prominent lamppost—an affluent (if melancholy) mother and child on one side, ragged road workers on the other.

Victorian notions concerning the governing ideas proper to a modern commercial society informed not only the debate about economics and art, they underpinned aesthetic judgements themselves, notably in architecture where confident experts like Palmerston demanded government buildings in an Italianate (rather than a Gothic) style because the latter seemed backward and medieval, the former somehow contemporary and up-to-date.[5] More extreme were those who pushed Bentham's argument, that 'if the game of push-pin furnish more pleasure' than the arts and sciences then 'it is more valuable than either',[6] to its logical conclusion and actually gloried in what they considered Victorian Britain's artistic inferiorities, a sure sign, they believed, of her economic and political strength. Few articulated this so unashamedly as the Liberal MP and businessman, Samuel Laing, who—in a series of books based on extensive continental

---

[4] For these citations and some of the references which follow I am indebted to a brief but acute catalogue of an exhibition at Leeds City Art Galleries in 1986: T. Friedman, *Great Paintings of Victorian Daily Life* (Leeds, 1986), unpaginated.

[5] I. Webb, 'The Bradford Wool Exchange', *Victorian Studies*, 20 (1976), 50–2; C. Stewart, *The Stones of Manchester* (London, 1956), 36–7.

[6] J. Bentham, 'The Rationale of Reward' (1st publ. in English in 1825) in *The Works of Jeremy Bentham*, ed. J. Bowring, 11 vols. (Edinburgh, 1843), ii. 253.

travel published between 1836 and 1852—compared free, stable, economically developed, well-governed, and artistically unproductive Britain with
autocratic, unstable, backward, art-mad lands like Italy, Germany, Spain,
and France.[7] And if Laing's views were unusually fierce, milder versions of
the creed passed beyond polemics into the corridors of contemporary
power. Thus Henry Cole (the most influential mid-Victorian art administrator) put much effort into ensuring that the design-school system was
reformed after 1849 along strictly commercial lines. 'I do not', he told a
parliamentary committee, 'think that these schools were created for aesthetic purposes, or for general educational purposes.'[8] 'Protection to literature or science', argued the *Morning Chronicle* in 1850, 'is mischievous in
nearly the same way as protection to commerce. The let-alone system is
equally desirable for both.'[9] In other words, free enterprise was best—in
the production of novels no less than the production of coal.

A good deal of ambivalence was involved in this. Successful writers like
Dickens, Carlyle, and Tennyson supported 'free trade' in books (or the
removal of retail price maintenance), yet Dickens's 'manager', John Forster, argued publicly that the state should give more pensions to needy but
worthy writers down on their luck.[10] While almost everyone, therefore, had
to be seen to be operating within *laissez-faire* criteria, special interests were
seldom slow to demand special treatment. Thus G. H. Lewes (George
Eliot's partner) wanted 'no government largesse', but he did want writers
appointed to lots of professorships and public offices.[11] And even the
commercially minded Cole was shocked when Palmerston refused funds
for the purchase of the Soulages collection of medieval Italian majolica and
bronzes with the (reported) quip 'What is the use of such rubbish to our
manufacturers?'[12]

Generally speaking, the market constituted the chief generator of cultural activity in Victorian Britain. Different arts responded in different
ways. Literary production remained an essentially solitary activity, with

[7] B. Porter, ' "Monstrous Vandalism": Capitalism and Philistinism in the Works of
Samuel Laing (1780–1868)', *Albion*, 23 (1991), 253–68.
[8] Webb, 'Bradford Wool Exchange', 48–9.
[9] M. Lund, 'Novels, Writers, and Readers in 1850', *Victorian Periodicals Review*, 17
(1984), 16.
[10] Ibid. 18. Resale price maintenance was abolished in 1852 as 'contrary to the freedom
which ought to prevail in commercial transactions': J. A. Sutherland, *Victorian Novelists and
Publishers* (London, 1976), 40.
[11] 'The Condition of Authors in England, Germany, and France', *Fraser's Magazine*, 35
(1847), 294–5.
[12] A. Briggs, 'The Later Victorian Age', in B. Ford (ed.), *The Cambridge Guide to the Arts
in Britain*, vii. *The Later Victorian Age* (Cambridge, 1989), 36.

commercial publishers (producers of multiple copies) and libraries acting as intermediaries between writers and individual consumers, though the theatre depended upon collective activities such as ensemble performance and interpretation. Performance was also essential to music, the denomination 'musician' being applied more often to players than composers. Painters directly produced unique art works, though some also painted several copies of popular pictures (and engravings made available derivative versions to a wider market). Lastly, architects, unlike the others, could hardly exist at all without commissioning patrons capable of supplying the large sums needed to translate drawings and plans into bricks and stones.

2. LITERATURE

The novel was widely regarded as the art form most suited to the age, the 'vital offspring of modern wants and tendencies' as the *Prospective Review* put it in 1850.[13] The crucial development here was the way in which the dramatic growth of the reading public affected the production and marketing of fiction and of literary works generally. Not only that, but, as leading writers began more and more to come from professional family backgrounds, so the idea—however empirically vulnerable—of the 'professional' author started to take hold as part of an attempt to throw the cloak of dignity over the cruder imperatives of commerce and cash.[14]

The large sums earned by a handful helped to make authorship in general seem more respectable than before. Dickens consistently (and insistently) saw himself as a 'professional' writer—not at all the attitude in earlier years of either the aristocratic Byron or the would-be country gentleman Scott (even though the latter was eventually obliged to crank out novels at an almost industrial pace in order to pay off his debts).[15] The proportion of writers able to make a tolerable living from literature alone remained small. As a result, there were clergyman writers like Kingsley, Newman, and Hopkins, academics like Carroll and Charles Reade (who was also a barrister), officials like Macaulay, Trollope, and Arnold, lawyers like Francis Jeffrey and Wilkie Collins, businessmen like John Galt, men with

---

[13] 'Hearts in Mortmain, and Cornelia', *Prospective Review*, 6 (1850), 495.
[14] R. D. Altick, 'The Sociology of Authorship: The Social Origins, Education, and Occupations of 1100 British Writers, 1800–1935', *New York Public Library Bulletin*, 66 (1962), 389–404; D. Duman, 'The Creation and Diffusion of a Professional Ideology in Nineteenth Century England', *Sociological Review*, NS 27 (1979), 137.
[15] Sutherland, *Victorian Novelists*, 23; R. L. Patten, *Charles Dickens and his Publishers* (Oxford, 1978), 11–12; R. A. Gettmann, *A Victorian Publisher: A Study of the Bentley Papers* (Cambridge, 1960), 5.

private means like Fitzgerald and Beddoes. Women writers were sometimes supported by husbands; Browning was long supported by his wife. Many moved in and out of jobs as their literary earnings fell and rose. Ruskin's personal fortune shrank in later life until he was only able to get a decent income by relying on publications written long before with very different ends in mind.[16] Such economic elasticities meant that the number of persons who might reasonably be designated 'writers', though impossible to pin down with precision, undoubtedly grew substantially. The number of individual contributors to the numerous Victorian periodicals may well have exceeded 24,000, while one well-informed contemporary (Walter Besant) suggested that in 1888 there were 14,000 persons in London alone who made some kind of living from (mainly journalistic) writing—far more (relative to the overall population) than there had been in 1836.[17]

Contemporary debates regarding the social status of this gathering literary army were long and inconclusive. In 1847 G. H. Lewes had no doubts: 'literature has become a profession. It is a means of subsistence, almost as certain as the bar or the church.'[18] But only four years earlier an attempt to set up a Society of Authors to underpin this supposed new professionalism had—despite the transient involvement of Dickens, Bulwer-Lytton, and Thackeray—entirely failed. By the 1880s, when a second attempt proved more successful, its instigators saw authorship as at best 'a collection of professions' united only by a common concern for 'material interests'. As the *Observer* put it in 1884, because writing was about the only 'business' for which no formal training was required, 'like cab-driving and the small coal trade' it was often adopted only 'after all other avenues to a livelihood' had been closed.[19] The great majority of authors were indeed, desperate unknowns, like the penny-dreadful writer spotted in the 1860s with 'faded, threadbare coat ... buttoned high at the throat, either to conceal the dirtiness of his linen or the naked fact that his solitary possession in that material was at that moment undergoing the process of washing'.[20] Of the 143 unsolicited manuscripts sent to the conscientious house of Macmillan between 1868 and 1870 only six were accepted, and what was true of book publishers was true of periodicals

---

[16] J. W. Saunders, *The Profession of English Letters* (London, 1964), 175–8, 190–7; J. Sutherland, *Victorian Fiction: Writers, Publishers, Readers* (London, 1995), 151–64.

[17] P. L. Shillingsburg, *Pegasus in Harness: Victorian Publishing and W. M. Thackeray* (Charlottesville, Va., 1992), 6; Altick, 'Sociology of Authorship', 400.

[18] 'Condition of Authors', 285.

[19] Lund, 'Novels', 20; V. Bonham-Carter, *Authors by Profession* (London, 1978), 83, 122.

[20] J. Greenwood, *The Wilds of London* (1874) cited E. S. Turner, *Boys Will Be Boys*, 2nd edn. (Harmondsworth, 1976), 58.

too.[21] In almost every respect the new and expanding publishers, as much products of the industrial revolution as cotton-spinners, posed an entirely new kind of challenge to authors who, having freed themselves from aristocratic patronage and secured independence, now stood in relation to the publishing industry as did other workers who had nothing to offer but their labour. A lack of skill in drawing up contracts could, as in the case of the best-selling Mary Elizabeth Braddon, lead to frantic hack work in order to escape the clutches of rapacious publishers. 'I know', she told Bulwer-Lytton in the 1860s, 'that my writing teems with errors, absurd-ities, contradictions and inconsistencies', but Ward Lock's demands left no time for anything else.[22]

And just as injury could reduce a skilled artisan from modest competence to relentless poverty, so a host of potential disasters threatened authors: illness, drink, improvidence, sudden changes in taste, rows with publishers, writer's block. Some remained permanently in Grub Street, forced to work for penny periodicals at 9d. a hundred words or 2d. a poem. As the editor of the *Literary Gazette* gloomily noted in 1852, not one in a hundred 'suc-ceeded to the realisation of a moderate independence' and perhaps only one in five hundred earned as much as a tolerably successful divine, lawyer, or physician.[23] What kept so many British writers at least alive, and sometimes a good deal more, was the market created by the numerous periodicals of the time. (On the continent things were much worse and payments, especially for fiction, much lower.[24]) For some—as with Dickens during the publication of *Pickwick Papers* (1836–7)—fame could come early and overnight. For others—as with Thackeray—only after a long struggle. Between 1837 and 1847 Thackeray contributed 450 articles to twenty-two periodicals; his first real book, *The Paris Sketch Book* (1840), earned him £50; in 1843 *The Irish Sketch Book* produced £385; he continued hand-to-mouth until *Vanity Fair* began to appear in 1847. Yet in the few years before his death in 1863 he was probably making £7,200 a year from literary activities (perhaps £350,000 in modern terms)—an extraordinary achieve-ment after so grinding a start.[25]

The most consistently substantial earners were Dickens, Trollope, and George Eliot. All were efficient minders of their own business interests. Yet

[21] Sutherland, *Victorian Novelists*, 210.

[22] M. Sadleir, *Things Past* (London, 1944), 77. Braddon's *Lady Audley's Secret* (1862) was one of the great Victorian best sellers.

[23] N. Cross, *The Common Writer: Life in Nineteenth-Century Grub Street* (Cambridge, 1985), 38, 43.

[24] [Lewes], 'Condition of Authors', 286–90.

[25] Shillingsburg, *Pegasus in Harness*, 36–47; Patten, *Dickens and his Publishers*, 230.

each adopted a very different approach to publishing. Trollope started slowly and did not resign from the Post Office until 1867 when he had already published nineteen novels. He used a number of different publishers, sold his copyrights outright if he could, liked to disguise high artistic sensibility behind smokescreens of breezy commercialism, and during his time of greatest success between 1862 and 1874 made £4,500 a year. Even so, he ended on a downward note, in part because his popularity faltered in the 1870s but in part also because commercial miscalculation led him in the 1860s to publish with less reputable firms.[26] And although the resulting moral—that quality imprints mattered—should have been engraven upon every successful novelist's heart, too many continued to allow greed to outrun long-term perspicuity.

George Eliot was not among them. Like Trollope hers was a comparatively slow start. In 1857 at the age of 38 she earned £443—a good, though not an enormous, sum. But (with one famous exception) she stayed with the same publisher (John Blackwood) throughout her writing career. She did not sell copyrights outright and after 1860 dealt on a royalty basis. The success of *Adam Bede* (1859), *The Mill on the Floss* (1860), and *Silas Marner* (1861) led George Smith to offer £10,000 for *Romola* to be published in parts in the *Cornhill Magazine*. But Eliot, though businesslike, was not rapacious, and Blackwood (to whom she later returned) was quickly mollified. Because she believed that artistically *Romola* would read better if divided into fewer than the sixteen instalments Smith had proposed, she reduced her fee by £3,000 in order to achieve this. So calm, measured, and high-minded an approach paid dividends in the long run. Her masterpiece, *Middlemarch* (in parts 1871–2, in book form 1872), made £9,000 in eight years, and by 1873 her total annual income had reached a steady £5,000, about half of it from investments based on previous literary receipts.[27]

Dickens was the biggest earner of all and in many ways the most imaginative exploiter of his talents, resorting to serials, three-volume publication, periodicals, Christmas books (popular Victorian compilations), collected editions, cheap editions, reprints, foreign rights, all with carefully judged expertise. While Dickens was earning £400 from each of the nineteen parts in which *Dombey and Son* was issued (1846–8), Thackeray was getting 'only' £60 per part for *Vanity Fair* (1847–8). In 1847 Dickens received £5,726 from his two main publishers, in 1865–6 £12,000 from

[26] A. Trollope, *An Autobiography*, ed. F. Page (London, 1950), 167–8; M. Sadleir, *Trollope: A Commentary*, 3rd edn. (London, 1945), 301. The 1842 Copyright Act (5 & 6 Vict., *c*.45) gave protection for forty-two years or seven years after the author's death (whichever was the longer) and remained in force until 1911.

[27] Bonham-Carter, *Authors by Profession*, 108–14.

Our Mutual Friend at a time when £3,000 a year was coming in from his proprietorship of the magazine *All the Year Round* and about another £3,000 from other sales. Dickens simply sold and sold and sold. He (and perhaps another half-a-dozen writers) could dictate terms to publishers. And he, too, was the king of the American lecture circuit, that enormously rewarding by-product of literary success. On returning from his 1867-8 tour he put £20,000 in the bank (Thackeray in the 1850s had been paid £2,400 a 'season'), while readings in Britain produced large amounts on top.[28]

The wide variety of contracts which Victorian publishers offered meant that only businesslike authors could maximize their earnings. Outright sales of copyright yielded the largest initial payments but could prove disappointing if sales exceeded expectations. Charles Lever (always in need of cash), Trollope, and Mrs Gaskell favoured this method, though the last might well have earned more by following the 'half-profits' system by which—after allowing for costs—receipts were split between author and publisher. Also common were copyright sales for limited periods and commission publishing whereby (usually desperate) authors paid all costs and 10 per cent to the publisher but then took all the profits. The modern royalty system was, however, uncommon before the 1880s, though George Eliot adopted it in the 1860s, while Charles Reade's popular *It is Never Too Late to Mend* was published in 1856 by Ticknor & Fields on a royalty basis.[29]

Few writers were, however, able to negotiate from a position of strength. Poets in particular found it difficult to earn much. Tennyson's success was exceptional and even he did not hit gold until the first series of *Idylls of the King* (1859) yielded £11,500 in five years, that is, a decade *after* his appointment as Poet Laureate. In 1865 alone he made £12,000 from literature. By contrast, the books of Dorset dialect verse by the enormously talented William Barnes, though often reprinted, did very little to augment his modest income as, first, a schoolmaster, and then a clergyman.[30] Nor should occasional bonanza payments for individual novels, like the £10,000 for Disraeli's *Endymion* (1880) or the £5,000 for Wilkie Collins's *Armadale* (1866), disguise the fact that the mass of Victorian fiction attracted much

[28] Sutherland, *Victorian Novelists*, 23; Patten, *Dickens and his Publishers*, 185-9, 230; D. Gray, review of Patten in *Victorian Studies*, 23 (1980), 416-18.

[29] J. G. Hepburn, *The Author's Empty Purse and the Rise of the Literary Agent* (London, 1968), 12; J. Feather, *A History of British Publishing* (London, 1988), 170; Bonham-Carter, *Authors by Profession*, 110, 93.

[30] J. S. Hagen, *Tennyson and his Publishers* (London, 1979), 79-80, 109-18; A. Chedzoy, *William Barnes: A Life of the Dorset Poet* (Wimborne, 1985), 118, 145-7, 161-2.

lower rates. Mid-century novels by *popular* authors operating well above hack level were paid for at prices varying from £100 to £500; first novels were usually never paid for at all.[31] The careers of two well-known and 'successful' writers make the point. Robert Bell knew Dickens, Thackeray, and Trollope, wrote novels and essays, but never earned more than £600 a year. And while this was not to be despised, it never allowed Bell to keep up the appearance of a prosperous man of letters. More striking still is the case of James Payn, whose novels rolled off the production line with metronomic regularity (*Lost Sir Massingberd* of 1864 being the best known) and who was as knowledgeable about finance as any writer. Yet even in his best years he never exceeded £1,500—very much less than the incomes of the bishops and barristers with whom, as a 'gentleman', he liked to compare himself.[32]

The labour involved in such a life is hard to exaggerate. Payn produced about 160 volumes including forty-six novels, eight collections of short stories, seventeen books of essays, and four memoirs full of wit and vitality. Mrs Oliphant, who was never at ease with publishers, was also prodigiously busy and in a career of fifty years turned out a hundred novels, as well as numerous biographies and hundreds—possibly thousands—of articles. Trollope reckoned that three tolerable books was as much as anyone could do in two years. Payn thought nine months the minimum for a three-volume novel 'worth reading', though a competent painter could, he believed, turn out three pictures in the same time and earn a good deal more. Short pieces of fiction like Trollope's *Harry Heathcote of Gangoil* (1874) could sometimes be done in a month and Rhoda Broughton produced her best seller *Not Wisely But Too Well* (1867) in a dazzling six weeks. But few could keep up such a pace and none could do so consistently.[33]

The amounts which even eminent writers left in their wills, while considerable, were hardly enormous by the measure of success in other fields. Dickens left £93,000, but Browning 'only' £16,774 and Thackeray about £18,000. The publishers George Routledge and George Bentley left £94,000 and £85,846 respectively.[34] One of the troubles was that, while even annual earnings of £3,000 were vast by working-class standards, literary workers living by the pen aspired to high levels of social status.

[31] Patten, *Dickens and his Publishers*, 232; R. C. Terry, *Victorian Popular Fiction, 1860–1880* (London, 1983), 40–1; [Lewes], 'Condition of Authors', 290.

[32] Cross, *Common Writer*, 123, 240; [Lewes], 'Condition of Authors', 286; Terry, *Victorian Popular Fiction*, 34–9. In the 1860s the annual incomes of the Bishops of Lincoln and Durham were £5,000 and £8,000 respectively.

[33] Terry, *Victorian Popular Fiction*, 133, 69, 41.

[34] Sutherland, *Victorian Novelists*, 23; Gettmann, *A Victorian Publisher*, 152; Shillingsburg, *Pegasus in Harness*, 32.

Dangerously large sums were spent trying to maintain the style of the prosperous middle classes. The bohemian, George Augustus Sala, insisted in 1874 that no man of letters with £2,000 a year could 'save anything substantial'.[35] And while this may have been nonsense, many writers believed it to be true. Dickens spent very freely, Thackeray very very freely. Harrison Ainsworth, whose novels commanded £2,000 and more in the 1840s, saved nothing and ended his life still writing furiously for less than £50 a time. Even the supposedly cautious Trollope thought £1,400 a year necessary for any kind of comfort in Ireland where costs were comparatively low. By the time he was earning £4,500 his expenditure patterns had come to be based on the assumption that £3,000 was needed to maintain a suitable style of life ('but I have ever been too well inclined to spend freely that which has come easily').[36] While, therefore, the new mass literary market may well have helped to produce Victorian Britain's greatest artistic achievements, it made few writers prosperous, let alone rich, though certainly it attracted many moths to the flame.

Growth in the market for 'respectable' fiction was, in any case, rather more limited than the rise in the number of books published might suggest. Between 1840 and 1870 the British population increased by 40 per cent, the number of books published annually by 400 per cent. Between 1800 and 1825 about 580 books appeared each year, by mid-century over 2,600, by 1900 6,044.[37] But even if, by 1880, about 380 new novels were being published every year, modern fiction counted for less, commercially speaking, than staples like grammars, cookery books, Shakespeare, Bunyan, and the Bible. The middle-class market at which most novels were aimed was rather like Victorian 'democracy'—growing, but still far from all-embracing. Given that the respectable novel-reading public is now thought to have grown from 50,000 in 1830 to 120,000 in 1890, optimistic references by mid-century publishers to 'literature for the millions' take on a distinctly exaggerated air.[38] Contemporaries, however, certainly thought they were witnessing dramatic growth. The *Bookseller* in 1860 hailed the triumph of

[35] G. A. Sala, *The Life and Adventures of George Augustus Sala*, 2 vols. (London, 1895), ii. 309.

[36] Sutherland, *Victorian Novelists*, 152–60; Trollope, *Autobiography*, 127, 167–8.

[37] J. Holloway, 'Literature', in Ford (ed.), *Cambridge Guide to the Arts*, vii. 87; M. Plant, *The English Book Trade*, 2nd edn. (London, 1965), 445–7. Between 1841 and 1871 the proportion of males and females in England and Wales returned by the Registrar General as 'literate' rose from 67.3 to 80.6% and from 51.1 to 73.2% respectively: M. Sanderson, *Education, Economic Change and Society in England 1780–1870*, 2nd edn. (London, 1991), 19.

[38] Cross, *Common Writer*, 206; Sutherland, *Victorian Novelists*, 12, 62, 64, 75; Saunders, *Profession of English Letters*, 199, 203; R. D. Altick, 'English Publishing and the Mass Audience in 1852', *Studies in Bibliography*, 6 (1954), 12.

George Smith's *Cornhill Magazine* (which serialized novels and was at first edited by Thackeray): 'It has opened our eyes to the great fact of there being a very large, and hitherto overlooked mass of readers for literature of high class. Whoever believed that a hundred thousand buyers could be found, month after month.'[39]

Two things underpinned such trends. The first was the remarkable adventurousness of even the respectable audience for fiction. Readers took in their stride Dickens's *Great Expectations* (1861), Wilkie Collins's *The Woman in White* (1860), Mrs Henry Wood's *East Lynne* (1861), and Mary Elizabeth Braddon's *Lady Audley's Secret* (1862). Tennyson declared himself steeped in Miss Braddon: 'I am reading every word she ever wrote'.[40] Of course certain novels sold better than others and few people would have thought in precisely the same terms of, for example, *East Lynne* as of *Great Expectations*. But the creation of exclusive hierarchies was not a notable Victorian literary trait, however much it might have been so in other spheres. Gladstone, for example, was once spotted in the library of his club deep 'in the perusal of a book', and 'when eventually he put the book down and left the room, the engrossing volume proved to be ... [Rhoda Broughton's] *Red as a Rose is She*' (1870).[41]

Publishing was becoming big business. Substantial capital was required. George Smith spent £32,280 on the first four years' literary expenses of the *Cornhill* and £4,376 on illustrations, besides all the other costs of production. By the 1860s his firm's 'annual volume of trade' had risen to £600,000, though this included the operations of a lucrative banking and Indian agency which allowed him to plough money into publishing. Eventually in the early 1870s Smith became English agent for the German Apollinaris mineral water, made £1.5m profit from the venture, and used much of it to finance that wonderfully Victorian project, the *Dictionary of National Biography* (first published 1885–1900).[42] Even a more dubious character like Henry Colburn, who was widely regarded as dishonest and uninterested in either literary or production standards, could prove highly innovative, in his case in the use of massive advertising.[43] As publishers became

[39] Sutherland, *Victorian Novelists*, 43. Sales soon fell.

[40] Terry, *Victorian Popular Fiction*, 4.

[41] Ibid. 5. While Gladstone's detailed diary does not actually list *Red as a Rose*, it does record his reading Broughton's *Second Thoughts* (1880) and *Belinda* (1882–4): *The Gladstone Diaries*, ed. H. C. G. Matthew and M. R. D. Foot, 14 vols. (Oxford, 1968–94), x. 78, and xi. 313.

[42] Sutherland, *Victorian Novelists*, 43–4, 74; J. Glynn, *Prince of Publishers: A Biography of George Smith* (London, 1986), 114, 190–4; B. Q. Schmidt, 'The Patron as Businessman: George Murray Smith 1824–1901', *Victorian Periodicals Review*, 16 (1983), 3–14.

[43] J. Sutherland, 'Henry Colburn, Publisher', *Publishing History*, 19 (1986), 59–63.

more businesslike, so did their relationships with authors, who in turn responded with a new, though not universal, sense of efficiency. Trollope produced great novels with the speed of potboilers, Dickens laboured to organize *Dombey and Son* to suit publishing requirements, Bulwer-Lytton felt guilty about the hasty books of his youth, Thackeray crafted *Henry Esmond* with unprecedented care: 'and in the late 1850s we have with George Meredith and George Eliot artists more interested in narrative control and order than any who had hitherto written in English'.[44]

The characteristic mid-Victorian three-volume novel (issued at the huge price of one and a half guineas or 31s. 6d., well above the weekly wages of all but the most skilled artisan) stood at the top of a complex and variegated pyramid consisting of part publication (weekly or monthly in paper covers), serialization in weekly or monthly periodicals, initial publication in one or two volumes, rapid republication in 6s. volumes, slightly later republication as 2s. 'yellowbacks' for sale at railway-station bookstalls operated by W. H. Smith, and—for the really successful—collected editions of various kinds. Eliot's career reveals the variety of channels by which a successful writer could reach the public: *Scenes of Clerical Life* first appeared in *Blackwood's Magazine* (1857) at 2s. 6d. each issue, *Adam Bede* (1859), *The Mill on the Floss* (1860), and *Felix Holt* (1866) as three-deckers at 31s. 6d., *Romola* in the *Cornhill* (1862–3) at 1s. an issue, *Middlemarch* (1871–2) and *Daniel Deronda* (1874–6) in bi-monthly and monthly part-numbers respectively at 5s. each, and a complete 'Cabinet Edition' in twenty volumes was produced between 1878 and 1885.[45]

The economics of publishing meant that three-decker novels could be produced in small impressions and still make money. *Adam Bede* was a runaway success on initial sales of 3,250 at 31s. 6d. over five months and then another 11,500 in a two-volume version at 12s. over the next two years. In the 1850s the average three-decker print-run lay between 500 and 1,000; selling 1,500 was 'really considered a triumphant speculation'.[46] Trollope estimated that an impression of as little as 600 selling 550 ('a good success for a novel') would yield £212 profit split between publisher and author, while Bentley believed that an edition of 2,000 selling 1,500 would produce £532.[47] In a difficult world, the three-decker was a comparatively safe speculation, with the result that publishers were encouraged to take risks with new authors because the system possessed a kind of built-in insurance against loss.

[44] Sutherland, *Victorian Novelists*, 62. [45] Ibid. 39.
[46] Ibid. 190; *The Times*, 9 Feb. 1854.
[47] Gettmann, *A Victorian Publisher*, 125–6; G. L. Griest, *Mudie's Circulating Library and the Victorian Novel* (Newton Abbot, 1970), 58–60.

Such commercial developments, themselves created by wider social and economic changes, affected not simply the income and status of authors but the nature of writing itself. Publication in parts achieved respectable popularity with the appearance of *Pickwick Papers* in 1836–7, but generally proved a failure for all but the most successful writers.[48] The precise format could vary, but *Pickwick*'s twenty monthly shilling parts (the last two published as a single bumper issue) remained the norm. This meant that a complete novel could be bought for a pound rather than 31s. 6d., a significant but not a spectacular saving which extended the relevant audience but still kept it firmly within the middle class. More purchasers meant more money for authors and publishers, who together also benefited from the highly commercial look of the product—*Vanity Fair*'s parts, for example, were sandwiched between puffs for Invisible Ventilating Perukes and Improved Elastic Chest Expanders. By the late 1850s serialization in periodicals was beginning to supersede separate publication in parts as the older quarterlies were being challenged by new monthly magazines. These cost a shilling, which meant that readers could now obtain an instalment and much else besides for the same price as a monthly part. And even if the *Cornhill*'s opening circulation of 100,000 did not last, it was still selling 30,000 in 1865, while *Macmillan*'s had settled at about 20,000. Further openings still were provided by the appearance of 2d. weekly periodicals publishing respectable fiction, notably those with which Dickens was associated such as *Household Words* and *All the Year Round*. As a result, writers with sufficient drawing power could now play off one editor against another. Eliza Linton's work appeared in thirty-five periodicals, Trollope's in ten, that of Wilkie Collins, Hardy, and Reade in almost as many.[49]

Part and serial publication redistributed power between publisher and author. Editors and proprietors interfered mercilessly in the texts supplied to them and often did so in mid-stream. In the 1860s Bradbury & Evans constantly told the editors of their *Once a Week* (a rival of *All the Year Round*) what they should do in quite trivial respects. The editor of *Fraser's Magazine* ordered Kingsley to shorten his novel *Yeast* in 1848 because readers were expressing fatigue. Trollope clashed with *Good Words* over *Rachel Ray* in 1863, as did Hardy with the *Graphic* over *Tess of the D'Urbervilles* (1891). Dickens himself, as editor of *Household Words*, kept offering advice to Mrs Gaskell during the serialization of *North and South*

[48] M. H. Handrea, 'Books in Parts and the Number Trade', in R. G. Landon (ed.), *Book Selling and Book Buying* (Chicago, 1978), 34–41; Sutherland, *Victorian Fiction*, 87–106.

[49] B. Q. Schmidt, 'Novelists, Publishers, and Fiction in Middle-Class Magazines: 1860–1880', *Victorian Periodicals Review*, 17 (1984), 145–52.

in 1854–5. A new element of great potential uncertainty was thus added to authorial preoccupations. Falling sales drove Dickens to trim the plot of *Martin Chuzzlewit* (1843–4) and to inject more Mrs Gamp when Mrs Gamp proved popular. Both Dickens and Thackeray wrote their serials as they went along (though the former developed an increasing need to see the story as a unity from an early stage); Trollope and Eliot completed whole novels before dividing them into parts.[50] But just as the spread of serialization in the 1860s interposed potentially powerful editors (as well as publishers) between writers and readers, so changes in printing technology, by increasing the supply of type, not only made publication in separate parts less economically necessary, but allowed authors to undertake more accurate corrections in proof and thus 'control' the appearance of their works in an entirely new way.[51]

The nature of contracts could also influence the artistic and psychological state of an author's mind. When the still relatively unknown Thackeray was offered a contract by Bradbury & Evans for *Vanity Fair* specifying no fixed number of parts, he found himself with little incentive to plan for any definite length. Lever in 1845 signed a contract with Chapman & Hall for *The Knight of Gwynne* providing for not less than twelve and not more than twenty parts, which at least made it possible to envisage some planning horizons, however flexible. The already-famous Dickens was able in 1846 to agree with Bradbury & Evans that *Dombey and Son* should appear in exactly twenty parts. Sometimes it mattered little: Lever, for example, could turn the tap off with little obvious effect upon the final product. Sometimes it mattered a lot: Thackeray's *Henry Esmond* (1852), for which he had a generous contract with Smith for initial publication in volume form, was continuously plotted in a way none of his earlier novels had been. On the other hand, there can be little doubt that Thackeray (and others) sometimes found the pressure of serial writing invigorating and that the resulting sense of continuous resolution could prove a strength rather than a weakness.[52] Serial publication and high sales created a unique and continuing dialogue between author and reader and did so within a context of notable excitement and public concern. Writers saw the importance of ending each episode at a point of tension—indeed it was for failing to do

[50] S. Elwell, 'Editors and Small Change: A Case Study of *Once a Week* (1859–80)', in J. H. Wiener (ed.), *Innovators and Preachers: The Role of the Editor in Victorian England* (Westport, Conn., 1965), 25–7; K. Tillotson, *Novels of the Eighteen-Forties*, 2nd impression (Oxford, 1956), 32, 35, 42; Saunders, *Profession of English Letters*, 196.

[51] A. C. Dooley, *Author and Printer in Victorian England* (Charlottesville, Va., 1992), 3–6, 148.

[52] Sutherland, *Victorian Novelists*, 102–10; Shillingsburg, *Pegasus in Harness*, 29–30.

this that Dickens berated Mrs Gaskell. Readers wrote to authors as publication unrolled and much of the story still remained to be written. They also, of course, either increased or cut their purchases.

Victorian fiction was, then, the outcome, not simply of unaided creative genius, but of unprecedentedly intense collaboration and compromises between authors and publishers. The new commercial circulating libraries generated a particularly important set of influences. The largest was that founded by Charles Edward Mudie in 1843. By 1875 Mudie's had 125 local agents and was also carrying on a vast postal trade. During the twenty-two months beginning in January 1858, 391,083 volumes were added to a stock two-fifths of which consisted of fiction. One-guinea-a-year subscribers were allowed to borrow one volume (*not* one novel) at a time and could change this as often as they liked. As a result, few readers actually bought three-decker novels at 31s. 6d.—the bulk of sales went to libraries and Mudie's purchasing power obliged publishers to stick with the three-decker whether they wanted to or not. When Mrs Henry Wood's *The Channings* appeared in 1862 Mudie took 1,000 copies, W. H. Smith (his nearest rival) 104, all the other London libraries and booksellers together 479. This enabled Mudie to obtain large discounts—up to 60 per cent—which in turn gave him a vested interest in keeping the price of novels to the public as high as possible. He could, and did, influence the size of editions, the format, the price, the date of issue, even the binding. But he also greatly influenced plot and—being like W. H. Smith a man of high moral 'tone'—the handling of 'delicate' matters, so that Victorian novelists, with some exceptions, found themselves obliged to respond to the public, not directly, but through its representative in the shape of the great librarian.[53]

More and more did publishers pressurize writers into reacting nimbly to 'market forces'. Bentley ordered Lever to change his approach in the 1840s and told Melville and Le Fanu what was needed to improve sales. Even the successful and touchy Bulwer-Lytton developed characters in *The Caxtons* (1849) along lines suggested by Blackwood. Neither Thackeray's *Henry Esmond*, nor Eliot's *Middlemarch*, nor Trollope's *Framley Parsonage* can be fully appreciated unless seen as partnership productions. With *Framley Parsonage* (1860)—written under pressure because Smith wanted a 'clerical novel' (for which there was a vogue) rather than the almost-complete *Castle Richmond*—Trollope hit upon a brilliantly successful formula which was to stand him in good stead thereafter. In a still more precise way Charles

---

[53] Feather, *History of British Publishing*, 154; Griest, *Mudie's Circulating Library*, 38, 77–8; Gettmann, *A Victorian Publisher*, 260; Sutherland, *Victorian Novelists*, 29.

Kingsley's *Westward Ho!* (1855) was transformed into the popular (Crimean) wartime best seller it became by means of constant dialogue between author and the publisher Macmillan: the autobiographical form was abandoned and what Macmillan called the 'preachment' reduced.[54]

Because Mudie's subscribers tended to borrow one volume at a time, they not only needed to be persuaded to continue to another, but to be presented with a one-volume text which, though partial, still possessed a certain cohesion of its own. Given the sheer length of the three-decker enterprise, this often led to repeated 'summaries', digressions, extended descriptions, multiple plots, even chats with the reader—what Meredith called the 'rattle of small talk'[55]—the whole frequently punctuated with wrenching devices of the 'But now to return to our tale' variety. Responding to what the market seemed to 'require', Chapman & Hall insisted that Mrs Gaskell add more text to her first novel, *Mary Barton* (1848), so as to stretch it to three volumes. What she added (especially chapter 37) hit so many nails bang on the head that it greatly diminished the notion that the novel was, in effect, a 'tragic poem'. Gissing too was well aware that his early novels were too long and he cut them in later revisions and translations. 'Far more artistic', he believed, was the method 'of merely suggesting; of dealing with episodes, instead of writing summaries ... hinting, surmising, telling in detail what *can* so be told, and no more'.[56] Rhoda Broughton's big-selling *Not Wisely But Too Well* (1867) and *Red as a Rose is She* (1870) were both the result of frantic last-minute padding. Ten extra chapters were added to *Cometh Up as a Flower* (1867) in order to reach even two volumes. Broughton clearly found plotting long works almost impossible and her shift in the 1890s to shorter one-volume novels suddenly revealed talents of insight and feeling which had previously been buried under the mass of words.[57]

Commercial imperatives, however, always imposed a complex range of effects. While the work of Broughton, Gissing, and others was often damaged by the pressures of vocabular inflation, prolix writers like Reade and Mrs Humphry Ward were sometimes very usefully required to cut texts in order to make three-volume publication possible. The popular novels of Mary Elizabeth Braddon were at once damaged *and* energized by publishing demands, her genteel genuflections to Mudie matched by an understanding of the human mind under emotion which seems almost to

[54] Gettmann, *A Victorian Publisher*, 156–60; Sutherland, *Victorian Novelists*, 6, 122–5, 144–51, 179–85.
[55] Gettmann, *A Victorian Publisher*, 255.
[56] Griest, *Mudie's Circulating Library*, 99–100; Gettmann, *A Victorian Publisher*, 254.
[57] Sadleir, *Things Past*, 85.

have been deepened by the necessity to write so often and so much.[58] Again, Mrs Oliphant's middle-brow 'Carlingford' novels, such as *Salem Chapel* (1863) and *Miss Marjoribanks* (1866), set among the aristocracy, professional families, and tradesmen of a provincial town show how the pressures of Victorian publishing were never entirely inimical to either astringency or well-wrought realism. However, by the mid-1880s the three-decker was under serious threat. Ten years later a changing market killed it off, by undermining the power of the circulating libraries at exactly the moment when artistic repugnance at its procrustean demands had become acute.[59]

Altogether greater than the sales of even popular authors like Eliot and Trollope were those of forgotten writers who hacked away in the less elevated reaches of the nineteenth-century publishing world. Blackwood sold 73,398 books by Eliot between 1866 and 1876. Mrs Henry Wood's *East Lynne* achieved sales of no less than 430,000 between 1861 and 1898. But G. W. M. Reynolds's *The Mysteries of London* (first published in parts in the 1840s) probably sold well over a million copies, while a number of popular periodicals and papers sustained circulations consistently in six figures. Only Dickens (of whose writings 4,239,000 'volumes' are supposed to have been sold in the dozen years after his death) could hold his own in such company.[60] At the top of this lower world stood 'improving' weekly journals catering for skilled workers and the growing lower middle class, notably the *Penny Magazine* (1832–45), the *London Journal* (1845–1912), and the *Family Herald* (1842–1939). In the mid-1850s the combined sales of the last two exceeded three-quarters of a million a week. Their sixteen closely printed pages included adventure stories, general fiction, answers to problems, an improving essay or two, household hints; and their vast circulations helped to create a pool of common material for private fantasy quite as powerful and far more ubiquitous than those produced elsewhere.[61]

---

[58] Griest, *Mudie's Circulating Library*, 101; Sadleir, *Things Past*, 78–9.

[59] Gettmann, *A Victorian Publisher*, 256–63.

[60] R. D. Altick, 'Best Sellers', in Altick, *The English Common Reader: A Social History of the Mass Reading Public 1800–1900* (Chicago, 1957), appendix B; id., 'Nineteenth-Century English Best Sellers: A Further List', *Studies in Bibliography*, 22 (1969), 197–206; id., 'Nineteenth-Century English Best Sellers: A Third List', *Studies in Bibliography*, 39 (1986), 235–41; A. Humphreys, 'G. W. M. Reynolds: Popular Literature and Popular Politics', in Wiener (ed.), *Innovators and Preachers*, 3–4.

[61] S. Mitchell, 'The Forgotten Woman of the Period: Penny Weekly Family Magazines of the 1840s and 1850s', in M. Vicinus (ed.), *A Widening Sphere: Changing Roles of Victorian Women* (London, 1977), 29–51; P. Anderson, *The Printed Image and the Transformation of Popular Culture 1790–1860* (Oxford, 1991), *passim*.

Distinctly lower was 'sensation' literature. Following on from the elec-trifying 'confessions' and 'dying speeches' which had formed the staple of the publisher, James Catnach, in the 1820s and 1830s came a tribe of successors—by mid-century perhaps ten such for every publisher working above the threshold—turning out Gothic fantasies like *Varney the Vampire* and *The Pirate's Bride*. Plagiarism was common, simplified versions of Dickens (notably crude slapstick Pickwicks) being especially popular. In many ways this sector was the most commercially innovative of all. It certainly pioneered many of the techniques later adopted by the high-class trade. Works were issued in weekly or fortnightly parts, though at 1d. or 2d. rather than 1s. or half-a-crown, and sales could exceed those of Dick-ens's parts by a factor of ten. Two opening issues were sold for the price of one. A free copy of the first issue of a new series was tipped into the last of a concluding one. Works were constantly reprinted and advertised on pos-ters, billboards, and by sandwich men. Some penny-dreadfuls went on virtually for ever: one version of *Black Bess* ran for more than 2,000 pages.[62]

Yet however forcefully a capitalist market was now able to shape the activities of publishers and authors alike, 'industry' itself remained a distant off-stage presence even in those Victorian novels which concern themselves with it at all. The North of England was seen as a great undifferentiated blot with 'giant chimneys overlooking all, blackening all with smoke. The rain coming down with a wiry persistency... the sky low, leadenhued'. Indus-trial workers were ant-like and indistinguishable: 'swarms of men and women... who pour forth from the factories at the sound of the bell'.[63] The mid-century wave of so-called industrial novels by Mrs Gaskell, Dickens, and others was soon over: by 1855 it had beaten itself out. Almost nothing distinctly *industrial* was to appear again until the 1890s: George Eliot's *Felix Holt* (1866) was about reform, Reade's *Put Yourself in His Place* (1870) about trade-union villainy, Gissing's *Demos* (1886) about the urban rather than the specifically industrial working class. Industrial pro-cesses remained obscure to most novelists and not least to Dickens, who never, for example, in *Little Dorrit* (1855–7), describes the engineer Doy-ce's crucial 'invention' at all. Few real industrialists appear in his pages. Even *Hard Times* (1854), his one novel centred on industry, never depicts the inside of a factory, unlike Mrs Gaskell's *Mary Barton* (1848). Nevertheless,

[62] Sutherland, *Victorian Novelists*, 5–6; Anderson, *Printed Image*, 162; Altick, *English Common Reader*, 287–93; L. James, *Fiction for the Working Man 1830–1850* (London, 1963), 50–2; Feather, *History of British Publishing*, 157; Saunders, *Profession of English Letters*, 202.
[63] Harriet Parr, *Maude Talbot* (1854), cited M. F. Brightfield, *Victorian England in its Novels*, i. 269; Harriet Frances Thynne, *The Adventures of Mrs Hardcastle* (1869), cited ibid. i. 272.

Dickens did gradually develop a sustained critique of industrialism in general, though not a subversive one (no novelist did that). While Mrs Gaskell, for all her perception, believed that the horrors of industry were but a misunderstanding which might be patiently broken down, Dickens knew his main task to be that of keeping human feeling alive in a mechanical age, not of transforming mechanization as such or even pretending (like Ruskin) that it could somehow all be undone. On the one hand, Dickens found his longing for a simpler more humane past constantly challenged by the excitement he felt in the new technology; on the other, he saw the machine as a symbol for the sins of society as a whole. For all Dickens's faith in progress, machines in novels like *Dombey and Son* stand eloquent witness to what the terrible union of moral indifference and economic power could bring about.

Like most Victorian novelists Dickens felt more at home when dealing with capitalism in general than industrialism in particular. And without ever being crudely deterministic he believed that capitalism's contemporary manifestations played a significant part in transforming evil, greed, materialism, and crime into more than mere abstract phenomena floating in some timeless void. The most powerful organizing concept in his later novels is the recurring metaphor of society as one huge market-place, with social relations (not excluding marriage and friendship) mediated through predominantly economic frames of reference.[64] Money itself is the theme of all his novels: 'getting, spending, owing, bequeathing provide the intricacies of his plots; . . . there is hardly a story without at least one character in whom the love of money is a master humour'.[65] Its very centrality allowed Dickens (and others like Reade) to use it both as a *deus ex machina* to provide moments of extraordinary release when money transfigures poverty and as a generator of those happy endings in which bags of gold enable characters to slide into that workless prosperity (what Orwell called 'a sort of radiant idleness'[66]) which the industrious Dickens so often seems to extol. As his novels developed in depth and sensibility, so the view of money and 'finance' changes. In the early books the typical financier is not a stockbroker but a small operator in mortgages and loans. Though companies are already often shady (the United Metropolitan Improved Hot Muffin and Crumpet Baking and Punctual Delivery Company in *Nicholas Nickleby* (1838–9) is a notable example), money remains most influential at

---

[64] J. M. Brown, *Dickens: Novelist in the Market Place* (London, 1982), 17, 23.

[65] H. House, *The Dickens World*, 2nd edn. (London, 1942), 58–60.

[66] G. Orwell, 'Charles Dickens' (1st publ. 1940), in *The Collected Essays, Journalism and Letters of George Orwell*, ed. S. Orwell and I. Angus, 4 vols. (London, 1968), i. 446.

an individual level. With *Little Dorrit* (1855–7) and *Our Mutual Friend* (1864–5) the fortunes of almost everyone hang upon the careers of big financial capitalists, the whole thing is an intricate *system*, the world of investment no longer bears any relation at all to the world of work.

Money stood so central to fictional preoccupations because the rising prosperity of the middle classes could, in individual cases, so easily be destroyed by illness, rash investments (as Tennyson and Thackeray found to their cost), or bad luck. Debt was a recurring theme, for, as Trollope noted in the fourth chapter of *Framley Parsonage*, 'there is no cholera, no yellow-fever, no small-pox, more contagious'. Bankruptcy features prominently for the same reason, in, among many others, Dickens's *Dombey and Son* (1847–8), Thackeray's *The Newcomes* (1853–5), Reade's *Hard Cash* (1863), George Eliot's *Middlemarch* (1871–2), and Hardy's *The Mayor of Casterbridge* (1886). Because unwise speculation could so easily undermine middle-class confidence, financial swindles provided novelists not only with potentially exciting devices for pushing characters abruptly up or down the economic ladder, but with metaphors for society as a whole. The two best-known fictional swindlers of the time constitute but the tips of a large literary iceberg, though even they differ in revealing ways. Dickens's Merdle in *Little Dorrit* (1855–7) is a subtler and more illuminating character than Trollope's Melmotte in *The Way We Live Now* (1875). The latter, painted in crude, bold colours, is harsh and overbearing, but largely a caricature. Merdle, by contrast, is a reserved, dull man, with little to say for himself, energized only when in direct contact with money and the power it brings. Trollope sees his swindler battening upon the good old England of embarrassed squires; Dickens's more sinister figure hovers over the nation as a whole.

The writing of plays stood even closer to capitalist finance, and Victorian playwrights long suffered rather than benefited as a result. In the 1840s £50 to £100 an act for a new West End play was on the high side; elsewhere the sums were much lower. Tom Taylor was paid only £200 for *The Ticket-of-Leave Man* which ran for 407 performances at the Olympic in the 1860s and remained one of the most popular of all Victorian melodramas.[67] The status of playwrights was low compared with that of star actors: parallels with carpenters and shoemakers were common. In 1843 Bulwer-Lytton reckoned that a play took him at least half as long as a novel to write, but (even if successful) yielded much less than half the cash.[68] Not until 1860 did a

[67] M. R. Booth, *Theatre in the Victorian Age* (Cambridge, 1991), 142–3.
[68] J. R. Stephens, *The Profession of the Playwright: British Theatre 1800–1900* (Cambridge, 1992), pp. xiii, 48.

breakthrough take place and then almost by accident. When in that year the
Irish playwright, Dion Boucicault, took his *Colleen Bawn* to Benjamin
Webster at the Adelphi, he suggested he share profits rather than be paid
a fixed sum. Within twelve months he had received £10,000.[69] Although it
took time for others to take the hint, Boucicault (by far the most professional dramatist of his time) had effectively introduced book-publishing
remuneration methods into the theatre and thereby greatly increased the
prospects of those at the top of the tree. F. C. Burnand, for example, made
£2,000 out of *Ixion* (1863) and at least as much from *Black-Eyed Susan*
(1866). Charles Reade, at a time when his novels were in decline, cleared a
staggering £20,000 from *Drink* in 1879 (his most successful novel earned no
more than a fifth of that). By the last quarter of the century a small band
(the 'Dramatic Ring')—including Sydney Grundy, Henry Arthur Jones
(who got £18,000 over the years from *The Silver King*), and Arthur Wing
Pinero (£30,000 the richer from *The Second Mrs Tanqueray*)—had begun to
find it possible to make a prosperous living out of playwriting alone.[70]

    That such dramatists were few in number had less to do with the fact
that mid-Victorian plays possessed small literary merit (a good many
meritless novelists did well enough) than with the economics of the contemporary theatre. Whereas the production of novels was a co-operative
venture between writers and publishers, the theatre was long dominated by
star actors and managers, often, indeed, they were one and the same. This
meant that once theatrical finances began to improve as touring possibilities
were extended by the railways, long runs appeared in London, and audiences became more respectable (something Queen Victoria did much to
encourage), the prime beneficiaries proved to be not writers at all, but
impresarios and a very few leading actors and actresses.[71] However, acting
in general (though a growing occupation) remained ill-paid, most actors,
then as now, finding it impossible to get regular work—many 'rested', some
starved.[72] Wages for the novice remained static until the end of the century
at perhaps 15s. or £1 a week. A 'good' touring company in the 1890s paid
25s. for small parts, £2 or £3 for 'a line of business' (actors specializing in

---

[69] A. Nicoll, *A History of Late Nineteenth-Century English Drama 1850–1900*, 2 vols.
(Cambridge, 1946), i. 69; Stephens, *Profession of Playwright*, 55.
[70] Nicoll, *English Drama*, i. 69; Stephens, *Profession of Playwright*, 52, 77.
[71] M. R. Booth, *Theatre in the Victorian Age*, 7–9, 13, 18–19, 40; Nicoll, *English Drama*, i.
5–9; Booth, 'Going on Stage', in J. Altholz (ed.), *The Mind and Art of Victorian England*
(Minneapolis, 1976), 119.
[72] M. Baker, *The Rise of the Victorian Actor* (London, 1978), 83; G. Taylor, *Players and
Performances in the Victorian Theatre* (Manchester, 1989), 10; Booth, 'Going on Stage', 107,
113.

particular roles such as villains or 'heavy men'), and £5 for a lead. Even in London, payment outside the West End was not much better, though rates in the 1890s (but not the 1880s) probably represented a small improvement on those of half a century before. For such sums run-of-the-mill actors had to provide costumes, pay for digs, and carry an enormous workload. Henry Irving played 428 parts in his first thirty months on stage in the 1850s, Squire Bancroft took on forty new roles in thirty-six nights at Cork in 1861. If by the late 1880s a 'first-rate' West End actor was getting as much as £50 a week, a select handful of stars—often involved in management—could earn very much more.[73]

Until the 1890s (when financial 'backers' first appeared) manager-lessees dominated the business, choosing and casting actors, selecting administrative staff, paying salaries, picking plays (and changing their texts), and sometimes acting too. Tolerably large resources were needed—probably a minimum of £2,000 (often borrowed) in the London of the 1860s. Costs at the top end of the business could be high: Kean's 1850s Shakespeare performances at the Princess's involved 550 persons, Irving in 1881 used thirty gasmen and ninety carpenters. Even so, until the 1880s the basic cost of operating an average London theatre was not excessive. Rents were not yet exorbitant, wages (save for stars) were modest. With a house two-thirds full a manager could clear £40 a night. Of course some went bankrupt: F. B. Chatterton failed in mid-*Cinderella* in the late 1870s owing £40,000. Others operated at the fringes of respectability, their whole existence (as Lever noted in 1861) 'passed in promises, excuses, evasions, and explanations'. But there was also very good money to be made. Wilson Barrett recorded average profits of £2,067 a year at the Grand Theatre Leeds in the early 1880s, mostly from pantomime. In the 1870s and 1880s the Bancrofts retired with over £174,000 and George Conquest, W. H. Kendal, and J. L. Toole died worth, respectively, £64,000, £66,000, and £80,000.[74]

The obvious directness and extent of the theatre's commercial imperatives, and the powers and profits these gave to managers, ensured that those who actually wrote the plays tended, with rare exceptions, to find themselves at the end of a very long financial queue indeed. In only one other field of mid-Victorian cultural endeavour did the creative artist fare even worse—that of music.

[73] Booth, *Theatre in the Victorian Age*, 118–19; id., 'Going on Stage', 114–16; Baker, *Rise of the Victorian Actor*, 133.

[74] Booth, *Theatre in the Victorian Age*, 28–37, 41; C. Lever, *One of Them* (London, 1861), 194; Baker, *Rise of the Victorian Actor*, 118.

3. MUSIC

The Victorians, it seemed, could do anything with music—except compose it. Nineteenth-century Britain was awash with music: that which has survived was foreign, that which was British is largely forgotten. Of the many operas, oratorios (at least 150), symphonies (over 60), concertos (over 90), concert overtures (over 100) known to have been produced by British and Irish composers between 1800 and 1860 virtually nothing has lasted save a few hymns, some church music by S. S. Wesley, a handful of hackneyed songs, some piano pieces by John Field.[75] And, leaving Gilbert and Sullivan aside, much the same could be said for the twenty years thereafter. In this qualitative sense the famous jibe, first produced about 1914, that England was 'Ein Land ohne Musik' was true. Yet in every other sense the Victorians were deeply musical. The number of music editions copyrighted increased from 151 in 1835 to 8,063 in 1901, the number of pianos manufactured from 23,000 in 1850 to 75,000 in 1910, the percentage of London parish churches maintaining choral services rose from five in 1858 to thirty-eight in 1882, the number of professional musicians (most of them performers or teachers) increased sixfold between 1841 and 1901.[76] Few communal events were complete without music. One observer writing in 1887 thought it no exaggeration 'to say that with the exception perhaps of natural science . . . there is no branch of human knowledge, or of human art, in which the change that the half-century of the Queen's reign has wrought, is so marked as it is in love of music'.[77]

Neither love nor enthusiasm nor ubiquity, however, generated much on the creative side. Considerable energy has been devoted to demonstrating that Victorian composition was not as feeble as is often claimed. Most of this, while occasionally unveiling pieces of modest merit, has been unconvincing stuff. While one authority believes that the 'English Romantics' of the 1830s and 1840s—Michael Balfe, John Barnett, William Sterndale Bennett, Edward Loder, and the like—were poised to emulate the achievements of their literary counterparts, another considers the period one of thin and brazen borrowings.[78] Rosy-tinted spectacles have detected 'renaissances' here, there, everywhere. The 1840s are supposed to have

[75] N. Temperley, 'Domestic Music in England 1800–1860', *Proceedings of the Royal Musical Association*, 85 (1958–9), 31.

[76] N. Temperley, 'The Lost Chord', *Victorian Studies*, 30 (1986), 7.

[77] F. Hueffer, 'English Music during the Queen's Reign', *Fortnightly Review*, NS 41 (1887), 899.

[78] N. Temperley, 'Introduction', in Temperley (ed.), *Music in Britain: The Romantic Age 1800–1914* (London, 1981), 1–5; J. Sachs, 'London: The Professionalization of Music', in A. Ringer (ed.), *Man and Music: The Early Romantic Era* (London, 1990), 217–18.

experienced take-off in the shape of Henry Bishop (the first musician knighted by a sovereign), the emergence of the singing-class movement, and Vincent Novello's first cheap music publications. More generally, if only slightly less unconvincingly, 1880 has been seen as an *annus mirabilis* with the foundation of the Guildhall School of Music, the appearance of Grove's *Dictionary*, and performances of Villiers Stanford's 'Evening Service' and Hubert Parry's *Prometheus Unbound*. But when some commentators begin to hail Sullivan, Parry, and Stanford as the chief 'architects of a renaissance', Sterndale Bennett as 'the biggest figure of the mid-century', and Alexander Mackenzie and Frederick Cowen as representing 'the achievements of Victorian music at their highest', it would seem that the sound of barrel-scraping is drowning out all else.[79] Mackenzie himself claimed in 1886 that, 'excepting Verdi, Gounod and Brahms, of whom only the last may be said to be in full activity' (Verdi's *Othello* appeared the next year and his *Falstaff* in 1893), Parry, Stanford, Sullivan, and Cowen were 'the peers, if not more than the peers, of their musical counterparts in other countries'.[80] So much for Grieg, Tchaikovsky, Dvořák, and Bruckner, or the early masterpieces of Mahler and Richard Strauss.

In the first half of the century there was much talk of the worthy Cipriani Potter (or 'Botter' as Beethoven called him—'he visited me a few times, he seems to be a good fellow') and even more of Sterndale Bennett, hailed by Mendelssohn and Schumann as a great hope for the future.[81] Then a little later the energetic George Alexander Macfarren mounted a campaign to write music in a distinctly English idiom and, in effect, to do in England what other nationalist musical movements were doing elsewhere, notably in Russia. He took up patriotic themes for operas like *Robin Hood* (1860) and *The Soldier's Legacy* (1864); he was much influenced by folk-song and adopted a bluff diatonic style; he used musical 'tags' as a kind of primitive leitmotiv. Wagner conducted his overture *Chevy Chase* in London in 1855 and thought it possessed a 'peculiarly wild, passionate character', though he found 'Macfarrinc' himself 'pompous [and] melancholy' (and Potter 'an elderly amiable contrapuntist').[82] And that was about the measure of it. Potter and Macfarren toiled mightily, but to little effect. Sterndale Bennett's

[79] M. Kennedy, 'Music', in Ford (ed.), *Cambridge Guide to the Arts*, vii. 283; F. Howes, *The English Musical Renaissance* (London, 1966), 20, 32, 39, 51.

[80] Kennedy, 'Music', 288.

[81] P. M. Young, 'Orchestral Music', in Temperley (ed.), *Music in Britain*, 364–5; J. R. Sterndale Bennett, *The Life of William Sterndale Bennett* (Cambridge, 1907), 54.

[82] N. Temperley, 'Musical Nationalism in English Romantic Opera', in Temperley (ed.), *The Lost Chord: Essays on Victorian Music* (Bloomington, Ind., 1989), 143–57; Kennedy, 'Music', 276.

talent withered amidst the deserts of teaching and administration. Even the single-minded Hugo Pierson, who emigrated to Germany in 1839 to escape the English musical scene, failed to live up to early promise. The most truly original Victorian works produced before Elgar are to be found either in the specialized Anglican church music of S. S. Wesley and a handful of others or among those light operas of Arthur Sullivan and W. S. Gilbert directed to a conservative middle-class audience whose values they gently mock but in reality applaud.

A satisfactory reason for this failure is difficult to find. Not that developments abroad were invariably more impressive. After all, Austria produced no major composer between Schubert's death in 1828 and the rise of Bruckner in the late 1860s. But for a country as economically and politically powerful as Britain it was a curious and conspicuous failure none the less. Some general disadvantages are obvious enough. Of all the Victorian arts music was least in touch with contemporary trends in thought and most clearly lived 'a life below stairs in the social complex'.[83] Composers were rigidly good-mannered—all 'solid reputable citizens and ratepayers of the United Kingdom, model husbands and fathers' as Arnold Bax later put it[84] (but then Haydn had been respectable enough). In general, too, the musical scene was suffused with a knee-jerk deference to continental models which, while understandable, proved unhelpful. The profession was long dominated by Italians and Germans. Little English music was played at concerts: only ten works by five composers at all the Philharmonic Society's concerts between 1850 and 1870. Until the 1880s almost all the operas presented at London's two chief venues—Her Majesty's Haymarket and Covent Garden—had, by immutable tradition, to be given in Italian: Balfe's *Bohemian Girl* (1843) was eventually done in 1858 as *La Zingara*, Wagner's *Der fliegende Holländer* (1843) in 1870 as *L'Olandese dannato*.[85]

Macfarren blamed everyone and everything in sight: slavish love of foreigners, a feeble aristocracy, a 'foreign court', even spelling the word programme in a French way (rather than program).[86] What, however, even he could not deny was that, in a pre-recording age, the undoubted Victorian increase in demand for music meant an equivalent increase in the number

[83] S. Banfield, 'The Artist and Society', in Temperley (ed.), *Music in Britain*, 17.

[84] A. Bax, *Farewell, My Youth* (London, 1943), 28.

[85] H. Raynor, *Music and Society since 1815* (London, 1976), 107; D. Burrows, 'Victorian England', in J. Samson (ed.), *Man and Music: The Late Romantic Era* (London, 1991), 268; Kennedy, 'Music', 278; M. Hurd, 'Opera: 1834–1865', in Temperley (ed.), *Music in Britain*, 315; N. Burton, 'Opera: 1865–1914', ibid. 343.

[86] G. A. Macfarren, ' "The English are not a Musical People" ', *Cornhill Magazine*, 18 (1868), 344–57.

of musicians. In England and Wales numbers rose from about 6,600 in 1841 or 4.4 per 10,000 population to 38,600 in 1891 or 13.3 per 10,000. Most of these were teachers and many of them women (by 1891 almost half).[87] Except for a few, teaching was a cut-throat affair. As no formal qualifications were required, the market was overcrowded and the pay low. Permanent situations worth as little as £70 and £40 a year attracted 176 and 97 applicants respectively in 1893.[88] Outside cathedral towns—where an organist was 'respected and admired' and might visit 'on equal terms his most worthy neighbours'—such posts were rare.[89] Even a gifted composer like Sterndale Bennett was forced to teach until he dropped: in 1848 at the age of 32 he taught the piano for 1,632 hours in addition to his duties at the new Queen's College in Harley Street. He taught wherever he could—in Maidstone, Ipswich, Brighton, anywhere. A typical day involved leaving home at 4 a.m., travelling to some distant school, teaching for nine hours, and returning at 11 p.m. Concerts and composing had to be fitted in as best they might. As a result, the social standing of musicians was low. 'A musician', noted an Oxford don in a pamphlet entitled *What Shall We Do with Music?* (1856), 'let him be ever so talented and exemplary in moral conduct, ranks scarcely above an ordinary artizan'.[90] Public perceptions were shaped by job specifications like that in 1868 for the 'Gloucester County Asylum: Assistant Carpenter Wanted. Wages £30 per annum, with board, lodging, and washing. Must be a Musician and be able to play at sight.' Small wonder that Elgar, from his twenty-second to twenty-seventh year bandmaster of the staff of a lunatic asylum, should have been patronized by his father-in-law when in 1889 he married the daughter of a major-general.[91] Hugo Pierson's father, a royal chaplain, was shocked by his son's wish to compose: to him musicians were not gentlemen and no gentleman would wish to be a musician. John Stainer was brought up in a cultivated home and possessed both artistic and literary ability, something not generally associated with English musicians at the time. Too often, indeed, a kind of canny commercialism did duty for artistic talent. Typical was Sir George Smart, at once a 'cautious and acquisitive man of business' and an 'astute juggler of engagements who gave value for money in a

---

[87] C. Ehrlich, *The Music Profession in Britain since the Eighteenth Century* (Oxford, 1985), 235–6; C. K. Salaman, 'On Music as a Profession in England', *Proceedings of the [Royal] Musical Association*, 6 (1880), 115–17.

[88] Ehrlich, *Music Profession*, 123–5.

[89] Salaman, 'On Music as a Profession', 111; Burrows, 'Victorian England', 268.

[90] Sterndale Bennett, *Life of William Sterndale Bennett*, 196–7; Ehrlich, *Music Profession*, 42.

[91] Ehrlich, *Music Profession*, 52; Burrows, 'Victorian England', 291.

competitive world with his own interests securely at heart'. He persuaded a Viceroy of Ireland to make him a knight, played the organ at Queen Victoria's coronation, and, as a sideline, sold pianos on commission.[92]

As regards music, professionalization amounted not to either high earnings or monopoly powers, but to a shift from a situation of patronage to one of somewhat rickety independence. By the 1850s amateurs had ceased to be taken seriously as remunerated performers, and successful musicians had become commercial entrepreneurs developing new methods for the management and promotion of concerts. At the popular end of the market composers could reach almost industrial rates of production. Charles Coborn (who wrote 'Two Lovely Black Eyes') saw himself as 'a tradesman supplying a public want', while Joseph Tabrar ('Daddy Wouldn't Buy Me a Bow-Wow') claimed—somewhat improbably—to have written 17,000 songs between the 1860s and the mid-1890s.[93] And as, in effect, performing tradesmen, players tried constantly to improve their conditions and pay. They had little success until the last decade of the century when a number of competing organizations—some with vocational aspirations like the élitist London Orchestral Association, some with a trade-union bias like the Amalgamated Musicians' Union—began to establish themselves.[94] However, with musicians in general enjoying low social esteem, composition (never, in any case, very rewarding financially) can hardly have seemed a particularly attractive enterprise.

Formal training was in short domestic supply. The most promising composers went to Germany: Charles Neate and Cipriani Potter belonged briefly to Beethoven's circle in Vienna, Sterndale Bennett, Hugo Pierson, Arthur Sullivan, even the ballad romanticists William Wallace and Michael Balfe, all spent substantial periods in Germany, as later did Stanford and, more briefly, Parry.[95] Superficially all this might seem very like the prolonged and frequent visits of Victorian painters to Italy. In reality it was very different. While the painters sought unmediated understanding of classical and renaissance art, which they could then transform into distinctly native forms, the composers were actually taught by German musicians along German lines and, more often than not, emerged as dutiful

[92] Banfield, 'The Artist and Society', 19; P. Charlton, *John Stainer and the Musical Life of Victorian Britain* (Newton Abbot, 1984), 10; A. V. Beedell, *The Decline of the English Musician 1788–1888* (Oxford, 1992), 119–20.

[93] W. Weber, *Music and the Middle Class: The Social Structure of Concert Life in London, Paris and Vienna between 1830 and 1848* (London, 1975), 11, 37–8; D. Russell, *Popular Music in England, 1840–1914: A Social History* (Manchester, 1987), 92.

[94] Ehrlich, *Music Profession*, 146.

[95] N. Temperley, 'Solo Song: Britain and the United States', in G. Abraham (ed.), *The New Oxford History of Music*, ix. *Romanticism 1830–1890* (Oxford, 1990), 771–87.

shadows of some Germanic original. Alexander Mackenzie is a perfect example: his piano quartet of 1873, while vigorous and often interesting, is entirely Schumannesque in idiom—though Schumann had been dead almost twenty years. For long neither the facilities provided by the Royal Academy of Music founded in 1822 nor by Oxford and Cambridge amounted to much. The Oxbridge chairs of music were virtually unsalaried, no real teaching was provided until the 1860s and 1870s, and even then mostly for non-residents. The Academy too was chronically underfunded, though after more than forty years of existence it is estimated that one player in six employed in the five major London orchestras (all of them shifting and overlapping affairs) had been trained there.[96] Many musicians were in fact 'trained' by family and friends or in cathedral choirs—John Stainer is a good example—and, indeed, families of musicians developed along much the same lines as families of carpenters. However, in the last quarter of the century, an astonishing expansion of formal, though at first rather feeble, training did take place, with the foundation in 1875 of Trinity College, London, in 1876 of the National Training School (replaced in 1883 by the Royal College of Music), and in 1880 of the Guildhall School in London. For its part, the state gave little help. Gladstone admittedly took the trouble to appear at the opening of the Royal College, but only to deliver a speech so vacuous (he would have been much better informed about literature or painting) that Stanford dismissed it as 'charming piffle, but piffle none the less'.[97] With the bulk of those passing through such places destined to teach, Trinity College inaugurated the great British obsession with music examinations: by 1885 5,000 were sitting its tests and the musician's career had begun its ceaseless quest for 'qualifications'.[98] The drive behind this was a desire to control entry and create a true profession. But economic and social realities torpedoed such aspirations, with the result that musicians were obliged to pursue an endless paper chase without enjoying any of the expected benefits.

What made life so difficult was not simply the low rates of pay but the scarcity of regular employment. In 1889 George Bernard Shaw thought music the worst-funded of all the arts, lacking as it did 'constant and enlightened patronage such as the upper classes accord to racing, millinery, confectionery, and in a minor degree to literature and painting'.[99] Serious

[96] Charlton, *John Stainer*, 85–95; B. Rainbow, 'Music in Education', in Temperley (ed.), *Music in Britain*, 29–39; Ehrlich, *Music Profession*, 80.

[97] Ehrlich, *Music Profession*, 108.

[98] Ibid. 113–17. In 1888 the Associated Board of the Royal Schools launched the external examination system which still exists today.

[99] J. M. Golby (ed.), *Culture and Society in Britain 1850–1890* (Oxford, 1986), 236–7.

creative work brought virtually no direct financial reward. Even the few safe jobs were poorly paid. Stainer got £120 a year from Magdalen College Oxford in 1860 for playing the organ and training the choir, S. S. Wesley £60 from Hereford Cathedral in 1832. By the late 1850s cathedrals paid about £150 (plus a house), London parish churches £50; even by the 1890s few organists and choir masters got much above £300.[100] In 1849 Wesley published an angry pamphlet in which he bitterly demanded that a public which could regularly find a thousand guineas for one of Landseer's paintings might think it possible to find the £500 a year necessary to enable cathedral organists to drop their endless free-lance teaching: 'Before our Palestrinas can find a home at Cathedrals, the difficulties of musical composition must be appreciated, and our artists allowed to rank with men of true eminence in other walks of life.'[101]

Capitalist considerations inevitably shaped both the character of the mid-Victorian musical enterprise and the manner in which its profits were distributed. The owners of new halls, like the St James's Hall opened in 1858 and the Crystal Palace after its removal to Sydenham in 1852, promoted concert series primarily in order to fill empty seats with paying customers. The former mounted the famous Monday 'Pops', the latter the weekly concerts conducted by August Manns, which, by the 1880s, had become the most adventurous and best in London. Music publishers did the same. Chappell & Co partly financed St James's Hall and promoted the 'Pops'. Boosey & Co started the London ballad concerts in 1867. Novello (who had an enormous catalogue of ecclesiastical scores) promoted oratorios and the like (indeed, the mid- to late Victorian popularity of Bach's *St Matthew Passion* owed more to Novello's efforts than to the better-known Mendelssohn revival of 1829).[102] By the 1860s London's art-music public was more broadly based than that of any other European city. By the 1870s a new concert world had been established in a recognizably modern form both in London and the provinces. But while a number of separate 'taste publics' certainly existed—those who preferred the elevated concerts of the Philharmonic Society, those who preferred Louis Jullien's showy and

[100] Banfield, 'The Artist and Society', 28; Charlton, *John Stainer*, 22; P. Chappell, *Dr S. S. Wesley 1810–1876: Portrait of a Victorian Musician* (Great Wakering, 1977), 20; Ehrlich, *Music Profession*, 44, 124.

[101] S. S. Wesley, *A Few Words on Cathedral Music and the Musical System of the Church* (London, 1849), 68–9, also 52 and 61.

[102] R. Nettel, *The Orchestra in England* (London, 1946), 203–16; P. A. Scholes (ed.), *The Oxford Companion to Music*, 10th edn. revised J. O. Ward (Oxford, 1970), 229–30; D. B. Scott, *The Singing Bourgeois: Songs of the Victorian Drawing Room and Parlour* (Milton Keynes, 1989), 122–3.

eclectic presentations, those who preferred tunes that could be whistled in the streets—they all functioned within a broadly inclusive musical culture marked more by catholicity than by rigid divisions.[103] A vast middle ground had become common property. *Il trovatore*, for example, was known not only to fashionable metropolitan audiences, but to the galleries of countless provincial theatres, to brass bands, even (in a markedly altered form) to the poverty-stricken barrel-organ audiences of the streets. The kind of music performed in parlours and drawing-rooms encompassed songs like 'The Holy City' (of concert hall origin), 'Kathleen Mavourneen' (written for the parlour), and 'I dreamt that I dwelt in Marble Halls' (opera). Amateur pianists tackled anything from 'A Maiden's Prayer' to the simpler works of Beethoven, Chopin, and Mendelssohn. Brass bands in particular—far more than the middle-class choral societies—mingled light and art music in a peculiarly rich way: by the 1870s Wagner was already common in their variegated repertoires.[104]

Music halls too were becoming big business and many musicians performed promiscuously in a wide range of venues. By 1866 London had thirty-three major halls with an average capacity of 1,500 and capitalization of £10,000, though some were much bigger. Singing stars and a few comic turns were the chief beneficiaries: in 1885 one West End hall was paying about £200 a week to artistes. By the late 1850s the first agencies catering for music-hall performers appeared, a dozen years earlier than those for opera singers and virtuoso instrumentalists.[105] The manager of Covent Garden enjoyed average profits of £15,000 a year from opera in the 1870s and already in 1866 Hallé's Manchester concert season was making a profit of more than £2,000. Sheet-music and instrument retailing expanded greatly, so that in the 1880s most towns of even 10,000 inhabitants had at least one music shop: in 1890 Bradford (population 266,000) had fifty-six.[106]

In every sense music was being exposed to the demands of a competitive, hard-headed, and rapidly developing commercial society. But while a new

---

[103] Weber, *Music and the Middle Class*, 7–12, 21, 29, 44, 100; E. D. Mackerness, *A Social History of English Music* (London, 1964), 201; Raynor, *Music and Society*, 109–12; Banfield, 'The Artist and Society', 16.

[104] R. Middleton, 'Popular Music and the Lower Classes', in Temperley (ed.), *Music in Britain*, 79; Russell, *Popular Music*, 5–6, 102–4, 147, 187–92.

[105] Russell, *Popular Music*, 76–7; P. Bailey, 'A Community of Friends: Business and Good Fellowship in London Music Hall Management c.1860–1885', in Bailey (ed.), *Music Hall: The Business of Pleasure* (Milton Keynes, 1986), 38; P. A. Scholes, *The Mirror of Music 1844–1944: A Century of Music Life*, 2 vols. (London, 1947), i. 202–3.

[106] R. Pearsall, *Victorian Popular Music* (Newton Abbot, 1973), 222; M. Kennedy, *The Hallé Tradition: A Century of Music* (Manchester, 1960), 32; Russell, *Popular Music*, 141.

musical world was being created in which a growing middle-class audience demanded substantial repertories performed repeatedly over long periods rather than a succession of new works, the advent of a glut of run-of-the-mill musicians in the half-century after 1840 meant that, in general, pay rates fell.[107] The few really large incomes were amassed by singers: even the best-known instrumentalists (most of them foreign) earned comparatively modest amounts. The £120 a year offered to Charles Hallé in 1849 to conduct the 'Manchester concerts' meant that he had to rely on piano pupils for the bulk of his income (his orchestral players got between £10 and £42). Sterndale Bennett's salary in 1866 as Principal of the Royal Academy of Music was £150 plus fees, for which he was obliged to 'be on the spot at stated times every day'. Composing as such earned its British practitioners almost nothing at all: between 1836 and 1871 Sterndale Bennett got an average of £36 a year.[108] In comparison with the incomes of leading novelists and painters this was small change. In the performing arts the creative side was poorly rewarded and, indeed, so was the performing side (save for a few stars). Business managers took the lion's share. In writing and painting, where no performer intervened, commercialization distributed its financial benefits more evenly. Once performers were involved, a society which rarely allocated wealth to its initial producers preferred to concentrate attention upon the 'appealingly re-creative rather than the uniquely creative individual'.[109]

4. PAINTING

Victorian painting presents a host of ambiguities. Once despised, its overall standing now ranks much higher than that of Victorian music, though still much lower than that of Victorian literature. What, in the present context, above all distinguished its practitioners was the money the most successful could earn—far, far more than their musical and more even than their literary equivalents. As incomes increased, so numbers and respectability increased also: estimates suggest perhaps a few hundred active artists in 1850, by 1892 almost 5,000. Whereas in the 1830s all but a handful had seen themselves as superior craftsmen who produced to order, by the end of the century contemporary paintings were being valued as expressions of indi-

[107] A. Ringer, 'The Rise of Urban Musical Life between the Revolutions, 1789–1848', in Ringer (ed.), *Man and Music*, 10; J. Rosselli, 'Italy: The Centrality of Opera', ibid. 195; Ehrlich, *Music Profession*, 162–3.
[108] Raynor, *Music and Society*, 29; Ehrlich, *Music Profession*, 44–50; Kennedy, *Hallé Tradition*, 25–7; Sterndale Bennett, *Life of William Sterndale Bennett*, 351, 412–13.
[109] Ringer, 'Urban Musical Life', 10.

vidual and independent personality.[110] But though the photographs reproduced in F. G. Stephens's *Artists at Home* in 1884 do indeed show lavish
studios framing well-dressed men of property wearing deliberate and
exquisite artistic uniforms of velvet jackets and embroidered caps, in social
terms much of this remained comparatively skin deep. It was after all less
than forty years since a third of Royal Academicians had been sons of
tradesmen and only William Dyce among them had possessed a degree.
Nor did even those few mid- and late Victorian artists who had begun to
enjoy aristocratic hospitality do so as anything other than 'interesting'
guests, invariably—and pointedly—invited without their wives.[111]

None the less, the steady social climb of the later nineteenth century was
as deliberate as it was broadly successful. High prices tempted some
painters to work with manic speed so as to capitalize on a popularity which
might at any moment disappear. Frank Holl, for example, drove himself to
nervous breakdown and an early grave in 1888 by producing twenty or
more of his literal and forceful portraits a year in order to pay for two grand
houses designed by the fashionable architect Norman Shaw. Between 1865
and 1868 Lawrence Alma-Tadema painted fifty-five pictures (about half of
them substantial oils, portraits, and water-colours); between 1871 and 1877
he averaged thirteen a year of his meticulous studies of figures in historical
settings. William Frith—a painter whose popularity did wane late in life—
coupled a wonderfully middle-class domesticity (splendid house, govern-
ess, sons at Harrow) with a second hidden household for a mistress and
seven children.[112] His picture of 1853, *The Sleepy Model*, characteristically
shows the girl fully clothed and himself dressed as if on the way to his
stockbroker. In much the same mode the art critic, Marion Harry Spielmann, never missed an opportunity to persuade his readers in the *Graphic*,
the *Pall Mall Gazette*, and the *Magazine of Art* that British painters were
uncontaminated by continental bohemianism, that they were 'gentlemen',
that they treated their models with decorum.[113]

In the 1860s the Volunteer Corps of Artists Rifles provided proof of
respectability: in silver-grey uniforms and singing their marching song,
'Cum Marte Minerva', William Morris, Dante Gabriel Rossetti, Holman

[110] M. B. Huish, 'Whence Comes the Great Multitude of Painters?', *Nineteenth Century*, 32 (1892), 720; J. Maas, *Victorian Painters* (London, 1969), 257.

[111] P. Gillett, *The Victorian Painter's World* (Gloucester, 1990), 32–3.

[112] J. Treuherz and others, *Hard Times: Social Realism in Victorian Art* (London, 1987), 73–4; V. G. Swanson, *Sir Lawrence Alma-Tadema: The Painter of the Victorian Vision of the Ancient World* (London, 1977), 24; Gillett, *Victorian Painter's World*, 96.

[113] J. F. Codell, 'Marion Harry Spielmann and the Role of the Press in the Profession-alization of Artists', *Victorian Periodicals Review*, 22 (1989), 10–13.

Hunt, Leighton, and Millais paraded in the gardens of Burlington House to demonstrate their willingness to repel military (as well as cultural) invasion from France.[114] At the top of the artistic tree perched a few very fine characters indeed. Charles Eastlake moved easily in royal circles. So did Landseer, who affected an aristocratic drawl 'till it became a second nature'.[115] Francis Grant, President of the Academy 1866–78, was a minor country gentleman himself and a noted rider to hounds. G. F. Watts thought his surname insufficiently 'distinguished', while 'Ned' Jones turned himself into Edward Burne-Jones at the age of 32.[116] Knighthoods were scattered more generously than in literature or music, baronetcies appeared in the last decades of the century, and in the year of his death (1896) Leighton was made a baron (as Tennyson had been a dozen years before). Leighton's death was a national event: prior to burial in St Paul's the body lay in state at the Academy and on the coffin were his palette, brushes, and mahlstick, his many honours on a cushion beneath.[117] Alma-Tadema's appetite for distinctions was greater still and more actively sought. His powers, noted a fellow artist, 'only gave him pleasure when extrinsic evidences are awarded him . . . He could make a necklet of orders and crosses for his wife, and still wants more.' Once established such men could name their terms; the lordly Leighton, for example, set aside days when selected dealers could visit his studio and be met not by him but by a servant discreetly carrying a list of prices that were as high as they were non-negotiable.[118]

The financial heyday of the successful Victorian painter lasted from the 1850s to the 1880s. Rewards at the top of the market rose substantially, driven in part by the increasing commercialism of the reproduction trade. While in 1846 the *Art-Union* journal was amazed at Landseer's getting almost £7,000 from four pictures (£2,400 for the paintings and £4,450 for the copyrights), by 1860 not an eyebrow would have been raised by this.[119]

[114] L. and R. Ormond, *Lord Leighton* (New Haven, 1975), 53.

[115] D. Robertson, *Sir Charles Eastlake and the Victorian Art World* (Princeton, 1978), 112; *A Victorian Canvas: The Memoirs of W. P. Frith*, ed. N. Wallis (London, 1957), 101; R. Ormond, *Sir Edwin Landseer* (London, 1981), 8–16.

[116] Gillett, *Victorian Painter's World*, 18–19, 57–8.

[117] Ibid. 57–8; P. Fuller, 'Fine Arts', in Ford (ed.), *Cambridge Guide to the Arts*, vii. 163. Also buried in St Paul's were Landseer, Turner, Millais, Alma-Tadema, Poynter, and Holman Hunt (Maas, *Victorian Painters*, 14).

[118] *Autobiographical Notes of the Life of William Bell Scott*, ed. W. Minto, 2 vols. (London, 1892), ii. 216; Gillett, *Victorian Painter's World*, 55; J. F. Codell, 'The Artist's Cause at Heart: Marion Harry Spielmann and the late Victorian Art World', *Bulletin of the John Rylands University Library of Manchester*, 71 (1989), 148.

[119] G. Reitlinger, *The Economics of Taste*, 3 vols. (London, 1961–70), i. *The Rise and Fall of Picture Prices 1760–1960*, 91; J. Maas, *Gambart: Prince of the Victorian Art World* (London, 1975), 20, 41–3; Robertson, *Sir Charles Eastlake*, 206.

The moderately successful genre painter, Charles Robert Leslie, made more money in the last decade of his life (the 1850s) than in the whole of his previous career. The Pre-Raphaelites did well from the start: the £150 the 20-year-old Millais got for *Christ in the House of his Parents* in 1849 would have astonished Turner and Wilkie at the same age, while Rossetti (a less 'popular' artist) was making £3,000 a year in his early forties. Indeed, the progress to modest (sometimes immodest) prosperity that so often forms the theme of artistic biographies in the third quarter of the century bears a remarkable congruity to the Victorian notion of the self-made man. Small wonder that Samuel Smiles's *Self-Help* in 1859 already included a chapter on 'Workers in Art', in which Martin, Leslie, Etty, and others were awarded the medal of Victorian Endeavour first class for their 'unflagging industry and indomitable perseverance'.[120]

By the middle of the century the prices of the most desired contemporary paintings had begun to match and not infrequently exceed those of the 'equivalent' old masters. In the 1870s, for example, Van Eyck's *The Three Martyrs at the Sepulchre* went for £336 and Titian's *Man in a Red Cap* for £94. 10s., as against £5,932 for Landseer's *The Otter Hunt*, £10,500 for Holman Hunt's *The Shadow of the Cross*, and £7,350 for Edwin Long's *The Babylonian Marriage Market*.[121] Prices of a thousand pounds a picture became common for a growing number of successful painters working in a variety of styles and dealing with a variety of subjects: Holman Hunt (religion), Leighton (historical, classical), Alma-Tadema (ditto), Landseer (animals, scenes of Highland life), Millais (Pre-Raphaelite brilliance, then sentimentality and portraits), Tissot (fashionable society), Frith (modern life), and many more. At the height of his fame Millais earned between £20,000 and £40,000 a year (well over a million pounds in current terms). Frith repeatedly collected £5,000 and more from dealers. Holman Hunt (who took advice from Dickens on what he should charge) sold a replica of *The Light of the World* to the statistician-shipowner, Charles Booth, for 12,000 guineas. Hunt, who depended entirely on painting and had negligible help from studio assistants, left £163,000, though he always moaned in public about money and claimed that 'flourishing artists do not gain more than one-third of what is gained by men of the same standing in other professions'. At least three Victorian artists died worth more than

[120] Gillett, *Victorian Painter's World*, 26; Reitlinger, *Economics of Taste*, i. 143; B. Denvir, *The Late Victorians: Art, Design and Society, 1852–1910* (London, 1986), 7; S. Smiles, *Self-Help: With Illustrations of Conduct and Perseverance*, popular edn. (London, 1897), ch. 6, pp. 154–201, at p. 184.

[121] D. Farr, *English Art 1870–1940* (Oxford, 1978), 355–7; Robertson, *Sir Charles Eastlake*, 124–8, 171, 189–90; Reitlinger, *Economics of Taste*, i. 99.

£200,000: John Linnell, John Gilbert, and Landseer (who in 1865 alone earned £17,352).[122]

Most successful artists tended to react to this mid-Victorian bonanza by combining conspicuous expenditure with a distinctly commercial approach. Just as Trollope listed the exact sums produced by his books, so Frith—who discussed his art with the satisfaction of a self-made businessman—recorded many of the prices earned from youth onwards. The success of Frith's brilliant 'modern life' pictures such as *Ramsgate Sands* (1854), *Derby Day* (1858), and *The Railway Station* (1862) persuaded other artists to try a similar approach, some of whom, like George Elgar Hicks and William Maw Egley, also kept meticulous account books noting the price of every picture and drawing sold.[123] John Linnell's highly developed business sense enabled him to amass a fortune from his idiosyncratic, sometimes brilliant, sometimes feeble, invariably repetitive ideal landscapes. Alma-Tadema (see Plate 8) was the shrewdest of all: 'he carefully supervised the ownership of copyright to his paintings, and never allowed anybody to make money from his work unless he was also to benefit'.[124] And while there had always been businesslike painters—Rubens is an obvious example—the economic and cultural atmosphere of Victorian Britain encouraged the financial exploitation of artistic gifts as never before. Some artists, having hit upon a saleable formula, stuck to it like limpets: Thomas Sidney Cooper, who went on turning out well-mannered cows and sheep until his nineties, boasted that he could finish two such pictures 'every morning before breakfast'. Portraits provided the quickest returns: they took less time than detailed classical scenes or contemporary panoramas, though their prices undoubtedly fluctuated according to an artist's reputation for grander works. Yet, in the end, nothing was certain: even the hard-headed Frith, having saved little in his glory days, died in 1909 aged 90 with an estate of only £1,310.[125]

The majority of artists never of course earned enormous sums, though the rise in prices at the top undoubtedly helped to increase rewards elsewhere. The Artists' General Benevolent Institution (founded in 1814) received many applications from distressed painters, from miniaturists

[122] W. Holman Hunt, 'Artistic Copyright', *Nineteenth Century*, 5 (1879), 424; Maas, *Victorian Painters*, 14; Reitlinger, *Economics of Taste*, i. 95; Ormond, *Sir Edwin Landseer*, 12.

[123] Wallis (ed.), *A Victorian Canvas*, 13–14, also 48, 54, 55, 58; Maas, *Victorian Painters*, 12, 146; C. Wood, *Victorian Panorama: Paintings of Victorian Life* (London, 1976), 12.

[124] Maas, *Gambart*, 155; id., *Victorian Painters*, 42–4; Swanson, *Sir Lawrence Alma-Tadema*, 34; C. Wood, *Olympian Dreamers: Victorian Classical Painters 1860–1914* (London, 1983), 123.

[125] Wood, *Victorian Panorama*, 204–5; A. Noakes, *William Frith: Extraordinary Victorian Painter* (London, 1978), 126, 152.

(who had once earned £500 a year) ruined by photography, from water-colourists ruined by lithography, though few from those specializing in landscapes or marine and figure painting. Even the outstanding Ford Madox Brown—painter of those two great Victorian icons, *Work* (1852–65) and *The Last of England* (1855)—was selling pictures in the 1850s for £5: the marvellous *English Autumn Afternoon* (1852–4) took him many months and fetched nine guineas. His diary is full of worries about how to feed his family. And although *Work* was eventually bought by a dealer for £1,320, Brown's fortunes remained low until he was commissioned in the late 1870s to paint murals in Manchester Town Hall.[126]

By contrast, successful painters lost little time in cocooning themselves within commissioned houses designed to serve both as a confirmation of their success and a stage upon which to play to a gallery of colleagues, patrons, and friends. The architect, Norman Shaw (himself a Royal Academician), was much in demand. J. C. Horsley RA began the trend with some Shaw alterations in 1860; then followed (among many more) E. W. Cooke RA 1861, F. W. Goodall RA 1870, Marcus Stone RA 1876, Luke Fildes RA 1877, Edwin Long RA 1878 and 1888, Frank Holl RA 1881.[127] Herkomer took a dozen years in the 1880s and 1890s to build a bizarre house in Hertfordshire called Lululaud in honour of his wife—Romanesque outside, Gothic inside, it cost £75,000. Leighton's house in Kensington was—and still is—like a restrained and tasteful Hollywood set. Alma-Tadema's cost £70,000 simply to 'improve', showed few signs of restraint, and—together with its owner's paintings—clearly provided much of the visual inspiration for film directors like Cecil B. De Mille. Appropriately for the great bravura painter of marble there was so much marble that the many distinguished visitors invited to recitals by Caruso and Tchaikovsky were asked to wear slippers so as not to damage the floors.[128] Not only, therefore, did the mid-Victorian art boom allow its beneficiaries to create houses mirroring the opulence of their pictures, it also allowed them to turn their own personalities into works of art, to become not merely artists but 'artistic' as well.

---

[126] C. A. Kent, ' "Short of Tin" in a Golden Age: Assisting the Unsuccessful Artist in Victorian Britain', *Victorian Studies*, 32 (1989), 494–5; *The Diary of Ford Madox Brown*, ed. V. Surtees (London, 1981), 82; Maas, *Gambart*, 149–50; J. Treuherz, 'Ford Madox Brown and the Manchester Murals', in J. H. G. Archer (ed.), *Art and Architecture in Victorian Manchester* (Manchester, 1985), 119, 171.

[127] H.-R. Hitchcock, *Architecture: Nineteenth and Twentieth Centuries*, 4th (2nd integrated) edn. (Harmondsworth, 1977), 294; A. Saint, *Richard Norman Shaw* (London, 1976), 153–5.

[128] Gillett, *Victorian Painter's World*, 112–15; Swanson, *Sir Lawrence Alma-Tadema*, 24–7.

Crucial in making this possible was a small group of dealers, who, about the middle of the century, began to deal in contemporary paintings (previously artists had tended to sell directly). In part this reflected worries about old master fakes, in part a more general shift in taste. The three most famous Victorian dealers (though there were many others) included only one Englishman, Thomas (later Sir Thomas) Agnew, whose firm began operations in Manchester and later expanded to London and Liverpool. In 1851 it had assets worth £27,000 and was making profits of £4,000 a year; ten years later the assets had risen to £61,000. By then Agnew's two major rivals, the Belgian Ernest Gambart (see Plate 8) and the German Louis Flatow, were also well-established, the former with capital of £100,000 in 1866, the latter with perhaps £60,000.[129] Effectively 'picture merchants', Gambart and Flatow were brilliant showmen who believed that large prices attracted attention and that pictures should be exploited in as many ways as possible. Flatow was loud-mouthed and near-illiterate, but possessed an uncanny flair for picking subjects that would 'go'. He offered Frith £4,500 for *The Railway Station* before it was finished, paid another £750 for 'exhibition rights', and reputedly cleared £30,000 in the form of resale, reproduction payments, exhibition fees, and so forth. Gambart, a suaver individual, bought Holman Hunt's *Finding the Saviour in the Temple* for 5,500 guineas, made £4,000 from exhibition fees, £5,000 from engravings, and finally sold the picture for another £1,500. By creating enormous interest, dealers could put such pictures singly into a room, and, charging perhaps a shilling or so admission, realize very substantial sums: 21,500 people, for example, paid to see *The Railway Station* in London, while other pictures were sometimes taken on provincial and international tours as well (a version of Holman Hunt's *The Light of the World* proved notably popular in New Zealand and Australia).[130]

Gambart and Flatow were, above all, outstandingly creative entrepreneurs: Flatow once took 14,020 gross steel pens from the manufacturer and collector, Joseph Gillott, in return for six Dutch old masters. Gambart, in particular, was reliable and honest and prepared to take a long view. The young Alma-Tadema inveigled him into his studio in 1864, Gambart saw a picture, bought it, and announced 'turn me out twenty-four other pictures of this kind and I will pay for them at progressive prices, raising the figure

---

[129] Maas, *Gambart*, 42–3, 135, 201; L. S. King, *The Industrialization of Taste: Victorian England and the Art Union of London* (Ann Arbor, Mich., 1985), 25–6, 183; J. Seed, ' "Commerce and the Liberal Arts": The Political Economy of Art in Manchester, 1775–1860', in J. Wolff and Seed (eds.), *The Culture of Capital* (Manchester, 1988), 53.

[130] Noakes, *William Frith*, 74–5; Maas, *Victorian Painters*, 164; id., *Holman Hunt and the Light of the World* (London, 1984), *passim*.

after each half dozen'. And when the contract was complete in 1868 a new one was made for another forty-eight, again at rising prices. Other painters, like Linnell, also had multi-picture contracts with Gambart, while the dealer's success in exploiting the work of the strong-minded Holman Hunt was masterful in every respect.[131] Capitalism in art had, as in so many other spheres, effectively squared the financial circle, in that most painters taken up by a good dealer got better results than they could ever have achieved by handling sales themselves.

The ability of dealers and artists to obtain substantial rewards depended in large part upon the dynamic growth of the Victorian reproduction industry. New electrotyping developments were making it possible to produce much bigger editions of steel engravings without loss of detail, while reductions in glass duty lowered the price of frames. Whereas previously the market for a five-guinea proof in a two-guinea frame had been small, Gambart and others were able to sell two-guinea proofs in 5s. frames to a much wider (though still a largely middle-class) public. Gambart's exploitation of Rosa Bonheur's famous *Horse Fair* showed what could be done. He bought the picture and copyright in 1855 for £1,600 and paid £800 to have it engraved. The first 2,000 proofs, priced at varying amounts from twelve guineas (for 'Artist's Proofs') downwards, yielded an amazing £23,000, which was then augmented by selling ordinary prints struck repeatedly thereafter from steadily deteriorating plates.[132] Small wonder that artists like Frith and Holman Hunt became highly expert at working copyrights through dealers. Already by 1847 half of Landseer's income was coming from copyright fees on engravings: eventually he received £60,000 from one publisher alone.[133]

The print explosion was driven, not by critics or a cultural élite, but by a comparatively broad section of the middle class which was therefore able to influence art in much the same way as the book-buying public was able to affect the character of the novel. High print sales had the effect of increasing the prices of original pictures, as happened with Landseer. Indeed, pictures as such, though they might still appear to be finished products, were more and more often becoming stages in a commercial sequence leading from the first impulse to the production (and appreciation) of multiple copies.

[131] Maas, *Gambart*, 45–7, 58; Swanson, *Sir Lawrence Alma-Tadema*, 14–17; L. Ormond, review of Maas, *Gambart* in *Victorian Studies*, 21 (1978), 271.
[132] Maas, *Gambart*, 30, 159–60; Reitlinger, *Economics of Taste*, i. 98–9; A. Dyson, *Pictures to Print: The Nineteenth-Century Engraving Trade* (London, 1984), 67.
[133] Reitlinger, *Economics of Taste*, i. 149–50; Noakes, *William Frith*, 68; Maas, *Gambart*, 238–9; Ormond, *Sir Edwin Landseer*, 12; C. Lennie, *Landseer: The Victorian Paragon* (London, 1976), 244.

410 MONEY AND MENTALITIES

Already in the 1830s the London Art Union had started to provide institutional underpinning for this print-driven extension of interest in the fine arts by soliciting subscriptions of a guinea a year (the same minimum Mudie demanded) in return for an annual engraving of a famous painting by a British artist and the chance to win original pictures in a lottery. Under the dynamic leadership between 1840 and 1868 of George Godwin (a kind of cultural Mr Pooter) it attracted a steady 12,000 to 14,000 subscribers and, most important of all, allowed the lottery winners to choose their own paintings up to a certain sum (usually about £300 to £400). By 1860 the cumulative amount spent had reached £138,662 on prize paintings, £64,623 on engravings, and £30,000 on other art products.[134] However, the appearance of chromolithography in the mid-1880s, by making it possible to reproduce in hundreds of thousands and sell the results at a shilling, brought this particular gravy train to a halt. Although sales increased enormously—Luke Fildes's *The Doctor* (1891) reputedly sold a million in the United States alone[135]—artists lost as a result. Whereas the tight control and relatively high prices of the mid-Victorian years had proved an ideal combination for artist and dealer alike, mass production, when it came, greatly increased the power of those who actually manufactured the multiple copies and thus their share of the profits too.

If by the end of our period art taste was unquestionably being fashioned by middle-class sensibilities, already in the first half of the century collections including a substantial proportion of contemporary works had been formed by a few notable patrons with industrial or commercial interests—Robert Vernon's fortune had, for example, come from horse dealing during the Napoleonic Wars, John Sheepshanks's from industry, Joseph Gillott's from the mass production of pens and nibs. But it was men like the Manchester industrialist Daniel Grant (who happily spent his horse-race winnings on pictures by Etty), Charles Meigh, a potter from Hanley, Charles Birch, a Birmingham colliery owner, George Knott, a city grocer, Sir Coutts Lindsay, a merchant banker, and the engineer Isambard Kingdom Brunel, who, somewhat later, came to constitute the most authentic patrons of a now-maturing industrial age. As F. G. Stephens, a member of the Pre-Raphaelite Brotherhood turned critic, noted in 1871, 'the so-called middle class of England has been that which has done the most for English art. While its social superiors "*praised*" Pietro Perugino, neglected Turner,

[134] King, *Industrialization of Taste*, 1–2, 41, 45, 141–4, 158; A. King, 'George Godwin and the Art Union of London 1837–1911', *Victorian Studies*, 8 (1964), 101–30.
[135] Wood, *Victorian Panorama*, 101–2.

let Wilson starve...the merchant princes bought of Turner, William Hunt, Holman Hunt, and Rossetti'.[136] In and out of each other's offices, factories, and houses, local collectors created and sustained a remarkable series of distinct but not dissimilar culture circles. Thus, while in New-castle the members of a close-knit business community not only controlled municipal affairs but developed a high degree of consensus in favour of Pre-Raphaelite pictures, their contemporaries in Birmingham preferred very different styles. Self-made businessmen often proved especially innovative because of a willingness to weed out early dross and replace it with more exciting material: 'brilliant and daring in their rise to the top...they were not afraid to admit their mistakes in the art market'.[137] By contrast, the purchases of super-rich plutocrats like Edward Hermon, Sam Mendel, Albert Levy, Henry William Bölckow, and Thomas Holloway had, by the 1870s and 1880s, become little more than passive expressions of metropo-litan fashion and dealers' advice. For Holloway and his like only the grandest would do, hence the popularity of painters like Alma-Tadema and Edwin Long, master producers of what were in effect high bourgeois versions of earlier grand aristocratic styles. However, outside such rarefied circles, the most widely diffused aesthetic impact of the middle classes upon the character of Victorian art can be summed up by the word 'domesticity', which, in turn, tended to mean smaller pictures and domestic themes. 'An old man reading his Bible', noted a writer in *Blackwood's Magazine* in 1869, 'is thought to be more the right sort of thing than a saint gazing into heaven.'[138]

The overall effect of this was, however, more complex than the original impetus. Most obviously it encouraged the kind of domestic realism cap-tured at its best in Frith's modern-life paintings and at its worst by artists without number. But it also encouraged, almost recreated, a love for meticulous still-life painting, so much so, that a minor school of so-called 'bird's nest' painters headed by William Henry Hunt was kept in constant work. Given that this was so, it is unsurprising that Ruskin's greatest impact upon picture-buying should have lain, not in his praise for late Turners or the aesthetics of certain Pre-Raphaelites, but in his emphasis

---

[136] Maas, *Victorian Painters*, 164; F. G. Stephens, 'English Painters of the Present Day. XXI—William Holman Hunt', *The Portfolio*, 2 (1871), 38.

[137] D. S. MacLeod, 'Mid-Victorian Patronage and the Arts: F. G. Stephens's *The Private Collections of England*', *Burlington Magazine*, 128 (1986), 601. Since this chapter was written, D. S. MacLeod has published her invaluable *Art and the Victorian Middle Class: Money and the Making of Cultural Identity* (Cambridge, 1996).

[138] [J. B. Atkinson], 'The London Art Season', *Blackwood's Edinburgh Magazine*, 106 (1869), 230.

upon the moral worth of detailed craftsmanship in general.[139] Indeed, it was exactly the lack of 'hard work' of this literal kind that drove Ruskin to denounce Whistler for having flung 'a pot of paint in the public's face' by charging 200 guineas for a picture (*The Falling Rocket*) that had allegedly taken only two days to complete. Though Whistler won only a farthing's damages in the ensuing libel action in 1878, it was above all this episode that marked the beginning of the end of that intense, reciprocal, and comprehensive relationship between artist and public so characteristic of the mid-Victorian age.

Among the most evident manifestations of this special and temporary mid-Victorian reciprocity between culture makers and a growing (but still limited) body of middle-class culture consumers was a fondness for sentimentality: childhood, the happy cottage, home sweet home, all were grist to the mill. By the same token, a reticence about 'disagreeable' things constrained even the work of social realists like Holl, Fildes, and Herkomer. Representations of motherhood, for example, possessed deep iconic popularity, but pregnant women hardly feature in paintings at all. Yet, if the middle class's preference for Frith over Titian may now seem strange, at least nineteenth-century patronage tended to avoid the cultural necrophilia so evident in certain other periods—not least our own. In 1856 the novelist, Wilkie Collins (brother of the Pre-Raphaelite painter Charles Allston Collins), caught the conjoined confidence and philistinism of it all with breezy precision.

These rough and ready customers were not to be led by rules or frightened by precedents. . . . Sturdily holding to their own opinions, they thought incessant repetitions of Saints, Martyrs, and Holy Families, monotonous and uninteresting—and said so . . . They wanted interesting subjects; variety, resemblance to nature; genuineness of the article, and fresh paint; they had no ancestors whose feelings, as founders of galleries, it was necessary to consult . . . so they turned their backs valiantly on the Old Masters, and marched off in a body to the living men.[140]

What the new collectors did share with their aristocratic forerunners was a willingness to go beyond participating in the creation of new styles and to demand, in addition, that painters be prepared to undertake such precise and specific adjustments to their pictures as customers might require. In this respect the Victorian art world was a transitional one: the status of painters rose but the tradition of the artisan craftsman willing to take orders from patrons survived until the very end of the century when the 'Art-for-

---

[139] Maas, *Victorian Painters*, 171; Gillett, *Victorian Painter's World*, 28–9.
[140] Wilkie Collins, *A Rogue's Life* (serialized in *Household Words* in 1856, 1st publ. in book form, 1879), ch. 5.

Art's-Sake' movement began to tilt the balance in favour of greater artistic autonomy. Mid-Victorian painters willing to respond in detail to what individual buyers wanted included the successful as well as the marginal. Of course there were exceptions, though few consistent ones. Not many buyers had the courage to ask grandees like Leighton to alter anything. Sargent was notoriously resistant and would hit back by changing his pictures in the opposite direction to that required. Far more, however, saw their art as something necessarily mediated through public response and therefore neither fixed nor 'finished'. The wealthy landscape painter, John Linnell, was happy enough in the 1850s to have Gambart lay down subjects 'comprising good and well defined foreground with figures and animals and other accessories . . . what is called sketchy to be avoided'.[141] In 1860 Gambart reported to Gillott that Clarkson Stanfield, one of the most distinguished of Victorian sea painters, had uncomplainingly 'repainted the sky in the Dutch picture which he has much improved—also worked on the water'.[142] Madox Brown undertook all sorts of changes to *Work* after the collector, Thomas Plint, wanted one of the young women on the left to be 'holy-looking . . . with a book or two and tracts'.[143] James Leathart, the Gateshead industrialist, refused in the 1870s to pay for Rossetti's *Sir Tristram and La Belle Iseult* until Sir Tristram's neck had been 'reduced in thickness and his hair in quantity', which Rossetti duly did. Similarly, Abraham Solomon removed certain 'objectionable features' from his now-lost *Drowned! Drowned!*, while Herkomer cheered up the workhouse with flowers and happier looks when he transformed the engraving *Old Age* (1877) into the oil-painting *Eventide* (1878). In 1853 even the touchy Holman Hunt altered the face of the (fallen) woman in one of his most famous pictures because its first owner found it too 'painful': he softened the face and then, significantly, offered to change the title from *The Awakening* to *The Awakened Conscience*.[144]

The pressures of public taste and the broad sympathies which many painters shared with the new urban middle classes shaped both their critiques and their celebrations of Victorian society. Moral judgements tended towards the conventional, as the many pictures of spendthrifts—

---

[141] Maas, *Gambart*, 58.

[142] Maas, *Victorian Painters*, 61; id., *Gambart*, 130.

[143] J. Wolff, 'The Culture of Separate Spheres' in Wolff and Seed (eds.), *Culture of Capital*, 124; C. Arscott, 'Employer, Husband, Spectator: Thomas Fairbairn's Commission of *The Awakening Conscience*', ibid. 161–2.

[144] MacLeod, 'Mid-Victorian Patronage', 601; Treuherz and others, *Hard Times*, 10–11; T. S. R. Boase, *English Art 1800–1870* (Oxford, 1959), 285–6; Arscott, 'Employer, Husband, Spectator', 159–60.

The Last Day in the Old Home (1861) by R. B. Martineau is a powerful example—make clear. Gambling attracted particular opprobrium: Elmore's *On the Brink* (1865) and Frith's *The Salon d'Or, Homburg* (1871) neatly mix financial and other kinds of decadence into a powerful cocktail of condemnation. Frith's five-picture series of 1878 'The Road to Ruin' moves from Cambridge to Ascot, to arrest for debt (with wife and children in attendance), 'struggles' in a broken-down lodging, and eventual 'ruin' prior to suicide. Two years later Frith painted another series called 'The Race for Wealth'—a remarkable pendant to Trollope's *The Way We Live Now* of 1875. Indeed, the tendency to depict 'realities' as Victorian pre-conceptions wished them to be, informed nineteenth-century art no less than nineteenth-century literature. Just as the actual details of industrial work were rarely described in contemporary novels, so painters too tended to treat industry tangentially, if at all, not least because they found it pictorially so difficult to reconcile the ideal with the real. William Bell Scott's *Iron and Coal* (*c*.1861) is unusual in depicting men actually involved in an industrial process (though the chief 'man' is in fact Sir Walter Trevelyan who commissioned the picture); Madox Brown's *Work* is allegorical; Herkomer's *On Strike* (1891), by definition, about inaction rather than activity. Industrialization as a physical presence was something middle-class patrons either wished to avoid or to see only in some highly unspecific way. So strong was this feeling, that, when local businessmen came to commission Madox Brown to paint murals in Manchester Town Hall celebrating civic and commercial pride, they insisted he paint historical rather than contemporary scenes even with regard to topics like Science, Education, and Mechanical Invention.[145]

Because Victorians wanted to be touched but not pained, a comprehensively oblique pictorial vocabulary was deployed in order to suggest rather than capture the grimmer shores of life: sad letters = emigration, resting workers = factory exploitation, pale convalescents = disease, funerals = death. Before the 1870s only a handful of pictures went anywhere near to touching the heart of such matters—some by Frederick Walker, perhaps some by Richard Redgrave—and only one (Henry Wallis's static and brutally moving representation of exploited death in *The Stonebreaker* of 1857–8) to the heart itself. Then, for a brief interlude of twenty years, a group of social realists, of whom Fildes, Holl, and Herkomer were the chief, produced a (comparatively small) number of powerful depictions of poverty painted more starkly than anything before in Britain. Why this should have happened just then is difficult to say. It preceded the onset of

[145] Treuherz, 'Ford Madox Brown and the Manchester Murals', 175.

the 'Great Depression' and probably had more to do with developments in graphic art—all three undertook commissions for the new illustrated periodicals of the time where their engravings greatly impressed Van Gogh—than with any independent response to hard times as such.[146] All three produced powerful paintings, notably Fildes's *Applicants for Admission to a Casual Ward* (1874), Holl's *Newgate—Committed for Trial* (1878), and Herkomer's *Hard Times* (1885), but all three were also quick to refocus themselves upon more fashionable and rewarding work such as portraiture.[147] If, therefore, developments in illustrated journalism (of which the foundation in 1869 of the *Graphic* was the most important) inspired the realists to create pictorial parallels of contemporary polemics like Andrew Mearns's *The Bitter Cry of Outcast London* (1883), the impetus soon died away.

An increasing number of exhibitions enabled the new 'culture public' to see original contemporary works in large numbers and thus diminished—more directly than engravings could do—the limitations of availability from which paintings suffered in comparison with the multi-copy novel. The Royal Academy's Summer Exhibition remained supreme, with a peak attendance in 1879 of no less than 391,197. Artists fought to have their work displayed: 6,876 items were rejected in 1865. It has been estimated that, in 1852, 4,756 works were formally exhibited throughout London as a whole, in 1881 no less than 8,419.[148] Exhibitions of contemporary art were also mounted in provincial towns: the ambitious Manchester Art-Treasures Exhibition of 1857 (visited by more than a million people) included a large contemporary section containing works by Leighton, Egg, Turner, Wilkie, Haydon, Etty, Frith, Goodall, Landseer, Millais, Holman Hunt, Madox Brown, and many others.[149] While the broader art public depended upon engravings, exhibitions, and critics for information, critics, in their turn, were also subject to complex networks of influence and fashion. The resulting symbiosis between artists, exhibition organizers, critics, patrons, and public gave mid-Victorian art a powerfully mutual character that was at once a strength (intelligibility, confidence, common sympathies) and a weakness (timidity, superficiality, playing to the gallery). What, however,

[146] Treuherz and others, *Hard Times*, 12.

[147] Gillett, *Victorian Painter's World*, 118–26.

[148] Ibid. 13; H. E. Roberts, 'Exhibition and Review: The Periodical Press and the Victorian Art Exhibition System', in J. Shattock and M. Wolff (eds.), *The Victorian Periodical Press: Samplings and Soundings* (Leicester, 1982), 92–6.

[149] G. P. Landow, 'There Began to be a Great Talking about the Fine Arts', in Altholz (ed.), *Mind and Art*, 126; Boase, *English Art*, 273; J. Steegman, *Victorian Taste* (London, 1970), 234–5; U. Finke, 'The Art-Treasures Exhibition', in Archer (ed.), *Art and Architecture*, 102–26.

such a state of things unambiguously meant was that leading painters were neither obscure nor marginal figures but key members of that unitary public culture of which G. M. Young wrote so persuasively, not least when recalling how he had found himself 'standing on a railway platform one day in the summer of 1896 when a man, certainly not of the aesthetic class (I guessed him to be a Gravesend pilot), opened his paper and exclaimed to a friend, "Millais is dead" '.[150] By then, however, the comparatively broad-based pictorial taste which Millais and the pilot represented had already begun to perish too.

5. ARCHITECTURE

Unlike Victorian novelists and painters, architects needed very large sums of money in order to realize their ideas. In their case patrons combined the roles which publishers and readers together occupied in the field of literature. But like the novelists and painters, Victorian architects also inhabited a specific time and place. New building techniques and materials, a transition from craftsmen to contractors, the growth of middle-class demand, the need to design building types for an industrializing and urbanizing population, all pressed hard upon them and added to the complexities created by their own often bewildering discoveries in the field of architectural history. Coherence of style gave way under such pressures. And the rapid expansion of an as-yet scarcely organized architectural profession encouraged the appearance of imposters of all kinds, so that Victorian architects 'had bitter personal experience of unrestrained competition, and their stylistic individualism was a necessary part of the struggle of each for survival'.[151] In a general sense, therefore, the unbridled private enterprise of the age actually helped to create the acute contrasts of High Victorian styles (with their strident personal mannerisms and lack of aesthetic direction). However, at the level of the individual architect it is easier to identify influences emanating from a contemporary crisis of artistic belief than from any directly economic imperatives, though a mingling of the two certainly helped to generate—in architecture as elsewhere—a characteristically Victorian conjunction of material optimism and spiritual disquiet. Thus an architect like the idiosyncratic and opulent Gothicist, William Burges, represented an optimistic strain, as can be seen in his castle building at Cardiff and Castell Coch (1868–81) for the wealthy Marquess of Bute and in the brilliantly realized St Fin Barre's

[150] G. M. Young, *Victorian Essays* (London, 1962), 206.
[151] P. Thompson, *William Butterfield* (London, 1971), 366–78.

Cathedral in Cork (1865–79). Equally, William Butterfield represented—like the poet, Gerard Manley Hopkins, with whom he corresponded—those Victorians for whom a state of persistent unease was only kept in check by religious faith, as his savage masterpiece, All Saints, Margaret Street, London (1850–9), so powerfully reveals.

Unlike all other art producers, architects began in the nineteenth century to see themselves *and* to be seen by others as belonging to a recognized profession. This artistic singularity occurred largely because money lay so central to their activities, even though only a small part of it remained in their hands. The number of architects rose substantially: in 1850 there may have been as few as 500 'proper' architects in the whole country, just under half of whom—the members of the Institute of British Architects founded in 1834—constituted an élite.[152] The explosion in the number and complexity of the building types required by an increasingly mature industrial society (hotels, factories, libraries, railway stations, hospitals, schools, offices, banks, town halls, markets, department stores) increased the demand for architectural skills and made specialization possible well beyond churches and country houses. H. and A. Saxon Snell, for example, concentrated on hospitals, C. J. Phipps and Frank Matcham on theatres, Rowland Plumbe on artisan housing. At the same time, the growth of official building regulations helped to establish the architect as a natural intermediary between client and builder, while the development of large-scale contracting demanded a continuous supply of detailed drawings and plans.[153] By the last quarter of the century numbers had increased substantially, perhaps by as much as 400 in each decade (mainly on the bread-and-butter side). Indeed, as early as 1861 it is possible to identify 638 'architects' in London directories, a third of them fellows or associates of the Institute.[154] Those at the top designed churches, great houses, and public buildings; the next rank obtained good commercial and medium domestic work; then came the old-style 'surveyors and architects' with highly varied practices; and at the bottom a long tail of fringe practitioners drawing elevations for speculative builders or preparing drainage plans for local authorities.[155] Dickens's Seth Pecksniff in *Martin Chuzzlewit* (1843–4) occupied the more dubious reaches.

[152] J. Summerson, 'Architecture', in Ford (ed.), *Cambridge Guide to the Arts*, vii. 43.
[153] A. Saint, *The Image of the Architect* (New Haven, 1983), 66–8; J. Summerson, *The London Building World of the Eighteen-Sixties* (London, 1973), 13; A. J. Paas, *Thomas Worthington: Victorian Architecture and Social Purpose* (Manchester, 1988), 115–45.
[154] Summerson, *London Building World*, 18–19.
[155] R. Dixon and S. Muthesius, *Victorian Architecture*, 2nd edn. (London, 1985), 251.

The brazen plate upon the door (which being Mr Pecksniff's, could not lie) bore this inscription, 'PECKSNIFF, ARCHITECT', to which Mr Pecksniff, on his cards of business, added 'AND LAND SURVEYOR'. In one sense, and only one, he may be said to have been a Land Surveyor on a pretty large scale, as an extensive prospect lay stretched out before the windows of his house. Of his architectural doings, nothing was clearly known, except that he had never designed or built anything; but it was generally understood that his knowledge of the science was almost awful in its profundity. Mr Pecksniff's professional engagements, indeed, were almost, if not entirely, confined to the reception of pupils; for the collection of rents, with which pursuit he occasionally varied and relieved his graver toils, can hardly be said to be a strictly architectural employment. His genius lay in ensnaring parents and guardians, and pocketing premiums.

Yet, despite the survival of such practitioners, architects did take significant, if partial, steps towards professionalization. Though at first many were themselves the sons of architects, by the end of the century recruitment was coming from a wider range of backgrounds with respect to occupation, though perhaps a more exclusive one with respect to status.[156]

Already by the 1830s architects had emerged as recognizable professionals designing and supervising the erection of buildings. Gradually certain specialized activities began to fall away to separate groups such as civil engineers and quantity surveyors, a clear sign of the increasing complexity of the construction industry. More buildings were now architect-designed and, with the decline of old-style aristocratic patronage, competition between architects became more widespread. Indeed, it was precisely the belief that such competition should be constrained to the benefit of practitioners which underlay the drive towards professional status. At the same time, the importance of being able to face commissioning committees of middle-class men primarily concerned with cost obliged architects to increase their managerial skills.[157] As fast as they could, successful architects shed less congenial tasks such as rent-collecting, surveying, and the like. With this greater concentration upon adopting the role of cultural intermediary the essential characteristics of professional status began to appear: 'ethics', standard charges, accepted conditions of employment and definitions of responsibility, effective training, a range of relevant journals, national associations.[158] In 1837 the Institute obtained a charter and in 1866 became the Royal Institute of British Architects. A ginger group, the

---

[156] Summerson, *London Building World*, 20; B. Kaye, *The Development of the Architectural Profession in Britain* (London, 1960), 47, 53.

[157] Dixon and Muthesius, *Victorian Architecture*, 11; F. Jenkins, 'The Victorian Architectural Profession', in P. Ferriday (ed.), *Victorian Architecture* (London, 1963), 39–41, 45–6.

[158] Thompson, *William Butterfield*, 58.

Architectural Association (founded in 1847 as a forum for discussion), lost no time in demanding formal education and examinations, as well as detailed architect-driven regulations to govern the complex and highly contentious competitions which were becoming so marked a feature of Victorian patronage. In 1863 the Institute organized its first (voluntary) examinations—though it did not become necessary to pass before being elected an associate until 1882—just as the greatest of all Victorian depressions in the building industry was beginning to make the exclusion of the unqualified a matter of especially pressing concern.[159] Although a bitter controversy in 1892 between those who saw architecture as a profession and those (notably Norman Shaw) who saw it as an art ended in a draw, the future lay with the professionals who, in this respect at least, succeeded in formally establishing their craft in a way that writers, painters, and musicians have never been able to do.[160]

What this meant in terms of income was sufficiency rather than wealth. Already in the eighteenth century a move towards percentage fees had begun, with 5 per cent of total costs plus expenses becoming typical. But until the Institute started to make itself felt in the 1840s, fees remained complex, obscure, and subject to dispute, though William Butterfield, who commenced work in 1840, was always able to insist on 5 per cent.[161] At the same time it was becoming professionally less acceptable to dabble in speculative building or in contracting to supply materials as Adam and Chambers had done. What kept the profession afloat financially and allowed its members to become more specialized was the sheer quantity of building work undertaken in Victorian times. About the middle of 1846 no less than 400 new churches alone are known to have been under construction, with the result that even an obscure provincial practitioner like E. H. Shellard of Manchester could have twenty-nine in hand at one time. Another typical run-of-the-mill architect, William Caldbeck, who designed local banks and commercial premises in mid-century Ireland, was earning almost £1,000 a year in his late thirties.[162] While a handful of leading men were able to amass substantial fortunes, Butterfield, who at his

[159] J. Summerson, *Victorian Architecture* (New York, 1970), 20; Jenkins, 'Victorian Architectural Profession', 47; Kaye, *Development of the Architectural Profession*, 125–7; H. J. Dyos, 'The Speculative Builders and Developers of Victorian London', *Victorian Studies*, 11 (1968): supplement, p. 660.

[160] Kaye, *Development of the Architectural Profession*, 140; Saint, *Image of the Architect*, 61–8.

[161] H. Colvin, 'The Beginnings of the Architectural Profession in Scotland', *Architectural History*, 29 (1986), 176–8; Thompson, *William Butterfield*, 62.

[162] D. Cole, *The Work of Sir Gilbert Scott* (London, 1980), 38; M. Craig, 'The Account Book of William Caldbeck, Architect', *Architectural History*, 27 (1984), 421–8.

peak in the 1870s had enjoyed a gross income of £2,200 a year, was not among them, leaving only £16,214 on his death in 1900. However, Anthony Salvin (who came from a landed family) left £70,000 in 1881; Alfred Waterhouse, whose gross income from his London and Manchester offices in 1866–7 totalled £7,776, left £164,000 in 1905; Sydney Smirke, famous for his rich palazzo style, left £80,000 in 1877; and Sir George Gilbert Scott, after having operated by far the largest practice of his time, left £130,000 (less than one might have expected) when he died in 1878.[163] Though such sums greatly exceeded the £380 a year net earned between 1860 and 1900 by the austere Philip Webb (who employed only a couple of assistants), they unsurprisingly fell far short of the one million pounds left by the great builder, Thomas Cubitt, in 1855.[164] The onset of professionalization, therefore, while it raised the standing and income of averagely competent architects, did nothing to propel the leading men beyond the financial heights already inhabited by their painter and writer equivalents. Indeed, the available evidence strongly suggests that the leading painters earned most of all.

As those who commissioned buildings gradually evolved from patrons into clients, so architects were obliged to become more efficient and businesslike. As a result, they also achieved a new artistic dominance: Butterfield, though notably fierce, was still prepared for intelligent debate, Charles Voysey (born forty-three years later in 1857 and a designer of houses for the successful upper middle class) insisted that 'all artistic questions you must leave to me to decide'.[165] And all this was rendered the more effective because the architects' rising status made it possible to treat clients with unprecedented *bonhomie*. While Butterfield was friendly enough with ecclesiological patrons like Sir Benjamin Webb, Alexander Beresford-Hope, and Sir William Heathcote, he never forgot their elevated social position. The Norman Shaw–Philip Webb–Charles Voysey generation was much more assertive and, by being so, helped prod urban and industrial clients into a new artistic adventurousness. Until well into the third quarter of the century the great majority of the buildings most influential in shaping the High Victorian style were commissioned by aristocrats and landed gentlemen: certainly an extreme architect like

[163] Thompson, *William Butterfield*, 25, 45, 64; J. Allibone, *Anthony Salvin: Pioneer of Gothic Revival Architecture* (Cambridge, 1988), 150; C. Cunningham and P. Waterhouse, *Alfred Waterhouse 1830–1905: Biography of a Practice* (Oxford, 1992), 46; Dixon and Muthesius, *Victorian Architecture*, 11.
[164] J. Brandon-Jones, 'Philip Webb', in Ferriday (ed.), *Victorian Architecture*, 262–3; Dixon and Muthesius, *Victorian Architecture*, 57.
[165] Thompson, *William Butterfield*, 54.

Samuel Sanders Teulon—probably the most dynamically 'ugly' of his day—relied almost entirely on an aristocratic clientele. Butterfield too—a close runner-up some would say—received but a single commission from a manufacturer. Gradually, however, changing economic relativities, the appearance of socially as well as artistically confident practitioners, and an active architectural press together helped to produce novel alignments of taste, with the result that wealthy middle-class clients began to look to Norman Shaw and his circle for houses with which to proclaim a new (if largely borrowed) sense of cultural assertiveness.[166]

The sphere in which the Victorian architect's growing efficiency proved most necessary was that of corporate patronage. Committees demanded detailed submissions. They demanded (but did not always get) accurate costings. They abhorred unpleasant surprises. Collectivities of 'equals', such as Oxbridge colleges, were especially difficult to please—as both Butterfield and Waterhouse discovered. But it was a field too lucrative to ignore. Indeed, a few architects, like Thomas Worthington of Manchester, obtained three-quarters or more of their commissions from corporate clients, both secular and ecclesiastical.[167] Municipal bodies vied with one another to build impressive town halls. In 1825 Manchester put up a modest classical building for £25,000. In 1877 Waterhouse's Gothic replacement was opened at a cost of almost a million pounds, to symbolize, as a contemporary put it, 'the opulence of the city' and 'the great principle of self-government'.[168] Birmingham started building to a design by Joseph Hansom in 1832. Liverpool trumped this by adding municipal offices (1860–6) to its eighteenth-century hall and putting up the greatest of all Victorian municipal masterpieces, H. L. Elmes's stunning neo-classical St George's Hall (1841–56). Then Leeds built an exuberant palazzo-style town hall by Cuthbert Brodrick (1853–8) and Manchester devoted the years 1866–77 to Waterhouse's design. It all resembled nothing so much as a game of architectural leap-frog organized into several divisions: great cities at the top, places like Halifax (1859–63) and Bolton (1866–73) in the middle, even market towns like Diss in Norfolk competing energetically with a corn hall in 1854 capable of holding 300 people or almost one in ten of its inhabitants.[169]

All this gave much additional work to architects. What they liked less were the competitions becoming popular for large public commissions.

[166] Ibid. 6, 16, 53; Saint, *Richard Norman Shaw*, 144–9.
[167] Paas, *Thomas Worthington*, 115.
[168] Seed, ' "Commerce and the Liberal Arts" ', 73; Dixon and Muthesius, *Victorian Architecture*, 168.
[169] Dixon and Muthesius, *Victorian Architecture*, 148–55.

Competitions in the provinces were often genuinely open, involved a gamble for dubious rewards, but occasionally allowed unknowns to make a name. Those for national projects, though often limited by invitation, were noted for wrangling, recrimination, even farce. That for new Whitehall offices in the late 1850s was marked by all three. First the winning architects were rejected in favour of a government practitioner, then he in turn was replaced by Gilbert Scott (who had originally come third), then Scott was forced to abandon a Gothic design in favour of an Italianate one. And much the same happened in 1866 when a limited competition was held for new lawcourts in the Strand. After bitter disputes, George Street was declared the winner, but was immediately obliged to change his plans to suit a modified site. So stressful did the whole affair become that it is generally agreed that Street died under the strain in 1881 a year before the building was finished. Small wonder that professional bodies tried to impose rules. In 1850 the Architectural Association produced a report on the matter. In 1872 the Institute issued a code requiring qualified assessors, strict and fixed specifications, money premiums, and compensation for winners whose designs were not used. The effect was mixed—an accurate reflection of the growing but still limited power of architects as a profession.[170]

Vigorous growth and continuing limitations were, indeed, the mixed architectural results of unprecedented economic and urban change. The need for modern factories, warehouses, and offices provided opportunities of an entirely new kind. Although the earliest such buildings were often put up by contractors alone, architects came into their own from about the 1830s onwards as industrialists began to see themselves as acceptable public figures and 'architecture' as a way of claiming prestige for their enterprises. Warehouses and offices, in particular, were soon tackled by architects of considerable ability. In the middle third of the century an Italianate palazzo style became the accepted one for banks, insurance offices, and warehouses too, though local variations reflected the lively regionalism of Victorian life. Edward Walters set the tone in Manchester with his Italianate Schwabe Warehouse of 1845. Bradford and the rest of Yorkshire followed, but Bristol had a liking for Byzantine, while in Nottingham T. C. Hine designed the Adams & Page Warehouse to look like a French château.[171] And with its regular rows of good-sized windows and the prestige of original association with the commercial aristocracy of Renaissance Italy, the style favoured for the new specially constructed office buildings pos-

---

[170] Summerson, *London Building World*, 21; id., *Victorian Architecture*, 93–5, 113–15; Boase, *English Art*, 251–2; Kaye, *Development of the Architectural Profession*, 109–15.
[171] Summerson, 'Architecture', 72–5; Paas, *Thomas Worthington*, 3.

sessed both real and symbolic attractions as far as businessmen were concerned. Not until the 1860s and 1870s did Gothic make even a brief commercial appearance, most notably in the shape of Waterhouse's twenty-seven terracotta buildings for the Prudential Assurance Company of which that in London's High Holborn (1876–9 with later additions) was—and still is—the most prominent.[172]

More generally too, the Gothic style (or more properly, styles), though certainly popular, proved somewhat less ubiquitous in the secular field than is sometimes thought. Charles Barry's brilliant new Palace of Westminster, begun in 1837 (after the destruction by fire of the old Palace in 1834) and not completed until 1867, did little to popularize its loosely 'perpendicular' approach. Indeed, for all its Gothic detail, it is far from being Gothic in the principles of its design, A. W. N. Pugin (though Barry's most important collaborator on the project) going so far as to remark to a friend as they passed the (admittedly incomplete) building 'All Grecian, Sir: Tudor details on a classic body'. While, therefore, the construction of the new Houses of Parliament constituted one of the very few points in the nineteenth century at which the arts of architecture and painting jointly occupied the minds of public men for a common purpose, it is significant that the building actually erected, after a competition specifying Gothic and Elizabethan as the only permissible styles, was at best Gothic in a highly modified and unusual sense.[173]

While leading architects proved highly adaptable when faced with new opportunities and new materials, they remained ambivalent so far as the organization of their own offices and the training of their successors were concerned. Certainly some practices became very substantial. Gilbert Scott's was so big and employed so many assistants that the great man must sometimes scarcely have known with which commission he was dealing, in a career involving nearly 500 churches, thirty-nine cathedrals and minsters, twenty-five universities and colleges, and many other buildings besides. If Scott's office was brilliantly organized and always on time, Street, by contrast, kept everything in his own hands, took on too much, and was invariably late. A characteristic Victorian mania for hard work as well as for hard cash drove all but a handful of rugged individualists like Webb into accepting too many commissions at once. Indeed, precisely because individual toil and application could often produce a great deal,

---

[172] Dixon and Muthesius, *Victorian Architecture*, 125–31; H.-R. Hitchcock, *Early Victorian Architecture in Britain*, 2 vols. (London, 1954), i. 375; Cunningham and Waterhouse, *Alfred Waterhouse*, 111.

[173] Dixon and Muthesius, *Victorian Architecture*, 155–8; Steegman, *Victorian Taste*, 119–23, 129–37.

the majority of offices remained small: E. B. Lamb never had more than two assistants, William Burges rarely more than six.[174] What was new was the greater attention given to management and to costs. Waterhouse, though he never employed many assistants and had no partners (apart from his son after 1891), ran a practice of pioneering efficiency, with his staff so well trained they could be relied upon to get details right and always produce 'Waterhouse' work. A highly successful businessman, Waterhouse was not only prepared to build within strict budgets, but to accept cost restrictions as a limiting factor from the start and reduce the splendour of his buildings accordingly. Many of the most successful architects in this respect— Waterhouse himself and Butterfield are notable examples—became increasingly skilful in ensuring that contractors built strictly to estimate without affecting the quality agreed. Supervision was, therefore, necessarily precise, and little, if anything, was left to inspired craftsmen working in the Ruskinian mould.[175]

Because such rapid modernizing developments coincided with comparatively slow changes in the way in which architects were trained, the profession was able to respond effectively to a new economic environment while retaining the close personal contacts which only a comparatively small group of mutually acquainted individuals could sustain. This is not to suggest that all architects knew one another, but that the survival of pupillage as the chief method of training generated lines of influence and relationship which disappeared once more modern systems of formal education were introduced. The majority of Victorian architects began their careers as pupils for about five years in an established office. Skills, attitudes, preferences were handed down in apostolic succession. Among Scott's pupils were William White, George Frederick Bodley, Sir Thomas Graham Jackson, and George Street. Street's pupils included Philip Webb and Norman Shaw. Shaw's office nurtured Ernest Newton and W. R. Lethaby, who lived until 1922 and 1931 respectively.[176] While this produced a distinct sense of coherence, it also encouraged cultural incest. As Shaw succeeded Webb as Street's principal assistant and then set up in

---

[174] Boase, *English Art*, 240; Saint, *Image of the Architect*, 68–9; id., *Richard Norman Shaw*, 143–4; E. Kaufman, 'E. B. Lamb: A Case Study in Victorian Architectural Patronage', *Art Bulletin*, 70 (1988), 314; J. M. Crook, *William Burges and the High Victorian Dream* (London, 1981), 80–1.

[175] Cunningham and Waterhouse, *Alfred Waterhouse*, 140–7; Thompson, *William Butterfield*, 71–4.

[176] Dixon and Muthesius, *Victorian Architecture*, 14; Jenkins, 'Victorian Architectural Profession', 46; Kaye, *Development of the Architectural Profession*, 102–3; Thompson, *William Butterfield*, 343.

partnership with W. E. Nesfield whose fellow-pupil in the office of William Burn he had previously been, one detects the existence of perhaps rather too many magic circles for the profession's ultimate good.

More formal systems of education made slow progress. In 1840 King's College London began to provide classes on the 'Arts of Construction in Connection with Civil Engineering and Architecture'. In 1841 University College London appointed a professor of architecture. From 1847 the Architectural Association encouraged self-help groups to meet and provide mutual support. But all this, together with occasional lectures at the Royal Academy, acted more as a supplement than an alternative to office training, which, almost until the end of the century, remained the main road to success.[177] At the same time, the more artistic and inspirational aspects of the profession were emphasized by the way in which so many young architects rounded off their studies by following the painters and the musicians to the continent. Some went immediately, others had to wait until they had enough money. Waterhouse went at the age of 23, Scott not until he was 30, Street not until he was 31.[178] While, therefore, architects proved themselves in many ways the most rapidly modernizing of the culture producers of the time, the close network of personal relationships which their training methods and comparatively small numbers made possible and the powerful influence of those who insisted that architecture must not be merely technological makes it reasonable to locate most of them—in the 1890s perhaps even more than the 1840s—firmly within the orbit of high art.

The businesslike nature of mid-Victorian cultural endeavour owed much to the peculiar resonances generated by a maturing industrial economy and by the social order which accompanied it. Developments in printing, publishing, and the marketing of books had a profound effect upon writers of all kinds. Novels were written to a certain length, plotted in certain ways, devoted to certain themes because commerce demanded three-deckers or serialization or adherence to Mr Mudie's moral code. Music was composed and performed in particular ways to suit the needs of music publishers, growing concert audiences, and cut-throat impresarios. The style and presentation of paintings were as much designed to appeal to newly rich industrialists or subscribers to the Art Union as were the actual subjects with which they dealt, while the appearance of highly capitalized art dealers,

---

[177] Jenkins, 'Victorian Architectural Profession', 46; Kaye, *Development of the Architectural Profession*, 93–8, 102–3; Saint, *Richard Norman Shaw*, 187–8.
[178] Cunningham and Waterhouse, *Alfred Waterhouse*, 13.

developments in engraving techniques, and the publication of illustrated magazines greatly expanded the market for pictures in general. Notable, too, was the manner in which the spatial imperatives and economic priorities of an urbanizing society accorded architects opportunities they had never enjoyed before, with technical innovations and the requirements of new economic entities like manufacturing industries and insurance companies calling forth an architectural inventiveness no less exciting—and no less 'Victorian'—than that stimulated by contemporary perturbations in religious organization and belief. Those creative artists at the top of the tree became richer and the opportunities for those in the middle became greater. Musical creativity proved the least financially rewarding because music, for its realization, requires performers, who, together with producers and actor-managers in the theatre, creamed off most of the available profits. Not that the status awarded or the incomes attained in any field invariably match the sensibilities of later generations. We may now think that the best Victorian novels inhabit some ultimate cultural Parnassus, but, despite much reconsideration, we still consign the best Victorian pictures to the nursery slopes. However, at the time, painters probably earned most of all. And for a society which accepted money as perhaps the clearest measure of approval, the supremacy of the painters shows how much its values, attitudes, and judgements belonged to a particular time and a particular place.[179]

[179] The high regard in which contemporary and near-contemporary painters were held is shown by the twenty-six artists' names inscribed on the exterior of Hull City Hall (built just after the end of our period). The immortals there recorded unsurprisingly include Titian, Rembrandt, Michelangelo, Rubens, and Velázquez. With them, however, are to be found, not just Turner, but Millais, Leighton, Landseer, and Watts as well.

CHAPTER 12

Godly People

1. DENOMINATIONAL LANDSCAPES

Never was Britain more religious than in the Victorian age. Contemporaries agonized over those who did not float upon the flood of faith. We marvel at the number that did. The episcopal Church of England and the presbyterian Church of Scotland each fought to safeguard their established status—the ecclesiastical equivalent of economic protectionism. Dissenters demanded free trade in souls as well as corn. The vital impulses which flowed from the Evangelical Revival of the late eighteenth and early nineteenth centuries rendered belief more dynamic, but more problematic too. Because the kind of faith the Victorians encouraged was the kind it is possible to lose through conscientious design as much as by accident, those who worried most about their feelings of 'honest doubt' often found themselves forever mimicking the language and thought processes of the Christianity they were leaving behind. Equally characteristic was the statistical temper in which Victorians approached the manifestations of belief. How many people, they wanted to know, went to church; how big was the pool of belief; who, in sectarian terms, led the field?

Certainly the number of distinct denominations was large. For some this was a sign of enterprise, for others one of damaging disunity. Splits were the order of the day. The Methodists divided repeatedly after John Wesley's death in 1791. Even groups as small as the Peculiar People of Kent and Essex (founded in 1838 and, in obedience to James 5: 14, scornful of medical aid) succeeded in generating schisms of bitter irreconcilability.[1] A broad measure of coherence can, however, be sustained if the English Christian cake is cut into four major slices: Anglicanism, old Dissent dating from the sixteenth and seventeenth centuries (Baptists, Congregationalists, Quakers, and so on), new Dissent (predominantly Methodist), and Roman Catholicism. The first constituted the establishment. The second and third,

---

[1] A. Smith, *The Established Church and Popular Religion 1750–1850* (London, 1970), 49.

though sharing a position of Nonconformity (in the case of Methodism, reluctantly so) towards that establishment, diverged from one another in significant theological and organizational ways. The fourth was becoming more important as a result of Irish immigration. Wales, Ireland, and Scotland maintained distinct denominational patterns of their own, sometimes subtly, often radically, different from those of England. In Wales Dissenters constituted a clear majority, notably in the shape of the Calvinistic Methodist Connexion, which, though part of Methodist new Dissent, rejected Wesley's Arminianism (the notion that all might be saved) in favour of Calvinist notions of a predestined elect. The Irish had the Anglican and (until January 1871, established) Church of Ireland, though three-quarters of them were Catholics and half the remainder Presbyterians. In Scotland Presbyterianism dominated, and was represented not only by the established Church of Scotland (whose 'establishment' involved far less subservience to the state than was the case south of the border), but by a vast range of non-established rivals, many of them small, a couple very substantial indeed.

TABLE 12.1 *Denominational statistics for England, 1838–1901*

	Church of England		All Methodists	
	000s	Density	000s	Density
1838/41	755	7.9	436	4.5
1851	875	8.1	490	4.4
1861/3	995	8.3	514	4.1
1880/1	1,225	7.9	631	4.0
1900/1901	1,945	9.4	733	3.5
	Congregationalists		All Baptists	
	000s	Density	000s	Density
1838/41	127	1.4	100	1.1
1851	165	1.5	140	1.3
1861/3	180	1.6	153	1.2
1880/1	n.a.	n.a.	201	1.3
1900/1901	257	1.3	239	1.2

Notes: Density = % of population aged 15 and over. Estimates of the 'Catholic population' in *England and Wales* (with those for 'mass attenders' in parentheses) are: 1851 = 7.8 (4.2); 1891 = 7.2 (3.9).

Church of England and Methodists: 1841, 1851, 1861, 1881, 1901.

Congregationalists and Baptists: 1838, 1851, 1863, 1880 (Baptists only), 1900.

Source: A. D. Gilbert, *Religion and Society in Industrial England* (London, 1976), 27–48.

But if religious bodies—aware of the competitive nature of the market for souls—fully shared the Victorian passion for counting things, each church counted in its own way, with the result that even the best data have more useful things to say about temporal changes within denominations than about comparisons between them. Protestant Dissenters were the most scrupulous and included only persons in full membership (a status they carefully defined). Roman Catholics claimed to count the 'Catholic population' and 'mass attenders', procedures as nebulous as they were imprecise. The Church of England, by counting Easter Day communicants, fell somewhere in between. The outcome, as regards England, is shown in Table 12.1. These Anglocentric relativities undergo significant changes when a *British* perspective (which, of course, still excludes Ireland) is adopted, though the same caveats apply (Table 12.2).

Such broad-brush statistics disguise almost as much as they reveal. By definition, Scottish Presbyterians were overwhelmingly confined to

TABLE 12.2 *Denominational statistics for Britain, 1840–1900*

	Episcopalians of all kinds		Scottish Presbyterians of all kinds	
	000s	Density	000s	Density
1840	821	6.9	503	4.2
1850	953	7.1	603	4.5
1860	1,078	7.2	723	4.9
1870	1,206	7.2	822	4.9
1880	1,332	7.1	949	5.0
1890	1,614	7.5	1,053	4.9
1900	2,089	8.4	1,164	4.7

	'Nonconformists'		Roman Catholics	
	000s	Density	000s	Density
1840	835	7.1	305	2.6
1850	1,021	7.6	846	6.3
1860	1,136	7.6	1,179	7.9
1870	1,290	7.6	1,213	7.3
1880	1,465	7.8	1,459	7.7
1890	1,635	7.6	1,691	7.9
1900	1,803	7.2	2,016	8.1

Notes: Catholic figures are for 'Catholic population', not 'mass attenders'. 'Nonconformists' are those not included under the other denominational categories.
Density = % of population aged 15 and over in Britain.

Source: R. Currie, A. Gilbert, and L. Horsley, *Churches and Churchgoers* (Oxford, 1977), 25.

Scotland, where, indeed, they maintained a very high density among those aged 15 and over: no less than 32.4 per cent in 1851. Yet, at the same time, the chronic fissiparousness of Presbyterianism in general meant that the established Church of Scotland attracted a substantially smaller proportion of worshippers north of the border than did the Church of England within its home territory to the south (perhaps 32 per cent compared to 47 per cent in 1851).[2] Again, denominations with strictly defined membership criteria were inevitably 'larger' than these figures suggest because their substantial followings of regular adherents or attenders were kept outside the main statistical gates. Thus in 1851 there were, for example, about 165,000 fully enrolled Congregationalists in England, who, however keen on going to chapel, could not possibly have accounted for the 1.2 million Congregational 'attendances' known to have taken place on one particular Sunday in that year. The same was true of other Dissenting bodies, notably the Methodists who dominated English Nonconformity in numerical terms. With about 490,000 members in 1851, they recorded more than 2.4 million attendances in England and Wales, of which almost two-thirds took place in Wesleyan chapels and a fifth in those of the largest group of seceders, the Primitive Methodists, famed for their fundamentalism and comparatively demotic social base.[3]

The year 1851 appears so often in Victorian religious statistics because it witnessed the only official attempt ever made to collect denominational data in Britain. This so-called 'religious census' was undertaken quite separately from the normal decennial census. Instead of counting heads (as was done in Ireland from 1861 onwards with regard to denominational affiliation), an attempt was made to count the number of 'attendances' at places of worship on Sunday 30 March and the extent of the seating accommodation provided. The results generated great excitement at the time (21,000 copies of the report were sold)[4] and have provided great confusion ever since. The statistician in charge, Horace Mann, tried to make sense of the raw data by means of sweeping assumptions designed in part to render the position of the Church of England as favourable as possible, in part to make the number of *attendances* yield the number of *individual persons* who had attended—which in fact cannot be done.

    [2] C. G. Brown, *The Social History of Religion in Scotland since 1730* (London, 1987), 63. See also below, Ch. 14, s. 2.
    [3] D. M. Thompson, 'The Religious Census of 1851', in R. Lawton (ed.), *The Census and Social Structure* (London, 1978), 274. The Primitives had appeared about 1810. Other significant Methodist groups include the New Connexion (1797), the Bible Christians (1819), and the Wesleyan Methodist Association (1836).
    [4] *Hansard*, cxxxv. 32 (11 July 1854).

The English and Welsh census (that in Scotland was less complete) dealt two shocks to the mid-Victorian psyche. It was found that large numbers of people simply stayed at home and that Anglicanism attracted less than half of all attendances. Just under a quarter of the population worshipped with the Church of England on 30 March; just over a quarter worshipped elsewhere; half did not worship at all. And if in parts of continental Europe such proportions would have occasioned a degree of godly jubilation, in England they occasioned melancholy gloom, made gloomier still by what were now officially sanctioned rankings in the three-nation British church-going league: Wales first, Scotland second, England last.[5]

While Mann's conclusion that 'a sadly formidable portion of the English people are habitual neglecters of the public ordinances of religion' was widely accepted, in historical terms the levels recorded in 1851 are, in fact, anything but low. Not only that, but the established church was still attracting 3.4 times as many attendances in England and Wales as the next largest denomination (the Wesleyans) and these were spread more evenly throughout the country than those of its competitors. If, therefore, in practical terms, the Church of England had already become a voluntary organization rather than a quasi-comprehensive national one, it remained much the largest religious institution of the time.[6]

Analysis of the least unsatisfactory measure provided by the census, the so-called Index of Attendance (the percentage which total attendances formed of total population), reveals distinct regional and denominational differences. The established church was weakest in Cornwall and all counties (save Westmorland) north of the Wash, in all of which its index was below the average Anglican figure of about 28 to 29 per cent for England and Wales as a whole. Congregationalists only managed to exceed 10 per cent in Essex, Suffolk, Dorset, and Hampshire; Baptists only in Bedfordshire, Huntingdonshire, Cambridgeshire, Buckinghamshire, Suffolk, Leicestershire, and Gloucestershire. Methodists of all kinds reached 15 per cent in no less than eleven English counties: Cornwall, the three Yorkshire Ridings, Durham, Cheshire, Lincolnshire, Norfolk, Derbyshire, Nottinghamshire, and Staffordshire. But while such relativities and distributions left the establishment in a denominationally unique position in England generally, in Wales its performance was worse even than in Nonconformist Cornwall.

[5] B. I. Coleman, *The Church of England in the Mid-Nineteenth Century: A Social Geography* (London, 1980), 7; H. McLeod, 'Introduction', in McLeod (ed.), *European Religion in the Age of Great Cities 1830–1930* (London, 1995), 13–17.

[6] J. D. Gay, *The Geography of Religion in England* (London, 1971), 55; Coleman, *Church of England*, 7.

Great efforts have been devoted to trying to make sense of the regional patterning of Victorian religious observance. Almost all—notably the suggestion that Methodism became strongest where old Dissent and the Church of England were weakest—founder upon the rocks of local particularism. In some counties, like those running from Kent to Somerset, such 'infilling' does indeed seem to have occurred. In others, like those in the North Midlands, it clearly did not.[7] And while overall it is possible to identify zones of high religious performance where both the Church of England and Nonconformity did well and zones of low performance where both did badly, individual localities could often behave in highly unpredictable and idiosyncratic ways. Thus industrial towns in the East Midlands differed dramatically in religious atmosphere from those in the West Riding; mining villages in Cornwall from those in Durham; south Lancashire cotton towns from those in north-east Lancashire. Even counties where Dissent was absolutely or relatively strong possess few common elements. In some, both Dissent and Anglicanism were strong: Bedfordshire, Huntingdonshire, Leicestershire, the North Riding. In some, Dissent alone was strong: Cornwall, Lincolnshire, Nottinghamshire, Derbyshire, the West and East Ridings (as well as Wales). In some, Dissent was weak but the Church of England weaker still: Cheshire, Staffordshire, Lancashire, Northumberland, Durham. Sometimes, what seems like a simple pattern was not in fact simple at all. For example, while churchgoing was often low in the large industrial towns of the North of England, this almost certainly owed less to industrialization as such than to regional patterns of religious enthusiasm stretching back to the Reformation and even beyond.[8]

Up to 1840 the growth of Dissent outstripped that of the population. From then until the 1880s the two were in balance. Thereafter the former fell behind. While the peak years for absolute membership occurred as late as 1906 for Methodists, 1907 for Baptists, and 1908 for Congregationalists, the peaks for membership relative to population were achieved much earlier—in 1841, 1880, and 1863 respectively.[9] By contrast, the Church of England, after a century of decline, experienced a remarkable period of

[7] F. Tillyard, 'The Distribution of the Free Churches in England', *Sociological Review*, 27 (1935), 1–18; K. D. M. Snell, *Church and Chapel in the North Midlands* (Leicester, 1991), 3, 28, 47–50.

[8] H. McLeod, 'Class, Community and Region: The Religious Geography of Nineteenth Century England', in M. Hill (ed.), *A Sociological Yearbook of Religion in Britain*, 6 (1973), 32, 41; Thompson, 'Religious Census of 1851', 260–1.

[9] D. Bebbington, *Victorian Nonconformity* (Bangor, 1992), 24–5; A. D. Gilbert, *Religion and Society in Industrial England: Church, Chapel and Social Change, 1740–1914* (London, 1976), 32, 37.

recovery from about 1830 until perhaps the outbreak of the First World War, during which the number of churches and clergy and the rate of participation by lay people probably increased more rapidly than did the population as a whole. Though by no means all the ground lost during the first two-thirds of the eighteenth century was made up, these years constitute the one prolonged period during which the Church of England improved its quantitative position. The reasons for this had much to do with the way in which increasing suburbanization created a growing middle-class demand for the establishment's mixture of social cachet, dignified services, and theological fluidity. While, therefore, the members of the mid-Victorian generation witnessed a vigorous multifaceted sectarian life, they also witnessed a process by which the established churches in England and Scotland for a time succeeded in increasing their relative numerical standing within Protestantism as a whole.[10] Not that the means adopted to achieve this were without risk. Denominational rivalry, for example, led to the construction of so many new churches that eventually a moment of gross overprovision came when increasingly empty buildings may well have begun to deter those with no very intense commitment to attend. Already, indeed, by the 1890s there were signs that even in some suburban districts (Croydon is an example) Anglican numbers were no longer keeping pace with population growth.[11]

Local differences notwithstanding, in certain respects Victorian denominational life did follow distinctly national paths. As regards the Church of England, two developments stand out: the growth of ecclesiastical parties or factions and the gathering pace of reform. While such parties had always existed, by the middle of the nineteenth century their character had changed and their disputes intensified. Most observers followed W. J. Conybeare in identifying three main groups, though many Anglicans remained vaguely neutral. The Evangelical or Low Church party stressed biblical literalism, friendship with Dissenters, conversion experiences, and plain services. High Churchmen looked to Catholic (but not generally to Roman Catholic) ecclesiastical traditions and liked elaborate liturgies. Broad Churchmen were liberal in theology and emphasized the importance of a truly national establishment. The first owed much to the emotionalism of the late eighteenth- and early nineteenth-century Evangelical Revival, the second to the Oxford Movement which had appeared in the 1830s as a protest against state interference in church affairs and been associated with

---

[10] Gilbert, *Religion and Society*, 27–9; Brown, *Religion in Scotland*, 65.
[11] R. Gill, *The Myth of the Empty Church* (London, 1993), 72–92; J. N. Morris, *Religion and Urban Change: Croydon 1840–1914* (Woodbridge, 1992), 179–82.

a series of tracts stressing the Catholicity of the Church of England (hence the name Tractarians), the third to developments in contemporary biblical, theological, and scientific studies. In 1853 one writer claimed that, out of the 17,000 clergymen who could be classified (1,000 could not), 38 per cent were Evangelical, 41 per cent High, and 21 per cent Broad. Twenty years later, a rather different split was suggested: 50 per cent High (of whom less than a fifth were extremely so), 25 per cent Low, 7 per cent Broad, and 18 per cent 'Nondescripts'.[12] The truth probably lay somewhere in between.

Looking back from today it is the agreement between the High and Low Church positions—over personal holiness, the divine inspiration of scripture, the uncompromising supernaturalism of Christianity—which strikes the observer. But at the time the differences seemed altogether more prominent. Upon one thing, however, there was virtual unanimity: the importance of reforming the abuses of the early nineteenth-century establishment. A series of Acts of Parliament beginning in the 1830s diminished those inequalities between dioceses, parishes, and parsons which had long characterized the established church in England and Wales (and indeed Ireland too). Episcopal incomes were more closely aligned by an act of 1836. In 1838 the commutation of tithes to cash payments partially mollified all those who resented being required to support financially a church to which they did not belong. In 1838 pluralism (the simultaneous holding of several benefices) was restricted. Also in the 1830s an Ecclesiastical Commission was set up for 'making better provision for the cure of souls' by augmenting poor livings, improving finances, and giving grants for buildings. Eight new dioceses were founded to meet the demands of a changing society: Ripon (1836), Manchester (1847), Truro and St Albans (1877), Liverpool (1880), Newcastle (1882), Southwell (1884), Wakefield (1888). Between 1840 and 1876 at least 1,727 new churches were constructed in areas of need and another 7,144 substantially restored at a cost of £25m, the bulk of it raised from private sources.[13] The Commissioners aimed to limit the size of parishes to 4,000 souls and between 1819 and 1895 created over 3,600 new parishes with this in view.[14] The provincial convocations of Canterbury and York, in which bishops and other clergy (some

[12] [W. J. Conybeare], 'Church Parties', *Edinburgh Review*, 98 (1853), 338; R. F. Littledale, 'Church Parties', *Contemporary Review*, 24 (1874), 304.

[13] *Returns Showing the Number of Churches (including Cathedrals) in every Diocese in England, which have been Built or Restored at a Cost exceeding £500 since the year 1840*, H[ouse of] C[ommons Paper] 1876 (125), lviii. 658.

[14] P. J. Waller, *Town, City, and Nation: England 1850–1914* (Oxford, 1983), 223–5. In the 1890s Protestant parishes in Berlin regularly had populations of 60,000 and more (McLeod, 'Introduction', 11).

of them elected) met annually and which had been effectively suspended since 1717, were revived in 1854 and 1861 respectively. Reforming bishops like Blomfield of Chester (1824–8) and London (1828–56) and Wilberforce of Oxford (1845–69) and Winchester (1869–73) prodded and dragged their priests into greater efficiency as well as greater spirituality. Wilberforce mounted three-day annual conferences for his rural deans, travelled without ceasing, demanded high standards, and between 1857 and 1860 held an unprecedented 217 confirmations for 18,747 candidates. Whereas in 1831 only 44.0 per cent of parishes nationally had been served by resident incumbents, by 1879 the proportion had reached 88.1 per cent, with Wilberforce's Oxford diocese recording 83.7 per cent as early as 1866.[15]

While much remained to be done, the history of the Church of England in the half-century after 1840 was one of success. In the city of York, for example, the number of Sunday services rose from thirty in 1837 to sixty-eight in 1901. In rural Lincolnshire the period 1830–75 saw 'more clergy, more resident incumbent clergy, spacious new parsonage houses, bigger incomes, old churches restored and new ones built'.[16] By the 1880s it would no longer have been possible—even in a remote North Yorkshire parish—for a new incumbent to encounter the state of things found by the Revd J. C. Atkinson at Danby in the late 1840s: a rickety altar table covered with filthy baize, a 'dirty shabby surplice, flung negligently over the altar-railing, itself paintless and broken, and the vestment with half its length trailing on the dirty, unswept floor'.[17] In 1854 Bishop Selwyn told a Cambridge congregation that 'a great and visible change' had taken place over the previous dozen years: 'It is now a rare thing to see a careless clergyman, a neglected parish, or a desecrated church.'[18] In 1859 a Baptist observer conceded ruefully that the anti-establishment hostility of contemporary Dissent was in large part a reaction against an Anglican Church which had never before shown 'such signs of vigour, such evidence of awakening life'.[19] As affluence spread, so the local parish church became more and more attractive to young ambitious Nonconformists who wished to attend

[15] M. A. Crowther, *Church Embattled: Religious Controversy in Mid-Victorian England* (Newton Abbot, 1970), 169–71; P. Virgin, *The Church in an Age of Negligence: Ecclesiastical Structure and Problems of Church Reform 1700–1840* (Cambridge, 1989), 290, 210–11; D. McClatchey, *Oxfordshire Clergy 1777–1869* (Oxford, 1960), 31.
[16] E. Royle, *Nonconformity in Nineteenth-Century York* (York, 1985), 14–17, 20; J. Obelkevich, *Religion and Rural Society: South Lindsey 1825–1875* (Oxford, 1976), 120.
[17] J. C. Atkinson, *Forty Years in a Moorland Parish* (London, 1891), 44–5.
[18] G. A. Selwyn, *The Work of Christ in the World: Four Sermons preached before the University of Cambridge* (Cambridge, 1855), 7.
[19] Gilbert, *Religion and Society*, 168.

pleasing services, avoid minute chapel supervision, and benefit from the
social standing of the establishment.[20]

In one important respect, the Church of England and Dissent had
derived much of their vigour from a common source, the Evangelical
Revival, itself as much a collection of responses to the emergence of modern
urban society as a theological system. Stressing conversion, activism, the
Bible, and the atoning death of Christ upon the cross, Evangelicals—true to
Lord Shaftesbury's dictum that 'Satan reigns in the intellect; God in the
heart of man'[21]—distrusted analytical religion, their general cast of mind
prefiguring, indeed preshaping, that kind of 'Victorianism' of sobriety, self-
improvement, and respectability which manifested itself so powerfully
through the temperance and sabbath observance movements of the mid-
century period.

The 1840s and 1850s constituted the high point of pan-denominational
Evangelicalism. In 1846 the newly formed Evangelical Alliance adopted a
nine-point doctrinal statement designed to encompass sympathetic Anglicans and all but the most irreconcilable Dissenters. But because the
Alliance was more the product of an efflorescence of anti-Catholicism
than anything more positive, Evangelical co-operation soon faded, not least
because of Anglican irritation over the triumphalism displayed by Dissenters
when celebrating in 1862 the 'Great Ejectment' of Puritan clergymen from
the established church two centuries before.[22] Yet even this falling apart
was deeply paradoxical, for it coincided with a diminution of theological
differences within Protestantism as a whole. Especially notable was the
virtual collapse of strict Calvinism outside (and even to some extent inside)
Scotland. By the middle of the century few believed that only those
predestined to salvation would be saved and the Arminian notion of
potential general redemption had moved well beyond its fastnesses in
Methodism and certain sections of the establishment.[23] That denominational rivalry, none the less, failed to abate suggests that its engines were not
driven by theology alone.

While, therefore, non-Anglican Protestants in England and Wales grew
in confidence throughout much of the nineteenth century (a development

---

[20] J. Cox, *The English Churches in a Secular Society: Lambeth, 1870–1930* (New York,
1982), 253–4.
[21] E. Hodder, *The Life and Work of the Seventh Earl of Shaftesbury*, popular edn.
(London, 1892), 527.
[22] G. Parsons, 'From Dissenters to Free Churchmen: The Transitions of Victorian
Nonconformity', in Parsons (ed.), *Religion in Victorian Britain*, i. *Traditions* (Manchester,
1988), 73–4; Gilbert, *Religion and Society*, 169; Bebbington, *Victorian Nonconformity*, 21–3.
[23] D. W. Bebbington, *Evangelicalism in Modern Britain: A History from the 1730s to the
1980s* (London, 1989), 16–17.

reflected by a changing nomenclature, from Dissenter in the early part, to Nonconformist in the middle part, to Free Churchman in the later part of the period), they lost neither a keen appreciation of sectarian differences nor a sense of competition with the establishment. As social structures became less favourable to Nonconformity (the replacement of the artisans of early industrialization by the factory workers of a more mature economy proved especially significant), so what were becoming increasingly middle-class denominations sought 'compensation' by building more expensive and ornate churches and by adopting richer liturgical forms. Contemporary estimates suggest that the number of Baptist, Congregational, and Method-ist chapels in England and Wales rose from 16,491 in 1851 to 20,375 in 1874.[24] As John Angell James put it in 1856, Dissent, once the religion of barns, was being 'infected with the ambition of becoming the religion of cathedrals'.[25]

More expensive buildings and more elaborate rituals were accompanied by a move towards formal professionalization. As more ministers became full-time experts, so they demanded higher incomes. As more members were 'born in' rather than converted from without, so the consolidation of organizational structures became an end in itself. Increasing middle-class penetration led to a sharper sense of hierarchy between sects. Leading Methodist New Connexion families (Ridgeways, Firths, Fowlers) per-ceived a gulf between themselves and the Wesleyan Reformers, who in turn were a little above the Free Methodists. While Congregational man-ufacturers (Salts, Leverhulmes, Unwins, Colmans, Crossleys) saw them-selves as the cream of the middle classes, the Unitarian élites were undoubtedly the real Brahmins of Dissent. But if growing respectability meant that rougher terrains were being abandoned to groups like the Brethren and the Salvation Army, it evinced little in the way of friendly recognition from the Church of England. The Anglican cleric and novelist Charles Kingsley continued to dismiss Baptist pastors as 'muck enthroned on their respective dung hills'. And when W. F. Freeman announced his conversion to Methodism in 1876, he was briskly told that his family's long-standing doubts about his sanity had thereby been fully confirmed.[26]

---

[24] Gilbert, *Religion and Society*, 145–9; H. S. Skeats, 'Statistics Relating to the Support of Religious Institutions in England and Wales', *Journal of the Statistical Society*, 29 (1876), 33; H. Davies, *Worship and Theology in England from Newman to Martineau* (Princeton, 1962), 65–113.

[25] R. W. Dale, *Life and Letters of John Angell James*, 2nd edn. (London, 1861), 560.

[26] I. Sellers, *Nineteenth-Century Nonconformity* (London, 1977), 13; K. D. Brown, *A Social History of the Nonconformist Ministry in England and Wales 1800–1930* (Oxford, 1988), 9.

Such reactions were prompted as much by fear of Nonconformist strength as dislike of Nonconformist theology. Both Baptists and Congregationalists were becoming organized as distinct sects rather than loose agglomerations of worshipping communities. The feeble Baptist 'Union' of 1813 was strengthened in 1832 and, under the leadership of J. H. Hinton (secretary 1841–66), transformed into an effective denominational force. Similarly, the low-key Congregational Union set up in 1831 was reconstituted under the secretaryship of Algernon Wells (1837–50) and given a more centralized structure still in 1871. In 1876 those few English Presbyterians who had not drifted into Unitarianism joined a growing band of emigrant Scots to form the Presbyterian Church of England with about 46,000 members. The other major representatives of old Dissent—the Quakers and the Unitarians—though both included many rich and philanthropic individuals, remained (at about 15,000 each) numerically small. Indeed, in 1851 the Latter-day Saints or Mormons, who had first arrived from the United States in 1837, attracted more worshippers than the Quakers, though numbers soon fell as members began to emigrate to the new Zion being established by Brigham Young at Salt Lake City in Utah.[27]

While the relative growth of old Dissent fell back gradually after the 1840s, Wesleyan Methodism experienced an altogether more dramatic attrition, the outcome in part of tensions generated by the autocratic figure of Jabez Bunting (secretary since 1814 and president on several occasions from 1820 onwards). Discontent with his iron control eventually burst out in a series of bitter pamphlets entitled the *Fly Sheets*, which began to appear in 1845. In 1849 three dissident ministers were expelled and a fourth was thrown out the following year. Numbers dropped sharply: by 54,000 (or 16.3 per cent) in 1850–1, 21,000 in 1851–2, and then more slowly. And although this exodus left power for a time in the hands of Bunting's supporters with their Tory politics and strict vision of Methodism as a *via media* between the Church of England and Dissent, and though Wesleyanism continued to be the largest and most powerful Nonconformist denomination, it was never again to experience the glad confident mornings of the years before 1845.[28]

In general, however, the period from the 1830s to the 1880s was a tolerably successful one for Dissent, in large part because of the peculiar congruities which gave sense to the relationship between its values and

<hr/>

[27] Sellers, *Nineteenth-Century Nonconformity*, 11; O. Chadwick, *The Victorian Church*, 2 vols. (London, 1966–70), i. 400–21, 436–9; Gilbert, *Religion and Society*, 40–1; R. Currie, A. Gilbert, and L. Horsley, *Churches and Churchgoers: Patterns of Church Growth in the British Isles since 1700* (Oxford, 1977), 207–8.

[28] Chadwick, *Victorian Church*, i. 382–6; Currie, Gilbert, and Horsley, *Churches and Churchgoers*, 141.

those of society as a whole.[29] At the heart of Dissent's synthesis of religion, politics, and economics lay a commitment to individualism—itself the dominant secular philosophy of the time. And even if not all Dissenters were Evangelicals, the great majority proclaimed a redemption in which the unique soul rather than the community of believers stood most immediately to the Lord. Politically too, Nonconformists upheld the liberty of the individual, a stance which made easier their alliance with Gladstone from the 1860s onwards and which was itself, at least in part, the creation of a middle-class leadership and working-class following together strongly committed to the principles of *laissez-faire* and (like the *General Baptist Magazine* of 1854) bitterly antagonistic to 'the oppressive weight of taxes that grind nations to the dust'.[30]

However, in the last quarter of the century such views suffered serious erosion under the impact of biblical and historical criticism, theological innovation, and changing attitudes to social reform. In religious terms a crucial shift took place towards an emphasis upon the love rather than the wrath of God, just at the time when the complexities of urban industrial society were eroding the consensus in favour of individual responsibility and self-help. Leading Nonconformist ministers, like the Wesleyan Hugh Price Hughes and the Baptist John Clifford, adopted less antagonistic attitudes to the role of the state, though they often found it difficult to carry their congregations with them. At the same time the growing integration of a new generation of Dissenters into secular society at large (attendance at Oxford and Cambridge, playing cards, going to the theatre) blurred the moral edge which had formerly provided Nonconformists with clear attitudes, clear aims, and reinforcing relationships.

The history of Victorian Roman Catholicism similarly illuminates some of the key social and intellectual preoccupations of the time. In particular, a substantial increase in numbers helped to draw from Protestants a congeries of anti-popery fears old and new—about Jesuitical machinations, the Scarlet Woman, about outsiders generally and the Irish in particular. In 1770 there may have been about 80,000 Catholics in England and Wales. By 1851 perhaps three-quarters of a million could be identified as such. Immigration from Ireland generated most of the increase, though perhaps a fifth of Irish immigrants were Protestants.[31] Changes in the size of the

[29] R. Helmstadter, 'The Nonconformist Conscience', in P. Marsh (ed.), *The Conscience of the Victorian State* (Hassocks, 1979), 135–72.

[30] Bebbington, *Victorian Nonconformity*, 62.

[31] E. Norman, *The English Catholic Church in the Nineteenth Century* (Oxford, 1984), 6; G. Connolly, 'Irish and Catholic: Myth or Reality?', in R. Swift and S. Gilley (eds.), *The Irish in the Victorian City* (London, 1985), 231–2.

Irish-born population (Table 12.3) provide a cloudy measure of what was involved—cloudy because, as time went on, second- and third-generation Irish (who obviously make no appearance in statistics of this kind) became more and more numerous.

TABLE 12.3 *Irish-born population in Britain, 1841–1881*

	1841	1851	1861	1871	1881
England and Wales	291,000	520,000	602,000	566,000	562,000
% of total population	1.8	2.9	3.0	2.5	2.2
Scotland	128,000	207,000	204,000	207,000	218,000
% of total population	4.9	7.2	6.7	6.2	5.8
Britain	419,000	727,000	806,000	773,000	780,000
% of total population	2.3	3.5	3.5	3.0	2.9

Source: Figures for 1841–61 from S. Gilley and R. Swift, 'Introduction', in Swift and Gilley (eds.), *The Irish in the Victorian City* (London, 1985), 13; for 1871–81 from *Thom's Official Directory of the United Kingdom...for the Year 1888* (Dublin, 1888), 566.

Catholic immigrants placed great pressure on ecclesiastical resources: in 1851 Catholics were unique in attracting more attendances on census Sunday than they provided sittings. Huge investment in buildings and manpower meant that by 1890 there were in England and Wales 1,335 Catholic chapels compared to 586 forty years before and 2,478 priests compared to 826. In Yorkshire alone, the number of priests rose from sixty-three serving sixty-one chapels in 1850 to 191 serving 154 chapels half a century later.[32] Indeed, by the 1870s the provision of parochial priests in parts of Britain was more generous than in Ireland: 1 priest to 1,005 Catholics in the archdiocese of Edinburgh as against 1 to 1,611 in the ecclesiastical province of Cashel in Ireland.[33]

While the numerical impact of the Irish upon Catholicism in Britain is clear enough, their impact upon the vitality of the church was more ambiguous. Indeed, the shock of large-scale immigration momentarily reduced a thriving native institution to crisis and confusion. However, from the 1840s onwards, heroic efforts by priests and lay people began to

[32] Thompson, 'Religious Census of 1851', 273–4; J. D. Holmes, *More Roman than Rome: English Catholicism in the Nineteenth Century* (London, 1978), 102; J. F. Supple, 'The Catholic Clergy of Yorkshire, 1850–1900', *Northern History*, 21 (1985), 213.

[33] B. Aspinwall and J. F. McCaffrey, 'A Comparative View of the Irish in Edinburgh in the Nineteenth Century', in Swift and Gilley (eds.), *Irish in the City*, 140–1 (though their Irish ratio figures are incorrect); K. T. Hoppen, *Elections, Politics, and Society in Ireland 1832–1885* (Oxford, 1984), 173.

improve matters, so that, by the 1880s, probably between 50 and 60 per cent of all baptized Catholics in England and Wales (of whom there were nearly 1.5 million—three-quarters of them Irish by birth or descent) were attending mass on Sundays with a substantial degree of regularity.[34] At more or less the same time the ceremonials that were attracting such attendances were themselves undergoing profound change as the un-adorned British and Irish observances of former times gave way to the more lavish ultramontane[35] liturgical and spiritual practices already firmly established in most parts of the European continent. Even a ruggedly old-fashioned churchman like Bishop Briggs of Beverley, who in 1850 could still brusquely refer to the Pope as 'our Chief Bishop Pius', had no doubts about spreading the new Rome-centred devotions to his diocese. The first plaster statue—one of Our Lady—did not appear in a London church until 1844. Within ten years they were to be found everywhere.[36]

Also from the 1840s onwards a small number of distinguished Anglicans joined the Roman church, of whom two clergymen, John Henry Newman and Henry Edward Manning, were the most prominent. But while New-man gave English Catholicism great intellectual distinction and Manning became its ecclesiastical leader as Archbishop of Westminster in 1865, the friction between them created difficulties as well as opportunities, even if, at parish level, a high degree of co-operation was maintained between the various groups: calm traditionalists, boisterous ultramontanes, English and Irish also.[37] In 1850 Pope Pius IX appointed a full hierarchy of bishops to replace the missionary vicars-general by whom the church in England and Wales had been governed since the sixteenth century. And it was over the three decades or so that followed that British Catholicism was to acquire all those features which made it distinctive among Victorian churches: cent-ralization and clericalism, discipline in doctrine, and exclusivity in the claims and style of living it prescribed.

[34] Connolly, 'Irish and Catholic', 225–54; id., 'The Transubstantiation of Myth: Towards a New Popular History of Nineteenth-Century Catholicism in England', *Journal of Ecclesiastical History*, 35 (1984), 78–104.

[35] This term denotes the greater papal control over the worldwide church characteristic of the nineteenth century and also the gaudier Catholic devotions and imagery which accompanied it—both at variance with the Gallicanism or Cisalpinism of the preceding 150 years.

[36] J. F. Supple, 'Ultramontanism in Yorkshire, 1850–1900', *Recusant History*, 17 (1985), 274–86; S. Gilley, 'Catholic Faith of the Irish Slums: London, 1840–70', in H. J. Dyos and M. Wolff (eds.), *The Victorian City: Images and Realities*, 2 vols. (London, 1973), ii. 837–53.

[37] J. F. Supple-Green, 'The Catholic Revival in Yorkshire 1850–1900', *Proceedings of the Leeds Philosophical and Literary Society*, Literary and Historical Section, 21/3 (1990), 203–95.

Equally characteristic was Catholicism's unusual ability to maintain a presence among the poor, largely because of the way in which Irish immigrants saw their religion as a broad inclusive cultural phenomenon. Traditions of mass attendance mattered less; indeed these had not been especially high in early nineteenth-century Ireland.[38] None the less, attendance rates of 50 to 60 per cent in late Victorian British towns could only have been attained if a significant proportion of manual workers and their families went regularly to mass. But the church's influence ranged well beyond the formally devout, for non-practising Catholics—mostly Irish aliens in a strange land—often remained strongly Catholic in a social sense. They championed priests against Protestant attack, they disliked marrying 'outside' the church, they were suspicious of taking help from Protestant charities. In short, Catholicism was the only Christian form of religion which succeeded in integrating the bulk of its adherents into a working-class environment.[39]

For Anglicans and Nonconformists, industrialization destroyed existing patterns. For Catholics the coincidence of industrial change, growing towns, Irish immigration, and an expanding denominational community, not only supplied but encouraged the exploitation of a host of remarkable and unprecedented opportunities. Working-class Catholics certainly felt more at home in their religion than did many of their Protestant (or, indeed, Catholic continental) counterparts—less alienated, more integrated. Their priests responded with affections at once autocratic and relaxed. The socialist Robert Blatchford thought them the 'most devoted and the most unselfish of all clergymen'. Investigators working on Charles Booth's survey of London in the 1890s were struck by the enthusiasm and joy of congregations, by the way in which many priests obviously liked their parishioners and praised them. At Bermondsey all three priests admired 'the generosity of their people, poor and struggling'. The very tone of voice of Father Buckley of Southwark was distinctly un-Protestant: 'our people are noisy, but there's not much else the matter with them'.[40]

The one other religious body about which such things might also be said was the small Jewish community. By 1851 there were perhaps 30,000 Jews in the United Kingdom (two-thirds of them in London), by 1882 perhaps

---

[38] S. Gilley and R. Swift, 'Introduction', in Swift and Gilley (eds.), *Irish in the City*, 10; D. W. Miller, 'Irish Catholicism and the Great Famine', *Journal of Social History*, 9 (1975), 81–98.

[39] H. McLeod, *Religion and the Working Class in Nineteenth-Century Britain* (London, 1984), 39; id., *Class and Religion in the Late Victorian City* (London, 1974), 72.

[40] R. Blatchford, *A Reply to the Encyclical of the Pope* (Manchester, 1892), 19; McLeod, *Class and Religion*, 75–7.

60,000. Only thereafter did a comparatively substantial immigration take place, with about 150,000 foreign Jews settling in the British Isles between 1881 and 1914. What distinguished mid-Victorian Jewry were its increasing (but by no means universal) prosperity and the manner in which many of the members of its small but prominent economic élite sustained—especially in London—a sense of communal solidarity with their less fortunate fellows. And though Jewish Emancipation was not granted until 1858 (almost thirty years after Catholics had been allowed to sit in parliament), the manner in which Jews combined ethnic intuitions, communal cohesion, and a sense of 'otherness' in British society was closer to the experiences of contemporary Catholics than to those of any other significant religious group of the time.[41]

The growth of Victorian Catholicism gave intense catalytic boosts to the forces of anti-popery, just as these were also deriving renewed energy from creeping Protestant disappointment that a period of rapid expansion was starting to fade and from the needs of the Tory Party to find a focus for recovery after the defeats of 1829–32. The intense denominationalism of Victorian religion meant that anti-Catholicism became both a uniting and a dividing force. It could unite all Protestants in some areas and at some times. Equally it could divide them—as in mid-century Northamptonshire where Tory Anglicans noisily accused Dissenting Liberals of being 'soft' on Rome or at the Hull election of 1852 when Liberals tried to attract support by becoming even shriller than their opponents in the condemnation of popery and all its works.[42]

The first great outburst of anti-Catholicism after the Emancipation excitements of 1829 was generated in 1845 by Peel's proposal to increase state funding for the Catholic seminary at Maynooth in Ireland from £9,000 to £26,360 a year and to place that funding on a more secure basis than hitherto. The widespread agitation that ensued was orchestrated by Tories disturbed by Peel's refusal to trudge along the bigoted paths of yesteryear and by Evangelicals anxious to create a pan-Protestant alliance on terms congenial to themselves. Over 10,000 petitions with 1,284,296 signatures were presented against the proposal.[43] 'Sir', a Norfolk countryman

[41] G. Alderman, *Modern British Jewry* (Oxford, 1992), 3, 8–11, 103–4, 110; T. M. Endelman, 'Communal Solidarity among the Jewish Elite of Victorian London', *Victorian Studies*, 28 (1985), 491–526; H. McLeod, *Religion and Society in England, 1850–1914* (London, 1996), 45–7.

[42] D. G. Paz, 'Bonfire Night in Mid Victorian Northants', *Historical Research*, 63 (1990), 316–28; Hull Election Poster (1852) in author's possession.

[43] J. Wolffe, *The Protestant Crusade in Great Britain 1829–1860* (Oxford, 1991), 199. St Patrick's College at Maynooth in County Kildare had been established in 1795 with

told his vicar, 'if them there Papishers come here, I have loosed one of the bricks in my cottage floor where I can hide my Bible.'[44] An Evangelical Alliance was founded to co-ordinate a broad Protestant crusade. But while many Dissenters opposed Peel because they disliked any state support for religion, Anglicans took so different a view that, only weeks after Peel's announcement, the so-called voluntaryists seceded to form their own Protestant Dissenters' Anti-Maynooth Conference.[45] The restoration of the English hierarchy in 1850 brought anti-papist frustrations to a head. The new archbishop, Nicholas Wiseman, might sensibly have adopted less triumphalist tones in announcing his appointment than he did, but the Whig Prime Minister, Lord John Russell, did nothing to douse the flames. Russell, genuinely appalled by papal pretensions but also desperate to establish a more secure political place for himself, abandoned decades of broad-mindedness by producing a public letter to the Bishop of Durham on the eve of Guy Fawkes Day dripping with rancorous energy.[46]

I agree with you in considering 'the late aggression of the Pope upon our Protestantism' as 'insolent and insidious' . . . But I rely with confidence on the people of England . . . which looks with contempt on the mummeries and superstition, and with scorn at the laborious endeavours which are now making to confine the intellect and enslave the soul.

In fact, the 'laborious endeavours' were largely those of aggressive Protestantism. Russell introduced an Ecclesiastical Titles Bill in February 1851, designed to punish any cleric outside the established church who assumed a British territorial title, by delivering a bizarre speech touching upon the existence of an ultramontane plot to interfere with 'the temporal and civil concerns of the State'.[47] The bill, though it occupied a vast amount of time, was passed with large majorities. The new Catholic bishops ignored it. No one was ever prosecuted under it. Gladstone repealed it in 1871. Yet the excitements it reflected and engendered were very revealing. Serious anti-Catholic riots broke out in November 1850 in

government help in the hope that Irish priests would no longer be trained in continental (and increasingly revolutionary) Europe. When Peel introduced his bill on 3 Apr. 1845 he also proposed that the annual grant be made a permanent charge on the consolidated fund and that an additional non-recurrent £30,000 be provided for buildings.

[44] O. Chadwick, *Victorian Miniature* (Cambridge, 1991: 1st publ. 1960), 86.

[45] E. R. Norman, *Anti-Catholicism in Victorian England* (London, 1968), 46–7.

[46] Wiseman's pastoral letter of 7 Oct. and Russell's letter to the Bishop of Durham (4 Nov.) are in *English Historical Documents 1833–1874*, 12/1, ed. G. M. Young and W. D. Handcock (London, 1956), 364–9.

[47] *Hansard*, cxiv. 187–211 (7 Feb. 1851); G. I. T. Machin, 'Lord John Russell and the Prelude to the Ecclesiastical Titles Bill, 1846–51', *Journal of Ecclesiastical History*, 25 (1974), 277–95.

Liverpool, Birkenhead, and genteel Cheltenham. Between October and December 2,626 English memorials to the Queen protesting against the hierarchy attracted 887,525 signatures. *The Times* demanded to know if 'an Italian priest' was to be allowed 'to restore a foreign usurpation over the consciences of men'. Anglican bishops brought a kaleidoscope of adjectives to bear: York called Pius's actions 'unparalleled', Chichester preferred 'audacious', London 'subtle', Oxford 'indecent'.[48] On Guy Fawkes Day 1850 an Essex curate preached about the undoubted connections between the 'advance of Popery', 'the manifest judgements of God upon us in the famine and cholera', and 'the numerous defections that have taken place from our own Church'.[49]

While the so-called 'Papal Aggression' was no more aggressive than English involvement in the establishment of a Protestant bishopric in Ottoman Jerusalem had been in 1841, Pius IX had certainly succeeded in setting ajangle some very frayed nerves indeed. What gives the episode an especially sharp sense of paradox was its temporal closeness to the Great Exhibition of 1851, that symbol of mid-Victorian confidence and strength. Probably the very same people who on Sundays thrilled to sectarian harangues that owed much to Foxe's *Book of Martyrs* of 1559 on Mondays became thoroughly up-to-date in order to glory in the machinery and artefacts so marvellously displayed beneath the glass dome of the Crystal Palace. 'When your party', wrote the hero of Kingsley's novel *Yeast* (1851) to a Catholic convert, 'compare sneeringly Romish Sanctity, and English Civilization, I say, "Take you the Sanctity, and give me the Civilization!... Give me the public economist... and take your saints and virgins" '.

Such attitudes were whipped into spasmodic frenzy by a growing band of anti-Catholic lecturers who toured Britain in the 1850s and 1860s. A few were honest men, like the former monk, Alessandro Gavazzi. Most were rogues like the former Dominican, Giacinto Achilli, and the soi-disant Baron de Camin. Almost all depended financially upon admission fees. Their lurid handbills advertised travesties of the mass, 'the secrets of the confessional', and 'wafer Gods' to be 'sold at 1d. each at the doors'. The most famous was the Irishman, William Murphy, who arrived in England in 1862, caused riots wherever he went, was taken up by enthusiastic Evangelicals, and told his listeners that 'every Popish priest was a murderer,

---

[48] D. G. Paz, 'Popular Anti-Catholicism in England, 1850–1851', *Albion*, 11 (1979), 331–59; Holmes, *More Roman than Rome*, 76; G. I. T. Machin, *Politics and the Churches in Great Britain 1832 to 1868* (Oxford, 1977), 218–19.

[49] Norman, *Anti-Catholicism*, 69–70.

a cannibal, a liar, and a pickpocket'.[50] At the same time a small group of
MPs, chief among them Charles Newdigate Newdegate and George Whal-
ley, kept up a parliamentary barrage in favour of official inspections of
convents, in their eyes centres of viciousness and vice. Although two
notorious 'scandals' concerning girls supposedly forced to take the veil
failed to reveal much in the way of dirt, Newdegate succeeded in getting
a parliamentary committee appointed to inquire into the state of monas-
teries and convents. This proved disappointingly fair-minded and actually
recommended legal changes in favour of monks and nuns.[51] However, in
1868 Disraeli could still hope to make parliamentary waves by telling the
Commons that 'High Church Ritualists and the Irish followers of the Pope
have been long in secret combination, and are now in open confederacy'.[52]
And six years later Gladstone could still become so agitated about the
recent declaration of the doctrine of papal infallibility that he published
angry pamphlets arguing that English Catholics could henceforth owe at
best a qualified allegiance to their country and Queen.[53] But though sales
were large (145,000 copies of *Vatican Decrees* were printed in less than two
months), Gladstone's efforts—targeted primarily at Catholic opponents of
infallibility for failing to say publicly what they asserted in private—did not
ignite the country in the way that Russell had done in 1850. Nor, indeed,
did the restoration of the Catholic hierarchy in Scotland in 1878 cause
much of a stir. If not quite asleep, the anti-Catholic patient had, it seems, at
least calmed down.

The reasons for this are complex: lack of unity among Protestant milit-
ants, the belief that popular feeling no longer needed organizing, unclarity
in the relations between 'Protestantism' and 'Protectionism', the vigour of
Catholic counter-attacks, a growing perception that Disraeli's use of sectarianism was entirely cynical. Most important of all was Britain's success
in transforming itself into a religiously open civic society during the half-
century between the 1820s and 1870s without having to resort to disestablishment (except in Ireland), something which continental countries with

[50] Supple-Green, 'Catholic Revival in Yorkshire', 212–13; Machin, *Politics and the
Churches*, 253–4; Norman, *English Catholic Church*, 20–1; D. G. Paz, *Popular Anti-Catholicism
in Mid-Victorian England* (Stanford, Calif., 1992), 25–8; W. L. Arnstein, *Protestant versus
Catholic in Mid-Victorian England: Mr Newdegate and the Nuns* (Columbia, 1982), 88–107.

[51] G. F. A. Best, 'Popular Protestantism in Victorian Britain', in R. Robson (ed.), *Ideas
and Institutions of Victorian Britain* (London, 1967), 128–9; Arnstein, *Protestant versus
Catholic*, 62–5, 108–22.

[52] *Hansard*, cxci. 924 (3 Apr. 1868). Disraeli's novel *Lothair* (1870) sheds further light on
this theme.

[53] *The Vatican Decrees and their Bearing on Civil Allegiance: A Political Expostulation*
(London, 1874) and *Vaticanism: An Answer to Replies and Reproofs* (London, 1875).

Catholic majorities singularly failed to do. None the less, many of the effects of anti-Catholicism remained visible. The Catholic Church in Ireland was confirmed in its hostility to British politicians. The potential strength of Tory populism was underlined. The opposition to any endowment of Catholicism reinforced Dissenting pressures in favour of a *de facto* secularization of the state. The language of nationalism was developed in a direction that was to prove receptive to the new imperial doctrines of the later nineteenth century.[54] And the ways in which the Irish were perceived in Britain changed also. During the first third of the century they had been distrusted because they were Catholics; by the middle third they were distrusted because they were Catholics *and* un-English in culture; by the end, they were distrusted predominantly on cultural grounds. Thus, as the British themselves gradually became more 'secular', so they stopped disliking the Irish because they were Catholics (something that was a matter of choice) and started disliking them simply because they were Irish (something that was not).[55]

Wales experienced little organized anti-Catholicism (not least because Catholics were thin on the ground). However, Scotland—where disputes within the anti-Catholic camp were partly the outcome of a collision between feelings of 'Britishness' and 'Scottishness'—saw a good deal. While a common Protestant identity often helped to promote a sense of cross-border solidarity, an important element within the Free Church of Scotland led by James Begg regarded the world in militantly Scottish terms.[56] Overall, however, the Protestant–Catholic divide proved deep enough to push Scottish–English differences into a lesser category of significance. Because of this, it is important not to let the undoubted particularities of the religious experiences of Victorian Scotland and Wales disguise the existence of certain important religious phenomena common to Britain as a whole. Although Scottish denominational structures centred upon various types of Presbyterianism, they were also (as in England) based on the opposing notions of establishment and dissent. In 1843 about two-fifths of the clergy and laity left the Church of Scotland to set up the Free Church, mainly over differences regarding patronage. Four years later various groups that had broken away in the eighteenth century came together to form the United Presbyterian Church. While the Free Church at first supported the idea of a 'purified' establishment, the United Presbyterians opposed establishments as such. And it was this disruption within

[54] Wolffe, *Protestant Crusade*, 247–317; id., *God and Greater Britain: Religion and National Life in Britain and Ireland 1843–1945* (London, 1994), 214–53.

[55] Paz, *Popular Anti-Catholicism*, 79–80.

[56] Wolffe, *Protestant Crusade*, 310–11. See below, Ch. 14, ss. 2 and 4.

the Church of Scotland that led in 1844 to the setting up in England of the important Anti-State Church Association, which in 1853 changed its name to the Society for the Liberation of Religion from State Patronage and Control. By the 1870s the greater part of the Free Church too had become voluntaryist, largely because disestablishment had come to be seen as a necessary preliminary to that unity of Scottish church and nation which could alone, many believed, secure a restoration of national greatness.[57] This was a characteristically split development, with integration into broadly British non-Anglican attitudes about state churches undertaken for reasons that were distinctly Scottish in nature and origin.

The mid-century decline of strict Calvinism was also both a Scottish and an English phenomenon. But while in England the chief attack was mounted by theologians with liberal inclinations, in Scotland Calvinism was undermined by Evangelicals who stuck closely to biblical literalism and a belief in eternal punishment.[58] Evangelicalism too proved a common thread joining Scottish Presbyterianism, English Nonconformity, and sections of the Church of England. 'English' church leaders were, indeed, often not actually English at all, like the Wesleyan, Hugh Price Hughes, the great Baptist preacher, Alexander Maclaren, or even A. C. Tait who became Archbishop of Canterbury in 1868. Newer denominations like the Methodists and the Salvation Army straddled national borders. A growing realization of the importance of 'doing something' about the working-class's lack of religious enthusiasm hit churchmen throughout Britain at much the same time and in much the same ways. By the 1860s worship in the Church of Scotland was becoming less austere: hymn-singing was spreading to almost all branches of Presbyterianism and even organs were beginning to make a tentative appearance.[59]

In an overall British context, Victorian religion can, indeed, be seen to have generated dual and often contradictory effects. At times it did much to develop and maintain specifically Welsh, Irish, Scottish, and English concepts of self-realization. Thus Nonconformity came to seem characteristically Welsh; Catholicism had long possessed distinctly Irish resonances; and

[57] D. M. Thompson, 'Scottish Influences on the English Churches in the Nineteenth Century', *Journal of the United Reformed Church History Society*, 2 (1978), 32; D. W. Bebbington, 'Religion and National Feeling in Nineteenth-Century Wales and Scotland', in S. Mews (ed.), *Religion and National Identity* (Oxford, 1982), 500; G. Parsons, 'Church and State in Victorian Scotland', in Parsons (ed.), *Religion in Victorian Britain*, ii. *Controversies* (Manchester, 1988), 108–23.

[58] G. Parsons, 'Victorian Britain's Other Establishment: The Transformations of Scottish Presbyterianism', in Parsons (ed.), *Religion*, ii. 125–9.

[59] A. L. Drummond and J. Bulloch, *The Church in Victorian Scotland 1843–1874* (Edinburgh, 1975), 184.

in England and Scotland established churches just about sustained themselves as national entities (though in Scotland it was Presbyterianism *as a
whole* which tended to be seen as the national faith). At other times important trends and influences of a religious nature—Evangelicalism, liturgical
change, anti-Catholicism, theological scholarship—contributed significantly
to the formation and consolidation of more uniformly British (though not
United Kingdom) notions of awareness, perception, and identity.

2. WHO THEY WERE AND WHAT THEY DID

Common to all churches was a characteristically Victorian preoccupation
with status and relative wealth, with, in effect, class. The 1851 census
showed that Anglicans, Quakers, and Unitarians worshipped mainly on
Sunday mornings when many of those tired from manual work were still in
bed, that Congregationalists and Baptists were evenly divided between
morning and evening, that Methodists mostly worshipped in the evening
(having sometimes attended Church of England services in the morning).
Congregationalists saw themselves as quintessentially middle-class. Some
regretted this. Others rejoiced. In 1848 Algernon Wells thought their
'preaching, buildings, ministers, manners, notions, and practices' all had
'on them the air and impress of English middle-class life'. Ten years later
the minister of fashionable Cavendish Street Chapel in Manchester noted
how 'every man seemed to be looking at me over the top of a money-bag'.[60]
While statistical findings support the common perception that Primitive
Methodists were less elevated than Wesleyans, they also show that even the
Primitives' presence on the lowest social rungs declined after the 1870s.
Indeed, throughout the second half of the century the numerical core of
Dissent came firmly from around (or just below) the lower end of the
middle classes, though the composition of individual congregations could
differ very markedly. As suburbs grew, so many chapels moved to where, as
a Wesleyan noted in 1859, 'the seat-holders are gone'.[61]

Patterns of regular worship were, however, also to be found among those
skilled artisans among whom a kind of benign Smilesian reciprocity of
influences seems to have operated by which, as the Congregationalist,
Thomas Binney, noted in 1855, 'the Evangelical form of Christian ideas'
produced a faith well fitted to sustain 'those things which contribute to the

---

[60] Helmstadter, 'Nonconformist Conscience', 152–3; K. S. Inglis, *Churches and the
Working Classes in Victorian England* (London, 1963), 100.

[61] C. D. Field, 'The Social Structure of English Methodism', *British Journal of Sociology*,
28 (1977), 206–10; R. Dennis, *English Industrial Cities of the Nineteenth Century* (Cambridge,
1984), 282; Inglis, *Churches and the Working Classes*, 63–4.

satisfaction and embellishment of life' and was then, in turn, itself sustained by them.[62] A detailed survey undertaken by the *Daily News* in London a decade and a half after the end of our period showed that 11.7 per cent of adults worshipped regularly in poor districts, 16.1 per cent in upper working-class districts, and 36.8 per cent in the wealthy suburbs.[63] Not that 'class' invariably informed denominational choice. For many people it was religion rather than economic standing that provided the primary point of reference. They saw themselves as Primitive Methodists rather than working-class, Baptists rather than shopkeepers.

However that may be, within congregations of all kinds it was the better-off who provided the bulk of the leadership. Some chapels, indeed, were little more than extensions of local factory hierarchies. If Dissenters were rarely found among the aristocracy and landed gentry, almost every denomination attracted wealthy businessmen. Yet the precise relationship between religion and entrepreneurial impulses is difficult to pin down. The Society of Friends, for example, encompassed a wide range of attitudes. Some successful businessmen like William Isaac Palmer (of Huntley & Palmer, biscuit-makers) combined economic success and rigorously 'plain' (to use the Quaker term) styles of living. Some like William White (of White & Pike, printers) were 'plain' and devout, but entrepreneurial failures. Then there were men who remained Quakers but became 'worldly' and yielded to none in the ruthlessness of their financial practices, like the four sons of William Bryant of the match manufacturers Bryant & May. Others resigned from the Society entirely. Indeed, almost any combination of attitudes and behaviour seems to have been possible.[64]

Contrary to accepted stereotypes, many businessmen were, however, not Dissenters at all, but Anglicans. Cotton masters, for example, easily surpassed the landed and professional classes as builders of Anglican churches. A study of the family backgrounds of late Victorian businessmen shows Quakers, Wesleyans, and Congregationalists supplying more entrepreneurs than might statistically have been expected, Baptists, Primitive Methodists, and Catholics less.[65] When, however, one looks to affiliation rather than background, Anglicans (and Unitarians) also join the above-average cat-

---

[62] Bebbington, *Evangelicalism*, 127.

[63] McLeod, *Class and Religion*, 26–7.

[64] Obelkevich, *Religion and Rural Society*, 195; D. J. Jeremy, 'Important Questions about Business and Religion in Modern Britain', in Jeremy (ed.), *Business and Religion in Britain* (Aldershot, 1988), 12–13; T. A. B. Corley, 'How Quakers coped with Business Success: Quaker Industrialists 1860–1914', ibid. 164–87.

[65] J. Garnett and A. C. Howe, 'Churchmen and Cotton Masters in Victorian England', in Jeremy (ed.), *Business and Religion*, 79–80; A. C. Howe, *The Cotton Masters 1830–1860* (Oxford, 1984), 61–72.

egory. Nor should entrepreneurial religious commitment be seen as merely an unctuous attempt to attract public esteem. While motives remain ultimately irrecoverable, by no means all devout princes of industry were obvious hypocrites. The responsibilities as well as the rights of wealth were widely appreciated. Commercial crises convinced many of the moral as well as practical differences between speculation and investment. Alfred Marshall's *Principles of Economics* (1890), which famously rejected the classical view that self-interest constituted the only efficient economic force and urged businessmen to adopt 'economic chivalry' instead, employed imagery and language which had long been the common coin of debate in religious circles generally and Evangelical circles in particular.

Unlike the rural gentry, though, Anglican entrepreneurs showed no very great interest in ecclesiastical patronage.[66] When in 1874 patronage was abolished in the Church of Scotland there were still many south of the border who believed that much of the English establishment's peculiar excellence flowed from the independence of its pastors as guaranteed by the wide variety of means by which they were appointed. Above all, the fact that so many advowsons (or rights of presentation to benefices) were in lay hands prevented, it was widely claimed, the Church of England from being dominated by a clerical élite. Indeed, the proportion of benefices to which bishops could appoint, though growing, remained comparatively small: 19.9 per cent in 1878 compared to 11.8 per cent in 1835.[67]

The appointment of bishops themselves was a matter of discussion between prime ministers and Queen Victoria, who could never be disabused of the idea that she was 'head' of the church in a more than merely constitutional sense. The Queen held strong views and liked broad-minded liberal clerics. Some prime ministers—notably the devout Salisbury—gave in; others—notably the equally devout Gladstone who believed that 'we politicians are children playing with toys in comparison to that great work of . . . restoring belief '[68]—argued her into irritation. After Disraeli's resignation in 1880 the notion of appointing bishops on political grounds slowly began to fade. At the parochial level, too, patrons such as the crown, the lord chancellor, and Oxford and Cambridge colleges were becoming somewhat more responsible in their efforts to seek out worthy and respectable

---

[66] Garnett and Howe, 'Churchmen and Cotton Masters', 80.

[67] Chadwick, *Victorian Church*, ii. 207; M. J. D. Roberts, 'Private Patronage and the Church of England 1800–1900', *Journal of Ecclesiastical History*, 32 (1981), 201–2, 209–10. In the Church of Ireland there was little private patronage (W. E. Vaughan, *Landlords and Tenants in Mid-Victorian Ireland* (Oxford, 1994), 14).

[68] J. Morley, *The Life of William Ewart Gladstone*, 3 vols. (London, 1903), ii. 524.

men.[69] Curiously, however, the one 'abuse' that was never mentioned was the universal neglect of the wishes of parishioners themselves. Financial and moral irregularities caused far more anguish. Not only could advowsons be bought and sold, but the right of the next presentation could be bought separately and patrons could present almost anyone in holy orders, not excluding themselves. In 1878 over 12 per cent of the 6,228 livings in private hands had patron-incumbents, another 10 per cent were held by persons with the same surnames and many others by close relatives with different names.[70] Some ecclesiastical operators found it possible to build up impressive networks of clerical clients and kin. William Rowe Lyell, who became Dean of Canterbury in 1845 and was an averagely upright man, succeeded in obtaining preferment for himself worth £64,000 (over his lifetime) and for eight relatives worth £169,000—a total of £233,000 in all.[71] But despite growing disquiet, few reforms were introduced before the Benefices Act of 1898. And even its provisions were modest: sales by auction more or less outlawed, certain dubious financial transactions disallowed, bonds of resignation (by which incumbents agreed to resign when asked) abolished.

Social and economic developments proved more powerful agents of change. Already before the agricultural depression beginning in the mid-1870s parish land was becoming separated from advowsons. As a result, the traditional view that a close relationship should exist between land and the Church of England became more difficult to sustain. This had, in any case, long been more common in fiction than reality. The kind of village in which church services were regularly graced by a squire in the best pew, respectable farmers in theirs, then benches of labourers in smocks, and in which congregations sat 'with a stolid attentiveness, not liking to be absent because of the squire... but in no way sorry to be there' was becoming increasingly rare. Indeed, by 1860 only a tenth of all Leicestershire villages had a resident squire at all.[72] Neither the idea that attendance was automatically high in the countryside nor the notion that the Church of England exercised some deep hold over the rural population can be sustained. Village parsons complained of the 'irreligion' of their flocks, per-

[69] M. D. Stephen, 'Gladstone's Ecclesiastical Patronage 1868–1874', *Historical Studies*, 11 (1964), 145–62.

[70] Chadwick, *Victorian Church*, ii. 209. Purchasers of the next presentation only could not, however, appoint themselves.

[71] C. Dewey, *The Passing of Barchester* (London, 1991), 43–4.

[72] Chadwick, *Victorian Church*, ii. 151; D. M. Thompson, 'The Churches and Society in Nineteenth-Century England: A Rural Perspective', in G. J. Cuming and D. Baker (eds.), *Popular Belief and Practice* (Cambridge, 1972), 270.

haps not as often as their colleagues in towns, but often enough.[73] Until well into the twentieth century most villages remained intensely local places. The church was kept locked and the practice of putting up sheets with service times in the porch so that strangers might be informed hardly known. Yet it was, above all, from this closed and highly circumscribed village milieu that the late Victorian Church of England continued to take many of its governing habits and ideas—and many of its problems too.

This failure to adjust to changing circumstances was neither confined to the Church of England nor of recent vintage. Although low levels of religious practice had long been a gift presented by the countryside to the towns, rapid population growth gave these a greater prominence than before. 'More especially in cities and large towns', declared the organizer of the 1851 census, 'it is observable how absolutely insignificant a proportion of the congregations is composed of artizans'.[74] Similar conclusions emerged from other systematic inquiries: newspaper surveys of 120 English and Scottish towns in 1881, Charles Booth's study of late Victorian London (which concluded that 'the great mass of the people remain apart from all forms of religious communion'), and Richard Mudie-Smith's splendid *Daily News* investigation of 1902.[75] Impressionistic evidence pointed the same way. Not three out of a hundred mid-century costermongers had ever been inside a church according to Henry Mayhew, who also noted the typical comments of one who had 'heerd a little about our Saviour,—they seem to say he were a goodish kind of a man; but if he says as how a cove's to forgive a feller as hits you, I should say he know'd nothing about it.'[76]

A virtual industry—still flourishing—grew up to explain why this should be so. Charles Kingsley confidently knew the answer in 1848 when he insisted that 'It is our fault. We have used the Bible as if it was a mere special constable's handbook—an opium-dose for keeping beasts of burden patient while they were being overloaded.'[77] As Edward Miall put it in 1849, once inside a chapel 'the poor man is made to feel that he is a poor man, the rich is reminded that he is rich'.[78] Some had no qualms about keeping the poor at arm's length. Others felt ashamed of their prejudices, like the Dulwich vicar who admitted to thinking, while in a third-class railway carriage, that 'If Heaven is worse than this I don't want to go there'.[79]

---

[73] McLeod, 'Class, Community and Region', 38–9.

[74] Gay, *Geography of Religion*, 58.

[75] G. Parsons, 'A Question of Meaning: Religion and Working-Class Life', in Parsons (ed.), *Religion*, ii. 73–5; Chadwick, *Victorian Church*, ii. 235–6.

[76] H. Mayhew, *London Labour and the London Poor*, 4 vols. (London, 1861–2), i. 21, 40.

[77] Chadwick, *Victorian Church*, i. 353.

[78] E. Miall, *The British Churches in Relation to the British People* (London, 1849), 211.

[79] R. O'Day, 'The Men from the Ministry', in Parsons (ed.), *Religion*, i. 274.

Small wonder that for many earnestly religious Victorians mission fields abroad seemed to provide the most hopeful opportunity for mass evangelization. Developing the aims of the major missionary societies founded around the end of the eighteenth century, they drew up increasingly ambitious plans for the conversion of all the peoples of the earth, the heroic grandeur of which was matched only by an equally heroic insensitivity. Indeed, Christianity and Anglo-Saxon cultural and economic 'success' were offered to 'lesser peoples' as a single unsplittable package. On handing the Kabaka of Buganda a Bible in 1881 a Church Missionary Society representative declared it to be 'the key to the secrets of England's greatness and glory'. However, even many of those in Africa, Asia, and elsewhere who responded most enthusiastically to missionary endeavour (and many responded very negatively) proved themselves no less selective and subversive in their uses of Christianity than did the poor inhabitants of the slums of Glasgow, Manchester, or Leeds.[80]

Both could see that worship and its appurtenances were rarely designed to make them feel at ease. In many churches in Britain the best seats were, for example, reserved for those prepared to pay. Indeed, pew-renting was one of the most ecumenical aspects of Victorian religion—common to Anglicans, Dissenters, Scottish Presbyterians, and Catholics alike.[81] Prices varied greatly. At Rotherham's main Independent chapel in the 1870s one pew went for five guineas, one for £2, and the rest then followed down to 10s. At an Anglican chapel of ease outside Sheffield 580 sittings cost 2s. a year while 120 were free. The Wesleyan Park Chapel (also in Sheffield) charged: first row 9s. 6d., second row 8s., third row 6s. 6d., fourth row 5s., fifth row 4s., with seats in the corners at 3s. In nineteenth-century Glasgow pew rents first rose as accommodation failed to match growing congregations, and then fell when the new Free Church started an ambitious building programme of its own. It was all a matter of supply and demand. By 1851 just over half the sittings throughout England and Wales had been appropriated by one means or another.[82] But while the renting system was often wheeled-out as a neat monocausal explanation for working-class

---

[80] R. Hyam, *Britain's Imperial Century 1815–1914* (London, 1976), 50–2, 56–7; E. A. Ayandele, *The Missionary Impact on Modern Nigeria 1842–1914* (London, 1966), 3–152.

[81] Inglis, *Churches and the Working Classes*, 50–4. Almost all pre-1800 Anglican parish churches did not charge, though pews were often 'appropriated' by the better-off without payment.

[82] E. R. Wickham, *Church and People in an Industrial City*, 5th edn. (London, 1964), 49, 76, 79; C. G. Brown, 'The Costs of Pew-Renting: Church Management, Church-Going and Social Class in Nineteenth-Century Glasgow', *Journal of Ecclesiastical History*, 38 (1987), 347–61; P. A. Welsby, 'Church and People in Victorian Ipswich', *Church Quarterly Review*, 164 (1963), 212.

absence, its decline towards the end of the century produced no flood of new recruits.

The gulf between the churches and the poor was marked out by more than charging for pews. Working men spoke of clerical hypocrisy, excessively 'educated' ministers, over-subtle theology, of being seldom visited in their houses, of boring sermons. Many more said simply that 'they were very tired, and they liked a walk in the afternoon'.[83] The clergy, especially the Anglican clergy, seldom grasped that it was their social behaviour—the way they talked, dressed, moved their bodies, lectured, frowned—rather than their social ideas which kept the people from church. The 'settlements' set up in slum areas from the 1880s onwards where young well-to-do men lived for a time under clerical guidance to 'give an example' achieved little. The socialist ideas of a few unrepresentative churchmen achieved less, not least because many of the most articulate working men were ardent Gladstonians, strong believers in low taxation and the minimal state.[84] Individual priests and ministers, especially when obviously holy men, attracted local support. Though this rarely lasted for long, it is significant that Catholic priests were often especially admired for their willingness to enter the worst of places to visit the sick and the dying. 'Many a man that's not a Catholic', remarked one of Mayhew's costermongers, 'has rotted and died without any good person near him'.[85] By contrast, Evangelical missionaries, like William Jackson active in Birmingham in the 1840s, too often combined insensitivity and confidence in a way that can only have repelled. Calling on a couple whose baby had just died, he reminded them of former sinfulness and how 'God in His mercy had spared them and visited them with another warning... by taking their infant to Himself'.[86]

This 'gloomy' and widely accepted picture of the Victorian churches' impact upon working people has, reasonably enough in certain respects, been put together by viewing the landscape from a particular perspective and through lenses fashioned by particular kinds of analysis. However, even quite modest adjustments can effect considerable alterations. Thus, while most of the four out of five British citizens who can be designated working-class failed to attend, let alone join, any church, the majority of those who

[83] Chadwick, *Victorian Church*, ii. 266–7.

[84] E. R. Norman, *Church and Society in England 1770–1970* (Oxford, 1976), 127, 159, 163–5; Inglis, *Churches and the Working Classes*, 143–74; E. F. Biagini, *Liberty, Retrenchment and Reform: Popular Liberalism in the Age of Gladstone, 1860–1880* (Cambridge, 1992), 84–138.

[85] Mayhew, *London Labour*, i. 21.

[86] G. Robson, 'The Failures of Success: Working Class Evangelists in Early Victorian Birmingham', in D. Baker (ed.), *Religious Motivation* (Oxford, 1978), 389.

did attend were undoubtedly manual workers and their families. In Scotland many congregations—arguably a majority—were dominated by working people, specifically by skilled workers. In England, much the same was true of the industrialized regions of the Midlands and North. This, indeed, helps to account for one of the thorniest problems the 'pessimist' case has had to face since fuller statistical evidence has become available showing that overall church membership actually increased in relation to population during most of the Victorian period and that decline has largely been a twentieth-century phenomenon.[87] Significant regional differences in attendance levels also suggest that in certain areas the proportion of working people going to church must have been very substantial indeed. Above all in Wales a strong working-class presence remained a feature of religious life until 1914 and even beyond.[88]

Distress that not more people worshipped was of course widespread at the time. And while some of the recruiting tactics adopted in response proved more vigorous than sensitive, they generally 'spoke to the condition' both of the growing middle class and the better-off sections of the working class which together provided the bulk of congregations in towns and cities of every kind. Such people furnished the new members without which denominations atrophy and die. It was they who responded to the conversionist strategies common to almost all churches: revivalist meetings, Anglo-Catholic ceremonial, Roman Catholic missions, Salvation Army marches, Wesleyan Central Hall meetings, Christian Endeavour Societies, Bands of Hope, organizations devoted to the creation of Pleasant Sunday Afternoons. And it was among them too that the Gladstonian message about the importance of good husbandry by the state mingled with Smiles's teaching about good husbandry by individuals to create a Christianity whose middle-class values could be (and were) adapted downwards without compromising skilled working-class integrity or independence.

Collectivist notions made altogether less impact. They offended those intent upon self-help and were too vague to attract the masses of un-

[87] Brown, *Religion in Scotland*, 81–3, 154, 165; id., 'Did Urbanization Secularize Britain?', *Urban History Yearbook* (1988), 1–14; H. McLeod, *Religion and Irreligion in Victorian England* (Bangor, 1993), 29–31; A. Hoppen, 'Presbyterians in Victorian Hull', *Journal of the United Reformed Church History Society*, 5 (1995), 349–52; Thompson, 'Churches and Society', 272–3; P. T. Phillips, *The Sectarian Spirit: Sectarianism, Society, and Politics in Victorian Cotton Towns* (Toronto, 1982), 14, 79, 169, 176–7; P. Hillis, 'Presbyterianism and Social Class in Mid-Nineteenth Century Glasgow', *Journal of Ecclesiastical History*, 32 (1981), 47–64.

[88] Snell, *Church and Chapel*, 26–7; Coleman, *Church of England*, 37; Inglis, 'Patterns of Religious Worship', 80–1; W. R. Lambert, 'Some Working-Class Attitudes towards Organized Religion in Nineteenth-Century Wales', *Llafur*, 2 (1976), 4–17.

employed poor. Certainly the Christian Socialists of the 1850s, such as
F. D. Maurice and J. M. Ludlow, and the later High Church Radicals, like
Stewart Headlam who founded the minuscule Guild of St Matthew in
Bethnal Green in 1877 and Henry Scott Holland whose Christian Social
Union started work in 1889, did have an impact, but it was upon middle-
class religious activists rather than upon those outside. On practical questions—health legislation, factory inspection, limits upon hours of work—
the church socialists had little to contribute. What they did do was persuade
bishops into uttering well-intentioned vacuities at the very moment when
the Church of England was entering its long numerical decline. Prominent
Nonconformist ministers trod similar paths, some, like the Wesleyan,
Hugh Price Hughes, being especially good at clothing unexceptionable
ideas in fiery-sounding rhetoric. And though the Catholic Archbishop
Manning cut a somewhat more convincing figure when supporting strikers,
his views too lacked both consistency and bite. The only truly Radical
Catholic bishop—Bagshawe of Nottingham (who delivered two virulently
anti-capitalist pastorals in 1883 and 1884)—was universally dismissed as
eccentric if not actually deranged.[89]

More effective in keeping religion before the public eye were preaching
and revivalism, whether of the American or the home-grown variety.
Middle-class Victorians loved sermons, the longer the better. A typical
mid-century Anglican Evangelical like the Revd W. W. Andrew of Ketter-
ingham in Norfolk thought one and a quarter hours a proper length, while
John Angell James of Birmingham's Carr Lane Independent Chapel kept
going for hours at a stretch by sucking upon oranges thrown to him by
friends below the pulpit. Almost every denomination had its oratorical stars
and 'sermon-tasting' was rife among the devout. The Baptist, Edward
Clodd, who came to London in 1855, visited several preachers each Sunday, not only Baptists, but Congregationalists, Unitarians, Broad Anglicans, High Anglicans, and many others too.[90]

When transferred to large halls, open fields, or meetings specifically
dedicated to spiritual renewal, sermons could become powerful instruments of conversion, sometimes long-lasting, often not. The initial revivalist impulse came from a confluence of early Methodism and importations
from North America. Both Charles Finney (an unorthodox Presbyterian)
and the Methodist James Caughey toured England in the 1840s and helped

[89] Inglis, *Churches and the Working Classes*, 311–12; Norman, *English Catholic Church*,
155–7, 197–8.
[90] Chadwick, *Victorian Miniature*, 91; Davies, *Worship and Theology*, 286; E. Clodd,
Memories (London, 1916), 9–11; D. Bowen, *The Idea of the Victorian Church* (Montreal,
1968), 140–1.

to inaugurate a new phase of more 'organized' revivalism—well-prepared, planned in advance, and based on the notion that all might be saved.[91] A contemporary description of one mid-century Primitive Methodist revival in Lincolnshire captures the flavour of this transitionary period.

.Several courses of special service have been held, which, under the blessing of Jehovah, have been very effective, and showers of saving grace have been vouchsafed. The consciences of the guilty have been grappled with; a free, full, and present salvation has been urged; and though we have had some dreadful conflicts with the powers of darkness, the hosts of Israel have been more than victorious.[92]

The thirty years beginning about 1850 saw this new organized revivalism at its height. Its most impressive native exponent was the Baptist, Charles Haddon Spurgeon, who preached in chapels, the open air, and in the magnificent Metropolitan Tabernacle built for him near the Elephant and Castle at a cost of £31,000, and whose combination of feeling, tears, laughter, and modest learning lightly worn was expertly presented rather than unusual in itself. When, therefore, the American evangelists, D. L. Moody and I. D. Sankey, first toured the British Isles between 1873 and 1875, they came to land already prepared. If anything, Moody's preaching was probably less powerful than Spurgeon's. What gave it unprecedented effect was the brilliance of Sankey's singing and tunes. Comfort after death, ultimate salvation, and, above all, the reuniting of families in the hereafter formed the core of Sankey's message.

> Meet me there, oh meet me there,
> No bereavements we shall bear,
> There no sighings for the dead
> There no farewell tear is shed;
> We shall, safe from all alarms,
> Clasp our loved ones in our arms.[93]

Powerful too were the musical and religious endeavours of the Salvation Army, effectively a new sect created by the revivalist zeal of William Booth, an Anglican, who, having moved through various Methodist groups, became an independent preacher in 1861 and began holding meetings in tents reminiscent of early Methodist revivalism. 'One young woman shook

---

[91] J. Kent, *Holding the Fort: Studies in Victorian Revivalism* (London, 1978), 9–37.

[92] R. W. Ambler, *Ranters, Revivalists and Reformers: Primitive Methodists in Rural Society: South Lincolnshire 1817–1875* (Hull, 1989), 73.

[93] The words for this item in Sankey's *Sacred Songs and Solos* were actually by E. G. Taylor (Kent, *Holding the Fort*, 230).

her head, saying, "No, not tonight", but soon was on the ground pleading mightily with God.... One brother said, "Oh, Oh! if this ain't heaven, what'll heaven be?" '[94] By 1878 the term Salvation Army, the uniforms, the military nomenclature, had become established. Though none of this was entirely novel, Booth's organizational abilities and personal magnetism gave his movement an unusually high profile in the streets of late Victorian towns. Although most of its members were lower middle-class, the Army could sometimes reach further down the social scale than all except the Catholics. It was cheery, happy, and loud. It aroused great dislike and its parades were often attacked by publican-inspired louts marching under the title of the Skeleton Army. But though the Army proved numerically successful (50 corps and 88 officers in 1878; 1,006 corps and 2,260 officers in 1886), its impact upon slums can easily be exaggerated. East London, with a population of almost a million, yielded all of 3,123 weekly attendances in 1886 and still only 6,376 in 1903. In an effort to overcome such apathy, Booth eventually abandoned his earlier lack of interest in social questions ('What does it matter if a man dies in the workhouse ... if his soul is saved?') in favour of dramatic attacks upon the evils of overcrowding and disease. But although his *In Darkest England and the Way Out* (1890) caused a sensation, it left the masses unmoved. They never read it, and even those who did were not always immediately beguiled by the harsh schemes of social engineering such as 'farm colonies' and compulsory emigration by which Booth hoped to solve 'the Problem of the Unemployed'.[95]

Revivalism was not, however, confined to fundamentalist Protestants. Already by the 1840s Catholic priests belonging to orders such as the Passionists, the Rosminians, and the Redemptorists were conducting emotional 'missions' on a parochial level. Redemptorists in particular could deliver hell-fire sermons with enough brimstone to make even the extremest Evangelical envious. But, while using methods familiar to all, Catholic revivalism also drew inspiration from internal sources, notably the seventeenth-century French example of St Vincent de Paul. Thus the Rotherhithe mission of 1861 ended with a huge meeting in the open with indulgences offered for kissing a 10ft cross that bore a red thorn crown and had scourges and a lance and sponge attached to it. In turn, High Church Anglicans borrowed much from Rome, with revivals that stressed the sacraments, the renewal of baptismal vows, and were parish-based. Indeed, the impact of their Twelve Days London Mission of November 1869

---

[94] Inglis, *Churches and the Working Classes*, 181, also 175–214.
[95] Chadwick, *Victorian Church*, ii. 293; R. Mudie-Smith (ed.), *The Religious Life of London* (London, 1904), 25; Inglis, *Churches and the Working Classes*, 176, 199–200.

explains why so many Evangelicals welcomed Moody and Sankey as authentic Protestant counterweights to recent ritualistic success.[96]

Whether the disproportionate presence of women in congregations was the result of a particular response to revivalism is uncertain. The fact of their greater enthusiasm, however, is not. Women made up 57 per cent of Church of Scotland communicants in 1874. In London and York at the end of the century two-thirds of Anglican, three-fifths of Catholic, and just over half of Nonconformist congregations were female.[97] Evidence from late Victorian Bradford suggests that the much-lamented absence of the working classes in reality meant the absence of working-class men. And even Nonconformity, though it attracted a comparatively high proportion of males, was more successful in gaining them as adherents than as members.[98] However, once international comparisons are made, it is the high rather than the low level of male participation which deserves comment. In large parts of France about 5.5 women attended for every man. In Britain the figure was nearer 1.3.[99]

The prominence of women members was not, however, reflected in the prominence of women leaders. By the 1850s even the Primitive Methodists and Bible Christians had abandoned their initial enthusiasm for female preachers. Women made enormous contributions to the Church of England as district visitors and Sunday School teachers, but were rigidly excluded from its representative bodies until 1919. Specifically female organizations like the Mothers' Union (founded in 1876 and 200,000-strong by 1900) were acceptable, but excursions into mainstream 'male work' were not. The female diaconate, so strong in Protestant Germany, never played more than a minor role in Victorian Anglicanism.[100] Nor did a brief efflorescence of middle-class female preaching in the 1860s last for long. Even those women most publicly dedicated to evangelization tended to regard themselves as 'the weak vessels' and their activities, above all, as a precious sign that 'God

[96] G. Parsons, 'Victorian Roman Catholicism', in Parsons (ed.), Religion, i. 172; id., 'Emotion and Piety: Revivalism and Ritualism in Victorian Christianity', ibid. 223–6; Gilley, 'Irish Slums', 839; Kent, Holding the Fort, 236–94.

[97] Brown, Religion in Scotland, 251; E. Royle, Modern Britain: A Social History 1750–1985 (London, 1987), 331; Bebbington, Evangelicalism, 128.

[98] H. McLeod, 'Varieties of Victorian Belief', Journal of Modern History, 64 (1992), 330; Bebbington, Victorian Nonconformity, 32–3.

[99] McLeod, Class and Religion, 30; J. Obelkevich, 'Religion', in F. M. L. Thompson (ed.), The Cambridge Social History of Britain 1750–1950, 3 vols. (Cambridge, 1990), iii. 341.

[100] McLeod, 'Varieties of Victorian Belief', 328–30; Obelkevich, 'Religion', 341–2; C. M. Prelinger, 'The Female Diaconate in the Anglican Church', in G. Malmgreen (ed.), Religion in the Lives of English Women, 1760–1930 (London, 1986), 161–92.

hath chosen the weak things of the world to confound the things which are mighty' (1 Cor. 1: 27).[101]

More significant in providing a lasting context for female endeavour were the religious orders for women in the Catholic and, to a lesser extent, the Anglican Church. Indeed, the Victorian revival of communal life in the Church of England began among women: six sisterhoods were founded 1845–51, nine 1851–8, fifteen 1870–1900. Their numbers were, however, overshadowed by those of the Catholic sisters and nuns, of whom there were 3,000 in England by 1873 and about 10,000 by the century's end.[102] Joining a convent was one of the few assertions of independence which a Victorian woman could make, and contemporary Protestant critics who saw convent life as a denial of freedom profoundly misunderstood its character. But, though convents could be ruled by women, they remained part of a male-dominated ecclesiastical organization and themselves mirrored the social divisions of the time. Over a third of those recruited came from working-class backgrounds and half of these entered houses which distinguished between richer 'choir' nuns and poorer 'lay sisters', the latter often little more than domestic servants. Even the so-called 'undivided' orders were generally marked by clear, if less explicit, distinctions. Yet there were some exceptions, notably the Franciscan Missionaries of St Joseph founded in 1871 by Alice Ingham, a cotton carder, in which all posts rotated and even illiterates could become heads of houses, under the title not of Mother Superior but of 'Good Mother', and the Sisters of the Cross and Passion founded by Elizabeth Prout (the daughter of a cooper) in the 1850s.[103] Far from inhabiting some remote planet, most Victorian nuns managed to combine, in an unusually complex manner, a capacity for independence with submission to the dominant norms of the day.

Attempts to make regular worship more attractive constituted a key strategy for those willing to look beyond sporadic revivalism. Hymn-singing started to spread in the Church of England from the 1820s onwards and soon became perhaps the greatest bond between Protestants of almost every kind. During the 1850s and 1860s over 400 collections were published in England alone, with the famous *Hymns Ancient and Modern* first appearing

---

[101] O. Anderson, 'Women Preachers in Mid-Victorian Britain', *Historical Studies*, 12 (1969), 470–3, 478–80, 483.

[102] S. P. Casteras, 'Virgin Vows: The Early Victorian Artists' Portrayal of Nuns and Novices', in Malmgreen (ed.), *English Women*, 131; S. O'Brien, ' "Terra Incognita": The Nun in Nineteenth-Century England', *Past & Present*, 121 (1988), 110.

[103] S. O'Brien, 'Lay Sisters and Good Mothers: Working-Class Women in English Convents, 1840–1910', in W. J. Sheils and D. Wood (eds.), *Women in the Church* (Oxford, 1990), 453–63.

in 1861.[104] A good deal of adjustment and modification took place. 'Rock of Ages' was sung by many who rejected its full-blooded Calvinism. 'Nearer my God to Thee' (written by a Unitarian) was often altered to give it a more Christological thrust. Old shockers like 'There is a fountain filled with blood' were eased out and A. M. Toplady's brilliant line 'When my eye-strings break in death' (in 'Rock of Ages') was silently neutered to 'When mine eyelids close in death'. The sentiments expressed bolstered contemporary notions of authority and hierarchy. They recommended charity rather than justice and deferred the rewards of the righteous poor to the life hereafter. Often the tunes mattered more than the words and the spread of hymn-singing was accompanied by the spread of organs and the disappearance of the raucous instrumental bands of former times.

Most other developments in worship took a generally 'Catholic' line. In the Church of England the half-century beginning in 1830 saw a trend towards the use of choirs, more frequent services, congregational responses, and the replacement of pews by benches. Sermons eventually became shorter, buildings less grubby. Nonconformists too began to use set prayers in place of extempore ones, as well as choirs and organs. Hugh Price Hughes even set up a Methodist sisterhood. Scottish Presbyterians were especially active: by the 1880s services in both the established and the Free Church would have struck eighteenth-century observers as dangerously elaborate.[105]

While the majority of Anglican parishes followed a moderate line—more dignity and reverence but nothing too gaudy—the appearance of 'ritualism' in the late 1840s introduced a quite deliberately 'Catholic' note in certain places. While early nineteenth-century High Churchmen had stressed things like frequent communion, new-model ritualists (responding more or less equally to certain forms of mid-Victorian taste and to the notion that colourfulness would attract the poor) wanted ornate services conducted in ornate churches by ornately attired priests. Though much of this began to get under way in the 1840s, colonization was slow and it always remained a minority affair. As late as 1888 less than 16 per cent of Anglican churches used vestments, less than 3 per cent used incense.[106] However, the general location of extreme practices in towns (where a multiplicity of Anglican churches led to liturgical competition) gave them a prominence which could easily lead to violent protest and even to riots, as at Exeter in 1845

[104] J. Obelkevich, 'Music and Religion in the Nineteenth Century', in Obelkevich, L. Roper, and R. Samuel (eds.), *Disciplines of Faith* (London, 1987), 554.
[105] Chadwick, *Victorian Church*, i. 518–22, ii. 326–7; Parsons, 'From Dissenters to Free Churchmen', 99–101.
[106] Chadwick, *Victorian Church*, ii. 318–19, 514–15.

and 1848, East Grinstead in 1848 and 1857, Pimlico in 1850–1, and East London in 1859–60. When the Revd W. J. E. Bennett built St Barnabas at Pimlico in 1850 with rood screen, stone altar, and lots of stained glass, and in it deployed surpliced choirs, candles, incense, and the like, plain-clothed policemen had to be posted inside to prevent disorder.[107] Whether any of this—as opposed to the personal sanctity of Anglo-Catholic clerics like Robert Dolling and Charles Lowder—attracted working people is doubtful, though it certainly attracted sections of the middle class.

What ritualist practices like lighted candles on altars and the use of unleavened bread did succeed in doing was drive maddened Protestants to seek redress in the courts. In the 1830s parliament had abolished the High Court of Delegates (the supreme tribunal for ecclesiastical affairs) and transferred its jurisdiction to the Judicial Committee of the Privy Council, which knew little of church or canon law. Curious and contradictory judgements began to be handed down, some of them mildly amusing like that authorizing the use of lit candles but only when needed for the purposes of providing light. A royal commission on ritual, set up in 1867, produced four unhelpful reports. Extreme ritualists ignored decisions which went against them. Queen Victoria was much distressed. Archbishop Tait of Canterbury determined that something should be done. But as long as Gladstone remained Prime Minister the state held back.[108]

Then, in February 1874, Disraeli returned to office. As he had not expected to win the election and had few legislative plans he gave a fair wind to Tait's Public Worship Regulation Bill. When enacted, this turned out to be a disaster. Its procedures were blunt, its wording imprecise. Five clergymen were sent to gaol. Four were soon released. But the Revd S. F. Green of Miles Platting remained incarcerated from 19 March 1881 until 14 November 1882—considerably longer than the roughly contemporaneous imprisonment of Charles Stewart Parnell in Kilmainham Gaol—because no one could find a way of getting him out.[109] Soon bishops began to veto prosecutions. Some Evangelicals, most of them laymen, complained that this meant that the wishes of a Protestant parliament and nation were being ignored. In this they were, of course, quite correct. Indeed, not the least interesting aspect of the failure to pursue ritualism with persistent

[107] G. Parsons, 'Reform, Revival and Realignment: The Experience of Victorian Anglicanism', in Parsons (ed.), *Religion*, i. 52; Davies, *Worship and Theology*, 122–3.
[108] P. T. Marsh, *The Victorian Church in Decline: Archbishop Tait and the Church of England 1868–1882* (London, 1969), 116–26; Parsons, 'Reform, Revival and Realignment', 53–5; Chadwick, *Victorian Church*, ii. 308–27.
[109] Marsh, *Church in Decline*, 185–6, 226–33, 277, 284; Chadwick, *Victorian Church*, ii. 348; J. Bentley, *Ritualism and Politics in Victorian Britain* (Oxford, 1978), *passim*.

vigour is what it reveals about the growing clericalization of the Church of England during the last decades of the Victorian age.

For many people, however, religion meant something very different from the tenets propagated by the clergy. On the one hand, what might loosely be called semi-pagan attitudes played a powerful part in certain popular beliefs. On the other, a diffuse, vague, and undogmatic Christianity attracted large numbers who went to church rarely if at all. The former existed mainly in the countryside, the latter almost everywhere. A parson on the North Yorkshire moors found much local interest in holy wells, magical cures, and witches among 'sensible, clear-headed, intelligent people'. Another in rural Norfolk noted in 1846 how one woman had wounded another in order to draw blood from someone 'known' to be a witch. In mid-Victorian Lincolnshire the devil—clearly seen as a person— was always referred to obliquely ('Old Nick', 'Old Sam'). The sacred universe 'inhabited' by many agricultural labourers and small farmers was not only fluid, pluralistic, and lacking any unifying principle, but peopled by beings and forces of a distinctly naturalistic kind.[110]

Villagers might go to the parish church on Sunday mornings and to the Methodists in the afternoon, but then put up a 'kern baby' (a straw doll) or a horse shoe over the door or ask permission of the 'old Gal' (the spirit of elder trees) before chopping elder wood. Though Christianity and this kind of 'paganism' were intellectually exclusive, the logic by which they were comprehended in the popular mind was usually 'both/and' not 'either/or'. Folk religion stretched along a wide spectrum, from certain kinds of popular Protestantism, through the use of Christian symbols and rites in curing diseases, to beliefs utterly remote from any orthodoxy. In particular, dreams required interpretation, and in this folk religion touched close to those mainstream believers (notably Methodists) who found visions and dreams of pressing Christian concern.[111] Roman Catholicism too, particularly in rural Ireland and among Irish immigrants, was often popularly intermingled with a range of beliefs far removed from the teachings of the official church: in fairies, the evil eye, changelings, holy wells, banshees.[112] Anglicanism, however, being singularly devoid of the kind of paraphernalia capable of bridging the gap between a transcendental deity and ordinary villagers, rarely succeeded in touching the popular mind in anything like the same way.

[110] Atkinson, *Forty Years*, 52, 60–3, 74–5, 97, 234–5; Chadwick, *Victorian Miniature*, 85–6; Obelkevich, *Religion and Rural Society*, 259–312.

[111] Obelkevich, *Religion and Rural Society*, 306–7, 232, 254.

[112] Hoppen, *Elections*, 211–24; R. Samuel, 'The Roman Catholic Church and the Irish Poor', in Swift and Gilley (eds.), *Irish in the City*, 284–7.

More widely spread still was the desire to give a religious dimension to rites of passage, something in which the Church of England (with its ubiquity and manpower) did, however, excel. Indeed, the unrivalled popularity of its 'occasional services' probably constituted the church's greatest parochial achievement in the Victorian period. The modern harvest festival (as, indeed, the modern Christmas) was invented in the nineteenth century and proved enormously popular, not least among those who rarely went to church but wanted to mark seasonal change, recall imagined rusticities, and sing rousing hymns. In 1894 some 85 per cent of all marriages in England and Wales still took place under religious auspices. Working people regarded christenings and church weddings as 'lucky'. Victorian London combined the nation's lowest levels of church attendance with the greatest incidence of Anglican marriages.[113] Few working people were secularists, but many dealt with the churches and the supernatural on their own terms, taking what they needed and ignoring the rest. 'These people's idea of Christianity', said an East London missionary, 'is "Doing the best you can and doing nobody any harm". They appear to think that if they don't get to heaven, there was little chance for anybody'.[114] Charles Booth found the same: small interest in doctrine but a generalized belief in Christ the Good Shepherd, a confidence that 'good people' would be taken care of in the life to come, a conviction that the Bible was a uniquely worthwhile book, and that children in particular should be exposed to its teachings.[115]

In the end, contemporary perceptions of the churches as special and holy entities were perhaps most seriously undermined by the clergy's eagerness to convert the indifferent by means of enthusiastic (and often uncritical) participation in secular pursuits. The last three decades of the century saw an involvement in clubs, societies, and associations so great and pervasive that at times it seemed as though many clerics had come to believe that the cheery comradeship of cricket and bicycling could, unaided, carry weak and sinful humanity to the glory of eternal life. By the 1890s the thirty-one Anglican and fifty-five major Nonconformist places of worship in Lambeth alone were supporting fifty-eight thrift societies, fifty-seven mothers' meetings, thirty-six temperance societies for children and nineteen for adults,

---

[113] F. Knight, *The Nineteenth-Century Church and English Society* (Cambridge, 1995), 86–105; Obelkevich, *Religion and Rural Society*, 158–60; J. Kent, 'Feelings and Festivals: An Interpretation of some Working-Class Religious Attitudes', in Dyos and Wolff (eds.), *Victorian City*, ii. 865–6; Chadwick, *Victorian Church*, i. 517; O. Anderson, 'The Incidence of Civil Marriage in Victorian England and Wales', *Past & Present*, 69 (1975), 52–5; Cox, *English Churches*, 90–105.

[114] McLeod, *Class and Religion*, 49–50.

[115] Cox, *English Churches*, 93–4.

thirty-six debating clubs, twenty-seven girls' clubs, twenty-five sports teams, twenty-five penny banks, twenty-one clothing clubs, seventeen Boys' Brigade and Church Lads' branches, and much more besides.[116] St Mary's Free Church of Scotland in Govan had Sunday schools with 1,137 members, Sabbath Forenoon Meetings with 469, a Literary Society with 185, male and female fellowships with 213; it had 420 enrolled in its temperance meeting; it organized 292 home workers and ran a Penny Savings Bank which registered 19,000 transactions a year.[117]

That Victorian men were obviously attracted by the clerical life is clear enough. Between 1841 and 1891 the number of clergymen in the Church of England rose from 14,613 to 24,232 and in the major Methodist groups from 1,877 to 3,552. In 1851 the Church of Scotland and the Free Church together had 1,860 ministers, forty years later they had 2,853. Congregationalist ministers increased in number from 2,338 in 1866 to 2,782 in 1882, Catholic priests in Britain more than threefold between 1845 and 1891.[118] Overall, however, the population grew faster still. Whereas Anglicans, Methodists, and Catholics in England and Wales provided one cleric for every 914 inhabitants in the mid-1840s and 1 for every 883 in 1861, by 1901 the ratio was 1 for every 1,004. Even so, the citizens of England, Wales, and Scotland consistently enjoyed the services of more clergymen—were, as some might say, more 'priest-ridden'—than the inhabitants of any other European country save Italy and Spain. Certainly the Irish, notorious for allegedly being knee-deep in priests, got along well enough with much lower levels of provision with regard to ecclesiastical personnel.[119]

For Anglican clerics (much the largest group) the long eighteenth century from 1700 to 1840 had seen an enormous rise in income: for those with benefices at least 400 per cent and perhaps (taking the effects of pluralism and private means into account) as much as 700 per cent. By the 1830s the median income of English incumbents was £275, of Welsh £172. But, while this was higher than it had been before, many still thought it less than the minimum needed (perhaps £400) to sustain the style of a gentleman.[120] Then, during the four decades beginning about 1840 incomes generally stood still, and the agricultural depression had a disastrous effect from the mid-1870s onwards, especially upon the tithe-

---

[116] Cox, *English Churches*, 58, 299–301.
[117] Brown, *Religion in Scotland*, 147–8.
[118] Currie, Gilbert, and Horsley, *Churches and Churchgoers*, 196–212.
[119] J. Harris, *Private Lives, Public Spirit: A Social History of Britain 1870–1914* (Oxford, 1993), 151; Hoppen, *Elections*, 171–3. Though the Irish figures are constructed differently from the British, the point can hardly be doubted.
[120] Virgin, *Age of Negligence*, 71–4, 90–3.

dependent clergy of the countryside. Until the 1850s handbooks on professional careers spoke optimistically of clerical remuneration. Thereafter they became gloomy. While the mean pay of curates did rise from about £73 in 1853 to £129 in 1873, a substantial increase in the number of curates meant that the median income of parochial clergymen as a whole registered no significant change.[121]

The majority of English and Welsh clergy outside the established church had always been obliged to rely on spiritual rather than material rewards. Catholic priests (who did not, of course, have to support wives and children) received as little as £25 plus maintenance in the Leeds diocese in 1863, much less than their counterparts in Ireland.[122] Nonconformist ministers, with a few notable exceptions, were also poorly paid. In 1853 the Congregational Union proudly claimed that only a tenth of its ministers received less than £70—and Congregationalists were better off than most. Baptist clergymen hovered around £65, with some getting much less. Wesleyans laid down salaries centrally, but many local congregations (in 1879 a third) proved unable to pay. In the 1860s married Wesleyan ministers were supposed to get £117, Primitive Methodists £50, and Bible Christians £40. The £36 paid by the Gainsborough (Lincolnshire) second Primitive Methodist circuit to its minister in 1852 put him on a level with farm labourers. All too often Nonconformist ministers found themselves desperately dependent upon a few prominent individuals. In 1844 four-fifths of Eliakim Shadrack's income at Dursley (Gloucestershire) came from five Congregational families. When one moved, he was down to £65.[123] It was difficult for a man with a family to live respectably on such sums and remain optimistic while giving comfort to the sick and dying, holding services, travelling the countryside, preaching, and providing Christian example. Small wonder that Dissenting denominations experienced a chronic haemorrhage of men out of the ministry, as emigration, disillusionment, and illness between them generated high levels of 'early retirement'.[124]

Nonconformists recruited ministers from the lower middle and skilled working classes. The Congregationalists were the most elevated, the Primitive Methodists the least. Between 15 and 20 per cent in virtually all the

---

[121] Ibid. 99–103; Chadwick, *Victorian Church*, ii. 167–8; A. Haig, *The Victorian Clergy* (London, 1984), 8–12, 223–5, 298–301, 319–29; W. T. Gibson, 'The Professionalization of an Elite: The Nineteenth-Century Episcopate', *Albion*, 23 (1991), 248.

[122] Chadwick, *Victorian Church*, ii. 251; Hoppen, *Elections*, 224–32.

[123] K. D. Brown, 'An Unsettled Ministry? Some Aspects of Nineteenth-Century Nonconformity', *Church History*, 56 (1987), 218–21; id., *Nonconformist Ministry*, 148–9, 152–5.

[124] Brown, 'An Unsettled Ministry?', 205–11.

sects were themselves the sons of ministers. Very few were graduates. In 1870 only one in a hundred Baptist ministers had any university experience.[125] Although a traditional Dissenting stress upon 'the call' (rather than training) held back the establishment of denominational colleges, formal arrangements for those wishing to be ordained were gradually introduced, by, for example, Wesleyans in 1834 and Primitives in 1868. In 1870, when half of all their ministers were still 'untrained', the Baptists were already running ten colleges.[126]

The educational backgrounds of Anglican clergymen moved in the opposite direction. The increasing attractiveness of secular careers meant that a smaller proportion of Oxbridge graduates sought ordination. Indeed, by 1862 one ordinand in four had not attended a university at all. After expanding in the eighteenth century, the proportion of graduate clergy began to fall in the years after 1850. In 1841 86 per cent of ordinands came from Oxford and Cambridge (and 7 per cent from Dublin and Durham). In the 1860s only 65 per cent and 9 per cent respectively did so. During the 1840s almost three-quarters of all Oxbridge graduates still became priests. By the mid-1870s, as the two ancient English universities transformed themselves from ecclesiastical into secular institutions, only a half did so. And the decline in recruitment was most marked among those with first-class degrees.[127] Much snobbishness, however, continued, to be directed at degreeless ordinands. As J. T. Baylee (the Principal of one of the new Anglican training colleges) bitterly pointed out in 1860, Peter the Fisherman would have stood little chance of ordination at the hands of any member of the mid-Victorian episcopal bench.[128]

The combined influences of the Evangelical and Tractarian Movements gradually transformed clergymen into exclusively religious specialists. Fewer Anglican priests became magistrates, more resided in their parishes. From the 1860s onwards that ultimate badge of clericalism—the dog collar—became common.[129] While Dissenting ministers continued to be

[125] Brown, *Nonconformist Ministry*, 19–55; C. Binfield, *So Down to Prayers: Studies in English Nonconformity 1780–1920* (London, 1977), 241; O'Day, 'Men from the Ministry', 267–8.

[126] R. O'Day, 'The Clerical Renaissance in Victorian England and Wales', in Parsons (ed.), *Religion*, i. 207–8; id., 'Men from the Ministry', 267–8.

[127] Gilbert, *Religion and Society*, 133; Parsons, 'Reform, Revival and Realignment', 25; Chadwick, *Victorian Church*, i. 522; Haig, *Victorian Clergy*, 30–2, 51. Because many Oxbridge matriculants did not take degrees at this time the proportion of those *admitted* to the two universities who became priests was lower—perhaps a half in the 1840s and less than two-fifths in the 1870s.

[128] Haig, *Victorian Clergy*, 143.

[129] Gilbert, *Religion and Society*, 131–4; J. L. Altholz, 'The Warfare of Conscience with Theology', in Altholz (ed.), *The Mind and Art of Victorian England* (Minneapolis, 1976), 61.

subjected to lay pressure, the priests of the establishment increased their influence within an institution that was growing more clericalist by the day. In the Roman community, too, priests and especially bishops were coming to wield considerably more power than had been the case forty years before.[130]

As theologians attempted to respond to what they considered to be the imperatives of a new age, this growing clericalism gave notable institutional authority to their efforts and to the manner in which they chose to interpret the relationship between religious and secular thought. In the 1830s and 1840s the debate about *laissez-faire* had already assumed important theological dimensions. Evangelicals in particular had formulated a variety of politico-economic analyses based upon different views of divine providence. Those who believed in 'general' providence or the operation of overall natural laws had opposed state activism, while more extreme fundamentalists who claimed that providence operated 'specially' by *ad hoc* interventions in terrestrial affairs had been prepared to countenance similar interventions on the part of human authorities.[131] What, however, such early and mid-century Evangelicals did not disagree about was the central truth of the doctrine of the atonement, the idea that Christ died on the cross as a substitute for sinful mankind. For them the world was to be seen essentially in terms of depravity—men and women separated from a transcendental God by original sin with only Christ's redeeming blood capable of ransoming them. In the 1850s this heavy stress upon human sinfulness started to weaken as the focus of theology moved from the centrality of the atonement towards an emphasis upon the comforting doctrine of the incarnation as expressing the love, mercy, and fatherhood of God. The drama of redemption was now increasingly conceived—by theologians and others—in terms of the redeeming participation of the divine in human affairs. Punishment began to be seen as reformative rather than vindictive, while incarnational thinking tended to emphasize the practical fellowship of all mankind.[132]

As a result, churchmen adjusted their attitudes to hell. Already in the 1840s and 1850s Nonconformist divines, like the Congregationalists Edward White and Baldwin Brown, questioned whether the ungodly would in fact suffer everlastingly. By the 1870s new hymns rarely mentioned hell at

---

[130] Brown, 'An Unsettled Ministry?', 215–17; Roberts, 'Private Patronage', 220; Obelkevich, 'Religion', 314–17.

[131] B. Hilton, 'The Role of Providence in Evangelical Social Thought', in D. Beales and G. Best (eds.), *History, Society and the Churches* (Cambridge, 1985), 215–33.

[132] G. Parsons, 'Social Control to Social Gospel', in Parsons (ed.), *Religion*, ii. 59; Davies, *Worship and Theology*, 196–8.

all and Methodists of various kinds were talking of death in terms of 'peace and sleep'.[133] Even the Baptists faltered sufficiently on hell-fire to induce Spurgeon to leave their Union in 1888. The publication the following year of a book of essays by moderate High Anglicans entitled *Lux Mundi* showed how much things had changed. The atonement itself was now interpreted in heavily incarnational terms, divine punishment was seen as reformative, and the literalness of the Bible qualified. Reactions to such developments ranged from a digging-in of heels, through uncertainty, to adjustment and reform. Apart from a few stalwarts like Spurgeon, the response of official Christianity was to adapt. On the one hand, many clerics found it easy—deceptively easy perhaps—to incorporate mid-Victorian evolutionary theory into their theological systems. On the other, church services became shorter and 'brighter', and much effort was devoted to turning Christ into 'Saviour and Friend', rather like a popular minister of religion—smiling but grave, learned, full of help, understanding, and fun.[134]

Although widespread and unambiguous numerical retreat did not take place until after 1900, its arrival was foreshadowed by the inability of the late Victorian churches to recruit with anything like their former vigour. The problem lay not so much in a leakage of existing adherents as in the absence of new ones. More important than any internal 'crisis of faith' was that 'crisis of plausibility' which had begun to erode the place of organized religion within a wider society decreasingly predisposed to take a religious view of things. By the early twentieth century the wealthy suburbs which had seen the greatest growth in participation over the previous fifty years, though they remained the epicentres of activism, were beginning to experience the greatest *proportional* decline.[135] Universal concepts like 'secularization' provide only a very partial explanation for this. After all, the United States of America, which also felt the effects of nineteenth-century industrial and urban growth, has maintained much higher levels of church attendance well into our own day. Yet perhaps it is the United States that constitutes the exception, for the British (though not until much later the Irish) experience has proved by far the more common in Europe as a whole. However that may be, it remains the case that signs of numerical erosion did not become unambiguously apparent until after the end of our period.

[133] Parsons, 'From Dissenters to Free Churchmen', 105; G. S. R. Kitson Clark, *An Expanding Society: Britain 1830–1900* (Cambridge, 1967), 104; R. Currie, *Methodism Divided* (London, 1968), 119–20.

[134] Obelkevich, 'Religion', 334–5; Currie, *Methodism Divided*, 125; Brown, *Nonconformist Ministry*, 50–2. For the relationship between religion and evolutionary thought, see below, Ch. 13, s. 3.

[135] McLeod, *Religion and Society*, 178–9.

The years between 1846 and 1886 witnessed the coming to maturity of the dramatic religious growth of the late eighteenth and early nineteenth centuries. Maturity, however, invariably generates problems of its own. And in the case of the mid-Victorian churches it led, by all sorts of predictable and unpredictable routes, to eventual senescence and decline.

CHAPTER 13

The Evolutionary Moment

I. SPENCER, DARWIN, AND OTHERS

The characteristics of any past age are revealed not simply by political and social developments, but by the manner in which contemporaries tried to explain their situation in time and place and by the language and concepts in which such explanations were formulated and discussed. In the case of mid- and late Victorian Britain the ambiguous and slippery notion of 'evolution'[1] generated perhaps the most striking cluster of concepts around which the governing ideas of the time were put together and assessed. Indeed, the appearance of views of society constructed out of an engagement with certain kinds of evolutionary analysis constitutes a division between the later Victorian period and what had gone before at least as significant as the movement towards electoral democracy or the development of the party system.

Already in the eighteenth century the idea of evolution had begun to acquire a variety of new biological meanings suggesting the existence of patterns of internal organic organization independent of—or at least divorced from—the influence of any external 'creator' or 'creative force'. Two tendencies were at work here. On the one hand, evolutionary thinking acquired a more focused character at the hands of scientists like the German biologist, Karl Ernst von Baer, who argued in the 1820s that the development of embryos involved the production of varied and complex structures out of earlier states of homogeneity and simplicity.[2] On the other, evolution was also increasingly being pressed into service as a broad term to describe any historical process or sequence of events. Colonial expansion, for example, led people to make overt comparisons between

---

[1] Neither 'evolution' nor 'Darwinism' were ever uncontested words (J. Moore, 'Deconstructing Darwinism: The Politics of Evolution in the 1860s', *Journal of the History of Biology*, 24 (1991), 353–408).

[2] P. J. Bowler, *Evolution: The History of an Idea* (Berkeley, Calif., 1984), 122–3.

the existence of 'primitive' types of social organization in the past and their 'survival' into the present. And it was such modes of comparative analysis which, when combined with a growing interest in German historical thought, helped to create a mounting dissatisfaction with those doctrines of early nineteenth-century utilitarianism emphasizing the fundamental likeness of all men and women in all times and hence with the plausibility of theories of society deduced from psychological assumptions about humanity as a whole.

The key mid- and late nineteenth-century figures in this new comparative endeavour—the lawyer Sir Henry Maine, the anthropologists General Pitt-Rivers, J. F. McLennan, and E. B. Tylor, the philosopher and sage Herbert Spencer—placed as they were amidst the ruins of utilitarianism, performed the remarkable feat of reasserting the essential unity of mankind, not by means of theories of human identity as such, but by explaining obvious differences as no more than different stages in the same universal and evolutionary process.[3] They believed themselves to be involved in the working out of rapid and profound change: 'they knew that their society was travelling, and they wanted to know the route and destination'.[4] Modern geological research, in particular, seemed to provide a method and an encouragement, having, during the early nineteenth century and above all in the writings of Charles Lyell, come to emphasize the continual operation of natural laws as sufficient cause for observable change, and having also introduced a large and expansive time-scale into the study of past ages. As Maine wrote in 1871, 'If indeed history be true, it must teach that which every other science teaches, continuous sequence, inflexible order, and eternal law'.[5]

Cutting across much of this, but also drawing considerable inspiration from Lyell's geological researches, was the work of Charles Darwin, whose book on *The Origin of Species by means of Natural Selection, or the Preservation of Favoured Races in the Struggle for Life* appeared in 1859. Already well before this it had of course been possible to buttress general speculations of an evolutionary kind with a variety of popular scientific arguments. In particular, *The Vestiges of the Natural History of Creation* (1844)—the work, it later emerged, of the amateur naturalist, Robert Chambers—had caused a sensation by broadening Lyell's concept of uniform geological laws and thereby greatly extending the potential claims of Victorian

[3] Id., *The Invention of Progress: The Victorians and the Past* (Oxford, 1989), 33.
[4] J. W. Burrow, *Evolution and Society: A Study in Victorian Social Theory* (Cambridge, 1966), 100.
[5] H. Maine, *Village-Communities in the East and West* (London, 1871), 266.

naturalism (that view of the world and of man which excluded the hypo-thesis of some controlling or directing force outside nature itself).[6]

What, however, Darwin did in *The Origin* was to put forward a new and crucial mechanism by which the evolution of species might be explained—namely natural selection or the differential survival in nature of such genetic variations as arise and are beneficial to the being in question under its conditions of life. The work had so enormous an impact that its author soon became the increasingly protesting victim upon whom all sorts of evolutionary speculations were indiscriminately lumbered. The more nerv-ous thought his views were turning the whole world upside down, polit-ically no less than intellectually (and certainly Darwin was happy to see his book, which might have been made ready earlier, appear during the relatively stable late 1850s rather than during the years of Chartist agitation and violence). *The Times*, noticing Darwin's later *The Descent of Man* in 1871, deplored the propagation of such 'disintegrating speculations' at the very moment when Paris was aflame with Communard incendiarism.[7] And even though Darwin himself did not use the actual word evolution at all until the fifth (1869) edition of *The Origin* (and then with some hesitation), few readers could have doubted the more obvious implications of his work. Indeed, it was precisely because evolutionary ways of thinking had already become so ubiquitous and elastic, that Darwin's most original contribu-tion—natural selection—was itself rapidly absorbed into a range of (not always compatible) systems of thought. This was why, certainly by the 1860s if not earlier, the idea of evolution had come, not only to imply a view of affairs in which flux rather than permanence represented reality in nature, but to acquire notions of linear direction and 'progress' as well.

Into this maelstrom of ideas dropped—perhaps oozed is a better word—the voluminous writings of Herbert Spencer. After enjoying a prodigious reputation for insight and synthesis, these were already being exiled to the lumber-room of redundant Victoriana by the time of Spencer's death in 1903. But it remains the case that the general formulation of some of the key notions commonly seen as 'Darwinian' should more properly be assigned to Spencer than to Darwin.[8] This does not mean that Darwin took much in the way of technical inspiration from non-scientists like Spencer (or indeed

---

[6] R. M. Young, *Darwin's Metaphor: Nature's Place in Victorian Culture* (Cambridge, 1985), 44–6, 88–92.

[7] A. Desmond and J. Moore, *Darwin* (London, 1991), 581. In *The Variation of Animals and Plants under Domestication* (1868) and elsewhere Darwin stressed that evolution was a multi-causal affair which depended on far more than natural selection alone.

[8] D. R. Oldroyd, *Darwinian Impacts* (Milton Keynes, 1980), 125, 207; P. Crook, *Darwin-ism, War and History* (Cambridge, 1994), 41–3.

Malthus), merely that—as a child of his time—he, too, inevitably found himself operating in an intellectual environment increasingly shaped by ideas of energy, struggle, and competition.[9]

By the 1850s Spencer (a self-made intellectual who was contributing to numerous important periodicals and becoming increasingly known in educated circles) had already lighted upon a jumbled fund of scattered facts and speculations including the 'tendency to individuation' of Coleridge and Schelling, Lamarck's theory that evolution takes place as a result of the inheritance by progeny of the characteristics acquired by their ancestors in direct response to environmental conditions (one of the main objects of attack in Darwin's *Origin*), von Baer's formula of 'the development of every organism as change from homogeneity to heterogeneity', and the theories of the Belgian zoologist, Milne-Edwards, concerning the 'physiological division of labour'.[10] A search for mutual echoes between zoology and economics appealed especially to Spencer, whose object it soon became to produce a theory in which evolution could provide a total explanation for all phenomena—with the single but significant exception of those occurring in the inaccessible realms of the 'Ultimate Cause' or, as Spencer liked to call it, 'The Unknowable'. What Spencer did was to extend the so-called 'laws' of evolution to all spheres of existence—social, organic, and physical—and to inject into the whole affair the clear and unambiguous notion of 'Progress' which, he argued as early as 1857, 'is not an accident, not a thing within human control, but a beneficent necessity'.[11] And it was Spencer who introduced the phrase 'survival of the fittest' (later, perhaps unwisely, adopted by Darwin himself), who popularized the Lamarckian version of evolution, and who, because of his intense belief that nature and society obey the same laws, made valiant and persistent attempts to subsume natural selection into an overall view of life.

Spencer, relying on a mixture of intuition and highly selective plunderings from others, devoted nearly forty years to the writing of his

[9] S. Gordon, 'Darwin and Political Economy: The Connection Reconsidered', *Journal of the History of Biology*, 22 (1989), 437–59; but see also Young, *Darwin's Metaphor*, 23–55.

[10] Burrow, *Evolution and Society*, 188–96.

[11] 'Progress: Its Law and Cause', *Westminster Review*, NS 11 (1857), 484. Spencer's final definition of evolution reveals his interest in both physics and biology no less than his eclecticism: 'An integration of matter and concomitant dissipation of motion; during which the matter passes from an indefinite, incoherent homogeneity to a definite, coherent heterogeneity; and during which the retained motion undergoes a parallel transformation'. Inevitably, this was parodied, especially neatly by the Revd T. P. Kirkman: 'Evolution is a change from a nohowish, untalkaboutable all-alikeness, to a somehowish and in-general-talkaboutable not-all-alikeness, by continuous somethingelsifications and sticktogetherations' (J. R. Moore, *The Post-Darwinian Controversies* (Cambridge, 1979), 165, 375).

multi-volume *System of Synthetic Philosophy* (1860–96). Here was offered a detailed rationale for human progress, a map, and—despite certain quali- fications—a hope for the future. Here too the theories of *laissez-faire* capitalism were justified as being in tune with necessary and natural evolutionary processes. Although Spencer's intense belief in individualism to some extent preceded his supposedly 'scientific' theories, the framework in which it was eventually elaborated and argued shows the enormous power which science and scientific models had begun to exercise over mid- and late Victorian students of politics and society. As a result, politics became, in Spencer's case, charged with deterministic inflexibility—the great law of evolution quite simply forbidding trade unions, church estab- lishments, public health legislation, poor laws, or the protection of trade as unnatural interferences in the working-out of cosmic processes. Slow and gradual change alone could prove permanent; struggle was unavoidable until the eventual age of peace and harmony arrived; premature reform (before human evolution had fully prepared the way) merely delayed the golden dawn. And because Spencer's theory postulated, not consistent progress, but the possibility of frequent bouts of 'dissolution', so political leaders must needs be constantly watchful to prevent any dangerous 'inter- ferences' that might encourage such temporary reversions to more primit- ive states. For Spencer, the upheavals of the late Victorian years, with their strikes and unrest, their colonial wars and dangerous compromises with collectivism, marked just one such set of barbaric reactions to a premature increment of freedom.[12] Spencer and his followers were, however, by no means alone in providing so explicitly directional a reading of evolution, for even the ambiguities of Darwin's own arguments, especially in his letters and in *The Descent of Man* were capable of creating a blurring of necessary distinctions between biological and social evolution, while his adoption of Spencer's phrase 'the survival of the fittest' involved all sorts of implica- tions of which he was possibly unaware. It is, therefore, unsurprising that less acute contemporaries should have merged the views of the two men into a grand if inconsistent unity to encompass also those older evolutionary traditions from which, for example, anthropologists like McLennan and Tylor had taken their inspiration.

Darwin's very language might, indeed, sometimes have almost been designed to attract that wider popular audience from which he formally protested to shrink and which, by its very extent and catholicity, helped to conflate his own tolerably specific theories with much vaguer and broader

---

[12] D. Wiltshire, *The Social and Political Thought of Herbert Spencer* (Oxford, 1978), 135–64, 192–224.

concepts of evolution. Thus he cites proverbs of profit and loss. He talks of many a mickle making a muckle, of the race being to the swift, of progress through competition, of handsome is as handsome does, of reflecting that in the midst of life we are in death.[13] And so too did some even of his most rigorous scientific followers, with, for example, Michael Foster, the Cambridge physiologist, speaking of mammals as 'living up to their physiological incomes' (while cold-blooded creatures 'saved' for the future) and referring to wise and unwise investments in the animal economy.[14]

Evolutionary models and evolutionary ways of thinking achieved, therefore, a very high prominence both among the public and among scientists themselves. Even in so seemingly distant a field as chemistry, important spectroscopic work undertaken in the 1860s and 1870s led William Crookes to formulate a scheme of 'elemental evolution' inspired by reading Spencer (not Darwin).[15] More striking still—as the writings of John Hughlings Jackson show—was the way in which clinicians studying the functioning of the nervous system and of the brain now made use of evolutionary ideas. Jackson, who held several influential medical appointments in London between 1862 and 1906, made important contributions to the age-old debate concerning cerebral localization or whether the various parts of the brain possess relatively distinct mental, behavioural, and physiological functions. On taking up the topic in the 1860s he was much struck by Spencer's evolutionary arguments in favour of a form of localization less rigid than that postulated by the phrenologists, who, despite their errors, had earlier raised crucial issues concerning the relationship of mind and brain. In particular, Jackson's observations of epileptic convulsions were closely informed by Spencer's theories (which feature much more prominently in his writings than those of Darwin).[16]

The influence of Spencer's evolutionism went both deeper and broader than this, for it gave Jackson a unifying conception within which to contrive a general approach to the structure, functioning, and diseases of the nervous system as a whole. More specifically, Jackson was much impressed by Spencer's frequent assertion that evolution did not refer only to the development of species towards 'higher forms', but that the prevalence of

---

[13] C. C. Gillispie, *The Edge of Objectivity* (London, 1960), 303.

[14] G. L. Geison, *Michael Foster and the Cambridge School of Physiology* (Princeton, 1978), 350.

[15] Crookes's Presidential Address to Section B (Chemistry) in *Report of the Fifty-Sixth Meeting of the British Association for the Advancement of Science ... 1886* (London, 1887), 558–76.

[16] R. M. Young, *Mind, Brain and Adaptation in the Nineteenth Century*, new impression (Oxford, 1990), 197–248.

unhelpful conditions could and did produce 'dissolution' or a regression towards more primitive stages.[17] With repeated acknowledgements to Spencer, Jackson published in the 1880s a series of papers setting out a model of the nervous system as consisting of three evolutionary levels, in which the lowest related to innate, stereotyped performance, the middle to acquired adaptive behaviour, and the highest to abstraction, discrimination, and communication.[18] Jackson deduced from this that, by analogy with evolutionary dissolution, the process of decay in nervous disease involved sequential damage to the levels, with the removal of the inhibitions of the higher levels and centres in the brain resulting in uncontrolled action by the lower. 'Dissolution', as he put it in his Croonian lecture of 1884,

being the reverse of the process of evolution...is a process of undevelopment...Hence the statement, 'to undergo dissolution' is rigidly the equivalent of the statement, 'to be reduced to a lower level of evolution'. In more detail: loss of the least organised, most complex, and most voluntary, implies the retention of the more organised, the less complex, and the more automatic.[19]

In consequence, the elaborate 'positive' symptoms of mental illness (illusions, hallucinations, delusions) are not, Jackson argued, the outcome of the activity of nervous elements damaged by any pathological process, but arise during activity on the still-intact lower evolutionary levels. A whole school of dissolutionary neurophysiology grew up, and Jackson's picture of individuals as the mental epitomes of their ancestral states (to which they could all too easily revert) provided scientific ammunition to those who saw social unrest as a return to the anarchy of primitive times. Jackson, who ended his life with the expression 'Thank heaven we have a House of Lords' often upon his lips, was well aware of the analogy and likened his account of neurological dissolution to the destruction of the nation's 'governing body', which would, in its turn, ensure both 'the loss of services of eminent men' and 'the anarchy of the now uncontrolled people'.[20]

Jackson's neurological conception of the individual corresponded closely with those speculations concerning social regression which formed so constant a part of Spencer's analysis, and which, like much contemporary

[17] J. H. Jackson, *Neurological Fragments with a Biographical Memoir by James Taylor* (London, 1925), 10–11.
[18] The general relationship of such views to Freud's system of id, ego, and super-ego, and to Pavlov's unconditioned reflex, conditioned reflex, and second signal system, highlights the existence of a broadly common matrix for ideas in neurology, psychiatry, and psychology.
[19] 'Evolution and Dissolution of the Nervous System' in *Selected Writings of John Hughlings Jackson*, ed. J. Taylor, 2 vols. (London, 1931), ii. 46.
[20] Ibid. ii. 47.

evolutionary social theory, recognized that seemingly irrational, absurd, and superstitious practices might well possess useful functions, albeit as part of a process towards an eventual (perfect) state in which they were to have no role. In particular, Jackson's pattern of neurological levels bore a close resemblance to the new anthropological doctrine of 'survivals', in itself a neat way of explaining the continued existence among advanced cultures of 'primitive' practices which seemed to serve no social function but could now be satisfyingly designated as simple relics of past times. Survival-hunting, indeed, became a major industry in Victorian Britain and proved of interest not only to anthropologists, but also to folklorists and to imaginative writers like Thomas Hardy, whose Wessex novels provide an extended commentary on the physical and psychic tensions created by the juxtaposition of 'survivals' (of custom, belief, sense of place) and present predicaments.[21]

Sir John Lubbock, a disciple of Darwin, who came to anthropology by means of evolutionary biology, noted in *The Origin of Civilization* (1870) that the 'study of the lower races of men', apart from its directly imperial relevance, could illustrate 'much of what is passing among ourselves, many customs which have evidently no relation to present circumstances, and even some ideas which are rooted in our minds, as fossils are imbedded in the soil'.[22] Though others, such as McLennan (author of the important *Primitive Marriage* of 1865) and Tylor, may have owed less to biological inspiration, their work too was presented within a comparative and broadly evolutionary framework. As Reader in Anthropology at Oxford, Tylor hoped that the appreciation of 'survivals' as no more than primitive relics would hasten their rejection and speed the course of social improvement. But while Tylor and Lubbock gave the story an overarching context of progress, however painful and slow, others (like Spencer and Jackson) stressed the constant dangers of regression, of sliding back, of chaos and dissolution.[23]

2. PROGRESS, DISSOLUTION, HOPES, FEARS

The relationship between evolutionism and theories of progress was, indeed, an extraordinarily complicated one, involving as it did an inter-mingling of scientific, philosophical, religious, and political considerations.

[21] E. B. Gose, jun., 'Psychic Evolution: Darwinism and Initiation in *Tess of the D'Urbervilles*', *Nineteenth-Century Fiction*, 18 (1963), 261–72.

[22] J. Lubbock, *The Origin of Civilization and the Primitive Condition of Man* (London, 1870), 1.

[23] Burrow, *Evolution and Society*, 228–59.

Darwin himself was no simple neutral and disinterested propounder of detached scientific hypotheses, and those who claimed to be extending his ideas into a wider conceptual world were not invariably bringing dishonest intellectual paternity suits against a wronged and misunderstood sage.[24] In part this flowed from the fact that, in natural selection, Darwin really had no satisfactory mechanism at all, lacking as he did genetics and molecular biology; but in part also from a personal inability to apply his vision with the full unremitting intensity of its own internal logic. Words like 'selection', 'favoured', 'struggle', 'preservation' (all of them present in the very title of his most famous book) strike a particular note right from the start. Natural selection is described as 'acting', as having 'visual powers' and 'skills'.[25] A kind of watery optimism keeps breaking through. 'It is apparently', he wrote in *The Descent of Man*, 'a truer and more cheerful view that progress has been much more general than retrogression; that man has risen, though by slow and interrupted steps, from a lowly condition to the highest standard as yet attained by him in knowledge, morals and religion'.[26] But while he tended to express himself with moderation—and never, for example, adopted the harsh racialist attitudes that were becoming fashionable in certain circles—he remained convinced that those agencies of population pressure, struggle for existence, encroachment and extinction of races, which were no less important to his theory of natural selection than they had been to Malthus, had all profoundly shaped the development of mankind. The tantalizing hints presented in *The Origin* were followed by intensive reading in the 1860s among a wide range of writers on social evolution—Spencer, Tylor, McLennan, Lubbock, Bagehot, and the eugenicist Francis Galton—many of whom were already either extending Darwin's own ideas or incorporating them into pre-existing evolutionary blueprints of their own. Unremittingly the emphasis was on the favourite problem of mid- and late nineteenth-century social theorists: the causes of progress and retrogression in human history.[27]

What is especially striking, and what, almost more than anything else, marks so many of these writers as men of a certain generation, was the way in which evolution provided them with an explanation, even a law, of progress, while at the same time giving a scientific or pseudo-scientific edge to all sorts of intellectual and political doubts. As early as 1862 the

[24] Bowler, *Invention of Progress*, 94–7.

[25] Young, *Darwin's Metaphor*, 93–4.

[26] C. Darwin, *The Descent of Man and Selection in Relation to Sex*, 2nd edn., 2 vols. (London, 1888), i. 224.

[27] J. C. Greene, 'Darwin as a Social Evolutionist', *Journal of the History of Biology*, 10 (1977), 1–27.

botanist, Joseph Hooker, was convinced that neither democracy nor repub-
licanism could 'resist the effects of Natural Selection'. 'This to me', he told
Darwin, 'is no question of what is good or bad, but of what must ever be,
and I do hold that a Govt. must always eventually get into the hands of an
individual, or a family . . . or there is no truth in Natural Selection'. On the
other hand, Thomas Huxley (Darwinism's most ardent scientific gladiator)
had come to believe that 'State Socialism'—for which he had 'little enough
time'—might actually prove to 'be a product of Natural Selection' on the
grounds that 'the societies of Bees and Ants exhibit socialism *in excelsis*'.[28]
That the evolutionary idea was, it seems, becoming more Janus-faced than
ever had, appropriately enough, two important effects. In the first place,
facing in different directions was precisely what rendered it more and more
generally applicable. In the second place, its very ambiguities served to
increase the tensions and anxieties of those already troubled by the circumstances of the world in which they lived.

The cause of progress was, as a result, defended with a more and more
desperate fidelity. Myths were manufactured to show that the supposedly
obscurantist arguments of Bishop Wilberforce at the British Association
meeting at Oxford in 1860 had been triumphantly exposed by upright truth
in the shape of Thomas Huxley.[29] Fierce denunciations were poured over
the head of the 8th Duke of Argyll, who, besides being an ornament of
government, was also a leading proponent of the anti-evolutionary theory
of cultural degeneration according to which contemporary 'savages' (and
perhaps others too) were seen, not as survivals of primitive man, but as
degenerate versions of more civilized ancestors. At times, indeed, evolution
seems to have been pressed into service simply because, for those with at
best an attenuated religious faith, it alone seemed capable of giving some
kind of coherence to the cosmic drama, a coherence at least of process if not
one of ends.

Yet, even in so dashing an application of evolutionary methods to human
affairs as Walter Bagehot's *Physics and Politics, or Thoughts on the Application
of the Principles of 'Natural Selection' and 'Inheritance' to Political Society*
(1872)—in no way the least interesting of its author's works—fears of
regression and of disintegration in the carefully established equilibrium of
modern British constitutional practice break the surface of optimism with
menacing regularity. Characteristically, Bagehot saw human development

---

[28] J. A. Rogers, 'Darwinism and Social Darwinism', *Journal of the History of Ideas*, 33
(1972), 271–2.
[29] J. R. Lucas, 'Wilberforce and Huxley: A Legendary Encounter', *Historical Journal*, 22
(1979), 313–30; Desmond and Moore, *Darwin*, 492–9.

in progressive and evolutionary terms, out of which he produced a general description of the growth of early civilization: a period of rigid 'fixed law' providing order and stability, followed by a crucial step in which the 'cake of custom' is broken by those few societies in which a sufficient amount of variability has, none the less, been retained. Despotism, though ideal for the first condition, smothers the second which can only flow from some 'standing system of semi-free discussion'. And here the findings of contemporary historians, notably E. A. Freeman, concerning the nature of early 'Teutonic' political life, enabled Bagehot to place his own country among those very few nations which had successfully negotiated the difficult passage from despotism to adaptive progress and growth. Even so, there was no room for complacency. Like a dark cloud on a summer afternoon stood the never-banishable prospect that even so polished a race as the Anglo-Saxons might suddenly slip and fall into a dissolutionary abyss.

We see frequently in states what physiologists call 'atavism'—the return, in part, to the unstable nature of their barbarous ancestors. Such scenes of cruelty and horror as happened in the great French Revolution, and as happen, more or less, in every great riot, have always been said to bring out a secret and suppressed side of human nature; and we now see that they were the outbreak of inherited passions long repressed by fixed custom, but starting into life as soon as that repression was catastrophically removed, and when sudden choice was given. The irritability of mankind, too, is only part of their imperfect, transitory civilization and of their original savage nature. They could not look steadily to a given end for an hour in their prehistoric state; and even now, when excited or when suddenly and wholly thrown out of their old grooves, they can scarcely do so.[30]

However tendentious some of Bagehot's borrowings may have been, the very fact of his turning to the sciences for an answer to crucial questions concerning the origins of social life, and to evolutionary sciences in particular, shows how deeply these had incorporated themselves into the general thought patterns of the time.

Those who shared Bagehot's fears about the masses and about democracy (and it is noteworthy that he expressed them shortly after the Second Reform Acts of 1867–8) found added cause for unease in the agrarian agitation of the 1870s, in the increasing violence of the Irish countryside during the Land War of 1879–82, and in the industrial unrest of the 1880s. The information about poverty, distress, despair, and occasional discontent, thrown up by new examinations of urban life produced for some, however mistakenly, the uncomfortable feeling of sitting upon a social

---

[30] *The Collected Writings of Walter Bagehot*, ed. N. St John-Stevas, 15 vols. (London, 1965–86), vii. 104–5. The text first appeared in the *Fortnightly Review* for 1867–72.

volcano, with the lower classes cast in the role of destructive and primitive savages. Remedies were increasingly being sought along scientific and evolutionary lines. Some hoped that the creation of a greater sense of national and racial identity might provide an antidote to class conflict and social disintegration. Occasionally rightly, but mostly wrongly, a conviction was growing that, in the words of Charles Kingsley, 'physical science is proving more and more the immense importance of Race; the importance of hereditary powers, hereditary organs, hereditary habits, in all organised beings, from the lowest plant to the highest animal'.[31] But while an evolutionary thrust could—as in contemporary suspicions of the Irish—add an extra charge to all sorts of insular prejudices, these also owed much to a wider and more complex set of influences, their intensification coinciding with despair in missionary circles over the intractability of the native 'material' in places like Basutoland, Nigeria, and New Zealand, and with what (already in 1862) Cobden denounced as the declining humanitarianism of the ruling class made manifest by a revival of cruel sports, by increasing demands for corporal and capital punishment, and by 'the tendency to condone slavery and to appeal to the devilish standard of mere intellectual superiority as a justification for the injustices inflicted on the African race'.[32]

While, therefore, Victorian racialism as well as the more aggressive forms of imperialism drew a good deal of inspiration from allegedly scientific arguments, such arguments rarely had much to do with Darwinism properly interpreted. Indeed, because Darwin's theories clearly suggest that the various peoples of the earth are no less mutable and inter-related than species of animals, it offered no legitimate help to those wanting proof of the superiority of one 'race' over another.[33] This did not, however, mean that vulgar and more general versions of evolutionary thinking had no effect on those seeking to justify Britain's imperial domination of 'lesser breeds' in Africa, Asia, and elsewhere. 'Primitive' peoples, it was argued, were little higher than brutes. They required discipline, order, even the lash. And when anyone began to question the validity of such notions—and many did—new and easy responses were now at hand in the shape of mantras derived from evolutionary debate about 'man's fighting instincts', the 'herd instinct', and, best of all, the 'survival of the fittest'.[34]

---

[31] 'The Natural Theology of the Future' (1871) in Kingsley's *Scientific Lectures and Essays*, new edn. (London, 1890), 324.
[32] W. L. Burn, *The Age of Equipoise: A Study of the Mid-Victorian Generation* (London, 1964), 69, 183.
[33] D. A. Lorimer, *Colour, Class and the Victorians* (Leicester, 1978), 144–5.
[34] R. Hyam, *Britain's Imperial Century 1815–1914* (London, 1976), 79.

Not that all scientists accepted Darwin's view of the matter. Dr James Hunt, the moving genius behind the Anthropological Society of London—perhaps the most brazen epicentre of racial theorizing during the 1860s—was staunchly anti-Darwinian, believing as he did in the multiple origin of races. Hunt, an unabashed applier of science to politics, attacked equality as a 'mere dream and all systems based on it' as 'mere chimeras'. He thought races were separate and unequal and so little capable of adapting to differing physical circumstances that black people could never even hope to match the achievements of *Homo Victorianus*. Although the Society lay outside the mainstream of contemporary scientific endeavour (notwithstanding the curious membership of the evolutionist and future socialist, A. R. Wallace) its activities highlight the variety of different ways in which the new religion of science could penetrate mid-Victorian minds.[35]

Growing fears that the social unrest of the 1870s and 1880s was both the outcome of genetic decline and the herald of worse to come encouraged the production of new political remedies. Though Spencer, whose purist individualism bore the marks of an earlier generation, was now being left behind, his fame was still sufficient to secure his adoption as patron saint by the anti-collectivist Liberty and Property Defence League founded by Lord Elcho in 1882. This body, which included a curious collection of idiosyncratic libertarians as well as employers' federations distracted by the legislation of Gladstone's second ministry, dispatched squads of 'liberty missionaries' on tandem tricycles to inflame the nation against the radical land tax theories of Henry George. Spencer gave his blessing, but his own growing gloom at the rising tide of war and imperialism—the wages of collectivist sin and clear manifestations of dissolution—contrasted sharply with the febrile optimism of his self-appointed followers. Some of these, such as Auberon Herbert (the son of Lord Carnarvon), saw evolution leading to the withering away of the state and hence to beneficial anarchism. Others co-operated with right-wing feminists in opposing union-inspired legislation to ban women from certain unpleasant occupations or to regulate the hours of shop assistants—both issues which split the poor.[36]

If all of this was small, though occasionally fizzy, beer, the evolutionary approach had already begun to yield some altogether fiercer doctrines. These revolved around a loose congeries of perceptions: demands for genetic improvement of the population stock, the application of Darwinian

[35] R. Rainger, 'Race, Politics, and Science: The Anthropological Society of London in the 1860s', *Victorian Studies*, 22 (1978), 51–70.

[36] E. Bristow, 'The Liberty and Property Defence League and Individualism', *Historical Journal*, 18 (1975), 761–89; M. W. Taylor, *Men against the State: Herbert Spencer and Late Victorian Individualism* (Oxford, 1992), 158–9, 193–4, 207–8.

'struggle' to groups rather than individuals, and a realization of the social dangers and opportunities afforded by imperial expansion. As early as 1864, A. R. Wallace (with Darwin the joint originator of the concept of natural selection) had argued that once men and women had become sociable, then natural selection operated on societies rather than individuals.[37] Bagehot too (as he said in *Physics and Politics*) had come to believe that progress resulted from evolutionary struggle between groups, tribes, and races, with the fittest predominating. External struggle seemed, therefore, to demand internal cohesion in the pursuit of national efficiency and international supremacy. Although in outline such ideas bore certain similarities to the earlier arguments of writers like Carlyle and Kingsley who had combined attacks on *laissez-faire* for its brutalization of working people with strong views on the inferiority of 'lesser' (usually black) races, they undoubtedly possessed a more modish look, decked out as they now were in the characteristically scientific language of late Victorian discourse and thought.[38]

A key text was the book *Social Evolution* (1894), the success of which enabled its author, Benjamin Kidd, to retire from the Civil Service. Kidd blamed Spencer for failing to defuse socialist class antagonism and for merely fobbing off workers with platitudes about immediate sacrifice for subsequent benefits. Only the state (which Spencer feared) could, he believed, bring about internal harmony by placing all citizens on a more equal footing 'in the rivalry of life'. Once all were ranged equitably under starter's orders, then struggle could be transferred to the rivalry between nations in which only the fittest would survive. Elevating the qualities of energy and resolve at the expense of reason (and with it socialism, reason's child), Kidd saw religion as the only force capable of justifying the subordination of present demands to future needs and thus plugging the gap opened up by the failure of Spencer's evolutionary altruism. In the end, therefore, he rejected both socialism and individualism in favour of centralized state action aimed at the encouragement of national and racial efficiency, demonstrating thereby that reaction as well as progressivism could nurture and encourage the growth of collectivist mentalities.[39] But while those who still argued in favour of individualism—for state action being best when it was least—were being made to seem more and more marginal, the habit of looking to biological models for political and social insight retained its force, not least because evolutionary concepts had now

[37] Burrow, *Evolution and Society*, 114–15.
[38] B. Semmel, *Imperialism and Social Reform* (London, 1966), 29–31.
[39] D. P. Crook, *Benjamin Kidd: Portrait of a Social Darwinist* (Cambridge, 1984), 49–68.

come to acquire a truly 360-degree capacity to validate almost any available point of view—socialist, imperialist, liberal, or conservative.[40]

One group in particular began to seek enlightenment from the genetic aspects of evolutionary thought. The leading figure here was Francis Galton, a half-cousin of Darwin and founder of the so-called science of eugenics or race improvement. Believing that mental as well as physical characteristics were the product of heredity, he used sophisticated statistical techniques to provide mathematical arguments for the applicability of scientific breeding to human populations. Having been given 'freedom of thought' by *The Origin of Species*, he began to discuss the distribution and nature of psychological and ethical characteristics along broadly racial lines. Civilization, he believed, tended to encourage the survival of the 'unfit' by preventing natural selection from eliminating the weak and the mentally inferior, with the result that contemporary British society had become marked by 'a sort of intellectual anarchy, for the want of master minds'.[41] Though his book *Hereditary Genius* (1869) was not well received in the scientific community (Darwin, however, was full of praise) Galton's message continued to be hammered home so effectively that, by the 1880s and 1890s, it had achieved a wider acknowledgement. What it amounted to was the irrelevance of environmental solutions—poor laws, factory laws, sanitation laws—to social problems, for it was only heredity that determined the capacities and capabilities of individual human beings. However, unlike the Spencerians, Galton did not see state 'interference' as necessarily against the iron laws of evolution. On the contrary, he favoured elaborate state action involving a national biographical index and the provision of 'eugenic certificates' to encourage the breeding habits of the intelligent at the expense of those of the feckless and poor.[42]

Considerable scientific credence seemed to be given to such views in the 1880s by August Weismann's chromosome theory of heredity, which, by postulating an unbroken line of descent between the germ cells of successive individuals, made variability depend, not on environmental factors at all, but merely upon the endless permutation and combination of different chromosomes. Eugenic anxiety grew. At the popular extreme, Victoria Martin's *The Rapid Multiplication of the Unfit* (1891) bewailed the burden that paupers placed on society; in the curiously entitled *A Plea for the*

[40]　G. Jones, *Social Darwinism and English Thought* (Brighton, 1980), 54–77.

[41]　F. Galton, 'Hereditary Talent and Character', *Macmillan's Magazine*, 12 (1865), 166.

[42]　R. S. Cowan, 'Francis Galton's Statistical Ideas', *Isis*, 63 (1972), 509–28; A. R. Buss, 'Galton and the Birth of Differential Psychology and Eugenics', *Journal of the History of the Behavioral Sciences*, 12 (1976), 47–58; R. J. Richards, *Darwin and the Emergence of Evolutionary Theories of Mind and Behavior* (Chicago, 1987), 169–75.

Unborn (1897) Henry Smith praised mothers who smothered deformed babies; while Dr John Berry Haycraft argued, in *Darwinism and Race Progress* (1895), that 'if we stamp out Infectious Diseases we perpetuate Poor Types'. Eventually, even the Malthusian League, founded in 1877 to uphold 'the fundamental principles of Malthus and Darwin' by encouraging family limitation among working people, overcame its opposition to centralized action and nervously supported a measure of state regulation to ensure differential procreation on class lines.[43]

Galton's ablest follower was Karl Pearson, who, after studying in Germany where he was converted to evolution and to socialism, was in 1884 appointed Professor of Applied Mathematics at University College London. Pearson's socialism was highly idiosyncratic. He denounced class struggle and, in common with many other evolutionists, believed that only the slow education of the governing classes to a 'higher social morality' could bring about permanent improvement. He rejected religion in favour of a 'rational motive for conduct' and internationalism in favour of a strongly expressed 'patriotism'. His veneration of the state made Kidd's views seem insipid. Soon he was advocating 'physical selection' (or allowing the 'unfit' to die of their disabilities) as the sovereign solution to contemporary discontents. External struggle, economic and military, would, he believed, favour the fit and the efficient, and only nations which allowed socialism à la Pearson to produce a homogeneous and united people could hope to prosper in harsh and warlike times.[44]

Eugenics, like so many of the movements of thought generated under evolutionary influences, was a broad church and thus capable of appealing not only to those who agreed with Galton and Pearson, but also to certain Fabian socialists who liked its scientific and potentially bureaucratic character, but who, on the whole, hoped to deploy it in favour of the deprived— a very different and highly modified version of the creed. That eugenics, with its emphasis on the importance of educational qualifications and mental ability rather than traditional privilege or manual labour, should have held particular attractions for the growing professional middle class is hardly surprising. Indeed, both 'conservative' and 'radical' eugenicists were united in their more or less equal suspicion of the social residuum ('the army of the biologically unfit'), on the one hand, and, on the other, of big business with its vested interest in the multiplication of the unfit as a pool of surplus labour.

[43] A. McLaren, *Birth Control in Nineteenth-Century England* (London, 1978), 142–54.
[44] Semmel, *Imperialism*, 35–52; G. R. Searle, *Eugenics and Politics in Britain 1900–1914* (Leiden, 1976), 9–44.

At the same time, however, the growing importance of science and technology—of which the evolutionary debate was a part—did not go unchallenged. Nor did those hymns to physical and mental achievement which rose, like secular incense, from the massed ranks of the new scientific priesthood, meet with universal admiration. To some at least, Huxley's boast that single-handed science had dispelled 'local ignorance and prejudice' and strengthened the nation against 'political or social anarchy' seemed at once ridiculous and untrue.[45] Matthew Arnold saw instead the onward march of the middle-class Philistines, while Ruskin bewailed the lack of aesthetic sensibility displayed by science in general and by many of its devotees (Darwin prominent among them) in particular.

Science as a pursuit was, none the less, attracting an increasing number of practitioners of all kinds. The size of the audiences at the annual meetings of the British Association (founded in 1831 to spread an appreciation of science among a wider audience) rose substantially in the 1850s, 1860s, and 1870s.[46] As interest grew, so did the strength of formal and informal networks of influence. Strings, it seemed, were being pulled beyond the public gaze, not always, some thought, for the public good. The small and intimate X Club founded in 1864 exercised a powerful voice in scientific affairs. Its members, who included Huxley, Lubbock, Hooker, and the physicist Tyndall, occupied key positions, and, in their love of schoolboy badinage, strenuous physical exertion, 'devotion to science, pure and free, untrammelled by religious dogma', represented a distinct and increasingly important strand within the British scientific enterprise.[47] Tyndall, Hooker, and Huxley also belonged to 'The Club', an exclusive dining society established in 1764 and by the 1880s catholic enough to include Gladstone and the Lords Kelvin, Rosebery, and Salisbury in its membership. Huxley and Tyndall seem, indeed, to have been inveterate joiners, being also active (as was Lubbock) in the Metaphysical Society, which, throughout the 1870s, provided a forum for orthodox and heterodox opinions alike. At its meetings eclectic and highly articulate voices—among them those of Gladstone (once again), Bagehot, A. J. Balfour, the atheistical mathematician W. K. Clifford, Cardinal Manning, Robert Lowe, the Catholic philosopher W. G. Ward, Ruskin, Leslie Stephen, and Tennyson—boomed

---

[45] Huxley's essay on 'Science' in T. H. Ward's jubilee compilation, *The Reign of Queen Victoria: A Survey of Fifty Years of Progress*, 2 vols. (London, 1887), ii. 322–3.

[46] A. Ellegård, *Darwin and the General Reader* (Gothenburg, 1958), 64.

[47] R. M. McLeod, 'The X Club: A Social Network of Science in Late-Victorian England', *Notes and Records of the Royal Society*, 24 (1970), 305–22. The words quoted are those of the mathematician, T. A. Hirst.

across the chasms now increasingly dividing the realms of belief, of aesthetics, and of the study of nature and of man.[48]

What for a considerable time kept such groups from falling apart was a typically Victorian combination of occupational affinity, actual kinship, free discussion, and social comradeship. The new upper middle-class intellectual aristocracy of the time was a closely inter-related coterie. Its characteristic attitude was one of critical but confident disinterestedness; its characteristic doctrine that 'the world could be improved by analysing the needs of society and calculating the possible course of its development'; its characteristic venue the Alps, where, from the 1850s onwards, the intelligentsia was to find a ruggedly congenial vacation habitat.[49] The love of mountaineering reflected a complex set of emotions: a new attitude to nature, a love of physical exertion, a search for the transcendental beyond orthodox religion, even a quest for scientific discovery. The Alpine Club, founded in 1857, helped to strengthen feelings of community and brotherhood both on the glaciers and in everyday life. Soon the Alps were swarming with British academics—lawyers, scientists, writers, and physicians. Over the years, John Tyndall, best known for his important research on heat, climbed with his fellow X Club members (Lubbock, Huxley, Hirst, and Frankland), with the geologist A. C. Ramsay and the lawyer Vaughan Hawkins, with the politician W. E. Forster, and with many other notables. Tyndall and Leslie Stephen, possibly the Alpine Club's most prominent agnostics, both admitted to almost religious experiences among the peaks. Tyndall felt an influence that seemed to proceed 'direct to the soul... I was part of it and it of me, and in the transcendent glory of Nature I entirely forgot myself as man'. Stephen, on a lazy day near Evian, 'became for a strictly limited period, a convert to Buddhism'.[50]

As members of a self-conscious élite, scientists shared not only common interests but, to some extent, common politics as well. Like so many other intellectual adherents of traditional English liberalism, they suffered acute bouts of revulsion and despair at what they considered Gladstone's self-advertisement, lack of steadiness, and pandering to ignorant democracy. Irish Home Rule provided the men of science, as it did the men of property (and the two could not now always be distinguished), with a proximate

[48] A. W. Brown, *The Metaphysical Society: Victorian Minds in Crisis, 1869–1880* (New York, 1947), *passim*.

[49] N. G. Annan, 'The Intellectual Aristocracy', in J. H. Plumb (ed.), *Studies in Social History* (London, 1955), 250. Eventually, however, the Metaphysical Society did fall apart as the mid-Victorian consensus disintegrated.

[50] D. Robertson, 'Mid-Victorians among the Alps', in U. C. Knoepflmacher and G. B. Tennyson (eds.), *Nature and the Victorian Imagination* (Berkeley, Calif., 1977), 112–36.

occasion for desertion. And even if motives were necessarily mixed, their 'science' and the kind of attitudes to human affairs which that engendered could and did furnish both the cause and the rhetoric of disenchantment. Huxley, convinced as he was that 'government by average opinion is merely a circuitous method of going to the devil', saw Gladstone as a benighted religious fanatic, who, 'if the working-men were . . . to vote by a majority that two and two made five, tomorrow . . . would believe it, and find them reasons for it which they had never dreamed up'.[51] Hence his Unionism; hence too the controversies with Gladstone on the accuracy of the Genesis order of creation and (more bitter still) over the story of the Gadarene swine. Huxley's famous lecture of 1893 on 'Evolution and Ethics', usually seen as a semi-humanistic recantation of strict evolutionary logic—a kind of dogged plea for mankind amidst the neutral forces of the cosmic process— was in fact a last desperate attempt to rescue evolution and natural selection from those who were beginning to use them to justify new and more collectivist versions of liberalism or even socialism itself. Far from depoliticizing the authority of evolutionary science, Huxley was using it to justify those modified *laissez-faire* policies with which old-style liberals like himself were still hoping to solve the problems of the times, not least those caused by economic downturns and by Irish discontents.[52]

The Unionism of the nominally Protestant Irishman Tyndall was perhaps less unexpected. But he too had once been a Liberal Party supporter and in some ways a radical one. His view of science was notably democratic and his staunch unbelief not a commodity much in demand among his new Conservative allies. In sheer rancour, however, his anti-Gladstonianism stood high among the bitter Home Rule harvests of late Victorian years. For Tyndall (who saw scientific men like himself as 'occupied with the veracities of nature'), Gladstone, having 'prostituted great abilities . . . to illustrate the unveracity of man', had himself become, quite simply, the 'wickedest man of our day and generation'.[53] Lubbock, effectively science's parliamentary representative as MP for London University, also lost no time in joining the Liberal Unionists. Indeed, by the late 1880s it had become almost impossible to walk the corridors of scientific power without being told that Gladstone was a politician as shifty as he was dangerous.

[51] L. Huxley, *Life and Letters of Thomas Henry Huxley*, 2 vols. (London, 1900), i. 353, ii. 124–6.

[52] M. S. Helfand, 'T. H. Huxley's "Evolution and Ethics" ', *Victorian Studies*, 20 (1977), 159–77.

[53] *The Times*, 13 Feb. 1890; A. S. Eve and C. H. Creasey, *Life and Work of John Tyndall* (London, 1945), 242–3, 264–7.

Among more 'imaginative' evolutionists, a similar high whine of emotionalism is to be found, and often for the same reasons. Tennyson, whose fears of man's reversion to beast status had long been acute, lashed the new order in 'Locksley Hall Sixty Years After' (1886), a work which, notwithstanding the complex relationship between poetic sentiment and a poet's beliefs, clearly stood in sharp and deliberate contrast to the optimism of the original 'Locksley Hall' of 1838. Gladstone's public response, a mild and complacent catalogue of the benefits of progress, showed concern rather than comprehension. For Tennyson, however, evolution no longer offered the wider hope and science itself stood revealed as the grim harbinger of random futility. Immediate anxieties over Hibernian horrors—agrarian outrages, murders, boycotts, and the like—reinforced the sense of cosmic disillusion.

> France had shown a light to all men, preach'd a Gospel, all men's good;
> Celtic Demos rose a Demon, shrieked and slaked the light with blood . . .
>
> Do your best to charm the worst, to lower the rising race of men;
> Have we risen from out the beast, then back into the beast again? . . .
>
> Is there evil but on earth? or pain in every peopled sphere?
> Well, be grateful for the sounding watchword 'Evolution' here,
>
> Evolution ever climbing after some ideal good,
> And Reversion ever dragging Evolution in the mud.

In more bathetic vein, Swinburne, once the rhapsodist of godless evolution in his masterpiece 'Hertha' (1868), emerged, twenty years later, as the curiously appropriate laureate of Unionism.[54]

> What are these that howl and hiss across the strait of westward water?
> What is he who floods our ears with speech in flood?
> See the long tongue lick the dripping hand that smokes and reeks of slaughter!
> See the man of words [Gladstone] embrace the man of blood! [Parnell]
>
> ('The Commonweal: A Song for Unionists')

From a very different ethical standpoint, the Catholic bard of married bliss, Coventry Patmore, in a piece starkly entitled '1880–85', brooded over the 'murder of Gordon' and the betrayal of truth into the hands of mass democracy.

---

[54] 'The Commonweal—A Song for Unionists' 1st publ. in *The Times*, 1 July 1886, and collected in Swinburne's *A Channel Passage* (1904).

Lo, how the dross and draff
Jeer up at us, and shout,
'The Day is ours, the Night is theirs!'
And urge their rout
Where the wild dawn of rising Tartarus flares.
Yon strives their leader [Gladstone], lusting to be seen.
His leprosy's so perfect that men call him clean!

Evolution, as a concept, was being applied in novel and disturbing political directions: towards imperialism and eugenics, on the one hand, and towards a new collectivist liberalism, on the other. The reaction of many of the leading scientists to the rising demands for women's rights is particularly revealing. Although, at its broadest, opposition to such demands drew upon a remarkably eclectic body of opinion, much of its rhetoric and many of its arguments were based upon a comparatively clear and often science-based conception of the supposed differences of temperament, physique, and intellect between male and female. Late Victorian scientific research was in fact a powerful influence in causing a distinct intellectual discontinuity in the feminist argument, with the strong evolutionary thrust of the 1860s and 1870s providing a particularly notable barrier. Although in 1869 J. S. Mill had already devoted much of his *The Subjection of Women* to refuting 'arguments from nature', it soon became obvious that the tide of scientific opinion about sex roles was well on the way to dousing any new feminist brushfires *The Subjection* might have started.[55] Darwin's chapters on 'Secondary Sexual Characters' in *The Descent of Man* laid down two of the basic ground-rules for the ensuing debate: that women had in the past produced few eminent poets, scientists, musicians, painters, and so forth, and that, while 'it is generally admitted that with woman the powers of intuition, of rapid perception, and perhaps of imitation, are more strongly marked than in man ... some, at least, of these faculties are characteristic of the lower races, and therefore of a past and lower state of civilization'.[56] Galton's anthropometric laboratory in London proved to the satisfaction of much of the scientific establishment that a deficiency of brain weight hopelessly deprived women of the mental resources available to men. Spencer, in turn, believed the restriction of women to their traditional roles to be part of a natural evolutionary order according to which the biological necessity of perpetuating the species must, at least for the time being, take precedence over any other inclina-

[55] F. Alaya, 'Victorian Science and the "Genius" of Woman', *Journal of the History of Ideas*, 38 (1977), 261–80.
[56] Darwin, *Descent of Man*, ii. 352.

tions that might be entertained. Along rather different lines, the physiologist, George Romanes, also set out to demonstrate the unavoidable fact of female mental inferiority, and in doing so presented, like all the others, the curious spectacle of an evolutionist crying halt to any further development on the part of one half of the human race.[57]

Not only women, however, but the majority of people outside the élites of the time had reason to harbour suspicions about the more pessimistic late Victorian versions of evolutionary thought. Some, when they considered the matter at all, simply distrusted the despotic and authoritarian uses to which evolutionary arguments were now being put. Some too may still have remembered the 1830s when earlier brands of evolutionism—often imported from France—had presented an altogether more Radical front in political terms, only to be subverted, first by Chambers and then by Darwin himself.[58] Almost all, however, would have agreed with the analysis, though not of course the disdainful language, put forward by Sir Henry Maine in 1885, to the effect that a very wide gulf regarding evolution had opened up between the intellectuals and the 'multitude'.

The central seat in all Political Economy was from the first occupied by the theory of Population. This theory has now been generalised by Mr Darwin and his followers, and, stated as the principle of the survival of the fittest, it has become the central truth of all biological science. Yet it is evidently disliked by the multitude, and thrust into the background by those whom the multitude permits to lead it.[59]

But if the socially differential response to science in general and to evolution in particular was becoming very marked, popular concern for the ape-ancestry of man ensured that evolutionary arguments continued to attract a wide (though also often a bemused) audience. Contemporary accounts testify to the frequency of surprised encounters by the intelligentsia 'with barbers, butlers, dockers, vapid young ladies and men on Clapham omnibuses who may know almost nothing of what Darwin, Spencer or Huxley are saying, but they know that evolution is important and part of enormous sweeping changes in the view of man and the universe'. In this sense at least, evolution (as John Morley noted) had by the 1870s, if not earlier, 'passed on from the laboratory and the study to the parlour'.[60]

[57] G. J. Romanes, 'Mental Differences between Men and Women', *Nineteenth Century*, 21 (1887), 654–72.
[58] A. Desmond, *The Politics of Evolution: Morphology, Medicine, and Reform in Radical London* (Chicago, 1989), 1–24.
[59] H. Maine, *Popular Government* (London, 1885), 37.
[60] S. Budd, *Varieties of Unbelief: Atheists and Agnostics in English Society 1850–1900* (London, 1977), 128; J. Morley, *Recollections*, 2 vols. (London, 1918), i. 88.

In trying to appeal to such wider audiences, those who considered evolution and biological analogies powerful specifics against collectivism were irritated when others began to use exactly the same weapons to put forward very different views of politics and society. On both sides, however, propagandists found it easier to deploy fashionable 'scientific' arguments than to construct careful intellectual links. Thus Annie Besant's efforts in the 1880s to rescue Social Darwinism from the reactionaries, her pronouncement that 'I am a Socialist because I am a believer in Evolution', her view that socialism performed for politics the function that Darwinian evolution performed for biology, were vague aspirations rather than logical borrowings. The same was true of the Webbs' use of Social Darwinist language in their effort to give the evolutionary and social implications of Positivism and Idealism a more scientific focus.[61] Rather more interesting, though not a great deal less tendentious, were the scientific, political, and religious conjunctures which enabled A. R. Wallace to engineer a somewhat different kind of marriage between scientific naturalism and social reform.

For a scientist, Wallace came from an unusually humble background. As a young man he had been deeply influenced by the utopian socialism of Robert Owen and the rationalist phrenology of George Combe. Like so many Victorian evolutionary naturalists, he was convinced that the past held the key to the future and that the theory of evolution must therefore be applied to the question of human origins. In 1864, in the first important interpretation of the significance of evolution for mankind since the publication of *The Origin of Species*, he suggested that human evolution had passed through two distinct phases: a period of merely physical development during which the various races had appeared, and then, 'when mind had evolved to the point where it could begin to take over the task of adaptation, the influence of natural selection had been transferred to the various mental faculties' which now distinguished men and women 'so clearly from the brutes'.[62] Thus the advent of mind had effected 'a grand revolution' in nature and enabled humanity to transcend the constraints of the physical environment. Eventually the 'higher' races would, Wallace argued, displace the 'lower', and an increasingly perfect adaptation would produce a 'single homogeneous race, no individual of which will be inferior to the noblest specimens of existing humanity'. Although Wallace contrasted the individualism of animals with the 'natural assistance' of human

    [61] W. Wolfe, *From Radicalism to Socialism: Men and Ideas in the Formation of Fabian Socialist Doctrines, 1881–1889* (New Haven, 1975), 262–6.
    [62] J. R. Durant, 'Scientific Naturalism and Social Reform in the Thought of Alfred Russel Wallace', *British Journal for the History of Science*, 12 (1979), 40.

societies, and transferred the influence of natural selection from the individual to the group, this did not take him along the road followed by Galton and Kidd. On the contrary, after a period of intense admiration for Spencer, Wallace's long-standing regard for the values of the so-called primitive societies he had encountered in the Malay and Amazon regions led him to recognize something few other Social Darwinists were ever able to see, namely, that the 'fittest' in the struggle for life were not of necessity the 'best'.

By 1869 Wallace had, in any case, become desperate to escape from total and unremitting naturalism and, like a significant number of his contemporaries, managed to perform this Houdini-like deliverance by integrating spiritualism into his philosophy and by proposing that 'infinite gradations of existence' possessing 'intelligence and will-power' had guided the development of man in past times. Wallace's dazzling combination of Darwinism, spiritualism, and socialism did not, however, impede his admiration for Galton's work on heredity or for Weismann's denial of the influences of education and environment, any ensuing dilemmas being neatly resolved by the suggestion that, only after certain social reforms had been carried out (female emancipation prominent among them), could that process he called 'human selection'—by which the biological improvement of mankind would be rendered inevitable—commence its operations. Wallace's views were of course complex and confusing, and it is not surprising that eugenicists sometimes thought of him as a possible supporter. In the final analysis, what his writings show is the extraordinary malleability of Victorian evolutionism and how it could enable even so errant a scientist as Wallace to stay in touch with a view of man and society that remained— sometimes despite his own best endeavours—a broadly naturalistic one.[63]

Wallace's combination of evolution and progressive politics was becoming increasingly common during the last decades of the nineteenth century. The so-called 'new liberalism' which emerged at this time, with its stress on social reform, reflected as clearly as anything the declining attractions of Benthamite utilitarianism in the face of Darwin and biological inquiry. The consequent intellectual transformation, the work notably of later thinkers such as D. G. Ritchie, J. A. Hobson, and L. T. Hobhouse, owed more to a dialogue between scientific evolutionism and the legacy of J. S. Mill than to fears that socialists might squeeze liberals out of the political arena. Although the evolutionary view adopted was that which stressed the inclination of organisms towards collaboration, any total merger of individual and social claims was rejected for fear of producing a monolithic

[63] Ibid. 31–58.

society. What the new liberals did was to deduce from evolution a tendency towards increased co-operation, while from older (often conservatively inclined) organic views of society they took the idea of locating the prime communal agency in the state rather than in any simple accumulation of individuals. The extent of their intellectual journeyings did not, however, blind them to a recognition of two crucial influences: Darwin, as Hobhouse acknowledged, had shown how natural selection might be used to harmonize a mass of otherwise disconnected facts of organic life, while Spencer— for all his 'faults'—had constructed a philosophy, not 'as philosophy too often is, opposed to science, but itself the sum or synthesis of the sciences'.[64]

The general impact of evolution, both directly and indirectly, was wider still. Traditional assurances about a knowable universe demonstrated through deductive laws were increasingly being challenged by biology as also by mathematics, physics, and chemistry. Randomness, or at best probability, was replacing rigorously deduced certainty. While this had disturbing consequences for some, it proved a liberating discovery for certain late Victorian social scientists working in fields such as economics, psychology, and political studies. With tentativeness enthroned, attempts to discover complete systems of economic, psychological, or social laws could now, they believed, be abandoned in favour of an empirical and piecemeal arrangement of problems in a ladder of importance determined simply by the state of knowledge and the amount of data available. Evolutionary thinking was, therefore, both part of positivistic Victorian science *and* the means of escape towards strictly conditional views of knowledge and of law. By 1874 W. S. Jevons was arguing for the treatment of economic and social problems by means of sophisticated probability theory, while the economic writings of Alfred Marshall mark a clear departure from established determinism. Evolution, indeed, provided Marshall with a theory in which individualism increasingly gives way to the greater rewards to be derived from mutual responsibility. And just as biology depended upon a complex set of interdependent and evolutionary forces, so, Marshall maintained, should the enormous mass of facts required for economic analysis oblige economists to avoid simplistic assignments of causality.[65] And even if the links connecting the arguments put forward by the new liberals and by social scientists like Jevons and Marshall with the reforming Liberal Party programmes of

[64] M. Freeden, *The New Liberalism: An Ideology of Social Reform* (Oxford, 1978), 78 (also generally).
[65] R. N. Soffer, *Ethics and Society in England: The Revolution in the Social Sciences 1870–1914* (Berkeley, Calif., 1978), 9–10, 69–88.

1906–14 were never less than circuitous and indirect, there can be little doubt that versions of evolutionism contributed to the validation of planned and state-led reforms and thus, eventually, to the implementation of political and social change under Asquith and Lloyd George.

3. MATTERS OF BELIEF

Within the realm of religious belief the response to evolution was, above all, a matter of distinct, though not unconnected, levels of discourse. If, on closer examination, it is difficult to pin down loss of faith directly to scientific influences, science—by the general issues it raised and by the manner in which the evolutionary debate of the 1860s coincided with fierce arguments about the historical truth of the Bible—was widely seen as playing a prominent role in the general unsettlement of educated British minds. Even so, there doubtless continued to sit in the pews many 'worshippers who had never heard of Tylor, were indifferent to Darwin, mildly regretted what they heard of Huxley and, if they thought about it at all, knew that their faith rested upon moral considerations inaccessible to the physical sciences'.[66] Others, however, saw things differently, and certainly some scientists seemed to be claiming a great deal—like the mathematician, W. K. Clifford, whose reading of Darwin and Spencer produced a violent conversion from Anglo-Catholicism to scientific naturalism. 'It is idle', wrote Clifford in 1874, 'to set bounds to the purifying and organizing work of science. Without mercy and without resentment she ploughs up weed and briar; from her footsteps behind her grow up corn and healing flowers; and no corner is far enough to escape her furrow'.[67]

But if a conflict between science and religion constituted one of the stock debating points of the time, an even greater growth industry clustered around the numerous and varied attempts at reconciliation, in large measure because, although Darwin's ideas may have initially struck many contemporaries as rebarbative, Darwin himself was very much an integral part of that educated mid-Victorian élite that was more and more obviously beginning to dominate the universities, the public schools, the Civil Service, and the upper reaches of the established church. What, above all, characterized the thinking of those belonging to this élite was a kind of disinterested rationality capable of encompassing a comparatively wide spectrum of beliefs, ranging from Broad Church Christianity, on the one hand, to various sorts of agonized doubt and even complete unbelief, on the

[66] O. Chadwick, *The Victorian Church*, 2 vols. (London, 1966–70), ii. 35.
[67] W. K. Clifford, 'Body and Mind', *Fortnightly Review*, NS 16 (1874), 736.

other. Unlike Wallace and Huxley, Darwin's family and educational background (wealthy intellectual household, Shrewsbury School, Christ's College Cambridge) placed him firmly among this important and self-conscious group, which, given the modest higher administrative needs of mid-Victorian society, was small enough to allow face-to-face contact, personal friendship, and shared experiences to provide the chief means of understanding between those who found themselves within its ranks.[68] Until the 1880s the principal agenda of such men was one of reform: for each individual, the object most needing reform was that which was nearest to hand. For some this meant the ancient universities, for others the Civil Service, for others the public schools, for yet others the Church of England (where Broad Churchmen benefited from the special favour of Queen Victoria).[69] For Darwin, the object of reform was science and in particular the interpretation of biological environments, of their origins, the changes they had undergone, the changes they might still experience. While, therefore, Darwin's reformist enterprise was perhaps the most drastic of all those under way in the middle years of the Victorian period, it was far from being unique. If anything, the seeming snugness of its fit within the framework of ideas and projects favoured by the intellectual élite of the time persuaded many contemporaries of the necessity—and even, at least on superficial acquaintance, the easy possibility—of formally aligning Darwin's notions to modern up-to-date thinking of every kind, religious as well as secular.

As a result, bearers of eirenical (and often contradictory) tidings pressed in from every side. In 1865 over 700 'men of science' signed an anodyne declaration announcing belief in a Supreme Being, in the truth of His actions and teachings, and in the agreement between science and the scriptures.[70] As Godwin Peak—the chief character in Gissing's novel

---

[68] In post-1854 'reformed' Oxford there were about 350 college fellows of whom only a minority did much teaching (C. Kent, *Brains and Numbers: Elitism, Comtism, and Democracy in Mid-Victorian England* (Toronto, 1978), 12). In 1861 Oxford and Cambridge had about 2,400 students between them and of these only a small proportion could have counted themselves among the social and intellectual élites of the time (R. D. Anderson, *Universities and Elites in Britain since 1800* (London, 1992), 22). For the smallness of the higher Civil Service in these years, see above, Ch. 4, s. 3.

[69] C. Harvie, *The Lights of Liberalism: University Liberals and the Challenge of Democracy 1860–86* (London, 1976); S. Rothblatt, *The Revolution of the Dons: Cambridge and Society in Victorian England* (London, 1968); C. K. Fry, *Statesmen in Disguise: The Changing Role of the Administrative Class of the British Home Civil Service 1853–1966* (London, 1969); O. J. Brose, *Church and Parliament: The Reshaping of the Church of England 1828–1860* (Stanford, 1959); D. Bowen, *The Idea of the Victorian Church: A Study of the Church of England 1833–1889* (Montreal, 1968); T. W. Bamford, *Rise of the Public Schools* (London, 1967).

[70] W. H. Brock and R. M. McLeod, 'The Scientists' Declaration', *British Journal for the History of Science*, 9 (1976), 39–66.

Born in Exile (1892)—noted, a large class of persons clung to some form of religious dogma, but, while realizing that 'bishops, priests, and deacons no longer hold it with the old rigour, and that one must be "broad"; these are clamorous for treatises which pretend to reconcile revelation and science. It's quite pathetic to watch the enthusiasm with which they hail any man who distinguishes himself by this kind of apologetic skill, this pious jugglery.' Even Darwin's unbelieving corpse could not avoid burial in Westminster Abbey in 1882 accompanied by a large collection of ecclesiastical and secular notables, by a bizarrely inappropriate hymn about nature's ways being always those of 'pleasantness' and 'peace', and by a funeral sermon in which Canon Farrar (later Dean of Canterbury) proclaimed his failure to detect 'one trace of materialism' in the writings of the great departed.[71]

At their simplest and least penetrating such 'reconciling' activities involved no more than a stark separation of science and religious belief into distinct intellectual compartments. This was the view of Gladstone, whose capacity for unscrambling complex relationships was as powerful as it could be misleading. After a brief flirtation with the notion that the idea of biological evolution, 'if it be true', would enhance 'the proper idea of the greatness of God', in 1881 he delivered to Tennyson, Froude, and Tyndall the chaste precept: 'Let the scientific men stick to their science, and leave philosophy and religion to poets, philosophers, and theologians'.[72] No less revealing were some of the contemporary attempts to fuse religion and evolutionary science into one homogenized whole. There were Calvinists, for example, who rejoiced that natural selection exalted chance over design, confirmed faith both in the arbitrary election of the chosen and in the spontaneous, unpredictable, and often tragic nature of the universe. Clergymen could be found who welcomed evolution as opening up new and glorious prospects of immortality. One distinguished botanist bewildered Darwin by announcing that natural selection made intelligible the birth of Christ and redemption by grace. More acute were those, like Sir Alexander Grant (Principal of Edinburgh University), who placed Darwin within a tradition of natural theology stretching back at least to the writings of William Paley.[73] There were also many intelligent and deeply religious

[71] *The Times*, 27 Apr. 1882; *The Life and Letters of Charles Darwin*, ed. F. Darwin, 3 vols. (London, 1887), iii. 360–1; Desmond and Moore, *Darwin*, 673.

[72] P. Magnus, *Gladstone: A Biography* (London, 1954), 233; Brown, *Metaphysical Society*, 106. When once Gladstone visited Down House he spent most of the time lecturing Darwin about Bulgaria. Before leaving he asked what evolution had in store. Did the future belong to America as the Eastern civilizations decayed? After mulling it over, Darwin ventured 'Yes' (Desmond and Moore, *Darwin*, 626).

[73] G. Himmelfarb, *Darwin and the Darwinian Revolution* (London, 1959), 325–6; A. Grant, 'Philosophy and Mr Darwin', *Contemporary Review*, 17 (1871), 274–81.

men, such as Baden Powell and Frederick Temple, for whom evolution provided a firmer, more tenable framework of law and a grander view of the Creator than those generated by images of a constantly meddling, flamboyant, miracle-working, and—in the end—petty God. Despite its subtleties, such theologically liberal broad-mindedness never quite got to the heart of the matter, and perhaps the only really authentic 'Christian Darwinism' was that expounded by a handful of very orthodox theologians, notably the Free Church of Scotland minister, James Iverach, and the Anglican High Church priest, Aubrey Lackington Moore. Moore, in particular, put forward a fearless, honest, and profound vision of the benefits of choice conferred by Darwinism upon religion. He saw the Christian revelation of God as both final and progressive: 'final, for Christians know but one God, and do not "look for another"; progressive, because Christianity claims each new truth as enriching our knowledge of God, and bringing out into greater clearness and distinctness some half-understood fragment of its own teaching'. 'It seems', he wrote in 1889, 'as if, in the providence of God, the mission of modern science was to bring home to our unmetaphysical ways of thinking the great truth of Divine immanence in creation'.[74]

Equally clever men saw the matter differently. Unbelief, they accepted, was on the increase, whether stoked by the findings of science or by an ethical revulsion from the doctrines of the atonement, everlasting damnation, or original sin. Yet—and despite the high personal probity of scientists like Darwin, Huxley, and Clifford—they doubted the viability of the new agnostic or atheistic naturalism as a vehicle for moral choice or standards. The philosopher and future Tory Prime Minister, A. J. Balfour, pinned down the naturalists with lepidopterist precision.

Their spiritual life is parasitic: it is sheltered by convictions which belong, not to them, but to the society of which they form a part; it is nourished by processes in which they take no share. And when those convictions decay, and those processes come to an end, the alien life which they have maintained can scarce be expected to outlast them.[75]

· Balfour's use of the word 'spiritual', which in late nineteenth-century thought had come to assume a dense accumulation of meanings sometimes excluding Christian doctrine but preserving issues and problems of human life previously addressed by traditional faith, focuses attention on one of the most interesting of all Victorian attempts to grapple with the problems of science and religious belief. This was the work of a group of individuals, who, while dissatisfied with the limitations of the Christianity in which they

[74] Moore, *Post-Darwinian Controversies*, 268–9.
[75] A. J. Balfour, *The Foundations of Belief* (London, 1895), 83.

had been reared, found the scientific naturalism of the time too confining for the scope of their ideals and aspirations. They objected to the new secular triumphalism, to that 'religion of science' described by Beatrice Webb as 'an implicit faith that by the methods of physical science and by these methods alone, could be solved all the problems arising out of the relation of man to man and of man towards the universe'.[76] Thus the Cambridge philosopher, Henry Sidgwick, believed that evolutionary thinkers committed the cardinal error of confusing what is or what will be with what ought to be. Able to find no ethical criteria in nature, Sidgwick clung to non-empirical postulates of a deity and of human immortality so that the cosmos of duty might not fall into chaos. Wallace too was unable to see social evolution as necessarily a guarantee of moral correctness, while the psychologist, F. W. H. Myers, desperately sought within the enduring materialism of matter and energy some possibility of immortality, of the human soul surviving death. Even George Romanes, once among the most arrogant apostles of scientific naturalism, eventually moved towards a highly personal religious interpretation of humanity and nature. His final partial reconciliation with the Church of England was much celebrated at the time and might, indeed, be considered to mark the failure of formal late Victorian naturalism to come to terms with the great and unavoidable fact of death.[77]

The intense preoccupation with questions of death and immortality on the part of individuals ground down between the millstones of belief and doubt explains much of the contemporary interest in spiritualism and psychical research as possible sources of quasi-religious enlightenment. Already by the 1860s a combination of this growing sense of reluctant doubt and of hopes that ways might be found to experience 'death without dying' was producing an efflorescence of interest in all forms of spiritualist inquiry.[78] In middle-class homes, in Mechanics' Institutes, among domestic servants, raps and table movements conveyed 'evidential messages' as mediums seemed to be experiencing clairvoyant visions of a world beyond the here and now. The Society for Psychical Research, established in 1882, was able to attract the support of Gladstone (who thought its type of activity 'the most important work, which is being done in the world'), of two bishops, eight fellows of the Royal Society, as well as of Ruskin and

[76] B. Webb, *My Apprenticeship* (London, 1926), 83 (writing about her state of mind in the 1870s).

[77] F. M. Turner, *Between Science and Religion: The Reaction to Scientific Naturalism in Late Victorian England* (New Haven, 1974), 38–163.

[78] L. Barrow, *Independent Spirits: Spiritualism and English Plebeians 1850–1910* (London, 1986), 96–145, 229–46.

Tennyson.[79] Sidgwick was a founder member and collaborated with A. J. Balfour in investigating psychical phenomena in the hope that they might discover an empirical basis for belief in human immortality. Wallace, in turn, believed that spiritualism brought man's total being under the governance of rational cosmic law, while Myers looked to psychical research as the possible foundation for a new 'religion' and Romanes sought empirical evidence for immortality from a programme of psychical observation and experimentation. They were not alone. Other prominent scientists were deeply interested: the physicist Oliver Lodge, the electrical engineer Cromwell Varley, the mathematician Augustus de Morgan, and the chemist William Crookes (who even joined Madame Blavatsky's theosophical movement).[80] Nor is the reason for so complicated and eclectic a set of enthusiasms hard to find. The three or four decades after 1860 were for many a crisis time of polar opposites: between science and faith, between naturalism and supernaturalism, between order and chaos. Spiritualism, with its combination of fraud and precision, of mood and measurement, at once provided a metaphor for the very crisis itself and a unique vehicle for possible reconciliation. Science and belief, many had come to believe, could now best be reconciled upon the medium's couch in heavy shuttered late Victorian drawing-rooms.

4. MATTERS OF IMAGINATION

Nowhere, perhaps, was the ambivalent message of evolution more strikingly interpreted by Victorians than in the works of those imaginative writers sensitive to its adaptive possibilities. Before the 1860s, Tennyson, whose 'In Memoriam' (written 1833-50) presents God as directing evolution towards beneficent ends, and Browning, whose scintillating 'Paracelsus' (1835) sees in the very fact of human imperfection a promise of development still to come, had found it possible to blow upon powerful poetic trumpets of pre-Darwinian evolutionary optimism and hope. It had been left to Clough and to Arnold to express the contrary virtues of acquiescent endurance in a universe of trivial repetitions and endless processes. With the appearance of Darwin's special biological brand of accidental neutrality, Tennyson, for one, became much disturbed. Soon he was nervously asking Darwin, 'Your theory of evolution does not make

[79] A. Gauld, *The Founders of Psychical Research* (London, 1968), 32–149.

[80] J. Oppenheim, *The Other World: Spiritualism and Psychical Research in England, 1850–1914* (Cambridge, 1985), 268–9, 278–89, 335–52, 474–5; W. H. Brock, 'William Crookes', in *Dictionary of Scientific Biography*, ed. C. C. Gillispie, 15 vols. (New York, 1970–80), iii. 474–82.

against Christianity?' and was no more than momentarily pacified by the politely negative reply.[81] Yet the deepening of Tennyson's political and social despair seemed to bring with it a counterbalancing move towards intellectual resolve in the shape of a return to more traditional orthodoxies. In this sense 'Locksley Hall Sixty Years After' was an act almost of exorcism. 'De Profundis' (completed in 1880), on the other hand, uses evolutionary language to encompass both physical reality and spiritual truth. In conversations during the 1880s Tennyson claimed to have found solace in Wallace's 'rescue' of the intellect from the clutches of natural selection and to have deduced therefrom that the spiritual being of humanity 'is something superadded' to merely brute natures generated by evolutionary change. Three years before his death he read the poem to a friend, and, on coming to the last section ('The Human Cry'), his voice 'growing tremulous...he broke down and sobbed aloud as he finished the prayer'

> We know we are nothing—but Thou wilt help us to be.
> Hallowed be Thy name—Halleluiah![82]

For Browning, by contrast, evolution had never been so consistent a preoccupation. And although poems such as 'Prince Hohenstiel-Schwangau' (1871) show some continuing concern, it is clear that he regarded the Darwinian theory primarily as an isolated hypothesis with slight bearing on his own metaphysical system and in no sense a threat to his belief in the existence and activity of a creating and guiding God.[83]

A more widespread interest, though not a deeper understanding, was reflected in the popular novels of the time. Snide attacks on science in general—as in F. G. Walpole's *Lord Floysham* (1886) in which a character twits: 'Science is inherently progressive in consequence of scientists rarely, if ever, agreeing with one another. What one advances, another contradicts, and this leads to the survival of the fittest'—jostled with ridicule, outraged denial, and amused contempt. Not all the writers involved are forgotten, R. D. Blackmore, a devout Anglican as well as the author of *Lorna Doone* (1869), let fly against those who equated mind with 'tadpole's spawn'. Wilkie Collins sneered with the best, as did—of all people—the popular melodramatic novelist Marie Corelli. Disraeli's *Lothair* (1870) and Charles Reade's *Put Yourself in his Place* (1870) were, respectively, mysterious and caustic in the ways they represented scientific novelties to substantial

[81] L. Stevenson, *Darwin among the Poets* (Chicago, 1932), 96.
[82] W. Ward, *Problems and Persons* (London, 1903), 217, 225; Stevenson, *Darwin among the Poets*, 55–116.
[83] Stevenson, *Darwin among the Poets*, 117–82.

audiences.[84] An equally large, if perhaps somewhat more thoughtful, public read those novels of faith and doubt of which *Robert Elsmere* (1888) by Mrs Humphry Ward remains the most notable. In this dramatic (though prolix) representation of the mental plight of a clergyman losing his faith, science forms only one among those hammer-blows driving men of sensibility towards disbelief—historical research, biblical criticism, philosophical speculation. Ward, none the less, ascribes to it a crucial role in helping to spread 'doubt': 'Evolution—once a germ in the mind— was beginning to press, to encroach, to intermeddle with the mind's other furniture'.

Notable too is the manner in which the evolutionary temper helped to shape the thinking of some of the foremost critical writers of the time. For example, John Addington Symonds, best known for his work on the *Renaissance in Italy* (1875–86), put forward an ingenious 'Application of Evolutionary Principles to Art and Literature' in which art is seen as exhibiting 'qualities analogous to those of an organic complex under- going successive phases of germination, expansion, efflorescence, and decay ... independent of the volition of the men who effected them'.[85] And in much the same way the famous conclusion to Walter Pater's *Studies on the History of the Renaissance* (1873) depicts art in evolutionary terms, freeing itself from matter in a continuing and evolving journey through (successively) architecture, sculpture, bas-relief, painting, poetry, and music.

More truly Darwinian were Pater's difficulties in preferring one formally perfected artistic school to another. Believing that 'all periods, types, schools of taste, are in themselves equal', he located the critic's task not in the assignation of works to schools (the mere artistic equivalent of the outdated biology of Linnaeus), but in elucidating the unique qualities which distinguish each particular work of artistic creation. Darwinism helped Pater to overcome (if not to resolve) the critical dilemma posed by the necessity of reconciling a personal isolated response to art with the requirements of traditional and historical comprehension. The manner in which he set art (in conjunction with science) against morality, philosophy, and religion finds a strong contemporary echo in Oscar Wilde's *fin de siècle* comment that 'There is no such thing as a moral or an immoral book. Books are well written, or badly written. That is all.' 'There is no such thing as a

[84] L. J. Henkin, *Darwinism in the English Novel 1860–1910* (New York, 1940), 76–93; Oldroyd, *Darwinian Impacts*, 309–32.
[85] J. A. Symonds, *Essays Speculative and Suggestive*, 3rd edn. (London, 1907), 37 (1st publ. 1890).

moral or an immoral organism', Darwin might have said, 'Organisms are well adapted, or badly adapted. That is all.'[86]

For more revealing instances of the powerful way in which evolution could encourage a metamorphosis of artistic sensibility one can, by way of example, turn to four very different writers: George Eliot, Rider Haggard, George Meredith, and Thomas Hardy. Eliot, herself a keen student of contemporary intellectual movements, was in her day often taken to task for the multitude of scientific allusions in her works. But in her two late and perhaps greatest novels, *Middlemarch* (1871–2) and *Daniel Deronda* (1876), the problems and opportunities raised by Darwin enter into the very substance of the fictional project as a whole. A study of processes and relationships of an unambiguously Darwinian kind underpins both books, as does a driving belief in the presence of permanent yet hidden laws in the natural world. Indeed, for Eliot—and for many of her nineteenth-century readers—evolutionary notions of significant repetition and variation probably supplied the essential principle according to which *Middlemarch* was actually put together. In its turn, *Daniel Deronda* is no less clearly situated within the debate about race and culture sparked off in the 1870s by the publication of *The Descent of Man*, with Eliot responding directly to that book's chapters on 'Sexual Selection' in a fictional exploration of the relations between women and men—their nature, limits, origins, and opportunities.[87]

Because, in his own way, Rider Haggard was also gnawingly concerned with matters of process and purpose, Darwin's concept of natural selection from random variations led him to highlight the tension he felt between a desire to see a God-directed principle of order within the universe and a realization that any such principle was quite possibly itself the outcome of no more than mechanical accident. Again and again the devil is given the best tunes, as when in *Jess* (1887) the wicked Anglo-Boer, Frank Muller, rejects the idea of purpose: 'Bah, a God! I snap my fingers at him. Chance is the only God. Chance blows men about like the dead grass, till death comes down like the veldt fire and burns them up.' A powerful obsession with the evolutionary immensity of time was superadded to Haggard's awareness of flux and change, and helped give humanity and insight to much even of his unashamedly 'imperial' writing. As a result, *King Solomon's Mines* (1886) and the other African books do, indeed,

[86] A. D. Culler, 'The Darwinian Revolution and Literary Form', in G. Levine and W. Madden (eds.), *The Art of Victorian Prose* (New York, 1968), 224–46. Wilde's comment is in the preface to *The Picture of Dorian Gray* (1891).

[87] G. Beer, *Darwin's Plots: Evolutionary Narrative in Darwin, George Eliot and Nineteenth-Century Fiction* (London, 1983), 149–235.

repudiate the most vulgar presumptions of the imperial idea, for, just as evolution had awoken Symonds to the sophistry of cultural absolutism, so Haggard's relativism freed him from condescension and from disparaging black peoples. In fact, Haggard's involvement with evolutionary change and process gave no prominence at all to such popular Victorian themes as the value of competition, the survival of the fittest, or the providential necessity of war.[88]

In the case of Meredith, especially Meredith the nature poet, the impact was even more direct. Like Haggard, he saw himself torn 'between the bogs of optimism and pessimism'. But a belief in progress (perceived from the laws of growth in nature rather than by intuitive means) provided Meredith with a more constant guiding star. An early rejection of Christianity was followed by persistent suspicion of 'priestcraft and priests' and of traditional moral systems. For Meredith, only evolutionary development, rightly understood, could banish the selfishness which sought sensual refuge in the setting-up of an external power allegedly transcending nature. Consciousness, however, marked the limits of natural selection. Thereafter, Meredith believed, men and women must themselves take a hand in the agonizing process of creation. This qualified view, very reminiscent of Wallace, filled Meredith with exhilaration, because, while allowing for the retention of older biological and predatory elements, it defined each person's task as the overcoming and harnessing of such primitive 'egoisms' in the search for a higher and ultimately selfless goal.[89] An acute sense of these evolutionary polarities informs his work. On the one hand, violence and horror stand at the very heart of the natural world.

> Earthward swoops a vulture sun,
> Nighted upon carrion:
> Straightway venom winecups shout
> Toasts to One whose eyes are out:
> Flowers along the reeling floor
> Drip henbane and hellebore:
> Beauty, of her tresses shorn,
> Shrieks as nature's maniac.

On the other hand, Meredith found it possible—even out of such saturnalias of death (quoted here from 'The Woods of Westermain' in *Poems and Lyrics*, 1883)—to derive revival and rebirth.

---

[88] A. Sandison, *The Wheel of Empire: A Study of the Imperial Idea in some Late Nineteenth and Early Twentieth-Century Fiction* (London, 1967), 25–47.

[89] Stevenson, *Darwin among the Poets*, 183–236.

Behold, in yon stripped Autumn, shivering grey,
Earth knows no desolation.
She smells regeneration
In the moist breath of decay.

('Ode to the Spirit of Earth in Autumn' in *Modern Love*, 1862)

In the end, evolution promised the greater hope. Asked, in the year of his death, to cite a favourite passage from among his verse, Meredith significantly chose lines from 'The Thrush in February' (published in *A Reading of Earth*, 1888):

Full lasting is the song, though he,
The singer, passes: lasting too,
For souls not lent in usury,
The rapture of the forward view.

Perhaps the most profound of all contemporary artistic responses to Darwinism came from Thomas Hardy. It is important to remember that Darwin's vision, though it tore away the pacific mask that life can wear, was tragic rather than hysterical: 'We behold the face of nature bright with gladness . . . we do not see or we forget, that the birds which are idly singing round us mostly live on insects or seeds, and are thus constantly destroying life'. Darwin never rose to the melodrama of Tennyson's 'Nature red in tooth and claw' or to the Grand Guignol of Meredith or of scientific disciples like Romanes, who, in 1892, described the 'teeth and talons whetted for slaughter, hooks and suckers moulded for torment—everywhere a reign of terror, hunger, and sickness, with oozing blood and quivering limbs'. In this respect Hardy proved a more reliable translator, as also in his reception of the slow move throughout *The Origin* from a static hierarchical view of nature towards Darwin's great final image of 'a tangled bank, clothed with many plants of many kinds, with birds singing on the bushes, with various insects flitting about, and with worms crawling through the damp earth' and then to the reflection 'that these elaborately constructed forms, so different from each other, and dependent upon each other in so complex a manner, have all been produced by laws acting around us'.[90]

The concrete result of Hardy's initial engagement with Darwin can best be seen in a poem such as 'Hap' written as early as 1866.

If but some vengeful god would call on me
From up the sky, and laugh: 'Thou suffering thing,

[90] S. E. Hyman, *The Tangled Bank: Darwin, Marx, Frazer and Freud as Imaginative Writers* (New York, 1962), 28–33. The quotation is from the final paragraph of *The Origin of Species*.

Know that thy sorrow is my ecstasy,
That thy love's loss is my hate's profiting!'

Then would I bear it, clench myself, and die,
Steeled by the sense of ire unmerited;
Half-eased in that a Powerfuller than I
Had willed and meted me the tears I shed.

But not so. How arrives it joy lies slain,
And why unblooms the best hope ever sown?
—Crass Casualty obstructs the sun and rain,
And dicing Time for gladness casts a moan . . .
These purblind Doomsters had as readily strown
Blisses about my pilgrimage as pain.

Here Hardy encounters precisely the same difficulty that had dogged Darwin throughout *The Origin*, namely, how to express the idea of 'un-design' without using terms that imply the opposite. For a poet this problem of language was of course especially acute, and Hardy, too, in phrases such as 'Crass Casualty' and 'dicing Time', found himself driven into a kind of defusing personification—evidence of how conditions of artistic representation and of language place virtually insuperable barriers in front of any accurate expression of the Darwinian world-view.[91]

However, it is in the later novels that Hardy moves from the mere borrowing of specific notions towards a confrontation with one of the deepest turns in Darwin's theme—the realization of the importance of the dynamics of the living organism's interior system. Thus, although individuals may be of small significance against the backdrop of nature, their responses to the environment (their interior life) become more and more important to us as a result of our awareness that such reactions are a key to the movement of life itself.[92] Already in *The Return of the Native* (1878) it is obvious that Hardy is intent on underpinning those coincidences (or more accurately those accidents) which carry the story along by the use of a patterned rather than a causal inevitability. Already too, anthropological relationships between personality and landscape constitute a central theme. Again and again Hardy emphasizes the evolutionary connections of all life, the relatedness of man and 'lower' forms, over the mere 'survival of the fittest'. Of course conflict is present, notably the tragic struggle of natural man to survive in a world where civilization is changing nature's ambiguous rules. Yet an overall notion of creative evolution remains consistently central to Hardy's artistic enterprise as a whole.

[91] Beer, *Darwin's Plots*, 29–76.
[92] P. Meisel, *Thomas Hardy: The Return of the Repressed* (New Haven, 1972), 16–17.

Tess of the D'Urbervilles (1891) provides perhaps the most complex and brilliant working-out of Hardy's evolutionary imagination. His delicate sense of the relationship between past and present owes an obvious debt to evolutionary models. The understanding of culture, not only as Angel Clare seems to cultivate it, but as something closer to a modern anthropological definition, comes from the same general source. The fact that Tess herself is not merely in direct contact with nature, but is involved in her own (historical) culture, adds a layer of evolutionary mediation to any comprehension of her predicament. A feeling for humanity's place in the ebb and flow of evolution and a grasp of the ritual requirements of each individual's relationship to nature enable Hardy to make Tess sympathetic, not simply as a victim of civilization, but as a woman caught in the movements of history, environment, and self.

The last stanza of 'In Tenebris II', written as Hardy was in the depths of depression in the 1890s, was one he himself liked to quote, not least, perhaps, because it provides so suitably ambiguous a commentary on the whole business of the mid- and late Victorian reception of evolutionary ideas.

Let him in whose ears the low-voiced Best is killed by the clash of the First,
Who holds that if way to the better there be, it exacts a full look at the Worst,
Who feels that delight is a delicate growth cramped by crookedness, custom, and fear,
Get him up and be gone as one shaped awry; he disturbs the order here.

The adaptations of evolution which manifested themselves in Victorian Britain had parallels elsewhere. In America the crudities of Social Darwinism evoked a particularly enthusiastic response. In France and Germany both reactionaries and liberals struck evolutionary attitudes. Around the notion of evolution, and especially around the ideas enunciated by Darwin, there clustered ever-thickening layers of interpretation, theory, and generalization. Dissolved by many different aesthetic, political, and metaphysical solvents, these came to form an indispensable part of that congeries of concepts, that totality of (often unquestioned) beliefs, within which mid- and late Victorian men and women sought their bearings and their place.

Hardly a field of thought remained untouched. Historians began to see the past as a living organism. Critics explored the evolution of literary types. Legal experts unravelled the law as a growing social institution. Anthropologists and sociologists looked to natural selection in their examination of social forms. Defenders of wealth demonstrated the 'unfitness' of the poor and the inevitability of progress under the élite leadership of the 'fit'. *Laissez-faire* liberals strove to prevent all interference with natural cosmic evolutionary laws. New liberals invoked evolutionary co-operation and meliorism. Socialists equated class conflict with the struggle of biological groups. Poets rhapsodized a creative life-force. Novelists absorbed both the matter and the style of evolutionary conceptualization. Solid volumes appeared on *The Evolution of Morality* (1878), *The Evolution of Religion* (1894), *The Evolution of Modern Money* (1901), *The Evolution of Immorality* (1901), *The Evolution of the Soul* (1904). When the great Victorian Scotsman, James Murray of the *Oxford English Dictionary*, was asked to give the Romanes lecture in 1900 he chose as his theme 'The Evolution of English Lexicography'. Some of this was crude, and—even when it was not—dealt more in analogy and metaphor than in direct application. But then no set of ideas can reach so wide an audience without adjustment and change. And though the 'evolutionary moment' was never more than a phase, so thoroughly were mid- and late Victorian minds laundered by its governing ideas that these have ever since remained irrevocably woven into the fabric of British thought and British life.

PART IV

England and Beyond

CHAPTER 14

A British Nation? The Experiences of Scotland and Wales

1. BRITAIN: A LOP-SIDED AFFAIR

The legislative steps which led to the creation of the United Kingdom of Great Britain and Ireland on 1 January 1801—namely, the very different acts of union with Wales (1536), Scotland (1707), and Ireland (1800)—were less comprehensive than is commonly supposed. Late Victorian disputes over Home Rule disguise the fact that the 'new' kingdom's actual, as distinct from its supposed, condition was always one of quasi-devolution. That, in the event, it often proved difficult to give formal recognition to this state of things had less to do with the smaller nations—Ireland, Scotland, Wales—than with England's overweening and relatively increasing power, wealth, and size. In 1841 80.2 per cent of Britain's and 55.7 per cent of the United Kingdom's inhabitants lived in England. Sixty years later these figures had grown to 82.5 and 73.6 per cent respectively. Given the absence of demands for regional autonomy within England, this presented devolutionists of all kinds with almost insuperable difficulties. Home Rule, therefore, was at heart always more an English problem than an Irish, Scottish, or Welsh one.

It was of course natural for London-based politicians to see matters differently and to believe that the growth of a 'British' identity would help to bind together at least all those on the larger island. Nor were they entirely mistaken in doing so, for the wars against the American colonists (1775–83) and revolutionary France (1793–1815) certainly generated powerful integrative effects: they impressed people with the idea that the differences between them were less than the differences which separated them all from the citizens of other lands. Yet almost every phenomenon which can be identified as encouraging a sense of Britishness possessed fissiparous as well as integrative qualities. Once anti-Scottish prejudices faded south of the border, anti-Irish prejudices seamlessly took their place. Industrialization may have brought a broadly common experience to

Lancashire, Clydeside, and South Wales, but it also created new barriers between country and town.[1] Better communications made it easier to reach remote parts of the kingdom. But they also made it easier to inflate theoretical animosities with the oxygen of actual (and very often rebarbative) contact, as many travellers' accounts show.[2]

And while the development of empire overseas did much to increase feelings of Britishness, this was by no means devoid of disintegrative ambiguities. Many Scots, for example, found comforting niches within the imperial enterprise—and Glaswegians boasted tirelessly of inhabiting an imperial city—but they still complained when early Civil Service reforms seemed to penalize Scottish graduates in the race for well-paid jobs in India and elsewhere.[3] Not only that, but an experience of empire could sometimes, as J. S. Mill pointed out,[4] lead to a greater understanding of the political and economic demands of the smaller nations within the United Kingdom (though Mill, too, could be stoutly Anglocentric when it suited his argument).

Looked at from one perspective, nineteenth-century religion certainly seemed to bind the British closer together. The Evangelical movement affected churches throughout the United Kingdom in broadly similar ways: more feeling, more emphasis on public morality, more anti-Catholicism. There were also clear parallels between the growth of Dissent in England, Wales, and Scotland, in all of which established churches lost ground to other Protestant groups.[5] Looked at from another perspective, denominationalism not only became more rather than less intense during the Victor-

[1] L. Colley, *Britons: Forging the Nation* (New Haven, 1992), 17, 145; E. Evans, 'Englishness and Britishness: National Identities, *c.*1790–*c.*1870', in A. Grant and K. J. Stringer (eds.), *Uniting the Kingdom? The Making of British History* (London, 1995), 223–43.

[2] H. D. Inglis, *A Journey throughout Ireland during the Spring, Summer, and Autumn of 1834*, 5th edn. (London, 1838); T. Carlyle, *Reminiscences of my Irish Journey in 1849* (London, 1882); C. Smout, 'Tours in the Scottish Highlands from the Eighteenth to the Twentieth Centuries', *Northern Scotland*, 5 (1983), 99–121. George Borrow's account of his Welsh tour of 1854 published as *Wild Wales* (1862) does, however, reveal considerable affection for the people and their language.

[3] C. Harvie, *Scotland and Nationalism: Scottish Society and Politics 1707–1994*, 2nd edn. (London, 1994), 62.

[4] 'And those Englishmen who know something of India, are even now those who understand Ireland best' (J. S. Mill, *England and Ireland* (1868) in *Collected Works of John Stuart Mill*, ed. J. M. Robson and others, 33 vols. (Toronto, 1963–91), vi. 519).

[5] D. W. Bebbington, 'Religion and National Feeling in Nineteenth-Century Wales and Scotland', in S. Mews (ed.), *Religion and National Identity* (Oxford, 1982), 501–2; C. G. Brown, 'Protest in the Pews: Interpreting Presbyterianism and Society in Fracture during the Scottish Economic Revolution', in T. M. Devine (ed.), *Conflict and Stability in Scottish Society 1700–1850* (Edinburgh, 1990), 88–9.

ian period, but often expressed itself in distinctly national modes. Presbyterianism bound Scotland to Ulster but separated it from England. The Calvinistic Methodists were an entirely Welsh body. Even non-Roman episcopalianism varied across national boundaries. The Church of Ireland was strongly Protestant in character. The Church of England (with which the Irish Church was 'for ever' united in 1801) experienced bouts of Anglo-Catholic activity and in Wales operated almost as a distinct entity. The Episcopal Church in Scotland was completely separate: numerically marginal, but socially significant. Nor was there much Britishness evident among those who laboured in God's vineyards overseas. Anglican missionary societies were largely English, Presbyterian societies largely Scottish: their activities lacked co-ordination and their mission stations possessed strikingly English or Scottish atmospheres.[6]

Even the few unambiguously British or United Kingdom institutions of the time displayed strong particularist tendencies. The army's regimental system became more localized. Debates at Westminster often widened rather than lessened national differences. The royal family may, from the 1840s onwards, have become devotees of the Scottish Highlands (though the Prince of Wales much preferred Sandringham to Balmoral), but Queen Victoria visited Ireland only four times in over sixty years and Wales less often still. As the century wore on prime ministers with almost no direct experience of Ireland (Gladstone, Disraeli, Salisbury, Rosebery) replaced prime ministers with substantial Irish connections (Melbourne, Peel, Russell, Palmerston, Derby). And though the Post Office did indeed function uniformly throughout the kingdom, the banking system in Scotland differed from that elsewhere. Ireland's separate administrative structures were retained after the Union and were still controlled, in the first instance, from Dublin Castle rather than Whitehall. The administration of Scotland, almost totally neglected by London in the eighteenth century, became characterized by *ad hoc* particularism in the nineteenth. Even supposedly fully absorbed Wales was able to display a few administrative peculiarities during the half-century before specifically Welsh legislation reappeared in the shape of the Sunday Closing Act of 1881.[7] And while political parties adopted the same labels throughout the kingdom, Conservatism and Liberalism in Scotland and Ireland differed greatly from their English counterparts.

---

[6] K. Robbins, *Nineteenth-Century Britain: Integration and Diversity* (Oxford, 1988), 95.
[7] K. O. Morgan, *Wales in British Politics 1868–1922*, 3rd edn. (Cardiff, 1980), 41. Thus certain official authorities—the Registrar-General, the Home Office, the Court of Chancery—treated Wales as a distinct unit for a number of purposes.

Scotland and England were also distinct countries in a broad cultural sense. Separate legal codes touched their inhabitants from cradle to grave. Men and women married according to distinctive legislation. Property was dealt with differently. The poor law operated differently, as did local administration in general. Complex statutes required endless fine-tuning in order to make it possible to deal with the problem of Scottish criminals who escaped to the south. In death too, different rites were used to send Christians to eternity. And should the manner of death require an inquest, then this would be carried out under separate regulations.[8] Different school and university systems affected English and Scottish children. The major sports of Association Football and Rugby were organized by independent national bodies and the first England–Scotland soccer match in 1872 opened up new and fruitful areas of conflict for the future.[9]

While it had undoubtedly become possible for those living in the minimal British state of early and mid-Victorian times to assert a set of multiple and interlocking loyalties—to be at once a citizen of Edinburgh, a Lowlander, a Scot, and a Briton—the key dates according to which the various nations divided up their contemporary (let alone their historical) experiences were distinctly their own: 1846 and Corn Law repeal in England, 1843 and ecclesiastical disruption in Scotland, 1847 and disputes over Blue Books on education in Wales, 1845–50 and the Great Famine in Ireland. When, therefore, new and more conscious forms of nationalism began, in the later nineteenth century, to collide with the Anglicizing tendencies of an emerging interventionist welfare state, the pragmatic multi-layered accommodations of former years became more and more difficult to sustain.

The use of language reveals much about the realities which lay behind public attitudes. And it is a curious feature of Victorian political discourse that no word was ever found to describe all the inhabitants of that United Kingdom so widely believed to be indissoluble. 'English' was commonly used for all those living on the 'mainland', and Gladstone so used it in his Midlothian speeches of 1879. When this became irritating to the Scots and Welsh, 'British' was adopted, but in turn rejected by all but a minority in Ireland.[10] Shakespeare of course called England 'this scepter'd isle': it is not. Disraeli called himself Prime Minister of England: he was not. The

---

[8] M. A. Crowther, 'Response: North of the Border', *Scottish Historical Review*, 73 (1994), 100–2 [Response to R. J. Morris and G. Morton, 'Where was Nineteenth-Century Scotland?', ibid. 89–99].

[9] Robbins, *Nineteenth-Century Britain*, 165. The first matches between England and Wales and Scotland and Wales were held in 1879 and 1882 respectively.

[10] H. C. G. Matthew, *Gladstone 1875–1898* (Oxford, 1995), 213; W. E. Gladstone, *Political Speeches in Scotland, November and December 1879* (London, 1879), 52.

Scottish poet Thomas Campbell urged 'Ye mariners of England' to 'guard our native shores'. H. T. Buckle's *History of Civilization in England* (1857–61) includes a substantial section on Scotland—as does this volume in the 'New Oxford History of England'. Confusion as well as hegemonic Anglo-Saxon attitudes lay and lie behind such things. For J. R. Seeley it was *The Expansion of England* (1883) that demanded explanation, for Charles Dilke it was the existence of a *Greater Britain* (1869). A. V. Dicey put forward not Britain's, but *England's Case against Home Rule* (1886). When Joseph Chamberlain talked about patriotism to the Glasgow University students who had elected him rector he meant the wondrousness of England and the English (as pained voices from the audience pointed out). When it suited them, certain Ulster Protestants insisted they were really British and that Ulster, as one put it in 1852, was 'not Irish at all'.[11] Wales was regularly written out of the script altogether, as when Peel declared his support for those religious establishments which connected 'Protestantism with the State in the *three* countries'.[12]

Two conspicuous feelings informed the attitudes of the English political and cultural classes towards the other parts of the kingdom: that the English were at once superior and constantly being imposed upon. Gladstone, though proud of his Scottish background, lectured the Scots and Irish Members of Parliament in 1872 about 'that part of the United Kingdom which had hardly been mentioned ... namely, that portion called England'.[13] But while Gladstone combined occasional querulousness with unusual and growing sympathy for the aspirations of the non-English lands (even though as late as 1881 he still knew less about Ireland's agrarian problems than about Balkan nationalism), others operated in an unambiguously negative mode when looking at Scotland or Wales, let alone at Ireland. Because notions of ethnicity constituted an important part of the mental furniture of educated Victorians, specific characteristics were regularly assigned to 'races' with all the breezy confidence which only a marriage of romanticism and science can generate. *The Times*, always keen to lecture lesser breeds beyond the Tweed or Offa's Dyke, called Wales 'a small country ... with an indifferent soil, and inhabited by an unenterprising people' and accused the Scots of sullenly keeping out all those 'English influences which might have done them good'.[14] 'Thank

[11] J. Loughlin, 'Joseph Chamberlain, English Nationalism and the Ulster Question', *History*, 77 (1992), 202–19.

[12] G. Kitson Clark, *Peel and the Conservative Party: A Study in Party Politics 1832–1841* (London, 1929), 328. My italics.

[13] *Hansard*, ccix. 1879 (12 Mar. 1872).

[14] *The Times*, 14 Sept. 1866 and 4 Dec. 1856.

God', declared the *Economist* in the revolutionary year of 1848, 'We are Saxons' and thus, unlike the 'savage Celt' and 'flighty Gaul', neither 'deplorably excitable' nor 'furiously wild'.[15] Nor does one have to go to the further shores of educated opinion to find Victorian intellectuals who believed all or some of these things. Matthew Arnold, while by no means unfriendly, patronized contemporary Celts as dreamy poets clinging to the past and rejecting the electric attractions of 'progress' and 'material civilization'.[16] J. S. Mill hoped that Welshmen and Scottish Highlanders would abandon their unprogressive desire to stand outside the English mainstream of the state. The Catholic historian, Sir John (later Lord) Acton, a close friend of Gladstone, saw Celts as either 'stationary or retrogressive' waiting idly 'for a foreign influence to set in action the rich treasures which in their own hands could be of no avail'.[17]

With such opinions providing the common coin of discourse among liberal intellectuals, it is hardly surprising that parliamentarians rarely found it necessary to focus upon the incomprehensible affairs of the lesser nations save when an O'Connell, a Parnell, a famine, or a small majority obliged them to do so. As long as the Scots remained quiet, Scottish business at Westminster was rushed through in the small hours by MPs anxious to get to their beds.[18] When in 1877 the Liberal leader, Hartington, was obliged to visit Scotland, he appealed desperately to colleagues to 'give me a safe sentence or two on Scottish matters' about which he was, in most respects, ignorant.[19] The Liberal governments which held a virtual monopoly of power between 1846 and 1874 had an unerring eye for nonentities when appointing Viceroys and Chief Secretaries of Ireland. And when in 1870 Gladstone at last offered the latter position to someone of substance he sugared the pill by insisting that no 'vast or extraordinary efforts' would be required.[20] Salisbury treated the Scottish Secretaryship (which he created

[15] *Economist*, 29 Apr. 1848, p. 477.

[16] P. Dodd, 'Englishness and the National Culture', in R. Colls and P. Dodd (eds.), *Englishness: Politics and Culture, 1880–1920* (London, 1986), 11–13; C. Harvie, 'Nineteenth-Century Scotland: Political Unionism and Cultural Nationalism, 1843–1906', in R. G. Asch (ed.), *Three Nations—A Common History? England, Scotland, Ireland and British History c.1600–1920* (Bochum, 1993), 214.

[17] J. S. Mill, *Considerations on Representative Government* (1861) in *Collected Works of John Stuart Mill*, ed. J. M. Robson and others, xix. 549; Acton's 'Mr Goldwin Smith's Irish History', *Rambler*, NS 6 (1862), 197–8.

[18] J. G. Kellas, *Modern Scotland: The Nation since 1870* (London, 1968), 173–4, 272.

[19] I. G. C. Hutchison, *A Political History of Scotland 1832–1924: Parties, Elections and Issues* (Edinburgh, 1986), 143.

[20] K. T. Hoppen, *Elections, Politics, and Society in Ireland 1832–1885* (Oxford, 1984), 259–61.

in 1885) even more disdainfully. 'The work', he told its first holder, the Duke of Richmond, 'is not very heavy—the dignity (measured by salary) is the same as your present office—but measured by the expectations of the people of Scotland it is approaching to Arch-angelic . . . It really is a matter where the effulgence of two Dukedoms and the best salmon river in Scotland will go a long way.'[21]

Small wonder that legislation designed to deal with Scottish (and Irish) affairs was often defective, sometimes heroically so. The senior Scottish law officer, the Lord Advocate, was rarely sufficiently talented or important to overcome the casualness of his colleagues. The Scottish Reform Act of 1832 was riddled with problems and inconsistencies. Key terms regarding property—like 'owner' and 'possession'—were simply transferred from the parallel English bill though they meant quite different things (if indeed they meant anything at all) north of the border. As a result, franchise abuses grew rather than diminished and many Scottish constituencies were swamped by fictitious or 'faggot' voters.[22] Social legislation was also badly mangled when the authorities in London, with more zeal than insight, tried to introduce uniform procedures throughout the realm. The 1848 Public Health (Scotland) Bill had to be abandoned entirely when its deficiencies became manifest, with the result that the 'big six' Scottish cities were for a time obliged to use private legislation to deal with matters of public health. In 1866 the Scottish Poor Law authorities complained that four key health acts passed since 1856 had failed in Scotland because of problems over Scots law. Enforcement of the Sanitary Act of 1866 depended ultimately upon decisions of the Court of Queen's Bench which, as any moderately informed lawyer might have known, possessed no jurisdiction in Scotland, where, as a result, the act could not be implemented at all.[23] A series of housing acts passed between 1868 and 1882 encountered similar problems, while the Scottish Education Bill of 1872 was only rendered effective by means of last-minute amendments. Not until the 1860s did public health conditions in Scotland reach those attained in England and Wales in 1848 and not until the 1890s did Scottish legislation really catch up. Even the 1885 bill setting up the post of Secretary for Scotland was poorly drafted. Incompetencies of this kind were, however, merely the outward and visible

[21] H. J. Hanham, 'The Creation of the Scottish Office, 1881–7', *Juridical Review* (1968), 229. Richmond actually held three dukedoms, those of Richmond, Lennox, and Gordon.

[22] Hutchison, *Political History*, 35; W. Ferguson, 'The Reform Act (Scotland) of 1832: Intention and Effect', *Scottish Historical Review*, 45 (1966), 105–14.

[23] Robbins, *Nineteenth-Century Britain*, 154; G. F. A. Best, 'Another Part of the Island: Some Scottish Perspectives', in H. J. Dyos and M. Wolff (eds.), *The Victorian City: Images and Realities*, 2 vols. (London, 1973), i. 392.

signs of a deeper neglect. The insight and attention regularly devoted, for example, to the affairs of the Church of England were not matched elsewhere. Indeed, the Great Disruption of the Church of Scotland in 1843 had almost as much to do with the government's casual approach—to Peel's ministers it all seemed incomprehensible, the work of fanatics—as with Evangelical intransigence.[24]

In any case, not even those comparatively few links of comprehension and mutual sympathy which did develop within the United Kingdom gave forth entirely consolidating rays. Anti-Catholicism helped to bind the three British nations together against Ireland. Equally, however, Ireland's disaffections sometimes called forth responsive echoes of a distinctly anti-English nature from Scotland and Wales. Loosely similar agitations in Wales, the Scottish Highlands, and Ireland may have given late nineteenth-century agrarian discontents a somewhat less localized dynamic than before, but they did nothing to encourage the growth of British or United Kingdom identities. If attempts to set up a Celtic League in the 1880s to promote 'common political objects' failed, the example of Ireland's Gaelic Athletic Association and Gaelic League exercised a powerful influence upon those in Scotland and Wales who feared that their own traditions were being ground down by the remorseless Anglicizations of the time.[25]

In many, though not all, other respects the differences between Scotland and Wales were, however, considerable. Scotland possessed certain institutions of nationhood: its own legal system, religious establishment, educational arrangements. Wales, while displaying a more distinctive linguistic individuality, did not. But as the century wore on it became clear that both had retained—or recreated—a capacity to sustain cultural identities sharply different from that of their greater neighbour. Indeed, being themselves much more than regions, they contained regions of their own, though there is little agreement about the exact number and extent of these. In the case of Scotland some authorities suggest three: the Highlands, the Western Lowlands, the Eastern Lowlands. Others (geographers especially) prefer the Highlands, Central Lowlands, and Southern Lowlands. Economists and demographers propose no less than six, sometimes even seven, regions. But within the context of the Victorian age it is the divisions created by

[24] M. Lynch, *Scotland: A New History* (London, 1991), 398, 401, 415; Hanham, 'Creation of the Scottish Office', 211; T. C. Smout, 'Scotland 1850–1950', in F. M. L. Thompson (ed.), *The Cambridge Social History of Britain 1750–1950*, 3 vols. (Cambridge, 1990), i. 248.
[25] J. Hunter, 'The Gaelic Connection: The Highlands, Ireland and Nationalism, 1873–1922', *Scottish Historical Review*, 54 (1975), 192; L. P. Curtis, jun., *Anglo-Saxons and Celts: A Study of Anti-Irish Prejudice in Victorian England* (Bridgeport, Conn., 1968), 115; J. Davies, *A History of Wales* (London, 1993), 454.

industrialization that make most sense: rural Highlands, a central belt with heavy industries, and a rural area to the south.[26] The bulk of population growth between 1801 and 1871 took place in the central-belt counties which increased their share of Scotland's population from 41 to 58 per cent. However, the rural districts followed no common pattern, with large falls in most of the Highlands and the Borders but growth in North-East Aberdeenshire and, to an even greater extent, in the Outer Hebrides where the very absence of modernization postponed the advent of demographic decline.[27] In Wales, too, older divisions between North and South were accentuated by industry's concentration in the latter, with the result that the proportion of the total population living in Glamorgan and Monmouthshire rose from 20 to 63 per cent between 1801 and 1911.[28]

In economic terms industrialization in Scotland and Wales followed roughly similar paths. Both countries achieved considerable industrial prominence, so much so that by mid-century the world's two largest iron works were to be found at Gartsherrie to the east of Glasgow and Dowlais in Glamorgan. In the period 1860–4 Scotland and Wales produced 13.0 and 17.5 per cent respectively of total British coal production by weight and 25.5 and 21.8 per cent of pig iron by weight.[29] But while the Scots concentrated, above all, upon the metal, engineering, and textile sectors, by the end of the century South Wales had become, first and foremost, a land of coal. And it was coal and mining generally which rendered Welsh employment patterns increasingly distinct (Table 14.1), not least because, by the 1870s, it was becoming clear that the Welsh iron industry was not keeping up to date. In the medium term Wales was lucky that coal, now liberated by the railway from close geographical dependence on iron, proved more than able to fill the gap. Employment in the Glamorgan coal fields alone rose from 38,000 men in 1861 to 117,000 in 1891 and 220,000 in 1911.[30] At the very moment, therefore, when the overall British economy was experiencing difficulties and even downturn, the Welsh coal industry was expanding very rapidly indeed.

[26] H. Kearney, *The British Isles: A History of Four Nations* (Cambridge, 1989), 151, 167; Smout, 'Scotland 1850–1950', 212, 215–16.

[27] M. Anderson and D. J. Morse, 'The People', in W. H. Fraser and R. J. Morris (eds.), *People and Society in Scotland*, ii. *1830–1914* (Edinburgh, 1990), 10; R. H. Campbell, *Scotland since 1707: The Rise of an Industrial Society*, 2nd edn. (Edinburgh, 1985), 136; A. Slaven, *The Development of the West of Scotland 1750–1960* (London, 1975), 136.

[28] P. Jenkins, *A History of Modern Wales 1536–1990* (London, 1992), 236.

[29] B. R. Mitchell, *British Historical Statistics* (Cambridge, 1988), 247–8, 281–2. The coal production of North Wales (estimated as about 2% of British output) has been added to Mitchell's South Wales figures.

[30] Jenkins, *History of Modern Wales*, 222–3, 228.

TABLE 14.1　　*Occupational distribution of labour force in Scotland, Wales, and England, 1841 and 1901* (%)

	1841			1901		
	Scotland	Wales	England	Scotland	Wales	England
Agriculture						
Males	30.9	36.6	27.5	14.2	14.3	10.6
All	24.3	30.2	21.3	11.5	12.1	7.7
Metals and engineering						
Males	5.4	7.5	7.1	15.3	10.6	12.8
All	3.8	6.0	5.5	11.0	8.7	9.5
Textiles and clothing						
Males	22.4	9.0	18.1	8.2	3.6	9.8
All	26.4	9.0	21.2	16.7	7.4	17.0
Mining and quarrying						
Males	3.5	15.1	3.9	9.5	29.1	6.6
All	2.6	12.0	3.0	6.8	23.0	4.7
Other manufacturing						
Males	7.3	4.4	9.4	12.2	7.2	13.5
All	5.8	3.9	7.7	12.4	7.0	12.1
Transport and services						
Males	12.1	10.5	15.5	20.7	18.1	25.7
All*	23.5	25.1	26.9	26.6	28.2	33.6
Other sectors						
Males	18.4	16.9	18.5	19.9	17.1	21.0
All	13.6	13.8	14.4	15.0	13.6	15.4

* Domestic service alone amounted to: Scotland 1841 = 17.5, 1901 = 12.1; Wales 1841 = 20.7, 1901 = 14.2; England 1841 = 19.6, 1901 = 15.4.
Source: C. H. Lee, *British Regional Employment Statistics 1841–1971* (Cambridge, 1979), Series A.

Whereas Scottish industrialization took place largely in areas which possessed at least some historically significant towns, the urban society of South Wales was a new creation. Welsh industrial towns were raw frontier places even by Victorian standards. In 1801, when Glasgow and Edinburgh already boasted 160,000 people between them, Cardiff had fewer than 2,000: by 1891 it had 129,000. So great was the demand for labour in Glamorgan and Monmouthshire that, after about 1860, those in rural Wales seeking a better life had no need to look outside their own country, not to England, not to America. Nineteenth-century Welsh migration overseas, despite romantic afflations about tiny settlements in Patagonia and rather larger ones in Pennsylvania, was a modest affair. During the

1880s England's loss by emigration amounted to 23 and Scotland's to 58 per 10,000 inhabitants, Wales's to 11 per 10,000, even though movement away from Welsh rural areas was (at about 100,000 in all) much higher than it had been in previous decades.[31] And thereafter came a period during which Wales generated no net emigration at all.

2. SCOTLAND: SOCIETY AND RELIGION

Scotland, with in 1871 3.36 million people compared to Wales's 1.42 million, operated on a larger economic scale. Its industrial base was broader and more regionalized. Because shipbuilding and the classic heavy metal industries were confined to the Clyde—by the end of the century over a third of British maritime tonnage was produced there—the district around Glasgow became stamped by a distinctive male-dominated working-class culture. Quite different was Dundee where the jute mills pursued international competitiveness by using low-paid female labour and where in consequence unemployed husbands found themselves doing the housework: 'He used', recalled one woman, 'to have the hoose spotless . . . an' ma denner a' made.'[32] Edinburgh, by contrast, despite its breweries and printing works, was strongly professional, as, to a lesser extent, was Aberdeen.

By the end of our period Scotland had become, after England, the most urbanized and industrialized country in Europe. But, as was not the case in England, its male workers were heavily (and increasingly) concentrated in capital goods industries dependent upon exports and susceptible to cyclical fluctuations. Therefore, even though the Scottish economy was more diversified than the Welsh, it lacked both a strong service sector and an adequate range of industries catering for domestic markets. If the Welsh industrial economy came to depend disproportionately on coal, Scottish prosperity was especially vulnerable to falling export demand, not least because newer industries like chemicals, vehicles, and electrical equipment were slow to develop north of the border.[33] But the very size of the major Scottish towns and the wealth of their growing middle classes disguised the

---

[31] G. A. Williams, *When was Wales? A History of the Welsh* (London, 1985), 178. Between 1881 and 1891 Glamorgan (pop. 1881 = 511,433) alone gained 77,417 people by *net* immigration (P. N. Jones, 'Population Migration into Glamorgan 1861–1911', in P. Morgan (ed.), *Glamorgan County History*, vi. *Glamorgan Society 1780–1980* (Cardiff, 1988), 174–6).

[32] S. and O. Checkland, *Industry and Ethos: Scotland 1832–1914* (London, 1984), 22; *Odyssey: Voices from Scotland's Recent Past*, ed. B. Kay (Edinburgh, 1980), 38.

[33] T. M. Devine, 'The Paradox of Scottish Emigration', in Devine (ed.), *Scottish Emigration and Scottish Society* (Edinburgh, 1992), 12; Slaven, *Development of the West of Scotland*, 10–11.

dangers that lay ahead. By 1891 Glasgow had become one of Britain's and indeed the empire's leading cities, its 658,000 people outnumbering those of the next two Scottish cities—Edinburgh and Dundee—combined. In the same year more than half of Scotland's people lived in towns with over 5,000 inhabitants, the proportion in settlements over 2,000 (65.4 per cent) being, in Europe, second only to that of England.[34] And not only was income per head in Scotland higher than in Wales (though the gap narrowed after 1880), but the middle classes were particularly prosperous. While manual earnings in industry were below British averages in 1886 and notably so in the textile sector, income tax assessments per head of population suggest that in 1880 Edinburgh was the third richest city in Britain (behind only London and Manchester), that Glasgow came fifth, and that Aberdeen and Dundee were comfortably ahead of places such as Sheffield and Leeds.[35]

Scotland's experience of emigration was also very different from that of England, even more so from that of Wales. Although Scotland came second only to Ireland in the nineteenth-century league table of European countries sending people to North America, its industrial base also attracted substantial immigration, notably from Ireland itself. None the less, Scotland's long history of migration seems to have meant that industrialization, far from reducing outward movement by providing new opportunities at home, actually helped to sustain a continuing exodus. During the forty years after 1861 about a quarter of the population's natural increase was diverted by net emigration and over the longer period 1830–1914 perhaps two million Scots left for destinations overseas and somewhat less than half that number for other parts of the United Kingdom. While these were substantially higher rates than those recorded by either England or Wales,[36] two aspects of Scottish emigration are often overlooked: that the movement was even more a Lowland than a Highland one and that after 1860 the typical Scots emigrant was an urban dweller endowed with distinctly

---

[34] Smout, 'Scotland 1850–1950', 244; J. Doherty, 'Urbanization, Capital Accumulation, and Class Struggle in Scotland, 1750–1914', in G. Whittington and I. D. Whyte (eds.), *An Historical Geography of Scotland* (London, 1983), 245–6.

[35] C. H. Lee, *The British Economy since 1700: A Macroeconomic Perspective* (Cambridge, 1986), 131; T. C. Smout, *A Century of the Scottish People 1830–1950* (London, 1986), 110–14; R. H. Campbell, *The Rise and Fall of Scottish Industry 1707–1939* (Edinburgh, 1980), 80, 83, 190; N. Morgan and R. H. Trainor, 'The Dominant Classes', in Fraser and Morris (eds.), *People and Society*, ii. 106.

[36] Devine, 'Paradox of Scottish Emigration', 6; M. Flinn (ed.), *Scottish Population History from the 17th Century to the 1930s* (Cambridge, 1977), 449; Anderson and Morse, 'The People', 15–17; Morris and Morton, 'Where was Nineteenth-Century Scotland?', 92.

marketable skills.[37] In the face of such losses the growing manpower needs of Scottish industry could only be met by an influx from Ireland so enormous that the proportion of Irish-born in Scotland rose far higher than in England and Wales—in 1851 it reached a peak of 7.2 per cent (compared with 2.9 per cent to the south) and it remained above 5 per cent until 1891.[38] And though perhaps a quarter of Irish immigrants were Protestants, the arrival of large numbers of Catholics unleashed a good deal of prejudice: 'They have eaten up our public charities, filled our prisons, crowded the calendar of crime, and destroyed the appearance and character of many an old Scots village.'[39] Indeed, anti-Catholic and anti-Irish sentiments, by appealing to Scots who agreed on little else, proved key elements in helping to create new and distinctively Victorian feelings of Scottish identity, nationhood, and nationalism.

For some in Scotland as elsewhere the whole industrial experience had seemed rebarbative from the start. The arrival of the Irish sullied it further. And while ruralist romanticism in England never achieved much purchase (arguments about gentrification notwithstanding) the political and intellectual cultures of Victorian Scotland were deeply marked by suspicions about industrialization and all its works. The city civilizations of Glasgow and Edinburgh failed to produce any significant urban literature, their middle classes preferring to escape from industrial realities into the thin sentimentalism of the so-called 'kailyard' writers whose works idealized the folkways of the Lowland village and small town.[40] While, therefore, parts of Scotland and Wales experienced the industrial revolution in its rawest forms, the national cultures of both countries were shaped by invented traditions of the pastoral far more than by the imperatives of city, factory, or mine. Characteristically, the nature of the Scottish Poor Law system continued to reflect rural misgivings about industrial modernity. Reformed

[37] M. Gray, 'Scottish Emigration: The Social Impact of Agrarian Change in the Rural Lowlands, 1775–1875', in D. Fleming and B. Bailyn (eds.), *Perspectives in American History VII* (Cambridge, Mass., 1973), 96–7; Devine, 'Paradox of Scottish Emigration', 2–3.

[38] W. W. Knox, 'Whatever Happened to Radical Scotland?', in R. Mason and N. Macdougall (eds.), *People and Power in Scotland* (Edinburgh, 1992), 229; L. M. Cullen and T. C. Smout, 'Economic Growth in Scotland and Ireland', in Cullen and Smout (eds.), *Comparative Aspects of Scottish and Irish Economic and Social History 1600–1900* (Edinburgh, [1977]), 12; H. J. Hanham, *Scottish Nationalism* (London, 1969), 49.

[39] Cited Campbell, *Scotland since 1707*, 144, from W. Wylie's *Ayrshire Streams* (1851).

[40] R. Anderson, 'In Search of the "Lad of Parts": The Mythical History of Scottish Education', *History Workshop*, 19 (1985), 84. 'Kailyard literature', from kailyard or kitchen garden: a term applied to a clutch of novelists and short-story writers who emerged in the 1880s and 1890s around William Robertson Nicoll and J. M. Barrie. They specialized in sentimental tales of rural Scotland with titles like *Beside the Bonnie Brier Bush* (1894) by 'Ian Maclaren' (John Watson) and *The Lilac Sunbonnet* (1894) by S. R. Crockett.

in 1845 it remained quite different from either the old or new English and Welsh Poor Laws. Its weak centralization, tenderness towards parish communities, and overall parsimony came from the most approved Scottish middle-class stock. Outdoor relief continued, as did a largely voluntary assessment system. The few poor houses erected caused little fuss for the simple reason that it was difficult—after 1859 almost impossible—for ablebodied indigents to get relief within their walls: and what the eyes of the public could not see their hearts did not grieve over. The fact that Scottish paupers were subjected to less demeaning tests of eligibility than their English counterparts was small consolation to all those completely debarred from relief of any kind. In short, Scotland's poor relief system was as unsuited to factory workers as to Highland crofters. However, its impressively low costs certainly helped to render its faults invisible and its virtues manifest to all those dedicated to the notion of the minimal state.[41]

One of the chief influences sustaining the parochial character of the Scottish Poor Law was that of Presbyterianism. And indeed religion in general constituted perhaps the key point of distinction between the nations of the Victorian United Kingdom. In almost every important sense Wales and Scotland were less divided by religion than England, though the Scots' love of institutional splinterings sometimes disguised the fact. If almost all Britons worshipped the same God and responded to parallel theological and liturgical influences, they did so in rather different ways. In Wales and Scotland religion played an even more powerful part in creating feelings of national identity than in England. However, like so much else, religion presented a Janus face when it came to matters of national distinctiveness, with the growing uniformity generated by Evangelicalism and liturgical revival being matched by outbursts of raw localist triumphalism—as when in the 1840s a meeting at Coupar Angus was moved by an 'irresistible tide of Scottish feeling and enthusiasm' to protest against any dilution of Calvinist orthodoxy.[42]

From the middle of the eighteenth century onwards Scottish Presbyterianism, once almost entirely represented by the established Church of Scotland, had experienced such repeated fractures that, by the 1830s, over a third of all non-episcopal Protestants were Dissenters.[43] The reasons

[41] A. Paterson, 'The Poor Law in Nineteenth-Century Scotland', in D. Fraser (ed.), *The New Poor Law in the Nineteenth Century* (London, 1976), 171, 178; Lynch, *Scotland: A New History*, 393; M. A. Crowther, 'Poverty, Health and Welfare', in Fraser and Morris (eds.), *People and Society*, ii. 269–70; R. Mitchison, 'Scotland 1750–1850', in Thompson (ed.), *Cambridge Social History*, i. 205–6.

[42] Bebbington, 'Religion and National Feeling', 499.

[43] C. G. Brown, ' "Each take off their several way"? The Protestant Churches and the Working Classes in Scotland', in G. Walker and T. Gallagher (eds.), *Sermons and Battle Hymns: Protestant Popular Culture in Modern Scotland* (Edinburgh, 1991), 73.

for this, though important to those involved, were not great enough to make any of the resulting sects abandon Presbyterianism as such. It was as if English Nonconformists had all remained Anglicans of a sort while rejecting the guidance of the Archbishop of Canterbury. The rows remained family rows, but were all the more bitter for that. Indeed, the Scottish sects constituted, as Robert Louis Stevenson pointed out, nothing so much as 'a large family of sisters', who, though thinking 'almost exactly the same thoughts', were divided from one another by the thickest of 'chalk lines'.[44] While, therefore, the complaints of Scottish Dissenters were less substantial than those of their English counterparts, their fierceness of argument was often extreme.[45]

A particularly bitter row had long been boiling with regard to the right of lay patrons to appoint ministers. While in England ecclesiastical patronage was widely accepted as an adjunct of establishment (indeed, in an episcopal church, lay patronage was seen as a valuable counterweight to bishops), in Scotland, where kirk sessions 'called' ministers, it was not. Its reintroduction by the British parliament in 1712 contrary to the provisions of the Act of Union gave a national twist to a primarily religious argument. By the 1830s it was clear that power within the Church of Scotland was slipping from emollient 'moderates' to those who, under the leadership of the distinctly craggy Thomas Chalmers, combined fundamentalist beliefs with a deep hatred of patronage. In May 1843 the church experienced an unparalleled split when, in the so-called Great Disruption, 474 of the 1,195 ministers left, together with nearly half of all worshippers.[46] The fact that many of them physically walked out of the church's annual assembly to set up a new Free Church in a different hall gave the occasion an especially dramatic charge.

Those who founded the new church did so not because they opposed established churches, but because they rejected the 'intrusion' of ministers by secular patrons. 'Though we quit the Establishment', said Chalmers, 'we go out on the Establishment principle; we quit a vitiated Establishment, but would rejoice in returning to a pure one ... We are the advocates for a

[44] *Edinburgh: Picturesque Notes* (1879), ch. 4, in R. L. Stevenson, *Ethical Studies and Edinburgh: Picturesque Notes* (London, 1924), 159–60 (Tusitala ed.).

[45] G. I. T. Machin, *Politics and the Churches in Great Britain 1832 to 1868* (Oxford, 1977), 114. Rather than tithes, baptisms, marriages, and burials, Dissenting grievances in Scotland tended to concern matters such as appointments to academic posts and the imposition of certain minor local taxes.

[46] This is the final count given in S. J. Brown, 'The Ten Years' Conflict and the Disruption of 1843', in Brown and M. Fry (eds.), *Scotland in the Age of the Disruption* (Edinburgh, 1993), 21—but estimates vary slightly.

national recognition and national support for religion—and we are not Voluntaries.'[47]

Chalmers deluded himself. The effect of the Disruption was to weaken rather than strengthen the force of Presbyterianism as a whole, a process from which, in the longer term, the Free Church was to suffer the most. At first, however, all seemed set for a glorious future. By the time of the religious census of 1851 the Free Church was, astonishingly, attracting almost as many attendances as the establishment: 31.7 of the total as opposed to 32.9 per cent. At enormous cost it built an alternative parochial structure throughout Scotland. In parts of the Highlands and Islands almost everyone entered its ranks and in Glasgow and Edinburgh too it constituted the largest denomination.[48] The result was a curiously spatchcock institution consisting, on the one hand, of prosperous middle-class men and women in the large towns ready and willing to respond to the church's ceaseless calls for cash and, on the other, of poor crofters and cottars in the Hebrides who associated the established church with landlordism and all its works. This proved to be a volatile and unstable mixture. While crofters clung to the puritanical fundamentalism which popular (but unordained) local leaders had long preached to them and were impressed by the initial Radicalism of a few Free Church ministers, the urban middle classes shared in a general contemporary drift from strict Calvinism and, as time went on, found Chalmers's view of religious establishments less and less relevant to their needs.[49]

However great was the Disruption of 1843, that year actually marks the end of the era of mighty Scottish religious splinterings. Henceforth reunions counted for more than the comparatively minor splits of late Victorian times. In 1847 a number of groups that had seceded from the Church of Scotland in the eighteenth century came together as the United Presbyterian Church, which, unlike the Free Church, followed most English Dissenters in favouring complete voluntaryism and disestablishment. By 1851 its 19 per cent of attendances gave it a strong third place in the Scottish denominational league. Soon the Church of Scotland also began to show signs of having been stimulated by the events of 1843 into mounting a significant revival of its own.[50] By the 1860s powerful elements within the

---

[47] H. Watt, *Thomas Chalmers and the Disruption* (Edinburgh, 1943), 306.

[48] J. Wolffe, *God and Greater Britain: Religion and National Life in Britain and Ireland 1843–1945* (London, 1994), 65; C. G. Brown, *The Social History of Religion in Scotland since 1730* (London, 1987), 38–9; P. L. M. Hillis, 'The Sociology of the Disruption', in Brown and Fry (eds.), *Age of Disruption*, 45–7.

[49] J. Hunter, *The Making of the Crofting Community* (Edinburgh, 1976), 100–3; Brown, *Social History of Religion*, 127–8.

[50] Brown, *Social History of Religion*, 61, 64.

Free Church were beginning to abandon Chalmers's half-way house and make common cause with the United Presbyterians in demanding that the Church of Scotland be disestablished. And when in 1874 Disraeli's government finally abolished patronage, the Free Church rendered itself ridiculous by complaining that the thing it had demanded in 1843 was now reprehensible on the grounds that its established rival might thereby gain in credibility.[51] Yet because the major Presbyterian denominations found that they were all participating in certain general religious developments—less dour services, less lily-white Calvinism, less moralistic intrusiveness, an active working-class involvement—so a future of further reunions now became possible.

The intensiveness of Presbyterian activity tends to obscure the relatively greater nineteenth-century numerical achievements of two of Scotland's lesser denominations, the Episcopalians and the Roman Catholics. The former became the fastest growing sect in the later nineteenth century largely by abandoning many of their distinctly Scottish characteristics and turning themselves into a mildly Caledonian version of the Church of England. Retaining the loyalty of many lairds, the Episcopal Church replaced its former rural strength in the North-East by aggressive urban evangelization among immigrants from England and from Ireland too.[52] Yet Roman Catholicism, which depended even more heavily upon immigrants, was already by 1851 attracting twice as many attendances as the Episcopalians: forty years later almost one in every twelve Scots was a Catholic.[53] The traditional anti-Catholicism and revulsion at the poverty-stricken character of the immigrants which made Scotland a centre of the anti-Popish cause in turn encouraged Catholic priests to corral their flocks safe from harm within citadels that became, in effect, the joint work of those without and those within.[54] Given such successes on the part of Episcopalians and Catholics it is remarkable how few—then or since—have taken any trouble to try to understand why (immigration aside) the two most dynamic of late Victorian Scotland's major denominations should have

[51] Hutchison, *Political History of Scotland*, 116–17; J. P. Parry, *Democracy and Religion: Gladstone and the Liberal Party, 1867–1875* (Cambridge, 1986), 220–1; Kellas, *Modern Scotland*, 60–1.

[52] Brown, *Social History of Religion*, 49; id., 'Religion, Class and Church Growth', in Fraser and Morris (eds.), *People and Society in Scotland*, ii. 318; Robbins, *Nineteenth-Century Britain*, 79–80.

[53] Wolffe, *God and Greater Britain*, 65; Brown, *Social History of Religion*, 46.

[54] Machin, *Politics and the Churches*, 254; T. Gallagher, 'The Catholic Irish in Scotland: In Search of Identity', in T. M. Devine (ed.), *Irish Immigrants and Scottish Society in the Nineteenth and Twentieth Centuries* (Edinburgh, 1991), 22.

been those with the shallowest roots in the dominant Scottish culture of the time.

3. WALES: RELIGION AND CULTURE

The dynamics of Victorian Wales favoured more rather than less Welshness in religious life. This was a comparatively recent phenomenon and perhaps for that very reason was able to generate such passion, excitement, and dramatic effect that religion became the most important single factor encouraging the growth—at first in a very inchoate form—of national feeling in Wales. It was not until the century beginning about 1750 that Wales turned into the Nonconformist country which almost everyone perceived it to be by the end of our period. Old Dissent, in the shape of Baptists and Congregationalists, expanded, especially in the increasingly urban South. In the rural areas an entirely new group, the Calvinistic Methodists, who had little to do with Wesley and were confined to Wales, emerged formally out of the Church of England during the second decade of the nineteenth century. And though the three denominations differed in many respects, their shared Evangelical fervour, linguistic dispositions, and generally exclusive view of the atonement provided the crucial—though not the only—inspiration for that particularly Welsh combination of Protestantism, language, and social culture that was to evolve from conception to stereotype over a period of less than a hundred years.

If this was a rapid, it was, however, far from being a simple process. In 1750 there had been few districts where the majority of worshippers had abandoned the Church of England. By 1851 Anglicans were in a minority almost everywhere. The chief reason for this was that, even more than in England, the established church in Wales was caught by the industrial revolution with institutional arrangements of a hopelessly unsuitable kind.[55] Dissent proved far more responsive to changing circumstances in both urban and rural areas, so that, by the middle of the nineteenth century, it had—though still of course divided into separate denominations—become the major religious force in Wales. Whereas in 1800 there had been 967 Anglican and 402 Dissenting places of worship, fifty years later the latter had increased almost sevenfold to 2,695, the former only very modestly to 1,110.[56] Wales was acquiring a wholly new theological topo-

---

[55] Davies, *History of Wales*, 319; D. G. Evans, *A History of Wales 1815–1906* (Cardiff, 1989), 80–1; Jenkins, *History of Modern Wales*, 190–1.

[56] I. G. Jones, *Explorations and Explanations: Essays in the Social History of Victorian Wales* (Llandysul, 1981), 36.

graphy dotted with chapels bearing biblical names like Calfaria (Calvary), Hebron, Zion, and Ebenezer. In 1811, when the Calvinistic Methodists became a distinct sect, perhaps a fifth of the people were Dissenters. Forty years later Dissent was in a clear majority, though certainly not the enormous one of 80 per cent which some interpreters of the 1851 census have claimed.[57]

What is beyond doubt is that by the middle of the nineteenth century the Welsh had become by far the most energetic church-goers in Britain. In England religious bodies provided seating for just over half the total population: in Wales they did so for more than three-quarters. Some places were wondrously supplied. Aberdaron at the tip of Caernarvonshire's Lleyn Peninsula had a population of 1,239 in 1851 and eight places of worship, with seating for more than 1,600. And the people who entered such places recorded an 'index of attendance' a good third higher than that recorded in England.[58] This extraordinary numerical achievement was given additional force by the fact that the similarities between the major Dissenting denominations were greater than the differences. There was general agreement about theology and, as time went on, something of a consensus concerning political and social questions. Indeed, the major nineteenth-century sects all contributed more or less equally to the devel-opment—perhaps invention is a better word—of a coherent Nonconform-ist Wales in which sabbatarianism, temperance, education, Liberalism, and the Welsh language became joint pillars of godly righteousness. As late as the end of the century the great bulk of Dissenters worshipped in Welsh-speaking congregations and even those who did not (numerous especially among the Wesleyans, though there too still in a minority in 1871) adopted an almost identical package of attitudes.[59]

This Nonconformist culture was at once newer and less pervasive than is sometimes supposed. Rather than sustaining hallowed practices and pat-terns of life, the Nonconformist sects were in many respects ruthless modernizers, the children as well as heralds of industrialization. The kind of popular semi-magical religiosity that had long flourished in rural Wales—as in rural England, Ireland, and Scotland—fell victim to a desire for biblical orthodoxy and prudish propriety. Sunday fairs, holy wells, seasonal customs, indigenous games and sports were all denounced in a

[57] Robbins, Nineteenth-Century Britain, 84; Davies, History of Wales, 427.

[58] Jones, Explorations and Explanations, 21, 25; id., 'The Elections of 1865 and 1868 in Wales', Transactions of the Honourable Society of Cymmrodorion (1964), 46. The 'index of attendance' is a statistical device more useful for making comparisons than measuring absolute levels: see above, Ch. 12, s. 1.

[59] Bebbington, 'Religion and National Feeling', 492.

determined clerical campaign against wantonness, drunkenness, and law-lessness, in the course of which Welsh Dissenting ministers came to resemble none so much as the priests of Catholic Ireland whose zeal to replace popular religious traditions with new model orthodoxies was no less intense.[60] But while both priests and ministers gained many victories, a realm of cussed independence remained beyond their grasp. Many people in Wales went to neither church nor chapel. A good deal of subterranean grumbling went on. Popular religiosity did not entirely fade away. And, perhaps most interesting of all, in the 1850s and 1860s rural as well as industrializing Wales swung away from chapel and towards civil marriages to such an extent that, for almost the next century, registry office weddings were—for reasons that are still unclear—far commoner in Wales than in any part of England.[61]

If religion provided much of the grammar with which the nineteenth-century Welsh and Scots were able to develop new idioms of national identity, it was not alone in doing this. Education, history, and linguistic individuality also played important roles. But, while in Scotland educa-tional debates were concerned with the advantages and disadvantages of adapting existing Scottish institutions to an expanding British environ-ment, in Wales they dealt with the creation of specifically Welsh institu-tions where none had existed before. And because the first genuinely national controversy in modern Wales was generated by the publication of the findings and recommendations of officially appointed education commissioners in 1847, educational concerns began to achieve a special place in the Principality's political and social consciousness. The three commissioners—young, able, cocksure—produced reports which, in their criticisms of existing arrangements, merely summarized opinions that had long been widely accepted.[62] However, the three had also been asked to inquire into the 'moral and religious progress' of the 'poorer classes', and it was their comments about the ubiquity of pilfering, drunkenness, and licentiousness and their sneers against the Welsh language for its role in severing 'the people from intercourse which would greatly advance their civilization' that produced a sudden, bitter, and public reaction throughout

[60] Jenkins, *History of Modern Wales*, 195; Davies, *History of Wales*, 392; I. G. Jones, *Mid-Victorian Wales: The Observers and the Observed* (Cardiff, 1992), 131; id., 'Merioneth Politics in Mid-Nineteenth Century', *Journal of the Merioneth Historical and Record Society*, 5 (1965–8), 289; Hoppen, *Elections*, 211–24.

[61] O. Anderson, 'The Incidence of Civil Marriage in Victorian England and Wales', *Past & Present*, 69 (1975), 72–8.

[62] E. T. Davies, *A New History of Wales: Religion and Society in the Nineteenth Century* (Llandybie, 1981), 21; Jones, *Mid-Victorian Wales*, 103–65, 186–98.

almost all sections (and more especially the Nonconformist sections) of Welsh society.[63]

By dubbing the episode *Brad y Llyfrau Gleision* or the Treachery of the Blue Books the commissioners' critics neatly linked it with the ancient Treason of the Long Knives (*Brad y Cyllill Hirion*) by which Hengist and Horsa had supposedly killed the British (that is, Welsh) leaders and secured through their plot a first threshold in Celtic Britain. Because many of the witnesses who had told the commissioners about proletarian immorality were Anglicans, Nonconformist leaders (worried also by the advantages which the Church of England enjoyed in the provision of schools) were encouraged to adopt more nationalistic stances than before. Language, religion, and ethnicity began, in other words, to take on that mutually supportive colouring so characteristic of modern Wales. If, however, Sunday schools rarely remained anything other than 'truly Welsh', the system introduced under the 1870 Education Act was at first 'wholly English', and it was only during the twenty years that followed that distinctively Welsh institutions supported by public funds began to appear.[64] The establishment of university colleges at Aberystwyth (1872), Cardiff (1883), and Bangor (1884)—though at first with little in the way of government money—at last silenced complaints that, unlike the Irish and the Scots, the Welsh could obtain no higher education at home. It was not, however, until 1889 that the Welsh Intermediate Education Act made it possible to set up a type of school peculiarly adapted to Welsh needs, controlled by the new (Liberal and Nonconformist dominated) county councils, undenominational, and paid for by a mixture of local rates and Treasury aid.[65]

The manner in which such schools and colleges were set up reflected the contradictions created by a society attempting to pursue cultural individuality and popular Victorian utilitarianism at one and the same time. The Aberystwyth College, soon to be associated with the Welshness of Wales, was seen by its founders not only as a distinctly Welsh institution, but as a means for popularizing the notion that the hope of Wales lay in 'nearer approximation to England in general culture and in commercial enterprise'.[66] Having suppressed many demotic local traditions, mid-

[63] Bebbington, 'Religion and National Feeling', 494; Wolffe, *God and Greater Britain*, 108–9; P. Morgan, 'From Long Knives to Blue Books', in R. R. Davies and others (eds.), *Welsh Society and Nationhood* (Cardiff, 1984), 199–215.

[64] G. E. Jones, *Modern Wales: A Concise History*, 2nd edn. (Cambridge, 1994), 285–7; Robbins, *Nineteenth-Century Britain*, 141.

[65] Jenkins, *History of Modern Wales*, 313; Davies, *History of Wales*, 448. In 1880 the ratios of university students to population were: Scotland 1:840, Ireland 1:3,121, Wales 1:8,200 (ibid., p. 447).

[66] E. L. Ellis, *The University of Wales Aberystwyth 1872–1972* (Cardiff, 1972), 15.

Victorian Welsh Nonconformity sometimes, indeed, seemed almost determined to give the impression of wanting to dress itself from head to toe in ideological garments tailored in metropolitan England and to push the past away in favour of new emphases upon industriousness, progress, and self-improvement.[67] But while utilitarianism never lost its powerful hold over educated Welsh minds, romantic and historicist ways of thinking eventually convinced many Nonconformists that concepts of nationhood and national identity possessed strong attractions of their own. As was the case with other 'suppressed' nations in Europe, this process involved a good deal of both fake and genuine history, much of it, ironically, first bundled together by Anglican clergymen of antiquarian bent. Though often accused of being *yr hen fradwres* (the old traitress), Anglicanism had, in fact, responded earlier than Dissent to the idea of Wales as a historical nation in its own right.[68] But while the church also undoubtedly reformed itself with great energy from the 1830s onwards—and in 1870 Gladstone appointed the first Welsh-speaking Bishop of St Asaph since 1727—it was Dissent which, not altogether deservedly, soon acquired the best ideological tunes. As a result, the church, with less than a third of all mid-nineteenth-century worshippers, found it more and more difficult to defuse arguments in favour of decoupling it from the apparatus of the state. Eventually in 1887 Welsh disestablishment became Liberal Party policy (though Gladstone remained delphic for a few more years) and was finally implemented shortly after the Great War.

The dominant Nonconformist vision of what nineteenth-century Wales should be (and to some extent already was) depended upon notions of historical and linguistic tradition, on the one hand, and of hard-headed profit and loss, on the other. What kept such opposites from flying apart was the fact that the one was as recent and modern as the other. The truth of this can be seen with especial force in the case of the eisteddfod movement. Revived in the eighteenth century by Welsh exiles in London, early eisteddfodau had been vigorously supported by Church of England landed gentry and equally strongly encased in colourful historical garments concocted under the influence of Iolo Morganwg (*anglice* Edward Williams 1746–1826), a master at combining fabrications and genuine discoveries into notably glittering displays. Especially remarkable was his invention of the gorsedd or guild of bards, whose members, at once poets, antiquarians, and historians, were to constitute a popular élite capable of deploying a usable past in order to build an attainable and unmistakably Welsh future.[69]

---

[67] Evans, *History of Wales*, 127.   [68] Williams, *When Was Wales?*, 204.
[69] Ibid. 165.

In 1819 Iolo succeeded in grafting the gorsedd on to the eisteddfod. Although the first bards were, in poetical terms, an undistinguished lot, this did little to undermine the growing popularity of eisteddfodau or the appearance of those features for which they were soon to become notable: extended prize essays, evening concerts by professionals, long patriotic and presidential speeches, competitions for crafts and trades. When in the late 1840s the chapels—partly in reaction to the Blue Books affair—began to embrace them as worthwhile institutions, eisteddfodau entered into the mainstream of Nonconformist consciousness. They ranged from small local affairs to grand national meetings and became so popular that 512 individual events are *known* to have taken place in the industrial county of Glamorgan alone between 1824 and 1900.[70] Closely related was the growing notion of Wales as a 'land of song'. Curwen's simplified singing method was promoted in a special journal, *Cerddor y Tonic Solffa* (*The Tonic Sol-fa Musician*), and enthusiastically adopted. By the 1860s ambitious choral societies were putting on performances of Handel, Haydn, and Mozart, all of them soon regarded as honorary Welshmen. *Hen Wlad Fy Nhadau* ('Land of my Fathers'), composed in 1856 by Evan and James James of Pontypridd, was sung with such passion at the Chester Eisteddfod of 1868 and was soon so widely accepted as a kind of national anthem that eventually even English-speaking Welshmen and women seemed to find little difficulty in accepting that the land of their fathers had been, as the song put it, exclusively peopled by warriors, singers, and bards.[71]

In the process of Nonconformity's aligning itself with and then colonizing the romantic vision of the Welsh past, new myths were created, notably that of the long-pedigreed classical *gwerin*, whose virtues were said to distinguish the Welsh countryside.[72] And because this concept of a serious, artistic, democratic, and successful rural society offered something to everyone (encouragement to Radicals, comfort to self-made men) it soon became almost an article of Welsh faith. Nor did Nonconformity's partiality for utilitarianism ever disappear. Until the 1890s annual National Eisteddfodau (first held in 1858) provided a regular platform for those

[70] Davies, *History of Wales*, 345–6; Evans, *History of Wales*, 226; Jenkins, *History of Modern Wales*, 314; G. Ashton, 'Literature in Welsh, *c.*1770–1900', in Morgan (ed.), *Glamorgan County History*, vi. 348–9.

[71] Evans, *History of Wales*, 223–4; Robbins, *Nineteenth-Century Britain*, 169–70; Davies, *History of Wales*, 417.

[72] Jones, *Modern Wales*, 211. The term *gwerin* has no English equivalent. In the late 19th-cent. view, 'the *gwerin* was a cultivated, educated, often self-educated, responsible, self-disciplined, respectable but on the whole genially poor or perhaps small-propertied people, straddling groups perceived as classes in other, less fortunate societies' (Williams, *When Was Wales?*, 237).

intent on celebrating both the English connection and contemporary notions of material progress, on supplying, as it were, rhetorical contradictions of the Arnoldian idea of Wales as the home of impractical dreams. When in 1866 a breakaway and less Anglophile *Eisteddfod y Cymry* (The Eisteddfod of the Welsh) was held at Neath, it proved a dismal failure.[73]

However much the cause of the Welsh language owed to Nonconformist leaders—and it owed a great deal—such men could hardly avoid a degree of linguistic ambiguity given the impact of English ideas and Victorian values upon nineteenth-century Wales. On the one hand, a minister could complain bitterly in 1851 that census forms were all printed in English and not in 'the best language now in the whole earth' and another could insist in 1858 that 'God has some great end in view in defending the Welsh people and their language in their native land'. On the other, many clergymen were impressed by what they regarded as the prestige and economic advantages associated with use of the English tongue.[74] To an extent, therefore, the cultural renaissance that took place in the 1880s and 1890s was a reaction against, as well as a product of, the Nonconformist vision of Wales. Its scholarly and disciplined interest in the Welsh past marked a new departure and though its main organizational vehicle, Cymru Fydd (The Wales To Be), at first confined itself to cultural affairs, the political implications behind its programme were soon obvious to all.[75] If politics is the use of words, then it is significant that nearly all the Welsh words for terms like 'nationalism' and 'nationalist' appeared for the first time in the comparatively calm 1850s and 1860s, ready-minted, as it were, for the storms that were to come.[76] By 1881 Osborne Morgan (the mainstream Liberal MP for Denbighshire) was talking to the Commons in a new tone when he told them that 'in dealing with Wales you are really dealing with an entirely distinct nationality', more distinct, indeed, than the Irish or the Scots because separated 'not merely by race and by geographical boundaries, but a barrier which interposes at every turn of life—I mean the barrier of language'.[77]

[73] Evans, *History of Wales*, 228; Davies, *History of Wales*, 420–1.

[74] Jones, *Explorations and Explanations*, 20; id., *Communities: Essays in the Social History of Victorian Wales* (Llandysul, 1987), 226; id., *Mid-Victorian Wales*, 66–9; Davies, *History of Wales*, 419.

[75] Evans, *History of Wales*, 315–16; K. O. Morgan, *Rebirth of a Nation: Wales 1880–1980* (Oxford, 1981), 100–2; Jenkins, *History of Modern Wales*, 317.

[76] G. Williams, 'Wales—the Cultural Bases of Nineteenth and Twentieth Century Nationalism', in R. Mitchison (ed.), *The Roots of Nationalism: Studies in Northern Europe* (Edinburgh, 1980), 123.

[77] *Hansard*, cclx. 1761 (4 May 1881).

However that may be—and consciousness of Welsh political nationality was still inchoate in comparison to that of Irish political nationality—the great fact of continuing linguistic particularism gave Wales a unique place among the non-English nations of the United Kingdom. By 1901, when reliable comparative data become available, about half the Welsh people could speak Welsh whereas only 4.9 per cent of Scots could speak Gaelic and 14.4 per cent of the Irish speak Irish. And while perhaps two-thirds had spoken Welsh as recently as the 1840s and while there were fewer mono-glots than before, absolute numbers did not reach a peak until 1911, when 977,366 persons were recorded as being able to speak Welsh.[78]

Why did the Welsh language decline so much more slowly than Scots Gaelic or Irish in the later nineteenth century? Partly of course because it had still been much stronger in the comparatively recent past; partly because Wales escaped the economic and cultural tragedies of the great Irish and the lesser Highland famines of the 1840s; partly because Non-conformist leaders, despite fitful waverings, were generally supportive rather than hostile. However, the chief explanation for the continuing vitality of Welsh and the vigour with which it became a printed as well as a spoken language (some 8,500 books and numerous newspapers and periodicals were published during the nineteenth century—many under Nonconformist auspices)[79] is to be found in Wales's experience of indus-trialization. In Ireland there was heavy emigration and little industry out-side Belfast. In Scotland industrialization did not prevent either emigration from the Gaelic-speaking Highlands or from the country generally. In Wales the growth of industry was so dramatic in relation to the size of the economy that large-scale emigration simply never occurred. By being given the opportunity to colonize their own country the Welsh were not forced to abandon their language along with their homes. As a result, there emerged a sufficiently large Welsh-speaking urban population with wide enough margins of prosperity to support flourishing cultural institutions of every kind.[80] Of course the distribution of Welsh speakers still greatly favoured the rural areas, but the strength sustaining the language as a nationwide phenomenon came largely from the intensity of industrialization

[78] H. Pelling, *Social Geography of British Elections 1885–1910* (London, 1967), 346; Robbins, *Nineteenth-Century Britain*, 31; Morgan, *Wales in British Politics*, 315.

[79] Williams, 'Wales—Bases of Nationalism', 121.

[80] G. Williams, 'Language, Literacy and Nationality in Wales', *History*, 56 (1971), 10; B. Thomas, 'The Industrial Revolution and the Welsh Language', in C. Baber and L. J. Williams (eds.), *Modern South Wales: Essays in Economic History* (Cardiff, 1986), 6–21; id., 'A Cauldron of Rebirth: Population and the Welsh Language in the Nineteenth Century', *Welsh History Review*, 13 (1987), 418–37.

in Wales. It was not long, however, before this very intensity began to create rather different effects. From the start, English immigrants had been attracted to Wales by the prosperity of the iron and coal industries. Until the end of the century such immigrants had been, in almost every sense, successfully incorporated and absorbed. After 1900 their increasing numbers made this much more difficult.[81] But if in linguistic terms industrialization did, indeed, prove to be a Trojan horse, the kind of society which eventually emerged in South Wales remained vigorous, occasionally violent, and—in all but language—indisputably Welsh.

4. SCOTLAND: IDENTITIES, REGIONS, LAND

Victorian Scotland sustained its myths of social cohesion no less energetically than Wales. In Scotland's case these revolved with especial energy around the idea that Scottish education was not only better than English education, but more egalitarian as well. The glories of the eighteenth-century Scottish enlightenment and the eminence of nineteenth-century science in Scotland gave strength to the former claim while mantra-like repetition turned the latter into a standard axiom of public platforms and after-dinner speeches throughout the Victorian empire. The phrase 'lad of parts' was much used to suggest the ease with which poor Scottish labourers could climb educational ladders to learning, riches, and esteem. First recorded late in the century, it encapsulated much older attitudes, though it is significant that these did not attract extreme public enthusiasm until such bases in fact as they had ever possessed began to tarnish and fade.[82] In 1868 one expert urged the readers of *Fraser's Magazine* to 'go into any Scottish family...a shepherd's, or a gardener's, or a village shoe-maker's, and the chances are that some member of the family has had a university education'.[83] A year earlier Daniel Fearon, sent by the Schools Inquiry Commission for England to look at education north of the border, reported excitedly that the influence of Scottish universities was keenly felt 'in the Islands as well as the Highlands; among the shepherds of the Grampians and the fishermen of Argyleshire [*sic*], as well as among the weavers of Paisley, and the colliers of Ayr and Dumfries'.[84] Victorian

---

[81] D. W. Howell and C. Baber, 'Wales', in Thompson (ed.), *Cambridge Social History*, i. 340.

[82] Anderson, 'In Search of the "Lad of Parts"', 89, 84.

[83] A. C. S[ellar], 'School and University System in Scotland', *Fraser's Magazine*, 78 (1868), 342.

[84] *Report on certain Burgh Schools, and other Schools of Secondary Education, in Scotland, by D. R. Fearon*, H[ouse of] C[ommons Paper] 1867–8 [3966–V], xxviii. 5.32.

novels too sometimes give the impression that Scottish farms were peopled exclusively by learned grammarians with a taste for classical literature, like Sandy Mackaye (in Kingsley's *Alton Locke* of 1850) who undertook Greek exercises in cowbyres and spent his few idle moments turning long passages of Virgil into 'good Dawric Scotch'.[85]

The notion of the 'lad of parts', like many self-congratulatory myths, did not, however, flourish without some anchorage in reality. In certain respects Scottish education was, indeed, more democratic than that elsewhere. A larger proportion of boys went to school and university than in England, and universities recruited from a wider (but only a somewhat wider) social spectrum than did their English counterparts.[86] But in so far as such things were true, they were true of the countryside rather than the towns and not even of all parts of the countryside.[87] Poorer children in urban areas did altogether less well, precisely because the Scottish educational system had originally been designed to meet the needs of a pre-industrial middle-class clientele. Excited talk about shepherds at universities was much exaggerated, though the recorded presence of three shepherds at Scottish universities in the 1860s deserves a passing salute.[88] And because such 'lads of parts' as did exist were for the most part sons of teachers, tenant farmers, and shopkeepers it was men of this kind rather than sons of farm labourers or unskilled factory workers who can rightly be said to have enjoyed career opportunities (especially entry into the professions) not to be found elsewhere in the United Kingdom.

Because such career patterns seem to have diminished during the later years of the century—in 1892 the Royal Commission on Labour found little trace of them[89]—it is tempting to connect this in some way with the Anglicization of the Scottish universities which is supposed to have occurred at the same time. Certainly the universities, by abandoning the uniform arts curriculum (with its strong philosophical emphasis) and by enrolling students less young than before, were losing some, but by no means all, of their distinctiveness. Yet at school level such trends are harder to find, not least because the effects of the Scottish Education Act of 1872

[85] C. Kingsley, *Alton Locke: Tailor and Poet* (London, 1869), 25 (ch. 3).

[86] R. Anderson, 'Education and Society in Modern Scotland', *History of Education Quarterly*, 25 (1985), 462; id., *Education and Opportunity in Victorian Scotland: Schools and Universities* (Oxford, 1983), 339–40; Kellas, *Modern Scotland*, 82; H. Corr, 'An Exploration into Scottish Education', in Fraser and Morris (eds.), *People and Society*, ii. 300–1.

[87] Robbins, *Nineteenth-Century Britain*, 134; Anderson, *Education and Opportunity*, 9–10, 160–1.

[88] Anderson, 'In Search of the "Lad of Parts"', 92.

[89] Smout, 'Scotland 1850–1950', 266.

were very different from those of the English (and Welsh) Act of 1870. Because all Presbyterians agreed upon the implications of the religious provisions of the 1872 act, the English division between voluntary and board schools was entirely avoided. As a result, Presbyterian churches of various kinds dominated the Scottish local boards, which, for a time at least, remained more powerful than the newly formed Scotch [*sic*] Education Department in London. Indeed, the moment that department began to show signs of greater activity, it was briskly passed in 1885 from the control of those whose prime task was the administration of English education to that of the Secretary for Scotland.[90]

In the educational field, therefore, Victorian Scotland was concerned largely with the preservation, and Victorian Wales with the creation, of distinctiveness. With regard, however, to other and more general matters of identity the Scots proved no less—indeed perhaps more—inventive than the Welsh. Whereas in Wales the comparative strength of the Welsh language made it possible to launch what amounted to a new cultural enterprise, it was the very weakness of Gaelic in Scotland which allowed romantic imaginations to create an entirely spurious image of the Highlands and then to superimpose that image upon the idea of Scotland as a whole.

For centuries the great majority of the people outside the Highlands and Islands had of course spoken not Gaelic, but Scots—for some a separate language, for others a dialect of English. But Scots, with its apparently rough and demotic character and unromantic Lowland emplacements, proved ill-suited to the needs of those who wanted to fashion grand myths about the Caledonian past. Instead, once Jacobitism had faded and new theories of landscape had transformed the Highlands from havens of dullness and damp into the headquarters of sublimity, it was Gaelic's very marginality that made it easy to furnish the north-western parts of Scotland with all the theatrical props which romantic feelings of national identity required. At the very same time, however, economic tragedies in the early and mid-nineteenth century broke the confidence of the Highland people themselves in their own language and culture to a degree never experienced in Wales, so that by 1891 there were only 250,000 Gaelic speakers left in a country of four million people.[91]

    [90] Anderson, *Education and Opportunity*, 342–3; Kellas, *Modern Scotland*, 57; Lynch, *Scotland: A New History*, 398; Robbins, *Nineteenth-Century Britain*, 135–6.
    [91] Robbins, *Nineteenth-Century Britain*, 38–41; Kellas, *Modern Scotland*, 7; V. E. Durkacz, *The Decline of the Celtic Languages* (Edinburgh, 1983), 137–43; C. W. J. Withers, *Gaelic Scotland: The Transformation of a Cultural Region* (London, 1988), 333; W. Ferguson, *Scotland 1689 to the Present*, new impression (Edinburgh, 1978), 364.

Idealized models of Highland life and history were wheeled out with so much enthusiasm throughout the early nineteenth century that it was not long before fiction was doing convincing duty for fact. The first great impresario was Sir Walter Scott, the most popular European writer of his day. The Celtic Society, an association of lairds and lawyers which he helped to set up in Edinburgh in 1820, smoothly glossed over genuine Highland problems (land hunger, poverty, emigration) in favour of bogusly antique literature, romance, and the kilt. Two years later Scott played a key role in George IV's visit to Scotland—the first formal royal visit since 1633. The fat king, kitted out as 'chief of chiefs' in kilt (banned until 1782 for its Jacobite associations) and flesh-coloured tights, became the instrument for letting loose upon the world a cult of tartanry, bagpipes, and spurious genealogy which clearly (as its long-term success shows) answered deep national needs in a way that feelings of 'North Britishness' were never able to do. For Tories like Scott those elements of distinctiveness which might have generated a degree of public pressure against London governments— education, religion, the law—were too dangerous to touch. The Highlands, by contrast, could be made to provide alternative symbols at once distant and safe: they were quiescent, militarily defeated, their inhabitants exiled or in the army, their social structures in ruins.[92]

Scott encouraged his fellow-countrymen and women to see themselves as individuals whose reason might be on the side of the Union but whose emotions were not. This made it possible for a surprisingly wide range of people to express sentiments of national identity simply by focusing upon the fripperies which the new imaginary Highlands so readily supplied. That, by the second quarter of the nineteenth century, romanticism— once so revolutionary a force—had, in effect, been rendered safe for common Caledonian consumption was confirmed when Queen Victoria bought Balmoral in 1848 and began a long career of Highlandolatry, when Landseer and Faed turned their brushes to *The Monarch of the Glen* and *The Last of the Clan*, when tourists and sportsmen began to visit the Highlands to rhapsodize and to slay. The more Scottish culture embraced a Celtic area which had had most of its linguistic and cultural teeth pulled, the more easily a sanitized vision of 'Scottishness' impressed itself upon the consciousness of the Lowland majority.[93]

---

[92] Durkacz, *Decline of the Celtic Languages*, 195–6; Lynch, *Scotland: A New History*, 355; M. Pittock, *The Invention of Scotland: The Stuart Myth and the Scottish Identity* (London, 1991), 100.

[93] N. T. Phillipson, 'Nationalism and Ideology', in J. N. Wolffe (ed.), *Government and Nationalism in Scotland* (Edinburgh, 1969), 186; Pittock, *Invention of Scotland*, 103; Smout, 'Tours in the Scottish Highlands', 110–11; Lynch, *Scotland: A New History*, 355.

What gave such developments added power was their plasticity, even ambiguity. If, at a superficial level, the Lowlands themselves seemed almost 'invisible', this was only because they provided the crucial vantage-point from which the necessary mythical observations could be made: straining to see far-away landscapes one does not notice the place at which one stands. Certainly Victorian Scots found it difficult to produce comparably powerful metaphors of industrial and urban society, though the late nineteenth-century self-image of Glasgow as imperial Presbyterian super-city was not without its admirers.[94] But it was always the Lowlanders who remained in ideological control, ready to turn off the tap of admiration should Highlanders fail to play their allotted parts. The attitudes of William Forbes Skene, a Lowland lawyer influenced by Scott, were typical. Schol-arly up to a point, active in the cause of Highland famine relief in the 1840s, Skene (who lived until 1892) possessed a mind which epitomized the duality that enabled many in the Scottish middle classes to 'sentimentalise the world of the "old" Highlands and, at the same time, vigorously and stridently condemn the way of life' of their contemporary inhabitants.[95] Remarks like those of an Aberdeen professor of anatomy in 1876 contrast-ing the 'Scandinavian blood and larger heads' of the people—'industrious, careful, and pushing'—of his own region with 'the naturally lazy, super-stitious, Gaelic-speaking race of the north-west coast',[96] while common coin among Lowlanders, in no way undermined enthusiasm for the founda-tion of empire-wide clan societies from the 1870s onwards or for the War Office's bizarre decision of 1881 to dress Lowland regiments (including those with battle honours against Highlanders) in tartan trews. And even if the late Victorian popularity of the cult of Robert Burns constituted a kind of Lowland antidote to tartanry, it, too, was no less rooted in the rural longings of those who had come to live in towns.[97]

[94] Pittock, *Invention of Scotland*, 100; Anderson, 'In Search of the "Lad of Parts"', 84; M. Lynch, 'Introduction: Scotland 1850–1979', in Lynch (ed.), *Scotland, 1850–1979: Society, Politics and the Union* (London, 1993), 7. Sport—largely an urban phenomenon—also became important as a late 19th-cent. focus for feelings of Scottish identity.

[95] T. M. Devine, *Clanship to Crofters' War: The Social Transformation of the Scottish Highlands* (Manchester, 1994), 167.

[96] *Report of the Royal Commissioners appointed to inquire into the Universities of Scotland*, iii. HC 1878 [C. 1935–II], xxxiv. 16 (Evidence of Professor Struthers).

[97] Lynch, *Scotland: A New History*, 356–7; H. J. Hanham, 'Mid-Century Scottish Nationalism: Romantic and Radical', in R. Robson (ed.), *Ideas and Institutions of Victorian Britain* (London, 1967), 148; C. Withers, 'The Historical Creation of the Scottish High-lands', in I. Donnachie and C. Whatley (eds.), *The Manufacture of Scottish History* (Edin-burgh, 1992), 150.

Indeed, the whole historiography of Victorian Scotland (which, to an extent, this book cannot but follow) is heavily distorted by a kind of nostalgia which sees to it that the countryside attracts more attention than the towns and the Highlands more than the Lowlands. That, economically speaking, Victorian Scotland as an entity possessed many similarities with England and that by 1900 it stood high among the industrialized nations of Europe are truths too often obscured by the hegemonic mists of nineteenth- and twentieth-century ruralist romanticism. Even in agricultural terms, Scotland, taken as a whole, does not stand out within Queen Victoria's United Kingdom. Nor, indeed, does Wales to any very substantial extent. Both were far more like one another and like England than either was like Ireland. In 1885 the percentage of farms above five but not exceeding fifty acres (a rough indication of the size of the small to middling farmer class) were as follows:[98] Scotland 41.4, England 43.4, Wales 50.2, and Ireland 71.0. Of course not all districts, even in the Lowlands, were characterized by large commercial farms, but nineteenth-century Scottish agriculture outside the Highlands was notable for its modernizations and efficiencies, so much so that output (by value) in the western Lowlands, having quadrupled between 1790 and 1840, doubled again over the next thirty years, and did so by means of increases in productivity scarcely equalled in most industrial sectors.[99]

Such advances involved a widespread degrading of substantial portions of the agricultural workforce from occupiers of land to mere labourers.[100] But while the attractions of industry undoubtedly played a large part in generating a decline of 40 per cent in the number of farm labourers in Scotland between 1851 and 1891, they also meant that wages in agriculture remained much higher than in Ireland and slightly higher even than in England and Wales.[101] Local labour shortages and the system of annual hirings at feeing fairs ensured that labourers, though still very much the

---

[98] Based on *Returns of the Number of Allotments detached from and attached to Cottages and of Agricultural Holdings in Great Britain*, HC 1886 (C. 4848), lxx. 476, and *The Agricultural Statistics of Ireland for the year 1885*, HC 1886 (C. 4802), lxxi. 8. Figures are % of all agricultural holdings above one acre.

[99] Slaven, *Development of the West of Scotland*, 78.

[100] Mitchison, 'Scotland 1750–1850', 176.

[101] About 1860 a farm-labouring family of two adults and three children would, when the man was in employment, have had a 'surplus' each week, after paying for food and clothing (poor quality housing might have been provided), of 5s. 6d. in Scotland, 3s. 6d. in England and Wales, and 1s. 10d. in Ireland. Such very rough orders of magnitude (which smooth out regional variations) can be calculated from data in F. Purdy, 'On the Earnings of Agricultural Labourers in Scotland and Ireland', *Journal of the Statistical Society*, 25 (1862), 436, 454, 465, 467.

underdogs of the agrarian world, were not so consistently powerless as their counterparts elsewhere. 'There's a story of a feeing market, that the farmer and the loon [boy] met, and argued a while. The farmer said, "Weel, I'll along an' get your character, laddie"—And of course he got the loon's character and went back to fee the loon. "Ah", the loon said, "But I've got your character, an' I'm no comin!" '[102] Overall, however, even if small farm enterprises in counties like Aberdeenshire remained viable and the distinctions between tenants and labourers were not always clear-cut—the same man might move from farmer's child, to day labourer, to (with the help of luck and remorseless thrift) tenant himself—by the middle years of the nineteenth century a much smaller part of the agrarian population possessed established rights to occupy land than had been the case a hundred years before. Cottars who rented small plots from farmers as sub-tenants were diminishing in number and, indeed, all those below the farmer class were becoming less and less differentiated economically despite the survival of local peculiarities regarding payment in kind, accommodation provision, and the like.[103]

The distinctions and tensions between small, let alone middling and large, farmers and labourers were the more considerable because many 'small' farmers in Victorian Scotland were, by the standards of contemporary Ireland, not really small at all. Indeed, to anyone familiar with the agrarian history of nineteenth-century Ireland the manner in which historians of Victorian Scotland casually apply the term to men with holdings of thirty, fifty, even eighty and more acres of tolerable land[104] seems exceeding strange, for in Ireland a tenant with eighty such acres would have been the envy of the neighbourhood. Whatever, therefore, kailyard romantics may suggest, tensions between farmers and labourers were a regular feature of Lowland life.[105] Nor were Lowland tenants consistently satisfied with the manner in which they were treated by their landlords. Throughout the 1880s tenants of all kinds in the north-eastern counties protested bitterly about proprietorial refusals to lower rents in difficult times. As a character

[102] I. Carter, 'Class and Culture among Farm Servants in the North-East, 1840–1914', in A. A. MacLaren (ed.), *Social Class in Scotland: Past and Present* (Edinburgh, [1976]), 112.
[103] I. Carter, *Farmlife in Northeast Scotland 1840–1914* (Edinburgh, 1979), 110–15, 179; T. M. Devine, 'The Making of a Farming Elite? Lowland Scotland 1750–1850', in Devine (ed.), *Scottish Elites* (Edinburgh, 1994), 62; Slaven, *Development of the West of Scotland*, 77.
[104] M. Gray, 'The Regions and their Issues: Scotland', in G. E. Mingay (ed.), *The Victorian Countryside*, 2 vols. (London, 1981), i. 87; Slaven, *Development of the West of Scotland*, 61; I. Carter, 'The Peasantry of Northeast Scotland', *Journal of Peasant Studies*, 3 (1976), 162–3.
[105] J. P. D. Dunbabin, *Rural Discontent in Nineteenth-Century Britain* (London, 1974), 130–54.

in William Alexander's *Johnny Gibb of Gushetneuk* (1871)—that great novel of nineteenth-century Scottish rural life—puts it: 'I'm weel seer it was never the arreengement o' Providence that the man that tills the grun an' spen's the strength o' 's days upon't sud be at the merciment o' a man that never laid a han' till't, nor hardly wair't a shillin' upon't, to bid 'im bide or gyang.'[106]

Stereotypical distinctions between exploited demoralized Highland crofters and happy hard-working Lowland farmers paint a false picture. The Lowlands experienced bitter disputes between labourers and farmers, between small and large farmers, between tenants and landlords. During the last quarter of the century Lowland agriculture, especially outside the cattle districts of the North-East, suffered a series of devastating blows: collapsing wheat prices, falling wool prices, bad harvests.[107] More seriously, population losses in the rural Lowlands were quite as severe as in the Highlands, quite as driven by broad economic and social developments, and quite as uncontrolled by legal constraints. Between 1851 and 1891 the number of men engaged in agriculture fell far more steeply in the Lowlands than the Highlands. During the next forty years the opposite was the case. In other words, the legislation of 1886 making crofter (but not other) evictions virtually impossible seems to have had no direct effect upon levels of agrarian employment as such. But because the Lowland 'Clearances' were piecemeal, slow, unsystematic, and less 'romantically' located, they have never attracted either much opprobrium or much analysis. When, during the passage of the Crofters Bill in 1886, two MPs tried to extend the bill's provisions beyond the seven 'crofting counties' of Shetland, Orkney, Caithness, Sutherland, Ross and Cromarty, Inverness, and Argyll, they were easily and predictably defeated even though there were smallholders in and around Aberdeenshire quite as poor as those to the north and the west.[108]

The Highlands assumed a disproportionate place in the perceptions of contemporaries and of later generations, not only because of romantic myth, but because it has proved temptingly simple to summarize the nineteenth-century experiences of their inhabitants under three highly charged headings: 'the Clearances', the 'Highland Famine', the 'Crofters'

[106] W. Alexander, *Johnny Gibb of Gushetneuk*, 21st edn. (Edinburgh, 1937), 244–5 (ch. 43).

[107] Carter, *Farmlife*, 170–1; G. Whittington, 'Agriculture and Society in Lowland Scotland, 1750–1850', in Whittington and Whyte (eds.), *Historical Geography of Scotland*, 150; Smout, 'Scotland 1850–1950', 263.

[108] Smout, *Century of Scottish People*, 59–60; Devine, *Clanship to Crofters' War*, 40; id., 'Making of a Farming Elite?', 70; Carter, *Farmlife*, 56–64, 174–5; M. Gray, 'North-East Agriculture and the Labour Force, 1790–1875', in MacLaren (ed.), *Social Class in Scotland*, 93.

War'. The first gives an exaggerated coherence to a range of important but disparate events, the second was a famine from which remarkably few people died, the third consisted of a series of minor skirmishes which a background of greater disturbances in Ireland persuaded the government to handle with remarkable legislative generosity and tact.

It is a paradox that the clearances of 1800–55, though they had a very considerable and immediate impact upon local populations, produced their greatest political and ideological effects only after they had come to an end. Their immediate cause lay in attempts to provide sounder economic structures for a poverty-stricken society whose social arrangements had been shaped by the increasingly redundant priorities of clanship and military obligation. Intermediate agrarian groups such as tacksmen (who rented large tracts and then sublet to smaller agriculturalists) were squeezed out. The great majority of Highland tenants began to rent directly from landlords in so-called crofter settlements consisting of a nucleus of arable land divided into separate smallholdings of perhaps five acres each surrounded by hill pasturage varying in quality and extent and held in common. The crofting system, in other words, was no ancient arrangement, but a product of the late eighteenth-century gospel of agricultural improvement. In itself, however, it provided a poor living for tenants and a poor return for proprietors—as late as 1881 the rents of 87 per cent of all holdings on Skye averaged less than £6 a year.[109]

It was during the Napoleonic Wars that the manufacture of kelp (an extraction of an alkaline ash from seaweed) became attractive as rising demand from the soap and glass industries could no longer be met by foreign alternatives. Prices increased tenfold to reach a peak of £20 a ton in 1810. Landowners, anxious to use the bulk of their acres for something more profitable than crofting, forced tenants to move to the coast and work either in the (extremely unpleasant) kelp manufactories or in fishing. Buoyant wool prices made it profitable to graze new and more productive breeds of sheep on the cleared land, while the increasing adoption of potato culture meant that the people could now be fed from a smaller number of acres than before.[110]

The first major clearances were those famously associated with the Duke of Sutherland between 1807 and 1821. Ironically, they were introduced not because of the financial distress of the landowner, but as a result of his enormous wealth, for Sutherland's clearances involved huge 'investments'

---

[109] Hunter, *Making of the Crofting Community*, 30; Gray, 'Regions and their Issues: Scotland', 88; Devine, *Clanship to Crofters' War*, 234; Dunbabin, *Rural Discontent*, 182.
[110] Campbell, *Scotland since 1707*, 128–33.

designed to make the new arrangements viable. Several thousand families were cleared—1,123 (or 5,700 persons) in the 1819–20 season alone. By then, however, the kelp market was beginning to collapse.[111] Attempts to set up textile enterprises also failed and the prices of sheep and cattle weakened substantially. Because, however, the population continued to grow, landlords—by now themselves often under great financial pressure—moved from what might be called a costly and subsidized system of clearances to one entirely devoid of any justification save that of self-interest. From the 1820s onwards, evictions rose and reached a mid-century peak as estate policies came to be linked less to resettlement plans of the Sutherland variety than to schemes (in effect compulsory schemes) for emigration. The fact that about two-thirds of all Highland properties were sold between 1800 and 1850—many of them to tycoons of various kinds—meant that the majority of landlords were now new men, who, while they lacked traditional notions of tenurial relationships (though, in truth, such notions have often been overadmired), certainly did not lack the deep purses required to pay the transatlantic fares of the thousands of cleared tenant families forced to set sail for new worlds overseas.[112]

The local impact of the final clearances was rendered the greater by famine in the Highlands in the late 1840s. This, like the Great Irish Famine of the same period, was brought about by successive annual potato failures caused by a fungal blight (*phytophthora infestans*) for which there was then no known cure. The Scottish famine was, however, much smaller in scale than the Irish. In Ireland over a million people died and a million emigrated. In the Highlands very few died and several thousand emigrated. The areas sufficiently dependent on the potato to be seriously affected were confined to the Hebrides and the coastal districts of Argyll, Inverness, and Ross. The number of people 'at risk' has been estimated at anything between 67,000 and 150,000: perhaps 100,000 would be a reasonable figure.[113] Because the blight reached Scotland later than Ireland, relief measures were better prepared and more efficiently handled under the direction of the talented and forceful government commissioner, Sir Edward Pine Coffin, a veteran of famine relief in Ireland, Mexico, and

---

[111] E. Richards, *A History of the Highland Clearances*, 2 vols. (London, 1982–5), i. 306; Campbell, *Scotland since 1707*, 132.

[112] Lynch, *Scotland: A New History*, 372; Smout, 'Scotland 1850–1950', 261–2; id., *Century of Scottish People*, 62; Richards, *History of Highland Clearances*, i. 408–20; Devine, *Clanship to Crofters' War*, 58–9.

[113] Flinn (ed.), *Scottish Population History*, 426; Smout, *Century of Scottish People*, 12; T. M. Devine, *The Great Highland Famine* (Edinburgh, 1988), 46; id., *Clanship to Crofters' War*, 148.

India.[114] The Highlands' romantic associations were also fully exploited by fund-raisers anxious to contrast Highland 'poetry and music, and national literature' with the vices of 'unruly and turbulent' Hibernia. Indeed, it is quite possible that the destitute crofters of 1846–9 were better fed and sustained than many factory workers driven into unemployment by the urban depression of 1846–7. And while the population of Ireland fell by 28 per cent in the forty years after 1851, that of the Highlands did so by 9 per cent, rather *less* than the fall in comparable areas of the Scottish Lowlands.[115]

An important though ironic effect of the Highland Famine was the manner in which it revealed that crofters were far from being at the bottom of the local scale of things. Of course no one would claim that a holding of five arable acres and the right to run an equal number of cattle on the hill amounted to riches. But it certainly amounted to much more than cottars and landless labourers could lay claim to. In Glenelg in Inverness-shire, for example, more than a third of the people occupied no land at all in the 1840s and even those who did were as often cottars sub-renting from crofters as direct crofting tenants themselves. The hardships of the late 1840s pressed most severely upon those with the least access or with no access at all to land and many cottars lost their small potato patches when crofters expanded their own holdings. The 8th Duke of Argyll was not alone in believing that only the 'fittest' Highlanders should survive: and the fittest often proved to be crofters. Indeed, a detailed study of certain Highland parishes shows that the proportion of cottars and squatters in the population fell from about half in the 1840s to a fifth or less four decades later.[116]

Historians have often been puzzled as to why, having accepted the clearances and the famine with comparative quiescence, crofters should in the 1870s and 1880s have mounted a spirited campaign for greater rights in the shape of the so-called Crofters' War. The explanations usually canvassed—a more active press, poor harvests, the sympathy of Celtic revivalists, the impact of Irish agitations—though relevant, lack a certain analytic bite. What actually provided the dough upon which such yeast-like

[114] Flinn (ed.), *Scottish Population History*, 431, 434–5; Devine, *Great Highland Famine*, 39, 89, 111–14.
[115] Devine, *Great Highland Famine*, 119; Mitchison, 'Scotland 1750–1850', 206; Smout, *Century of Scottish People*, 64.
[116] M. Gray, *The Highland Economy 1750–1850* (Edinburgh, 1957), 198; Devine, *Clanship to Crofters' War*, 54–5, 193–7, 200; Duke of Argyll, *Crofts and Farms in the Hebrides* (Edinburgh, 1883). Argyll was a keen student of evolutionary science, though an opponent of Darwin's idea of natural selection by random variations.

factors were able to act were, first, the crofters' greater sense of economic and social identity, and, secondly, tenacious memories of their own and their parents' former occupation of land now given to sheep and to deer. And while crofters were not of course in any absolute sense 'prosperous', the increasing marginalization of cottars and labourers meant that they could now present a more homogeneous and politically coherent front than before.

In 1882 a series of mildly violent demonstrations against rent increases, reductions in common grazing, and so forth, was inaugurated by the famous crofting outbreak known as the 'Battle of the Braes' on Skye. The dispatch of police and soldiers yielded colourful copy for sympathetic journalists. A kind of modest imitation of events in Ireland ensued, with a Highland Land Law Reform Association pursuing a strategy loosely based on that of the Irish Land League.[117] Commentators pointed out that the protests were led by young adults brought up in the more prosperous 1860s and 1870s, who, while retaining their parents' attachment to the land, had not themselves experienced the demoralization of the Clearances and the Famine. The timing of the protests could not have been better. Ireland had obtained a radical Land Act in 1881 and Gladstone was himself moving towards an ideological acceptance of the crofters' historicist notion of land occupation and rights. In February 1883 a royal commission to inquire into the condition of crofters and cottars was appointed under the chairmanship of Lord Napier, a former Civil Servant in India where traditional tenurial complexities had long pressed upon official minds. Its report, published in April 1884, while radical, did not meet all the agitators' demands. Significantly, while the justified complaints of cottars that they had been overlooked were simply ignored, those by crofters with less than six acres (who, the commission had felt, were too poor to deserve support) were rapidly met. The Crofters Act of 1886 neglected the cottars but—in an unusual departure for Victorian governments—granted crofters not only substantial reductions in rent but virtually inalienable rights to hereditary occupation as well.[118] As in Ireland, those with land benefited, those without did not. But while in Ireland tenants were gradually offered more and more favourable terms on which to purchase their holdings and assume complete responsibility for them, Highland crofters remained tenants, paying minuscule rents, regarding the land as culture symbol rather than

[117] Richards, *History of Highland Clearances*, i. 472–505; Smout, *Century of Scottish People*, 71–5; J. G. Kellas, 'The Crofters' War 1882–1888', *History Today*, 12 (1962), 281–8.
[118] Devine, *Clanship to Crofters' War*, 222–3, 229; Hunter, *Making of the Crofting Community*, 162–4.

economic opportunity, and generally farming with remarkable lack of knowledge and skill.[119]

5. WALES: LAND AND POLITICS

In Wales, though rural matters also loomed large, the agrarian landscape lacked the dramatic divisions which existed in Scotland between Highlands and Lowlands. The North-West of Wales fattened livestock, the more fertile North-East made butter and cheese, the South too was characterized by dairy production. But neither these distinctions nor those between the poorer hill farmers and their more prosperous counterparts in the valleys prevented the development of a comparatively concordant mentality among tenant farmers of various kinds, partly, perhaps, because the mean size of holdings in 1885 was, at forty-seven acres, less than the sixty acres of both England and Scotland.[120] Characteristically, Welsh farms were 'mixed', though they became more pastoral in the 1870s in efficient response to changes in meat and cereal prices. And because dependence on the potato, while it existed among the very poor, was far less common than in Ireland or the Scottish Highlands, Wales escaped famine (though lesser food shortages did from time to time occur).[121] Landlords resembled those in England. They granted abatements of rent in hard times, they liked to behave paternalistically—a habit seen by its beneficiaries as economically useful but psychologically irritating—they even, though decreasingly, showed an interest in the history and culture of Welsh Wales. The largest among them tended to invest heavily in improvements, though this too did not necessarily make them popular, for not all farmers liked being forced into efficiency.[122] All in all, there can be little doubt that the agricultural economy advanced markedly in Wales after the mid-1850s and did so without the consistently bitter discords evident in Ireland and in large parts of Scotland too.

This is why the agrarian conflicts of Wales during the second half of the nineteenth century were relatively less widespread and intense than they have sometimes been made to seem by Victorian radicals and nationalist

---

[119] E. A. Cameron, 'Politics, Ideology and the Highland Land Issue, 1886 to the 1920s', *Scottish Historical Review*, 72 (1993), 77–9.

[120] D. W. Howell, *Land and People in Nineteenth-Century Wales* (London, 1977), 68.

[121] Ibid. 3, 106–7; id., 'Farming in South-East Wales *c*.1840–80', in Baber and Williams (eds.), *Modern South Wales*, 283, 288; A. Conway, 'Welsh Emigration to the United States', in Fleming and Bailyn (eds.), *Perspectives*, 194.

[122] Jenkins, *History of Modern Wales*, 286–7; Jones, *Modern Wales*, 159; Evans, *History of Wales*, 200; Howell, *Land and People*, 50–1.

historians. The vigour of the nineteenth-century Welsh-language press, the ease with which landlords could be depicted as Anglican aliens, and the existence of an extensive menu of minor complaints made it a simple matter to gather together a series of fragmented and modest episodes under the grand (but rather misleading) banner of the Welsh Land War. But to call the landlords of Wales—as the Revd Thomas Gee's *Baner ac Amserau Cymru* (*The Banner and Times of Wales*) did in 1886—'devourers of the marrow of their [tenants'] bones' was never much more than an exercise in polemical exaggeration.[123]

Particular excitement was generated by the eviction of a handful of tenants in the 1850s and 1860s because they had voted against their land-lords' wishes. In fact, only four electoral contests were ever clearly identi-fied as having involved such coercive retaliation: Merionethshire in 1859, Cardiganshire, Caernarvonshire, and Carmarthenshire in 1868. And the twelve evictions known to have occurred in the most notorious case (that of Merionethshire) caused so high a degree of consternation precisely because of their exceptional character and because the landlords concerned turned out to have been foolish enough to evict the uncle of a famous politician and the mother of a famous Nonconformist minister.[124] Ten years later the Revd Michael D. Jones (the minister in question) claimed that sixty-nine tenants had been evicted in Wales after the general election of 1868, a contest famously described by Lloyd George as having 'shattered' the 'political power of landlordism...as effectively as the power of the Druids'.[125] Others, however, who thought such figures exaggerated, believed proprietorial interference had been as nothing 'compared with the systematic intimidation of the Dissenting Preachers'.[126] And certainly the clergy had been very active indeed, though more perhaps as articulators of communal feelings than as imposers of unwelcome and rebarbative authority. Whatever the truth of the matter, these evictions—modest compared to those of Scotland and Ireland—certainly provided Radicals with powerful ammunition for decades to come, their memory being still mint-fresh in the 1880s when agrarian disturbances broke out in parts of rural Wales.[127] What was, however, most remarkable about these later

[123] Howell, *Land and People*, 42.

[124] M. A. Jones, 'The Background to Emigration from Great Britain in the Nineteenth Century', in Fleming and Bailyn (eds.), *Perspectives*, 80; Conway, 'Welsh Emigration', 209; Davies, *History of Wales*, 430; Morgan, *Wales in British Politics*, 20–1; Jones, 'Merioneth Politics', 275, 286–7, 303, 313. The politician was Tom Ellis.

[125] Morgan, *Wales in British Politics*, 22–7.   [126] Howell, *Land and People*, 64–5.

[127] M. Cragoe, 'Conscience or Coercion? Clerical Influence at the General Election of 1868 in Wales', *Past & Present*, 149 (1995), 140–69; D. W. Howell, 'The Regions and their

episodes was that they were driven not so much by fierce antagonisms between tenants and proprietors as by intense Nonconformist dislike of having to pay tithes to the representatives of the Anglican Church. In Ireland the Tithe War of the 1830s had long ago yielded emollient legislative compromises, while in Scotland the more modest teind imposts had never been much of an issue. In Wales, however, the tithe question achieved wide public prominence in the 1880s precisely because landlords had recently begun to grant substantial rent abatements in response to the agricultural problems of the day, something which encouraged Radicals to argue that what had become sauce for the proprietorial goose should without delay be made into sauce also for the Anglican gander.[128]

Though Welsh farmers, no less than others, disliked paying taxes of any kind, it was religious differences more than close-fistedness as such which gave the Welsh tithe disputes their particular charge: farmers in south-east England, for example, though more heavily tithed, proved much less obstructive. Yet, however much the Welsh Land War may have tried to dress itself in garments first tailored in Ireland and Scotland—a Land League, collisions with the police and army, thunderous speeches by secular and spiritual agitators—it always remained comparatively modest in both degree and extent. As one magistrate put it, 'Welsh farmers cannot play the Irish game there are too few of them they are not united enough and they are too close to striking distance of the party of law and order'.[129] Indeed, the most notable similarity with events elsewhere lay in the way in which landless labourers were ignored and overlooked. Although a good deal of Welsh sentimentalism has developed about the closeness between farmers and their labourers, the undoubted existence of rigid social barriers separating various sections of the rural community belies claims about the egalitarian character of the Welsh countryside.[130] By the early 1890s the Welsh Land War had, in any case, come to an end. The wispy nature of its agrarian achievements should not, however, disguise its political importance, for what had taken place was not a land war at all but an agitation

Issues: Wales', in Mingay (ed.), *Victorian Countryside*, i. 74; Jones, 'Elections of 1865 and 1868', 41–2.

[128] P. O'Donoghue, 'Causes of the Opposition to Tithes, 1830–38', *Studia Hibernica*, 5 (1965), 7–28; A. A. Cormack, *Teinds and Agriculture: An Historical Survey* (London, 1930); Dunbabin, *Rural Discontent*, 211–14. Refusals to pay tithes were not matched by refusals to pay rents (Howell, 'Regions and their Issues: Wales', 75).

[129] Dunbabin, *Rural Discontent*, 229; Howell, 'Regions and their Issues: Wales', 74–5.

[130] Howell, 'Regions and their Issues: Wales', 78; id., *Land and People*, 93; R. Nash, 'Family and Economic Structure in Nineteenth-Century Wales', *Welsh History Review*, 11 (1982), 135–49.

orchestrated by a group of fiercely patriotic Welshmen to promote the Liberal cause in Wales. And this they achieved to so considerable a degree that, by the end of the century, the power of the landed proprietors no longer counted for much and the Liberalness of Wales, first fashioned in the 1860s, had come to seem as fixed and impressive as Snowdon itself.

In political terms the history of mid- and late Victorian Wales is, indeed, characterized above all by a powerful confluence of national sentiment, Nonconformist consciousness, and Liberal politics, with the linguistic closeness of the Welsh words for 'freedom' (*rhyddid*) and 'Liberals' (*Rhydd-frydwyr*, literally 'men intent upon freedom') carrying an especially potent charge. This confluence did not, however, begin to flow with any urgency until the 1860s and did not attain full flood until the 1880s and 1890s. The processes involved were neither simple nor linear, with the focus of debate turning, first, from the aggrieved nationalism of the Blue Books period towards an emphasis upon slandered Nonconformity, and only later towards an understanding of the political strength which could be derived from a close amalgamation of national and religious feelings of various kinds.[131]

Until the Reform Act of 1867 the Tories held a majority of Welsh seats. Thereafter they were in a permanent minority. In 1868 they won ten out of thirty-three seats, in 1880 four out of thirty-three, in 1885 four out of thirty-four, in 1892 three out of thirty-four. At the same time the number of Nonconformist MPs steadily rose. The first was returned as late as 1852. Double figures were reached in 1885 with fourteen members: in 1892 there were twenty-one of whom sixteen spoke Welsh.[132] The much-trumpeted Liberal electoral breakthrough of 1868—when only three Nonconformist MPs were successful, the Tories held almost a third of the seats, and Whig landlords still dominated the Liberal representation—was, therefore, no more than a step along the path.[133] Even so, at least some of the retro-spective importance given it by later generations can be justified, for the 1860s in general constitute a key decade during which the surviving impact of earlier nineteenth-century agitations such as those associated with

[131] P. Morgan, 'Pictures for the Million of Wales, 1848: The Political Cartoons of Hugh Hughes', *Transactions of the Honourable Society of Cymmrodorion* (1994), 79–80. I owe the linguistic point—and much else besides—to the kindness of Howell Lloyd.

[132] F. W. S. Craig, *British Parliamentary Election Results 1832–1885* (London, 1977), 622; Evans, *History of Wales*, 302–3; Davies, *History of Wales*, 428; Jenkins, *History of Modern Wales*, 323, 332.

[133] Robbins, *Nineteenth-Century Britain*, 109; J. Morgan, 'Denbighshire's *Annus Mirabilis*: The Borough and the County Elections of 1868', *Welsh History Review*, 7 (1974), 64; K. O. Morgan, 'Gladstone and Wales', *Welsh History Review*, 1 (1960), 66.

Chartism and the Rebecca disturbances was transformed (partly by the bitter reactions produced by the Blue Books and partly by that realignment of working-class politics evident throughout mid-century Britain) into potentially powerful forms of respectable Radicalism. In addition, the activities in Wales during the 1860s of the Liberation Society (a body demanding disestablishment in every part of the United Kingdom) created a new religious agenda upon which both Nonconformists and Radicals could agree.[134]

The greatest symbolic event of 1868 was the victory in the Merthyr constituency of a Congregationalist minister, whose career, attitudes, and influence so neatly epitomized the period that some have called the two decades that followed 'the age of Henry Richard'.[135] London-based and secretary of the Society for the Promotion of Permanent and Universal Peace set up in 1816 to make international lions lie down with lambs, Richard possessed good contacts with metropolitan Radicalism and a capacity for adopting tones of high morality unlikely to offend entrenched interests in Wales itself. Above all he found it easy to generate an attractive rhetoric that was both distinctly national and politically safe.[136] A famous speech of 1868 reveals his gift for talking to the 'real people' of Wales and for deploying 'Welsh' and 'Nonconformist' as synonymous terms.

The people who speak this language [Welsh], who read this literature, who own this history, who inherit these traditions, who venerate these names, who created and sustain these marvellous religious organizations, the people forming three fourths of the people of Wales—have not they a right to say to this small propertied class . . . We are the people and not you?[137]

Although Richard sat for an industrial constituency, the transformation of the 'ill-formed and half-expressed aspirations entertained by Welsh Nonconformists in 1868' into a 'national programme' was driven, above all, by the rural and small-town engines of Welsh Liberalism.[138] It was these that made possible the creation of a new party-political agenda in which disestablishment, tithes, evictions, and the like counted for more than trade unions, factory strikes, or truck payments. Political power was taken from the landed gentry, not by the urban working classes and their leaders, but by farmers, shopkeepers, journalists, Nonconformist ministers, and profes-

---

[134] Jenkins, *History of Modern Wales*, 275; Evans, *History of Wales*, 152–3; Jones, *Modern Wales*, 240–1; Jones, *Mid-Victorian Wales*, 157.

[135] I. G. Jones, 'The Merthyr of Henry Richard', in G. Williams (ed.), *Merthyr Politics: The Making of a Working-Class Tradition* (Cardiff, 1966), 28.

[136] R. Wallace, *Organise! Organise! Organise! A Study of Reform Agitations in Wales, 1840–1886* (Cardiff, 1991), 82–5; Jones, 'Merthyr of Henry Richard', 28–57.

[137] Morgan, *Wales in British Politics*, p. v.   [138] Ibid. 28.

sional men.[139] What such people demanded was that more parliamentary and government attention be given to Wales and its problems, that a greater sense of Welsh nationhood be encouraged, but that talk of Home Rule be confined to threats that something nasty might follow if certain modest concessions were not made.

In the 1880s Richard's informal leadership passed to the unlikely figure of Stuart Rendel, a rich English Anglican arms manufacturer and member of parliament for Montgomeryshire, who made himself popular by adopting every cause dear to Nonconformist hearts. Friendship with Gladstone gave him a certain prestige as well as strong motives for keeping his followers loyal to the leadership. As Welsh Liberal members came to see themselves as a distinct (but not a separate) group, so they became better organized and more effective, though they cannot be said to have embodied with any close faithfulness that amalgamation of religion and national feeling which was largely responsible for their presence at Westminster in the first place. They supported Gladstone in the Home Rule split of 1886. They obtained minor concessions such as the Sunday Closing Act of 1881 and, from a Conservative government, the more substantial Welsh Intermediate Education Act of 1889.[140] They persuaded Gladstone to utter increasingly sweet words about Wales and its aspirations. In 1870 he had strongly opposed Welsh disestablishment. By 1881—though unwilling 'to set up an extravagant theory of nationality with regard to either Wales, Ireland, or Scotland'—he was suggesting that 'respectful regard' should be given to Welsh opinion. By 1887 disestablishment had become 'ripe for decision'. In 1891 he voted and even (though not without equivocation) spoke in its favour.[141] In return, the bulk of Welsh members remained loyal and true, never sighting a leaking Liberal Party boat without impulsively denying any intention of sinking it.

6. AMBIVALENT STATES

If in Wales the Irish Home Rule issue passed almost rippleless over the political seas, in Scotland it caused major storms. Dominance by Liberals was longer established in Scotland: since 1832 they had returned the

[139] Morgan, *Rebirth of a Nation*, 48; D. A. Pretty, 'Richard Davies and Nonconformist Radicalism in Anglesey, 1837–68', *Welsh History Review*, 9 (1979), 433.

[140] H. J. Hanham, *Elections and Party Management: Politics in the Time of Disraeli and Gladstone* (London, 1959), 177–8; E. W. Williams, 'Liberalism in Wales and the Politics of Welsh Home Rule 1886–1910', *Bulletin of the Board of Celtic Studies* [of the University of Wales], 37 (1990), 193–5; M. Barker, *Gladstone and Radicalism: The Reconstruction of the Liberal Party in Britain 1885–94* (Hassocks, 1975), 126–7; Jenkins, *History of Modern Wales*, 332; Davies, *History of Wales*, 452; Morgan, *Wales in British Politics*, 71, 115–16.

[141] Morgan, *Wales in British Politics*, 34–5, 81–2, 91–2; *Hansard*, cclx. 1772 (4 May 1881).

majority of members by deploying a powerful amalgam of religion, self-help ideology, occasional scepticism about the landed aristocracy, and an ability to identify Liberalism with Scottish ethnic consciousness.[142] 'I am a Liberal', claimed one supporter, simply 'because I am a Scotchman'.[143] Between 1832 and 1885 the Conservatives never held more than three of the twenty-three (or after 1867 the twenty-six) burgh seats, and they won none at all at the general elections of 1857, 1859, 1865, and 1880. Yet Toryism never entirely folded its Scottish tents. It retained some rural strength and was kept alive, especially in towns with Irish immigrant communities, by strong injections of populist anti-Catholic prejudice. For this, however, it had to pay a (temporary) price, in that the kinds of prosperous middle-class suburbanites who in England flocked to Disraeli after 1867 seem to have been somewhat repelled by blatant quasi-Orangeism —but only until Gladstone's decision to support Irish Home Rule in 1886 repelled them even more.[144]

By the time both parties had set up specifically Scottish organizations in the 1870s, political debate north of the border was in the process of acquiring an increasingly distinct Scottish character.[145] The first issue to assume transcendent importance was the disestablishment of the Church of Scotland, something which the United Presbyterians had always desired and which a growing element in the Free Church had also begun to demand. For Gladstone the party-political aspects of the matter were a good deal more complex than those of its Welsh equivalent, for in Scotland many moderate Liberals supported the establishment. At the general election of 1885, he therefore decided that it was less risky to offend Scottish Radicals than Scottish moderates, on the grounds that the latter were more likely to be frightened into voting Conservative than the former.[146] He talked of placing disestablishment 'in a long vista' and of waiting until a sufficient unanimity had emerged to render the proposal a 'genuine offspring of Scottish sentiment and Scottish conviction'.[147] But while he

[142] Smout, 'Scotland 1850–1950', 230–1; Hutchison, *Political History*, 1, 103–5.

[143] A. Taylor Innes in *Why I am a Liberal*, ed. A. Reid (London, [1885]), 64.

[144] Hutchison, *Political History*, 120–5.

[145] Ibid. 112; M. Fry, *Patronage and Principle: A Political History of Modern Scotland* (Aberdeen, 1987), 89, 91, 96; D. W. Urwin, 'The Development of the Conservative Party Organisation in Scotland until 1912', *Scottish Historical Review*, 44 (1965), 97–101; Robbins, *Nineteenth-Century Britain*, 107; J. G. Kellas, 'The Liberal Party in Scotland 1876–1895', *Scottish Historical Review*, 44 (1965), 2–12.

[146] Hutchison, *Political History*, 157–61; A. Simon, 'Church Disestablishment as a Factor in the General Election of 1885', *Historical Journal*, 18 (1975), 791–820; G. I. T. Machin, *Politics and the Churches in Great Britain 1869 to 1921* (Oxford, 1987), 156–9.

[147] Matthew, *Gladstone 1875–1898*, 213–14.

clearly did not expect the Scots to produce such unanimity in the near future, the public admission that a united national demand might carry sufficient moral weight to change government attitudes had important implications for the other great question of the day, namely, Irish Home Rule. Whatever the differences between the two cases, Gladstone's willingness, 'unprecedented and rarely repeated, to make metropolitan politics available to the claims of the numerically inferior constituent nationalities of the United Kingdom' was as important as it was original.[148]

If during the second half of the nineteenth century the idea of a separate national identity became more prominent in Scotland and Wales, it did so without posing any immediate threat to the existence of the United Kingdom. Both countries sustained forms of politics that were more than simply regional. Both experienced periodic bouts of discontent about the manner in which their affairs were handled in London. Yet in both cases complaints were overwhelmingly focused upon the notion of equality rather than upon those of separation or exclusion. The first organization to draw attention to Scottish 'rights' (the 1853–5 National Association for the Vindication of Scottish Rights) combined demands that the Act of Union be more fully and fairly implemented with pedantic complaints about incorrect heraldic usages, in a manner that was to become characteristic of successor movements throughout the next hundred and more years. Indeed, the Association's thirty-one-point 'Statement of Grievances' furnished almost a complete programme for the future: under-representation in parliament, unfairly low levels of public expenditure, the ignorance of metropolitan governments concerning Scotland, as well as a host of lesser but still bitterly resented matters ranging from the non-recognition of Scottish degrees to the improper display of emblems and flags.[149] And much the same sort of approach marked most of Scotland's other mid- and late Victorian nationalistic manifestations, notably the building of a series of monuments to William Wallace in the 1850s and 1860s and the erection of a memorial in 1881 on Culloden Moor inscribed to the memory of the 'Brave Clans who fought for SCOTLAND AND PRINCE CHARLIE'.[150]

In Wales politico-cultural movements like Cymru Fydd (founded in 1886) possessed greater ideological coherence, but they, too, operated at the margins of political effectiveness. While some Gladstonians in both Scotland and Wales eventually began to talk favourably about Home Rule

[148] Ibid. 214. Gladstone eventually issued a public commitment to Scottish disestablishment in June 1889.

[149] Fry, *Patronage and Principle*, 206; Hutchison, *Political History*, 91–2; Bebbington, 'Religion and National Feeling', 499; Hanham, 'Mid-Century Scottish Nationalism', 164–6.

[150] Wolffe, *God and Greater Britain*, 143; Pittock, *Invention of Scotland*, 116–19.

'all round', only eccentrics—however charismatic—like the Jacobite Theodore Napier in Scotland or the ardent Francophile Robert Ambrose Jones (Emrys ap Iwan) in Wales espoused Home Rule with undeviating enthusiasm.[151] Thus, although Tom Ellis, the leading Welsh Liberal of the 1890s and a founding member of Cymru Fydd, gave a famous speech at Bala in September 1890 in favour of a Welsh parliament, he none the less allowed himself to be persuaded to become the United Kingdom party's chief whip four years later—'grasping the Saxon gold' as a less flexible contemporary put it.[152] In Scotland, too, mainstream Gladstonians found it easy to dabble with the idea of Home Rule precisely because their commitment to it was anything but fierce.[153] Occasional concessions, like the revival in 1885 of the office of Secretary for Scotland, helped to keep devolutionist demands at a low level of political force. So long as the success of the industrial sectors in Scotland and Wales continued to provide what seemed like living proof of the benefits to be derived from the British connection, so long did devolutionism remain the enthusiasm of the few. But because the concepts of distinct Scottish and Welsh cultural and political identities never disappeared—even during the age of high imperialism—the agenda of grievances originally drawn up in the mid- and late nineteenth century was able to achieve a much greater prominence once the old industries of South Wales and the Clyde began to fail.

In 1886 Gladstone predicted that the controversy over Irish Home Rule would encourage 'the sense of nationality, both in Scotland and in Wales...[to] take a wider range than heretofore'.[154] In cultural terms this 'wider range' had been evident long before 1886. In the political sphere the seed which Irish Home Rule helped to sow within Britain itself took several decades to germinate. But when it did, the shape and vigour of the resulting plant owed much to the fact that Victorian concepts of Britishness had never achieved complete hegemony over the minds of those who lived in Scotland and in Wales.

---

[151] Evans, *History of Wales*, 316–17; Hanham, *Elections and Party Management*, 85; Morgan, *Rebirth of a Nation*, 113.

[152] Davies, *History of Wales*, 460.   [153] Hutchison, *Political History*, 171–3.

[154] W. E. Gladstone, *The Irish Question. I—History of an Idea. II—Lessons of the Election* (London, 1886), 36.

CHAPTER 15

The Island of Ireland

1. CONTEXTS

From the perspective of British and even more so of English history, nineteenth-century Ireland has been seen primarily as the home port of a troublesome pirate ship, the SS *Irish Question*. Apart from stereotypical notions suggesting that it was also a land remarkable for the violence, religious intensity, laziness, and jollity of its inhabitants, neither the mid-Victorian nor subsequent generations in Britain have known much about the island of Ireland itself. And it is precisely out of this smooth avoidance of any real engagement with the close and reciprocal connections between developments within Ireland and the changing nature of the Irish Question that many of the misunderstandings and complications of modern Irish–British relations have grown.

The Act of Union of 1800 which injected 100 (after 1832, 105) Irish MPs into the Westminster parliament created, not only an Irish Question for Britain, but a British Question for Ireland. Given that Ireland was the smaller entity—and in population and economic terms it became both absolutely and relatively smaller still as a result of the Great Famine of the late 1840s—this was to prove an especially pressing problem for its politicians and for its people generally. Successive generations of historians have rightly drummed out the message that British politics became obsessed, even shaped, by Irish considerations during the last quarter of the nineteenth century. However, far less attention has been given to the equally important fact that all aspects of Irish life, not least the political, were constantly obliged to react and reverberate to the imperatives and the dominance of the larger island.

Not that such reverberations were ever either simple or direct. In both its Catholic and Protestant modes Irish religious life, for example, though locally distinct, owed much to wider contemporary enthusiasms for Evangelicalism and cultural modernization. However, as regards economic and social matters, similar kinds of alignment were less possible because the strong survival in Ireland of an agrarian sector, the comparative lack of industries, and the effects of famine, population collapse, and massive emigration continued to subject almost the whole of the island to problems that elsewhere in the United Kingdom had (certainly by the middle of the nineteenth century) become problems of comparatively modest import and concern. In politics things were perhaps more complicated still, with the impact of one of modern Europe's most innovative politicians, Daniel O'Connell (master equally of British constitutional practices and prodigious peasant mobilizations), epitomizing, in an especially compelling manner, the often contradictory nature of the nineteenth-century Irish experience.

It was O'Connell who first made plain the potential power of peaceful mass agitation and of harnessing the Catholic clergy to the cause of popular politics. But while his successful campaign for Catholic Emancipation—in 1829 Roman Catholics had at last been allowed to sit in parliament[1]— showed the effectiveness of his approach, his complete failure to obtain repeal of the Union (his next and greater goal) showed its weaknesses and deficiencies. Not until the second half of the century did it become clear that two additional ingredients were required before O'Connell's political mixture could reach higher degrees of inflammability. The first of these was the reappearance of revolutionary nationalism and the creation of a particular (though often nervous) set of relationships between it and constitutional politics. The second was the transformation of agrarian discontent into a coherent force capable of reformulating political priorities in almost all parts of Ireland. O'Connell had always been opposed to violence of any kind and had, indeed, displayed a consistent admiration for the young Queen Victoria and for characteristically British ideologies such as utilitarianism. As an owner of property in Kerry, he had also never quite managed or wanted to rid himself of a landlord's suspicion of rural radicalism, a suspicion which those prominent in the politically amorphous agrarian protests of the early nineteenth century occasionally reciprocated: 'Emancipation has done nothing for us. Mr O'Connell and the rich Catholics go to Parliament. We die of starvation just the same.'[2]

By the end of O'Connell's career—he died in 1847—a small number of his followers had grown weary of their leader's moderation and lack of sympathy for the new kind of cultural nationalism they were themselves

---

[1] In 1829 Catholics with the required qualifications were also allowed to become voters in Britain, as they had been in Ireland since 1793.

[2] A. de Tocqueville, *Journeys to England and Ireland*, ed. J. P. Mayer (London, 1958), 132.

constructing on the most approved continental models. Although from almost exclusively Anglo-Irish or middle-class Catholic stock, these Young Irelanders (as they began to call themselves in the 1840s) took an intense interest in that emphasis upon Celtic literary, historical, and linguistic identities that was also beginning to make its mark in Scotland and Wales. Some of them, notably John Mitchel, John Martin, and William Smith O'Brien (all of them Protestants), combined such thinking with a willingness to consider the use of physical force in order to achieve their ends. And, indeed, in 1848 Smith O'Brien put himself at the head of an armed rising, which, though distinctly feeble and easily suppressed, marked—in a country where symbols mattered a great deal—the symbolically important reintroduction of revolutionary violence into political life.[3]

A preoccupation with nationalist (and, indeed, with Unionist) mobilization has obscured the fact that Irish politics were as much concerned with the local and everyday as with grand issues such as repeal, Home Rule, or independence. Given that the parish pump was, in many respects, the true symbol of politics in nineteenth-century Ireland, what needs to be explained is not why at certain periods nationalist advances faltered, but why broad nationalist or unionist movements from time to time succeeded in overcoming the localism and fissiparousness that constituted the basic condition of political society as a whole. O'Connell's success in diverting his countrymen and women away from purely local issues—better roads, better sewers, jobs for relatives, favours of all kinds—proved only temporary. After his death localist imperatives asserted themselves again. Not that this reduced the political temperature. It merely proved that in normal times it is often easier to become agitated about the immediate and the mundane than about the distant and the abstract.

Paradoxically it was the Catholic clergy O'Connell had attracted to his cause, who, soon after his death, proved instrumental in weakening the national impulses he had generated. Having tasted political influence, they proved reluctant to let go. But, once deprived of the kind of strong secular leadership O'Connell had provided, their power, though it did not perhaps diminish, became incoherent as individual bishops and priests followed priorities of their own.[4] However, if in the political sphere the clergy found it difficult to discover a safe anchorage, they undoubtedly made dramatic progress in defining and increasing their role as spiritual and religious professionals.

[3] K. B. Nowlan, *The Politics of Repeal* (London, 1965), 11–13, 109–15, 138–40, 209–16.
[4] K. T. Hoppen, 'Priests at the Hustings: Ecclesiastical Electioneering in Nineteenth-Century Ireland', in E. Posada-Carbó (ed.), *Elections before Democracy: The History of Elections in Latin America and Europe* (London, 1996), 117–38.

By 1834, when a royal commission estimated that about 80 per cent of the Irish population was Catholic—the rest being split more or less equally between various types of Presbyterianism and the (Anglican) Church of Ireland—certain key leaders of the Catholic Church were already actively engaged in a great project of reform and renewal which would further help to translate the Church's numerical strength into a political, social, and cultural predominance. This was a long process and involved increasingly autocratic episcopal action designed to reduce those clerical laxities which had inevitably developed during the years before 1800 when the church had been at best tolerated, at worst persecuted, by an exclusively Protestant state. At the same time the measure of religious control which priests themselves exercised over their flocks was extended by a powerful campaign to do away with those unorthodox folk practices—belief in magic charms and holy wells, exuberant observances of local festivals, supposedly 'pagan' celebrations of the passing of seasons—which had come to play an important role in rural life. Two aspects of this campaign of modernization are especially remarkable: first, that it was so successful, and, second, that its clerical proponents so closely mirrored the activities of their Protestant counterparts (for both Anglicans and Presbyterians were just as busily engaged upon the twin tasks of clerical reform and spiritual sanitization). In this particular sense, therefore, Evangelical revival (with its emphasis on purity, enthusiasm, and rigour) proved in Ireland to be almost as much a Catholic as a Protestant phenomenon.

As a result, all of the churches in Ireland experienced a period of reinvigoration during the first half of the nineteenth century from which they emerged not only stronger and livelier, but also better equipped to do vigorous combat with each other. The Church of Ireland clergy lost their polite eighteenth-century quietude. The Presbyterians, who had formerly (though to a lesser degree than Catholics) suffered for dissenting from the Anglican establishment, began to see themselves as Protestants first and Nonconformists second. The Catholic priesthood, once notably deferential towards the state and anxious to avoid argument, assumed a new sense of political and spiritual drive. Therefore, just as the various denominations were becoming more and more hostile towards one another, so all of them began more and more to share one new thing, namely, Victorian earnestness—together with all the strengths and weaknesses which that implied.

On the Catholic side the process was, at least to begin with, a gradual one, for, in a society where the sacred and the profane, the orthodox and the magical, the modern and the traditional, had long been closely intermingled, there could be no immediate and total acquiescence in official church reforms, however forcefully presented and authoritatively urged.[5] That this so-called 'devotional revolution' took more than fifty years to establish itself owed much to the character of the priesthood's location within society as a whole. Although contemporary Protestant and later nationalist observers have shared a tendency to see all priests simply as 'peasants'—for the first a term of reproof, for the second one of praise—this is a profoundly misleading view and shows little understanding of the gradations that existed within nineteenth-century Irish society. All the available evidence makes it clear that the cost of a clerical training alone excluded the mass of the rural poor. Contemporary ordinands admitted as much when they designated their fellows as products of the 'middling order . . . the agricultural . . . or the commercial order'. They saw themselves as 'the sons of persons in business and trade . . . of the comfortable, middle, and humble farmers in the country'.[6] Now, although Ireland was of course a predominantly agrarian country (in 1841 less than 14 per cent of the people lived in settlements of 2,000 inhabitants or more and even in 1861 the proportion was still below a fifth[7]) it was not, at least not before the Great Famine, one dominated numerically by the sort of tenant farmers most likely to contribute young men to the priesthood. That priests were, indeed, the products of an élite group becomes clear when Irish rural society is seen as a pyramid, the base of which consisted, not of tenant farmers of any kind, but of labourers who worked the land. Excluding perhaps 7,000 or 8,000 landlords who actually owned the soil—a few of them very rich, many of them, in the 1840s, greatly in debt—Table 15.1 represents in round numbers the general state of things with regard to adult males, each of whom was, of course, usually required to support a considerable number of dependants as well as himself. What is immediately obvious is that Irish agriculturalists consisted predominantly of labourers and of cottiers (the latter renting cabins and very small potato plots from farmers and paying for these partly by labour service) and that probably no more than a quarter were farmers in any reasonable meaning of the word.

[5] E. Larkin, 'The Devotional Revolution in Ireland', *American Historical Review*, 77 (1972), 625–52; K. T. Hoppen, *Elections, Politics, and Society in Ireland 1832–1885* (Oxford, 1984), 171–232.

[6] *Eighth Report of the Commissioners of Irish Education Inquiry*, H[ouse of] C[ommons Paper] 1826–7 (509), xiii. 969; *Report of Her Majesty's Commissioners appointed to inquire into the management and government of the College of Maynooth*, HC 1854–5 [1896], xxii. 406.

[7] *Irish Historical Statistics: Population, 1821–1971*, ed. W. E. Vaughan and A. J. Fitzpatrick (Dublin, 1978), 27. In 1861 the proportion of people in England and Wales living in places with populations of 2,500 and above was 58.7% (C. M. Law, 'The Growth of Urban Population in England and Wales, 1801–1911', *Transactions of the Institute of British Geographers*, 41 (1967), 129–30).

TABLE 15.1 *Adult Males and rural social structure in Ireland, c.1841*

	N	%
Rich farmers (mean holdings 80 acres)	50,000	2.9
'Snug' farmers (mean holdings 50 acres)	100,000	5.9
Family farmers (mean holdings 20 acres and rarely employing outside labour)	250,000	14.7
Cottiers (mean holdings 5 acres)	300,000	17.7
Labourers (often with no land)	1,000,000	58.8

Source: J. S. Donnelly, jun., 'The Social Composition of Agrarian Rebellions in early Nineteenth-Century Ireland', in P. J. Corish (ed.), *Radicals, Rebels and Establishments: Historical Studies XV* (Belfast, 1985), 152. For slightly different figures, see C. Ó Gráda, *Ireland before and after the Famine*, 2nd edn. (Manchester, 1993), 78.

2. THE GREAT FAMINE

The Great Famine that was set in train during the autumn of 1845 changed these relativities and thus also the priesthood's social standing within society as a whole. But these were of course no more than second-order effects. To many of those in the mid-century countryside the famine's major consequences were, quite starkly, disease, agony, death, and departure. That the famine possessed an economic 'background' does not mean that its horrors were either necessary or inevitable, though Ireland had of course experienced severe economic and social strains in the years before 1845. Over the previous century population growth had averaged 1.3 per cent a year, far greater than that of countries like France (0.4 per cent). Only England and Finland (1.0 per cent each) came close. By the early 1840s Ireland—unlike England still an overwhelmingly agricultural country—had 8.3 million people. England had 15 million. And already well before the famine, population and other pressures had created a culture of emigration, with more than 1.5 million people leaving Ireland between 1815 and 1845 alone. This was a massive outflow for the time.[8]

What also struck almost everyone who commented upon Ireland during the first half of the century was the heavy dependence of its people upon a single food, namely, the potato, though it was not obvious to them (nor has it been obvious to historians) whether this was the cause or the result of population growth. On the eve of the famine two million acres were devoted to potato culture, a third or so of all tilled land. About three million people ate little else and many others consumed large quantities, as did

[8] C. Ó Gráda, *The Great Irish Famine* (London, 1989), 13–15.

farmyard pigs and hens. Adult males often ate about 12 to 14 lb. a day for much of the year. Given that, in strictly nutritional terms, the potato provides an extremely good diet, a regime of this kind augmented by a little skimmed milk or buttermilk, could, if not interrupted by shortages, sustain remarkably impressive levels of growth and health.[9] Be that as it may, the overall economy was undoubtedly weakened by its almost exclusive dependence on agriculture, a dependence that grew rather than diminished as a result of the collapse after 1815 of the domestic textile industry. Not that either the jeremiads of the Malthusians or the *local* food shortages of years like 1816–19, 1822, and 1831 were then—or should now be— regarded as imperatively precise indicators that reliance upon a single source of food was bound to lead to disaster. While the Irish economy was certainly a vulnerable one, the disease that struck the potato crop in the late 1840s had never struck before and could not realistically have been anticipated.

As in the Scottish Highlands, though beginning a year earlier, the potato crop was destroyed by a fungal disease (*phytophthora infestans*) commonly at the time called the blight. As no cure was discovered until the 1880s, the effects were devastating. The first signs were reported in September 1845, and that season's crop was about one-third short. In 1846 three-quarters was lost. Yields were better in 1847, but little had been planted by despairing people who had eaten their seed potatoes. In 1848 yields were only two-thirds of normal.[10] Although matters improved thereafter it was not until 1850 that the worst can be said to have passed and even then agricultural dislocation and large-scale emigration (which only reached its peak in 1851) continued for several years more.

The Conservative administration under Peel, which remained in power until June 1846, initially reacted with modest promptitude. Local relief committees were encouraged and given substantial grants, and £100,000 was spent buying Indian meal (or maize)—a diet not unknown to the Irish poor—for distribution should prices rise to unusual heights. In the eyes of eternity this may not have been a great deal, but, given the long-standing prejudice of governments towards Ireland, it was more than might have been expected. None the less, it was an approach which Peel, had he remained in office, would almost certainly have abandoned in the face of the worsening conditions that were to follow. This was because, like the members of Lord John Russell's Whig cabinet of 1846–52, Peel had come

---

[9] C. Ó Gráda, *Ireland: A New Economic History 1780–1939* (Oxford, 1994), 83–4, 105–10.

[10] P. Solar, 'The Great Famine was No Ordinary Subsistence Crisis', in E. M. Crawford (ed.), *Famine: The Irish Experience 900–1900* (Edinburgh, 1989), 114.

to share a particular set of loosely related attitudes towards Ireland, which, while neither simple nor unambiguous, had little time for substantial economic interventions by the state. With regard to the famine, two (not entirely reconcilable) propositions flowed from this kind of approach. In the first place, the Corn Law crisis had strengthened the general belief that there should be no interference with market forces. Yet, in the second place, long years of engagement with Irish poverty in the 1830s and 1840s had persuaded most Whigs and most Conservatives of the Peel variety to see public works as better long-term means of famine relief than food hand-outs, even though such works might also involve a measure (they hoped a lesser measure) of government intervention and expenditure.[11] Nor were such confusions confined to politicians. Equally large areas of potential contradiction occupied the minds of economic theorists of all kinds—classical economists, members of the more radical Manchester School, those who looked to John Stuart Mill. Although here, too, the weight of opinion was against large-scale government spending, there was much disagreement about the efficacy or otherwise of active administrative inter-ventions designed to strip away those 'traditional' social and economic structures which, it was widely held, still massively impeded the workings of a free market in Ireland.

The practical difficulties and confusions created by the broad thrust of specifically economic analyses were rendered more striking still by a reli-gious mode of thought highly pervasive at the time. This was providen-tialism, or the belief that human affairs are closely regulated by a divine agency for the good of mankind. While providentialism, like *laissez-faire*, took a variety of forms, its general impact was to intensify the widespread view that the potato blight had been sent by God for ascertainable pur-poses. While many poor Catholics in Ireland certainly saw the famine as a 'visitation of God', it was Protestants who responded most eagerly to providentialist suggestions that the famine constituted a special 'mercy' calling sinners both to Evangelical truth and to the dismantling of all artificial obstacles to divinely inspired spiritual (and economic) order.[12]

With such a set of ideas to hand, those in power found it easy to place the Catholic Irish in the dock. Whig-Liberal cabinet ministers like Earl Grey, Charles Wood, and Sir George Grey, and Civil Servants like Charles Trevelyan (the most senior London administrator dealing with famine

[11] G. L. Bernstein, 'Liberals, the Irish Famine and the Role of the State', *Irish Historical Studies*, 29 (1995), 513–36.

[12] P. Gray, 'Ideology and the Famine', in C. Póirtéir (ed.), *The Great Irish Famine* (Cork, 1995), 86–103; id., 'Potatoes and Providence: British Governments' Responses to the Great Famine', *Bullán: An Irish Studies Journal*, 1 (1994), 75–90.

problems) neatly spliced together certain congenial economic and religious views so as to make the lowest possible amounts of expenditure seem at once economically prudent and morally correct. The pattern of government action that resulted from such an approach reflected a congeries of related priorities: to spend as little state money as possible, to make the Irish bear the costs of relief until the pips squeaked, to create conditions favourable to the operations of a free market in labour and in land.

Even the most parsimonious of intentions did, however, from time to time, crumble in the face of starvation and death. A scheme introduced by Peel in March 1846 to provide public work for the poor (to be paid for by 'persons of property in the distressed districts') was continued under Russell, but was soon so overwhelmed that state funding had to be provided. By the spring of 1847 no less than 720,000 people were being employed on relief projects. However, given that all those incapable of physical exertion were of course automatically excluded, it was clear that more needed to be done. In February 1847 a Temporary Relief Act was rushed through parliament so that soup kitchens might be set up to provide food of a kind (there were bitter rows as to what exactly this should consist of) at subsidized prices or, if absolutely necessary, free of charge—though four months earlier Russell had told a colleague that 'it must be thoroughly understood that we cannot feed the people'.[13] And even now it was hoped that much of the cost would ultimately be found by local ratepayers, with the Treasury doing no more than supplying repayable loans. Although by early July an incredible three million persons were being fed each day, the winding down of the public-works scheme meant that many starving people probably found it impossible to get relief of any kind.[14]

Then in the summer of 1847 the Irish Poor Law Extension Act switched the main burden of relief from the soup kitchens to the Poor Law system as a whole. Predictably, the recently built workhouses proved quite inadequate and were soon so overrun that the horrors within them presented what one observer bleakly called 'a picture of demi-savage life'.[15] As a result, large numbers of people had to be given outdoor relief, contrary to the principles laid down when the Poor Law had been introduced to Ireland in 1838. Indeed, as late as July 1849 some 784,000 individuals were still being so relieved. To ministers, however, such tergiversations mattered less

[13] C. Kinealy, *This Great Calamity: The Irish Famine 1845–52* (Dublin, 1994), 75; G. Ó Tuathaigh, *Ireland before the Famine 1798–1848* (Dublin, 1972), 214.

[14] J. S. Donnelly, jun., 'The Soup Kitchens', in W. E. Vaughan (ed.), *A New History of Ireland*, v. *Ireland under the Union*, 1. *1801–70* (Oxford, 1989), 309–10.

[15] *Copies or Extracts of Correspondence relating to the State of Union Workhouses in Ireland*, 3rd ser., HC 1847 (863), lv. 445.

than the way in which throwing the burden on the Poor Law system and upon Irish taxpayers allowed them to proclaim to the world that, so far as they were concerned, the famine was now over.

Although much admirable work was done by private charities and large sums were received from non-government sources in Britain and Ireland, the experience of hunger and of the diseases which followed hunger (notably typhus, relapsing fever, and various conditions then bundled under the term 'dysentery') was widespread, terrible, and deep.[16] The constabulary reported a massive increase in crime, though this was overwhelmingly 'against property', rather than 'against the person' or 'the public peace', as starving cottiers and labourers desperately stole food or anything that could be sold for money with which to buy food.[17] Only eye-witness accounts can, however feebly, even begin to capture the measure of the tragedy. 'Being aware', wrote a magistrate in December 1846 concerning a visit to Skibereen in west Cork,

that I should have to witness scenes of frightful hunger, I provided myself with as much bread as five men could carry, and on reaching the spot I was surprised to find the wretched hamlet apparently deserted. I entered some of the hovels to ascertain the cause, and the scenes which presented themselves were such as no tongue or pen can convey the slightest idea of. In the first, six famished and ghastly skeletons, to all appearances dead, were huddled in a corner on some filthy straw . . . their wretched legs hanging about, naked above the knees. I approached with horror, and found by a low moaning they were alive . . . in a few minutes I was surrounded by at least 200 such phantoms, such frightful spectres as no words can describe, either from famine or from fever. Their demoniac yells are still ringing in my ears, and their horrible images are fixed upon my brain.[18]

Some landlords did their best to help the poor who lived about them. One such proprietor recorded in January 1847 how, even in a county like Derry where things were not as desperate as in the West,

the moment I open my hall door in the morning until dark, I have a crowd of women and children crying out for something to save them from starving. The men, except the old and infirm stay away, and show the greatest patience and resignation . . . The only reply to my question of what do you want, is, I want something to eat . . . We are also visited by hordes of wandering poor who come from the mountains, or other districts less favoured by a resident gentry, and worst of all, Death is dealing severely and consigning many to an untimely tomb.[19]

---

[16] L. M. Geary, ' "The Late Disastrous Epidemic": Medical Relief and the Great Famine', in C. Morash and R. Hayes (eds.), 'Fearful Realities': New Perspectives on the Famine (Dublin, 1996), 49–59.

[17] Hoppen, Elections, 368.

[18] C. Woodham-Smith, The Great Hunger: Ireland 1845–9 (London, 1962), 162.

[19] Public Record Office of Northern Ireland (Belfast), Dawson Papers MS T2603/1.

In their own way the statistics are no less chilling. Here the best estimates suggest that the number of 'excess' deaths from the famine (that is, deaths which would not otherwise have occurred) amounted to about 1.1 million. Although deaths were highest in the western counties—over 40 per cent took place in the province of Connacht where only 17 per cent of the population had lived in 1841—no significant correlation has been discovered between excess mortality and the local extent of potato cultivation. More successful in explaining differences in the impact of the disaster are general economic variables such as income per head, levels of literacy, housing quality, and the distribution of farms below twenty acres in size.[20] This suggests that, while the famine undoubtedly affected labourers and cottiers most severely, only those farmers with substantial holdings managed to emerge either relatively unscathed or, in a few cases, stronger than ever before. It was also small farmers and labourers who constituted the bulk of the 2.1 million people who left Ireland in the years between 1845 and 1855, more than half of them to seek a new life in the United States. With the exception of one or two areas such as south Ulster and north Connacht, the relationship between emigration and excess mortality was, however, an inverse one because many of those in the most death-ridden districts simply found it impossible to summon up either the energy or the cash that was required.[21] Although emigration had been common in parts of Ireland long before 1845, the famine drove people away in unprecedented numbers. Those that survived the passage set up communities abroad distinguished—especially in the United States—by long devotion to bitter memories of exile and loss, memories that became bitterer still as the passage of time began to match the passages of distance suffered by the multitudes that had left their homeland during and immediately after the Great Hunger of 1845–9.

Perhaps only an authoritarian state committed to the welfare of the poor at all costs could have alleviated suffering and death much more effectively. The problem, after all, lay not only in a general failure of food supply but in the inability of the poor potato eaters to buy food. Dramatic acts—which were never remotely probable in the circumstances of the time—such as the compulsory slaughter of livestock or the banning of grain exports would have faced the government with even fiercer and politically more damaging antagonisms because (as is often forgotten) the chief beneficiaries of the

---

[20] J. Mokyr, *Why Ireland Starved: A Quantitative and Analytical History of the Irish Economy, 1800–1850*, revised edn. (London, 1985), 261–77.

[21] J. S. Donnelly, jun., 'Excess Mortality and Emigration', in Vaughan (ed.), *New History of Ireland*, v/1. 353; K. A. Miller, *Emigrants and Exiles: Ireland and the Irish Exodus to North America* (Oxford, 1985), 199–200, 291–7, 569, 582.

unrestrained workings of market forces were not the landlords, but certain substantial Irish farmers and merchants who showed little inclination to swap places with the poor. Nor is it likely, given the class interests involved, that any Dublin-based government would have done much better. Indeed, it is quite possible that an O'Connellite administration might have proved less rather than more effective. Yet, when all is said and done, claims that the £7m eventually supplied by the central authorities was a remarkably large amount for the minimalist mid-Victorian state to find possess only a restricted plausibility. Not only was far more money than that raised in Ireland itself, but when minimalist mid-Victorian ministers felt truly roused, the cash could be found quickly enough—almost £70m, for example, for the Crimean War.[22]

It was especially damaging for Ireland that the famine should have occurred just as balanced-budget finance was becoming a dominant theme in *British* politics. Not that the cabinet and the Civil Servants in London lacked accurate information. Indeed, the sheer quantity of information probably helped to turn unsympathetic hearts more unsympathetic still. Nor was there a lack of concrete suggestions for alternative methods of distributing and financing relief, though few of those actually put forward would, in the circumstances, have yielded significant improvements. Officials in Dublin Castle and elsewhere in Ireland grew desperate and weary as their warnings and reports were ignored. Some were sacked, others (like Edward Twisleton, the Chief Poor Law Commissioner) resigned in disgust. What ministers lacked was insight and understanding, not energy and commitment. Distinctly reluctant to 'intervene' financially, they were ever busy with suggestions for dramatic acts of social engineering. If Ireland could not be turned into an industrial country—and, notwithstanding the costs of industrialization, the famine was a grim reminder of what a lack of industry could entail—then an agenda might at least be adopted to refashion it along the best English agricultural lines, with beneficent landlords, prosperous tenants, and deferential labourers. If only, therefore, intermediate classes like small tenant farmers and cottiers could be eliminated, then—so ministers liked to argue—all might still be made well.

It was those who thought in this way and believed also that the Scottish clearances had produced splendid results who most eagerly gave their support to the clause (the so-called Gregory clause) in the 1847 Poor Law Extension Act excluding from relief anyone occupying more than a quarter

[22] J. S. Donnelly, jun., 'The Administration of Relief, 1847–51', in Vaughan (ed.), *New History of Ireland*, v/1. 329; Mokyr, *Why Ireland Starved*, 292.

of an acre of land. To receive help, small tenants and cottiers were now obliged to give up their holdings to their landlords. As landlords were responsible for paying the rates on holdings valued at £4 and less and therefore already prejudiced against small tenants, the pressure on such people was thereby rendered doubly great. Small wonder that the number of individuals belonging to families dispossessed of their holdings between 1846 and 1854 exceeded half a million.[23]

More starkly than ever before, rural society was divided by the famine into haves and have-nots, with the line of separation falling most sharply between those occupying twenty or more acres and those with either less or with no land at all. Thus did the famine itself, the social engineering of the authorities, and the attitudes and behaviour of the proprietors and stronger farmers all combine to effect a settlement of those power struggles which had, for almost a century, constituted the dominant theme of agrarian life. Not that, in the longer run, any of this did much for the reputation of Irish landlords in Britain, for ministers, though quick to seek ways of reconstructing the Irish countryside, were no less quick to denounce what Russell called the 'lynch law' of landlords attempting to do the same. Themselves notably tight-fisted, ministers complained constantly that Irish landlords were not paying their proper share.[24]

For the small band of intellectual revolutionaries in Ireland the disaster supplied a unique polemical resource, though the masses of the poor seem to have viewed it as a scourge sent from God for sins unknown and unknowable. Only in the longer run did John Mitchel's savage comment in *The Last Conquest of Ireland (Perhaps)* of 1860 that 'The Almighty, indeed, sent the potato blight, but the English created the Famine' become a key text, especially for those who had emigrated and for their offspring who had never known Ireland directly at all. The more immediate mood was better captured by the doomed young poet, James Clarence Mangan (himself a cholera victim in June 1849), in a vision of 'endless Funerals' turning the earth into 'one groanful grave'.[25]

> It was as though my Life were gone
> With what I saw!
> Here were the FUNERALS of my thoughts as well!
> The Dead and I at last were One!

---

[23] J. S. Donnelly, jun., 'Mass Eviction and the Great Famine: The Clearances Revisited', in Póirtéir (ed.), *Great Irish Famine*, 155–6.

[24] Ibid. 163.

[25] From Mangan's poem 'The Funerals' (1849), in C. Morash (ed.), *The Hungry Voice: The Poetry of the Irish Famine* (Dublin, 1989), 143–4.

3. A POST-FAMINE WORLD: LAND, RELIGION, POLITICS

That the Great Famine constituted the major social and economic caesura of nineteenth-century Irish history is clear.[26] In the decades that followed the countryside underwent a series of transformations which eventually helped to establish what amounted to a new social order. These changes did not occur at once and the time-scales involved provided an important backdrop to many of the political developments of the time. Their precise character and meaning have been matters of dispute. Older historical accounts were painted in two simple colours: black (landlords) and white (tenants). Landlords were seen as all-powerful, tenants as their playthings, with only legislation—like Gladstone's Land Acts of 1870 and 1881— capable of curbing proprietorial wickedness.[27] Later and more detailed examinations of relevant sources greatly modified this picture, first by showing that landlords and tenants never constituted anything like mono- lithic groups, and then by remedying a glaring deficiency of earlier accounts, namely, the entire omission from historical consideration of the landless labourers who, until the 1850s, constituted the demographically largest element in rural society. In particular, the 'rediscovery' of those with the least access to land undermined claims that all that mattered both before and after 1850 was the conflict between farmers and landlords, for it showed that nineteenth-century labourers and cottiers suffered far greater exploitation at the hands of farmers than the latter experienced from land- owners. The Devon Commissioners, who examined the Irish land question in the early 1840s, were told again and again how labourers were 'oppressed by farmers', made 'dependent as slaves', 'more wretched than the Fellahs of Egypt or the blacks of Cuba'. As a witness from County Louth put it, 'Every class in this country oppresses the class below it, until you come to the most wretched class . . . There is no exaction practised by their super- iors that they do not practise upon those below them.'[28] During the famine itself labourers and cottiers received little compassion from larger farmers. Indeed, magistrates complained of the time courts had to spend in hearing farmers' complaints against labourers caught stealing tiny amounts of food.[29] Nor is there much evidence to suggest that such antagonisms

---

[26] This (perhaps obvious) point has not always been undisputed. But see K. O'Rourke, 'Did the Great Irish Famine Matter?', *Journal of Economic History*, 51 (1991), 1–22; C. Ó Gráda, *Great Irish Famine*, 65–76.

[27] J. E. Pomfret, *The Struggle for Land in Ireland, 1800–1923* (Princeton, 1930); E. R. Hooker, *Readjustments of Agricultural Tenure in Ireland* (Chapel Hill, NC, 1938).

[28] Hoppen, *Elections*, 95.

[29] J. S. Donnelly, jun., *The Land and the People of Nineteenth-Century Cork: The Rural Economy and the Land Question* (London, 1975), 87–9, 101.

disappeared thereafter. Instead, the famine's especially savage impact upon the 'people of no property' meant that it was the landless themselves who suffered the greatest demographic attrition, with a particularly rapid fall in numbers taking place in the three decades after 1845. Thus, while in 1841 farmers and their 'assisting relatives' had together constituted only two-fifths of the occupied adult male farming population (the rest being cottiers, labourers, and the like), by 1881 they had come to constitute three-fifths, that is, a clear majority.[30] Mid-Victorian Ireland, therefore, witnessed a growing numerical—as well as economic—triumph on the part of farmers, with the result that tenants found it increasingly easy to realign the 'land question' in such a way that only their aspirations were discussed and attended to.

After the famine the population of Ireland continued to decline in a way unmatched in any other European country: from 6.6 million in 1851 to 4.7 million forty years later. This was largely a rural phenomenon, with emigration obviously playing the most important role: about 4 million people left Ireland between 1850 and 1914.[31] Those who remained behind adopted a variety of strategies to help them make the best of changing circumstances. In particular, the pre-famine practice of dividing farms between a number of sons (and often transferring some land before fathers had died) was replaced by the practice of impartible inheritance according to which a single child took over the land and that usually only on the father's death. Already before 1850 many eastern farmers had begun to select a single male heir who was then found a suitable dowried wife by means of a formal 'match', so that marriage became above all a symbol of the pooling of property.[32] With the numerical retreat of the labourer/ cottier class this practice grew greatly in popularity, although it was not until the last third of the century that impartible inheritance spread to the agriculturally least-developed western parts of the country. Because now only one heir could succeed and could wed but one spouse, non-inheritors found themselves excluded from the marriage market. And although it was above all emigration which allowed this system to flourish, there can be little doubt that the Catholic Church's ability to furnish a coherent and (in sexual terms) increasingly puritanical set of psychological supports for those who stayed behind also helped to lubricate the machine.

[30] Hoppen, *Elections*, 105.
[31] Ó Gráda, *Ireland: New Economic History*, 224–5.
[32] D. Fitzpatrick, 'Marriage in Post-Famine Ireland', in A. Cosgrove (ed.), *Marriage in Ireland* (Dublin, 1985), 120–1. Although very few Irish farmers owned their holdings before the end of the century, many were allowed by landlords to hand on their farms to kin.

By any standards the post-famine rise in rural celibacy was dramatic, with eastern counties affected first and the trend becoming especially rapid from the 1880s onwards. By 1901 almost a quarter of all males aged between 45 and 54 had never been married (the figure in 1841 had been a tenth). But while marriages became scarcer, the mean age of marriage (once much canvassed as an explanation for falling population), though it rose towards the end of the century, changed comparatively little before then. What remains less clear is whether the practice of celibacy was adopted as a precondition for material betterment (the only path to prosperity, as it were) or whether—as some have argued—it was selected by already prosperous farmers as one among a range of possible strategies aimed at achieving security in old age by, in this case, accumulating, not children, but cash with which to pay for hired help instead.[33]

What is perhaps most remarkable about the post-famine Irish countryside is that, despite the huge loss of people, the number of farmers fell comparatively little after 1850. Much the same of course happened in England, though there in a context shaped by economic and demographic developments of a very different kind. But while Irish farms remained small by British (let alone English) standards, the average size did increase, so that, by the end of the century, those over thirty acres had come to constitute almost a third of all holdings rather than a sixth as in 1841. And it was precisely the farmers with larger holdings of this kind who were now finding it more and more possible to influence the political life of the county constituencies (which returned 64 of Ireland's 105 MPs). Thus, while the electorate of O'Connell's time in the 1820s, 1830s, and 1840s had included many very poor agriculturalists, after the Irish Franchise Act of 1850 only those occupying holdings with a rateable value of £12 a year or more—usually men paying at least £15 a year in rent—were entitled to register as county voters. Not only, therefore, was the electorate now more homogeneous than before, but within its ranks farmers of a substantial kind had come to possess the overwhelming voice.[34]

The landlord class, for its part, emerged from the famine in a strengthened rather than a weakened condition, partly as a result of another piece of attempted social engineering introduced by Russell's government. Although many proprietors had effectively gone bankrupt during the famine, legal constraints at first made it impossible for their estates to be sold. Peel urged the Whig administration to change the law and allow new and

[33] Ó Gráda, *Ireland: New Economic History*, 214–16.
[34] Hoppen, *Elections*, 91, 103–6; id., 'Politics, the Law, and the Nature of the Irish Electorate, 1832–1850', *English Historical Review*, 92 (1977), 746–76.

more energetic owners to enter the market. Ministers like the Chancellor of the Exchequer, Charles Wood, had, in any case, long been committed to sweeping away all those landlords they considered at once lazy and inefficient. Indeed, to Wood as to Peel, 'free trade in land' was the logical climax to a famine crisis that had made 'free trade in corn' so vital in 1846. But while the Encumbered Estates Act of 1849 certainly made sales possible—almost a quarter of all land changed hands under its auspices—the majority of purchasers were not the hoped-for British capitalists but Irish landlords who had survived the famine in good financial shape and were now able to make use of low prices to increase the size of their estates.[35]

In aggregate Irish landlords were enormously wealthy, though, as with farmers, this wealth was unevenly distributed. Twenty years after the famine about 2,000 of them, each with 2,000 acres or more, owned two-thirds of the soil. Together they enjoyed a gross annual rental in the region of £10 million at a time when the peacetime royal navy cost about £7 million a year. They continued to extract a large surplus from agriculture—about £340 million between 1850 and 1879.[36] Gross rents were not, however, the same as net incomes. Not only did landlords have to pay taxes and the cost of managing their estates, most were also burdened with mortgage interest payments and the often substantial jointures assigned to younger sons, daughters, widows, and the like. The result was that usually only about a half of gross rental was actually available to allow landlords to maintain the style of living thought appropriate to their rank. And while in law they enjoyed almost limitless rights over their properties, practical exigencies rendered these less complete than theory or overeager equations between 'rights' and 'behaviour' have tended to suggest. For example, rents did not function in an economic void, while large-scale evictions could severely reduce revenues. As a result, though most farmers did not have leases and held their land only 'from year to year', the number of families put out of their holdings once the effects of the famine had worn off was much less than many students of Irish history formerly supposed (though higher than in England or Wales): perhaps 3 to 4 per cent of all tenants during the whole period from 1855 to 1880. Nor was proprietorial

[35] J. S. Donnelly, jun., 'Landlords and Tenants', in Vaughan (ed.), *New History of Ireland*, v/1. 348–9; P. G. Lane, 'The Impact of the Encumbered Estates Court upon the Landlords of Galway and Mayo', *Journal of the Galway Archaeological and Historical Society*, 38 (1981–2), 45–68.
[36] W. E. Vaughan, 'An Assessment of the Economic Performance of Irish Landlords, 1851–81', in F. S. L. Lyons and R. A. J. Hawkins (eds.), *Ireland under the Union: Varieties of Tension* (Oxford, 1980), 187; id., *Landlords and Tenants in Mid-Victorian Ireland* (Oxford, 1994), 217–18.

absenteeism especially damaging or even widespread. Indeed, many of the most benevolently run estates belonged to wealthy landlords, who, because they owned land in many different counties or in Britain too, were inevitably unable to reside on more than one property at a time.[37]

None the less, tensions arose out of a clash between the farmers' increasing insistence that they be granted certain things by law and the landlords' that these should remain no more than concessions. A national Tenant League active in the 1850s laid down the demands which were to form the core of the farmers' case for decades to come, the so-called 3 Fs—fair rent, fixity of tenure, and free sale or the ability of tenants to 'sell' an 'interest' in their holdings upon peaceably giving these up to their successors, something which, if allowed, would represent a recognition that tenants somehow possessed property rights in land they did not own. Farmers' leaders claimed free sale to be an ancient 'right'. In truth, like so many similar claims, it was neither very old nor very precise, though its assertion undoubtedly reflected the widespread existence among farmers of two particular beliefs: that their ancestors had been wrongly deprived of land and that, in consequence, they now deserved some share in its ownership.

Historians continue to dispute the relative financial experiences of landlords, tenants, and labourers during the post-famine years. Early accounts simply saw landlords as rich and tenants as poor. A first wave of revision presented a picture in which (for reasons that were never explained) landlords actually allowed overall rents to fall dramatically behind the increasing value of agricultural produce and thus, in effect, permitted the lion's share of a growing rural prosperity to fall into the hands of the men who farmed the soil.[38] On both a priori and empirical grounds so drastic a revisionism has always had its problems, not least because the considerable prowess with which post-famine landowners conducted their electoral affairs creates unease about the suggestion that the same men should have been prepared to forgo the electric attractions of hard cash and money in the bank. The case depends crucially upon the accuracy of certain estimates concerning changes in the value of agricultural output, rent, and labour costs. And in this respect a second wave of revision has put forward a view which makes more sense of the political and social developments of the time by suggesting that between 1856/8 and 1871/3, though total agricultural output increased by 12.5 per cent and overall rent by not much less than a

---

[37] B. L. Solow, *The Land Question and the Irish Economy, 1870–1903* (Cambridge, Mass., 1971), 56–7; Vaughan, *Landlords and Tenants*, 20–9, 229–31; Hoppen, *Elections*, 109, 127–8.
[38] Vaughan, 'Assessment of Economic Performance', 173–99; id., *Landlords and Tenants*, 247–50.

fifth, tenants' net income rose by no more than 7.7 per cent. In other words, despite a good deal of ingenuity in adapting to market forces, notably by moving from tillage to pasture (that is, from crops to milk and meat) Irish farmers' profits fell behind the rise in output and rent during that part of the quarter-century after the Great Famine (1856/8 to 1871/3) which can most reliably be determined by opening and closing groups of years tolerably free of unusual disturbances likely to affect underlying trends.[39] Although some individuals were doubtless less successful than others, landlords as a group not only remained wealthy, but were at first considerably more surefooted than farmers in benefiting from the prosperity of the times.[40]

Given that this was so, it is not surprising that Irish farmers were scarcely overjoyed with their experience of post-famine life. And while more than sudden economic decline was required to turn resentment into revolt—the 1859–64 depression, for example, produced little disorder[41]— the potential for such a development was never far below the surface in a society long marked by periods of severe rural unrest. What was needed was the construction, even if only for a short time, of something approaching a universal discontent coincident with the availability of effective political leadership. Although neither existed at first, the economic coherence of the electorate established in 1850 had at least created a situation in which it might eventually prove possible to mobilize voters in favour of political and agrarian revolt in an unprecedentedly effective way. Not only that, but Gladstone's first Land Act in 1870, which granted legal recognition to certain limited demands, itself (somewhat paradoxically) encouraged the gradual spread of new rural resentments. Disappointment at its feeble concessions was almost universal, while its unintended effect of increasing indebtedness—the recognition of tenant right had made it easier to borrow—rendered farmers more susceptible to any sudden decline in prices that might thereafter occur.

The worldwide agricultural depression of the late 1870s, coinciding as it did with a series of disastrous harvests, triggered a crisis which abruptly snatched back from farmers what had been a very recent return to something like the comparative prosperity of the mid-1850s and created among them a state of deep anxiety that the economic roller-coaster was once again

<hr/>

[39] M. Turner, *After the Famine: Irish Agriculture, 1850–1914* (Cambridge, 1996), 196–216.

[40] Donnelly, *Land and People*, 173–218; Hoppen, *Elections*, 106–7; id., 'Landlords, Society, and Electoral Politics in Mid-Nineteenth Century Ireland', *Past & Present*, 75 (1977), 62–93.

[41] J. S. Donnelly, jun., 'The Irish Agricultural Depression of 1859–64', *Irish Economic and Social History*, 3 (1976), 33–54.

heading in a downward direction. The safety-valve of emigration was also severely constricted by the American slump of 1874–9, with the result that an unusually large number of young men remained 'captive' at home— frustrated, discontented, and ready to vent their rage if given leadership and opportunity.[42] As the value of agricultural output fell from £48.4m in 1876 to £37.2m in 1879,[43] so farmers of all kinds found it difficult to repay their debts and needed little encouragement from those who had given them credit (especially shopkeepers in the country towns) to look to land-lords for reductions in rent. What, however, rendered this new confluence of discontents so much more formidable than before was the existence of effective political leadership on the tenant side. The first inchoate violence that erupted in Connacht in 1879 was, therefore, not simply allowed to burn itself out, but was harnessed to an agitation whose implications and effects were soon to reverberate throughout the island as a whole.

What the strong leadership of Michael Davitt and Charles Stewart Parnell succeeded in doing was to prevent various sectional interests from flying apart until certain substantial concessions had been won. And if, in the event, these concessions proved to be both sectional and incomplete, that, for some at least of the most powerful elements on the tenant side, was perhaps their greatest charm. While violence and evictions reached levels unknown since the famine period, more noteworthy still was the manner in which different sections of non-landlord rural society were, if only briefly, prepared to support a single agitation. Although, therefore, it was the prosperous farmers and their shopkeeper allies in the towns who dominated the *leadership* of the Land League set up in 1879, such men proved, at least for a time, to be the officers of an army remarkable for its ability to recruit from a very wide social range indeed.[44]

It was not long, however, before the contradictory priorities of different sections of the farming community came into play once more. While the smaller men of the west (who would have found it difficult to make ends meet even if they had paid no rent at all) demanded more land, those with bigger holdings aspired to reductions in rent. And it was Gladstone's delivery of a second Land Act in 1881 incorporating machinery designed to meet only the latter expectation that brought these differences into a state

---

[42] J. Lee, *The Modernisation of Irish Society 1848–1918* (Dublin, 1973), 66.

[43] Turner, *After the Famine*, 108.

[44] P. Bew, *Land and the National Question in Ireland 1858–82* (Dublin, 1978), 98–114, 174–5; S. Clark, *Social Origins of the Irish Land War* (Princeton, 1979), 246–304; D. E. Jordan, *Land and Popular Politics in Ireland: County Mayo from the Plantation to the Land War* (Cambridge, 1994), 199–223; C. Townshend, *Political Violence in Ireland: Government and Resistance since 1848* (Oxford, 1983), 105–80.

of bitter collision. It also obliged landlords—rather than the minimal state—to pay for many of the economic ravages of the time because most of the arrears accumulated after 1877 were never made good and a succession of amending statutes exercised a consistently downward effect upon the amounts tenants were required to pay. During its first twenty years of operation the new Land Court set up under the 1881 act reduced the rents of about 60 per cent of all occupiers (farming almost two-thirds of the cultivated land) by an average of 22 per cent. Even on so well-run an estate as that of the Duke of Devonshire in Cork and Waterford, receipts dropped sharply in 1883–5 and again in 1886–7.[45]

Indeed, so far had the balance of advantage shifted in their favour that most farmers at first responded unenthusiastically to the various land-purchase acts which, beginning with Ashbourne's Tory Act of 1885, eventually provided substantial state funding to those interested in buying their holdings. With the Conservatives—more prepared than the Liberals to make taxpayers provide loans to help buy out hard-pressed landlords—in power for all but a handful of years between 1886 and 1905, money was no longer in short supply. Irish farmers, however, became determined to hold out for better and better terms. In the 1880s and 1890s only about 60,000 applied for loans with which to buy their holdings. Eventually in 1903 Wyndham's Act made an offer few could refuse. By 1913 about £125m of government money had been lent, £101m since 1903. Whereas, therefore, in 1870 only 3 per cent of farmers owned their farms, 46 per cent did so by 1908, and by the time of the Great War perhaps as many as three-quarters.[46] Politics had effectively short-circuited economics (as well as the minimal state). Proprietors, squeezed by falling rents and a collapsing land market and faced with heavy encumbrances, became increasingly desperate to turn their fields into cash. It was, however, to be the last occasion on which the landed gentry of the South of Ireland succeeded in drawing upon the credit of their English connections and loyalties. From then on, the account was closed.

Although Irish agriculture experienced many vicissitudes after the 1880s, its overall performance in relation to British—but less so to

---

[45] M. Turner, 'Rural Economies in post-Famine Ireland c.1850–1914', in B. J. Graham and L. J. Proudfoot (eds.), *An Historical Geography of Ireland* (London, 1993), 329; L. Proudfoot, 'The Management of a Great Estate: Patronage, Income and Expenditure on the Duke of Devonshire's Irish Property, c.1816 to 1891', *Irish Economic and Social History*, 13 (1986), 44.

[46] K. T. Hoppen, 'Landownership and Power in Nineteenth-Century Ireland: The Decline of an Elite', in R. Gibson and M. Blinkhorn (eds.), *Landownership and Power in Modern Europe* (London, 1991), 175–6; Turner, 'Rural Economies', 328–30; M. J. Winstanley, *Ireland and the Land Question 1800–1922* (London, 1984), 41.

continental European—agriculture was moderately impressive.[47] Just as important, however, from the political point of view, was the gradual transformation of Irish farmers from tenants into the owners of their holdings. Having won the economic war, they continued (though very much on their own terms) to support a variety of nationalist political movements, into whose affairs they now quickly introduced all the many conservatisms so dear to the hearts of those who own property and especially of those who own land.

Ireland's overwhelmingly rural character manifested itself in mental and cultural as well as in economic and political ways. Indeed, a strong ruralism shared by landlords, tenants, priests, nationalists, and men of letters constituted a unifying thread amidst the many splinterings of Irish life. 'I am not fond', noted the novelist Martin Ross, 'of anything about towns'[48]—a view that was widely generalized to encompass a deep distrust of England as the baleful contemporary headquarters of both urbanism and unbelief. And while it would be misleading to suggest that the slowly growing band of Irish separatists had no place for industry in their vision of the future, the new Ireland of their dreams was almost always—as so often among the suppressed nationalities of late-nineteenth-century Europe—portrayed in terms of an idealized conception of 'traditional' rural values and attitudes of mind. What gave their musings an especially potent charge was the fact that the concentration of industry in the North-East of Ireland made it easy to equate industrialism with forces—notably Protestantism and Unionism—which nationalists liked to denounce as alien, hostile, and 'British'. By 1881 only 18.8 per cent of Ireland's occupied population worked in the industrial sector, compared to 42.3 per cent in England and Wales and 45.5 per cent in Scotland.[49] Of course many Irish men and women did eventually become industrial workers—but not until they had left the land of their birth.

More and more was Belfast turning into what in Irish terms was a very special kind of place: a Victorian metropolis of a recognizable British type with, already by the 1880s, the majority of its workforce engaged in industrial occupations, notably engineering and shipbuilding. Soon to overtake Dublin as the largest urban centre in Ireland, Belfast—together with the area immediately around it—co-operated most closely in economic

---

[47] M. Turner, 'Agricultural Output and Productivity in Post-Famine Ireland', in B. M. S. Campbell and M. Overton (eds.), *Land, Labour and Livestock* (Manchester, 1991), 426–8; Ó Gráda, *Ireland: New Economic History*, 255–72.

[48] L. P. Curtis, jun., 'The Anglo-Irish Predicament', *Twentieth Century*, 4 (1970), 60.

[49] S. A. Royle, 'Industrialization, Urbanization and Urban Society in Post-Famine Ireland, c.1850–1914', in Graham and Proudfoot (eds.), *Historical Geography*, 264. 'Industrial sector' here includes manufacturing, building, and mining.

matters with industrial regions in Britain. By the end of the century the South of Ireland so lacked significant industries of any kind apart from a few food and drink undertakings that about two-thirds of all Irish industrial exports probably originated in Belfast and its hinterland.[50] In the end, however, it was not really the process of industrialization, but Protestant control of that process, that gave the north-eastern Ulster economy its unique and, to many southern nationalists, its alien character. To an important degree (and long before 1921) the manner in which the Belfast region developed economically can be said to have helped to pave the way for the partition of Ireland and the creation of the Northern Ireland state.

Perhaps unsurprisingly, therefore, the most enthusiastic nineteenth-century Irish ruralists were to be found among Catholic priests, themselves the products of a middling farmer milieu in which the terms 'city' and 'sin' were widely regarded as interchangeable. But while in the spiritual and moral spheres they increasingly succeeded in acquiring that sense of professionalism and exclusiveness which had constituted the main thrust of pre-famine attempts at religious modernization, their political activities followed a very different pattern, with a period of ineffective high-profile involvement in the 1850s and 1860s giving way to one during which the clergy, with some reluctance and occasional complaint, took second place to Parnell and his associates.

As far as Irish Catholicism was concerned, the third quarter of the nineteenth century was dominated by a single powerful personality, that of Paul Cullen, Archbishop of Armagh 1849–52 and then of Dublin until his death in 1878. Created a cardinal in 1866 Cullen completed the religious reform programme already under way on his appointment. He enjoyed powerful contacts in Rome and was gradually able to fill the episcopal bench with deferential and like-minded disciples, keen, as he was, to put up impressive church buildings, introduce the practices of an increasingly ultramontane spirituality (grander ceremonials, Marian devotions, total obedience to the papacy), and make sure that the laity did what it was told.[51] Given that the famine had greatly reduced the prominence within congregations of the labourers, cottiers, and very small farmers most sympathetic to the unreformed religious practices of former times and

[50] L. M. Cullen, *An Economic History of Ireland since 1660* (London, 1972), 162.

[51] E. Larkin, *The Making of the Roman Catholic Church in Ireland, 1850–1860* (Chapel Hill, NC, 1980); id., *The Consolidation of the Roman Catholic Church in Ireland, 1860–1870* (Dublin, 1987); id., *The Roman Catholic Church and the Home Rule Movement in Ireland, 1870–1874* (Dublin, 1990); id., *The Catholic Church and the Emergence of the Modern Irish Political System, 1874–1878* (Dublin, 1996); id., *The Roman Catholic Church and the Creation of the Modern Irish State 1878–1886* (Dublin, 1975).

that, in social terms, the clergy now reflected the increasing power of the middling to large tenant class, this proved a far easier task than it might otherwise have been. In addition, the enormous population loss of the late 1840s greatly improved the ratio of parochial priests to Catholic people—from 1:2,773 in 1845 to 1:1,476 in 1871—and thus the degree of close supervision which priests could maintain over their flocks in every area of life.[52]

Many of the moral propositions of this 'reformed' Irish Catholic ideology, though rooted in rural society, became almost as widely accepted by townspeople as by farmers and those close to them. That, however, in their attitude to matters like marriage, priests were in fact as much responding to as shaping general changes in the deep social and economic imperatives of post-famine Irish society is made clear by the manner in which Protestants differed little from Catholics with regard to celibacy, large families, and sexual puritanism. In truth, despite certain obvious differences, the cultural thrust of late nineteenth-century religious experience in Ireland was common to all the major denominations, as can be seen, for example, in the universal lack of complaint over the failure to extend England's divorce legislation of 1857 across the Irish Sea.[53] And just as certain key aspects of Catholic ultramontanism were imported from abroad, so Ulster Evangelicals four times invited the American revivalists Moody and Sankey to their province to underpin the effects of one of the most dramatic events in modern Irish religious history—the revival of 1859, with its dynamic preaching, conversions, convulsions, weepings, and speaking in tongues.[54]

However, as Catholics became more confident and Protestants more defensive, so inevitably the stockades marking the boundaries between the two grew more prominent. Both sides adopted exclusive approaches to marriages between Protestants and Catholics and to education. Both proved successful in keeping their people safe from 'contamination' by the other side. But the disestablishment of the Church of Ireland in 1869 showed clearly that minorities were going to find it more and more difficult to hang on to their religious privileges. 'We were told', recalled the Church

[52] Hoppen, *Elections*, 171, 181; E. Hynes, 'The Great Hunger and Irish Catholicism', *Societas*, 8 (1978), 137–56.

[53] D. Fitzpatrick, 'Divorce in Modern Irish History', *Past & Present*, 114 (1987), 185–7, 195; R. E. Kennedy, jun., *The Irish: Emigration, Marriage, and Fertility* (Berkeley, Calif., 1973), 191; A. C. Hepburn, 'Catholics in the North of Ireland, 1850–1921', in Hepburn (ed.), *Minorities in History: Historical Studies XII* (London, 1978), 92–5.

[54] S. J. Connolly, 'Religion, Work-Discipline and Economic Attitudes: The Case of Ireland', in T. M. Devine and D. Dickson (eds.), *Ireland and Scotland 1600–1850* (Edinburgh, 1983), 46; P. Gibbon, *The Origins of Ulster Unionism* (Manchester, 1975), 45–65.

of Ireland Bishop of Ossory in 1899, 'that the Act of 1869 would kill jealousy, and draw all Christian folk together. The very opposite has been the case... all Ireland has been divided into hostile camps, with clerical sentries pacing between.'[55]

If in social and cultural terms the authority of Catholic priests and bishops grew in a linear fashion after 1850, in politics it followed a roller-coaster path. During the famine itself, though political debate had continued, its sparks had been deadened by the overwhelming catastrophe of the times. In June 1847, a month after O'Connell's death, the Catholic Archbishop of Cashel had noted how 'every feeling of decent spirit and of truth has vanished, and instead there is created for us a cringing lying population, a Nation of Beggars'.[56] With the kind of effective lay leadership that O'Connell had provided now lacking, the 1850s and 1860s turned out to be decades during which priests pursued political goals on their own account, something which, in the event, allowed the inherent localisms of Irish politics to assume dizzier heights than ever before. Like pressure-cookers from which the O'Connellite valve had been removed, constituencies now flourished amidst a culture in which local notables, such as shopkeepers, priests, and property owners, led what amounted to rival electoral armies based more upon kinship and the cash nexus than upon anything else.

At a national level post-famine politics revolved, however loosely, around three related matters: farmers' efforts to bend rural society to their own imperatives by means of a Tenant League, the continuation of Catholic agitation in the shape of a Catholic Defence Association, and the reaction to such developments on the part of a vigorous and revived Protestant Conservatism. Although all of these were authentically 'Irish' (not least the last), they were none of them nationalist in any real sense, and much the same was true of the Independent Irish Party which emerged as a parliamentary reflection of agrarian and Catholic aspirations, only to collapse into ineffective confusion before the 1850s had come to an end.[57] Groping for a political programme, Catholic bishops alighted upon the twin issues of educational change (or more sectarianism at state expense) and the disestablishment of the Church of Ireland, neither of them capable of generating much

[55] D. Bowen, *The Protestant Crusade in Ireland, 1800–70* (Dublin, 1978), 257.

[56] D. A. Kerr, *'A Nation of Beggars'? Priests, People, and Politics in Famine Ireland, 1846–1852* (Oxford, 1994), 41.

[57] J. H. Whyte, *The Independent Irish Party 1850–9* (Oxford, 1958); K. T. Hoppen, 'National Politics and Local Realities in Mid-Nineteenth Century Ireland', in A. Cosgrove and D. McCartney (eds.), *Studies in Irish History presented to R. Dudley Edwards* (Dublin, 1979), 190–227.

enthusiasm among the people at large. With the reappearance in the late 1850s of violent separatism in the shape of the Fenian movement, it became more important than ever for the Church to help put together a form of constitutional politics likely to elicit mass support and inoculate the more restless sections of the laity against revolutionary—and potentially anticlerical—infections of various kinds. The church-inspired National Association of 1864 was the outcome of such preoccupations, and its programme of disestablishment, mild agrarian reform, and better funding for Catholic education reflected a compromise between clerical ideals and the politics of the possible. However, such successes as might be put to its credit owed as much to British as to Irish circumstances. On the one hand, its opportunistic alliance with the largely Nonconformist Liberation Society over disestablishment made its activities part of a wider United Kingdom campaign; on the other, Gladstone's eventual decisions in favour of disestablishment and land reform broke the Irish political log-jam far more effectively than the Association had ever succeeded in doing on its own.[58]

The only national political entity which proved successful in extracting immediate benefits from the political turbulences of the 1850s and 1860s was Irish Conservatism, an almost entirely Protestant affair. Led by able men, producing far earlier than its opposite number in England an effective electoral organization (the Central Conservative Society founded in 1853), dextrously tapping Protestant fears as well as a passing degree of Catholic disenchantment with the Liberal Party, the Conservatives succeeded at the general election of 1859 in winning a majority of seats in what was an overwhelmingly Catholic country with a predominantly Catholic electorate. Perhaps, therefore, it would be at least as useful to try to understand Irish constitutional politics in this period in terms of Conservative revival as in terms of the much more frequently cited nationalist 'inadequacies' of the Tenant League, the Independent Party, and the National Association. Indeed, in many ways, Protestant political culture proved more rugged than its Catholic counterpart. Not only did Conservatism succeed in drawing nourishing sustenance from the prevailing localism of the mid-century period, it also proved able, when required to do so in the 1880s, to reinvent itself and—under the flag of 'Unionism'—adopt a new and distinctly more free-wheeling and piratical stance than hitherto.[59]

For its part, the cause of revolutionary separatism was kept alive—although for years without much success—by the Irish Republican Broth-

---

[58] Government policies towards Ireland in the period 1868–86 are discussed more fully in Chs. 16 and 17.

[59] Hoppen, *Elections*, 278–332; id., 'Tories, Catholics, and the General Election of 1859', *Historical Journal*, 13 (1970), 48–67.

erhood set up in 1858 and by its American offshoot, both of them commonly subsumed under the general style of the Fenian movement. The IRB was a secret oath-bound society (and thus condemned by the Catholic Church), though, like most such organizations in Irish history, it was quickly infiltrated by government spies. At first the only groups from which it attracted significant support were urban artisans and shopworkers, and even these were often more interested in the opportunities for communal recreation it offered (gymnastics, boxing, and the like) than in its amateurish attempts at military mobilization.[60] Before long, however, the willingness of some Fenian leaders to water down their exclusive adherence to armed revolution and join the land agitation growing out of the agricultural depression of the 1870s helped create a brief interlude during which agrarianism, constitutionalism, Catholicism, and republican separatism were able to coalesce and together overcome the powerful particularisms which otherwise tended to shape the priorities of Irish political life.

Gladstone's success in disestablishing the Church of Ireland in 1869 and passing a symbolically important but practically innocuous Land Act in 1870 angered many Protestant Conservatives because too much, and many tenant farmers because too little, had been conceded. These contradictory reactions quickly brought into being a Home Rule movement which soon took on an overwhelmingly Catholic character when all but a handful of its early Protestant supporters realized that there was little future in cutting themselves adrift from British attachments and support. Towards the end of 1873 a formal Home Rule League was established, led by one of the few Protestants who did not run away, the lawyer Isaac Butt, formerly a pillar of intransigent Conservatism but now convinced that the Union required adjustment and perhaps a good deal more than that. At the general election of 1874 fifty-nine MPs were returned on Home Rule 'principles', though many proved no more than fair-weather friends anxious simply to catch a favourable electoral breeze.[61] Nor was Butt's gentlemanly leadership effective, especially when the Disraeli administration of 1874–80 took little interest in Irish affairs. What changed everything was the advent of depressed times.

Already certain Fenians had come to realize that exclusive attachment to the politics of violence held out little prospect of immediate success. In 1873 the IRB decided it would 'support every movement calculated to

---

[60] R. V. Comerford, 'Patriotism as Pastime: The Appeal of Fenianism in the Mid-1860s', *Irish Historical Studies*, 22 (1981), 239–50; id., *The Fenians in Context: Irish Politics and Society 1848–82* (Dublin, 1985).

[61] D. Thornley, *Isaac Butt and Home Rule* (London, 1964), 176–211.

advance the cause of Irish independence consistently with the preservation of its own integrity'.[62] This was the first of several so-called 'new departures' by which the forces of revolutionary and constitutional nationalism (including the former's financially important American wing) were able to enter into an effective, though often uneasy, marriage of convenience. At Westminster a few advanced Home Rulers began to 'obstruct' proceedings by holding up all kinds of business in order to draw attention to their cause. After a by-election in April 1875 they were joined by a recruit in every way greater than themselves, the Protestant Wicklow landlord, Charles Stewart Parnell, whose confidence, abilities, and cunning were soon to make him the most formidable Irish politician since O'Connell.[63]

The depression of the late 1870s became politically significant, therefore, not simply because a sudden drop in incomes created discontent, but because an effective leadership was in place to take advantage of a situation that might otherwise have run into the well-worn sands of confusion and dispute. By the time a full-scale Land War between tenants and proprietors broke out in 1879, Parnell had already achieved a powerful position in Home Rule affairs. By collaborating with American Fenians and more immediately with Michael Davitt (the most effective exponent of the aspirations and discontents of small farmers) Parnell was able, partly by luck and partly by deploying some awesomely tuned political skills, to assume control of a combined agrarian and nationalist movement in which the former constituent was for a time to prove the dominant one.

Bad harvests and falling prices made it difficult for tenants to pay their rents. Evictions rose to levels not experienced since famine times (see Plate 5). Rural violence, as measured by the official enumeration of 'agrarian outrages', began to increase in 1879 and reached a peak in the twelve months ending in June 1882.[64] After starting in Connacht (hitherto the least disturbed part of Ireland), the agitation spread rapidly to the whole of the southern and to some of the northern parts of the country. And though it was not long before the different forces which had coalesced behind Davitt and Parnell began to fall apart once more, what is, in the end, remarkable about the Land War of 1879–82 is not its ultimate disintegration, but that it proved possible to sustain a united front at all. That during the early 1880s the small farmers of the west were prepared, however briefly, to follow the lead of the rich and hated graziers, that the local

[62] T. W. Moody, *Davitt and Irish Revolution 1846–82* (Oxford, 1981), 123; R. F. Foster, *Modern Ireland 1600–1972* (London, 1988), 403–5.

[63] R. F. Foster, *Charles Stewart Parnell: The Man and His Family* (Hassocks, 1976); F. S. L. Lyons, *Charles Stewart Parnell* (London, 1977).

[64] Moody, *Davitt*, 562–8.

branches of the Land League attracted not only a representative membership from the whole spectrum of tenants but also labourers so long hostile
to farmers of all kinds, is evidence that something unusual and important
had taken place, even if its meaning could as yet be perceived only as
through a glass darkly.[65]

Gladstone's 1881 Land Act granted the 3 Fs and proved attractive to
many farmers. Parnell, since 1880 the leader of a substantial party at
Westminster, adopted the ingenious device of urging tenants to 'test' the
act, thus enabling them to enjoy its advantages without entirely undermining his own attacks upon its insufficiencies. He was rescued from
having to make a less opaque response by his arrest and imprisonment in
Kilmainham gaol in October 1881. It was not long, however, before it
became clear that both he and the government had reached an impasse.
Gladstone feared that agitation was becoming endemic, Parnell that his
control over it was in danger of falling into other hands should he remain in
goal. In May 1882, he was released after having come to an unofficial
agreement with the government (the so-called Kilmainham Treaty): he to
counsel peaceful behaviour, it to alleviate arrears of rent. Parnell, like
O'Connell primarily a political rather than an agrarian operator, was now
able to devote himself more intensely to the great aim of his life, namely,
Home Rule or the granting of a substantial measure of political and
administrative devolution to Ireland. The Land League, banned in October
1881, was replaced by the National League, which, though drawn from
much the same personnel, was dominated by parliamentarians and primarily committed to constitutional rather than purely agrarian activities.

At the general election of 1885 the Home Rule Party won every seat
outside north-east Ulster and Dublin University. Its 86 MPs constituted
the first modern political party in the United Kingdom: its leader exercised
iron discipline and its less prosperous members were paid (at first out of
party funds). The overall result of the election (Liberals 335, Conservatives
249, Home Rulers 86) gave Parnell considerable power. He could either
double the Liberal majority or destroy it utterly as circumstances might
dictate. Although a few Conservatives had dropped hints that some kind of
alliance with Parnell might be possible, the announcement by Gladstone's
son on 17 December 1885 that his father had been 'converted' to Home
Rule changed everything. Whatever Gladstone's motives may have been—
and they were complex and included considerations that went far beyond

[65] S. Clark, 'The Social Composition of the Land League', *Irish Historical Studies*, 17
(1971), 447–69; id., 'The Importance of Agrarian Classes: Agrarian Class Structure and
Collective Action in Nineteenth-Century Ireland', *British Journal of Sociology*, 29 (1978),
22–40; Jordan, *Land and Popular Politics*, 199–263.

Ireland—his decision succeeded in attaching Parnell's forces to the Liberal Party with rods of steel, so much so that constitutional nationalism's freedom of action with regard to British party politics was to remain closely circumscribed for thirty years and more.[66]

With Irish support Gladstone became Prime Minister for the third time in February 1886. His diary shows him working on a 'definitive settlement' for Ireland from the day he assumed office, this to consist not only of a Government of Ireland (or Home Rule) Bill, but of a new land-purchase measure as well. When introduced in April the former at once revealed the enormous technical, administrative, and financial difficulties which any kind of devolution involved.[67] There was to be an Irish legislature with an executive reporting to it, but with a string of 'imperial' matters excluded from its jurisdiction: defence, foreign affairs, customs and excise, the Post Office, and much else besides. Eventually even Gladstone was forced to think again about his initial proposal that Irish representation at Westminster should cease. In the end, however, the Conservatives could not be won over and enough Liberals voted against the bill to ensure its defeat in June by twenty votes. The resulting general election in July ushered in two almost-solid decades of Unionist supremacy over United Kingdom affairs.

By then Parnell (the last years of whose career form an inseparable pendant to the events of 1886) was firmly locked into his alliance with the Liberals. His room for manœuvre severely circumscribed, he adopted a policy of cloudy inertia well-suited to the complex circumstances of the time and to his own equally complex character. Long absences from Ireland—from 1886 onwards he lived permanently with his mistress, Mrs O'Shea, at Eltham in south-east London—enabled him to achieve a degree of aloofness from the second phase of the Land War, the so-called Plan of Campaign launched in 1886 by his lieutenants John Dillon and William O'Brien in the face of renewed economic difficulties.[68] Although some initial successes were achieved, the campaign proved an expensive failure, with Parnell, wisely from his own point of view, giving it just enough support to maintain an image of sympathy but not so much as to become too closely identified with its eventual collapse. However, in December 1889 Mrs O'Shea's husband, a shifty character who had long known about his wife's liaison, filed suit for divorce and named Parnell as co-respondent.

---

[66] Lyons, *Charles Stewart Parnell*, 170–311.

[67] H. C. G. Matthew, *Gladstone 1875–1898* (Oxford, 1995), 239–58. For a more detailed discussion of these matters and of Home Rule as an episode in British politics, see below, Ch. 17, s. 3.

[68] S. Warwick-Haller, 'Parnell and William O'Brien', in D. G. Boyce and A. O'Day (eds.), *Parnell in Perspective* (London, 1991), 65–70.

In November 1890, when the case came for trial, Gladstone, under pressure from his Nonconformist supporters, told Parnell's associates that the 'Chief' would have to go. Already, too, a number of Catholic bishops in Ireland had begun to make threatening noises and had only been held back by Archbishop Walsh's sensible advice that they had better wait and see what the Home Rule MPs themselves would do. After a week of bitter debate at Westminster these split 45 to 27 against Parnell (if those absent could have voted the result would have been 54 to 32).[69] Parnell, though always popular in Ireland as a whole, had never been a genial or emollient party leader, quite the reverse. Now that a clear decision had to be made, his parliamentary followers thought the Liberal alliance more important than his own continued presence among them.

For some years Parnell had been in indifferent health and the bitter political warfare that now broke out between his supporters and the anti-Parnellite majority proved too much for him. His physical degeneration became obvious; his increasingly extreme speeches coarse and repetitive; his appearance—he had always been a knowingly handsome man—distinctly unkempt. He was only 45 years old when he died on 6 October 1891. To the end he had remained, and in this of course he differed greatly from O'Connell, pretty much an archetypal Anglo-Irish landed proprietor. For a man from his background, his nationalism and fiercely anti-English feelings were, indeed, the only 'eccentric' things about him. He rode to hounds, played cricket with passion, maintained a decent style—at a dinner with Victor Hugo in Paris in 1881 he was the only Irishman in evening dress[70]—and hoped, by converting Irish landlords to his point of view, to help them regain their 'proper' role as the true leaders of their country's political life. Though the precise contours of his thinking are almost impossible to identify (the phrases 'Home Rule' and 'Irish nation', for example, were never clearly defined) there is ample evidence to suggest that cautious political and social conservatism represented a more authentic mode than did those occasional bursts of radical rhetoric characteristic especially of his last years.

In choosing to project nationalism as a political and not as a cultural force, Parnell rather grandly bypassed many of the passions of his time. And if the kind of nationalism represented by the Gaelic Athletic Association (founded in 1884)—romanticism, ruralism, and Fenianism mixed up with an enthusiasm for ethnically 'pure' Gaelic games—unsurprisingly left

[69] E. Larkin, *The Roman Catholic Church in Ireland and the Fall of Parnell 1888–1891* (Liverpool, 1979), 191–232; F. S. L. Lyons, *The Fall of Parnell 1890–91* (London, 1960), 118–49; id., *Ireland since the Famine* (London, 1971), 192.
[70] R. F. Foster, *Paddy and Mr Punch: Connections in Irish and English History* (London, 1993), 73.

him cold, its growing popularity just as certainly had the potential for leaving his kind of politics out in the cold as well. Where, however, his thinking proved entirely in tune with that of almost all other Irish nationalists was in its inability to grasp the increasingly irreconcilable nature of Ulster Protestant opposition to what nationalists hoped to achieve. That the 1880s proved to be the decade during which Irish Conservatism turned into Irish Unionism, and in so doing acquired a far more clearly Ulster-driven character than before, was too easily dismissed by nationalists as no more than a little local difficulty. Yet when the general election of 1886 took place during the sacred Orange month of July the Unionists were able to present a notably forceful front. Newspapers were full of reports that Orangemen were planning to buy guns and the first leader of the Ulster Unionist MPs, Edward Saunderson, was already urging his followers to drill, arm, and put uniforms on.[71]

By then Irish considerations had begun to reshape the character of British politics, just as British power had long influenced Irish affairs. The Liberal split over Home Rule affected all parts of the United Kingdom. Under Lord Salisbury the Conservatives renamed themselves Unionists as an earnest of their commitment to the kingdom's continued integrity. For them Irish nationalist demands were to be resisted not least because they seemed to constitute the thin end of a wedge that might eventually be used to prise apart the great Victorian empire that was their pride and joy and the source of so many middle- and upper-class jobs. For Gladstonian Liberals the very same Irish demands were, in part at least, to be *granted* for an almost identical reason—that concessions would pacify Ireland and thus remove a set of grievances capable of destabilizing both the United Kingdom and the empire overseas. In a curious way, therefore, both Conservatives and Liberals had now, under the impress of the Home Rule movement, come to see Ireland as a 'special' kind of place to be either controlled or mollified according to rules quite different from those applicable in England, Scotland, or Wales. This marked a dramatic change from the earlier disposition of men like Peel, Russell, and Palmerston to work towards making Ireland an undifferentiated part of a united polity. Its effects were potentially very great, not least because 'treating Ireland as a "special" place' gave so many hostages to fortune that it eventually became more rather than less difficult to resist the most special demand of all—independence for Ireland and the break-up of the Union itself.

[71] D. C. Savage, 'The Origins of the Ulster Unionist Party, 1885–6', *Irish Historical Studies*, 12 (1961), 203; P. Buckland, *Ulster Unionism and the Origins of Northern Ireland 1886–1922* (Dublin, 1973), 2–3; A. Jackson, *Colonel Edward Saunderson: Land and Loyalty in Victorian Ireland* (Oxford, 1995), 73–118.

CHAPTER 16

Gladstone and Disraeli 1868–1880

1. GLADSTONE SPRINTING

The period 1868–80 was remarkable for the starkness with which political differences were epitomized by dramatic confrontations between its two leading men. Even when the behaviour of the ministries led by Gladstone and Disraeli converged under the impress of circumstances, the passion of colliding philosophies and rhetoric usually managed to disguise the fact. Not that the general election of 1868, which cleared the way for such things, was itself either especially fierce or especially novel in character. If more constituencies were fought than at any election since 1832, this was because extensive franchise reforms always made it necessary to survey the political map anew. In almost every other respect contests followed familiar lines. There was much electoral violence. About eighty seats remained under the control of landed patrons, while in the industrial North factory owners were emerging as political godfathers in their own right.[1] The Tory campaign showed few signs of imperialist stridency. Religion still counted for much (and Disraeli, despite attempts to rally the 'Protestant' vote, lacked finesse in that department). Most of the members returned came from the usual backgrounds: aristocracy, landed gentry, and (but no more than before) the purple of commerce. Even the overall result looked remarkably like that of 1865: the Conservatives merely held twenty seats less (274 as against 294) and the Liberals twenty more (384 as against 364).[2] It was hardly an earthquake. The Tories had not been rewarded for passing the reforms of 1867–8; the Liberals, though they won handsomely, do not seem to have greatly benefited from the extended franchise as such.

[1] H. J. Hanham, *Elections and Party Management: Politics in the Time of Disraeli and Gladstone* (London, 1959), 406–12; P. Joyce, 'The Factory Politics of Lancashire in the Later Nineteenth Century', *Historical Journal*, 18 (1975), 525–53.

[2] England showed the least change, while in Wales the Liberal majority rose from 4 to 13 and in Scotland (whose 60 MPs in 1868 included only 7 Conservatives) from 33 to 46. It should be stressed that it is not possible in this period to fix such numbers with absolute precision.

Given that Gladstone's chief electoral device had been the active mobilization of public opinion behind a clearly articulated set of proposals, the Liberal majority of about 110 allowed him to embark upon an unprecedented programme of legislation designed to confirm the voters' faith in his reputation for financial orthodoxy and cautious reform. Although at first he regarded only Ireland and retrenchment as immediate priorities, his overall approach marked a new departure in the sense that neither Russell, nor Derby, nor Palmerston, nor Aberdeen, nor Melbourne, nor Grey had ever considered legislation to be the main function of government.

Gradually, however, so much went awry that the frequently hailed triumphs of Gladstone's first administration produced comparatively few political benefits for their author. When legislation united his party (as over Irish disestablishment) it yielded little or no party advantage after the event. When it divided the party (as over education) bitter Liberal malcontents long continued to roam the landscape seeking revenge. When it sought to remedy a 'great wrong', it could prove notably ineffective and—as happened in the case of the first Irish Land Act—anger rather than pacify its supposed beneficiaries (the tenants). When it seemed to promise dramatic action—as with Civil Service and university reforms and the abolition of purchase in the army—the practical results were generally modest, sometimes even minimal. When—as with the Judicature Act of 1873—it dealt with important technical matters, only a few experts were impressed. Nor did controversial laws concerning the secret ballot, trade unions, and the drinks trade fare any better. Their supporters soon forgot the kindness. Their opponents neither forgot nor forgave. In such circumstances Disraeli's lazy 'policy', of moving slowly and doing little, eventually enabled him to play the victorious tortoise to Gladstone's overenergetic hare.

The opening fanfares were, however, everything that Gladstone might have hoped for, something of especial importance to a man who saw the premiership begun in December 1868 as, not only his first, but also perhaps his last.[3] The fifteen-strong cabinet turned out to be more radical than might have been expected. Though some have categorized almost half its members as Whigs,[4] this was not really the case in any efficient sense of that term. Gladstone himself was certainly no Whig and only Clarendon at the Foreign Office and Hartington as Postmaster-General were unambiguously such, with Granville (Colonial Secretary) and Kimberley (Privy Seal) being, in effect, minor aristocrats who owed political allegiance to Glad-

[3] H. C. G. Matthew, *Gladstone 1809–1974* (Oxford, 1986), 168.
[4] Ibid. 174; E. J. Feuchtwanger, *Democracy and Empire: Britain 1865–1914* (London, 1985), 59–60; R. Shannon, *The Crisis of Imperialism 1865–1915* (London, 1974), 77.

stone alone. The Lord President, Earl de Grey (from 1871, Ripon), was a free-wheeling radical quasi-Peelite, while Bright's presence at the Board of Trade constituted both a genuflection to the left and a recognition that Nonconformists might at last be allowed to sit around the cabinet table. Overall, indeed, the ministry's tone was set by a conjuncture of Peelites, High Churchmen, and unclassifiable reformers—such as Argyll (India), Cardwell (War Office), Bruce (Home Office), Hatherley (Lord Chancellor), and Fortescue (Ireland)—on the one hand, and meritocrats—like Lowe (Exchequer), Goschen (Poor Law Board), and Childers (Admiralty)— on the other.[5] And though a number of junior appointments certainly reinforced the impression that this was something more than a retread of Palmerstonianism, Gladstone's unprecedentedly wide consultations regarding minor offices revealed the ominous fact that the new Prime Minister knew next to nothing individually about his rank-and-file followers in parliament. Palmerston had maintained 'easy contact with the small fry' in the tea-room; Gladstone not only shunned the place, but fled Westminster altogether when the hour for dinner arrived.[6]

On the whole, cabinet members displayed comparatively little naked ambition. The Prime Minister was unassailable and personal relations (always excluding the irascible Lowe) were amiable enough. Within a general context of economic retrenchment the main aim was to create what mainstream Liberalism regarded as a legitimate order based upon the maximization of personal opportunities. Apart from one or two minor nudges towards a more positive social policy, the ideological thrust of Gladstone's thinking at this time was firmly concentrated upon placing all citizens under such conditions as would allow them to make the most of their talents and stations in life. But while this kind of Liberalism appealed especially to Gladstone's most ardently respectable followers in the middle and lower ranks of society,[7] political circumstances did not always make it easy to keep the genie of collectivist intervention in the bottle quite as firmly as the Prime Minister would have liked.

Gladstone wisely chose to begin by tackling what was *at the time* a comparatively manageable topic, as well as the one on which he himself was most urgently committed, namely, Ireland. The disestablishment of

---

[5] J. P. Parry, *Democracy and Religion: Gladstone and the Liberal Party, 1867–1875* (Cambridge, 1986), 279–80.

[6] J. Morley, *The Life of William Ewart Gladstone*, 3 vols. (London, 1903), ii. 173; Matthew, *Gladstone 1809–1874*, 177, 219, 233; id., *Gladstone 1875–1898* (Oxford, 1995), 272–3.

[7] E. F. Biagini, *Liberty, Retrenchment and Reform: Popular Liberalism in the Age of Gladstone, 1860–1880* (Cambridge, 1992), 84–138.

the (Anglican) Church of Ireland was, indeed, the only major issue capable of uniting all sections of the Liberal Party, while, in parliamentary terms, Irish land reform turned out to be less difficult to handle than might have been expected (largely because of the ramshackle nature of Conservative opposition to it). Disestablishment, in particular, had all the advantages of symbolic importance and practical insignificance. Of course, as with land, some MPs feared (and others hoped) that Irish innovations would cross the sea to England, Scotland, and Wales. However, only extreme optimists and extreme pessimists maintained such illusions for very long.[8]

The Church Bill of 1869 was the Prime Minister's work from the start and the Land Bill of 1870 rapidly became so. Not since Peel had such important pieces of legislation been handled in this manner. The former called forth a particularly classic example of Gladstone's skill at repainting erstwhile contradictions in retrospective shades of logic and inevitability. On this occasion the trick was performed by the pamphlet *A Chapter of Autobiography* published on 23 November 1868. In it Gladstone first pictured himself as having, already by the late 1830s, been 'alive to the paradox' posed by the Irish establishment with its huge endowments and modest membership. Then he recorded his having written privately in 1863 to a close friend to the effect that he 'had made up his mind on the subject, and that he should not be able to keep himself from giving public expression to his feelings'. Finally, he brushed away the awkward fact that in 1865 he had actually voted against Dillwyn's Commons motion demanding disestablishment with the (somewhat airy) argument that 'it is not the duty of a Minister to be forward in inscribing on the Journals of Parliament his own abstract views' on a matter 'remote' and 'not within the range of practical politics'.[9]

Within less than three years the issue had, none the less, conveniently become 'ripe' (a favourite Gladstone term), just in time to provide a crucial unifying theme with which to bind Liberals together after the débâcle of 1866–7. With Disraeli still Prime Minister, Gladstone pushed motions on disestablishment through the Commons in the spring of 1868 as part of a wider strategy designed to project an image of himself as somehow already in overall command. Given such an approach, it was inevitable that disestablishment would constitute his ministry's first major legislative enterprise.

Those Whigs, those few Roman Catholic intellectuals, and the single Irish Catholic bishop (Moriarty of Kerry) who favoured concurrent endow-

[8] The Anglican Church in Wales was eventually disestablished in 1920, the Church of England remains more or less as it was, while the (Presbyterian) Church of Scotland continues to enjoy its own low-key version of establishment.

[9] *A Chapter of Autobiography* (London, 1868), 18, 40, 44–5.

ment (or providing state cash for a number of denominations) were disappointed to find that disestablishment was to be total. In Gladstone's view, once an established church could no longer represent a complete 'religious nationality' then the only alternative was the opposite extreme of voluntaryism. Matters, therefore, soon settled into a conflict over what might be called 'severance terms'. When the Lords attempted to improve these a clash between the two Houses of Parliament seemed imminent. The Queen and Archbishop Tait of Canterbury worked hard for a compromise. Gladstone (it was to become something of a habit at difficult moments) fell ill and negotiations were left in the hands of the more emollient Granville, with the result that all major problems were resolved towards the end of July 1869 and a bill passed which included the great bulk of Gladstone's original scheme. The Church of Ireland obtained terms better than its feeble claims merited: some £16m were taken away and then £10m given back again. The most revolutionary aspect of the settlement was that the balance was to be made available for 'non-religious' causes: the relief of poverty, agricultural improvement, higher education, and so forth.[10] Both parties in parliament remained happily united throughout. On the second reading the government had a majority of 118 in a House of 622, with only six Liberals and four Conservatives voting against their whips.[11] It was as if an irritating tooth had been pulled. A major, if rather abstract, complaint on the part of Irish Catholics was removed. British Nonconformists hoped the process would continue elsewhere. Most Anglicans, once the initial shock had worn off, realized that it would not. In short, a great multitude had—very skilfully—been fed with no more than a handful of fishes and loaves.

Gladstone's swift and intense immersion in the details of the land question in Ireland—the second item on his agenda of Irish reforms—allowed him to dominate the ensuing legislation much as he had done over disestablishment. Unfortunately this was a somewhat more complicated business. What Irish tenants wanted was to own the land they occupied and sort out certain deep conflicts of interest between those with large and those with small holdings. However, Gladstone (like almost all Britons of his class) believed not only that landlords were part of the natural rural order, but that no equitable solution was possible without their enthusiastic participation. Not that even this was enough for all his ministers. Some became alarmed at the remotest thought of 'attacking' property, Lowe announcing that 'he would rather give up everything than consent to put

[10] P. M. H. Bell, *Disestablishment in Ireland and Wales* (London, 1969), 110–212.
[11] G. I. T. Machin, *Politics and the Churches in Great Britain 1869 to 1921* (Oxford, 1987), 24.

his hand in one man's pocket, and rob him for the benefit of another'.[12] In response, Gladstone took care to present himself to his colleagues as a natural conservative driven by unwelcome pressures to do something tolerably modest about Irish land. This (to him) congenial guise had the further effect of rendering his mind peculiarly susceptible to a recently published pamphlet given him by the eminent Civil Servant, Sir Charles Trevelyan, in the summer of 1869. Simply entitled *The Irish Land* this was the work of George Campbell, an administrator and judge in India, who, drawing upon a knowledge of customary tenures in Asia, had portrayed the popular Irish stress upon similar extra-legal customs in what might broadly be called 'traditional' terms. By appealing to recent historicist interest in 'primitive' tenurial arrangements Campbell's pamphlet spoke to Gladstone's pressing need to find an Irish solution which could be put forward as somehow in tune with organic local imperatives, as, in other words, an ultimately conservative rather than a merely radical proposal.[13]

The bill that was passed in the summer of 1870 gave legal sanction to the so-called 'Ulster Custom', by which departing tenants in good standing received generous 'compensation' from in-coming tenants, not only for unexpired improvements, but simply for quitting the land peaceably. However, in districts where the custom did not operate, only compensation for improvements would be required by law. Because the majority of tenants held without a lease, the eviction of non-leaseholders was to be made difficult except on grounds of non-payment of rent. Finally—at Bright's insistence—some mouse-like clauses were added providing ungenerous assistance for those wishing to purchase their holdings.

As an immediate 'solution' the Land Act of 1870 was a failure. Its main provisions were easily circumvented by proprietors with even half their wits about them: rents could be raised high enough to allow eviction, leases containing restrictive covenants could be forced on unwilling tenants, all sorts of other dodges and stratagems were quickly discovered.[14] Retrospectively, however, it can be seen to have heralded the beginnings of the collapse of the landlord class in Ireland. As far as perceptive Tory die-hards like the 3rd Marquess of Salisbury were concerned, Irish landlords, having proved themselves incapable 'of holding their own in the open fight of politics', were now a wounded and enfeebled class.[15] More generally, the

[12] E. D. Steele, 'Gladstone and Ireland', *Irish Historical Studies*, 17 (1970), 82.
[13] Id., *Irish Land and British Politics: Tenant-Right and Nationality 1865–1870* (Cambridge, 1974), 104–5; S. B. Cook, *Imperial Affinities: Nineteenth Century Analogies and Exchanges between India and Ireland* (New Delhi, 1993), 55–62.
[14] K. T. Hoppen, *Ireland since 1800: Conflict and Conformity* (London, 1989), 94.
[15] *Hansard*, ccii. 76 (14 June 1870).

act had breached, as was widely pointed out at the time, 'that great monopoly which the age . . . steadfastly maintains . . . the right of private property itself'.[16]

If, however, the Land Act pleased hardly anyone else, it certainly pleased its author. Gladstone believed a great deed had been done, a community of interests brought into being, a proper course taken as regards the development of Irish politics. In other words, normal service regarding Ireland could (with the exception of the university question) now be resumed. For ministers like Kimberley this meant musings to the effect that ultimately 'the true source of Irish unhappiness is the character of the Irish race'.[17] For Gladstone it meant attacks on the new Home Rule movement. 'So far as my research has gone', he told a Scottish audience in September 1871,

we have not had the advantage of hearing all that is to be said [about Home Rule]. I have seen nothing, except that it is stated there is a vast quantity of fish in the seas that surround Ireland, and that if they had Home Rule they would catch a great deal of these fish. [Much laughter and cheers.] But there are fish in the sea which surrounds England and Scotland. England has no Home Rule, and Scotland has no Home Rule, but we manage to catch the fish. [Cheers and laughter.][18]

If over Ireland the special alliance between Catholics, Nonconformists, and the bulk of Liberal Anglicans that Gladstone had done so much to create worked smoothly and effectively, over education in England and Wales it fell apart to such an extent that in certain key Commons divisions Gladstone found himself in the same lobby as the Conservatives. This was because schooling in England and Wales was not only a matter of deep religious and sectarian significance but one of directly local concern to the bulk of MPs and peers. For decades a modest system of state aid for what were essentially denominational schools had grown up, though under it many children (the statistics are unreliable) had received no instruction at all. Clearly something more comprehensive was required, if only to render Britain strong amidst the international rivalries of the time. 'Civilized communities', remarked the minister introducing the Education Bill in February 1870, 'are massing themselves together, each mass being measured by its force; and if we are to hold our position among . . . the nations of the world we must make up the smallness of our numbers by increasing

---

[16] J. R. Seeley, 'The English Revolution of the Nineteenth Century III', *Macmillan's Magazine*, 22 (Oct. 1870), 447.

[17] ' "A Journal of Events during the Gladstone Ministry, 1868–74" by John, First Earl of Kimberley', ed. E. Drus, *Camden Miscellany XXI*, Camden 3rd ser. 90 (London, 1958), 9–10.

[18] *The Times*, 27 Sept. 1871.

the intellectual force of the individual'.[19] More specifically, as Gladstone himself pointed out, German successes in the Franco-Prussian War which broke out in August 1870 seemed, among much else, to award 'a marked triumph to the cause of systematic popular education'.[20]

Notwithstanding the urgency of such reasoning, sectarian and financial imperatives required that any proposals must needs be at once cautious and cheap. This would not, however, be easy given the manner in which battle lines had been sharpened by the almost simultaneous foundation in 1869 of a National Education Union supporting the existing denominational system and a National Education League favouring universal and unsectarian (some preferred the term 'secular') schooling, the latter especially notable for providing Joseph Chamberlain with the means of entering national political life.

A bill was eventually introduced in February 1870 by W. E. Forster, the Vice-President of the Council, in a speech remarkable for its frankness. 'Our object', he announced, 'is to complete the present voluntary system, to fill up gaps, sparing the public money where it can be done without, procuring as much as we can the assistance of the parents, and welcoming ... the co-operation and aid of those benevolent men who desire to assist their neighbours.'[21] The voluntary sector would, it emerged, not only survive but be given a short period in which to apply for additional building grants (a torrent of successful applications predictably ensued). In districts with insufficient provision, elected boards were to be established to run schools funded out of the rates. Elsewhere voluntary schools would continue to receive Treasury money to cover a proportion of their costs. Neither those who desired a complete state system nor those who wanted only sectarian voluntary schools were pleased.

Most contentious of all were the clauses which permitted boards to provide denominational instruction (from which parents could withdraw their children).[22] In this matter almost all the trouble that followed can be laid at the Prime Minister's door. Forster had originally wanted to allow only non-denominational religious instruction. Gladstone took a more rigid view. Ideally he would have liked fully dogmatic denominational

---

[19] *Hansard*, cic. 465–6 (17 Feb. 1870).

[20] [W. E. Gladstone], 'Germany, France, and England', *Edinburgh Review*, 132 (Oct. 1870), 564.

[21] *Hansard*, cic. 443–4 (17 Feb. 1870).

[22] Severe difficulties were also produced by clause 25 which allowed boards to use rates to pay the fees of poor children at their own *or* at voluntary schools, though Nonconformist critics only spotted this possible subsidy for the voluntary sector after the bill had been enacted.

teaching. Failing that he rejected liberal pan-Christian vagueness in favour of the other extreme, namely, completely secular state-funded education, with the churches themselves to be responsible for any religious teaching that might be demanded or supplied.[23] Although this last alternative (voluntaryism) was not without a measure of popularity, the intermediate Forsterian position was much more widely supported among Nonconformists as well as among Anglicans of a Broad and (in many cases) of a Low Church persuasion. Preoccupied with Irish land, Gladstone complained (and not without justice) that 'men are decided, not between two courses, or even three, but four or five'.[24] Three months later, however, a crucial amendment was accepted from W. F. Cowper-Temple to the effect that in board schools 'no religious catechism or religious formulary which is distinctive of any particular denomination shall be taught'. This and a few other changes ensured that the bill passed into law. It also, however, ensured that large numbers of Dissenters remained angry at having—as they saw it—failed to secure much more than half a loaf. This was because the Cowper-Temple clause did not really prevent the teaching of denominational religion as such. It merely banned catechisms and 'formularies'. Loopholes were quickly discovered by ingenious glossists, among them Gladstone who was fond of arguing that, though the Nicene and Athanasian Creeds could hardly now be taught, the Apostles' Creed ('acknowledged by the great bulk of Christendom') remained quite acceptable.[25] The League, therefore, continued to complain, especially when its sophisticated attempts to control elections to the new boards proved far less successful than had been expected. Committees of prominent men in major cities condemned the government and discontent among significant sections of Nonconformist opinion hurt Liberal candidates at by-elections and at the general election of 1874.

In terms of numbers and the spread of educational provision the act of 1870 was of lasting importance. By 1883 there were 3,692 board schools, which, especially in the larger towns, signified a reduction in the influence of the established church.[26] Above all, the act had an impact in an area which to mid-Victorians mattered almost as much as godliness, namely,

[23] Matthew, *Gladstone 1809–1874*, 203.

[24] *Correspondence on Church and Religion of William Ewart Gladstone*, ed. D. C. Lathbury, 2 vols. (London, 1910), ii. 138.

[25] Morley, *Life of Gladstone*, ii. 307–8.

[26] N. J. Richards, 'British Nonconformity and the Liberal Party 1868–1906', *Journal of Religious History*, 9 (1977), 390–1. However, in 1883 there were also no less than 11,589 Anglican schools and in 1903, when the 1870 act was eventually superseded, a clear majority of children were still being educated in voluntary schools (Machin, *Politics and the Churches*, 38).

finance. In 1870 the central education vote stood at £1.6m or 4.1 per cent of government expenditure excluding debt charges. By 1885 it had risen to £5.1m or 8.6 per cent. Local authority spending on education rose from £2.2m in 1875 (no earlier figures are available) to £3.2m in 1885 or from 5.4 to 7.3 per cent of the overall sums. Indeed, if it were possible to add the (unknown) amounts spent locally in Scotland and Ireland it is probable that by 1885 the total figure would not have been far short of the £11.4m then being devoted to the Royal Navy—a novel and remarkable state of affairs.[27] Soon the system was developing its own momentum as more and more politicians began to see how it might benefit them. The Tory Education Act of 1876 gave a nudge towards compulsory attendance, its author, Lord Sandon, being particularly keen to increase numbers at voluntary schools in rural areas in order to prevent the spread of boards, which, he believed, afforded 'the platform and the notoriety specially needed by the political Dissenting Ministers (many of them, to my mind, the most active and effective revolutionary agents of the day)'.[28] Eventually in 1880 compulsion became general, though not yet quite universal, while in 1891 the remaining fees were effectively abolished for pupils at voluntary and board schools alike.

Outside England and Wales the matter of schooling was either less contentious (Scotland) or frozen into a condition of suspended religious truce (Ireland). In Ireland the supposedly non-denominational 'national' system of 1831 had been effectively transformed into one where the state paid the money and the churches called the tune. In Scotland the broad measure of theological agreement which continued to exist among Presbyterians even after the Disruption of 1843 gave the relationship between the churches and education a specifically Caledonian slant. This made it possible to enact a Scottish Education Bill in 1872, which, by placing all parochial and many other schools within a national rate-aided system with scope for religious instruction, encouraged the rapid closure of the great majority of the schools run by Presbyterian Churches—now satisfied that their religious requirements were being fully met by the public sector, and at little cost to themselves.[29]

If Gladstone was almost as dissatisfied as many of his supporters with the 1870 Education Act, he was at first even less attracted by the idea that further reforms be forced upon the Universities of Oxford and Cambridge.

---

[27] B. R. Mitchell, *British Historical Statistics* (Cambridge, 1988), 588, 612. Although local expenditure on education in Ireland was minimal, that in Scotland had by 1893 reached £1.5m a year (ibid. 626, 638).

[28] P. Smith, *Disraelian Conservatism and Social Reform* (London, 1967), 249.

[29] D. J. Withrington, 'Towards a National System, 1867–1872: The Last Years in the Struggle for a Scottish Education Act', *Scottish Educational Studies*, 4 (1972), 107–24.

Already in the 1850s he had disliked the legislation breaking the Anglican exclusivity of the student body. In 1866 he had voted to preserve it still in the case of dons. Eventually, however, he reluctantly accepted that further moderate change might prevent worse in the future and allowed the 1871 University Tests Act to open most academic posts to all men upon equal terms. Both universities, however, continued to function and teach in much the same way as before. Indeed, given the rising demand among the well-to-do, Oxbridge students may well have become more rather than less socially exclusive during the decades between 1870 and the outbreak of the Great War.

This combination of energetic surface disturbance and submarine stability applied—at least in the short and medium terms—to many of the changes introduced by the ministry of 1868–74. The famous Order in Council of June 1870 reorganizing the Civil Service is a notable case in point. The service was now divided into two rigidly distinct parts. Entry into the superior or policy-making section was controlled by examinations fashioned to suit the ethos of Oxford and Cambridge—classics and mathematics obtained the highest marks—while entry into the lower section depended upon competence in bookkeeping, copying, and (a nice touch) English history. But although recruitment was now by 'open competition', the changes which ensued were at first hardly more substantial than those ushered in by the Northcote-Trevelyan reforms of 1855.[30] The differentiated system kept non-graduates in their place. The Foreign Office refused to participate at all. Certain specialized departments (notably Education) continued to recruit by nomination. The Home Office only joined in after a three-year delay and did not actually admit any open entrants until 1880. Sceptical as he was about any sudden adoption of the 'principle of indiscriminate open competition', Gladstone thoroughly approved of such caution. What mattered was getting the 'best men', which for the Chancellor of the Exchequer, Robert Lowe, no less than for Gladstone himself, meant those who had enjoyed 'the education of public schools and colleges and such things, which gives a sort of freemasonry among men which is not very easy to describe, but which everybody feels'.[31]

Because few members of the cabinet had much direct experience of the armed forces, attitudes were perhaps a little less tender to privilege there than in the Civil Service. Yet the immediate effects of the military reforms introduced between 1869 and 1872 were no less innocuous. They were,

---

[30] See above, Ch. 2, s. 2, and Ch. 4, s. 3.
[31] *Hansard*, cvc. 497 (9 Apr. 1869); *Third Report from the Select Committee on Civil Services Expenditure*, H[ouse of] C[ommons Paper] 1873 (352), vii. 672.

however, a good deal more complicated, in part because defence was inherently a many-sided business, in part because the outbreak of the Franco-Prussian War cast a lurid and confusing glow upon the proceedings. Although the Tory government of 1866–8 had been notably parsimonious in military matters,[32] the new Secretary for War, Edward Cardwell (like Gladstone, a one-time Peelite), was determined to be more parsimonious still. Gladstone was delighted: 'It is really like seeing a little daylight after all these years, and a return to reason from what has been anything but reason.'[33] Bitter opposition from military interests—'Changes are always bad' muttered a senior officer[34]—merely helped to convince Cardwell that economical improvements were not enough. In 1869 he abolished flogging in peacetime. Then in 1870 he launched both an Army Enlistment Act to make it possible for men to enrol for shorter periods (usually six years in the colours and six in reserve) and a War Office Act designed to place the Commander-in-Chief firmly under War Office control. The first, though it increased the size of the reserve, entirely failed to produce either a steady flow or a better class of recruits. The second passed easily through parliament for the simple reason that it actually contained little that was new. The Commander-in-Chief, the Duke of Cambridge, complained bitterly that he now had to move from Horse Guards to the War Office (his writing paper was headed 'Horse Guards' until he retired) and the Queen (his first cousin) was equally unenthusiastic. But in practice little changed. On the one hand, the 'subordination' of the post of Commander-in-Chief was already well established; on the other, the duke, because of his experience and royal connections, remained an immensely powerful figure with limitless tenure and with responsibilities that had actually been increased rather than diminished by Cardwell's legislation.[35]

Although Cardwell had decided upon the course he wished to follow well before the outbreak of the Franco-Prussian War, that conflict placed the government's military policy in striking relief, not least because it seemed to persuade Gladstone, the great critic of Palmerstonian bluster, to toy with the idea of putting on the mantle Palmerston had let fall. Already in 1866 he had wanted to censure Bismarck's bellicose conduct. In 1869 he had scolded Clarendon for supporting Belgium with insufficient vigour. In July 1870 he had wished to put more pressure on the French to draw back than Granville (his new Foreign Secretary) thought fit. And when eventually he heard that Bismarck intended to annex Alsace-Lorraine he

[32] R. Millman, *British Foreign Policy and the Coming of the Franco-Prussian War* (Oxford, 1965), 145, 152.

[33] E. M. Spiers, *The Army and Society 1815–1914* (London, 1980), 179.

[34] Ibid. 181.   [35] Ibid. 186–7.

tried to persuade the cabinet to issue a formal protest. This it repeatedly refused to do, Granville reminding him of how Palmerston had 'wasted the strength derived by England from the great war by his brag. I am afraid of our wasting [it]... by laying down general principles when nobody will attend to them.'[36] Gladstone, however, would not let go and proceeded to take the extraordinary step of publishing in the *Edinburgh Review* for October an anonymous article—his authorship was at once universally known—in which he publicly criticized his own government's foreign policy, described that of France as motivated by 'a spirit of perverse and constant error', questioned Bismarck's 'scrupulousness and integrity', and concluded by talking of 'Happy England' endowed by God with a 'streak of silver sea' to separate it from the squabbles of less fortunate peoples.[37] Many contemporaries no doubt agreed. But it was a bizarre performance on the part of a British Prime Minister, let alone one who had persistently condemned Palmerston's braggadocio, denunciations, and threats. A senior colleague, Lord Kimberley, confided to his diary the opinion that Gladstone could not 'guide safely the foreign relations of this country'.[38]

Gladstone's aggressiveness in 1870 renders all the more surprising the failure of Cardwell's reforms to direct the British army towards those great advantages which continental forces were supposed to enjoy—professional competence, skill, adaptability, efficiency. Generally (though not invariably) successful in 'minor' colonial engagements, the late Victorian army proved altogether less impressive in major conflicts such as the South African War of 1899–1902. If Cardwell's initial emphasis upon shorter enlistment and War Office reorganization achieved comparatively little, his later decisions to abolish the purchase of commissions and introduce 'territorialization', as it was called, proved no more immediately significant. The latter involved the division of the United Kingdom into sixty-six districts in each of which two line battalions, two militia battalions, and a certain number of part-time Volunteers were to be based. This was supposed to help recruitment by associating regiments with particular localities, though success in this respect was at first patchy. At the centre of the plan stood the idea that one of the line battalions would remain at home (to recruit, reorganize, etc.) while the other served overseas. From the start,

---

[36] Lord E. Fitzmaurice, *The Life of Granville George Leveson Gower Second Earl Granville*, 2 vols. (London, 1905), ii. 63.

[37] [Gladstone], 'Germany, France, and England', 564, 576, 588; D. Beales, 'Gladstone and his First Ministry', *Historical Journal*, 26 (1983), 997; D. Schreuder, 'Gladstone as "Troublemaker": Liberal Foreign Policy and the German Annexation of Alsace-Lorraine, 1870–1871', *Journal of British Studies*, 17/2 (1978), 106–35.

[38] [Kimberley], 'Journal of Events during the Gladstone Ministry', 32.

however, theory outran practice and 'home' battalions were often so starved of men that many became little more than paper establishments.[39]

The abolition of the system of purchasing commissions in the infantry and cavalry was more contentious but equally insubstantial. Although Gladstone was at first far from impressed by the proposal, he was won round by the counter-productive violence of those military men in the Commons who held up Cardwell's legislation at every turn and who (rather than the Irish) deserve to be acknowledged as the true pioneers of parliamentary obstruction.[40] In fact, the 'colonels', as they became known, completely misunderstood Cardwell's thinking on the matter, which sprang much more from anger at the illegal size of purchase payments than from any desire to change the social composition of the officer corps. But so bitter was the opposition in the Lords that ministers eventually decided to secure abolition by persuading the Queen to cancel the royal warrant which alone made purchase possible, thus forcing their opponents to acquiesce lest the compensation originally promised be withdrawn. In the event, the abolition of purchase did little good and even some harm. On the one hand, because pay was not increased and expenses were not reduced, exactly the same kind of men continued to become officers; on the other, one of purchase's few advantages—the possibility of rapid promotion—was lost as Cardwell's hopes for advancement by merit were torpedoed with such effectiveness that henceforth seniority alone was taken into account.[41]

Nor was the navy handled to better effect, being allowed to remain technologically backward, reactionary in outlook, and organizationally confused. Cardwell's opposite number at the Admiralty, Hugh Childers, achieved little save the easing of promotion blockages by forcibly retiring—with generous compensation—all officers over a certain age.[42] Indeed, not the least remarkable aspect of the government's military reforms was the substantial expenditure required to prop them up. Childers's early retirement scheme involved a great increase in pensions; the new depots required for localized regiments cost £3.5m; compensation for the abolition of purchase a massive £8m; and there was a good deal more besides.[43]

As all these pounds were being spent, the Chancellor of the Exchequer remained energetic in the saving of pence. A couple of months before his

---

[39] E. M. Spiers, *The Late Victorian Army 1868–1902* (Manchester, 1992), 2–28.

[40] Indeed, the parliamentary struggle over the Army Bill was much more bitter than that over the Irish Land Bill.

[41] Spiers, *Army and Society*, 190–5.

[42] There had never been a purchase system in the navy.

[43] N. A. M. Rodger, 'The Dark Age of the Admiralty, 1869–85', *Mariner's Mirror*, 61 (1975), 331–44; 62 (1976), 33–46 and 121–8; Spiers, *Army and Society*, 191, 195.

appointment Lowe had told a friend 'I wish they would make me Chancellor of the Exchequer. I think I possess the faculty for saying No as well as anyone, and in that and not in super finance lies the real secret of financial prosperity.'[44] In the beginning it all seemed easy. The 1869 budget was a triumph. A recent military campaign in Abyssinia was paid for by collecting the revenues early, which then also made it possible to abolish various commodity duties and reduce the income tax from 6d. to 5d. in the pound. Much the same happened in 1870 when another penny was taken from income tax and Lowe told the Commons that 'the secret of all this success is the simplest in the world—it is nothing on earth but economy'.[45] But by the spring of the following year the additional military costs already mentioned and the start of a succession of colonial campaigns—the Red River expedition in Canada in 1870, the Looshai expedition of 1871–2 in northeast India, the Ashanti War of 1873–4—were beginning to create problems.

Nemesis came in the unlikely shape of the poor and desperate matchgirls of the East End of London. In 1871 Lowe believed he could minimize increases elsewhere by introducing a tax on each box of matches sold. This would have the advantage of forcing the poor (who escaped most direct taxes) to make a contribution as well as the rich—something Gladstone too always considered an important fiscal principle.[46] Lowe even told the Commons of the witty motto he had hit upon for the match tax stamp: *ex luce lucellum* (from light, a little gain). He also proposed to put income tax up by 1d. and increase succession duty. It was of course these last things which really annoyed the well-to-do, who thereupon lost little time in throwing their support behind the pitiful demonstrations mounted outside parliament by matchgirls egged on by their self-interested employers. A humiliated Lowe (even the Queen had intervened) was quickly forced to withdraw and to increase income tax by 2d. instead—perhaps not quite what most of the well-heeled instant humanitarians had had in mind. No longer much of an asset to the ministry, Lowe now found that, even when buoyant revenues (buoyant, that is, because of inflation) allowed him to cut income tax to 4d. in 1872 and 3d. in 1873, he still received more criticism for having in 1871 underestimated future government income than praise for having subsequently cut the amount direct taxpayers were required to pay.

In the end it was a pair of financial scandals in 1873 which brought Lowe's tenure as Chancellor to a close. Not only had an overzealous official at the Post Office (for which the Treasury was ultimately responsible) indulged in

---

[44] J. Winter, *Robert Lowe* (Toronto, 1976), 244–5.

[45] *Hansard*, cc. 1644 (11 Apr. 1870).

[46] Gladstone and Lowe were also united in their belief that charities should not escape taxation (Winter, *Robert Lowe*, 246–7).

some creative accounting, but insufficient care had been taken over awarding a contract for carrying mail to Zanzibar. Such faults made Lowe look foolish, though he blamed everyone but himself. With the government already in political trouble Gladstone decided upon drastic action. Lowe was shunted to the Home Office and Gladstone became Chancellor as well as Prime Minister. Back in his old office he began to dream his old dream of scrapping income tax altogether. When the defence departments refused to make this possible, he called an election on what turned out to be the unsuccessful platform of abolishing the tax if returned to office. By now Gladstone was in a bitter mood. Lowe had proved a disappointment, an ineffective ally against extravagance and 'wretchedly deficient' in controlling expenditure.[47] 'Outstripping others', Lowe was told in a caustic letter, 'you reach the goal or conclusion, before them, and being there, you assume that they are there also. This is unpopular.'[48] But what nearly broke Gladstone's heart was the way in which he could not avoid having to entrust a surplus of £5.5m to Disraeli's Conservative administration after the general election of 1874. 'Is it not disgusting', wrote Mrs Gladstone to her son Herbert, 'after all Papa's labour and patriotism and years of work to think of handing over his nest-egg to that Jew?'[49]

If, in the event, the financial policies of Disraeli's administration of 1874–80 diverged more in emphasis than in principle from those of its predecessor,[50] this was true also of other areas of government concern, notably the regulation of trade unions. In early 1867, legal decisions in *Hornby* v. *Close* and *R.* v. *Druit* had reversed the previous assumption that peaceful picketing involved no criminal conspiracy and had also left the unions without vital protection against corrupt officials.[51] The minority Conservative administration then in office had at once appointed a royal commission which delivered its findings to Gladstone's ministers in 1869. While the majority report was cautious, though by no means antipathetic to the union case (by far the most hostile member was the old 'patriotic' Radical, J. A. Roebuck), the minority report was overtly sympathetic. At first the cabinet was lukewarm about taking action. Nor did the campaign

[47] *Political Correspondence of Mr Gladstone and Lord Granville 1868–1876*, ed. A. Ramm, Camden 3rd ser. 2 vols. 81–2 (London, 1952), ii. 407.
[48] Winter, *Robert Lowe*, 295.
[49] G. Battiscombe, *Mrs Gladstone: The Portrait of a Marriage* (London, 1956), 158.
[50] P. R. Ghosh, 'Disraelian Conservatism: A Financial Approach', *English Historical Review*, 99 (1984), 268–96.
[51] J. Spain, 'Trade Unionists, Gladstonian Liberals and the Labour Law Reforms of 1875', in E. F. Biagini and A. J. Reid (eds.), *Currents of Radicalism: Popular Radicalism, Organised Labour and Party Politics in Britain, 1850–1914* (Cambridge, 1991), 109–33; Biagini, *Liberty, Retrenchment and Reform*, 148–64.

mounted by the new Trades Union Congress (which had held its inaugural meeting in 1868) prove either immediately effective or widespread.[52] But because the unions could not be left in legal limbo, a Trade Union Act was passed in 1871, effectively reversing *Hornby* v. *Close* and giving unions secure status as registered societies, though an accompanying Criminal Law Amendment Act was less friendly in tone and placed tight restrictions on the activities which those in dispute with their employers could legally mount. What, however, rendered this second law more severe even than had been intended were coercive additions introduced by Tory peers and unexpected interpretations made by Mr Justice Brett in the so-called Gas Stokers' Case of 1872. During 1873 the cabinet moved slowly to the view that further legislation was required and in November seems to have agreed to the heads of a bill which would have done much of what Disraeli's government eventually did in its Conspiracy and Protection of Property Act and Employers and Workmen Act of 1875.[53] These substantially eased the difficulties of the unions—largely through the instrumentality of amendments pressed upon Disraeli's Home Secretary, R. A. Cross, by the Liberal opposition. What this whole episode in the end reveals is not a Liberal front-bench rigidly hostile to union aspirations being succeeded by sympathetic Tories, but a growing feeling in both parties—but especially on the Liberal side—that in dealing with trade unionists it was as important to assign rights as to demand obligations.

Of no less intense and certainly more widespread concern was the question of alcoholic drink and its regulation. Here Gladstone's ministry found itself subjected to sustained pressure from the variegated ranks of temperance. But though this reached a peak around 1870/71—when the main temperance organization, the United Kingdom Alliance, attracted the vast annual income of £100,000—the irreconcilable differences between those who wanted total prohibition and those who favoured some lesser restriction dissipated the effectiveness of the overall campaign. State control was in any case repugnant to believers in strict *laissez-faire* and Gladstone was well aware that neither drinkers nor the drink trade were without political influence. Eventually one of his less able ministers, the Home Secretary H. A. Bruce, unveiled a bill in 1871 which would have made it possible for magistrates to introduce fairly strict limitations on opening hours and the granting of licences. This was too much for the trade

[52] Initially the TUC was a modest affair. Serious rifts among union leaders were only healed when the third Congress of 1871 was able to attract an attendance of forty-nine unions claiming a membership of almost 290,000. Three years later these figures had risen to 153 and 1.2 million respectively.

[53] Matthew, *Gladstone 1809–1874*, 214.

and too little for the Alliance. The bill collapsed, though its intentions were accorded a very shadowy afterlife in the form of a much weaker measure passed the following year.[54]

In political terms this had important results. While it is a considerable exaggeration to suggest that the drinks trade became entirely Conservative in sentiment, the number of Liberal publicans (and there had been many) certainly declined as did that of Liberal brewers. As pubs were important—perhaps the most important—centres of popular relaxation and exchange, this was not without significance. Henceforth too the Tories could convincingly pose as the champions of the beer-drinking working man. Indeed, even Bruce's feeble 1872 act was greeted by sporadic rioting on the part of those who believed it to have been inspired by the doctrine that there should be one law for the rich (drinking in their clubs and at home) and another for the poor. In 1874 Disraeli's Home Secretary lost no time in producing a legislative homage to such feelings in the shape of an Intoxicating Liquors Act. This restored longer opening hours because, as he airily explained, the problems of excessive drinking could only be effectively tackled within the context of more general changes to the condition of working people as a whole. Pubs were now able to open in London from five in the morning until half-past midnight and elsewhere almost as long, while Sunday hours remained more restricted. And even though the United Kingdom Alliance complained loud and long, neither it nor the movement in general ever recovered. Of course much local agitation continued; many teetotal pledges were still taken; and Nonconformity became, if anything, more dedicated than before. But in political terms temperance had become a fading force.[55]

It was the misfortune of the 1868–74 administration that many of its most unsatisfactory initiatives were accompanied by much critical publicity, while its successes often concerned matters of small interest to the public at large. Thus the Ballot Act of 1872, which at last introduced secret voting, caused no general enthusiasm. For some years the issue had been dead and only Gladstone's desire to get Bright into his cabinet had driven it up the ladder of ministerial priorities.[56] Nor, outside legal circles, was there much enthusiasm for the important Judicature Act of 1873 designed to consolidate the many overlapping and contradictory jurisdictions of the time. But then Gladstone himself was not very excited about such things

[54] A. E. Dingle, *The Campaign for Prohibition in Victorian England* (London, 1980), 30–3.

[55] Smith, *Disraelian Conservatism*, 208–13; Dingle, *Campaign for Prohibition*, 59–179.

[56] B. L. Kinzer, *The Ballot Question in Nineteenth-Century English Politics* (New York, 1982), 101–3.

either. He never really shed his early doubts about secret voting, was never greatly interested in licensing reform, and, when it came to the government's legal proposals, contented himself with telling the Lord Chancellor to save as much money as possible.[57]

By April 1872 the administration was in enough trouble to allow even a tired and lately supine Disraeli to seem convincing when he derided ministers for having become no more than a 'range of exhausted volcanoes'.[58] In 1872 and 1873 a series of scandals concerning appointments and financial matters did nothing for the government's claims to either probity or competence. Nor was it particularly cheering that during the 1868–74 parliament's lifetime as a whole no less than thirty-two seats were lost to the Conservatives at by-elections (as compared to a mere ten which moved the other way). An attempt at a third round of Irish reforms in 1873 brought additional difficulties. Irish Catholics had long argued that they lacked acceptable university facilities. Early in 1873 an Irish University Bill was brought forward. Its contents showed the impossibility of pleasing all the denominational parties concerned—for both Episcopalians and Presbyterians were also affected. Proponents of secular education thought the measure conceded too much. The Irish bishops thought it insufficient. The bill, with its provision that 'sensitive' disciplines such as theology, philosophy, and modern history should not be taught at all in the proposed university system, deserved to be defeated, as indeed it was by a majority of three—with of course many Liberals voting against.[59] The government resigned. Disraeli astutely refused to take office, so as to allow ministers to twist a little longer in the winds of unpopularity. There was nothing for it but to come back in again. Gladstone took on the Exchequer, while Bright, who had resigned as President of the Board of Trade in 1871 partly on grounds of ill health and partly because of administrative incapacity, returned as Chancellor of the Duchy of Lancaster in order to rally Dissent in a last desperate stand. It was all to no avail. Suddenly in early 1874 Gladstone went to the country—only to find that the country had grown tired of him and his ministry.

---

[57] *The Gladstone Diaries*, ed. H. C. G. Matthew and M. R. D. Foot, 14 vols. (Oxford, 1968–94), vii. 517 (29 June 1871); Dingle, *Campaign for Prohibition*, 76; R. A. Cosgrove, 'The Judicature Acts of 1873–5', *Durham University Journal*, 31 (1976), 196–206.

[58] Less than two years later, during the 1874 election campaign, he blandly transformed the same 'exhausted volcanoes' into overactive purveyors of 'incessant and harassing legislation' (R. Shannon, *The Age of Disraeli 1868–1881: The Rise of Tory Democracy* (London, 1992), 139, 173).

[59] Parry, *Democracy and Religion*, 353–68.

2. DISRAELI STROLLING

It was not as if the Conservatives had done much to help themselves. For more than three years after the defeat of 1868 Disraeli remained politically lethargic. Senior colleagues became so dissatisfied they even held a plotters' meeting in January 1872 attended by, among others, Hardy, Cairns, Pakington, Ward Hunt, Marlborough, Noel (the chief whip), Northcote, and Manners. Although nothing came of it, only the last two remained loyal throughout. Yet behind the sluggishness and confusion a good deal of moderately important organizational work was being undertaken by John Gorst. Conservative Central Office was set up in 1870 and new associations were established in many constituencies. The rhetorical flourishes about Tory democracy which had been issued to make retrospective sense of 1867 were quietly abandoned and the National Union of Conservative and Constitutional Working-Men's Associations set up in the year of reform soon dropped 'Working-Men' from its title. At a time when a few percept-ive minds in Britain and the continent had already begun to perceive signs that the middle classes were becoming more and more satisfied and less and less radical, this was perhaps just as well.

In a context of increasing political uncertainty Disraeli's famous speeches of 1872 before large audiences at Manchester and the Crystal Palace in April and June—events he neither enjoyed nor much repeated—were intended to generate broad-brush feelings rather than deliver precise policies. Disraeli actually said little that was new. In so far as he presented any kind of social policy, this was either unremarkable or designed not for social ends as such but as part of a long-standing strategy of constitutional resistance, according to which minor concessions might occasionally be necessary in order to help protect the sacred core. Repeatedly he made it plain that he would have nothing to do with financial experimentation. The 'great problem', as he told his Crystal Palace audience, was how to improve the condition of the people 'without violating those principles of economic truth upon which the prosperity of all states depends'. Soon he was even daring to criticize Gladstone for spending too much on the Ashanti War.[60] If, however, the importance and originality of the speeches were once upon a time treated with exaggerated respect, it would be wrong to go entirely to the opposite extreme. Of course the references to social matters were bland. Of course the discussions of empire were vague, comparatively brief, and anything but belligerent. But it was the close combination of the two subjects which

[60] Ghosh, 'Disraelian Conservatism: A Financial Approach', 290; id., 'Style and Sub-stance in Disraelian Social Reform, c. 1860–80', in P. J. Waller (ed.), *Politics and Social Change in Modern Britain* (Brighton, 1987), 59–90.

created both contemporary and subsequent resonances. This does not mean that the combination was immediately efficient as regards policy, though it certainly was efficient in helping to refashion the manner in which the Tory Party was generally perceived. The social reforms of 1874–80 may have turned out to be comparatively modest and the image of belligerence was only later thrust upon Disraeli by a Gladstone bubbling over with indignation about Bulgaria, but the idea of Toryism as a national creed 'identifying itself with the country's greatness, appealing to the masses first as Britons, but attending to their vital needs at the same time as it nourished their patriotic pride' married traditional and novel thinking in a way that was to remain significant for another hundred years.[61]

In the short term the speeches mattered above all as signs that life had not entirely departed from the opposition leadership and it may well be that they inspired none so effectively as Disraeli himself. When his beloved wife, Mary Anne, died on 15 December 1872 some of his colleagues feared he might leave public life. But, having re-established control over his party and come once again from the shadows, he had no intention of abandoning the limelight. By now the Liberals were in any case providing their own opposition and there was little to do but wait and make as few mistakes as possible. On both sides the 1874 election campaign was, as a result, a curiously subdued and negative affair.[62] As printed in *The Times*, Gladstone's address devoted two columns to his fiscal proposals and ten lines to the franchise, the game laws, land laws, education, licensing, and the trade unions. If the public was being promised quieter and cheaper times, the promise had come too late. 'We had exhausted our programme', admitted one cabinet member, '& quiet men asked, What will Gladstone do next? Will he not seek to recover his popularity by extreme radical measures?'[63] Among Liberals there was confusion and discord. In thirty-four constituencies unofficial candidates stood against official Liberals and a dozen or more seats were lost as a result.[64] Indeed, the whole affair involved Liberal disintegration more than anything very positive on the other side. The suddenness with which Gladstone had called the election left both parties at sea. The crucial word in Disraeli's famous promise of 'a little more energy in foreign affairs' was of course 'little'—as the appointment of the 15th Earl of Derby as Foreign Secretary soon made clear. However, unlike the Liberals, Conservative candidates fought a smooth and well-concerted

[61] Smith, *Disraelian Conservatism*, 161.

[62] R. Blake, *Disraeli* (London, 1966), 534–7; R. Jenkins, *Gladstone* (London, 1995), 375–9.

[63] [Kimberley], 'Journal of Events during the Gladstone Ministry', 43.

[64] W. H. Maehl, 'Gladstone, the Liberals, and the Election of 1874', *Bulletin of the Institute of Historical Research*, 36 (1963), 67.

campaign. And their addresses (by accident as much as design) followed more or less coherent lines: defence of the Church of England, an end to Gladstone's domestic hyperactivity, more religious teaching in schools, opposition to Home Rule, relief for local taxpayers, and the vaguest of vaguenesses on foreign affairs.[65]

Even so, the extent of the Tory success astonished everyone. After the 1868 election the Liberals had enjoyed an overall majority of more than a hundred. This now changed into a Conservative one of about fifty. In England alone a Liberal majority of thirty had become a Conservative one of 112. Of the 170 English county seats, the Liberals now held less than a sixth and in the boroughs the Tories had registered enough gains to reach a position of equality. In Wales and Scotland modest gains were also made (though these proved transitory), while the return of some fifty-seven so-called Home Rulers in Ireland increased the effective Conservative majority in the Commons well beyond its nominal fifty or thereabouts.[66] It was a stunning success. The pattern laid down at the general election of 1847—that whoever provided the majority it was not the Conservatives—was broken. Having (with the 14th Earl of Derby) re-established the Conservatives as a party of legislative success in 1867, Disraeli now did the same with respect to electoral affairs. By not standing in the way of middle-class dissatisfactions both he and the party were increasingly able to profit from the slow anti-Liberal shifts that were taking place in leafiest suburbia. This surprised them as much as, perhaps even rather more than, anyone else.

The new cabinet was broadly based and generally able. Its relative talent showed how far the party had progressed since the embarrassing search for ministers in 1852. A real 'find' was R. A. Cross, the Home Secretary, a representative of the industrial, commercial, and professional Conservatism of the provinces, though as a product of Rugby and Trinity Cambridge he could be hailed as 'middle class' only in comparison with the aristocrats who surrounded him. His selection for so senior a post may, in any case, have been semi-fortuitous, one of those lucky accidents from which Disraeli was rarely slow to benefit. Notable too was the manner in which the appointments of Lord Salisbury to the India Office and Lord Carnarvon to the Colonies marked the formal end of those hostilities over reform which had troubled Conservative affairs since 1867. Disraeli was now simply too powerful for the 'diehard' Salisbury to be able to make sense of staying out

[65] Parry, *Democracy and Religion*, 390–1.

[66] This was so despite the fact that a substantial number of the Home Rulers returned in 1874 were really closet Liberals who had decked themselves out in new colours simply in order to save their seats.

even if, as he told his wife, 'the prospect of having to serve with this man again is like a nightmare'.[67]

The presence of Carnarvon and Salisbury also meant that two men of decidedly High Church views had entered the cabinet. This created considerable difficulties when Disraeli decided to launch his ministry with an opportunist attempt to play the 'Protestant' card. Ever since the Oxford Movement of the 1830s and 1840s the Church of England had been troubled by the activities of an Anglo-Catholic party anxious, among other things, to 'restore' a more medieval liturgy and introduce practices such as auricular confession and benediction more usually associated with Rome. Many Anglicans found such 'ritualism' repugnant, but it was difficult to stop. Eventually in April 1874 the Archbishop of Canterbury, A. C. Tait, introduced a Public Worship Regulation Bill designed to curb 'excesses'. Disraeli at once began to treat this more or less as a government measure, partly because he thought it would be popular and partly because he knew that Gladstone would feel obliged to lead the High Church defence in the Commons. Salisbury, however, fought so successfully against the bill in the Lords that an exasperated Disraeli was driven into publicly denouncing his own Secretary for India as nothing less than 'a great master of gibes and flouts and jeers'.[68] Though many recognized that this was no more than the pot calling the kettle black (for both men were verbal pyrotechnicians of a high order), it was unusual even in so comparatively robust a political age. The Liberals, however, were also divided, with Gladstone's future Home Secretary, Sir William Harcourt, strongly supporting Tait or—as Gladstone privately put it—showering 'slimy, fulsome, loathsome eulogies upon Dizzy... aimed at me'.[69]

While the Public Worship Regulation Act turned out to be a damp squib, the fact that Disraeli devoted so much of his new government's time to the matter hardly suggests that he had many more urgent or exciting projects to implement. Indeed, as Cross discovered to his surprise, Disraeli had no great plans at all as regards either foreign or domestic affairs to unveil at his first cabinet meeting. Compared to Gladstone's initial burst of speed, comparatively little was done in 1874: the licensed trade was rescued from Bruce's rather moth-eaten bondage, ritualism was attended to, a minor measure favouring Anglican endowed schools was passed, and Fiji was taken into imperial care. 'The government', as Sir Charles Dilke put it, merely 'perplexed the publicans, persecuted the parsons, disgusted the

---

[67] Lady G. Cecil, *Life of Robert, Marquis of Salisbury*, 4 vols. (London, 1921–32), ii. 46.
[68] J. Bentley, *Ritualism and Politics in Victorian Britain* (Oxford, 1978), 73.
[69] *Political Correspondence of Gladstone and Granville 1868–1876*, ed. Ramm, ii. 457.

Dissenters, and annexed the Cannibal islands'.[70] Even if a useful Factory Act reducing working hours and an act abolishing patronage in the Church of Scotland are added, the harvest remains unimpressive at a time when legislation was coming to be seen (by Liberals perhaps more than by Conservatives) as an increasingly important part of a government's duty. While all politicians naturally pursue party advantage—and certainly the Patronage Bill had the happy effect of driving a nasty wedge between Gladstone and more rigid Liberal upholders of church establishments— Disraeli's conduct during the first session of the new parliament seemed driven by little else. But, then, the feebleness of the Liberal opposition provided temptations difficult to resist. Immediately after the election Gladstone had wanted to resign as party leader. His colleagues had persuaded him to stay. For about a year he remained in desultory command. Eventually in January 1875 he was replaced by a duo: Hartington in the Commons and Granville in the Lords. But he still remained in parliament, where his presence did nothing to make his successors feel at ease.

A major aspect of Disraeli's attempt to keep things quiet domestically was the avoidance of significant constitutional issues: in other words, no more reform acts and things of that kind. Less problematic, however, was 'social' legislation, distinguishable in contemporary eyes from 'political' legislation by being generally marginal and low-key. In 1875 one Conservative MP revealingly talked of 'suet-pudding legislation; it was flat, insipid, dull, but it was very wise and very wholesome'.[71] Not that there was anything like a Conservative social programme. Disraeli, not by nature a legislative politician at all, simply left relevant ministers to proceed as the need arose. They in turn produced a series of rather haphazard bills, the timing and contents of which were dictated more by circumstance than anything else.

This did not mean that all Conservatives lacked interest in social affairs or that sporadic sympathy for paternalistic reforms of various kinds had entirely died away. What, however, it did mean was that in general terms economic orthodoxies had now come to encase the Tory heart almost as firmly as the Liberal. Indeed, on some questions Conservatives took the harder line, notably in relation to local taxation which they thought wildly excessive and wasted upon the idle poor. And it is revealing that when depressed times seriously undermined the living standards of working people in the late 1870s Disraeli firmly rejected plans for additional expenditure. 'Her Majesty's Government', he told parliament in December 1878,

---

[70] P. W. Clayden, *England under Lord Beaconsfield* (London, 1880), 110.
[71] *Hansard*, ccxxv. 1064 (7 July 1875).

'are not prepared—I do not suppose any Government would be prepared—with any measures which would attempt to alleviate the extensive distress which now prevails'.[72]

This, then, was the context within which the oft-acclaimed Conservative social reforms of the 1870s were enacted. Although the peak of activity was reached in 1875, even the measures passed in that year—with the possible exception of the more or less cross-party Trade Union Acts—reflect a fairly undeviating adhesion to a species of modified *laissez-faire*, according to which the state should at most lay down certain guidelines for improvement which other bodies could then either choose to adopt or entirely ignore. An act designed to render friendly societies (important working-class institutions which provided mutual insurance benefits for their four million members) financially secure was a mouse-like affair combining requirements that certain minimal information be given to members with pointed reminders that this should not be taken to imply any kind of state guarantee. The same kind of thinking lay behind Cross's Artisans Dwellings Act, which empowered municipal councils to draw up improvement schemes for districts certified as unhealthy and provided them with loans for the purpose. The great majority of councils proved unsurprisingly reluctant to incur additional expense or face the problems of temporary rehousing (which Cross had more or less ignored). Indeed, by 1881 only ten of the eighty-seven towns in England and Wales to which the act applied had made any attempt to implement its provisions. Similarly, the Sale of Food and Drugs Act, though it contained clauses designed to reduce the dangerous adulteration common at the time, did not oblige local authorities to appoint the analysts who alone could have produced real improvements. Nor was the immensely detailed Public Health Act anything more than a consolidating measure, lacking, as it did, efficiently original principles of any kind.[73]

Sometimes, indeed, the government only took action when placed under great public pressure to do so. The Merchant Shipping Acts of 1875 and 1876 are cases in point. Sailors led notoriously dangerous lives and ship owners made only just enough safety provisions to prevent their vessels from actually sinking beneath the waves. The case for reform had been vigorously adopted by the Liberal member, Samuel Plimsoll. Shipping interests were, however, predominantly Conservative. In 1875 the incompetent President of the Board of Trade, C. B. Adderley, introduced a measure which pleased no one. As parliamentary time was short Disraeli announced that it would be postponed, whereupon Plimsoll stage-managed

---

[72] *Hansard*, ccxliii. 79 (5 Dec. 1878).   [73] Smith, *Disraelian Conservatism*, 218–30.

a famous 'scene' on the floor of the House. In the event, neither the temporary holding bill which this produced nor the more substantial legislation of the following year actually *compelled* owners to use the load line which Plimsoll had made the centre of his campaign.[74]

The immediate reason behind Disraeli's eagerness to postpone shipping legislation in 1875 had been a wish to find time for an Agricultural Holdings Bill, itself somewhat imperfectly designed to secure for tenants the benefit of any unexhausted improvements they may have made to their farms. This appealed to the Prime Minister on two counts: it was relatively innocuous but could, none the less, be pressed into service against those who accused the Tories of being no more than the landed gentry assembled at Westminster. And it was during its passage that he most clearly enunciated the principles lying behind the government's overall approach.

Permissive legislation is the characteristic of a free people. It is easy to adopt compulsory legislation when you have to deal with those who only exist to obey; but in a free country, and especially in a country like England, you must trust to persuasion and example as the two great elements, if you wish to effect any considerable change in the manners and customs of the people.[75]

After 1875 there was not a great deal even of such lawmaking. The Rivers Pollution Act of 1876 was feeble in the extreme. The Education Act of the same year was designed to prevent the spread of school boards into the squirearchical countryside. The Prisons Act of 1877 ran against the grain only in so far as it centralized the system under a Prison Commissioner.

Although the immediate practical effects of the social legislation of 1874–7 were modest, perceptions as regards the way a ministry should allocate its time did undergo some adjustment and change. Certain things began to seem less rebarbative and precedents of a kind were established. But there was little public concern and less excitement. If Plimsoll rather unusually managed to raise some steam, even he proved a good deal less successful than, for example, Dr Edward Kenealy, who in February 1875 defeated both Liberal and Conservative candidates at the Stoke-on-Trent by-election on a platform entirely devoted to the cause of a confidence trickster who had amassed widespread support for his claim to be the rightful heir to the Tichborne family fortune. Tichborne societies were established throughout the land; newspaper columns were full of the affair; endless court cases ensued; thousands paraded in London and the provinces; in distant Naples the San Carlo Opera announced a new work—

---

[74] Smith, *Disraelian Conservatism*, 232–40.   [75] *Hansard*, ccxxv. 525 (24 June 1875).

Roger di Ticciborni.[76] In comparison, contemporaries reacted tepidly to the social legislation which many later Conservatives have often claimed to be deeply significant, even epoch-making. By January 1876 Disraeli had, in any case, grown weary in the extreme, telling his Foreign Secretary that it would be a mistake 'to pledge ourselves' to more domestic lawmaking— 'We can't have too much foreign. It's the taste of the day.' Small wonder, then, that the Conservatives made so little of their social record during the 1880 election campaign, despite Gladstone's jibes about their 'singular' inefficiency 'in the work of domestic legislation'.[77]

Not that the history of the Liberal Party in these years can be said to present a picture of consistent unity or success. Religious issues continued to be divisive, though in opposition it did eventually become easier to bring about a reconciliation, if only because public expectations were less intensely directed at those out of than at those in office. For almost a year after the election of 1874 the party in parliament was 'led' by a Gladstone distressed that the moral charge between himself as Prime Minister and righteous public opinion had been short-circuited. Ambivalence surrounded his partial and then complete withdrawal from the leadership. That these actions were sincere can hardly be doubted. That they were also by no means innocent of hopes about returning under more suitable circumstances is highly probable.[78] Although any judgement as to when such circumstances might reasonably be thought to have come about presented obvious difficulties, Gladstone's innate sense of context enabled him to develop in such matters a highly convenient theory of political timing. 'The real test', he wrote later, 'may be stated in one word: the ripeness or unripeness of the question.'[79] But while of course the arrival of future 'ripeness' was a matter for him to announce and others to accept, it was never perceived as inevitable—hard work would be required to bring it about.

During 1874 Gladstone's chief interests revolved, as so often, around religious affairs. The rejection of the Irish University Bill had snapped his political alliance with the forces of Irish Catholicism. Long suspicions of Rome had been intensified by the First Vatican Council's declaration of the doctrine of papal infallibility in 1870. In October 1874 a measured defence

[76] D. Woodruff, *The Tichborne Claimant: A Victorian Mystery* (London, 1957), *passim*; R. McWilliam, 'Radicalism and Popular Culture: The Tichborne Case and the Politics of "Fair Play", 1867–1886', in Biagini and Reid (eds.), *Currents of Radicalism*, 44–64.

[77] M. Swartz, *The Politics of British Foreign Policy in the Era of Disraeli and Gladstone* (London, 1985), 30; T. Lloyd, *The General Election of 1880* (Oxford, 1968), 47; Ghosh, 'Disraelian Conservatism: A Financial Approach', 295.

[78] Matthew, *Gladstone 1875–1898*, 1–7.

[79] T. A. Jenkins, *Gladstone, Whiggery and the Liberal Party 1874–1886* (Oxford, 1988), 24.

of Anglican High Churchmanship in the *Contemporary Review* was peppered with violent criticisms of British Roman Catholics for their subservience to the papacy. A month later he published his famous pamphlet *The Vatican Decrees in their Bearing on Civil Allegiance: A Political Expostulation*, in which he roundly asserted that Catholics could now offer at best a very incomplete loyalty to the British state. It sold in vast numbers, produced replies (plus a second pamphlet from Gladstone) and generated a good deal of excitement all round. If its sarcastic tone caused Catholics to close ranks, a great many Nonconformists were delighted and began to forgive the 'betrayals' over education and temperance. Yet it soon also became clear that, despite much enthusiasm and public vitriol, the issue had not brought about any fundamental change in Gladstone's own relationship with the public at large, though it had perhaps begun to do so. Nor would all British Liberals have been reassured had they known of the warm thanks sent to Gladstone by Bismarck (then still engaged in his *Kulturkampf* against Catholicism in Germany), who, in a mischievous parody of Gladstonian language, declared himself pleased 'to see the two nations which in Europe are the champions of liberty of conscience, encountering the same foe'. In the very month of publication Gladstone still felt disconsolate enough to tell Granville that in 'politics I see no daylight ... Nothing will rally the party but a cause.'[80]

As the new Liberal leader in the Commons, Hartington offered precisely the kind of calm 'responsibility' which many MPs thought Gladstone lacked. He could, he told an audience at Lewes, find 'no particular fault' with the Conservatives. He believed the Liberals would 'now probably for a considerable period [be] removed from office' and did not obviously grieve over the thought.[81] Though his languorous manner hid a sharp ambition, it looked as if he was determined to recreate a kind of mirrored version of the 1850s and 1860s, with himself playing Derby to Disraeli's Palmerston. And while this may not have posed many immediate challenges to the government, it did heal some Liberal wounds and allow Hartington—with a good deal of cunning—to move safely towards the adoption of some surprisingly radical positions in connection with domestic affairs. Extension of the county franchise, redistribution of seats, local government reform in rural areas, and some land reforms had, for example, all been accepted within the party by 1879. In foreign affairs, however, the new leaders (Granville continued to lead in the Lords) proved less successful, partly because their

[80] H. C. G. Matthew, 'Gladstone, Vaticanism, and the Question of the East', in D. Baker (ed.), *Studies in Church History*, xv. *Religious Motivation* (Oxford, 1978), 436–7; *Political Correspondence of Gladstone and Granville 1868–1876*, ed. Ramm, ii. 460–1.

[81] Jenkins, *Gladstone, Whiggery*, 49.

penchant for 'responsible' opposition left them with even less freedom of manœuvre than in domestic matters and partly because of Gladstone's activities in connection with the Bulgarian massacres. As early as January 1875 one of Gladstone's oldest friends had felt sure that the former Prime Minister would 'soon become *désœuvré* and take to prowling around the political pen, from which he has excluded himself and snuffing for an entrance'.[82] What needs to be stressed, however, is not so much that Gladstone did eventually succeed in snuffing his way back, but that Hartington's leadership continued to give forth an impression of success almost until the very end.[83]

Gladstone had, none the less, begun to show mild signs of renewed political activity well before the Bulgarian issue erupted. Once it was under way he even decided to speak at the inaugural meeting of Chamberlain's National Liberal Federation in May 1877, not because of an interest in organization but because so few other party platforms were open to him. By then the two men had, in any case, come to a kind of unspoken alliance of convenience in which both hoped to use the other to further mutually irreconcilable ends.[84] Already in October 1876 Chamberlain—busily disengaging himself from the Midlands to become an essentially metropolitan politician—could not 'help thinking' that Gladstone 'is our best card ... If he were to come back for a few years (he can't continue in public life for very much longer) he would probably do much for us.'[85] However, the trouble from Chamberlain's point of view was that (as he himself soon recognized) the forces of Radicalism in parliament were deeply fragmented.[86] But if, in the longer run, only Gladstone—not Chamberlain or Hartington—was to succeed in developing those larger themes capable of attracting both Radical and moderate Liberals, this was as yet by no means clear.

3. FOREIGN AND IMPERIAL AFFAIRS

Foreign affairs constituted the most important platform upon which the politics of the 1870s were resolved and, to some extent, clarified. Here one of the chief party problems—how best to present a distinct approach—was

---

[82] *Letters of Frederic Lord Blachford Under-Secretary of State for the Colonies 1860–1871*, ed. G. E. Marindin (London, 1896), 360.

[83] P. Jackson, *The Last of the Whigs: A Political Biography of Lord Hartington* (Cranbury, NJ, 1994), 59–95.

[84] P. T. Marsh, *Joseph Chamberlain: Entrepreneur in Politics* (New Haven, 1994), 116–21.

[85] R. Quinault, 'Joseph Chamberlain: A Reassessment', in T. R. Gourvish and A. O'Day (eds.), *Later Victorian Britain, 1867–1900* (London, 1988), 69–92, 312–14; P. Adelman, *Victorian Radicalism: The Middle-Class Experience 1830–1914* (London, 1984), 96–7.

[86] D. Judd, *Radical Joe: A Life of Joseph Chamberlain* (London, 1977), 78.

rendered especially severe because there were men on both sides whose understanding of Britain's role in the world differed little if at all. Change, however, there was, in the shape of a modest shift away from broadly consensual diplomatic minimalism towards a more active quasi-Palmerstonian style which became known as Beaconsfieldism, after the title Disraeli adopted on moving to the House of Lords in August 1876. To Gladstone other countries represented alternative theatres for the playing-out of a seamless moralism. For Disraeli they possessed an exotic particularity which gave foreign policy a superior kind of political importance. 'Look at Lord Roehampton', he makes a character say in his novel *Endymion* (1880), 'He is the man. He does not care a rush whether the revenue increases or declines. He is thinking of real politics: foreign affairs; maintaining our power in Europe.'[87] It did not matter that Disraeli's knowledge of geography was deficient, that he tended to work by fits and starts, that many of his most famous utterances were vague to the point of meaninglessness. Because foreign affairs occupied a special place in his political mentality and because he understood that gestures could have an importance all their own, he was gradually able to make the influence of his idiosyncratic personality felt in altogether unexpected ways.

For at least the first two years after the election victory of 1874 Disraeli was finding his way, though even then, in the so-called 'War in Sight' crisis of May 1875 (when Britain and Russia told Bismarck to damp down some anti-French agitation in Germany which the iron chancellor had himself got up), he was able to secure a quite unwarranted reputation for decisive authority. Much the same happened in connection with the purchase later in the same year of a minority interest in the Suez Canal Company for £4m from the bankrupt Khedive of Egypt. This gave no kind of control and little legal power of any kind—though it was a good investment. Yet Disraeli managed not only to clothe it in cloak-and-dagger excitement, but to persuade people that it represented a key step within a considered imperial plan. Gladstone became furious and attacked the episode in the Commons to no very great effect. Hartington, more astutely, had no doubt that the public would see it as, above all, a 'most successful coup'.[88]

It was, however, above all developments in south-eastern Europe that provided the new element which made it possible for politicians to re-

---

[87] Derby's letter to Salisbury of 23 Dec. 1877 is worth recalling: 'He [Disraeli] believes thoroughly in "prestige" as all foreigners do, and would think it (quite sincerely) in the interests of the country to spend 200 millions on a war if the result was to make foreign States think more highly of us' (Blake, *Disraeli*, 636).

[88] J. P. Rossi, 'The Last Whig: Lord Hartington as Liberal Leader, 1875–80', *Canadian Journal of History*, 21 (1986), 170; Jackson, *Last of the Whigs*, 71.

arrange both the relationships between themselves and the links which bound them to the public at large. Turkish weakness, rising nationalism, pan-Slav identity, Russian sympathies, and Habsburg nervousness all ensured that any sudden shifts in equilibrium would be difficult to contain without involving a whole array of interested parties well beyond the region itself. What, in the British context, soon became especially notable was how Balkan affairs allowed Gladstone and Disraeli each to make a mark and to record what could, at least with the eyes of faith, be regarded as a distinct political success.

In July 1875 an insurrection against Ottoman rule broke out in Herze-govina and Bosnia. Russia and Austria had 'vital' regional interests at stake. Autonomous Serbia and tiny Montenegro became anxious over the fate of their Slav cousins. Germany fretted about disputes between its two fellow-members of the *Dreikaiserbund*.[89] Britain remembered the Crimea and the dangers of Turkish collapse and Russian expansion. France worried about being left on the sidelines. At first Disraeli was not especially concerned. He had no sympathy with petty foreign nationalisms: 'Fancy autonomy for Bosnia, with a mixed population: autonomy for Ireland wd. be less absurd.'[90] But when the crisis developed and Gladstone assumed a notably anti-Turkish stance, Disraeli began to display all the by now traditional British fears of Russia as a European and even more as an Asiatic power.

In December 1875 Austria and Russia (where for the moment forces antipathetic to pan-Slav sentiment held sway) drew up a Note usually named after the Austrian Foreign Minister, Count Andrassy, with the aim of putting pressure upon the Turks to introduce reforms. Germany had given its prior agreement, and France, Italy, and Britain were asked to sign as well. This Disraeli did, but with considerable reluctance. He resented not having been involved from the start and was far from delighted when Gladstone hailed Britain's adhesion as a master stroke of pacific diplomacy. The Porte as usual made all sorts of promises which it then failed to keep. Indeed, in this and other respects, the development of the Eastern Question in the mid-1870s constituted a remarkably faithful reprise of the events leading up to the Crimean War.

In May 1876 the revolt against Ottoman rule spread to the Bulgars. The cruelty of the Turkish response became known in Britain some weeks later and almost immediately a critical reaction set in. Disraeli did not help to

---

[89] The 'Three Emperors' League' of 1873 began as a Russo-German agreement for mutual aid if one or the other was attacked, and was completed by an Austro-Russian agreement to consult together if aggression threatened.

[90] W. F. Monypenny and G. E. Buckle, *The Life of Benjamin Disraeli*, 6 vols. (London, 1910–20), vi. 13.

defuse this by referring to accounts of massacres in papers like the *Daily News* as 'coffee-house babble' and talking sarcastically of the savage customs common in remote and primitive regions. Bland reports from the pro-Turkish ambassador at Constantinople, Sir Henry Elliott, chimed in all too well with his own prejudices. When, by the end of August, denials had become useless, Disraeli blamed everyone but himself. It helped little at the time to be able to point out that initial claims of 25,000 deaths were exaggerated (12,000 was soon accepted as a more accurate figure). Nor has it much helped Disraeli's subsequent reputation that perhaps 'only' 4,000 may actually have been killed, that massacres of this type were all too common, or that no one in the West got very excited when widespread Muslim resistance to the eventual Berlin settlement of 1878 was crushed with very considerable brutality by Austrians and Russians alike.[91]

To begin with, Gladstone surveyed the agitation that arose over the Bulgarian massacres from without. The lead was taken by others, notably W. T. Stead, the young editor of the *Northern Echo*, and three Oxford men: Bishop Fraser, Canon Liddon, and the historian E. A. Freeman. These last represented High Church Anglicanism, which, with its sympathy for Eastern Christians (Bulgars among them), was to be prominent in the campaign, while Stead stood for the numerically more significant ranks of provincial Nonconformity. Although Gladstone had certainly displayed signs of dissatisfaction with his retirement, he had not been obsessively waiting about for just any opportunity to create a stir. Even in this case he began by supporting the territorial integrity of the Ottoman Empire (as his Crimean involvements might have suggested), though his thoughts had also begun to move well beyond their usual concern with religious matters in general towards a more specific engagement with Eastern Orthodoxy as such. Eventually, however, the depth and width of the campaign persuaded him into excited action. 'Good ends', he told Granville, 'can rarely be attained in politics without passion: and there is now, the first time for a good many years, a virtuous passion.'[92] In late August he began to write the pamphlet which simultaneously marked his own entry into the agitation and his chief claim to its leadership: *The Bulgarian Horrors and the Question of the East*. It was finished in a few days and published on 6 September. For Gladstone the act of writing clearly released all sorts of tensions and gave him hopes that the moral relationship between himself and the 'masses' broken in 1874 might soon be restored. The evening before publication he

    [91] R. Millman, *Britain and the Eastern Question 1875–1878* (Oxford, 1979), 162; Blake, *Disraeli*, 592; Shannon, *Age of Disraeli*, 280.
    [92] R. Shannon, *Gladstone and the Bulgarian Agitation 1876* (London, 1963), 106–7.

consulted Granville and an extremely unenthusiastic Hartington. The three men then set off to see a farce at the Haymarket Theatre. A friend of Disraeli's noticed three empty seats in front of him: 'into one of the stalls came Ld. Granville; then in a little time, Gladstone; then, at last Harty-Tarty! Gladstone laughed very much at the performance; H.-T. never even smiled.'[93]

Newspapers at once reprinted the pamphlet. Many pirated versions were also produced. In a little over three weeks some 200,000 copies of the official edition were sold. It is not now easy to see why. Compared to *The Vatican Decrees* the text is restrained, with only occasional wild words ('fell satanic orgies' perhaps the wildest) to spice up the worthy yards of sober analysis. And as with the Pale of the Constitution speech of 1864 there was quite enough tortuousness to permit subsequent extrication. One winged passage, however, took flight: 'Let the Turks now carry away their abuses in the only possible manner, namely by carrying off themselves. Their Zaptiehs and their Mudirs, their Bimbashis and their Yuzbashis, their Kaimakams and their Pashas, one and all, bag and baggage, shall I hope clear out from the province they have desolated and profaned'.[94] An already lively agitation became livelier still, with—broadly speaking—the provinces, some Radicals, and most Nonconformists being anti-Turk; clubland, metropolitan 'society', the upper classes, and all (save some High Church) Anglicans either uninterested or anti-Russian. In a period of less than six weeks nearly 500 demonstrations took place throughout Britain demanding a repudiation of the government's pro-Turkish policies and a great National Conference was held in London attended by 'undoubtedly the most brilliant array of intellectual figures ever brought together to intervene in a question of politics in England'.[95]

Such rapidly generated intensities could, however, hardly be sustained, and by the end of December the campaign began to run out of steam. Gladstone's second pamphlet, *Lessons in Massacre*, was published in January 1877 and sold only 7,000 copies. Later in the year Granville reported that provincial audiences no longer cared 'twopence about the Eastern Question'.[96] Most Liberal leaders, who disliked popular enthusiasms in general and Gladstone's encouragement of them in particular, heaved a sigh of relief. From the start of the Bulgarian agitation, Hartington had been hostile, Granville lukewarm, Bright semi-detached, while Harcourt, Childers, and Goschen had stood aloof. Only Argyll had shared Gladstone's

[93] Monypenny and Buckle, *Life of Disraeli*, vi. 61.
[94] Morley, *Life of Gladstone*, ii. 554.   [95] Shannon, *Bulgarian Agitation*, 26.
[96] *The Political Correspondence of Mr Gladstone and Lord Granville 1876–1886*, ed. A. Ramm, 2 vols. (Oxford, 1962), i. 51.

passion. When, therefore, in May 1877 Gladstone moved the first of a set of Commons resolutions on the East, he found himself going down to ignominious defeat.[97]

Though soon over, the Bulgarian agitation left several important legacies. Disraeli's government did not emerge unmarked and never again recovered its early confidence. The failure of the campaign to achieve its immediate aims persuaded Gladstone, now once again convinced of his moral connection with the public at large, that work remained to be done and to be done publicly. The affair also reinforced his growing belief that truth and honesty were more generally to be found among the masses than the social élite. From the 'upper ten thousand', as he began to call them in 1876, 'there has never on any occasion within my memory proceeded the impulse that has prompted... *any* of the great measures which in the last half century have contributed so much to the fame and happiness of England'. And whence came this superiority of the popular judgement in politics? It came, he told the readers of the *Nineteenth Century* in 1878, simply and powerfully from 'moral causes' and from those alone.[98]

The government's foreign policy showed no evidence of responding to any of this. Towards the end of March 1877 the Turks rejected yet another call for reform (the London Protocol) upon which the Russians at last did what many had long expected and declared war. The Turks were better equipped and resisted strongly. Disraeli—carried away by the exuberance of distant warfare—was soon talking wildly of invading Russian Armenia and capturing Tiflis.[99] Divisions in the cabinet grew. Disraeli was now openly anti-Russian, though his Foreign Secretary, Derby, still favoured conciliation. As High Churchmen, Salisbury and particularly Carnarvon were not unsympathetic to the plight of the Bulgars. With pardonable exaggeration the Prime Minister told Queen Victoria that 'in a Cabinet of twelve members, there are seven parties, or policies, as to the course which should be pursued'.[100] However, as time went on, so the anti-Russian group became stronger, and Salisbury in particular moved steadily towards Disraeli's belligerent position, not because he had much time for the Porte but because of fears about Russia controlling the Straits.

[97] Shannon, *Bulgarian Agitation*, 118–20, 268–70; Jackson, *Last of the Whigs*, 74–81.

[98] Morley, *Life of Gladstone*, ii. 557; 'A Modern "Symposium": Is the Popular Judgement in Politics More Just than that of the Higher Orders?', *Nineteenth Century*, 4 (1878), 185–6.

[99] M. S. Anderson, *The Eastern Question 1774–1923: A Study in International Relations* (London, 1966), 196.

[100] Monypenny and Buckle, *Life of Disraeli*, vi. 194.

When eventually the key Turkish fortress of Plevna fell on 9 December 1877 difficult decisions could no longer be avoided. Derby was sunk in gloom. Salisbury, having resolved his own position, indulged in sepulchral jokes. On 20 January 1878 Russian troops reached Adrianople. Disraeli urged the Turks to continue resistance and hinted at possible British aid. Derby told the Porte to cut its losses as no help would be forthcoming. Three days later the cabinet decided to order the fleet to Constantinople. Derby and Carnarvon resigned. Then the decision was withdrawn. Derby and Carnarvon came back. By 27 January the Russians were at the gates of the Ottoman capital. Almost at once an armistice was signed. On 8 February the Royal Navy was once more ordered to Constantinople. War seemed near, especially when Russia imposed on Turkey the pan-Slavist Treaty of San Stefano, unacceptable to London for many reasons (most particularly its provision for an autonomous Bulgaria stretching south of the Balkans to the Aegean). On 27 March the cabinet decided to call up the reserve and move troops from India to the Mediterranean.[101]

Now Carnarvon and Derby (who was near collapse and drinking heavily) resigned for the second and final time. They did so, however, for rather different reasons: Carnarvon was simply anti-Turkish, Derby was by nature a non-interventionist. As their departure was not co-ordinated, it caused Disraeli little trouble and a good deal of relief. A minor reshuffle took place in which Salisbury took over the Foreign Office, where his steady grasp of both detail and strategy soon became apparent. In a circular of 1 April he reasserted British demands concerning San Stefano while simultaneously holding out the prospect of negotiation. Bismarck, embarrassed by the breakdown of the *Dreikaiserbund*, offered himself as an 'honest broker' and a disgruntled Russia was obliged to accept. In late May an Anglo-Russian protocol solved most of the major difficulties. Russia gave way regarding Bulgaria, which was now to be divided into two, the northern part to be an autonomous principality, the southern part (Eastern Rumelia) to remain, with certain safeguards, subject to Turkish rule. In response, Britain agreed to a modest amount of Russian territorial expansion, having itself bullied the Sultan into handing over Cyprus in the optimistic belief that the island would furnish a base from which British power could be exercised in the region as a whole. With Bulgaria divided, Britain and Austria hoped that Russian influence would be reduced. And, indeed, their hopes were realized—but for a quite unexpected reason. Independent Bulgaria quickly fell out with its northern Slav patron and thus—to Western astonishment—turned itself into a bulwark against,

---

[101] K. Bourne, *The Foreign Policy of Victorian England 1830–1902* (Oxford, 1970), 130–2.

rather than a tool of, Russian expansionism, with the result that, a few years later, it was allowed to acquire Eastern Rumelia after all.

Most, though by no means all, of the major points at issue having been resolved, an international congress met at Berlin in June 1878. There was much wrangling and ill-informed poring over large-scale maps. Salisbury noted that 'what with deafness, ignorance of French and Bismarck's extraordinary mode of speech', Disraeli had only 'the dimmest idea' of what was going on. Yet even the super-efficient Salisbury sometimes faltered, as when, pleading for the cause of the Lazes people near Batum on the Black Sea, he suddenly quite forgot the name of 'cette intéressante tribu' as Bismarck sarcastically described them.[102]

Disraeli returned claiming to bring 'peace with honour'. Some thought that he should call an election. But the premature ending of a parliament was widely disliked and he carried on. His triumph was, in any case, largely a product of sleight of hand, Salisbury's restraining presence having paradoxically ensured that, even after March 1878, Derby's extremely cautious approach prevailed. Certainly peace had been made to come about—a considerable achievement in itself—and there was to be no war between major powers for almost as long a period as had followed the Congress of Vienna in 1815. Certainly Russia had been kept out of Constantinople and the south-east Balkans. Certainly, too, the *Dreikaiserbund* now looked unimpressive: Austria and Russia were at loggerheads, each resentful of Germany for not helping them more. But when Disraeli told the Queen that she was now 'the arbiter of Europe' he was romancing.[103] Not only did the Balkan settlement soon disintegrate, but it was not long before the diplomatic fluidity of the previous two decades began to solidify into arrangements in which Britain was to play no part.

Even so, neither the official Liberal leadership nor Gladstone was able to make much of a mark in 1878. The most immediately obvious manifestations of public engagement had shifted from criticism of Turkey to an excited Russophobia. Disaffected Radicals, old-fashioned Liberals, prize eccentrics like Lord Stratheden (chairman of the National Society for the Resistance of Russian Aggression and, it was said, 'the greatest bore in Europe'), even Tichbornites on the lookout for fresh fields, all mounted demonstrations to protest against tsarist expansionism. Soon after Russia had declared war on Turkey Disraeli's secretary had gone 'to feel the pulse of the holiday-makers' at the London Pavilion. 'There was one song, very

---

[102] R. W. Seton-Watson, *Britain in Europe 1789–1914* (Cambridge, 1937), 537–8.
[103] W. N. Medlicott, 'Bismarck and Beaconsfield', in A. O. Sarkissian (ed.), *Studies in Diplomatic History and Historiography* (London, 1961), 250.

badly sung', he reported, 'but tumultuously cheered at the end of each verse'.[104]

> We don't want to fight, but by Jingo if we do
> We've got the ships, we've got the men, and got the money too.
> We've fought the Bear before, and while we're Britons true,
>   The Russians shall not have Constantinople.

Even though The Great Macdermott's Jingo song was profoundly inaccurate—at least as regards the men and the ships—it was soon being howled out at anti-peace rallies in a mood, not merely of belligerence, but of anti-Gladstonianism as well, so much so that police detachments of up to a thousand men had to be mobilized in London alone during February and March.[105] Anti-Russian demonstrations were held all over the country and the windows of Gladstone's house in Harley Street were smashed by a Jingo mob. Respectable Liberal opinion was outraged. To the Radical, George Holyoake, the whole thing looked as if it had been got up by 'the habitués of the turf, the tap-room, and the low music halls, whose inspiration is beer, whose politics is swagger, and whose policy is insult to foreign nations'. Others talked pointedly of meetings attended by 'every gambler on the Stock Exchange, every toady of Baron Rothschild, every Jew Pedlar'.[106] Chamberlain detected 'an underground current of which we know nothing because it exists amongst a class which is not represented on the Liberal Association & which ordinarily takes no part in politics'.[107] But while this was a percipient enough analysis of certain kinds of latent Toryism and of the way in which Britain was sharing in a European swing towards populist conservatism, the moment of excitement soon passed away, sooner even than had the Bulgarian agitation two years before.

In the colonial sphere, disputes arose more out of almost semi-automatic collisions between governments and oppositions than out of any deep-seated ideological distinctions. In 1867–8 the Tories had mounted an Abyssinian expedition and the Liberals had criticized it; in 1873 the Liberals launched a campaign against the Ashanti which many Conservatives found it easy to attack. Between late 1868 and early 1874 there was much talk of Britain being overextended, and Granville at the Colonial Office antagonized white settler administrations by insisting that they bear a greater share of local defence costs. But although a few troops were here and there withdrawn, in most other respects things continued much as before. Once other powers seemed to be showing an interest in, for

---

[104] Swartz, *Politics of British Foreign Policy*, 61.   [105] Ibid. 76, 188.
[106] H. Cunningham, 'Jingoism in 1877–8', *Victorian Studies*, 14 (1971), 429–53.
[107] Marsh, *Joseph Chamberlain*, 123.

example, the Malay peninsula, no strong efforts were made to curb the expansionist tendencies of colonial officials on the spot—a process which continued smoothly when the Conservatives returned to power in 1874. The same happened in the case of Fiji where chronic instability, the presence of other Europeans, attempts by local rulers to seek external alliances, and free-booting British representatives made it more and more difficult to resist annexation. Certainly the view offered by the new Colonial Secretary, Carnarvon, in July 1874 had nothing especially 'Conservative' about it: 'There are English settlers in such numbers, English capital is so largely embarked and English interests are so much involved in the peace of the islands, that it would not be safe to fold our arms and say we would not have anything to do with the islands.'[108]

Contemporary developments in West Africa make the point more clearly still. Throughout the 1860s select committees and individual MPs repeatedly recommended that Britain reduce its commitments in the area. In June 1870 Granville declared his willingness to give the Gambia to France. Yet neither this nor any other abandonment was ever actually implemented, quite the reverse. In 1872 the government acquired, for cash down, a series of Dutch forts along the Gold Coast and in the following year mounted a full-scale war against the Ashanti who were pressing down towards the sea from the north. And just as Carnarvon was to annex Fiji in 1874 without Disraeli knowing much about it, so in August 1873 Kimberley at the Colonial Office and Cardwell at the War Office went ahead with punitive measures in West Africa after only the most exiguous consultations with the cabinet. Gladstone was at first aghast at the financial implications. However, the success of a quick, efficient, and cheap expedition under the dynamic Garnet Wolseley soon overcame his doubts.[109] If imperialism could be advanced by such means, Gladstone was not going to stand in its way.

Disraeli, for his part, displayed no greater or more sustained interest in colonies as such, though he sometimes liked to pretend otherwise. Occasional mutterings by Gladstone about withdrawal did of course make it easy for Disraeli to introduce some ringing phrases into his Crystal Palace speech of 1872 to the effect that there had 'been no effort so continuous, so subtle, supported by so much energy, and carried on with so much ability and acumen, as the attempts of Liberalism to effect the disintegration of the Empire of England'.[110] However, not only were such declara-

---

[108] R. Hyam, *Britain's Imperial Century 1815–1914: A Study of Empire and Expansion* (London, 1976), 340.

[109] W. D. McIntyre, *The Imperial Frontier in the Tropics, 1865–75* (London, 1967), 143, 147; Matthew, *Gladstone 1809–1874*, 190.

[110] Monypenny and Buckle, *Life of Disraeli*, v. 194.

tions undermined by simultaneous endorsements of 'self-government' (code for saving money), but colonial affairs played a very subordinate role in the speech as a whole. In practice, therefore, the new Conservative administration of 1874 stuck to paths already well-trodden by its Liberal predecessor. Garrisons continued to be reduced where possible. In January 1875 Northcote, as Chancellor of the Exchequer, wanted to do away with the force in Hong Kong, in order to save £100,000 a year and demonstrate 'that our Colonies are supports to the Mother Country,—not as some would have it, causes of embarrassment and weakness to her'. In a similar vein Carnarvon sternly warned the first government of Fiji to avoid 'all possible expenditure that is not necessary'.[111] Yet at the same time—and just as with the Liberals—a combination of disdain for foreigners and fear of international competition often pushed ministers in a clean opposite direction. When, for example, Portugal refused to 'sell' Delagoa Bay in southern Africa, Carnarvon thought it curious 'to observe the tenacity with which these wretched little countries cling to their Colonial possessions which they neither can nor try to develop'. And even the low-key Earl of Derby did not in July 1874 'like the notion of letting foreigners come so near us. We shall want New Guinea some day for ourselves.'[112]

What Disraeli did have a liking for was an imperialism of the grand stroke designed to impress politicians and public alike. Harcourt neatly captured this when discussing the Suez Canal share purchase of 1875.

There was something Asiatic in this mysterious melodrama. It was like 'The Thousand and One Nights', when, in the midst of the fumes of incense, a shadowy Genie astonished the bewildered spectators. The public mind was dazzled, fascinated, mystified. We had done we did not know exactly what—we were not told precisely why—*omne ignotum pro magnifico*.[113]

Not that the gestures were always of Disraeli's own making, as when Queen Victoria badgered him into arranging that she be declared Empress of India in 1876. By not consulting the opposition over the matter Disraeli caused a row. Forster privately ranted about not being able to 'have the privilege and honour of being governed by a Jew without paying for it'. Hartington got unusually solid Liberal support for a motion declaring it 'inexpedient to impair the ancient and royal title of Sovereign by the addition of the designation "Empress"'.[114] Even so, the violence of Gladstone's reaction proved too strong for most stomachs. It also drove the Queen's increasingly

---

[111] Swartz, *Politics of British Foreign Policy*, 11.   [112] Ibid. 15, 21.

[113] *The Times*, 31 Dec. 1875, reporting a speech by Harcourt at Oxford. The tag is from Tacitus: 'Everything unknown (is taken to be) magnificent'.

[114] Jackson, *Last of the Whigs*, 72–4; Rossi, 'The Last Whig', 172.

pathological dislike of him and his policies into new and destructive realms of fantasy and rage. Gleefully Disraeli told Derby that only posterity could now 'do justice to that unprincipled maniac ... extraordinary mixture of envy, vindictiveness, hypocrisy, and superstition; and with one commanding characteristic—whether preaching, praying, speechifying, or scribbling—never a gentleman!'[115]

However, in 1879 Disraeli's relaxed approach to running a government eventually forced imperial affairs upon parliamentary and public attention in a manner highly damaging to the Conservatives. The history of southern Africa had long been a complicated one, with Boers, British settlers, black peoples, and the Colonial Office all helping to create problems to which only the most confident could see a solution. The discovery of gold and diamonds in the late 1860s encouraged those who wanted to expand British territory. After unsuccessful efforts to bring about a confederation between the four colonies of the Cape, Natal, Basutoland, and Griqualand West, on the one hand, and the two Boer republics of Transvaal and the Orange Free State, on the other, Carnarvon appointed Sir Bartle Frere (an Indian Civil Servant who knew nothing of Africa) as Governor and High Commissioner in the spring of 1877 and simultaneously annexed the now almost bankrupt Transvaal. The Boers' sense of national identity grew in response. Frere was a born expansionist and read his unclear instructions with the eyes of imperial faith. A strong contemporary resurgence of militancy among the black nations of the region worried the Boers (who had long been encroaching on 'native' land) and persuaded Frere that he could at one stroke mollify the Transvaalers and solidify British power by attacking the powerful kingdom of the Zulus. When in November he was instructed to meet 'the Zulus in a spirit of forbearance and reasonable compromise', he simply ignored this and chose instead to interpret undoubted ambiguities in earlier messages as implying the contrary.[116]

On 11 December 1878 Frere sent an ultimatum to Cetewayo, the great Zulu chief, which he knew would be rejected. On 22 January 1879 a Zulu army, moving with great speed, destroyed a force of about 1,200 defending General Lord Chelmsford's temporary base camp at Isandhlwana. The news of the disaster reached London in mid-February. Few defeats have created so sudden and so violent a shock. To be beaten by French or Russian soldiers was bad enough. To be beaten by black men—at a time when racialism was becoming an ever more prominent aspect of colonial endeavour—was beyond comprehension. The government reacted with

[115] P. Magnus, *Gladstone: A Biography*, 4th impression (London, 1960), 244–5.
[116] Blake, *Disraeli*, 665–9; B. Porter, *The Lion's Share*, 2nd edn. (London, 1984), 94–8.

feeble indecision. It neither recalled Frere nor backed him to the hilt. Between them Disraeli and the new Colonial Secretary, Sir Michael Hicks Beach, persuaded their colleagues that a severe reprimand (bizarrely combined with expressions of confidence) would meet the point. From the Liberal side Harcourt made the appropriate response by reading to the House an imaginary letter: 'My dear Sir Bartle Frere; I cannot think you are right. Indeed, I think you are very wrong; but then, after all, I feel you know a great deal better than I do. I hope you won't do what you are going to do; but if you do, I hope it will turn out well.'[117] Not until July was Cetewayo defeated and captured at the battle of Ulundi, his army destroyed, his kingdom broken up. With the Zulu threat removed, the Boers quickly recovered and in 1881 those of the Transvaal defeated the British at Majuba Hill and regained self-government subject to something vaguely described as British 'suzerainty'.

In political terms the South African débâcle was rendered more damaging still by the almost simultaneous explosion of difficulties in Afghanistan. The relationship between India and its north-western neighbour had long been characterized by tension and controversy. For some years Whitehall had tended to follow those senior officials in India who believed that Afghanistan should be left to its own devices, the policy of 'masterly inactivity' as it became known. However, by the mid-1870s excessive fears of Russian incursion had combined with Disraeli's predilection for oriental intrigue to produce something of a change. When, therefore, in 1876 the Indian Viceroyship fell vacant, Disraeli—admittedly after offering it to three others—appointed the 2nd Lord Lytton, the son of the novelist, Bulwer-Lytton, and himself the author of bad verse under the pseudonym 'Owen Meredith'. This was certainly romantic and at first it seemed as if it might be successful as well. The new Viceroy began cautiously enough, even after he had been given to understand that 'masterly inactivity' had now been firmly struck from the imperial menu. When, however, he did begin to act, he was soon pursuing a more vigorous path than Disraeli could ever have bargained for.

In July 1878 a Russian delegation was received at Kabul by the Amir, Sher Ali, who had previously refused to accept agents proposed to him by the Viceroy. Lytton sent a British mission. It was stopped at the border. An ultimatum was issued and ignored. Three British armies then invaded. Sher Ali died and was succeeded by his son, Yakub Khan, who signed the Treaty of Gandamak on 26 May 1879 ceding control over the passes between India and Afghanistan and accepting British direction of his

---

[117] *Hansard*, ccvl. 84–5 (31 Mar. 1879).

foreign policy and a British minister at Kabul. This was not at all what Disraeli had expected (though his plans had never been clearly stated). Then on 3 September the British minister, Sir Louis Cavagnari, and all his staff were killed by mutinous Afghan soldiers in Kabul. General Roberts conducted another brilliant campaign and entered Kabul in triumph on 13 October. Making the best of an extremely bad job, Disraeli, who wanted no repetition of Harcourt's jibes about his treatment of Frere, gave Lytton effusive public support. In private, however, he was well aware that the government's standing had suffered a further serious blow.[118]

4. ANOTHER LIBERAL TIDE

Before much could be done about the future of Afghanistan the government was defeated at a general election held in April 1880, which had itself been preceded by a notable public campaign in which the twin imperial confusions of 1879 had played a prominent part. Gladstone's failure to enthuse the Liberal Party over Bulgaria had persuaded him that another major push was needed in order to improve the moral tone of political life and his own standing as morality's champion. He had never been happy with his Greenwich constituency. Perhaps something less metropolitan and less stridently Radical would better meet his needs. In due course he became convinced that he should accept an invitation to stand for the Scottish county seat of Midlothian, which had been narrowly won by a Conservative in 1874 and might well prove a more congenial place from which to launch a bid for popular support. It was small and its 3,280 registered electors were unusually select (only 15 per cent of its adult males being enfranchised compared to an average of 55 per cent in boroughs). Midlothian also possessed a substantial aristocratic Liberal interest of the old-fashioned sort led by Lord Rosebery, whose agents would be able to 'organize' Gladstone's return along traditional lines.[119] In other words, the place entirely matched those conservative inclinations out of which Gladstone was so often able to fashion materials of a distinctly unconservative kind.

After a scientific survey had revealed that the Liberals would almost certainly win the seat, Gladstone announced his candidature in January 1879. With relations between himself and Disraeli worsening almost by the day, he was above all determined to smash Beaconsfieldism and to do so by attaching 'the proceedings of 1876–9 by a continuous process to the

[118] T. A. Heathcote, *The Afghan Wars 1839–1919* (London, 1980), 103–41; Blake, *Disraeli*, 662.

[119] Matthew, *Gladstone 1875–1898*, 46–7.

dissolution' of parliament.[120] With such hopes in his mind, in an atmosphere of colonial troubles, and in the middle of a widespread outbreak of political speech-making during the autumn recess he left Liverpool by train for Scotland on 24 November 1879 to begin a fortnight's ceaseless campaigning in Midlothian and the surrounding districts.

Although the use of electoral platforms to put a case to the nation was not new, the delivery of a large number of connected speeches over a short period was distinctly novel. Under the Telegraph Act of 1868 (passed, incidentally, by a Tory administration) news agencies such as the Press Association and the Exchange Telegraph had been encouraged to expand their activities by being charged favourable rates, and it was to their reporters that Gladstone's speeches were now consciously addressed.[121] Yet, however important such innovations undoubtedly were, it was only direct contact with physical audiences which enabled Gladstone to lift the complexities of his language to dazzling—if intermittent—heights of impact, fervour, and excitement. Dramatic settings helped to create an atmosphere which few other leading politicans could generate. 'You can hardly imagine', reported Gladstone's daughter Mary of their entry into Edinburgh, 'the wild beauty and excitement of one of these galloping drives, the lurid light of the torches and bonfires, the brilliant glare of the electric lights and fireworks, the eager faces and waving hands and shouting voices'.[122] Standing as he did outside the cousinship of Whiggery and with little interest in party bureaucracies, Gladstone depended upon words—and increasingly upon words reported in the press—to achieve high political visibility. Whereas Chamberlain sought power through organization, Gladstone sought it through language. For him, therefore, Midlothian represented a counterweight to Chamberlain's caucus system, not a development from it.[123]

Gladstone's message was simple: Beaconsfieldism was rotten in every respect. Preliminary notes made before his arrival in Scotland indicate the all-embracing nature of the attack: 'Indictment agt. the Govt.—abroad—everywhere!'[124] The first Midlothian speech of 25 November set the plan in motion when he told his listeners that 'What we are disputing about is the whole system of Government, and to make good that proposition that it is a whole system of Government will be my great object in any addresses that I

[120] Morley, *Life of Gladstone*, ii. 587.
[121] H. C. G. Matthew, 'Rhetoric and Politics in Great Britain, 1860–1950', in Waller (ed.), *Politics and Social Change*, 43–4.
[122] *Mary Gladstone (Mrs Drew): Her Diaries and Letters*, ed. L. Masterman (London, 1930), 183.
[123] Matthew, *Gladstone 1875–1898*, 50.
[124] Swartz, *Politics of British Foreign Policy*, 114.

may deliver in this country.'[125] Two matters were, however, made to stand out amidst the universal nature of the condemnation, namely, the old Gladstonian favourites of foreign affairs and finance. On 27 November at West Calder six 'right principles of foreign policy' were announced: 'to foster the strength of the Empire by just legislation and economy at home', 'to preserve to the nations of the world...the blessings of peace', to 'maintain...the concert of Europe', to 'avoid needless and entangling engagements', 'to acknowledge the equal rights of all nations', and to ensure that 'the foreign policy of England should always be inspired by the love of freedom'.[126] And just as these points harked back to Bulgaria and beyond that to Alsace-Lorraine, Schleswig-Holstein, and Italy, so the attacks on Conservative finance encapsulated the rage which Gladstone had long felt about Disraeli's behaviour as Chancellor of the Exchequer and as Prime Minister. Reasserting the patrimony of Peel he declared that 'even worse than mismanagement of finance is destruction or disparagement of the sound and healthy rules which the wisdom of a long series of finance Ministers...has gradually and laboriously built up, to prevent abuse ...and to take care that the people shall not be unduly burdened'.[127] Reading the speeches today it is difficult to raise much enthusiasm for the acres of financial detail. Not only, however, were they delivered in an atmosphere of peculiar receptivity, but Gladstone took his customary care to scatter about sufficient colourful phrases to sustain the interest of both his immediate and more general audiences. Appealing to the same emotions that had been aroused over Bulgaria he asked his listeners to 'Remember the rights of the savage, as we call him. Remember that the happiness of his humble home, remember that the sanctity of life in the hill villages of Afghanistan among the winter snows, is as inviolable in the eye of Almighty God as can be your own.'[128]

On one important point Gladstone was strikingly silent. He had virtually no economic (as opposed to fiscal) remedies to offer at a time when distress pressed upon many. In part this was because his chief local supporters had no wish to hear such things: indeed, they had been much impressed by a recent warning delivered by Gladstone to the inmates of a London work-house against 'luxurious living' and the poisonous notion of a labourer being persuaded to think 'he could do better for himself by making himself a charge upon' the community.[129] In part it was because Gladstone's own

---

[125] W. E. Gladstone, *Political Speeches in Scotland, November and December 1879* (London, 1879), 50.

[126] Ibid. 115–17.   [127] Ibid. 147.   [128] Ibid. 94.

[129] D. Brooks, 'Gladstone and Midlothian: The Background to the First Campaign', *Scottish Historical Review*, 64 (1985), 51.

deepest convictions left him with little comfort to offer even the depressed farmers of Midlothian: 'I hope it may *perhaps possibly* be my privilege and honour to assist in procuring for you *some* of those provisions of necessary liberation from restraint; *but* beyond that, it is your own energies, of thought and action, to which you will *have* to trust.'[130]

If Gladstone had little to say about knife-and-fork questions, Disraeli had even less. Economic historians now deny the reality of a homogeneous 'Great Depression' in these years and in this they are correct. But a series of bad harvests had certainly produced severe difficulties and prices overall fell almost consistently for fourteen years after 1873. Unemployment too may well have risen (the statistics are unhelpful). Above all, there can be no doubt that contemporaries thought that a depression was under way. As the party in office the Conservatives inevitably suffered most. A Farmers' Alliance was formed in July 1879 and began to put up candidates at by-elections demanding government assistance and a return to protection. Disraeli made it plain that this was impossible. Like Gladstone he was quite unwilling to mount any kind of rescue operation for those in distress.[131] As he had little else to offer either, it is not surprising that his party was defeated. Even so, it seems to have been less a case of the Conservative vote falling (though it did so in Scotland) than one of the Liberal vote going up.

Although on both sides there was much speech-making, an unenthusiastic and aged Disraeli kept himself aloof. Hartington actually spoke more often than Gladstone, while significant contributions were also made by Bright, W. H. Smith, and Northcote. The final result stood that of 1874 on its head. The Liberals rose from 243 to 351 seats, the Conservatives fell from 352 to 239 (the Irish Home Rulers, though now a more determined band, experienced little numerical change). Especially noteworthy was the Liberal gain of thirty-eight county seats in England and Scotland, not least because both Gladstone and Hartington had deliberately stood for—and won—county constituencies.[132] Disraeli blamed bad times and wished too late that he had gone to the country eighteen months earlier: 'six bad harvests in succession... like Napoleon, I have been beaten by the elements!'[133] The Queen, whose partisanship was becoming intense, wanted anybody but Gladstone. However, on 12 April a trusted intermediary, Lord Wolverton, informed Granville and Hartington of Gladstone's belief that circumstances demanded his own return as Prime Minister. On the same

---

[130] Gladstone, *Political Speeches*, 101. My italics.

[131] Lloyd, *General Election of 1880*, 58–62.

[132] J. Parry, *The Rise and Fall of Liberal Government in Victorian Britain* (New Haven, 1993), 279.

[133] Lord R. Gower, *My Reminiscences*, 2 vols. (London, 1883), ii. 354–5.

day Gladstone told Argyll that the unexpectedly decisive Liberal majority called for 'skilled and strong hands'.[134] On 22 April Hartington was summoned to Windsor. He recommended that Gladstone be sent for. The Queen required him to persevere. Hartington then consulted Gladstone who explained that he would, of course, support a Hartington administration as an independent MP but that 'promises of this kind... stood on slippery ground, and must always be understood with the limits which might be prescribed by conviction'. This, being interpreted, meant that he might well cause trouble if denied the lead. Eventually Granville and Hartington in separate interviews managed to reconcile the Queen. Her private secretary saw them shortly afterwards: 'Granville kissed his hand with a smile like a ballet girl receiving applause. And Hartington threw himself into a chair with "Ha! Ha!" '[135] Only three weeks had gone by since Victoria had declared that she would 'sooner *abdicate* than send for or have anything to do with that *half-mad fire-brand* who would soon ruin everything, and be a *Dictator*'.[136]

Gladstone not only came back on his own terms, but—despite having carefully distanced himself from the party hierarchy—was now actually taking office as a declared 'Liberal' for the first time. (In 1868 he had still called himself a 'Liberal-Conservative', that is, a Peelite.) To Bright he had written even before kissing hands of his sense of destiny.

It is a great and wonderful time. Toryism or Conservatism will rise again from its ashes, but I hope upon different lines, the lines of Party not the lines of Beaconsfield. You and I probably both think we see the hand of God manifest in what has been going on. For my own part, I seem to have had a thousand signs of it, from day to day. I rejoice in it from the bottom of my soul.[137]

During the campaign Disraeli had produced a manifesto in the shape of a letter to the Duke of Marlborough. In it he had tried to steer the debate towards a consideration of Ireland where Home Rule was challenging 'the expediency of the Imperial character of this realm'. Gladstone was unimpressed. His own brand of moral Liberalism would, he thought, prove as inspirational in Ireland as it had been elsewhere. Indeed, the 'true supporters of the Union' were, he believed, those who sought 'to bind the three nations by the indissoluble tie of liberal and equal laws'.[138] In October 1879 the Land League had been established in an agriculturally depressed Ire-

[134] Jenkins, *Gladstone, Whiggery*, 131–2. [135] Ibid. 136–7.
[136] Magnus, *Gladstone*, 270.
[137] Swartz, *Politics of British Foreign Policy*, 118.
[138] F. W. Hirst, 'Mr Gladstone's Second Premiership, 1880–1885', in W. Reid (ed.), *The Life of William Ewart Gladstone* (London, 1889), 636.

land with Charles Stewart Parnell as president. On 17 May 1880 Parnell became leader of the Home Rule Party in the House of Commons. Whatever Gladstone's expectations may or may not have encompassed, the question of Ireland was about to re-enter the British political arena with new and unexpected force and with the most profound implications for his own future career.

CHAPTER 17

Shifts and Realignments 1880–1886

1. LEADERS, PARTIES, POLICIES

What the Liberal administrations of April 1880–June 1885 and February–July 1886 actually did was the reverse of what the Midlothian campaigns had suggested. The handling of foreign and colonial matters proved a sorry disappointment. Gladstone entirely failed to breathe continuing life into the notion of a concert of Europe (designed to prevent international imbalances through co-operation between the powers), and, far from keeping imperialism in check, his governments rendered the world map redder still. By contrast, much was achieved in two areas little touched upon by Liberals during the election of 1880—Ireland and domestic affairs generally—though the failure of Home Rule in 1886 and misleading comparisons with the administration of 1868–74 have tended to disguise the fact. There was, in other words, a particularly severe disjunction between intention and performance in the years between 1880 and 1886.

The same cannot be said with regard to the development of Gladstone's political personality. Here all was continuity—and what was being continued owed more to the recent years of opposition than to those of the previous premiership. Three things stand out: astonishing energy interspersed with occasional hypochondria, increasingly strident condemnations of selfishness on the part of the élite, repeated statements that retirement was nigh. In September 1881 Bright was told that the burdens of office had been assumed only as 'a special and temporary mission', that while much had already been done regarding 'India, the Eastern Question, and perhaps finance', there still remained the Transvaal and, above all, Ireland which had come 'upon us unawares, looming very large'.[1] In truth, Ireland had been looming large for some time, but Gladstone's satisfaction with his own earlier Hibernian reforms had of late rendered it almost as invisible to him

---

[1] T. A. Jenkins, *Gladstone, Whiggery and the Liberal Party 1874–1886* (Oxford, 1988), 230–1.

as it had long been to many of his contemporaries. Soon, however, Ireland became the chief 'speciality' 'obliging' Gladstone to remain in office. He began to see himself as 'chained to the oar',[2] and whenever the chain seemed in danger of rusting—as during the calmer days of 1883 and 1884—he set about buffing the metal so as to render the manacles more conspicuous. In October 1882 he was again telling ministers of his reluctance to 'remain on the stage like a half-exhausted singer'; a month later that, once certain necessary changes in parliamentary procedure had been made, he would certainly retire.[3] Within days, however, this was being postponed to the next Easter, then to the autumn, until in December Gladstone declared himself prepared to 'mortgage another piece of my small residue of life', this time on behalf of franchise reform. In January 1885 the talk was again of going at Easter; by May of waiting until the end of the session; and so it went on.[4]

All of this, while 'genuine' enough, served a variety of useful purposes. Above all, it allowed Gladstone to sustain a general air of uncertainty about the future, which, though it destabilized the business of government, made it difficult for Liberal challengers to mount successful campaigns against him or, indeed, against one another. The truth was that virtually every other leading man in the party needed Gladstone more than the Prime Minister needed any of his lieutenants. The Whigs—still powerful beyond their numbers and still intent, as one of them put it, 'to separate the real deliberate wishes and opinions of the people from the thirst for plunder'[5]— looked for guidance to Hartington (who had led the party in the Commons after Gladstone's withdrawal in 1875) and Hartington pleaded with Gladstone not to retire lest Radicalism be unleashed in his wake. Hartington was loyal, ambitious, fitfully cunning, and wholly unimaginative, but above all desperate to maintain a place near the centre of power for those like himself who he believed had ensured that British reforms had 'been made not by the shock of revolutionary agitation, but by the calm and peaceful process of constitutional acts'.[6] Because of this, Whiggery in the early 1880s was in no sense a secessionist mentality. It still provided a means of advancement

---

[2] Ibid., also Gladstone to Mrs Thistlethwayte, 14 Aug. 1882, *The Gladstone Diaries*, ed. H. C. G. Matthew and M. R. D. Foot, 14 vols. (Oxford, 1968–94), x, p. xxviii.

[3] J. L. Hammond, *Gladstone and the Irish Nation* (London, 1938), 327–8; *The Political Correspondence of Mr Gladstone and Lord Granville 1876–1886*, ed. A. Ramm, 2 vols. (Oxford, 1962), i. 451, 458.

[4] Jenkins, *Gladstone, Whiggery*, 231–2; H. C. G. Matthew, *Gladstone 1875–1898* (Oxford, 1995), 102–5.

[5] Earl Cowper, 'What is a Moderate Liberal to Do?', *Nineteenth Century*, 18 (1885), 358.

[6] B. Holland, *The Life of Spencer Compton, Eighth Duke of Devonshire*, 2 vols. (London, 1911), i. 406; Jenkins, *Gladstone, Whiggery*, 183–9.

for ambitious politicians and its adherents were even, for example, prepared to accept quite substantial Irish reforms so long as these could be portrayed in exclusively Irish terms. They also tended to exaggerate the strength of Radicalism at Westminster. Radical numbers in parliament may at times have seemed impressive—amounting to possibly about a hundred or so of the 338 Liberals returned for non-Irish seats in 1880, though estimates differ widely—but there was little sense of unity or overall coherence. There were old Radicals like Bright, new 'moral' Radicals like Morley, new hard-nosed Radicals like Chamberlain, cynical Radicals like Labouchere who thought his colleagues 'a contemptible set of weak humbugs',[7] the list could be extended almost indefinitely. As a result, most Radicals (like most Whigs) wanted Gladstone to remain in place as the least unacceptable ringmaster currently available.

What kept Gladstone in a fit state to master the situation he faced was a combination of enormous energy and indomitable will. He had celebrated his seventieth birthday in December 1879 but his actions belied the repeated predictions of departure. Until the end of 1882 he was Chancellor of the Exchequer as well as Prime Minister. As Leader of the House of Commons he arranged its business and attended with remarkable regularity. As the main force behind much, especially Irish, legislation he carried an extraordinary burden, which, by its very size, 'overpersonalized the government, held back able men, and encouraged attention to the particular rather than the general'.[8] Yet, despite complaints and sharp stress-related illnesses, it did not break him. In January, February, and March 1881 he steered the Irish Coercion Bill through a turbulent House. Then he introduced a budget. Then he immediately launched the complicated and controversial Irish Land Bill and guided it through no less than fifty-eight difficult sittings. Again, in July 1882—the month of the Egyptian crisis— he spent 148 hours on the Treasury bench, often until early into the morning. His continuing sense of drive came in part of course from innate character, but increasingly it flowed also from Gladstone's growing commitment to a very personal brand of 'progressive' politics. This had nothing to do with what might broadly be called social issues, on which he remained very cautious. Rather, it concerned his vision of political morality and the location of that essential quality among the masses rather than the 'classes'. On some issues, therefore, the Prime Minister, who never shared the sense

[7] M. Barker, *Gladstone and Radicalism: The Reconstruction of the Liberal Party 1885–1894* (Hassocks, 1975), 6.

[8] Matthew, *Gladstone 1875–1898*, 163. Because both the Foreign and Colonial Secretaries were in the Lords, much of their business in the Commons also fell on Gladstone's shoulders.

of pessimism beginning to attract many leading figures of the day, could find himself the most radical man in his own cabinet.

All this was combined with undiminished fiscal rectitude, with deeply deferential behaviour towards the Queen (whose biased, though not always ill-informed, interventions Gladstone endured with the fortitude of a saint), and with a lingering nostalgia for the practices of former days. It also, rather surprisingly, coincided with a period of comparative reticence out of doors. After the great Midlothian campaigns, the burdens of office inevitably reduced public speechifying. Yet the degree of reticence was remarkable all the same. A huge demonstration at Leeds in October 1881 was Gladstone's only direct meeting with the electorate until August 1884. The resulting vacuum was, however, to some extent filled by the popular cult which had begun to turn what had formerly been one politician among many into '*Mr* Gladstone', the 'Grand Old Man'. Inexpensive biographies began to appear, as did an impressively varied iconography: statuettes, plates, jugs, mugs, embroideries, engravings, and even chamber pots for the Tory country house market. Large organized groups of visitors (up to 1,400 strong) 'called' at his Flintshire residence at Hawarden, watched the Prime Minister fell a tree, presented silver axes, and were then treated—for Gladstone was ever the dedicated old trouper—to a few impromptu words. Indeed, in 1884 Lord Randolph Churchill mocked Gladstone as 'the greatest living master of the art of personal political advertisement...Every afternoon the whole world is invited to assist at the crashing fall of some beech or elm or oak. The forest laments in order that Mr Gladstone may perspire.'[9]

The defeated Conservatives naturally faced greater problems. Many feared that the victory of 1874 had been a fluke after all. Disraeli continued to lead from the Lords, and not without spirit. But he remained ambiguous about who should succeed him. On his death in April 1881 the party followed the feeble example the Liberals had set in 1875 by dividing the lead between Sir Stafford Northcote in the Commons and the Marquess of Salisbury in the Lords. Salisbury—by no means an automatic or widely acclaimed choice—was that unusual species of Tory, an intellectual. But his lineage, demeanour, and respectably bearded looks rendered this less disagreeable in party circles than it might otherwise have been. Although cleverness set him apart from his followers, he fully shared their fears about the rise of democracy. Intent on preserving the privileges of property, education, and established religion, he was deeply pessimistic about being

[9] D. A. Hamer, 'Gladstone: The Making of a Political Myth', *Victorian Studies*, 22 (1978), 29–50.

able to do more than postpone their inevitable collapse. Yet, as a true class warrior, he consistently operated upon the assumption that what others called 'the people' simply did not exist as 'an acting, deciding, accessible authority'.[10]

After Disraeli's death things at first went badly for the Conservatives. Salisbury fluffed his chances in the Lords. His lead on crucial matters like the Irish Land Bill of 1881 and the Arrears Bill of 1882 was unimpressive. When he was firm his followers wanted compromise; when he was flexible they demanded unyielding resistance. By the autumn of 1883 prominent Tories like the Duke of Richmond and Earl Cairns were ignoring his advice. A small council of peers even met to 'consider' the leadership.[11] In the Commons Northcote faced greater difficulties still, especially in dealing with a Prime Minister whose private secretary he himself had once been. His moderation depressed back-benchers who could, as one said, see nothing but 'the hands of perplexity travelling up and down the sleeves of irresolution'.[12] 'One can never dine in Tory company', noted a Liberal observer, 'without hearing Sir S. Northcote slighted ... [yet] they admit he is indispensable to them.'[13] While Northcote wanted to work for a major Whig secession from the government by holding to the centre ground, Salisbury (who knew the Whigs disliked him) favoured a more combative style. At first neither approach showed much promise. Few doubted the sensible expediency of Northcote's line, but many doubted its chances of speedy success and suspected that Northcote himself was a kind of closet Peelite. For a time the Tories wanted the Whigs more than the latter wanted to leave the Liberal Party, and Salisbury had good reason to suspect that, even in the event of a Liberal split, the beneficiaries would prove to be almost anyone—Hartington, Northcote, Churchill—rather than himself. Already, indeed, by November 1882 a Tory MP had written him off as 'the coming man' who had simply failed 'to come'.[14]

Gradually such perceptions began to change. Northcote remained sensibly dull. But Salisbury's reputation increased as foreign and imperial affairs (by now his established specialities) became more prominent, as his brilliant handling of franchise reform in 1884–5 highlighted North-

[10] [Lord Salisbury], 'Disintegration', *Quarterly Review*, 156 (1883), 571.

[11] P. Marsh, *The Discipline of Popular Government: Lord Salisbury's Domestic Statecraft, 1881–1902* (Hassocks, 1978), 29–30.

[12] A. Jones, *The Politics of Reform 1884* (Cambridge, 1972), 68.

[13] *The Diary of Sir Edward Walter Hamilton 1880–1885*, ed. D. W. R. Bahlman, 2 vols. (Oxford, 1972), ii. 590 (7 Apr. 1884).

[14] J. France, 'Salisbury and the Unionist Alliance', in Lord Blake and H. Cecil (eds.), *Salisbury: The Man and his Politics* (London, 1987), 221.

cote's lack of flair, and as Ireland eventually enabled him to clothe unexceptional Tory policies in language more trenchant than the party had recently been accustomed to hear. Even as regards party organization and the general nature of Tory support in the country at large, Salisbury was able to turn things to his advantage. A long struggle for control of the National Union of Conservative Associations was eventually resolved in his favour. This was important, not because the National Union mattered a great deal, but because various leading men had decided to use it as a battleground for power and influence. The most pugnacious was Churchill who eventually in 1884 joined the Salisbury camp. All of this put Salisbury in an excellent position to benefit from certain significant and connected developments regarding Conservatism generally. As early as June 1882 he had himself noted the growth of 'a great deal of Villa Toryism which requires organization'.[15] And although not exactly keen on mingling with humbler supporters, he differed from his predecessors in a willingness to undertake provincial speaking trips and to appear at numerous (and doubtless boring) urban functions of a political kind.[16] Salisbury thus played an important role in that long (and by no means problem-free) process by which Victorian Conservatism was transformed from the political arm of the landed interest into something like a party of property in general. Important too was the foundation in 1883 of the most successfully deferential Tory organization that has ever existed (an extreme claim to be sure), the Primrose League, named after what is said to have been Disraeli's favourite flower. This soon had an enormous membership—perhaps as large as a quarter of a million by 1886 and much bigger thereafter—completely overshadowing all other British political organizations at the time (though Ireland of course was another matter).[17] Its 'medieval' hierarchy of ranks (knights companions, knights almoners, dames, vavasours, even Primrose buds) appealed to middle-class Tories in town and country alike. It also mobilized women far more successfully than 'progressive' organizations were able to do. Though it counted for nothing in the battle for the leadership, it stood ready to deliver support to whoever would eventually succeed in climbing unaccompanied to the top of the greasy pole. And by early 1885 it was clear that this was likely to be Salisbury.

[15] J. Cornford, 'The Transformation of Conservatism in the Late Nineteenth Century', *Victorian Studies*, 7 (1963), 52.

[16] E. H. H. Green, *The Crisis of Conservatism: The Politics, Economics and Ideology of the British Conservative Party, 1880–1914* (London, 1995), 105.

[17] M. Pugh, *The Tories and the People 1868–1935* (Oxford, 1985), 27; Green, *Crisis of Conservatism*, 117, 125–7.

These struggles for supremacy took place within a complicated and disorderly parliamentary world. In particular, the obstructive tactics adopted by some Home Rule members in the 1870s were being pursued with increased vigour. Matters reached a crisis in the famous forty-one-and-a-half-hour sitting of 31 January to 2 February 1881 on the Coercion Bill. Eventually the Speaker consulted Gladstone and unprecedentedly brought the debate to an end, though thirty-six Irish MPs were suspended in the process. In the autumn of 1882 formal procedures were drawn up to prevent filibustering. These included the principles of the *clôture* and the *guillotine*, which, though never actually enforced during Gladstone's second ministry, thereafter had the effect of taking more and more power away from back-benchers and delivering it to the executive.[18]

Speaker Brand's firmness with respect to the Home Rulers may well have been designed to compensate for his feeble handling of rows concerning the attempts by Charles Bradlaugh, Liberal MP for Northampton, to take his seat. Bradlaugh represented a combination of beliefs which, though eminently Victorian in some respects, was not much canvassed in polite society. Though his election address had been positively Gladstonian in its denunciation of 'our present seriously extravagant National Expenditure', though he strongly disapproved of remarriage after divorce and exuded an air of utmost respectability, he was an atheist, a republican, and an advocate of birth control.[19] He also wanted to affirm rather than swear the oath before taking his seat, a practice already admitted in courts of law. Brand foolishly submitted the matter to the House, upon which Bradlaugh, a very reluctant hero, decided he would take the oath after all, but then torpedoed any chance of success this might produce by writing to *The Times* to say that oaths meant nothing to him. Between 1880 and 1886 he repeatedly tried to take his seat and occasionally even managed to do so for short periods. Just as repeatedly, he was ejected, only to be sent back to Westminster by the voters of Northampton. Two select committees deliberated to no effect. In 1883 an Affirmation Bill was defeated after a brilliant speech from Gladstone in its favour. Bradlaugh was even briefly imprisoned. The whole affair was agony to the Liberal Party. The government could not rely on its regular majority. Members were deeply split, Gladstone nobly, if ineffectually, fought on behalf of a man whose opinions he deplored. At last in 1886 a new Speaker (A. W. Peel) simply allowed Bradlaugh to take the oath after all—and in 1888 affirmation itself was made lawful.

[18] Matthew, *Gladstone 1875–1898*, 171–3.
[19] W. L. Arnstein, *The Bradlaugh Case: A Study in Late Victorian Opinion and Politics* (Oxford, 1965), 30 (and generally).

If the Liberals were divided on the Bradlaugh affair, Gladstone remained a commanding figure throughout. Not so Northcote, whose lack of decisiveness was cruelly exposed. Because almost all Conservatives despised Bradlaugh, Northcote's 'responsible' approach proved neither successful nor popular. The most strident discontent came from a handful who soon became known as the 'Fourth Party' (fourth, that is, after the Conservatives, Liberals, and Home Rulers). Their number never rose above three and a half: Lord Randolph Churchill, John Gorst (the disillusioned organization expert), Sir Henry Drummond Wolff (an amusing minor diplomat), with the fraction supplied by Salisbury's nephew, A. J. Balfour, who was never more than a semi-detached adherent but whose connections were useful and whose languid manner disguised a fitfully firm resolve (as the Irish discovered when he became Chief Secretary in 1887). The Bradlaugh case attracted first Wolff's and then Churchill's attention and in effect called the new 'party' into being. Churchill, the third son of the Duke of Marlborough, was certainly the sharpest, ablest, and loudest of the inner trio. His contributions to the Bradlaugh debate displayed all the characteristics he was soon to make peculiarly his own: an ability to breath new life into old prejudices, quickness in controversy, ambition, and, above all, kaleidoscopic opportunism. Intervening vigorously over a wide range of topics, the contents of his speeches mattered less to him than the sheer business of political activity. Ireland provided especially frequent opportunities for bravura displays—now strongly Unionist, now in concert with the Home Rulers, now in opposition to them. Throughout, Churchill depicted himself as the chief proponent of 'Tory Democracy' and in doing so turned what had been a chimerical notion under Disraeli into a fraudulent one.

The Fourth Party's platform was entirely guided by tactical imperatives. In private, Churchill, who loved to shock, described it as 'chiefly opportunism'.[20] His most notable *démarche* began in the spring of 1883 ostensibly as a critique of the Tories' inadequate organization and of Northcote's unworthiness to wear 'Elijah's [that is, Disraeli's] mantle'. Although Gorst knew a good deal about organization and masterminded efforts to win control of the National Union as a counterweight against the 'old Gang's' control of the Central Committee, Churchill knew little and cared less. This made it as easy for him to generate a party crisis as—quite suddenly— to bring the crisis to an end by means of an agreement with Salisbury in July 1884. Gorst was effectively ditched. Churchill joined the highest ranks of Tory leaders. And Salisbury gained an ally now bound to him by explicit rather than merely implicit bonds.

[20] R. F. Foster, *Lord Randolph Churchill: A Political Life* (Oxford, 1981), 107.

There was little in this to disturb the government. Indeed, a general lack of Conservative bite helped ministers (contrary to much received opinion) to pass some considerable domestic legislation. Of course the chief motive behind Gladstone's return to office had been the destruction of Disraeli's legacy with respect to foreign and imperial matters, a task, he believed, fit only 'for skilled and strong hands'.[21] But while such priorities clearly shaped the attitudes of the cabinet in general and of Gladstone in particular, the ministry's successes lay more obviously at home than abroad—and this even though many of the bills passed in 1880–5 ran far less with the grain of contemporary Liberalism than had been the case in 1868–74.

The cabinet itself was something of a retread: ten of the initial fourteen were old hands. Hartington, as the leading Whig in the Commons, was given the appropriately important posts of Secretary for India (1880–2) and Secretary for War (1882–5). The Radicals did less well. In 1880 only Chamberlain of the 'new men' was admitted (as President of the Board of Trade), with Dilke not coming in until five months after Bright had left in 1882. And just as a general sense of pragmatism ensured that no single sectarian tendency dominated, so the Prime Minister's talk of retirement helped to create a kind of amicable desultoriness and a reluctance to reach painful decisions. The Whigs, though still capable of sporadic resolution, had exchanged the 'intellectual daring and political initiative of the Russell era' for the 'grey conventionality of Hartington: moderately competent, politically respectable, but sterile'.[22] At the other end of the spectrum, Bright had long been a very exhausted volcano indeed, Chamberlain created so much distrust in Gladstone's mind that his presence was more an irritant than anything else, while the gifted Dilke was to be driven from high politics by a famous divorce scandal in 1885–6.

Such things may have deprived the ministry's legislative record of coherence; they did not, however—especially to begin with—deprive it of either significance or practical success. In an attempt to splinter the Tory alliance between English landlords and their tenants, a series of modestly useful measures was offered to the farming community. In 1880 the malt tax was finally removed. The Ground Game Act of the same year gave occupiers certain concurrent rights with landowners to kill rabbits and hares, while the Agricultural Holdings Act of 1883 prevented proprietors from contracting out of an earlier act of 1875 with respect to compensation due to tenants for unexhausted improvements. And as if to match the warning shots fired at landowners, the Employers' Liability Act of 1880,

---

[21] J. Morley, *The Life of William Ewart Gladstone*, 3 vols. (London, 1903), ii. 615.
[22] Matthew, *Gladstone 1875–1898*, 106.

by making it slightly easier for workers to sue employers, signalled at least a minor interference with freedom of contract. Indeed, taken together with Irish land legislation and technical acts dealing with bankruptcy and patent law, such measures gave the ministry a surprisingly collectivist—or, to use a contemporary term, 'constructionist'—air.

Especially striking was the Corrupt Practices Act of 1883, not only the first really effective attempt to regulate the wilder excesses of nineteenth-century electioneering, but an unambiguous interference with what many still regarded as virtually a 'free trade' in votes. Unlike its feeble predecessor of 1854, it combined good intentions with sound drafting, limiting the amounts candidates could spend, making it easier to punish those who indulged in bribery, and effectively shifting the task of canvassing from the shoulders of paid (often overpaid) agents to those of volunteers. Corruption may have dribbled on for a while, but 1883 marks an altogether more dramatic watershed in the culture of Victorian elections than the Secret Ballot Act of 1872.[23] Also of considerable practical as well as symbolic significance were the Burials Act of 1880 (a concession to Dissenters), the final abolition of flogging in the army in 1881, and the Married Women's Property Act of 1882. The last of these not only placed wives upon a complete equality with unmarried women as regards earnings and property, but constituted—rather like the Irish Land Act of 1881—a case of unsatisfactory lawmaking from Gladstone's first administration having to be revised and extended in his second.

Though more successful than is often allowed, the 1880–5 ministry's legislative activities did not lack blunders. A disgruntled Chamberlain was forced to withdraw his Merchant Shipping Bill in July 1884 after heavy opposition from shipowners and a lack of enthusiasm on the part of cabinet colleagues.[24] More striking still was the complete failure to implement that widespread decentralization which Gladstone repeatedly declared both timely and important. Local government bills for Ireland, the English counties, and London were promised at the beginning of each session, but only the last was ever submitted to parliament and it too was soon abandoned. Particularly damaging was the government's failure to milk political benefits from those major enactments that were eventually passed into law. The 1881 Irish Land Act, the 1883 Corrupt Practices Act, and the 1884–5 franchise reforms were all large-scale measures of the greatest

[23] K. T. Hoppen, 'Roads to Democracy: Electioneering and Corruption in Nineteenth-Century England and Ireland', *History*, 81 (1996), 553–71; C. O'Leary, *The Elimination of Corrupt Practices in British Elections 1868–1911* (Oxford, 1962), 159–208.

[24] R. Jay, *Joseph Chamberlain: A Political Study* (Oxford, 1981), 89; P. T. Marsh, *Joseph Chamberlain: Entrepreneur in Politics* (New Haven, 1994), 171–3.

importance. Yet they elicited comparatively few Liberal huzzas. On Ireland the going had become distinctly harder since 1869–70, while abolishing corrupt practices made existing MPs—the beneficiaries of traditional electioneering—feel more anxious than virtuous, and franchise reform worried the Whigs more than it pleased the Radicals. Small wonder, then, that almost all the cabinet (with the notable exception of the Prime Minister) felt exhausted when the government was finally defeated in 1885 on an amendment to the budget. 'Cabinet at noon', noted Rosebery on 9 June, 'All in high spirits except Mr G. who was depressed.'[25] Unlike his colleagues, who behaved as if the school holidays were about to start, Gladstone had come to see the events of the previous five years in terms of destiny and high drama, as—in a phrase Disraeli might have envied—nothing less than 'a wild romance of politics with a continual succession of hairbreadth escapes and strange accidents pressing upon one another'.[26]

In other respects, too, the ministry found it difficult to gain the bonuses which some at least of its achievements might reasonably have elicited. This was especially true of that old Gladstonian favourite, finance. Sermons demanding fiscal rectitude had constituted a staple part of the Midlothian diet. Gladstone, gleeful in May 1880 that 'We have not a sixpence to give away',[27] even held office as Chancellor as well as Prime Minister until December 1882 when the burden became too great and Childers took over. But despite all the talk of modest and balanced budgets an impression of profligacy was created by the ceaseless voting of additional funds to meet the cost of foreign entanglements. In 1882 the Egyptian crisis forced the government to introduce a vote of credit for £2.3m and to increase the income tax from 5d. to 6½d. over the financial year as a whole. In December 1884 a newspaper campaign about the dangers posed by a *rapprochement* between France and Germany led to a vote of £5.5m for naval expenditure. Most dramatic of all was the announcement in April 1885 that an additional £11m would be required to meet new difficulties in Afghanistan and the Sudan. Such increases dented Gladstone's claims to prudence. And the fact that income tax levels now actually reached greater heights than under the despised Disraeli made matters worse: an average of 5.7d. for the five financial years ending April 1885, as compared to 3.3d. for the six years ending April 1880.[28] Nor did Gladstone help by constantly and publicly bemoaning the absolute growth of estimated budget expenditure—from £73m in 1873 to almost £85m in 1881 (despite a fall in prices) and then to

[25] Jenkins, *Gladstone, Whiggery*, 241.

[26] *Gladstone to his Wife*, ed. A. Tilney Bassett (London, 1936), 246.

[27] *Political Correspondence of Gladstone and Granville 1876–1886*, ed. Ramm, i. 124.

[28] B. R. Mitchell, *British Historical Statistics* (Cambridge, 1988), 645.

£100m in 1885. What, however, neither he nor anyone else at the time realized was that central government spending remained—for what was still the only world power—remarkably low in relation to the economy as a whole, the proportion it bore to Gross National Product being exactly the same in 1885 as it had been twenty years before, namely, 7.9 per cent.[29]

Despite his fiscal sophistication, Gladstone clearly saw it as no part of a government's duty to 'take a view' of the economy as a whole. Detailed information was collected on the performance of the Egyptian economy, but the cabinet had none on that of Britain 'save the odd comment on the buoyancy or otherwise of indirect taxes'.[30] Although Ireland constituted something of an exception to such minimalism, the phenomenon known as the 'Great Depression' did not. Just as Gladstone had told Midlothian farmers in 1879 that they must look to themselves for help in difficult times, so he believed the same to be true for all citizens. Indeed, when the Salisbury administration in 1885 bowed to public demands and set up a royal commission on depression in trade and industry the Gladstonians adamantly refused to have anything to do with it. Although relative agricultural decline and the increasingly (sub)urban nature of Conservative support made it unlikely that Britain would soon follow the continent's return to protectionism, it suited Gladstone to exaggerate the extent to which free trade was under attack in order to unite the disparate forces which acknowledged his lead.

Not that he had much to fear from the legions of the 'left'. Craft unions had expanded steadily throughout the late 1870s and into the 1880s, but unions recruiting less skilled workers fell back once the boom of the early 1870s came to an end. By 1888 there were about 750,000 union members (a tenth or so of all adult male manual workers) as opposed to perhaps a million in 1874.[31] But while unions continued to be fierce in industrial disputes, they were relatively gentle in the political sense. Indeed, the 'Address to the Workmen of the United Kingdom' produced by the Parliamentary Committee of the TUC in 1885 made Chamberlain's highly circumscribed Radicalism seem strong by comparison.

In so far as the more doctrinaire forms of progressivism in the 1880s deserve attention at all they do so less for their impact upon events than for their future potential and colourful variety. The handful of individuals who fought the good fight represented an enormous range of beliefs and canvassed an enormous range of remedies. A few (a very few) had read Marx,

[29] Matthew, *Gladstone 1875–1898*, 166.   [30] Ibid. 163.
[31] H. A. Clegg, A. Fox, and A. F. Thompson, *A History of British Trade Unions since 1889*, 3 vols. (Oxford 1964–94), i. 1–3.

who died in 1883 with his major book still not translated into English. Rather more were influenced by the American Radical, Henry George, whose *Progress and Poverty* appeared in an English edition in 1881, the year in which he came to preach its message in the United Kingdom. But George's programme was confined to a modified form of land nationalization and had limited revolutionary appeal. Such formal organizations as existed enjoyed similarly restricted support, not least among manual workers. Federations, leagues, and societies split from one another in the fashion of small religious sects. In 1881 H. M. Hyndman, a product of Eton and Trinity College Cambridge, established the Democratic Federation. Soon he adopted a socialist position (though a highly individual one combining certain Marxian concepts with more populist strands of native radicalism) and changed its name to the Social Democratic Federation. Hyndman's fiercest and most consistent assumption was a hatred of liberalism in general and the Liberal Party in particular. Indeed, he had at one time been a Tory (of sorts) and was prepared to accept Tory subsidies to run a couple of candidates at Hampstead and Kennington during the general election of 1885 when they jointly attracted fifty-nine votes (though John Burns did better with 598 in Nottingham). Already in the previous year one of his most enthusiastic followers, the artist, poet, and craftsman, William Morris (who rejected Hyndman's state socialism), had broken away and founded the short-lived—and even smaller—Socialist League. After news of Hyndman's acceptance of 'Tory gold' leaked out another exodus produced the Socialist Union. Only the Fabian Society founded in 1884 possessed much staying power and it soon became more concerned with the empirical study of social problems than with raising the consciousness of working people as such.

In terms of numbers, socialism in the mid-1880s was a modest affair: many leaders and a tiny stage army of followers. The best estimates suggest that the total membership of all known bodies came to some 3,000—and this at a time when the Primrose League had a quarter of a million adherents and was growing by the week.[32] No wonder the Russian anarchist, Kropotkin, finding himself lecturing to 'ridiculously small audiences' in England in 1881, concluded that 'for one who held advanced socialist opinions, there was no atmosphere to breathe in'.[33] Yet despite such meagre realities, some members of the establishment believed that red sedition presented a serious threat. The widespread belief that a depression

[32] H. Pelling, *The Origins of the Labour Party 1880–1900*, 2nd edn. (Oxford, 1965), 229; Pugh, *Tories and the People*, 27.
[33] P. Kropotkin, *Memoirs of a Revolutionist* (New York, 1899), 440–1.

was under way had certainly brought about a serious decline in business confidence, indeed in confidence generally. Signs of disorder like the violent London demonstrations of February 1886 and November 1887, the unrest in Ireland, and Fenian bombings in England touched nerves which had lost their mid-century calm. Prosecutions in 1881 and 1882 of those associated with an anarchist German-language paper called *Freiheit* for rejoicing at the assassination of Tsar Alexander II broke a tradition of non-interference with political refugees. A system of regular secret surveillance of foreign revolutionaries was begun and the various developments in undercover police activity which had marked the late 1870s were greatly expanded. A metropolitan Criminal Investigation Department (CID) had been set up in 1878 with some 240 men. Three years later the first tentative moves were undertaken to establish what became known in 1887 as the Special Branch, a body modelled, in large part, on Irish police procedures and using senior personnel trained in Ireland (which had long possessed a national and quasi-military force).[34] Not only did all this mark a distinct shift in tone as regards the maintenance of law and order, it also stood quite contrary to Gladstone's notion of the minimal state.

More characteristic of the Prime Minister's increasing tendency to wrap radical measures in soothing traditional detail were the major franchise reforms introduced in 1884–5. In retrospect these seem to fit neatly into that lengthy process by which the ruling élite jerkily doled out highly circumscribed increments of electoral democracy. However, at the time they were regarded as striking, dramatic, perhaps even revolutionary. What they certainly were not was any kind of response to pressure from without—for there was no pressure to speak of when, in 1880, Gladstone first promised to extend the electorate. Though the Whigs were suspicious throughout, in December 1883 Hartington showed a keen grasp of realities when he engineered a crisis designed, first, to keep Gladstone in place, secondly, to block the Radicals, and, finally, to accelerate redistribution so as to prevent the calling of an election on a new franchise but in unchanged constituencies—a conjunction widely considered unfavourable to the Whigs (and indeed to the Conservatives as well).[35] Hartington also tried to ensure that Ireland (where Home Rule was in the ascendant) would be treated separately. Here he did not, however, succeed, for a single Representation of the People Bill was introduced in February 1884 to deal with the

[34] B. Porter, 'The *Freiheit* Prosecutions, 1881–1882', *Historical Journal*, 23 (1980), 833–56; id., *The Origins of the Vigilant State: The London Metropolitan Police Special Branch before the First World War* (London, 1987), 19–67.

[35] Jenkins, *Gladstone, Whiggery*, 184–8; P. Jackson, *The Last of the Whigs: A Political Biography of Lord Hartington* (Cranbury, NJ, 1994), 162–6.

United Kingdom as a whole, the first time this had been done. Though the bill included many complicated proposals touching voters' qualifications, essentially it created a uniform householder and lodger franchise based on that introduced for the English boroughs in 1867. An amendment to extend the vote to women attracted a respectable degree of support, though it was still defeated by 271 votes to 135.

The bill passed the Commons but was at first rejected by the Lords where the Conservatives (and Whigs) declared they would proceed only if acceptable redistribution proposals were put forward by the government. Chamberlain now mounted a 'Peers versus People' campaign. Demonstrations were held in various parts of the country: that at Hyde Park on 21 July attracted 100,000 and was watched (and perhaps even slightly legitimized) by the Prince and Princess of Wales. But the business lacked fire. Though Gladstone himself indulged in some outdoor activity (largely neglected since 1880) sustained interest was inconsiderable.[36] Eventually an agreement was reached that inter-party discussions be held to resolve the impasse. These took place in November 1884 between Gladstone, Hartington, and Dilke, on the one side, and Salisbury and Northcote, on the other. From the start, Hartington and Northcote found it difficult to keep up with the others who indulged in enjoyable quicksilver debate whilst sitting amidst a disorder of constituency maps on floor and furniture. Gladstone's cruel picture reflected a wider truth about the Conservative leadership: 'Lord Salisbury took the whole matter out of the hands of Northcote, who sat by him on the sofa like a chicken protected by the wings of the mother hen.'[37]

Salisbury adopted a remarkably drastic line over redistribution. Although he had come to accept that the outright opposition to reform he had presented in 1867 was no longer feasible, there is little evidence to suggest that his approach in November 1884 was part of any coherent strategy. The subject was complicated and Salisbury's ultimate success owed more to luck than planning. As finally agreed, the Redistribution Act engineered the most extensive reform of the constituencies since 1832. Previously most had returned two or more members; now all but a handful were to return only one. This benefited the Conservatives, for, by disaggregating large city-wide constituencies into smaller units (many of them suburban in character), the act allowed the middle classes to translate their increasingly Tory votes into additional Tory seats.[38] The over-representation of the South-East was reduced, and the under-representation of London re-

---

[36] Jones, *Politics of Reform*, 162–5; W. A. Hayes, *The Background and Passage of the Third Reform Act* (New York, 1982), 186–8.

[37] Jones, *Politics of Reform*, 82.

[38] Hayes, *Third Reform Act*, 282–3. See above, Ch. 8, s. 3.

medied. Traditional differences between town and country became blurred, though to whose advantage was at first unclear. Indeed, it is difficult to know who 'won'. Certainly many Tories at first believed they had 'lost'. Perhaps it is fairest to conclude that there were gains for almost everyone—except the Whigs who had wanted fewer seats for Ireland, the preservation of small boroughs, and the maintenance of two-member constituencies. Gladstone, as was not infrequently the case, had begun by sharing the Whigs' traditional pieties.[39] As he did not, however, press his views very hard, in the end only the preservation of a few two-member constituencies in medium-sized towns survived as a relic of his emotional, but largely ineffective, electoral antiquarianism.

Of course many men—and all women—were still denied the parliamentary vote. Few leading politicians had ever wanted anything else. But a mighty step had been taken none the less, all the mightier when combined with the reforms introduced by the Corrupt Practices Act of 1883. Between 1861 and 1871 the proportion of adult males entitled to vote in the United Kingdom had grown (largely because of the legislation of 1867–8) from 16.7 to 30.3 per cent. By 1891 it had risen to 61.0 per cent.[40] In Britain agricultural labourers, smallholders, and some others obtained the vote. In Ireland even many medium-sized farmers were now admitted to the register for the first time. The absolute numbers involved were larger than ever before. Between 1861 and 1871 the United Kingdom electorate had risen from about 1.31 million to 2.53 million. Immediately after the legislation of 1884 it stood at 5.68 million.[41] Disraeli is rightly given much credit for the reforms of 1867–8. Yet Gladstone's achievement in 1884–5, although less obviously dynamic in the strictly party sense, was no less significant—both as electoral engineering and political choreography.

For his part, Chamberlain found Gladstone's success in introducing reforms of various kinds almost as aggravating as his own failure in that department. Because his immediate following in the Commons never amounted to more than twenty-five or so members, his primary strategy was aimed not at filling the cabinet with other 'Radicals' (most of whom he dismissed as 'crotchet-mongers' or 'windbags'), but at concentrating the representation of Radicalism at the higher levels in his own hands.[42] In

---

[39] *Hansard*, ccxciv. 373 (1 Dec. 1884).

[40] K. T. Hoppen, 'The Franchise and Electoral Politics in England and Ireland 1832–1885', *History*, 70 (1985), 210, 215, 217 (with figures recalculated along United Kingdom lines).

[41] B. M. Walker, 'The Irish Electorate, 1868–1915', *Irish Historical Studies*, 18 (1973), 400–3. (This article also supplies useful data for England, Wales, and Scotland.)

[42] Jenkins, *Gladstone, Whiggery*, 194.

March 1883, having become convinced of the necessity of raising the temperature, he seized the occasion of some remarks by Salisbury (fully his equal in verbal offensiveness) to denounce the Tory leader as

the spokesman of a class; of the class to which he himself belongs, 'who toil not, neither do they spin'; whose fortunes . . . have . . . grown and increased, while they have slept, by levying an unearned share on all that other men have done by toil and labour to add to the general wealth and prosperity of the country.[43]

What, however, such an approach actually meant was that when, in 1885, Chamberlain eventually unveiled a general political blueprint of his own— the famous 'Unauthorized Programme'—his main targets of attack turned out to be some very old punchbags indeed: the House of Lords, the monarchy, the established church, and the landed classes in general.

In a series of speeches in January of that year he began by listing what he thought the most immediately needful reforms: manhood suffrage, the abolition of plural voting, payment of MPs, the extension of local government, compulsory land purchase, and graduated taxation. The language was often extreme and there was much talk of state intervention, but the details were usually left vague. Far from being 'socialist' (as some fevered contemporaries claimed), the Programme, which was published more fully in September, actually constituted an alternative to socialism—the rights claimed being those of individuals not of classes. What it amounted to was old Radicalism's 'assault on privilege, traditionalism, and the irresponsible power of "sinister interests"' repackaged in the wrappings of the new electoral 'democracy' created in 1884.[44] As an unkind critic from the Social Democratic Federation put it, the Chamberlainite Radical was merely 'the "Artful Dodger" who went up and down this country telling the people to take hold of the landlord thief, but to let the greater thief, the capitalist, go scot-free'.[45]

Chamberlain followed the launch of his Programme with unprecedented electoral speechifying, which, unlike the bulk of Gladstone's Midlothian campaigns (previously considered the height of demagogy), was not confined to a single constituency. Gladstone, in turn, produced an election address of striking 'moderation', whereupon Chamberlain (who still relied on the Prime Minister as protection against the Whigs) was obliged to tone down earlier suggestions about his unwillingness to join any future ministry not dedicated to the principles he had now so publicly espoused. In the event, the Liberals' considerable election gains in the counties in November 1885 probably owed little to Chamberlain's policies, while the unexpectedly

[43] *The Times*, 31 Mar. 1883.   [44] Jay, *Joseph Chamberlain*, 76.
[45] Clegg, Fox, and Thompson, *History of Trade Unions*, i. 53.

strong Conservative performance in London, Lancashire, and the English boroughs as a whole may well have been generated by a reaction against them.[46] By the end of the year it had become clear that Chamberlain had lost influence within the party, that the initiative remained with Gladstone, and that he rather than the Radicals—whether old or new—was now in a position to dictate the agenda for the coming parliament.

2. FOREIGN AND IMPERIAL AFFAIRS

If the government's domestic record was one of modest achievement, the great Midlothian promises about the 'right policy' to be adopted overseas never found much purchase in reality. There were many reasons for this, some personal, some ideological, some structural, some no more than accidental. As Foreign Secretary Granville proved suavely incompetent. He avoided making decisions and reading dispatches. 'With a smile and a quick little epigrammatic phrase' he would, recalled Lord Cromer, 'elude one's grasp and be off without giving any opinion at all'.[47] Indeed, Granville's feebleness encouraged Gladstone to keep foreign affairs largely to himself, so much so that the cabinet was often expected to do no more than confirm decisions already taken by a man sometimes so preoccupied with Irish business that little psychological calm was left over for anything else.

When aroused, Gladstone talked much of 'the high office of bringing Europe into concert, and keeping Europe in concert' as a task 'specially pointed out for our country to perform'.[48] He favoured collective action, but was prepared to intervene alone if persuaded that in doing so Britain could be said to embody the 'moral force' of Europe as a whole. Sometimes it suited others to let him believe that such was, indeed, the case. And because this happened most strikingly at the very beginning of the ministry, over the question of the borders of Montenegro and Greece (where the Berlin settlement had still not been fully implemented), Liberal politicians were too easily persuaded that 'concert' policies would always prove both righteous and effective. In reality, Bismarck, who thought Gladstone a 'mad professor' ('ein verrückter Professor'), had simply paid lip-service to the concert idea in order to render it innocuous. After 1880–1 Gladstone's distinctive notion—'the definition of a common objective, consultation by diplomatic discussion or conference as to a programme of action,

[46] H. Pelling, *Popular Politics and Society in Late Victorian Britain*, 2nd edn. (London, 1979), 6–7.
[47] Earl of Cromer [Evelyn Baring], *Modern Egypt*, 2 vols. (London, 1908), i. 392.
[48] W. E. Gladstone, *Political Speeches in Scotland, March and April 1880* (Edinburgh, 1880), 221.

execution of plans by concerted diplomatic pressure'—was abandoned by all the other major powers, not only in practice (as had long been the case), but even in pretence.[49]

Of course there was still an international striving for peace. Indeed, Bismarck's alliance system and his continuous efforts to divide potential opponents were largely devoted to that end. But the mechanisms most effectively deployed owed little to British initiatives. This was not merely because British statesmen proved 'inadequate', but because the assumptions behind Liberal foreign policy in general and Gladstonian foreign policy in particular embodied a view of international relationships singularly out of phase with developments elsewhere. Gladstone's concert notion supposed not that European countries should abandon their differences for their mutual benefit, but that there were ultimately no differences of substance to be abandoned at all. Behind the superficial appearance of what he believed to be transient discord, Gladstone perceived a kind of deeper Platonic reality in which equilibrium was sustained by free trade, a universal perception of progress, and by what amounted to a self-balancing mechanism, rather like that which supposedly kept the economy in order. Unfortunately continental countries saw things differently. They maintained large armies, occasionally fought large wars, worse still, they abandoned free trade.

Bismarck's brilliant short-term domination of international relations, though the antithesis of everything Gladstone stood for, was greatly helped by some of the policies which Gladstone adopted and the decisions his government made. A fairly high degree of British diplomatic incompetence simultaneously annoyed the French over their occupation of Tunis in 1881 and the Italians who greatly resented that occupation.[50] In the following year Britain's own invasion of Egypt gave Bismarck further opportunities for stirring up trouble between Britain and France. But because Gladstone steadfastly believed that Britain had no enemies and sought none, he was able to meet Bismarck's wild rages against Victorian liberalism with comparative indifference. Bismarck wrongly interpreted this as contempt and became wilder still.[51] Matters were not helped by Gladstone's addiction to moral rhetoric. Especially notorious was an outburst of March 1880 to the effect that 'Austria has ever been the unflinching foe of freedom in every

---

[49] W. N. Medlicott, *Bismarck, Gladstone, and the Concert of Europe* (London, 1956), 314–15.

[50] K. Bourne, *The Foreign Policy of Victorian England 1830–1902* (Oxford, 1970), 139.

[51] Matthew, *Gladstone 1875–1898*, 159. Gladstone seems to have been more or less unaware of Bismarck's 'ideological war against Gladstonianism' (P. Kennedy, *The Rise of the Anglo-German Antagonism 1860–1914* (London, 1980), 157–66).

country of Europe . . . There is not an instance—there is not a spot upon the whole map where you can lay your finger and say, "There Austria did good" '.[52] By the time Salisbury briefly took over as Prime Minister in June 1885 he could, without excessive exaggeration, sneer that the Liberals had 'at least achieved their long desired "Concert of Europe". They have succeeded in uniting the continent of Europe—against England.'[53]

In the imperial sphere the cabinet also lacked general ideas of a practical or effective kind. Though its members might, nevertheless, have successfully adopted a policy of carefully calibrated pragmatism, their actual behaviour was marked by confusion, muddle, and inconsistency. The handling of the South Africa question exhibited what might be called the 'mild' version of this infirmity. In Midlothian Gladstone had denounced the annexation of the Transvaal. On assuming office he prevaricated and told the Boer leaders (who were to suffer much from his terminological gymnastics) that 'we have to deal with a state of things which has existed for a considerable period, during which obligations have been contracted . . . which cannot be set aside'.[54] Incompetent local administrators made matters worse and in December 1880 an armed Boer rebellion began. Gladstone and his Colonial Secretary, Lord Kimberley, persuaded the cabinet to mount a vigorous response, though Gladstone assumed from the start that this would be followed by a 'generous peace'. Only Chamberlain, then as much a 'little Englander' as he was ever to be, provided any serious cabinet opposition. But if Gladstone ever believed that he was combining firmness and liberality in fruitful measure he was mistaken, for in the end he achieved the worst of all worlds—concessions without gratitude.

Instructions to local officials that they combine the carrot with the stick fell on deaf ears, none deafer than those of Sir George Colley, the Governor of Natal. On 27 February 1881 his small force of 554 soldiers was attacked by Boer forces at Majuba Hill. He was killed and another 266 men were either killed, wounded, or taken prisoner. It was a small enough affair as battles go, but it aroused typically imperialist rage both within and outside parliament. From Gladstone it evoked an equally typical diary reflection: 'Sad Sad news from South Africa: is it the Hand of Judgement?'[55] The subsequent unveiling of the 'generous' approach he had long privately advocated was now made to look like the product of military defeat. After

---

[52] *The Annual Register . . . for the Year 1880* (London, 1881), 47.

[53] Lady G. Cecil, *Life of Robert, Marquis of Salisbury*, 4 vols. (London, 1921–32), iii. 136.

[54] D. M. Schreuder, *Gladstone and Kruger: Liberal Government and Colonial 'Home Rule' 1880–85* (London, 1969), 59; R. Robinson and J. Gallagher, *Africa and the Victorians: The Official Mind of Imperialism* (London, 1961), 65.

[55] *Gladstone Diaries*, ed. Matthew and Foot, x. 25 (28 Feb. 1881).

some very bad-tempered negotiations the Pretoria Convention was signed in August 1881. This recognized the 'independence' of the Transvaal subject to British 'suzerainty', which seemed to mean control over foreign policy and some influence over the Boers' treatment of black peoples. But it was all wonderfully vague—Kimberley had even consulted an eminent lexicographer as to what the word 'suzerainty' actually meant—certainly vague enough to serve as a capacious cloak with which to disguise a calculated retreat.[56]

After Majuba Hill Gladstone undoubtedly handled the political fall-out skilfully. He kept the cabinet together and managed to deflect repeated Conservative attacks. In February 1884 the London Convention gave further concessions to the Transvaal and silently removed the word 'suzerainty' which had seemed so important three years before (though rows over the term were soon to reappear). But if the Boers had been granted much, they were still dissatisfied, repeatedly ignoring the frontiers that had been agreed and expanding into 'native' lands. They also continued to resent Britain's economic power, its residual local influence, and its contempt for their own culture and beliefs.

The 'harsher' side of the government's imperial infirmity became evident in the handling of Egyptian affairs. Nominally governors in the name of the Ottoman Empire, the Khedives of Egypt had developed a polity which, while effectively independent of Constantinople, had become increasingly subordinate to Western financiers and Western governments. In 1879 Khedive Ismael, a genuine if not always competent modernizer, was deposed at the instigation of various European powers worried by the size of his country's debt and replaced by his docile son Tewfik. At the same time the Egyptian finances, which had already come under a degree of international management, were put under the so-called Dual Control of officials from Britain and France. So humiliating a process, together with the manifold corruptions of Egyptian life, created a complex set of reactions, some of them nationalist, some particularist, others religious and ethnic. What amounted to *coups* were staged in 1881 and 1882 by an army officer, Colonel Arabi, who not only led those local factions opposed to Turkish influence, but became the focus of national and nationalist sentiment itself the product of complex mixtures of resentment against foreign infidels and against the influence of Western ideas upon Muslim faith and traditions.[57]

[56] Matthew, *Gladstone 1875–1898*, 154–5; Schreuder, *Gladstone and Kruger*, 221.
[57] G. N. Sanderson, *England, Europe and the Upper Nile 1882–1899* (Edinburgh, 1965), 14.

Egypt had long interested the British both for strategic and economic reasons. Ironically it had been Palmerston who (in 1859) had most trenchantly warned against turning interest into occupation. 'We do not want Egypt', he had insisted,

for ourselves any more than any rational man with an estate in the north of England and a residence in the south, would have wished to possess the inns on the north road. All he could want would have been that the inns should be well kept, always accessible, and furnishing him, when he came, with mutton-chops and post-horses.[58]

The trouble was that, by the 1870s, the inn was fast running out of chops and had ceased—at least in Western eyes—to be well kept. Yet Gladstone continued to believe that Britain should remain aloof. He publicly condemned Disraeli's acquisition of Suez Canal shares in 1875. Two years later he published an article in the *Nineteenth Century* criticizing proposals that Britain take over both the canal and Lower Egypt generally.[59] And his Midlothian speeches of 1879–80 made it clear that he had not changed his mind.

Yet within two years of returning to office the Liberals had thrown such caution entirely to the winds. The reasons for this are complicated. Certainly money played a part. By 1880 the United Kingdom took 80 per cent of Egypt's exports and supplied 44 per cent of its imports. A third of the country's total debt was in the hands of British bondholders and Egyptian and Turkish bonds had long accounted for a substantial proportion of all foreign securities issued in London.[60] As a result, there existed in the Home Counties a charmed circle of the great and the good capable, without obvious impropriety, of effecting a 'harmonious union between personal and national interests'.[61] That Gladstone himself was an Egyptian bondholder at one remove[62] was, however, much less significant than his fascination for matters of finance in general, whether at home or abroad. On occasion, indeed, he devoted far more cabinet time to discussions of the minutiae of Egyptian taxation than, for example, to more substantial questions of peace and of war.

[58] E. Ashley, *The Life and Correspondence of Henry John Temple, Viscount Palmerston*, 2 vols. (London, 1879), ii. 337–8.

[59] 'Aggression on Egypt and Freedom in the East', *Nineteenth Century*, 2 (1877), 149–66.

[60] M. Swartz, *The Politics of British Foreign Policy in the Era of Disraeli and Gladstone* (London, 1985), 127.

[61] A. G. Hopkins, 'The Victorians and Africa: A Reconsideration of the Occupation of Egypt, 1882', *Journal of African History*, 27 (1986), 380.

[62] Matthew, *Gladstone 1875–1898*, 135–6.

Repeated warnings from British 'men on the spot' that Dual Control was breaking down and the Egyptian Exchequer plunging into collapse persuaded important elements in the cabinet (notably Hartington, Northbrook—a member of the Baring family—and, increasingly, Chamberlain) that strong measures were needed, though Gladstone at first remained cautious. When in February 1882 Tewfik found himself forced to accept a 'nationalist' ministry, Britain collaborated with France in securing its dismissal after only three months. In May British and French naval forces arrived off Alexandria to protect their respective 'interests'. On 11 June an anti-Western riot took place in the town in which some fifty Europeans (six of them British-born) were killed. Although Arabi had in no sense fomented the riot, the cabinet immediately gave the impression of behaving as if led by a Palmerston inflamed by the fate of Don Pacifico.[63] On 3 July Admiral Seymour was given authority to prevent the Egyptians from increasing the defences of Alexandria. Eight days later Seymour chose to interpret loose orders in an extreme way and (shortly after the French had recalled their own ships) bombarded the place. On 20 July it was decided to send a British military force. Only Bright resigned. Chamberlain, now as keen on invasion as anyone, remained in the cabinet, where, five months later, he was to be joined by his fellow Radical, Sir Charles Dilke, a man whose imperial pedigree was of a more substantial and altogether less recent character than his own.

In mid-August the largest British force deployed between the Crimean and the Boer Wars landed under General Wolseley. Arabi declared a jihad but was overwhelmingly defeated at Tel-el-Kebir on 13 September. Not only was there little censure of such militarism at home—though Frederic Harrison declared he could hear 'a hollow and ghostlike laugh of derision' from Disraeli's burial vault[64]—but in the short term the government actually gained in popularity and cohesion. Gladstone himself was exceeding pleased with Wolseley's success, not least because much of the expense could be charged to the Indian Exchequer. Although his administration had in fact blundered into war, rather as Aberdeen's had done in 1854, he could see no similarities—'for [now] we are pleased with our army, our navy, our admirals, our Generals, and our organization'.[65] Already in June, Dilke had noted that 'our side in the Commons is very jingo about Egypt. They badly want to kill somebody. They don't know who.'[66] For his part Gladstone

[63] M. E. Chamberlain, 'The Alexandria Massacre of 11 June 1882 and the British Occupation of Egypt', *Middle Eastern Studies*, 13 (1977), 14–39.

[64] Id., 'British Public Opinion and the Invasion of Egypt, 1882', *Trivium*, 16 (1981), 23.

[65] Matthew, *Gladstone 1875–1898*, 138.

[66] J. S. Galbraith and A. L. al-Sayyid-Marsot, 'The British Occupation of Egypt: Another View', *International Journal of Middle East Studies*, 9 (1978), 484.

wanted to kill Arabi, having, like most other mid-Victorian Liberals, decided that no movement led by a professional soldier could possibly be 'popular'. In late September he bizarrely declared that he would be 'very glad' if the colonel could 'be hung without *real* inclemency'.[67] But it was not to be. After a court martial (at which he was defended by lawyers dispatched by a small band of British sympathizers) Arabi was exiled to Ceylon where the Governor-General Sir Arthur Gordon—himself the son of a former Prime Minister, Lord Aberdeen—showed what he thought of such bloodthirstiness by putting on a public dinner in honour of his distinguished guest.[68]

If Gladstone eventually felt some pangs of guilt over Arabi, he had few doubts about the enterprise as a whole. He told the Commons that free institutions would be slow to spread from 'Christian races' to 'a Mohammedan people'. 'Before God and man' he declared it to have been 'an upright war, a Christian war'.[69] None the less, the actions of his government had undoubtedly opened the door to riskless trouble-making on the part of powers such as Germany, not least because France had already come to believe that Britain had stolen a march on it in Egypt and was—up to a point—happy to listen to German suggestions about 'compensation'. As Bismarck's son elegantly put it, the aim now was 'to squash Gladstone against the wall, so that he can yap no more'.[70]

The invasion of Egypt was, therefore, a matter of great European significance and not (like the Transvaal) merely an imperial affair. Bismarck was able to use it to consolidate his policy of controlled tension between the powers and as a block to Anglo-French *rapprochement*. The concert was now not only dead, but seen to be dead. The 'liberal alliance' between Britain and France was seriously fractured and the way prepared for the Franco-Russian alliance of the early 1890s. The Gladstone government had adopted a position completely at variance with its professed principles. Over the next forty years some sixty-six promises were issued by official spokesmen that Britain's control over Egypt (formally indirect but in practice almost colonial) would be brought to an end. But the 'right' moment never seemed to come and all the promises were broken.

Such bellicose popularity as the administration gained from the invasion was to be blown away amidst the sands of the Sudan. In July 1881

[67] *Political Correspondence of Gladstone and Granville 1876–1886*, ed. Ramm, i. 429.
[68] Chamberlain, 'Alexandria Massacre', 33.
[69] D. Steele, 'Britain and Egypt 1882–1914', in K. M. Wilson (ed.), *Imperialism and Nationalism in the Middle East* (London, 1983), 2–4.
[70] *The Holstein Papers*, ed. N. Rich and M. H. Fisher, 4 vols. (Cambridge, 1955–63), iii. 131.

Mohamed Ahmed had declared himself to be the Mahdi (literally 'one who guides [from God] in the right way') and had raised the standard of revolt in the vast territory of the Sudan then nominally part of the Khedive's dominions. Even more fiercely than traditionalists in Egypt itself, the Mahdi's followers resented the Westernizing tendencies of the Egyptian administration and the increasing employment of Christian officials in high places. However, both Gladstone's ministers and the 'men on the spot' thought it a matter of small importance. The Khedive, who did not, was therefore casually allowed to mobilize a scratch punitive force of 10,000 men under a British officer, Hicks Pasha, only to have it annihilated in November 1883. Most of the Sudan was now in the Mahdi's hands. In January 1884 the London government decided to evacuate what was left and appointed Major-General Charles Gordon to organize this. Like the Mahdi, Gordon was a highly complex character who espoused religion in its most fundamentalist form. Abroad he had courted danger and glory in China, at home he worked tirelessly among poor boys in 'ragged schools'. He was not, however, much interested in the everyday practicalities of life. Indeed, his own departure from London introduced a note of farce which thereafter never entirely abandoned what was to become a deeply tragic enterprise. At Charing Cross he discovered he had neither a timepiece nor cash, so General Wolseley handed over his own watch and all the money in his pockets while Lord Granville personally rushed off to buy the appropriate railway ticket.

Gordon's orders were not as clear as they might have been and were, moreover, changed after he had begun his journey. In February he arrived at Khartoum. His various suggestions for attempting a reconstruction of government in the Sudan were rejected largely because they involved giving office to a notorious slaver called Zobeir. After March he was increasingly endangered and also out of telegraphic contact (some suspected deliberately), though he continued to be heard from indirectly in 'many odd ways'.[71] The cabinet spent the spring and summer in anxious debate. Slowly Whig pressure for action began to tell and in September Wolseley was appointed to command a relieving force. While complaining endlessly about the slowness and inefficiency of the politicians, the new commander seemed in no great hurry himself.[72] Gordon, besieged in Khartoum, was killed on 26 January 1885, two days before Wolseley's advance guard arrived outside the city walls.

[71] Gladstone to Northbrook, 14 Aug. 1884, Matthew, *Gladstone 1875–1898*, 145.

[72] A. Preston, 'Wolseley, the Khartoum Relief Expedition and the Defence of India, 1885–1900', *Journal of Imperial and Commonwealth History*, 6 (1978), 254–80.

On 5 February the news reached London. The outcry put earlier reactions to Isandhlwana and Majuba Hill into the shade. One MP denounced Gladstone (who took to his bed with diarrhoea) as 'that Anti-Christ whose advent was foretold as the prelude of the end of the world'.[73] The Queen sent a notorious telegram to Granville, Hartington, and Gladstone *en clair*: 'These news from Khartoum are frightful, and to think that all this might have been prevented and many precious lives saved by earlier action is too fearful.' But despite the frenzy, despite Gordon's death becoming one of the great metaphorical and actual (in G. W. Joy's famous painting) icons of late Victorian imperialism, Gladstone was able to ride out the immediate storm with relative ease once a censure motion had been defeated by fourteen votes. Feelings of honour made it impossible, Gladstone believed, to resign and he persuaded a reluctant cabinet to stay on. He himself soon began to look remarkably refreshed. Worried mostly about Ireland, the catastrophe of Gordon seems almost to have acted as a restorative. For a while there was no more talk of retirement and important decisions about the Sudan were reached with unprecedented dispatch.

The simultaneous explosion of another imperial crisis (and its comparatively speedy resolution) helped to divert public attention from the Sudan. In the months after the 1880 election it had seemed as if the government had at last succeeded in settling Britain's complicated relationship with Afghanistan. Lord Ripon, the new Viceroy of India, had recognized Abdur Rahman (a nephew of Sher Ali) as Amir. He in turn acknowledged British control over his foreign policy but was not required to accept a British Resident in Kabul. The new Amir (who ruled until 1901) proved ruthless and able and it looked as if Gladstone could at last point to an instance of Midlothian reticence having been successfully implemented abroad. However, the continued expansion of Russia caused renewed difficulties. On 30 March 1885 Russian forces defeated an Afghan army at Penjdeh close to what was generally understood to be the Afghan-Turcoman frontier. Although at first Granville reacted with something close to panic—'it is too dreadful', he declared, 'jumping from one nightmare into another'[74]—he and Gladstone soon succeeded in deploying a well-judged mixture of firmness and flexibility. In the Commons Gladstone once again struck a Palmerstonian stance and threw the opposition into confusion by speaking in favour of war credits. When in May pacific feelers were extended to St Petersburg, Salisbury, having no alternative to suggest, could only point out, with more wit than utility, that 'the Government go into every danger

[73] B. Porter, *The Lion's Share*, 2nd edn. (London, 1984), 115.
[74] W. L. Langer, *Alliances and Alignments 1871–1890*, 2nd edn. (New York, 1950), 313.

with a light heart, and then they make up for it by escaping with a light foot'.[75] In the event, the final settlement reached under his own minority administration in September 1885 followed exactly the lines suggested by Gladstone four months before: Penjdeh itself was more or less given up but the approaches to the important Afghan town of Herat were protected by denying Russia the crucial Zulficar Pass. It was a rare and almost total Liberal success. The setting up of a 'protectorate', with all its military implications, had been avoided and the defence of India substantially removed from the realm of political controversy.

Whether that more extended episode known as the 'Scramble for Africa' (a term coined by *The Times* in September 1884) should also be judged a success for Gladstone's administrations is more difficult to say. Midlothian notwithstanding, expansion in Africa (and parts of Asia and Oceania) did not cease in the 1880s. Salisbury's remark that, when he left the Foreign Office in April 1880 no one gave a thought to Africa but when he returned in June 1885 few talked of anything else, says more about the myopia of 'experts' in London than about the situation on the ground.[76]

It has been vigorously argued that the invasion of Egypt—by galvanizing France into responsive colonial action (first encouraged and then joined by Germany)—set the 'Scramble' in motion.[77] But while the invasion undoubtedly encouraged an increase in colonial activity, crucial French decisions and actions concerning Tunis and West Africa had in fact been made well before the summer of 1882. By then the French, as well as King Leopold of the Belgians and others, had also already started to express acquisitive interest in the Congo Basin, while expansion of various kinds in southern Africa had long been both lively and infectious. The 'causes' of the 'Scramble' did not, therefore, grow out of a single event. Instead, economic circumstances, the appearance of new industrial nation states protecting themselves with tariffs, the decline of certain commodity prices, and a heightened sense of commercial competition all helped to produce a widespread feeling of anxiety and alarm. In particular, European business-men were beginning to argue in favour of pre-emptive colonial strikes. Already in 1881, for example, Manchester merchants were complaining so bitterly about French expansion that (in their eagerness to preserve Africa from the protectionism of others) they quite overlooked their own long-held suspicions of costly colonial entanglements.[78] At the same time,

---

[75] *The Times*, 6 May 1885.   [76] Lady G. Cecil, *Marquis of Salisbury*, iv. 310.

[77] Notably by R. Robinson and J. Gallagher in their *Africa and the Victorians*.

[78] B. M. Ratcliffe, 'Commerce and Empire: Manchester Merchants and West Africa, 1873–1895', *Journal of Imperial and Commonwealth History*, 7 (1979), 294–5; A. G. Hopkins, *An Economic History of West Africa* (London, 1973), 124–66; P. J. Cain and A. G. Hopkins,

political and economic crises within Africa itself persuaded certain indigenous groups to look for external help against their neighbours.[79]

As the French made moves in West Africa and the eyes of others were roving along the coast behind Zanzibar, so groups of mercantile freebooters found it profitable to tour the interior with bundles of printed treaty forms ready for the ill-informed signatures of local chiefs. In order to contain the French along the Congo basin Britain reached an agreement with that most ramshackle of colonial nations, Portugal, acknowledging certain moth-eaten Portuguese claims in the area. But the other powers refused to recognize the treaty, which was also denounced by British merchants on free-trade grounds and eventually abandoned in June 1884. Germany ignored it from the start and raised its own flag, first over the desolate outpost of Angra Pequena near Walfisch Bay and then in August over the whole of what was to become known as South-West Africa.

Eventually an international conference met to discuss these matters in Berlin between November 1884 and February 1885. Britain did well to have its unimpressive claims along the Lower Niger recognized. Germany, too, received a variety of benedictions with regard to recent excursions into Togoland and the Cameroons. France gained 'rights' over the Upper Niger and parts of Gabon. Complex interlocking jealousies allowed the greatest gain of all to go to the most unlikely player, King Leopold, whose private-enterprise International African Association was awarded the huge territory which, under the name of the Congo Free State, was later to be so savagely exploited by his representatives. Although annexations continued for another decade or so, the conference, by paying careful attention to the self-interest of the participating powers, proved remarkably successful in reducing the impact of colonial disputes upon international relations and in restraining maverick treaty collecting throughout tropical Africa as a whole. What amounted to loose 'rules' governing future activity were laid down, in particular, that effective occupation should be the chief title to annexation and that 'spheres of influence' should be recognized as well as territorial acquisitions as such.

For Britain itself the whole process of expansion and of forestalling expansion by others had generated an almost unstoppable momentum. Somaliland, Nigeria, North Borneo, part of New Guinea, and various Pacific islands were acquired as 'protectorates', Bechuanaland was annexed

'The Political Economy of British Expansion Overseas, 1750–1914', *Economic History Review*, 33 (1980), 485–6.

[79] J. Sturgis, 'Britain and the New Imperialism', in C. C. Eldridge (ed.), *British Imperialism in the Nineteenth Century* (London, 1984), 90.

outright, and Egypt brought under informal control. Radicals like Chamberlain were becoming more imperialist by the month.[80] Gladstone, never anti-empire as such but still by conviction anti-imperialist, was finding it more and more difficult to sustain the distinction in practical terms. Only in East Africa was he able to postpone expansion and even that required a good deal of effort. 'Terribly have I been puzzled & perplexed', he told Dilke in December 1884, 'on finding a group of the soberest men among us to have concocted a scheme such as that touching the mountain country behind Zanzibar with an unrememberable name [Kilimanjaro]. There *must* somewhere or other be reasons for it, which have not come before me.'[81] Small wonder that perceptive observers like the colonial governor, Sir Hercules Robinson, thought it 'strange... that the Government which came in on the platform of curtailing Imperial responsibilities should be likely to add more to them than any previous Ministry'.[82]

Gladstonians dealt with the 'problem' (for so a good many of them still saw it) of continuing colonial expansion in two ways. The first was common to almost all of them and was expressed in assertions like that of the *Manchester Guardian* of 7 April 1884 to the effect that 'the conquests which we make are forced upon us'.[83] The second—Gladstone's own preferred line—took the form of adopting extremely relaxed attitudes towards acquisitions by other powers so long as these did not interfere with Britain's own spheres of influence. This was why the 'Scramble' proved such a relatively painless affair in European terms—to Bismarck's evident surprise. German claims in Togoland, the Cameroons, Zanzibar, Samoa, and New Guinea were conceded without fuss. Not only was Gladstone's mind often on other things, but he took the view that the possession of colonies would probably induce a heightened sense of responsibility and co-operation all round. Whatever might or might not happen to native peoples, he was convinced that a 'colonial' Germany would become 'our ally and partner in the execution of the great purposes of Providence for the advantage of mankind'. So comforting a view was not, however, shared by all his cabinet colleagues. Although few of them felt that Germany should have no colonies at all, they acquiesced for negative rather than positive reasons and resented Bismarck's taste for blackmail and opposition to liberal principles.[84]

[80] Jay, *Joseph Chamberlain*, 92–3.
[81] *Gladstone Diaries*, ed. Matthew and Foot, xi. 259.
[82] Robinson to J. X. Merriman, 3 Jan. 1884, *Selections from the Correspondence of J. X. Merriman 1870–1890*, ed. P. Lewsen (Cape Town, 1960), 155 (Van Riebeck Society Publications, 41).
[83] Porter, *Lion's Share*, 111.   ·   [84] Kennedy, *Anglo-German Antagonism*, 181–2.

3. IRISH QUESTIONS

From the point of view of the administrations of 1880–6 one problem proved especially (and rather unexpectedly) prominent—that of Ireland. Though primarily domestic in character, this also possessed an imperial dimension, both in the sense that any change in Ireland's constitutional status would inevitably have implications elsewhere and in the sense that manifestations of discontent long regarded as typically Irish were no longer confined to Ireland alone. Although ministers were not unaware of this, they rarely moved beyond the simplest of generalizations—condemning Kruger and Parnell in the same breath or applying the terminology of Home Rule to Egyptian affairs. In part this was the result of simple ignorance, in part the outcome of the cloudy manner in which local situations seemed to mirror one another. Afrikaner nationalism may well have been 'weaker' than that of Ireland in the 1880s, but the two phenomena depended upon not entirely dissimilar mixtures of religion, economic interest, cultural identity, and re-creations of the past. The *Genootskap van Regte Afrikaners* (Association of True Afrikaners) founded in 1875 by the Revd S. J. du Toit (as also his later *Afrikaner Bond*) foreshadowed, however loosely, bodies like the Gaelic Athletic Association and the Gaelic League set up in 1884 and 1893 respectively. Jan Hofmeyr's *Boere Beschermings Vereeniging* (Farmers' Association) of the 1870s can be compared with the Irish Land League, not least because agrarian agitation in southern Africa suffered from divisions between large (and moderate) and smaller (and more extreme) farmers very like those evident in Ireland during and after the Land War of 1879–82.[85] But because the complications of Irish and Afrikaner history were almost equally incomprehensible to the majority of Victorians, such imperial comparisons as were made tended to be superficial and unhelpful. Fenian violence temporarily persuaded the Colonial Office to view all things South African through Irish spectacles. Derby worried about creating 'another Ireland in South Africa'.[86] But, in general, neither politicians (Gladstone being something of an exception, at least with regard to Ireland–India comparisons) nor Civil Servants made much of an effort to dig below easily viewable surfaces in order to examine the— sometimes similar, sometimes very different—realities that lay beneath.

This did not make them any less irritated by the interest which Irish nationalists took in the affairs of the 'lesser' peoples of the empire. In the 1870s support had been expressed for the Boers. In 1881 Parnell said that

[85] Schreuder, *Gladstone and Kruger*, 27–30, 298–9, 372–3, 480–2; P. Bew, *Land and the National Question in Ireland 1858–82* (Dublin, 1978), 91–190.

[86] Schreuder, *Gladstone and Kruger*, p. vii.

he stood 'as an Irishman in sympathy with gallant people who were struggling for their independence'. Other Home Rule MPs said much the same.
Some, notably F. H. O'Donnell, focused on 'native' matters and thereby
greatly annoyed an imperial government itself much given to proclaiming
similar concerns. At least two Nationalist MPs belonged to the London
Indian Organization. Another visited the subcontinent in early 1882 to
investigate conditions there, at a time when some of his own colleagues
were in prison at home. Three years later the Indian National Congress was
founded. Though extremely moderate at first and anxious to distinguish
itself from Hibernian extremism, its leaders found it difficult to let the Irish
example slip entirely from their minds.[87]

Gladstone, for whom nationalism was a privilege which the Montene-
grins, for example, had *earned*, not a right to be demanded by Egyptians,
Afrikaners, or Irishmen, returned to office in April 1880 with little more in
the way of an Irish policy than Disraeli had possessed six years before.[88]
While his appointment of the heavyweight, W. E. Forster, as Chief Secretary for Ireland—though the insignificant Earl Cowper was made Viceroy—
showed that he took Ireland seriously, it also showed a keen desire to keep
Chamberlain out of an office he very obviously desired. Difficult decisions,
it was clear, needed to be made without delay because agricultural distress
had already led to the foundation of the Land League in 1879 and was now
in the process of generating that amalgam of agrarianism and nationalism
upon which the maverick Protestant landlord, Charles Stewart Parnell
(elected leader of the Home Rule Party in May 1880), was to base the
most powerful Irish political movement since the days of O'Connell.

Forster at once decided he would not renew the existing coercion
legislation (which gave unusual powers to the state and particularly to the
army and police) when it expired in the summer of 1880—a bold step later
regretted. But he found it difficult to overcome the long-standing Liberal
neglect of Ireland in policy matters and therefore tried to buy time by
introducing a range of minor reforms and setting up a royal commission on
land.[89] The immediate centrepiece of this strategy was the Compensation
for Disturbance Bill, a temporary measure designed to provide some help
for tenants of small farms evicted because they *could* not (rather than *would*
not) pay their rents. But even though evictions were undoubtedly increasing (the gross number of families evicted rose from 463 in 1877 to 2,110 in
1880 and then to 5,201 in 1882), the bill pleased almost no one, Gladstone

[87] A. O'Day, *The English Face of Irish Nationalism* (Dublin, 1977), 158–66.
[88] On Ireland generally, see above, Ch. 15.
[89] A. Warren, 'Forster, the Liberals and New Directions in Irish Policy 1880–1882',
Parliamentary History, 6 (1987), 99.

alone giving it some rather ill-focused support.[90] Opposition from Whigs and others in the Commons encouraged the Lords—where three junior ministers actually resigned—to reject the measure in August 1880 by 282 votes to 51. Having tried to buy time, Forster was now left with an empty purse and nothing to show for it.

The autumn of 1880 saw a distinct increase in the intensity of Parnell's agitation and a good deal of confused cabinet debate. Gladstone, who had begun to look more closely at Ireland, opposed Forster's latest idea that renewed coercion be combined with agrarian reform. Chamberlain talked of resignation if the former were imposed; Hartington warned against the latter. The absence of a clear policy in these months undermined the government's standing in Ireland. Amidst much excitement and confusion—and ministers could hardly be blamed for treating with alarm a campaign which was 'as near a revolutionary movement as anything seen in the United Kingdom between 1800 and 1914'[91]—British politicians took insufficient notice of the fact that the Land League also lacked a clear and widely accepted programme. There were deep splits between farmers of various kinds. There were jealousies between traders in towns and farmers as a whole, between farmers and the many labourers who held little or no land, and between revolutionaries and constitutionalists. Yet, again and again, it was the two steps forward, one step back approach of the administration which allowed Parnell and his lieutenants to prevent their own agrarian-nationalist coalition from falling apart.

Altogether characteristic was the way in which even a failed Compensation for Disturbance Bill seemed to demand some coercive counterweight, in this case the prosecution of Parnell and thirteen others for conspiracy. The trial stumbled along through December 1880 and January 1881, when the jury failed to agree. Nothing had been achieved save an increase in popularity for Parnell and the League. Intimations that the trial might well collapse, as well as advance news that the royal commissions examining agricultural distress in Ireland (under Lord Bessborough) and in the United Kingdom as a whole (under the Duke of Richmond) would recommend substantial reforms, provided the backdrop to a series of chaotic cabinet meetings in November and December 1880. Ministers began by accepting renewed coercion, though Gladstone continued to demur, not least because of the expense involved. Then, on the last day of the year, it was agreed that some kind of land reform should also be introduced, its precise nature being,

[90] T. W. Moody, *Davitt and Irish Revolution 1846–82* (Oxford, 1981), 563; A. Warren, 'Gladstone, Land and Social Reconstruction in Ireland 1881–1887', *Parliamentary History*, 2 (1983), 155.

[91] Matthew, *Gladstone 1875–1898*, 190.

however, left so obscure that Forster was driven to asking the Prime Minister what it was they had all decided upon. Gladstone could not or would not help, replying oracularly that 'We are pledged to take the Land Act [of 1870] for a starting point and develop it. Each man has his own interpretation.'[92] Indeed, in some respects the cabinet proved itself more divided than the Land League: there were forward and moderate parties and divisions between those (such as Argyll, Gladstone, Forster, and Hartington) who wanted to proceed by changing tenurial arrangements and those (such as Bright and Childers) who preferred land-purchase schemes.

Forster inaugurated the cabinet's revised stick-and-carrot approach by introducing a severe Protection of Person and Property Bill in January 1881. Despite dramatic and unprecedented obstruction by Home Rule members it passed into law on 2 March. Under its provisions the executive obtained, in A. V. Dicey's words, 'the absolute power of arbitrary and preventative arrest, and could without breach of law detain in prison any person arrested on suspicion for the whole period for which the Act continued in force'.[93] But while coercion was an old story, the Land Bill introduced by Gladstone on 7 April 1881 was a very substantial and innovative legislative carrot indeed. In essence it established the principle of co-partnership in the land between proprietor and tenant by granting the latter the famous '3 Fs'—fair rent, fixity of tenure, and free sale. Though the bill did not apply to leaseholders or to many tenants in arrears of rent, its key novelty—a Land Court which at once began to reduce rents substantially—undoubtedly constituted a very severe interference in the principle of freedom of contract. Landlords complained bitterly and the Duke of Argyll, fearing that Hibernian precedents might cross the sea to Scotland, resigned from the cabinet.

Gladstone was not only aware of such worries, he sympathized with some of them. In order, therefore, to persuade the Whigs and also perhaps himself of the government's moderation he continued to deploy generous helpings of ambiguity. A good deal of needlessly equivocal language was inserted into the bill and he himself skirted around the contradiction between the measure's support for the survival of smallholdings and the economic case for larger farms by simply refusing 'to enter into the economical part of the subject' at all.[94] He weakened the purchase clauses

---

[92] Warren, 'Forster', 104.

[93] A. V. Dicey, *Introduction to the Study of the Law of the Constitution*, 5th edn. (London, 1897), 221.

[94] *Hansard*, cclx. 918 (7 Apr. 1881). The notion of 'fair rent' was never precisely defined, being (according to the bill) what 'in the opinion of the [Land] Court...a solvent tenant would undertake to pay one year with another'. The eventual act found even this too much and gave no hint of any kind (Hammond, *Gladstone and the Irish Nation*, 238–9).

because of his belief that the health of rural society depended upon the presence of a landlord class and because any substantial scheme would, he thought, be expensive and require the creation of fully representative local government structures (as yet absent in Ireland) to make it work. The controversy as to whether the '3 Fs' were or were not being granted to their fullest extent was, he told the Commons, something he could not further discuss, adding mysteriously that 'The "three F's" I have always seen printed have been three capital F's; but the "three F's" in this Bill, if they are in it at all, are three little f's'.[95]

The bill presented Parnell with as many problems as it did the Liberals. Squeezed between those who wanted to reject it on grounds of inadequacy and those keen to take half a loaf, he only just managed to escape intact. In the event, the measure's successful passage (it became law in August 1881) was greatly helped by the incompetence of the Tory opposition. Churchill's violent amendments rapidly became tiresome and his ironic third-reading speech congratulating Parnell is remembered chiefly for having called forth Gladstone's jibe that he was merely a kind of flea 'whose office it is to bite, and who does not even produce in his victim the consciousness of being bitten'.[96] In the Commons Northcote found himself undermined by the enthusiasm shown by Conservative members from Ireland for Gladstone's proposals, which (conscious of the electoral realities at home) they supported by a majority of two to one. Nor in the Lords did Salisbury, who privately expressed renewed reservations about the calibre of Irish landlords, manage matters with any greater degree of success.[97]

Parnell proved more dangerous. He and his chief lieutenants realized that the new act might mollify enough of their followers to decouple the agrarian engine from the Home Rule train. A neat solution was eventually found: farmers were told to 'test' the act by taking thousands of cases to the new Land Court. At the same time speeches of a more and more extreme kind were delivered in order to demonstrate the incorruptibility of Parnell's nationalism. Urged on by Forster, Gladstone deliberately provoked Parnell by telling a large public meeting at Leeds on 7 October that 'the resources of civilization' were by no means exhausted should it 'appear that there is still to be fought a final conflict in Ireland between law on the one side and sheer lawlessness upon the other'. Parnell hit back in words which, if exaggerated, carried enough truth to wound when he denounced the Prime

[95] *Hansard*, cclxiii. 1419 (cited Matthew, *Gladstone 1875–1898*, 195–6).
[96] Foster, *Lord Randolph Churchill*, 90.
[97] Hammond, *Gladstone and the Irish Nation*, 216–17; Marsh, *Discipline of Popular Government*, 19–22. For Salisbury's views on Irish landlords after the 1870 Land Act, see above, Ch. 16, s. 1.

Minister as 'this masquerading knight-errant, this pretending champion of the rights of every other nation except those of the Irish nation'.[98] On 13 October Parnell was arrested under the recent Coercion Act and so were many others over the days that followed. A week later the Land League was proclaimed illegal.

Thus did the government allow itself to be goaded into a confrontation from which only its opponents could gain any long-term advantage. Chamberlain, once the foremost spokesman for conciliation, had begun to talk about 'war to the knife between a despotism created to re-establish constitutional law, and a despotism not less completely elaborated to subvert law and produce anarchy as a precedent to revolutionary change'.[99] Of course the agrarian agitators also faced serious problems and the 'No Rent' manifesto issued over the names of Parnell and others proved an embarrassing flop. But the simple fact of imprisonment disguised such failures by saving Parnell from having to respond directly to the enthusiasm of many tenants for the 1881 act. That the future might now lie with less exclusively agrarian agitations also suited him well enough, for he himself had always favoured the primacy of the political (Home Rule) over the socio-economic (land reform) aspects of the nationalist campaign. As he told his mistress, Katharine O'Shea, 'Politically it is a fortunate thing for me that I have been arrested, as the movement is breaking fast, and all will be quiet in a few months, when I shall be released.'[100]

And released he was soon to be. Forster's hope that coercion would induce acquiescence proved unfounded. No progress could be made as long as the chief men on one side were locked up in Kilmainham Gaol. Chamberlain swung back to a more conciliatory line and (with the cabinet's knowledge) opened up complex communications with the Irish leadership through Captain O'Shea (Katharine's unsavoury husband and a Home Rule MP). In response, Parnell provided a declaration (which did not remain secret for long) to the effect that, once certain adjustments had been made to the Land Act (such as extending its provisions to leaseholders and those in arrears) then this would be regarded in Ireland as 'a practical settlement of the Land Question and would I feel sure enable us to co-operate cordially for the future with the Liberal Party'.[101] On 2 May 1882 it

---

[98] Morley, *Life of Gladstone*, iii. 61; F. S. L. Lyons, *Charles Stewart Parnell* (London, 1977), 166–8.

[99] P. Adelman, *Victorian Radicalism: The Middle-Class Experience, 1830–1914* (London, 1984), 106.

[100] K. O'Shea, *Charles Stewart Parnell: His Love Story and Political Life*, 2 vols. (London, 1914), i. 207.

[101] Hammond, *Gladstone and the Irish Nation*, 277; Marsh, *Joseph Chamberlain*, 153–4.

was decided to release Parnell. On the same day Forster (who had strongly opposed the move) resigned, never to hold office again.

Almost immediately the whole affair was overshadowed by a still more dramatic event. Gladstone once again 'overlooked' Chamberlain and chose as Forster's replacement Lord Frederick Cavendish, who was not only Hartington's brother but was married to Mrs Gladstone's niece. On 6 May Cavendish and the Irish Under-Secretary, T. H. Burke, were killed while walking in Phoenix Park near Dublin by murderers wielding surgical knives. Parnell was shocked and offered to resign as leader of his party. Outrage was expressed on all sides. But the truly remarkable aspect of the murders was not how much but how little practical impact they had upon the course of events. Even when Cavendish's successor, G. O. Trevelyan, and a new Viceroy, Lord Spencer, brought in an understandably tough Crimes Bill on 11 May, Parnell, far from resigning, carried on much as before. On the government side, too, normal service was soon resumed. The promised Arrears Bill was enacted in August. In October Parnell successfully launched a new organization, the National League, more under his own personal control than the Land League had ever been and also rather more focused on the constitutional issue of Home Rule than on agrarian reform.[102] Gladstone himself, though severely shaken, stuck grimly to the path the so-called Kilmainham Treaty had laid down, believing, as he now did, that Parnell offered the best hope for a peaceful and reasonable settlement in Ireland, that if he went 'no restraining influence will remain', that, quite simply, there was no alternative to co-operation of some kind.[103]

What of course Gladstone was still unprepared to concede was 'Home Rule', though neither he (nor indeed many Home Rulers) quite knew what the term meant. In November 1882 he insisted that there was 'not the least chance of any question as to any sort of assembly (for Ireland) in Dublin', but conceded that a measure of devolution might remove the Irish sense of grievance and—for him a no less important point—make it possible to force Ireland to carry the full cost of the changes it so insistently demanded.[104] Clearly Gladstone was beginning to align agrarian and local government reforms into an integrated political and financial approach. Although cool towards extensive state-assisted land purchase, he believed that, were it to be introduced, an increase in local economic and political

[102] K. T. Hoppen, *Elections, Politics, and Society in Ireland 1832–1885* (Oxford, 1984), 277, 475–81.
[103] Morley, *Life of Gladstone*, iii. 70.
[104] *Political Correspondence of Gladstone and Granville 1876–1886*, ed. Ramm, i. 461; ii. 9–11.

responsibility would become absolutely necessary. And when eventually Trevelyan brought forward a complex (and abortive) purchase scheme in 1884 the Irish executive too insisted that it should be preceded by proposals for a system of responsible and representative local government.[105]

For a time the coercive policies introduced after the Phoenix Park murders proved highly effective. Officially tabulated 'agrarian outrages' declined from 4,439 (including 22 homicides) in 1881 to 762 (and no homicides) in 1884—and evictions fell at the same time.[106] When, therefore, Chamberlain began in December 1884 to reveal details of what soon became known as the 'Central Board' scheme, his moves were less the product of any immediate crisis in Ireland than of the doldrums besetting his own political career. The scheme (which was not as novel as many thought) assumed its final shape during indirect and rather cloudy discussions between Chamberlain and Parnell via Captain O'Shea (Gladstone in early 1885 sensibly used the far more reliable Mrs O'Shea as his intermediary). It provided for the establishment of representative local government in the Irish counties and the creation of what was termed a 'Central Board'.[107] On 17 December 1884 Chamberlain (who of course had no official responsibility for Irish matters as such) wrote about his ideas to a Radical Walsall solicitor called W. H. Duignan, who had shown an interest in Ireland and had conducted fact-finding tours of the country by tricycle in 1883 and 1884. Anxious to make a mark, Duignan, with Chamberlain's consent, showed the letter to interested parties—an exceedingly numerous group, as it turned out. Gladstone soon became a convert, if not a very committed one. Parnell, whose ostensible agreement had been obtained through O'Shea, was, however, less enthusiastic, fearing not that the scheme conceded too little, but rather that it conceded too much and might therefore (as Chamberlain hoped) take the wind out of the Home Rule sails. But while the plan was, indeed, bureaucratically advanced, it was much less so politically. It also marked the absolute limits to which Chamberlain would go. 'I can', he told Duignan, 'never consent to regard Ireland as a separate people [sic] with the inherent rights of an absolutely independent community ... Accordingly, if Nationalism means separation, I, for one am prepared to resist it.'[108]

---

[105] Until 1898 county government in Ireland remained in the hands of unelected grand juries, though increasing responsibilities had, over the years, been given to the partly elected Poor Law boards set up after 1838.

[106] National Archives (Dublin), 'Irish Crime Records' (printed but not published).

[107] C. H. D. Howard, 'Joseph Chamberlain, Parnell and the Irish "Central Board" Scheme', Irish Historical Studies, 8 (1953), 324–61.

[108] J. L. Garvin and J. Amery, The Life of Joseph Chamberlain, 6 vols. (London, 1932–69), i. 579.

By early 1885 Chamberlain's proposals had been sucked into discussions as to what should be done once the existing coercive legislation expired in the coming summer. Spencer wanted fierce continuation, Chamberlain substantial abandonment. On 9 May the cabinet rejected the Central Board scheme, all the commoners (save Hartington) voting in favour and all the peers (save Granville) against. On 15 May Gladstone told the Commons that certain unspecified crime proposals would shortly be introduced. Complicated misunderstandings then ensued over the possibility of further land legislation, and some days later Dilke and then Chamberlain and then Shaw Lefevre handed in their resignations. On 21 May the *Pall Mall Gazette* published a detailed report of the cabinet's differences. The three resignations were neither accepted nor withdrawn, but remained in suspense until 8 June when the administration was defeated on the budget in a division which saw no less than seventy Liberal members absent and unpaired. Next day the ministers decided to resign, though it took a fortnight of cross-party discussions, concerning the future behaviour of what on paper remained a Liberal majority, before Salisbury took office at the head of a minority Conservative government. In a circular to colleagues on 16 June Gladstone (now well into his seventies) did not 'perceive, or confidently anticipate, any state of facts' which might prevent retirement at the end of the current parliament.[109] Over the next thirteen months he was to fight two general elections, put forward a dramatic settlement of the Irish Question, and split his party beyond repair.

The events of June 1885 marked both the final emergence of Salisbury as uncontested leader of his party and the short-lived culmination of some recent Tory efforts to attract parliamentary support from the Home Rule camp. Churchill had long been fishing in Irish Nationalist waters and had made attacks upon Liberal coercion something of a personal speciality. On 20 May he had announced at the St Stephen's Club that a Tory administration would not renew coercion because there was 'every reason to hope ... that the time of great popular disorder in Ireland had passed away'. And even before Salisbury kissed hands a formal agreement had been reached that the Tories would abandon coercion and that the Home Rulers in return would abstain from disrupting government business in the Commons.[110]

From the start, the Tory/Home Rule understanding was a rackety affair. Coercion was indeed allowed to lapse—to the disgust of Spencer whose

[109] *Gladstone Diaries*, ed. Matthew and Foot, xi. 358.
[110] A. O'Day, *Parnell and the First Home Rule Episode 1884–87* (Dublin, 1986), 51–4; Foster, *Lord Randolph Churchill*, 177–81.

later support for Gladstone's Home Rule proposals was forged in his hatred of Salisbury's perfidy during the summer of 1885. In addition, the Tories (more ready than Liberals to throw money at problems if landlords stood to benefit) introduced the first substantial Irish land-purchase scheme in the shape of Ashbourne's Act which soon put Gladstone's earlier legislation on the matter entirely in the shade.[111] The pact's most remarkable aspect was, however, also its most ambiguous. To the post of Viceroy, Salisbury appointed his old High Church companion-in-arms, Lord Carnarvon, who had recently developed sentiments of sympathy for Irish demands. On 1 August, with Salisbury's knowledge, Carnarvon held a secret meeting with Parnell at an empty house in London. Nothing very remarkable took place. Parnell offered a few bromides about the nature of any future Irish legislative body. Carnarvon seems to have conveyed almost nothing beyond signalling his own personal sympathies.[112] Yet, however cynical all the chief actors (save Carnarvon) may have been, the very fact that such a meeting was allowed to take place at all was remarkable in itself.

What Salisbury wanted was Irish support in parliament and also at the next general election. What Parnell wanted was to ensure that, from an Irish perspective, both major party groupings remained in play for as long as possible, especially as the Conservatives virtually controlled the Upper House and took a line on education distinctly more attractive to his Catholic followers than that of most Liberals. It was also not uncongenial to him that Salisbury (though, like all his colleagues save Carnarvon, resolutely opposed to Home Rule itself) held a very low opinion of Ulster Conservatives, whose support for the 1881 Land Act and admiration for Northcote annoyed him more or less equally. Indeed, Ulster 'Unionism' first emerged in its modern form not over Home Rule, but as a result of Salisbury's failure to 'remember' Ulster when concluding the pact with Gladstone which made the franchise reforms of 1884–5 possible. In early October 1885 Salisbury treated an audience at Newport in Monmouthshire to a speech of dazzling elasticity in which garlands of welcome were thrown in almost every direction, the 'integrity of Empire' being coupled with 'prosperity, contentment and happiness' in Ireland and sympathy tendered to an

---

[111] £5m was advanced to tenants over forty-nine years at 4% and a further £5m added by another Conservative act in 1888. Over 25,000 farmers bought their holdings under these two measures, as compared to about 6,500 under the Disestablishment Act's purchase clause and the Land Acts of 1870 and 1881 combined (F. S. L. Lyons, *Ireland since the Famine* (London, 1971), 174; J. Vincent, 'Gladstone and Ireland', *Proceedings of the British Academy*, 63 (1977), 215).

[112] O'Day, *First Home Rule Episode*, 75–7; A. B. Cooke and J. Vincent, *The Governing Passion: Cabinet Government and Party Politics in Britain 1885–86* (Brighton, 1974), 281–2.

impressively diverse range of opinions on Hibernian affairs generally.[113] However, below the surface of short-term expediency, Salisbury and Churchill were already hard at work preparing the very different Irish syllabus they were jointly to expound the following year.[114]

On the Liberal side, the summer and autumn of 1885 saw a concentration upon considerations of leadership, with rather more attention being devoted to the future of church establishments than to Home Rule. But as Chamberlain became more and more angry over the failure of his Central Board initiative so Gladstone began to conflate the question of party leadership with that of Ireland. Characteristically he seemed to be casting about for a good reason for remaining at the centre of events, in which respect Ireland clearly possessed all the potential of a new Bulgaria, even though (perhaps because) its geographical closeness and integration into the imperial system presented awesome problems of a political, constitutional, and emotional kind. Already in August Hartington had come to think Gladstone's 'state of mind about Ireland' so 'alarming' that he spoke out forcefully against Parnell's self-government demands in a speech otherwise intended to undermine Chamberlain's 'Radical Programme'.[115] Publicly, however, Gladstone at first chose to assert the continuation of his leadership not through the medium of Irish affairs, but—a general election being imminent—by means of a manifesto published on 18 September, in which, despite much windy vagueness, he firmly took the Whigs' part against Chamberlain.

Both Gladstone and Hartington expected the forthcoming election to produce a large Liberal majority. The latter believed this would force the Irish to accept whatever was offered them and that they could therefore safely be offered a good deal—short of Home Rule. Indeed, in a speech at Belfast on 5 November he was prepared to contemplate 'very bold Irish reforms, all tending in the direction of decentralisation'.[116] For Gladstone, confidence in victory and in Parnell's electoral strength had begun to generate more complicated thoughts: that a 'great and critical problem in the national life' might soon demand the making of big and imaginative decisions and the suspension of all talk of his own retirement.[117] Gladstone, Derby reported to Granville in early October,

---

[113] A. Jackson, *The Ulster Party: Irish Unionists in the House of Commons 1884–1911* (Oxford, 1986), 25–6, 37.

[114] W. C. Lubenow, *Parliamentary Politics and the Home Rule Crisis: The British House of Commons in 1886* (Oxford, 1988), 132.

[115] Holland, *Life of Spencer Compton*, ii. 77; O'Day, *First Home Rule Episode*, 88–9; Jenkins, *Gladstone, Whiggery*, 208–14; Jay, *Joseph Chamberlain*, 113.

[116] Jenkins, *Gladstone, Whiggery*, 258–9.

[117] To Spencer, 30 June 1885, *Gladstone Diaries*, ed. Matthew and Foot, xi. 366.

said he had been studying the subject [of Ireland] a good deal; that he had come to the conclusion that the Union was a mistake:...that he did not hold the popular theory that a single executive could not co-exist with two independent legislatures ...He did not believe the Irish irreconcilable: thought they would have accepted moderate terms till R. Churchill came into power: now nothing less than a Parliament of their own would satisfy them: the question was becoming urgent: the Irish were better organised than ever: we could not get on with eighty or ninety of them in the House of Commons—the state of that body now was a disgrace, and it would be worse in the new Parliament.[118]

As Derby's account suggests, Gladstone's journey towards Home Rule was neither abrupt nor simply self-interested. There was no single moment of decision as there had been over disestablishment, no deep inner struggle. And precisely because this was so, Gladstone quite failed to realize how big a thing Home Rule would be for those he hoped to convert. The Tories, he believed, had destroyed all prospects of a 'moderate' settlement. If for many Liberals this left resistance as the only option, for him it left only concession, with Parnell cast in the role not of revolutionary, but of bulwark against revolution. In particular, Gladstone's own linkage of land reform and the necessity of locally devolved institutions in Ireland now allowed him to see the move to Home Rule as a perfectly 'natural' transposition.

Of course it is tempting to argue that, in practice, nothing mattered but personal relationships, personal rivalries, personal victories, and personal defeats. And, indeed, the very detail in which the operation of British politics at the highest levels in 1885 and 1886 has been studied has persuaded some that such was the case, that the trees of pragmatism always counted for more than the woods of conviction, and that the 'Irish Question' was no more than 'the temporary and particular name given in the 1880s to a continuous and permanent existential problem which party managers inflict upon themselves'.[119] In such a view the 'Home Rule' episode of 1885–6 should be seen, above all, as the most successful party purge in modern British history, with Gladstone brilliantly inventing ceaseless ways of ditching Liberal rivals to both his right and his left in order to prevent them from breaking up the party over the question of property. This 'realism' (some might call it cynicism) is not without evident virtues. In particular, its stress on the importance of political relationships has restored a vital element to historical analysis. Not only, however, has much also been rendered unnecessarily obscure, but the public language of politics has been unnecessarily subverted by conspiratorial reminders that

[118] Lord E. Fitzmaurice, *The Life of Granville George Leveson Gower, Second Earl Granville*, 2nd edn., 2 vols. (London, 1905), ii. 465.
[119] Cooke and Vincent, *Governing Passion*, 18.

public words are never more than veils flung over an infinity of private intrigues. In fact, it does now seem clear that Gladstone had begun to move decisively towards an acceptance of Home Rule as an efficient and worthy political cause well before the general election of late 1885 and that, in doing so, he was committing no violence towards his own record on Ireland over the previous four years.

After much prompting, Parnell eventually supplied (via Mrs O'Shea) a 'Proposed Constitution for Ireland' on 1 November.[120] Although this was moderate in tone, Gladstone gave a non-committal reply and refused to enter into a public auction for the Irish vote.[121] Privately, however, he began to formulate his own plans on the matter almost at once, so quickly indeed that within a fortnight he produced three impressively specific memoranda from which, in effect, have derived all British legislative attempts at Home Rule, whether for Ireland, Scotland, or Wales.[122]

Two key ideas lay at the core of Gladstone's thinking at this stage: the belief that he needed time to 'educate' his party and the expectation that this would be made available by a massive Liberal majority at the forthcoming general election. While, therefore, his election manifesto proposed specific, though very modest, changes in areas such as local government, voter registration, and parliamentary procedure, the whole question of Ireland was dealt with in terms of Delphic obscurity. Most other Liberal candidates simply ignored Home Rule altogether, barely a score declaring themselves even broadly sympathetic.[123] Having received nothing from Gladstone, Parnell had little choice but to back the Conservatives. But he waited as long as he dared before issuing a statement on 21 November calling upon the Irish in Britain to oppose the Liberals, who were now vituperatively denounced as 'perfidious, treacherous, and incompetent'. What difference this—and similar advice from the Catholic clergy—made is difficult to assess. Disappointed Liberals spoke of losing twenty seats as a result. Almost certainly they were exaggerating.

At the general election that followed (24 November to 18 December), the Liberals, in a reversal of traditional patterns, did well in the counties and the Conservatives in the towns where the recent redistribution allowed them to dominate many of the new single-member constituencies. The provision of additional seats in London had a similar effect. In rural areas the newly enfranchised agricultural labourers voted Liberal, not so much because of Chamberlain's promises about their being given 'three acres and

---

[120] Printed in Hammond, *Gladstone and the Irish Nation*, 422–3.
[121] Matthew, *Gladstone 1875–1898*, 226.
[122] Printed in *Gladstone Diaries*, ed. Matthew and Foot, xi. 429–30.
[123] Lord Ebrington, 'Liberal Election Addresses', *Nineteenth Century*, 19 (1886), 606–19.

a cow', but because they hated the entrenched interests of rural Conservatism: parsons, land agents, prosperous farmers, and the like.[124] A larger proportion of seats was contested than ever before (outside Ireland only twenty returned their members unopposed). The results, however, pleased almost no one, at least not immediately. Parnell obtained his expected success and now led a parliamentary force of 86. With the Liberals returning 334 and the Conservatives 250 members, Salisbury had failed to escape from his minority chains. On the Liberal side Chamberlain was the chief loser and now saw himself in imminent danger of disappearing down the ravine which had opened up between his expectations and the fact that among Radical members his own following still constituted a minority. It needed no deep insight for Gladstone to realize, first, that he could not now lead a government relying exclusively on Liberal MPs, and, secondly, that the possibility of a calm interval for 'educating' his party about Home Rule had vanished. Only for Hartington and the 'moderates' (not yet fully aware of Gladstone's opinions) did the election seem to promise better things. With Chamberlain and the Radicals thwarted, their own prospects looked brighter than for some time.

Aware of the dangers ahead, Gladstone briefly tried to persuade the Conservatives to take up Home Rule themselves. Whether this was based upon any real hope that the Tories would mix high-mindedness with self-interest (getting rid of Irish MPs from Westminster etc.) or simply a procedure for clarifying his own mind and forcing Salisbury to make a decisive move is unclear: probably both considerations mattered, but at different levels of consciousness. Salisbury, who had no wish to replicate what he had always denounced as Tory spinelessness in 1829, 1846, and 1867, was delighted to be able to stand on firmer ground at last. 'Gladstone', he told Churchill, 'has written to Arthur [Balfour] a marvellous letter saying that he thinks "it will be a public calamity if this great subject should fall into the lines of party conflict"—& saying he desires the question should be settled by the present Government. His hypocrisy makes me sick.'[125]

On 17 December, a couple of days after the approach to Balfour, two newspapers published information supplied by Gladstone's son, Herbert, to the effect that his father had indeed decided to support Home Rule, the famous 'Hawarden Kite'. Herbert had received many requests for clarification and the initiative seems to have been entirely his own. Presumably he

[124] Pelling, *Popular Politics*, 6–7; A. Simon, 'Church Disestablishment as a Factor in the General Election of 1885', *Historical Journal*, 18 (1975), 818–19.

[125] Salisbury to Churchill, 24 Dec. 1885, Marsh, *Discipline of Popular Government*, 85.

flew the kite (named after Gladstone's country house) in the hope that it might 'clear the air', reveal the Conservatives' total negativism, and counteract the apparent intention of Chamberlain and Dilke to keep Salisbury's government in office and thus shelve, first Ireland, and then perhaps Gladstone as well. The timing, however, made it seem as if an unprincipled and opportunist bid was being made for Irish support. Gladstone himself reacted calmly and, over the next weeks, played his cards with considerable skill. In particular, he avoided giving pledges to the Home Rulers and in due course succeeded in taking advantage of an amendment to the Address put forward by Chamberlain's acolyte, Jesse Collings, to defeat the government on 27 January 1886 by 329 votes to 250—though ominously some seventy Liberals (including Bright) abstained and eighteen (including Hartington) voted with the Conservatives. Within forty-eight hours the Queen had commissioned Gladstone to form a new administration.

In terms of the immediate context, Gladstone had behaved with rare skill. He had brought down Salisbury's ministry on a non-Irish issue and thus given few hostages to fortune. He had exposed a good deal of parliamentary incompetence on the other side. He had obtained support from an increasingly desperate Parnell on what seemed like cheap terms—hints rather than promises.[126] But in other respects the obstacles that lay ahead remained as formidable as ever: the House of Lords, Ulster, the Liberal Party itself. No wonder some have doubted the genuineness of his commitment and argued that, while Ireland was a great imperative, the nature of his activities in February and March 1886 suggests that, at least for a time, he believed further land reform to constitute a greater priority than Home Rule.[127] In fact, Gladstone saw the two things as inextricably connected, and, while in no way unaware of the difficulties facing him (though Ulster did not much engage his thoughts), seems to have believed that the provision of a clear-cut opportunity for a comprehensive settlement would of itself somehow yield a satisfactory result.[128]

While the Irish Nationalists greeted Salisbury's defeat on 27 January with enthusiasm, a Liberal noted how it 'was received with almost complete silence by our own men'.[129] Hartington in particular viewed the kite with deep distaste, though, after refusing to serve in Gladstone's new administration, he at first played a cautious waiting game. He worried that Chamberlain could still be persuaded to support Home Rule. He realized that

[126] O'Day, *First Home Rule Episode*, 139.

[127] Vincent, 'Gladstone and Ireland', 226–8.

[128] J. Loughlin, *Gladstone, Home Rule and the Ulster Question 1882–93* (Dublin, 1986), 80–4; Matthew, *Gladstone 1875–1898*, 234–7.

[129] Lubenow, *Parliamentary Politics*, 4.

only by letting Gladstone try and fail would it be possible to persuade the new 'popular' electorate to accept the necessity of further sharp coercion in Ireland. Above all, he hoped that failure might at long last bring about the Prime Minister's oft-heralded retirement.[130] Gladstone, in turn, must have been heartened by the comparative ease with which his new ministry was put together. By not actually insisting on a Home Rule loyalty oath (though a vague document on the matter was tendered to those offered a place), he ensured that only the most irreconcilable stayed out: Hartington, Derby, Northbrook, Goschen, Bright. The fact that Chamberlain took cabinet office signalled weakness rather than strength. Damaged by the election and deprived of close support from Dilke (now discredited by the Crawford divorce scandal), Chamberlain accepted the insultingly minor appointment of President of the Local Government Board. Gladstone had begun by offering the Admiralty. This was declined. 'Then what office would you prefer?'—'The Colonial Office'. 'Oh', said the Prime Minister, 'a Secretary of State', with which he raised his head and tacitly dismissed the notion as absurd.[131] Worse still, from Chamberlain's point of view, was Gladstone's selection of the much more junior Radical, John Morley (now hot for Home Rule), for the key post of Chief Secretary for Ireland. The most substantial convert of all was Spencer. Eight months earlier he had led the opposition to the Central Board. Now the Conservatives' opportunism over coercion had undermined his faith in imperial government and he was ready to try Home Rule as the only viable alternative.

Eventually Chamberlain forced the issue of Ireland at a cabinet on 13 March. By then the process by which Gladstone was privately subordinating land purchase to Home Rule was already well under way. Details were, however, kept secret as long as possible, and not until 20 March was the Government of Ireland Bill printed for cabinet distribution. Six days later Chamberlain and Trevelyan resigned. Chamberlain's subsequent claims that he was inspired by a desire for a united empire and believed that Home Rule would make such unity impossible are difficult to sustain. After all, his record on Irish devolution was then still as strong as his commitment to imperial cohesion had been weak. Perhaps he genuinely opposed the withdrawal of Irish MPs from Westminster and believed that his kind of Radicalism would wither without the existence of a powerful imperial parliament. What he certainly did believe was that, in whatever way Gladstone's Irish plans might eventually work out, he himself would be able to take over from the old man. 'Either Mr G will succeed and get the

---

[130] Jenkins, *Gladstone, Whiggery*, 272–3.
[131] Hammond, *Gladstone and the Irish Nation*, 475.

Irish question out of the way or he will fail. In either case he will retire from politics and I do not suppose the Liberal Party will accept... even John Morley as its permanent leader.'[132]

From the moment of forming his third administration Gladstone worked steadily on the details of a 'definitive' Irish settlement. The aim was to achieve social order by the joint means of further land reforms and a measure of self-government. One without the other would be insufficient; both were necessary. Notes made for his opening speech on Home Rule listed five 'conditions for a good plan', namely, '(1) Imperial unity. (2) Political equality. (3) Equitable distributions of burdens. (4) Reasonable safeguards for minority. (5) It must be a settlement.'[133] The fourth point was shorthand for buying off the (largely Protestant) landlords, not for conciliating Ulster Unionists, of whose increasingly strident activities Gladstone took little notice. And 'buying off the landlords' meant a purchase scheme, which in turn (by a circuitous but compelling logic) made some kind of statutory Irish body necessary to provide that degree of local financial and political responsibility without which the required expenditure could not safely be contemplated.

What the land-purchase proposals amounted to was a dramatic abandonment of earlier caution on the matter, not least as regards finance. If the 1881 Land Act had been designed to 'save the principle of property from shipwreck' (as Gladstone was later to claim),[134] the 1886 plan was aimed at the creation of *two* stabilizing groups: an aristocracy now integrated into the community as natural leaders and a new class of peasant proprietors grateful to an imperial authority for its very existence. Huge, if vaguely assessed, sums were to be provided to underwrite a scheme of great practical complexity. Because purchase was to be voluntary, costs were difficult to assess. First the appalling figure of £120m was mentioned, then £60m, with the bill itself proposing £50m (though Gladstone believed it might well be more).[135] Liberals (let alone Conservatives) expressed themselves much shocked. Cheese-paring Radicals, who had long counted Gladstone as an ally, denounced him as a traitor to the noble idea of the minimal state. Others simply objected to so much being spent on landlords and Irish landlords at that. Indeed, for many Liberals the purchase bill was the really rebarbative part of Gladstone's package. 'Every Radical', wrote one, 'will hail with delight the prospect of being able to support with a free

---

[132] Marsh, *Joseph Chamberlain*, 232.

[133] British Library, Gladstone Papers Add. MS 44672 (8 Apr. 1886).

[134] W. E. Gladstone, 'Mr Forster and Ireland', *Nineteenth Century*, 24 (1888), 454.

[135] Matthew, *Gladstone 1875–1898*, 246; Loughlin, *Gladstone, Home Rule and Ulster*, 80–94.

conscience the home rule scheme. [But] with a land purchase jockey, many of us could not back the Irish horse, and those who did would feel like men riding into the Bog of Allen.'[136] But though it was temporarily shelved, Gladstone never doubted the measure's central necessity and fully intended to reintroduce it once significant progress had been made on Home Rule.

The Government of Ireland Bill was introduced on 8 April just over a week before the Land Purchase Bill, in the forlorn hope that it would remain uncontaminated by the latter's expected unpopularity. Although Gladstone had not found it easy to come up with a suitable plan, he treated the technical difficulties (which have continued to haunt all subsequent labourers in the same vineyard) with great—perhaps excessive—confidence. He had gained much from examining various existing constitutional models, notably that delineated in the British North America (i.e. Canada) Act of 1867, and his thinking remained firmly imperial throughout. 'The principle that I am laying down', he told the Commons on 8 April,

I am not laying down exceptionally for Ireland. It is the very principle upon which... we have not only altered, but revolutionized our method of governing the Colonies. I had the honour to hold Office in the Colonial Department... 51 years ago.... England tried to pass good laws for the Colonies, at that period; but the Colonies said—'We do not want your good laws; we want our own'. We admitted the reasonableness of that principle, and it is now coming home to us from across the seas.[137]

The powers the bill proposed to give to a unicameral Irish 'legislative body', though considerably greater than those possessed by the provincial assemblies in Canada, were, however, less than those of the Canadian dominion parliament.[138] Matters of defence, foreign policy, and international trade were the chief items over which London was to retain control.[139] The legislative body was to consist of two 'orders' which would deliberate together but could vote individually and exercise a species of temporary veto over one another. The first order was to consist of the twenty-eight Irish representative peers and seventy-five other persons elected for ten years on a comparatively exclusive ($£25$ occupier) franchise,

[136] G. D. Goodlad, 'The Liberal Party and Gladstone's Land Purchase Bill of 1886', *Historical Journal*, 32 (1989), 631.
[137] *Hansard*, ccciv. 1081 (8 Apr. 1886).
[138] J. Kendle, *Ireland and the Federal Solution: The Debate over the United Kingdom Constitution, 1870–1921* (Kingston and Montreal, 1989), 44–5.
[139] The proposed Irish body was not to be allowed to establish any religion or impose customs duties and excise duties connected with the customs. Navigation, coinage and legal tender, weights and measures, and copyright were also to remain under the imperial parliament.

with candidates having to be men of reasonable substance. This, like the land-purchase scheme, was designed to 'protect' the minority. The second order was to consist of the existing 103 Irish MPs plus another 101 members elected along similar lines. After a good deal of wavering, Gladstone had decided that it would be best to exclude Irish members from Westminster altogether. But while this was one of the few aspects of the bill which many of its opponents may well have found attractive, it presented so many difficulties that he was later forced to change his mind. Indeed, a continuing series of complications (on the whole handled with great dexterity) showed how very hard it was to draw up a systematic plan when the constitution whose powers were to be devolved was not itself systematically stated in law.[140]

Despite the great labour which had gone into the bill much remained vague, though in the excitement of debate this was by no means always apparent. The roles of the Irish Privy Council and the Viceroy were, for example, left undefined, and much the same was true of the executive organs of the new legislature. But on only one major point was there a real dispute between Gladstone and Parnell—that of finance. Here much posturing and bidding went on, not because of any informed economic analysis (hard facts were in singularly short supply), but because both men thought it important to be seen to have struck a good bargain. Initially Gladstone suggested that Ireland should bear one-thirteenth of imperial costs. Then this was changed to one-fourteenth, and eventually to one-fifteenth. There, however, he stuck firm and all Parnell's demands for something nearer one-twentieth fell on deaf ears. Curiously, in the bill itself the proportion was actually expressed in fixed money terms unalterable for thirty years, a provision which, in the light of subsequent inflation, would have represented an amazing bargain for the Irish and would not have come up for renegotiation until—of all years—1916.[141]

As regards political reactions, the details mattered less than the mere fact that 'Home Rule' was being seriously proposed at all. Politicians on all sides urgently realigned their relationships in response to what had been announced. Chamberlain and Gladstone indulged in a good deal of shadow-boxing, the former demanding concessions, the latter going through various conciliatory motions, neither of them wishing to accept the blame for a split. As Churchill mischievously put it: 'Gladstone is pretending to make up to Joe in order to pass his Bill; and Joe is pretending to make up to Gladstone in order to throw out his Bill. Diamond cut diamond.'[142]

[140] Matthew, *Gladstone 1875–1898*, 249.
[141] Ibid. 251–3; Loughlin, *Gladstone, Home Rule and Ulster*, 69–76.
[142] Jay, *Joseph Chamberlain*, 139–40.

Hartington, for his part, cherished lively hopes of recapturing the party for a policy of moderate reforms short of Home Rule and then heading a vaguely Palmerstonian administration capable of attracting support from almost all parts of the House. But while, in the immediate context of Gladstone's proposals, many Liberal sceptics enthusiastically danced a pragmatic quadrille, their opposition and criticism were also often the products of longer disillusionments. Unlike Gladstone, the Whigs had lost their mid-century optimism about the conservative effects of reform. South Africa, Egypt, and now Ireland all seemed to demonstrate the increasing unacceptability of Gladstone's traditional Liberal approach. Just as diplomatic developments had rendered the notion of a concert of Europe irrelevant to contemporary conditions, so (according not only to the Whigs but to certain Radicals and mainstream Liberals also) changing imperial fortunes had begun to require a tougher stance both in Ireland and elsewhere. Salisbury, however, was determined that the destruction of Gladstone should take place under his own rather than under Whig auspices. And with Churchill's help he proceeded to raise the temperature so high that Hartingtonian compromises became impossible. Essentially this involved drenching opposition to Home Rule with such reactionary flavours that only a figure like himself could be seen to possess plausible claims to its leadership.

Already on 22 February Churchill had visited Belfast and—in a complete reversal of his earlier references to 'foul Ulster Tories'—told loyalists that in these dark days 'there will not be wanting to you those who on all hands in England are willing to cast in their lot with you, and who, whatever the result may be, will share your fortunes and your fate'. To which, some weeks later, he appended the more famous coinage that 'Ulster will fight; and Ulster will be right.'[143] Nor was Salisbury's defence of Orange resistance in his Crystal Palace speech of 2 March any less uncompromising. Although, therefore, the Tory leader appeared on a platform with Hartington in April, he remained determined to isolate the anti-Home Rule Liberals so as to render impossible any hopes they might retain about dominating a Unionist alliance at cabinet level. With this in mind he delivered a virulent speech to a London audience on 15 May. The best way to govern Ireland, he declared, was twenty years of coercion. The best solution to Irish problems was massive emigration. Some 'races'—he only mentioned 'Hottentots' and 'Hindoos' but no one doubted he meant Hibernians also—were inherently incapable of self-government.[144]

[143] Jackson, *Ulster Party*, 117; *The Times*, 23 Feb. 1886; Foster, *Lord Randolph Churchill*, 258.
[144] *The Times*, 17 May 1886; also R. Shannon, *The Age of Salisbury 1881–1902: Unionism and Empire* (London, 1996), 193–203.

On 31 May, not long after Gladstone had denounced those who disagreed with him as representing 'Class and the dependants of Class',[145] Chamberlain held a meeting with fifty MPs in Committee Room 15 of the House of Commons (ironically the same room where, four-and-a-half years later, the Irish Nationalists were to depose Parnell) at which a dramatic declaration from Bright against Home Rule was read and forty-six of those present pledged themselves to vote against the bill. The next day Hartington successfully urged another fifty-eight to do the same.[146] In the early hours of 8 June the debate on the second reading came to an end with a pleading exhortation from the Prime Minister.

Go into the length and breadth of the world, ransack the literature of all countries, find, if you can, a single voice, a single book . . . in which the conduct of England towards Ireland is anywhere treated except with profound and bitter condemnation. . . . Think, I beseech you, think well, think wisely, think, not for the moment, but for the years that are to come, before you reject this bill.[147]

It was not enough. When, shortly afterwards, the members voted by 341 to 311 against Home Rule it was found that no less than 94 Liberals had gone into the lobby against Gladstone and another half-dozen or so had abstained.[148] Among the 94 Chamberlain's followers were in a distinct minority.

Although Hartington and others wanted the government to resign in favour of Salisbury and thus allow a possible regrouping of Liberal forces under new leadership, Gladstone had little difficulty in persuading the cabinet to dissolve, with the result that another election was held only seven months after the last.[149] The Liberals' election expert, Francis Schnadhorst, was full of optimism—fatally so. His advice to move quickly made it difficult to find suitable (or indeed any) candidates in certain constituencies. The Conservative/Liberal Unionist alliance worked smoothly, sitting Liberal Unionists being allowed a free run. The Conservatives won 316 seats, the Liberals 191, the Liberal Unionists 78, and the Irish Nationalists 85. Scotland, Wales, and Ireland all produced Home Rule majorities, in aggregate by almost three to one. Only England—with its own rather different, but no less intense, sense of national identity—stood in the way.

[145] W. E. Gladstone, *Speeches on the Irish Question in 1886* (Edinburgh, 1886), 176.
[146] Lubenow, *Parliamentary Politics*, 17.
[147] *Hansard*, cccvi. 1239–40 (7[sic] June 1886).
[148] W. C. Lubenow, 'Irish Home Rule and the Social Basis of the Great Separation in the Liberal Party in 1886', *Historical Journal*, 28 (1985), 128.
[149] J. Parry, *The Rise and Fall of Liberal Government in Victorian Britain* (New Haven, 1993), 302.

Gladstone showed little interest in the mechanics of electioneering, but used the occasion to resurrect the glories of Midlothian. With undiminished energy he developed the theme of class division he had so clearly enunciated just after the defeat of the bill. He ended the campaign with a speech in Liverpool, in which he listed ten major reforms enacted during the previous half-century and insisted that 'on every one of them, without exception, the masses have been right and the classes have been wrong'.[150] By now he seemed more than a politician or even a statesman in the eyes of those who heard and remained faithful: he had become a symbol, an icon. The Irish Nationalist MP, T. P. O'Connor, saw him after the Liverpool speech as he went into the streets, his starched collar limp and the back of his black coat wet with sweat 'as if he had stood out in the open under a heavy shower of rain'. O'Connor records the magnificent face, the splendid eyes, the broad shoulders, the sense of vigour 'not weakened by 76 years of life' so electrifying the crowd that it was almost like 'the trailing of a miraculous saint among masses of idolaters'.[151]

In the Commons the alignment in 1886 between fears over the safety of property, on the one hand, and opposition to Home Rule, on the other, was by no means as exact as has sometimes been supposed. Of course the bulk of the Radicals remained with Gladstone, while the great bulk of the Whigs took to their heels. But most of those who left did so because of a particular objection to Home Rule and a distaste for that populist worship of the masses which seemed to have become Gladstone's instant recourse in adversity rather than from any consistent reactionary stance on domestic issues generally. In any case, Gladstone was by no means unsuccessful in retaining the support of 'moderate' Liberals. Even in Scotland, where desertions were numerous, some of the most 'right-wing' Liberals—townsmen as well as lairds—stayed in his camp.[152] Leaving Home Rule aside, the differences between many Gladstonians and Liberal Unionists remained comparatively small. Liberal Unionist leaders (to Gladstone's astonishment) continued to sit in their customary seats on the opposition benches. And not until 1911 did Liberal Unionists become eligible to join the Carlton Club. Indeed, of the original ninety-four defectors only one (Goschen) ever sat as a Conservative and no less than thirteen eventually returned to the fold.[153]

[150] Gladstone, *Speeches on the Irish Question*, 294.
[151] T. P. O'Connor, *Memoirs of an Old Parliamentarian*, 2 vols. (London, 1929), ii. 43–4.
[152] I. G. C. Hutchison, *A Political History of Scotland 1832–1924: Parties, Elections and Issues* (Edinburgh, 1986), 163–4; Lubenow, *Parliamentary Politics*, 284–6.
[153] Lubenow, *Parliamentary Politics*, 287–9; id., 'The Liberals and the National Question: Irish Home Rule, Nationalism, and their Relationship to Nineteenth-Century Liberalism', *Parliamentary History*, 13 (1994), 119–42.

Outside Westminster the Home Rule crisis helped to crystallize a greater displacement and undoubtedly played a part in accelerating the shift of middle and upper middle-class voting support from the Liberal to the Conservative side. The drift of the better-off into Toryism had been detectable as early as 1868. After 1886 (in part because of the Third Reform Act, in part because of Home Rule) it became pronounced. For some erstwhile Liberals Home Rule merely completed a process of disillusionment with Gladstone's handling of a succession of crises stretching back two decades and more. For Whigs, Home Rule threatened their most cherished principles: the rule of law, the sanctity of property, the might of Britain overseas. Among intellectuals a similar, if rather more ambiguous, set of reactions took place. On the one hand, the disenchantment with Gladstone of men like Huxley, Tyndall, Tennyson, Browning, Lecky, Seeley, Froude, Goldwin Smith, Jowett, and Spencer helped add a note of intellectual polish to Conservatism's new amalgam of social élitism, high reaction, and suburban anxiety. On the other, it looked back to a golden age—between 1832 and 1867—before an 'excessive' democracy, unleashed ironically by the Conservative hands of Disraeli, had contaminated the intelligence of public men. At the same time the unique duality of Ireland as both a domestic and an imperial concern meant that the congeries of political ideas which now centred upon Salisbury's Conservative Party became more strongly connected than ever with those strident attitudes to empire, which, though not new in themselves, had achieved a greater prominence and importance in the preceding decade.[154] As John Morley had begun to recognize almost twenty years before being appointed Chief Secretary in 1886, the matter of Ireland was, indeed, coming to 'wrap up' nearly all 'the controversies of principle' of the time: 'the functions of the State, the duties of property, the rights of labour, the question of whether the many are born for the few'.[155]

While, therefore, Gladstone's election victory of 1880 had at first seemed to represent a peculiar local exception to that collapse of classical Liberalism so evident during the 1870s in continental countries such as Italy, Austria, Germany, and France, the events of 1886 to some extent integrated British political developments into those of a wider European whole. Whatever the differences between Salisbury's attitudes and those of Conservatives elsewhere, the arrival of 'mass politics' throughout Western Europe in the 1880s generally favoured right-wing governments and, in

[154] T. Dunne, 'La Trahison des clercs: British Intellectuals and the First Home Rule Crisis', Irish Historical Studies, 23 (1982), 134–73.

[155] J. Morley, 'Old Parties and New Policy', Fortnightly Review, 10 (1868), 327.

addition, pushed a significant number of Liberals—Chamberlain was anything but unique—into alliances with the very reactionaries they had once so fiercely denounced.

Among British political leaders generally only Salisbury gained: he was to lead the Conservative Party for another sixteen years, thirteen of them as Prime Minister. Hartington's hopes for centrist moderation were gradually boiled down into little more than defensive conservatism. Chamberlain's original aspirations 'simply vanished into thin air'.[156] By contrast, Gladstone, though he soon found that Home Rule offered no sure foundations for the kind of Liberalism he had come to favour, was still left with a party strong enough to be able to attract a comparatively wide range of opinion and support. Above all, however, the events of 1886 nailed British politicians of almost every kind to the Irish cross. This did not mean that henceforth Ireland was always uppermost in their thoughts, far from it. But it did mean that Ireland effectively became the hinge upon which both major parties now turned. The Conservatives (or Unionists as they began to call themselves) had, in effect, been transformed into political vampires, dependent for life-giving doses of unity and cohesion upon Home Rule—the very thing they despised—remaining the great question of the day. The Liberals (save in 1906–10) were to find it impossible to form a government without the support of those Irish MPs whose presence at Westminster they wished either to erase or at least to reduce.

Gladstone believed that the introduction of the first Home Rule Bill represented 'one of those golden moments of our history—one of those opportunities which may come and may go, but which rarely return, or, if they return, return at long intervals, and under circumstances which no man can forecast'.[157] Over forty years later King George V told Ramsay MacDonald: 'What fools we were not to have accepted Gladstone's Home Rule Bill. The Empire now would not have had the Irish Free State giving us so much trouble and pulling us to pieces.'[158] What would have happened had Gladstone 'succeeded' in 1886 cannot be known. But, more than one hundred years later, the return of the 'golden moment' is still awaited, much as men of old awaited favourable portents in the sky. And Ireland continues to hang heavily over British politics, with British politicians too little and Irish politicians perhaps too much aware of the histories and precedents crowding around the constitutional and other problems with which—despite Gladstone's efforts—they are still condemned to deal.

[156] Jay, *Joseph Chamberlain*, 145–8.   [157] *Hansard*, cccvi. 1237 (7 June 1886).
[158] K. Rose, *King George V* (London, 1983), 242.

Maps

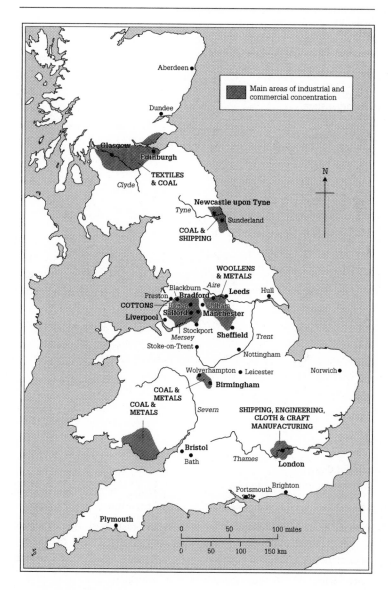

Aberdeen

Dundee

Glasgow
Edinburgh

**TEXTILES
& COAL**

Clyde

	Main areas of industrial and commercial concentration

N

Newcastle upon Tyne

Tyne

Sunderland

**COAL &
SHIPPING**

**WOOLLENS
& METALS**

Blackburn   *Aire*   **Leeds**   Hull

Preston   **Bradford**

COTTONS   Bolton   Oldham

Liverpool   **Salford**   **Manchester**

Stockport

Mersey   **Sheffield**   *Trent*

Stoke-on-Trent

Nottingham

Wolverhampton   Leicester   Norwich

**COAL &
METALS**

**COAL &
METALS**   *Severn*

Birmingham

**SHIPPING, ENGINEERING,
CLOTH & CRAFT
MANUFACTURING**

Bristol

Bath   *Thames*   **London**

Portsmouth   Brighton

Plymouth

0	50	100 miles
0	50	100	150 km

MAP 1. Mid-nineteenth-century industrial and urban Britain, showing towns with more than 50,000 inhabitants in 1861 (those with more than 100,000 are shown in **bold**). NB: No Welsh towns exceeded 50,000 until 1871

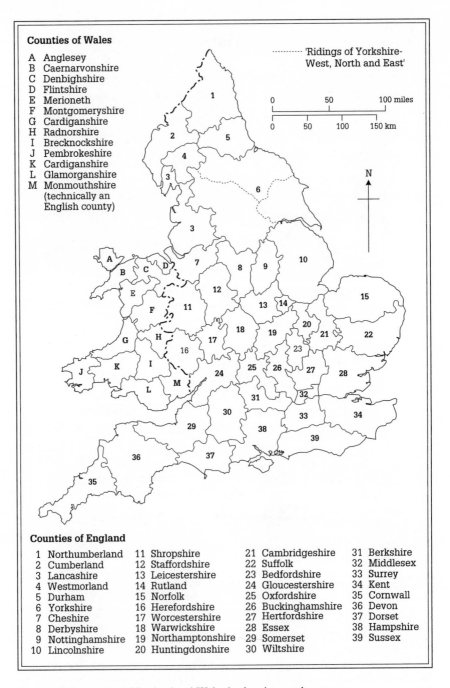

Counties of Wales

A Anglesey
B Caernarvonshire
C Denbighshire
D Flintshire
E Merioneth
F Montgomeryshire
G Cardiganshire
H Radnorshire
I Brecknockshire
J Pembrokeshire
K Cardiganshire
L Glamorganshire
M Monmouthshire
(technically an
English county)

-------- 'Ridings of Yorkshire-
West, North and East'

N

Counties of England

1 Northumberland	11 Shropshire	21 Cambridgeshire	31 Berkshire
2 Cumberland	12 Staffordshire	22 Suffolk	32 Middlesex
3 Lancashire	13 Leicestershire	23 Bedfordshire	33 Surrey
4 Westmorland	14 Rutland	24 Gloucestershire	34 Kent
5 Durham	15 Norfolk	25 Oxfordshire	35 Cornwall
6 Yorkshire	16 Herefordshire	26 Buckinghamshire	36 Devon
7 Cheshire	17 Worcestershire	27 Hertfordshire	37 Dorset
8 Derbyshire	18 Warwickshire	28 Essex	38 Hampshire
9 Nottinghamshire	19 Northamptonshire	29 Somerset	39 Sussex
10 Lincolnshire	20 Huntingdonshire	30 Wiltshire	

MAP 2. The counties of England and Wales in the nineteenth century

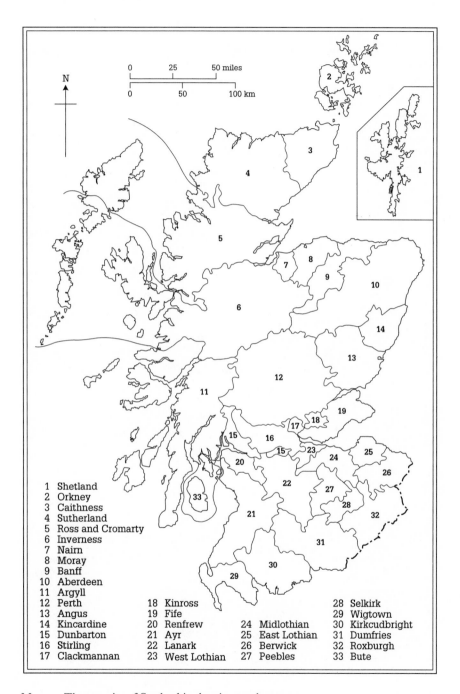

MAP 3. The counties of Scotland in the nineteenth century

1 Shetland
2 Orkney
3 Caithness
4 Sutherland
5 Ross and Cromarty
6 Inverness
7 Nairn
8 Moray
9 Banff
10 Aberdeen
11 Argyll
12 Perth
13 Angus
14 Kincardine
15 Dunbarton
16 Stirling
17 Clackmannan

18 Kinross
19 Fife
20 Renfrew
21 Ayr
22 Lanark
23 West Lothian

24 Midlothian
25 East Lothian
26 Berwick
27 Peebles

28 Selkirk
29 Wigtown
30 Kirkcudbright
31 Dumfries
32 Roxburgh
33 Bute

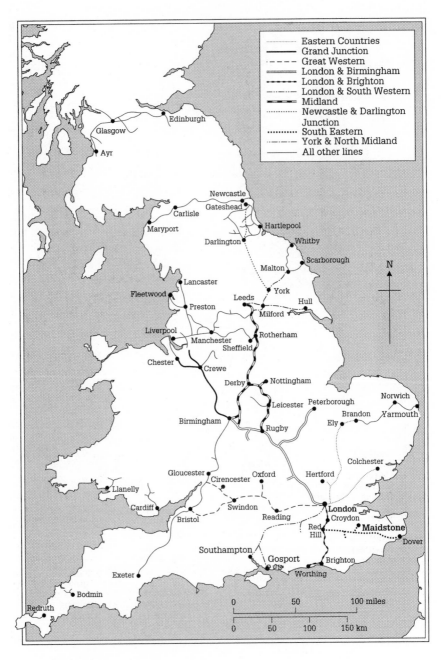

Legend:
- Eastern Countries
- Grand Junction
- Great Western
- London & Birmingham
- London & Brighton
- London & South Western
- Midland
- Newcastle & Darlington Junction
- South Eastern
- York & North Midland
- All other lines

N

Edinburgh
Glasgow
Ayr

Newcastle
Gateshead
Carlisle
Maryport
Hartlepool
Darlington
Whitby
Scarborough
Malton
Lancaster
Fleetwood
Leeds
York
Hull
Preston
Milford
Liverpool
Rotherham
Manchester
Sheffield
Chester
Crewe
Derby
Nottingham
Leicester
Peterborough
Norwich
Brandon
Yarmouth
Birmingham
Ely
Rugby
Colchester
Gloucester
Oxford
Hertford
Cirencester
Llanelly
Swindon
Cardiff
Reading
London
Bristol
Croydon
Red Hill
Maidstone
Dover
Southampton
Gosport
Brighton
Exeter
Worthing
Bodmin
Redruth

0   50   100 miles
0 50 100 150 km

MAP 4. The British railway system in 1845

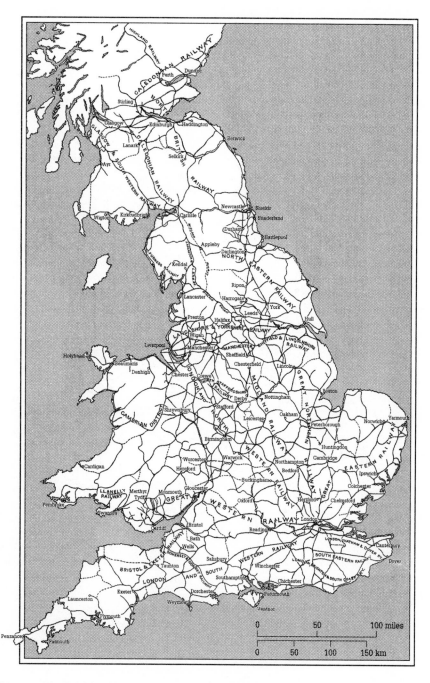

MAP 5. The British railway system in the early 1870s

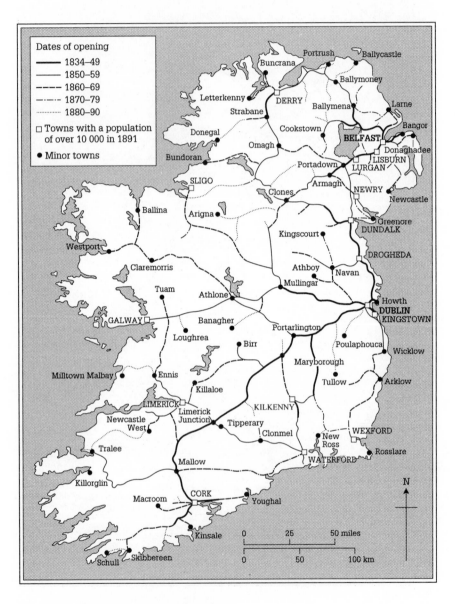

MAP 6. The Irish railway system 1834–1890

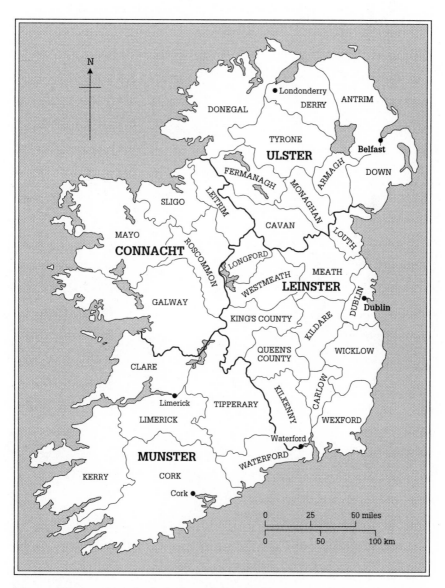

MAP 7. The counties and principal towns of Ireland in the nineteenth century, showing towns with more than 20,000 inhabitants in 1861 (those with more than 100,000 are shown in **bold**)

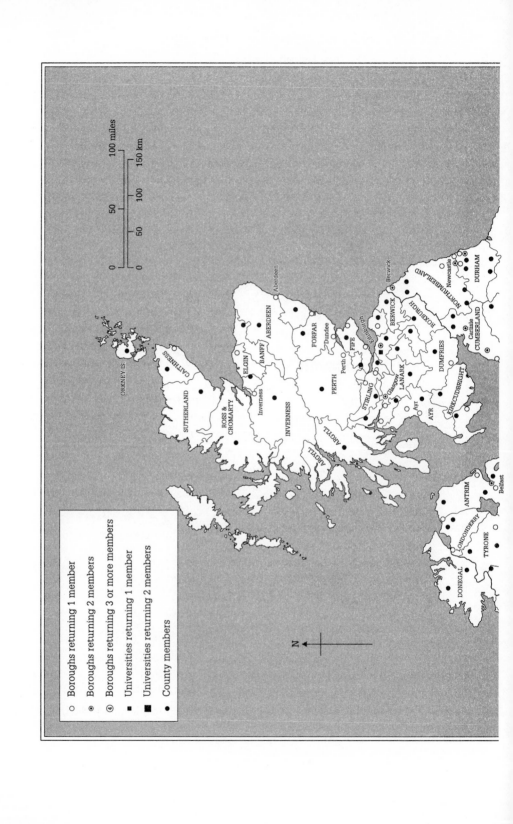

○	Boroughs returning 1 member
⊙	Boroughs returning 2 members
⊕	Boroughs returning 3 or more members
■	Universities returning 1 member
■	Universities returning 2 members
●	County members

N

0   50   100 miles

0   50   100   150 km

ORKNEY IS.

CAITHNESS

SUTHERLAND

ROSS & CROMARTY

Inverness

INVERNESS

ARGYLL

ARGYLL

ELGIN

BANFF

ABERDEEN

Aberdeen

FORFAR

Dundee

PERTH

Perth

FIFE

Edinburgh

STIRLING

Glasgow

LANARK

Ayr

AYR

KIRKCUDBRIGHT

DUMFRIES

BERWICK

Berwick

ROXBURGH

NORTHUMBERLAND

Newcastle

DURHAM

Carlisle

CUMBERLAND

DONEGAL

LONDONDERRY

TYRONE

ANTRIM

Belfast

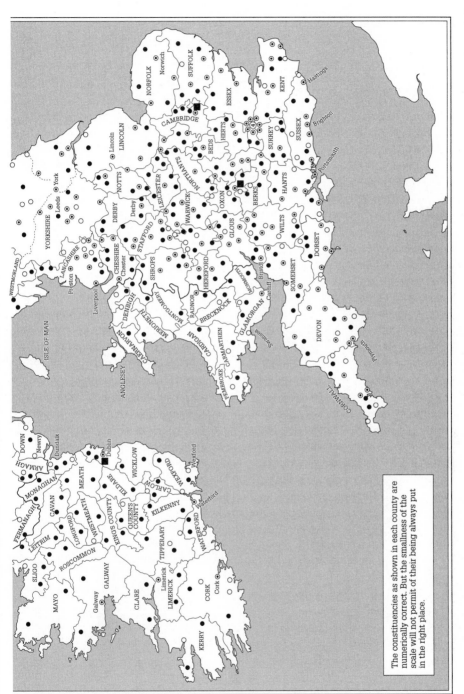

The constituencies as shown in each county are numerically correct. But the smallness of the scale will not permit of their being always put in the right place.

MAP 8. Parliamentary representation after the Reform Acts of 1832. NB: some (comparatively minor) adjustments took place over the period 1832–1884

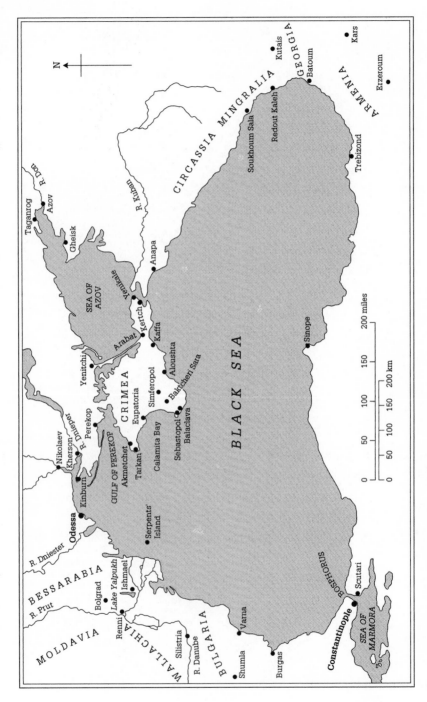

MAP 9. The Black Sea area at the time of the Crimean War

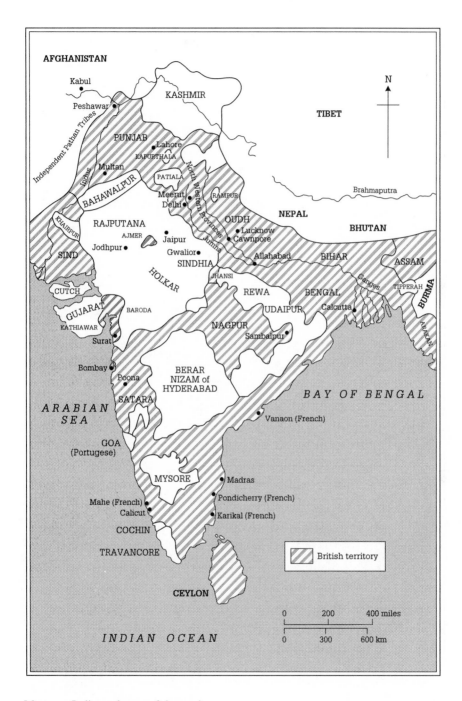

AFGHANISTAN

Kabul

Peshawar

Independent Pathan Tribes

Indus

KASHMIR

TIBET

N

PUNJAB

Lahore

KAPURTHALA

Multan

BAHAWALPUR

PATIALA

North Western Provinces

Brahmaputra

KHAIRPUR

RAJPUTANA

AJMER

Jaipur

Meerut
Delhi

RAMPUR

NEPAL

BHUTAN

OUDH

Lucknow
Cawnpore

SIND

Jodhpur

Gwalior

SINDHIA

Jumna

Allahabad

BIHAR

ASSAM

HOLKAR

JHANSI

REWA

Ganges

BENGAL

TIPPERAH

CUTCH

GUJARAT

BARODA

UDAIPUR

Calcutta

BURMA

KATHIAWAR

Surat

NAGPUR

Sambalpur

ARAKAN

Bombay

Poona

BERAR
NIZAM of
HYDERABAD

BAY OF BENGAL

SATARA

ARABIAN
SEA

Vanaon (French)

GOA
(Portugese)

MYSORE

Madras

Mahe (French)

Calicut

Pondicherry (French)

Karikal (French)

COCHIN

British territory

TRAVANCORE

CEYLON

0   200   400 miles

0   300   600 km

INDIAN OCEAN

MAP 10. India on the eve of the mutiny

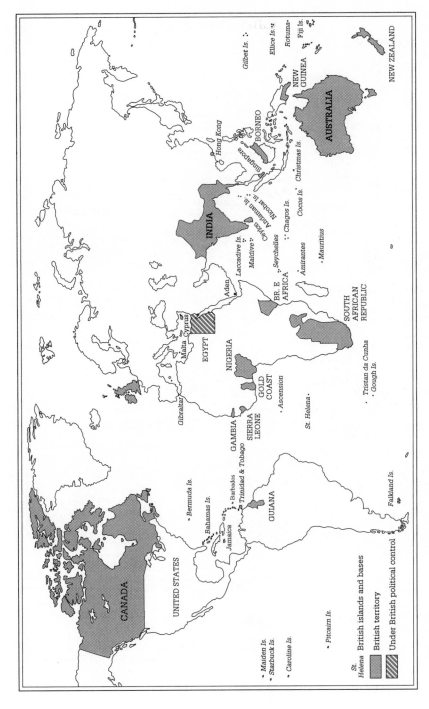

MAP 11. The British Empire by the 1890s

Chronology

Publication dates are for first publication in book form.

Date	*Politics*	*Legislation* (see also *Politics*)
1846	Corn Laws repealed (by 9 & 10 Vict., c. 22) Peel resigns and Russell becomes Prime Minister	272 Railway construction bills enacted (a record)
1847	General election	'Ten Hour' Factory Act (10 Vict., c. 29) Irish Poor Law Extension Act (10 Vict., c. 31) Poor Law Act (10 & 11 Vict., c. 109)
1848	Chartist demonstration on Kennington Common Smith O'Brien's rising in Ireland	Public Health Act (11 & 12 Vict., c. 43)
1849	Disraeli becomes Conservative leader in Commons Annexation of the Punjab	Navigation Acts repealed (by 12 & 13 Vict., c. 29) Encumbered Estates (Ireland) Act (12 & 13 Vict., c. 77)
1850	Palmerston's 'Civis Romanus Sum' speech Tenant League founded in Ireland London Protocol on Schleswig-Holstein (confirmed by Treaty of London 1852)	Irish Franchise Act (13 & 14 Vict., c. 69)
1851	Palmerston resigns as Foreign Secretary	Ecclesiastical Titles Act (14 & 15 Vict., c. 60)
1852	Derby forms minority Tory ministry (Feb.) General election Aberdeen forms Whig-Peelite ministry (Dec.)	Patent Law Amendment Act (15 & 16 Vict., c. 83)
1853	Gladstone's first budget	Compulsory Vaccination Act (16 & 17 Vict., c. 100)
1854	Britain declares war on Russia (Crimean War 1854–6) Battles of Balaclava and Inkerman	Oxford University Act (17 & 18 Vict., c. 81) Corrupt [Electoral] Practices Act (17 & 18 Vict., c. 102)

People, projects, events	Publications and the Creative Arts	Date
Irish Famine (1845–9) worsens Evangelical Alliance founded	E. Lear, *A Book of Nonsense* Mendelssohn conducts *Elijah* in Birmingham	1846
Formation of United Presbyterian Church in Scotland	C. Brontë, *Jane Eyre* E. Brontë, *Wuthering Heights*	1847
Queen Victoria visits Balmoral for first time	C. Dickens, *Dombey and Son* E. Gaskell, *Mary Barton* T. B. Macaulay, *History of England* (–1861) J. S. Mill, *Principles of Political Economy* W. M. Thackeray, *Vanity Fair*	1848
Cholera epidemic in London	M. Arnold, *The Strayed Reveller* J. Ruskin, *The Seven Lamps of Architecture*	1849
Roman Catholic hierarchy restored in England and Wales R. Stephenson's Menai Straits bridge opens to rail traffic Founding of Amalgamated Society of Engineers	C. Dickens, *David Copperfield* C. Kingsley, *Alton Locke* A. Tennyson, *In Memoriam* (becomes poet laureate) H. Spencer, *Social Statics* J. Millais, *Christ in the House of His Parents* (painting) W. Butterfield, All Saints, Margaret Street, London	1850
Great Exhibition in Hyde Park Foundation of Owens College, Manchester Census of religious attendance in Britain	G. Borrow, *Lavengro* W. Thomson formulates the two great laws of thermodynamics in communications to the Royal Society of Edinburgh (–1854) E. Landseer, *The Monarch of the Glen* (painting) J. Paxton and G. H. Stokes, Mentmore Towers (–1854)	1851
King's Cross station (designed by L. Cubitt) completed	W. M. Thackeray, *Henry Esmond* F. Madox Brown, *The Last of England* (painting)	1852
C. H. Spurgeon begins preaching at Exeter Hall, London Queen Victoria takes chloroform during birth of Prince Leopold	M. Arnold, *Poems* E. Gaskell, *Cranford* R. S. Surtees, *Mr Sponge's Sporting Tour* J. Martin, *The Great Day of His Wrath* (painting, 1851–) C. Brodrick, Leeds Town Hall (–1858)	1853
Publication of Northcote-Trevelyan Report on Civil Service	C. Patmore, *The Angel in the House: The Betrothal* A. Tennyson publishes *The Charge of the Light Brigade* W. H. Hunt, *The Scapegoat* (painting)	1854

Date	Politics	Legislation (see also Politics)
1855	Palmerston becomes Prime Minister Stamp duty on newspapers abolished New South Wales, Victoria, and Newfoundland obtain responsible government	Metropolis Management Act (18 & 19 Vict., c. 120) Limited Liability Act (18 & 19 Vict., c. 133), further Act in 1856 (19 & 20 Vict., c. 47)
1856	Annexation of Oudh Treaties of Paris end Crimean conflict *Arrow* incident War with Persia (−1857) South Australia, Tasmania, and New Zealand obtain responsible government	County and Borough Police Act (19 & 20 Vict., c. 69) Cambridge University Act (19 & 20 Vict., c. 88)
1857	General election Indian Mutiny	Matrimonial Causes [Divorce] Act (20 & 21 Vict., c. 85)
1858	Irish Republican Brotherhood (IRB) founded Derby forms minority Tory ministry Britain extends possessions around Hong Kong	Property Qualification of MPs Act (21 & 22 Vict., c. 26) Jewish Disabilities Act (21 & 22 Vict., c. 48) Public Health Act (21 & 22 Vict., c. 97) Local Government Act (21 & 22 Vict., c. 98) India Act (21 & 22 Vict., c. 106)
1859	Conservative Reform Bill defeated General election Liberal meeting in Willis's Rooms Palmerston returns as Prime Minister	
1860	Anglo-French (Cobden-Chevalier) Free Trade Treaty Second Maori War (−1870) British troops burn emperor's Summer Palace at Peking	Food and Drink Adulteration Act (23 & 24 Vict., c. 84)
1861	Public Accounts Committee established Paper duty abolished Threat of war with USA over *Trent* incident	Bankruptcy and Insolvency Act (24 & 25 Vict., c. 134)

People, projects, events	Publications and the Creative Arts	Date
Hyde Park demonstrations against restrictions on Sunday trading *Daily Telegraph* commences publication	E. Gaskell, *North and South* H. Spencer, *Principles of Psychology* A. Trollope, *The Warden* F. Leighton, *Cimabue's Celebrated Madonna* (painting, 1853–) T. Deane and B. Woodward, University Museum, Oxford (–1860) Wagner conducts concerts in London	1855
H. Bessemer's steel-making process introduced W. H. Perkins prepares first aniline dye ('mauve')	C. Reade, *It is Never Too Late to Mend* H. Irving's debut on the London stage	1856
Financial crisis R. Burton and J. Speke sent by Geographical Society to search for the equatorial lakes of Africa Science Museum, South Kensington, founded	R. M. Ballantyne, *Coral Island* C. Dickens, *Little Dorrit* T. Hughes, *Tom Brown's Schooldays* A. Trollope, *Barchester Towers* H. Wallis, *The Stonebreaker* (painting) Manchester Art Treasures Exhibition	1857
Ireland–Newfoundland telegraph cable completed Leeds Town Hall (designed by C. Brodrick) opened by Queen Victoria Darwin and Wallace present papers to Linnean Society on evolution by natural selection	T. Carlyle, *Frederick the Great* (–1865) W. P. Frith, *Derby Day* (painting, 1856–) New Royal Opera House, Covent Garden, opens	1858
First overseas cricket tour—to Canada and USA Fears of French invasion lead to creation of volunteer force *Irish Times* commences publication	C. Darwin, *The Origin of Species* C. Dickens, *A Tale of Two Cities* G. Eliot, *Adam Bede* J. S. Mill, *On Liberty* A. Tennyson, *Idylls of the King* (–1885) C. Barry, Halifax Town Hall (–1863)	1859
Last major bare-knuckle boxing contest in England (Sayers *v.* Heenan) J. Swan invents electric lamp London University establishes degrees in science *Cornhill Magazine* founded under Thackeray's editorship	D. Boucicault, *The Colleen Bawn* (play) W. Collins, *The Woman in White* G. Eliot, *The Mill on the Floss* *Essays and Reviews* [ed. J. Parker] W. Dyce, *Pegwell Bay* (painting, 1858–)	1860
Post Office Savings Bank opens HMS *Warrior*, first all-iron warship, completed Prince Consort dies (14 Dec.)	C. Dickens, *Great Expectations* H. Maine, *Ancient Law* J. S. Mill, *On Representative Government* C. Reade, *The Cloister and the Hearth* Mrs H. Wood, *East Lynne*	1861

Date	Politics	Legislation (see also Politics)
1862	Self-governing colonies permitted to raise defence forces British-built Confederate raider *Alabama* sails from Birkenhead and attacks US shipping Gladstone undertakes northern speaking tours	Police and Public Health (Scotland) Act (25 & 26 Vict., c. 101)
1863		Security against Violence [Garotters'] Act (26 & 27 Vict., c. 44)
1864	Garibaldi visits England Gladstone supports franchise reform in Pale of Constitution speech London Conference on Schleswig-Holstein fails	First Contagious Diseases Act (27 & 28 Vict., c. 85), others follow in 1866 (29 Vict., c. 35) and 1869 (32 & 33 Vict., c. 96), see 1886
1865	General election Palmerston dies (18 Oct.) and Russell returns as Prime Minister Reform League founded	Colonial Laws Validity Act (28 & 29 Vict., c. 63) Urban [Poor Law] Chargeability Act (28 & 29 Vict., c. 79)
1866	Liberal Reform Bill defeated Derby forms minority Tory ministry	Exchequer and Audit Departments Act (29 Vict., c. 39) Sanitary Act (29 & 30 Vict., c. 90)
1867	Fenian rising in Ireland (Second) Reform Act for England and Wales (30 & 31 Vict., c. 102) Foundation of National Union of Conservative and Constitutional Associations	British North America Act (30 Vict., c. 3) Factory Acts Extension Act (30 & 31 Vict., c. 103)
1868	Disraeli succeeds Derby as Prime Minister Boundary [of Constituencies] Act (31 & 32 Vict., c. 46) (Second) Reform Acts for Scotland (31 & 32 Vict., c. 46) and Ireland (31 & 32 Vict., c. 49—Note: an Irish Franchise Act had been passed in 1850, see Legislation)	Abolition of Compulsory Church Rates Act (31 & 32 Vict., c. 109)

People, projects, events	Publications and the Creative Arts	Date
J. W. Colenso (Bishop of Natal) causes storm by denying authenticity of the Pentateuch Construction of Thames Embankment starts (–1874) 'Revised Code' introduces 'payment by results' for schoolteachers International Exhibition, South Kensington Distress in Lancashire caused by 'cotton famine'	M. E. Braddon, *Lady Audley's Secret* G. Meredith, *Modern Love* A. L. Egg, *Travelling Companions* (painting) W. P. Frith, *The Railway Station* (painting) G. G. Scott, Foreign Office, London (–1873)	1862
W. Whiteley opens his department store in Bayswater Football Association established in London	C. Kingsley, *The Water-Babies* C. Lyell, *The Antiquity of Man* J. S. Mill, *Utilitarianism* C. Brodrick, Grand Hotel, Scarborough (–1867) G. G. Scott, Albert Memorial, London (–1872)	1863
First County Cricket championship Metropolitan Railway (pioneer of the Underground) opens in London	J. H. Newman, *Apologia pro Vita Sua* A. Trollope, *The Small House at Allington*	1864
Rebellion in Jamaica, Governor Eyre recalled W. Booth leads his first Christian Mission meeting (forerunner of Salvation Army) *Pall Mall Gazette* and *Fortnightly Review* commence publication W. Whymper climbs the Matterhorn	L. Carroll, *Alice's Adventures in Wonderland* C. Dickens, *Our Mutual Friend* J. Ruskin, *Sesame and Lilies* W. Burges, St Fin Barre's Cathedral, Cork (–1879)	1865
Collapse of Overend & Gurney Bank precipitates financial crisis Foundation of Amateur Athletic Club (later Association) 'Sheffield Outrages' (intimidation of non-union workers)	E. Gaskell, *Wives and Daughters* C. Kingsley, *Hereward the Wake* D. G. Rossetti, *Monna Vanna* (painting)	1866
First worldwide 'Lambeth Conference' of Anglican bishops J. Lister introduces antiseptic system for surgery The 'Manchester Martyrs' executed 8th Marquess of Queensberry supervises production of new rules for boxing Fenian explosion at Clerkenwell (12 killed)	W. Bagehot, *The English Constitution* A. Trollope, *The Last Chronicle of Barset*	1867
Last public execution First Trades Union Congress meets Press Association founded	W. Collins, *The Moonstone* C. Dilke, *Greater Britain* W. Burges, Cardiff Castle (restoration, –1881) G. G. Scott, Midland Hotel, St Pancras, London (–1874)	1868

Date	Politics	Legislation (see also Politics)
	General election Disraeli resigns before parliament meets Gladstone forms a Liberal ministry	
1869	Church of Ireland disestablished (by 32 & 33 Vict., c. 42)	Trades Unions Funds Protection Act (32 & 33 Vict., c. 61)
1870	I. Butt founds Home Government Association in Ireland Gladstone's first Irish Land Act (33 & 34 Vict., c. 46) Elementary Education Act for England and Wales (33 & 34 Vict., c. 46) Conservative Central Office founded	Army Enlistment Act (33 & 34 Vict., c. 67) First Married Women's Property Act (33 & 34 Vict., c. 93), see 1882
1871	London Convention annuls Black Sea clauses of main Treaty of Paris (1856) Treaty of Washington settles various Anglo-American problems Gladstone speaks at Aberdeen against Home Rule	University Tests Act (34 Vict., c. 26) Trade Union Act (34 & 35 Vict., c. 31) Criminal Law Amendment Act (34 & 35 Vict., c. 32) Army Regulation Act (34 & 35 Vict., c. 86)
1872	Disraeli delivers Crystal Palace speech C. Dilke declares republican views in Commons (Secret) Ballot Act (35 & 36 Vict., c. 33) Scottish Education Act (35 & 36 Vict., c. 62)	Licensing Act (35 & 36 Vict., c. 94)
1873	Gladstone resigns after defeat on Irish University Bill, but Disraeli declines to take office Ashanti War (–1874) Foundation of Home Rule League in Ireland	Judicature Act (36 & 37 Vict., c. 66)
1874	General election Disraeli returns as Prime Minister	Factory Act (37 & 38 Vict., c. 44) Public Worship Regulation Act (37 & 38 Vict., c. 85)
1875	Gladstone resigns Liberal leadership in Commons, succeeded by Hartington Government buys minority interest in Suez Canal	Artisans Dwellings Act (38 & 39 Vict., c. 36) Public Health Act (38 & 39 Vict., c. 55) Sale of Food and Drugs Act (38 & 39 Vict., c. 63) Conspiracy and Protection of Property Act (38 & 39 Vict., c. 86)

People, projects, events	*Publications and the Creative Arts*	*Date*
National Education League founded Charity Organization Society founded	M. Arnold, *Culture and Anarchy* R. D. Blackmore, *Lorna Doone* J. S. Mill, *The Subjection of Women*	1869
Civil Service reforms introduced Royal Commission on Scientific Instruction appointed under chairmanship of 7th Duke of Devonshire (reports 1871–5) B. Jowett becomes Master of Balliol College, Oxford	B. Disraeli, *Lothair* J. Lubbock, *The Origin of Civilization* D. G. Rossetti, *Poems* A. Waterhouse, Eaton Hall, Cheshire (–1883)	1870
Abolition of purchase of army commissions Local Government Board set up Chair of Experimental Physics established at Cambridge Rugby Football Union founded Bank Holidays introduced Stanley finds Livingstone English FA cup competition established	L. Carroll, *Through the Looking-Glass* C. Darwin, *The Descent of Man*	1871
J. Arch founds National Agricultural Labourers' Union First FA cup final (Wanderers beat R. Engineers 1–0) First football international (goalless draw between England and Scotland)	G. Eliot, *Middlemarch* T. Hardy, *Under the Greenwood Tree* C. Rossetti, *Sing-Song: A Nursery Rhyme Book* J. A. McN. Whistler, *Arrangement in Grey and Black No. 1: The Artist's Mother* (painting)	1872
D. L. Moody and I. Sankey begin revival tour of Britain (–1875)	J. Clerk Maxwell, *Treatise on Electricity and Magnetism* J. S. Mill, *Autobiography* W. Pater, *Studies in the History of the Renaissance*	1873
First strike by agricultural labourers in England Tichborne claimant found guilty of perjury Foundation of Yorkshire College, Leeds Foundation of International Exhibition Co-operative Wine Society	W. E. Gladstone, *The Vatican Decrees* T. Hardy, *Far from the Madding Crowd* L. Alma-Tadema, *The Picture Gallery* (painting) J. Tissot, *The Ball on Shipboard* (painting) G. Street, Law Courts, Strand, London (–1882)	1874
London main drainage system completed London Medical School for Women opens M. Webb first to swim English Channel	G. Meredith, *Beauchamp's Career* A. Trollope, *The Way We Live Now* W. S. Gilbert and A. Sullivan, *Trial by Jury* (opera)	1875

Date	Politics	Legislation (see also Politics)
1876	Queen Victoria declared Empress of India Bulgarian atrocities agitation	Elementary Education Act (39 & 40 Vict., c. 79) Merchant Shipping Act (39 & 40 Vict., c. 80)
1877	Sir B. Frere appointed high commissioner in South Africa The Transvaal annexed National Liberal Federation founded Gladstone visits Ireland	Prisons Act (40 & 41 Vict., c. 21), the same for Ireland (c. 49) and for Scotland (c. 53)
1878	Disraeli (now Beaconsfield) attends Berlin Congress Britain acquires Cyprus British troops enter Afghanistan	Factory and Workshops Act (41 Vict., c. 16)
1879	Zulus defeat British detachment at Isandhlwana Treaty of Gandamak with Afghanistan 'Land War' in Ireland (–1882) Irish National Land League founded Gladstone begins Midlothian campaigns	
1880	General election Gladstone returns as Prime Minister Parnell elected chairman of Home Rule Party Bradlaugh affair begins First South African War begins (–1881)	Burials Act (43 & 44 Vict., c. 41) Employers Liability Act (43 & 44 Vict., c. 42)
1881	Britain recognizes the Transvaal Republic Disraeli dies (19 Apr.) Conservative leadership shared between Salisbury and Northcote Gladstone's second Irish Land Act (44 & 45 Vict., c. 49) Revolt in Egypt led by Arabi Pasha Parnell arrested and Land League proscribed	Peace Preservation (Ireland) Act (44 & 45 Vict., c. 5)
1882	Kilmainham 'Treaty' between government and Parnell Murder of Lord F. Cavendish (Chief Secretary) in Dublin Invasion of Egypt	Prevention of Crime (Ireland) Act (45 & 46 Vict., c. 25) Ancient Monuments Protection Act (45 & 46 Vict., c. 73) Second Married Women's Property Act (45 & 46 Vict., c. 75), see 1870
1883	E. Baring appointed British Agent in Egypt (–1907) Mahdist rebellion in the Sudan Primrose League founded	Corrupt and Illegal [Electoral] Practices Act (46 & 47 Vict., c. 51)

People, projects, events	Publications and the Creative Arts	Date
Presbyterian Church of England founded W. Morris, *Sigurd the Volsung* F. Holl, *The Firstborn* (painting) H. Richter conducts concerts in London	G. Eliot, *Daniel Deronda* W. E. Gladstone, *The Bulgarian Horrors*	1876
Society for the Protection of Ancient Build- ings founded All-England Lawn Tennis Championship first played at Wimbledon	W. H. Mallock, *The New Republic* D. G. Rossetti, *Proserpine* (painting) Wagner and Richter conduct three-day series of Wagner concerts in London	1877
Roman Catholic hierarchy restored in Scot- land Development of Gilchrist-Thomas steel- making process	T. Hardy, *The Return of the Native* W. F. Yeames, *And When Did You Last See* *Your Father?* (painting) Whistler-Ruskin libel action W. S. Gilbert and A. Sullivan, *HMS Pina- fore* (opera)	1878
Public granted unrestricted access to gal- leries at British Museum First London telephone exchange First women students at Oxford	G. Meredith, *The Egoist* R. L. Stevenson, *Travels with a Donkey* W. H. Crossland, Royal Holloway College, Egham (−1887)	1879
First Test Match played in England (Eng- land *v.* Australia) Captain C. Boycott's name enters English language	B. Disraeli, *Endymion* F. Leighton, *Captive Andromache* (paint- ing) J. L. Pearson, Truro Cathedral (−1910) Guildhall School of Music founded	1880
Natural History Museum, South Kensing- ton, opens Flogging abolished in British army, follow- ing abolition in Royal Navy (1879)	Revised Version of New Testament pub- lished L. Alma-Tadema, *In the Tepidarium* (painting) W. S. Gilbert and A. Sullivan, *Patience* (opera)	1881
Opening of Regent Street Polytechnic Foundation of Society for Psychical Research Electric trams begin operations in London	H. A. Jones, *The Silver King* opens at Prin- cess Theatre, London R. L. Stevenson, *New Arabian Nights* A. J. Moore, *Dreamers* (painting) W. S. Gilbert and A. Sullivan, *Iolanthe* (opera)	1882
W. Thomson lectures to Royal Institution on the size and nature of atoms Boys' Brigade founded	[A. Mearns], *The Bitter Cry of Outcast Lon- don* J. R. Seeley, *The Expansion of England* R. L. Stevenson, *Treasure Island* E. Poynter, *The Ides of March* (Painting) Royal College of Music founded	1883

Date	Politics	Legislation (see also Politics)
1884	Foundation of Fabian Society London Convention on the Transvaal Wolseley sent to rescue Gordon in the Sudan (Third) Reform (Representation of the People) Act (48 Vict., c. 3)	
1885	Gordon killed in Khartoum Salisbury forms minority Tory ministry Redistribution of Seats Act (48 & 49 Vict., c. 23) General election 'Hawarden Kite' (H. Gladstone announces his father's conversion to Home Rule)	Criminal Law Amendment Act (48 & 49 Vict., c. 69) Irish Land Purchase Act (48 & 49 Vict., c. 73)
1886	Gladstone returns as Prime Minister First Home Rule Bill defeated Liberal Party splits General election Salisbury returns as Prime Minister with Liberal Unionist support	Contagious Diseases Acts repealed (by 49 Vict., c. 10), see 1864

People, projects, events	Publications and the Creative Arts	Date
Gaelic Athletic Association founded in Ireland Royal Commission on the Housing of the Working Classes appointed under the chairmanship of C. Dilke (reports 1884–5)	H. Spencer, *The Man versus the State* E. Burne-Jones, *King Cophetua and the Beggar Maid* (painting) W. Q. Orchardson, *Marriage de Convenance* (painting) C. Villiers Stanford, *Savonarola* (opera)	1884
Irish dynamiters damage Westminster Hall Cruft's Dog Show first held, London	H. Rider Haggard, *King Solomon's Mines* W. Pater, *Marius the Epicurean* A. W. Pinero, *The Magistrate* opens at Belgravia (Royal Court) Theatre, London H. von Herkomer, *Hard Times* (painting) W. S. Gilbert and A. Sullivan, *The Mikado* (opera)	1885
Colonial and Indian Exhibition, London Unemployed riot in West London Severn Railway Tunnel opens *English Historical Review* founded	G. Gissing, *Demos* T. Hardy, *The Mayor of Casterbridge* R. L. Stevenson, *Kidnapped* and *Dr Jekyll and Mr Hyde* J. Millais, *Bubbles* (painting)	1886

List of Cabinets

RUSSELL'S FIRST CABINET

formed July 1846

Prime Minister and First Lord of the Treasury: Lord John Russell
Lord Chancellor: Lord Cottenham
Lord President: Marquess of Lansdowne
Lord Privy Seal: Earl of Minto
Chancellor of the Exchequer: Sir C. Wood
Home Secretary: Sir G. Grey
Foreign Secretary: Viscount Palmerston
Secretary for War and Colonies: Earl Grey
First Lord of the Admiralty: Earl of Auckland
President of the Board of Trade: Earl of Clarendon
President of the Board of Control: Sir J. C. Hobhouse (cr. Lord Broughton 1851)
Chancellor of the Duchy of Lancaster: Lord Campbell
First Commissioner of Woods and Forests: Lord Morpeth (Earl of Carlisle 1848)
Chief Secretary for Ireland: H. Labouchere
Postmaster-General: Marquess of Clanricarde
Paymaster-General: T. B. Macaulay

Changes

July 1847: Labouchere succeeded Clarendon as President of the Board of Trade (his successor as Chief Secretary for Ireland was not in the cabinet). *August 1847*: Macaulay resigned (his successor as Paymaster-General was not in the cabinet). *January 1849*: on the death of Auckland, F. T. Baring became First Lord of the Admiralty. *March 1850*: Carlisle succeeded Campbell as Chancellor of the Duchy of Lancaster. *June 1850*: on Cottenham's retirement the Great Seal remained in commission until the appointment of Lord Truro as Lord Chancellor in July 1850. *February 1851*: Russell resigned, but resumed office a fortnight later. *October 1851*: Lord Seymour, Fox Maule, and Earl Granville entered the cabinet as First Commissioner of Works, Secretary at War, and Paymaster-General. *December 1851*: Granville succeeded Palmerston as Foreign Secretary. *February 1852*: Fox Maule succeeded Broughton as President of the Board of Control.

DERBY'S FIRST CABINET

formed February 1852

Prime Minister and First Lord of the Treasury: Earl of Derby
Lord Chancellor: Lord St Leonards

Lord President: Earl of Lonsdale
Lord Privy Seal: Marquess of Salisbury
Chancellor of the Exchequer: B. Disraeli
Home Secretary: Spencer Walpole
Foreign Secretary: Earl of Malmesbury
Secretary for War and Colonies: Sir J. Pakington
First Lord of the Admiralty: Duke of Northumberland
President of the Board of Trade: J. W. Henley
First Commissioner of Works: Lord John Manners
Postmaster-General: Earl of Hardwicke

ABERDEEN'S CABINET

formed December 1852

Prime Minister and First Lord of the Treasury: Earl of Aberdeen
Lord Chancellor: Lord Cranworth
Lord President: Earl Granville
Lord Privy Seal: Duke of Argyll
Chancellor of the Exchequer: W. E. Gladstone
Home Secretary: Viscount Palmerston
Foreign Secretary: Lord John Russell
Secretary for War and Colonies: Duke of Newcastle
First Lord of the Admiralty: Sir James Graham
President of the Board of Control: Sir C. Wood
Secretary at War: Sidney Herbert
Minister without Portfolio: Marquess of Lansdowne

Changes

February 1853: Russell ceased to be Foreign Secretary and remained in the cabinet as Minister without Portfolio; the Earl of Clarendon became Foreign Secretary. *June 1854*: a new office of Secretary for the Colonies was created and given to Sir G. Grey; Newcastle remained Secretary for War; Granville became Chancellor of the Duchy of Lancaster with a seat in the cabinet, and Russell succeeded him as Lord President. *January 1855*: Russell resigned.

PALMERSTON'S FIRST CABINET

formed February 1855

Prime Minister and First Lord of the Treasury: Viscount Palmerston
Lord Chancellor: Lord Cranworth
Lord President: Earl Granville
Lord Privy Seal: Duke of Argyll
Chancellor of the Exchequer: W. E. Gladstone
Home Secretary: Sir G. Grey

Foreign Secretary: Earl of Clarendon
Secretary for War: Lord Panmure (formerly Fox Maule)
Colonial Secretary: Sidney Herbert
First Lord of the Admiralty: Sir James Graham
President of the Board of Control: Sir C. Wood
First Commissioner of Works: Sir W. Molesworth
Postmaster-General: Viscount Canning
Minister without Portfolio: Marquess of Lansdowne

Changes

February 1855: Gladstone, Herbert, and Graham resigned; Sir G. Cornewall Lewis became Chancellor of the Exchequer, Lord John Russell became Secretary for the Colonies, and Wood became First Lord of the Admiralty; R. V. Smith entered the cabinet as President of the Board of Control. *March 1855*: the Earl of Harrowby entered the cabinet as Chancellor of the Duchy of Lancaster. *July 1855*: Canning left the cabinet on appointment as Governor-General of India; Russell resigned; Molesworth became Colonial Secretary (his successor as First Commissioner of Works was not in the cabinet). *October 1855*: on Molesworth's death, H. Labouchere entered the cabinet as Colonial Secretary. *November 1855*: Argyll became Postmaster-General; Lord Stanley of Alderley entered the cabinet as President of the Board of Trade. *December 1855*: the Earl of Harrowby succeeded Argyll as Lord Privy Seal; M. T. Baines succeeded Harrowby as Chancellor of the Duchy of Lancaster and entered the cabinet. *February 1858*: the Marquess of Clanricarde succeeded Harrowby as Lord Privy Seal and entered the cabinet.

DERBY'S SECOND CABINET

formed February 1858

Prime Minister and First Lord of the Treasury: Earl of Derby
Lord Chancellor: Lord Chelmsford
Lord President: Marquess of Salisbury
Lord Privy Seal: Earl of Hardwicke
Chancellor of the Exchequer: B. Disraeli
Home Secretary: Spencer Walpole
Foreign Secretary: Earl of Malmesbury
Secretary for War: General J. Peel
Colonial Secretary: Lord Stanley
First Lord of the Admiralty: Sir J. Pakington
President of the Board of Trade: J. W. Henley
President of the Board of Control: Earl of Ellenborough
First Commissioner of Works: Lord John Manners

Changes

June 1858: on the resignation of Ellenborough, Stanley became President of the Board of Control, and was succeeded as Colonial Secretary by Sir E. Bulwer-Lytton. *August 1858*: the office of President of the Board of Control was abolished, its place being taken by a new secretaryship for India to which Stanley was appointed. *February 1859*: Walpole and Henley resigned, and were succeeded by T. H. Sotheron-Estcourt and the Earl of Donoughmore.

PALMERSTON'S SECOND CABINET

formed June 1859

Prime Minister and First Lord of the Treasury: Viscount Palmerston
Lord Chancellor: Lord Campbell
Lord President: Earl Granville
Lord Privy Seal: Duke of Argyll
Chancellor of the Exchequer: W. E. Gladstone
Home Secretary: Sir G. Cornewall Lewis
Foreign Secretary: Lord John Russell (cr. Earl Russell 1861)
Secretary for War: Sidney Herbert (cr. Lord Herbert of Lea 1860)
Colonial Secretary: Duke of Newcastle
First Lord of the Admiralty: Duke of Somerset
Secretary for India: Sir C. Wood (cr. Viscount Halifax 1866)
Chancellor of the Duchy of Lancaster: Sir G. Grey
Chief Secretary for Ireland: E. Cardwell
Postmaster-General: Earl of Elgin
President of the Poor Law Board: T. Milner-Gibson

Changes

July 1859: Milner-Gibson became President of the Board of Trade, and was succeeded as President of the Poor Law Board by C. P. Villiers. *May 1860*: Argyll remained Lord Privy Seal and became in addition Postmaster-General in place of Elgin who had gone on a mission to China. *August 1860*: Lord Stanley of Alderley replaced Argyll as Postmaster-General. *June 1861*: on the death of Campbell, Lord Westbury became Lord Chancellor. *July 1861*: Herbert resigned, and was succeeded as Secretary for War by Cornewall Lewis; Grey became Home Secretary and Cardwell Chancellor of the Duchy of Lancaster (the latter's successor as Chief Secretary for Ireland was not in the cabinet). *April 1863*: on the death of Cornewall Lewis, Earl de Grey became Secretary for War. *April 1864*: Newcastle resigned, Cardwell became Secretary for the Colonies and the Earl of Clarendon became Chancellor of the Duchy of Lancaster. *July 1865*: Westbury resigned, and Lord Cranworth entered the cabinet as Lord Chancellor.

RUSSELL'S SECOND CABINET

formed October 1865

Earl Russell became Prime Minister and First Lord of the Treasury, and the Earl of Clarendon succeeded him as Foreign Secretary; G. J. Goschen entered the cabinet as Chancellor of the Duchy of Lancaster in January 1866. On the resignation of Sir C. Wood in February 1866, Earl de Grey became Secretary for War. Otherwise the cabinet remained unchanged after Palmerston's death.

DERBY'S THIRD CABINET

formed June 1866

Prime Minister and First Lord of the Treasury: Earl of Derby
Lord Chancellor: Lord Chelmsford
Lord President: Duke of Buckingham
Lord Privy Seal: Earl of Malmesbury
Chancellor of the Exchequer: B. Disraeli
Home Secretary: Spencer Walpole
Foreign Secretary: Lord Stanley
Secretary for War: General J. Peel
Colonial Secretary: Earl of Carnarvon
First Lord of the Admiralty: Sir J. Pakington
President of the Board of Trade: Sir Stafford Northcote
Secretary for India: Viscount Cranborne
Chief Secretary for Ireland: Lord Naas (Earl of Mayo 1867)
President of the Poor Law Board: Gathorne Hardy

Changes

March 1867: Carnarvon, Peel, and Cranborne resigned; the Duke of Buckingham became Colonial Secretary, Pakington became Secretary for War, and Northcote became Secretary for India; the Duke of Marlborough, H. T. L. Corry, and the Duke of Richmond entered the cabinet as Lord President, First Lord of the Admiralty, and President of the Board of Trade. *May 1867*: Walpole resigned the Home Secretaryship and remained in the cabinet as Minister without Portfolio; Hardy became Home Secretary.

DISRAELI'S FIRST CABINET

formed February 1867

B. Disraeli became Prime Minister and First Lord of the Treasury, and G. Ward Hunt took his place as Chancellor of the Exchequer; the Earl of Mayo left the cabinet to become Viceroy of India (his successor as Chief Secretary for Ireland was not in the cabinet). Otherwise the cabinet remained unchanged after the Earl of Derby's resignation.

GLADSTONE'S FIRST CABINET

formed December 1868

Prime Minister and First Lord of the Treasury: W. E. Gladstone
Lord Chancellor: Lord Hatherley
Lord President: Earl de Grey (cr. Marquess of Ripon 1871)
Lord Privy Seal: Earl of Kimberley
Chancellor of the Exchequer: Robert Lowe
Home Secretary: H. A. Bruce
Foreign Secretary: Earl of Clarendon
Secretary for War: E. Cardwell
Colonial Secretary: Earl Granville
First Lord of the Admiralty: H. C. E. Childers
President of the Board of Trade: John Bright
Secretary for India: Duke of Argyll
Chief Secretary for Ireland: Chichester Fortescue
Postmaster-General: Marquess of Hartington
President of the Poor Law Board: G. J. Goschen

Changes

July 1870: W. E. Forster (Vice-President, Education) entered the cabinet; Granville became Foreign Secretary (following Clarendon's death); Kimberley became Colonial Secretary; Viscount Halifax became Lord Privy Seal. *January 1871*: Fortescue succeeded Bright (resigned) as President of the Board of Trade; Hartington became Chief Secretary for Ireland (his successor as Postmaster-General was not in the cabinet). *March 1871*: Goschen succeeded Childers (resigned) as First Lord of the Admiralty; James Stansfeld became President of the Poor Law Board. *August 1872*: Childers rejoined the cabinet as Chancellor of the Duchy of Lancaster. *October 1872*: Lord Selborne succeeded Hatherley as Lord Chancellor. *August 1873*: Bruce (cr. Lord Aberdare) succeeded Ripon as Lord President; Lowe succeeded Bruce as Home Secretary; Gladstone succeeded Lowe as Chancellor of the Exchequer (combining the office with the premiership). *September 1873*: Bright rejoined the cabinet as Chancellor of the Duchy of Lancaster, in place of Childers (resigned).

DISRAELI'S SECOND CABINET

formed February 1874

Prime Minister and First Lord of the Treasury: B. Disraeli
Lord Chancellor: Lord Cairns (cr. Earl Cairns 1878)
Lord President: Duke of Richmond
Lord Privy Seal: Earl of Malmesbury
Chancellor of the Exchequer: Sir Stafford Northcote
Home Secretary: R. A. Cross

Foreign Secretary: (15th) Earl of Derby
Secretary for War: Gathorne Hardy
Colonial Secretary: Earl of Carnarvon
First Lord of the Admiralty: G. Ward Hunt
Secretary for India: Marquess of Salisbury
Postmaster-General: Lord John Manners

Changes

August 1876: Disraeli succeeded Malmesbury (resigned) as Lord Privy Seal (combining the office with that of the premiership) and went to the House of Lords as Earl of Beaconsfield; Sir Michael Hicks Beach, Chief Secretary for Ireland, entered the cabinet. *August 1877*: W. H. Smith succeeded Ward Hunt (deceased) as First Lord of the Admiralty. *February 1878*: Hicks Beach succeeded Carnarvon (resigned) as Colonial Secretary (his successor as Chief Secretary for Ireland was not in the cabinet); the Duke of Northumberland became Lord Privy Seal in place of Disraeli. *April 1878*: Salisbury succeeded Derby (resigned) as Foreign Secretary; Gathorne Hardy (cr. Viscount Cranbrook) succeeded Salisbury as Secretary for India; F. A. Stanley succeeded Gathorne Hardy as Secretary for War; Viscount Sandon succeeded C. B. Adderley (not in cabinet) as President of the Board of Trade and entered the cabinet.

GLADSTONE'S SECOND CABINET

formed April 1880

Prime Minister and First Lord of the Treasury: W. E. Gladstone
Chancellor of the Exchequer: W. E. Gladstone
Lord Chancellor: Lord Selborne (cr. Earl of Selborne 1881)
Lord President: Earl Spencer
Lord Privy Seal: Duke of Argyll
Home Secretary: Sir W. V. Harcourt
Foreign Secretary: Earl Granville
Secretary for War: H. C. E. Childers
Colonial Secretary: Earl of Kimberley
First Lord of the Admiralty: Earl of Northbrook
President of the Board of Trade: Joseph Chamberlain
Secretary for India: Marquess of Hartington
Chief Secretary for Ireland: W. E. Forster
President of the Local Government Board: J. G. Dodson
Chancellor of the Duchy of Lancaster: John Bright

Changes

May 1881: Lord Carlingford (Chichester Fortescue) succeeded Argyll (resigned) as Lord Privy Seal. *May 1882*: Spencer, while retaining his seat in the cabinet, became Viceroy of Ireland; Forster resigned as Chief Secretary for Ireland (his successors were not in the cabinet). *July 1882*: Bright resigned as Chancellor of the Duchy of Lancaster and was succeeded by Kimberley who combined the office with that of Colonial Secretary. *December 1882*: Gladstone resigned the Chancellorship of the Exchequer to Childers; Hartington succeeded Childers as Secretary for War; Kimberley succeeded Hartington as Secretary for India; Kimberley was succeeded as Colonial Secretary by Lord Derby and as Chancellor of the Duchy of Lancaster by J. G. Dodson; Dodson was succeeded as President of the Local Government Board by Sir Charles Dilke. *March 1883*: Carlingford succeeded Spencer as Lord President and combined that office with that of Lord Privy Seal. *October 1884*: G. O. Trevelyan succeeded Dodson (resigned) as Chancellor of the Duchy of Lancaster; *November 1884*: C. J. Shaw-Lefevre (Postmaster-General) was brought into the cabinet. *March 1885*: the Earl of Rosebery was brought into the cabinet, taking over from Carlingford as Lord Privy Seal.

SALISBURY'S FIRST CABINET

formed June 1885

Prime Minister and Foreign Secretary: Marquess of Salisbury
First Lord of the Treasury: Earl of Iddesleigh (Sir Stafford Northcote)
Lord Chancellor: Lord Halsbury
Lord President: Viscount Cranbrook
Lord Privy Seal: Earl of Harrowby
Chancellor of the Exchequer: Sir Michael Hicks Beach
Home Secretary: Sir R. A. Cross
Secretary for War: W. H. Smith
Colonial Secretary: F. A. Stanley
First Lord of the Admiralty: Lord George Hamilton
President of the Board of Trade: Duke of Richmond
Secretary for India: Lord Randolph Churchill
Viceroy of Ireland: Earl of Carnarvon
Postmaster-General: Lord John Manners
Vice-President (Education): E. Stanhope
Lord Chancellor of Ireland: Lord Ashbourne

Changes

August 1885: Richmond was appointed to the new post of Secretary for Scotland; he was succeeded as President of the Board of Trade by Stanhope (whose successor as Vice-President (Education) was not in the cabinet). *January 1886*: Smith became Chief Secretary for Ireland while retaining his seat in the cabinet.

GLADSTONE'S THIRD CABINET

formed February 1886

Prime Minister and First Lord of the Treasury: W. E. Gladstone

Lord Privy Seal: W. E. Gladstone
Lord Chancellor: Lord Herschell
Lord President: Earl Spencer
Chancellor of the Exchequer: Sir W. V. Harcourt
Home Secretary: H. C. E. Childers
Foreign Secretary: Earl of Rosebery
Secretary for War: H. Campbell-Bannerman
Colonial Secretary: Earl Granville
First Lord of the Admiralty: Marquess of Ripon
President of the Board of Trade: A. J. Mundella
Secretary for India: Earl of Kimberley
Secretary for Scotland: G. O. Trevelyan
Chief Secretary for Ireland: John Morley
President of the Local Government Board: Joseph Chamberlain

Changes

April 1886: Chamberlain resigned and was succeeded by James Stansfeld; Trevelyan resigned (his successor as Secretary for Scotland was not in the cabinet).

Bibliography

The works listed below will allow the reader to seek more detailed information about the topics with which this book deals. The emphasis is upon comparatively recent books, though certain articles of importance—especially if not yet absorbed into the literature—have also been included. Although some items relate to more than one of the sections into which this bibliography has been divided, very few are mentioned more than once. Limitations of space have restricted the amount of detail it has proved possible to give concerning individual items in those many volumes of collected essays published in recent years.

All books were published in London unless otherwise stated. SESH = 'Studies in Economic and Social History' (introductory works of about a hundred or so pages published under the auspices of the Economic History Society).

I BIBLIOGRAPHIC AND REFERENCE WORKS

The fullest (but increasingly outdated) general guides are L. M. Brown and I. R. Christie, *Bibliography of British History 1789–1851* (Oxford, 1977) and H. J. Hanham, *Bibliography of British History 1851–1914* (Oxford, 1976). G. R. Elton, *Modern Historians on British History, 1485–1945: A Critical Bibliography* (1970) makes up for its age by the confidence of its judgements. J. L. Altholz, *Victorian England 1837–1901* (Cambridge, 1970) is also still useful.

These are best supplemented by the Royal Historical Society's *Annual Bibliography of British and Irish History* and the Historical Association's *Annual Bulletin of Historical Literature*.

Writings on Irish history published 1936–78 were listed annually in the September issue of *Irish Historical Studies* 1938–79, and thereafter—under the auspices of that journal—on microfiche (for 1979–83) and then in separate booklets. See also *Irish Historiography 1936–70*, ed. T. W. Moody (Dublin, 1971) and *Irish Historiography 1970–79*, ed. J. Lee (Cork, 1981).

Information about relevant periodical publications is carried annually in the *English Historical Review* (to 1993 in the July issue and thereafter in the September issue), the *Scottish Historical Review* (October issue), and the *Welsh History Review* (December issue).

R. C. Richardson and W. H. Chaloner, *British Economic and Social History: A Bibliographical Guide*, 3rd edn. (Manchester, 1995) is valuable, while the *Economic History Review* carries lists of periodical publications each year in the February issue. *Irish Economic and Social History* covers all relevant Irish materials in its annual issue published in the autumn.

The unprecedentedly comprehensive 'Royal Historical Society British Biblio-graphies' (general editor J. S. Morrill) are available (1997) from Oxford University Press on CD-ROM (and may also appear—at least in part—in hard copy form).

Parliamentary Papers are usefully introduced in two publications by P. and G. Ford, *A Guide to Parliamentary Papers*, 3rd edn. (Shannon, 1972) and *Select List of British Parliamentary Papers 1833–1899* (Shannon, 1969).

B. R. Mitchell, *British Historical Statistics* (Cambridge, 1988) is excellent, while C. Cook, *British Historical Facts 1830–1900* (1975) provides lists of office holders and much else besides.

II GENERAL WORKS

Two good introductory texts meet in the middle of our period: E. J. Evans, *The Forging of the Modern State: Early Industrial Britain 1783–1870*, 2nd edn. (1996) and K. Robbins, *The Eclipse of a Great Power: Modern Britain 1870–1992*, 2nd edn. (1994). A. Briggs, *The Age of Improvement 1783–1867*, corrected edn. (1979), though showing its age, has worn extraordinarily well. Solid studies are N. Gash's almost entirely political *Aristocracy and People: Britain 1815–1865* (1979), D. Read's more rounded *The Age of Urban Democracy: England 1868–1914*, 2nd edn. (1993), and E. J. Feuchtwanger's *Democracy and Empire: Britain 1865–1914* (1985). R. K. Webb approaches *Modern England from the Eighteenth Century to the Present*, 2nd edn. (1980) from a fruitfully transatlantic angle. D. Beales, *From Castlereagh to Gladstone 1815–1885* (1969) remains useful, while M. Bentley provides an interesting (if allusive) study of attitudes in *Politics without Democracy 1815–1914: Perception and Preoccupation in British Government*, 2nd edn. (1996).

A splendid overview is supplied by G. Kitson Clark, *The Making of Victorian England* (1962), a social perspective by G. Best, *Mid-Victorian Britain 1851–1875* (1971), a political approach by M. Pugh, *The Making of Modern British Politics 1867–1939*, 2nd edn. (1993), and a world context by R. Shannon, *The Crisis of Imperialism 1865–1915* (1974) and B. Porter, *Britannia's Burden: The Political Evolution of Modern Britain 1851–1990* (1994).

The relevant volumes of the original 'Oxford History of England'—E. L. Woodward, *The Age of Reform 1815–1870*, 2nd edn. (Oxford, 1962) and R. C. K. Ensor, *England 1870–1914* (Oxford, 1936)—still have much to offer, especially the latter. The most finely attuned examination of professional middle-class mid-Victorian mentalities is W. L. Burn's marvellous *The Age of Equipoise: A Study of the Mid-Victorian Generation* (1964).

III DIARIES, LETTERS, DOCUMENTS

On the **Liberal side** *The Gladstone Diaries*, ed. H. C. G. Matthew and M. R. D. Foot, 14 vols. (Oxford, 1968–94) constitute a key—if at times dense and decept-ively mundane—source embellished by large helpings of relevant correspon-dence. Useful too are *The Prime Ministers' Papers: W. E. Gladstone*, ed. J. Brooke and M. Sorensen, 4 vols. (1971–81), *The Political Correspondence of Mr Gladstone and Lord Granville 1868–1876*, ed. A. Ramm, 2 vols., Camden 3rd ser. 81–2 (1952), *The Political Correspondence of Mr Gladstone and Lord Granville 1876–1886*, ed. A. Ramm, 2 vols. (Oxford, 1962), '"A Journal of Events during the Gladstone Ministry, 1868–74" by John, First Earl of Kimberley', ed. E. Drus, *Camden Miscellany XXI*, Camden 3rd ser. 90 (1958), *The Letters of the Third Viscount Palmerston to Laurence and Elizabeth Sulivan 1804–1863*, ed. K. Bourne, Camden 4th ser. 23 (1979), and (for a back-bench viewpoint) *The Parliamentary Diaries of Sir John Trelawny, 1858–1865*, ed. T. A. Jenkins, Camden 4th ser. 40 (1990) and 'The Parliamentary Diaries of Sir John Trelawny, 1868–73', ed. T. A. Jenkins, *Camden Miscellany XXXII*, Camden 5th ser. 3 (1994).

Light is thrown on the **Conservative side** by the edition of *Benjamin Disraeli Letters*, ed. M. G. Wiebe and others, 5 vols. to date (Toronto, 1982–) which has reached 1851, and also by *Derby, Disraeli and the Conservative Party: Journals and Memoirs of Edward Henry, Lord Stanley 1849–1869*, ed. J. Vincent (Hassocks, 1978) and *A Selection from the Diaries of Edward Henry Stanley, 15th Earl of Derby... between September 1869 and March 1878*, ed. J. Vincent, Camden 5th ser. 4 (1994)—the 15th Earl became a Liberal in 1880 and a Liberal Unionist in 1886.

The Greville Memoirs 1814–1860, ed. L. Strachey and R. Fulford, 8 vols. (1938) record the—rather gossipy—views of C. C. F. Greville, Clerk to the Council 1821–59, who had friends on both sides of the political divide. Some of Queen Victoria's more important letters are printed in *The Letters of Queen Victoria*, ed. A. C. Benson, Lord Esher, and G. E. Buckle: 1st series 1837–61, 3 vols. (1907), 2nd series 1861–85, 3 vols. (1926–8), 3rd series 1886–1901, 3 vols. (1930–2).

Selections of **contemporary documentary materials** are provided in *English Historical Documents XII (1) 1833–1874*, ed. G. M. Young and W. D. Handcock (1956), *English Historical Documents XII (2) 1874–1914*, ed. W. D. Handcock (1977), and *The Nineteenth-Century Constitution*, ed. H. J. Hanham (Cambridge, 1969).

The relevant volumes of *Parliamentary Debates* (commonly called *Hansard*) constitute an invaluable source (though for our period debates were not reported verbatim).

IV MID-VICTORIAN SOCIETY

Useful **general works** are E. Royle, *Modern Britain: A Social History 1750–1985*, corrected impression (1988) and F. Bédarida, *A Social History of England 1851–1990*, 2nd edn. (1991). More specifically angled interpretations are offered in H. J. Perkin, *The Origins of Modern English Society 1780–1880* (1969), F. M. L. Thompson, *The Rise of Respectable Society: A Social History of Victorian Britain, 1830–1900* (1988) which engages an important, though slippery, theme, and J. Harris, *Private Lives, Public Spirit: A Social History of Britain 1870–1914* (Oxford, 1993). *The Cambridge Social History of Britain 1750–1950*, ed. F. M. L. Thompson, 3 vols.

(Cambridge, 1990) includes some excellent essays under three themes: 'Regions and Communities', 'People and their Environment', and 'Social Agencies and Institutions'.

The affairs of the **countryside** feature prominently in J. V. Beckett, *The Aristocracy in England 1660–1914*, revised edn. (Oxford, 1989) and D. Cannadine, *The Decline and Fall of the British Aristocracy* (New Haven, 1990)—both of which discuss much else besides—and also in F. M. L. Thompson, *English Landed Society in the Nineteenth Century* (1963), G. E. Mingay, *Rural Life in Victorian England* (1977), A. Howkins, *Reshaping Rural England: A Social History 1850–1925* (1991), A. Armstrong, *Farm Workers: A Social and Economic History 1770–1980* (1988), and J. P. D. Dunbabin, *Rural Discontent in Nineteenth-Century Britain* (1974). G. E. Mingay (ed.), *The Victorian Countryside*, 2 vols. (1981) is well illustrated and includes valuable essays on agriculture, country towns and industries, landed society, labouring life, politics, and regions.

Urban developments receive wide-ranging attention in P. J. Waller's excellent overview *Town, City and Nation: England 1850–1914* (Oxford, 1983) and in A. Briggs, *Victorian Cities*, 2nd edn. (1968)—which contains chapters on Manchester, Leeds, Birmingham, Middlesbrough, and London, M. Wolff and H. J. Dyos (eds.), *The Victorian City: Images and Realities*, 2 vols. (1973)—includes pioneering essays arranged under headings such as 'Numbers of People', 'Shapes on the Ground', 'Ideas in the Air', and 'A New Earth', R. Dennis, *English Industrial Cities of the Nineteenth Century: A Social Geography* (Cambridge, 1984), D. J. Olsen, *The Growth of Victorian London* (1976), J. H. Johnson and C. G. Pooley (eds.), *The Structure of Nineteenth-Century Cities* (1982) which examines both shapes on the ground and shapes in society, and D. Fraser and A. Sutcliffe (eds.), *The Pursuit of Urban History* (1983) which includes essays on Victorian housing, working-class households, the middle classes, and the petty bourgeoisie. C. M. Law provides important statistics in 'The Growth of Urban Population in England and Wales 1801–1911', *Transactions of the Institute of British Geographers*, 41 (1967).

The nature and influence of various **urban élites** are addressed in D. Cannadine, *Lords and Landlords: The Aristocracy and the Towns* (Leicester, 1980), R. J. Morris, *Class, Sect and Party: The Making of the British Middle Class 1820–50* (Manchester, 1990), F. Crouzet, *The First Industrialists: The Problem of Origins* (Cambridge, 1985), A. Howe, *The Cotton Masters 1830–1860* (Oxford, 1984), R. H. Trainor, *Black Country Elites: The Exercise of Authority in an Industrialized Area 1830–1900* (Oxford, 1993), and L. Davidoff and C. Hall, *Family Fortunes: Men and Women of the English Middle Class* (1987). W. J. Reader looks at *Professional Men: The Rise of the Professional Classes in Nineteenth-Century England* (1966). Economic borderlands are the subject of G. Crossick (ed.), *The Lower Middle Class in Britain 1870–1914* (1977), with essays on religion, clerks, housing, and shopkeepers. W. D. Rubinstein provides details about 'The Size and Distribution of the English Middle Classes in 1860' in *Historical Research*, 61 (1988) and about plutocrats of all kinds in *Men of Property: The Very Wealthy in Victorian Britain* (1981).

The world of **manual workers** is examined both in general works such as J. Belchem, *Industrialization and the Working Class: The English Experience, 1750–1900* (Aldershot, 1990), R. Price, *Labour in British Society* (1986), and J. Benson, *The Working Class in Britain 1850–1939* (1989) and in more focused studies such as G. Stedman Jones, *Outcast London: A Study in the Relationship between Classes in Victorian Society* (Oxford, 1971), G. Crossick, *An Artisan Elite in Victorian Society: Kentish London 1840–1880* (1978), P. Joyce, *Work, Society and Politics: The Culture of the Factory in later Victorian England* (Hassocks, 1980), especially good on power relationships, and R. Q. Gray, *The Aristocracy of Labour in Nineteenth-Century Britain* (SESH 1981). Working-class autobiographies are presented in *Useful Toil: Autobiographies of Working People from the 1820s to the 1920s*, ed. J. Burnett, new impression (1984), and analysed in D. Vincent, *Bread, Knowledge and Freedom: A Study of Nineteenth-Century Working Class Autobiography* (1981).

Key pioneering articles on the **standard of living** are reprinted in A. J. Taylor (ed.), *The Standard of Living in Britain in the Industrial Revolution* (1975). The conclusions presented by P. H. Lindert and J. G. Williamson in 'English Workers' Living Standards during the Industrial Revolution', *Economic History Review*, 36 (1983) and Williamson's *Did British Capitalism Breed Inequality?* (1985) have been undermined by C. H. Feinstein in 'The Rise and Fall of the Williamson Curve', *Journal of Economic History*, 48 (1988). Feinstein makes important positive contributions in 'What Really Happened to Real Wages? Trends in Wages, Prices, and Productivity in the United Kingdom 1880–1913', *Economic History Review*, 43 (1990) and 'A New Look at the Cost of Living 1870–1914', in J. Foreman-Peck (ed.), *Essays in Quantitative Economic History* (Cambridge, 1991). E. H. Hunt analyses *Regional Wage Variations in Britain 1850–1914* (Oxford, 1973), while a new approach—based on biological data—is put forward in R. Floud, K. Wachter, and A. Gregory, *Height, Health and History: Nutritional Status in the United Kingdom 1750–1980* (Cambridge, 1990). Diet generally is examined by J. Burnett in *Plenty and Want: A Social History of Diet in England from 1815 to the Present*, 3rd edn. (1989). The same writer also contributes *Idle Hands: The Experience of Unemployment 1790–1990* (1994). J. H. Treble in *Urban Poverty in Britain 1830–1914* (1975) and P. Johnson in *Saving and Spending: The Working Class Economy in Britain 1870–1939* (Oxford, 1985) look at very different areas of working-class experience, while W. H. Fraser, *The Coming of the Mass Market 1850–1914* (1981) casts light on consumption patterns generally.

Housing—a key aspect of living standards—is briefly introduced in R. Rodger, *Housing in Urban Britain 1780–1914* (SESH 1989) and more fully in J. Burnett, *A Social History of Housing 1815–1985*, 2nd edn. (1986). The situation at the lower ends of the social scale is discussed in A. S. Wohl, *The Eternal Slum: Housing and Social Policy in Victorian England* (1977), M. J. Daunton, *House and Home in the Victorian City: Working-Class Housing 1850–1914* (1983), and E. Gauldie, *Cruel Habitations: A History of Working-Class Housing, 1780–1918* (1974), while the upper end receives attention in M. Girouard, *The Victorian Country House*, new edn. (1979), J. Franklin, *The Gentleman's Country House and its Plan 1835–1914*

(1981), and J. Gerard, *Country House Life: Family and Servants 1815–1914* (1994). More work needs to be done on what lay between.

For **public health** issues, see F. B. Smith, *The People's Health 1830–1910* (1979) and A. S. Wohl, *Endangered Lives: Public Health in Victorian Britain* (1983), as well as studies of two major administrators: R. A. Lewis, *Edwin Chadwick and the Public Health Movement* (1952), S. E. Finer, *The Life and Times of Sir Edwin Chadwick*, revised edn. (1980), and R. Lambert, *Sir John Simon 1816–1904* (1963).

The **family and population** are the subjects of essays in A. S. Wohl (ed.), *The Victorian Family: Structures and Stresses* (1978), and of M. Anderson, *Family Structure in Nineteenth-Century Lancashire* (Cambridge, 1971), J. A. Banks, *Prosperity and Parenthood: A Study of Family Planning among the Victorian Middle Classes* (1954), J. A. Banks, *Victorian Values: Secularism and the Size of Families* (1981), and J. Walvin, *A Child's World: A Social History of English Childhood 1800–1914* (1982).

Women's experiences constitute the subject of an increasing number of works. These include general studies—J. Lewis, *Women in England 1870–1950: Sexual Divisions and Social Change* (Brighton, 1984) and the essays in M. Vicinus (ed.), *Suffer and Be Still: Women in the Victorian Age* (Bloomington, Ind., 1972) and M. Vicinus (ed.), *A Widening Sphere: Changing Roles of Victorian Women* (Bloomington, Ind., 1977)—studies of employment and related matters—E. Richards, 'Women in the British Economy since about 1700', *History*, 59 (1974) and the essays in A. V. John (ed.), *Unequal Opportunities: Women's Employment in England 1800–1918* (Oxford, 1986)—and important (if inconclusive) statistical revisions such as E. Higgs, 'Women, Occupation and Work in the Nineteenth Century Censuses', *History Workshop*, 23 (1987). Middle-class women are the subjects of P. Branca, *Silent Sisterhood: Middle-Class Women in the Victorian Home* (1975) and L. Holcombe, *Victorian Ladies at Work: Middle-Class Working Women in England and Wales 1850–1914* (Newton Abbot, 1973), marriage and its associated legal and political problems of P. Jalland, *Women, Marriage and Politics 1860–1914* (Oxford, 1986), J. Perkin, *Women and Marriage in Nineteenth Century England* (1989), M. L. Shanley, *Feminism, Marriage, and the Law in Victorian England, 1850–1895* (1989), and L. Holcombe, *Women and Property: Reform of the Married Women's Property Law in Nineteenth-Century Britain* (Oxford, 1983), and loving relationships of M. J. Peterson, *Family, Love, and Work in the Lives of Victorian Gentlewomen* (Bloomington, Ind., 1989) and F. Barret-Ducrocq, *Love in the Time of Victoria: Sexuality, Class, and Gender in Nineteenth-Century London* (1991).

Leisure activities of various (and increasingly commercialized) kinds were a prominent feature of mid-Victorian life at all levels and are discussed in two broad-ranging works, P. Bailey, *Leisure and Class in Victorian England* (1978) and H. Cunningham, *Leisure in the Industrial Revolution c.1780–c.1880* (1980), as well as in more specific studies such as R. Carr, *English Fox Hunting* (1976), D. C. Itzkowitz, *Peculiar Privilege: A Social History of English Foxhunting 1753–1885* (Hassocks, 1977), W. Vamplew, *The Turf: A Social and Economic History of Horse*

Racing (1976), C. Chinn, *Better Betting with a Decent Feller: Bookmakers, Betting and the British Working Class, 1750–1990* (Hemel Hempstead, 1991), M. Clapson, *A Bit of a Flutter: Popular Gambling and English Society* c. *1823–1961* (Manchester, 1992), J. Lowerson, *Sport and the English Middle Classes 1870–1914* (Manchester, 1993), J. A. Mangan, *Athleticism in the Victorian and Edwardian Public School* (Cambridge, 1981), W. Vamplew, *Pay Up and Play the Game: Professional Sport in Britain 1875–1914* (Cambridge, 1988), T. Mason, *Association Football and English Society 1863–1915* (Brighton, 1980), P. Bailey (ed.), *Music Hall: The Business of Pleasure* (Milton Keynes, 1986), J. S. Bratton (ed.), *Music Hall: Performance and Style* (Milton Keynes, 1986), and J. K. Walton, *The English Seaside Resort: A Social History 1750–1914* (Leicester, 1983).

V THE STATE

Wide-ranging discussions of **contemporary views of the state** are to be found in S. Checkland, *British Public Policy 1776–1939* (Cambridge, 1983), W. H. Greenleaf, *The British Political Tradition*, 3 vols. in 4 (1983–7)—i. 'The Rise of Collectivism', ii. 'The Ideological Heritage', iii. 'A Much-Governed Nation'— G. Sutherland, *Studies in the Growth of Nineteenth-Century Government* (1972), O. MacDonagh, *Early Victorian Government 1830–1870* (1977), P. Marsh (ed.), *The Conscience of the Victorian State* (Hassocks, 1979)—essays on Whig, utilitarian, Nonconformist, Conservative, imperial, and Gladstonian aspects—and J. T. Ward, *The Factory Movement 1830–1855* (1962).

The broad **constitutional and administrative manifestations of the state** are analysed in G. H. Le May, *The Victorian Constitution: Conventions, Usages and Contingencies* (1979), F. Hardie, *The Political Influence of Queen Victoria*, 2nd edn. (1938), E. A. Smith, *The House of Lords in British Politics and Society, 1815–1911* (1992), N. Chester, *The English Administrative System 1780–1870* (Oxford, 1981), O. MacDonagh, 'The Nineteenth-Century Revolution in Government', *Historical Journal*, 1 (1958), P. W. J. Bartrip, 'State Intervention in Mid-Nineteenth Century Britain', *Journal of British Studies*, 23 (1983), J. Prest, *Liberty and Locality: Parliament, Permissive Legislation, and Ratepayers' Democracies in the Mid-Nineteenth Century* (Oxford, 1990), R. J. Lambert, 'Central and Local Relations in Mid-Victorian England', *Victorian Studies*, 6 (1962), A. Brundage, *England's 'Prussian Minister': Edwin Chadwick and the Politics of Government Growth 1832–1854* (1988), and P. W. J. Bartrip, 'British Government Inspection 1832–1875', *Historical Journal*, 25 (1982).

For the **Civil Service and government departments**, see G. K. Fry, *Statesmen in Disguise: The Changing Role of the Administrative Class of the British Home Civil Service 1853–1966* (1969), E. Hughes, 'Civil Service Reform', *History*, 27 (1942), G. Kitson Clark, ' "Statesmen in Disguise": Reflexions on the History of the Neutrality of the Civil Service', *Historical Journal*, 2 (1959), R. Prouty, *The Transformation of the Board of Trade 1830–1855* (1957), J. Pellew, *The Home Office 1848–1914* (1982), R. Jones, *The Nineteenth-Century Foreign Office: An*

Administrative History (1971), B. L. Blakeley, *The Colonial Office 1868–1892* (Durham, NC, 1972), and H. Roseveare, *The Treasury: The Evolution of a British Institution* (1969).

Social welfare issues and institutions are discussed in G. Finlayson, *Citizen, State and Social Welfare in Britain 1830–1990* (Oxford, 1994), D. Roberts, *Victorian Origins of the British Welfare State* (New Haven, 1960), D. Fraser (ed.), *The New Poor Law in the Nineteenth Century* (1976)—essays on settlement, medical services, education, urban and rural areas, and the Scottish Poor Law, M. E. Rose, *The Relief of Poverty 1834–1914*, 2nd edn. (SESH 1986), and M. A. Crowther, *The Workhouse System 1834–1929* (1981).

For **education**, see G. Sutherland, *Elementary Education in the Nineteenth Century* (1971), J. Hurt, *Elementary Schooling and the Working Classes 1860–1918* (1979), J. Lawson and H. Silver, *A Social History of Education in England* (1977), R. D. Anderson, *Universities and Elites in Britain since 1800* (SESH 1992), M. Sanderson, *The Universities and British Society 1850–1970* (1972), T. W. Bamford, *Rise of the Public Schools* (1967), and (more generally) C. Harvie, *The Lights of Liberalism: University Liberals and the Challenge of Democracy 1860–86* (1976).

Studies of **policing and crime** include C. Emsley, *Crime and Society in England 1750–1900* (1987), V. A. C. Gatrell, 'The Decline of Theft and Violence in Victorian and Edwardian England', in V. A. C. Gatrell, B. Lenman, and G. Parker (eds.), *Crime and the Law* (1980), C. Steedman, *Policing the Victorian Countryside: The Formation of English Provincial Police Forces 1856–80* (1984), T. A. Critchley, *A History of Police in England and Wales*, revised edn. (1978), C. Emsley, *The English Police: A Political and Social History* (Hemel Hempstead, 1991), and V. Bailey (ed.), *Policing and Punishment in Nineteenth-Century Britain* (1981).

For the **military**, see s. VIII.

VI POLITICS AT THE CENTRE

General works and studies of particular ministries include N. Gash, *Reaction and Reconstruction in English Politics 1832–1852* (Oxford, 1965), A. Hawkins, ' "Parliamentary Government" and Victorian Political Parties *c*.1830–80', *English Historical Review*, 104 (1989), J. B. Conacher, *The Aberdeen Coalition, 1852–1855* (1968), A. Hawkins, *Parliament, Party and the Art of Politics in Britain, 1855–59* (1987), P. M. Gurowich, 'The Continuation of War by Other Means: Party and Politics, 1855–1865', *Historical Journal*, 27 (1984), and D. F. Krein, *The Last Palmerston Government* (Ames, Ia., 1978).

Particular topics and episodes: W. O. Aydelotte, 'The House of Commons in the 1840s', *History*, 39 (1954) and J. R. Bylsma, 'Party Structure in the 1852–1857 House of Commons', *Journal of Interdisciplinary History*, 7 (1977) analyse MPs' voting patterns. The politics of finance are addressed in H. C. G. Matthew, 'Disraeli, Gladstone, and the Politics of Mid-Victorian Budgets', *Historical Journal*, 22 (1979) and P. R. Ghosh, 'Disraelian Conservatism: A Financial Approach', *English Historical Review*, 99 (1984). Religious considerations loom large in J. P.

Parry, *Democracy and Religion: Gladstone and the Liberal Party 1867–1875* (Cambridge, 1986), while the politics of reform (though not the details, for which see VII) receive allusive attention in M. Cowling, *1867: Disraeli, Gladstone and Revolution* (Cambridge, 1967) and A. Jones, *The Politics of Reform 1884* (Cambridge, 1972). Salisbury's domestic preoccupations are examined in P. Marsh, *The Discipline of Popular Government: Lord Salisbury's Domestic Statecraft, 1881–1902* (Hassocks, 1978). Although many of the works in this section touch upon the Liberals' (and especially Gladstone's) Irish involvements, a number of specific studies deserve particular mention, notably, J. L. Hammond, *Gladstone and the Irish Nation* (1938), which, though seriously out-of-date, still offers the only broad sweep, J. Vincent, 'Gladstone and Ireland', *Proceedings of the British Academy*, 63 (1977), spritely but partial, and some revealing articles by A. Warren, 'Gladstone, Land and Social Reconstruction in Ireland 1881–1887', *Parliamentary History*, 2 (1983) and 'Forster, the Liberals and new Directions in Irish Policy 1880–1882', ibid. 6 (1987). Especially important are two very different and controversial analyses of the Home Rule crisis itself (the former a close reading of day-by-day events, the latter concentrating on division lists): A. B. Cooke and J. Vincent, *The Governing Passion: Cabinet Government and Party Politics in Britain 1885–86* (Brighton, 1974) and W. C. Lubenow, *Parliamentary Politics and the Home Rule Crisis: The British House of Commons in 1886* (Oxford, 1988).

Works dealing specifically with the **Tory Party** include B. I. Coleman's useful conspectus *Conservatism and the Conservative Party in Nineteenth-Century Britain* (1988), studies of party organization and mentality such as R. Stewart, *The Politics of Protection: Lord Derby and the Protectionist Party 1841–1852* (Cambridge, 1971), R. Stewart, *The Foundation of the Conservative Party 1830–1867* (1978), R. Shannon, *The Age of Disraeli 1868–1881* (1992), R. Shannon, *The Age of Salisbury 1881–1902* (1996), E. J. Feuchtwanger, *Disraeli, Democracy and the Tory Party* (Oxford, 1968), and E. H. H. Green, *The Crisis of Conservatism: The Politics, Economics and Ideology of the British Conservative Party, 1880–1914* (1995). See also J. B. Conacher, *The Peelites and the Party System 1846–1852* (Newton Abbot, 1972) and P. Smith, *Disraelian Conservatism and Social Reform* (1967).

For the **Liberal Party** the following should be consulted: T. A. Jenkins, *The Liberal Ascendancy 1830–1886* (1994), excellent overview, J. Parry, *The Rise and Fall of Liberal Government in Victorian Britain* (New Haven, 1993), vigorously anti-Gladstonian, P. Mandler, *Aristocratic Government in the Age of Reform: Whigs and Liberals 1830–1852* (Oxford, 1990), D. Southgate, *The Passing of the Whigs 1832–1886* (1962), rather old-fashioned, J. Vincent, *The Formation of the Liberal Party 1857–1868* (1966), path-breaking and moving well beyond Westminster, M. Bentley, *The Climax of Liberal Politics: British Liberalism in Theory and Practice 1868–1918* (1987), T. A. Jenkins, *Gladstone, Whiggery and the Liberal Party 1874–1886* (Oxford, 1988), and D. A. Hamer, *Liberal Politics in the Age of Gladstone and Rosebery* (Oxford, 1972).

More specifically **biographical studies** are numerous. Two older 'life and times' biographies contain a good deal of meat and are still useful: J. Morley, *The*

Life of William Ewart Gladstone, 3 vols. (1903) and W. F. Monypenny and G. E. Buckle, *The Life of Benjamin Disraeli*, 6 vols. (1910–20). The deepest modern studies of Gladstone (at once both more and less than 'biographies') are H. C. G. Matthew, *Gladstone 1809–1874* (Oxford, 1986) and H. C. G. Matthew, *Gladstone 1875–1898* (Oxford, 1995)—which in essence contain the introductions to various volumes of the *Gladstone Diaries* (see s. III). R. Jenkins, *Gladstone* (1995) is a good recent single-volume biography, while R. Shannon, *Gladstone 1809–1865* (1982) provides interesting, though generally dyspeptic, insights into its subject's earlier years. R. Blake's excellent *Disraeli* (1966) is worth comparing with P. Smith's more recent and tauter *Disraeli: A Brief Life* (1996). Other useful—and sometimes more than useful—works on individual politicians include N. Gash, *Sir Robert Peel: The Life of Sir Robert Peel after 1830*, 2nd edn. (1980), J. Prest, *Lord John Russell* (1972), M. E. Chamberlain, *Lord Aberdeen: A Political Biography* (1983), E. D. Steele, *Palmerston and Liberalism 1855–1865* (Cambridge, 1991), J. Winter, *Robert Lowe* (Toronto, 1976), P. Jackson, *The Last of the Whigs: A Political Biography of Lord Hartington* (Cranbury, NJ, 1994), P. T. Marsh, *Joseph Chamberlain: Entrepreneur in Politics* (New Haven, 1994), R. Jay, *Joseph Chamberlain: A Political Study* (Oxford, 1981), R. F. Foster, *Lord Randolph Churchill: A Political Life* (Oxford, 1981). D. Read's *Peel and the Victorians* (Oxford, 1987) examines a reputation rather than a career.

VII POPULAR, LOCAL, AND ELECTORAL POLITICS

The political impact of various **popular movements and organizations** is examined generally in D. G. Wright, *Popular Radicalism: The Working-Class Experience 1780–1880* (1988) and P. Adelman, *Victorian Radicalism: The Middle-Class Experience 1830–1914* (1984), while late Chartism and its aftermath receive more specific, if very varied, treatment in D. Goodway, *London Chartism 1838–1848* (Cambridge, 1982), J. Saville, *1848: The British State and the Chartist Movement* (Cambridge, 1987), M. C. Finn, *After Chartism: Class and Nation in English Radical Politics 1848–1874* (Cambridge, 1993), T. R. Tholfsen, *Working Class Radicalism in Mid-Victorian England* (1976), N. Kirk, *The Growth of Working-Class Reformism in Mid-Victorian England* (1985), and M. Taylor, *The Decline of British Radicalism 1847–1860* (Oxford, 1995). Other movements and individuals are discussed in P. Hollis (ed.), *Pressure from Without in Early Victorian England* (1974), their more violent manifestations in J. Stevenson, *Popular Disturbances in England 1700–1870* (1979) and D. Richter, *Riotous Victorians* (1981). Important new light is shed upon Gladstone's working-class admirers by E. F. Biagini in *Liberty, Retrenchment and Reform: Popular Politics in the Age of Gladstone 1860–1880* (Cambridge, 1992) and by essayists in E. F. Biagini and A. J. Reid (eds.), *Currents of Radicalism: Popular Radicalism, Organised Labour and Party Politics in Britain 1850–1914* (Cambridge, 1991).

H. Pelling, *The Origins of the Labour Party 1880–1900*, 2nd edn. (Oxford, 1965) looks at early socialist stirrings, while the rise of the '**Labour Movement**' generally is examined in R. Harrison, *Before the Socialists: Studies in Labour and Politics 1861–1881* (1965), K. D. Brown, *The English Labour Movement 1700–1951* (Dublin, 1982), and E. H. Hunt, *British Labour History 1815–1914* (1981).

For **trade unions**, see H. A. Clegg, A. Fox, and A. F. Thompson, *A History of British Trade Unions since 1889*, i. *1889–1910* (Oxford, 1964), which includes some earlier material, W. H. Fraser, *Trade Unions and Society: The Struggle for Acceptance 1850–1880* (1974), A. E. Musson, *British Trade Unions 1800–1875* (SESH 1972), and J. Lovell, *British Trade Unions 1875–1933* (SESH 1977).

The **press** receives concentrated attention in A. J. Lee, *The Origins of the Popular Press in England 1855–1914* (1976), S. Koss, *The Rise and Fall of the Political Press in Britain*, i. *The Nineteenth Century* (1981), and L. Brown, *Victorian News and Newspapers* (Oxford, 1985), while a campaign heavily dependent on newspaper publicity is assessed in B. Harrison, *Drink and the Victorians: The Temperance Question in England 1815–1872*, 2nd edn. (Keele, 1994) and A. E. Dingle, *The Campaign for Prohibition in Victorian England: The United Kingdom Alliance 1872–1895* (1980).

Studies of **local political life** include D. Read, *The English Provinces c. 1760–1960: A Study in Influence* (1964), G. R. Searle, *Entrepreneurial Politics in Mid-Victorian Britain* (Oxford, 1993), which ranges fruitfully between centre and localities, D. Fraser, *Urban Politics in Victorian England* (Leicester, 1976), J. Garrard, *Leadership and Power in Victorian Industrial Towns 1830–1880* (Manchester, 1983), E. P. Hennock, *Fit and Proper Persons: Ideal and Reality in Nineteenth-Century Urban Government* (1973), P. J. Waller, *Democracy and Sectarianism: A Political and Social History of Liverpool, 1868–1939* (Liverpool, 1981), and essays on Manchester, Leeds, and Bradford in D. Fraser (ed.), *Municipal Reform and the Industrial City* (Leicester, 1982).

Electoral politics more closely defined have attracted attention at both a national and a more local level. C. Seymour, *Electoral Reform in England and Wales: The Development and Operation of the Parliamentary Franchise 1832–1885* (New Haven, 1915; repr. Newton Abbot, 1970) still constitutes the essential starting-point. F. B. Smith, *The Making of the Second Reform Bill* (Cambridge, 1966) and W. A. Hayes, *The Background and Passage of the Third Reform Act* (New York, 1982) analyse crucial legislation. Further information on the **franchise**, much of it modifying earlier views, can be found in J. Davis, 'Slums and the Vote', *Historical Research*, 64 (1991), J. Davis and D. Tanner, 'The Borough Franchise after 1867', *Historical Research*, 69 (1996), K. T. Hoppen, 'The Franchise and Electoral Politics in England and Ireland 1832–1885', *History*, 70 (1985), M. E. J. Chadwick, 'The Role of Redistribution in the Making of the Third Reform Act', *Historical Journal*, 19 (1976), and H. C. G. Matthew, R. I. McKibbin, and J. A. Kay, 'The Franchise Factor in the Rise of the Labour Party', *English Historical Review*, 91 (1976). H. Pelling, *Social Geography of British Elections 1885–1910* (1967) is an encyclopaedic constituency study useful for earlier periods also. The working-out of the **electoral system at the local level** is examined further in R. W. Davis, *Political Change and Continuity 1760–1885: A Buckinghamshire Study*

(Newton Abbot, 1972), R. J. Olney, *Lincolnshire Politics 1832–1885* (Oxford, 1973), and T. J. Nossiter, *Influence, Opinion and Political Idioms in Reformed England: Case Studies from the North-East 1832–1874* (Hassocks, 1975). D. C. Moore, *The Politics of Deference: A Study of the Nineteenth-Century English Political System* (Hassocks, 1978) makes considerable use of the **pollbooks** which provide unofficial details of personal voting in many constituencies before the advent of the secret ballot in 1872, as does J. R. Vincent, *Pollbooks: How Victorians Voted* (Cambridge, 1967). The politics of the **ballot** are discussed in B. L. Kinzer, *The Ballot Question in Nineteenth-Century English Politics* (New York, 1982), while the **electoral system as a whole** in the 1860s, 1870s, and 1880s is best approached through H. J. Hanham's excellent *Elections and Party Management: Politics in the Time of Disraeli and Gladstone* (1959). Also useful are T. Lloyd, *The General Election of 1880* (Oxford, 1968), M. Pugh, *The Tories and the People 1868–1935* (Oxford, 1985), good on the Primrose League, and J. Cornford, 'The Transformation of Conservatism in the Late Nineteenth Century', *Victorian Studies*, 7 (1963).

Electoral corruption and expenditure generally receive attention in W. B. Gwyn, *Democracy and the Cost of Politics in Britain* (1962), K. T. Hoppen, 'Roads to Democracy: Electioneering and Corruption in Nineteenth-Century England and Ireland', *History*, 81 (1996), and C. O'Leary, *The Elimination of Corrupt Practices in British Elections 1868–1911* (Oxford, 1962). On **electoral violence**, see D. Richter, 'The Role of Mob Riot in Victorian Elections, 1865–1885', *Victorian Studies*, 15 (1971) and K. T. Hoppen, 'Grammars of Electoral Violence in Nineteenth-Century England and Ireland', *English Historical Review*, 109 (1994).

VIII CRIMEAN WAR AND INDIAN MUTINY

The broad **military context** can be established from E. M. Spiers, *The Army and Society 1815–1914* (1980), G. Harries-Jenkins, *The Army in Victorian Society* (1977), H. Strachan, *Wellington's Legacy: The Reform of the British Army 1830–54* (Manchester, 1984), J. Sweetman, *War and Administration: The Significance of the Crimean War for the British Army* (Edinburgh, 1984), A. R. Skelley, *The Victorian Army at Home: The Recruitment and Terms and Conditions of the British Regular, 1859–1899* (1977), E. M. Spiers, *The Late Victorian Army 1868–1902* (Manchester, 1992), and B. Bond (ed.), *Victorian Military Campaigns* (1967) which includes essays on the Sikh Wars 1845–9, the Third China War 1860, the Abyssinian Expedition 1867–8, the Ashanti Campaign 1873–4, the South Africa War 1880–1, and the Egyptian Campaign 1882.

For the **Crimean War** and its effects, see M. A. Anderson, *The Eastern Question 1774–1923* (1966), A. P. Saab, *The Origins of the Crimean Alliance* (Charlottesville, Va., 1977), N. Rich, *Why the Crimean War?* (Hanover, NH, 1985), D. M. Goldfrank, *The Origins of the Crimean War* (1994), better on Russia than on the other powers, D. Wetzel, *The Crimean War: A Diplomatic History* (Boulder, Colo., 1985), A. D. Lambert, *The Crimean War: British Grand Strategy 1853–56* (Manchester, 1990) which argues—with mixed success—for taking a geographically wider view of the conflict, P. W. Schroeder, *Austria, Great Britain, and the Crimean War* (Ithaca, NY, 1972), O. Anderson, *A Liberal State at War: English Politics and Economics during the Crimean War* (1967), a model historical analysis, J. B. Conacher, *Britain and the Crimea 1855–56* (1987), and J. R. Vincent, 'The Parliamentary Dimension of the Crimean War', *Transactions of the Royal Historical Society*, 5th ser. 33 (1981).

For the **Indian Mutiny** (its context, development, and effects), see C. A. Bayly, *Indian Society and the Making of the British Empire* (Cambridge, 1966), E. Stokes, *The Peasant and the Raj: Studies in Agrarian Society and Peasant Rebellion in Colonial India* (Cambridge, 1978), M. Edwardes, *The Red Year: The Indian Rebellion of 1857* (1973), J. A. B. Palmer, *The Mutiny Outbreak at Meerut in 1857* (Cambridge, 1966), S. N. Sen, *Eighteen Fifty-Seven* (Calcutta, 1957), H. Chattopadhyaya, *The Sepoy Mutiny, 1857: A Social Study and Analysis* (Calcutta, 1957), R. C. Majumdar, *The Sepoy Mutiny and the Revolt of 1857*, 2nd edn. (Calcutta, 1963), S. B. Chaudhuri, *Civil Disturbances during the British Rule in India (1765–1857)* (Calcutta, 1955), S. B. Chaudhuri, *Civil Rebellion in the Indian Mutinies (1857–1859)* (Calcutta, 1957), R. Guha, *Elementary Aspects of Peasant Insurgency in Colonial India* (Delhi, 1983), E. Stokes, *The Peasant Armed: The Indian Revolt of 1857*, ed. C. A. Bayly (Oxford, 1986), R. Mukherjee, *Awadh in Revolt 1857–1858: A Study of Popular Resistance* (New Delhi, 1984), T. R. Metcalf, *The Aftermath of Revolt: India 1857–1870* (Princeton, 1965), and A. Hawkins, 'British Parliamentary Alignment and the Indian Issue 1857–1858', *Journal of British Studies*, 23/2 (1984). S. B. Cook presents a fascinating analysis of wider imperial connections in *Imperial Affinities: Nineteenth Century Analogies and Exchanges between India and Ireland* (New Delhi, 1993).

IX THE ECONOMY

Works of a **general nature** engaging with broad matters of degree and timing include P. Mathias, *The First Industrial Nation: An Economic History of Britain 1700–1914*, 2nd edn. (1983), C. H. Lee, *The British Economy since 1700: A Macroeconomic Perspective* (Cambridge, 1986), and F. Crouzet, *The Victorian Economy* (1981).

Good translations of the sometimes esoteric work of the **econometricians** into more comprehensible forms are available in R. Floud and D. McCloskey (eds.), *The Economic History of Britain since 1700*, 3 vols., 2nd edn. (Cambridge, 1994), vols. i–ii of which deal with the period to 1939 and include important essays on population, agriculture, services, investment, living standards, industrialization, technical change, foreign trade, and the economy in general. C. H. Feinstein provides relevant statistics in *National Income, Expenditure and Output of the United Kingdom 1855–1965* (Cambridge, 1972). Though still useful, the findings of P. Deane and W. A. Cole in *British Economic Growth 1688–1959*, 2nd edn. (Cambridge, 1969) are beginning to show their age and should be corrected and supplemented by those in R. C. O. Matthews, C. H. Feinstein, and J. C. Odling-Smee, *British Economic Growth 1856–1973* (Oxford, 1982). The economic effects of **industrialization** are discussed in N. F. R. Crafts, *British Economic Growth during the Industrial Revolution* (Oxford, 1985), E. A. Wrigley, *Continuity, Chance and Change: The Character of the Industrial Revolution in England* (Cambridge, 1988), and the essays in and especially the introduction to J. Mokyr (ed.), *The British Industrial Revolution: An Economic Perspective* (Boulder, Colo., 1993). Two brief introductions to cycles and the timing of the **climacteric** are R. Church, *The Great Victorian Boom 1850–1873* (SESH 1975) and S. B. Saul, *The Myth of the Great Depression 1873–1896*, 2nd edn. (SESH 1985), while more detailed and up-to-date information is available in the articles referred to in Ch. 9 n. 8.

The **agricultural economy** is examined in J. D. Chambers and G. E. Mingay, *The Agricultural Revolution 1750–1880* (1966), the massive G. E. Mingay (ed.), *Agrarian History of England and Wales*, vi. *1750–1850* (Cambridge, 1989), E. L. Jones, *The Development of English Agriculture 1815–1873* (SESH 1968), and C. S. Orwin and E. H. Whetham, *History of British Agriculture 1846–1914* (1964).

For **transport**, see P. S. Bagwell, *The Transport Revolution from 1770* (1974), M. J. Freeman and D. H. Aldcroft (eds.), *Transport in Victorian Britain* (Manchester, 1988), essays on railways, urban transport, shipping, and the like, J. R. Kellett, *The Impact of Railways on Victorian Cities* (1969), T. R. Gourvish, *Railways and the British Economy 1830–1914* (SESH 1980), and G. R. Hawke's ingenious, if ultimately unsuccessful, attempt to measure precisely the economic impact of railways in *Railways and Economic Growth in England and Wales 1840–1870* (Oxford, 1970).

Particular industries receive attention in R. Church (ed.), *The Dynamics of Victorian Business* (1980), essays on coal, iron, engineering, shipbuilding, railways, cotton, wool, and construction, D. A. Farnie, *The English Cotton Industry and the World Market 1815–1896* (Oxford, 1979), R. Church, *The History of the British Coal Industry*, iii. *1830–1913: Victorian Pre-Eminence* (Oxford, 1986), D. McCloskey, *Economic Maturity and Industrial Decline: British Iron and Steel, 1870–1913* (Cambridge, Mass., 1973), S. Pollard and P. Robertson, *The British Shipbuilding Industry 1870–1914* (Cambridge, Mass., 1979), R. C. Floud, *The British Machine Tool Industry 1850–1914* (Cambridge, 1976), I. C. R. Byatt, *The British Electrical Industry 1875–1914* (Oxford, 1979). An important article of more general import is R. Samuel, 'Workshop of the World: Steam Power and Hand Technology in Mid-Victorian Britain', *History Workshop*, 3 (1977), on the subject of which, see also G. N. von Tunzelmann, *Steam Power and British Industrialization to 1860* (Oxford, 1978).

Trade has attracted—sometimes rather technical—attention in R. Davis, *The Industrial Revolution and British Overseas Trade* (Leicester, 1979), A. G. Kenwood and A. L. Lougheed, *The Growth of the International Economy 1820–1990*, 3rd edn. (1992), an introductory text, S. B. Saul, *Studies in British Overseas Trade 1870–1914* (Liverpool, 1960), A. H. Imlah, *Economic Elements in the 'Pax Britannica': Studies in British Foreign Trade in the Nineteenth Century* (Cambridge, Mass.,

1958), and D. McCloskey, *Enterprise and Trade in Victorian Britain* (1981), which includes essays not only on trade but also on entrepreneurship and the economy as a whole.

The related—and sometimes equally knotty—matter of **investment** at home and overseas is analysed in C. Feinstein and S. Pollard (eds.), *Studies in Capital Formation in the United Kingdom 1750–1920* (Oxford, 1988), P. L. Cottrell, *Industrial Finance 1830–1914: The Finance and Organization of English Manufacturing Industry* (1980), M. Collins, *Banks and Industrial Finance in Britain, 1800–1939* (SESH 1991), P. L. Cottrell, *British Overseas Investment in the Nineteenth Century* (SESH 1975), and M. Edelstein, *Overseas Investment in the Age of High Imperialism: The United Kingdom 1850–1914* (1982). See also s. XVII.

Entrepreneurship and Britain's economic success or lack of it have been much debated in, among other works, S. Pollard, *Britain's Prime and Britain's Decline: The British Economy 1870–1914* (Cambridge, 1988), W. P. Kennedy, *Industrial Structure, Capital Markets and the Origins of British Economic Decline* (Cambridge, 1987), rather unrealistically severe, D. H. Aldcroft (ed.), *The Development of British Industry and Foreign Competition 1870–1914* (1968), ten essays on major industries, and P. L. Payne, *British Entrepreneurship in the Nineteenth Century*, 2nd edn. (SESH 1988). A more broadly cultural approach has been taken in M. J. Wiener's critical but unconvincing *English Culture and the Decline of the Industrial Spirit 1850–1914* (Cambridge, 1981), by W. D. Rubinstein, whose *Capitalism, Culture and Decline in Britain 1750–1990* (1993) stresses Britain's financial successes, and by the contributors to B. Collins and K. Robbins (eds.), *British Culture and Economic Decline* (1990).

X THE BUSINESS OF CULTURE

Two collections of essays address the topic as a whole: J. Wolff and J. Seed (eds.), *The Culture of Capital: Art, Power and the Nineteenth-Century Middle Class* (Manchester, 1988), and B. Ford (ed.), *The Cambridge Guide to the Arts in Britain*, vii. *The Later Victorian Age* (Cambridge, 1989).

Literature: authorship and authors generally are discussed in J. W. Saunders, *The Profession of English Letters* (1964), N. Cross, *The Common Writer: Life in Nineteenth-Century Grub Street* (Cambridge, 1985), V. Bonham-Carter, *Authors by Profession* (1978), J. R. Stephens, *The Profession of the Playwright: British Theatre 1800–1900* (Cambridge, 1992), and R. D. Altick, 'The Sociology of Authorship: The Social Origins, Education, and Occupations of 1100 British Writers, 1800–1935', *New York Public Library Bulletin*, 66 (1962).

For the relationship between writers, publishers, agents, readers, etc., see J. A. Sutherland, *Victorian Novels and Publishers* (1976), important and original, J. A. Sutherland, *Victorian Fiction: Writers, Publishers, Readers* (1995), R. D. Altick, *The English Common Reader: A Social History of the Mass Reading Public 1800–1900* (Chicago, 1957), L. James, *Fiction for the Working Man 1830–1850* (1963), A. C. Dooley, *Author and Printer in Victorian England* (Charlottesville, Va., 1992),

J. Feather, *A History of British Publishing* (1988), M. Plant, *The English Book Trade*, 2nd edn. (1965), and J. G. Hepburn, *The Author's Empty Purse and the Rise of the Literary Agent* (1968).

Individual publishers and the publishing experiences of individual writers can be further studied in R. A. Gettmann, *A Victorian Publisher: A Study of the Bentley Papers* (Cambridge, 1960), J. Glynn, *Prince of Publishers: A Biography of George Smith* (1986), R. L. Patten, *Charles Dickens and his Publishers* (Oxford, 1978), J. M. Brown, *Dickens: Novelist in the Market Place* (1982), P. L. Shillingsburg, *Pegasus in Harness: Victorian Publishing and W. M. Thackeray* (Charlottesville, Va., 1992), J. S. Hagen, *Tennyson and his Publishers* (1979), and A. Trollope, *An Autobiography*, ed. F. Page (1950). The importance of circulating libraries is made clear in G. L. Griest, *Mudie's Circulating Library and the Victorian Novel* (Newton Abbot, 1970), while another aspect of commercialism is discussed in N. Russell, *The Novelist and Mammon: Literary Responses to the World of Commerce in the Nineteenth Century* (Oxford, 1986).

For the theatre, see also M. R. Booth, *Theatre in the Victorian Age* (Cambridge, 1991), A. Nicoll, *A History of Late Nineteenth-Century English Drama 1850–1900*, 2 vols. (Cambridge, 1946), M. Baker, *The Rise of the Victorian Actor* (1978), and G. Taylor, *Players and Performances in the Victorian Theatre* (Manchester, 1989).

Music: the relevant works tend to be rather general in character. The following contain useful essays: N. Temperley (ed.), *Music in Britain: The Romantic Age 1800–1914* (1981), N. Temperley (ed.), *The Lost Chord: Essays in Victorian Music* (Bloomington, Ind., 1989), A. Ringer (ed.), *Man and Music: The Early Romantic Era* (1990), and J. Samson (ed.), *Man and Music: The Late Romantic Era* (1991). Other general studies of interest include C. Ehrlich, *The Music Profession in Britain since the Eighteenth Century* (Oxford, 1985), important, C. Ehrlich, *The Piano: A History*, new edn. (Oxford, 1990), F. Howes, *The English Musical Renaissance* (1968), H. Raynor, *Music and Society since 1815* (1976), A. V. Beedell, *The Decline of the English Musician 1788–1888* (Oxford, 1992), follows the international pere-grinations of a family of musicians, W. Weber, *Music and the Middle Class: The Social Structure of Concert Life in London, Paris and Vienna between 1830 and 1848* (1975), E. D. Mackerness, *A Social History of English Music* (1964), and M. Kennedy, *The Hallé Tradition* (Manchester, 1960).

On individual musicians, see J. R. Sterndale Bennett, *The Life of William Sterndale Bennett* (Cambridge, 1907), P. Charlton, *John Stainer and the Musical Life of Victorian Britain* (Newton Abbot, 1984), P. Chappell, *Dr S. S. Wesley 1810–1876* (Great Wakering, 1977), and on 'popular' music, D. Russell, *Popular Music in England 1840–1914: A Social History* (Manchester, 1987), D. B. Scott, *The Singing Bourgeois: Songs of the Victorian Drawing Room and Parlour* (Milton Keynes, 1989), and the works on music hall in s. IV.

Painting: the most useful general studies are: T. S. R. Boase, *English Art 1800–1870* (Oxford, 1959), D. Farr, *English Art 1870–1940* (Oxford, 1978), J. Maas, *Victorian Painters* (1969), wide-ranging and valuable, and G. Reynolds, *Victorian Painting* (1966). Two of the few truly contextual studies are: P. Gillett, *The*

Victorian Painter's World (Gloucester, 1990) and D. S. MacLeod, *Art and the Victorian Middle Class: Money and the Making of Cultural Identity* (Cambridge, 1996).

On particular types of painting, see C. Wood, *Victorian Panorama: Paintings of Victorian Life* (1976), J. Treuherz and others, *Hard Times: Social Realism in Victorian Art* (1987), C. Wood, *Olympian Dreamers: Victorian Classical Painters 1860–1914* (1983).

The role of dealers is clarified in J. Maas, *Gambart: Prince of the Victorian Art World* (1975). Details about prices are given in G. Reitlinger, *The Economics of Taste*, 3 vols. (1961–70), i, and about particular aspects of commercialism in A. Dyson, *Pictures to Print: The Nineteenth-Century Engraving Trade* (1984) and L. S. King, *The Industrialization of Taste: Victorian England and the Art Union of London* (Ann Arbor, Mich., 1985).

Much can be gleaned from works on (or memoirs by) individual artists such as V. G. Swanson, *Sir Lawrence Alma-Tadema: The Painter of the Victorian Vision of the Ancient World* (1977), L. and R. Ormond, *Lord Leighton* (New Haven, 1975), D. Robertson, *Sir Charles Eastlake and the Victorian Art World* (Princeton, 1978), C. Lennie, *Landseer: The Victorian Paragon* (1976), R. Ormond, *Sir Edwin Landseer* (1981), A. Noakes, *William Frith: Extraordinary Victorian Painter* (1978), *A Victorian Canvas: The Memoirs of W. P. Frith*, ed. N. Wallis (1957), and *The Diary of Ford Madox Brown*, ed. V. Surtees (1981).

Architecture: a general impression can be gained from R. Dixon and S. Muthesius, *Victorian Architecture*, 2nd edn. (1985). Also useful are C. Stewart, *The Stones of Manchester* (1956), on the buildings of one city, J. H. G. Archer (ed.), *Art and Architecture in Victorian Manchester* (Manchester, 1985), essays on painting, patronage, and exhibitions, as well as buildings, J. Summerson, *The London Building World of the Eighteen-Sixties* (1973), P. Ferriday (ed.), *Victorian Architecture* (1963), essays on professionalization and on particular practitioners such as Burges, Street, and Webb, A. Saint, *The Image of the Architect* (New Haven, 1983), on professionalization, training, and the contemporary standing of architects, and B. Kaye, *The Development of the Architectural Profession in Britain* (1960).

Good studies of individual practitioners include A. Saint, *Richard Norman Shaw* (1976), P. Thompson, *William Butterfield* (1971), A. J. Paas, *Thomas Worthington: Victorian Architecture and Social Purpose* (Manchester, 1988), D. Cole, *The Work of Sir Gilbert Scott* (1980), J. Allibone, *Anthony Salvin: Pioneer of Gothic Revival Architecture* (Cambridge, 1988), J. M. Crook, *William Burges and the High Victorian Dream* (1981), and C. Cunningham and P. Waterhouse, *Alfred Waterhouse 1830–1905: Biography of a Practice* (Oxford, 1992).

XI RELIGION

While O. Chadwick, *The Victorian Church*, 2 vols. (1966–70), though best on the Church of England, is the only tolerably **comprehensive work**, the essays in vols. i, ii, and iv of G. Parsons and J. R. Moore (eds.), *Religion in Victorian Britain*, 4 vols. (Manchester, 1988) together provide an excellent overview including, as they do, pieces on various denominations, the clergy, theology, establishments and disestablishment, 'doubt', biblical criticism, and science and religion which move well beyond purely English concerns. More **denominationally bound** are E. R. Norman, *Church [of England] and Society in England 1770–1970* (Oxford, 1976), D. M. Thompson (ed.), *Nonconformity in the Nineteenth Century* (1972), documents, I. Sellers, *Nineteenth-Century Nonconformity* (1977), C. Binfield, *So Down to Prayers: Studies in English Nonconformity 1780–1920* (1977), E. R. Norman, *The English Catholic Church in the Nineteenth Century* (Oxford, 1984), J. D. Holmes, *More Roman than Rome: English Catholicism in the Nineteenth Century* (1978), G. Connolly, 'The Transubstantiation of Myth: Towards a New Popular History of Nineteenth-Century Catholicism in England', *Journal of Ecclesiastical History*, 35 (1984), an important revisionist piece, and G. Alderman, *Modern British Jewry* (Oxford, 1992). More wide-ranging is D. W. Bebbington, *Evangelicalism in Modern Britain: A History from the 1730s to the 1980s* (1989).

The **social aspects** of Victorian religion can be studied further in a wide variety of publications. The fullest statistics are in R. Currie, A. Gilbert, and L. Horsley, *Churches and Churchgoers: Patterns of Church Growth in the British Isles since 1700* (Oxford, 1977), though useful details are also provided in B. I. Coleman, *The Church of England in the Mid-Nineteenth Century: A Social Geography* (1980) and J. D. Gay, *The Geography of Religion in England* (1971). A. D. Gilbert, *Religion and Society in Industrial England: Church, Chapel and Social Change 1740–1914* (1976) is a key work. **Rural religious practices** are splendidly elucidated in J. Obelkevich, *Religion and Rural Society: South Lindsey 1825–1875* (Oxford, 1976). In the same context A. Everitt looks at *The Pattern of Rural Dissent: The Nineteenth Century* (Leicester, 1972), while K. D. M. Snell studies a whole locality in *Church and Chapel in the North Midlands* (Leicester, 1991). F. Knight, *The Nineteenth-Century Church and English Society* (Cambridge, 1995) ranges more widely. For **urban developments** see H. McLeod, *Religion and the Working Class in Nineteenth-Century Britain* (SESH 1984), K. S. Inglis, *Churches and the Working Classes in Victorian England* (1963), H. McLeod, *Class and Religion in the Late Victorian City* (1974), on London, J. N. Morris, *Religion and Urban Change: Croydon 1840–1914* (Woodbridge, 1992), J. Cox, *The English Churches in a Secular Society: Lambeth 1870–1930* (New York, 1982), and E. R. Wickham, *Church and People in an Industrial City*, 5th edn. (1964), on Sheffield. C. G. Brown has written both an important article 'Did Urbanization Secularize Britain?', *Urban History Yearbook* (1988) and an extremely useful *Social History of Religion in Scotland since 1730* (1987).

Three books examine the **clergy**: B. Heeney, *A Different Kind of Gentleman: Parish Clergy as Professional Men in Early and Mid-Victorian England* (Hamden, Conn., 1976), A. Haig, *The Victorian Clergy* (1984), and K. D. Brown, *A Social History of the Nonconformist Ministry in England and Wales 1800–1930* (Oxford, 1988).

The **political side of things** is amply laid out in two books by G. I. T. Machin, *Politics and the Churches in Great Britain 1832 to 1868* (Oxford, 1977) and *Politics*

and the Churches in Great Britain 1869 to 1921 (Oxford, 1987), is studied locally in
P. T. Phillips, *The Sectarian Spirit: Sectarianism, Society and Politics in Victorian
Cotton Towns* (Toronto, 1982), and is subjected to exciting and wide-ranging
analysis in B. Hilton, *The Age of Atonement: The Influence of Evangelicalism on
Social and Economic Thought 1785–1865* (Oxford, 1988).

Miscellaneous but important topics are examined in H. Davies, *Worship and
Theology in England from Newman to Martineau* (Princeton, 1962), B. M. G.
Reardon, *Religious Thought in the Victorian Age: A Survey from Coleridge to Gore*,
2nd edn. (1995), J. Kent, *Holding the Fort: Studies in Victorian Revivalism* (1978),
R. Carwardine, *Transatlantic Revivalism: Popular Evangelicalism in Britain and
America 1790–1865* (Westport, Conn., 1978), J. Wolffe, *The Protestant Crusade in
Great Britain 1829–1860* (Oxford, 1991), D. G. Paz, *Popular Anti-Catholicism in
Mid-Victorian England* (Stanford, Calif., 1992), and S. O'Brien, ' "Terra Incog-
nita": The Nun in Nineteenth-Century England', *Past & Present*, 121 (1988).

XII THE EVOLUTIONARY MOMENT

Important **contextual studies** are: J. W. Burrow, *Evolution and Society: A Study
in Victorian Social Theory* (Cambridge, 1966), P. J. Bowler, *Evolution: The History
of an Idea* (Berkeley, Calif., 1984), and A. Desmond, *The Politics of Evolution:
Morphology, Medicine, and Reform in Radical London* (Chicago, 1989).

For the work and impact of **Darwin**, see, in the first place, two of his own books:
*The Origin of Species by Means of Natural Selection, or the Preservation of Favoured
Races in the Struggle for Life*, 1st edn. (1859) and *The Descent of Man and Selection
in Relation to Sex*, 1st edn. (1871). A. Desmond and J. Moore, *Darwin* (1991) is the
best biographical study. Also useful are R. M. Young, *Darwin's Metaphor: Nature's
Place in Victorian Culture* (Cambridge, 1985), D. R. Oldroyd, *Darwinian Impacts*
(Milton Keynes, 1980), J. Moore, 'Deconstructing Darwinism: The Politics of
Evolution in the 1860s', *Journal of the History of Biology*, 24 (1991). **Social
Darwinism** is analysed in G. Jones, *Social Darwinism and English Thought*
(Brighton, 1980) and D. P. Crook, *Benjamin Kidd: Portrait of a Social Darwinist*
(Cambridge, 1984). **Physiological and psychological impacts** are examined in
R. M. Young, *Mind, Brain and Adaptation in the Nineteenth Century*, new impres-
sion (Oxford, 1990) and R. J. Richards, *Darwin and the Emergence of Evolutionary
Theories of Mind and Behavior* (Chicago, 1987) and **religious aspects** in J. R.
Moore, *The Post-Darwinian Controversies: A Study of the Protestant Struggle to
Come to Terms with Darwin in Great Britain and America 1870–1900* (Cambridge,
1979) and F. M. Turner, *Between Science and Religion: The Reaction to Scientific
Naturalism in Late Victorian England* (New Haven, 1974).

The interactions between evolutionary ideas and **political and social theory**
are more closely discussed in S. Gordon, 'Darwin and Political Economy', *Journal
of the History of Biology*, 22 (1989), D. Wiltshire, *The Social and Political Thought
of Herbert Spencer* (Oxford, 1978), M. W. Taylor, *Men versus the State: Herbert
Spencer and Late Victorian Individualism* (Oxford, 1992), M. Freeden, *The New*

Liberalism: An Ideology of Social Reform (Oxford, 1978), and R. N. Soffer, *Ethics and Society in England: The Revolution in the Social Sciences 1870–1914* (Berkeley, Calif., 1978).

For the responses to evolution in general and Darwinism in particular by **imaginative writers**, see L. Stevenson, *Darwin among the Poets* (Chicago, 1932) and L. J. Henkin, *Darwinism in the English Novel 1860–1910* (New York, 1940), both rather dated though still worth consulting. Altogether more sparky are S. E. Hyman, *The Tangled Bank: Darwin, Marx, Frazer and Freud as Imaginative Writers* (New York, 1962), P. Mensel, *Thomas Hardy: The Return of the Repressed* (New Haven, 1972), and G. Beer's deeply considered *Darwin's Plots: Evolutionary Narrative in Darwin, George Eliot and Nineteenth-Century Fiction* (1983).

XIII A UNITED KINGDOM?

Although some interesting studies of the United Kingdom's multinational character have recently appeared, there is little agreement even on such fundamental matters as the number of the national entities involved. See K. Robbins, *Nineteenth-Century Britain: England, Scotland and Wales: The Making of a Nation* (Oxford, 1988), L. Colley, *Britons: Forging the Nation* (New Haven, 1992), H. Kearney, *The British Isles: A History of Four Nations* (Cambridge, 1989), R. G. Asch (ed.), *Three Nations—A Common History? England, Scotland, Ireland and British History*, c. *1600–1920* (Bochum, 1993), and A. Grant and K. J. Stringer (eds.), *Uniting the Kingdom? The Making of British History* (1995).

XIV SCOTLAND

General and political studies include M. Lynch, *Scotland: A New History* (1991), S. and O. Checkland, *Industry and Ethos: Scotland 1832–1914* (1984), T. C. Smout, *A Century of the Scottish People 1830–1950* (1986), W. Ferguson, *Scotland 1689 to the Present*, new impression (Edinburgh, 1978), M. Fry, *Patronage and Principle: A Political History of Modern Scotland* (Aberdeen, 1987), I. G. C. Hutchison, *A Political History of Scotland 1832–1924: Parties, Elections and Issues* (Edinburgh, 1986), and J. G. Kellas, *Modern Scotland: The Nation since 1870* (1968). Two books directly address the matter of **nationalism**: H. J. Hanham, *Scottish Nationalism* (1969) and C. Harvie, *Scotland and Nationalism 1707–1994*, 2nd edn. (1994), while the political and other uses to which Scottish history has been put are analysed in M. Pittock, *The Invention of Scotland: The Stuart Myth and the Scottish Identity* (1991) and I. Donnachie and C. Whatley (eds.), *The Manufacture of Scottish History* (Edinburgh, 1992).

For **economic and social developments**, see R. H. Campbell, *Scotland since 1707: The Rise of an Industrial Society*, 2nd edn. (Edinburgh, 1985), R. H. Campbell, *The Rise and Fall of Scottish Industry 1707–1939* (Edinburgh, 1980), T. M. Devine (ed.), *Scottish Elites* (Edinburgh, 1994), A. A. MacLaren (ed.), *Social Class in Scotland* (Edinburgh, [1978]), R. A. Cage (ed.), *The Working Class in Glasgow*

1750–1914 (1987), R. Q. Gray, *The Labour Aristocracy in Victorian Edinburgh* (Oxford, 1976), and W. H. Fraser and R. J. Morris (eds.), *People and Society in Scotland Volume II* (Edinburgh, 1990), excellent essays on towns, the countryside, class, women, education, religion, and employment. **Education** is critically examined by R. Anderson in *Education and Opportunity in Victorian Scotland: Schools and Universities* (Oxford, 1983) and 'In Search of the "Lad of Parts"': The Mythical History of Scottish Education', *History Workshop*, 19 (1985). **Regional studies** include A. Slaven, *The Development of the West of Scotland 1750–1960* (1975) and M. Gray, *The Highland Economy 1750–1850* (Edinburgh, 1957).

In a corpus of writings overconcerned with the Highlands, **rural matters** receive attention in T. M. Devine, *Clanship to Crofters' War: The Social Transformation of the Scottish Highlands* (Manchester, 1994), T. M. Devine, *The Great Highland Famine* (Edinburgh, 1988), J. Hunter, *The Making of the Crofting Community* (Edinburgh, 1976), excellent, E. Richards, *A History of the Highland Clearances*, 2 vols. (1982–5), P. Gaskell, *Morvern Transformed: A Highland Parish in the Nineteenth Century* (Cambridge, 1968), C. W. J. Withers, *Gaelic Scotland: The Transformation of a Cultural Region* (1988), and I. Carter, *Farmlife in Northeast Scotland 1840–1914* (Edinburgh, 1979).

For the complexities of **religion** in Scotland, see C. G. Brown, *A Social History of Religion in Scotland since 1730* (1987), S. J. Brown and M. Fry (eds.), *Scotland in the Age of the Disruption* (Edinburgh, 1993), and two books by A. L. Drummond and J. Bulloch, *The Church in Victorian Scotland 1843–1874* (Edinburgh, 1975) and *The Church in late Victorian Scotland 1874–1900* (Edinburgh, 1978).

XV WALES

The best and most balanced **general history** is P. Jenkins, *A History of Modern Wales 1530–1950* (1992), though D. G. Evans, *A History of Wales 1815–1906* (Cardiff, 1989) and G. E. Jones, *Modern Wales: A Concise History*, 2nd edn. (Cambridge, 1994) are also useful. Lively, but written to a tighter and at times polemical agenda, are G. A. Williams, *When was Wales? A History of the Welsh* (1985) and J. Davies, *A History of Wales* (1993).

More exclusively **political** are K. O. Morgan, *Wales in British Politics 1868–1922*, 3rd edn. (Cardiff, 1980), K. O. Morgan, *Rebirth of a Nation: Wales 1880–1980* (Oxford, 1981), and R. Wallace, *Organise! Organise! Organise! A Study of Reform Agitations in Wales 1840–1886* (Cardiff, 1991).

Economic and social issues are examined in three books of essays by I. G. Jones, *Explorations and Explanations: Essays in the Social History of Victorian Wales* (Llandysul, 1981), *Communities: Essays in the Social History of Victorian Wales* (Llandysul, 1987), and *Mid-Victorian Wales: The Observers and the Observed* (Cardiff, 1992), as also in C. Baber and L. J. Williams (eds.), *Modern Wales: Essays in Economic History* (Cardiff, 1986), D. W. Howell, *Land and People in Nineteenth-Century Wales* (1977), and E. L. Ellis, *The University of Wales Aberystwyth 1872–1972* (Cardiff, 1972).

For the **Welsh language**, see G. Williams, 'Language, Literacy and Nationality in Wales', *History*, 56 (1971) and B. Thomas, 'A Cauldron of Rebirth: Population and the Welsh Language in the Nineteenth Century', *Welsh History Review*, 13 (1987).

Religion and its reverberations are discussed in E. T. Davies, *A New History of Wales: Religion and Society in the Nineteenth Century* (Llandybie, 1981), D. W. Bebbington, 'Religion and National Feeling in Nineteenth-Century Wales and Scotland' in S. Mews (ed.), *Religion and National Identity* (Oxford, 1982), and M. Cragoe, 'Conscience or Coercion? Clerical Influence at the General Election of 1868 in Wales', *Past & Present*, 149 (1995).

Glamorgan County History, vi. *Glamorgan Society 1780–1980*, ed. P. Morgan (Cardiff, 1988) contains excellent essays on politics, popular movements, factory reform, trade unions, coal, landscape, towns, migration, religion, and culture generally, while G. Borrow's *Wild Wales* (1862) is a sympathetic account of the writer's Welsh travels in 1854.

XVI IRELAND

For all sorts of reasons nineteenth-century Ireland has attracted more attention than Scotland or Wales.

Among **general histories** R. F. Foster, *Modern Ireland 1600–1972* (1988) is excellent over the longer run, while J. C. Beckett, *The Making of Modern Ireland 1603–1923*, 2nd edn. (1981) is still useful. Studies of rather shorter periods include F. S. L. Lyons, *Ireland since the Famine*, new edn. (1973), K. T. Hoppen, *Ireland since 1800: Conflict and Conformity* (1989), J. Lee, *The Modernisation of Irish Society 1848–1918* (Dublin, 1973), and P. O'Farrell, *England and Ireland since 1800* (Oxford, 1975). The two relevant—and massive—volumes of *A New History of Ireland*, namely v. *Ireland under the Union I 1801–70* (Oxford, 1989) and vi. *Ireland under the Union II 1870–1921* (Oxford, 1996), both ed. W. E. Vaughan, contain many excellent essays on all aspects of nineteenth-century Ireland—political, social, economic, religious, and cultural.

The **Great Famine** is placed in context by C. Ó Gráda, *Ireland: A New Economic History 1780–1939* (Oxford, 1994), L. M. Cullen, *An Economic History of Ireland since 1660* (1972), and J. Mokyr, *Why Ireland Starved: A Quantitative and Analytical History of the Irish Economy, 1800–1850*, revised edn. (1985) and is—very variously—described and analysed in C. Ó Gráda, *The Great Irish Famine* (SESH 1989), M. E. Daly, *The Famine in Ireland* (Dublin, 1986), C. Woodham-Smith, *The Great Hunger: Ireland 1845–9* (1962), C. Kinealy, *This Great Calamity: The Irish Famine 1845–52* (Dublin, 1994), C. Póirtéir (ed.), *The Great Famine* (Cork, 1995), P. Gray, 'Potatoes and Providence: British Governments' Responses to the Great Famine', *Bullán: An Irish Studies Journal*, 1 (1994), G. L. Bernstein, 'Liberals, the Irish Famine and the Role of the State', *Irish Historical Studies*, 29 (1995). Population statistics are provided in W. E. Vaughan and A. J. Fitzpatrick (eds.), *Irish Historical Statistics: Population, 1821–1971* (Dublin, 1978) and emigration is analysed in K. A. Miller, *Emigrants and Exiles: Ireland and the Irish Exodus to North America* (Oxford, 1985) and in essays in the *New History of Ireland* volumes.

Although it is virtually impossible to disentangle the land question from **political developments generally** in nineteenth-century Ireland, works in which the latter constitute the dominant element include D. G. Boyce, *Nationalism in Ireland*, 2nd edn. (1991), K. B. Nowlan, *The Politics of Repeal: A Study in the Relations between Great Britain and Ireland, 1841–50* (1965), K. T. Hoppen, *Elections, Politics, and Society in Ireland 1832–1885* (Oxford, 1984), C. Townshend, *Political Violence in Ireland: Government and Resistance since 1848* (Oxford, 1983), P. Gibbon, *The Origins of Ulster Unionism: The Formation of Popular Protestant Politics and Ideology in Nineteenth-Century Ireland* (Manchester, 1975), D. A. Kerr, *'A Nation of Beggars'? Priests, People, and Politics in Famine Ireland, 1846–1852* (Oxford, 1994), J. H. Whyte, *The Independent Irish Party 1850–9* (Oxford, 1958), R. V. Comerford, *The Fenians in Context: Irish Politics and Society 1848–82* (Dublin, 1985), D. Thornley, *Isaac Butt and Home Rule* (1964), R. F. Foster, *Charles Stewart Parnell: The Man and his Family* (Hassocks, 1976), F. S. L. Lyons, *Charles Stewart Parnell* (1977), C. C. O'Brien, *Parnell and his Party 1880–90*, corrected impression (Oxford, 1964), and L. P. Curtis, jun., *Coercion and Conciliation in Ireland 1880–1892* (Princeton, 1963). In turn, the **land question** plays the dominant role in: T. W. Moody, *Davitt and Irish Revolution 1846–82* (Oxford, 1981), S. Clark and J. S. Donnelly, jun. (eds.), *Irish Peasants: Violence and Political Unrest 1780–1914* (Manchester, 1983), J. S. Donnelly, jun., *The Land and the People of Nineteenth-Century Cork* (1975), W. E. Vaughan, *Landlords and Tenants in Mid-Victorian Ireland* (Oxford, 1994), M. Turner, *After the Famine: Irish Agriculture 1850–1914* (Cambridge, 1996), P. Bew, *Land and the National Question in Ireland 1858–82* (Dublin, 1978), S. Clark, *Social Origins of the Irish Land War* (Princeton, 1979), D. E. Jordan, *Land and Popular Politics in Ireland: County Mayo from the Plantation to the Land War* (Cambridge, 1994), and B. L. Solow, *The Land Question and the Irish Economy 1870–1903* (Cambridge, Mass., 1971).

For **Religion and the Churches**, see the excellent brief introduction by S. Connolly in *Religion and Society in Nineteenth-Century Ireland* (Dundalk, 1985) and also D. Bowen, *The Protestant Crusade in Ireland, 1800–70* (Dublin, 1978), D. H. Akenson, *The Church of Ireland: Ecclesiastical Reform and Revolution 1800–1885* (New Haven, 1971), D. Bowen, *Paul, Cardinal Cullen, and the Shaping of Modern Irish Catholicism* (Dublin, 1983), and the extensive writings of E. Larkin (whose books provide a detailed but largely episcopally orientated account of contemporary Irish Catholicism), especially 'The Devotional Revolution in Ireland, 1850–75', *American Historical Review*, 77 (1972), *The Making of the Roman Catholic Church in Ireland 1850–1860* (Chapel Hill, NC, 1980), *The Consolidation of the Roman Catholic Church in Ireland 1860–1870* (Dublin, 1987), *The Roman Catholic Church and the Home Rule Movement 1870–1874* (Dublin, 1990), *The Catholic Church and the Emergence of the Modern Irish Political System 1874–1878* (Dublin, 1996), and *The Roman Catholic Church and the Creation of the Modern Irish State 1878–1886* (Dublin, 1975).

748 BIBLIOGRAPHY

XVII FOREIGN AND IMPERIAL AFFAIRS

On **foreign affairs** some older works still repay attention, notably L. D. Steefel, *The Schleswig-Holstein Question* (Cambridge, Mass., 1936), R. W. Seton-Watson, *Britain in Europe 1789–1914: A Survey of Foreign Policy* (Cambridge, 1937), A. J. P. Taylor, *The Struggle for Mastery in Europe 1848–1918* (Oxford, 1954), and W. N. Medlicott, *Bismarck, Gladstone and the Concert of Europe* (1956). Useful works of more recent vintage include K. Bourne, *The Foreign Policy of Victorian England 1830–1902* (Oxford, 1970), with documents, P. Hayes, *Modern British Foreign Policy: The Nineteenth Century 1814–1880* (1975), M. E. Chamberlain, *'Pax Britannica': British Foreign Policy 1789–1914* (1988), D. Beales, *England and Italy 1859–60* (1961), P. Kennedy, *The Rise of the Anglo-German Antagonism 1860–1914* (1980), B. Porter, *Britain, Europe and the World: Delusions of Grandeur*, 2nd edn. (1987), K. A. P. Sandiford, *Great Britain and the Schleswig-Holstein Question* (Toronto, 1975), R. Millman, *British Foreign Policy and the Coming of the Franco-Prussian War* (Oxford, 1965), M. Swartz, *The Politics of British Foreign Policy in the Era of Disraeli and Gladstone* (1985), R. T. Shannon, *Gladstone and the Bulgarian Agitation, 1876* (1963), on domestic reverberations of foreign events, and R. Millman, *Britain and the Eastern Question 1875–1878* (Oxford, 1979). See also s. VIII.

General studies of **imperial affairs** include R. Hyam, *Britain's Imperial Century 1815–1914* (1976), B. Porter, *The Lion's Share: A Short History of British Imperialism*, 3rd edn. (1996), and C. C. Eldridge, *Victorian Imperialism* (1978). The following have a more specific focus: R. Robinson and J. Gallagher, *Africa and the Victorians: The Official Mind of Imperialism* (1961), W. P. Morrell, *British Colonial Policy in the Age of Peel and Russell* (Oxford, 1930), C. C. Eldridge, *England's Mission: The Imperial Idea in the Age of Gladstone and Disraeli 1868–1880* (1973), B. Semmel, *The Governor Eyre Controversy* (1962), D. A. Lorimer, *Colour, Class and the Victorians: English Attitudes to the Negro in the Mid-Nineteenth Century* (Leicester, 1978), W. D. McIntyre, *The Imperial Frontier in the Tropics 1865–75: A Study of British Colonial Policy in West Africa, Malaya, and the South Pacific* (1967), G. N. Sanderson, *England, Europe and the Upper Nile 1882–1899* (Edinburgh, 1965), and A. G. Hopkins, 'The Victorians and Africa: A Reconsideration of the Occupation of Egypt, 1882', *Journal of African History*, 27 (1986).

Economic and financial interpretations of British imperialism (the authors of which rarely agree) include P. J. Cain and A. G. Hopkins, *British Imperialism: Innovation and Expansion 1688–1914* (1993), P. J. Cain, *Economic Foundations of British Overseas Expansion 1815–1914* (SESH 1980), D. K. Fieldhouse, *Economics and Empire 1830–1914* (1973), L. E. Davis and R. A. Huttenback, *Mammon and the Pursuit of Empire: The Political Economy of British Imperialism 1860–1912* (Cambridge, 1986), P. K. O'Brien, 'The Costs and Benefits of British Imperialism 1846–1914', *Past & Present*, 120 (1988), and A. Offer, 'The British Empire, 1870–1914: A Waste of Money?' *Economic History Review*, 46 (1993). See also s. VIII.

Index

Note: Titled persons are cited under the styles most commonly used, with cross-references where appropriate.

Chamberlain, Joseph (*cont.*)
  on Salisbury 654
  and second Gladstone
    administration 646, 647
  and third Gladstone
    administration 682
Chambers, Robert (1802–71),
  writer 473
Chartism 66, 128
  agitation (1848) 129–31
  differences within 129
Childers, Hugh Culling Eardley
  (1827–96), politician 593, 623
  and navy 604
  and Ireland 670
children:
  attitudes towards 316, 328–30
  care of 318
  health of 330–1
  numbers desired 86, 317
  protection of 108, 141, 330
  and work 330
  see also families
China 156, 167, 183, 201–2
Christian Socialists 457
Churchill, Lord Randolph Henry
  Spencer (1849–94), politician 643
  and Fourth Party 261, 645
  on Gladstone 641
  and Ireland 671, 675, 677, 686
Church of England:
  Anglicans abroad 370
  and business 450–1
  clerical incomes 44–5, 466–7
  clergymen 39, 41, 44, 96, 435, 453,
    466–9
  in countryside 452–3
  demands for disestablishment
    of 448, 534
  and education 599–600
  episcopal appointments 451–2
  established 427
  and evangelicalism 436
  parish churches 394

parties within 433–4
and patronage 451–2
pew renting 454
reform and revival of 432–6, 452,
  498
regional distribution 431–2
and religious orders 461
and revivalism 459–60
and rites of passage 465
ritualism (Anglo-Catholicism)
  in 145–6, 369, 433–4, 462–4, 515,
  613
statistics 428–31
styles of worship 462–3
and suburbanization 433
in Wales 530, 532, 534, 552
and working classes 456–7,
  463
Church of Ireland 428, 515, 582–3
  disestablishment of 219–20, 582–3,
  593–5
  revival of 562
Church of Scotland 526–30
  and disestablishment 556–7
  established 427, 527–8
  Great Disruption (1843) of 447–8,
  520, 527–9
  ministers 466
  and patronage 451, 527
  Presbyterianism 428
  numbers 430, 528
  revival of 528–9
  worship 448, 462
  see also Presbyterians
Civil Service:
  earnings in 45
  expenditure on 110, 120–1
  and graduates 514
  Indian 45, 112
  and intellectual élite 497–8
  nature 111
  personnel 95, 154–5
  reforms of 45, 100, 111–13, 139,
  199, 601

Dickens, Charles (*cont.*)
  works by 104, 373, 377, 378–9, 382,
    383–5, 389–91, 417–18
diet 344–7
  changing patterns 84–5
  of children 330
  food adulteration 615
  food costs 73, 85
  food preparation 337, 345
  mass-produced foods 346
  mealtimes 329, 345–7
  nutritional status 88–9, 345
  regional differences 345
Dilke, Sir Charles Wentworth
    (1843–1911), politician 517, 613
  and franchise reform 284, 652
  and imperial affairs 660
  and Ireland 675, 681
  and second Gladstone
    administration 646
Disraeli, Benjamin, Earl of
    Beaconsfield (1804–81), prime
    minister 268, 641
  administration (1874–80) of 610–19
  and agricultural distress 136, 144,
    146
  attacks Gladstone's first
    administration 609
  and Bentinck 143–5
  budgets 138, 148–51, 205
  and Bulgarian agitation 621–4
  and centralization 105
  and Congress of Berlin 626
  Conservative leader in
    Commons 135–8, 148
  and Derby 135–7, 148–50, 297–8,
    212
  and economic and financial
    affairs 119, 136, 205, 214, 610,
    614–15, 635
  and foreign affairs 183, 233, 236,
    611, 620–6
  and the franchise 147, 215, 208–9,
    219, 237

  on Gladstone 630
  and imperial affairs 158, 610–11,
    628–32
  and Indian Mutiny 194
  and Ireland 636
  and Jewish emancipation 207
  and landed interest 26
  notions of party, 133, 138
  on Palmerston 198, 218
  as novelist 373, 376, 503
  and protection 13, 135–7
  public speeches (1872) 261, 610–11,
    628
  and Queen Victoria 629
  and ritualism 446, 463, 613
  and Second Reform Act 248–53,
    255
  search for allies 132, 135, 138, 212
  and social legislation 614–17
  see also administrations
Disruption, Great (in Church of
    Scotland) 447–8, 520
Dissenters, *see* Nonconformists
divorce 100, 199–200, 320–1
  see also marriage
doctors (medical) 41, 42, 43
domesticity 57–8
  in art 411
  and country houses 334–5
  domestic equipment 337–8
  furniture etc. 336, 340–1
  household manuals 336
  households 317, 329, 331–2, 333,
    336–7
  lighting and fuel 337–8
  plumbing 338
  versions and cult of 316, 335,
    336
drink (alcoholic) 608
  consumption 353
  licensing laws 100, 354, 607–8
  temperance movements 354–5,
    607–8
  see also public houses